Yearbook on

International

Communist Affairs

1972

Yearbook on International Communist Affairs

1972

EDITOR: Richard F. Staar

ASSOCIATE AREA EDITORS:

East Europe and Soviet Union	Milorad M. Drachkovitch
Western Europe	Lawson A. Pendleton
Africa and Middle East	Lewis H. Gann
Western Hemisphere	William E. Ratliff
Asia and Pacific	Yuan-li Wu
Front Organizations	Witold S. Sworakowski

STAFF MEMBERS: Valerie I. Bloom, Eric P. Stromquist,
Robert F. Turner, Edith R. Wyden

HOOVER INSTITUTION PRESS
Stanford University
Stanford, California
1972

The Hoover Institution on War, Revolution and Peace, founded at Stanford University in 1919 by the late President Herbert Hoover, is a center for advanced study and research on public and international affairs in the twentieth century. The views expressed in its publications are entirely those of the authors and do not necessarily reflect the views of the Hoover Institution.

Hoover Institution Publications 118
Standard Book Number 8179-1181-2
Library of Congress Card Number 67-31024
Printed in the United States of America
© 1972 by the Board of Trustees of the
Leland Stanford Junior University

Yearbook on International Communist Affairs 1972

Advisory Board

CONTENTS

Western Hemisphere

Asia and the Pacific

International Communist Front Organizations

PREFACE

The objective of the 1972 *Yearbook on International Communist Affairs*, the sixth consecutive volume to be published, is to provide once again a comprehensive survey covering the calendar year 1971 about the organizational structure, internal development, domestic and foreign policies, and activity of communist parties throughout the world. Most of the materials are based on primary sources.

Profiles of individual communist movements include, as far as available data permit, the following information on each party: founding date; domestic conditions under which the party operates; membership figures; electoral support and participation, if any, in government; organization and leadership; the role of auxiliary organizations; domestic political programs and activities; decisions on key problems of communist ideology, strategy, and tactics; views and positions on major international issues; orientation within the international communist movement; and principal party communications media. Pro-Chinese, Castroite, Trotskyist, and other rival communist movements are treated whenever applicable. Insofar as they affect policies and activities of major communist movements, certain pro-communist parties and groups are noted, as are some guerrilla organizations (particularly in Latin America and Africa) and heterogeneous elements of the so-called New Left. In general, the organizational structure and the policies of these groups are treated only peripherally.

In the specific case of Africa, when selecting parties for inclusion in this *Yearbook*, we have only chosen orthodox Marxist-Leninist movements. Groups referred to by Soviet sources as "revolutionary-democratic," like the PAIGC (Partido Africano de Independência da Guiné e Cabo Verde), MPLA (Movimento Popular de Libertação de Angola), FRELIMO (Frente de Libertação de Moçambique) have been excluded, even though these three movements engage in armed struggle with Soviet support, follow a pro-Soviet course in international affairs, and were represented by official delegates at the Twenty-fourth Congress of the Communist Party of the Soviet Union, held in March-April 1971 at Moscow.

Communist-ruled countries present a particular problem as a result of the entwined interrelationship between government and party. In these profiles, therefore, the focus is on the position and functioning of each party, while policies pursued by the communist-ruled states are treated predominantly within the context of official party programs and attitudes.

The section on International Communist Front Organizations includes a brief historical background, structure, policy lines, internal issues, and developments of the major fronts and their role within the overall world communist movement. It is followed by a Chronology, Selected Bibliography, and Index of Names. The Documents section has been dropped again, but significant data contained in major documents are incorporated in the *Yearbook* profiles.

*　　*　　*

Members of the staff and several associate area editors were responsible for most of the research and writing of the *Yearbook*. Profiles were contributed also by Dorothy C. Atkinson, Ivan Avakumovic, Edward J. Bacciocco, Jr., Dennis L. Bark, George Charney, John K. Emmerson, Bennett Kovrig, George Lerski, Carla Liverani, Kay McKeough, H. J. M. Mennes, James F. Morrison, Michel G. Nabti, Nicholas C. Pano, B. Marie Perinbam, Marin Pundeff, Lynn Ratliff, Nelly Stromquist, and Zdenek L. Suda. Full names and affiliations of each outside contributor appear at the end of his or her profile. Ellen Leung assisted in the processing and filing of research material.

Special appreciation is due to the Curators of the Hoover Institution and to members of its Readers' Services and Serials Departments, as well as to all those organizations—government and private—which made available source material and translations. We are indebted particularly to the copy editor, Jesse M. Phillips, for putting the manuscript in its final form.

Richard F. Staar

*   *   *

Note on Sources

Sources are cited throughout the text, with news agencies normally identified by generally accepted initials. Abbreviations are also used for the following widely quoted publications:

Yearbook on International Communist Affairs	*YICA*
World Marxist Review (Toronto, Canada, edition)	*WMR*
and its *Information Bulletin*	*IB*
International Meeting of Communist and Workers' Parties (1969)	*IMCWP*

EASTERN EUROPE
AND THE
SOVIET UNION

Albania

The Albanian Communist Party was founded on 8 November 1941. At the party's First Congress in November 1948 the name was changed to the Albanian Party of Labor (Partia e Punës e Shqipërisë; APL). As the only legal political party in Albania, the APL exercises a monopoly of power. All 264 seats in the national legislature, the People's Assembly, are held by candidates of the Democratic Front, which is the party-controlled political alliance of the APL and the mass organizations.

Membership. In 1971, according to official party statistics, the APL had a total of 86,985 members, consisting of 68,858 full members and 18,127 candidates (*Zëri i Popullit*, 4 November). Membership increased by 20,658 between the party's Fifth Congress in November 1966, and the Sixth Congress in November 1971. Slightly more than half of this gain was made during 1970-71. The population of Albania is 2,150,000 (estimated 1971).

It was revealed at the Sixth Congress (*ibid.*, 2 November), that 1,323 members and 434 candidates had been expelled from the party between 1967 and 1970, while 1,047 members had been demoted to candidate status. These figures do not include the several thousand communists expelled but reinstated prior to the Sixth Congress. These data indicate that the party purge in conjunction with the "revolutionization" movement (Ideological and Cultural Revolution) apparently was not so extensive as had been suggested in the APL theoretical journal, *Rruga e Partisë* (March 1969), which put the membership in early 1969 at about 50,000.

In accordance with the desire of the Albanian leadership to infuse the party with "new blood" and help bridge the "generation gap," the APL conducted a massive recruiting drive during 1969-71. A special effort was made to increase representation of women, young persons, workers, and peasants. Reportedly, more women were admitted during 1967-71 than in the period from 1941 through 1966. In 1971, women comprised 22.05 per cent of the membership. In social composition, laborers accounted for 36.4 per cent; peasants, 29.7 per cent; and white collar workers, 33.9 per cent. (*Zëri i Popullit*, 4 November.) This was the first time that laborers were the largest group. It is expected that their percentage will continue to rise during the 1970s.

Organization and Leadership. The APL's Sixth Congress, on 1-7 November 1971, produced no major changes in party leadership. Enver Hoxha, the leader of the party since its founding, was reelected first secretary. The only noteworthy change occurred at the Central Committee plenum on 25-26 January, when Politburo member Haki Toska replaced Deputy Premier Xhafer Spahiu as a secretary of the Central Committee (Tirana radio, 27 January). Spahiu, who was elected to the Secretariat at the Fifth Congress, had succeeded Toska as a deputy premier in November 1970. Spahiu's election to Politburo candidate membership at the Sixth Congress seemed to indicate that this shift within the leadership had administrative rather than political overtones.

The Congress reelected all incumbents in the Politburo, which in November 1971 consisted of thirteen full members: Abdyl Këllezi, Adil Çarçani, Beqir Balluku, Enver Hoxha, Haki Toska, Hysni Kapo, Kadri Hazbiu, Koço Theodosi, Manush Myftiu, Mehmet Shehu, Ramiz Alia, Rita Marko, Spiro Koleka; and four candidates: Petrit Dume, Pilo Peristeri, Pirro Dodbiba, and Xhafer Spahiu. Three candidates—Këllezi (chairman, State Planning Commission), Hazbiu (Interior minister), and Theodosi (Industry and Mining minister)—were promoted to full membership. Agriculture minister Dodbiba and Deputy Premier Spahiu were elected candidates. (*Zëri i Popullit*, 8 November.) Dodbiba's appointment came as a surprise after the poor agricultural performance during the Fourth Five-Year Plan (1966-70).

Reflecting the increase in party membership, the Central Committee was expanded from 97 to 110 members (71 full members and 39 candidates. It is noteworthy that 58 of the 61 full members elected at the Fifth Congress were reelected. Eleven candidates were promoted to full membership. Only two of the new members lacked previous experience in the party's central organs. Of the 39 candidates, 16 were holdovers and 23 were newcomers. Women comprised 30.8 per cent of the new candidates but only 15.4 per cent of the total membership of the Central Committee. (*Ibid.*)

The composition of the Secretariat remained unchanged, with Hoxha as first secretary and Toska, Kapo, and Alia as secretaries. Membership of the Central Control and Auditing Commission increased from 17 to 21, and Ibrahim Sina was reelected chairman. (*Ibid.*)

Among the most remarkable characteristics of the top leadership during the past decade have been its stability and cohesiveness. No Politburo member has been dropped since 1960, and there have been relatively few dismissals from the Central Committee. This situation is in marked contrast to that in the lower- and middle-level party organs, where extensive leadership changes have occurred, especially since 1966, in connection with the "revolutionization" movement and Hoxha's calls for a "rejuvenation" and "proletarianization" of party cadres.

The Ideological and Cultural Revolution ("Revolutionization" Movement). Enver Hoxha devoted a major part of his report at the Sixth Congress to analysis of the goals and achievements of the "revolutionization" movement initiated in 1966. In general, he was pleased with the results:

> The great process of comprehensive revolutionization which has taken place in our country, particularly following the Fifth Congress, has further strengthened the position of socialism in Albania, has encouraged the militant spirit and revived the entire life and creativity of the party, and has given an unprecedented impulse to the creative initiative of the masses and to the rapid development of the people's economy and culture. (*Zëri i Popullit*, 2 November 1971.)

At the same time, Hoxha called upon the Albanian people for greater efforts to eliminate problems which threatened success of the "revolutionization" program.

One of the chief sources of concern to the APL leadership was the attitude and behavior of a "small segment" of young people who had come under the "harmful influences" of foreign films and radio and television broadcasts. Their "mod" clothes, long hair, vulgar language, boorish deportment, and petty vandalism had reached a point where the party felt constrained to address itself to the problem (*ibid.*, 28 April; *Rruga e Partisë*, August), which the leadership, during 1971, sought to deal with in a constructive and moderate manner. Musicians were encouraged to compose more "rhythmic" songs, youth preferences given greater consideration in radio programing, popular music festivals encouraged, and more state-subsidized vacations for students authorized. A major share of responsibility for criticism and reeducation of "misguided" elements among the young generation was delegated to the Union of Albanian Working Youth (see *Zëri i Rinisë*, 9 June; *Zëri i Popullit*, 20 November). Mindful of the "counterrevolutionary" and "bourgeois" attitudes that emerged among the young in Eastern Europe and the Soviet Union during the 1950s and 1960s, the APL seems prepared to take the necessary steps to ensure the "ideological purity" of the younger generation in Albania, where 42 per cent of the population is under fourteen years of age.

While hailing the country's progress, Hoxha told the Sixth Congress that there were still problems to be overcome. These involve such aspects of the "revolutionization" movement as emancipation of women, "workers' control," eradication of religious and other "feudal-bourgeois" influences, and the campaign against bureaucratism (*Zëri i Popullit*, 2 November).

Concern for the material and moral welfare of the individual ("socialist humanism") was the major theme of the Central Committee plenum on 25-26 January. The plenum instructed the government to upgrade medical services in rural areas and improve working conditions in factories and on farms, condemned voluntary abortions (which apparently have increased markedly because of the women's emancipation movement), and urged economic enterprises to take appropriate steps to prevent pollution of rivers and streams (*Rruga e Partisë*, February).

During 1971 the APL strongly emphasized the concept of "people's war." Beqir Balluku, deputy premier and People's Defense Minister, made major policy statements on this matter at the Central Committee plenum on 29 June-1 July and at the Sixth Congress. In his congress address Balluku noted that Albania had embraced the doctrine of "people's war" during the 1960s. The major elements in this doctrine, he said, were "the organization of the people's armed forces and the arming and training of the entire population without exception, under the absolute guidance of the party" (*Zëri i Popullit*, 3 November). Premier Mehmet Shehu had earlier sought to justify this policy:

> Under the actual conditions in which Albania is living, working, and building socialism, [with] the country strategically surrounded by imperialist and revisionist enemies, the military training of the youth and of all the people becomes absolutely necessary. (*Zëri i Rinisë*, 19 December 1970.)

Economy. According to official reports on the Fourth Five-Year Plan (1966-70), industrial production in 1970 was 83 per cent greater than in 1965, substantially above the 50 to 54 per cent planned increase. Agricultural output in 1970 was 33 per cent higher than in 1965—less than half the 71 to 76 per cent projected growth. National income rose by 55 per cent between 1965 and 1970, exceeding the 45 to 50 per cent increase foreseen by the plan. (*Zëri i Popullit*, 5 November.)

The Fifth Five-Year Plan (1971-75) established equally ambitious goals for the Albanian economy. Industrial production in 1975 is expected to be 61 to 66 per cent above the 1970 level. The projected increase in agricultural output for the period is 65 to 69 per cent, and national income is expected to rise by 55 to 60 per cent. (*Ibid.*)

According to the plan, heavy industry will grow at twice the rate of light industry between 1971 and 1975. Approximately 66 per cent of the investment fund is earmarked for industrial development, while only 12 per cent has been allocated to agriculture. The plan stipulates that 80 per cent of the growth in farm output will result from increased labor productivity. (*Ibid.*) Given the low morale of the peasants, the shortage of trained cadres in the countryside, insufficient mechanization, administrative shortcomings, the resistance of the peasants to modern techniques, and other problems (see, e.g., *ibid.*, 20 April), it would be surprising if agricultural goals were realized.

To help combat peasant apathy, a system of state-subsidized social security, including pensions and workers' compensation for collective farm members, was established in October 1971. In addition, the debt incurred by collective farms for rural electrification was canceled. (Tirana radio, 21 October.)

Albania's first computer center, which will be involved with economic planning, was inaugurated in November (*Bashkimi*, 3 November). The Vau i Dejes ("Mao Tse-tung") hydroelectric plant on the Drin River began operations in October (Tirana radio, 28 October). With an installed capacity of approximately 200,000 kw, this plant will double Albania's previous power-generating capacity. Work began on the Fierza hydroelectric station, with planned capacity twice that of the Vau i Dejes plant, and on the Elbasan metallurgical complex, which is to include the country's first steel mill (*ibid.*, 16 and 28 October).

Political Developments. At the Sixth Congress, Hoxha announced that the Albanian constitution, in force since 1950, will be superseded. Haxhi Lleshi, the head of state, explained:

> Since the proclamation of the constitution, as a result of the country's transition through the stages of reconstruction and the construction of the economic basis of socialism into the stage of the complete construction of socialist society, profound revolutionary changes have occurred. These changes were particularly great following the construction of the economic basis of socialism, especially after the party's Fifth Congress. As a consequence, many of the laws approved during this time are more advanced than the constitution itself. (*Zëri i Popullit*, 4 November 1971.)

The drive to decentralize political and economic administration continued to encounter opposition from the central bureaucracy. Some of the most serious resistance to this movement during 1971 came from the Industry and Mining, Education and Culture, Construction, and Agriculture ministries (*ibid.*, 28 July). The APL leadership, however, made it clear that it had no intention of retreating on this issue (*ibid.*, 2 and 27 November).

Foreign Relations. Albania during 1971 established diplomatic relations with Greece (Tirana radio, 6 May), Iran (*ibid.*, 24 May), Norway (*ibid.*, 29 May), Chile (*ibid.*, 12 September), and Peru (*ibid.*, 15 December), and raised its representation to embassy level with Yugoslavia (*ibid.*, 5 February) and Ethiopia (*ibid.*, 10 February). At year end, Albania maintained diplomatic ties with 53 countries.

Albanian-Chinese Relations. Despite the Chinese decision to invite U.S. President Nixon to Peking, the absence of a Chinese Communist Party (CCP) delegation at the APL's Sixth Congress, and political infighting among Chinese leaders, there was no evidence of any serious strain in Sino-Albanian relations during 1971.

Albanian-Chinese exchanges continued at a high level throughout the year. The most important Chinese delegation to visit Albania was headed by Li Te-sheng, candidate member of the CCP Politburo and director of the Political Department in the People's Liberation Army. During his sojourn, 15-22 August, Li repeatedly and with great vigor in his public statements (Tirana radio, 16-22 August) condemned "U.S. imperialism" and "Soviet revisionist social-imperialism." Coming a month after the Chinese invitation to Nixon, and at a time when the Soviet Union through its East European allies (*New York Times*, 14 August) had issued warnings concerning the dangers inherent in the formation of a pro-Chinese "bloc" in the Balkans, the Li visit probably was intended to reassure the Albanians. Either by design or coincidence, Agriculture Minister Pirro Dodbiba, the highest-ranking Albanian visitor to China in 1971, spent the month of August there (NCNA, 1 and 30 August).

China's failure to send a delegation to the APL's Sixth Congress was apparently due to a 1969 CCP policy decision to stop sending delegations to congresses and conferences of foreign communist parties. There is no evidence of intention to snub Tirana. On the contrary, the Chinese leadership reaffirmed its solidarity with the Albanians. The CCP Central Committee sent two warm messages of greeting and support to the Sixth Congress (*Zëri i Popullit*, 3 and 9 November), published the full text of Hoxha's report (NCNA, 9 November), organized several meetings to honor the congress and the thirtieth anniversary of the APL (*ibid.*, 8 and 9 November), authorized publication of a Chinese translation of the official history of the APL (*ibid.*, 7 November), and issued a set of postage stamps to commemorate the APL anniversary (*ibid.*)

For their part APL leaders lavishly praised the Chinese for economic and technical aid provided to Albania "in the true spirit of proletarian internationalism" and declared that Sino-Albanian friendship and cooperation remained the cornerstone of Albania's foreign policy (e.g., *ibid.*, 2 and 5 November).

Sino-Albanian cooperation continued throughout the year. Albania played a major role in the campaign that led to replacement in October of the Republic of China by the People's Republic of China in the United Nations. China and Albania manifested common policies toward the Vietnam war, "U.S. imperialism," the India-Pakistan War, "Soviet revisionist social-imperialism," and "national liberation movements" (*ibid.*; NCNA, 8 November). Reportedly, Albania was provided with Chinese-manufactured MIG-21 aircraft (*Washington Post*, 2 March).

Albanian-Soviet Relations. During 1971, relations between Albania and the Soviet Union continued to be strained. In January an editorial in the APL newspaper asserted that, since the Soviet Union had become a "capitalist-imperialist power," the struggle against the Soviets must be escalated from the ideological to the political-diplomatic level (*Zëri i Popullit*, 5 January). The Soviet Union, however, continued to make conciliatory gestures (e.g., *Pravda*, 11 January). In his report to the Twenty-fourth Congress of the Communist Party of the Soviet Union (CPSU), General Secretary Leonid Brezhnev declared: "As far as Albania is concerned, we continue to be ready to restore normal relations with that country. This would be useful for both our countries and for the common interests of the socialist states." (*Ibid.*, 31 March.) The APL rejected Brezhnev's overture in a lengthy and bitter commentary on the CPSU congress (*Zëri i Popullit*, 17 April). Besides rejecting a rapprochement on the state and party levels, Albania condemned the attacks which Brezhnev and others had made against China and the "Marxist-Leninist" movement at the congress. Hoxha reiterated his position on normalization of Albanian-Soviet relations at the APL's Sixth Congress:

> Of late the Soviet leaders have pretended to want to "normalize" relations with our country. This is nothing but demagoguery.... We shall not allow ourselves to be intimidated by their saber rattling or deceived by the olive branch they wave. They have great political, ideological, and economic debts to repay Albania. There can be normalization only when the Soviet peoples and true Bolsheviks intervene to establish Marxist-Leninist revolutionary justice in respect to these questions. (*Ibid.*, 2 November.)

A similar rancor was displayed by the refusal of the Albanian-Soviet Friendship Society to accept a congratulatory message from its Soviet counterpart on the occasion of Albania's national holiday (Moscow radio, 30 November). For the most part, this bitterness stemmed from the Albanian fear that the Soviet Union might take drastic action to thwart the growing Chinese influence in the Balkans.

Albanian-Greek Relations. Resumption of Albanian-Greek diplomatic ties in May ended the technical state of war that had existed between the two countries since 1940, and represented another important move by Albania to strengthen its relations with the Balkan states. This development had been foreshadowed in 1970 by the conclusion of a trade agreement (February) and the reestablishment of telecommunications links (November). Spokesmen for both governments expressed an interest in further expanding their relations (*Zëri i Popullit*, 14 May 1971; *Eleutheros Kosmos*, Athens, 15 August). A major irritant was removed when the Greek undersecretary of state for foreign affairs indicated that his country had given up its claim to Northern Epirus, the 1900-square-mile region in southern Albania which contains a very small Greek minority (*New York Times*, 14

November). The flight to Corfu and request for asylum in Greece by 33 Albanian fishermen (*ibid.*, 10 August) apparently had no serious impact on Albanian-Greek relations.

Relations with Eastern Europe. Albania and Yugoslavia upgraded their diplomatic representation to ambassadorial level in February 1971. After this promising development, prospects for further normalization were somewhat clouded by Hoxha's stinging attack on the Yugoslav self-management system (*Zëri i Popullit*, 2 November) and by the growth of nationalist and separatist sentiment among the Albanians in Yugoslavia's Kosovo region (*East Europe*, October; Tanyug, Yugoslav news agency, 21 and 22 December). While Albanian-Yugoslav cultural contacts increased, these mainly involved the Kosovo Albanians. Albanian-Yugoslav trade in 1971 was scheduled to rise by 60 per cent over the 1970 level, and confidence was expressed in Belgrade that volume was capable of further growth (Tanyug, 18 April).

The Yugoslavs were surprised by Hoxha's condemnation of their self-management system. Although probably intended to underscore the ideological differences between the two countries and to discourage any attempt to steer the Albanian workers' control movement in the direction of the Yugoslav system, the attack provoked an angry retort (*ibid.*, 4 November). Both states moved to alleviate the situation (*ibid.*, 10 and 11 November; Tirana radio, 27, 28 November), but relations remained complicated by the emergence of "Albanian separatist nationalism" in Kosovo (Tanyug, 22 December) and the developing separatist sentiment in other areas of Yugoslavia (*Washington Post*, 17 December).

Albanian-Bulgarian relations, suspended since July 1968, were quietly resumed on the chargé d'affaires level in 1971. This left Bulgaria as the only Balkan state with which Albania did not exchange ambassadors. Bulgarian party leader Todor Zhivkov in a speech at the Tenth Congress of the Bulgarian Communist Party described the Albanian leadership as "bogged down in a quagmire of opportunism and anti-Sovietism" (BTA, Bulgarian news agency, 20 April) but also stated that his country would "continue to make efforts to normalize and improve relations" with Albania.

Only Romania among Warsaw Pact member states has maintained cordial relations with Albania. These ties are primarily cultural. Most probably at the behest of the CPSU, the Romanian Communist Party—which alone among the East European ruling parties had sent a delegation to the Fifth Congress of the APL—was not represented at the Sixth Congress of the Albanian party. Commenting on the third anniversary of the Soviet-led invasion of Czechoslovakia, an Albanian broadcast alleged that the Czechoslovaks had made known their feelings by refusing to participate in Soviet-Czechoslovak friendship organizations and displaying "negative reactions" at sports events and other public gatherings (Tirana radio, 20 August). Albania's ties with Poland, Hungary, and East Germany during 1971 remained limited.

Relations with Western Europe and the United States. Most countries of Western Europe—especially Austria, France, and Italy—continued to improve their relations with Albania in 1971. These contacts, however, are primarily cultural. An important role in promoting relations with Western Europe is played by friendship societies which Albania has established in the countries with which it has ties. The societies sponsor exhibits of Albanian art and crafts, showings of Albanian films, and lectures dealing with Albanian history and culture.

Albania also has shown interest in expanding its commercial ties with Western Europe. It has begun to participate in many of the major trade fairs and international expositions and to invite West European businessmen to visit Albania. Prospects for an appreciable increase in trade remain dim for the present, owing both to the quantity and quality of goods available for export and the Albanian desire to avoid large trade deficits (*Die Presse*, Vienna, 8 July).

Since 1969 tourism has been encouraged. It is estimated that some 10,000 tourists, mostly West Europeans, visited Albania in 1970 (*ibid.*) There probably will not be any rapid growth of tourism in the near future, since hotel space and other tourist facilities are still scarce (*New York Times*, 31 January 1971; *Christian Science Monitor*, 31 August).

Albania has taken steps to improve its relations with Western Europe, but does not seem to be interested in a rapprochement with the United States. The press was especially harsh in its criticism of the U.S. role in the Vietnam war (e.g., *Zëri i Popullit*, 4 February and 2 November). Hoxha branded "U.S. imperialism" as the "chief enemy of all peoples" and the "biggest oppressor and exploiter of other countries" (*ibid.*, 2 November). While it appears that Albania is not following China's lead in formulating its policy toward the United States, a significant thaw in Sino-American relations could result in a modification of Albania's hard-line stance. Unclassified scientific data has been made available by the United States to Albania and other communist-ruled states, with which it has no diplomatic ties (*Washington Post*, 27 January).

International Communist Movement. During 1971 six ruling communist parties—the Soviet, Bulgarian, Czechoslovak, Mongolian, East German, and Polish—held congresses. The APL apparently was not invited to any of these gatherings. Albania's status in the world communist movement was even more pointedly demonstrated when only one ruling party, the North Vietnamese, sent a delegation to the APL's Sixth Congress. Its presence was probably due to the desire to preserve the communist united front in the Indo-china War.

The Sixth Congress provided a forum for the "Marxist-Leninist parties and forces" and also an opportunity to ascertain the support Albania enjoyed within the communist movement (*Zëri i Popullit*, 1-9 November). In addition to the North Vietnamese, representatives were present from the National Liberation Front of South Vietnam; the communist parties of New Zealand, Indonesia ("Delegation of the PKI Central Committee"), Malaya, and Sudan (Revolutionary Command Council); the Albania-based "Communist Party of Poland"; and "Marxist-Leninist" and pro-Chinese parties or groups in Argentina, Australia, Austria, Belgium, Brazil, Ceylon, Chile, Denmark, Ecuador, France, Great Britain, Italy, Japan, Netherlands, Norway, Peru, Spain, Sweden, and West Germany.

Greetings or messages of solidarity were sent to the congress by the Chinese Communist Party, the Communist Party of Thailand, the Communist Party of Burma, and various "Marxist-Leninist" and pro-Chinese groupings in Czechoslovakia, the Dominican Republic, Finland, Honduras, Iran, Iraq, the Malagasy Republic, San Marino, Switzerland, and Uruguay.

Publications. The APL central organ prints a daily, *Zëri i Popullit*, and a monthly theoretical journal, *Rruga e Partisë*. Another major publication is *Bashkimi*, the daily organ of the Democratic Front. The Union of Albanian Working Youth publishes *Zëri i Rinisë* twice weekly.

Western Illinois University   Nicholas C. Pano

Bulgaria

The Bulgarian Communist Party (Bulgarska Komunisticheska Partiya; BCP), which assumed the name "BCP (Narrow Socialists)" in 1919, dates its origin from 1891 when the Bulgarian Social Democratic Party was formed. In 1903, a faction split off in a conflict over the "narrow" versus "broad" interpretation of Marxism. Since 1891 the party has also had the designations "Bulgarian Workers' Social Democratic Party," 1894-1903; "BWSDP (Narrow Socialists)," 1903-19; "BCP (Narrow Socialists," 1919-38; "Workers' Party," 1938-44; and "Bulgarian Workers' Party (Communists)," 1944-1948. The Workers' Party, formed in 1927 as a front for the BCP, was outlawed between 1924 and 1944. The BCP dates its transition to Leninism and "bolshevization" from the 1917 revolution in Russia.

A negligible organzation of 1,923 members in 1912, the BCP became Bulgaria's second-largest party by 1920 as a result of the debacles the country had suffered in the Balkan wars and World War I. Under the regime of the largest party, the Bulgarian Agrarian People's Union (Bulgarski Zemedelski Naroden Suyuz), the BCP took the position that the Union represented the "rural bourgeoisie," and fought it as implacably as it did the urban parties. In the rightist coup détat against the peasant government of June 1923, the BCP decided on a course of "neutrality" but was quickly reversed by the Comintern and ordered to stage an uprising in cooperation with the Union's left wing. The abortive insurrection of September 1923 resulted in decimation of BCP cadres throughout the country and flight of its leading functionaries (Vasil Kolarov, Georgi Dimitrov, et al.) to the Soviet Union. During the underground period it recovered some strength and by 1942, under Dimitrov's guidance from Moscow, it joined the left wing of the Agrarian Union, "Broad" Socialists, and other groups in forming the so-called Fatherland Front (Otechestven Front; FF) coalition as a vehicle for seizing power. This occurred on 9 September 1944, mainly because of the Soviet declaration of war against Bulgaria only four days earlier and the arrival of the Red Army. The coalition began to break up almost immediately over BCP policies aimed at monopoly rule. By 1948 only one other party, a fragment of the Agrarian Union under leaders subservient to the BCP, still survived. Since then the FF has been retained by the BCP as an umbrella organization over the Agrarian Union (120,000 members), the Dimitrov Communist Youth Union (Dimitrovski Komunisticheski Mladezhki Suyuz, with 1,161,000 members), the central body for the trade unions, and other mass organizations.

The main events during 1971 included the Tenth BCP Congress (20-25 April), which produced a new program and changes in statutes, elected a Central Committee, adopted "Directives on the Socio-Economic Development of the People's Republic of Bulgaria during the Sixth Five-Year Plan (1971-75)," and approved the draft of the new Bulgarian constitution. Adoption of the constitution by popular referendum (16 May) was followed by national and local elections (27 June). In numerical strength, BCP membership was 699,476 (*Rabotnichesko Delo*, 21 April) representing an increase of more than 88,000 from the Ninth Congress, in November 1966, and some eight per cent of the country's population (about 8.6 million in 1971). In social composition, 40.1 per cent of BCP members were blue-collar workers, 28.1 per cent white-collar workers, and 26.1 peasants. Also announced at the Tenth Congress was the policy to admit more persons under thirty years of age; almost 75 per cent of those admitted since 1966 were said to be young people, primarily Communist Youth Union members.

In the National Assembly, the BCP controls 287 deputies (including 21 affiliated with the Communist Youth Union) out of 400 as established by the new constitution. The remainder comprise 100 Agrarians and 13 "not affiliated with any party." (For names and affiliations see *ibid.*, 8 June.) Elections were conducted with one candidate for each electoral district. In local councils, the BCP secured 37,777 seats (out of 53,665), the remainder going to Agrarians (10,637) and those with no party affiliation (5,251). The vote for official candidates reportedly came to 99 per cent of the total.

Leadership and Organization. In 1971 the BCP top leadership remained essentially unchanged. Todor Zhivkov, first secretary since 1954, was reelected by the Tenth Congress, as was also the Politburo consisting of himself, Stanko Todorov, Boris Velchev, Boian Bulgaranov, Zhivko Zhivkov (not related to Todor), Ivan Mikhailov, Ivan Popov, Pencho Kubadinski, Tano Tsolov, Todor Pavlov, and Tsola Dragoicheva. Some changes came at the next level: Luchezar Avramov, candidate Politburo member, was dropped from all party and government posts; Venelin Kotsev, a Central Committee secretary under Todor Zhivkov, became a new candidate Politburo member (the other continuing candidates were Angel Tsanev, Ivan Abadzhiev, Kostadin Giaurov, Krustiu Trichkov, and Peko Takov); Abadzhiev was also named a secretary under Zhivkov (the other continuing secretaries are Boris Velchev, Stanko Todorov, Venelin Kotsev, and Ivan Prumov); Peniu Kiratsev, a Central Committee member, was added to the secretaries; Roza Koritarova was dropped from the secretariat (the other two continuing members were Vladimir Bonev and Georgi Bokov). On 7 July Todor Zhivkov assumed the chairmanship of the new State Council created by the constitution, retaining the post of BCP first secretary, while Stanko Todorov became premier (a post held by Zhivkov since 1962) and relinquished the functions of party secretary. On 6 July Georgi (Grisha) Filipov, a Central Committee member, was named a party secretary.

Organizationally, the BCP consisted of the above-named top bodies, the Central Committee of 147 members (up from 137) and 110 candidate members (87 before) (names in *Rabotnichesko Delo*, 26 April), the 107-member Central Control and Audit Commission (with Stoian Karadzhov reelected chairman), and some 24,000 primary and other local organizations. According to BCP statutes, its "reserve" is the Communist Youth Union, described as the "first helpmate in its work toward the communist upbringing of the young generation" and operating "under the direction of the BCP." The Union's first secretary is Encho Moskov (born in 1941, a party secretary in Iambol), who replaced Ivan Panev (*ibid.*, 4 December).

Party Internal Affairs. The opening months of 1971 were highlighted by the preparations for the Tenth Congress of the BCP. Originally scheduled to begin eight days earlier, the congress was postponed to 20 April "to allow more time for discussion of the draft program" and other documents (*Rabotnichesko Delo*, 27 March). The real reason for postponement, however, undoubtedly was to provide time after the conclusion of the Twenty-fourth Congress of the Communist Party of the Soviet Union (CPSU), (on 30 March-9 April), for Bulgarian leaders to return from Moscow. hold a Central Committee meeting on 13 April, and, if necessary, revise plans and documents for their own congress in the light of decisions at the CPSU congress. The BCP Ninth Congress in 1966 had similarly been scheduled after the CPSU Twenty-Third Congress, and the BCP then lengthened the interval between congresses from four to five years as the CPSU had done.

The Tenth Congress was attended by 1,553 delegates and representatives from 89 communist, socialist, and other left-wing parties or revolutionary movements. Top billing among the foreign delegations, of course, went to that of the CPSU, consisting of party head Leonid Brezhnev, who stayed from 19 to 25 April; Vladimir Shcherbitski, Politburo member and Ukrainian premier, two lesser CPSU functionaries, and Soviet ambassador Aleksandr Puzanov. Notably absent among the foreign party representatives were the Yugoslav communists, who sent only an observer, and the Chinese communists, who ignored the congress altogether. However, both the North Vietnamese party and the National Liberation Front of South Vietnam were represented. Among the BCP delegates, the party organization in Sofia was represented by the largest number (245), followed by Plovdiv (127), Varna (75), and Burgas (72). Women present totaled 373 or 24 per cent. Delegates having higher education were 939 or 60.3 per cent. Including those with more than elementary education, the percentage was 85.3. In age distribution, 169 delegates were under 30 years, some 350 from 30 to 40, another 669 from 41 to 50, a total of 263 from 51 to 60, and 107 over 60. (*Ibid.*, 22 April.)

The congress had a five-point agenda: Central Committee accountability report, Central Control and Audit Commission report, adoption of the new party program, approval of directives for the country's socio-economic development in 1971-75, and election of new leading party bodies. The congress also heard addresses from many foreign representatives.

The Central Committee's accountability report, read by Todor Zhivkov, dealt in seven segments with the international situation and the tasks of the party and the state in the area of foreign policy; efforts of the party to build the "material and technological foundations of socialism" and to intensify economic processes; development of science, education, and artistic culture; the improvement of administration over society and expansion of "socialist democracy;" "care for man" as the party's "basic concern"; expansion of the party's role as leading and directing force; and the new party program. (*Ibid.*)

In his analysis of the international situation, Zhivkov predictably found capitalism in a deepening general crisis and socialism winning the global conflict through the operation of "the three mighty currents of the revolutionary process at present," namely, the world socialist system, the international working class, and the national liberation movements. Also predictably, Zhivkov reaffirmed his fidelity to the Soviet Union, "the Red giant standing tall on one-sixth of the earth, strong, peace-loving, fraternally generous, and ready to come to the assistance of any nation fighting for its freedom and independence." Since the Ninth Congress, Zhivkov said, Czechoslovakia came close to being taken out of the world socialist system by "anti-socialist and right-wing revisionist forces" in the country, but the "internationalist assistance" which the U.S.S.R., Bulgaria, and other socialist countries sent had saved Czechoslovakia for "our fraternal family."

In regard to the country's economy, Zhivkov declared that "the most important" indexes of the 1966-1970 plan were fulfilled and that the total industrial production had risen 67 per cent over 1965, with the result that the ratio between industrial and agricultural production had changed from 74:26 to 80:20. He admitted that production had fallen short of the plan targets in pig iron, steel, rolled iron, steel pipes, chemical fertilizers, paper, artificial fibers, cement, trucks, meat, and other commodities. In March, Luchezar Avramov also indicated that production in industry and agriculture had fallen short by 300 and 1,400 million leva, respectively.

In the field of science, education, and culture Zhivkov stressed the importance of expanding scientific research and development programs and the number of scholars engaged in research (about 13,000 in 1971). The percentage of the national income invested in them during 1969 was 1.8 (0.5 in 1960). In the area of the social sciences he found that there had been success in overcoming "one of the most important weaknesses," namely "schematicism and a superficial attitude to facts and phenomena," and noted the resurrection of sociology. In education, the task ahead was to continue reforms to make the country's high schools "polytechnical" and open them to 85 per cent of young people by 1975. In regard to literature and the arts, Zhivkov hinted at problems in the relations between the State Committee for Art and Culture and the creative unions of writers, artists, and others. He stressed that the committee must, as a state organ, make all essential decisions on the cultural front. He also emphasized that "active, principled, and militant" criticism was needed to apply the "class and party yardstick" to literature and the arts.

The passages Zhivkov devoted to improvement of administration over society and expansion of "socialist democracy" were vague and repetitious of earlier formulations. Also general and quite brief were references to the proposed new constitution, presumably because it was not a strictly BCP affair. On the other hand, the "care for man," a topic recently emphasized in BCP propaganda, drew much comment, some of it from the draft directives for the sixth Five-Year Plan. The minimum monthly wage of 60 leva (just over 30 dollars) established by the fifth Five-Year Plan will be increased, so as to bridge the gap between urban and much lower rural wages. Personal income will continue to be determined mainly by the socialist principle "from each according to his ability, to each according to his work."

Zhivkov gave much more attention to "further elevation of the party's role as leading and directing force." He stressed that the Central Committee, in guiding party and state, made collective decisions. Twenty-six plenums and 12 national conferences had been held with party and government functionaries since 1966. In attracting new blood, Zhivkov said that BCP should "resolutely free itself of members who lack or have lost the qualities of communists, demonstrate ideological confusion, allow anti-party actions to occur, or seek personal gain through membership in the party." The BCP should use sociological and other studies to assess its own processes and those of society. Such studies have suffered from "old methods and faddist preoccupations" in scientific form as well as "primitivism and cliché approaches." The study of problems in party work, which lags behind the other social sciences, must be placed on a broader foundation. BCP ideological activity should address itself not only to combating ideological laxity in the country, bourgeois propaganda from abroad, and divisive work by right and left opportunists, but to curbing negative aspects of "our current reality" such as egoism, heartlessness, bureaucratism, conceit, favoritism, stealing, and misuse of public funds for private gain.

In regard to changes in the BCP statute, Zhivkov proposed dropping the statement on the party's main tasks since they were detailed in the new BCP program. Between party congresses, the Central Committee "makes concrete and develops their decisions" and confirms (rather than appoints, as previously) editorial boards of the central press. He proposed a period between congresses to coincide with five-year economic plans and precede national elections; improving BCP structure in factories with more than 800 communists and in the largest villages. Zhivkov explained that it was high time the party adopted a new program since it operated on the basis of a "Programmatic Declaration" from 1919, decisions of the Fifth Congress in 1948, and Central Committee plenum of April 1956. All these had long been implemented. Needed was a program for building an advanced socialist society, showing future directions for development. In drafting it, he acknowledged, the 1961 CPSU program had been of "enormous help." His report and the BCP program was unanimously approved by the congress.

A lengthy document, the program consists of an introduction and five chapters dealing with the transition from capitalism to socialism, the victory of socialism in Bulgaria, building of an advanced socialist society, the leading role of the party in that stage, and communism as the "end goal." (For text see *ibid.*, 29 April.) The introduction and first two chapters review the BCP past and analyze relations between imperialism and socialism as a "struggle without mercy, without pity, in which the question 'who—whom?' on a global scale shall be decided in favor of socialism." In the socialist camp, revisionists and renegades are said to be distorting basic Marxist-Leninist principles, denying the leading role of the working class, reducing or rejecting the leading role of the party, and sowing "social democratic illusions" to disarm the party in the face of "a class enemy armed to the teeth." In the imperialist camp, the tendency toward left opportunism concealed in "ultra-revolutionary phraseology" allegedly creates the danger of pushing the masses into adventures, without a "sober, strictly objective Marxist-Leninist assessment of all class forces in a given country and on a global scale." It separates the party from the proletariat. Both tendencies have as their common feature nationalism, which becomes especially malignant and dangerous if it infects ruling communist parties. After citing Georgi Dimitrov's dictum that the touchstone of proletarian internationalism is the attitude toward the CPSU and the Soviet Union, the program declares that the U.S.S.R. has the most powerful and advanced economy. Hence, it is "the decisive force for the growth of socialism as a global system." The BCP "prime responsibility and daily task" remains cultivation of fraternal ties with the CPSU and friendship with the peoples of the Soviet Union.

The third and longest chapter outlines building of an advanced or mature socialist society as "the main immediate historic task of the BCP." An advanced socialist society is described as the highest and concluding stage in the development of socialism, as the first phase of communism. In that stage, socialism becomes the leader in the scientific and technological revolution and achieves a leap in the development of forces of production through mechanization, automation, optimal concentration and specialization of production and administration, and increasing integration with the other socialist countries. Agriculture becomes increasingly transformed into a variety of industrial work. State and cooperative forms merge into a single ownership by all the people. The growing needs of individuals continue to be satisfied on the basis of the socialist principle "From each according to his ability, to each according to his work." Dictatorship of the proletariat grows into a state of all the people, self-government receives wide application, and socialist democracy reaches its height. The role and importance of the BCP, as leading and directing force, grows even further as it becomes the vanguard of the people and the party of all. Under BCP leadership, the advanced socialist society is built "under the banner of proletarian internationalism, in implacable struggle against any and all manifestations of nationalism, anti-Sovietism, and 'left' or right opportunism."

According to the program, BCP tasks in the economy at this stage are to complete the material-technical basis for socialism and continue intensification of the economy by the fullest use of the latest achievements from the scientific-technological revolution. These will include broader mechanization and automation, electrification, application of chemistry, concentration and specialization of production, integration of science with production, optimalization in territorial location of productive forces, and improvement of inter-branch and intra-branch structure throughout the economy. In regard to structure of society, the party will remove gradually intra-class and inter-class differences to establish social homogeneity. In the area of "forming the new man," the factor of personal material interest will preserve its fundamental importance. At the same time, the element of "spiritual interest" will be advanced by fostering socialist consciousness and socialist ethics. Of exceptional importance is inculcation of proletarian internationalism and socialist patriotism as well as the struggle against both nationalism and nihilism. In education, the unified labor-polytechnic secondary school is to become compulsory for all, providing general education as well as training in technology under the slogan "Study and work, work and study." In literature and art, socialist realism will prevail.

In government, the BCP will continue to apply democratic centralism as the "basic principle for administration over society." At the same time socialist democracy is to expand, among other ways, by gradual introduction of elections for public officials. The state will continue to hold its central place as "principal instrument" of the party and will increasingly turn into an agency of all the people, while retaining its basic "features and functions as a state of the dictatorship of the proletariat." Its strength as an organization will constantly grow, and coercion by the state will be maintained against all persons who turn to overt or covert forms of struggle against the socialist system. The Fatherland Front, the Communist Youth Union, the Bulgarian Agrarian People's Union, and the trade unions will develop along the established lines.

The fourth chapter on the leading role of the BCP stipulates that, while the party of the working class gradually becomes the vanguard of the entire people, it will continue to implement "a clearly expressed class policy of the proletariat." Its principles, aims, tasks, and approach are "consistently class-party ones." BCP importance in the coming stage will be marked by "still greater growth as the leading and directing force." Any rejection or underestimation of the party's leading role would inevitably result in "retreat from class-party positions, manifestations of anti-socialist frenzy, harm to the people's interests, threat of deformation of the socialist system, and restoration of capitalism."

The last and very brief chapter of the BCP program outlines communism as the end goal, to which building of an advanced socialist society is the prelude. In familiar phrases, communism is described as a classless social system in which conditions of economic plenty will make possible the application of the principle "From each according to his ability, to each according to his needs." Work, no longer a duty, becomes a natural and free expression of creative impulse for the good of society. Money and market disappear. Personal relations are free from materialism and are built on mutual love, friendship, and respect. Science is completely in the service of man and production. Society functions through self-government. Nations draw ever closer together until "complete merger in the future." Society passes "from the kingdom of necessity into the kingdom of freedom." Communism, this depiction of the millenium concludes, is "the beautiful future of all peoples."

The congress also adopted unanimously directives for the sixth Five-Year Plan (1971-75), based on the formulations in Zhivkov's report and the new BCP program (text, *ibid.*, 28 April). The main socioeconomic task of the plan is to secure a "fuller satisfaction of the growing material and spiritual needs of the people and raise socialist consciousness." A paraphrase from earlier plans, this task is to be accomplished by more of the same: fullest use of the scientific-technological revolution, accelerated industrialization, increased productivity of labor, rapid economic growth. Support of scientific research and development is to reach 2.5 to 3 per cent of national income. Industrial production will rise by 55 to 60 per cent, which in turn is to result primarily (70 to 80 per cent) from increased labor productivity. Production in the consumer industries will grow by 50 per cent, with special attention to overcoming shortages in "certain basic merchandise groups." Agricultural production should increase by 17 to 20 per cent, some 40 to 45 of this to be contributed by greater labor productivity. Institutions of higher education are to reach by 1975 an enrolment of 120,000 and graduate about 65,000 students. Finally, in regard to meeting consumer needs, a beginning is to be made "toward liquidation of the discrepancy" between purchasing power and "the merchandise stocks both in volume as well as in type." By 1975, per capita production will be (in kilograms) 55 of meat and meat products, 11 for fish, 37 of sugar and sugar products, 135 for vegetables; 159 eggs; some 4.7 square meters of wool cloth; about 2.2 pairs of shoes; half a refrigerator; and 0.14 automobiles per family. Communism, which requires abundance to apply the principle "To each according to his needs," will not be in sight at the end of the sixth Five-Year Plan.

Government Changes. The new constitution, approved by referendum of 16 May (text, *ibid.*, 9 May), was enacted, like the new BCP program to which the preamble refers, to fit the new stage of building an advanced socialist society. In 10 chapters and 143 articles, it stipulates that

Bulgaria is a "socialist state of the workers from town and village headed by the working class," that the "leading force in society and in the state is the BCP," and that "the BCP directs the building of an advanced socialist society in close fraternal cooperation with the Bulgarian Agrarian People's Union" (Article 1). The commitment to Soviet fidelity and the socialist camp, in effect acceptance of the "Brezhnev doctrine," is incorporated in the preamble and provisions that Bulgaria "belongs to the world socialist community." This tie "is one of the principal conditions for its independence and all-round development" (Art. 12), and the economy "develops as part of the world socialist economic system" (Art. 13).

The most important change in government structure is introduction of a State Council with functions similar to, but greater than, the superseded Presidium of the National Assembly. Elected by the National Assembly and operating continuously, the State Council "unites the making of decisions with their implementation" and links legislative activity with the executive (Art. 90). Twenty-two specified functions include scheduling elections, convoking the National Assembly, introducing legislation, interpreting laws, providing general direction for defense and security of the country, appointing and dismissing members of the State Committee on Defense and high-ranking officers of the armed forces, representing the country in foreign relations, ratifying and denouncing treaties, supervising the Council of Ministers, and exercising control over administration (Art. 93).

The National Assembly elected under the new constitution chose leader of the Agrarian Union Georgi Traikov as president and Central Committee member Roza Koritarova and non-party member Georgi Kulishev as vice-presidents. The State Council under Zhivkov comprises 22 members, including candidate Politburo member Krustiu Trichkov as first deputy chairman, Agrarian Union governing council member Georgi Andreev, candidate Politburo member Peko Takov, and Writers' Union president Georgi Dzhagarov as deputy chairmen; Central Committee member Mincho Minehev as secretary; and other BCP leaders (list, in *Rabotnichesko Delo*, 9 July). At the same time, a new Council of Ministers emerged with Politburo member Stanko Todorov as chairman; Politburo member Tano Tsolov and Agrarian Union governing council member Petur Tanchev as first deputy chairmen; Politburo members Pencho Kubadinski, Zhivko Zhivkov, Ivan Popov, as well as Central Committee members Sava Dulbokov and Mako Dakov as deputy chairmen; and 22 ministers and chairmen of state committees (list, *ibid.*). The above plus the finance minister, Dimitur Popov, and the minister of labor and social welfare, Misho Mishev (both Central Committee members) comprise a ten-man Bureau of the Council of Ministers, with power to make decisions on behalf of the parent body.

On this occasion, nine ministers were dropped (Luchezar Avramov had been replaced earlier as foreign trade minister by Ivan Nedev, when the BCP Congress relieved him of all posts). The most important of these changes involved replacement of internal affairs minister Angel Solakov by candidate Politburo member and lieutenant-general Angel Tsanev. No reasons were given until a plenum on 4-6 October went over a wide range of party and government affairs. It announced that Solakov had been dismissed from the Central Committee for "gross errors in style and methods of work, incompatible with party principles and party ethics" (*ibid.*, 7 October). No specific charges have been made to date against Solakov. In other personnel changes, Central Committee member and foreign affairs minister Ivan Bashev died on 13 December in a skiing accident and was succeeded by another Central Committee member and first secretary of the BCP district committee for Vidin, Petur Mladenov. In the Committee for Art and Culture, the party leader's daughter, Liudmila Zhivkova, was appointed a deputy chairman in late December.

The October plenum also announced that the Central Committee, henceforth, would be informed regularly about Politburo and Secretariat activity, which had not been done previously. The public also was promised information on "the more important decisions of the Politburo, State Council, and Council of Ministers." The plenum further decided, on a Politburo motion, to set up four

Central Committee commissions for party and state management, the economy, ideology, and international relations. It approved but did not reveal their membership and charged the Politburo with regulating their work. The plenum announced three future meetings over the next few months to discuss trade unions, agriculture, and the 1972 economic plan.

BCP Domestic Activity. The first four months of 1971 were spent in preparation for the Tenth Congress. The Politburo conducted meetings with key groups: representatives of the so-called creative intelligentsia (3 March), the Agrarian Union's governing council (18 March), "revolutionary cadres" (23 March), the Communist Youth League (26 March), and the "heroes of socialist labor" (13 April) in order to show democratic centralism in action on the eve of the congress. May and June were taken up with enactment of the new constitution, elections, and reorganization of top government agencies in structure and personnel. In July the Central Committee, Council of Ministers issued a joint decree on socioeconomic development for Sofia (text in *Rabotnichesko Delo*, 2 July). Next, the party celebrated its 80th anniversary (2 August); then came Zhivkov's 60th birthday (7 September); and the following month, it mourned the death of his wife (23 October).

The last months of the year saw an outburst of activity. The plenum of 4-6 October had discussed the question of "reorganization of the scientific front and higher education" and issued a lengthy outline of changes (text, *ibid.*, 10 October). The plan involves establishment of new centers for scientific research and development, stressing basic research and "unified centers for science and training of cadres" which combine research with education as well as expansion of scientific and educational facilities. An immediate result was elevation of the Teachers' College at Turnovo to the country's second university on 15 October. Another plenum one month later approved the economic plan and budget for 1972, enacted by the National Assembly in December. The same plenum issued a comprehensive decree on improving economic education of workers (text, *ibid.*, 18 November). The Central Committee issued another joint decree with the Council of Ministers on recycling of secondary raw materials, i.e., scrap and waste, which reflects the shortage of "primary" raw materials (text, *ibid.*, 21 November). The party's concern with problems among youth was emphasized by Zhivkov's appearance at the Communist Youth League's plenum (3 December), which approved personnel changes to enliven the organization beset by banality and political apathy. He also attended a Politburo meeting with university students in Sofia (7 December) on the eve of Student Day, interrupting a visit to Poland (see below).

The Central Committee sponsored establishment of a "Georgi Kirkov Society for Dissemination of Scientific Knowledge" at a conference held on 3-4 December and addressed by Georgi Bokov, editor in chief of *Rabotnichesko Delo* and president of the Journalists' Union. This society will carry on the ideological struggle against "Western imperialist centers of mass information and propaganda" and function as "a subsystem in the overall network uniting ideological institutions and organizations" throughout the country. The last major activity before year's end was a Politburo decision outlining improvement of programs for physical fitness, sports, and domestic tourism (text, *ibid.*, 22 December).

BCP Foreign Activity. In the area of foreign policy, contacts with other communist parties and international propaganda, the year began with a visit by a Czechoslovak party-government delegation led by first secretary Gustav Husák, and premier Lubomír Štrougal (communiqué in *Rabotnichesko Delo*, 15 January). The visit reportedly passed "in a spirit of complete mutual understanding" and established identity of views on foreign and domestic policies. The following day, *Rabotnichesko Delo* published extensive parts of the official analysis, entitled "Lessons from the Crisis Developments in the Czechoslovak Communist Party and Society after the 13th Congress of CPC" in 1966 and adopted by the CPC Central Committee in December 1970. As expected,

Zhivkov led the BCP delegation (including Todor Pavlov, Krustiu Trichkov, and Konstantin Tellalov) to the Twenty-fourth CPSU congress. He delivered an address pledging friendship "for centuries," and toured parts of the U.S.S.R. during his long stay (29 March-10 April). In May, he led a BCP delegation (with Ivan Abadzhiev and Georgi Dzhagarov) to the Fourteenth CPC congress (24-29 May). Stanko Todorov represented the BCP at the Sixteenth Congress of the Mongolian People's Revolutionary Party in June, while Zhivkov led a delegation to the Eighth Congress of the Socialist Unity Party of (East) Germany. In August, Zhivkov took part in the meeting of Soviet and East European leaders at the Crimea, where announcement of U.S. President Nixon's visit to China was presumably discussed. Somewhat of a surprise was Brezhnev's visit to Sofia (26-27 September) after an official trip to Yugoslavia, presumably to reassure BCP leaders that no particular concessions had been made to Tito in regard to the Macedonian question. On 23-27 November, Stanko Todorov paid an official visit to Hungary; on 30 November, he and Zhivkov made a trip to Moscow (returning the same day) to confer with Brezhnev, Podgorny, and Kosygin. Zhivkov and Grisha Filipov were BCP delegates to the Sixth Congress of the Polish United Workers' Party (5-11 December). Todorov led a party-government delegation on an important visit to North Vietnam (21-27 December). It included Ivan Abadzhiev, Mako Dakov, and Army chief-of-staff Colonel General Atanas Semerdzhiev.

Among these visits and contacts with ruling communist parties, some were of considerable importance, although details surrounding them have for the most part remained a secret. Of such obvious importance was the Zhivkov-Todorov visit to Moscow. Brief reports in the press (e.g., *ibid.*, 1 December) indicated only standard points of reference, like current international developments, Soviet-Bulgarian economic relations, and CMEA coordination and integration. As usual, they reaffirmed "complete mutual understanding on all questions." More extensive were comments on Todorov's high-level visit to Hanoi (*ibid.*, 20 through 29 December), undertaken as a demonstration of "fraternal friendship and fighting solidarity" with North Vietnam as well as an occasion to discuss aid Bulgaria provides. The Bulgarian-Vietnamese Declaration issued at the end of the visit (text, *ibid.*, 29 December) reviewed at length the world situation, developments in Indochina, and North Vietnam's determination to "continue and intensify the struggle on three fronts—military, political and diplomatic—until complete victory." Talks were said to have taken place in "an atmosphere of fraternal friendship, mutual understanding, and complete identity of views on all questions discussed." Conclusion of agreements were announced for military and non-military aid "without compensation," exchange of goods, and long-term credits from Bulgaria. To stress commitment for the Vietnamese struggle, Todorov granted an interview with two Bulgarian journalists and further explained the visit and BCP policy (text, *ibid.*, 1 January 1972).

In relations with Yugoslav communists, the Macedonian question continued to create tension. Scholars and propagandists on the Bulgarian side of the border hold that the Macedonians are historically and linguistically Bulgarian; those on the Yugoslav side deny it. On the government level, however, Todorov reiterated during his visit to Hungary the position formulated in particularly tense circumstances after the 1968 invasion of Czechoslovakia that Bulgaria had "no territorial claims on any country." (For the original reassurance see *ibid.*, 29 September 1968.)

Regarding non-ruling parties and leftist groups, Zhikov gave an interview in June to the organ of the Italian Communist Party, *L'Unità*. He explained at length BCP policies and achievements. Kostadin Giaurov traveled to Brussels for an exchange of views with the Belgian party. On 2-4 September the deputy secretary-general of the French Communist Party, Georges Marchais, visited Sofia in apparent preparation for the visit of French Foreign Minister Maurice Schumann later in the year. Also in September, a BCP delegation led by Venelin Kotsev visited Syria. By far the most amazing development involving BCP foreign relations occurred in Sudan. During a power struggle between leftist and rightist Sudanese officers in July, Bulgarian and Soviet representatives in Khartoum intervened on the side of the former, supporting the secretary-general of the Sudanese Communist Party, Abd al-Khaliq Mahjub, who had helped carry out a successful coup. After General Numairi recovered power, Mahjub was executed and Bulgarian ambassador Stoian Zaimov and a Soviet diplomat were expelled from the country. The BCP Central Committee issued an obituary for Mahjub, describing him as the outstanding leader of Sudanese communists for more than twenty years and declaring that the BCP "deeply mourns the heavy loss and lowers its battle flags" to his memory (*ibid.*, 29 July).

Publications. The daily *Rabotnichesko Delo* (Workers' Cause), edited by Secretariat member Georgi Bokov, is the central organ of the BCP. The Central Committee publishes also *Novo Vreme* (New Times), a theoretical monthly, edited by Nikolay Iribadzhakov, and *Partien Zhivot* (Party Life), a monthly journal on internal party matters, edited by Petko Rusev. More specialized nationwide publications are *Politicheska Prosveta* (Political Education) and *Ikonomicheski Zhivot* (Economic Life) biweeklies of the Central Committee, and the youth publications *Narodna Mladezh* (People's Youth) and *Mladezh* (Youth), organs of the DCYU. In propaganda themes, a great deal of space has been devoted to the struggle in Vietnam, including Bulgarian relations with North Vietnam and the National Liberation Front in South Vietnam, the trial of U.S. communist Angela Davis, the "great China chauvinism of Mao's clique," and Zionism as a world-wide movement and an ally of "U.S. imperialism" in the Middle East.

California State University, Northridge   Marin Pundeff

Czechoslovakia

The Communist Party of Czechoslovakia (Komunistická strana Československa; KSČ) celebrated its fiftieth anniversary in November 1971. It was founded at a constituent congress in Prague, in November 1921, by left-wing elements of the socialist movement who had seceded from the Czechoslovak Social Democratic Party, under the impact of the Russian October Revolution of 1917. Unlike other ruling communist parties in Central and Eastern Europe, the KSČ seized power by a coup d'état (February 1948). Since then, it has held the monopoly of government in the country. The claim of the KSČ to the leading political role is explicitly recognized in the preamble of the 1960 constitution of the Czechoslovak Socialist Republic. The party rules through the channel of the National Front of Working People, a formalized coalition of political parties and mass organizations, in which it commands a majority. The National Front has the exclusive right to nominate candidates for elections of all levels, and no political activity is tolerated outside the National Front. President of the Republic Ludvík Svoboda and Federal Premier Lubomír Štrougal are both members of the KSČ.

Following a constitutional reform of October 1968, Czechoslovakia was transformed into a federation of two ethnic units: the Czech Socialist Republic and the Slovak Socialist Republic. However, the organizational structure of the communist party does not parallel the federal type of the Czechoslovak polity. There is a separate Slovak party organization—the Communist Party of Slovakia (KSS)—but without a corresponding unit in the Czech Socialist Republic. After a few hesitant steps, such as creation of a "Bureau for Party Work in the Czech Lands" in 1968, the KSČ returned to the model of "assymetric centralism." Thus a state with a federalist constitution is ruled by a centralist Communist Party.

Party Organization. The top organs of the KSČ are the Central Committee and the Presidium. In May 1971 the party held a congress in Prague. Officially, this was the Fourteenth Congress because the present leadership does not recognize the validity of the congress convened in August 1968, which had condemned the Soviet military intervention in Czechoslovakia. The 1971 congress brought but minor changes in the party organization: it tacitly abandoned the road to the federalization of the KSČ (the Bureau for Party Work in the Czech Lands was not renewed); changed the title of the chief executive official from First Party Secretary to Secretary-General, in accordance with a change previously effected by the Communist Party of the Soviet Union (CPSU); extended the interval between the congresses from four to five years; and reintroduced the institution of the candidature to party membership which the Thirteenth Congress in June 1966 had abolished. The proposal for a significant revision of the party statutes, worked out on the initiative of the reformist leadership in 1968, was not considered by the congress.

Leadership. The purge of the party from the "revisionist elements" associated with the policies of the former First Secretary Alexander Dubček continued selectively in 1971. This process, officially labeled "normalization," ran parallel with a struggle between the current leadership and a group of right-wing hard-liners who tried to take the advantage of the presence of the Soviet troops in the country for a complete return to the dogmatist course of the pre-1968 regimes of Klement Gottwald and Antonín Novotný. The congress in May 1971 seems to have stabilized the position of the Secretary-General Gustav Husák and his associates. It replaced 76 out of 137 Central Committee members. On the one hand, the remaining supporters of the "Prague Spring" were eliminated; on the other, numerous dogmatist opponents of the present line were equally ousted. The new Party Presidium consists of eleven full members: Vasil Bil'ák, Peter Colotka, Karel Hoffmann, Gustav Husák, Alois Indra, Antonín Kapek, Josef Kempný, Josef Korčák, Jozef Lenárt, Lubomír Štrougal, and Ludvík Svoboda, and two candidate members: Miloslav Hruškovič and Václav Hůla. The Secretariat is led by the Secretary-General Husák and consists of eight secretaries: Vasil Bil'ák, Jan Fojtík, Miloslav Hruškovič, Alois Indra, Josef Kempný, František Ondřich, Oldřich Švestka, and Václav Svoboda and two Secretariat members: Jozef Lenárt and Miroslav Moc. Milos Jakeš remained as chairman of the Party Control and Auditing Commission. The congress also confirmed Jozef Lenárt in the office of the First Secretary of the Communist Party of Slovakia. The position of the head of the Bureau for Party Work in the Czech Lands was not filled.

Membership. After a mass purge among the rank-and-file members of the KSČ, carried out in 1970, the membership declined by 27.8 per cent, as compared to the figure for January 1968. The strength of the party effectives changed little during 1971. According to an official statement, the KSČ still had "almost 1,200,000 members" (*Život strany*, no. 6, March 1971). Despite the purge, the KSČ remains one of the strongest parties of the world measured *per capita*; it includes about 8.4 per cent of the entire population (in the U.S.S.R. only 2 per cent), as recorded by the 1970 census. Workers comprise 26.1 per cent of the membership, compared to 42.5 per cent in 1952 and 36 per cent in 1962 (*ibid.*). The population of Czechoslovakia is 14,467,000 (estimated 1970).

Domestic Affairs. Next to the party congress, the long overdue national election, held in November 1971, was the major domestic political event of the year. The election turnout, close to 100 per cent in the 1964 elections, was slightly higher (99.45 per cent as compared to 99.41 in 1964) and the percentage of votes cast in favor of the candidates of the National Front slightly lower (99.81 compared to 99.94). These results, unusual even for a centrally ruled polity with a communications monopoly, were interpreted by the leadership as an expression of the popular endorsement of its policies of "normalization." It may be assumed that the outcome of the elections has been used by Husák and his followers as an argument in their dealing with the Soviet controlling power, to prove that the process of the return to "normalcy" has made good progress.

On other evidence, however, it would seem that the crucial problems of the KSČ, created by the arrested reform movement of the late 1960s, remained through 1971. There were indications of the leadership's serious concern about the continuing opposition to the new course and to the Soviet interference, both among the party membership and the population at large. The leaders went to great length to justify their policies. A document entitled "Lessons from the Crisis Development of Party and Society since the 13th Party Congress", released by the Central Committee, was given very wide publicity (*Rudé právo*, 14 January 1971). It presented the short-lived reformist regime of 1968 as a conspiracy to undermine the socialist order in Czechoslovakia, but it put also a part of the blame on the dogmatist and conservative leaderships which had preceded Dubček, because of their reluctance to carry out the rehabilitations of the victims of Stalinist justice and other indispensable changes. Entirely new in the document was the assertion that the KSČ leaders had taken a "truly Marxist-Leninist and internationalist stand" after the Soviet military intervention in 1968. Interpreted as an explicit approval given to the Soviet-sponsored action of the five Warsaw Pact countries, this claim would contradict known historical facts. The document also affirmed that "thousands of Czechoslovak Communists as well as non-Communists had appealed to the fraternal parties for help against the counterrevolutionary forces," an affirmation which had been vehemently denied in August 1968 by all party groups and segments. This "invitation thesis" was obviously supposed to legitimate the Soviet invasion and, by implication, the political line imposed by the Kremlin.

Another symptom of the continuing party crisis could be seen in the political trials which took place in Czechoslovakia during 1971 (and early in 1972) despite previous pledges by the secretary-general to the contrary. The prosecution affected several journalists and artists for views which they expressed publicly during or after the Soviet intervention. Prominent party officials have not yet been arrested or tried, although the press hinted several times at such a possibility. It was felt that the sentences handed down to Czech and Slovak intellectuals during the year might have been also intended to disarm the hard-line opposition. A confrontation with this group resulted in the dismissal of the minister of education of the Czech Socialist Republic, Jaromír Hrbek, a staunch dogmatist (Prague radio, 8 July).

The year saw further steps toward the liquidation of the heritage of the 1968 reformist course. The party, which gave up its one-time intention to restructure its organizational pattern to match the federalist constitution of the state, proceeded to the curtailing of the powers of the two ethnic units in matters of economy and security. The freedom to pursue cultural activities of the ethnic minorities, particularly the German, considerably increased in 1968, was restricted and their organizations were purged (Bratislava radio, 30 March). Purges continued in both Czech non-communist parties, the Socialist Party and the People's Party (*Svobodné slovo*, 6 February; *Lidová demokracie*, 20 February). Religious freedoms, too, were subjected to further restrictions; no activity outside pastoral and liturgical functions was permitted. Pro-regime religious organizations, such as "Pacem in Terris," disbanded in 1968, were reconstituted (*Katolícke noviny*, 10 January). The rehabilitation process of the victims of Stalinist justice was practically stopped in 1971, but very few previous decisions of the rehabilitation courts have been reversed (Bratislava radio, 15 March).

The first results of the 1970 population census, published in 1971, showing an unusually low increase, seemed to testify to the severity of the exodus following the Soviet invasion and suggested that the officially admitted total of 53,000 refugees fell far short of the actual number (*Statistický přehled*, no. 3, March). Strict limitations on travel to non-communist countries were maintained all through 1971, but border formalities with the Warsaw Pact nations were considerably simplified, though not always on the basis of reciprocity (*Rudé právo*, 17 January 1972).

Mass Organizations. The Czechoslovak mass organizations continued during 1971 toward what the party considered to be "normalization." The centrist Jan Piller, who in 1970 replaced the reformist Karel Poláček as chairman of the Revolutionary Trade Union Movement, was in turn relieved and succeeded by a conservative member of the party Presidium, Karel Hoffmann (Prague radio, 11 March). A Czechoslovak Peace Movement delegation traveled to the Soviet Union in June. The International Union of Students held its Tenth Congress in Bratislava in February, with the Czechoslovak National Union of Students as host. The congress reflected many of the political conflicts which at present divide the various leftist and communist fellow-traveler organizations in the world (*Rudé právo*, 4 February).

Culture, Education and Youth. During 1971 the Husák leadership continued its efforts to bring scientific and artistic life in Czechoslovakia under the closest possible control of the party.

After the dissolution of the artists' unions unwilling to compromise with the new course, the union of scientists in the Czech lands was disbanded and a new body put into its place (Prague radio, 1 June). Pressure was particularly strongly felt among the writers and in the dramatic arts. Also journalism was subjected to very tight supervision. Newspapers and periodicals were forbidden to accept contributions from a great majority of correspondents and free-lance reporters, because of the "negative" position of the latter, and a special discriminatory system of remuneration was introduced in the mass media sector (*Novinář*, no. 2, February). The programs of the publishing houses were radically revised, translations from non-communist literature were restricted and a *de facto* censorship system installed. A number of Czech- and Slovak-language artistic and literary periodicals disappeared during the year. In the world of films, too, the party carried out personnel changes which promised a return to topics with a propagandistic slant, committed to the ideology of socialism in Soviet interpretation (*Tvorba*, 2 June).

The class and political background of the applicants for enrollment in the institutes of secondary and higher education, which the reformist Action Program of 1968 had declared irrelevant and discriminatory, was again introduced as the main criterion for admission. The Czechoslovak press recognized, however, that in 1971 the students opposing the pro-Soviet course still remained in majority (*Mladá fronta*, 3 February). The politicization of education in Czechoslovakia was further reinforced by increased stress upon the ideological training of teachers of all levels (*Učitelské noviny*, 15 April).

Armed Forces. Not much was heard during 1971 of the Soviet army contingent stationed in Czechoslovakia since August 1968. The strength of this force was estimated at some 80,000 men. The Czechoslovak army, on the other hand, continued to be one of the most important objects of the "normalization" efforts by the party. These efforts consisted in reasserting the unity of the political and the military command authority—i.e., unlimited party control of the armed forces—and in reimposing the principle of unreserved commitment to the cause of socialist proletarian internationalism—i.e., unqualified obedience to the Soviet supreme leadership embodied in the Warsaw Pact. Of the two concerns, the latter might appear even more serious than the former, as the trial of General Václav Prchlík, held in March 1971, would suggest. General Prchlík, formerly chief of the security, justice, and army policy division of the Central Committee of the KSČ, criticized in July 1968 the structure of political and strategic decision-making within the Warsaw Pact organization, which in his opinion gave a quasi-monopoly to the representatives of the Soviet Union. The Higher Military Court in Príbram, Bohemia, condemned Prchlík to three years in prison (Prague radio, 26 March). Prchlík has been so far the only political and governmental representative to be prosecuted for actions taken prior to the Soviet military intervention.

The inner security system in Czechoslovakia was completed in 1971 by the reactivation of the Auxiliary Police Force, which had been introduced in 1952 but had been dormant since 1967. The APF had 61,000 members at the time of its reactivation (*Pravda na víkend*, 8 January). At the end of the year, the Ministry of Defense lost jurisdiction over the Border Guards, which since 1966 had been considered a part of the armed forces and had received full military training. The Border Guards were transferred under the authority of the Ministry of Interior (ČETEKA press release, 22 December).

Economy. The consolidation of the Czechoslovak economy during 1971, or—more precisely—the avoidance of a much feared economic deterioration after the events of 1968, has been one of the arguments which the party leadership never failed to invoke in support of the adopted course. Prices of a number of consumers' goods were reduced in the spring (*Rudé právo*, 29

April) and the prices of automobiles followed in early summer (*Pravda*, 8 June). Also the harvest of 1971 turned out to be good on the whole, despite serious apprehensions because of the weather (Prague radio, 21 August). These positive features were stressed in the official evaluation of the overall economic performance, but at the same time several negative factors were singled out which might impair the fulfilment of the target figures of the Fifth Five-Year Plan (1971-75): decline in general productivity of labor, great labor turnover, rising costs of construction work, failure to meet the deadlines in the implementation of various capital investment projects, etc. (*Hospodářské noviny*, 24 December). Industrial production in 1971 rose by 7 per cent, which was 1.1 per cent more than the plan had foreseen. The manufacturing of capital goods increased by 7.2 per cent, the production of consumers' goods by 6.2 per cent. The employment in the socialist sector of the industry was up by 54,000 jobs, which fell 4,000 jobs short of the projected plan figure. Nominal wages and salaries rose by 3.7 per cent although the plan expected only 2.5 per cent. Average wages in absolute figures reached 2,009 Kčs per month. Foreign trade closed with a favorable balance, both with the socialist and the capitalist countries. Living costs declined by 0.4 per cent and savings deposits increased by 12 per cent. The draft federal budget for 1972 was based on 118.8 billion Kčs revenue and 115.35 billion Kčs expenditure, both figures slightly under those for 1971 (*Rudé právo*, 20 December).

In accordance with the overall trend toward the liquidation of the 1968 reforms, the Party imposed restrictions on private initiative in the economy which had been encouraged by the New Economic Model approved by the Thirteenth Congress in 1966 (Prague radio, 13 February). In Slovakia, the party declared its intention to collectivize the remaining 10 per cent of arable land which remained in private hands after the collectivization of the late 1950s, but the difficulties of such an operation were openly admitted (*Pravda*, 7 May).

Foreign Affairs. Czechoslovak foreign policy during 1971 was dominated by concern to remain as much as possible in line with the foreign policy of the Soviets. This was reflected in dealings both with the socialist countries and with the rest of the world. The principles of the foreign policy of the Husák leadership were explicitly defined in the KSČ Presidium report, approved at the Central Committee plenary session of 21 October, which reiterated the old dogmatic thesis that the attitude toward the Soviet Union was the main touchstone of the progressive and socialist stand of any country. On these grounds, the Czechoslovak press continued to criticize communist governments opposed to Moscow, particularly that of China. However, an improvement in the relations with China occurred when after an interval of two years a new Chinese ambassador was appointed to Prague (Prague radio, 2 June). Regardless of this change, the Czechoslovak media joined in the Soviet-led campaign against the new U.S. policy toward China. They charged that China had abandoned all principles and denied the existence of class conflict on a global scale. At the same time they stressed that small nations could play no significant role in the conflict between the great powers—an obvious hit at the relatively independent China policy of Romania (*Rudé právo*, 31 July).

The major issue in the international relations of Czechoslovakia in 1971 concerned the regularization of diplomatic contacts with the Federal Republic of Germany and mutual recognition. The issue appeared to be seriously complicated by the divergent views of the two partners on the most proper form of repudiation of the 1938 Munich treaty. In protracted negotiations, the West German side was willing to declare the treaty simply null and void, while the Czechoslovak representatives insisted on the recognition of its being null and void *ab initio*. However intricate these differences, it would seem that the slow progress of the negotiations was due to the lack of interest on the Soviet side in an early agreement between Czechoslovakia and West Germany rather than to any inherent difficulty in reconciling the two positions. Reports on the talks held toward the end of the year in Germany supported this view (Prague radio, 19 November). At the same time Czechoslovak leaders remained in contact with the party and government of East Germany (*Rudé právo*, 13 November).

During 1971, several important treaties on economic cooperation and trade were signed with a number of countries. Economic relations with the CMEA nations were in the forefront of interest. The Czechoslovak mass media often labeled these relations as integrative, although a true economic integration within the CMEA area, for instance in the terms of the ambitious Khrushchev project of 1962, remained as remote as ever. Czechoslovakia signed a bilaterial agreement with the Soviet Union on the coordination of production in the engineering, chemical, and electrotechnical industries early in the year (*Pravda*, Bratislava, 22 January). On 11 January work was begun on the Czechoslovak section of the pipeline which is to supply Western Europe with natural gas from the Soviet Union (Prague radio, 11 January). Toward the end of the year, another agreement was concluded between the two countries, on the use of a standardized type of atomic reactor for the production of energy (*Jaderná energie*, no. 12, December). The CMEA International Investment Bank granted a credit of 77.5 million rubles to Czechoslovakia (Bratislava radio, 12 November). Czechoslovakia, East Germany, and Hungary began to work out a plan for a large automobile plant in Slovakia, with an output up to 600,000 cars per year (Budapest radio, 18 January). This plan did not advance very much during 1971. Long-term trade agreements were concluded with Bulgaria (*Rudé právo*, 11 January), Hungary (Prague radio, 23 January), Romania (*ibid.*, 30 January), Yugoslavia (Bratislava radio, 26 January), and Poland (Prague radio, 2 March). Economic ties with Poland were further strengthened by a bilaterial treaty later in the year (Prague radio, 14 August). Trade agreements were also concluded with Chile (*Rudé právo*, 9 June) and Spain (*ibid.*, 6 October).

International Communist Movement. The share of the KSČ in the activities of the international communist movement during 1971 continued to be rather modest. The wish to avoid undesirable confrontations with views not quite orthodox imposed considerable caution. Although in a smaller measure, some fraternal parties kept on questioning the legitimacy of the Soviet move against the Czechoslovak reformist course in 1968. Such was the case of the Italian Communist Party (PCI), whose press carried in 1971 an interview with the former Federal Assembly Chairman and Presidium member Josef Smrkovský. Expelled from the party in 1970, he lives in retirement. In the interview, he testified that an enquiry by the National Assembly in August 1968 had established that not a single politician or party official was able to corroborate the so-called invitation thesis; everybody denied having appealed for help to the allied parties or governments or having complained about any "counter-revolutionary plots" in Czechoslovakia prior to the Soviet intervention. The publication of the interview led to a sharp exchange between the KSČ and the PCI (*Vie Nuove Giorni*, no. 22, 16 September; *Rudé právo*, 25 September). Relations between the two parties did not improve when Czechoslovak police arrested and later expelled the free-lance contributor of the official daily of the PCI *L'Unità*, Ferdinando Zidar (*L'Unità*, Rome, 9 February 1972).

In order to counteract the effect of these critical positions in the international communist movement, the Husák leadership used every opportunity to endorse the Soviet action in Czechoslovakia, notably at the CPSU congress in Moscow (Bratislava radio, 1 April), the congress of the Communist Party of Bulgaria (*Rudé právo*, 22 April), the congress of the Socialist Unity Party of (East) Germany (Prague radio, 14 June), and the congress of the Polish United Workers' Party (*Rudé právo*, 6 December).

Czechoslovak party leaders and mass media stepped out of their reserve only rarely. They joined in the criticism of the Romanian absence from the meeting of the communist parties in the Crimea in August (*Smena*, 11 and 17 August), possibly more out of the desire to please the Soviet policy makers than because of any deep involvement in the issue. The reports in the Western press about the critical speech by party secretary and Presidium member Vasil Bil'ák addressed to the Romanian, Hungarian, Polish, and East German parties at the KSČ Central Committee session on 21 October (*Corriere della Sera*, Milan, 14 February 1972), appear quite plausible but there has been little corroboration from any official Czechoslovak source so far.

Publications. The main organ of the KSČ is the daily *Rudé právo*. The official daily of the KSS is *Pravda* (Bratislava). There is no periodical addressed specifically to the communist organizations in the Czech lands. The quasi-official theoretical party weekly is *Tribuna*; its Slovak counterpart is *Predvoj*. *Tvorba* is a weekly with a long tradition but whose line has changed considerably several times since its foundation in the 1920s. It has its readership chiefly among educated party members. The fortnightly *Zivot strany* brings organizational news and instructions for party workers on all levels. The daily sponsored by the Revolutionary Trade Union Movement is *Práce*, which has a Slovak version *Práca* with an independent editorial office in Bratislava. The Czechoslovak Socialist Youth Union publishes its daily *Mladá fronta* in Prague and *Smena* in Bratislava.

University of Pittsburgh   Zdeněk L. Suda

Germany: German Democratic Republic

The Socialist Unity Party of Germany (Sozialistische Einheitspartei Deutschlands; SED) was founded on 21 April 1946 by a forced merger of the Communist Party of Germany (KPD) and the Social-Democratic Party of Germany (SPD) in the Soviet zone of occupation. Although at the time the SED was constituted 53 per cent of its members were Social Democrats, the communists soon assumed control over the party apparatus. A resolution adopted in July 1948 declared that the SED was to become "a party of a new type," modeled after the Communist Party of the Soviet Union (CPSU). The change was effected by the time a constitution had been drafted and the German Democratic Republic (GDR) was formally created in October 1949.

Government and Party Structure. From the birth of the GDR, the communist party has been in absolute control over life in East Germany and its loyalty to the Soviet Union has been unmatched by any socialist country of Eastern Europe. Allegiance was unquestioned under the long-term leadership of Walter Ulbricht, first secretary of the SED and chairman of both the State Council and National Defense Council. Multiple authority gave Ulbricht uncommon power until 3 May 1971, when he resigned his party post, citing age and ill health as a reason. He passed the mantle to Erich Honecker, who as an expert on security and military matters and as a prominent member of the Politburo had long figured in speculation about Ulbricht's successor.

Elections are regularly scheduled in East Germany, but the outcome is predictable, since voters receive ballots of a "National Front" single list of candidates. The last general election, held on 14 November 1971, brought out 98.48 per cent of the eligible electorate of 11,400,000 and 99.85 per cent cast their votes for listed candidates to the People's Chamber (Volkskammer) and 15 district assemblies. With 564 candidates for 434 seats in the Volkskammer, those not chosen were retained as reserve deputies. Politburo member Friedrich Ebert, reporting on the elections to a subsequent plenum of the SED Central Committee called the near unanimous results "impressive proof of the stability of our socialist state and social system" (*Neues Deutschland*, 20 November).

The Eighth Congress of the SED was held on 15-19 June 1971 in East Berlin. Elections to the leading bodies of the party—the Politburo, the Secretariat, and the Central Committee—were part of the proceedings. Erich Honecker was unanimously confirmed in his new position as first secretary, the post to which he had acceded only a few weeks before the congress. "In recognition of his achievements" Walter Ulbricht was elected chairman of the SED (a position especially created for him), and was retained as a full member of the Politburo. No incumbents were eliminated from this powerful body, but its size was increased from 14 members to 16 to produce this line-up: Erich Honecker,* Hermann Axen,* Friedrich Ebert, Gerhard Grüneberg,* Kurt Hager,* Günter Mittag,* Erich Mückenberger, Alfred Neumann, Albert Norden,* Horst Sindermann, Willi Stoph (also premier of the GDR), Walter Ulbricht, Paul Verner,* Herbert Warnke, newcomer Werner Krolikowski, and Werner Lamberz* (promoted from candidate status). The number of candidate members was raised from six to seven with newcomers Erich Mielke and Harry Tisch chosen to serve with incumbents Georg Ewald, Walter Halbritter, Werner Jarowinsky,* Günter Kleiber, and Margarete Müller. The Secretariat was composed of the men whose names above are followed by an asterisk; the only notable changes were the elimination of Walter Ulbricht and the election of Horst Dohlus as a "member of the Secretariat" (a new title that sets him apart from the regular "secretaries"). The congress elected a Central Committee consisting of 135 full members and 54 candidates; about half of the candidates were newcomers.

At the congress it was announced that the delegates represented 1,845,280 SED party members and 64,579 candidates and that the total of 1,909,859 was organized in 72,207 basic party organizations and branches. The population of East Germany is 17,004,000 (estimated 1970).

Together with the SED, the following four parties constitute the National Front: the Christian Democratic Union of Germany (Christliche Demokratische Union Deutschlands; CDU), headed by Gerald Götting, who is also chairman of the Volkskammer; the National Democratic Party of Germany (National-Demokratische Partei Deutschlands; NDPD), headed by Dr. Lothar Bolz; the Liberal Democratic Party of Germany (Liberal-Demokratische Partei Deutschlands; LDPD), headed by Manfred Gerlach; and the Democratic Peasant Party of Germany (Demokratische Bauernpartei Deutschlands; DBD), headed by Ernst Goldenbaum. Each of these parties holds 52 seats in the Volkskammer, while the SED has 127 representatives.

A number of mass organizations also are allowed a political role, but their views never differ from those of the SED. The most important are represented in the Volkskammer and include the Free German Trade Union Federation (FDGB), which has 7.1 million members; the Free German Youth (FDJ), 1.7 million; and the Democratic League of Women (DFB), 1.3 million. Additional mass organizations serve general or specific interests. For example, the German-Soviet Friendship Society fosters friendly relations with the Soviet Union and promotes its views. The Society for Sport and Technology (GST) enrolls approximately 500,000 young people and instills "socialist soldierly virtues" to prepare them for service in the People's Army.

Party Internal Affairs. Party interest in 1971 revolved around the change in leadership and the Eighth Congress.

A little more than a month after resigning as SED party chief, Walter Ulbricht lost his second important post, when the Volkskammer (on 24 June) elected Erich Honecker as chairman of the National Defense Council. East Berlin radio reported on the Volkskammer session and finished with this statement: "Previously, Walter Ulbricht was chairman of the GDR National Defense Council." Political analysts could hardly be faulted for predicting that loss of the largely ceremonial post of chairman of the State Council would follow and complete Walter Ulbricht's retirement. Therefore it was a surprise when the Volkskammer in November unanimously reelected Ulbricht to a new four-year term as the GDR's nominal head of state. West Berlin's *Der Tagesspiegel* (27 November) ventured the opinion that Ulbricht was not given an option, but was forced to stay in office because of Soviet insistence on the need to "demonstrate the unanimity of the past and present leadership of the SED" in order to "conceal the fact that the GDR and the SED still only fulfill the functions of Soviet foreign policy." Similar views were expressed in the West German press on various occasions during the year. The big daily *Frankfurter Allgemeine Zeitung*, for instance, described the SED at the time of the congress as "without a will of its own, not even a shade ot it" and as "completely subordinated to the Soviet 'brother party.' "

When Ulbricht resigned as party chief in May, the transfer of power initially was described as smooth and harmonious. Later stories told of Ulbricht's unwillingness to step down before the congress convened, of his intransigence which endangered an "orderly transition," and of a "mild shove" used to counter his objections. When Honecker in his speech to the SED congress in

June placed strong emphasis on the need for collective decision-making within the party, some analysts interpreted it as an oblique rebuke to Ulbricht, who had grown inclined to ignore or overrule his colleagues and who in the last months of his party rule had even been accused of "slight delusions of grandeur" (*Manchester Guardian Weekly*, 18 September).

The retention of Ulbricht as head of state in all probability only delayed a long-rumored shuffling of positions among party and government functionaries. Particular speculation involved Politburo member Horst Sindermann, who in May was named deputy chairman of the Council of Ministers, placing him in line to succeed Premier Willi Stoph, who was said to be slated to take Ulbricht's place on the State Council. Sindermann has moved up rapidly and his close contacts with Honecker date back to the time when both men held leading positions with the FDJ.

The Eighth Congress. The Eighth Congress was attended by 2,047 delegates with voting rights, 74 present in an advisory capacity, and 790 guests. Among the guests were delegates from "94 Communist, Workers' national democratic and Left-wing Socialist parties from 83 countries" (*WMR*, September). More than 60 per cent of the delegates were workers, and 79 per cent were of working-class origin; 10.5 per cent were cooperative farmers and 26.6 per cent members of the intelligentsia; 42.3 per cent were in the age group between 41 and 50 years, and 12.6 per cent were under 25 years of age; women delegates numbered 569, or two per cent more than at the Seventh Congress; 60 per cent of the delegates had attended party schools, and 1,805 had received high government awards for their contribution to the building of a socialist society in the GDR (*Neues Deutschland*, 18 June).

East German observers characterized the congress as "business-like and moving," emphasizing the "realistic evaluations, the wise pro's and con's, and the simple and clear language" prevailing in reports and discussions (*ibid.*, 22 June). In contrast, Western observers stressed the fact that the convention was postponed by 24 hours only two days before its scheduled opening and that the "circulatory disturbance" suffered by Walter Ulbricht hours before he was to deliver the opening address necessitated having his speech read for him. (*Economist*, 19 June).

The SED lauded the congress as "a further indication of the Party's complete unity and cohesion and the consistency of its policies," although it acknowledged that in order to "continue building developed socialism" the party would have to "raise its militancy, step up its theoretical, ideological, political and organizing activity, and encourage greater initiative on the part of its members." Collective leadership was identified as the most important principle to guide all party committees, because it alone "guarantees the adoption of correct decisions and prevents subjectivism," and provides a "realistic and earnest approach" based on personal responsibility; it would also simplify realization of the SED's congressional keynote promise—"to do all in its power for the good of the working class and the people." (*WMR*, September.)

Domestic Views and Activities. *The Economy*. The GDR operates under a "socialist economic system" of a centrally planned economy in accordance with the directives of five-year plans. A draft of the rive-year plan for 1971-75 was submitted for public discussion in May 1971 and forecast "Steady GDR Progress, But No Sensations" (headline in *Democratic German Report*, East Berlin, 2 June). The amended directive was submitted to the Eighth Congress by Premier Willi Stoph and published as a special supplement to *Neues Deutschland* (23 June). It projects considerable growth for all areas of the economy, although some rates of growth—notably for national income, productivity, and industrial production—are scaled down slightly from the previous five-year plan. On the other hand, investments are raised above their past targets, in view of the fact that they far exceeded their earlier quotas. The main task outlined for the future is to raise the "material and cultural standard" of the population by providing a greater supply of consumers' goods, 500,000 new housing units, and extra funds for social needs or subsidies that will assure the maintenance of low prices for basic foods, cheap transportation, and minimal rents. Previous shortcomings are implied by a new emphasis on the need for "proportional development," the introduction of more modern technological procedures, and a search for maximum effectiveness by "socialist rationalization." The directive also foresees intensification of socialist economic integration in Eastern Europe under the aegis of the Council for Mutual Economic Assistance (CMEA) to the point of "gradual adaptation and interdependence of the national economic structures." The development of joint research and production projects with the Soviet Union is listed as a specific GDR goal.

The new directive gives evidence of dissatisfaction with past achievements, even though the GDR has for years enjoyed the highest standard of living of any country in the Eastern Bloc, including the Soviet Union. This record notwithstanding, serious current economic difficulties were announced by party chief Honecker in a sobering report delivered to the SED Central Committee plenum in September. Honecker stated that economic progress must be weighted against a number of "negative factors" and named serious "distortions in fulfilling contracts in industry and the balance sheet for power, materials, and labor." He discussed the 1971 problems of agriculture and the poor harvest caused by extreme heat and drought, which caused a drop in crop production of at least 20 per cent, equivalent to the feed needed to produce a million tons of milk and 500,000 tons of meat. "Never before in the history of our agriculture have we registered such extensive losses due to the vagaries of nature," Honecker asserted in explaining the need for imports to make up for the deficits. (ADN, East German news agency, 17 September; *Neues Deutschland* 18 September.)

While Honecker in his address to the plenum dealt with specific imbalances in the economy—manpower shortages and lagging production of consumers' goods and power in addition to agricultural misfortunes—the SED's chief ideologist, Politburo member Kurt Hager, used the occasion to question the country's official basic economic theories as laid down in the book *Political Economy of Socialism and Its Application in the GDR*, published under party supervision in 1969. Hager's criticism was directed at the tendency to "formalize" economic processes and to give their form precedence over their substance. (*Neues Deutschland*, 20 September.)

Before the Volkskammer adopted the economic plan for 1972 and the long-range plan for 1971-75 on 20 December, the party and government jointly announced that retail prices would not be increased during the duration of the plans and that lower- and medium-priced goods must be made available to the people "in appropriate assortments and qualities" (*ibid.*, 19 November).

Other Domestic Issues. Both the Eighth Congress and the five-year plan concerned themselves with education and culture, the needs of the very young and the old, health and recreation, and the duties and privileges of trade unions, youth organizations, and the women of the GDR.

The basic goal of the "developed socialist system of education" is to raise the young to become "responsible socialist citizens" with extensive training and an appreciation of culture. To achieve it, the long-range plan provides for a ten-year secondary polytechnical education for all. The country also seeks to teach its children to "love socialism passionately and hate imperialism," and to cultivate esthetic and moral values in order to make them "unassailable to all the influences of bourgeois decadence and immorality." (Excerpts from congress speech by Education Minister Margot Honecker, *Deutsche Lehrerzeitung*, no. 27, July). Heavy emphasis was also put on expansion of the nursery school system, which by 1975 should have facilities for approximately 70 per cent of all children of preschool age, and on the provision of vocational training for virtually all the young people not going on to a school of higher education.

To exert proper influence on the young was partly the task of the FDJ, the communist youth organization, which celebrated its twenty-fifth anniversary in March and convened its Ninth Parliament (congress) in May. In 1971 the FDJ adopted guidelines for its own activities in the universities—particularly the need for immediate contact with first-year students—under this heading: "Consolidation of Stable Socialist Convictions and Development of Understanding for the Major Concern of the Third University Reform and for the Place of the FDJ in this Process" (*Junge Generation*, July). Effectiveness of the university reforms had earlier been claimed by Erich Honecker in his congress speech praising "unity of research and teaching" and "new leadership forms [that] promote socialist democracy" (*Neues Deutschland*, 16 June).

The FDJ did not concentrate its attention on one group of young people. It was seeking to extend its influence over vocational trainees, and declared that it was assuming greater responsibility for the very young children of the Ernst Thälmann Young Pioneer Organization. FDJ training is so strict that its "exemplary" older members are in demand for the border brigades of the National People's Army, a service for which absolute loyalty and political reliability are prerequisite (*IWE Tagesdienst*, West Berlin, 6 October).

Although the National People's Army was characterized as an efficient fighting force, every citizen was exhorted to show awareness of the need for greater defense efforts. General Heinz Hoffmann, Minister of Defense, writing in the SED theoretical journal *Einheit* (June), declared that "national defense in the coming years will take on increasingly a total social character, will reach out into all spheres of national life, and will increasingly confront every citizen with the problems and demands which they involve." Hoffmann, not unlike the GDR Minister of Education, stressed that the young must be taught readiness to "give their lives in defense of socialism" and "hate of imperialism and its system" because "the enemy will increasingly attempt to influence our youth in order to weaken their faith in socialism."

In the fields of art and culture, politics remained close to the surface and some remarkable assertions were made. In 1970, when the world celebrated the 200th anniversary of Beethoven's birth, East Germany saw his music "come alive only through integration into the culture of the socialist community." In 1971, the GDR Minister of Culture tried to claim the art of Albrecht Dürer exclusively for his countrymen and to deny the artist's home town Nuremberg in West Germany the right to hold commemorative celebrations in his honor. He argued that only in the socialist German state could Dürer works be seen in their true significance and that they had "nothing in common with the anti-humanistic, aggressive system of imperialism" of the Federal Republic of Germany. The Minister of Culture then used his own assumptions to deduce that they provided proof of the falsehood of "cultural convergence theories" and a common German culture. (*Neues Deutschland*, 6 February).

Christian-Marxist cooperation or state-church relations were topics discussed with more than routine interest on the occasion of the tenth anniversary of the meeting between Walter Ulbricht and church leaders (9 February 1961), which had concluded that there was "such a wide area of agreement between the humanist and social aims of the original Christianity and the humanist and social aims of Socialism, that cooperation becomes imperative" (*Democratic German Report*, 10 February 1971). Politburo member Paul Verner praised the "effectiveness of the direction-giving, normative, community-creating power" displayed ten years before as the basis for complete independence of the churches of the GDR from the "all-German grip" or the "presumptuous domination" exerted by the Evangelical Church of Germany (*Evangelischer Nachrichtendienst in der DDR*, East Berlin, 10 February). Verner's statement referred to the formation of the Federation of Evangelical Churches in the GDR and its 1969 declaration of complete independence from the all-German organization.

Relations with West Germany. Erich Honecker submitted a five-point program for peace and security in Europe to the Eighth Congress, which included the "establishment of normal relations with the Federal Republic of Germany [FRG], according to the rules of international law." In spite of its expression of basic intent, Honecker's speech was hardly conciliatory: "Ruling circles in the FRG seek to support their revanchist line about 'inner-German' relations with the deceitful allegation that a united German nation still exists. This is, of course, not the case." (*German Democratic Report*, 30 June.) Honecker predicted that the "process of delineation" between the two German states would "become increasingly deeper" and insisted that relations could "only be based on the principles of peaceful coexistence between sovereign states with different social orders." He addressed a special warning to believers in convergence theories: "If there are those in the West who think to swallow the GDR and liquidate our social system, it is well to remind them that the GDR is a stable socialist state and an inseparable part of the powerful socialist community." (*Neues Deutschland*, 16 June.)

On other occasions the East Germans accused the Bonn government of resorting to mere "variations of revanchism" which would operate under the "counter-revolutionary motto of 'transformation through rapprochement' and have West German imperialism penetrate the socialist order of the GDR and restore capitalism" (*Horizont*, no. 17, April).

East German military spokesmen saw the FRG intensifying "psychological warfare" through the use of the "most cunning means of ideological influence" and preparing for "a smooth transition from covert to overt aggression at any time." They observed an increase in the "mobility of the Bundeswehr's combat troops and the firing power of their heavy weapons" and other signs that "prove clearly that the 'new Ostpolitik' and the forward strategy in planning are closely interwoven" in a pattern of aggressive preparedness (*Volksarmee*, no. 33, August).

In the course of the year the GDR made many additional charges against West Germany. Among them were "abuse of the Olympic ideal" in connection with the planning for the Olympic Games in Munich in 1972 (*Neues Deutschland*, 14 April); attempts to block East German participation in international activities, including the Universal Postal Union (ADN, 8 April); provocation of border incidents with the purpose of defaming the GDR (*ibid.*, 2 August); efforts to prevent the successful conclusion of four-power talks on West Berlin (*ibid.*, 3 August); promotion of discrimination against the GDR in Africa (*ibid.*, 20 October); use of the Baltic Sea as a "runway for NATO" and promotion of NATO to "undermine détente in Europe" (*Neues Deutschland*, 7 November); and refusal to consider repeated demands by the countries of the Eastern Bloc to curb the "provocative activities" of Radio Free Europe broadcasting from Munich (ADN, 3 June).

With world attention focused on negotiations over Berlin, the contested city assumed unprecedented importance in 1971 for the future of East Germany. For many years the GDR had insisted that West Berlin was an "independent political unit, located on the territory of the GDR," and that West Germany had "no rights whatsoever" in the city. Furthermore East Germany had enjoyed the "sovereign" rights of controlling the movement of all "persons and goods" along the access routes between West Germany and West Berlin since the Soviet Union had conceded these rights by treaty in 1955.

The Quadripartite Agreement on Berlin signed by the four powers responsible for Germany—the United States, Great Britain, France, and the Soviet Union—on 3 September 1971, called for concessions on the part of all interested countries. The Soviet Union had to admit four-power responsibility for the flow of unimpeded civilian traffic between the FRG and West Berlin, thus canceling the rights of unlimited control which the GDR had enjoyed for 16 years. In turn, East Germany's status was enhanced by the fact that for the first time since World War II it was mentioned in a four-power agreement by name. East Germany was also given some decision-making powers, when the four powers stipulated that details on access to the city were to be worked out by direct negotiations between officials of the GDR, the FRG, and West Berlin.

When both East and West Germany signed the access agreement in December, after deadlocks over contested points were settled by compromise, the *New York Times* (18 December) reported on the event: "It was the first major political agreement reached between the two countries since they were established in the ruins of a defeated and divided Germany a quarter-century ago.... For the East Germans, the agreement was a major step forward in asserting their legitimacy as a nation and in their drive to get diplomatic recognition from the West." *Neues Deutschland* (12 December) stressed the progress toward détente in Europe inherent in the completion of the agreement and editorialized: "For the first time the FRG government has had to recognize the state frontiers with the FRG and West Berlin in a treaty with the GDR, it being understood as a matter of course that Berlin is the capital of the GDR, that transit traffic passes over the GDR's sovereign territory, and that the FRG respects the right of our state to issue visas. Anybody can see that the agreement makes full allowance for the GDR's sovereign rights and safeguards its legitimate interests."

The GDR and the Soviet Bloc. Most western experts agree that one of the most important consequences of the change in SED leadership in 1971 was the ever closer cooperation between East Germany and the Soviet Union in all areas of endeavor. In his speech to the SED congress, Honecker pridefully acknowledged that consultations between the governments and the ruling parties of the two countries had "intensified systematically" and led to unprecedented unanimity on ideology and foreign policy. *Neues Deutschland* (22 June) reported that the congress had with ease pinpointed the most important foreign political task facing the GDR—the all-round strengthening of the alliance with the Soviet Union and the community of socialist states. The newspaper called the "demonstration of friendship and socialist internationalism" greeting the speech by Soviet party secretary Brezhnev a "highlight" of the SED congress and reiterated the Central Committee's declaration that "all East German achievements would be unthinkable without the close fighting union with the CPSU."

East German expressions of appreciation or virtual eulogies for the Soviet Union were common throughout the year. A sample quotation, taken from the official report of the GDR delegation to the CPSU congress will illustrate the trend: "With all clarity did the Twenty-fourth Congress of the CPSU demonstrate the historic rule of the CPSU as the vanguard of the builders of communism in the U.S.S.R., tempered in battle, the leading force in the international revolutionary process of our epoch, the vanguard for the progress of the whole of mankind" (ADN, 4 May).

A tendency toward closer integration of the GDR with the member countries of the Warsaw Pact and the CMEA could also be observed in 1971. Particularly important was the CMEA meeting held in Bucharest late in July, where decisions were reached for economic cooperation of "a new type" providing for a "complex program" that would be the "collective treasure of the experiences of all participating countries" (Willi Stoph, interview with *Einheit*, September). One of the most significant facets of this program would be the adoption of a convertible currency, a move intended for implementation over a period of 15 to 20 years (*New York Times*, 31 July).

Premier Willi Stoph at the time of the CMEA meeting characterized socialist economic integration as a "long-term balanced process noted for its diversity of form" and insisted that socialist integration was "equally an economic, scientific-technical, and ideological problem" (TASS, 27 July). He further noted that "experience in cooperation shows that a part of multilaterally coordinated tasks is implemented on the basis of bilateral treaties, while bilateral cooperation, particularly with the U.S.S.R., yields essential elements for the development of multilateral relations." Such pronouncements fit in with the observations by a U.S. expert, who sees the GDR as "a centripetal force reinforcing alliance cohesion" and deviating from this course only by expressing "preferences for a tighter bilateral relationship with the Soviet Union" (Robert Gerald Livingston in *Foreign Affairs*, December).

To coordinate foreign policy, the foreign ministers of the Warsaw Pact nations met on 30 November-1 December in the Polish capital. The weekly *Horizont* (no. 1, January 1972) reported that the conference had discussed the need to perfect the socialist defense system to counter NATO, but had noted some progress toward improvement of the political situation in Europe. Earlier in the year the Warsaw Pact nations were allegedly urging an increase in military aid for developing countries to allow them to "repel imperialist aggression" and "advance along the road of non-capitalist development" (*IWE Tagesdienst*, 30 June).

International Views and Positions. The five-point program for peace submitted to the SED congress advocated the "early summoning of a European Security Conference," and expressed "GDR readiness to join the United Nations" and "GDR readiness for normal diplomatic relations with all states." All three issues had been promoted for several years, but some variations in approach occurred in 1971. For instance there was a noticeable lull around the middle of the year in GDR propaganda in favor of a European security conference. Analysts observed a parallel lag of interest in the Soviet Union and attributed it to Soviet anticipation that the United States would reduce its military commitments in Europe even without the endorsement of military cutbacks by such a convention. But GDR interest perked up at the end of the year after invitations to a consultative meeting in Brussels early in 1972 had been issued by the Belgian League for European Security and Cooperation. The GDR then shifted to an active promotion of "the people's movement for European security," noting even the "keen support of church circles." The GDR Committee for European Security charged, however, that there were plans to "discriminate against the GDR in connection with the security conference by giving it a lesser status" instead of granting equal rights of participation to all European states. (ADN, 2 December.)

Regarding membership in the United Nations and the establishment of diplomatic relations with all countries, the GDR accused West Germany of impeding East German progress. It tried to substantiate its charges by citing West Germany's "arrogant demand that relations with the GDR—a sovereign state—and its equal membership in the United Nations and participation in other international organizations and agreements be dependent on prior establishment of 'inter-German relations,' a formula wholly at odds with international law" (Foreign Minister Otto Winzer in *WMR*, August). To aid its cause, the GDR appealed to the U.N. General Assembly and U.N. special organizations, trying to substantiate its right to participation in the world organization. Late in the year the GDR protested its exclusion from a planned environmental protection conference in Stockholm and pointed out that such states as Denmark, Norway, and Iceland had abstained from voting for the first time and that affirmative votes for the participation of all interested countries were cast by 34 states, many of them formerly reluctant to vote for inclusion of the GDR (*Neues Deutschland*, 17 December).

Although the GDR continued to lack a voice in the most important international forum, the list of countries according East Germany full recognition lengthened again in 1971. At the end of the year 30 states—more than half of them not under communist rule—had established diplomatic relations and public pressure for recognition was building in such Western nations as France, Great Britain, Denmark, Switzerland, and the Netherlands. The price paid by the GDR for promoting its international image was high, however, and some of the tactics backfired. The Central African Republic, for instance, in August 1971 broke off relations only 16 months after recognition had been granted. President Bokassa of the CAR explained that relations were severed because promised East German development aid had remained "nonexistent." In Zambia, East German hopes for full recognition were crushed when the Foreign Minister announced the closing of the GDR trade mission in September. The *Zambia Daily Mail* (13 September) accused the East Germans of interfering in domestic affairs and of "fomenting trouble wherever they could," and suggested that the Germans had been acting on orders from the Soviet Union: "They went about doing the dirty work of their masters until they were caught red-handed."

In contrast, East Germany was getting increasingly more involved in the political, economic, and cultural life of the Arab states of the Middle East—especially Iraq, Yemen, Sudan, Syria, and Egypt—which had granted full recognition to the GDR in 1969 and 1970. An elite corps of policemen in uniforms similar to those seen in East Germany, for instance, appeared in the streets of Cairo shortly after the East German Minister of the Interior, General Friedrich Dickel, paid a visit to the Egyptian capital and revealed the existence of a cooperative agreement "for the exchange of expertise and the training of police" (*al-Ahram*, Cairo, 22 February). A few months later the *Egyptian Gazette* (Cairo, 23 May) printed the denial by a spokesman of the Egyptian Ministry of the Interior concerning rumors that East German experts were serving in the U.A.R.'s security service. Reports of unusual East German interest in Arab information media were confirmed when the Iraqi and East German journalists' associations signed a five-year agreement on press, radio, and television cooperation in August 1971.

World events produced East German reactions normally identical with those of the Soviet Union. The GDR invariably supported Soviet foreign interests, such as the treaty of friendship and cooperation between India and the U.S.S.R., which *Neues Deutschland* (11 August) lauded as an event of "overwhelming significance" and a "safeguard for peace." Late in the year the GDR—which has long zealously campaigned for diplomatic recognition by India—fully supported Indian involvement in the armed conflict in Pakistan. Subsequently, early in 1972, East Germany became the first nation outside the Indian subcontinent to recognize the new nation of Bangladesh.

When U.S. President Nixon's plans to visit China were announced in July, *Neues Deutschland* delayed comment for two weeks, but then editorialized critically (29 July): "Nixon has grandiloquently described his forthcoming visit to Peking as a 'journey for peace.' Public opinion rightly wonders whether the aim is to pursue the old aggressive policy of imperialism with new more flexible methods." The political weekly *Horizont* (no. 32, August) later asserted that efforts for U.S.-Chinese rapprochement were not based on a desire for peace but were to serve as a diversion from internal crises in both countries—the consequences of the Cultural Revolution in China and dissension over the Indochina war in the United States. Both countries allegedly were motivated by "pure anti-Sovietism," but China was held guilty of special hypocrisy for "contact with Washington via a secret line" and public denunciation of imperialism while trying to "establish China as the third world power." *Horizont* further asserted that all suspicions were confirmed by the attitude of West German politicians, who were suddenly acting like friends of China, whereas they "usually excel in anti-communism and in opposing any détente." Their new mood was said to result from "betting on a change in the 'weather' in favor of their aggressive, strategic goals regarding the socialist states, particularly the GDR," another newspaper explained (*National Zeitung*, East Berlin, 1 August).

The announcement of Nixon's plan to visit Moscow in 1972 was hailed by the SED party organ as a move that "foils the plans of Peking's leaders to use their latest flirtation with Washington for the establishment of an anti-Soviet bloc." But *Neues Deutschland* (13 October) also provided this interpretation for the intended trip: "It shows that there is no basic issue of international politics which can be solved without the Soviet Union."

In spite of the many charges leveled against China, East Germany viewed the admission of that country to the United Nations with "profound satisfaction." Self-interest was displayed, however, by speculation on the possibility of additional admissions and the following recommendation: "The time has surely come to remove all the discriminatory measures imposed by imperialism, in contravention of international law, on other states. The time has come to fully and finally enforce the universality of the world organization." (ADN, 27 October.)

Publication of the Pentagon Papers in June provided the impetus for East German charges that the United States was seeking to "revitalize" militarism or the "long bankrupt policy of strength" (*Neues Deutschland*, 12 June); that all political credibility had been destroyed by the revelation that the United States had "provoked this war [in Vietnam] according to plan"; that "U.S. presidents deliberately deceived Americans"; that the "secret papers reveal the predatory tactics of imperialists"; and that publication of the papers was motivated by the desire to blame past U.S. administrations while "exonerating" the Nixon administration and "saving it by providing it with a new image" of apparent peaceful pursuit (*Neues Deutschland*, 17 and 23 June; domestic television 3 July).

Generally, East Germany in 1971 condemned only its foreign enemies of long standing. An exception was Sudan, a country with which the GDR had established full diplomatic relations in 1969. This did not deter the Germans from reacting vehemently to the "hysterical anti-communist drive" and the "murder and persecution of our Sudanese comrades" when President Ja'far al-Numairi jailed or executed every Sudanese communist who could be rounded up following an abortive communist coup in July. *Neues Deutschland* (28 July) warned the government of Sudan that only by ending the persecution and consolidating all "patriotic forces" could it "fight successfully against imperialism and neo-colonialism and secure national independence and social advancement."

Great Britain was denounced for the "slander campaign instigated by the Conservative government against the U.S.S.R." which held the Soviets "responsible for strikes by British workers, the difficulties of shipbuilders on the Clyde, and the sanguinary unrest in Northern Ireland" (*Berliner Zeitung*, East Berlin, 28 September). "Brutality" in internment camps in Northern Ireland and the "inhuman, undemocratic order, devoid of all freedom," used by British forces and "their extreme right-wing helpers ... not choosy in their methods" were repeatedly scored by East German media (*Neues Deutschland*, 10 August, 19 November).

Iceland and Malta received considerable favorable attention by the East German press in 1971, because their new governments were "steering a course against NATO" (ADN, 13 July).

International Party Contacts. In 1971 the SED participated in numerous bilateral and multilateral meetings with representatives of foreign communist parties. The scope of inter-party contacts was also illustrated by the attendance of representatives of 91 parties at the SED congress.

Only a few contacts were noteworthy for deviating from the established norm, such as the unusual publicity given to the activities of the (West) German Communist Party (DKP), including the extensive coverage of its congress, held in Düsseldorf in November. The Communist Party of Finland assumed an unexpectedly prominent role after the Finnish government submitted identical proposals to both the GDR and the FRG in September suggesting negotiations on the possible conclusion of state treaties and the establishment of diplomatic relations. An SED delegation, headed by Politburo member Hermann Axen, went to Helsinki in November to discuss these proposals. Helsinki radio (12 November) reported on Axen's discussion with the president of Finland and other government officials: "Axen said the GDR understood the principle of equality contained in the Finnish proposal, according to which talks should be held simultaneously with the two German states. Axen added that the GDR has given an affirmative reply to this offer for negotiations, with the complete sovereignty of all sides in mind." A lengthy communiqué issued at the conclusion of talks between the SED representatives and leaders of the Communist Party of Finland contained this statement: "The Communist Party of Finland reiterates its view, repeatedly expressed in the past, that Finland must on no account make the establishment of diplomatic relations with the GDR dependent on the attitude of the FRG" (ADN, 13 November).

Occasions for multilateral contacts were provided at home by such events as the annual "Baltic Week," held in Rostock in July, or abroad by attendance at congresses of fraternal parties, of which the CPSU congress was the most important.

Publications and Broadcast Media. The official organ of the SED Central Committee, *Neues Deutschland*, is the most important daily newspaper in East Germany (circulation about 800,000). In April 1971 *Neues Deutschland* was hailed on the occasion of its twenty-fifth anniversary, as a "collective propagandist agitator and organizer in the struggle for building socialism in the GDR." In July, Honecker announced the appointment of Joachim Herrmann as editor in chief, replacing Rudolf Singer (who was named chairman of the State Broadcasting Committee). The SED also publishes the *Berliner Zeitung* (circulation 500,000) and dailies in major cities of the GDR. In addition, officially approved material appears in publications of the other National Front parties and mass organizations. Two of them, the CDU's *Neue Zeit* and the FDJ's *Junge Welt*, got new editors in chief in 1971. The SED deals with party questions in the semimonthly *Neuer Weg* and with the theory and practice of scientific socialism in the monthly *Einheit*.

A new radio station, Stimme der GDR (Voice of the GDR), began transmission on 15 November and simultaneously "Deutschlandsender" and "Berliner Welle" ceased broadcasting. *Neues Deutschland* (4 November) carried this announcement: "The new station will acquaint listeners primarily with the policy of our state on all international questions. It will not only cover international events and developments of interest in the socialist world, primarily in the Soviet Union, but will also feature popular international music and entertainment." That East German authorities were concerned about information media was also indicated by an SED decision that only newspapermen from the GDR could work in the FRG for East Germany; even members of the West German communist party could no longer be accredited correspondents (Hamburg radio, 19 April).

Edith Wyden

Hungary

Hungarian communists formed a party in November 1918 and briefly held power, but after 1919 the movement virtually disappeared. Near the end of World War II, communists organized again and gained control of the country in 1947, taking the name of the Hungarian Workers' Party in 1948. On 1 November 1956 the name was changed to the Hungarian Socialist Workers' Party (Magyar Szocialista Munkáspárt; HSWP).

Party Affairs. The HSWP holds a monopoly of political power in Hungary. Party membership numbers about 670,000. The population of Hungary is 10,354,000 (estimated 1971).

The current leadership, elected in November 1970 at the party's Tenth Congress, is headed by János Kádár as first secretary, an office he has held without a break since 25 October 1956. Other secretaries include György Aczél, Béla Biszku, Zoltán Komócsin, Rezsö Nyers, Miklós Ovári, and Arpád Pullai. The thirteen member Politburo consists of Aczél, Biszku, Kádár, Komócsin, Nyers, Antal Apró, Valéria Benke, Lajos Fehér, Jenö Fock, Sándor Gáspár, Gyula Kállai, Dezsö Nemes, and Károly Németh. The Central Committee numbers 105 members. Kádár remains unchallenged in his position. Prominent lieutenants appear to be Biszku, with responsibility for domestic and party affairs; Komócsin, as foreign policy expert; and Nyers who has played a leading role in the economic reform known as the New Economic Mechanism (NEM).

One of Kádár's predecessors, Mátyás Rákosi, who led the party during Hungary's absorption into the Soviet bloc, died early in 1971 in the Soviet Union and was given private burial in Budapest. Recent party histories have charged him with "sectarianism," violations of "socialist legality," and promotion of a personality cult. Such accusations serve to disassociate the current party line from the "distortions" of the Stalinist era.

During 1971 the HSWP Central Committee met five times in plenary session: on 28 January, 29 April, 4 August, 3 November, and 1 December. Ideological and cultural issues were discussed at a special national conference of party workers and communications media representatives in Budapest on 10-11 May (*Népszabadság*, 12 May). János Brutyó, chairman of the Central Control Committee, disclosed in an interview (*ibid.*, 4 July) that disciplinary proceedings had been initiated in 1970 against 5,181 party members and that 29 had been expelled for political reasons. Most cases allegedly arose from "money grubbing" and abuses of authority, but there were 37 cases indicative of the party's concern for its democratic image involving suppression of and retaliation against criticism. Among current party problems are the maintenance of morale and dedication of members and the recruitment of young manual workers and intellectuals into its aging and increasingly bureaucratized membership.

Mass Organizations and Interest Groups. A network of mass organizations in the Hungarian political system continues to serve the dual function of mobilizing support for official policy and articulating sectional interests. While such organizations are no longer exclusively the agents of party control, their performance as independent pressure groups in the Western sense is extremely limited.

The Patriotic People's Front (PPF), with some 4,400 committees and 120,000 registered members, coordinates the political activities of party members and non-members. In a report to the PPF National Council on 18 February, Secretary-General István Bencsik stated that the principal task was fostering "socialist democracy" in governmental and social activities. (Budapest Radio, 28 February). During the year, the PPF performed its principal periodic function of supervising nomination procedures and mobilizing the population for the general elections.

The National Trade Union Council (SZOT) is headed by Politburo member Sándor Gáspár as secretary-general. The SZOT and the individual trade unions have in recent years demonstrated an increased degree of independence in pursuing the interests of their members, a task that acquired new significance under the NEM policy of decentralizing economic management. Criticism of wage and price policies, work conditions, fringe benefits, and "enterprise democracy" is frequently voiced at union meetings, and officials have emphasized the unions' dual role of serving both the general interest of society and the "legitimate interests of a smaller community" (Népszava, 16 January). Under the new labor code, a division of responsibility operates at the enterprise level between union locals and management, industrial branch level between trade unions and ministries, and highest level between SZOT and the Council of Ministers. Strong criticism of official policies and statements was voiced when the National Union of Food Industry Workers attacked new wage regulations (Magyar Hirlap, 12 January). Later the trade union daily Népszava (10 February) rebuked a minister for allegedly unfounded complaints regarding the printing industry. The National Congress of Trade Unions (4-8 May) debated a number of controversial issues, notably problems faced by union locals in exercising their rights.

Other mass organizations that held congresses during 1971 included the National Council of Hungarian Women (MNOT), National Association of Industrial Cooperatives (OKISZ), National Organization of Artisans (KIOSZ), and Communist Youth League (KISZ). The MNOT conference discussed party and government resolutions on improvement of the social and economic position of women. Industrial cooperatives, numbering 1,107 with 316,000 members, play a major role in the economy. Although their output increased by 77 per cent over the past five years, the deputy prime minister complained at the congress of their neglect of the underdeveloped service sector in favor of more profitable production (Magyar Hirlap, 13 October). Official concern over the restlessness of young people was emphasized in connection with the KISZ congress (8-11 December), which provided a forum for assurances of understanding and support by party and government leaders and exhortations to the young to involve themselves in the building of socialism. Mass organizations remain under direct or indirect HSWP control. Only those representing sectional economic interests appear to act as pressure groups as well as more orthodox safety valves and agents of mobilization.

Government and Administration. At the 1970 party congress, in addition to reasserting its confidence in NEM viability, the HSWP had endorsed a cautious liberalization of the political system through controlled decentralization, all under the guise of developing "social democracy." The National Assembly passed a bill on councils that supported this policy. Defining local government councils as "autonomous administrative organs of the state, realizing the power of the people and functioning on the basis of democratic centralism" (Budapest radio, 10 February), the bill was aimed at increasing the councils' independence, initiative, and efficiency and at the same time improving the effectiveness of central direction. The reform reduced the central government's role to general guidance and supplying of material support. Longer (four year) budgetary allocations extended the councils' economic autonomy. By linking certain council revenues to the performance of enterprises under their jurisdiction, the bill also was aimed at an indirect improvement of economic management. This experiment in decentralization was an outgrowth of HSWP policy for economic modernization and legitimization of its rule through broader popular participation in public affairs. Parameters for council activities, however, are to be centrally determined as before. The HSWP Central Committee referred to the council bill as part of the gradual transformation of governmental administration and declared that the next task of socialist construction would be to improve efficiency in the bureaucracy through better definition of authority and increased responsibilities for administrators (*Népszabadság*, 4 November).

A major manifestation of "socialist democracy" during the year was the holding of elections to both National Assembly and local councils. This was to be the last instance of simultaneous voting at two levels of government, since a new law promulgated in October 1970 provides for a staggering of the four-year term. Thus, in 1971 council members were elected for only two years. Another new feature was the relaxation of nomination procedures. Whereas previously PPF sponsorship had been the deciding factor at nomination meetings, candidates supported by at least a third of those attending were automatically placed on the ballot. Extensive publicity was given to this new democratic option in order to mobilize popular involvement for an essentially predictable political process. The party newspaper (*ibid.*, 26 March) even reprimanded some PPF officials in Budapest for overly authoritarian conduct of nomination meetings. On the other hand, the requirement that all candidates adhere to the PPF program remained in force. Kádár told an election rally that "candidates' personalities are very important, but what is most important, what is decisive, is the policy, the program" (*ibid.*, 21 April).

At nomination meetings organized by the PPF between 15 and 31 March, 49 multiple candacies were registered in 352 parliamentary electoral districts (compared with 9 in the 1967 election) and 3,016 multiple candacies for 68,946 local council seats. In the elections, held on April 25, 98.7 per cent of the voters exercised their franchise and the PPF received 99.1 per cent of the valid votes (99.7 per cent in 1967). This means that 68,996 persons crossed off all names on the ballot. (*Ibid.*, 28 April.) Since many of the multiple candacies had represented official PPF candidates, the extent to which voters took advantage of the electoral reform remained unclear, but a number of "spontaneously" nominated candidates were elected. The new National Assembly had some 100 non-party members, compared with about 80 in 1967 (*Magyar Nemzet*, 25 April). In occupations, a marginal decline took place in deputies from the party apparatus, the mass organizations, and the agricultural sector. Slight increases from the industrial sector and the intelligentsia were registered.

At its constituent meeting on 12 May the National Assembly elected the Presidential Council and Council of Ministers with few changes in personnel (*Népszabadság*, 13 May). Pál Losonczi was returned as chairman of the Presidential Council (i.e., head of state) and Jenö Fock as premier. One of four deputy premiers, Antal Apró, was replaced by former minister of finance, Péter Vályi. Apró became speaker of the National Assembly, replacing Gyula Kállai, a former premier who kept several offices as member of the Presidential Council and Politburo and president of the PPF. The finance ministry went to an experienced civil servant, Lajos Faluvégi, and two other major portfolios changed hands—heavy industry and light industry.

Neither the election nor the constituent session made any significant alteration in the government. This was in keeping with HSWP emphasis on NEM consolidation and the modest role played by parliament. Despite frequent official assertions of the National Assembly's growing importance and expertise, its deliberations have continued to reflect the concept of government by consensus. Convened for brief, two-day sessions in June, September, and December, the Assembly functioned mainly as a forum for communication and ratification of government policies; few deputies took any active part in its largely formal deliberations. During the year the Assembly approved various economic and budgetary measures and a new youth bill. Also it elected a committee to prepare a revision of the 1949 constitution to "incorporate the social, political, economic, and cultural achievements of the past two decades" and to "express in the constitution the tasks of the complete building of socialism" (Budapest radio, 24 June).

The New Economic Mechanism. Launched by the HSWP in 1968 to lift Hungary's economy out of the doldrums of the mid-sixties, the NEM reform program remains the most radical attempt at economic modernization within the Soviet bloc. At the same time, according to official party interpretation, NEM represents not a specifically Hungarian road to socialism (which would have obvious connotations of Titoism) but a Marxist-Leninist policy for building socialism which takes into account the national framework (Kádár interview, Budapest radio, 17 March 1971). Broadly, NEM seeks an ongoing decentralization of authority and provides incentives for competitiveness in domestic and foreign markets. Despite positive results, its radical departure from earlier orthodoxy has occasioned certain stresses of readjustment, some of which approached a critical point in 1971.

A report on fulfillment of the 1970 plan showed improved performance. National income rose by 5 per cent, per capita real wages in industry registered a 4 per cent increase over 1969, and real income (including increased social benefits) rose by 6 to 7 per cent (*Népszabadság*, 7 February). Retail prices remained relatively stable with an average increase of 1.2 per cent. Industrial production rose by 7 per cent and per capita production by 6.8 per cent, reflecting a healthy improvement in productivity which nevertheless stood at half the level of the more developed states. Expansion was most notable in the favored chemical and precision engineering branches. Although agricultural production declined by 5 per cent, largely as a result of bad weather, the peasants' real income also advanced. Two negative aspects were an unfavorable balance of foreign trade and growth in incompleted investments. The report on the five-year plan for 1966-70 indicated satisfactory performance in most sectors. (*Ibid*., 20 March.)

Despite this favorable overall record, the economy continued to suffer from a number of problems. In view of the manpower shortage, modernization of industrial plant and processes will be necessary in order to achieve the desired improvement in productivity, requiring in turn a high level and efficient utilization of investments. The manpower shortage and inadequate incentives for private artisans have also retarded the development of the service sector (*ibid*., 24 April). Fulfillment of the domestic and export demand on agriculture has continued to be hindered by inadequate mechanization and marketing, the most acute shortages arising in the supply of meat. Selective government subsidies, development of county marketing centers, official encouragement of private plot farming, and vertical integration of food production are some of the measures aimed at alleviating the situation.

Social stresses attributable to NEM have compelled the HSWP and the government to pursue a continuous publicity campaign in its defense. An important corollary has been the relatively open debate on its merits and shortcomings. The permissive and competitive climate engendered by NEM has led to instances of excessive profitseeking at both individual and enterprise levels. So-called money-grubbing practices are regularly denounced by the press. In response, the government has imposed restrictions on secondary employment ("moonlighting") and real estate speculation—the latter by limiting a family's holdings to two plots or residences (*ibid*., 9 July; *Magyar Hirlap*, 25 September).

The more delicate issue of wage differentiation and bonuses tends to bring the NEM goal of increasing productivity into conflict with the public's more immediate concern for the standard of living. A new basic wage system, introduced in February, established uniform standards for the classification of workers, employees, and managers and an expanded wage scale (*Népszabadság*,

30 March). This created tensions within enterprises and aroused egalitarian reactions in the labor movement. Selective wage increases in the educational and health sectors and for Budapest's transport workers only exacerbated the debate on differentiation criteria. The government has instituted tighter central regulation over annual premiums, particularly for upper management, and has hinted at higher taxation of incomes from secondary employment, but remains committed to its policy of productivity incentives.

The labor code guarantee of freedom of employment has, in an increasingly market-oriented and manpower-poor economy, led to an annual industrial labor turnover of over 30 per cent. Certain councils have taken the ostensibly temporary but nonetheless unpopular step of setting up compulsory labor exchanges for specified categories of workers. Partly as a result, manpower turnover declined slightly during 1971 (Budapest radio, 18 December).

Social stresses concomitant with the NEM appear to have been caused by rising expectations of consumers, labor, and government planners. That the economy faced serious trouble was made clear at an extraordinary conference of top party, government, and enterprise officials on 22 October, where Premier Fock referred to grave deficiencies in investments, manpower management, and foreign trade. Unfinished projects, he said, accounted for an intolerable 80 per cent of annual investments. The government would have to take steps both to accelerate the rate of completion and to scrutinize new projects more closely. In manpower, the foreseeable stabilization in the number of working-age people, together with the high rate of labor turnover, necessitated remedial measures, including incentives to retain pensionable workers in the labor force. Blaming agricultural cooperatives for enticing workers away from the state sector and into their ancillary industrial activities, Fock announced that such diversification would be checked (a decree to this effect was announced on 2 December). The major economic shortfall noted by Fock was a rapidly worsening trade deficit, the first eight months of 1971 having produced the highest deficit in Hungary's history. Exports to the non-socialist countries especially had suffered a sizable decline. Fock took pains to emphasize, however, that corrective measures should not be construed as a "restrictive policy." (Ibid., 23 October.) The meeting was significant not only for the frank revelation of shortcomings, but also for the decision of the party and government to debate these problems openly.

The 1972 budget responded to the weaknesses outlined by Fock. Finance Minister Faluvégi reported to the National Assembly that in many respects—industrial and agricultural production, consumption, and even housing—the economy had performed better than was expected (ibid., 21 December). On the other hand, he indicated that in 1972 the level of investments could not rise and that authorities would exercise greater selectivity in credit policy. Further, he repeated earlier threats to stop unprofitable production. Also speaking on the budget, Politburo member Nyers stated that the government's decision to reestablish economic equilibrium necessitated a slight deceleration in the growth of the national income, but stressed that the trade imbalance would have to be corrected mainly by increased exports rather than a drastic reduction in imports of consumers' goods.

Ideology and Culture. In recent years ideological debate in Hungary has focused on socioeconomic issues, arising in part from NEM, and on the significance of patriotism in a socialist society. The viability of the political system and of the HSWP "national unity" policy, which stresses cooperation rather than indoctrination, has remained unchallenged. Even so, in 1971 the country's foremost Marxist scholar, György Lukács, communicated to a foreign journalist his profound pessimism regarding the prospects for genuine socialist democracy within the bureaucratic-authoritarian systems of the Soviet Union and Eastern Europe (L'homme et la société, Paris, April-June). Lukács died on 4 June. A subject of wide debate during the year was the apparent popularity among some young people of a Guevarist radicalism which charges that revolutionary socialist principles have been abondoned in favor of a crass materialism by much of Hungarian society and, by implication, its leaders. A report on "political crimes" noted—along with a general decline and cautious behavior on the part of former "class enemies"—a new source of dissent on the "extreme left" (*Népszava*, 3 July). Although this fashionable radicalism has become an embarrassment to the HSWP, as have the somewhat opportunistic egalitarianism of the trade unions and the increasing disparities in wealth, the party line remained anchored to the middle-of-the-road pragmatism and cautious reformism elaborated in the 1960s.

On a more academic level, debates continued on the inclusive but elusive "working class" concept (*Társadalmi Szemle*, June). Clearly, it requires some reappraisal in an officially classless society that is nevertheless socioeconomically differentiated and marked by imperfect social mobility. The question acquires greater relevance in the educational sphere, where statistics show a disproportionate representation of children of the intelligentsia in academic high schools and universities (*ibid.*, May). Here the problem is to increase the number of manual workers' children without reintroducing the discriminatory admission policies abolished in 1962 at the HSWP's Eighth Congress. High school students' political profiles are still taken into account, and their political education, including a subject called "Fundamentals of Our World-View" is receiving new emphasis as is the ideological and pedagogical elaboration of "Marxist ethics."

The ever-present themes of the nation and nationalism—although highly sensitive in respect to Hungary's relations with the Soviet Union and the neighboring socialist countries—surfaced in various debates. The concern voiced by the prominent writer Gyula Illyés for the survival of the Hungarian people within and outside the country's borders (he noted in this context an endemically high suicide rate) drew the orthodox criticism that he had overemphasized national consciousness at the expense of socialist consciousness (*Népszabadság*, 14 February). The fifth "Conference on Socialist Patriotism" dealt extensively with that third of all Hungarians who live outside the country, with the historical and now reappearing phenomenon of nationalism in Eastern Europe, and with the consequences these have for Hungary's relations with her neighbors (*Magyar Nemzet*, 20 October).

HSWP cultural guidelines, expounded principally by Gyorgy Aczél, remained unaltered (*Társadalmi Szemle*, November). They proclaim Marxist hegemony rather than monopoly and appear in practice as the "three T's"—the supported, tolerated, and prohibited artistic categories. In addition to these rather vague and flexible limitations, the "Cultural Fund" instituted under NEM had exercised influence by taxation of "trash" and the subsidizing of more elevating works (*Magyar Hirlap*, 7 November). At a national sociographic conference on 29-30 November it was claimed that today's literary sociographers, unlike their predecessors in the political opposition of the 1930's, remain in the socialist mainstream with works such as the "Discovery of Hungary" series, but their probing quasi-sociological studies occasionally test party tolerance.

The major development in church affairs was the sudden departure of Cardinal Mindszenty for exile on 28 September after fifteen years in the U.S. Embassy at Budapest. He undertook never to return and, following a visit to the Vatican, retired to Vienna. The government granted him a pardon, without dismissing the charge of treason for which he was sentenced in 1949. His departure facilitated a further normalization of relations with the Vatican. On 1 October the Vatican abrogated its 1957 decree reserving for itself the right to allow Hungarian priests to participate in political life. This right thus reverted to the bishops, whose freedom of action is circumscribed by HSWP's limited flexibility in religious matters. The compromise—which apparently included restrictions on Mindszenty's public life in exile—seemed to favor the government.

International Relations. Economic affairs figure prominently in Hungary's international relations since 40 per cent of the national income is derived from foreign trade. The first eight months of 1971 showed an adverse balance of 3,284 million foreign exchange forints with the socialist countries and another 3,003 million with the non-socialist countries (*Statisztikai Havi Közlemények*, [Monthly Statistical Bulletin], Budapest, no. 9), as against a total adverse balance of 3,142 million for all of 1970, prompting the minister of foreign trade to urge improvements in technical standards of Hungarian products, marketing techniques, and market research (Budapest radio, 1 November).

Economic integration of member countries of the Council for Mutual Economic Assistance made little progress in 1971. One revealing instance of lack of coordination is the excess capacity of the machine industries in the CMEA countries, which produce goods not in demand either within the bloc or, for reasons of technical inferiority on the world market (*Külkereskedelem*, [Foreign Commerce], Budapest, October). The principal result of the CMEA meeting at Bucharest on 27-29 July was agreement on a "complex program" which, in essence, recognizes the diversity in size, structure, and mechanism of member economies and aims merely at further development of the existing pattern for voluntary cooperation and specialization (*Népszabadság*, 7 August). One subsequent multilateral agreement on production specialization, devised by CMEA's standing committee on machine industry and involving seven Hungarian enterprises, was hailed as an application of the program (*Világgazdaság*, [World Economy], Budapest, 12 October).

In the main, Hungary's trade relations with socialist countries remained bilateral. A number of cooperative agreements highlighted Soviet-Hungarian trade (which accounts for roughly a third of all Hungarian trade), including the bauxite-aluminum industry, computer technology, and passenger cars (although the Hungarian enterprise producing parts for the Soviet Zhiguli (Fiat) automobile went bankrupt). Trade with Mainland China, stagnant in recent years, increased substantially: in the first quarter of 1971, imports and exports rose by some 57 per cent and 308 per cent respectively over the corresponding figures for 1970 (*Statisztikai Havi Közlemények* no. 4).

Chronic shortages of energy have imposed a constant quest for new foreign sources. The major development in 1971 was a preliminary agreement on the long-delayed Adria pipeline. Necessitated by the Soviet Union's inability to increase its oil exports, and conceived as a Yugoslav-Hungarian-Czechoslovak project, the pipeline when completed in 1975 will supply Middle Eastern oil, probably from Iraq, to the three countries (*Világgazdaság*, 8 October). Other agreements will provide hydroelectric power from Romania in addition to natural gas and, by 1975, link Hungary to the pipeline bringing natural gas from Siberia to Western Europe.

Trade with the industrialized Western countries has been growing rapidly but not entirely to Hungary's advantage in either its trade balance or its export structure. Besides redressing the balance, Hungary seeks to increase the proportion of exported industrial and finished goods, overcome trade restrictions by long-term agreements, gain membership in the General Agreement on Trade and Tariffs (GATT) organization and most-favored-nation status with the United States, and enter cooperative agreements particularly where they bring technological innovations (*Külkereskedelem*, August-September 1971). In spite of the Common Market's trade barriers, Italy and West Germany are (along with Austria) Hungary's major Western trading partners. A contract was signed with West Germany in July to provide equipment valued at $37 million for the Tisza Chemical Combine olefin works. Algeria, Chile, Japan, China, and Canada were among countries visited by Hungarian delegations in search of new markets. A trade exhibit at Toronto was the first such Hungarian venture overseas.

A good record in repaying foreign loans facilitated negotiation in 1971 of a new five-year credit for $50 million from a Western consortium. It will be used for development of export-oriented branches of industry (*Népszabadság*, 3 December). Earlier, the Hungarian National Bank issued $25 million in bonds on the Eurobond market, presumably to cope with the unfavorable balance of payments. Tourism, an important source of hard currency, increased by 32 per cent over 1970.

Partly to increase tourism and also for political reasons, the government is pursuing rapprochement with the sizable Hungarian population abroad.

The foreign policy orientation of the HSWP remains essentially indistinguishable from that of the Soviet Union. Sino-American negotiations have prompted charges that China, in the words of Gyula Kállai, is "trying to turn [the United Nations] into a platform of anti-Soviet and anti-Socialist policy and thus adopting a common stand with the world's reactionary forces" (Budapest radio, 21 December). China also contributed to momentarily strained relations between Hungary and her Balkan neighbors. The visit of Romanian party leader Nicolae Ceauşescu to Peking in June and reports of a projected visit by Chinese Premier Chou En-lai to Albania, Yugoslavia, and Romania gave rise to speculations about an anti-Soviet Tirana-Belgrade-Bucharest axis. Categorical denials were made that the Chinese line, distinguishing between the interests of the superpowers (and implying a contradiction between the interests of the Soviet Union and Eastern Europe), could supersede the class viewpoint (*Népszabadság*, 18 July; *Magyar Hirlap*, 13 August). Such press comments, together with Warsaw Pact maneuvers in central Hungary, were open to an anti-Romanian and anti-Yugoslav interpretation.

Even less equivocal was the unprecedented rebuke to Romania voiced by Komócsin before the National Assembly on 24 June: "It is a matter of fundamental concern to us that both the people of our country and those of Romania—including the Hungarian minority living there—should realize that the fate and the future of our people are inseparable from socialism" (*Népszabadság*, 25 June). There were sharp responses from Bucharest and Belgrade, but following Brezhnev's visits to the Yugoslav capital and to Budapest, the polemics subsided and relations between Hungary and the two states returned to normal. A notable feature of Komócsin's address involved his exceptional reference to the 1.5 million Hungarian minority in Romania; the status of minorities and the duty of a socialist state to protect their cultural identity appear to be no longer proscribed subjects (*Elet és Irodalom* [Life and Literature], Budapest, 20 November). Elsewhere in Eastern Europe, the HSWP has warmly endorsed the communist regimes of Czechoslovakia and Poland. In March-April, a party delegation led by Kádár attended the Twenty-fourth Congress of the Communist Party of the Soviet Union and made the customary expressions of solidarity.

In relations with the West, the HSWP has followed the soviet lead by denouncing "American imperialism" in Southeast Asia and the Middle East. It advocated on every suitable occasion, notably at the meeting of the Warsaw Pact foreign ministers in December, convocation of a European security conference. The Hungarian head of state Pal Losonczi, visited Austria on June 28-July 2 and was in Africa in December which had the more immediate purpose of improving economic relations.

Publications. HSWP organs include the Budapest daily newspaper *Népszabadság* [People's Freedom] circulation 755,000; the theoretical monthly *Társadalmi Szemle* [Social Review] 36,000; and the monthly organizational journal *Pártélet* [Party Life] 95,000. Among other important publications are the dailies *Magyar Hirlap* [Hungarian News] and *Magyar Nemzet* [Hungarian Nation], the latter published by the Patriotic People's Front, and the National Trade Union Council's *Népszava* [People's Voice]. All are published in Budapest.

University of Toronto   Bennett Kovrig

Poland

The communist movement in the Polish People's Republic goes under the name of the Polish United Workers' Party (Polska Zjednoczona Partia Robotnicza; PUWP). Its origins date back to December 1918 and the founding of the Communist Workers' Party of Poland, which operated underground after being outlawed in early 1919. The name was changed to the Communist Party of Poland in 1925. For reasons not entirely clear the Comintern dissolved the party in 1938, and many of its leaders perished in the great Soviet purge. In January 1942 the party reappeared as the Polish Workers' Party. It quickly dominated the "national unity" coalition government that followed the advance of the Red Army into Poland. In 1948 it induced the left-wing remnants of the old Polish Socialist Party to merge with it as the Polish United Workers' Party.

Since then the PUWP has controlled all political activities in Poland through the "National Unity Front," ostensibly a coalition of the PUWP and two communist-controlled "independent" parties—the United Peasant Party (Zjednoczone Stronnictwo Ludowe; UPP) and the Democratic Party (Stronnictwo Demokratyczne; DP), officially representing the peasantry and the working intelligentsia and small entrepreneurs, respectively. To make the government appear as broadly representative as possible, three Catholic groups have been allowed to include candidates in the single list elections: (1) "Pax," founded in 1945 by Bolesław Piasecki, who sees no incompatibility between Christianity and the social and economic policies of the PUWP, though he rejects its atheism and supports an independent existence for the Catholic church; (2) the Christian Social Association split off from Pax in 1956 under Jan Frankowski, after Piasecki insisted on a hard Stalinist line; and (3) "Znak," a Catholic intellectual group associated with the church hierarchy. In mid-1971, Polish media referred to representation (secretary general Józef Szwajner) of a fourth Catholic "group" in the Sejm, or parliament: "Caritas," a charity association. (For results of the most recent, June 1969 elections, see *YICA* 1970, p. 61).

Membership. On 5 December the PUWP daily *Trybuna Ludu* printed the Central Committee report on party activity between the fifth and sixth PUWP congresses. It noted that as of 30 September party membership, including candidates, stood at 2.27 million. The total represented a drop of 50,000 from the 2.32 million enrolled at the end of 1970, due to somewhat tighter membership standards and the "individual talks" held with about half of the PUWP membership during the summer. As of 30 September, the social composition of the party was reported as: workers, 40.1 per cent; peasants, 11.0 per cent; white-collar workers, 43.2 per cent; and other, 5.8 per cent. Party members comprise not quite 7 per cent of a population estimated at 32,800,000 (1971).

Organization and Leadership. The PUWP is organized hierarchically, with the lower units subordinated to the next higher. There were about 72,600 civilian and 3,500 military primary party units in 1971. The next level is formed by district organizations, and the third echelon comprises province organizations. The highest authority is the congress. The Sixth Congress in December, was called a year early because of the need to legitimize policy changes introduced by the new leadership under First Secretary Edward Gierek. It elected a Central Committee, and the latter chose a Politburo, Secretariat, and Central Party Control Commission. Additional changes in the composition of the top PUWP organs took place after the Sixth Congress, as Gierek continued to consolidate his position and attempted a major revitalization of the party (see below for details).

Mass Organizations. The PUWP relies heavily on mass membership and other smaller and specialized organizations to (1) increase its legitimacy, (2) disseminate propaganda and mobilize support for its political and economic objectives, (3) mold socialist attitudes and control mass behavior, (4) provide a party-controlled substitute for every organization normally found in modern society and preempt the field for any potential opposition organizations, (5) undermine existing organizations not yet under party control (e.g., the Catholic church), and (6) mobilize the population for socially useful work over and above their regular employment. The publications, mass meetings, rallies, campaigns, and other activities of these organizations provide an important supplement to the direct work of the PUWP activists and press.

The most important of these mass organizations are the various trade unions (with over 10,100,000 members in 23 occupational groups) coordinated by the Central Council of Trade Unions (Centralna Rada Związków Zawodowych; CCTU). The CCTU has been headed by Władysław Kruczek since 15 January, when Ignacy Loga-Sowiński was forced to resign in the wake of continued worker unrest. The trade unions play a particularly important role in mobilizing workers to fulfill economic tasks decided on by the party and the central planning apparatus. They were given responsibility for preparing a draft labor code, completed in May and submitted to a government study commission. Despite subservience to the party, there has been an increasing tendency for unions to represent more actively the interests and demands of the workers, especially so after December 1970. The Gierek leadership is clearly interested in increasing the degree to which trade unions, the nearly 7,500 workers' councils, and the more than 8,000 workers' self-government organizations serve as channels of feedback communication to top party levels.

Within the CCTU are separate specialized associations for government employees, health service personnel, and primary and secondary school teachers. The rest of the intelligentsia has its own associations which provide social services to members, mobilize them to build socialism, and exercise control over the quality and political content of their work. Politically the most important of these are the Association of Polish Journalists, the Association of Polish Lawyers, the Polish Writers' Union, and the Association of Authors.

In rural areas, apart from the UPP and the CCTU farm workers' union, there is a Peasant Self-Help Cooperative "Samopomoc Chłopska" with over 2,500 separate co-ops and a network of more than 35,000 agricultural circles with more than 2,600,000 members, established to improve the quality of village life and encourage cooperation as well as introduction of improved farming techniques. The Central Union of Agricultural Circles (Centralny Związek Kółek Rolniczych; CUAC) coordinates the work of the local circles. In July UPP member Aleksander Schmidt replaced Franciszek Gesing as CUAC chairman after Gesing, also a UPP member had been elected to the Council of State.

The two most important youth organizations are the Socialist Youth Union (Związek Młodzieży Socjalistycznej), headed by Andrzej Zabiński, with about 1,290,000 members (of which 10.5 per cent are also PUWP members), and the Rural Youth Union (Związek Młodzieży Wiejskiej), headed by Zdzisław Kurowski, with about 1,073,000 members (of which 8.6 per cent are also PUWP and 3.7 per cent UPP members). These two organizations operate clubs, summer camps, and youth publications. They also serve as recruiting pools for the PUWP and UPP and provide a training ground for future party activists.

The Polish Students' Association (Zrzeszenie Studentów Polskich), headed by Stanisław Ciosek, with over 200,000 members (about 86 per cent of all full-time students) constitutes the student government organization, administering scholarship programs, work experience internships, and sports, travel, and social programs for the students. The Union of Polish Scouting (Związek Harcerstwa Polskiego), with over 2,000,000 members and some 73,000 leaders, combines the traditions of international scouting with the function of teaching socialist values and norms. There is also a Military Youth Circle organization. The Women's League (Liga Kobiet), with a little under 400,000 members, is headed by Maria Milczarek and has been active in educating women about various problems of family life, practical economics, and socialist values.

ZBoWiD, the Union of Fighters for Freedom and Democracy (Związek Bojowników o Wolność i Demokrację), is headed by General Mieczysław Moczar and has around 338,000 members in some 4,200 circles. It is a patriotic veterans' organization. The ORMO or Volunteer Militia Reserve (Ochotnicza Rezerwa Milicji Obywatelskiej) with 379,400 members assists the regular militia in crowd control and other police work requiring extra manpower. The League for Defense of the Country, headed by Zbigniew Szydłowski, is a civil defense organization with about 2,300,000 members in almost 38,000 circles.

Several other more specialized groups serve the same functions as the mass organizations: the Society for Ties with Poles Abroad "Polonia" promotes the interests of "People's Poland" among émigrés; the Society for a Secular School promotes elimination of religious education from schools; the Society for the Propagation of Secular Culture and the Society of Atheists and Freethinkers oppose all forms of religious belief; the Society of Children's Friends works with teachers and parents to ensure proper care of children and has also promoted school construction and supervised after school recreation; the Society for the Popularization of Knowledge promotes education among adults and young working people. There are eight associations of national minorities and 18 associations for friendship with people of other countries. One major mass organization, the Society for De-velopment of the Western Territories, was disbanded during 1971 after declaring that "the tasks which we were given have been fully accomplished."

According to the official view, Poland is not yet a completely classless society because private enterprise is still allowed in both town and countryside. The National Unity Front, and the other two parties pledged to follow the leadership of the PUWP, provides the mechanism through which "progressive" classes cooperate in the tasks of preparing Poland for socialism. The UPP has over 413,000 members, of whom about 72 per cent are peasants and the rest intelligentsia, workers, or craftsmen. At the UPP Central Committee plenum in February, former chairman Czesław Wycech resigned along with two of the three deputy chairmen. Stanisław Gucwa was elected to replace him. The Democratic Party has some 88,000 members; about 39 per cent are craftsmen or private entrepreneurs (8.6 per cent) and the rest working intelligentsia. The DP chairman continues to be Zygmunt Moskwa. The National Unity Front itself underwent a change in leadership during June with appointment of a noted non-party scientist and Polish Academy of Sciences president, Professor Janusz Groszkowski, to succeed former Council of State Chairman Marian Spychalski. This appointment broke the tradition that the National Unity Front chairman be a PUWP member and head of state. The National Unity Front played an important role during 1971 by mobilizing people to discuss the PUWP Sixth Congress guidelines in the pre-congress campaign in order to obtain non-party people as well as party members to express their views and become involved in revitalization of the Polish socioeconomic and political system.

Party Internal Affairs. Following the riots and change of top party and government leadership in December 1970 (for the leadership lineup see *YICA*, 1971, p. 57), new PUWP First Secretary Gierek was faced with three major interrelated problems: consolidating his position within the party, alleviating continued worker unrest and drastically increasing popular support, and gaining the confidence and support of the Soviet Union and other member states in the Council for Mutual Economic Assistance (CMEA). The first two problems resulted in leadership changes for the party and government at all levels both before and after the Sixth Congress (6-11 December 1971).

The first major personnel change on 24 January was replacement as interior minister of Kazimierz Świtała by General Franciszek Szlachcic, a career officer in the security service who had served five years as militia commander in Silesia when Gierek was party leader there. Dozens of lesser changes were reported to have taken place in the Interior Ministry, presumably to ensure control by the new leadership. In mid-June, Deputy Minister (and Major General) Ryszard Matejewski, who headed the secret police, was reported to have been replaced with no reasons given. A few days later two deputy department directors and two division chiefs in the ministry were dismissed and arrested on charges of embezzlement and maintaining contacts with criminal elements.

The first changes within the top party leadership took place at the Central Committee plenum of 6-7 February when Stanisław Kociołek and Ignacy Loga-Sowiński (replaced as trade union chief on 15 January) were forced to resign from the Secretariat. After a long discussion about the December events, two former members of the Politburo under Gomułka were removed from the Central Committee—Zenon Kliszko for errors in cadre policy, ideological matters, and dealing with the situation at Gdańsk during the riots; and Bolesław Jaszczuk for errors in economic policy. Former First Secretary Gomułka was only suspended from Central Committee membership, in view of his absence because of ill health and because the party recognized his "previous merits and services to the party and the country." He was found guilty of "serious mistakes in the management of the Party in recent years, which resulted in a weakening of its links with society, the emergence of irregularities in economic development and finally, in an open political crisis and inappropriate methods applied during that crisis." The resignation of Antoni Wałaszek, former first secretary of the Gdańsk party organization, from the Central Committee was also accepted and four candidate members were elevated to fill the three new vacancies and the existing one left by the 1969 death of Adam Kruczkowski.

At the plenum of 16 April, Stanisław Kania (head of the Central Committee administration department) was appointed to the Secretariat and soon began to take over Moczar's duties in the area of defense and security matters. At the next plenum, 24-25 June, both Artur Starewicz (the last Jewish member of the Secretariat) and Moczar were relieved of their posts on the Secretariat. The latter had just been elected chairman of the government's audit agency, the Supreme Control Chamber. Although this was clearly a demotion, he still retained a Politburo post (until December 1971), membership on the Council of State, and his ZBoWiD position. The last important pre-congress change in central party organs involved removal of Zenon Nowak from the chairmanship of the Party Control Commission at its 26 June session. Later appointed ambassador to the Soviet Union, Nowak was replaced by Deputy PCC Chairman Stefan Misiaszek.

At the voivodship level, by year's end over half the 19 first party secretaries were new. The March-April report and election campaigns also produced important changes in composition of the PUWP ruling bodies, reflecting an attempt by the new leadership to renew and invigorate the organization. A surprising number of people were elected to party office for the first time—46 per cent of factory committee members and executive officers in primary party organizations, 20 per cent of the membership on district committees, 39 per cent on voivodship committees, and 70 per cent of the 1,815 delegates to the Sixth Congress. The objective of increasing significantly the number of workers and peasants elected to the PUWP bodies was also achieved at all levels.

At the Sixth Congress, election of the new Central Committee (enlarged from 94 to 115) also reflected this attempt at renewal. Of the 87 remaining old members, 29 including Gomułka were not elected as congress delegates and therefore became ineligible for Central Committee membership. Of the 49 old members attending the congress, all 49 were reelected to the Central Committee. Three were dropped including Franciszek Wachowicz, former Kielce first secretary and a Moczar supporter. In addition to the 49 carry-overs from the previous Central Committee, 23 were advanced from candidate membership, and 43 were elected for the first time. Of the 93 candidate members, 25 were carry-overs and 68 elected for the first time.

The first meeting of the new Central Committee approved a number of important changes in the Politburo and Secretariat. Dropped from the Politburo were the last three important party leaders under Gomułka: Józef Cyrankiewicz (also retired as chairman of the Council of State at the next Sejm session), Stefan Jędrychowski (removed as foreign minister), and Mieczysław Moczar (who retained chairmanship of the Supreme Control Chamber). The Politburo was expanded from 10 to 11 members, with election of Henryk Jabłoński (minister for general and higher education and a leader of the old Polish Socialist Party before its 1948 merger with the PUWP), Mieczysław Jagielski (Planning Commission chairman and permanent CMEA representative), Wojciech Jaruzelski (national defense minister)—all three former candidate Politburo members, and Franciszek Szlachcic (soon replaced as interior minister). Gierek, Babiuch, Jaroszewicz, Kruczek, Olszowski, Szydlak, and Tejchma were reelected to the Politburo. Central Committee secretaries Stanisław Kania, Kazimierz Barcikowski, and Zdzisław Grudzień (who replaced Gierek as first secretary of the Katowice voivodship organization in late 1970) were elected and Józef Kępa reelected candidate Politburo members.

The Secretariat also expanded from 7 to 9 plus Andrzej Werblan (deputy Sejm speaker) and Ryszard Frelek (Central Committee foreign affairs department head) became *members* of the Secretariat. Stanisław Kowalczyk (Central Committee heavy industry and transportation department head and former economic secretary of the Katowice voivodship party organization under Gierek during 1960-68), Jerzy Łukaszewicz (on the secretariat of the Warsaw city party organization), and Franciszek Szlachcic (heretofore interior minister) were the new secretaries. Reelected were Gierek, Szydlak, Babiuch, Tejchma, Kania, and Barcikowski. Stefan Olszowski (to become minister of foreign affairs) was not reelected.

At the Sejm session held 21-22 December, following the Sixth Congress, a number of ministerial changes were made. Interior Minister Franciszek Szlachcic (appointed to the Politburo and Secretariat) was replaced by Wiesław Ociepka (former Silesian miner, youth leader, and head of the Central Committee administration department). Stefan Jędrychowski stepped down as minister of foreign affairs to become finance minister, succeeding Józef Trendota, and was succeeded in the foreign ministry by Stefan Olszowski. Andrzej Giersz was replaced by Aloyzy Karkoszka (first secretary of the Gdańsk voivodship party organization) as minister of building and the building materials industry. Stanisław Wroński (head of Książka i Wiedza publishing house and Soviet-Polish Friendship Society chairman) became culture minister, vacant since Motyka had been removed in October.

With some exceptions, the net effect of these government and party personnel changes was to put into office men who were younger, more energetic, more flexible, and less tarnished by work during the Gomułka period than those replaced.

Domestic Attitudes and Activities. The new leadership elected at the Central Committee plenum of 20 December 1970 had made several early attempts to deal with the highly volatile situation following the riots (See *YICA*, 1971, pp. 63-64). Nevertheless, these measures were insufficient to restore order completely, as sporadic strikes and slowdowns continued in the coastal cities well into January. A strike of major proportion took place in the Łódż textile mills on 12-16 February, forcing the party into an even more thorough self-analysis of its policies, more extensive leadership changes, and eventually a decision to abandon for the moment introduction of the controversial new system of "material incentives." During the Łódż strike the party agreed to roll back food prices to the 12 December 1970 level, a decision made possible only after the Soviet Union agreed to give Poland extensive credits (reportedly $500 million, including $100 million in convertible currency). These last major decisions in combination with the extensive talks by striking workers and the top party leadership, important developments at the Central Committee plenum of 6-7 February, and the new atmosphere created by continued efforts by the new leaders to communicate to the public their reform efforts provided the basis for growing support.

The 6-7 February plenum devoted most of its attention to an evaluation of the "December events" and current tasks of the party. In addition to personnel changes discussed above the plenum agreed to appointment of a second commission to investigate further the December events, support the policy of increasingly broad consultation with economic and social activists and experts in defining tasks of the current year and of the 1971-75 period, and convene the Sixth Congress at an earlier date than foreseen by the party statutes. In his analysis of the underlying causes of the December crisis, Gierek emphasized that the old leadership had been intolerant of criticism, leading to a distortion of information with which it had been supplied so that "More and more, social and economic reality was misunderstood." He also emphasized the interrelationship between such a style of rule and the resulting economic stagnation and "crisis of confidence." Other speakers also emphasized the importance of improving the economic situation in the country and raising the standard of living and the idea that the development of the economy is not an end in itself but a means of satisfying social needs (see below for details of the evolving economic strategy). Several speakers stressed the need to maintain close ties with the Soviet Union. "Poland may develop only as a socialist state, inseparably allied with the Soviet Union, with our neighbors and allies," Gierek declared; "this is truth number one." (See international section below.)

Evolution of the new leadership's economic, social, and political policies continued through the plenum of 16 April, which included a report by Gierek on the Twenty-fourth Congress of the Communist Party of the Soviet Union (CPSU) in which he said that the CPSU assumes that the satisfaction of the needs of the working people is the primary objective of production in socialism and that the achievement of a higher Polish standard of living is dependent on "the links of the Polish economy with the Soviet one and those of other countries of the Council for Mutual Economic Assistance."

The plenum of 24-25 June was interesting not only because of changes in personnel, but because of the emerging outlines of a new economic plan for 1971-75 and introduction of new procedures for discussion. The plenum had been preceded by the work of a wide range of experts and by broad public and party discussion, including a series of Politburo meetings on selected social and economic problems. During the plenum four working teams were set up to discuss different sets of problems contained in the paper read by Jaroszewicz, thus creating an opportunity for much more widespread participation in the discussion and a greater depth of analysis.

The plenum of 4 September set the date for the Sixth Congress and accepted the guidelines prepared for the pre-congress discussion, entitled "For the Further Socialist Development of the Polish People's Republic." In his speech Gierek noted that the traditional form of pre-congress theses had been abandoned in favor of the guidelines, because the theses had very often proven "difficult for the party and public to understand" and were "more in the nature of information about what was going to be done than something which encouraged people to think, discuss, and act." The guidelines were conceived not as "a final program which should be distributed and popularized," but rather as a set of goals and assumptions whose details were "open to any essential changes and corrections." Gierek emphasized that the party's action program "should always be the result of discussion," which provides "the main guarantee of the correctness and effectiveness of our policy."

The guidelines were organized into four main parts. The first analyzed the current social and economic situation in Poland, including a brief discussion of the major shortcomings of the past five years. Blame for the party's failure to use the achievements of science and technology effectively, "to improve significantly central planning, harmonize consistently the tasks of the economy as a whole, increase economic effectiveness, and create conditions for the stimulation of social initiative" or "to coordinate socioeconomic concepts with society's needs" (i.e., neglect of consumers' goods was placed on the errors of the past leadership rather than on the PUWP, whose ability to correct the situation was seen as "proof of our party's political strength." The December events were attributed to "errors in economic and social policy, which was based on subjectivism, deformation of Leninist principles, and the party and government leadership's isolation from the masses."

The second part outlined the aims and directions of socioeconomic development for 1971-75, including sections on the general aims and directions of the economy, tasks connected with "meeting the people's needs," industry, agriculture and foodstuffs, and modernization and improvement of the management system. The basic aim of socioeconomic policy was defined as "a constant increase in consumption and a continuous improvement in the living, social, and cultural conditions of the population. This objective is to be pursued through increased productivity and effectiveness of management, reconstruction and modernization of the economic structure of our country, scientific-technical progress, and improvement of our economic system as a whole." Even more interesting was the suggestion that the role of government would concentrate increasingly on economic policy-making and implementation. The guidelines defined the main functions of government as "the programing and planning of socioeconomic development, the creation of conditions for its pursuit, and the control of its implementation." It was also emphasized that the economic decision-making authority of local plant managers and the local government organs would be increased. Central planning is to remain the keystone of the economic system, but in order to increase its effectiveness it is to concentrate on "the basic socioeconomic goals and the means of achieving them"; on "ensuring the priority of public interests over particular interests"; on ensuring that the latest planning methods are used throughout the system; and on eliminating unnecessary bureaucracy in planning.

The third part of the guidelines dealt with "development of socialist democracy and the increase of civic consciousness," with separate sections for the political system, the training and education of youth, science, culture, and the role of mass information and propaganda media. In addition to emphasizing the leading role of the PUWP, the guidelines stressed the importance of increasing the role and authority of the Sejm and of the local government organs, and that of the trade unions and organs of worker and peasant self-government, cooperatives, and other social organizations. It was also noted that the existing system of socialist law would be further improved to bring it into line with the tasks of a modern socialist state and that a new constitution would be drafted in view of the level of development achieved by the Polish People's Republic and "the increase in the social awareness of the broadest mass of citizenry." Considerable attention was paid to improvements in the educational system which "must mold the ideological attitude of youth" and to the role of the press, radio, and television, whose primary task is "to increase the effectiveness of ideological-educational and political influence on the shaping of socialist awareness." The guidelines also noted that the party would work out an improved system for "passing on to society prompt and factual information." The media are also to play a greater role in exposing "negative facts and shortcomings in socioeconomic life" but only within "the field of criticism extended by the party."

The last part of the guidelines dealt with the leading role of the PUWP. Great stress was laid on the need to improve political qualifications of the party membership and "to make up for the backlog and shortcomings in intra-party ideological political work." Individual conversations with the rank and file are to become a permanent feature of party life. Emphasis was also placed on the need to increase the two-way flow of information in order to achieve intra-party democracy and "openness of party life." The Central Committee is to be kept regularly informed on the work of the Politburo, Secretariat, and government, which are to make "greater use of the press, radio, and television, both for passing on quick and accurate information to the public about their intentions and activities and for intensifying general ideological upbringing and propaganda work."

In contrast to previous theses, there was no special section on the international situation or Polish foreign policy, though brief mention was made in the Introduction to the party's basic policy of "unity with the fraternal communist parties, mainly with the CPSU, and its solidarity with all forces of progress and national liberation."

Although the guidelines seem to have been read and discussed far more extensively and critically than past theses, it is clear from a poll conducted by the Polish state radio and TV opinion polling center (with results announced 14 November) that the reading and discussion were by no means universal during the two months after the guidelines were made public. Of those polled, 64 per cent had not yet read the guidelines and an additional 14 per cent had only glanced at them. A full 47 per cent of the sample had not participated in the pre-congress discussion. Only 13 per cent had actually taken part in discussions at meetings, the other 40 per cent having only informally talked about the guidelines with relatives or friends. Within the PUWP, UPP, DP, and at places of work, however, extensive discussions—often critical—took place, and there was almost daily coverage of the guidelines in the press. *Trybuna Ludu* noted on September 10 that the inauguration of the pre-congress campaign of discussion at all levels within the party "marked the return to the practice—neglected in the past—of organizing national discussions among the party activists on questions of vital importance for the party and nation."

Elections of delegates to the Sixth Congress were completed on November 20. Of the 1,815 delegates, 308 were elected directly by the largest factories in the country, 81 by the armed forces, and the remainder at 19 voivodship conferences.

The plenum of 18 November approved a report by the Central Committee on its activity between the fifth and sixth congresses and resolved that the report be sent to the delegates elected to the forthcoming congress. The plenum also decided on the unprecedented step of "communicating" the report to the delegates at the previous, Fifth Congress. The second item on the agenda was a Politburo report on recent talks with party leaders from the Soviet Union, the German Democratic Republic (GDR), and Czechoslovakia.

The Sixth Congress convened on 6 December, with representatives of 70 communist, workers', and socialist parties from other countries (compared with 39 foreign delegations at the 1968 congress). First Secretary Gierek presented the three-hour-long Central Committee report on "The Tasks of the Party in the Further Socialist Development of the Polish People's Republic," a comprehensive analysis of past failures and future party tasks in every area of life. At the beginning of the report he noted four conclusions that the party had drawn from the "December events:"

(1) "The problems of the working people must always remain at the center" of the party's attention with socialist construction bringing about "a systematically felt improvement of material and cultural living conditions of the masses." (2) "We must be guided in all our activities by the principle that the working class is the main social force of socialism, and constant contact with it is a condition for successful development of our system." (3) "Socialist construction requires a systematic raising to a higher level of the party's leading role, consistent observance of Leninist methods of party

work and a constant contact with reality.'' (4) One must not allow occurrences of conflict which obstruct progress and offer a scope of action for the opponents of socialism under contemporary conditions of world-wide struggle and rivalry between socialism and capitalism. He argued that the party must both carry on ''an uncompromising struggle against revisionism'' and overcome ''the dogmatic ossification, as well as subjectivism, which is characterized by lack of faith in the working class and in the creative abilities of the nation and which ignore reality and lead to the isolation of the party from the masses.''

In addition to criticizing more recent years of rule by the old leadership, Gierek also criticized the 1956-59 period when ''the basic weakness of party policy [was] the fact that the necessary elimination of defined dogmatic and sectarian errors, and the restoration of the (previously violated) observance of socialist laws, was accompanied by a compromise with revisionism and with other ideological tendencies alien to our party. The harmful effects of all this was noticeable in the later period, becoming the foundation of the attacks on the fundamental system and ideological and political principles of our socialist state.''

The second day of the congress was devoted to plenary discussion of the Central Committee report on PUWP activities since the Fifth Congress and of Gierek's report on future tasks, speeches of several foreign delegates, including CPSU leader Leonid Brezhnev, and a report by Premier Piotr Jaroszewicz on the main directions of socioeconomic development in Poland for 1971-75. On the third day the delegates, as previously planned, broke up into 19 working groups to discuss basic congress documents (i.e., reports already presented and noted above) and the suggestions and proposals made during the precongress discussion. The report of the Central Audit Commission was also released. The fourth day again included plenary discussion and speeches. It was later reported that 75 per cent of the delegates either spoke or submitted their views in writing during the congress. On the fifth day, members of the Central Committee, Central Audit Commission, and Central Party Control Commission were elected. On the final day of the congress the newly elected Central Committee met in its first plenary session to choose a Politburo and Secretariat.

At noon, the last session of the congress began. Gierek in his closing speech promised that specialized plenums for working out detailed plans to implement decisions of the congress would soon be held and said that the work of the congress would be put before the entire nation during the campaign preceding forthcoming elections to the Sejm so that it might be confirmed by non-party citizens as well. Two major resolutions were passed: ''For the Further Socialist Development of the Polish People's Republic,'' with three sections corresponding to the last three parts of the precongress guidelines, and ''On Security and Co-operation in Europe,'' restating the party's position on international affairs and calling for early convening of a European security conference. There were also a few amendments made to the PUWP statutes aimed at tightening up requirements for party membership, increasing the responsibility of officials to the organizations which elect them, and expanding the role of the basic party organization meeting.

Following the sixth congress, a press conference was held for 200 Polish and foreign journalists. In the next few days the delegates met with the groups from which they had been elected to discuss the decisions reached. Then on 20 December a Central Committee plenum discussed ''the tasks of the party authorities and organizations in implementing the conclusions resulting from the pre-congress discussion and the congress resolutions.''

The Economy. The new leadership's economic policy took shape slowly during 1971, beginning with the recognition that more had to be done to improve the standard of living and to bring about the increase in productivity that would make such improvement possible. Although the party leadership was quick to recognize the need for significant revisions in the draft of the 1971-75 plan, the full nature and extent of reforms did not become clear until mid-year. The basic outlines of the new economic policies can be summarized as follows:

(1) Acceptance of the fundamental principle that the economy is to serve the needs of society, including the goal of bringing about a continual and "systematically felt improvement of the material and cultural living conditions of the masses." The party rejected the ideal (attributed to the Gomułka leadership) of economic development as en end in itself, to which the needs of the people had to be subordinated. Economic planning and social policy were to be seen not as fragmentary and improvised activities, but as interrelated means of achieving long-range goals of social justice and economic and social well-being.

(2) Acceptance of the principle of balanced growth. Long-range as well as short-range needs of society have to be taken into account. Although increasing living standards is important, investment cannot be neglected either. The new economic policy calls for maintaining (and even increasing) the high rate of economic growth while making possible increased consumption through greater economic efficiency, expanding consumers' goods imports, and shifting investment somewhat from producers' goods production to consumers' goods, but excessive consumption has to be avoided. In 1971-75 investments are to constitute about 24 per cent of national income, and national income is to increase by 38 to 39 per cent (compared with 34 per cent in 1966-70), which means a 33 per cent per capita increase. Investments in industry are to increase by 53 per cent over the last five-year plan.

(3) Greater participation by experts in economic planning. In contrast to Gomułka who was accused of autocratic decision-making from above, ignoring public opinion, and rejecting the advice of experts, the new leadership has emphasized that it does not have all the answers to the problems of economic and social organization and policy and has called upon an unprecedented range of experts to provide policy advice. In late February the Politburo decided to establish a party-government Commission on the Modernization of Management and the Functioning of the Economy. Its membership of 230 was divided into 10 teams and requested to provide continual consultation with the government and party. Its work was to be divided into three stages: (a) critical assessment and diagnosis of the situation, (b) definition of a course of action and final goals, and (c) making proposals for "concrete system solutions."

(4) A full employment policy. Gomułka's "planned unemployment," was abandoned. The old policy was officially expected to result in an increase of unemployment from 100,000 to 350,000 as a result of the deliberate failure to plan enough investment or direct it in such a way that all of those coming on to the labor market in the 1971-75 period would have jobs. About 3.5 million new workers are expected to join the labor force. The new leadership promised to provide the full 1.7 million new jobs required through increased investment, expansion of services and other jobs requiring minimum investment, special funds for areas with surplus workers, encouragement of early retirement and reduction of overtime, and expansion of part-time work and cottage industries. In March a special fund was established to create additional jobs. The party apparently sees the problem of full employment as a key to its youth policy as well as being increasingly important for women.

(5) Increased wages and consumption. At the end of the year it was announced that real wages during 1971 had increased by 5 per cent and that consumption was up 7.4 per cent, the highest increase in 12 years. Peasant incomes were also up considerably, with a 15 per cent increase in cash income from sales of agricultural produce. The new five-year plan called for an increase of real wages of 17 to 18 per cent (twice as much as in 1966-70), or about 3.5 per cent a year. Consumers' goods production is to increase by 42 per cent (compared with 36 per cent in 1966-70), while producers' goods production will increase by only 51 per cent compared with 57 per cent in the previous five-year period. Food production is also to increase substantially. Although the five-day work week was rejected for the present, the party agreed to plan toward a situation where everyone has at least one free Saturday a month, with precedence for those whose work is most

onerous. High priority is to be given to returning the miners to a normal work week. One other important group was singled out for special attention, with the announcement that the salary of teachers will be increased by 40 per cent over the five-year period. (The average teacher earns about 1,700 zloty per month, compared with a national average of 2,464 and from 5,000 to 6,000 for coal miners and steel workers.) One other important development in the consumption area was the decision in July to reduce prices on some additional consumers' goods and to reduce or abolish customs duty on food and clothing.

(6) Increased outlays for housing. As early as January it was announced that outlays for new housing construction and preparation of new apartment building sites would be increased substantially. The new policy called for a 10 per cent increase in housing construction in 1971 and an overall increase of 25 per cent for the 1971-75 period compared with 1966-70, or some 1,075,000 new apartments. The long-range goal is a separate apartment for every family by the end of the decade. A decision was also made to encourage construction of private individual houses to relieve communal construction. Five additional prefabricated housing factories were purchased from the Soviet Union and Germany during the year. The first began production in August.

(7) A decision to launch mass motorization. Although Gierek had talked about the possibility of producing a small inexpensive family car as early as January, the new leadership went beyond that and accepted the principle that motorization is a desirable part of improved living conditions. An agreement was signed with Fiat in October for an entirely new car in Poland by 1974. The new factory will produce 150,000 cars per year, compared with the 70,000 cars at present sold each year on the Polish market. The party also agreed to undertake construction of an adequate highway net and other facilities required for motorization.

(8) Improvements in health, welfare, and pensions. In February the government announced higher pensions for 470,000 persons who had worked for more than 10 years. Maternity leave was extended from 12 to 16 weeks for the first child and 18 weeks for subsequent children. Outlays were also increased for health, orphanages, recreation, sports, culture, and tourism. In April it was announced that all foreign medicine heretofore available only for dollars could now be purchased for zloty. A campaign was launched in May to expand the summer rest and recreation possibilities for the maximum number of children and young persons. The most important development in health and welfare policy, however, was the decision to extend health insurance coverage to Poland's 6,500,000 private farmers as of 1 January 1972.

(9) Modernization of the economy and increasing efficiency of the economic system. Although the same basic system of economic planning will be retained, important changes should make possible a more rapid improvement in living standards called for by the new leadership. Labor productivity is to be increased by the more effective use of fixed assets and new investment in modern equipment as well as more efficient investment and a shortening of the investment cycle. More emphasis will be placed on more effective utilization of science and technology. Workers are to play a more important role in enterprise decision-making.

(10) Increased foreign trade and importation of technology. The new leadership has expressed a strong interest in engaging not only in increased trade with other countries, but also in joint cooperative ventures in almost any area. Although the PUWP has emphasized the importance of close ties with the Soviet Union, Czechoslovakia, the GDR, and other socialist states and has stressed its growing economic dependence on them, it has also emphasized that the only real barriers to increased trade and cooperation with the West lie with Common Market (EEC) restrictions on Polish exports. Foreign trade policy will become more rational, with individual firms having more freedom to initiate, carry through, and benefit from foreign transactions.

(11) A new agricultural policy. The aim is apparently to increase confidence in the government on the part of the Polish peasant, who still owns 89 per cent of the arable land, and to provide

additional incentives for more farm production. On the symbolic level the leadership almost completely stopped referring to the transitional nature of the present private landholding system and promised to support both socialist farms and economically effective peasant farms. To underscore this change the government passed a law that at last makes it possible for a large number of persons who have been farming land for five years or more to get title to it and, therefore, become eligible for government credits. Another law makes it easier to buy, sell, and inherit land. A third law reduces the higher tax on larger holdings—in order to encourage increase in their average size (presently 4.5 hectares). The government also raised prices paid farmers for milk and livestock in March, and in April it announced the end of obligatory deliveries of agricultural products (in effect, a tax in kind) as of 1 January 1972. As noted above, social insurance protection is also to be extended to private farmers at the beginning of 1972. In the 1971-72 period plant production should increase by 17-20 per cent and animal production by 19 to 21 per cent as a result of greater investment in machinery, fertilizers, agricultural education, rural services, and electrification and increased incentives.

Revitalization of the Party and Government. A persistent theme throughout 1971 was the need to revitalize the party and the nation's economic and governmental institutions and overcome the persistent problem of the passivity, indifference, lack of commitment, and incompetence of local party authorities, government officials, and the management of economic enterprises. Finding ways of injecting initiative and a sense of responsibility at the local level was seen as a key to solving the nation's economic ills. Two types of solutions seem to have been adopted by the party: (1) increased party democracy with more rank-and-file participation in deliberations and decision making at all levels of the party and increased latitude for discussion and criticism, and (2) a new cadres policy that emphasized tighter standards for party membership, better training, continued accountability for proper attitudes and behavior, and advancement and office tenure strictly according to performance.

In a special limited edition of the PUWP theoretical monthly *Nowe Drogi* for June, the official party report on the December riots accused Gomułka of heading a small leadership group that "did not tolerate any criticism and rejected any initiative other than its own ... These informal arrangements exercised control over the Politburo and the Central Committee," so that eventually "the unanimity of decisions of the Politburo and Central Committee were becoming ever more formal and illusory." Under Gomułka the Politburo was convened increasingly rarely and the Secretariat not at all. In a report to the 16 April plenum, Central Committee Secretary Babiuch said that under the new leadership, the Politburo had met 23 times in the 16 weeks preceding the plenum, including three meetings with the government Presidium and two with the leadership of the UPP, while the Secretariat met 12 times. He went on to note: "It has become the practice to invite comrades from the government and Party apparatus, who prepare material and who are responsible for the future implementation of decisions made, to take part in the discussion of individual problems."

At meetings of the Central Committee the new leadership also encouraged much more widespread participation than in the past, even dividing one plenum into four working teams. It also attempted to encourage participation and criticism from the rank-and-file at the primary party unit, district, and voivodship levels during the spring report and election campaign and during the pre-congress discussions of the guidelines in an effort to overcome passivity among the membership and shake up entrenched and unimaginative party bureaucrats and elected officers. The views of members in lower-level party organizations were asked on proposed leadership choices and subjects to be discussed at higher levels. The change in composition of party leadership groups served the purpose of providing an additional lever for the top echelon to use against middle-level bureaucrats, but also increased the degree of two-way communication between party and workers.

In cadre policy there was a clear increase in emphasis on improvement of the quality of key personnel as an essential element in achieving long-range party goals. Applicants for party membership were to be more thoroughly investigated, with more opinions solicited from non-party people as well as party members. Much more attention was also to be paid to the training and ideological-political qualifications of candidates and party members. During the summer approximately half of the party rank-and-file were brought in for "individual talks" regarding their commitment to party work, resulting in deletion from the party lists of 100,000 and the formal expulsion of 10,500 more. The emphasis, in short, was on increasing the quality rather than numbers, with the decrease in membership serving "to strengthen party unity and political discipline, to intensify the activity of party organizations, and to enhance the ranks of party membership." The Central Committee report to the Sixth Congress noted that the December 1970 events "proved [that] the numerical growth of the party is not invariably a correct indication of public support for its policies, and that the party's strength is not directly related to the number of its members." During 1971, the Gierek leadership also stressed frequently the importance of promoting and retaining people in office on the basis of their merits. In another development related to cadre policy, the new leadership reactivated the party's Higher School of Social Sciences, disbanded by Gomułka in 1968, and 107 regional party activists were admitted to the school for a three-year course.

There was also an important change in the style of party relations with the masses. In contrast to Gomułka's aloofness, Gierek and his associates devoted a great amount of time during 1971 to face-to-face campaigning among the masses. Gierek appeared before hundreds of groups of workers, students, intellectuals and peasants, waded into crowds and shook hands, and appeared on radio and TV on a scale unprecedented in Eastern Europe in an attempt to bring the party and government closer to the people. In his "dialogue with the people" Gierek continued to emphasize the theme first put forward in December 1970, of the need for cooperation among all the people of Poland. At the Sixth Congress he declared: "It is in the interest of the people always to strengthen the links between party and non-party people. The stimulation of social militancy of non-party people, the provision of information for them, and the reckoning with their views, and entrusting them with responsible tasks and functions is and will be the principle of our policy."

In keeping with the promise of making more information available to the public, the Politburo in March ordered the appointment of a press spokesman for the government. Włodzimierz Janiurek became undersecretary of state for information at the Council of Ministers to fulfill this function. On 3 June a new TV program, "Citizen's Tribune," was introduced similar to the ones that have been broadcast in Czechoslovakia and Hungary for some time. The program format consists of answers to questions (written or phoned in by the public) by party and government officials who are guests on the program that day.

Another theme stressed by the leadership was the importance of letters and complaints as "an important source of information about the real feelings and needs of the people, supplying many justified proposals about ways to solve social problems." On 31 July the Council of Ministers issued a resolution on complaints, emphasizing the importance of complaints "in consolidating and deepening the mutual confidence between the state and society," and aiming at more efficient handling, shortening the period in which some must be settled, and increasing the possibilities for Sejm deputies and people's council members to check on and facilitate the handling of complaints and suggestions. In September the Central Committee Secretariat issued a resolution on examination of letters and suggestions, calling for more care to be taken in answering complaints and for a more rapid and adequate response to "the signals of the working people." The resolution also stressed their importance as "a means of expressing public opinion and a source of information about the troubles and moods of the people" and as "one of the forms of strengthening the ties between party and society and of the people's participation in social control."

Another theme stressed by the party was that of increasing "social control" to combat passivity, laziness, stagnation, and abuse of authority. The press, radio, TV, workers self-management, trade unions, youth organizations and other social organizations, the Sejm, and the people's councils were all expected to increase their social control functions over the next five years.

Among other developments for increased democratization of government, in the case of the Sejm there was a marked increase in the number of sessions held and decisions made. Interpellations (i.e., questions from deputies addressed to government ministers) increased spectacularly, both in number and in importance. Sejm commissions also seem to have been more active, and two new ones were created for Full Employment and for Light Industry, Crafts, and Small Scale Production, reflecting the new leadership's policies. Much of the additional work revolved around the draft plan for 1971-75, which the Sejm was given an opportunity to discuss before its formal presentation for approval. At the lower levels of government (i.e., the people's councils), there were also signs of revitalization, with almost daily press reports on the removal of local officials. According to resolutions of the Sixth Congress, the scope of authority of the people's councils is to be increased and they are to be held more accountable for their actions. The role of the worker's self-government organs also increased somewhat in response to a special letter from the Central Committee Secretariat addressed in January to organs of workers' self-government, trade union leaders, and directors of enterprises, stressing the indispensibility of active participation in solving problems relating to improving the working and living conditions of enterprise employees.

Numerous statements by Gierek, Jaroszewicz, and other party and government leaders alluded to the need for a greater division of labor between party and government organs, and for greater delegation of authority by the Council of Ministers to the ministries and heads of central offices and local governments.

Party Policy toward Cultural Affairs and the Development of Socialist Attitudes. On the whole Gierek's cultural policy must be classified as very cautious. There was some easing of censorship, with considerably greater latitude for criticism—especially of the Gomułka period and of major targets, such as apathetic bureaucrats and economic problems. Certainly the press became more lively and interesting than before. The Gierek leadership called on the mass media to work both as "instruments for implementation of the party's program" and to play a greater role in exposing "the negative facts and shortcomings in socioeconomic life" but only within "the field of criticism extended by the Party." Some authors banned under Gomułka (e.g., poet Antoni Słonimski and author-composer Stefan Kisielewski) were allowed back into print, and such people as satirist Sławomir Mrozek and theater director Kazimierz Dejmek (director of the controversial play, "Dziady," which sparked the 1968 disturbances) reportedly have been invited to return to Poland. The appointment of Wincenty Kraśko as deputy premier for problems of education, culture, and youth is also interesting, as he has a reputation for moderation in cultural policies and has expressed more than once the view that the arts cannot be simply ordered about.

There was some reduction in the prison terms of the "mountaineer group" sentenced in 1970 for allegedly smuggling anti-government material into the country. At the same time, in July seven members of the "anti-state" youth group "Ruch," accused of actions in protest against Gomułka's rule, were found guilty and received sentences of from 10 months to three-and-a-half years.

In February the Politburo recommended that the Council of Ministers draw up a law to solve the problem of "social parasitism," directed primarily at black marketeers and prostitutes. The law, submitted to the Sejm for discussion in October, proved to be quite controversial. It provided for three stages in dealing with "parasites:" warning, committal to supervision, and committal to a labor center. There was also evidence of increased concern with drug usage and crime. In September, for example, Warsaw Radio announced an anti-hooligan campaign.

The guidelines and Sixth Congress resolutions placed usual stress on the importance of developing a socialist content of Polish culture with special emphasis on proper education and upbringing of youth and the key roles to be played by schools and youth organizations. In January a special Committee of Experts on Educational Reform was established on recommendation of the Politburo. Work of the 23 experts is directed by Professor Jan Szczepański, the well-known sociologist at the Polish Academy of Sciences. Another sign of continued concern with youth was an announcement that the Institute of Youth Studies of the central party school was preparing a "Report on Youth."

Anniversaries. Both the traditional May Day celebration and the 22 July National Day observances were relatively quiet. The only major innovation in the former was that major party and government leaders joined in the march for a few hundred feet before taking their places on the reviewing stand. The Gierek leadership used the holiday as another means of increasing personal contact with the workers through visits to plants and telephone greetings to workers at several important factories the day before the celebration. There were no parades or expensive shows on National Day, which was declared a day of rest. At the Sixth Congress some attention was paid to the fact that the thirtieth anniversary of the Polish People's Republic is to be celebrated before the next congress.

Relations with the Church. Relations between the state and the Catholic church continued to improve during 1971, although major differences still remain. There is strong evidence that Gierek sought better relations with the church as part of his broader program to achieve cooperation among all Poles. He declared in his report to the Sixth Congress: "We want the policy of our party to unite the entire community, workers, peasants, and intelligentsia, the old and the young, believers and nonbelievers, and to bind together all who are ready to aspire to the common end of building an affluent, socialist Poland." The guidelines also expressed the party's "appreciation and recognition" for "the quality of work and creative activities" of "citizen believers." Gierek was reported to have told journalists in late September: "There are cases where a man is a believer and, because of that, among other reasons, cannot be promoted in the government or economic hierarchy. I think that if he is really an honest man and moreover possesses good professional qualifications, then the question of whether he is a convinced Marxist should carry less weight than consideration of whether he is useful in his place of work and whether, given the proper chance, he could be more useful still."

The leadership announced in late January that the church is to receive title to the 4,700 churches and chapels and 2,200 other church-related buildings in former German territories, heretofore held by the government and only rented to the church. In June the Sejm passed a bill formalizing the transfer and providing for reimbursement of rent paid for the property retroactive to 1945. The government also began to take a more favorable attitude toward church construction (though it is still up to the local people's councils to issue building permits, approve construction plans, and allocate building materials), made it easier for the clergy to receive passports, and reduced the obstacles to publishing for Catholic institutions.

The government's position on the church was expressed in a September speech to "Pax" by Aleksander Skarzyński, director of the Religious Affairs Office. He said that the government was willing to offer its recognition of "the lasting character of the church's religious activity" and the social value of its institutional work, but that the church in return must recognize the permanent nature of the socialist system in Poland, maintain neutrality on the political attitudes of Catholics, and refrain from political activity of any kind. He also noted that the state finds it incomprehensible that the Vatican has not yet established Polish church administration in the recovered territories. (The Vatican insists on German ratification of the Bonn-Warsaw treaty first.) The church's position is that it wants an end to all church building restrictions so that it can achieve its goal of "1,000 new churches," exemption of priests from military service, agreement on procedures for nominating bishops, more freedom for church publications, and a complete end to harassment of the church and of believers.

There were several important meetings between church and state officials during 1971. On 3 March Premier Piotr Jaroszewicz met with the Primate of Poland, Stefan Cardinal Wyszyński. In April, Skarżyński went to Rome for talks with the Vatican. In November the Holy See's Monsignor Agostino Casaroli came to Warsaw for a continuation of the talks, amid speculation that Poland and the Vatican would soon enter into an accord modeled after the 1970 agreement establishing full diplomatic relations with Yugoslavia.

In other developments relating to the church, Cardinal Koenig of Austria visited Poland in May and praised Polish reconstruction efforts in the recovered territories. In late September, Cardinal Wyszyński went to Rome for the bishops' synod. On 17 October Father Maksymilian Kolbe, a martyr of Auschwitz was beatified.

International Activities. The major international problem faced by the new Polish leadership in 1971 was gaining confidence and support from the political leadership of the Soviet Union and the other communist-ruled states of Eastern Europe. Toward this end, PUWP leaders were in frequent communication and consultation with the Soviets, and met on several occasions with leaders from other East European states. The speeches of the Polish leaders were filled with statements of assurance—about the close fraternal ties that bind Poland and the Soviet Union in inseparable unity, the Polish commitment to promoting unity within the socialist camp, the importance of fighting revisionist tendencies, the links that tie all Polish aspirations to the socialist system, the importance of the unity of the international socialist system in its confrontation with ''imperialism'' and in the struggle for the progress of socialism, and so on. The Poles were also careful to emphasize that there was no anti-Soviet sentiment expressed during the December events and that the PUWP and the Polish working people were able to correct the situation themselves, thanks in part to Soviet understanding and support. Gierek also did his best to show how his policies in Poland reflected similar developments in the Soviet Union. The Polish leadership frequently emphasized its dependence on increased trade and division of labor within CMEA in fulfilling its economic goals for 1971-75. At the same time it stressed the importance of coexistence with the capitalist world and its desire for increased trade and economic cooperation with the West and with the ''third world.'' After restoring order on the domestic scene, the Polish leadership resumed the same basic foreign policy course it had taken before the December 1970 events. Again the convening of a European security conference was the major diplomatic objective, with sub-themes of a world disarmament conference, nuclear-free zones, and the non-proliferation of nuclear weapons. Another major target was ratification of the treaty signed in 1970 by Poland and the Federal Republic of Germany (FRG). Recognition for the GDR and the admission of the two Germanys to the United Nations were also frequent themes in the Polish press. The Vietnam war continued to receive major attention in the press. In a speech to the U. N. General Assembly in October, Foreign Minister Jędrychowski offered to put a Polish military contingent at U. N. disposal.

The Warsaw Treaty Organization and the CMEA. Poland took part in the usual WTO military maneuvers and consultations during 1971. At the CMEA session in Bucharest in July, Poland continued to push for more rapid progress in expanding trade, the international division of labor, and the role of the transferable ruble. Gierek attended the August meeting of CMEA party chiefs in the Crimea.

Relations with the Soviet Union. Whatever doubts the Soviet leadership may have had about Gierek must have been dispelled in the course of the year, given the skill with which the new Polish leadership dealt with the potentially explosive domestic situation and the continued close Polish ties with the Soviet Union and the rest of the socialist camp. Gierek engaged in an impressive number of consultations with the top Soviet leadership, visiting the Soviet Union at least seven times between December 1970 and the end of 1971. Soviet party leader Brezhnev was in Poland at least once, to attend the PUWP congress, where he remarked that "historical experience" had shown that "some failings and mistakes, even serious ones," may occur during socialist construction, but that these mistakes are the result, not of "the nature of socialism as a social system" or "its aims or principles," but rather "deviations from these principles." He went on to emphasize the importance of "the ability to take a critical view of one's own activity and to draw the necessary practical conclusions." He then expressed the "respect" of Soviet communists for "the principles and courageous approach of the PUWP in correcting the negative phenomena which occurred." He went on to say: "We clearly see the great and sincere concern for the interests of the working people, for constantly strengthening the ties with the mass of working people displayed by your party, by its central committee, headed by a true son of the Polish working class, our friend and comrade, Edward Gierek."

Soviet assistance—in the form of credit (reportedly as much as $500 million, including $100 million in convertible currency) and deliveries of grain and consumers' goods—was of key importance in helping the Polish leadership to emerge as well as it did from the December-February period of crisis. No doubt, the Polish leaders see Poland as inevitably dependent to a large degree on the Soviet Union and the other CMEA states for meeting its future economic development needs, and these ties as much as anything else explain their strong verbal support for the Soviet Union. Also, Poland currently enjoys quite favorable terms of trade with the Soviet Union and finds it advantageous to expand its trade there, especially in view of the difficulties in doing so with the West.

Poland's most important trading partner, the Soviet Union accounted for 37.7 per cent of imports and about 35.3 per cent of exports in 1970 (compared with 11.1 per cent and 9.3 per cent for the GDR, Poland's second most important trade partner). Poland is the Soviet Union's second most important trade partner (next to the GDR), the second-largest and most populous communist state in Europe (next to the Soviet Union) and the major buffer between the Soviet Union and Western Europe. According to the terms of the 1971-75 trade agreement signed on 29 December 1970, trade between the two countries is to expand by 67 per cent over the previous five year period.

First Secretary Gierek and Premier Jaroszewicz attended the CPSU congress in Moscow in late March and early April. In his speech Gierek emphasized the close ties between Poland and the Soviet Union and described the new CPSU program as one "directed toward man, a program designed to meet in better fashion the material and spiritual needs of the Soviet peoples."

Relations with the Chinese People's Republic. Polish relations with China remain cool, correct, but distant. There were numerous references in the press and in official speeches about the Polish desire to engage in normal, cooperative relations with China, but at the same time there was frequent criticism of Chinese positions. The Chinese communists did not attend the PUWP congress (nor did Albania), and in his speech to the congress Gierek referred to the "splitting" tendencies of the Chinese leadership.

Relations with Other Communist-ruled States. In the first 16 days of 1971, representatives of the Polish party leadership visited all of the communist-ruled states of Eastern Europe except Albania. Presumably the PUWP was trying to inform the other communist-ruled states about the situation in Poland and the intentions of its leadership and seeking their confidence and support. Further contacts followed later.

Perhaps the most interesting development was the increasing closeness of the ties among Poland, Czechoslovakia, and the GDR, whose previous "northern tier" relationship (developed in the mid 1960's) had deteriorated after 1968. In addition to frequent and increased exchanges of high-level delegations, on the symbolic level a clear pattern emerged, in the press and in speeches of Polish leaders, of referring to "the U.S.S.R., Czechoslovakia, the GDR," and then "other fraternal countries." At the end of the year, Poles, Czechoslovaks, and East Germans no longer needed visas or passports to visit one another's countries, regular domestic identification cards sufficing for visits of up to three months. Unlimited exchange of currriencies was also to be allowed. In the case of Polish-GDR relations, four new crossing points and one additional rail link were added to the five and two already in use, with the expectation that more Polish workers will cross over to work in GDR factories.

On 5 January Poland and the GDR signed a trade agreement for 1971-75 envisioning a 70 per cent increase in trade compared with 1966-70. A protocol for 1972, signed in December, included provisions on delivery of materials to Poland for construction of a second oil pipeline from the Soviet Union to Poland and the GDR. On 18-20 September the East German party first secretary, Erich Honecker, and GDR premier Willi Stoph visited Poland. Relations between Poland and the GDR seemed much warmer than when Gomułka and Ulbricht were in power.

On 3 March Czechoslovakia's foreign minister, Jan Marko, visited Poland. In May a PUWP delegation headed by Gierek attended the Czechoslovak party congress in Prague, where Gierek followed Brezhnev in addressing the delegates. On 13 August the Czechoslovak premier, Lubomír Štrougal, visited Poland for economic talks. On 1-3 October Štrougal and Czechoslovak party leader Husák came to Poland for talks.

Poland and Hungary signed a trade agreement for 1971-75 in February calling for a 40 per cent increase. Then on 15-16 May Gierek and Premier Jaroszewicz visited Budapest. Foreign Minister Jędrychowski followed on 20 May.

On 20 January Poland and Romania signed a 1971-75 trade agreement. In July the Romanian foreign affairs minister came to Poland for four days.

The foreign minister of Cuba visited Poland in June.

Relations with Yugoslavia. In addition to the January visit to Yugoslavia by Tejchma and Kania, on 21-24 October Jaroszewicz went to Belgrade for the first trip by a Polish premier since 1965. (Brezhnev's visit in September had laid the groundwork for improved Polish-Yugoslav relations.) The arrival was hailed as a turning point in Polish-Yugoslav relations and of great importance for Yugoslav relations with CMEA, and the substance of the talks was largely economic. In June a study delegation of the League of Communists of Yugoslavia visited Poland.

Relations with the Federal Republic of Germany. Polish-FRG relations suffered something of a letdown following the excitement at the signing of the Bonn-Warsaw treaty on 7 December 1970, finalizing the Oder-Neisse border and providing the basis for normalizing relations between the two states. Although some minor problems arose over repatriation of Germans living in Poland, the major disappointment for the Poles was the failure of the Germans to obtain early ratification of the treaty. The Poles were perhaps even more disappointed by the failure to get a greater increase in trade, the unwillingness of the Germans to provide favorable credit terms (a condition of Polish imports from Germany), the lack of success at working out joint cooperation between enterprises (because of the insistence on joint ownership of enterprises on the part of the private West German firms involved), and the failure to be accorded special GATT treatment. Nevertheless, Polish-FRG relations remained cordial, if somewhat strained. There were a number of visits by government officials and important private citizens between the two countries. A Frankfurt-Warsaw air link was inaugurated in April.

Relations with Other States. Despite all of the attention paid by the press to increased trade with other socialist states, Polish trade with the West seemed in 1971 to be expanding at an even more rapid rate, especially with countries outside the Common Market. Poland is anxious to do so with the West, but has made it clear that credit on favorable terms is a prerequisite. It has repeatedly called for elimination of import restrictions and trade discrimination by Western states (especially the EEC), but without much success. In October, Poland called for the establishment of an east-west trade center to further cooperation. In addition to continued attempts at promoting a European security conference, Poland devoted special attention in 1971 to cultivating relations with the states around the Baltic, and with Switzerland, Austria, and Italy. It also continued to cultivate better trade relations in Latin America, with special attention to Chile, Brazil, Colombia, and Peru. The Chilean foreign minister was in Poland during May as head of a seven-member delegation on a tour of eight communist countries. In June, a delegation of the Socialist Party of Chile came to Warsaw.

In April, Poland signed a 1971-74 trade agreement with Great Britain; in July a contract was signed between British Petroleum and the Polish Ciech enterprise providing British credit for the delivery of three million tons of oil a year over ten years (compared with 8.2 million tons a year from the Soviet Union in 1969) for a reported total of $500 million.

Important developments took place in Polish-American trade relations. In August, the U.S. government reversed an earlier stand and approved the sale to Poland of a license for the catalytic cracking method of oil refining. The following month the Poles announced that agreements had been reached for bottling Coca-Cola and Pepsi-Cola in 1972. In December, the U.S. secretary of commerce visited Poland after 11 days in the U.S.S.R. He discussed the possibilities for development of trade and scientific and industrial cooperation with Poland and indicated that U.S. credits would be made available for investments, in addition to most-favored-nation status and elimination of quotas. He also announced that a trade documentation center would be opened in Warsaw by the United States.

The Austrian foreign minister came to Poland in January followed by the French secretary of state for foreign affairs in late April and early May. The Polish foreign minister went to Japan at the end of April to discuss cultural and scientific exchanges—the first such visit ever by a high Polish official.

International Party Contacts. In addition to the extensive party-government contacts already noted, First Secretary Gierek headed the PUWP delegation to the Bulgarian party Congress on 20-21 April. In June, Politburo member and CCTU chairman Kruczek headed the PUWP delegation to the congress of the Mongolian People's Revolutionary Party. A PUWP delegation, headed by Politburo member and Central Committee secretary Edward Babiuch, visited Cuba on 27 May-2 June. In March, a PUWP delegation attended the congress of the Belgian Communist Party. In June and November there were visits by delegations from the French Communist Party and in September a visit from an Italian Communist Party delegation. A German Communist Party (DKP) delegation was in Poland 20-22 May.

Publications. The daily organ of the PUWP is *Trybuna Ludu* (The People's Tribune); its monthly theoretical journal is *Nowe Drogi* (New Roads). A monthly, *Zycie Partii* (Party Life), is directed at party activists, and a biweekly, *Chlopska Droga* (The Peasant's Way), is aimed at rural readers. The Central Committee agitation and propaganda department puts out the fortnightly *Zagadnienia i Materialy* (Problems and Materials). In addition there is a new party monthly, *Ideologia i Polityka* (Ideology and Politics). Seventeen dailies are published by voivodship party organizations. Two influential weeklies, *Polityka* and *Kultura* (Warsaw), deserve notice though they are not official PUWP publications.

* * *

The "Polish Communist Party in Albania." Kazimierz Mijał, a former PUWP Central Committee member, left Poland in February 1966 after he came under attack for organizing a Maoist faction within the party. Since then he has been active in Tirana, Albania, broadcasting in Polish "documents" allegedly originating with the "Central Committee of the Polish Communist Party in Poland" or from its organ, *Czerwony Sztandar* (Red Banner). No information is available about the size or composition of the alleged party, but it is assumed to be primarily a diversion supported by China and Albania. Mijał, who claims to be its first secretary, has taken a consistent Maoist position and has been highly critical of the PUWP as being "revisionist" and "compromised" and of its leaders as "slaves of Moscow." He can be expected to continue this line of attack against the new PUWP leadership.

University of Florida   James F. Morrison

Romania

The Romanian Communist Party (Partidul Comunist Român, RCP) was founded in 1921 by a group of left-wing social democrats and several radical peasants. Declared illegal soon thereafter, it went underground and emerged only at the end of World War II. It assumed power on demand of the Soviet Union in 1948, at which time the movement called itself the Romanian Workers' Party. In 1965, the original name was restored. As the only political party in the country, the RCP exercises a monopoly of power. A mass organization called the "Socialist Unity Front" was formed in November 1968, replacing the former "People's Democratic Front," which is active only during elections to the Grand National Assembly or parliament and to administrative bodies at lower levels. This renamed front organization, in which the RCP plays the leading role, but which includes representatives of major mass and civic organizations and also the national minority councils, provides a permanent organizational framework for broad strata of the population to participate in political life.

In 1970 Romania had a population of just over 20 million. The majority of the adult population, 58 per cent, worked in agriculture; industrial workers comprised 31 per cent; the remainder were office clerks, teachers, and other professionals. Industrialization of the country probably produced in 1971 a further increase of industrial workers, at the expense of the peasants. By ethnic origin, some 86 per cent is Romanian, 9 per cent Hungarian, 2 per cent German, and 3 per cent other nationalities.

Organization and Leadership. The supreme organ of the RCP is the party congress, held every four years, to which delegates are elected at county conferences. The Tenth Congress took place in August 1969. Between congresses, the Central Committee of 165 full members and 120 candidates is the governing authority. The 1969 congress elected Nicolae Ceauşescu as secretary-general. At that time the Central Committee elected a Standing Presidium consisting in 1971 of Emil Bodnaraş, Manea Mănescu, Ion Gheorghe Maurer, Paul Niculescu-Mizil, Gheorghe Pană, Gheorghe Rădulescu, Virgil Trofin and Ilie Verdeţ. It also elected a Secretariat in 1971 comprising Mihail Gere, Manea Mănescu, Paul Niculescu-Mizil, Gheorghe Pană, Vasili Patilineţ, Dumitru Popescu, and Virgil Trofin. There exists an Executive Committee, almost identical in composition with the combined Standing Presidium and Secretariat. The Standing Presidium is the policy-making body of the party. At lower levels, each county has a party committee, headed by a secretary. Some municipalities have committees equal in rank to those of the counties. They direct and supervise the work of primary party organizations in factories, towns, and villages. During 1971, much emphasis was placed on improvement of county committee efficiency.

Changes in party membership by occupational categories were shown in statistics published in the official party press (*Scînteia*, 20 March 1970 and 17 February 1971) (see table). The number of women increased from 20 to 23 per cent of the total. Fifteen per cent of the adult population belongs to the party.

The growth of industrial workers among party members and the simultaneous decline of peasants by now represents a steady trend. The main reason appears to be the progressive industrialization of the country. While the movement of peasants from the villages to cities contributes to a growth of factory party cells, the peasants remaining in rural areas show less eagerness to join the party. The special effort made in 1971 to increase peasant membership apparently failed. No mention of this has been made in the press.

Party Membership

Category	31 December 1969		31 December 1970	
	Number	Percent	Number	Percent
Industrial workers	867,800	43.4	926,440	44.3
Peasants	531,920	26.6	553,917	25.5
Intellectuals and white collar workers	400,000	20.0	437,000	23.0
Others	200,000	10.0	171,728	7.2
Total	1,999,720	100.0	2,089,085	100.0

Major Party Meetings. The Central Committee held five plenary meetings during 1971 which dealt with the following major problems: 10-11 February—reform and reorganization of trade unions as well as politico-ideological education of party cadres; 5-6 May—economy, agriculture and peasant needs; 15 July—strengthening ideology in party work; 3-5 November—adoption of party program, proposed on 15 July; 15 December—economic and social development plan for 1972.

All plenums were preceded by meetings of the Executive Committee, held jointly with the Council of Ministers. These sessions prepared proposals for the plenums as well as draft bills which, after approval by the plenum, were forwarded to the National Assembly. The real source of new legislation, hence, is the Executive Committee. A majority of its members also serve as government ministers. The plenum may introduce some minor changes to drafts, but the National Assembly simply rubber-stamps such proposals.

The party called several broad membership meetings, to mark special occasions or consider particular aspects of its activities, at which the top leadership presented reports and proposals. The most important of these were held on 7 May, for the fiftieth anniversary of the RCP; on 9 July for a party *aktif* discussion of ideological, political and cultural-educational activities; and on 23 December, when the party chief lectured communal party secretaries and chairmen of local peoples' councils (mayors). Ceauşescu also held several working sessions with writers, artists, students, teachers, university professors, and others to discuss their relationship to the party. The press did not give details, but it has been reported that some of these meetings led to confrontations in which the secretary-general insisted that intellectuals submit to party ideology and discipline.

Personnel Changes. The 10-11 February plenum promoted Manea Manescu to membership on the Standing Presidium. This brought to nine the number of top leaders. In connection with party and government programs, and after sharp criticism by Ceauşescu, members of the leadership engaged in self-criticism at plenums. Nevertheless, many persons on the first and second party levels were demoted and sent to work in province offices. The more spectacular demotions were those of Ion Iliescu (formerly secretary for youth affairs, from a secretaryship in the Central Committee), Florian Danilache (from chairman of the General Union of Trade Unions, February 11), and Ilie Rădulescu (chief of the propaganda section in the Central Committee, July 15).

Party-State Interlocking Directorate. Following the Soviet example, a person can simultaneously hold high party and government positions. This in practice creates a personal union between party and state. The Council of Ministers meets together with the party's Executive Committee, and most participants belong to both bodies. In high-level official dealings with other communist-ruled states, Romania normally is represented by Ceauşescu as RCP secretary-general and Maurer as premier, as in the case of Brezhnev and Kosygin in the U.S.S.R.

General Evaluation. Internal developments continued to indicate stabilization of economic and social conditions, with the population considering the slow but steady improvement in standard of living as a result of Ceauşescu's "wise" policy. The party leader has fostered this general feeling by participating in "working sessions" of county committees and visiting factories. By establishing personal rapport with the administration at lower levels as well as workers and peasants, Ceauşescu cleverly exploited these visits to distant areas for promotion of his "grass-roots" politics. He has intervened concerning local shortcomings and complaints of the population. Under these circumstances dislike of the party still prevails, particularly among peasants due to a stronger regime stand against the church, but there exist no centers of opposition.

Taking this paternalistic attitude toward workers and peasants, Ceauşescu has assured himself support from the great majority of the population. He, thus, has a free hand in dealing with intellectuals, members of the professions, and white-collar workers both in state and party administration. Since the 1968 ferment in Czechoslovakia, Romanian intellectuals have been striving for liberalization of the regime and elimination of "socialist realism" from literature and the arts. They attained advances in this direction, when the regime needed their support in mobilizing public opinion against Soviet pressure. By 1971, Ceauşescu obviously felt strong enough to ignore this group.

During a 9 July meeting with the party *aktif* on ideological, political, and cultural-education activities of the party, he explained that Marxist-Leninist ideology cannot tolerate return to practices of the bourgeois West. Without calling totalitarianism by name, he insisted that party ideology must dominate every domain of political, social, and economic life in a communist state. He announced that the party would henceforth take all measures to assure strengthening of ideology and discipline among the party aktif (*Scînteia*, 13 July). On 15 July the plenum voted resolutions later implemented by the government. Self-criticism, dismissals and resignations followed as evidence of a tougher domestic line.

Ceauşescu repeated his insistence on strengthening ideology and party discipline on 23 December in a speech to 5,000 communal party secretaries and chairmen (mayors) of local peoples' councils. The tone appeared milder, the principal objective being to simplify administrative operations and eliminate unnecessary red tape. (*Ibid.*, 25 December).

In foreign affairs, Ceauşescu still exploits hatred of the Soviet Union by Romanians. The unforgettable presence of the Red Army during World War II and U.S.S.R. annexation of purely Romanian territories provide a permanent antidote against Soviet machinations. Unlike other East European states, Romania does not have a pro-Moscow faction in its communist party. This situation creates an unadvertised, but strongly felt, spiritual link between Romania and Yugoslavia. The "Ceauşescu formula," coined in 1970, provided that Romania's relations with other socialist states must be based "on the principles of respect for national independence and sovereignty, equal rights, noninterference in internal affairs and mutual advantage"; it was upheld and repeated during 1971 on several occasions by Ceauşescu and his subordinates. The June visit to Peking of the Romanian party leader offered an occasion to have this formula confirmed by the Chinese.

Internal and external tranquility allowed Ceauşescu to launch another program which up to now is less clearly defined: education of a "Romanian socialist man." The party boss and his new education minister, Mircea Maliţa, speaking about this "new man," seemed to be sending up a trial balloon. Party and government activities suggested a paradoxical trend: farther away from Moscow but closer to Marxism-Leninism.

Domestic Affairs. *The Economy.* The press on 30 January published an official report on implementation of the 1970 economic plan. The total value of industrial production almost reached 297 million lei ($59,450 million, at an official exchange rate of six lei for one U.S. dollar) which meant 100.6 per cent over-fulfillment of the plan. Compared with 1969, the increase totaled 12 per cent. No figures appeared on money value of agricultural production. Only the volume production was given, with an average of 30 per cent below plan.

National income grew by 7 per cent, much below the planned 12 per cent. The flood in 1970 and a bad harvest explained this failure. Goods sold to the population rose in value by 8.6 per cent, among which food sales rose by 9.4 per cent, and industrial consumers' goods by 7.7 per cent. This indicates improvement of the living standard.

The total value of foreign trade in 1970 was 22.8 billion lei, an increase by 12.7 per cent over 1969, which exceeded the planned 11.5 per cent increase. Although exports grew by 13.5 per cent and imports by 12 per cent, the trade balance showed a deficit.

The 1971 economic plan, as accepted by the National Assembly in December 1970, was published early in 1971. Investments were raised by 13 per cent to 75.8 billion lei (about $12,630 million). Industry continued to absorb the largest amount of investments (1970, 38.2 billion lei; 1971, 42.9 billion). Agriculture will receive slightly more than in past years (1970, only 8.1 billion; 1971, some ten billion). In contrast to these increased allocations, investment for housing, education, and culture showed a decrease.

Investments in industry will be used almost entirely for construction of new plants, whereas the increase in agriculture will develop and modernize mechanization of agriculture, expanding irrigation and drainage, and combating soil erosion.

The December 1970 workers riots in Poland influenced a last-minute raise of investments that will serve the population directly. Housing, originally to be cut substantially, received only slight reduction to 93,000 new apartments from state funds or considerable government credits. Investments in food production also were raised only insignificantly, but Ceauşescu promised improvements during the year and kept his promise. Wages are to increase by not more than 3.5 per cent, which is low in comparison with 8 per cent achieved during 1970. Again, Ceauşescu later in the year increased wages to agricultural workers above the planned 3.5 per cent.

Foreign Trade. Romania produced a foreign trade deficit of 574 million lei in 1970 which caused great concern to the party leadership. Although much blame was placed on last year's floods which reduced export of agricultural products, the latter had been declining steadily. On 3-5 February a special conference on foreign trade had participation from highest state and party authorities. Ceauşescu presented a survey of Romanian foreign trade over the past five years and projections for 1971-1975. During 1966-1970, foreign trade increased by 75 per cent over 1965, and considerably exceeded the goal of 50 to 55 per cent. Nevertheless, during this five-year period, a deficit of 3.1 billion lei had accumulated. This resulted from an average 12.6 per cent increase of imports compared with an 11 per cent for exports. The quality of the latter is inferior, and customer specifications are not fulfilled. Ceauşescu blamed the General Inspectorate of Quality Control for these deficiencies.

To overcome these problems and increase exports, the party leader proposed that excessive centralism be eliminated, responsibility for exports be placed on producing enterprises, central organs, and ministries, and that monopoly exercised by the foreign trade ministry end. Ceauşescu also appealed to party elements in production centers for their active support in export operations.

Agriculture. Disastrous floods and a bad harvest the previous year had adverse influence on agricultural production in 1971. The flood required much attention by state and party leaders, bringing to their attention the essential needs of the peasants. Ceauşescu visited not only areas affected but made several trips to rural communities in various parts of the country. Listening to peasant grievances, he promised improvement. The party and government analyzed questions related to agricultural cooperatives and the peasants. Wages for workers on state farms and cooperatives were raised by 5 to 10 per cent; social security benefits were extended and improved; taxes on private plots were reduced. This provided the peasant with more money to spend for food and consumer products. It also assured Ceauşescu of peasant gratitude. By the end of the year, almost 1.2 billion lei of cooperative debts (payable in 1972) were canceled, which gave members a higher income. Despite this aid, farm income and living standards are still below those of the Czechoslovak, Hungarian, or Polish peasants.

Culture. At the Central Committee plenum of 10-11 February the new education minister Mircea Malița submitted a draft bill on education and professional qualifications for discussion. Malița said that many countries, including Romania, have concluded that investing in man is more important than investing in equipment. Due to rapid progress of technology, and increased need for technical and scientific information, the present school system is no longer adequate. The new educational system must be based on the idea that school will provide only the basic part of a person's education. Additional training must be obtained in special or periodic refresher courses, adjusted to individual needs to perform well on assignment and job. This new education method should not be rigid, but rather interesting and attractive in order to satisfy adults. The new sequence would include only preschool, school, and postgraduate education. The law would make it compulsory for all wage earners to improve their qualifications. Up to the end of the year, the proposal had not been made into law.

On 1 October, in a speech at the opening of the 1971/72 academic year, Ceauşescu dealt at length with ideological education, the leading role of the party in all domains, improvement of political activity in education, and "molding of the new man." He mentioned that the ten-year general education program would be implemented by the 1973/74 school year, and called for "gradual removal of distinctions between intellectual and manual work."

In his long speech at the party meeting for ideological, political, and cultural education activities on 9 July, Ceauşescu indicated displeasure with the literary production of poets, writers, playwrights, movie producers, and journalists. He demanded that they abandon a search for models in the West and find their inspiration in Marxism-Leninism.

In party-member and non-affiliated artistic circles these demands were strongly criticized orally, but journals gave only sporadic comments. Artists talked in cafes and at round-table discussions. In September, Ceauşescu held a meeting with members of the Writers' Association but little came out in the press. Supposedly in protest against party pressure on the writers, leading novelist Nicolae Breban resigned from editorship of the journal *Romania Literară*.

During the 3 November plenum several writers, including the Writers' Association president, Zaharia Stancu, participated in a discussion which returned to Ceauşescu's demands of 9 July. Writers assured the party leadership that they fully adhere to the principles contained in the leader's speech.

Youth. Ceauşescu's increased activity during the entire year also covered youth, for which he had shown little past interest. In February he attended the congress of the Union of Communist Youth, where he delivered a speech. Before the November plenum he took part in a preliminary meeting of the Union of Communist Youth and Union of Romanian Student Associations, at which he demanded that they adopt resolutions implementing the principles of ideological training that he proposed in his 9 July speech. It is somewhat unusual that the press did not report this preliminary meeting at all, and only much later did it become known.

Also in November, Ceauşescu had a meeting with students at Timişoara, where "a number of measures for youth" were worked out (*Scînteia*, 7 November).

On 2-3 December a joint plenum of the Union of Communist Youth and Union of Romanian Student Associations took place, at which the youth affairs minister, Marţian Dan, revealed serious shortcomings in the organizational life of young persons. He demanded "radical improvements." The plenum belatedly adopted the party's ideological program.

Romanian youth, both in high schools and universities, has little sympathy for the party. This is well known throughout the country, but the press abstains from discussing manifestations of opposition. No riots took place in schools or universities, but such acts as consistent turning of Ceauşescu's picture in class rooms to face the wall and similar deeds express the feelings of youth. The Union of Communist Youth, imposed at school on pupils, is not popular and its activities are minimal.

Trade Unions. With the growth of industry financed by significant state investments, work crews in factories are absorbing a large portion of the young people from villages. These recruits for the Romanian proletariat expanded over the last ten years from 17 to 31 per cent of the population. The 44 per cent among party members outnumbers the peasants in the party. Manipulated and socially engineered by the bureaucracy, this growing mass has concentrated in several major industrial centers. The worker's loyalty to the government is more or less taken for granted because, for those offered the opportunity, the social advancement from peasant to factory worker creates enough satisfaction and gratitude among these new proletarians.

The December 1970 events in Poland, during which similar new industrial workers became a menace to the ruling party, sounded an alarm at Bucharest. Ceauşescu was shrewd enough to perceive the similarity of conditions. He convinced the leadership that the party had to take energetic measures to prevent a repetition of the Polish events in his country. From this arose the sudden preoccupation with the need to "reform" the structure of trade unions, modernize labor legislation, and improve housing and food for industrial workers. During all of 1971, these industrial problems received priority in party activities.

Most of the Central Committee plenum on 10-11 February discussed and elaborated on reforming the General Trade Union Confederation. Ceauşescu extensively lectured the plenum on the need for greater participation in and democratization of trade unions, to strengthen the role of unions in enterprises (adopting here as a pattern the Yugoslav workers' councils), and to abandon paid trade union activists in favor of participation by persons in the production process in decision-making positions of trade unions. At the same time, Ceauşescu warned that trade unions must not become administrative organs and replace the administration of the enterprise.

The sharpness of Ceauşescu's criticism of the past trade union operations and their general federation, as well as the broad scope of planned reform, are indications of the leader's concern. The old apparatus worker Florian Danilache, chairman of the trade union Central Council, was replaced by Standing Presidium member Virgil Trofin. This happened in a manner significant for communist organizational matters. During his speech, Ceauşescu had advocated more democracy in trade unions. At the same time, he did not allow the unions to elect their new chairman but simply appointed him.

A few days later, on 16 February, a plenum of the trade union central council accepted in general terms the guidelines of the party plenum. It voted the theses and new draft statutes which were to be presented to the sixth congress of the Trade Union Confederation. These texts, together with Ceauşescu's speech at the February party plenum, were widely publicized in the press and on factory billboards with an appeal that workers voice criticism and proposals during debates in factories and in letters to newspapers. At the same time, Ceauşescu started a tour of factories. He gave speeches (but abstained from Gierek-style discussions in Poland), talked to workers, and appealed for improved production in order to fulfill the new five-year plan. These visits and speeches again were publicized widely in the press, as indication that the party was concerned with the well-being of the industrial workers, "the governing class" in the Romanian People's Republic. There appeared indeed hundreds of letters in the press which dealt with management-worker relations, the need for canteens, improvement of wages or pensions, and similar details. Little constructive criticism came out.

Between 10 and 13 March, conventions of the particular branch unions belonging to the federation took place. The theses and draft statute were broadly discussed and delegates to the congress elected. Trofin and some ministers participated in these conventions. There were no reports of opposition, only proposals voiced for inclusion in a future program of the federation for certain improvements and additions. Ceauşescu was praised for his concern with worker grievances, and the change from Danilache to Trofin seemed to have passed without notice. The party machine had done efficient work.

The congress rubber-stamped all drafts and proposals, as presented by the federation's Central Council, which in fact originated with party authorities. The newly elected Central Council includes probably more true workers and fewer "apparatchiks" than before. The congress voted resolutions on improvement of labor conditions and discussed the outline of the new Labor Code that is expected to appear in 1972.

Amnesty. Coinciding with the forthcoming Christmas and New Year's holidays, the State Council issued on 24 December 1970 a decree on amnesty. It was fulfilled early in 1971. The amnesty had been limited to offenses with prison terms up to five years. All offenders against the state security were excluded from the amnesty. Sentences up to one year in prison received pardons, and fines were canceled. Sentences between one and five years were reduced by half.

Foreign Relations—Communist-Ruled States. *U.S.S.R.* Renewal in 1970 of the Romanian-Soviet friendship treaty inagurated a period of "normalization" between the two countries and eased tensions. On 15 March 1971 a new Soviet ambassador, Vasilii Drozdenko, replaced Aleksandr Basov, who had witnessed Ceauşescu's road to party leadership during his six years in Bucharest. Although Romania emphasized continuation of an independent foreign policy, opposition to economic integration through the Council for Mutual Economic Assistance lessened. Hardening its political stance in ideological matters, the RCP reaffirmed Marxist-Leninist orthodoxy. The Romanian press carefully avoided anything that might displease the Soviets.

This lasted until Ceauşescu's visit to Moscow in March-April for the Twenty-fourth Congress of the Communist Party of the Soviet Union. In a speech on 1 April he reiterated his independent foreign and domestic policy by referring to Marxist theory. The manner in which the Soviet press reported this speech indicated that his hosts had been displeased.

When Romania celebrated the fiftieth anniversary of its communist party on 7 May, Brezhnev did not come to Bucharest. Ceauşescu again gave an elaborate speech in which he returned to his formula of "national independence, and sovereignty, full equality of rights, noninterference in internal affairs, and mutual advantage" as the basis of foreign policy. He continued by saying: "I have been asked in various interviews whether Romania is considering renouncing its support of these principles. . . . These principles are as necessary in contemporary human society, in the relations of cooperation in the world, as are water and air for the existence of mankind. How could we give up water and air? It would mean giving up life." (*Scînteia*, 8 May.) In a later part of this speech, he quoted Lenin and also the 1943 resolution on dissolution of the Comintern in order to support his present policy with experience of the past.

A few days after this celebration, President Gustav Heinemann of the Federal Republic of Germany visited Romania. At about the same time, Bucharest radio announced that Ceauşescu would travel to Peking in June. This announcement as well as the Heinemann visit provided the impetus for attacks against Romania by the Czechoslovak, Hungarian, and Polish newspapers. Although the Soviet press abstained from any comment, it reprinted critical remarks from other East European sources. Disapproval appeared when Ceauşescu, on his way home from East Asia, landed on 24 June in Moscow. A planned two-day layover became a three-hour refueling stop, with only Kosygin and Suslov at the airport to greet the Romanian state and party chief. The absence of Podgorny and Brezhnev emphasized the Kremlin's displeasure that Ceauşescu had dealt with the Chinese.

The flood of criticism in the East European press, with Hungarian articles particularly vicious, did not provoke Bucharest. Only the RCP secretary for inter-party relations, Niculescu-Mizil, responded, and he did so in a factual but emphatic manner (*ibid.*, 9 July). He indicated that Romania, as a sovereign state, has a right to its own foreign policy and treats all socialist states on the same equal level. By the end of July, when the government refused to allow Warsaw Pact forces to cross Romanian territory for military maneuvers in Hungary, the tension increased. Nevertheless, during a top-level CMEA meeting at Bucharest on 27-29 July, Romania took a conciliatory stand concerning the long-term economic integration plan of member states.

On 2 August there took place in the Crimea a meeting of first secretaries from communist parties in Eastern Europe, with participation of Brezhnev and Podgorny. Ceauşescu remained conspicuously absent. It never became known whether he was not invited or whether he declined an invitation. The announced subject of discussion at this conference was U.S. President Nixon's forthcoming visit to Peking and the situation in Sudan, where a counter-coup eliminated communists who had seized power. A communiqué issued after this meeting did not mention Romania but emphasized the importance of "the struggle against right-wing and left-wing opportunism and of rallying all progressive and national liberation forces in the anti-imperialist struggle."

Perhaps not by coincidence, on the day of the Crimea meeting the RCP newspaper deplored "pressure and blackmail" from unnamed quarters and reaffirmed Romania's intention to continue good relations with all states, "regardless of their social and political system" (*ibid.*, 2 August). Facing pressure with calm, Bucharest prepared for the worst. Announcing war games, several divisions were increased to full strength, but in fact no maneuvers took place.

On 22-25 September Brezhnev visited Tito. Due to the close collaboration between the latter and Ceauşescu, it was obvious that the Belgrade visit would have indirect meaning for Romania. Indeed, at a dinner given in his honor, Brezhnev dedicated a long passage of his speech to refuting the "invention of a so-called doctrine of limited sovereignty" which had been ascribed to him. It is too early to conclude that the Belgrade speech was a capitulation to Ceauşescu's "formula," but it did represent a complete reversal of the motivation behind the 1968 "fraternal socialist" military intervention in Czechoslovakia. Only the Chinese press devoted adequate attention to this reversal. Brezhnev snubbed Bucharest, stopping in Budapest and Sofia, but seeing Romania only from his airplane when on his way home from Yugoslavia.

After these visits to Yugoslavia, Hungary, and Bulgaria the pressure on Romania gradually eased. By the end of October, the U.S.S.R. and Romanian defense ministries exchanged military missions. Toasts at receptions in both capitals sounded as if no August crisis had ever taken place. "Normalization" continued to be the slogan for relations between these two neighbors.

Communist China. The entire year was marked by an increased exchange of visits by high state and party officials of Romania and China. On 22 March the Romanian foreign trade minister, Gheorghe Rădulescu, signed a protocol specifying the use of a $244 million loan granted to Romania in 1970 by China. This was noted in the East European press without special comment. Then, in May, it became known that Ceauşescu would visit Peking. Attacks against him appeared throughout the Bloc.

This visit lasted from 1 to 9 June, and Ceauşescu was the first leader of a communist-ruled state to have visited China since the beginning of the Sino-Soviet rift. He received a lavish reception, conferring with both Mao Tse-tung and Chou En-lai. During a banquet, Chou supported Romania's defense of its sovereign rights and aspirations to full independence in an explicit manner. This represented clear approval for the "Ceauşescu formula," which repeatedly had evoked Soviet disapproval. After Tito, Chou became the second representative of a communist-ruled state to give recognition of Ceauşescu's desire for independence from the Soviet Union. Agreements reached between the two countries during this visit strengthened political and economic ties between them.

Hungary. János Kádár's consistent role as Moscow's mouthpiece for attacking Romanian foreign policy created deep distrust between Budapest and Bucharest. During these press skirmishes, the Hungarian side raised complaints about treatment of its minority in Transylvania. Niculescu-Mizil again answered in *Scînteia.*

After Brezhnev's visit to Budapest on 25 September, the tension seemed to ease. However, the Romanian-Hungarian friendship treaty, which expired in 1968, has never been renewed. Although the signing of such a treaty between Romania and the U.S.S.R. in 1970 induced Poland and Bulgaria to follow suit, Hungary still avoided a reconciliation after Romanian refusal to participate in the 1968 Czechoslovak intervention. Only on 23 November did the Hungarian foreign affairs minister, János Peter, come to Bucharest for talks on renewal of the friendship treaty and improvement of economic relations. This visit supposedly will be followed in the future by a Kádár-Ceauşescu meeting to sign the treaty. This improvement is a by-product of "normalization" with the Soviet Union.

European Bloc Countries. Romanian relations with the German Democratic Republic (GDR) were reserved. The much-discussed state visit by the East Berlin leadership did not materialize. The appearance of West Germany's President Heinemann at Bucharest and Ceauşescu's trip to Peking produced further deterioration in relations with the GDR.

Contacts with Poland and Bulgaria reflected Romanian-Soviet "normalization." Ceauşescu bypassed Warsaw when he flew late in June to Helsinki, but sent Mănescu to Poland in early July as a first step in improving relations. The atmosphere of détente by year's end saw Ceauşescu in Warsaw at the Seventh Congress of the Polish United Workers' Party. Party leaders from other East European countries were there, and this could have served as an occasion to break the isolation in which Romania had found itself. In his speech on 7 December, Ceauşescu emphasized the need to reestablish unity of the world communist movement on a new basis. He warned that existing differences should not affect inter-state relations. Economic exchanges between Romania and Poland improved during 1971.

Bulgaria, having its own internal troubles, stayed out of the controversy over Ceauşescu's visit to Peking. By leaving Bucharest in peace, Sofia apparently wanted to create a better atmosphere for a projected détente with Yugoslavia.

Albania's relations with Romania were mentioned on several occasions in the Bucharest press as developing "normally."

Yugoslavia. Romanian contacts with this communist-ruled state are friendly and close. The mutual element of attraction is a common interest in preserving independence, particularly from the U.S.S.R. Reciprocal visits by high party and government officials have strengthened political and economic cooperation. The harnessing of the Danube at the Iron Gates and construction of the large ancillary power plant as a joint project can be considered a model for economic cooperation in Eastern Europe.

At the time of the mysterious consultation among communist party chiefs in the Crimea, in which neither Yugoslavia nor Romania participated, Foreign Minister Corneliu Mănescu was "vacationing" in Yugoslavia but found time for consultations with the new Premier, Dzemal Bijedić, and other high officials. According to reports from Yugoslav and Romanian news agencies, the discussions centered around political-economic cooperation and the international situation. Following this visit, Manea Mănescu, party secretary and chairman of the Economic Council, paid a visit to his Yugoslav counterparts.

Brezhnev's meeting with Tito in September was followed by the latter's visit to Ceauşescu at Timişoara on 23-24 November. A joint communiqué stressed peaceful coexistence, cooperation, and détente as objectives of foreign policy. Other reports from these talks indicate that both governments called for abandoning the practice of holding military maneuvers on the territory of other states. Little information on the Tito-Ceauşescu meeting appeared in the Soviet or other East European press.

Asian Countries. Romania's attitude toward Vietnam seems to be tightly dependent upon its relations with the U.S.S.R. Whenever relations deteriorate, the government and press in Bucharest come out with anti-U.S. attacks. Ceauşescu's visit to Hanoi and to the North Korean capital represented token manifestations of solidarity. At the same time, insignificant trade with both showed further reductions.

Ceauşescu's visit to Mongolia had different overtones. Here, it became obvious that the Romanian leader intended to improve old established relations. Rumors that he attempted to promote a Chinese-Mongolian rapprochement seem to be unfounded.

Foreign Relations—Non-Communist Countries. *United States.* In general terms, Romania's attitude toward the United States was friendly and correct, with one exception. Press attacks occur in connection with the Vietnam war and occasional visits by prominent delegations from Hanoi, when the newspapers speak about "imperialist aggression." Corneliu Mănescu conferred with U. S. Secretary of State William Rogers in New York on the occasion of the opening session of the United Nations. Romania is eager to increase trade with the United States, and this found support from a U.S. Senator. Walter Mondale introduced a bill which would grant most-favored nation status to Romania. Although this bill never came to a vote, Romania succeeded in obtaining credits from the Export-Import Bank. Exchanges of students and scholars began and progressed slowly.

West Germany. The visit of President Heinemann to Bucharest and several ministerial visits from both sides characterized relations between the two countries. Both sides are interested in expanding trade. A halt to repatriation of Germans from Romania produced the first difficulty in these relations. Also the German desire to obtain seasonal agricultural workers from Romania met with obstacles in Bucharest.

France. The French secretary-general of the foreign affairs ministry, Hervé Alphand (former ambassador to Washington), visited Bucharest during 28-31 January and conferred with Corneliu Mănescu as well as Ceauşescu. The Western press speculated that a European security conference, the Middle East situation, German *Ostpolitik*, and mutual trade relations represented major topics under discussion. Manea Mănescu later went to Paris for a meeting of the Franco-Romanian Mixed Economic Commission. On 15 November, Corneliu Mănescu arrived to spend five days in Paris and had conversations with President Pompidou and several ministers. A joint communiqué, issued on 19 November, mentioned that an "identity of views over a broad spectrum had become apparent" (*Scînteia*, 20 November). The *Financial Times* of London on 19 November, however, stated that Mănescu was seeking French support in securing Common Market preferential status for Romania.

Several other ministerial visits from both sides seemed to indicate that both states have an interest in extending and strengthening their relations.

Other Countries. The presidency of the U.N. Security Council, held by Corneliu Mănescu offered the Romanian foreign affairs minister possibilities to initiate relations with many countries on all continents. He made good use of this advantage. During 1971 he was very active not only in visiting such countries as Canada, Denmark, Sweden, Finland, and Greece, but also in receiving officials from many other states in Bucharest. This activity, combined with the widely known resistance of Ceaușescu to Soviet pressure, resulted in a growth of Romanian prestige throughout the world. Mănescu is an important member of Ceaușescu's team and, in addition to interpreting the leader's foreign policy, he helped to develop trade relations with non-communist states.

Warsaw Treaty Organization. A conference of foreign affairs ministers of Warsaw Pact members took place at Bucharest on 18-19 February, before the new tension between Romania and the Soviet Union. Andrei Gromyko participated and conferred with Ceaușescu on international affairs. The main subject of discussion of the conference was a European security conference. The communiqué said that preparation for a conference had progressed and also mentioned that a détente in Europe was developing (Bucharest radio, 19 February).

The 1971 maneuvers of Pact countries took place in Hungary with host, Czechoslovak, and Soviet units participating. They started on 3 August, one day after the Crimea conference of party leaders. As mentioned above, the Romanian government refused to grant transit rights for Soviet troops. It explained this action by claiming that permission could be given only by the National Assembly, at the time in recess.

During October, military missions from the Soviet Union and Romania exchanged visits. From their composition, it can be deduced that problems of ideological training in the respective armies were discussed.

On 26-29 October the Military Council of the Pact countries met in Warsaw, with Romania represented by Defense Minister Ion Ioniţa and several other generals. No details were reported from this conference.

Council for Mutual Economic Assistance. During the crisis in Romanian-Soviet relations, on July 27-29 a meeting of the CMEA Economic Council took place in Bucharest. It approved plans for further integration of member economies over the next five years. Romania accepted these plans, obviously maintaining its right to a later veto over specific unfavorable measures. The meeting also adopted a new convertible ruble, to be used for Bloc commercial transactions.

Inter-Party Relations. A stepped-up exchange of visits with foreign communist parties characterized 1971. Particularly, relations with non-ruling parties were cultivated. By "coincidence" on 2 August, the day of the Crimea conference for secretaries of East European parties, in which Ceaușescu did not participate, the Romanian party leader entertained a large group of West European party leaders and officials at a lavish reception on the same Black Sea shore, but in Romania.

During 23-25 November on initiative of the Italian Communist Party, a conference of European party representatives took place concerning the attitude to be adopted by parties toward the Common Market. Italian representatives urged changing the Common Market so as to permit a democratic "transformation of the community." They called for establishment of a new European economic unit, "from the Atlantic to the Urals." Romanian delegates, having a particular interest in achieving closer cooperation with the Common Market, participated in this conference.

Publications. The official organs of the RCP Central Committee are its daily newspaper *Scînteia* and a monthly ideological review, *Lupta de Clasa*, both published at Bucharest.

W. S. Sworakowski

Union of Soviet Socialist Republics

The Communist Party of the Soviet Union (Kommunisticheskaia Partiia Sovetskogo Soiuza; CPSU) derives from the Russian Social Democratic Labor Party which was founded in 1898 and split into Bolshevik ("majority") and Menshevik ("minority") factions at its Second Congress in 1903. Following the 1917 revolution which brought them to power, the Bolsheviks changed the title of the party at its Seventh Congress in March 1918 to the "All-Russian Communist Party (Bolsheviks)." After the country was renamed the Union of Soviet Socialist Republics, the party in 1925 became the "All-Union Communist Party (Bolsheviks)." The present designation was adopted in 1952 at the Nineteenth Congress. The CPSU is the sole political party given legal recognition in the U.S.S.R.

At the Twenty-fourth Congress (30 March-9 April 1971) party membership was reported to be 14,455,321 (including 645,232 candidates). A total of 14.2 million had been announced in late 1970. Efforts to strengthen the worker component in the party after the Twenty-third Congress, in 1966, increased its proportion slightly, to 40 per cent, according to the Credentials Committee report. White-collar occupations still claimed 45 per cent. Only 15 per cent of the party membership worked in agriculture during 1971, although 28 per cent of the total labor force was in this sector (*SSSR v tsifrakh v 1970 god*, Moscow, 1971, p. 99.). Women, numbering over three million in the party, made up a fourth of CPSU membership, over half of the population, and half of the labor force. Among the party's ethnic constituents, Russians predominated, providing 63 per cent of all members. The 1970 census (listing 91 nationalities) showed Russians to comprise 53 per cent of the population.

The party's youth auxiliary, the Communist Youth League (Komsomol), had over 28 million members in 1971. Since the Twenty-third Congress, when it became the only route to party membership for young people between the ages of 18 and 23, it has provided almost half of all CPSU recruits. (Party growth has been somewhat restricted in recent years, due to revived emphasis on the Leninist concept of a highly disciplined elite organization.) The CPSU membership of 14.4 million was slightly under 6 per cent of the 244 million population at the beginning of the year (*Pravda*, 7 May) and included 9 per cent of all adults, according to a Twenty-fourth Congress report.

Organization and Leadership. Though the party controls and directs public life, it is formally distinct from the parallel structure of state administration. The government forms a hierarchy of some 50,000 soviets (councils), with each of the 15 Union Republics and 20 Autonomous Republics headed by its own Supreme Soviet. Over all is the Supreme Soviet of the U.S.S.R. Forty-five per cent of the 2 million deputies chosen in the 13 June 1971 general elections for republic and lower-level soviets were party members, with the percentage rising substantially at higher levels (*Izvestiia*, 20 June). The CPSU has a broad base of primary party organizations which numbered 370,000 in March. The structure includes intermediate party committees, the 14 Central Committees of the Union Republics (there is no separate party organization for the Russian Republic), and finally the CPSU Central Committee. The last body is elected at the party congress; according to the statutes, it functions as the highest party organ between congresses. The locus of power lies in the Politburo, which meets weekly to decide basic questions of domestic and foreign policy; and in the Secretariat which supervises implementation of party directives by departments of the Central Committee and controls personnel appointments.

The party derives two-thirds of its income from membership dues that are scaled to individual earnings. Another important financial source lies in profits from party publications such as the daily newspaper *Pravda* (circulation, 9 million) and the Politizdat publishing house. The reported increase in party income of approximately 40 per cent since the Twenty-third Congress (*Pravda*, 1 April) is substantially above the membership increase of about 15 per cent for the same period.

The major event of the year in party life was the convening of the Twenty-fourth Congress, which had been postponed, apparently in connection with the belated new five-year plan, beyond the maximum four-year interval stipulated in party regulations. In order to permit future republic and national congresses to coincide with the economic planning cycle, party statutes were amended to provide that congresses will now meet at least once every five years. Lower-level party committees, including those of the 31,000 primary party organizations large enough to have a committee, are to convene conferences at least twice every five years. The vast majority of basic units will continue to hold annual review and election meetings. Further modification of party statutes was designed to facilitate establishment of primary party organizations in production sectors and strengthen other basic party units. The right of surveillance and control over administration activities—already held by their counterparts in production enterprises—was extended to primary party organizations in transport, communications, and supply as well as in all "planning organizations, construction bureaus, scientific research institutions, educational establishments, cultural, medical, and other institutions whose administrative functions do not extend beyond the framework of their own collectives." (See *Partiinaia zhizn'*, no. 9, for text of all changes.) Party units in such high-level agencies as ministries were warned not to interfere with the activities of subordinate institutions, but were instructed by the congress to "exert control over the work of the staff in fulfilling the party and government directives in observance of Soviet law." Party cards were to be recalled and reissued for the first time in seventeen years to permit a review of membership, strengthen party discipline, and provide opportunity for elimination of undesirable elements.

The 4,740 delegates to the Twenty-fourth Congress were elected on the basis of one delegate for every 2,900 party members. An additional 223 delegates without voting rights represented the same proportion of candidates for membership in the party. Slightly over one-fourth of the delegates (1,284) belonged to Supreme Soviets of republics or of the U.S.S.R. According to the report of Credentials Commission Chairman I. V. Kapitonov (*Pravda*, 3 April), the working class was represented on an unprecedented scale. The 1,195 workers were said to include "famous metallurgists and mining engineers." Agriculture had 870 delegates. About 1,700 representatives were party committee secretaries, most of them from higher party levels. The remainder included delegates from the sciences, the arts, and the military. The stenographic report of the congress, published later in the year, broke with previous practice in failing to provide data on the occupation or party branch affiliation of individual representatives.

The new Central Committee elected by the congress was expanded to 241 members (previously 195). Candidates, however, dropped to 155 (from 165). About 80 per cent of the former Central Committee members retained their seats. Those dropped include L. N. Efremov, member since 1952, who had been transfered from his post as first secretary of Stavropol in 1970 (*YICA*, 1971, p. 86), and former Komsomol leader S. P. Pavlov (*YICA*, 1969, p. 811). Both were elected to the less important Central Audit Commission. Most of the 88 new Central Committee members had assumed important government or party posts in recent years. Observers noted also the presence of Brezhnev protegés, indicating the mounting prestige and influence of the party general secretary (*New York Times*, 11 April). Included in this group were Georgii S. Pavlov and Konstantin U. Chernenko, functionaries of the Secretariat, and Georgii E. Tsukanov, who heads Brezhnev's personal staff. Among others advanced to full membership was Anatolii F. Dobrynin, ambassador to the United States.

At the congress, a plenum of the new Central Committee elected an enlarged Politburo of 15 members which included all eleven previous members. The presence once again of Brezhnev supporters among those added drew notice in view of the widespread support expressed for the principle of "collective leadership." Unlike lists published subsequently, the order of names announced by Brezhnev at the close of the congress and given below was non-alphabetical. Members of the old Politburo were followed by three former candidates promoted to full status and a newcomer was named last. Six former candidate members were not promoted but were retained in their positions. No new candidates were added. At the November plenum of the Central Committee, Mikhail S. Solomentsev (who replaced Gennadii I. Voronov as chairman of the RSFSR Council of Ministers in July) was named a candidate Politburo member and relieved of duties as secretary for heavy industry. Voronov, moved to chairmanship of the U.S.S.R. People's Control Committee, retained Politburo rank. Membership at the end of the year is shown in the accompanying list.

POLITBURO

Members:

Brezhnev, Leonid I.	General secretary, CPSU Central Committee
Podgornyi, Nikolai V.	Chairman, Presidium of the U.S.S.R. Supreme Soviet
Kosygin, Aleksei N.	Chairman, U.S.S.R. Council of Ministers
Suslov, Mikhail A.	Secretary, CPSU Central Committee
Kirilenko, Andrei P.	Secretary, CPSU Central Committee
Pel'she, Arvids Ia.	Chairman, Party Control Committee
Mazurov, Kirill T.	First deputy chairman, U.S.S.R. Council of Ministers
Polianskii, Dmitrii S.	First deputy chairman, U.S.S.R. Council of Ministers
Shelest, Petr E.	First secretary, Ukrainian Central Committee
Voronov, Gennadii I.	Chairman, RSFSR Council of Ministers (to July); thereafter: chairman, U.S.S.R. People's Control Committee
Shelepin, Aleksandr N.	Chairman, All-Union Central Council of Trade Unions

Grishin, Viktor V.	First secretary, Moscow City Party Committee
Kunaev, Dinmukhamed A.	First secretary, Kazakh Central Committee
Shcherbitskii, Vladimir V.	Chairman, Ukrainian Council of Ministers
Kulakov, Fedor D.	Secretary, CPSU Central Committee

Candidate members:

Andropov, Iurii V.	Chairman, Committee of State Security (KGB)
Ustinov, Dmitrii F.	Secretary, CPSU Central Committee
Demichev, Petr N.	Secretary, CPSU Central Committee
Rashidov, Sharaf R.	First secretary, Uzbek Central Committee
Masherov, Petr M.	First secretary, Belorussian Central Committee
Mzhavanadze, Vasilii P.	First secretary, Georgian Central Committee
Solomentsev, Mikhail S.	Chairman, RSFSR Council of Ministers (from July)

The position of Kosygin, who had been ranked ahead of Podgornyi in the Twenty-third Congress election announcement, drew widespread comment, as did the appearance of Kulakov, Central Committee secretary for agriculture since 1965, who achieved Politburo membership without prior candidate status.

The composition of the 10-man Secretariat, reelected by the Central Committee in April, remained unchanged, Headed by the General Secretary, the members were announced in the following order at the Congress: Brezhnev, Suslov, Kirilenko, Kulakov, Ustinov, Demichev, Kapitonov (Ivan V.), Ponomarev (Boris N.) Katushev (Konstantin F.), Solomentsev. The first four are Politburo members, the next two are candidates. As a result of Solomentsev's departure in November, the Secretariat was reduced to nine at the end of the year.

During its first plenum, the Central Committee confirmed Politburo member Pel'she as chairman of the Party Control Committee. The Central Audit Commission reelected Gennadii F. Sizov chairman. All of those elected to the highest party positions were members of the U.S.S.R. Supreme Soviet or its Presidium. The 25 key leaders on the Politburo and Secretariat form an inner circle to which there have been no additions since 1968. The group includes 15 Russians and four Ukrainians. Women held no top party positions and had less than 10 per cent of the seats on the Central Committee.

Just as the Twenty-fourth Congress produced minimal changes in CPSU leadership, the republic congresses held shortly before confirmed the thrust of continuity in upper party echelons. Few changes occurred among officials of republic bureaus and secretariats, though the promotion of several local KGB chairmen to membership in republic party bureaus drew comments, along with KGB chief Andropov's appearance at the head of the list of Politburo candidates. Republic Central

Committees showed a higher rate of turnover than the CPSU Central Committee. The Azerbaidzhan party organization, which had long been under attack (see *YICA*, 1971, p. 86; 1970, p. 88), replaced half of its Central Committee, as did the Belorussian branch of the party. The Ukrainian Central Committee, with a change of a third of its full membership, was one of the most stable.

Republic first secretaries remained unchanged: Anton I. Kochinian (Armenia), Geidar A. Aliev (Azerbaidzhan), Petr M. Masherov (Belorussia), Ivan G. Kebin (Estonia), Vasilii P. Mzhavanadze (Georgia), Dinmukhamed A. Kunaev (Kazakhstan), Turdakun U. Usubaliev (Kirghizia), Augustas E. Voss (Latvia), Antanas Yu. Snechkus (Lithuania), Ivan I. Bodiul (Moldavia), Dzhabar Rasulov (Tadzhikistan), Mukhamednazar Gapurov (Turkmenistan), Petr E. Shelest (Ukraine), and Sharaf R. Rashidov (Uzbekistan). On the lower krai and oblast level, 137 of the 141 first secretaries subject to election retained their positions during 1971. Notable personnel shifts included appointment in January of V. I. Stepakov as ambassador to Yugoslavia, replacement of Georgii I. Popov as Leningrad city first secretary by Boris I. Aristov, and the move of Pskov oblast First Secretary I. S. Gustov to deputy chairmanship of the Party Control Commission in November. L. N. Efremov (see above) was appointed ambassador to the German Democratic Republic (GDR) and relieved in October of his position as vice-chairman of the U.S.S.R. Council of Ministers. V. S. Tolstikov, ambassador to China, was removed from the Presidium of the U.S.S.R. Supreme Soviet at its November meeting.

Domestic Policies. The two main internal concerns of the party in 1971 were highlighted at the Twenty-fourth Congress. Brezhnev's report raised the vexed problem of the relationship of the party to state and society, while Kosygin's speech on the five-year plan focused attention on the economy. The issues, as both the reports and subsequent events made clear, were not unrelated. "The development of the party's role," advised *Partiinaia zhizn'* (no. 21), "proceeds primarily through the strengthening of its influence on the economic life of society." Appraisal of past economic performance and formulation of new directives for the ninth five-year plan, in conjunction with the problem of dissent in various social sectors, led to reconsideration of the nature and degree of party control essential to the attainment of official socioeconomic goals. On the theoretical level, this heightened ideological activity; in practice, it intensified the growing emphasis of recent years on control and led to reinforcement of control mechanisms through such techniques as the extension of the authority of primary party organizations discussed above.

Ideology. Under the original framework of Marxism-Leninism, the state was viewed as a repressive organ; no theory of a non-repressive state was elaborated. In a 1917 analysis, Lenin merely reiterated Engels's formula that the state would "wither away" as socialism developed. The party is thus faced with the necessity of maintaining a distinction between itself and the government, while directing state development. Lack of a precise definition concerning the relationship between the two has created a long-standing ambiguity that drew closer attention in 1971. In his report to the Twenty-fourth Congress, Brezhnev criticized shortcomings in theoretical work and noted that more study should be devoted to the close link "between party and state work in resolving the concrete tasks of communist construction." Earlier suggestions that the dictatorship of the proletariat was no longer necessary for internal development in the fully socialized U.S.S.R., where the state had become "an organ for expressing the interests and the will of all the working people," were rejected in a lengthy article in *Pravda* (18 June). Philosopher G. Glezerman of the party's Academy of Social Sciences disputed the view that class distinctions could be ignored under socialism.

The class content of modern societies in general came up for discussion in an interesting defense of Marxism-Leninism against a "bourgeois ideological attack" mounted by such disparate allies as J. K. Galbraith and Herbert Marcuse (*Leningradskaia pravda*, 19 May). The view of these analysts that modern social evolution has been changing the position of the workers as they move into the middle class—"the de-proletarianization thesis"—was firmly rejected. Western social scientists distort the concept of the proletariat, claimed the article, by limiting the class to hired manual labor, by distinguishing blue-collar workers from white-collar workers, and by failing to distinguish the different social classes and strata within the latter. Most white-collar workers, it asserted, belong to "the proletariat of the non-production sphere," which forms a growing part of the working class. The party's theoretical journal, *Kommunist* (no. 9), reminded its readers that only "bourgeois ideologues—past and present" denied the necessity, made clear by Lenin, for a dictatorship of the proletariat. Broader interpretation of the character of the proletariat strengthened arguments for extension of the authority of the party as its vanguard.

At a major conference on "The 24th CPSU Congress and the Development of Marxist-Leninist Theory," Politburo and Secretariat member Suslov stressed that the modern Soviet historical stage was marked by the successful functioning of a developed socialist society, with distribution according to quantity and quality of labor (*Pravda*, 30 September). The mature social relations typical of such a society, said Suslov, are based on the establishment of social, political, and ideological unity. Petr N. Fedoseev, director of the Institute of Marxism-Leninism and vice-president of the U.S.S.R. Academy of Sciences, implied party conformity to a Marxian developmental model in an address entitled "The Growth of the Party's Role is a Law of Socialist and Communist Construction."

The need for intensification of ideological training and economic education of party members was cited throughout the year in a variety of publications. Improved work among the armed forces was called for repeatedly in party military journals. At an October conference for ideological workers among the troops, reported in The Defense Ministry newspaper *Red Star* (*Krasnaia zvezda*, 17 October), party members in the armed forces were urged to set an example through personal "ideological tempering." The problem of ideological education among the expanding young sector of the population led to inauguration of a new program of instruction by the U.S.S.R. Ministry of Higher and Specialized Secondary Education. A five-year plan was adopted for communist education of students in higher institutions of learning during 1971-1975, with specific research topics assigned to each school.

Party and Soviet history continued to be touchstones of ideological developments, insofar as appraisals of past performance and leadership reflect current views on the party's proper sphere and functions. At the congress, Brezhnev declared that the party "attached immense importance to the accurate, unbiased presentation of the history of the [Soviet] state." He condemned preoccupation with past mistakes as well as attempts to whitewash the past. A fourth edition of the textbook history of the CPSU, extending coverage to include the Twenty-fourth Congress, stressed emphasis by the latter on growth in the role and authority of the party. Official treatment of Stalin during the year followed the middle course marked out earlier, retreating from the critical reappraisal begun in 1956 at the Twentieth Congress, but stopping short of full rehabilitation. In line with the current view that polemics on Stalinism are detrimental to the communist cause (*Kommunist*, no. 10), the thirteenth volume of the Soviet historical encyclopedia presented a cautious evaluation that balanced the former leader's achievements and errors. *Pravda* (May 8) drew attention to the "convincing conclusion" in the latest book of the new six-volume party history, that a strong military-industrial base had been created by the outbreak of World War II, despite some shortcomings in preparation. The most telling indicator of the party's current attitude to its past leadership, however, was the official reaction to the death of Nikita S. Khrushchev on September 11. The former party head, deposed in 1964, had been openly lauded in Marshal I. K. Bagramian's memoirs at the end of 1970, but was clearly the target of Brezhnev's reference to past "subjectivist errors," mentioned alongside the Stalinist "cult of personality" at the Twenty-fourth Congress. The brief public announcement and small private funeral raised little prospect of immediate rehabilitation for the man who had launched de-Stalinization.

Dissension and Control. That the participation of Soviet youth in such manifestations of discontent as demonstrations, underground literature, and public protests has caused apprehension can be inferred from the introduction noted above of more systematic political indoctrination in the universities and higher schools. The government sought to reduce dissatisfaction by raising student stipends. At the same time Brezhnev, speaking to an all-Union student rally, called for greater party control over education. Komsomol first secretary, Evgenii M. Tiazhelnikov, accented his speech to students with references to the indebtedness of Soviet youth to the party. (*Komsomolskaia pravda*, 21 October). The enthusiasm of some young Soviet citizens for popular Western music and "mod" youth styles drew critical comment in the press. Teachers were advised to warn parents to shield children from distorted impressions of foreign countries and to supervise any foreign correspondence. Misleading appearances of well-being abroad were to be corrected by instruction on the social injustice prevailing in non-socialist countries (*Uchitel'skaia gazeta* [*Teacher's Newspaper*], 25 May).

Foreign and domestic pressure for the right of Soviet Jews to emigrate to Israel resulted in an unprecedented authorization of departures—largely from Georgia and the Baltic states—estimated at up to 15,000 as compared with about 1,000 for the previous year (*New York Times*, 30 December). The change in exit visa policy was related by outsiders to the unfavorable world-wide publicity attracted by the Leningrad trial of Jews late in 1970. Continuing Jewish trials prompted a letter of protest on May 20 to the U.S.S.R. Supreme Soviet from the founders of the Soviet Committee on Human Rights, affirming the right of individuals to leave any country. Though some highly-trained Jewish activists were granted visas, party spokesmen stated—and the pattern of authorizations generally confirmed—that skilled workers vital to the economy would not be permitted to emigrate. Further evidence of problems with national minorities appeared in the Baltic countries, in the Ukraine, and among Turkic ethnic groups.

Lithuanian nationalism was involved in the May trial of Simas Kudirka, a sailor sentenced to ten years in a labor camp for an attempt to obtain political asylum on a U.S. ship. The party journal in neighboring Latvia acknowledged that the nationalities problem was not only complex, but politically sensitive (*Kommunist Sovetskoi Latvii*, Riga, no. 2). Voss, head of the Latvian party organization, revealed that Latvian nationalists denied the mutual benefits of friendship with other peoples of the U.S.S.R. and "especially with the Russians" (*Pravda*, 20 March). Ukrainian national sentiment posed a special challenge due both to its long tradition and to the size of the Ukrainian minority, which follows the Russians in the population with 41 million members. According to the underground Ukrainian press, a 14-year sentence was meted out to Ukrainian historian Valentin Moroz after a trial in which both the defendant and witnesses (including journalist Viacheslav Chornovil) refused to give testimony on the grounds that the secrecy of the proceeding was unconstitutional (*Ukrainskii visnik* [*Ukrainian Herald*], no. 4). Chornovil, previously imprisoned for compiling an account of illegal treatment of Ukrainian dissidents, was reported under arrest again early in January 1972 along with a group of suspected Ukrainian nationalists arrested in Lvov and Kiev. (*New York Times*, 19 January 1972). At the Ukrainian Writers Congress, attended by top republic party leaders in May, sharp attacks were directed at nationalism (*Literaturna Ukraina* [*Literary Ukraine*, Kiev], 20 May). The prolonged frustration of attempts by the Turkic Meshkhetian people to return to their home territory, from which they had been deported to Central Asia in 1944, led to their demand in 1971 for permission to emigrate to Turkey. Details were reported in the illegal *Kronika tekhushchihk sobytii* (Chronicle of Current Events) (no. 21) and in *The Economist* (9 October). The Meshkhetian problem is similar to that of the Crimean Tatars, who continue to trouble the authorities. Leaders of both groups were reported arrested during the year.

National antagonisms pose a long-range problem as the recent census indicated; minority nationalities showed greater relative increases in growth and rising birth rates, in the face of a declining Russian birth rate. The highest rates of population increase were in Central Asia, where the imprint of a long Islamic past is said to make difficult the eradication of unwelcome social and economic attitudes. Current party discussion of nationalities policy stresses the fusion of peoples in the U.S.S.R. into a "single multinational socialist culture" (*Voprosy istorii KPSS*, no. 7, 1971). Eighteen of the nationalities listed in the 1959 census were dropped in 1970, and several (including Jews, Karelians, Mordvinians) had decreased substantially. Assimilation, it was claimed at the Twenty-fourth Congress, has produced a "new historic community—the Soviet people," melded by a single economy, political system, and ideology into "monolithic unity." An article appearing in the republic press, though, insisted that talk of assimilation was premature and that the persistence of nationalist sentiment constituted a menace (*Sovetskaia Latviia*, Riga, 2 June).

Dissidence among the intelligentsia was another source of concern in 1971. At the congress, Brezhnev voiced the party's concern with the ideological content of literature and art but declared that "negative phenomena" were not widespread. Nonetheless, changes proposed in the statutes of the U.S.S.R. Union of Writers at its congress (29 June-2 July), indicated that the problem was taken seriously. The shift of union and republic writers' congresses to five-year intervals corresponded to the rescheduling of party congresses, and would provide for closer linkage between the party and the writers. Voting on admissions to the Writers' Union was no longer to be kept secret on all levels, and the directorship of the union was narrowed by establishment of a new Bureau to be elected from its Secretariat (*Literaturnaia gazeta*, June 30). Literature without, or in contravention of, official approval continued to appear in private circulation and was published abroad. Western journalists reported the existence of a monthly "Political Diary" (*Politicheskii dnevnik*), issued from the mid-sixties to 1970 or 1971 (*New York Times* and *Washington Post*, 21 August). Produced by and for a limited group of Soviet intellectuals describing themselves as "liberal socialists," it included material taken from the official press, from *samizdat* sources, and from foreign publications.

One issue of the journal discussed an unpublished poll of *Literaturnaia gazeta* readers which revealed that Aleksandr Solzhenitsyn, despite the suppression of his works, was one of the most popular writers among the literary community. The publication in the West of his latest novel, *August 1914*, was followed by a veiled defense of the author in the October·issue of *Novy mir*, the journal where his first work had appeared. The award of a State Prize in November to its former editor Aleksandr Tvardovskii, recently out of favor, was taken as a gesture of conciliation toward restless literary elements, but the first official comment on Solzhenitsyn's new work (*Literaturnaia gazeta*, 12 January 1972), describing it as most useful "for anti-Soviet elements," defined the limits of the gesture. Any writer who "helps our ideological adversaries to fight against socialism," declared Brezhnev at the congress, "deserves only public contempt." Tvardovskii's funeral in December occasioned the first public appearance since 1964 of Solzhenitsyn, who was still negotiating at the end of the year for the Moscow presentation of his 1970 Nobel award.

Another Soviet work published outside the country during the year, *A Question of Madness* by biologist Zhores Medvedev and his historian brother, described the 1970 attempt to put the outspoken scientist in a mental hospital (see *YICA*, 1971, p. 89) and its aftermath. An appeal sent by youthful dissident Vladimir Bukovskii to Western psychiatrists, requesting them to investigate the continuing Soviet practice of consigning civil rights advocates to psychiatric hospitalization

(*The Times*, London, 12 March), resulted in the arrest of Bukovskii at the end of March and his confinement in a mental institution. International attention and numerous protests at home concerning the political exploitation of psychiatric treatment prompted an *Izvestiia* denial of alleged abuses (24 October). Brought to trial later, Bukovskii was declared sane but sentenced to twelve years of imprisonment and inland exile.

A growing interest in religion among young people, often in connection with nationalist or neo-Slavophile sympathies, led to some increased activity in the campaign against religion (*Zaria vostoka*, Tbilisi, 31 August). Though the official policy of contained coexistence with the Russian Orthodox Church was generally maintained, such groups as Lithuanian Catholics and the widely dispersed Baptists were frequent targets. Noting the increased attention devoted in the press to atheist propaganda, *Sovetskaia Belorussiia* on 26 June sounded a common theme with a statement that religion remained the "major ideological enemy."

The need for supervision over various dissident sectors was clearly related to the authorization given primary party organizations to check on activities of scientific, academic, cultural, and medical institutions where members of the intelligentsia are employed. However, the recent appointment to the highest control agencies of both Voronov (head of the People's Control Committee) and Gustov (deputy chairman, under the aging Pel'she, of the Party Control Committee), who have backgrounds as agricultural experts, suggests that implementation of economic programs is another major function of current control policy.

The Economy. Draft directives for the ninth five-year economic plan were published on 14 February 1971 after considerable delay and after the opening of the first year of the plan. Central Committee endorsement was published in a decree over Brezhnev's signature, marking the first occasion since Stalin's death when the party head alone issued a Central Committee decree. The main objective of the plan was said to be "a substantial improvement in the material and cultural standard of living." The new orientation was related by some diplomats to the recent Polish disturbances, but state planning official Aleksei Goregliad stated in an interview in the Moscow party journal that increased material benefits for the population had been called for by the party leadership in early 1969 when a plan draft was rejected (*Moskovskaia pravda*, 21 February). The political implications of domestic complaints about recurrent shortages of food and consumers' goods, and about inadequate housing and services, were spelled out by Brezhnev at the congress. Asserting that past conditions had led millions to accept deprivation and poor quality, he stated that times had changed: "What was explainable and natural in the past [is] not acceptable under present conditions." His comment that some might "fail to understand this," suggested the possibility of disagreement between the "metal-eaters" (concerned primarily with heavy industry and defense) and the "consumerists" (backing increased investment in agriculture and light industry). In the discussion of the economy, which occupied a large part of Brezhnev's report to the congress and anticipated Kosygin's later report on the plan directives, the general secretary cited Lenin's observation that the ultimate funcion of "the production of means of production" was the supply of the consumer industry. The share of producers' goods in 1970 industrial output was said to be 74 per cent, while that of consumers' goods amounted to only 26 per cent.

Charges that the socialist system is incompatible with an efficient organization of labor and with worker incentives are disproved by the rapid advance of the Soviet economy, Kosygin told the congress. Socialism, he added, ensures an improvement in the standard of living. For the first time in the history of multi-year planning, but in line with the last few annual plans, the consumer sector was assigned slightly higher growth rates than was the heavy industrial sector, though the latter retained its primary role. In the final version of the plan, accepted by the Supreme Soviet after approval by the Politburo and by a November plenum of the Central Committee (which also endorsed foreign policy—see below), output of means of production was scheduled to grow by 46.3 per cent and consumers' goods by 48.6 per cent. The new plan placed greater emphasis on agriculture, a chronic problem despite the record 186-million-ton grain harvest in 1970; agricultural investment was raised in comparison with the previous plan by almost 70 per cent, to 129 billion rubles (out of a total capital investment raised 42 per cent to 501 billion), while an increase in agricultural output of 20 to 22 per cent was projected over the five-year period. The fact that previous investment in agriculture had produced unsatisfactory rates of return may be connected with the recent staffing of the supervisory control agencies with specialists in agriculture, just as Kulakov's appointment to the Politburo would appear linked to the increased attention given to agrarian problems.

Targets set by the plan were modest in comparison with previous plans and often close to actual earlier attainments. National income was expected to rise by 37 to 40 per cent during 1971-75, and real per capita income by 31 per cent. Almost all of the increase is to be derived from increased labor productivity. Since labor reserves in the country have been virtually exhausted, and demographic patterns indicate that the growth of the population in the age groups capable of work will be only about one per cent a year (*Voprosy ekonomiki*, no. 4), heavy emphasis has been placed on the necessity for increasing labor productivity through automation and mechanization. A discussion of productivity incentives (*ibid.*, no. 2) revealed that wages had dropped 21 per cent as a component of industrial production costs between 1958 and 1968, while industrial profits almost quadrupled. From Brezhnev's congress report to a "Political Diary" (no. 67, 1970) excerpt of *Fortune* magazine data on Western computers, Soviet sources showed a widespread interest in the updating of economic management. One proposal (*Pravda*, 28 October) envisaged a special government agency to run an automated computer control system for the entire country.

Though the Twenty-fourth Congress called for more efficient central coordination, the economic reform which introduced a degree of autonomy for enterprises in 1965 is to be extended throughout the economy. The need for improvement in the application of the reform, however, overshadowed references to achievement; the extension of party control over industry has been prescribed as a concomitant to extension of the new system (*ibid.*, 20 August). Despite talk of managerial flexibility and attention to cost accounting criteria, sustained public emphasis on consumer satisfaction (particularly evident during the late spring electoral campaign speeches) led to a joint party-government decree stipulating that the flow of a wide range of production goods in popular demand could not be reduced or halted by industry (*ibid.*, 29 October). Shortly after the end of the year, it was announced that the basic tasks of the 1971 annual plan had been fulfilled (*ibid.*, 23 January 1972). The grain harvest for the year was placed at 181 million tons, and agricultural performance in general was said to be satisfactory. Livestock reports were less encouraging, and severe winter weather raised prospects of continuing crop difficulties. Labor productivity was reported up by 6.3 per cent in industry and by 2.0 per cent in agriculture; average annual increases of 6.9 and 6.7 per cent respectively had been called for by the plan. Emphasis on iron and steel development within the heavy industrial sector, a development allotted an investment increase of close to 70 per cent, resulted in notable achievement. Due in part to a decline in U.S. output, the Soviet Union became the world's leading producer of steel in 1971 (*ibid.*, 29 January 1972). Defense expenditure for the year remained unchanged at 17.9 billion rubles, or 11.4 per cent of the annual budget.

In line with the announced aim of the plan to further develop foreign economic relations, Soviet ties with the other socialist-state economies were strengthened through an agreement on economic integration adopted in July by the eight members of the Council for Mutual Economic Assistance. Yugoslavia, an associate, agreed to some participation in the new plan for closer economic cooperation (*ibid.*, 7 August). Kosygin's report to the Supreme Soviet on the approved five-year plan in November expressed interest in more trade with other foreign countries and referred to welcome initial contacts exploring increased trade possibilities with the United States. Just as domestic economic policy reflected the internal political situation, the expansion of foreign trade was likely to depend on political relations with other countries.

Of special significance in the year of the Twenty-fourth Congress was an article in *Voprosy istorii* (no. 7), analyzing the Tenth Party Congress held fifty years earlier. Party historian and ideologist E. I. Bugaev noted that the 1921 congress had adopted a new economic policy (despite opposition of some party members) because of the political danger in popular discontent and the economic necessity of improving agricultural output. Other issues under consideration at the time included a party purge, the nationalities problem, resumption of trade with foreign countries, and Lenin's call for the "iron discipline of the party of the proletariat." For the CPSU, history was more than "past politics" in 1971.

International Views and Policies.[1] In evaluating Soviet foreign policy since the Twenty-fourth Congress, a plenum of the Central Committee on 23 November 1971 described it as one that "invariably combined a firm rebuff to imperialism and support for the revolutionary, liberation movement with consistent effort towards the peaceful coexistence of states with differing social systems" (*New Times*, Moscow, no. 49, December). This dual Soviet approach had been repeatedly challenged in the past by revolutionary groups critical of the second aspect, which in their view denoted an acceptance of the status quo. One of the Soviet Union's major critics, the Maoist leadership in China, appeared to be extending its diplomatic relations. Within a context of unabated Sino-Soviet polemics, the need for a dual U.S.S.R. approach to face this new development appeared more urgent. Not only was the Soviet Union faced with competition at the diplomatic level, but the new Chinese overtures (e.g., the invitation to U.S. President Nixon to visit China) offered the CPSU an opportunity to challenge Maoist "revolutionary purity" and, in the process, attract to its own side left-wing critics.

On the diplomatic level, 1971 was notable for the number of high-level foreign visits undertaken by top Soviet government and party leaders (see below) and an apparent attenuation in the U.S.S.R. stand on such issues as the status of West Berlin. On the ideological front, however, the year witnessed repeated criticism by CPSU spokesmen of all forms of Marxist-Leninist "deviation." It covered the spectrum from Marxist humanists—like Roger Garaudy and Ernst Fischer, of France and Austria respectively—to Trotskyists.[2] In his speech to the CPSU congress, Brezhnev noted that while the Soviet party had "done much to strengthen the cohesion and unity" of the world communist movement, the years since the 1966 congress had seen the most acute "attempts on various sides to attack Marxism-Leninism as the ideological-theoretical basis for the activity of the communist movement." He went on to add:

> The Chinese leadership went over to the establishment in a number of countries of splinter groupings under the signboard of the so-called "Marxist-Leninist" parties," and has clearly tried to unite them in some way as a counterweight to the international communist movement. The Trotskyites have now and again formed blocs with these groupings. Here and there tendencies towards nationalistic self-isolation have been stepped up, and both "Left" and Right-wing opportunism have been revived. (*IB*, no. 7-8, 1971).

While claiming that there was "ground to say that cohesion in the international communist movement" was being increasingly strengthened, Brezhnev warned that "negative phenomena [had] not yet been overcome everywhere." Claiming that the "fight against Right and 'Left'-wing revisionism,

---

[1]For details of CPSU relations with other communist parties see respective country surveys.

[2]See, e.g., *Agitator*, June; *Pravda*, 31 July; and *Literaturnaia gazeta*, 3 November.

against nationalism," continued to be urgent, he stressed: "It is precisely the nationalistic tendencies, especially those which assume the form of anti-Sovietism, that bourgeois ideologists and bourgeois propaganda have placed most reliance on in their fight against socialism and the communist movement." (*Ibid*.)

Criticism of nationalist phenomena found expression on a number of occasions by leading CPSU spokesmen. The subject was analyzed extensively in a lengthy report to an ideological conference in Moscow by Boris Ponomarev, who stated:

> In present conditions, special importance attaches to combating nationalism. Practice has shown the close interconnection between revisionist distortion and nationalist vacillation. Wherever revisionist departures from Marxist-Leninist theory are tolerated, the doors are opened, for the infiltration of petty-bourgeois nationalist ideology into the revolutionary movement. Conversely, every departure from proletarian internationalism to nationalist stances offers room for Right and "Left" revisionist activity. (*Kommunist*, no. 15, December; *IB*, no. 23-24, 30 December.)

Ponomarev noted that communists, "while supporting the general democratic and anti-imperialist content of the nationalism of oppressed nations and developing countries," were "aware of the fact that it may also be a vehicle for the ideology of the reactionary exploiting element endeavoring to hitch the young states to the imperialist chariot." He warned that "the line between the progressive anti-imperialist side of nationalism and its reactionary side [was] historically mobile," and added:

> Nationalist slogans can often change their sociopolitical orientation and turn from a weapon for national liberation into a weapon against the unity of the anti-imperialist forces, or even—as Maoism has shown—into a vehicle of hegemonic chauvinist policy against the main forces of the world revolutionary movement. (*Ibid*.)

Finally, Ponomarev emphasized that nationalism was "doubly dangerous" when it was of "an anti-Soviet complexion." He claimed that following the Twenty-fourth Congress "fraternal parties" had "stepped up the struggle against all types of anti-Sovietism," and added: "Subversion of the prestige of the CPSU and the Soviet Union—the main revolutionary force, the pioneer and standard-bearer of the new socialist era—injures the entire world revolutionary process." (*Ibid*.)

The Twenty-fourth Congress offered the CPSU an occasion to develop its dual foreign policy approach. In this connection, it is noteworthy that the number of non-communist foreign delegations attending was larger than at any previous CPSU congress. Out of a total of 101 delegations from 90 countries, there were 22 "national-democratic and left-wing socialist parties" represented, as compared with 12 at the Twenty-third Congress (1966) and only three at the Twenty-second Congress (1961). Foreign communist representation, in contrast, did not increase significantly—a total of 73 named delegations,[3] compared to 72 (in 1966) and 77 (in 1961). Aside from China and Albania, the other eleven ruling foreign communist parties sent delegations. Western Europe was represented by 21 communist parties, from Austria, Belgium, Cyprus, Denmark, Finland, France, Germany (three parties, two from West Germany and one from West Berlin), Great Britain, Greece, Ireland, Italy, Luxembourg, Norway, Portugal, San Marino, Spain, Sweden, Switzerland, and Turkey. The Middle East and Africa were represented by 10 communist parties—from Iran, Iraq, Israel, Jordan, Lebanon, Réunion, South Africa, Sudan, Syria, and Tunisia. The Western Hemisphere sent the greatest number of communist delegations (25), from Argentina, Bolivia, Brazil, Canada,

---

[3]Delegation attendance totals are complicated by the presence of unidentified parties—six (in 1971), four (in 1966), and six (in 1961). At the Twenty-fourth Congress one of the unidentified groups reported as having attended was a delegation from the monthly Prague-based publication, *World Marxist Review*; other delegations that are believed to have been included in the total were representatives of communist parties from Algeria and Nepal and a delegation from the World Federation of Trade Unions.

Chile, Colombia, Costa Rica, Dominican Republic, Ecuador, El Salvador, Guadeloupe, Guatemala, Guyana, Haiti, Honduras, Martinique, Mexico, Nicaragua, Panama, Paraguay, Peru, Puerto Rico, the United States, Uruguay, and Venezuela. Asia and the Pacific were represented by only 6 communist parties, from Australia, Ceylon, India, Japan, New Zealand, and East Pakistan.

Most of the delegations from "national-democratic and left-wing socialist parties" were African, including: the People's Movement for the Liberation of Angola, the Congolese Party of Labor (Democratic Republic of the Congo), the Democratic Party of Guinea, the African Independence Party of Guinea and the Cape Verde Islands (Portuguese Guinea), the Mauritanian People's Party, the Mozambique Liberation Front, the Supreme Revolutionary Council of Somalia, the African National Congress (South Africa), the Revolutionary Command Council of the Democratic Republic of the Sudan, the Tanganyika African National Union, the Arab Socialist Union (U.A.R.), and the Afro-Shirazi Party (Zanzibar). The Middle East sent representatives from four parties: the Ba'th parties of Iraq and Syria, the Kurdish Democratic Party (Iraq), and the National Front Party of the People's Democratic Republic of Yemen. There were three delegations from Asia: the Japan Socialist Party, the Laotian Patriotic Front, and the National Liberation Front of South Vietnam. European representation was limited to the Workers' and Small Farmers' Social Democratic League (Finland) and the Italian Socialist Party of Proletarian Unity. Only one such movement—the Socialist Party of Chile—came from the Western Hemisphere.

On the level of foreign communist party attendance, there were several noteworthy changes, as compared with the 1966 congress. The communist parties of Algeria, Iceland, Lesotho, the Netherlands, Morocco, and Nepal, which attended the 1966 congress, were not—officially, at least—listed as having participated in 1971. The Irish communists, who had been represented in 1966 by two delegations, this time sent a joint delegation as a result of the merger in March 1970 of the parties from the Republic of Ireland and Northern Ireland. The most significant addition was attendance by the Japan Communist Party (see below). Another "gain" was more formal than real—the legal German Communist Party, founded in 1968—was invited along with the illegal Communist Party of Germany. New Zealand, which was unrepresented in 1966, in view of the pro-Chinese alignment of its principal communist party, was represented in 1971, for the first time, by the pro-Soviet Socialist Unity Party founded in October 1966. Other new participants included communist parties from the Dominican Republic, East Pakistan, and Puerto Rico. The People's Progressive Party of Guyana, which attended the 1966 congress as a "national democratic party," was listed in 1971 as a regular communist party.

CPSU pursuit of a dual foreign policy, which extended to inviting to its congress both government parties and rival communist delegations, resulted in no serious incident such as took place in 1966 with the walk-out of the Algerian National Liberation Front (see *YICA*, 1966, p. 265). Considerable tension, however, appears to have been engendered by the presence of both communist and government delegations from Iraq and the Sudan—countries where relations between the government and local communists were strained (see below, and *Iraq* and *Sudan*).

Although an apparent attempt to cover up differences of opinion was made, several controversial issues continued to plague the communist delegations. Opposition to the 1968 Soviet-led invasion of Czechoslovakia was rekindled as a result of Gustáv Husák's defense of the action. While only one other delegate—Rodolfo Ghioldi (Argentina)—expressly referred to the invasion (see *Pravda*, 5 April), Husák's speech gave rise to repeated opposition in several parties' respective national organs, with one of the strongest reactions coming from the Italians (see *L'Unità*, Rome, 3 April). Several communist leaders, moreover, condemned the invasion indirectly by stressing the principles of "sovereignty, independence, and noninterference and self-determination" in the relations between socialist countries and communist parties. These principles were more or less strongly emphasized by leaders of delegations from Belgium, France, Great Britain, Italy, Japan, Mexico, Romania, San Marino, Spain, Sweden, Réunion, and Yugoslavia.

An issue closely related to that of communist party independence is the question of the Soviet Union's role as "leading center" of the socialist countries and of the world communist movement. This concept, explicitly renounced by Khrushchev in 1960, was revived by three Latin American delegations (Argentina, Paraguay, and Peru—see *Pravda*, 5, 9 and 8 April, respectively), and rejected by the chairman of the Communist Party of Belgium, Marc Drumaux. In his speech, Drumaux stated: "In the world communist movement, there is no leading center" (*ibid.*, 9 April). Another controversial issue, the question of different national "roads to socialism," elicited rival responses. On 31 March, CPSU Politburo member Masherov equated "any revision of Marxism-Leninism" and "any opportunism" with "direct apostasy and desertion to the camp of counterrevolution" (*ibid.*, 1 April); the next day, however, the Italian Communist Party's deputy secretary-general, Enrico Berlinguer, described his party's "endeavors, on the basis of its own experience and ideas, to make an original contribution to the elaboration of the common problems of socialism and socialist theory" (*ibid.*, 2 April). Berlinguer was followed by Yugoslav delegate Mijalko Todorović, who said:

> The variety of roads and the richness of forms of development of socialism are an expression of the breadth and intensity of the contemporary socialist transformation of the world. The differences which derive from this reality are an expression of the creative force and the consolidation of socialism in the conditions of a democratic exchange of opinions and of cooperation between equal and sovereign movements and countries. (*Ibid.*, 4 April.)

Criticism of the Chinese leadership was expressed by 19 foreign delegations—those of the ruling parties of Bulgaria, Czechoslovakia, Hungary, Mongolia, and Poland and those of communist parties in Argentina, Bolivia, Brazil, Denmark, El Salvador, the Federal Republic of Germany (the German Communist Party), India, Israel, Lebanon, Paraguay, Peru, Portugal, the United States, and Venezuela. No representative of national-democratic or left-wing socialist parties participated in the anti-Chinese polemics. While no other communist delegation spokesmen attempted to defend the Chinese leadership, several appeared to have expressed reservations about the Sino-Soviet conflict owing to their repeated emphasis on the need for unity among *all* socialist countries.

Eastern Europe. The two aforementioned elements—Chinese diplomatic overtures and the issue of national sovereignty—were reflected in Eastern Europe. Their interconnection made it all the more urgent for the Soviet Union to consolidate its advocacy of "limited sovereignty" for the area. In this endeavor, the Soviets attained mixed results and temporarily exacerbated their differences with the principal exponents of national independence—Romania and Yugoslavia.

Soviet-Romanian relations at the beginning of the year appeared to be improving. Although the essential features of Romanian foreign policy remained unchanged, there appeared to be a greater willingness to accept certain aspects of the Soviet line, especially on CMEA integration. This amity, however, was shortlived. The first reassertion of Romanian autonomy came in the speech to the Twenty-fourth Congress by Romanian president and party leader Nicolae Ceauşescu. While denying the right of any party to interfere in the internal affairs of another party, Ceauşescu stated that Romania would continue its policy of developing good relations with all communist states and parties and of strengthening economic and diplomatic ties with all countries, including those with different social systems (*Pravda*, 3 April). A month later, in a speech commemorating the fiftieth anniversary of the Romanian Communist Party, Ceauşescu stated: "I have been asked in interviews whether Romania is considering renouncing its support of [its foreign policy] principles. These principles are as necessary for contemporary human society, for cooperation in the world, as are water and air for the existence of mankind. How could we give up water and air?'' (*Scînteia*, 8 May.) In June he left for a twenty-five-day trip to Asia, including a nine-day visit to China—the first by a Warsaw Pact leader since Chinese-Soviet differences became public. Ceauşescu's warm reception in China initially evoked only a guardedly critical response from the Soviet Union, whose broadcasts to Romania stressed that country's obligation to consult with its allies on questions of foreign policy. Soviet disapproval was also shown during the Romanian president's brief stop in Moscow on 24 June, following his Asian tour. He was greeted by Kosygin and Suslov, although in terms of protocol he should have been welcomed by Brezhnev and Podgornyi. It had been reported that he would remain in Moscow for two days, but his visit lasted only three hours. Later in the summer, the Soviet Union increased its pressure on Romania in a campaign which ranged from real and rumored Warsaw Pact maneuvers in allied countries bordering Romania to criticism in the East European media.

On 2 August a conference of Warsaw Pact member states, without participation of Romania, took place in the Crimea. The discussion of ''unity of the socialist camp'' occurred amid rumors that Chinese Premier Chou En-lai would visit both Romania and Yugoslavia in the fall. This, coupled with Ceauşescu's conspicuous absence, made it seem likely that Romania had been a major topic of the meeting. Shortly thereafter, the campaign against Romania was stepped up. The Czechoslovak newspaper *Smena* (Bratislava, 11 August) warned that ''the policy of walking the tightrope would be paid for sooner or later,'' and the Hungarian *Magyar Hirlap* (Budapest, 13 August) refered to the emergence of an ''anti-Soviet axis'' stretching from Peking to the Balkans. On 14 August the East German *Neues Deutschland* warned that ''tolerance of Mao'' was in fact ''encouragement of his policies and a violation of principles of proletarian internationalism.''

During this time the Soviet Union did not engage in direct polemics against Romania, but it increased its criticism of the Chinese leadership and, in a number of theoretical articles, reinterpreted the principles of ''socialist, proletarian internationalism'' so as to proscribe the independent exercise of foreign policy. In the process, it extended the justification for intervention in the affairs of ''fraternal socialist states'' to apply even when such states followed an orthodox domestic policy.

Shalva P. Sanakoev, deputy editor in chief of the monthly *International Affairs*, in the June issue, wrote:

> Coordination of the fraternal countries' foreign policy efforts is dictated by the nature of socialist international relations and their underlying principles. The relations of friendship and fraternal mutual assistance in all spheres of social life, based on Marxism-Leninism and socialist internationalism, have made this close cooperation in foreign policy both possible and vitally necessary. Foreign policy coordination is one of the organic requirements of socialist internationalism and one of the main trends of its practical implementation.

In an *Izvestiia* (3 July) article, Sanakoev cited ''specific steps'' the Soviet Union and its allies had taken ''in defense of socialism in Czechoslovakia'' and emphasized:

> The following should be particularly stressed—that cooperation of the countries of socialism, including coordination of their foreign policy activities, has decisive significance in the struggle for construction of socialism and communism, for preservation of the proletarian gains of the peoples against all ideological and political diversion by international imperialism.

The next month Sanakoev, in an apparent attempt to dispel the Romanians' illusions that they were safe from intervention as long as they retained orthodox domestic policies, claimed that nonconformance in foreign affairs was a reliable warning sign of pending ''deformation of the internal system'':

> Is it, after all, possible to imagine a state having a socialist domestic policy but no socialist foreign policy, or vice versa? Experience shows that the degeneration of the political line followed by

state and party leaders, deformation of the internal system as a rule, starts with a departure from the fundamental Marxist-Leninist principles of foreign policy, the principles of internationalism. (*International Affairs*, no. 8, August.)

Soviet and East European pressure did not, however, modify significantly Romania's independent foreign policy line. The apparent effect was to bring about a close rapprochement with Yugoslavia. Polemics began to abate after celebration of Romania's National Day (23 August), and tension decreased further following the announcement on 10 September of Brezhnev's pending visit to Yugoslavia later in the month.

Soviet-Yugoslav relations tended during the year to parallel those between the U.S.S.R. and Romania, and were linked to Yugoslavia's growing rapprochement with China. At the beginning of the year there appeared to be a mutual desire to avoid polemical confrontations, and Soviet criticism of the "Yugoslav road to socialism" notably decreased. The period was marked by an official visit to Moscow (23-27 February) by the Yugoslav state secretary for foreign affairs, Mirko Tepavac. However, while the final communiqué noted that there had been "a useful exchange of views on Yugoslav-Soviet relations as well as on current international problems," there was no reaffirmation of the principles expressed in the Belgrade and Moscow declarations of 1955 and 1956 respectively.

Relations between the two countries started deteriorating again at the CPSU congress, attended by Mijalko Todorović, known as one of the most outspoken critics of the Czechoslovak invasion. Although his speech was relatively moderate, Yugoslav press reports on the congress were highly critical. They attacked what they saw as acceptance by the Soviet Union of the so-called limited sovereignty theory, which had justified the intervention in Czechoslovakia.

On 14 April the Swedish daily *Dagens Nyheter* published a report that the Soviet Union was giving support to the Ustashi, a Croatian extremist nationalist organization. Although the U.S.S.R. Embassy in Stockholm denied the allegations, there was no doubt that the Ustashi-oriented Croatian National Committee (under Branko Jelić) had reversed an erstwhile anti-communist line. Its organ *Hrvatska Država* began advocating strongly pro-Soviet views. The question of whether the U.S.S.R. was encouraging Croatian separatism in an effort to dismember the Yugoslav federation was a source of considerable tension in Soviet-Yugoslav relations throughout the year (see *Yugoslavia*).

Polemics between the two countries continued on other levels. On 24 March the Zagreb weekly *Vjesnik u srijedu* accused *Pravda* of misrepresenting the situation in Yugoslavia, especially when quoting Tito's speeches. In June, at the time of the Tepavac visit to China, the Yugoslav daily *Politika* (Belgrade, 9 June) accused Soviet authorities of encouraging the activities of Cominformist emigrés in Moscow. This, in turn, provoked a strong attack in *Izvestiia* (17 June). At the same time there were rumors of Soviet military maneuvers in Hungary, near the Yugoslav border, creating further tension (see, e.g., commentaries in *Večernje novosti*, Belgrade, 17 June, and *Vjesnik*, Zagreb, 19 June).

Brezhnev's decision to pay an unofficial visit to Yugoslavia coincided with a decline in polemics. Talks with the Yugoslav leadership (22-25 September) produced a joint statement, reaffirming the Belgrade and Moscow declarations: "The methods of constructing socialism, which reflect the experience of and specific aspects in the development of individual countries, are a matter for the peoples of the working classes in individual countries and need not contradict each other" (*Borba*, Belgrade, 26 September). Moreover, in a speech on 22 September, Brezhnev had claimed that "the so-called new doctrine of limited sovereignty" represented "an invention" (*ibid.*, 23 September). The extent to which the visit resulted in a genuine amelioration in relations was unclear. In the following months there continued to be evidence of strain in relations between Yugoslavia and Bulgaria, whose party first secretary, Todor Zhivkov, had declared at the CPSU congress: "The position of the Bulgarian Communist Party is identical with the position of the CPSU" (*Pravda*, 2 April).

Soviet relations with the other East European governments did not change noticeably. Support was offered for Czechoslovak policies of eradicating all remaining vestiges of the 1968 reform. Likewise, the new Polish leadership under Edward Gierek received Soviet encouragement, including considerable economic aid. Replacement of Walter Ulbricht by Erich Honecker in the East German party did not affect close ties with the CPSU. Brezhnev himself attended the Czechoslovak, East German, and Polish party congresses (May, June, and December respectively) and throughout the year there were numerous high-level contacts. Despite continuation of relatively unorthodox economic reforms in Hungary, the CPSU continued to retain cordial relations with the Hungarian Socialist Workers' Party. As noted above, Bulgarian views mirrored those of the Soviet Union. With regard to Albania, Soviet pronouncements during the year were characterized by repeated attempts to attain rapprochement at the expense of China. Soviet overtures, however, were rejected by the Albanian leadership.

Western Europe. During 1971, in its relations with West European states, the U.S.S.R. appeared to be concerned chiefly with developing its government interests. Continued opposition by West European communist parties to aspects of Soviet foreign policy, the foremost of which continued to be the 1968 invasion of Czechoslovakia, were largely ignored. The invasion, however, and Soviet-supported "normalization" in Czechoslovakia affected the parties' own national positions. The concept of "socialist internationalism" and its corollary, the doctrine of "limited sovereignty," harmed communist attempts to portray themselves as legitimate national spokesmen and forced them to disassociate themselves publicly from developments unacceptable to potential political allies or supporters.

The Czechoslovak issue was rekindled in mid-January with the publication in Prague of a party resolution on "lessons" from events surrounding the invasion. There was an immediate and strong reaction from the Italian Communist Party (PCI), whose newspaper *L'Unità* (15 January) commented that Italian communists could not remain silent, because sovereignty was "an inalienable right" which even in a communist state had nothing to do with its class and international character. Returning to the theme at a mass rally in Rome on 24 January to mark the PCI's fiftieth anniversary, Politburo member Gian Carlo Pajetta declared that national independence and sovereignty had to be defended "in all circumstances" and that internationalism did not exist unless "founded on the full rights of the nation." The PCI, he pledged, would continue to follow an independent Italian road to socialism. (*Ibid.*, 25 January.) Similarly the French Communist Party (PCF) newspaper *L'Humanité* (18 January), reiterating its original condemnation of the invasion, attacked the new document for redefining national sovereignty in a way incompatible with principles proclaimed by the world communist movement. Controversy over Czechoslovakia flared up again at the CPSU congress in April (see above) and the Czechoslovak party's congress in May. On both occasions the Italians were in the forefront among critics of development in that country. At the Czechoslovak congress, PCI delegate Sergio Segre refused to amend his speech containing criticism of the invasion and was barred from the rostrum; *L'Unità* (29 May) promptly published his message in full. The preceding day, PCI Secretary-General Luigi Longo confirmed in an interview with the party's weekly *Rinascita* that Segre had been instructed to convey publicly the Italian party's continuing disagreement with the Czechoslovak (and by implication Soviet) version of 1968 events. Two other European communist parties, the British and Spanish, refused to attend the congress when speeches they had submitted in advance were declared unacceptable by Czechoslovak party officials. The French party (*L'Humanité*, 29 May) labeled as "falsification" any interpretation of the Prague speech of PCF delegate and Politburo member Raymond Guyot as showing a weakening of the party's unequivocal disagreement with the invasion.

U.S.S.R. reaction to the above developments tended to be subdued, with the CPSU allowing the Czechoslovak party to carry the burden of defending the Soviet-led intervention. Differences between the CPSU and its West European communist critics were acknowledged only indirectly in the communiqués following high-level meetings. Thus, talks between PCF deputy secretary-general Georges Marchais and Soviet leaders in Moscow on 1-3 July were marked by "mutual understanding" but no agreement (*L'Humanité*, 6 July); the general secretary of the Communist Party of Great Britain, John Gollan, was reported only as having "exchanged views on certain problems of mutual interest for both parties" during his conversations on 23 July with Politburo member Arvids Pel'she (TASS, 23 July).

Conversely, U.S.S.R. attempts at furthering a policy of inter-state détente in Europe often was undertaken with little concern for positions of respective national communist parties. Thus, in conformity with a growing Spanish-Soviet rapprochement, an article on Spain in *Izvestiia* (8 February) was only moderately critical of the Franco government, showed little concern for opposition activity, and made only passing reference to Spanish communists. Brezhnev's visit to France on 25-30 October also was marked by numerous articles in the Soviet press stressing ties between the U.S.S.R. and France, indicative of the Soviet Union's readiness to do business with a bourgeois government at the expense of local communists in opposition. This was particularly striking in view of Brezhnev's position as CPSU general secretary, but a similar comment could be made on Kosygin's visits to Denmark (2-5 December) and Norway (5-7 December).

Middle East and Africa. The conflict between often irreconcilable communist international solidarity and Soviet foreign policy was seen most clearly in the CPSU response to developments in the Arab countries. Throughout 1971, Soviet relations with the Arab governments—which included such notable diplomatic achievements as the treaty of friendship and cooperation with the U.A.R. on 27 May—were clouded by suppression of local communists by their respective governments. In general the interests of Soviet foreign policy prevailed at the expense of ideological affinity, a choice partly motivated by increased Chinese diplomatic and economic activity in the area. As noted earlier, courting of the non-communist Arab political parties extended even to the CPSU congress. Whereas at the 1961 congress Arab participation was exclusively communist, and the 1966 congress had representation from only one non-communist party (the Algerian National Liberation Front), the 1971 congress included an equal number of communist and non-communist delegations (see above).

In pursuance of what the Twenty-fourth congress termed "inviolable Soviet-Arab friendship" (*IB*, no. 7-8, 1971), the Soviet Union was involved in a number of high-level contacts with Arab governments. On 13-19 January, Podgornyi visited the U.A.R.; a Syrian delegation, headed by Premier Hafiz al-Asad, conferred in Moscow with top government and party leaders on 1-3 February; at the end of May, and following the purge of pro-Soviet elements from the U.A.R. government and the Arab Socialist Union (ASU), Podgornyi returned to Cairo (25-28 May) accompanied by CPSU Secretary Boris Ponomarev. The visit was highlighted by the aforementioned treaty of friendship and cooperation, which *Pradva* (2 June) hailed as evidence that relations between the two countries were "rising to a new a higher level and moving into a qualitatively new stage." In June a Soviet delegation led by Vladimir Novikov, deputy chairman of the U.S.S.R. Council of Ministers and member of the CPSU Central Committee, visited Iraq. According to the communiqué, discussions were held on cooperation, international relations, and problems of "development of relations between the CPSU and the Iraqi Arab Socialist Ba'th Party" (*Pravda*, 26 June). Despite the Iraqi Communist Party's concurrent accusations against its government of "despotic policies of repressions and torture" (*L'Humanité*, 16 June), the Soviet delegation "assessed in a positive manner the anti-imperialist policy conducted by the Iraqi Republic and the Ba'th Party as well as the progressive socioeconomic transformations carried out in the country'' (*Pravda*, 26 June). In the second half of July, a CPSU delegation headed by Ponomarev attended the Egyptian ASU's general national congress which ratified the May expulsions of its pro-Soviet members. With virtual disappearance of the Algerian and Moroccan communist parties—neither of which was reported as having attended the CPSU congress—Soviet policy toward Algeria and Morocco became less vulnerable to the challenge of duality. Kosygin paid an official visit to both states between 4 and 11 October. Soviet affirmation of friendship toward these countries on this occasion was particularly opportune in view of growing Chinese activities in the Maghreb area, especially in Algeria.

The communist-backed coup d'état in Sudan on 19 July was welcomed by the Soviet Union, which referred to it as "an important event in the political life of the Arab world" (TASS, 21 July). The counter-coup three days later, which brought back to power the al-Numairi government, placed the U.S.S.R. in an awkward position. The Soviets, however, were spared the onus of trying to reestablish amicable relations with the Sudanese: al-Numairi's vehement denunciation of the Soviet Union, his rapprochement with China (which had not supported the coup), and the execution of many leading members of the Sudanese Communist Party gave the Soviet Union no such option.

Latin America.   The challenge to U.S.S.R. views and policies represented since the mid-1960's by Castroite revolutionary strategy appeared in 1971 to have subsided considerably. The two major factors affecting revolutionary options in the area were (1) the 1970 Marxist electoral success in Chile, which both confirmed the feasibility of a parliamentary road to power—a contention favored by most major pro-Soviet communist parties in Latin America—and disproved the Castroite advocacy of the inevitable need for violent tactics; and (2) growing Cuban economic dependence on the Soviet Union, estimated at some $500 million a year in aid. Within this context, U.S.S.R. policy toward Latin America focused primarily on development of diplomatic and economic relations, a concern partly motivated by the need to capitalize on the adoption of "anti-imperialist nationalism" by several Latin American governments. Despite disparagement of the phenomenon (*New Times*, no. 33), concern for developing intergovernmental relations could also be seen as a response to increasing Chinese links with Latin American countries.

In his speech at the CPSU congress, Brezhnev claimed that "great changes" were taking place in a number of Latin American countries (*IB*, no. 7-8). While he listed only Chile, Peru, and Bolivia—claiming that the first was following a "progressive line" while the other two were "fighting against enslavement by the US monopolies"—there was a notable decline during the year in Soviet criticism of the other Latin American states. This reticence extended also to commentary on the overthrow of the left-wing Bolivian government in August, Soviet news media limiting their account of events to factual reports. This response contrasted with that of Fidel Castro, who reiterated his earlier oft-expressed contention that the only feasible strategy in Bolivia was that of armed struggle.

Throughout the year the CPSU and the pro-Soviet communist parties in Latin America stressed the importance of the Chilean communists' use of united front tactics for the attainment of revolutionary goals. Two major meetings of the area's communist parties, held in spring and autumn (*WMR*, July; *El Siglo*, Santiago, 11 October), concluded that each country would find its own road to "victory." Opposition to violent tactics, such as those of the Uruguayan "Tupamaro" guerrillas, was underlined by the scant and general condemnation in Soviet publications. An article in the March issue of *Prostor*, the journal of the Kazakhstan Writers' Union, written by the Soviet delegate to the Twentieth Congress of the Communist Party of Uruguay, Politburo member Dinmukhamed Kunaev, mentioned the Tupamaros only twice, describing them as a "terroristic petty-bourgeois group" and as "pseudo-revolutionaries." That same month the Soviet ambassador to Brazil, in a press conference, criticized both Castroite tactics and the very concept of exporting revolutionary ideas.

Soviet-Cuban relations, which had been improving since Castro's qualified support in 1968 for the Soviet-led invasion of Czechoslovakia, were highlighted by several high-level contacts. Among the most notable were the visits of Kosygin to Havana (26-30 October) and Cuban President Dorticós to Moscow (21-28 December). The cordial welcome given to Kosygin contrasted with the cool reception during his earlier visit, in June 1967 (see *YICA*, 1968, p. 152). A joint communiqué noted that opinions had been exchanged on "topical problems of the world communist movement and national liberation movement and on the basic international problems of the time." It added that both sides had "expressed full unanimity in assessing the present international situation and social development throughout the world" (TASS, 1 November).

At the conclusion of the Dorticós visit the two sides "reaffirmed the appraisal of the present international situation which was unanimously set out" in the earlier communiqué (*ibid.*, 28 December). In a message to the Cuban government and party leadership—for the anniversary of the Cuban Revolution—the Soviet party and government noted "with great satisfaction the unswerving growth of friendship and close cooperation between Cuba and the Soviet Union," adding that "this was helped to no small degree by the [recent] visits of party and state figures" of the two countries (Moscow radio, 31 December). On another level, Soviet-Cuban solidarity was demonstrated by the arrest and alleged confession of Cuban poet Heberto Padilla (see *Cuba*). Despite criticism of this incident by a broad segment of left-wing opinion, *Komsomolskaia pravda* (2 June) attacked the "wave of propagandist hysteria" and offered its support for steps toward "normalizing the atmosphere in the milieu of Cuban literary and art figures."

Despite increasing U.S.S.R. diplomatic and economic ties with Latin American governments, CPSU relations with pro-Soviet communist parties continued to be cordial. In two countries, however, repercussions from the 1968 invasion of Czechoslovakia continued to be felt. The split in the Communist Party of Venezuela became final when two separate congresses were held in January, resulting in formation of a dissident communist party led by Pompeyo Márquez and Teodoro Petkoff —two leading critics of the invasion. Repercussions of the split extended beyond the borders of Venezuela, because a number of dissidents held leading posts in Soviet-controlled international front organizations, such as the World Federation of Democratic Youth and the International Organization of Journalists. In Mexico, the communist party continued to reiterate its opposition to the invasion and retained friendly relations with the Venezuelan dissidents, despite repeated attacks against the latter by the CPSU. In July, David Siqueiros, the most prominent supporter of the Soviet invasion of Czechoslovakia, was expelled by the Mexican party from its Central Committee for "activities contrary to the party's political line."

Asia. In his speech to the CPSU congress, Brezhnev claimed that the CPSU and the Soviet government had "done their utmost to bring about the normalization of relations with the People's Republic of China," but added:

> It will be recalled that the Chinese leaders have put forward an ideological-political platform of their own which is incompatible with Leninism on the questions of international life and the world communist movement.... Our Party has resolutely opposed the attempts to distort the Marxist-Leninist teaching, and to split the international communist movement and the ranks of the fighters against imperialism. (*IB*, no. 7-8, 1971.)

He continued the tradition of differentiating between inter-party and inter-government relations.

Regarding the latter he claimed that, as a result of Soviet initiative, there had been "signs of some normalization." He stated that negotiations over the border issues were "proceeding slowly" and noted that there had been an exchange of ambassadors at the end of 1970. He also added that "after a considerable interval" trade agreements were signed and that trade had "somewhat increased." (*Ibid.*)

Brezhnev's speech was preceded on 18 March by a Chinese ideological attack against the CPSU leadership, reminiscent of polemics exchanged at the height of Sino-Soviet conflict and stronger than any criticism since April 1970. The Soviet response was relatively mild. Radio broadcasts to China on the same day concentrated primarily on developing the claim that the Chinese attacks, which coincided with the celebrations of the Paris Commune centennial, served to further "imperialist" aims by detracting attention from the significance of the anniversary. A subsequent TASS statement in *Pravda* (22 March) claimed that the Chinese had "distorted Marxist-Leninist teachings" and the "principles of the Paris Commune." It added that the "imperialist states approved the new anti-communist action by the Chinese leadership" and did not "conceal their hopes" that it would lead to an aggravation of Sino-Soviet relations.

The exchanges in mid-March set the scene for a gradual deterioration in party relations. While continuing to stress that the CPSU "principled line" was one of "normalizing Soviet-Chinese relations" (Radio "Reace and Progress," 12 April), U.S.S.R. media accused the Chinese of deviations ranging from nationalism (*Novoe vremia*, Moscow, 28 May) to Trotskyism (Moscow radio, 14 July). The Soviet Union's initial reaction to the announcement of U.S. President Nixon's visit to China—and the prospect of a change in relations among the three powers—was a ten-day silence. On 25 July a long article in *Pravda*, by I. Aleksandrov (thought to be a pen name for a senior political figure) offered a cautious and relatively moderate response. A normalization of relations between Washington and Peking was favored, provided this did not develop into a "political combination against other states." By the time Aleksandrov published a second, lengthier article (*ibid.*, 4 September), the tone was quite different, representing in many respects the peak of anti-Chinese polemics since the 1969 fighting on the Ussuri River. It included a veiled threat of extending the doctrine of limited sovereignty to China:

> Of course, in waging a resolute ideological-political struggle against the great-nation chauvinist principles of Peking and its foreign policy, we are doing everything to defend the interests of the Soviet people [and] the interests of our friends and allies against any encroachment.

Aleksandrov concluded by arguing that Maoism was "objectively" allied with imperialism, racism, Trotskyism, and reformism, with which it was forming a "united front."

During this time, and throughout the rest of the year, the Soviet Union published what was reported by *Komsomolskaia pravda* (27 August) to be a "whole series of fundamental research works devoted to a critical examination of various aspects of the domestic and foreign policy of the present Peking leadership." On another level a sign of tension could be seen in the fact that, for the first time since World War II, the number of U.S.S.R. divisions facing China (33) exceeded the number in Eastern Europe (31). At the same time, the Soviets apparently attempted to incite the Chinese military against Mao Tse-tung. As evidence accumulated of a major purge in the Chinese army and of a possible anti-Mao conspiracy led by his nominated successor, Lin Piao, U.S.S.R. broadcasts addressed to the military increased correspondingly. A commentary in mid-November warned: "The purge always begins with the chiefs of the armed forces. But this is only the beginning. As in the past, hundreds of thousands of high and middle-ranking commanders will be replaced or persecuted. This has happened before, and it will happen in the future." (Moscow radio, 14 November.)

At the end of December, and in contrast to previous practice, Soviet media started leveling attacks against Premier Chou. An article in *Pravda* (22 December) accused the Chinese leadership of "betraying the national-liberation movement" by its support of the Pakistan government against insurgents in East Pakistan, and added: "Attention is focused on the fact that one of the main instigators of the unti-Indian and anti-Soviet campaign is none other than Premier of the [Chinese] State Council Chou En-lai." The *Pravda* article was complemented with a broadcast on the same day by Radio "Peace and Progress" referring to opposition in China against a Sino-American rapprochement, and such a rapprochement was interpreted as having been inspired by Chou En-lai.

The extent of pro-Soviet sentiment in other communist parties in Asia continued to be modest. Among the ruling parties that attended the CPSU congress, only the one from Mongolia could be counted on to align itself fully with Soviet views. The only significant pro-Soviet parties in non-communist Asian states were those from India and Ceylon, the latter a partner in that country's coalition government. Relations with the Communist Party of Australia, a strong critic of the invasion of Czechoslovakia, continued to deteriorate throughout the year. Moreover, by inviting the party's national secretary, Laurie Aarons, to the congress, the CPSU incurred the displeasure of the small pro-Soviet element among Australian communists. The group branded the action "unfraternal".

Relations with the Japan Communist Party (JCP) showed some signs of improvement. JCP attendance at the CPSU congress was the first such participation in ten years at a Soviet Union function. It was preceded by CPSU-JCP talks in Moscow on 15-19 March. The communiqué noted that talks were held in an atmosphere of "comradeship and frankness." It was agreed that differences between the parties should be settled on principles of independence, equality, and non-interference. Although not included in the communiqué, JCP delegation head Nishizawa Tomio stated on 20 March that the CPSU had agreed to withdraw support from the pro-Soviet "Voice of Japan" group. During the summer and early autumn, more inter-party talks were held. An August visit by a JCP delegation, led by Secretariat member Fujii Sadaharu, was followed on 19 August by another with JCP chairman Miyamoto Kenji. A month later Miyamoto returned for a longer stay (19-26 September). The communiqué referred to a "frank and comradely atmosphere," implying that differences continued to exist (Moscow radio, 27 September).

CPSU comments on North Korea during the year appeared exceptionally cordial. The tenth anniversary of the Soviet-North Korean friendship treaty evoked a warm response in *Izvestiia* (6 July):

> Relations between the Soviet Union and the DPRK [Democratic People's Republic of Korea], which are based on the principles of Marxism-Leninism and proletarian internationalism, are one of the living examples of relations of a new type between members of the socialist community enjoying equal rights.... Friendship between the Soviet Union and the DPRK is firm and inviolable, it is not of an ostentatious nature, and has survived the test of time.

CPSU Politburo member Kirill Mazurov attended the anniversary celebrations in Pyongyang, and his speech on that occasion reflected similar views (*Pravda*, 7 July). A delegation led by Politburo candidate member Sharaf Rashidov subsequently visited North Korea. On its return a broadcast to North Korea by Moscow radio (13 December) described it as "a heartening fact indeed" that relations between the two countries, "based on the principles of Marxism-Leninism and proletarian internationalism," were "growing and consolidating year by year." The extent to which the North Koreans subscribed to these views was not evident, and in the area of party relations the Korean Workers' Party tended to align itself more closely with independent parties such as the Romanian and Japanese. Even small incidents, such as the visit of a Soviet football coach to South Korea in September, provoked a strong reaction. The Korean Central News Agency (11 September) claimed that North Korean "people and public circles" regarded the visit as "something hardly understandable."

North Vietnam and the National Liberation Front of South Vietnam (NLFSV) continued to steer a middle course in the Sino-Soviet conflict. In contrast to its absence from the 1969 Moscow world communist party conference, the (North) Vietnamese Workers' Party sent a delegation to the CPSU congress. Its spokesman, First Secretary Le Duan, did not engage in Sino-Soviet polemics but expressed gratitude to China as well as the U.S.S.R. and other communist-ruled countries for their "massive help." Following the announcement of Nixon's intended visit to China, the Soviet Union attempted to capitalize on it by portraying Chinese policy as leading to a betrayal of the "Vietnamese liberation struggle." The U.S.S.R. also repeatedly stressed its own commitment and assistance to the Vietnamese communists (see, e.g., *Pravda*, 2 September). The visit of Podgornyi to Hanoi was described as "a new vivid expression of the growing friendship of the peoples of the Soviet Union and Vietnam" (*Pravda*, 11 October; *Izvestiia*, 12 October).

The growing rapprochement between the Soviet Union and India, exemplified by the 9 August treaty of peace, friendship, and cooperation and strong Soviet support for India against Pakistan, created a certain conflict of interest in view of the close CPSU ties with the opposition Communist Party of India. This situation does not appear, however, to have caused insurmountable problems. Podgornyi's visit to India coincided with the Ninth Congress of the Communist Party of India attended by CPSU Politburo member Dinmukhamed Kunaev.

Soviet relations with Prince Sihanouk's Royal Government of National Union of Cambodia and the National United Front of Kampuchea (NUFK), both in Peking, continued to be strained. The U.S.S.R. retained its embassy in Phnom Penh, and the only NUFK delegation to visit the Soviet Union (1-10 September) was invited by the Afro-Asian Solidarity Committee—not by either the CPSU or the U.S.S.R. government. In an interview, Sihanouk complained that the Soviets, although wanting to prevent his supporters from becoming pro-Chinese, were doing everything necessary to make them so (Agence France Presse, 10 September).

International Party Contacts. For CPSU contacts with foreign communist parties and movements, in addition to those noted above, see the profiles of individual countries.

Publications. The main CPSU organs are the daily newspaper *Pravda*, the theoretical and ideological journal *Kommunist* (appearing 18 times a year), and the twice-monthly *Partiinaia zhizn'*, a journal on internal party affairs and organizational party matters. *Kommunist vooruzhennikh sil* is the party theoretical journal for the armed forces, and *Agitator* is the journal for party propagandists, both appearing twice a month. The Komsomol has a newspaper, *Komsomolskaia pravda* (issued six times a week); a monthly theoretical journal, *Molodoi kommunist*; and a monthly literary journal, *Molodaia gvardia*. Each U.S.S.R. republic prints similar party newspapers and journals in local languages, and usually also in Russian.

Stanford University   Dorothy Atkinson
                                                                     Milorad I. Popov

Yugoslavia

The Communist Party of Yugoslavia was founded in June 1920.[1] At the party's Sixth Congress, in November 1952, the name was changed to League of Communists of Yugoslavia (Savez Komunista Jugoslavije; LCY). The LCY is the only political party in Yugoslavia and holds a monopoly of power through its leading role in the Socialist Alliance of Working People of Yugoslavia (Socijalistički Savez Radnog Naroda Jugoslavije; SAWPY), an organization which includes all mass political organizations and also individuals representing various social groups.

Organization and Leadership. The Ninth LCY Congress, held in March 1969, replaced the Central Committee with an annual Conference of the LCY. The Presidium was enlarged to 52 members, including first LCY secretaries in the six constituent republics and two autonomous regions of Yugoslavia. On recommendation of party leader Josip Broz Tito, the congress created a 15-member Executive Bureau of the Presidium to strengthen central leadership by providing a form of "collective leadership" in order to prevent factionalism. It included two leaders from every republic, one from each of the two autonomous regions, and Tito as chairman. Elected to the Executive Bureau, besides Tito, were Edvard Kardelj, Vladimir Bakarić, Krste Crvenkovski, Nijaz Dizdarević, Stane Dolanc, Stevan Doronjski, Kiro Gligorov, Fadilj Hodža, Cvijetin Mijatović, Miroslav Pečujlić, Budislav Šoškić, Mijalko Todorović, Miko Tripalo, and Veljko Vlahović. Because of intra-party dissension the LCY Conference (scheduled to convene in October 1971) was postponed to January.

The LCY claims a membership of 1,049,334 (*Borba*, 22 April). The population of Yugoslavia is 20,504,516 (census of 31 March 1971).

Party Internal Affairs. Despite Tito's claim at the Ninth Congress that the party would obtain "a far stronger leadership" and "eliminate all deviations more resolutely," the LCY passed "through what is perhaps its most serious crisis in its 50-year history" (*Večernje novosti*, Belgrade, 9 December). The reason was the inability of leaders to cope with rising nationalism, both in the country and within LCY organizations of different republics. The situation became aggravated due to multiple and unresolved economic and social problems. The most acute aspect of the crisis took place in Croatia, but it had repercussions elsewhere. At the same time, the basic difficulty of reconciling the need for centralized party discipline with partly institutionalized goals of decentralization in a social system based on the principle of workers' self-management was revealed.

Crisis in the Croatian LC. On two occasions, in April and December, internal problems of party leadership in Croatia assumed major proportions and required drastic intervention by Tito.

---

[1]Yugoslav communists claim April 1919 as the party's establishment, since a Unification Congress in Belgrade temporarily established a Socialist Workers' Party of Yugoslavia (Communists). It included both communist and non-communist elements, but this organization broke up in June 1920.

In the first instance, the so-called police affair, Croatian leaders appeared unified in their public attitude; in the second instance, on policy vis-à-vis the Croatian "national movement," the republic leadership openly split and had to be purged.

The still murky "police affair," with domestic and foreign political overtones, had its origins in allegations reportedly made by secret police organs in Belgrade. The leadership of the Croatian LC was accused of contacts with Ustashi émigrés in West Germany, especially a group located in West Berlin and headed by physician Dr. Branko Jelić. He changed his anti-communist attitude and began to claim Soviet support in efforts to subvert Yugoslavia by creating an independent Croatian state. At the request of Croatian party leaders, the LCY Executive Bureau made an investigation. Results were published on 24 March. The communiqué stated that "some aspects of enemy activities against the Socialist Federal Republic of Yugoslavia and some questions pertaining to work of security organs [had been examined] and some conclusions adopted about further tasks in that domain" (*Nedeljne Informativne Novine*, 18 April).

Two weeks later, on 7 April, after a meeting of the Croatian LC Central Committee, a more precise statement castigated "organized action to disqualify the political leadership of the Croatian Socialist Republic by spreading slanderous claims about alleged contacts between the leadership of the Socialist Republic of Croatia and the Ustashi emigration." While attacking the "unitarist, centralist and bureaucratic forces" within Yugoslavia, opposed to the political line established at the first LCY Conference, the communiqué particularly stressed that "disinformation" about Croatian leaders' behavior had been "also placed through some organs of the federal administration." The Croatian Central Committee requested further investigation into the matter (*Borba*, 8 April). A high-level commission of the Federal Executive Council (government) began to investigate official Croatian complaints. Transfer of the "police affair" from internal LCY circles to the public domain precipitated rumors and speculation. This prompted Tito to unusually harsh words in a speech on 14 April at Priština (Kosovo): "I do not believe that we have ever had such a situation as we have now in the League.... Our very existence is in question, our socialist state, our community. And where can we lay the responsibility for all this except on the Communists. That is how we must behave and anyone who does not conduct himself in this way—out with him from the League of Communists." (*Yugoslav News Bulletin*, New York, 20 April.)

To discuss the situation, the LCY Presidium met (28-30 April) at Tito's island retreat of Brioni. Sharp discussion and mutual recrimination particularly among the Croatian and Serbian party leaders characterized the meeting. Although proceedings were not published, the official communiqué issued after the session admitted "worsening of the situation and of relations within the LCY as well as sluggishness in implementation of decisions by the Ninth Congress and the first LCY Conference." Regarding the Croatians, the communiqué scored "increased subversive action of foreign enemies" aiming to "disqualify the political leaders of the Socialist Republic of Croatia [in order] to provoke political instability, intra-republic frictions and mistrust," while endorsing results of the government investigation that "neither organs of federal administration nor their services and individuals have taken part in any kind of plot." By upholding the loyalty of Croatian communist leaders and clearing the political police of conspiracy charges, the communiqué announced "full unity" in the Presidium on forthcoming LCY tasks. The necessity for a "more determined and more concrete struggle against all the aspects of nationalism" was emphasized, nationalism being described as a "platform for rallying all anticommunist forces" (*Novosti*, 3 May).

While the Brioni plenum appeared to have restored unity at the top, another kind of political contest in Croatia soon divided the ranks of that republic's communist leadership. The problem this time was how to cope with a strong and popular nationalist current that responded to constitutional reform (see below) and saw in it a step toward full Croatian state sovereignty. Proponents of the "national movement" included prominent intellectuals, some of them LCY members, who on 15 April launched *Hrvatski tjednik* (Croatian Weekly), organ of the prestigious literary-cultural organization "Matica Hrvatska." Circulation of this newspaper by fall reached the level of the best known among established communist weeklies in Croatia. The "movement" also received enthusiastic support from student activists at Zagreb University. In April the regular, communist-led slate was rejected by an unprecedented student vote and replaced by a new student-body leadership with marked nationalist proclivities. Public meetings in many localities throughout Croatia celebrated establishment of local organizations of Matica Hrvatska and gave the appearance of attempts to create a political party.

On both ideological aspects of the new movement and how to deal with it politically, the communist leadership divided. One faction led by older party stalwarts Vladimir Bakarić and Jakov Blažević, president of the republic's Assembly, denounced the movement and any LC leniency toward it; the other group, headed by Croatian LC president Savka Dabčević-Kučar and dynamic younger leader Miko Tripalo, advised flexibility in order to broaden the party's mass appeal and popular base. On 23 July two prominent and politically active younger professors at Zagreb University who also served as high functionaries in the Matica Hrvatska and members of the *Hrvatski tjednik* editorial board, Šime Djodan and Marko Veselica, were expelled from the LC. This seemed a victory for the Bakarić faction. Moreover, on 2 August the Croatian LC executive committee issued an Action Program which accused "some people" around Matica Hrvatska of striving to utilize it as "a cover for oppositional activities, for another political party," thus becoming "a conspiratorial group against both the Croatian LC and the LCY." The Program criticized ideas of a "national movement" and a "general Croat reconciliation" as contrary to class teaching of the LCY. The Program, however, received scant publicity and saw little implementation. The two factions, avoiding an open showdown, held two long secret meetings at a Zagreb villa during the summer but did not succeed in settling their differences. (A detailed description of these intra-party confrontations appeared in *NIN*, 19 December 1971 and 23 January 1972). This façade of unity and vigilance must have induced Tito, after a tour of Croatia, to declare that "all kinds of stories about Croatia [which maintain] that there is no unity, that the people think differently, that there is a blooming nationalism—are completely absurd" (*Vjesnik*, 16 September).

Despite these reassuring words, ferment in Croatia continued and reached a climax on 22 November with proclamation of a student strike at Zagreb University. It spread thereafter to other Croatian campuses, involving between 30,000 and 35,000 young people. Invoking the postulate of "Croatia as a sovereign, national state of the Croatian people," strikers proclaimed solidarity with the working class and blamed "bureaucratic forces" for constantly delaying solution of vital issues. The students demanded "radical decisions" by official organs to solve the foreign currency, banking and foreign trade problems (*Vjesnik*, 24 November). Other demands advanced before and during the strike included establishment of a Croatian army and membership for the Croatian Republic in the United Nations (*Politika*, 18 November). The strike ended on 3 December but the danger that it could spread to other segments of the population prompted both Savka Dabčević-Kučar and Miko Tripalo to denounce it.

More importantly, the strike moved Tito to launch significant political action. On 30 November, he convoked at his hunting lodge Karadjordjevo in Vojvodina the entire leadership of the Croatian LC. The meeting lasted twenty hours. It was followed during 1 and 2 December by a plenum of the LCY Presidium. Starting with criticism of the student strike and hinting that domestic and foreign enemies were behind it, Tito reproached Croatian leaders for not having prevented the strike and thereby having shown "lack of vigilance, complacency and rotten liberalism. Thus, the enemy could very easily accomplish his counterrevolutionary activities." Tito's main target was Matica Hrvatska: "We know that there exists the so-called revolutionary committee of fifty members—I call it counterrevolutionary—which directs all these activities.... This is an organization which works both legally and illegally, and its focal point is Matica Hrvatska.'' The same institution was also charged with having become a "very powerful parallel party," anti-socialist in its orientation, and opposed to Yugoslavia as a state, preferring the establishment of a "Pavelić type" state.[2] Tito condemned any idea of a Croatian "national movement" which "could only tend to put aside the Communist party" (*Borba*, 3 and 5 December).

Although names were omitted from this criticism of the Croatian LC leadership, it was obvious that a major purge would take place. During or immediately following a tense meeting of the Croatian LC central committee, held on 12-14 December with a police helicopter circling the building and helmeted militiamen stationed on Zagreb's main squares, a number of party leaders resigned. They included both Miko Tripalo and Savka Dabčević-Kučar (replaced by Milka Planinc); secretary of the Croatian LC's executive committee, Pero Pirker (replaced by Josip Vrhovec); a member of the same committee in charge of territorial defense, Marko Koprtla; president of Zagreb's party conference, Srećko Bijelić; head of the Croatian veterans organization, Ivan Šibl; president of the Croatian government, Dragutin Haramija (replaced by Ivo Perišin); and several cabinet members. Principal student leaders, among them the student prorector at Zagreb University, Ivan Zvonimir Cičak, and the president of the Zagreb student organization, Dražen Budiša, were arrested on 12 December. Several days of violent student street demonstrations and clashes with the militia followed. Resignations, expulsions, and removals during the second half of December affected hundreds of key officials at different levels of the party apparatus and state administration as well as in the mass media. The entire executive board of Matica Hrvatska resigned, and *Hrvatski tjednik* ceased to appear. On 12 January 1972, eleven prominent Croatian intellectuals (including Djodan, Veselica, and Vlado Gotovac, former editor of *Hrvatski tjednik*) were arrested and charged, among other political crimes, of having worked to overthrow by force or other unconstitutional means, the existing social order.

The gravity of these dramatic events or a rationalization for having unleashed them was expressed by Tito in his speech to the presidium of Yugoslav trade unions: "Had we not started this struggle and prevented this [separatism] ... shooting and civil war would perhaps have begun in six months and you know what that would mean. Could we have allowed it? As chief of state and LCY president, I could not have allowed someone else to come to restore peace and order. I have said that I would never allow this and that I would rather apply extreme means, and you know what these extreme means are." (Belgrade radio, 18 December.)

The LCY Organizational Dilemma. Events in Croatia exposed the LCY "ideological crisis," a main theme of Tito's speeches at Karadjordjevo, and its institutional-organizational "paralysis" (*NIN*, 23 January 1972). Both of these are interwoven, resulting from the general trend toward decentralization of social and economic life—and of the opposition to decentralization. The tendency toward self-centeredness of communist parties in the six republics and two autonomous regions had been strengthened at the expense of a unified and centrally-led LCY. The most important commissions of the party Presidium (LCY development, theoretical and ideological work, press, and the economic commission) met only once during 1971, neglecting to analyze important problems and offer nation-wide solutions. The commission on LCY statute questions met in April and concluded that violations of democratic centralism were particularly observable in the highest party organs. The same commission also noted a general decline in LCY membership. It complained about the small—and decreasing—percentage of workers in LCY ranks: from 31.1 per cent in 1968 to 29.6 per cent in 1970 (*Borba*, 22 April; *Socijalizam*, nos. 7-8, p. 836). The official LCY organ stated

[2]An allusion to the Independent Croatian State established by the Axis powers in April 1941, after dismemberment of Yugoslavia, and headed by Ante Pavelić.

that this represented a symptom of the "growing discrepancy between ideology and reality" (*Komunist*, 3 June).

Blaming communist "inertia" over the past several years for the present LCY predicament (and criticizing the 1952 congress of the party—which ratified and strengthened the new self-management system—as having contributed to weaken party firmness), Tito suggested in his 18 December speech to the trade union council a reorganization of the LCY on the basis of greater respect for democratic centralism. He said: "If the League of Communists continues to move in [the current] downward direction, this Yugoslavia would break up. It would break up, or rather it would be prey to someone, and it is only a question whose prey it would be. But the League of Communists must again become [the] cohesive force of our socialist community and a guarantee of its strength. It must not only be an ideological directing force, but at times must even be somewhat firmer toward those who fail to adhere to party policy, that is, the policy adopted and inaugurated by the top leadership."

Domestic Affairs. *Constitutional Reform.* On 28 February, the draft of the third set of amendments to the present constitution of April 1963 was officially announced. It contained 21 amendments numbered from twenty to forty (six amendments were enacted in April 1967 and thirteen in December 1968). On 2 March the LCY Presidium met to discuss them and inaugurated four months of public debate on the same topic. According to Edvard Kardelj, architect of all postwar Yugoslav constitutional laws and change, the reform intended to "reduce to the minimum the mechanism of the supranational state structure within the federation," while "essentially strengthening the position of individual republics and autonomous regions [and thus] setting up powerful barriers to the reemergence of any big-state centralism" (*Politika*, 3 March). The most significant innovation was the collective State Presidency. "A factor of political cohesion at the center" (Kardelj), with wide legislative and executive powers, it would adjust common interests of the republics and regions whose assemblies were to elect the membership.

Discussions about constitutional reform in parliament and the press and by professional, social, and political groups assumed an often harsh and contradictory character. For some parliamentary critics the State Presidency would diminish prerogatives of the Federal Assembly, while the government would be paralyzed by being responsible to the Assembly but controlled by the Presidency. In Croatia and Serbia the reform found both most ardent defenders and critics. For Miko Tripalo, the constitutional amendments confirmed the basic principle that "the republic, the nation is the source and the bearer of sovereignty." Hence, the federal organs would not enjoy any more automatic supranational prerogatives. In many instances, only unanimity of all republics and regions would bring forth binding federal decisions (*Domet*, Rijeka, no. 3; *Vjesnik*, 30 March).

Likewise, according to Zagreb University rector Ivan Supek, the amendments created the hope that "Croatian statehood with a Socialist content will see the day" (*Politika*, 25 March). On the other hand leading Serbian constitutional law experts viewed with apprehension what they saw as evolution of Yugoslavia from a federation to a confederation. In his analysis of constitutional amendments, Belgrade professor of law Dr. Stevan Vračar wrote about a "dramatic sharpening of the profound social crisis which the country has not experienced since the revolution." For him the reform was basically retrogressive because, in its confederalist essence, it would establish "six independent national states ... leading not only to weakening but to disintegration of the Yugoslav community" (*Student*, Belgrade, 13 April). Despite these or similar opinions and contradictory views, the Federal Assembly adopted on 30 June only a slightly revised text of constitutional amendments.

New State Administration. At a 29 July joint session of the five chambers in the Federal Assembly, the composition of the new State Presidency was announced. It had 22 members (eight presidents of republic and regional assemblies plus 14 persons elected by these assemblies) as well as Tito, elected on the same occasion chairman of the new collective Presidency for the next five years.

The following day, the Federal Assembly elected a new prime minister and 21 other members of the Federal Executive Council, using also a proportional republic-regional key: three per republic and two per region. Džemal Bijedić, a 54 year-old Moslem from Bosnia, became the new premier and replaced the Slovene, Mitja Ribičič.

Nationality Conflicts and Problems. The tendency toward "republican statism," a result of constitutional reform, revived old politico-ethnic problems and created new ones in all constituent parts of the country. While prewar royalist Yugoslavia had been beset by the "Croatian problem," Tito's Yugoslavia was faced during 1971 in particularly sharp form with both a Croatian *and* a Serbian problem (*Economist*, London, 21 August; *East Europe*, New York, October; *The World Today*, London, December; *Est et Ouest*, Paris, 1-15 February 1972). A majority of Croats greeted constitutional reform and aspired toward national sovereignty within and, for some, outside Yugoslavia, while demanding far-reaching institutional change in the economy (see below). A great number of Serbs viewed basic national problems in reverse order. Dispersal of Serbs among several republics contributed to uneasiness about results of confederacy. They were particularly alarmed by an upsurge of nationalism in Croatia and wondered what statehood would bring to over 700,000 Serbs living on the territory of that republic. In this connection a prominent deputy in the Croatian Sabor (Assembly) General Rade Bulat, a Serb and partisan leader in World War II, created a major controversy by proposing that the amended republic constitution establish a Council (Chamber) of Nationalities within the Sabor, assuring national and civil rights to the Serb minority. Another proposal to create an autonomous region, where a compact Serb population lives, was advanced by some leading members of "Prosveta" (Enlightenment), the main Serbian cultural association in Croatia (*NIN*, 22 August).

The "Serbian problem" was much in evidence also in the autonomous region of Kosovo, officially part of Serbia. With 73.8 per cent of its population of Albanian origin, the region has the fastest rate of population growth in the country. Complaints of discrimination by the Serbian minority, emigration by many Serbs from the region, Albanian-Serbian-Montenegrin brawls among students at Priština University, statements by certain officials that the region should become a full-fledged republic were discussed at an enlarged plenum of the Kosovar party the end of June. Albanian and Serbian leaders defended divergent viewpoints.

In Montenegro too, within and outside the party, a debate raged throughout the year on two issues: nature of the literary language (Montenegrin variant of Serbian or a separate Montenegrin language and literature); destruction of a little Serbian Orthodox chapel on Lovćen mountain, where the bones of the famous poet and prince, Petar Petrović-Njegoš, are buried, and construction at this place of a Njegos mausoleum designed by Croatian sculptor Ivan Meštrović. The Montenegrin Metropolitan of the Serbian Orthodox Church sued the government on this issue in April, and most Montenegrin intellectuals living in Serbia opposed destruction of the Lovćen chapel.

In Macedonia, the problem of "nationalist deviation" assumed aspects of an intra-party feud. A member of the LCY Executive Bureau and of the State Presidency, Krste Crvenkovski, became the target of veiled attacks. Accused in December of sharing republic statist views of Miko Tripalo, he was suspected also of being a supporter of a pro-Bulgarian line. Although Crvenkovski was defended by the Macedonian Central Committee (*Nova Makedonija*, Skopje, 15 December), the suspicion of local "nationalism" by party "unitarists" indicated the explosive nature of the nationality issue.

Hardly a single domain in public life remained free of nationality strife or recrimination. In April, Croatian members of the Association of the Fine Arts of Yugoslavia walked out of the congress in protest because headquarters were maintained in Belgrade. Political rather than literary quarrels negatively affected relations within the Alliance of Yugoslav Writers. Croatian and Serbian linguists were in full disagreement about the character and official use of the Serbo-Croatian language. Disputes arose about historical textbooks and their content. Croatian and Macedonian student representatives refused in May to sign a document issued by the Conference of Yugoslav Students, favoring constitutional amendments. The following month at a regular conference of the Yugoslav Student Union, Croatian delegates adamantly maintained their position even regarding the name of the organization. Sports events with competing teams from different republics often degenerated into physical clashes among players and spectators.

The Role of the Army. Domestic ferment and external uncertainty enhanced the role of the Yugoslav Army. Since enactment of the Law on All-People's Defense (12 February 1969), the two components of Yugoslavia's military system—the regular army of about 250,000 and the territorial defense units with 600,000 men (*Borba*, 4 June)—have been of domestic and foreign interest. Amendment 39 to the constitution (see above) formulated the principle of "total national defense" and stressed "the right and duty of the communes, regions and republics to organize territorial defense." Overlapping responsibilities between a centralized regular army and decentralized territorial forces created a confusing situation ("who would control whom in the reality of war or even domestic political crisis?"—*The Economist*, 21 August), in view of ideas about separate republic armies advanced in different parts of the country.

Warsaw Pact summer maneuvers in Hungary and Bulgaria were criticized by the Yugoslav press (*Borba*, 7 August; *Vjesnik*, 11 August). On the other hand, "Freedom—71" war games in the western part of Yugoslavia took place between 2 and 9 October. The regular army, territorial and civil defense formations, and other local all-people's defense units involved received maximal publicity. Commenting on the maneuvers, federal secretary for national defense General Nikola Ljubičić declared that "the state of affairs in international relations compels us to devote our constant and extraordinary attention to the strengthening of our defense capability" (Belgrade radio, 30 September). Chief of the General Staff General Viktor Bubanj stressed the originality of these maneuvers, in contrast to those held elsewhere in the world, because "all the people participate in these maneuvers together with their armed forces and employ all forms of resistance against the armored and mechanized forces of the aggressor" (*ibid.*).

The December events in Croatia (see above) placed special emphasis on the role of the army in case of major domestic unrest. On 11 December in Karadjordjevo, Tito received top army and territorial force leaders. He informed them about decisions by the LCY Presidium ten days earlier and received their pledge "to fight without compromise for the implementation of party policy" (Zagreb radio, 11 December). On 21 December, speaking at Sarajevo, Tito hinted about a possible domestic political role for the army and stated: "The task of our army is not merely to defend the territorial integrity of our country, but also to defend our socialism when we see that it is in danger and that it cannot be defended by other means" (*Narodna armija*, Belgrade, 24 December). He repeated the same warning the following day, while addressing an elite group of veterans in the Bosnian town of Rudo (*ibid.*).

Criticism, Censorship, and Social Problems. Political and institutional turmoil had its counterpart in the intellectual, ideological, and social arena. Widespread criticism of the regime in individual publications and reflected in the mass media prompted Tito to attack in his 1 May Labin speech journalists working in the press, radio, and television for "spreading lies and smearing leaders who were elected by the people." He added to the list university professors "who have been working against our system, teaching our youth to be hostile to our society'' (*Borba*, 3 May). A week later, in his closing speech to the Second Congress of Self-Managers, he extended these attacks to encompass "various so-called intellectuals" and "philosophers" whom he called "unphilosophers" (all Yugoslav radio stations, 8 May).

Hotbeds of dissent included universities, faculty and student publications, and some independent reviews and magazines. At the Ljubljana University in Slovenia, the student newspaper *Tribuna* was banned in early November for having criticized Tito's participation in Iran's 2,500th-anniversary celebration. In mid-September, both Albanian and Serbian editions of student organs at Priština University were temporarily proscribed. Repressive censorship was frequently used in Belgrade. On several occasions (30 April, 27 August) the outspokenly critical newspaper *Student*, which had included nationalist, Western-style New Left, and Maoist-oriented articles, was banned. This also happened to an issue of *Annals of the Law Faculty* (June) at Belgrade University, because of articles criticizing constitutional reform, and to the student satirical review *Stradija*. An issue of the Belgrade review *Kultura* (August) was banned for having reprinted a 1945 article by Nicholas Berdyaev, found offensive because of anti-Marxism and criticism of the Soviet Union. The organ of the Association of Belgrade Students, *Vidici*, was banned twice (August and November). The same happened to the 16 August issue of the most prominent Belgrade literary periodical, *Književne Novine*.

Particularly significant was the banning of the internationally known Zagreb philosophical magazine *Praxis* (nos. 3-4, May-August). The two incriminating articles in that issue contended that the middle class (through its bureaucratic and technocratic positions within Yugoslav society) had infiltrated the party, vitiated the system of workers' self-management, and had been instrumental in spreading such anti-socialist phenomena as nationalism and social inequality.

This last charge, much in evidence throughout the year, was widely discussed by the press, sociological reviews, and at the meetings of various mass organizations. Tito recognized this in his 18 December speech before the Trade Union Council: "Social inequalities have assumed enormous proportions in our country.... Therefore at times it seems to me that the socialist nature of our society is disappearing." He proclaimed the necessity of a "general struggle against enrichment" and assailed particularly the luxurious private villas on the Adriatic coast and weekend houses in suburban locations.

The Second Congress of Self-Managers. To examine the experience of two decades, the Second Congress of Self-Managers took place in Sarajevo on 5-8 May and was attended by some 3,300 delegates. Foreign guests included delegations from the Soviet Union and other East European countries. Edvard Kardelj delivered the main report. Prime Minister Mitja Ribičič also addressed the congress, and two of Tito's interventions highlighted events. Twenty-eight resolutions were passed.

Following the April crisis in the LCY and the Brioni meeting of its Presidium (see above), the congress reflected the grave and unresolved problems in Yugoslav society. It gave full support to the publicly debated constitutional reform, and Kardelj linked strengthening of workers' self-management with constitutional decentralization. For him and Ribičič, the main domestic problem was the conflict between self-managing and statist tendencies. According to Kardelj, centralization of income and funds outside working organizations (which should decide about their distribution) makes the worker feel expropriated and deprived of his self-managing rights. According to Ribičič, big business banks, insurance, and foreign trade organizations are emerging as new centers of economic power which absorb surplus-value from social work. "Our economic instability results from a still too high degree of dependence by the self-managing system on external, state and political decisions and sources of financial power that are alienated from the working man." Several resolutions suggested resolving the contradiction between state centralization at all levels and a genuinely decentralized self-managing system in favor of the latter. (An analysis of the congress appeared in *Socijalizam*, nos. 7-8, pp. 946-57.)

Economy. In his 1971 New Year's message, Tito had indicated that the major task ahead was to stabilize the economy (see *YICA*, 1971, p. 107). Two circumstances, one economic and the other political, worked against this stabilization.

Economic destabilizing factors were described as follows: "Yugoslavia is about to enter 1972 with an economy whose total spending has been three percent in excess of resources offered by the GNP. Consequences have included unpleasant price increases, a large balance-of-payments deficit, and a high degree of illiquidity, with an overall rate of inflation estimated at an annual 17 per cent." (*Quarterly Economic Review—Yugoslavia*, London, no. 4.) The government introduced various measures to combat these negative factors. On 23 January the currency was devalued by 20 per cent, reduced vis-à-vis the U.S. dollar from 12.5 to 15 dinars. This and other stabilization measures (such as freezing prices) failed to bring positive results, admitted on 9 April by Premier Ribičič and criticized on 14 April by Tito at Priština. The outgoing Ribičič cabinet took new interventionist steps on 26 July by placing additional limits on imports, investments, and consumer credit. The new Premier Bijedić decreed on 26 November a three-month price freeze and on 21 December decided again to devalue the dinar by 18.73 per cent, further reducing it vis-à-vis the dollar (from 15 to 17 dinars), indicating that the government fight against inflation remained ineffective (*Wall Street Journal*, 4 June).

The crucial political factor, with its as yet incalculable impact on the economy, was the constitutional reform. It limits the economic role of the federation and enhances prerogatives of individual republics and regions. The London *Economist* (21 August) described "the gloom and dismay of [Yugoslav market] integrationists, the jubilation of the victorious decentralisers, the general confusion and uncertainty about how far this process will go." The main points of contention involved financial decentralization and especially revision of the foreign exchange system, the future of federal banks in Belgrade, and the functioning of foreign trade organizations. Difficulties in reaching inter-republic agreement on transfer of certain obligations and resources from the federation to republics caused a delay in adopting the 1971 federal budget, approved by the Federal Assembly on 30 March after months of heated debate. The principal Croatian claim that foreign currencies should be owned by those who earn them (*Vjesnik*, 11 November) was challenged by the Belgrade economic weekly as leading toward financial separation among republics (*Ekonomska politika*, 15 November). Echoing fears of lesser developed republics and regions interested in continuation of federal aid, Macedonian premier Ksente Bogoev warned that "every concept of regionalism in the areas of foreign currency and trade would undermine the bases of the [Yugoslav] common market" (*Borba*, 21 November).

The strike of students and ensuing developments in Croatia (see above) prompted the Federal Executive Council to action. On 27 December, Premier Bijedić announced a new foreign exchange system: Instead of being legally bound to return all but 7 to 10 per cent of their foreign currency earnings to the central government, export firms would be allowed to retain as much as 20 per cent of their hard currency earnings (and up to 40 per cent in the case of the tourist industry).

Economic shortcomings stirred discussion in the press and professional journals, with the frequently expressed need for a new and more expertly devised economic reform to replace the one hastily introduced in 1965. The failure of that reform to deal with the problem of unemployment (in 1971, 8 per cent of the adult population, with about a million workers employed abroad) prompted Croatian economist Branko Horvat to explain rising nationalism as massive frustration because a fourth of the Croatian labor force is employed abroad (*Književne novine*, 8 May).

On the optimistic side, industry produced 11 per cent more than in 1970. Agricultural output was also higher, with a record wheat harvest of 5.6 million (48 per cent more than in 1970) and maize production of 7.3 million tons (5 per cent above 1970). Likewise, invisible trade earnings increased, especially in tourism and remittances from workers abroad. In June a $45 million loan came from the World Bank, and in August the International Monetary Fund extended another one of $83.5 million. The United States agreed to reschedule payment of $58.6 million in loans received by Yugoslavia between 1949 and 1959 that would have fallen due over the next two years (*Time*, 8 November).

Yugoslavia's foreign indebtedness at the beginning of 1971 amounted to more than two billion dollars (covering financial credits, equipment, processed material, and food). Between 16 and 17 per cent of earned foreign currency is used for repayment of interest on foreign credits (*Politika*, 26 November). In July the Federal Assembly amended legislation initially passed in 1967, liberalizing regulations for investment of foreign capital in Yugoslavia. This aimed at stimulating ventures with domestic firms and increasing the export potential (*Journal of Commerce*, New York, 23 June).

Foreign Affairs. *The Soviet Union.* A New York Times editorial (9 August) spoke of "the nervous state of Yugoslav-Soviet relations." This observation can be analyzed at three levels: indirect Soviet pressure and activities bordering on subversion; ideological disputes; and official state-party relations.

Tito noted the first aspect in his 1 May speech at Labin when he complained that intelligence services of some countries, which regarded Yugoslavia as "a thorn in their side," were exercising "unbelievable pressure" on the country. Former U.S. Undersecretary of State George W. Ball wrote about "minions of the KGB [Soviet secret service] active in agitating the various separatist movements in Yugoslavia" (*Newsweek*, 8 November), a contention made earlier by the *Economist* (21 August). The most intriguing development concerned a Croatian exile periodical, *Hrvatska Država* (Croatian State), published in West Berlin by Dr. Branko Jelić, whose sudden switch from anti-communism to a militant pro-Soviet posture has been noted (see above). In its February-March issue, an alleged Moscow correspondent of the magazine wrote an article entitled "Croatia in the East." He discussed "incorporation of Croatia into the defense concept of the Warsaw Pact" and reported on a conference of Croatian communists held at Kharkov which, among other things, raised the possibility of organizing paramilitary units.

An article by Major General S. Ilin in the official organ of the U.S.S.R. Defense Ministry (*Krasnaia Zvezda*, 12 March) mentioning "expansion of international tasks for the [Soviet] armed forces" was noted prominently in the Yugoslav press ("Fright on Demand," in *Politika*, 18 March). A heated press controversy erupted in June when the *Politika* correspondent relayed news about public lectures given in Moscow by pro-Cominform exiles, who attacked Yugoslavia's sociopolitical system and policies. The Soviet government newspaper *Izvestiia* (18 June) accused the correspondent of engaging in "crude fabrications, ill-intentioned distortions, and slander" having "an anti-Soviet taint." *Politika*'s editorial board gave full support to its correspondent. A few days earlier, it announced that the foreign ministry had protested the activity of anti-Yugoslav émigrés in Moscow. Attacks on pro-Cominformists and their agitation within and outside of Yugoslavia abounded in the Yugoslav press during the summer. The leading Belgrade weekly *NIN* (13 June) indirectly accused the U.S.S.R. of creating troubles inside Yugoslavia to defeat the self-management system.

As for the ideological dispute, the Yugoslav press (*Vjesnik*, 8 July) strongly reacted to a book written by Sergei P. Trapeznikov, the director of the science department in the Central Committee of the Communist Party of the Soviet Union (CPSU).[3] Entitled *At the Turning Points of History*,

---

[3] In his essay *Progress, Coexistence, and Intellectual Freedom* (New York 1968, Andrei D. Sakharov called Trapeznikov "one of the most influential representatives of neo-Stalinism at the present time;" Harrison E. Salisbury who annotated the above, called Trapeznikov "a close and long-time associate of Party Secretary Brezhnev."

the volume attacked the Yugoslav version of revisionism, the self-management system as "repetition of the old anarcho-syndicalist notions of Lasalle concerning worker 'self-management' or producers democracy." Trapeznikov stated: "We have entered a new era in which revisionism will be destroyed and shattered." Similarly, a *New History of the CPSU*, published at Minsk, justified the 1948 expulsion of the Yugoslav party from the Cominform (reported in *Vjesnik*, 8 September). On the Yugoslav side, two books criticized Soviet postulates in foreign and intra-party relations. *Socialism and Sovereignty* was written by a Macedonian member of the LCY Presidium, Slavko Miloslavlevski. The main theme was that "every country must remain independently responsible for its own history." The other volume was a revised edition of the *History of Marxism* by Predrag Vranicki, philosopher and editor of *Praxis* magazine. He argued that Stalinism still remained dominant in the Soviet Union and Eastern Europe.

Official relations with the U.S.S.R. underwent fluctuations during the year. On 10 February a new five-year trade agreement was signed for 1971-75, providing an increase to over $3 billion. On 23-27 February the federal foreign affairs secretary, Mirko Tepavac, paid an official visit to the Soviet Union. Despite rumors in the foreign press (*Le Monde*, 19 February) that Leonid Brezhnev would ask that Tito personally attend the Twenty-fourth Congress of the CPSU (30 March-9 April), the LCY delegation was led by LCY Executive Bureau member Mijalko Todorović.

Tensions during April coincided with suspicions that Soviet agents were encouraging Croatian separatism. U.S.S.R. pressure in the summer assumed the form of Warsaw Pact maneuvers close to Yugoslav borders and Soviet displeasure over the Yugoslav-Chinese rapprochement (see below). After an apparent change in U.S.S.R. attitude, came the announcement of Brezhnev's "unofficial friendly visit." Public speeches during the visit (22-25 September) and an official statement indicated that both sides desired better relations through compromise but left many problems unsettled. The statement, signed by Brezhnev and Tito, stressed the desire for close cooperation between the communist parties and governments. It indicated that "development of multiform Soviet-Yugoslav relations is based on principles set forth in the Belgrade Declaration of 1955, the Moscow Statement and Declaration of 1956, the Joint Soviet-Yugoslav Statement of 1965." Citing these documents represented vindication of Titoism, i.e., noninterference in internal affairs for any reason. However, at a banquet speech Brezhnev questioned the meaning of these declarations by saying that their principles should be implemented "under present-day conditions as widely and fully as possible" (*Borba*, 23 September). Despite such ambiguous words, and with the obvious intention of placating his hosts, Brezhnev on this same occasion denied existence of "the so-called new doctrine of limited sovereignty," decried "rumors of Soviet armies allegedly prepared to move into the Balkans," and assailed "various forces trying to drive a wedge" between the Soviet Union and Yugoslavia.

On the other hand, in a speech the next day before an audience of workers, Brezhnev admitted: "It is no secret that the current organization of Yugoslav social life does not seem acceptable to Soviet communists and the Soviet people" (*ibid.*, 24 September). The official statement also contained elements which may be viewed as Yugoslav concessions. One was "the heavy ideological phrasing" (*New York Times*, 27 September), such as "fidelity to the principles of socialist internationalism" or reference to Marx-Engels-Lenin teachings as "the only and invariable foundation today and in the future of the policy of the communist and workers' parties." Contacts at various levels between the CPSU and the LCY were repeatedly emphasized. Finally, endorsement of the Soviet foreign political line on those international issues enumerated in the Declaration hardly seemed compatible with official Yugoslav nonalignment. (Full text of statement in *New Times*, Moscow, no. 4, October.)

Summing up, if the Brezhnev visit alleviated fears of impending Soviet military intervention, it hinted also that the new cooperation tactic had been devised to better serve "the long-time Soviet attempt to re-absorb [Yugoslavia] into the Eastern bloc" (*World Today*, December).

China and Albania. Normalization of Yugoslav-Chinese relations made progress when Foreign Secretary Mirko Tepavac visited Peking on 9-15 June at the invitation of the government. The communiqué after talks with Premier Chou En-lai stated they had been conducted in "an atmosphere of frankness, understanding, and friendship" (*Borba*, 16 June). The Tepavac visit and reports of an impending Chou En-lai trip to some of the Balkan countries, including Yugoslavia, precipitated hostile comments by the East European press. In mid-August, the Hungarian paper *Magyar Hirlap* charged building of a Chinese-backed and anti-Soviet "Tirana-Belgrade-Bucharest" axis (which *Borba* on 16 August dismissed as "hallucination"). The East German *Berliner Zeitung* accused the Chinese of striving to "drive a wedge between socialist states in the Balkans." A little later in an interview given to the Zagreb daily *Vjesnik* (28 August), Chou En-lai warmly praised "the Yugoslav people" but added: "We are far away from Europe and, as you know, one of our popular proverbs says: 'Distant water cannot quench fire.' " In early September, a Chinese economic delegation headed by the light industry minister toured Yugoslavia and discussed increased trade relations. Yugoslavia was among co-sponsors of the Albanian resolution on admission of the People's Republic of China into the United Nations.

On 5 February, Yugoslavia and Albania decided to raise their respective diplomatic missions to embassy level. This event signified a formal end to over 20 years of hostile relations. In his opening speech to the Sixth Congress of the Albanian Party of Labor, First Secretary Enver Hoxha stated that relations with Yugoslavia were "developing in a good-neighborly spirit," despite "known ideological differences" (quoted in *Borba*, 2 November).

Eastern Europe. Yugoslavia maintained bilateral relations with all states of Eastern Europe in the form of numerous trade, scientific, and cultural contacts. Trade with the countries of the Soviet-Bloc accounted for about one-third of Yugoslav exports and imports. Sales to these countries increased by 17 per cent during the first nine months of 1971 (*Quarterly Economic Review*, no. 4). There existed, however, differences with respect to individual state and party relations. Closest ties existed with Romania, which Foreign Secretary Tepavac visited in May and Tito on 23-24 November. The communiqué mentioned "identity or great proximity of attitudes and viewpoints." Both sides favored accelerated preparations for a European security conference, called for elimination of foreign bases, withdrawal of troops to national borders, and dissolution of military blocs, and condemned U.S. intervention in Vietnam. (*Borba*, 26 November.) Polish Premier Piotr Jaroszewicz came to Yugoslavia in late October. Yugoslav Premier Bijedić was guest of the Hungarian government in December. High-level Polish and Hungarian party delegations toured Yugoslavia in January and February, respectively. An LCY delegation attended the Polish United Workers' Party congress in December.

Less satisfactory relations, from the party viewpoint, were those with Czechoslovakia and Bulgaria. An LCY delegation attended the congress of the Communist Party of Czechoslovakia in May but leading Yugoslav papers criticized the congress's unconditional following of Moscow's line. As for Bulgaria, no LCY delegation was present at the Tenth Congress of the Bulgarian Communist Party, held in late April, and the perennial Bulgarian treatment of Yugoslav Macedonia as part of Bulgaria caused sharp comments in the Yugoslav press.

Finally, after long stagnation Yugoslav-Greek relations improved: Foreign Secretary Tepavac made a stopover in Athens on 16 June, and the Greek undersecretary of foreign affairs visited Belgrade in early September. An official statement said that the two countries were "prepared to promote their cooperation in the political, economic, and cultural fields" (Tanyug, 10 September).

Western Europe and the United States. For both economic and political reasons, Yugoslav relations with Western Europe and especially with countries belonging to the European Economic Community were extensive. EEC members are Yugoslavia's principal trading partners, responsible for 31 per cent of exports and 40 per cent of imports (*The Economist*, 21 August). The large number of Yugoslav workers employed in the Federal Republic of Germany and Yugoslavia's interest in increasing trade and credit relations there explain the multiplicity of official contacts at different levels—involving ministers of labor, trade union officials, and business firms and including negotiations about indemnification of Yugoslav citizens stemming from World War II. Yugoslav-Italian relations, briefly disturbed in December 1970, were improved by Tito's official visit to Italy (25-29 March). In a Rome TV interview Tito declared that "relations between Yugoslavia and Italy could serve as an example of successful relations between countries with different social systems" (*Politika*, 25 March). On 29 March Tito met in the Vatican with Pope Paul VI, thus becoming the first communist chief of state to do so. On that occasion Tito reportedly made a strong case for the Arabs in the Middle East conflict (*New York Times*, 30 March). French Premier Jacques Chaban-Delmas and Foreign Minister Maurice Schumann paid an official visit to Yugoslavia on 22-24 April. The joint communiqué stated that the visit had "consolidated in a notable manner the traditional Yugoslav-French friendship." The two sides mentioned interest in the proposed conference on security and cooperation in Europe and stressed the situation in the Mediterranean as of great importance for peace. (Tanyug, 24 April.) A few days later the Yugoslav Army chief-of-staff, General Victor Bubanj, left for a visit to France. French Defense Minister Michel Debré visited Yugoslavia in early October.

The LCY also maintained contacts with the various West European communist parties, particularly those of Italy (high-level talks in April and June) and Spain (the same in May and September). An LCY delegation attended in March the Twentieth Congress of the Belgian Communist Party.

Yugoslav-U.S. relations were dominated by Tito's state visit to the United States (27 October-2 November). The two Nixon-Tito meetings were regarded as examples of "the era of negotiation" ushered in by the Nixon Administration. The joint statement issued at the end of the talks spoke of a "cordial, frank, and friendly atmosphere" of discussions and mentioned both "spheres of agreement" and "differences of opinion" (implying particularly the war in Vietnam and the Arab-Israeli conflict). A wide range of topics was discussed: Yugoslav-U.S. relations, European security, the Middle East, South and Southeast Asia, Africa, the developing countries, the international monetary situation. The statement mentioned that "President Tito acquainted President Nixon with his impressions from his recent meetings with the leaders of various countries," while "President Nixon confirmed the U.S. interest in Yugoslavia's independent and nonaligned position and policy." The two presidents also agreed to intensify economic relations, including industrial cooperation, joint investments, and cooperation in third markets. (*Ibid.*, 30 October.)[4]

A series of talks at government and business levels on economic topics was held during the year. The Yugoslav side was especially interested in obtaining new loans for various commercial and industrial projects, and in improving its negative balance of trade with the United States (during the first four months of 1971, Yugoslav exports to the United States increased by almost 21 per cent, but imports rose by 250 per cent (*Privredni Pregled*, Belgrade, 7 June). In September, a "study group" of the Yugoslav Army visited the United States at the invitation of the Defense Department.

The Nonaligned and Other Parts of the World. The official Yugoslav policy of nonalignment was promoted by Tito's highly publicized trips in October to Iran (13-17), India (17-20), and Egypt (20-21). On 18 October, Tito met with Indian Prime Minister Indira Gandhi, with whom he discussed his talks with Pakistan President Yahya Khan during his visit to Iran. Mrs. Gandhi

---

[4]After an extensive tour of the United States, including the space center at Houston and the Douglas aircraft factory in Long Beach, California, Tito visited Canada (2-7 November) and then the United Kingdom (7-8 November), where he held talks with Premier Pierre Trudeau and Prime Minister Edward Heath, respectively.

totally rejected the Pakistan viewpoint on the problems of East Pakistan (Bangladesh) and India-Pakistan relations, and Tito declared himself "impressed by her arguments and by the fullness and correctness of the picture she depicted." Both sides agreed on the necessity to make more concrete the decisions of the 1970 summit conference of nonaligned countries at Lusaka, Zambia (*YICA*, 1970, p. 112). They criticized the fact that the principle of unanimity among the 77-member group of developing countries made the documents they adopted "pale and insufficiently binding" (*Borba*, 19 October).

Tito's visit to Cairo (his nineteenth, and his second meeting with Egyptian President Anwar al-Sadat) resulted in his reiteration of full support for Egypt in its conflict with Israel. Tito declared that "the realization of a just and lasting solution [of the Middle East crisis] required elimination of all consequences of Israeli aggression and the withdrawal of all Israeli troops from Arab territories occupied after 4 June 1967, as well as the restoration of rights to the Palestinian people" (*ibid.*, 23 October).

Yugoslav interest in promoting bilateral trade relations and economic cooperation, as well as in implementing resolutions of the nonaligned summit at Lusaka, were manifest in the exchange of many delegations with Asian, African, and Latin American countries. In June, the Indonesian foreign minister and after him the Cambodian (representing the Peking-based government-in-exile) visited Yugoslavia; in September, a Japanese Diet delegation toured the country; at the end of October, Singapore Prime Minister Lee Kuan Yew came to Belgrade; and in early December, the Malaysian deputy prime minister had economic talks with Yugoslav officials. The same was true with regard to Africa: representatives of the Angolan People's Liberation Movement visited Yugoslavia in June and met with Yugoslav military leaders; the same month, talks on nonalignment took place in Algeria; the Sudanese defense minister visited Yugoslavia in July; Zambian and Tanzanian government delegations were in Yugoslavia during September; and Yugoslav Defense Minister Nikola Ljubičić toured several African countries in November. Two high-level Yugoslav trade and political delegations visited Latin American countries in July (Argentina, Uruguay, Brazil, Peru, and Venezuela) and in October (Panama, Peru and Brazil). The Chilean foreign minister paid a visit to Yugoslavia in May.

Contacts at different levels also were maintained with North Korea (whose first economic delegation arrived in Yugoslavia in May) and with North Vietnam. On 22 May, Yugoslavia and the Provisional Revolutionary Government of South Vietnam agreed to establish diplomatic relations at the ambassadorial level.

Publications. The chief organs of the LCY are *Komunist*, a weekly magazine, and *Socijalizam*, a theoretical monthly. The important daily newspapers are *Borba* (Belgrade) and *Vjesnik* (Zagreb), organs of the SAWPY bodies of Serbia and Croatia respectively, and *Politika* (Belgrade). The *Vjesnik* publishing house also puts out a weekly, *Vjesnik u srijedu*. The Yugoslav communist youth organization publishes a weekly, *Mladost*. Tanyug is the official Yugoslav news agency.

Milorad M. Drachkovitch

WESTERN EUROPE

Austria

The Communist Party of Austria (Kommunistische Partei Österreichs; KPÖ) was founded on 3 November 1918. A pro-Chinese Marxist-Leninist party was formed in 1966. The KPÖ enjoys legal status, but continues to play an insignificant role in Austrian political affairs. In the general elections of 10 October 1971 the KPÖ polled 1.4 percent (1970: 1.1 percent) of the total vote (*Volksstimme* 12 October). This was insufficient for KPÖ representation in the Austrian parliament, in which the KPÖ has been without seats since 1959.

The KPÖ did not publish membership figures in 1971. But Franz Marek (see below) estimated that membership had declined from 25,000 in 1970 to 15,000 (*Politique Aujourd'hui*, Paris, February). The population of Austria is 7,400,000 (estimated 1970).

The KPÖ continues to experience difficulties as a result of the rift within the party that arose following the invasion of Czechoslovakia. In 1971 the schism contributed not only to a decline in party membership, but produced a complicated picture of the communist movement in Austria. In effect there exist in Austria two communist parties. One of these is the KPÖ. The other, headed by former KPÖ members Franz Marek and Ernst Fischer, is composed of the "progressive" faction that was expelled from the KPÖ during 1970 (see *YICA*, 1971, pp. 119-123). The Marek group did not believe that conditions in Austria permitted "the formation of an autonomous Marxist-Leninist party" in 1971 (*Wiener Tagebuch*, February).

Consistent with the program of the party's Twenty-first Congress (1970), "principled criticism of modern state monopoly capital" remains the basis of the KPÖ's "ideological-political struggle" (Hans Kalt, *Pravda*, 25 May). Although this view is basically shared by the Marek group, his faction is equally concerned with stressing the "basic principles of independence, sovereignty, and equal rights" of the individual parties within the communist movement. In contrast to the KPÖ, Marek and his supporters continue to oppose the invasion of Czechoslovakia and to condemn Soviet domination of the international communist movement and KPÖ subservience to the politics of the Communist Party of the Soviet Union (CPSU) (*Wiener Tagebuch*, February, and *Volksstimme*, 13 March). Contrary to the Marek group, the KPÖ opposes joint action with the Austrian Socialist Party (Sozialistische Partei Österreichs; SPÖ), and condemns the Marek faction as "an appendage of the establishment" that systematically defames "the communist movement" (*Weg und Ziel*, April; *Wiener Tagebuch*, September and October).

The Communist Youth of Austria (Kommunistische Jugend Österreichs; KJÖ) is closely associated with the KPÖ and provides a major source of new party members. The KJÖ was founded in May 1970 to replace the party's Free Austrian Youth (Freie Österreichische Jugend; FÖJ), that supports the Marek faction. On the occasion of its first anniversary, the KJÖ was praised as "the logical conclusion" to the ideological struggle within the KPÖ. After a year in operation it had increased its membership and "won itself a solid, clearly defined place among the organized youth" of Austria. The KJÖ conducted more than 40 actions, supporting "reform" of the Austrian army, "freedom" for U.S. communist Angela Davis, and U.S. withdrawal from Southeast Asia. During the year the KJÖ collected 41,000 shillings for "medical supplies" for Indochina communist forces (*Volksstimme*, 12 March, 11 May). Another youth group, the Society of Democratic Students (VDS), also favors "a political alliance with the KPÖ." This was only possible, however, after the VDS eliminated the "right wing" (Marek and Fischer supporters) from its leadership at a special plenary session in November 1970 (*Weg und Ziel*, February).

Prior to the 1971 general elections in October the Marek faction supported formation of the "Aggressive Left" party, composed of FÖJ members. The "Aggressive Left" was an attempt to "draw the dissatisfied and discontented segments of the younger generation out of political inactivity." The Marek faction held that its formation would provide one of "the crystallization points for all those who want to work for a credible leftist alternative for Austria." (*Wiener Tagebuch*, October.)

The KPÖ-controlled Trade Union Unity organization (Gewerkschaftliche Einheit; GE) continues to work within the influential Austrian Trade Union League in an effort to influence trade union members (*ibid.*, June). Reflecting the schism within the KPÖ, the GE experienced a split in 1971 led by Marek supporter Egon Kodicek. In June Kodicek formed the "Study Group for Trade Union Unity," asserting that the GE rejected the "principles of autonomy and independence" (*Die Presse*, Vienna, 4 June; *Weg und Ziel*, June).

KPÖ and KJÖ members are active in several auxiliary organizations, such as the Austrian Peace Council, the League of Democratic Women, and the Austrian-Soviet Society. In an effort to generate support for diplomatic recognition of the German Democratic Republic (GDR), KPÖ members founded in October an "Austria-GDR Society" (*Volksstimme*, 31 October).

Leadership and Organization. The KPÖ did not hold a party congress in 1971, and no changes were announced in the party's leadership. Franz Muhri remained KPÖ chairman. The members of the Politburo are Muhri, Friedl Fürnberg, Kurt Hager, Leopold Horak, Hans Kalt, Franz Karger, Franz Leitner, Alois Peter, Erwin Scharf and Walter Wachs. The Secretariat is composed of Muhri, Kalt, Scharf, Wachs, and Heinrich Fritz. Central Committee secretaries are Kalt and Scharf. The Central Committee itself is composed of 64 members. The Chairman of the GE is Anton Hofer.

Party Internal Affairs. In an article commemorating the 1970 KPÖ congress, Politburo member Hans Kalt pointed to the alleged defeat of the Marek and Fischer group that had opposed the "principles of democratic centralism" and endorsed "open anti-Sovietism" (*Pravda*, 25 May 1971). Throughout 1971, KPÖ leaders provided numerous assurances that the party had "closed its ranks." But the attention devoted to assuring its members that the actions of the "rightist opportunists" had failed and that "decisive steps toward consolidation" had been taken belied the "numerous difficulties" that were still to be overcome (*Volksstimme*, 13 March).

The steps taken by the KPÖ in 1970 to modify its condemnation of the invasion of Czechoslovakia were almost completed in 1971. The Central Committee approved a resolution on 11 March in which the "revisionists" in the party (the Marek faction) were condemned for having sown "confusion" within the KPÖ with the "aid of the bourgeois mass media" (*ibid.*). The resolution, that was not unanimously approved (*Die Presse*, 25 March), rejected "essential formulations" in the initial condemnatory KPÖ declaration of 22 August 1968 as "incorrect", pointing out that "rightist opportunists" had exploited the intervention in an attempt to declare the Soviet Union guilty of "imperialism" and "aggression." The majority of the KPÖ members, the resolution stated, regarded the intervention as "necessary in order to protect socialism in Czechoslovakia, the security of the socialist countries, and world peace" (*Volksstimme*, 13 March).

In August party chairman Muhri acknowledged that there remained "a difference of views" within the KPÖ concerning the Czechoslovak events." But he stressed that events subsequent to the intervention had provided justification for the decision. "The decisive factor," he believed, was the "positive political solution of the problem by consolidating socialism, developing the economy, raising living standards, and advancing socialist democracy" in Czechoslovakia. For this reason the KPÖ now "categorically rejected the Fischer and Marek orientation on a break with the world Communist movement and the CPSU." (*WMR*, August.) While the KPÖ consistently criticized the "anti-Sovietism" of the Marek group und accused its members of becoming "neo-Trotskyites" (Franz Muhri, *Rudé Právo*, Prague, 13 February), Franz Marek castigated Muhri as a "mini-Černík" (*Politique Aujourd'hui*, February) and the *Wiener Tagebuch*, edited by Marek, kept up its criticism of the KPÖ.

The defeat of the "revisionist forces" permitted the KPÖ "to reassume its role as a revolutionary party of the working class" (Muhri, *Rudé Právo*, 13 February). But the KPÖ considered it necessary to strengthen the party as fast as possible. It conducted a concentrated membership drive in the spring aimed at recruiting "young people and employed workers" (*Weg und Ziel*, February). The party reported the enlistment of 547 new members, of whom more than 64 percent were blue-collar and white-collar workers and more than one half under thirty years of age (*WMR*, September). In a plenary session of the Central Committee on 14 October all members were called upon to discuss preparations for a new membership campaign scheduled for early 1972 (*Weg und Ziel*, November).

The discussion within the Society of Democratic Students concerning its proper role in the communist movement in Austria also reflected continuing difficulties. Although the "right wing" (the Marek group) was forced out of the VDS leadership in November 1970, "ideological differences were not reconciled." The VDS was particularly concerned with three issues: (1) the proper policy on higher education, (2) the question of the "character" of the SPÖ (Sozialistische Partei Österreichs; SPÖ) government and of VDS policy vis-à-vis the "Social Democratic Student Union" (VSStO), and (3) the proper position in the conflict of the KPÖ with the *Wiener Tagebuch* group and the FÖJ (*ibid.*, February).

The conclusions drawn by the VDS coincided with the position of the KPÖ. The VDS would seek to achieve "an alliance with the working class, while not talking abstract nonsense about 'reciprocal action between higher education and society.'" The VSStO, it believed, pursued "an opportunistic policy" in concert with the SPÖ that aimed at concealing "capitalistic rationalization." At the same time, however, the VDS would seek to "struggle jointly" with the VSStO. The VDS did not endorse phrasing questions of party policy in terms of "for" or "against" the Soviet Union, or in terms of "for" or "against" the intervention in Czechoslovakia. But it did support "a political alliance with the KPÖ." (*Ibid.*)

The KPÖ recognized that there were difficulties in the relationship between the party and intellectuals at the universities, and acknowledged that the responsibility was mainly the party's. But it warned that Marxism-Leninism was not a "world view" to be isolated from the tactics and strategy necessary for its "concrete realization." The KPÖ urged that students assist the KPÖ with "enterprise work," and with the "political struggle" at the universities. The party hoped to bring as many students as possible into the "revolutionary workers' movement…against the unity of state and big capital" and "where possible to neutralize where one cannot mobilize." (*Ibid.*, November.)

Domestic Attitudes and Activities. The KPÖ's basic program of action was defined by Politburo member Erwin Scharf at the Central Committee meeting on 19-20 January as "the struggle against the rising cost of living, to stop the price spiral and to reform the tax system." The aim was a "redistribution of the material benefits created by society in favor of the working people." (*Volksstimme*, 21 January.) The KPÖ viewed itself as the "only organized anti-capitalist leftist force" in Austria (*ibid.*, 2 February; TASS, 17 September).

The KPO devoted primary attention to the October elections. The watchword of the party conference on 27 February, attended by 460 delegates, was "Strengthen the Communist Party of Austria! Communists—to the Parliament!" (TASS, 27 February). The KPÖ believed that it stood an excellent chance to win seats in parliament because of the passage of a new election law in 1970, and because the Twenty-first Congress had ostensibly solved the crisis within the party (*Volksstimme*, 21 January). The KPÖ concentrated on "a struggle against creeping inflation [and] taxes that are burdening the population: a struggle for the renewal of democracy, which is naturally possible only if the power of big capitalism is suppressed" (Muhri, *Rudé Právo*, 13 February).

The election platform was issued on 11 September. It opposed inflation and cartels, supported housing construction, urged reduction of military service, the elimination of educational and political privilege, and condemned the influx of "foreign capital that places Austria at the mercy of monetary crisis." Support was also accorded a price freeze, a redistribution of wealth through tax reform, equality for women, automatic pensioning, measures against pollution, and agricultural reforms. It also endorsed active neutrality, international disarmament and peace, and establishment of a system of European security (*Volksstimme*, 11, 24 September and 9 October).

The KPÖ supported the organization of "action and movements... which affect the broadest masses" (Muhri, *Horizont*, East Berlin, May). Sixty percent of the party functionaries led activities "in factories, offices, and official agencies." Party members were urged to participate in discussions, to write leaflets and to contribute articles to "enterprise" newspapers concerning wage questions, "enterprise council" activities and issues related to "socialism, freedom, and democracy." The GE and the KPÖ were to join efforts in the enterprises while maintaining separate organizations. The resolution of the KPÖ conference of 303 enterprise functionaries on 3 April declared that all actions taken "in the interest of enterprise employees and within the trade unions" were to be linked to "political indoctrination, consolidation of [the] party, recruitment of new members, and promotion of [the] party press" (*Weg und Ziel*, June).

During the election campaign the KPÖ consistently condemned the SPÖ policy of "social partnership" between "big capitalist bosses and the association of Austrian trade unions." The KPÖ offered the alternative of "struggling for the socialist development of Austria" (Hans Kalt, *Pravda*, 25 May). The SPÖ, asserted Politburo member Walter Wachs, pursued reform policies "that do not affect the capitalist system" and obscured the "class character of Austria's society" (*WMR*, September).

The KPÖ received 60,705 votes (1.4 percent). This represented an increase of 38 percent over the total received in 1970. Although the party did not win any parliament seats, the election results were considered testimony to successful reestablishment of "unity and action" within the party (*Volksstimme*, 25 November). Particular tribute was paid to the "thousands of new worker voters" and the "young communists and members of the Communist Youth of Austria" (*ibid.*, 22 October). But while the KPÖ viewed the results as a major step "in the transformation of the capitalist exploitive order" (*ibid.*, 25 November), the *Wiener Tagebuch* concluded that the KPÖ "would have had deputies in parliament by now if it had not sacrificed its autonomy on the altar of normalization" with the Soviet Union (*Wiener Tagebuch*, September and November).

Following the election, party goals for the forthcoming period were announced at the plenary meeting of the KPÖ Central Committee on 14 October. In accordance with the resolution of the Twenty-first Congress, the party would continue to devote attention to the "problems in the enterprises and communities" and to "rights and demands of the working groups," and would "turn more strongly to the younger generation" (*Weg und Ziel*, November). It would also criticize "state-monopolist capitalism," the "capitalist integration policy of the SPÖ," and the alleged "superiority of socialism" (*Weg und Ziel*, 25 November). This was especially important because the SPÖ would not attempt to "restrict the boundless capitalist profit economy," "counter inflation," or contribute to tax reform. It would "continue the burdens of the working population through 'unpopular measures' in the interest of strengthening capitalism" (*Volksstimme*, 15 October).

International Views and Positions. The successful reestablishment of unity within the KPÖ was reflected in the party's endorsement of the "international class struggle" at the side of the Soviet Union (*Volksstimme*, 25 November 1971), which, moreover, did not "contradict the principles of the independence of each party and non-interference in internal affairs" (Muhri, *Pravda*, 13 July).

Paralleling the CPSU position on foreign policy issues, the KPÖ endorsed Soviet emphasis on "broad pan-European economic and scientific and technical cooperation" (*ibid*.), and rejected both criticism of the Czechoslovak party leadership and future discussion of the events of 1968 (*Volksstimme*, 13 March). The party praised the "determination in the class struggle" evidenced by the new party leadership in Poland that had successfully eliminated "confusion and ideological resignation" produced by "bureaucratic inaccessibility of individual leadership cadres" (*Weg und Ziel*, November).

The contention that there existed a "Brezhnev doctrine" was rejected by Central Committee member Heinrich Fritz (*Volksstimme*, 11 April). The KPÖ welcomed Brezhnev's endorsement of mutual and balanced force reductions in Europe and accused the United States of opposing such discussions. The positive response to Brezhnev's proposal indicated that the "wish for disarmament and détente" was very strong in the world today and that even NATO could no longer afford to reject the Soviet proposal as "unacceptable" (*ibid*., 19 May).

The existence of NATO was condemned by the KPÖ (*ibid*., 23 June) together with an asserted NATO violation of Austrian neutrality in April for shipping tanks from West Germany to Italy through Austria (*ibid*., 20 May). The KPÖ also denounced the U.S. Central Intelligence Agency for allegedly maintaining "ties" with the Austrian Defense Department (*ibid*., 21 March). The KPÖ welcomed the West German treaties with the Soviet Union and Poland and urged their ratification (*IB*, no. 5-6). The Berlin agreement was also endorsed (*Weg und Ziel*, October). At the same time Muhri emphasized that the treaties themselves "do not change the substance of West German imperialism" as a threat to Austria's neutrality (Muhri, *Rudé Právo*, 13 February).

The KPÖ condemned U.S. intervention in Vietnam (*Volksstimme*, 9 April), Austria's relations with West Germany and the United States, and opposed any connection with the European Economic Community. The KPÖ also opposed any increase in military expenditures in Austria at a time when "there are concrete prospects for a positive solution to the problems of European security" (*Horizont*, May). Hans Kalt viewed Brezhnev's visit to France in October as a major step toward "further consolidation of peace" (*Volksstimme*, 31 October). Erwin Scharf viewed the "anti-communist" attitude of the SPÖ as a decisive hindrance to the "full utilization of the possibilities" offered by neutrality "in the interests of peace and European security." He also endorsed a European security conference and recognition of the German Democratic Republic (*ibid*., 25 November).

The KPÖ welcomed Austria's recognition of China (*ibid*., 28 May) and China's admission to the United Nations (*ibid*., 28 October). The party supported "every effort" toward a "new unity" with China (*WMR*, August), but condemned the Chinese Communist Party and urged the "rallying of all revolutionary and anti-imperialist forces" to oppose its "splitting" activities (*Volksstimme*, 11 April).

International Activities and Party Contacts. The KPÖ praised the 24th Congress of the CPSU as a "striking demonstration of the international solidarity and growing unity of the world communist movement" that would contribute to "stronger party contacts and fraternal relations" (Muhri, *Pravda*, 13 July). Of special importance were meetings with the "fraternal parties in capitalist Europe." Particularly "closer links" with the (West) German Communist Party (DKP) had provided the KPÖ useful information concerning its experiences with the Social Democratic Party in West Germany. This exchange of information was facilitated by lectures given by visiting party leaders (*WMR*, August).

KPÖ representatives made numerous visits during the year. In February Hans Kalt visited Warsaw to interview Deputy Foreign Minister Adam Willman (*Volksstimme*, 23 February). A KPÖ delegation headed by Alois Peter attended the congress of the Bulgarian Communist Party in April (*ibid.*, 20 April). A Polish delegation visited Vienna in May for the first anniversary of the KPÖ youth organization, KJÖ (*ibid.*, 18 May). In June a delegation from the Rumanian Communist Party visited Vienna (AGERPRES, 11 June). Eighty members of the KPÖ involved with the publication of the party organs visited the editorial offices of *Népszabadság* in Budapest in October (*Volksstimme*, 28 October). A KPÖ delegation also attended the "Second Congress in Self-Administration" held by the League of Communists of Yugoslavia in May (*Weg und Ziel*, July). KJÖ member Fritz Podolsky attended the First Youth Conference of the West German party, held at Hannover in May (*Weg und Ziel*, July). At the end of the month KJÖ chairman Otto Podolsky attended the Ninth Parliament of the Free German Youth of the GDR (*ibid.*). In the same month KJÖ representatives were sent to the conference of the West European Youth Organization, in Mannheim. At that meeting resolutions were passed condemning NATO and endorsing a European security conference (*ibid.*).

Franz Muhri led a KPÖ delegation that attended the 24th Congress of the CPSU. His evaluation of the congress stressed that Soviet foreign policy was in full accordance with Austria's national interests, neutrality, and independence (TASS, 13 April). In June the KPÖ was represented at the congress of the Social Unity Party of (East) Germany (SED) (*Volksstimme*, 26 June). Erwin Scharf was a guest delegate at the congress of the DKP at Düsseldorf in November. In his remarks he praised the DKP for supporting ratification of West Germany's treaties with Poland and Russia "in the interest of relaxation of tensions and security in Europe" (*ibid.*, 25 November). A four-member delegation of the SED, headed by Politburo member Erich Mückenberger, met with KPÖ leaders in November in Vienna (*ibid.*, 1 December).

Friedl Fürnberg led a KPÖ delegation to Prague in May for the congress of the Communist Party of Czechoslovakia. Fürnberg lauded "international solidarity" and the leadership of the Soviet Union. But he also stressed that "communist parties must find their own way based on concrete conditions in their countries; however, not in national isolation but [by] drawing on the experience of all communist parties." (CETEKA, Czechoslovak News Agency, 27 May). In March, Fürnberg, Franz Muhri, and Erwin Scharf visited the Prague editorial offices of *World Marxist Review* at the invitation of the Czechoslovak party (*WMR*, April). In November a delegation from the Communist Party of Greece met with KPÖ Politburo members in Vienna. Both parties endorsed efforts to "secure the unity of the international communist and workers' movement on the basis of Marxism-Leninism." (*Volksstimme*, 28 November).

Publications. The official organ of the KPÖ is the Vienna daily newspaper *Volksstimme*. Its circulation is estimated at 40,000 on weekdays and 70,000 for the Sunday edition. Politburo member Hans Kalt is the editor in chief. The theoretical organ *Weg und Ziel* appears monthly; Hans Kalt heads the "editorial collective" in charge of this journal.

In May Kalt pointed out that the "right opportunist group" headed by Marek and Fischer, had been forced out of the "particularly strong positions in the party press" from which they had disseminated "erroneous views ... not in accordance with party decisions" (Hans Kalt, *Pravda*, 25 May). During 1971, however, Marek continued to edit and publish the independently financed *Wiener Tagebuch* on a monthly basis. The journal was founded in 1969 to provide a platform for those KPÖ members who disagreed with the KPÖ's domestic and foreign policies.

* * *

The Marxist-Leninist Party of Austria (Marxistische-Leninistische Partei Österreichs; M-LPÖ) was established in May 1966. It is pro-Chinese and enjoys legal status. Its membership numbers approximately 500. The M-LPÖ is headed by Franz Strobl as first secretary. The party's headquarters are in Vienna. (See *YICA*, 1971, pp. 125-26.)

The M-LPÖ maintains contacts with Marxist-Leninist groups in West Germany and has a particularly close relationship with the West German KPD/ML (Communist Party of Germany/Marxist-Leninist), which was formed at approximately the same time. In January a sizable portion of the M-LPÖ organ, *Rote Fahne*, was devoted to the activities of its West German counterpart.

The M-LPÖ scheduled its Second Congress for the spring of 1971. Although no information was available on the results of the congress, *Rote Fahne* wrote at the beginning of the year that the congress would deal with the following points: (1) analysis of party activity since its First Congress, held in March 1969, (2) questions of organization and training, (3) current problems of mass work and cooperation with leftists groups, (4) problems of proletarian internationalism, (5) questions of financial support, (6) election of a new Central Committee, central commissions, and party leadership, and (7) resolutions and messages of greeting (*Rote Fahne*, no. 125).

Stanford University   Dennis L. Bark

Belgium

The Communist movement in Belgium is represented by three parties. The oldest and largest of these is the Communist Party of Belgium (Parti Communiste de Belgique; PCB), founded in 1921. The others are a second Communist Party of Belgium (hereafter referred to as PCB-II), formed in December 1963 by dissidents from the PCB, and the Marxist-Leninist Communist Party of Belgium (Parti Communiste Marxiste-Leniniste de Belgique; PCMLB), established in November 1967 by dissidents from the PCB-II as the Communist Party (Marxist-Leninist) of Belgium until the current name was adopted on 28 June 1970. In addition to these three parties, there is a Trotskyist movement represented by the Socialist Young Guards (Jeunes Gardes Socialistes; JGS), a group aligned with the United Secretariat of the Fourth International. All four organizations enjoy legal status.

Although none of the above parties publishes figures, Western sources estimate that the PCB has between 11,000 and 12,500 members; the PCB-II and PCMLB are believed to have 50 and 150 members, respectively; while the JGS has a growing membership, which in 1971 was estimated at more than 500. The population of Belgium is about 10 million (estimated 1970).

Two of the communist parties, the PCB and the PCB-II, participated in parliamentary elections of 31 March 1968. For the Chamber of Representatives, the PCB polled 3.3 per cent of the total vote, losing one seat but retaining five. In the Senate, the PCB obtained 3.5 per cent of the vote, keeping two seats. No PCB-II candidates were elected. On 24 September 1971, Premier Gaston Eyskens dissolved parliament and called for elections on 7 November which advanced the normal date from May 1972. His government was returned to power. The PCB obtained 163,785 votes or 3.2 per cent and kept its five seats out of 212 in the Chamber of Representatives. It lost one of two seats in the 106-member Senate. The PCB-II lost all races which it had entered.

The PCB was the only communist party to participate in local elections on 11 October 1970. With the exception of western Hainaut, it "suffered reversals."

The PCB. Organization and Leadership. Since 1966 the PCB has been divided into two branches, Walloon and Flemish, each of which directs implementation of policy in its own region. The leaderships meet every year to make joint decisions, with each having veto power. The ratio of Walloon to Flemish members in the party, however, is five to one. All PCB parliamentary representatives are Walloons. Party policy of a national and international nature is decided at PCB congresses, normally held once a year, with lapses in 1969 and 1970.

The PCB leadership during 1971 was elected by the Twentieth Congress, held 19-21 March at Charleroi. A new 60-member Central Committee unanimously returned Marc Drumaux as its president. Vice-presidents Jean Terfve (President of the Walloon branch) and Jef Turf (president of the Flemish branch) also were reelected. The Politbureau comprises 12 members. The Secretariat includes Urbain Coussement, Albert de Coninck, Claude Renard, and L. Van Geyt. Jef Turf succeeded Jan Debrouwere as director of the communist press and political director of the party's Flemish language weekly, *De Rode Vaan*. Robert Dussart was appointed political director of the PCB French-language weekly, *Le Drapeau Rouge,* succeeding Claude Renard.

The PCB directs a youth organization, the Communist Youth of Belgium (Jeunesse Communiste de Belgique; JCB), and a student group called the National Union of Communist Students (Union Nationale des Etudiants Communistes). the party does not have its own labor union, but exerts some influence over the largest trade union, the General Workers' Federation of Belgium (Fédération Générale du Travail de Belgique; FGTB).

Domestic Views and Policies. The PCB in 1971 continued to advocate united action with other left-wing forces and focused its attention on the Belgian Socialist Party (Parti Socialiste Belge; PSB). The latter's former president, Léo Collard, had originally called for a regrouping of "progressive" forces (*rassemblement progressiste*) in May 1969 which the PCB endorsed and then adopted as one of its major themes. While pushing for unity, the PCB has nevertheless been extremely critical of PSB participation in the coalition government and frequently attacked its right-wing "reformist" elements. An article analyzing the work of the PCB Twentieth Congress, pointed out:

> We know today what big capital has obtained from Socialist participation in the government.... Its consequence is not to enhance the workers' struggle but to contain and delay it.... One of the major questions is to know how to distinguish the role of the right and the left of the PSB. (*Les Cahiers Marxistes*, June-August.)

While PCB President Drumaux reproached the Socialists for their lack of cohesion and militancy, he said it was necessary for communists to achieve a more intensive involvement, especially in workers' centers. He went on: "We must tell the Socialist and trade union left very frankly that it must agree to cooperate with us without gimmicks. For them to pretend not to hear us on the pretext that our electoral impact has remained insufficient[1] would be nothing more than a wait-and-see attitude, whereas the grand bourgeoisie is increasing its attacks against the workers." (*Ibid.*) In a 1 May speech Drumaux raised the question, "Is the Socialist Party going to continue in its international affairs to implement the policy of the bourgeoisie, or is it going to agree to go at least as far as Willy Brandt did last year?" (He chided the PSB for not sending a delegation to the congress of the Soviet party in Moscow.) Drumaux added that, if there could be no serious planning for a *rassemblement progressiste* at this time, the PCB would participate in concerted action with all the forces of the Left. (*Le Drapeau Rouge*, 7 May.)

In his report to the Central Committee during 2-3 October on the forthcoming elections, Drumaux accused the government of "laying a trap for the nation" by using the PSB to maintain illusions of the working class, weaken trade unions, and destroy prospects for an alternative left-oriented political solution. He said that to vote Socialist would represent a "step backward" in the struggle against monopolies and only reduce the chances for a progressive front. He asserted that to vote communist was the only way to vote for a prospective alliance of progressives, "because the socialist left needs a communist victory in order to get out of the mire into which it is presently sinking," (*Ibid.*, 8-14 October.) A broad political alliance capable of following a new policy against capitalist forces, which the PCB had called for at its congress, did not materialize. Relations with the PSB under its new president Edmond Leburton had not improved during the year. As a result the PCB also concentrated its efforts on the workers' movement and, at its congress, resolved to resist

[1]The PCB obtained approximately 3.2 per cent of the vote in the November parliamentary elections, compared with the 27 per cent for the PSB.

any attempts to weaken trade union organizations, i.e., attempts at integration by big business and its Social Democrat allies.

Drumaux spoke at great length of dangers in the workers' right-wing as well as dangers inherent in fighting right reformist elements. The PCB looked to the workers for implementation of its strategy of counter-power which had been developed in March 1970 at a discussion forum. (See YICA, 1971, p. 129) At the PCB congress, Drumaux stressed the importance of this concept which, he explained, represented a logical extension of worker control. It calls for establishment of action centers against monopolies, but should not be limited to enterprise framework. It should be applied to community councils, public institutions, universities and to the trade unions, especially the FGTB. Drumaux advocated this strategy, because "what is lacking is a determination by all opponents of big capital to unite on the basis of concrete action and draft a common program ... Yet this is the road to follow if opposition to power gradually is to be built up in different fields." (Les Cahiers Marxistes, July-August.)

The long-standing regional and language disputes were somewhat mitigated during the year due to recent constitutional changes which gave the regions of Wallonia, Flanders, and Brussels some degree of autonomy and significant powers in cultural and economic affairs. The PCB, which had opposed the amendments, alleged that the government was making a systematic effort to avoid implementing the principles set forth by the revised Constitution, namely, granting of real power to the regions had been put off indefinitely by means of political maneuvers. (Le Drapeau Rouge, 8-14 October.) The views of the party were summarized in documents prepared for the Twentieth Congress: the government had refused any concession of power to the decentralized economic organs, multiplied obstacles by creating the three political-economic regions and imposed on Brussels a territorial statute which was arbitrary, politically motivated, and unpopular (Ibid., 8 January). A major address in the Chamber of Deputies by PCB spokesman L. Van Geyt reiterated these views, claiming that the "famous pacquet" had deceived the people and that measures adopted by parliament essentially eliminated cultural autonomy as well as regional economic and, hence, political power (ibid. 23 July). The PCB congress adopted resolutions expressing these sentiments.

International Views and Policies. The PCB supported policies of the Communist Party of the Soviet Union (CPSU), as reflected in Drumaux's speech at the PCB congress in March, when he stressed the importance of struggle against anti-communist and anti-Soviet campaigns that attempt to isolate communists. He said, "There cannot be any communists falling for the debate of anti-Sovietism" (ibid., 26 March). In an article appearing in the fall (ibid., 3 September), he wrote of expanding rather than reducing PCB international relations, in particular those with the communist-ruled states, and especially the Soviet Union. The PCB concept of internationalism implied a struggle for unity in the international communist movement. No center of leadership exists, according to the article. While supporting the CPSU, Drumaux maintained his party's autonomy:

> Our party is autonomous and works out its own policy.... At present, the problem is to work for international unity while respecting the principle of autonomy of each party. We want the maximum of cohesiveness. We cannot accept that one or another communist party should not participate in this common effort. We hope that our relations with the Chinese Communist Party will be reestablished. (Ibid.)

The PCB considered admission of Red China into the United Nations a serious defeat for American strategy within the UN framework and a "triumph for peace" which should lead to other victories, namely, convocation of a European security conference. At its congress, the PCB resolved to demand that the Belgian government voice its unconditional consent to earliest convening of the latter, and decided to establish district committees for action and information on European security. Resolutions called for dissolution of existing military blocs, determined opposition to

NATO, and establishment of a European security system. The PCB attached great importance to its relations with communist parties in European capitalist countries for the purpose of reinforcing joint action against international trusts dominating Common Market institutions. It called for increased exchanges between communist parties active in trade unions throughout the Common Market area, regardless of their international affiliation.

While the PCB praised domestic policies adopted by the CPSU congress, the two parties also concurred on all major international issues. They strongly endorsed the solidarity of communist parties and the international movement. However, the PCB was not willing to change its stand on the question of Czechoslovakia. It had criticized the expulsion of Alexander Dubček from the Communist Party of Czechoslovakia and expressed disapproval of the tendency which had reasserted itself after the 1968 Soviet-led invasion. (See *YICA*, 1971, pp. 130-131). When the Communist Party of Czechoslovakia released a document entitled ''Lessons Drawn from the Crisis Development in the Party and Society since the 13th Congress of the Czechoslovak Party'' which tried to justify the 1968 invasion and subsequent ''normalization,'' the PCB said that it contributed nothing new to the situation. An editorial in *Le Drapeau Rouge* (22 January) noted that the document described progress in the economic and political sectors of the country as well as in the party itself. It presented replacement of Antonín Novotný in January 1968 as a necessary act, directed also against the tendency which he had inspired. But the editorial went on to state that the intervention in August 1968 was justified with arguments which were no more convincing today than they were then, adding: ''We repeat that we leave to the Communist Party of Czechoslovakia responsibility for its acts and judgments, likewise the choice of methods of justification, which evidently implies support of the workers.''

The PCB supported the new leadership in Poland, and praised Edward Gierek for reforms he had implemented. It noted that even under the threat of new strikes Gierek had maintained calm among the labor focce and made efforts to improve living conditions (*ibid.*, 29 January). Interviews with workers in various regions in Poland cited increased contact between workers and party, improved labor conditions, and better financial conditions (*ibid.*, 11 June). Generally, however, the PCB concentrated its efforts in 1971 on domestic issues and avoided debate within its ranks on intra-party problems of other countries, particularly in Eastern Europe.

International Party Contacts. PCB Central Committee member Jean Bonnet met with a delegation from the Communist Party of Greece during 9-10 January. Representatives from the League of Communists of Yugoslavia met with PCB officials at Brussels in late January to discuss various European issues, especially possibilities for a European security conference. The PCB participated in a solidarity rally for ''the peoples of South Vietnam'' on 29 January at Brussels, with Mme. Nguyen Thi Binh as a special guest. Delegations from more than 20 communist parties attended the PCB congress on 19-21 March in Brussels. Warm greetings were extended particularly by Soviet and East European delegates. During the congress, Dr. Jef Turf held talks with the delegation of the Socialist Unity Party of (East) Germany on the need for recognition of the German Democratic Republic. The CPSU and most communist parties sent messages of congratulation to the PCB on its fiftieth anniversary 4 September.

President Marc Drumaux and Central Committee member Bob Gordower represented the PCB at the CPSU congress. Politbureau members Robert Dussart and Jan Debrouwere led a PCB delegation to Romania, 18-28 September.

Publications. The PCB publishes a weekly, *Le Drapeau Rouge,* and three times a week the four-page bulletin *PCB Informations*. The party also prints a weekly in Flemish, *De Rode Vaan*. Since March 1969 the PCB has been issuing a quarterly, *Les Cahiers Marxistes,* whose purpose is to "contribute to the clarification of the unresolved problems of socialism and the international communist movement."

* * *

The PCB-II. Internal difficulties of the 50-member PCB-II were reflected in the frequency of its publication, *La Voix du Peuple*. While during 1968 it appeared weekly with 20 pages, it had become a bimonthly in 1970, and the last issue of the year had only four pages. In 1971 it began as a four or six-page bimonthly, but then came out irregularly with an issue number but no date. The only information on party internal organization or leadership appeared in a circular advertising general meetings to be held 1 May at Antwerp with Jacques Grippa, secretary of the Central Committee, presiding; and at Brussels, under Politbureau member Jean Vercheval.

The PCB-II continued its criticism of the Chinese Communist Party leadership. When U.S. President Nixon's visit to Peking was announced, the paper commented that it was not an accident but an element of the general policy of the "neo-revisionist Maoists who seized control in the August 1966 coup." The invitation, which it called the worst aggression since Hitler, was said to signify an accord had already been concluded between the revisionists in China and the "Yankee imperialists" (*La Voix du Peuple*, no. 3.) The journal criticized the former Gomulka leadership in Poland for its revisionism and right opportunism, expressing hope that the new government would reestablish the base of democratic centralism, maintain better communications with workers, and rebuild socialism in the country. It praised some of Gierek's reforms which directly affected the workers. (*Ibid.*, January-February).

The PCMLB. The PCMLB is recognized by the Chinese Communist Party (CCP). It controls the Belgium-China Association (Association Belgique-Chine) and what appears to be a small youth group, the Marxist-Leninist Communist Youth of Belgium (Jeunesse Communiste Marxiste-Leniniste de Belgique; JCMLB). Support for the party apparently originated for the most part from the mining region of Borinage. During the year, the PCMLB adhered to strict Maoist interpretations, and its weekly organ, *Clarté*, printed articles lauding China. A 22 June letter of congratulations on the CCP's fiftieth anniversary warmly praised Mao Tse-tung for his contributions to international Marxism-Leninism and his leadership. In August, a delegation of the PCMLB Central Committee visited China and had talks with CCP Central Committee member Keng Piao. Subsequently the PCMLB Politbureau issued a number of points on which it would concentrate in its struggle for revolution. These included a stronger fight against "imperialism" and "revisionism," and improved relations among Marxist-Leninist parties throughout the world. (*Clarté*, September.)

The PCMLB had entered into negotiations with another small Maoist group, centered around the weekly *L'Exploité* and led by Jacques Trifaux. A letter sent from the PCMLB Politbureau to this organization welcomed further dialogue, providing the latter pledged to put an end to the practice of "slandering and insulting the PCMLB party and its leaders" (*ibid.*, 1-15 October).

* * *

The Trotskyist movement in Belgium is primarily represented by the Socialist Young Guards (Jeunes Gardes Socialistes; JGS — in Flemish, Socialistische Jonge Wacht; SJW), a student group which in 1969 asked to be recognized by the United Secretariat of the Fourth International as a "sympathizing organization." Its views are expressed in a weekly Brussels publication, *La Gauche*, edited by United Secretariat leader Ernest Mandel. The JGS was successful in its efforts to form a Revolutionary League of Workers (Ligue Révolutionnaire des Travailleurs; LRT), which is the official Belgian section of the United Secretariat. *La Gauche* is considered the official organ of this new group.

The International Executive Committee, statutory leadership for the United Secretariat of the Fourth International, held its third meeting since the Ninth World Congress from 21 October to 1 November. A major item on the agenda included reinforcement of the central apparatus of the Fourth International. To achieve this, financial resources were increased substantially, the Permanent Committee strengthened, and some reorganization plans adopted. (*La Gauche*, 12 November.)

American Enterprise Institute   Kay McKeough
for Public Policy Research

Cyprus

The Communist Party of Cyprus (Kommounistikon Komma Kiprou) was founded in August 1926. Outlawed in 1933, it was revived in April 1941 as the Reconstruction party of the Working People of Cyprus (Anorthotikon Komma Ergazomenou Laou Tis Kiprou; AKEL). AKEL was outlawed again in 1955, when all Greek political organizations were proscribed, but has been legal since the proclamation of the Cypriot Republic in 1959. By far the strongest and best organized political party in Cyprus, AKEL currently has between 12,000 and 14,000 members. The population of Cyprus is 636,000 (estimated 1970). Virtually all AKEL support comes from among the Greek Cypriot majority (80 per cent) on the island.

Despite the party's overall strength and the generally favorable attitude of Archbishop Makarios, the president of the republic, AKEL has never held any cabinet posts and, for tactical reasons, has chosen to understate its influence at the government level in recent years. In the July 1970 parliamentary elections the party contested only nine of the 35 seats reserved for the Greeks, winning in all of them and receiving an aggregate 39.6 per cent of the popular vote. Its reluctance to make a genuine showing of electoral strength takes into consideration the fact that the 1959 Zurich and London agreements provide for the guarantor powers' intervention against a communist threat. In recent years the party has suffered embarrassment from improved Soviet-Turkish relations and has taken wavering positions on such questions as conciliation between Greek and Turkish Cypriots. Domestically, frictions with non-communist parties, renewed in 1968 by the Warsaw Pact intervention in Czechoslovakia, were further stimulated during 1971 by the Soviet Union's increasing interest in Cypriot affairs.

Leadership and Organization. The leading figures in AKEL are the secretary-general, Ezekias Papaïoannou, and his deputy, Andreas Fantis, both reelected in 1970 at the party's Twelfth Congress. The Politburo of the Central Committee includes Pavlos Georgiou, M. Poumbouris, Andreas Ziartides, Yiannis Sofikli, and Yinnis Katsourides. Secretariat members include Georgiou, Katsourides, and Dinos Konstandinou.

The total figure for all elements within the AKEL apparatus, including various fronts and allowing for overlapping memberships, is estimated at some 60,000. AKEL controls the island's principal trade union organization, the Pan-Cypriot Workers' Confederation (Pankipria Ergatiki Omospondia; PEO), which has some 36,000 members — more than half of all those holding membership in labor unions — and is an affiliate of the communist-front World Federation of Trade Unions. Andreas Ziartides is PEO secretary-general. The party also controls the United Democratic Youth Organization (Eniaia Dimokratiki Organosis Neolaias; EDON), which is headed by Panikos Paionidis. EDON claims to have 10,000 members and is believed to operate a branch in England. The EDON organization of secondary school students — known as PEOM — has an estimated 2,000 members, who are also members of EDON. EDON holds a seat on the Executive Committee of the communist-front World Federation of Democratic Youth. Other AKEL-dominated fronts include the Pan-Cypriot Confederation of Women's Organizations (Pankiprios Omospondia Gynekon Organosen; POGO); the Pan-Cypriot Peace Council (Pankiprios Epitropi Erenis; PEE), which is a member of the communist-front World Peace Council and is headed by Yiangos Potamitis; the Cypriot-Soviet Association, headed by Panos Taliadoros; and the Cypriot-German Friendship Society, headed by M. Papapetros. An adjunct to AKEL, the "Union of Cypriots in England," has an estimated 1,250 members.

Domestic Attitudes and Activities. AKEL has consistently exploited anti-colonialist sentiment in its protests against the restrictions placed on Cyprus by the Zurich and London agreements and against the continuing presence of British bases. On the other hand, because as a mass party it seeks to attract Turks as well as Greeks, AKEL has at no time more than half-heartedly supported the purely Greek objective of enosis — the union of Cyprus and Greece. (Under the present circumstances, enosis would probably result in the outlawing of AKEL.) Enosis was overwhelmingly popular among Greek Cypriots until the 1967 coup in Athens, and as a result AKEL's strength as a national party was for some time precariously balanced. Thereafter, AKEL began to stress its "patriotic" orientation and took credit for rising above partisan considerations to prevent an outbreak of hostilities on the island. The communists were happy to support Makarios's deemphasis of enosis and his advocacy of a "feasible" solution to the island's nationalities problem rather than a "desirable" one, envisaging a workable accommodation between Greek and Turkish Cypriots with at least a temporary abandonment of the goal of enosis. Firmly opposed to the 1967-68 talks between Greece and Turkey, which unsuccessfully sought a settlement, AKEL has actively supported the inter-Cypriot discussions which began in June 1968.

AKEL representatives were among some 70 leading Cypriot politicians called by Makarios on 27 January 1971 to discuss the intercommunal situation. An AKEL Politburo communiqué endorsed current government policies and deemed the inter-Cypriot talks the "best method of settling differences." Those in opposition, it said, were "basically the enemies of Cyprus," who could be expected to continue their "eforts to impose partitionist and divisive plans to achieve enslavement." *Kharavyi*, 17 February.) AKEL later asked the government to "put a permanent check" on extremist pro-enosis groups agitating against both the president and the communist party, but at the same time urged its members and organizations to "confront the provocations calmly and wisely" so as to "reinforce the internal front led by President Makarios." (*Ibid.*, 23 April.)

AKEL frequently addressed itself to alleged external designs to provoke conflict between Cypriots — between left and right, and between Turk and Greek. This "bid to create tension on the island," according to AKEL Deputy Secretary-General Fantis in an interview with a Soviet correspondent, was "part of a general plan for the assassination and abduction of leading political figures of the progressive and patriotic organizations," and "part of the general criminal plan of the aggressive NATO bloc" which was "hoping for a clash between Cypriot Greeks and Turks" so that it could use the situation to impose on Cyprus its own solutions "in the interests of the imperialist circles" and to "help implement their military-strategic and economic plans in the Middle East." The key influence in the NATO plans was attributed to the United States, which "by its entire policy toward Cyprus" was seeking "transformation of the island into a military base in the eastern Mediterranean." (Moscow radio, 19 January.)

AKEL applauded the announcement, in late April, of Makarios's first visit to the Soviet Union, from 2 to 9 June. The president, the party commented, "could be expected to seek Soviet support in dealing promptly with hostile intentions toward Cyprus." The visit was said to be coming at a particularly important time in view of Turkey's "blackmail for acceptance of inadmissible contitutional demands" and "threats to establish a separate Turkish Cypriot state and carry out an airlift between Turkey and Turkish areas on the island." (*Kharavyi*, 1 May.) Turkey's position on Cyprus was said by Papaïoannou, at an extraordinary plenum of the AKEL Central Committee and Control Committee called on 17 May, to have hardened under its new premier, Nihat Erim. The Turkish solution of "dual enosis," he said, would bring about the "partition of Cyprus and its military occupation by the imperialist states of NATO," and therefore must be averted through continuation of the inter-Cypriot talks. He indicated that, despite serious differences, some progress had been made in the talks, and an agreement could be achieved if the Turkish Cypriot leadership accepted in substance the concept of the unitary state and "abandoned any inclination to create a state within a state." (*Ibid.*, 19 May.) These views were conveyed to Makarios on 19 May be a five-member AKEL leadership delegation (*ibid.*, 20 May).

On the conclusion of Makarios's visit, a joint communiqué issued in Moscow upheld Cypriot independence and sovereignty, insisting that the Cyprus problem be "peacefully solved by the people of Cyprus in accordance with the United Nations Charter and resolutions." The Soviet side expressed its "firm and active opposition to any intervention, interference, use of force, or threat to use force against Cyprus," and reaffirmed Soviet support for the withdrawal of all foreign troops. (Nicosia radio, 9 June.) Papaïoannou lauded the "unselfish support and assistance" pledged by the Soviets to Makarios as "clear warning to all those planning intervention or aggression against Cyprus in its struggle for a completely independent, territorially integral, sovereign, unitary, and demilitarized nation" (*Kharavyi*, 15 June). For tactical reasons, AKEL ignored the fact that the Soviet Union has (albeit mildly) supported Turkey's advocacy of a federative or cantonal system in Cyprus which would give local autonomy to the Turkish Cypriots, and that the Soviet promise of support made no mention of either material aid or of any direct assistance in the event of "imperialist intervention." Makarios, for his part, appeared to be capitalizing on AKEL's strength to support his own move toward the Soviets, so as to counter pressure by Greece for an early settlement.

AKEL argued that, to avert implementation of the alleged "imperialist plan" for the "removal" of Makarios and "progressive" Cypriots — the enemies of the president and of AKEL being, in its professed view, synonomous — the government and people must look to the "decisive support of the powerful Soviet Union that has sustained Cyprus during all our critical moments like an impenetrable shield." Giving the joint communiqué a liberal interpretation which, notably, Makarios made no move to repudiate, Papaïoannou declared that the Soviets had "served notice to the imperialists" that Soviet protection was "not limited to words," adding that Moscow had "all the capabilities to enforce its declarations" and that the Soviet fleet in the Mediterranean was "not for tourist purposes, but for protecting the peoples struggling for their national independence and existence." (*Kharavyi*, 20 June.)

The text of a letter purported to have been sent by Greek Premier Yeoryios Papadopoulos to President Makarios on 18 June, reprinted in *Elevtheria* (Nicosia, 13 July) from the German magazine *Der Spiegel*, was seized upon by AKEL as substantiation of its fears of outside intervention. The letter suggested, in strong terms, that Makarios make concessions to the Turkish Cypriots, failing which the Greek government would "find itself forced to take those measures dictated by the national interest and the well-understood interest of Cypriot Hellenism, however bitter they may be." Makarios, whose failure to repudiate the letter suggested its authenticity, was said to have resisted the implied ultimatum, responding: "Thus far I have survived thirteen [Greek] premiers. I will survive the fourteenth also. I will seek aid from Moscow." (*Ibid.*) AKEL leaders met with Makarios on 13 July to reiterate the party's "unlimited support in the struggle to repulse all enemy plans against Cyprus so that the Cypriot people can solve their problem themselves without foreign intervention or pressure." AKEL, like the Soviets, favored reference of the nationalities problem to the U.N. Security Council in the event of the collapse of the talks. (*Kharavyi*, 14 July.) The party pressed Makarios to remain firm in insisting on "genuine" independence. There could not be a unitary and independent state with an independent Turkish "central organization," just as there could be no independent state so long as there existed "sovereign" British bases or U.S. "espionage radio stations" on the island. Only by totally demilitarizing the island could Cyprus prevent Turkey from raising the question of its "security" and at the same time thwart NATO plans for "solving" the Cyprus question "in the name of strategic import." (*Kharavyi*, 16 July.)

The Soviets, meanwhile, were stepping up anti-Western propaganda on the Cyprus issue, as well as their support of AKEL. On 21 July TASS carried excerpts from and *Pravda* the full text of an article by Papaïoannou declaring that the "imperialists" were planning to make a move against Cyprus by September. The visit to Cyprus, from 17 to 24 September, by a delegation of the Czechoslovak Communist Party, may have been intended as a demonstration of socialist bloc support of both AKEL and Makarios. A joint communiqué by AKEL and the Czechoslovak party declared: "The Cyprus problem must be settled through peaceful means by the Cypriot people themselves, without foreign intervention, on the basis of independence, sovereignty, and a unitary state in the interests of all the Cypriot people, Greeks and Turks alike" (*Kharavyi*, 28 September). In an interview with Moscow radio and television correspondents in Nicosia on 19 October, Papaïoannou said the strategic importance of Cyprus to the "imperialist aims" had increased with Malta's move to expel the British and NATO. The United States, he said, was "following in Hitler's footsteps" by "raising the communist bogey" in Cyprus with a view to "splitting the forces of the people," exploiting differences between Greek and Turkish Cypriots — "differences for which the imperialists themselves bear the main responsibility" — so as to "divert Cyprus from its unaligned policy and tie it to NATO."

It was not until 14 December, apparently, that AKEL made any public comment with regard to the reported return to Cyprus, a few months earlier, of the anti-communist Greek General Grivas, a persistent advocate of enosis who was recalled to Athens in 1967 from his position as commander of the Greek Cypriot National Guard. In a talk on Moscow radio, Fantis said that the "imperialists," having been "unable to achieve their goals as agreed upon at the NATO meeting in Lisbon in June 1971 regarding the imposition of a Cyprus settlement," had "changed tactics" while their aims remained the same. They had, he said, "resorted to the services of General Grivas," whose clandestine return to Cyprus was the "starting point and slogan" for an "unprecedented provocative and insulting campaign" against Makarios and the "patriotic forces" by Cypriot "tools of circles hostile to Cyprus and its cause," and for setting up "unlawful armed groups by his fanatic followers."

AKEL was clearly relieved when a new round of inter-Cypriot talks was announced, to begin in January 1972, following discussion of the problem in the United Nations. The party expressed reservations, however, over the inclusion of Greek and Turkish advisers in the forthcoming talks. (*Kharavyi*, 21 December.)

International Views and Positions.. Consistently pro-Soviet in international affairs, AKEL professes to view the United States as the major force preventing peace throughout the world. An article by Papaïoannou (*WMR*, May 1971), addressing itself to "neo-colonialism and the developing countries," purported to show that "U.S. monopoly capital" was "the largest world exploiter." The export of capital to developing countries, he wrote, was one of the economic bases of neo-colonialism and an important means of prolonging economic backwardness and dependence in the "Third World" countries. Neo-colonialism's "principal political weapon" was seen as a process whereby young and developing states were drawn into various political and economic blocs with former colonialists and granted military and other aid for the purpose of preventing these countries from charting a new road for their economies and to keep them in subordination to the world capitalist economic system. The "main ideological weapon" was anti-communism, which the neo-colonialists were said to be employing, by means of the "deliberate distortion of Marxist-Leninist theory and socialist construction," in an endeavor to split anti-imperialist forces.

According to the AKEL leader, most newly independent countries — and here he cited Cyprus — would have found it almost impossible to retain their independence without the support of the socialist countries and in particular the Soviet Union. Anti-Soviet, anti-communist propaganda conducted by the United States was designed to falisify the policy of cooperation between socialist countries and the "Third World." In Cyprus, he declared, the United States had expended large sums for anti-communist propaganda in order to promote the disunity of the people and to deceive U.S. public opinion by presenting the country as a "red danger."

Publications. AKEL's central organ is the daily newspaper *Kharavyi* (Dawn). Its theoretical organ is *Theoritikos Dimokratis* (Theoretical Democrat). AKEL also publishes a quarterly review, *Neos Dimokratis* (New Democrat); a monthly journal, *Nea Epochi* (New Epoch); and a weekly, *Neoi Kairoi* (New Times). The PEO publishes a weekly newspaper, *Ergatiki Vima* (Workers' Step). EDON publishes a newspaper, *Dhimokratia*, and a monthly, *Neolaia* (Youth).

Valerie Bloom

Denmark

The Communist Party of Denmark (Danmarks Kommunistiske Parti; DKP) was formed on 9 November 1919 by a left-wing splinter of the Social Democratic Party. It has been legal since its inception except during the German occupation in World War II. The party has some 5,000 members, out of Denmark's population of 4,900,000 (estimated 1970). Principal support comes from among industrial workers in Copenhagen and other major urban areas.

The DKP has failed to win any parliamentary seats since 1959, when right-wing secessionists formed the Socialist People's Party (Socialistisk Folkeparti; SF). Communist influence was further weakened by the emergence, in 1967, of the Left Socialists (Venstresocialisterne; VS), a radical offshoot of the SF. Defection of a VS representative to the DKP gave the party one parliamentary seat, which it held from January 1970 until the 21 September 1971 election, when it failed to poll the 2.0 per cent qualifying minimum, receiving 1.4 per cent of the vote (1.0 per cent in 1968). The Social Democrats, who increased their seats by 8 to 70, formed a minority cabinet with the backing of the SF, which increased its seats by 6 to 17. Like the DKP, the VS fell below 2.0 per cent (to 1.6) and lost the 4 seats it had won in 1968.

Leadership and Organization. DKP Chairman Knud Jespersen was reelected most recently at the party's Twenty-third Congress, in 1969. The Executive Committee (Politburo) of the Central Committee consists of Jespersen, Ib Nørlund (the secretary-general), Poul Emanuel, Villy Fuglsang, Preben Henriksen, and Per Kristensen. The Central Committee has 39 full and 13 candidate members. There is also a five-man Control Commission.

The DKP-affiliated Communist Youth of Denmark (Danmarks Kommunistiske Ungdom; DKU) probably has fewer than 2,000 members. In recent years it has had little success in stemming the flow of young leftists into proliferating Maoist, anarchist, and other movements — most of whom consider themselves more radical than the DKP, and less hampered by ideological restraints. Another DKP auxiliary is the politically insignificant League of Women (Kvindeudvalg).

Neither the communists nor their immediate competitors, the SF and VS, control any national labor unions. DKP members hold some key posts, however, including the presidency of the Danish Seamen's Union. The party has also had considerable success in infiltrating the Danish Trade Union youth organization and in a bid to organize an apprentice federation under its leadership. The DKP regularly sends delegates to the "Workers' Conferences of the Baltic Countries, Norway, and Iceland," held annually by trade unionists in Rostock, East Germany.

The party is influential in a number of friendship organizations, the most active of which is the Denmark-Soviet Union Association, whose chairman is DKP Central Committee member Alfred Jensen.

Domestic Attitudes and Activities. The return of the DKP to parliament was treated by the party leadership as a politically significant event. In the party monthly, *Tiden* (no. 6, 1971), a series of articles was introduced under the title, "The Communists in Parliament." They outlined positions taken by the party's sole legislator, Hanne Reintoft, as well as proposals introduced by her on such issues as employment, wages, taxes, housing, and social welfare. In addition, any statement made by her received prominent note in the party newspaper, *Land og Folk*.

During the parliamentary debate on a government-proposed new price law, the DKP upbraided the Social Democrats and the Socialists for allegedly failing to demand "just" price controls so that cost-of-living rises in essentials (food, housing) and fixed levies (taxes, rates) would not exceed industrial wage increases. According to the communists, the current "automatic cost-of-living regulating index," which compensated the worker for less than half the increase in his basic expenses, was geared to the interests of big business, and favored "speculators, swindlers, and monopolist gentlemen." A fair wage increase, Hanne Reintoft declared, should not come from increased prices, but from the capital gains (*Land og Folk*, 28-29 March editorial; 1 April). The new price law became effective on 2 April, lifting the temporary price freeze imposed in September 1970 and in turn precipitating a series of DKP warnings to consumers that a new wave of price increases could be anticipated.

Professing to be the sole party representing the interests of workers and the poor, the DKP accused the government of conducting, under the guise of a need to "rectify the balance of payments," a financial offensive against wage earners and pensioners by restricting consumption. Since the payments deficit had risen sharply despite restrictive measures, the communists argued, consumption was not sapping the economy. On the contrary, they said, the inflationary spiral was due to speculation in and loans on land, real estate, and other capital values. (*Land og Folk*, 18 May; from Central Committee statement, 16 May.)

The DKP has consistently agitated against the surtax on consumers' goods first imposed in 1967 and later increased to 15 per cent. Particularly the levy on foodstuffs is condemned by the party as discriminatory against the poor, and hence "asocial." A five-week DKP campaign of public meetings, street displays, and dissemination of literature culminated on 26 March when 28,308 signatures were delivered to the finance minister and claimed as indicative of "broad opposition" to the tax. (*Ibid.*, 21-22 and 27 March.) A DKP proposal for removal of the surtax on foodstuffs was introduced in parliament on 27 May. Both the Social Democrats and the Socialists joined the government in opposition to the communist bill, which was supported by only one Left Socialist — and even then with qualifications. (*Ibid.*, 28 May.)

DKP proposals for economic recovery were outlined by Ib Nørlund at a conference of 15 West European communist parties in London on 11-13 January. The main thrust of the proposals (*Tiden*, no. 1) concerned Denmark's need for extensive foreign trade, the struggle against "state monopoly capitalism and closed economic blocs," opposition to U.S. economic penetration under cover of "European" integration, and efforts to reverse the alleged betrayal by the Social Democrats of socialist economic tenets. The Social Democrats and the Socialists, Jespersen charged later, had "entered the ranks of administrators of capitalism," as evidenced during their coalition rule from 1966 to 1968 when they "gave us the added-value tax, proffered speculators a free hand, and defeated themselves through their attempts to steal the workers' modest cost-of-living [wage] increases" (*Land og Folk*, 29-30 August).

International Views and Positions. Denmark's entry into negotiations for membership in the European Economic Community provided the backdrop for DKP agitation in external affairs. Such membership was frequently compared to Denmark's affiliation in 1949 with NATO, through which the nation allegedly had surrendered its independence and jeopardized its security. The EEC, in this view, posed similar dangers on the economic and political fronts. (E.g., speech by Knud

Jespersen, *Land og Folk*, 6 May.) Developments during the year — on the one hand, the government's failure to stem economic deterioration, and on the other, divison among Social Democrats — were favorable to communist propaganda. Nonetheless, the DKP — as one of three tiny parliamentary groupings to the left of the Social Democrats and Socialists (the others being the two-member Left Socialists and a single-member offshoot, the Socialist Working Group) — appeared to make little pragmatic gain. Its campaigns, both inside and outside the parliamentary arena, were noteworthy more for their unique positions than for the influence they wielded.

The DKP professes to have supported all initiatives toward cooperation among the Northern countries which would "assure their common and individual independence" of NATO and the Common Market—said to be "imperialism's military and economic bloc formations." Thus the "Nordek" inter-Scandinavian customs union—negotiated by Denmark, Norway, Sweden, and Finland, and ratified by all but the Finns, who in March 1970 caused the Nordek plan to collapse by withdrawing abruptly—was endorsed by the DKP, albeit only insofar as it meant furthering the economic independence of the North as opposed to being a "steppingstone to the EEC." When the Nordic Council met at Copenhagen in mid-February 1971, the DKP attacked the Danish premier's proposal—which Finland and Sweden rejected—for reviving Nordek. Praising Finland for having broken off the original Nordek talks, the party now claimed that the Nordek concept was a cover for an attempt to "further the argument that EEC membership of Nordic countries would not preclude intimate cooperation among themselves." (*Ibid.*, 16 February, editorial.) Sweden's bid for a conditional affiliation with the EEC would have a considerable impact in Denmark and Norway, the DKP subsequently predicted. If Sweden could achieve favorable conditions without becoming an EEC member, why should Denmark and Norway join? The DKP appealed for joint Scandinavian negotiations with a view to a stronger, common front vis-à-vis the EEC. (*Ibid.*, 20 March.)

At a Central Committee meeting on 15-16 May, Jespersen spoke of making Denmark less vulnerable to the "vicissitudes" and "crises" of Western capitalism. Because Denmark had bound its trade and its politics to capitalism, even modest "tremors" in larger capitalist countries could trigger "earthquakes" in the Danish economy: as an instance, the DKP charged that the United States was attempting to "solve its monetary problems by forwarding the bill for the Vietnam war to the European peoples." In contrast, a new trade course based on long-term agreements with the "crisis-free" socialist countries was seen as assuring Denmark a sound economy as well as markets for its products and full employment. (*Ibid.*, 16-17 May.)

DKP propaganda against U.S. involvement in Southeast Asia followed the Soviet line closely, including condemnation of the "Nixon doctrine's plan to let Indochinese kill Indochinese" (*ibid.*, 1 April). Upon the publication by the *New York Times* of the "Pentagon papers," the DKP declared that Danish foreign policy was being conducted on the basis of "false and distorted information" and that the Danish government's arguments defending U.S. actions in Southeast Asia had been shattered by the revelation of the U.S. government's "dishonesty." In a message to the Danish foreign minister, Hanne Reintoft suggested that the government review its position in light of the new situation, with a view to "freeing the Danish people of joint responsibility for the genocide of the Indochinese populace." (*Ibid.*, 19 June). In a similar vein, Jespersen asserted that Denmark could disassociate itself from further U.S. "official crimes" only by withdrawing from NATO. Responding in an open letter to Social Democratic leader Jens Otto Krag's admission of having been "shaken" by the Pentagon papers, he suggested (unsuccessfully) a "free exchange of views" and urged the Social Democrats to press for condemnation of the United States and recognition of both the Provisional Revolutionary Government of South Vietnam and the Democratic Republic of Vietnam. (*Ibid.*, 20-21 June.)

International Communist Movement. The DKP continued in 1971 to maintain virtually un-questioning loyalty to the Soviet Union. Articles praising various aspects of Soviet life appeared frequently in the party newspaper, while adverse criticism was generally absent. Although the DKP has not formally retracted its mild disapproval of the 1968 Warsaw Pact invasion of Czechoslovakia, it apparently approves of the current Husák regime in that country. Moderately neutral in the early stages of the Sino-Soviet split, the DKP has since firmly aligned on the Soviet side and can be counted upon to speak out against Communist China at Moscow gatherings.

In his address to the Soviet party's Twenty-fourth congress, in April, Jespersen stated that during the intensified class struggle between socialism and imperialism, the class enemy, "led by circles in the U.S.," was making desperate attempts to split the communist movement. Such attempts, Jespersen contended, were supported by the Chinese leaders' open commitment to struggle against the communist movement and the Soviet Union -- despite the Soviet "desire to normalize relations with China." (*Land og Folk*, 7 April.) In a speech over Moscow radio (30 April), Jespersen extolled the new Soviet five-year economic plan, terming it a "booster to the Danish EEC alternative"; denied that Soviet influence within the world communist movement was waning and that pro-Soviet communist parties were directed from Moscow; held that the Soviet Union's position as the first socialist country gave it a natural "authority" in the international communist movement; and concluded by terming the Soviet Union "the people's guarantee of being able to opt for a world without war and imperialism."

In response to wide debate among Danes regarding the lot of Jews in the Soviet Union, the DKP published numerous articles upholding the Soviet claim that Jewish cultural traditions are respected and that any reported anti-semitism or persecution of Jews was the fabrication of Western propagandists. When, in July, a number of prominent Danish curchmen, artists, labor leaders, and politicians formed a group called "Denmark's Committee for the Soviet Jews," an editorial in *Land og Folk* (1) July) referred to it as the "Danish Anti-Soviet Associaton" and attacked the organizers as "professional anti-communists and Soviet-haters" who were seeking to capitalize on "cheap mendacious propaganda." The DKP singled out for defense the Soviet prosecution of Jews for airplane hijacking attempts -- a crime, it pointed out, no less punishable in Denmark. To the committee's plea for a free exit from the Soviet Union for all Jews, the DKP countered that "every month hundreds of Soviet Jews are given legal exit permits." In the same issue was a photograph of a classical Jewish theater group in the autonomous Jewish area of Birobidjan.

Publications. The DKP daily newspaper, *Land og Folk* (Land and People), is edited by Thorkild Holst and Erley Olsen. The monthly theoretical organ *Tiden* (Times) has an editorial committee headed by Secretary-General Ib Nørlund. It publishes articles in Danish translation from the *World Marxist Review*, this section being supervised by Politburo member Villy Fuglsang. *Fremad* (Forward) is the DKU organ.

*   *   *

Communist Splinter Organizations. To the left of the DKP are a number of small splinter groups, all formed since the Sino-Soviet schism. None have participated in national elections. They include the Communist League (Marxist-Leninist) -- Kommunistisk Forbund (M-L), or KFML -- and its apparent youth affiliate, the Communist Youth (Marxist-Leninst) -- Kommunistisk Ungdom (M-L) -- or KUML; the Communist Labor Circle (Kommunistisk Arbejdskreds; KAK) and the KAK-endorsed Communist Youth League (Kommunistisk Ungdoms Forbund; KUF); the Socialist Youth League (Socialistisk Ungdoms Forbund; SUF), which was expelled by the Left Socialists in 1969; and the Revolutionary Socialists (Revolutionaere Socialister). The Socialist Youth League and the Revolutionary Socialists are Trotskyist and are affiliated with the Fourth International. The rest are believed to be aligned with the Chinese communists, who recognize the KFML as the party representing Danish Marxist-Leninists and publish messages from it extolling developments in China (see, e.g., *Peking Review*, 30 July).

These splinter groups—among which the KFML and SUF are currently the most active—command all together the support of an insignificant segment of the population and remain isolated but vociferous sects with negligible political power. Comprising more youthful elements than the established parties, they are unanimous in rejecting policies of both the "traitorous" Social Democrats and the "revisionist" Socialists and the DKP, as well as in seeking to create a revolutionary counterforce to the political status quo. They vary, however, in their platforms for the overthrow of the present power structure and creation of a socialist state. Within each of these organizations there exist ideological and tactical differences, many of an extreme and seemingly irreconcilable nature. This factor, coupled with limited support and an increasing tendency to purge ranks of "anarchist" elements, has generally rendered them unable to effect any substantive political change.

Publications. The KFML publishes a monthly newspaper, *Kommunist*, and occasional "Marxist-Leninist study letters"; the KUML organ is *Rød Front* (Red Front). The KAK irregularly prints a mimeographed bulletin, *Kommunistisk Orientering*; the KUF issues a bulletin entitled *Ungkommunisten* (Young Communist). The SUF publishes a journal called *Klassekampen* (Class Struggle) ten times a year.

Valerie Bloom

Finland

The Communist Party of Finland (Suomen Kommunistinen Puolue; SKP) was founded in Moscow on 29 August 1918 by exiled members of the Finnish Social Democratic Party. It has been legal since 1944.

SKP membership has fallen off slightly in recent years. It was noted by the party in *World Marxist Review* (April 1971) that of 45,990 members, industrial, building, and municipal workers accounted for 58.5 per cent; pensioners, 12.7; housewives, 9.7; farmers, 7.2; office employees and service industry workers, 6.6; students, intellectuals, and others, 3.0; and small private employers, 2.3 per cent. The party comprises 17 district and 1,342 local organizations. The population of Finland is 4,679,000 (estimated 1970).

The SKP participates in national elections through the Finnish People's Democratic League (Suomen Kansan Demokraattinen Liitto; SKDL), an electoral front organization formed by the party on 29 October 1944. The 25-member SKDL leadership includes 17 SKP members. Communists are believed to comprise about a third and left-wing socialists most of the rest of the SKDL's supporters. The SKDL appears to draw a larger share of Finland's radical intellectuals than any other party. The latest parliamentary election, in March 1970, gave the SKDL 16.6 per cent of the vote and 36 of 200 seats, its lowest total ever and down 5 from 1966. Of this total, 33 seats are filled by SKP members. From July 1970 to 17 March 1971 the SKP participated in a center-left coalition government headed by Ahti Karjalainen, along with the Social Democratic Party (52 seats, down 3), the Center Party (36, down 13), the Swedish People's Party (12), and the Liberal Party (8). The SKDL held three of the 17 cabinet portfolios: Justice, Social Affairs, and Communications. Karjalainen formed a new government on 26 March without the SKDL, but that government resigned on 29 October and was succeeded by a caretaker cabinet to serve until 2 January 1972, when new elections were scheduled.

Leadership and Organization. Under a conciliation agreement reached at an extraordinary SKP congress in February 1970 between Aarne Saarinen's "reformist" majority and a "Stalinist" minority headed by Taisto Sinisalo, the party's 35 Central Committee posts were apportioned 20 to 15 in favor of the reformists. Saarinen and Erkki Salomaa retained their posts as chairman and vice-chairman, respectively, but the agreement created a second (and equal) vice-chairmanship for Sinisalo. Salomaa died in November 1971 and was replaced by Olavi Hänninen. Arvo Aalto, a reformist, retained the post of secretary-general which he captured at the 1969 congress from the veteran "Stalinist" Ville Pessi. The Politburo—enlarged from 12 members to 16 under the agreement and apportioned 10 to 6 in favor of the Saarinen forces—consists of Arvo Aulis Aalto, Arvo Hautala, Anna-Liisa Hyvönen, Olavi Hänninen, Markus Kainulainen, Erkki Kivimaki, Olavi Laine, Oiva Lehto, Ville Pessi, Aarne Saarinen, Erkki Salomaa, Jorma Simpura, Taisto Sinisalo,

Ossian Sjöman, Leo Suonpaa, and Erkki Tuominen. The eight members of the Secretariat are Aalto, Hänninen, Kivimäki, Lehto, Pessi, Saarinen, Ossi Nurminen, and Olavi Poikolainen.

The SKP holds eight of the 22 seats on the governing board of the unified 700,000-member Finnish Confederation of Trade Unions (SAK), to the Social Democrats' 12. There has been a growing power struggle between the Communists and the Social Democrats in the SAK leadership, with a similar trend among individual SAK unions.

Domestic Attitudes and Activities. Despite the conciliation agreement between the reformist and Stalinist factions of the SKP, the successes of the increasingly militant Stalinists led to a breakdown in the SKDL parliamentary front, and on 17 March 1971 the SKDL withdrew from the coalition government. Unable to hold the line against Stalinist opposition to the government's economic stabilization policies—the Stalinists controlling 15 of the 36 SKDL seats—and in the interests of preserving a united front, SKDL deputies joined in precipitating a government crisis by refusing to agree to relaxation of certain price controls. At the same time, the Stalinists' gains on the labor front led to a major strike from 8 February to 26 March by the 70,000-member SAK-affiliated Metalworkers' Union following its rejection of wage contract proposals based on the economic stabilization program. Both developments posed tactical difficulties for the Saarinen moderates, torn between a commitment to government cooperation and the directly conflicting demands of those unions under strong influence by the Stalinist elements of the SKP.

The abrupt decision to withdraw from the government threw the SKP leadership as well as its programmatic policies into disarray following the obvious victory scored by the minority. At a Central Committee meeting convened to discuss the new political situation, intraparty developments clearly dominated the proceedings. Secretary-General Aalto leveled strong criticism at the Sinisalo group, accusing it of preserving its own parallel organizations and of other activity "in deep conflict with the resolutions of the extraordinary party congress of February 1970 aimed at integration" (see *YICA*, 1971, p. 151). It was only by a relatively weak vote (20 to 10) that the Saarinen forces passed a resolution calling upon the party Politburo to take "rapid action to prevent increased disruption" (Helsinki radio, 22 April).

Saarinen commented later that while certain SKDL-SKP "miscalculations" had played a role in the government collapse, the basic cause was the increased influence of bourgeois elements in parliament as a result of leftist losses in the 1970 elections which, in his view, could have been averted by government policies "turned a degree or two to the left in order to answer better the needs of the poor and the working class." Saarinen favored a return to SKDL participation in the government insofar as an acceptable minimum program could be worked out with the other government parties. (*Kansan Uutiset*, 24 April.) Before this could be achieved, however, an effort must be made to avoid the further deterioration of relationships within the SKP leadership. He called for a "flexible, far-reaching, and broad-minded policy capable of distinguishing between friend and enemy, and of avoiding alienating friends with strict dogmatic views or revolutionary jingoism not in complete harmony with reality." Such a policy, he said, implied neither revisionism or reformism, but an adaptation of Marxism-Leninism to actual Finnish conditions. (*Kansan Uutiset*, 25 April.)

SKDL leader Ele Alenius characterized the government crisis as a situation in which the SKDL "ended up on thin ice and fell in." Henceforth, he said, the SKDL must "build bridges which will hold [it] up." Internal differences within the SKDL and SKP, he said, had been a major factor in the government collapse inasmuch as they "precluded the proper conditions for effective participation in government responsibility." SKDL parliamentary policy, moreover, had been dominated by the SKP, and noncommunist SKDL socialists had been "exceptionally loyal toward the SKP and its policies," even though it "sometimes seemed" that the SKP had "forgotten the existence of the SKDL and its politically varied membership when forming government policy." There was a pressing need, therefore, to clarify SKDL activity and more specifically define and distinguish SKDL policy and general direction. (*Ibid.*, 24 and 27 April.) Despite such statements, Alenius continued to deny rumors of plans for a new socialist party, such as had followed the SKDL's call for a "working-class policy seminar" to be held in late April. The seminar, he said, was only one of several SKDL initiatives to introduce "more varied exchanges of opinion and more purposeful discussion of the views and ideas of left socialists in order to further develop SKDL policy." Alenius spoke of the need to rally in the SKDL those who realized that "a true renewal of society cannot be accomplished without changing the order of society from capitalism to socialism," but who could not for "traditional, religious, or other personal reasons" join the communist party. (*Ibid.*, 23 April.)

After the collapse of the coalition, the SKP campaigned widely as an opposition party and predicted that the nation was heading for an economic crisis due to the excessive influence of "bourgeois rightists" in the government. Expressing what soon became the official SKP line, Arvo Aalto declared that the Centrists and Social Democrats, having failed to learn from the past, were continuing to practice a "day-to-day" policy and refusing to pursue necessary far-reaching social reforms. Because of the SKDL's presence in three governments between 1966 and 1971, he claimed, more had been done during that period "for the benefit of the people"—as regards national income, social security, education, medical care, housing construction, and industrial development—than at any other time in the 1950s or 1960s. (*Kansan Uutiset*, 21 June.)

As the internal situation in the SKP continued to deteriorate, the Central Committee met at the end of October in an effort to bring the conflicting factions together in time for the party's Sixteenth Congress, scheduled for March 1972. In a statement supported by all its members, the committee called upon the Politburo to draft joint recommendations based on "respect for differing viewpoints." (Helsinki radio, 24 October.)

International Views and Positions. The SKP claims to have held a "central position" in the post-World War II development of relations between Finland and the Soviet Union, as a result of which Finland has achieved "an international position unprecedented in its history." In 1971 the party denounced Finnish critics of the Soviet Union as being under the direction and protection of "international reactionary centers" which were seeking to "hinder and undermine" mutual friendship and economic cooperation. These elements allegedly were trying to provoke conflicts between the two countries by, for example, publishing "distorted documents such as Khrushchev's 'memoirs' " and smuggling "contraband" publications into the Soviet Union under the guise and protection of "religious" mail. (*Kansan Uutiset*, 30 May.) This charge paralleled Soviet allegations of Finnish "right-wing intrigues backed by reactionary circles abroad" such as appeared in *Novoye Vremya* (Moscow, nos. 26 and 31, 1971). Similarly, SKP organs joined with Soviet media in protesting criticism of conditions in the Baltic republics by conservative Finnish media. The SKP-controlled Finnish-Soviet Society expressed concern over the intensification of anti-Soviet publishing activity that "offends and blackens" the Soviet Union and "is indisputably contrary to the spirit of friendship and cooperation," and proposed the appointment of a permanent Finnish-Soviet information commission to include the Finnish-Soviet Society (Helsinki radio, 5 March).

The SKP professed to note, however, an improvement in ties between the government coalition parties and the Communist Party of the Soviet Union (CPSU) which, it declared, should have a positive influence in hindering opposition from the extreme right. The SKP advocated a long-range economic cooperative plan, including the appointment of specialists to Finland's trade mission in Moscow to set up procurement systems, and reciprocal commercial and apprentice exchange programs.

On the technical front, the party envisaged cooperative programs to increase the training of Finnish scientists in the Soviet Union. (Central Committee statement, *Kansan Uutiset*, 30 May.) The SKP delegation to the Soviet party congress, comprising Saarinen, Sinisalo, Tuominen, Simpura, and Poikolainen, met on 12 April with a CPSU delegation headed by M. A. Suslov and Arvids Pelshe. A joint communiqué spoke of the economic benefits to Finland deriving from close SKP-CPSU relations, which were said to have contributed directly to a number of cooperative measures subsequently negotiated at the state level. Saarinen upon returning to Finland predicted that this factor would once again "manifest itself" during the Finnish premier's impending visit to Moscow (*ibid.*, 16 April). Apparently it did: Karjalainen signed a ten-year trade, technical, and industrial treaty with the Soviets on 20 April and also discussed with them the question of closer links with the Council for Mutual Economic Assistance.

When the Finnish government, on 10 September, submitted to the East and West German governments identical draft treaties on diplomatic recognition which embodied provisions on neutrality and the mutual renunciation of force, the SKP Central Committee took the position that Finland should not make normalization of relations with the German Democratic Republic dependent upon any stand adopted by the Federal Republic of Germany: separate talks should begin as soon as either party was ready, and either treaty should be ratified upon the culmination of satisfactory talks between the negotiating parties. The SKP also urged the government to step up its efforts to have ambassadorial talks opened in Helsinki on the convocation of an all-European security conference. (Helsinki radio, 18 September.) The question of European security was discussed in Helsinki from 7-12 November by a high-level delegation of the East German communist party, headed by Politburo member Hermann Axen, and SKP leaders. A joint communiqué deemed the quadripartite agreement on West Berlin "an important step in the path of relaxation of tension," and considered that conditions existed for "the earliest possible start of multilateral preparations for a security conference of European states." (ADN, 13 November.) Axen met also with President Kekkonen, and announced that the East German government understood and accepted "the principle of equality contained in the Finnish proposal" (Helsinki radio, 12 November).

International Communist Movement. Firmly in the Soviet camp, the SKP continued to repudiate Maoist ideology and the policy of the leadership of China as "alien to Marxism-Leninism and to the national and international tasks of the communist workers' and national liberation movement." While "certain tactical changes" had taken place in Chinese policy, they had not revised its "faulty" basic line. The SKP, based on its policy of "peaceful coexistence between states and different social systems," supported China's seating in the United Nations, for example, but condemned its "anti-Soviet policy" as well as its "baseless doctrine of a superstate." (Central Committee statement; *Kansan Uutiset*, 18 September.)

Publications. The central organ of the SKP is the daily *Kansan Uutiset* (People's News), edited by Politburo member Jorma Simpura. The party's monthly theoretical journal, *Kommunisti*, is edited by Inkeri Lehtinen. The Sinisalo faction controls *Tiedonantaja*, a regional party organ issued in Uusimaa. *Folktidningen* (People's News) is published weekly in Swedish as the organ of the SKDL. It carries most SKP documents and is the voice of the SKP among the Swedish-speaking minority. Its editor is Mikael Romberg.

*   *   *

A small pro-Chinese party, the Finnish Association of Marxist-Leninists, was established in 1968. It poses no current threat to the SKP. With cells in Helsinki, Tampere, and Turku, it is fundamentally an extraparty organization although it does include some SKP and SKDL members. Maoist tendencies have thus far been unable to secure a political foothold in Finland (in contrast with the other Scandinavian countries), and the association's activities are generally limited to education and propaganda. It has, however, received the endorsement of the Chinese Communist Party, whose media carry statements of the Finnish group. The association issues a bulletin in Helsinki, *Punakaarti* (Red Guard).

Valerie Bloom

France

The French Communist Party (Parti Communiste Français; PCF) was founded in December 1920. Although confronted with growing dissent within its ranks and challenged by other small Marxist-Leninist organizations, the PCF remains the largest and electorally strongest left-wing party in France. Georges Marchais, deputy secretary-general, claimed a 400,000 membership (*L'Humanité*, 30 December 1970). However, the Paris monthly *Unir-Dé*bat (no. 49, 10 January), organ of a dissident PCF group, estimated membership at only 250,000 or 260,000. The non-communist *Est & Oeust* (no. 461, 1-15 February) placed membership at a maximum of 290,000. The population of France is about 51 million (estimated 1971). On 3 August, the Politburo and Central Committee moved to new headquarters at 2, place du Colonel-Fabien, Paris 19, designed by architect Oscar Niemeyer. A fund-raising drive brought in 1.5 million francs ($300,000) but 4 or 5 million more was needed (about $1,000,000).

The March local elections in 37,657 cities filled 462,023 councillor seats. Coalitions were left to local PCF organizations by the national leadership. On the first round, the PCF received 11.6 per cent or 2,140,085 of the votes (*Le Monde*, 16 and 17 March). Communist-led coalitions won in 39 municipalities, 37 on the first ballot, including Le Havre, de Colombes, Levallois-Perret, and Nimes. They also gained Arles, Amiens, Calais, Saint Dizier and Savigny. Thirty of these mayors were from the "red belt" of Paris, the outlying workers' suburbs, and four were from similar districts around other major cities. In the 90-seat Council of Paris, the PCF won 20 seats. In the fall Senate elections, where one-third of the 283-seat Senate was up for re-election, the single PCF candidate who faced reelection won and the PCF kept its 18 seats or 6.3 per cent of the full body.

Organization and Leadership. The national leadership of the PCF was elected at the Party's Nineteenth Congress, held 4-9 February 1970. Waldeck Rochet is secretary general and Georges Marchais, deputy. Due to Rochet's prolonged illness, Marchais serves in fact as actual party leader and spokesman. For the first time, it was stated that Rochet would never again serve in his post (*L'Humanité*, 24 August). The same Secretariat remains in office: Etienne Fajon, Roland Leroy, René Piquet, Gaston Plissonnier and André Vieuguet. The Politburo continues with Gustave Ansart, François Billoux, Guy Besse, Jacques Duclos, Etienne Fajon, Benoît Frachon, Georges Frischmann, Raymond Guyot, Henri Krasucki, Paul Laurent, Roland Leroy, Georges Marchais, René Piquet, Gaston Plissonier, Waldet Rochet, Georges Séguy, André Vieguet as members, and two candidate members, Claude Poperen and Madeleine Vincent. No changes in either the Secretariat or Politburo were reported in 1971.

Auxiliary Organizations. The primary PCF auxiliary organization is the General Confederation of Labor (Confédération Générale du Travail; CGT), the largest trade union in France. At the time of its last Congress, it claimed a membership of 2,300,000 (*L'Humanité*, 18 November 1969). Official government estimates, however, put CGT membership at between 1,300,000 and 1,500,000. The CGT is led by PCF Politburo members Georges Séguy (secretary-general) and Benoît Frachon (president).

The Movement of Communist Youth (Movement de la Jeunesse Communiste; MJC) initiated a campaign in June to attract 10,000 additional members and create 300 new centers. It comprises four groups—the Union of Communist Students of France (Union des Etudiants Communistes de France; UECF), the Union of Young Girls of France (Union des Jeunes Filles de France; UJFF), the Union of Communist Youth of France (Union de la Jeunesse Communiste de France; UJCF), and the Union of Farm Youth of France (Union de la Jeunesse Agricole de France; UJAF). The MJC held a national congress, together with its four component groups in December 1970. At that time, the following were elected to the National Bureau: Roland Favaro, secretary-general; Jean Michel Catala (sometimes spelled Cathala), deputy secretary-general; Gérard Molina, secretary-general of UECF; Nicole Garand, secretary-general of UJFF; Gérard Lanternier, secretary-general of UJCF; Michel Larrat, secretary-general of UJAF; and P. Barre, Elaine Bize, G. Bras, José Fort, Jackie Hoffmann, Jeanine Jambu, Michel Jouet, Jean-Claude Le Meur, Nicolas Marchand, Michel Navarro, Mireille Riou, Georges Troubat, Alain Therouse, Dominique Vidal, and Pierre Zarka. No changes were announced in 1971.

Since the events of May 1968, the PCF has made a special effort to consolidate itself in the educational trade unions. It gained control over the leadership of the National Union of University Teachers (Syndicat Nationale de l'Enseignement Supérieur; SNE-Sup— see *YICA*, 1970, p. 161.) Its secretary-general is Daniel Monteux. The struggle between the UECF, operating through a group called UNEF-Renewal (UNEF-Renouveau) and the Trotskyist Alliance of Youth for Socialism (Alliance des Jeunes pour le Socialisme; AJS), grouped within the tendency called Trade Union Unity (Unité Syndicale) to gain control of the powerful National Union of Students (Union Nationale des Etudiants de France; UNEF) culminated in an official split of the UNEF during 1971.

Since the April 1970 congress, the Unified Socialist Party (Parti Socialist Unifié; PSU) had tried to retain the UNEF leadership, assisted by Maoists aligned with *L'Humanité Rouge*. Relations between the two groups deteriorated and the latter withdrew support, leaving the PSU in a difficult position. Finally, under pressure from national headquarters, it resigned the leadership at a 10 January 1971 meeting (see *YICA*, 1971, p. 160, for background.) This left two opposing factions, the Unité Syndicale and the UNEF-Renouveau; the former made a motion to hold the 1971 congress at Dijon (an AJS-dominated region) in February; the latter proposed a later congress in Paris. The first motion carried 628-320. Another Unité Syndicale motion won. It set up a "permanent delegation" composed of three AJS members, two from UNEF-Renouveau and, theoretically, four from the PSU. Elected leader was Michel Sérac, a Trotskyist, and current UNEF president. *L'Humanité* contested the "delegation's" legality, and during February both factions tried to rally support from unions and leftist groups before the congress. On 14 February, 125 UNEF-Renouveau controlled "action committees" met and voted to hold a separate congress in March at Paris, and thus confirmed the UNEF split.

The congress opened in Dijon with delegations present from FEN (Fédération de l'Education Nationale), FO (Force Ouvriére), and CFDT (Confédération Français Democratique du Travail). The Socialist Party (Parti Socialiste) grouped within the UNEF in a faction called "Unity, Independence and Democracy" and an usual supporter of the Unité Syndicale faction, was absent. It had threatened to withdraw if two congresses were held. The CGT, SNE-Sup, UECF (see above) and UNCAL (Union National des Comités d'Action Lycéens) sent representatives to the UNEF-Renouveau congress in Paris. Guy Konopnicki emerged as leader of a 26-member Politburo, including 13 PCF members. He stated that the UNEF-Renouveau is not communist and that membership is open. It allegedly represents 21,000 members, while the UNEF (Unité Syndicale) claims 16,000 adherents (*Est & Oeust*, 1-15 April). The two split on the issue of student participation in university administration, the UNEF called this a "sellout," whereas UNEF-Renouveau endorsed it. The former is strong in Dijon, Grenoble, and Clermont-Ferrand; the latter in Aix, Nancy, and Orsay (*Le Monde*, 9 March). Both had petitioned the courts to determine which is the legitimate UNEF. The judgment ruled that neither could claim the legal status of UNEF (*ibid.*, 19 July). A group affiliated with the UNEF, the Union of Professional Schools (Union des Grandes Ecoles; UGE), formed an UGE-Renouveau faction which held its own congress on 13-14 February.

Other major PCF auxiliary organizations active in 1971 included the Union of French Women (Union des Femmes Françaises; UFF), the Peace Movement (Mouvement de la Paix), and the Movement for the Defense of Small Farmers (Mouvement de Défense des Exploitants Familaux; MODEF).

Party Internal Affairs. Since the 1968 Soviet-led invasion of Czechoslovakia, criticism of the PCF leadership has focused on its failure to extend condemnation of the invasion to include subsequent "normalization" imposed by the Soviet Union (see *YICA*, 1971, pp. 160-62, 164-66 for background). Two leaders of the dissent, prominent author and former Politburo member Roger Garaudy as well as World War II Resistance leader Charles Tillon were expelled from the party in 1970. Opposition in 1971 to PCF policies centered around two monthly publications *Politique Aujourd'hui* and *Unir Débat*, the weekly *Politique Hebdo*, and the literary *Les Lettres Françaises*.

Roger Garaudy remained a particularly active critic. His latest book, *Reconquest of Hope* (*Reconquête de l'espoir*), supplements previous works, and discusses the crisis of contemporary communism. It attacks such "crimes" as the "savage repression" of Polish workers in 1970, the Leningrad trials, and the anti-Solzhenitsyn campaign. Garaudy differentiates between the positive values of socialism and the negative nature of the Soviet version of socialism, which is the one exported to other countries. He ascribes its greatest fault to the lack of socialist democracy: "Concerning the workers' revolt in Poland, the misdeeds of importing the Soviet model appeared resoundingly.... The fundamental demand was for workers' self-management and self-government against bureaucratic centralism." (See also *Unir-Débat*, 10 March.) In his opinion, these mistakes were to be compounded by the Twenty-fourth Congress of the Communist Party of the Soviet Union (CPSU), which would produce a "dogmatic reaffirmation of bureaucratic centralism." To correct this fault, it was necessary to "begin the long march toward a self-managing socialism ... the reconquest of hope." He repeated these themes in an interview with *Der Spiegel* (Hamburg, 10 May), warning of the danger of re-Stalinization emanating from the CPSU congress, advising the PCF that if it does not publicly condemn developments such as those that took place in Czechoslovakia, it condemns itself to a slow death.[1] Despite these views, Garaudy has not ruled out the possibility of being readmitted to the party. When asked by *Der Spiegel* if he had made such a request, he replied: "No, not yet, because the conditions are not ripe. Perhaps the time will come when this question can be raised and possibly solved." To a similar question at a college debate in Paris, he answered: "One day, very calmly and very officially, I will reopen the issue of my reintegration, since I see some of my opinions making their way into the party." (*Le Monde*, 3 April.)

Garaudy's friend and ally, Louis Aragon, has remained a member of the party's Central Committee, but he frequently criticizes the PCF for supporting Soviet policies in his publication, *Les Lettres Françaises*. The first issue in 1971 (6-12 January) contained his list of "New Year's wishes," including very pointed ones for the imprisoned Jews of the Soviet Union, and for the Czechoslovaks who displayed a "Biafra spirit." He went on to criticize the systematic destruction of the University of Prague and the blows to creative work in Czechoslovakia. In discussing the new Polish leadership,

---

[1]Similar views were expressed in his article in *Le Nouvel Observateur*, 12 April.

he said: "Socialism has a positive meaning for those who fight against capitalist exploitation only if it keeps its promises when in power." In *Les Lettres Françaises* (5-11 May) editor Pierre Daix published a long, outspoken review of Czechoslovak author Pavel Kohout's new book, *Diary of a Counterrevolutionary*, which denounced the Soviet invasion and subsequent developments in that country. Daix praised the author as a "prophet and protagonist" of the Prague spring, and then he denounced the various stages of "normalization" since 1968. *Les Lettres Françaises* remained skeptical of news, particularly from Poland and Czechoslovakia, concerning literary and cultural figures; for example (issue of 7-13 April), it was highly indignant when Czechoslovak theater director Otomar Kreica was dismissed; the same issue printed four new poems of Polish poet Arnold Slucki, noting he had had to leave Poland in 1968 due to the regime's anti-Semitism there.

Garaudy, Tillon and other party dissidents formed a new protest group called the Centers for Communist Initiative (Les Centres d'Initiative Communiste; CIC) in December 1970).[2] They drew up a six-point "declaration of intent" in which they stated their aim "to carry on publicly the necessary debate and confrontation on all problems facing the communist movement and to prepare the effective instruments which are needed for victory of socialism" (*Initiative Communiste*, 25 February, reprinted in *Unir-Débat*, 10 February). The group's aim was not to set up a separate party, but to transform and democratize the PCF from within, although there was disagreement on the tactics. Some members advocated assistance from outside leftist groups. The declaration of intent pointed out that CIC differed from the PCF in that it was willing to "explore the failings of bureaucratic authoritarian regimes of Eastern Europe" on the basis of principle, and not just in reaction to particular events. Sixty-eight dissident activists endorsed this "declaration" at a 22 January meeting held in Paris and established a temporary ruling committee. The first national CIC meeting was held 1-2 May, at which time a national executive committee composed of eight delegates from Paris and another eight from the provinces was elected. The committee was to meet twice yearly. By the time of its second national meeting (20-21 November, also in Paris), the CIC had 1,300 members and 44 local centers. The membership includes 31 per cent PCF members, 58 per cent former PCF members, and 11 per cent communist sympathizers (*Le Monde*, 18 November).

Until CIC began its own weekly publication *Action* on 4 November, the journals *Politique Aujourd'hui* and *Politique Hebdo* served as its forum. *Unir-Débat*, many of whose subscribers were CIC members, urged its readers to read the CIC pamphlet entitled *Initiative Communiste*, publicized its activities, and later reprinted articles from *Action*. In June it was proposed that *Unir-Débat* merge with *Initiative Communiste*. The former would cover broad problems of a political, social and ideological nature for general distribution; the latter would concentrate on technical intraparty matters for PCF members only. After approval by *Unir-Débat* readership, the arrangement was put into effect in October.

Domestic Views. The PCF remains the strongest left-wing party in France (with more than 20 per cent electoral support), but it is not strong enough to attain power on its own. In consequence, the PCF intensified efforts during 1971 to portray itself as a legitimate and responsible political party, moderate in its criticism of government policies and reasonable in formulating alternatives. An increased drive to form a coalition with other left-wing parties followed.

The PCF took positions on all major domestic issues. At its 20-22 April plenum, the Central Committee proposed that all Frenchmen join a "sustained struggle" for seven national objectives.

[2]For an analysis of CIC, see *Politique Hebdo* (31 December 1970 and 4 February 1971). This publication supported CIC, but six months after its inception, it went bankrupt but was revived by a fund-raising drive. It began republishing in the fall of 1971.

These concerned taxation, housing, transportation, job opportunities for youth, disarmament, public health and social security, and popular representation in all elected assemblies. A month later, Marchais made a detailed criticism of the government's Sixth Economic Development Plan, charging that it had not been formulated democratically and that the "so-called policy of industrialization" would not raise the standard of living as intended but merely accentuate the power of monopolies, and particularly the multinational corporations (*L'Humanité*, 8 May).

In October, the PCF made public its own 200-page "Program for a Democratic Government and Popular Unity" which it would strive to implement either alone or in a government coalition. In presenting the program, Marchais said it was drawn up in response to the "current crisis" in French society. He claimed: "The workers are being kept out of management and the population cannot participate in making the political decisions which decide the nation's destiny.... Big capital commands, dominates, and rules the entire life of the nation. It is necessary to change course. The PCF offers its solution—the building of socialism in France." (*Ibid*., 12 October.) Six chapters of the program define a new economic policy, based on progressive nationalization in key sectors of the economy, democratic management and planning in enterprises, and price control in financial and industrial firms. Other proposals, grouped under the heading "To Live Better," can be traced back to the seven objectives published in April and other frequently expounded PCF recommendations. The program is silent on how these reforms would be financed. It guarantees rights and liberties of individuals and freedom of choice in elections: "The parties will exercise their activities freely within the framework of legality. The plurality of parties and the freedom of candidacy in elections are and will continue to be elements of French democracy." The right to form trade unions and to strike is assured. (*Ibid*.; *Le Monde*, 13 and 14 October carried excerpts.)

The interesting aspect of the program is less in content than in reasons for drafting. Relations between the Socialist Party and the PCF were strained, and the latter was attempting to reopen negotiations for a coalition based on a joint political program. By publishing the program, the PCF made clear that it still sought unity, based not on an electoral agreement but on a concrete political program. In presenting the program, Marchais said, "The PCF does not claim to want to secure the country's future alone. The policy we are proposing must be the work of a government of Democratic Popular Unity ... in which our party will have the place it deserves." (*L'Humanité*, 13 October.) In the program, the PCF even put forward how the "legislative contract" would work as a "guarantee of stability, efficiency, and cooperation" in relations between government and parliament and between government and the majority. (The program outlined procedures for dissolving the government, should it no longer represent the will of the majority.)

The Socialist Party remained cool to the program, and its leader commented: "It is too vast and unrealistic.... Five years is too short to materialize important changes in such a large sector as the economy." (*Le Monde*, 24-25 October.) Lengthy negotiations between the two parties had culminated in the December 1970 "balance sheet" which included many positive aspects of their talks as well as points of divergence. Socialists never ratified the document, preferring to do so after talks were resumed following their June congress. In January, the PCF nevertheless pressed for an electoral accord with the Socialist Party and other left-wing groups. After extensive communications and almost reaching an agreement, talks broke down. The obstacle had been the Socialist desire to seek broad coalitions, whereas the PCF disapproved of unity with "reactionaries" and refused to withdraw in favor of a candidate "most capable of carrying the day," should one be supported by "centrists" as well as Socialists. It was left to local PCF chairmen to form coalitions, and some 124 agreements were signed in the 192 cities: in fifty instances with François Mitterand's party, the Convention of Republican Institutions (Convention des Institutions Républicains; CIR) prior to the June 1971 Socialist congress (see below); and in 30 instances with the Unified Socialist Party (Parti Socialiste Unifié; PSU). It is noteworthy that in Marseille, the prominent Socialist

Gaston Defferre was reelected even though the PCF-Socialist Party coalition had broken down because Defferre preferred to seek alliances with some centrist groups. His coalition won 15 of 22 former communist district seats. Traditional rivalry caused a breakdown in talks at Toulouse, where the PCF failed to give its united support to the incumbent Socialist candidate Louis Bazerque. In a major upset, Gaullist candidate Pierre Baudis was elected (*ibid.*, 23 March, gave full results).

After the elections, Marchais sent letters to the Socialist leadership demanding a resumption of talks, based on the December 1970 "balance sheet," and he listed points which he wished to see considered at the congress. The latter opened on 11 June at Epinay-sur-Seine and proclaimed a new, enlarged Socialist Party which fused the traditional Socialist Party with François Mitterand's CIR and unaffiliated socialist groups. Two main issues arose at the congress. The first concerned the method by which the delegates would be elected to represent the new party. Six proposals were presented. After a bitter struggle, Mitterand barely defeated former Socialist Party leader Alain Savary by 43,926 to 41,757 votes. The second issue concerned collaboration with the PCF. Savary and Mitterand both made motions for reopening negotiations on the basis of a government program. The former called for more immediate talks, based on the "balance sheet," the latter wanted to postpone talks for six months and insisted on guarantees of independence and democratic elections in advance. Mitterand's proposal won, and he emerged as leader of the new party. The PCF immediately criticized the Socialists for "taking a step backward" by refusing to "unfreeze the situation" and insisting on guarantees, previously given. Nevertheless, the PCF was willing to work out the differences. Talks remained stalled and at the PCF Central Committee meeting in October, Roland Leroy asked: "Has [the Socialist party] or has it not decided to commit itself to socialist transformation of French society?" Mitterand seemed more cautious than Savary, preferring to consolidate his new party before concluding an agreement with the PCF. Although he always endorsed unity of left-wing parties, he is not easily pressured.

The PCF attitude toward other left-wing parties remained unchanged and showed a hardening of attitude toward extremist groups. After their "disorderly demonstrations" on Labor Day (1 May), Marchais severely criticized them and added: "We want order. We really want order. This is the reason we struggle." (*L'Humanité*, 3 May.) With a rejuvenation of the Radical Party led by Jean-Jacques Servan-Schreiber, there seemed little hope of reaching any kind of accord.

International Views. Although in the past George Marchais has stated that "the policy of the PCF is worked out and decided not in London, not in Washington, nor yet in Moscow, but in Paris" (*L'Humanité*, 22 July 1970), it is questionable whether the party has altered its pro-Soviet orientation. As indicated above, this has caused dissent within the party and adversely affected PCF negotiations for an alliance with the Socialist Party. The PCF has endorsed unity of the international Communist movement as well as the friendship and solidarity between the CPSU and other communist parties. At the same time, however, it attempted to show its independence by repeatedly supporting the principles of sovereignty, freedom of choice, and diversity for individual parties.

Marchais stressed these themes at the CPSU congress: "Between the CPSU and the PCF there has always existed a fraternity, a solidarity, and a cooperation that has never been contradictory.... The different forms of anti-Sovietism constitute a crime against the interests of the working class.... Soviet military strength constitutes a safeguard for peace." (*Ibid.*, 15 April 1971.) But he went on to say: "We also believe that the establishment and building of socialism in France must and will follow an original path in accordance with our national traditions and conditions.... It is impossible to build socialism without basing it upon general laws and without taking into account concrete historical characteristics of every country." He stressed the independence of the PCF: "It is precisely on the basis of general rules governing the struggle for socialism and of our country's specific conditions that we completely, independently formulate our own policy.... We are very attached to the principles of independence and sovereignty of every party, very attached to these principles in relations between fraternal parties." These statements were repeated in conversations with the Socialist Party during the remainder of the year.

Talks were held in Moscow during 1-3 July between CPSU and PCF leaders on a number of European problems, the building of socialism, and the consolidation of forces for world peace. The joint communiqué (*ibid.*, 10 July) endorsed principles of sovereignty and noninterference in the internal affairs of parties, principles laid down at the June 1969 International Meeting of Communist and Workers' Parties. The PCF approved international and domestic policies, accepted at the CPSU congress, and the two parties concurred on all major international issues and agreed to a joint struggle against all departures from unity of action in the fight against imperialism. In exchange for its support, the PCF was assured by the CPSU that the principles determined by the June 1969 meeting, and the "various forms according to each country's national specific traits and historical conditions" that socialism could take would be respected. The most difficult subject, Czechoslovakia, was avoided. The dissident publication *Unir-Débat* (10 July-10 August) strongly criticized Marchais for drafting the communiqué "as if the intervention had never occurred." It accused the PCF of being summoned to Moscow and allowed to use certain formulas to save face and enter into dialogue with the French Socialist Party. A document released in January by the Communist Party of Czechoslovakia and the CPSU congress were more difficult situations.

The document, entitled "Lessons drawn from the crisis development in the party and society since the Thirteenth Congress of the Czechoslovak Party," justified the 1968 invasion and the subsequent "normalization." After taking several days to consider its reply, the PCF answered:

> The PCF position is well-known. Our party voiced its opposition to the military intervention. It has always advocated a *political* settlement of the crisis.... Forces capable of achieving this existed. Nothing induces our party to modify its position. (*L'Humanité*, 18 January).

Then came criticism of the document, because it did not adhere to the principles which the PCF vigorously defended:

> Furthermore, this document introduces into the concept of the socialist states' national sovereignty elements which are not part of the International Communist Movement's principles, as jointly defined by the June 1969 Conference.... These principles are equally valid for relations between communist parties. Our party adheres resolutely to the letter and spirit of these principles. (*Ibid.*)

At the CPSU congress, Czechoslovak leader Gustáv Husák used his speech to justify the Soviet invasion, despite prior agreement by delegates not to mention the issue. Marchais quickly replied, as reported in a telephone interview with *L'Humanité* (2 April):

> Our delegation did not wish to recall the well known and unchanged position of the PCF on the military intervention in Czechoslovakia in August 1968. It is regrettable the Czechoslovak delegate devoted his greeting to an exposé on this question in which he was critical of our position. I add that the thesis formulated by the delegate seems foreign to the principles defined in common at the 1969 conference.

Marchais reminded Husák that the PCF was willing, "despite certain differences," to present a united front against imperialism; "the diversity in conditions of the struggle should by no means weaken action by the parties."

The dissident *Unir-Débat* (10 June) accused Marchais of "feigning protest" in his remarks and criticized him for praising only successes of the Soviets. Others suggested he might have blamed Brezhnev and not Husák for the intervention. Rather than precipitating a controversy and insulting the Soviet leader, Marchais preferred to keep silent. The "coolness of his remarks" and his reproach of Husák did not cause PCF absence from the Czechoslovak party congress at the end of May in Prague. Sending a PCF delegation to the congress angered party dissidents. They claimed that this action in fact recognized Husák, the result of the intervention and, hence, intervention itself (*Est & Ouest*, 16-30 April). After the British and Spanish communist parties had decided not to send delegations, the Italian Communist Party and the PCF together reportedly agreed to attend but not to send their top leaders.

The PCF then sent Raymond Guyot, which was a "slap at the Soviets" (*Unir-Débat* 10 June), since he is the brother-in-law of Arthur London, a prominent Czech imprisoned from 1952 to 1956. He wrote an autobiography, *L'Aveu*, subsequently filmed in France. The significance of sending Guyot was lost, however, when he read his opening address:

> In the recent period acknowledged differences have appeared between our two parties. As our [Nineteenth] Congress declared, we believe their existence must not lead to any weakening of the fundamental bonds which unite our communist parties.... This is the principle which inspires and will continue to inspire our line of conduct under any circumstances. (*L'Humanité*, 28 May).

He then reiterated PCF adherence to the principles of sovereignty and independence of individual parties and discussed general, non-controversial topics. An official greeting to the Czechoslovak party on its fiftieth anniversary repeated the themes of Guyot's address (*ibid.*, 14 May). The PCF message to the Polish United Workers' Party on its anniversary read: "Poland is coming to an end of errors that led to crisis, namely the lack of a spirit of responsibility and inertia of representatives" (*ibid.*, 22 July). It praised the Polish government for adopting measures to raise its standard of living and ending the "crisis of confidence" but added "it is necessary to hear more."

The PCF was elated by Brezhnev's state visit to France in October, his first trip to a West European country. A major part of Raymond Guyot's report on international affairs to a Central Committee meeting was devoted to this topic, and *L'Humanité* ran almost daily stories on its significance "as a major step in Franco-Soviet relations [which] would stimulate multiform cooperation between the two countries" (*ibid.*, 8 October). It hoped that Brezhnev's visit would activate preparation for a European security conference, and would underline the importance of recent European security agreements: the U.S.S.R.-Poland and U.S.S.R.-West German treaties, and the West Berlin agreement.[3] During the visit, official contact between Brezhnev and the PCF was limited to a visit to Lenin's former apartment in Paris by Brezhnev, although the party ran full-page articles on his activities and published an official welcome by Marchais (*ibid.*, 25 October). At a 4 November PCF rally in Paris, Politburo member Ansart gave a report on the "positive results" of the visit, citing the conclusion of a number of economic and commercial pacts, agreement on preconditions for the European security conference, "turning Europe toward peace ... liquidation of antagonistic military blocs, for the sensible reduction of the military charges that weigh on the people" (*ibid.*).

Party dissidents took the occasion of Brezhnev's visit to launch attacks against Soviet policies and the leader himself: "The true enemies of socialism are Brezhnev and his like. So Stalin has passed, so Brezhnev will pass and, with him, the methods of authoritarian centralism." They pointed out: "The profound political significance [of the visit] does not escape us.... If he is a welcome guest for Pompidou, Brezhnev gets no welcome from thoughtful Communists." (*Unir-Débat*, 10 October.)

The PCF "Government Program" adopted in October reaffirmed the party's position on these European security issues, calling for French recognition of East Germany, disengagement from

---

[3]The PCF endorsed the Berlin settlement as a step along the path of detente, security and cooperation in Europe (*L'Humanité*, 4 and 10 September). It called for immediate signing of the agreement, despite some "minor disagreement over details." And it criticized the Western powers, acting under pressure from the United States, for such "special and independent problems" as Berlin as preconditions for a European security conference.

the Atlantic alliance, and an immediate European security conference. It did not, however, demand French withdrawal from the European Economic Community. Instead, it advocated an extension of "little Europe" to include cooperation with Eastern Europe and revision of the Rome treaty (*ibid.*, 12 October). It continued to criticize the existing organization as a "mutilated response to the needs of contemporary economy." (*Ibid.*, 18 November.)

The PCF has supported the U.S.S.R. in the Sino-Soviet rift, and has generally ignored mention of China in its communiqués and journals. When U.S. President Nixon's visit to China was announced, however, *L'Humanité* (17 and 26 July) reprinted editorial comment from *Pravda*. After China was admitted to the United Nations, the PCF commented: "This dissipates an absurdity, puts into concordance the facts.... But, on the other hand, [the United States] believes the moment has come to play China against the U.S.S.R." (*Ibid.*, 26 October.) The PCF claimed that it had always advocated admission of China into the U.N., despite differences which existed between the communist parties of the two countries.[4] A direct confrontation with the Chinese government occurred when it refused to receive two PCF members of a French parliamentary delegation that was to visit Peking. The National Assembly president then reorganized the mission, excluding the PCF, which in turn criticized him and bitterly denounced the Chinese government for "interfering in French internal affairs and discriminating against faithful fighters against imperialism" (*ibid.*, 13 July).

International Party Contacts. The PCF was represented at the London meeting of European communist parties, 11-13 January 1971, by a delegation led by Jacques Denis. Earlier the same month, Politburo members Roland Leroy and Raymond Guyot met with members of the Communist Party of Spain. André Vieuguet and Claude Poperen saw leading members of the Portuguese Communist Party. (*L'Humanité*, 12 and 15 January, for joint communiqués). Cuban President Osvaldo Dorticos and Premier Fidel Castro received André Vieuguet and a PCF delegation on 4 February in Havana. Georges Marchais led the PCF delegation, including Gaston Plissonnier and Madeleine Vincent, to the CPSU congress (*ibid.*; 1 April lists the delegation). During the congress, PCF leaders met with First Secretary Edward Gierek of the Polish United Workers' Party and with Japanese and U.A.R. party officials. Gierek also met with Jacques Duclos in Poland on 24 March; on 11 June the Polish leader received Gaston Plissonnier and a PCF delegation. On 24 March the PCF and Socialist Vanguard Party of Algeria held consultations on problems of concern to petroleum-rich countries.

Paul Laurent and Robert Montdargent represented the PCF at the Bulgarian party congress in April. At the end of that month, Georges Séguy led a CGT group to Finland for talks with labor leaders. A Korean Workers' Party group was received 13 May in Paris by Georges Marchais. Twenty-seven countries sent representatives to the international scientific conference in May at Paris, which was sponsored by the Maurice-Thorez Institute and devoted to the centenary of the Paris Commune. On 24 May, Raymond Guyot arrived in Prague for the Czechoslovak party congress (see above). Roland Leroy headed the PCF delegation to the congress of the Socialist Unity Party in East Berlin, opening 15 June. Also in June, Politburo member Claude Poperen led a PCF delegation to the congress of the Mongolian People's Revolutionary Party.

On 20 June the PCF sponsored a rally of "solidarity with the Spanish people"; Etienne Fajon presided, and Jacques Duclos and Spanish party leaders Dolores Ibárruri and Santiago Carrillo

---

[4]The communiqué sent to the Chinese Communist Party on its 50th Anniversary reproached it for "the profound differences [which] have appeared between us, which are detrimental to our common cause ... the refusal to take joint action against imperialism for the sake of some particular view hinders greater and more rapid successes of the struggle." (*L'Humanité*, 1 July).

spoke. The rally marked the end of a PCF-sponsored campaign to raise money for Spanish workers. A high-powered meeting took place 1-3 July in Moscow between CPSU and PCF leaders (*ibid.*, 6 and 10 July for listing and communiqué).

Japanese Central Committee members met with the PCF 6-13 August to discuss Southeast Asian problems. Talks were held 30 August-6 September in Sofia between Georges Marchais and Bulgarian First Secretary Zhivkov (*ibid.*, 4 September for communiqué). PCF delegations visited collective and state farms in Russia, 15-25 September, and toured cooperatives in East Germany on 29 September. Representatives of the PCF met with West German communist party members at Saarbrücken on 17 September to discuss workers' problems in border factories, and the Free German Trade Union Federation was received for the first time in France by Georges Séguy during 20-27 September. A large open meeting calling for recognition of the German Democratic Republic and immediate convocation of a European security conference was held at the Mutualité Hall on 7 October. Friedrich Ebert and other top East and West German party leaders spoke; Jacques Duclos chaired the meeting. (*Ibid.*, 8 October.) Marchais consulted with Italian party leaders on a number of European problems during 16-17 November in Paris. Guy Besse represented the PCF at the Indian party congress earlier that month, and in mid-November it was announced that Jacques Duclos was soon to visit Chile at the invitation of President Allende. A delegation of the Israeli Communist Party (RAKAH) met with PCF leaders in Paris on 7-13 December.

Publications. The main publications of the PCF include its daily newspaper, *L'Humanité*; a weekly, *France Nouvelle*; a monthly theoretical organ, *Cahiers du Communisme*; a popular weekend magazine, *Humanité Dimanche*, which introduced a new format on 18 April to coincide with a circulation drive (estimated at 40,000); a peasant weekly, *La Terre*; an intellectual monthly, *La Nouvelle Critique*; a literary monthly, *Europe*; a bimonthly economic journal, *Economie et Politique*; a philosophically oriented bimonthly, *La Pensée*; and a historical quarterly, *Les Cahiers de l'Institut Maurice-Thorez*. In addition, the party has a number of province papers. The MJC publishes *Nous Les Garcons et Les Filles* and the monthly journals, *Avante Garde* and *Le Nouveau Clarté*. For intraparty work, the Central Committee has *La Vie du Parti*, a monthly dealing with organization propaganda, education, and other matters.

*   *   *

Trotskyists. The two major opposing Trotskyist groupings in France are the Communist League (Ligue Communiste) and the Internationalist Communist Organization (Organization Communiste Internationaliste; OCI). They are aligned with the United Secretariat and the International Committee of the Fourth International, respectively.

The Communist League was formed in April 1969 by militants of the banned Internationalist Communist Party, led by Pierre Frank, and former militants of the banned Revolutionary Communist Youth, centered around the publication *Rouge*. The league reportedly has about 1,200 members in the Paris area (*Le Monde*, 21-22 February), and its leaders include Pierre Frank, Alain Krivine, Daniel Bensaïd and Henri Weber (*ibid.*, 3-9 June, lists Politburo). One of the top priorities of the group are relations with workers and trade unions. It devoted much of its congress (29-31 May) at Rouen to an analysis of activities in factories and schools. Of those present at the congress some 25 per cent were teachers; 43 per cent were students; 65 per cent were under the age of twenty-five years (*ibid.*, 1 June). The league often collaborates with the PSU and groups centered around the publications *Unir-Débat* and *Politique Hebdo*. After lengthy negotiations, it finally signed a protocol 5 January which defined lines of a future merger with a Trotskyist group around *La Lutte Ouvrière* and included plans for fusion of this publication with the League's organ, *Rouge*.

At the Rouen congress Krivine said he wanted the League to "break loose from leftism and broaden its base." Weber added: "The first congress was the one for the struggle of Leninism, the rejection of ultra-leftism.... This is the congress of disengagement from the leftist movement." (*Ibid.*)

The league scored somewhat of a success because of the "Guiot affair" in February. It represented the only group able to organize mass support, protesting the arrest of a Paris university student named Raymond Guiot. Maoists had used the situation to increase militancy and gained only scattered support. Rallies organized by other leftist groups met with poor response. As a result, the league increased its student following. It received wide support from labor and left-wing groups when the trial of *Rouge* editor Charles Michaloux opened on 19 October in Paris. (He was found guilty the following month on four counts of defaming the police.)

On 16 May the Communist League mobilized 30,000 persons, including delegates from 12 foreign countries, for the centenary of the Paris Commune. This was a sizable show of strength, since the PCF appeal for a demonstration the following week brought out only 50,000 (*Le Monde*, 18 May). And on May Day 15,000 to 25,000 demonstrators from the league, the PSU, and other groups marched (as compared with 30,000 to 40,000 CGT participants later that day). Krivine told the PCF that it should take note of these numbers. In June 1970 the Communist League was active in creation of Red Help (Secours Rouge). Attempts by Maoists to gain control of the organization and manipulation of "ultra-left" groups caused four founding Trotskyist members to resign and the Communist League to withdraw its support. A national meeting to advertise Red Help was held on 29 October in Paris.

A minority group in the Communist League, comprising 200 to 300 members, primarily students from the south of Paris, announced its decision to leave the organization (*Le Monde*, 21-22 February). At a Central Committee meeting a week earlier it had been accused of preparing to set up its own group. On 24 February, former minority leaders Henri Maller and Isaac Joshua announced establishment of a new movement, "Revolution," and a monthly journal by the same name. *Rouge* (11 March) condemned the minority for its views and the split.

The other main Trotskyist grouping includes three different but related groups: (1) The Internationalist Communist Organization, banned in 1968 but legal since 4 July 1970, is led by Pierre Lambert, Stephane Just, and Charles Berg. It publishes *La Verité*, an irregular theoretical journal. (2) The Alliance of Youth for Socialism (Alliance des Jeunes pour le Socialisme; AJS) is headed by Charles Berg, reelected secretary-general at the second AJS congress on 2 November 1971. It originated from the Federation of Revolutionary Students, banned in 1968 but legal since 1970. Its slogan is "We Must Lead Youth from Revolt to Revolution." Its aim is to make itself known to workers, and it seeks unity of all organizations that support workers' organizations. It publishes a monthly, *Jeune Révolutionnaire*. (3) The Federation of Workers' Alliance Committees (Fédération des Comités d'Alliance Ouvrière supersedes another group, banned in 1968, which had gathered around the publication *Révoltes*. It is led by Stephane Just, and its principal publication is the weekly *Informations Ouvrières*.

Most of the communist parties and organizations, independent of the PCF, were banned on 12 June 1968 (see *YICA*, 1969, p. 319). During 1971, several of them reconstituted themselves under different names or were propagating their views in renamed journals. Nearly all non-PCF Marxist-Leninist groups are either pro-Chinese or Trotskyist in orientation. (For a genealogy of the development of most of these organizations see *L'Idiot International*, Paris and London, February 1970, and *YICA* from 1966 on; see *Est & Ouest*, 1-15 May 1971, p. 251, for a list of splinter and ultra-left organizations.)

Pro-Chinese Groups. Views of the banned Marxist-Leninist Communist Party of France (Parti Communiste Marxiste-Léniniste de France; PCMLF) were propagated during 1971 by the weekly

L'Humanité Rouge. The group around this publication reportedly numbers 2,500 (*Est & Ouest*, 1-15 May) and appears to be the only group to have support of the Chinese Communist Party leadership. Its influence has been waning after a series of defeats since 1968, a serious internal crisis in the spring of 1970, and splitting of the group into a number of factions (see *YICA*, 1971, p. 168). The publications director, François Marty, was killed 1 June 1971 in an automobile accident. He had helped found the PCMLF and had been publisher of *L'Humanité Nouvelle*, banned in 1968, but which appeared in 1971 on an irregular and clandestine basis.

Another major group is the Proletarian Left (Gauche Prolétarienne; GP), founded by leaders of the banned Union of Communist Youth (Union des Jeunesses Communistes Marxistes-Léninistes; UJCML), which has the monthly publication *La Cause du Peuple*. GP and its newspaper were banned on 27 May 1970, the editors were sentenced to prison terms, and leader Alain Geismer received an eighteen months' sentence for inciting to riot. On 24 November 1970 Geismer was given an additional two-year term for continuing activities of the banned group. On 7 July 1971 he was again in court on the same charge and sentenced to another eighteen months, to be served concurrently. With national support for the GP decreasing, autonomous groups were started in Montpellier, Grenoble, and the Normandy region (*Le Monde*, 28 January).

While *La Cause du Peuple* was being suppressed, the group first attempted to publicize its views in *L'Idiot International*. On 15 January some of its supporters launched a new monthly *J'Accuse*. It was under the patronage of Jean-Paul Sartre, Jean-Luc Godard, and Simone de Beauvoir. Beauvoir resigned as director of *L'Idiot International* in April. *J'Accuse* had the same spirit as *La Cause du Peuple*, being oriented toward workers, but was better edited.[5] Editors of the latter, Michel Le Bris, Jean-Pierre Le Dantec, and Michel Leiris, were released from prison in January and the publication reappeared. After several issues were not seized by the government, the editors planned to publish semimonthly under the slogan "For a New Justice, for Truth, for Liberty." During the summer *La Cause du Peuple* absorbed *J'Accuse*. Jean-Paul Sartre serves as director.[6]

Maoists had tried unsuccessfully to gain control of Red Help but only succeeded in splintering and weakening the group. They had hoped that the reappearance of *La Cause du Peuple*, their own vehicle for ideologies, would help them regain strength. However, in June the government cracked down on Maoist and "revolutionary" publications. Jean-Paul Sartre was arrested for libel; Jean Edern Hallier and the editors of *Tout*, *Révolution*, and *Rouge* were charged on several counts. Police began close surveillance of these groups, and arrests on miscellaneous charges took place during the fall.

Another significant Maoist group, Long Live the Revolution (Vive la Révolution; VLR), was formed in July 1969 by dissident ex-UJCML members. It functioned in Paris, particularly at universities, under the leadership of Roland Castro. With the slogan, "To Change Life," VLR attracted various Maoists groups, all advocates of "spontaneity" and believers in immediate revolution. A fortnightly publication, *Tout*, summarized VLR views: "What do we want? Everything." In the fall of 1970 VLR reoriented itself and chose a non-directed, loose structure. In April 1971 it dissolved itself: "We are no longer going to proclaim the revolution, we are going to make it.... We are beginning to take ourselves seriously." (*Le Monde*, 27 August). *Tout* last appeared in July. "Autonomous units of struggle" have been set up in local communities.

Several dozen other Maoist militants have organized a clandestine group, the New Popular Resistance (La Nouvelle Résistance Populaire), which advocates commando-type action to bring

---

[5]*Le Monde*, 28 January 1971, gives an analysis of Maoist publications.
[6]*New York Times Magazine*, 17 October 1971, p. 38, carries an interview with Sartre on his publishing activities.

about desired results. In 1971 it attacked the Jordanian Embassy allegedly to demonstrate French workers' support for the Palestinian revolution. Activities were curtailed by the arrest of one of its leaders, Bernard Liscia, and several "shock troopers" (*ibid.*, 29 October).

American Enterprise Institute
for Public Policy Research

Kay McKeough

Germany: Federal Republic of Germany

The Communist Party of Germany (Kommunistische Partei Deutschlands; KPD) was founded in 1918. Outlawed in August 1956 for being in conflict with the Basic Law of the Federal Republic, the party was ordered dissolved and membership in it was prohibited. Thereafter the KPD engaged in clandestine activities in West Germany from headquarters relocated in East Berlin and also carried on a persistent fight to regain legal status. Its role was drastically altered in September 1968 when the German Communist Party (Deutsche Kommunistische Partei; DKP) was established as a new and legal West German party. Both the KPD and the DKP, as pro-Soviet parties, face some competition from the growing number of extreme left-wing splinter groups, including no less than twenty pro-Chinese organizations.

No membership figures for the KPD are available for 1971, but it is generally assumed that they are a small fraction of the 7,000 estimated late in 1968, just before large-scale transfers to the DKP began. DKP membership, on the other hand, has been growing rapidly: at the party congress in November 1971 it was reported to have reached 33,410 at the beginning of the month, organized into 408 factory groups, 871 residential groups, and 23 university units. The total was exclusive of the Socialist German Workers Youth (SDAJ), the communist youth organization. The population of West Germany is 60,840,000 (estimated 1970).

The DKP's ability to attract new members has not been equaled by success at the polls, either at the national or state level. In the latest general election, in September 1969, the communist-organized leftist coalition, Action for Democratic Progress, received only 0.6 per cent of the vote. In 1971 the DKP staged intensive campaigns in state elections, but in all instances failed to gain the minimum 5 per cent prerequisite for representation in the state governments. In the balloting for the Landtag of Schleswig-Holstein (25 April), for instance, the DKP won the support of only 0.4 per cent of the electorate; in the Rhineland-Palatinate (21 March), 0.9 per cent; and in the city-state of Bremen (10 October), 3.13 per cent. In 1970 the DKP record had been similarly unimpressive in elections held that year in North Rhine-Westphalia (0.9 per cent), Lower Saxony (0.4), the Saarland (2.7), Bavaria (0.4), Hesse (1.2), and Hamburg (1.7).

The communists have registered somewhat greater success in local elections. In 1971 they won their first seats on the city council of Mannheim and the county administration of Esslingen, and *DKP Pressedienst* (Düsseldorf, 28 October) announced that communists were represented in a total of twenty-six local government bodies, including the large cities of Stuttgart, Nuremberg, and Bottrop.

The DKP in 1971 stepped up its efforts to gain influence within the labor unions and tried to propagandize among factory workers by means of a veritable flood of plant newspapers. Each individual publication—out of a total of 326—tried to highlight the grievances of workers in the immediate area and thus to provoke discontent and class awareness (*Welt am Sonntag*, Hamburg, 7 February). In fact, the draft theses prepared for submission to the DKP congress in November

1971 laid down general instructions for trade union activities: "Every communist has the duty to be an active labor union member and to win his fellow workers over to the labor unions" (*Unsere Zeit*, 7 August, special supplement).

Leadership and Organization. In 1971 the KPD organization seemed on the verge of being dismantled in spite of the persistent demands for lifting of the party ban. The most persuasive evidence was the request by Max Reimann, the long-term secretary-general of the KPD and in recent years almost its sole spokesman, for admission to membership in the DKP. Asked whether his entry into the DKP marked perhaps a merger of the KPD and DKP, Reimann denied that this was the case and added: "With my entry into the DKP I belong to only one party, and that is the DKP. Thus I am exercising no party functions outside it." (*Neues Deutschland*, East Berlin, 25 September.) Shortly after the KPD leader announced his decision, the DKP Presidium proposed that its upcoming party congress should elect him honorary president.

The DKP held its Second Congress in Düsseldorf on 25-28 November. Kurt Bachmann was reelected to the office of party chairman, Herbert Mies was again chosen as his deputy, and Max Reimann was named honorary president. All previous members of the Presidium retained their posts, and several new members were added. The new Presidium is composed of incumbents Bachmann, Mies, Kurt Erlebach, Ludwig Müller, Karl-Heinz Nötzel, Gerhard Deumlich, Hermann Gautier, Willi Gerns, and Manfred Kapluck, together with Georg Polikeit (former chief of Information Services) and newcomers Jupp Angenfort, Martha Buschmann, Kurt Fritsch, Heinz Lang, and Max Schäfer. Karl-Heinz Schröder was renamed Presidium secretary. The Secretariat, under the leadership of Herbert Mies and his deputy Hermann Gautier, included Werner Cieslak, Willi Mohn, Arno Rann, Karl-Heinz Schröder, and Robert Steigerwald. Virtually without exception, these leaders of the DKP are important former functionaries of the KPD. Twenty-one newcomers were elected to the Party Executive (i.e. Central Committee) of 91 members.

A report by the Interior Ministry on right and left-wing extremist political activities in the Federal Republic (Bonn, 5 April) included a number of interesting findings on the DKP. An analysis of the party's financial situation, for instance, would indicate expenditures far in excess of membership fees and apparent contributions. The report pointed out that DKP functionaries not only received training in West Germany, but also were sent regularly to East Berlin and Moscow for schooling. Concerning the KPD, it appears noteworthy that the Interior Ministry eliminated that party from its listing of important communist groups active in the Federal Republic.

A group that was included was the Socialist German Workers Youth (SDAJ), which in 1971 had an estimated membership of at least 10,000. At last clearly identified as the youth organization of the DKP, it grew noticeably more active and staged a major congress of its own at Recklinghausen in the Ruhr on 22-23 May under the slogan "Working Youth Versus Monopolies." Chairman of the SDAJ is Rolf-Jürgen Priemer, who was active in communist youth activities long before the SDAJ was founded in 1968.

Party Internal Affairs. Removal of the ban against it was the all-pervasive interest of the KPD in 1971. Chances for legalization received a serious setback in 1970 when the federal constitutional court in Karlsruhe banned dissemination of the draft program, which the party had prepared in 1968 to prove its desire to "achieve socialist reconstruction by peaceful democratic means." In June 1971, however, a provincial court in Flensburg ruled that confiscation of the copies of the draft program in 1968 had been illegal. Max Reimann interpreted the new decision optimistically: "A court of the Federal Republic has declared that the KPD's draft program of 1968 was not in violation of the constitution.... If the government retains the ban, it means new arbitrariness directed against our party.... The government should take advantage of the opportunity it has to revoke the ban.'' (Interview, *Friheten*, Oslo, 16-21 August.) Reimann also asserted that maintenance of the ban fed "revanchism and anti-communism" and implied government support of the "worst enemies of any democratic development" ("German Freedom Station 904," 12 August).

The DKP lent strong support to the KPD's cause with such allegations as the following: "The KPD prohibition is a constant threat to all democrats and a direct aid to the reactionary, neo-fascist forces of our country. Without repealing the KPD prohibition, the policy of the Brandt-Scheel government, seeking 'more democracy' and wanting peaceful, equal cooperation with the socialist states and other European states, remains questionable." (*Unsere Zeit*, 19 June).

The DKP outlined its ideology, tasks, and policies in the draft theses for its Second Congress (*Unsere Zeit*, 7 August, special supplement). The theses clearly reflected the major problem faced by the DKP: how to avoid violations of the constitution which would endanger its legality. This problem had a new urgency because the Interior Ministry reported in May that it was becoming increasingly evident that the goals of the DKP were identical with those of the illegal KPD. Of 663 high party functionaries of the DKP, the government revealed, at least 440 had belonged to the KPD before its prohibition and 523 had continued to be active afterward.

Aware of the dangers confronting its survival, the DKP refrained, in its theses, from calling for a dictatorship of the proletariat. Instead, it urged "anti-monopolistic forces, under the leadership of the working class, to struggle and win decisive influence in the state and society." Socialism was acknowledged as the party goal, but with the qualification that while the "development toward socialism does not take place automatically, neither can it be imported nor come about by a putsch or conspiracy." The party then formulated its approach to change: "The DKP strives for transformation on the basis of the democratic principles and rights proclaimed in the constitution." The DKP theses placed heavy emphasis on the need for "unity of action"—at the core of which would be cooperation between Social Democrats and communists—and termed such unity the "crucial issue in communist policy." The party declared further, that it would not be diverted from this orientation either by "stepped-up anti-communism in the Social Democratic leadership, or by the phony revolutionary phraseology of left-wing opportunist groups." (*Ibid.*)

The DKP's affirmation of unwavering adherence to unity seemed to clash with its earlier acknowledgment of the Social Democrats' "emphatic rejection of joint action with Communists" (*WMR*, May). The Social Democratic Party, in fact, on 26 February had resolved that "the Party Council, the Executive Board, and Control Commission expect from all members of the party unmistakable respect for decisions on the incompatibility of action groups with Communist organizations, no matter what direction." This *Unvereinbarkeitsbeschluss* (resolution on incompatibility), first promulgated in November 1970, was based on the following argument: "We are living in a world which we have to share with the communists. Since we have to coexist with them it is vital to ensure that we are not swallowed up by them." (*News From Germany*, Bonn, vol. 26, January/February/March/April 1971). The DKP assessed the Social Democratic position paper as a sign of "intensified anti-communism" and predicted future trouble from a move which "reactionary forces, primarily the CDU-CSU [Christian Democratic Union-Christian Social Union] leaders and the Springer press, acclaim," and alleged that "the anti-communist course of the Social Democratic leadership is fateful, because it heats up the political climate in which rightist extremism and neo-Nazism flourish" (*Neues Deutschland*, East Berlin, 2 March).

The DKP's first party school was established in Essen in 1971 and named in honor of Karl Liebknecht. According to Heinz Muelhaus, the temporary director, the school could accommodate eighteen resident students and accept additional non-residents for each class. Its purpose would be to train party members, primarily in scientific socialism. Courses for the party elite would be conducted by specialists such as Josef Schleifstein, head of the Institute for Marxist Studies at Frankfurt, and by guest lecturers from France and East Germany. During vacations, courses for young people would be offered, and before elections DKP candidates would study the special problems of local politics. Not all training would be theoretical; editors of communist publications, for instance, would be given instruction in the psychologically most effective presentation of communist propaganda. (*Handelsblatt*, Düsseldorf, 13 September.)

In April, the Institute for Marxist Studies sponsored what was claimed to be the "largest social science conference ever held in the Federal Republic," when 1,200 participants met in Frankfurt to discuss "Economic Theory—Political Strategy and Trade Unions." At the conclusion of the conference, Schleifstein commented: "What force besides Marxism in the Federal Republic is today in the position of being able to hold such an event? None!" (*Unsere Zeit*, 1 May).

In the summer the DKP sponsored a cultural and political forum held in Nuremberg at which "more than 400 writers, artists, scholars, workers, and students" discussed possible methods of "meeting the cultural requirements of the working class, the effects of monopolization of the mass media and other problems." The forum resolved to launch a movement to be called Democratic Action, which through "co-management of the mass media, among press, radio, and television staffs" would seek to improve the party's press and exhibitions. (*WMR*, August.)

Communist-controlled community action campaigns, built around local or regional grievances or domestic and foreign policy problems, flourished in 1971. For instance, ratification of the Moscow treaty was a theme in Düsseldorf, high rents and land speculation in Hamburg, the rising cost of automobile insurance in Munich, and the shortage of kindergartens in Nuremberg and Ludwigshafen. There were anti-pollution campaigns, anti-inflation protests, and highly effective "Roter Punkt" actions—the mobilization of private transportation during public transit delays or blockages.

Domestic Views and Activities. Domestically the DKP called for the greatest vigilance, and deputy party chief, Herbert Mies, explained the need:

> A strategic goal of West German imperialism is to intensify the exploitation of the working people and use the fruits of the technological revolution for strengthening the state-monopoly system and for building up its economic and military power. The slogan of "integrating" political organizations and the trade unions into the capitalist system serves these objectives. (*WMR*, May 1971.)

According to Mies, the West German government was motivated by its desire to extend its economic and political influence abroad, maintain the status quo in Europe, and "roll back socialism and prevent the growth of the national liberation movement." The only improvements the communist leader noticed under the Social Democratic government were the adoption of "more flexible tactics" by authorities and the resort to "new strategic concepts" by big capital "under the impact of a changing alignment of forces." According to Mies, the DKP had vowed to oppose the "reactionary, aggressive strategy of the ruling class" by unceasingly fighting for a "democratic renovation of state and society," according to this plan:

> Renovation will be initiated by eliminating neo-Nazism and its roots ... defeating the militarists' great-power policy ... extending the political rights of the working people, ensuring that they have a say in management and control, socializing the big corporations, putting the economy on a democratically planned basis and effecting progressive reforms in social security, education and culture.

These and similar domestic ideas were incorporated into the "Manifesto of the Düsseldorf DKP Congress," which appeared under the slogan "The Future Depends on Us—What the Future Brings Will Determine Our Deeds." (*Neues Deutschland*, 28 November.)

The DKP condemned West Germany's tax policies, claiming that it took money from the workers, "the simple people, and all those who create values," and put it in the pockets of the rich. It suggested that part of the fiscal problem could be alleviated if annual expenditures for arms were reduced by 15 per cent and if ties to the "bankrupt U.S. dollar" were severed, thus ending support for the "dirty U.S. war in Indochina." The communists also demanded immediate suspension of currency "offset" payments amounting to 3 billion German marks, and using the funds to strengthen the domestic economy for the benefit of the workers. (*DKP Pressedienst*, 18 August.)

"Unchecked exploitation" of the farmers was claimed by the communists, who cited the agricultural state of Schleswig-Holstein as an example and alleged that in 1970 50 per cent of the farmers sustained losses, 25 per cent labored just to break even, and a mere 25 per cent gained a satisfactory return. The DKP claimed to be the only party in the country interested in developing an agricultural program that would assure a decent existence for the farm population. (*Ibid.*, 14 October.) Special interest in the farmers was also evidenced by the DKP's publication of *Landrevue*, the only regular party newspaper in the Federal Republic to be keyed to this special interest group. The first issue (20 January 1971) contained articles comparing the farmers' lot in West Germany and the German Democratic Republic (GDR), discussed problems of territorial and administrative reforms pertaining to agriculture, and reported on the giant Badische Anilinund Sodafabrik, which is a big West German producer of fertilizers and other chemicals.

East-West German Relations. West German communist views on relations with the GDR in some ways grew more rigid in 1971 and in others tried to come to grips with changing international conditions. The aforementioned theses for the party congress concluded that it was the DKP's task to "repel all attacks against the GDR as attacks against its own interests," and claimed that West German recognition of the GDR had been denied because the "ruling monopolistic-capitalistic circles in the Federal Republic" feared that the "example of social security and steady social progress set by the GDR [would] make socialism the goal of the workers in the Federal Republic as well." The theses also characterized the GDR as a "stabilizer of peace" in Europe which served as a barrier to the "big-power drive of the West German imperialists and militarists" and provided "strong support for the struggle of workers, employees, intellectuals, and farmers in the Federal Republic for their social and political interests against big capital."

West German communists dropped their previous references to West Berlin as an "independent political unit" when it became obvious that four-power negotiations would lead to an agreement in 1971. The DKP draft program offered a new interpretation of the situation:

> West Berlin must no longer be a disturbing factor that upsets peace and European security. West Berlin is not a part of the Federal Republic. For this reason the Federal government must cease to claim rights there to which it is not entitled. The West Berlin issue can be resolved if the international agreements on its special status are respected and if the sovereign rights of the GDR are recognized.

The phraseology of the theses provided enough flexibility to allow the DKP Presidium to express approval of the quadripartite Berlin Agreement after it was signed by the United States, Great Britain, France, and the Soviet Union in August. A special DKP statement issued on 25 August gave the credit for the successful conclusion of the negotiations to the "persistent and patient efforts of the Soviet Union, acting in the closest possible coordination with the other socialist countries, particularly the GDR, for bringing about this agreement" (*DKP Pressedienst*, 25 August).

A few weeks later Kurt Bachmann took a critical stand on the attitude of the Federal Government and the Senate of West Berlin in the negotiations with the GDR. With intra-German agreements on traffic and the status of "enclaves" prerequisite to implementation of the four-power Berlin accord, the West German communists demanded that the Federal government "proceed from realities and immediately discontinue all attempts to discriminate against the GDR" (*ibid.*, 31 October). When the Germans finally reached a compromise on Berlin in December, the DKP welcomed the agreement and its "basis of recognition of the principles of full equality, non-discrimination

... and respect for the sovereign rights and legitimate interests of the GDR and the FRG'' (*ibid.*, 11 December).

International Views and Party Contact. The draft program for the DKP congress affirmed that the interests of the working class demanded a "consistent peace and détente policy" and implied that the communist party was the only consistent advocate of such a policy. Heading the communists' list of international moves considered mandatory for peace in Europe were the ratification and implementation of the treaties signed between the Federal Republic and the U.S.S.R. and Poland in 1970. Of only slightly lesser importance were the convening of a European security conference; the reduction of forces and arms in Central Europe and the simultaneous dissolution of the NATO and the Warsaw Pact military organizations; recognition of the GDR as a sovereign state under international law; and U.N. membership for both Germanies.

Throughout 1971 the DKP stressed its solidarity with the Soviet Union and its gratitude: "The Soviet Union bore and bears the main burden of the conflict with imperialism. That is only one of many reasons why the DKP ... views the question of the attitude toward the Soviet Union as a decisive criterion for every communist" (*Unsere Zeit*, 3 July). The closeness of the relationship was dramatically symbolized by the strength of the delegation sent to the DKP congress by the Communist Party of the Soviet Union (CPSU). Leading the delegation was CPSU Politburo member Arvids Pelshe, who was the target of uncommon demonstrations of fraternal approval and set a precedent as the first Soviet Politburo member ever to travel to West Germany on party business.

The similarly high-level East German delegation to the DKP congress was led by Politburo member Albert Norden and included several members of the Central Committee of East Germany's Socialist Unity Party of Germany (SED). It was probably a sign of changing times—and particularly of the progress of West Germany's *Ostpolitik*—that high-ranking party functionaries from the Soviet Union and the GDR were even allowed to enter the Federal Republic. The host party, in turn, reacted to this official evidence of increasing détente between East and West by polite, though unmistakable, praise of Chancellor Brandt's initiatives in Eastern Europe.

Earlier in the year, DKP leaders attended congresses of the CPSU and the SED and evaluated the proceedings as evidence that "socialism and peace are one" (*Unsere Zeit*, 3 July). Total faith in the East European parties as exemplary models was also expressed at the DKP congress. Deputy Chairman Mies gave this reason for his party's close ties with the socialist countries: "It is a basic principle of our policy and our *Weltanschauung* [that] the working class of our country can only understand and realize its role in changing society when it consciously uses the socialist achievements of the socialist countries for the improvement of its own position in the struggle" (*Neues Deutschland*, 27 November).

The DKP pledged its support in the fight against U.S. "war criminals" and "warmongers and murderers," and characterized as "helpers of the enemies of mankind" anyone remaining silent about "disgraceful" U.S. actions in Indochina. It proclaimed that the working population and young people of West Germany had "nothing in common with American imperialism, but everything with the workers, blacks, and students, who are fighting in the United States against race discrimination, and for peace, workers' rights, and social progress." (*Unsere Zeit*, 3 July).

Publications. The party organ of the DKP is the weekly *Unsere Zeit*; it is published in Düsseldorf by party chairman Kurt Bachmann and edited by Presidium member Gerhard Deumlich, and has a circulation of approximately 70,000. The party also issues the *DKP Pressedienst*, a general news service, and *DKP Informationen*, a publication of opinion, discussion, and documentation. The SDAJ distributes 20,000 copies of its monthly magazine, *Elan*, published in Dortmund. As previously noted, DKP plant newspapers have been proliferating and hundreds of thousands of copies find their way into West Germany's factories and shops. The KPD's most important medium in recent years has been "German Freedom Station 904" (Deutscher Freiheitssender 904), which beamed broadcasts to West Germany from its East German location. This radio station suddenly turned silent on 1 October 1971, although no announcement of a pending suspension of service was made.

*   *   *

In 1971 the Spartakus-Association of Marxist Students, which the Interior Ministry characterized as being in "close touch" with the DKP, gained considerably in political influence among students. Several small Spartakus groups were founded during the preceding two years—often by former members of the Socialist German Student Union—but it was only in 1971 that they became linked in a central organization, publicized throughout the country when Spartakus held its founding congress at Bonn in May. Christoph Strawe, who was elected chairman, had previously made a name for himself as leader of the Bonn group.

At the time of its congress, Spartakus claimed 500 members in 40 universities and colleges. Later a non-communist newspaper (*Handelsblatt*, 3 August) credited it with 1,500 members and with control of the student government or committees at the universities of Hamburg, Bonn, Karlsruhe, Göttingen, Freiburg, and Marburg, and at Hanover Technical University. Strawe stated in the Spartakus newspaper *Rote Korrespondenz* (no. 11, 1971) that his organization's goal was to achieve "democratic control of the universities and education" as part of a wider campaign to "change the social order in favor of the working class and achieve the overthrow of capitalism." In addition, Strawe came out in favor of cooperation with the DKP and support for that party's proposals on university reform.

Spartakus has made it clear that it is not prepared to cooperate with "left-sectarian" and "Maoist" groups. The West German government has identified 120 such groups, including 20 Maoist and 5 Trotskyist. Biggest among the Maoists is the Communist Party of Germany (Marxist-Leninist)—the KPD(ML), led by Ernst Aust. Its ideology is disseminated through the publication *Roter Morgen*, and its young members are organized in units of "Red Guards." In 1970 some dissidents broke away from the KPD(ML), organized independently around the publication *Rote Fahne*, and set up their own youth organization in competition with the Red Guards. A more serious split and opposition to the leadership of Aust developed within the KPD(ML) late in 1971 (*Christ und Welt*, Stuttgart, 31 December).

All the Trotskyist groups are small. The best-known leaders of the German segment of the Fourth International are Bernard Achterberg of the International Communists of Germany, in Kiel, and Herwarth Achterberg of the Group of International Marxists, in Mannheim. Trotskyist youths convened in Frankfurt on 29-30 May 1971 for the purpose of establishing the "Revolutionary Communist Youth" as a nationwide organization dedicated to the premise that "revolution requires an internationally centralized leadership." (*Intercontinental Press*, New York, 19 July).

Edith Wyden

Germany: West Berlin

The Socialist Unity Party of West Berlin (Sozialistische Einheitspartei Westberlins; SEW) was founded in November 1962 as the Socialist Unity Party of Germany-West Berlin. The reference to Germany was dropped from the name in 1969 because the party had come to consider itself an "independent political power."

Communist activity in West Berlin is legal, since the status of the city precludes application of the constitutional ban that outlawed the communist party in West Germany in 1956. The SEW, despite its claim of independence, looks for guidance and financial support to the ruling party in East Germany, the Socialist Unity Party of Germany (SED), of which it was officially a part until 1962. It tries to present a semblance of freedom of action by participating in West Berlin's elections and distributing its own newspaper. By scheduling numerous regular meetings or programs the party aims at enlisting popular support.

SEW membership in 1971 was approximately 7,000. The population of West Berlin is 2,135,000 (estimated 1969). The party's political influence continued to be negligible—the inevitable consequence of communist lack of representation in the city government. The party held hopes of changing this status in the elections of 14 March 1971, but with 33,930 votes, 2.3 per cent of the total, it again fell short of the minimum 5.0 per cent required for representation in the Senate, West Berlin's governing body. Nevertheless, the party expressed satisfaction at its gain of 4,000 votes (0.3 per cent) over the previous election in 1967.

Leadership and Organization. The SEW is headed by Gerhard Danelius, who was elected chairman at its first congress in 1966 and reelected at the second, in 1970. Erich Ziegler is his deputy. Party organization provides for a 13-member *Büro* and 47-member *Parteivorstand*, substantially equivalent to a Politburo and a Central Committee. Elected to the powerful Büro in 1970 were Danelius, Ziegler, Dietmar Ahrens, Dr. Karlheinz Kniestedt, Inge Kopp, Bruno Kuster, Horst Schmitt, Gert Ellert, Harry Flichtbeil, Peter Klaar, Hans Mahle, Emil Redmann, and Heinz Thomaszik. The first seven were also named to the Secretariat of the Parteivorstand. Else Dibbern was elected head of the Control Commission. All remained in office during 1971.

The SEW has a youth organization, the Free German Youth-West Berlin (Freie Deutsche Jugend-Westberlin; FDJ-W), which is particularly in evidence on May Day. The SEW shows serious concern for the "correct relationship of the party to youth" and puts great emphasis on party membership "rejuvenation" (*Konsequent*, West Berlin, March 1971).

Party Internal Affairs. The 1971 election campaign and its aftermath provided the SEW with repeated opportunities to state its guiding principles, which have remained virtually unchanged from those adopted by the Second Congress. According to Danelius (*WMR*, July 1971), the party has "consistently pledged parliamentary and extraparliamentary activity to restrict and eventually eliminate monopoly power" and to bring about sociopolitical change through "working class unity, through joint action by all those opposed to present-day capitalism." It rejects revolutionary change, but considers itself the "only genuine alternative" to the existing system in West Berlin. (*Die Wahrheit*, 11 March).

Even in defeat at the polls the SEW saw benefits deriving from the accumulated experience: "Our tactics and vigorous election campaign strengthened the party ideologically, politically, and organizationally, and won it new allies in the anti-imperialist struggle" (*ibid.*). The communists interpreted the election outcome as proving the necessity and practicality of self-criticism, which in turn would lead to major changes in organization. Desired results would include the improvement of "collective leadership activity" at the local and regional level and "broader collaboration of new forces through the creation of advisory councils for organizational questions, for social, economic, and financial policies, for youth and women's affairs, and for matters of education and culture." (*Berliner Extra-Dienst*, 31 March).

The SEW appealed to all workers of West Berlin to turn May Day—the party's most important day of the year—into "a great manifestation for peace, democracy, and socialism." It endorsed "maximum mobilization" to assure success, but made clear its unwillingness to demonstrate together with those "who misuse the red banner and in reality promote anti-Soviet policies." In explanation the party warned of the need to set up defenses against attempts by "right" and "left opportunists" to turn the May Day demonstrations into "an anti-union function," and stated that it was "not ready to replace Marxism-Leninism—the ideology of the working class and all progressive people—with Maoism." Alluding to additional problems which involved "attacks on its unity and cohesiveness," the SEW declared that it would not "permit the members of the party to be split according to age groups and to be played off against one another." (*Die Wahrheit*, 27/28 March.)

Further complaints were directed at the "small groups" which were said to pose as the "true Left," "genuine revolutionaries," and "principled communists," to call loudly for proletarian revolution, and to claim that they alone represented proletarian interests. The SEW was especially bitter at the support these groups received from "those who speak for the bourgeoisie, [including] some Social Democratic leaders." (*WMR*, July.) This seems of more than routine importance, because the communists' hope for cooperation with the Social Democrats had been dashed in 1970 when that party adopted a resolution specifically forbidding collaboration with them.

According to a non-communist West German newspaper, the SEW could take pride in the fair success of its Marxist evening school, opened in October 1970. The school enlisted East German specialists and other experts to lecture on socioeconomic and political subjects. (*Stuttgarter Zeitung*, 29 January.) In outlining post-election tasks, the party, listed "qualitative improvement" and increases in attendance at the school among the major aims of the SEW's "constructive policies" (*Die Wahrheit*, 27/28 March).

Domestic Attitudes and Activities. In 1971 the SEW continued to advocate the interests of the "West Berlin proletariat." The party's domestic policy, as outlined by its chairman after the elections, centered on achieving workers' rights at places of employment and in the economy and society, equal rights for women and young people, a democratic system of education, and rent control and tenants' protection (*Die Wahrheit*, 27/28 March).

Presenting itself as a "mediator" between East and West, the SEW intimated that in this role it could serve West Berlin's interests better than any other party. In contrasting their own capabilities with those of the parties represented in the Senate, the communists were most critical of the Christian Democratic Union (CDU) as always deserving "good marks when it was a question of heating up the cold war against the German Democratic Republic and thus preventing normal relations between West Berlin and the GDR'' (ADN, East German news agency, 10 March). The CDU, the communists charged, talked of a ''satisfactory settlement'' for West Berlin and of ''humaneness,'' but in fact looked upon the 2.2 million West Berliners only as ''pawns on the chessboard of revanchism and anti-communism,'' and was clearly a ''party of monopolies and super-concerns, of retreats and reaction, of cold war and expansion'' (*Die Wahrheit*, 2 February).

The Social Democratic Party (SPD), fared little better in the communist assessment. As the party controlling the Berlin Senate, it was criticized for having ''nothing to say'' to the workers, whose jobs allegedly were being rationalized out of existence or moved out of Berlin, thus rendering their future extremely insecure. The program submitted by the SPD after the elections was described by Danelius as an ''escalation of the previous policy of unreason, of nonrecognition of the realities and the geographical situation of our city,'' and also as a ''genuflection at the throne of the CDU.'' (*Ibid.*, 1 May.) The long-term whipping boy of the communists, the Springer publishing firm, was said to have almost ''succumbed to euphoria'' over the content of this program.

Relations with East Germany and West Germany. In 1971 the SEW seemed to propagate the foreign and domestic policies of the GDR even more than in previous years. Close public identification began early in the year with a highly publicized meeting between an SEW delegation and the East German premier, Willi Stoph, held in East Berlin on 4 February. The meeting was arranged at the request of Chairman Danelius. Subsequently the SEW tried to present itself as the carrier of a new ''Berlin offer'' by East Germany. The attempt failed when the mayor of West Berlin, Klaus Schuetz, reacted to Danelius's written request for a ''personal'' meeting—in which the communist party chief would report ''in detail'' on the substance of his talks with Stoph—by commenting: ''If the GDR leaders want to talk to us, they know where to find us.''

Since a personal meeting with the mayor was rejected, Danelius called a press conference to ''submit to the public a new proposal,'' which he described as ''highly significant for the normalization of the situation, the viability, and the future of the city'' (ADN, 16 February). His proposal was for the ''opening of immediate and direct negotiations between the Senate [of West Berlin] and the government of the GDR.'' Danelius then detailed what he considered the most urgent items for an agenda: (1) agreements and arrangements in the fields of economics, science and technology, and traffic policy, among others; (2) agreements to facilitate economic, scientific-technical, and cultural relations between West Berlin and all states, including the Federal Republic of Germany; (3) agreements on the transportation and transit of West Berlin citizens and goods to and from all states; (4) simplification of transit traffic; and (5) travel of West Berlin's citizens to the GDR, including its capital. (*Die Wahrheit*, 17 February.)

While in 1970 the SEW had continually called for recognition of the German Democratic Republic under international law, the communists shifted to a somewhat different approach in 1971: ''It is fortunate that the socialist GDR exists, where the capitalistic and big landowners have been expropriated and deprived of power forever, where the workers and working people under the leadership of the SED build a system free of exploitation and oppression [which] has no room for imperialist global strategists, for racial discrimination and hatred among people'' (*ibid.*, 27/28 March). Before the election, the communist party chairman put it this way: ''The SEW favors good relations with the GDR. Peace-loving West Berliners sense that West Berlin needs at long last good relations with the socialist world around them. Without them there will be no security for our city.'' (ADN, 10 March.)

In contrast to its praise of the GDR, the SEW heaped criticism on the Federal Republic. In an interview with the West German *Münchner Kurier* (23 February), Danelius claimed that ''revanchist interference'' obstructed progress toward a settlement of the status of Berlin; as in the past, he demanded that the Bonn government renounce all claims to the legality of holding its assembly meetings or permitting West German party conventions in the city. *Die Wahrheit* (27 May) similarly complained about West German "annexationist policies" and the "unlawful Federal presence" in West Berlin, while in *World Marxist Review* (July) there were references to "harmful provocations" that aimed to convert West Berlin into a "front-line city of the cold war."

The SEW welcomed signing of the quadripartite agreement on Berlin by the United States, Great Britain, France, and the Soviet Union and emphasized that "our party has made its contribution to this" (ADN, 24 August). The party also concluded that successful negotiations between socialist and capitalist states are feasible provided all sides muster good will; that the agreement was a defeat for the forces opposing peace, European security, and détente; that it represented a failure of efforts to incorporate West Berlin into the Federal Republic as the eleventh state; and that the hopelessness of all plans to abuse West Berlin as a "thorn in the flesh of the GDR" had been exposed. The SEW summed it all up with the declaration that the most important lesson learnt was that "the forces of peace and socialism are stronger than the forces of reaction and aggression." (*Neues Deutschland*, East Berlin, 8 September.)

The four-power agreement stipulated that details on transit and access to Berlin were to be worked out by direct negotiations between officials of East Germany, West Germany, and West Berlin. As delays developed over contested points, the SEW invariably blamed "procrastination" by West Berlin's Senate, while crediting East Germany with flexibility and "concessions." When the problems were resolved by compromise and agreements were signed, in December, the SEW hailed the result as progress toward détente in Europe and implied a major contribution of its own with this comment: "The struggle of our party has proven worthwhile" (*Die Wahrheit*, 11/12 December).

International Views and Activities. As a member in good standing of the pro-Soviet faction in the international communist movement, the SEW stressed its "links of fraternal friendship" with the Communist Party of the Soviet Union (CPSU) and the "trust and support offered by all members of the mighty community of socialist states" (*Die Wahrheit*, 11 March). At the Twenty-fourth Congress of the CPSU, the SEW leaders hailed the policies of the Soviet party, its fight against "imperialism," and for "peace and international cooperation," and its "opposition to all attempts to distort the teaching of Marxism-Leninism" (*ibid.*, 11 May).

After the quadripartite agreement was signed, the SEW not only considered it a "natural reflection" of the party's "efforts and demands," but stressed that it meant removal of "artificial barriers" to ratification of the Moscow and Warsaw treaties on renunciation of force signed by West Germany and the Soviet Union and Poland in 1970, and that it opened the way for an all-European security conference (Danelius, radio interview, East Berlin, 9 September).

Around the world, the SEW supported or condemned causes essentially according to positions taken by the Soviet Union. It endorsed, for instance "liberation movements" in Asia, Africa, and Latin America, blamed "British monopolies" for "colonial war" or "murder" in Northern Ireland, commented repeatedly on "imperialist aggression" in Vietnam and Cambodia and "Israeli provocations" in the Middle East, described NATO as the "obstacle" to peace in Europe, and protested the fate of communists in Sudan and "freedom-loving" persons in Spain and Greece.

Publications. The central organ of the SEW, *Die Wahrheit*, is published four times a week. Hans Mahle, the editor in chief, is a member of the party Büro. The SEW also publishes a theoretical journal, *Konsequent*.

*   *   *

The "Communist Party of Germany Development Organization" (KPD Aufbauorganisation, or KPD-AO), founded in West Berlin in March 1970, announced in mid-1971 that its choice of name had been a mistake and that it was reconstituting itself as the "true" Communist Party of Germany (Kommunistische Partei Deutschlands; KPD). Its membership is estimated at approximately 3,000 and is drawn largely from "red cells" at the Free University and other educational institutions in West Berlin. At the time of the adoption of the new name, the party's program was published in its newspaper, *Rote Presse Korrespondenz*.

The KPD explained the original name choice as an attempt to distinguish itself from the "irresponsible" Communist Party of Germany (Marxist-Leninist)—KPD(ML)—a pro-Chinese group based in the Federal Republic. Although affirming its own adherence to the ideology of Mao Tse-tung, the KPD charged that the KPD(ML) fails to grasp the basic issues of communism. (*Rote Presse Korrespondenz*, 30 July.)

Advocating change through revolution, the KPD believes that the SEW and the Communist Party in West Germany (Deutsche Kommunistische Partei; DKP) suffer from illusions when they hope to achieve power by parliamentary means. It accuses both these parties of serving the interests of the "monopolist bourgeoisie," "dividing the united front of the proletariat," and being "agents of modern revisionism" (*ibid.*).

In general, the extreme left in West Berlin, as in the Federal Republic, was in a state of flux and growing fragmentation during 1971. Various revolutionary groups claimed to be the guiding force of a "workers movement." Besides the KPD, those that vied for new members and a voice in West Berlin included the "Communist Student Federation" (KSV), the "Proletarian Left/Party Initiative" (PL/PI), the Spartakus group, and the KPD/ML. These and dozens of others expend most of their energy in polemics against one another.

Edith Wyden

Great Britain

The Communist Party of Great Britain (CPGB) was founded in 1920. Although the oldest and largest representative of communism in Great Britain, the CPGB continued in 1971 to be faced with increasing competition from other parties and groups advocating Marxism-Leninism (see below) and from a vocal and active "new left" movement.

The CPGB is a recognized political party in Great Britain. In 1971 it had 28,803 members, according to a party Executive Committee report drawn up for presentation to the Thirty-second Congress in November. This represented a decline since the previous congress, in November 1969, when the party had a membership of 30,607—the latter figure also reflecting a downward trend apparent since 1964. The population of Great Britain is 55,347,000 (census 1971).

Communist party candidates contend in elections for both national and local offices, although there have been no members in the House of Commons since 1950. In local elections in May 1971, the party defended 11 offices, only four successfully; it gained one new position for a net loss of six.

The CPGB. Organization and Leadership. The National Congress is the supreme authority of the CPGB and is responsible for policy adoptions. It meets biennially when called by the Executive Committee, but a special congress can be convened under extraordinary circumstances. The Thirty-second Congress was held on 13-16 November 1971. The National Congress elects the 42-member Executive Committee, which represents the highest authority between congresses. At its first meeting after a congress has been convened, the Executive Committee elects the party officers and the Political Committee. Whereas the Executive Committee meets every two months, the Political Committee holds sessions weekly or more frequently. Below the leadership level, the CPGB is organized into district committees, and further subdivided into area and borough committees and finally into party branches.

During 1971 the Political Committee consisted of Tony Chater, Gerry Cohen, Reuben Falber, John Gollan, Michael McGahey, Gordon McLennan, George Matthews, Alex Murray, Bert Pearce, Bert Ramelson, James Reid, Frank Stanley, William Wainwright, George Wake, and Jack Woddis. Party officers and department heads were John Gollan (general secretary), John Tocher (chairman), Reuben Falber (assistant secretary), Tony Chater (Press and Publicity), Gordon McLennan (Organization), Bert Ramelson (Industrial), Jack Woddis (International), Margaret Hunter (Women), Betty Matthews (Education), Vic Eddisford (Electoral), and Denis Elwand (national treasurer).

Fourteen members of the Executive Committee were replaced during the November Congress. The most popular member, judging from the voting to reseat him on the committee, was Jimmy Reid, who had led the Upper Clyde Ship-builders "workers' takeover" in August and had been elected rector of Glasgow University in October.

According to the Credentials Committee report, of the 422 delegates to the congress, 385 represented party branches—including 122 factory branches, 613 local branches, and 26 student branches—and 37 represented district committees. Among the more than 27 unions represented were the Amalgamated Union of Engineering and Foundry Workers (AEF; 73 delegates) and the Transport and General Workers' Union (31 delegates). (*Comment*, 18 December.)

The Young Communist League (YCL), affiliated to the CPGB since the latter's founding, is the party's youth organization. In 1971 the YCL was headed by National Secretary Tom Bell, who was reelected in May. Like the CPGB, the YCL has declined in membership, from 3,850 in 1969 to 3,200 in 1971.

The CPGB derives its greatest strength from the trade union movement and exercises perceptible influence there. Although increasingly challenged by other Marxist-Leninist groups—particularly the Socialist Labour League (SLL), a Trotskyist party—the CPGB continued in 1971 to contribute actively to industrial agitation with a measure of success disproportionate to its size and electoral support (see below). During the year the party continued in its attempts to attain influence within the Amalgamated Union of Engineering and Foundry Workers (AEF), Britain's second-largest union (about 1,280,000 members). The party was also active in promoting its Liaison Committee for the Defence of Trade Unions (LCDTU), an "umbrella organization" for unofficial rank-and-file bodies set up in many parts of the country and in key industries, which was founded in 1966.

Party Internal Affairs. The minority dissent against the CPGB's condemnation of the 1968 Warsaw Pact intervention in Czechoslovakia suffered a serious setback at the Thirty-second Congress. This was the opposition's first large test since the 1969 congress, at which time it mustered 29 per cent of the delegates in an unsuccessful attempt to defeat the Executive Committee's draft resolution. Before the 1971 congress, supporters of the faction claimed to have the backing of at least 40 per cent of the delegates (*The Guardian*, Manchester and London, 27 October), but an amendment to the Executive Committee's draft resolution on Czechoslovakia proposed at the congress by Sid French, one of the main spokesmen for the faction, could garner only 18 per cent. French, the Surrey district organizer, criticized the party leadership largely for its position on the intervention and subsequent events and for its "over-critical attitude" toward the Soviet Union. In addition, minority resolutions criticized the party's neglect of the industrial rank-and-file and the virtual disappearance of factory-based branches (contrasting with gains at the policy-making level in many unions), its electoral "illusions," its hope that a Labour government with more leftist policies would replace the Conservatives, and the efforts to appeal to the general public by the party organ *Morning Star* (which was said to be sacrificing space that should be given to political news and analysis, including "adequate treatment of developments in the socialist countries"). (*Ibid.*, 15 November.) To these charges *Morning Star* editor George Matthews replied that the CPGB was seeking increased contacts with other communist parties and greater unity within the communist movement. He added, however: "It is a perversion of the meaning of international solidarity to argue [that such unity] precludes public expression of disagreement of policy where it is considered necessary. (*Morning Star*, 16 November.) General Secretary John Gollan denied that the alleged incorrectness of the party's policy on Czechoslovakia was confirmed by the decline in membership. He told the dissenters: "We decide policy on the basis of principle, irrespective of the immediate effect, then fight to get maximum support" (*ibid.*). No supporter of the faction, often termed "pro-Soviet" or "Stalinist," appeared to have been elected to the new Executive Committee.

The divisions in the party were magnified in its youth wing. At its Twenty-eighth Congress, which opened in Scarborough on 24 April, the YCL was beset by district-level draft resolutions that challenged the organization's policies and leadership. The so-called "Stalinist" faction was able to average more than 40 per cent of the votes at the congress, according to a report in *The Times* (London, 5 July). A resolution calling for a new YCL program and leadership was proposed by delegates from Surrey (where the pro-Soviet faction is strongest in both the YCL and the CPGB) and was defeated by only eight votes in a 133-125 decision (*Morning Star*, 26 April). The congress elected the slate of new National Committee members recommended in a list prepared by the Standing Orders Committee, but overrode the retiring National Committee when, contrary to the wishes of the latter, it approved a resolution that the YCL change the character of its paper *Challenge* to a more campaigning form and style to win support from more young people (*ibid.*).

In a review of the YCL congress, CPGB National Organizer Gordon McLennan condemned procedural disputes and political differences that interferred with the progress of the meeting and forced an extension of the closed session at which YCL unity was debated. McLennan was critical of the political differences indicated by the submission of opposing draft resolutions on, for example, Czechoslovakia (one supported the YCL opposition to the 1968 intervention and another called for a reversal of this "highly opportunistic line") and on the YCL's criticisms of socialist countries (one sought greater disapproval of their non-socialist aspects and another attacked the continued "excessive" criticism). Although the retiring leadership was able to defeat the pro-Soviet faction's resolutions, the internal bickering caused McLennan to indicate that the party might seek greater controls over the league: "The Party, learning the lessons of the recent experiences of the YCL, including the 28th Congress, must radically improve at all levels its assistance to the League." According to a *Times* article on 5 July, the YCL had censured some of its London members and removed others from office in the wake of the congress.

The party organ *Morning Star*, over which there had been a running debate regarding its purpose and format, also appeared to suffer internal disagreements. Following the resignations of two members of its editorial staff within a month, *The Guardian* (11 October) and other British papers attributed the losses to political differences among the 30 editorial staff members, an estimated 40 per cent of whom were said to be "Stalinist hard-liners," with the majority supporting the more independent view of the CPGB leadership. The reply by the *Morning Star* (12 October) stated that while political differences were present in the resignations, the two were not forced to leave and their parting was "amicable."

Domestic Views and Policies. During 1971 the CPGB continued to advocate parliamentary means toward the attainment of its goals, urging repeatedly the "unity of the left" and attempting to legitimize itself in the public eye as a party committed to British democratic traditions (see *YICA*, 1969, pp. 365-66). At the same time the major thrust of the party's activities continued to be centered in the trade union movement.

The CPGB saw itself and Great Britain as faced with two major threats during the year: the Industrial Relations Act, which became law on 14 August, and Great Britain's expected entry into the European Common Market following parliamentary approval on 28 October and a treaty with other Common Market countries on 22 January 1972. The party's policy toward both was first to campaign for their defeat and afterward to work for their abrogation. To accomplish these goals, it sought to strengthen what it identified as a leftward trend in the unions and in the Labour Party. Its best potential for a leftward advance lay in the trade unions, as was explained at an Executive Committee press conference in London: "Above all, it is the forces of the Left in the unions, involved in the vital sphere of industrial struggle, who can contribute the most to this advance" (*Daily Telegraph*, London, 3 June). As in the past, the party cautioned against relying on left extremists. The Executive Committee's draft resolution on unity for the Thirty-second Congress stated: "Ultra-left ideas do not assist in the struggle against the right-wing; while temporarily attractive to some young people who desire change, they are essentially disruptive and unhelpful in the class struggle because they are based on political adventurism and lack of confidence in the working class and labour movement" (*Comment*, 14 August).

The party continued to support efforts to return the Labour Party to power. The draft resolution on unity (*ibid.*), outlined its approach to this campaign: "To win a Labour Government with new socialist policies requires the breaking of the right-wing political grip, a new leadership, and a continuous mass movement of pressure to ensure socialist policies are carried through." On 13 June the CPGB organized what it described as the "biggest national demonstration held by any political party for many years" to promote its anti-Conservative campaign. General Secretary Gollan told a rally of 7,000 people: "Never forget our aim is not only higher wages, trade union freedom, defeat of the Common Market and the like, but the conquest of political power and socialism." (*Morning Star*, 14 June). The CPGB Press and Publicity Department head, Tony Chater, castigated news directors of government-operated television networks for "straight political discrimination" in having refused to mention what he called the biggest demonstration of popular anger to date against the Conservatives' Common Market policy (*ibid.*, 15 June).

The Liaison Committee for the Defence of Trade Unions was active throughout 1971 in campaigning against the industrial relations legislation. A national LCDTU conference, held in London on 24 April, adopted a program by which delegates pledged to "make and abide by [their] own union rules in defiance of the [Industrial Relations Act]." Close to 700 delegates attended, representing 150 trade union branches, 31 trades councils, 53 shop stewards' committees, 19 union district committees, and two union national executive committees. The conference also demanded an unqualified commitment from the Labour Party that, if returned to power, it would repeal the act in the event that it had become law. (*Morning Star*, 26 April.) The enactment of the Industrial Relations Bill in August brought a promise from the LCDTU that the organization would launch a new phase in the "battle to retain free trade unions"—one characterized by "total non-co-operation and opposition to the Act" (*ibid.*, 6 August).

The LCDTU supported two general strikes—on 1 and 18 March—spearheaded by the AEF to demonstrate workers' opposition to the bill. Simultaneously with the second strike, which was supported by the Transport and General Workers' Union, the largest union in Britain (about 1,530,000 members), a Trades Union Congress (TUC)[1] decision opposed strike action against the bill as being counterproductive (see *Christian Science Monitor*, 20 March). The TUC advised the unions, instead, not to register under the terms of the bill, the enactment of which appeared imminent at that time. Although the CPGB also advocated non-registration (unregistered unions could not legally call a strike) and commended the TUC for having "by and large" adopted many leftist policies at its 1971 annual congress (*Comment*, 14 August), it continued to support strikes in protest against the bill.

The CPGB expressed satisfaction at the gains it registered in placing party members in official positions in the trade unions during the year. Communist influence in the Amalgamated Society of Woodworkers (ASW; about 175,000 members) was enhanced when early in 1971 the Amalgamated Union of Building Trade Workers (AUBTW; about 62,000 members) became affiliated with the ASW. Two of the five AUBTW members on the new joint Executive Committee were communists. In May an additional member was gained on the AUBTW Executive Committee (which continued to function separately) when a Labour Party member of the committee left his party to join the

---

[1] The TUC, an organization of 150 trade unions (with a total membership of almost 10 million), formulates the main policies of trade unionism and participates in discussion with other leading economic and industrial bodies, and with the Government, on matters dealing with wage earners and salaried employees. It is affiliated to the International Confederation of Free Trade Unions and nominates the British delegate to the International Labor Organization.

CPGB. The party made a concerted effort to gain control in the National Union of Mineworkers, but mid-year presidential elections defeated communist candidate Michael McGahey by a vote of five to four in favor of a Labour Party candidate. In May the CPGB seated one of its members, Joe Whelan, on the Executive Committee of the mineworkers' union.

International Views and Policies. The positions of the CPGB on international issues continued in 1971 to be dominated by the party's reaction to the 1968 Warsaw Pact intervention in Czechoslovakia and the subsequent "normalization" process. Highly critical of the intervention at the time, it has since extended its criticisms to what it identified as "deep aberrations" from Marxism in a number of communist countries.

A statement adopted by the Central Committee of the Communist Party of Czechoslovakia (KSČ) in December 1970 (entitled "Lesson Drawn from the Crisis Development in the Party and Society after the Thirteenth Congress of the KSČ") elicited from the CPGB a reaffirmation of its stance. On 6 February *Comment* carried excerpts from the statement together with a commentary by Tony Chater, who contended that the KSČ was attempting to form new conclusions despite a lack of new information to warrant such modifications. While most previous statements by the current KSČ leadership referred to events in 1968 as "*heading towards* an imminent counter-revolutionary danger," Chater asserted, the new document characterized these events as having "culminated in counter-revolution" (emphasis in original). The correctness of the CPGB's stance at its 1969 congress, he argued, was shown by the fact that no official request for the intervention had ever been made, despite the statement's assertion to the contrary.

This issue led to the CPGB's absence from the Czechoslovak party's congress in May-June. Having initially accepted an invitation to send a representative, the CPGB Executive Committee later declined when it was learned that the representative's speech, submitted in advance to the KSČ, would not be acceptable. The brief speech reportedly was to contain the following passage:

> As you know, our [1969] congress expressed the view that the military intervention ... was a grave mistake and a violation of the commonly agreed principles of the international Communist movement concerning relations between Socialist States and relations between Communist Parties. Nothing that has happened or been said since has changed our assessment. (*Morning Star*, 26 May.)

The CPGB participated with other West European communist parties in conferences designed to publicize their opposition to the Common Market and to formulate and coordinate activities to discredit the organization. The first such conference of the year was organized by the CPGB in London on 11-13 January. Twenty-seven delegates from fifteen countries attended, representing Austria, Belgium, Denmark, Finland, France, West Germany, Great Britain, Greece, Ireland, Italy, Netherlands, Norway, Spain, Sweden, and Switzerland. Though the main subject of the conference was "international firms"—"bastions of neo-colonialism" that should be nationalized, according to General Secretary Gollan—it dealt also with the question of the United Kingdom's entry into the Common Market. Gollan stated that the CPGB opposition was on the grounds of possible effects on the cost of living, balance of payments, agriculture, and Commonwealth trade; moreover, he said, "Parliament would be deprived of sovereign powers over a whole range of economic questions which would come under the domination of an undemocratic and uncontrolled super bureaucracy acting in the interests of the trusts." (*Ibid.*, 12 January.)

In August, leaders of the communist parties of four applicant countries to the Common Market (Denmark, Great Britain, Ireland, and Norway) met in Copenhagen and, in a joint communiqué, denounced the organization as a "threat to the sovereignty of nations," and agreed to unite their efforts to prevent its expansion (*Le Monde*, Paris, 19 August). A third meeting of West European communist parties to discuss problems posed by the Common Market was held in London in September and attended by representatives of the communist parties of Denmark, France, West Germany, Great Britain, Ireland, Italy, and the Netherlands. The parties of Belgium and Luxembourg greeted the event by telegrams but apparently did not send representatives. (*Morning Star*, 29 September.)

The CPGB frequently voiced its position on the unstable situation in Northern Ireland. A joint statement following a meeting in April of the CPGB and the Communist Party of Ireland condemned the British Government's failure to solve the crisis, calling for an end to the "misuse of the British Army as a police force" and for its gradual withdrawal from Northern Ireland, the release of political prisoners, and discussions that would lead to the unification of Northern Ireland and the Republic of Ireland (*ibid.*, 15 April). The Thirty-second Congress was not of one mind on the issue. It defeated a demand for immediate withdrawal of all troops from Northern Ireland. The majority opinion was that such a move would lead to a "holocaust" (*Guardian*, 16 November).

Among the major visits abroad by CPGB members, a two-man delegation led by Jack Woddis (International Department) was the guest of the League of Communists of Yugoslavia on 5-8 January. Both sides to the discussions agreed that there should be further development of relations between the two parties (Tanyug, Yugoslav news agency, 7 January). Harry Bourne, a member of the Executive Committee, stated during his attendance at the Eighth Congress of the Socialist Unity Party of (East) Germany that CPGB efforts to bring about recognition of the German Democratic Republic under international law had recently secured stronger support among broad sections of the British public (ADN, East German news agency, 17 June). In July, General Secretary Gollan met in Moscow with Arvids Pelshe, Politburo member of the Communist Party of the Soviet Union. Talks were held in a "comradely atmosphere," according to the joint communiqué (*Morning Star*, 24 July).

Publications. The London daily newspaper of the CPGB is the *Morning Star*. Other major party publications include *Comment*, which, beginning with its 27 February 1971 issue, changed from a weekly to a fortnightly magazine; *Marxism Today*, a monthly theoretical journal; and *Labour Monthly*, which provides commentary on political events. The YCL has an irregular monthly journal, *Challenge*, and a monthly theoretical organ, *Cogito*.

*   *   *

The SLL. Among the numerous Marxist-Leninist parties and groups that challenge the CPGB's leadership in the British communist movement, the largest and most influential (particularly in the trade union movement) appears to be the Socialist Labour League. The SLL was founded in 1959. It is an affiliate of the Trotskyist International Committee of the Fourth International.

The SLL is believed to have a membership of about 1,000. Its youth movement—the Young Socialists (YS)—claims 20,000 members and apparently is the largest Marxist-Leninist youth group ever to have existed in Great Britain.

The SLL is led by Gerry Healy as national secretary. Among others prominent in the SLL (which does not publish complete information on the composition of its leading bodies) are Michael Banda, editor of the league's daily newspaper, *Workers' Press*, and Tom Kemp and Cliff Slaughter, editors of *Fourth International*, a quarterly organ of the International Committee of the Fourth International, published in London. The YS is led by John Simmance. Aileen Jennings is editor of *Keep Left*, the monthly publication of the YS.

The SLL controls the All Trade Unions Alliance (ATUA), a group similar to the CPGB-controlled LCDTU. The main line of SLL domestic policy in 1971 continued to be oriented toward industrial agitation. The league's approach toward organized labor was somewhat different from that of the CPGB. While the latter was making inroads in the trade union movement at a relatively high level, the SLL concentrated its activities among the rank and file and the shop stewards. Like the CPGB, the SLL focused its attention on the engineering industry.

The SLL fought actively against the Industrial Relations Bill and favored the use of strikes for this purpose. The ATUA campaigned during the early months of 1971 for a general strike to begin on 3 May to protest the bill. It had, however, neither the strength nor the backing at the higher levels in the unions to create by itself a national strike.

The Young Socialists also were active in promoting SLL policies in the trade unions. A YS-sponsored conference in London on 14 February, attended by some 4,000 young people, passed a resolution calling for the replacement of bureaucracy in the trade unions by revolutionary leadership. The same resolution sought the replacement of the ruling Conservatives by the Labour Party, which in turn could be made to "retreat before the mass movement of the working class." At the annual meeting of the YS, held on 3-4 April in Scarborough as its Eleventh Congress, John Simmance called on members to mobilize workers in the unions to block what he termed the "retreat of the union leaders of the so-called 'left.' "

*   *   *

In addition to the CPGB and the SLL, there are numerous small Marxist-Leninist groups in Great Britain. None of these has been able to muster numerically significant support, with the possible exception of two groups that work closely together—the International Marxist Group (IMG) and the International Socialism Group (ISG). The IMG is the British section of the United Secretariat of the Fourth International. The IMG's national secretary is Pat Jordan, who also is editor of the group's monthly publication, *International*; Ernest Tate and Tariq Ali are frequent spokesmen. Two fortnightly publications, *Black Dwarf* and *Red Mole*, represent divergent factions within the IMG. The group associated with the *Red Mole* (which is edited by Tariq Ali) founded a new organization in 1970, the Spartacus League, which became the youth group of the IMG.

A conference organized by the Spartacus League in London on 20-21 February 1971 attracted some 400 young people. The following edition of the *Red Mole*, reporting on the conference, emphasized the "basic fact" that a "revolutionary party cannot be built until it has firm roots in the working class."

The ISG, in its efforts to organize labor during 1971, gave priority to the establishment of "fractions" or groups of workers under the control of party action committees. The primary targets of this aim were teachers, workers in automobile factories and power plants, printers, and draftsmen.

The Communist Party of Britain (Marxist-Leninist), was founded at an inaugural congress in April 1968. This pro-Chinese party, led by Reg Birch, a member of the Executive Council of the AEF, claims a membership of 400. It appears to be the only pro-Chinese party in Great Britain whose activities and statements are publicized by the People's Republic of China. The party organ, *The Worker*, in a special supplement dated Spring 1971, denounced what it called "capitulation to the employers." Calling for workers to unite and not be swayed by "public opinion," the article declared: "There will be no satisfactory settlement overall other than the complete defeat of the employers as a class: the destruction of the employers' class power and its replacement by the class power of the workers." The party held a rally in September to demand the withdrawal of British troops from Northern Ireland.

The Communist Federation of Britain (Marxist-Leninist), formed in September 1969, is an umbrella organization for various contending pro-Chinese groups. Little information is available on the group's leadership or on the extent of its support. Its organ is a monthly newspaper, *Struggle*. The views of the federation are also publicized in a quarterly magazine, *The Marxist*.

Eric Stromquist

Greece

The Communist Party of Greece (Kommounistikon Komma Hellados; KKE) was founded 18-22 November 1918 in Piraeus as the Socialist Workers' Party of Greece (Socialistikon Ergatikon Komma Hellados). The party joined the Comintern in 1920, and four years later assumed its present name. Outlawed during the communist insurgency in December 1947, the KKE has since maintained its leadership in East Europe; only a few Central Committee members operate in Greece to direct domestic activities, particularly among tobacco and factory workers, stevedores in the principal ports, and seamen. Abroad, the party has a large following among some 100,000 persons who left Greece at the end of the 1947-49 civil war and made their homes in various European countries. The KKE is believed to have some 27,000 members in Greece and 10,000 to 15,000 in exile. The population of Greece is 8,736,000 (estimated 1971).

Although an illegal party, the KKE until the coup of 1967 maintained an active political life through the United Democratic Left (Eniea Dimokratiki Aristera; EDA), a broad "progressive" electoral formation which it was instrumental in founding in 1951. The EDA, like all other political parties, was proscribed by the current government headed by Yeoryos Papadopoulos. Of some 6,000 communists arrested at the time of the coup, however, most have been released. Arrests and convictions have declined steadily, and the shift, in 1971, of many trials of alleged subversives from military to civilian courts has generally resulted in shorter sentences. To avoid detection, those communists still at liberty in Greece are organized in small cells whose members often have no knowledge of the composition or activities of other, parallel bodies.

The continuing reluctance of non-communist anti-government elements to collaborate with the KKE stems both from a general wariness of identification with the communists and from the fear that another civil war could lead to a communist takeover. Statements of KKE leaders do little to dispel such misgivings. While the party professes to have "no other ambition than to serve the cause of freedom of the Greek people, shoulder to shoulder with the other opponents of tyranny," it consistently pledges not only to occupy a position "*in the vanguard* of the struggle for economic and political demands" of the people, but actually to "*lead* them to a true democratic and progressive future." (New Year statement by KKE Chairman Apostolos Grozos, "Voice of Truth" radio, 1 January 1971; emphasis added.)

Leadership. Although Grozos is KKE chairman, it is the secretary-general, Konstandinos (Kostas) Koliyannis, who is the leading personality in the party. The Politburo of the Central Committee includes Grigoris Faragos, Nikolaos Kaloudhis, Leonidas Stringos, Panayotis Mavromatis, and (first name unknown) Hyphantis. One candidate Politburo member is Yerasimos Stefanatos. Leading KKE members currently imprisoned include Faragos, Kaloudhis, and Central Committee members Zinon Zorzovilis, Ioannis Yiannaris, Kostas Loules, Kharilaos Florakis, Mina Yiannou, Avra Partsalidhis, Loula Koukoulou, and Efstratios Tsambis.

Party Internal Affairs. The Koliyannis leadership, headquartered in East Germany, and with its principal following in the Soviet Union and East Europe, is seriously challenged by a less doctrinaire faction composed of two groups, under Dimitrios (Mitsos) Partsalides and Antonis Brillakis, who were purged by Koliyannis in 1968 at the KKE's Twelfth Plenum (the last meeting of the Central Committee of the unified party) and reached an agreement to cooperate in 1969. The dissidents are believed to have the allegiance of the majority of Greek communists and fellow travelers in Greece and West Europe, and substantial sympathy among Greek expatriates in East Europe, primarily in Romania and Czechoslovakia. Partsalides, as a Politburo member, headed the large KKE branch in Czechoslovakia which, following its condemnation of the 1968 Warsaw Pact invasion of that country—Koliyannis's approval of the event having widened the KKE division—was reorganized under a new leadership loyal to the secretary-general. Brillakis, a Central Committee member, headed the "Bureau of the Interior" responsible to the Politburo for operations inside Greece. He left Greece in the summer of 1968 to set up West European EDA headquarters in Rome, while Kharalambos Drakopoulos remained in Athens to head the bureau. In 1969, Koliyannis appointed Central Committee member Antonis Ambatielos to establish an EDA headquarters in Paris and named a new "Echelon of the Central Committee" to "replace" the Brillakis and Drakopoulos operations. It is difficult to gauge the nature of the relationship between the Partsalides-Brillakis-Drakopoulos forces, or their relative strengths. As is the case with the Koliyannis camp, the dissidents' organizations have been fragmented by the arrests of leaders and cadres. On 25 October 1971 the government announced the arrest, in Athens, of Partsalides, Drakopoulos, and 30 anti-Koliyannis cadres. Appeals for their release, reported in the Italian Communist Party organ *L'Unitá* (27 October), included the signatures of composer Mikis Theodorakis and actress Melina Mercouri.

The split within the KKE (for more details of which and related subsequent developments, see *YICA*, 1970, pp. 193-95 and *YICA*, 1971, pp. 190-92) is reflected within all organizations under party control. Largest and most important of these, next to the EDA, is the mass resistance organization called the Patriotic Anti-Dictatorial Front (Patriotikon Metopom; PAM), of which, like the EDA, there are pro- and anti-Koliyannis bases in Greece and branches throughout East and West Europe. In addition, there are the EDA's youth affiliate, the Lambrakis Democratic Youth (Demokratike Neolaia Lambraki; DNL), and numerous "anti-dictatorship" or "solidarity" committees, in Europe and elsewhere, whose supporters and sympathizers are actively wooed by both rival KKE factions. Theodorakis is a leading figure in the EDA, PAM, and DNL. He has a large following among prominent persons both in Greece and abroad, and, since his release from prison in 1970, has actively challenged Koliyannis.

Prospects for reunification of the KKE appear remote. Koliyannis accuses the dissidents of pursuing a policy alien to Marxism-Leninism, seeking to minimize the KKE's revolutionary character and remove it from the international communist movement, and capitalizing on positions and titles acquired through the party to subvert the EDA and PAM. The dissidents counter that the Koliyannis forces, having been in exile for more than twenty years, are incapable of comprehending—much less directing—the complex developments in Greece.

Since the split, Koliyannis has been attempting to rally sufficient support to hold the party's Ninth Congress, whose assured endorsement of his leadership and the purge of the dissenters would be a precondition. (The KKE's Eighth Congress was held in 1961.) His first move in this direction, a "Thirteenth Plenum" of KKE leaders loyal to him, held in January 1969 at an undisclosed location in East Europe, approved the purges; the second, a "Fourteenth Plenum," in April 1970, adopted theses to constitute the basis for pre-congress discussions among the rank and file. The theses presented a self-criticism: the Eighth Congress should have prepared the party not only for the peaceful path to socialism advocated by the "revisionist" Partsalides and Brillakis and their followers, but also for the eventuality of a nonpeaceful path; further, the leadership had failed to prepare the party and the masses ideologically, politically, and organizationally for resisting the 1967 coup (see *YICA*, 1970, p. 191).

Then, in early February 1971, Koliyannis convened a "Fifteenth Plenum," which adopted the draft of an amended party program for eventual congress ratification. It was evident from the new program (see below) that Koliyannis was seeking all possible allies and thus was adopting the tactic of his critics, which he had condemned as a dangerously "opportunist" dilution of communist purity and cited as justification for the ouster of Partsalides and Brillakis from the party leadership.

Domestic Views and Activities. The draft program of February 1971 embraced fundamental changes which took cognizance of existing political conditions in Greece. Reports and resolutions of the "Fifteenth Plenum" were broadcast over the party's "Voice of Truth" radio station between 13 and 22 February. An unexplained delay in the release of the text of the draft program, which was broadcast in installments from 26 to 28 February, may have indicated divergent views within the Koliyannis camp with regard to its provisions.

The program called for (1) the government's overthrow, (2) a subsequent "anti-imperialist democratic revolution" in preparation for a "socialist revolution," and (3) a later transition from a socialist to a communist state. According to the program, an "anti-imperialist democratic revolution" was required before Greece could pass over to socialism, and this revolution could only be achieved through "the struggle of the people themselves, under the leadership of the working class with its party, the KKE, at its vanguard." The revolution would not be the work of a single class or party, but of "all social classes and strata, parties, political groups, and popular organizations whose interests coincide with the materialization of this program and which are in favor of change." A worker-peasant alliance would constitute the foundation of the revolution, around which would gather the urban middle classes, national minorities, "progressive" intelligentsia, and "patriotic" army officers. Inasmuch as "ferocious resistance" was to be anticipated on the part of the "plutocratic oligarchy and the imperialists," the "anti-dictatorship front" could not rule out any form of struggle, "armed or otherwise."

Policy after the projected coup would be directed first to "delivering the country from the domination of foreigners," following which the KKE envisaged a "speedy transition from the democratic revolution to a socialist revolution." This socialist revolution would create a new, "higher form of democracy"—the "dictatorship of the proletariat"—in which "the wider participation of workers in the exercise of political power and in the construction of the new socialist community" would be able to "neutralize every attempt by imperialists to bring back a regime of exploitation." The program indicated that most Greek industry and commerce would be nationalized immediately after the overthrow of the government, and that the economy would then gradually be shifted to "socialist forms of production" by "making full use of the achievements of the scientific-technological revolution." Farmers, craftsmen, and artisans would all be persuaded to organize into cooperatives. In this way the entire means of production would be transferred to communal ownership. Greece—relieved of the "contradictions of capitalism" and its related "forms of exploitation"—would enter the path to communism, which was said to be the "final aim of the KKE," and the principle "from everyone according to his ability, to everyone according to his need" would prevail.

In his report to the plenum, Koliyannis described the bourgeois elements in Greece as fearing the "revolutionary initiative of the working class" and "its party, the KKE," and wanting to rely upon outside forces—primarily the United States and NATO—to overthrow the government. Their efforts were directed to "ensuring solutions that would serve their own class and narrow party interests after the fall of the junta at the expense of democratic liberties and popular and national interests." It was essential, he said, that a coup be accompanied by "concrete measures ... enabling the people to freely choose the type of government to replace the junta." The KKE program for an "anti-imperialist democratic revolution," accordingly, provided for restoration of all civil rights, legalization of the KKE, a general political amnesty, a purge of "fascist elements" in the army, replacement of existing police units, dissolution of "fascist and para-state organizations"; and the election of a constituent national assembly to vote for a new democratic constitution "consecrating the above principles."

On the tactics to be employed by party cadres at the present stage of the "anti-dictatorial struggle," Koliyannis said that the most fruitful forms were "collective demands, protests, representations to authorities, and assemblies turned into demonstrations against the dictatorship." Experience had shown, he said, that any "popular gathering, social event, or spontaneous mass resistance to police pressure" could be used to further the struggle. Although the KKE was opposed in general to "dynamic actions" by individual militants, it favored wildcat strikes and sitdowns. All such tactics, he suggested, could create a popular awareness of the "demagogy" of the government—with regard to its "imaginary gradual liberalization" policies and the "farce" of its "so-called consultative assembly," its continuing efforts to militarize the country, and its policies permitting domestic and foreign monopolists to conduct an offensive against the masses through bids to freeze wages, introduce anti-labor legislation, and embezzle insurance funds.

The Greek people, according to Koliyannis, were "shedding their illusions about the junta and its U.S. patrons," but the resistance struggle, because of its disunity, was not yet nationwide. Considering that "all classes and social strata, with the exception of the plutocratic oligarchy connected with foreign monopoly capital," and almost all parties, allegedly, were opposed to the government, an "objective opportunity" existed for coordination of the "anti-dictatorial struggle." Koliyannis reasoned that the basic impediment to opposition unity was anti-communism. It was only anti-communism, he said, which had "prevented the democratic forces from averting the 21 April [1967] fascist coup d'état" and the resulting conversion of Greece into a "field of imperialist intervention and unrestrained monopolistic exploitation."

Koliyannis leveled a personal attack against Andreas Papandreou (exiled former cabinet minister in the Center Union government headed by his father, the late George Papandreou, and leader of the "Pan-Hellenic Liberation Movement," or PAK) for his refusal to work with the communists. Papandreou, he said, was trying to isolate the KKE by "cultivating and imposing the idea that the political forces to be taken into consideration should be only those represented in parliament" at the time of the coup. Papandreou, further, had "exerted persistent efforts to monopolize the resistance and to place parties and organizations under his exclusive control," and was "facilitated in his policy by the apostates of the KKE, Partsalides and Brillakis." Koliyannis was here referring to a 1968 cooperative agreement between the PAK and the anti-Koliyannis faction of the PAM. Cooperative endeavors between the two had collapsed in 1970, however, amid reports that Papandreou was demanding a dominant personal role. Papandreou figured in subsequent, apparently unproductive, talks with both communist (anti-Koliyannis) and non-communist resistance groups. Following the PAK-PAM breakdown, the dissident PAM became party to a new "National Resistance Council"—the EAS—set up in London in February 1971, which included neither the Koliyannis KKE nor Papandreou. Other parties to the council were: a militant centrist organization, the "Democratic Defense," and two groups of ousted army officers, the "Defenders of Liberty" and the "Free Greeks."

There was no evidence during the year of any move by other resistance forces to take up the question of cooperation with the Koliyannis camp. The apparent absence of any commentary by them on the KKE Plenum or its proposed program suggested that the KKE had become further isolated from the reality of present Greek politics. The KKE dissidents, on the other hand, though with substantial popular support among Greek "progressives," have as yet failed to manifest any firm direction, either in ideology or in programmatic orientation, which would markedly distinguish them from other anti-government forces and favor their taking a leading role in the resistance. Their efforts to play down any "communist image" so as to win the broadest possible support could even have the adverse effect of alienating many communists in favor of the Koliyannis camp.

International Views and Positions. Unreservedly pro-Soviet in foreign affairs, the KKE continues to point to the United States as the source of every major threat to world peace. According to a "Fifteenth Plenum" resolution, "international imperialism," led by the United States, had not renounced its "aggressive" designs; it was still interfering in the internal affairs of Vietnam and other Indochinese countries, striving to "create new hotbeds of local wars" in the Middle East, and seeking to perpetuate tension around the "movement for European peace and security." Under the Papadopoulos government, said to be a "blind instrument of American imperialism," Greece was "selling out to foreigners the country's wealth" and transforming Greece into a "nuclear arsenal for the Americans and NATO" and a "springboard for their adventures against the socialist and Arab countries."

The KKE's draft program for the "anti-imperialist democratic revolution" called for restoration of national independence and sovereignty, abrogation of the 1953 Greek-U.S. agreement and others "incompatible with Greek sovereign rights," dissolution of foreign military bases and expulsion of all foreign military and secret services and missions on Greek territory, withdrawal of Greece from NATO and the Common Market, conversion of the Mediterranean and the Balkans into a non-nuclear zone, abrogation or revision of all agreements with "foreign monopolist capital," and nationalization of foreign enterprises in Greece.

In his report to the plenum, Koliyannis cited as evidence of Greece's direct involvement in "adventures associated with U.S. and NATO projects" the supply of U.S. arms to Greece, the frequent visits by U.S. and NATO officials, the "excessive" presence of the U.S. 6th Fleet in Greek ports and its "provocative" military exercises in the area, and the U.S. use of Greek bases for "spy flights and military missions."

The official visit by U.S. Vice-President Agnew in October was depicted by the KKE Politburo as underlining the U.S. intent to "continue to grossly intervene to shape the fate of Greece in accordance with its own interests." Calling for a broad expression by the people of their "anti-American and anti-imperialist" feelings, the KKE urged all opposing the government to "rid themselves of an anti-communist spirit" and of "delusions regarding the role of Washington and the NATO imperialists." ("Voice of Truth," 16 October.)

On the Cyprus issue, the KKE, like the Cypriot communist party, AKEL, has deemphasized the purely Greek goal of enosis—the union of Cyprus with Greece. Currently professing to uphold the independence of the island, the KKE accused the Greek government of "doing its utmost ... to facilitate the realization of U.S. and NATO adventurous plans in the Mediterranean and South East Europe" (*IB*, no. 5-6). The KKE charged, in June, that a new "conspiracy" was being plotted against the island, envisaging "the imposition on Cyprus of a tripartite occupation by the militarist regimes of Athens, Ankara, and NATO." This conspiracy could be repelled, however, with the "undivided help" said by the KKE to have been promised by the Soviets to Cyprus President Archbishop Makarios. (*Ibid.*, 24 June.) Subsequent KKE statements—notably similar to those appearing in the Soviet press—accused Papadopoulos of having given an "ultimatum" to Makarios demanding acceptance of a "NATO solution." The KKE also charged that the "aggressive and adventurist pursuits" of the United States and NATO were being "encouraged and intensified" by the "subversive, divisive, and anti-Soviet policy of the Chinese leadership." (*Ibid.*, 18 September.)

International Communist Movement. The KKE in 1971 continued its policy of strict allegiance to the Soviet Union, despite differences with the Communist Party of the Soviet Union (CPSU) that have emerged since, and as a result of, the KKE schism. Following his attendance at the CPSU's Twenty-fourth Congress, in March-April, Koliyannis depicted the Soviet Union as the "steadfast and sure protector of peace, freedom, and social justice," whose successes in the "struggle for the victory of communism" were a "source of inspiration to the oppressed and exploited peoples of the entire world" ("Voice of Truth," 30 March). The party has been embarrassed by the recent improvement in relations between the U.S.S.R. and East European communist countries and Greece, but, being financially dependent upon the Soviets, has been obliged to acquiesce in the growing contacts. In explaining its acquiescence the party points to the economic benefits to the Greek peasantry from increased trade with these countries. The Partsalides and Brillakis dissenters, for their part, refuse to compromise their condemnation of the Greek government. They openly oppose Soviet trade with Greece, for example, and appeal for international economic sanctions against the Papadopoulos government.

The Romanian, Italian, and Spanish communist parties are among those within the international communist movement which have openly supported the KKE dissenters. Many Western communist parties attempt either to appear neutral in the schism, or, outwardly at least, to ignore its existence.

Party Media. The central organs of the KKE, the newspaper *Rizospastis* and the theoretical journal *Neos Kosmos*, are published outside Greece. There are several party newspapers for Greek exiles living in socialist-bloc countries: *Elefteria* (Bulgaria), *Dimokratis* (Poland), *Laikos Agon* (Hungary), and *Neos Dromos* (Tashkent, U.S.S.R.). Clandestine publications within Greece are *Adhouloti Athina*, the organ of the Athens branch; *Rizospastis*, a domestic edition of the party's central organ; and *Odhiyiti*, issued by the KKE's youth group. The KKE radio station, "Voice of Truth," thought to be located in Leipzig, East Germany, broadcasts frequently to Greece. Rival versions of the EDA organ *Eleftheri Patrida* are published by the Koliyannis branch in Paris and the Brillakis faction in Rome. In Greece, the pro-Koliyannis PAM publishes *Lefteria*, and organs of the dissidents include *O Mahitis* and *Rizospastes-Makhetes*.

*   *   *

Splinter Groups. The KKE's long record of internal discord and factionalism is reflected by the existence of several Greek communist splinter groups. Followers of Nikolas Zachariadis, expelled as secretary-general under pressure from Moscow in 1956, form one group of dissidents; those of Markos Vafiadis, a commander of communist guerrillas, expelled from the party in 1958, comprise another. These factions represent the personal followings of the two rival communist leaders of the civil war period. In addition, there is the International Communist Party of Greece (Kommounistiko Diethnistiko Komma tes Ellados), which is the Greek section of the Fourth International; its organ is the monthly *Ergatike Pale*. A pro-Chinese faction also exists, with headquarters in Romania. Its leader is Polydoros Danielides, a former KKE Central Committee member; its views are made known through its bulletin, *Anagennesis*, and through Peking media.

Valerie Bloom

Iceland

The original communist party in Iceland was formed in 1930 by the secessionist left wing of the Social Democratic Party. In 1938 it absorbed a radical group of Social Democrats and became the United People's Party-Socialist Party (UPP-SP). The date of this reorganization, 24 October 1938, has since been regarded by the communists as the official founding date of their party. In 1965 the UPP-SP, some left-wing elements, and the small National Opposition Party joined in an electoral front called the Labor Alliance. In November 1968 the front became a "Marxist political party" under communist leadership, the UPP-SP was formally dissolved, and the new party was designated the Labor Alliance (LA).

The dissolution of the front split the Icelandic communist movement into three mainstreams: the LA; the Organization of Liberals and Leftists (OLL), comprising mostly non-communist elements of the front; and the Organization of Icelandic Socialists (OIS), comprising the hard-line, pro-Soviet elements. Membership figures have been closely guarded by the three new parties, each of which claims to represent Icelandic communists, but the LA has clearly retained by far the largest share of the some 1,000 former UPP-SP members. The population of Iceland is 206,000 (estimated, 1971). OLL strength has increased rapidly, while the OIS is politically insignificant.

Enjoying legal status since the inception of their party, the communists have twice been represented in the government: in the 1944-47 postwar coalition, and in 1956-58 under the front of the Labor Alliance. In the June 1971 parliamentary elections the LA received 17.1 per cent of the vote (17.6 in 1967) and 10 of the 60 parliamentary seats. (It received 10 seats in 1967, but in the interim two members defected to the OLL and one became an independent.) The OLL, in its first general election, received 9.0 per cent and 5 seats. The OIS entered no candidates. The LA and OLL joined with the Progressive Party (PP)—which polled 25 per cent of the vote (down 3.0 per cent) and 17 seats (down one)—in forming a leftist government to succeed the decade-old coalition of the conservative Independence Party (IP) and the Social Democratic Party (SDP). It was at the expense of the IP and the SDP (whose shares of the vote dropped, respectively, from 37.5 and 15.7 per cent to 36.2 and 10.5 per cent, and their seats from 23 and 9 to 22 and 6) that the OLL registered its success. The gains of the far left thus followed the trend indicated in the May 1970 municipal elections when the LA, the OLL (in its first municipal election), and the OIS received an aggregate of 21.1 per cent of the vote (14.3, 6.2 and 0.6, respectively) compared with the LA's 16.7 per cent in 1966.

In the new cabinet, formed on 10 July, the PP holds the post of the prime minister and the portfolios of Justice and Ecclesiastical Affairs (Olafur Johannesson), Foreign Affairs (Einar Agustsson), and Finance and Agriculture (Halldor Sigurdsson). The LA holds Fisheries and Commerce (Lúdvík Jósefsson) and Industries and Health and Social Security (Magnus Kjartansson), and the OLL, Communication and Social Affairs (Hannibal Valdimarsson) and Education and Statistics (Magnus Torfi Olafsson).

Leadership and Organization. *The LA.* The most recent LA congress, on 19-21 November 1971, reelected Ragnar Arnalds as Chairman and Adda Bára Sigfúsdóttir as Vice-Chairman. The new 30-member Central Committee, with its 10 deputies, reflected a substantial renewal inasmuch as new party regulations permit only a three-year term. In the case of the LA cabinet members Jósefsson and Kjartansson, however, a special resolution was passed naming them (additional) members of the Central Committee—without voting rights. The new Political Committee was to be elected by the Central Committee at its first meeting, in January 1972.

The OLL and OIS. The OLL is headed by Hannibal Valdimarsson, who resigned the chairmanship of the SDP in 1956 to head the LA front. Other OLL leaders include Bjorn Jónsson and Alfred Gislason. The OIS leader is Steingrímur Adalsteinsson.

Mass Organizations. The LA and OLL together play a leading role in the labor movement. Bjorn Jónsson in 1971 took over from Valdimarsson the chairmanship of the Icelandic Federation of Labor, which represents some 85 per cent of the country's 43,000 organized workers. Edvard Sigurdsson (LA) heads the largest single union, the General Workers' Union in Reykjavík.

The schisms in the communist movement have filtered down to the party's youth elements. The main auxiliary, known as "The Brigade," has declared its autonomy and removed the age limit for membership. The Brigade appears to be divided into doctrinaire (pro-OIS) and more liberal (pro-LA) factions, but also embraces militants with little apparent ideological allegiance, whose activities are assailed by both conservative and liberal Brigade members as well as by both LA and OIS.

Domestic Views and Activities. There was considerable maneuvering among the parties in the months leading up to the 1971 election. The OLL engaged in "current leftist dialogues" with the SDP and the Federation of Young Progressives (which included the radical left-wing of the PP), excluding the LA, which made a parallel effort to engage the SDP in electoral cooperation talks. Within each of the parties there existed factional bases of power which produced a complex crossfire of polemics that ruled out any formal cooperation among them. Talks between the SDP, LA, and OLL did eventually get under way after several months of preliminary consultations starting in 1970, but little ground was given from any quarter, and the talks only heightened existing antagonisms. The LA and PP accused OLL leader Valdimarsson of trying to split the PP by seeking association with its youth group, while the LA charged that the SDP had abandoned social-democratic policies and was bound to the IP.

The LA election campaign was launched on 25 April, when a 44-page edition of the party newspaper, *Thjodviljinn*, was devoted to conservation and the environment. The LA argued that these were political issues: "Attitudes toward them depend upon whether the individual is preferred to profits, whether social aspects are preferred to pecuniary ones, whether people consider that economic systems exist for the individual or the individual for the systems." The foremost issue in the campaign concerned the territorial waters. The LA, proposing unilateral action by Iceland to extend the existing 12-mile limit set by 1958 and 1961 agreements with England and West Germany, called for a 50-mile fishing limit and a 100-mile "anti-pollution zone" banning the dumping of industrial and chemical wastes. There was, in fact, little fundamental divergence between the parties on this question; all were agreed on extending the fishing limit and all were opposed to adoption of a quota system or other type of restriction. The IP-SDP government, however, was opposed to setting any specific date for an extension or unilaterally announcing the agreements null and void. It favored, instead, consultations with other nations and independent research, with a view to presenting Iceland's position at the Law of the Sea Conference, planned for 1973, and making an earlier decision only if conditions changed. The OLL and PP concurred with the LA on the immediate unilateral implementation of new limits.

In a post-election commentary, *Thjodviljinn* editorialized (17 June) that the nation had given its mandate to the 50-mile fishing limit and 100-mile anti-pollution jurisdiction, and had elected a parliamentary majority that was "morally bound to implement this without delay." Appointed by the president to form a government, the PP concentrated on uniting the leftist parties on the basis of their joint policy on the fishing limits issue despite their differences on other questions. The OLL, and Valdimarsson in particular, pressed for inclusion of the weakened SDP in discussions on a new cabinet—there were indications that Valdimarsson personally was hoping for an SDP-OLL merger—but the SDP rejected inclusion, largely because of the long-standing hostility between it and the PP.

The PP-LA-OLL coalition—formed only on 10 July—was an uneasy one from the outset, resting upon general accord on a single, albeit major, issue—the future of the island's primary source of income, its territorial waters. In joint policy formulation, concessions were made by all three parties, but the greatest influence appeared to accrue to the communist section of the coalition. By year's end, the Progressives were seen to be resisting communist pressure on a number of policy matters, and to be retreating somewhat from immediate post-election positions. The communists, in contrast, remained firm on adherence to agreements made, and inflexible as to possibly divergent interpretation of these agreements (see below).

International Views and Positions. The LA continued to advocate Icelandic neutrality and independence, an end to the "U.S. occupation" (the presence of the U.S. Iceland Defense Force, or IDF, at Keflavík), and the country's total withdrawal from the NATO alliance. By the beginning of 1971, with indications of possible combined gains for the LA, OLL, and PP in the June elections, however, statements by LA leaders had begun to suggest a new flexibility in the party's NATO policy. In a New Year's interview, for example, (quoted in *Morgunbladid*, Reykjavík, 7 January), Ragnar Arnalds said that were a new (leftist) government coalition able to reach agreement on withdrawal of the IDF and to take a generally "healthier position on the international scene," then Icelandic withdrawal from NATO would not necessarily be a precondition to LA participation in forming a cabinet.

The LA assailed the "do-nothing" policy of the IP-SDP government toward what it termed the penetration of Iceland by foreign monopoly capital. In his speech to the Nordic Council meeting, held at Copenhagen on 13-18 February, Kjartansson put the blame for the alleged penetration on the applications by Norway and Denmark for admission to the European Economic Community (EEC) and on the collapse of the "Nordek" plan for an inter-Scandinavian customs union. He appealed to other Nordic countries to support Iceland's position on fishing limits and ocean pollution. (*Thjodviljinn*, 16 February.) The party newspaper editorialized later that should England, Denmark, and Norway—already members of the European Free Trade Association (EFTA)—be successful in their efforts to join the EEC, EFTA would be dead. The eventual dissolution of EFTA in this way, it was said, would confirm the LA's longstanding contention that EFTA was simply an EEC anteroom. (*Ibid.*, 14 May.)

In a post-election statement, Arnalds said that the LA could not hope to have all of its policies implemented immediately and that the needed radical changes in Iceland's foreign policy would only be realized in stages (*Morgunbladid*, 15 June). The "government platform agreement," announced in mid-July after protracted consultations between the PP, LA, and OLL, advocated close relations among Nordic nations, support for the seating in the U.N. of Communist China and both German states, the right of self-determination of all nations, condemnation of the use of force anywhere by large powers against small nations, convocation of a European security conference, general disarmament, and the abolition of all military alliances. The document stated that disagreement existed among the parties on NATO membership (to which only the LA was clearly opposed). Therefore, NATO membership was to be maintained, although Iceland's position would be "constantly reviewed in light of changed conditions." The defense treaty with the United States, however, was to be taken up for review with a view to terminating the U.S. military presence by 1975. Iceland, further, would not join the EEC, but would seek special arrangements with it in tariff and trade matters on a reciprocal basis. On the fishing limits issue, the government platform called for abrogation of the existing agreements, and extension, not later than 1 September 1972, to 50-mile fishing and 100-mile anti-pollution limits. (*Thjodviljinn*, 15 July.) Arnalds characterized the platform agreement as a "compromise" and the "common denominator of the policy upon which all three parties can agree." While the LA "must be content" with continued membership in NATO, the agreement, on the other hand, contained "important policy changes in foreign affairs, both concerning the military base issue and general stands toward international issues." (*Ibid.*, 14 July.)

A policy platform adopted by the LA congress, in November, upheld the "independent" foreign policy which had replaced the "servility displayed by the former government." The document lent considerable emphasis to the LA's continuing assertion that the government platform agreement called for the unconditional withdrawal of the IDF during the current electoral term. (*Thjodviljinn*, 23 November.) (A more liberal interpretation of this clause, rejected by the communists, has been made on occasion by Foreign Minister Einar Agustsson. Agustsson currently appears to interpret the clause as intending that the IDF agreement was to be reviewed and abrogated *subject to* the findings of the review.) A ministerial committee comprising Einar Agustsson for the PP, Magnus Kjartansson for the LA, and Magnus Torfi Olafsson for the OLL was formed in October to deal with the military base issue. Following a review on the IDF question, expected to take several months, the Icelandic government was to ask the U.S. for bilateral talks.

As in previous years, the LA rarely took a position on international events that did not directly or indirectly affect Iceland. With regard to the Vietnam war, it charged the IP and SDP with "refraining from doing or saying anything that could be displeasing to the American politicians responsible for the most detestable genocide in history" (*Thjodviljinn*, 24 March). The publication of the "Pentagon Papers" prompted the LA newspaper to editorialize that Icelandic officials had "shown U.S. government authorities special trust, accepted all of their statements as the undisputed truth, and, on this basis, made decisions which had greatly changed national conditions" (*ibid.*, 3 July). The party, which has remained neutral in the Sino-Soviet schism, scored Iceland's "subservience" to the United States on the issue of relations with China. It was only this subservience, in this view, which had prevented the Icelandic government from "adopting common sense" and recognizing China. (*Ibid.*, 17 April.) The new government established diplomatic relations at the ambassadorial level with China on 8 December.

International Communist Movement. Iceland's communists maintained an isolationist posture in international communist affairs until 1968, avoiding important meetings and disassociating their organization from ideological schisms. The LA, under the current leadership, has adopted a far less impartial attitude, particularly with regard to Soviet policies. It has expressed continuing condemnation of the Soviet-led intervention in Czechoslovakia in 1968 and of Soviet activities there since. The strongest attacks in *Thjodviljinn* are penned by Magnus Kjartansson. For example, an article by him in the 9 March 1971 issue, recalling the Czechoslovak communist party's attempt in 1968 to lift censorship and sanction freedom of speech, stated that "Russian tanks ... broke the back of this freedom anew and represented the symbol of state power which [true] socialists intend to repel." Kjartansson was criticized by many veteran Icelandic communists, particularly those within the OIS, whose secession from the LA in 1969 was prompted by the reverberations of the events in Czechoslovakia. The LA organ was, however, not consistent in its treatment of developments behind the Iron Curtain, and hence came under fire from critics within and outside the party. Apparently the divergent strains in the newspaper's editorial policy caused the purge of its staff that was undertaken by its "governing board" in June. Kjartansson, who headed the paper for many years, chose to resign, purportedly to concentrate on his ministerial duties, and was replaced by the less controversial Svavar Gestsson. LA official policy on Czechoslovakia remained unequivocal, however; the party congress reiterated its stand "in support of a Czechoslovakia currently in bondage by the military occupation of a foreign power." (*Thjodviljinn*, 23 November.)

It had been a seeming departure from the party's generally isolationist posture within international communism when, in January, the LA sent a message to the London conference of fifteen West European communist parties, expressing interest in the work of the conference and asking to be invited to such meetings in the future. The message was delivered by the delegate of the Communist Party of Norway, who spoke in favor of the inclusion of the Icelandic communists in interparty deliberations.

Publications. The daily newspaper *Thjodviljinn* is the central organ of the LA. A theoretical journal, *Ny Utsyn*, is published biweekly. The OLL organ is *Nytt Land*. The OIS publishes *Ny Dagsbrun*. *Neisti* is the organ of the Brigade.

Valerie Bloom

Ireland

The Communist Party of Ireland (CPI) was founded in 1921, but its initial existence appears to have been short lived. It was refounded in 1933—a date adopted by present Irish communists as the original year of the party's founding. The organizational structure of the CPI was disrupted during World War II, partly as a result of the fact that the Republic of Ireland, in the south, declared itself neutral while Northern Ireland participated in the conflict. In 1948 the communists in the south founded the Irish Workers' Party (IWP) and those in the north the Communist Party of Northern Ireland (CPNI). At a special "Unity Congress" held in Belfast on 15 March 1970, the two parties reunited, founding once again a united Communist Party of Ireland. The party, now based in Dublin, held its Fifteenth Congress on 16-17 October 1971 in Belfast.

The CPI is estimated to have some 300 members and is somewhat larger in the south than in the north. The population of the Republic of Ireland is nearly 3,000,000 and that of Northern Ireland about 1,500,000 (estimated 1970).

Although the CPI is not strong in either the north or south and holds no seats in any legislative body, it wields influence in Irish politics disproportionate to its small size because of its association with the "Official" Irish Republic Army (IRA; see below) and to a lesser extent with the Civil Rights Association (CRA)—the latter an uneasy coalition of a wide range of political groups opposed to the Government of Northern Ireland. (The Government, situated on an estate—Stormont—in Belfast, is dominated by the Unionist Party, which is broadly similar to the British Conservative Party and supports the union of Northern Ireland and Great Britain.) The party also controls a small organization of young persons, the Connolly Youth Movement. It has minimal strength in the labor movement.

Leadership and Organization. In its current form the Communist Party of Ireland's leading body—the Executive Committee—is divided into two branches representing the south and the north. At the party's founding congress in March 1970 the following were elected to the Executive Committee: northern branch—Andrew Barr, Brian Graham, James Graham, Hugh Moore, Sean Morrissey, Hugh Murphy, Edwina Stewart, James Stewart, Betty Sinclair, and Bill Somerset; southern branch—Joseph Deasy, George Jeffares, Patrick McCarthy, Sam Nolan, Sean Nolan, Michael O'Reilly, Michael O'Riordan, Sean O'Rourke, Geoffrey Palmer, and Aodh Rafferty. The Executive Committee, meeting a week later, elected the following six-member Secretariat: Andrew Barr, Hugh Moore, Sam Nolan, Sean Nolan, Michael O'Riordan, and James Stewart. Michael O'Riordan was elected general secretary, while Andrew Barr became the party chairman.

Domestic Views and Policies. The fundamental goal of the CPI is the establishment of a united socialist republic in Ireland. To accomplish this task, the party advocates the formation of a "national liberation front" in which it seeks the participation of Protestants as well as the predominantly anti-Unionist Catholics. Many of the Protestants of Northern Ireland, however, find the prospect of unification unpalatable since it would mean losing the majority position they currently enjoy there. The CPI, mainly Catholic in the South and Protestant in the North, is thus faced with the problem that much of what is acceptable to Catholics antagonizes Protestants. It therefore attempts to unite the two sides, especially through the labor movement, on the basis of common grievances—inadequate housing and increased living costs—and opposition to the Common Market. It describes the current situation in both North and South as one whose ills are economic and largely the result of British "colonial" policy and offers socialism as the remedy.

The party also perceives the situation as extremely complex, and one that does not call for the "mindless militarism" of some of its competitors. While not eschewing violence, it prefers political methods to open warfare. This relative moderation has in recent years alienated the growing number of anti-Unionist militants who have come to prefer such groups as the Trotskyists, the "International Socialists" of the People's Democracy group (through which civil rights leader and Member of Parliament Bernadette Devlin achieved her popularity, although she no longer belongs), and, since 1970, the militant "Provisional" IRA.

At its Fifteenth Congress in October, the CPI reiterated its recently formulated program calling for the release of all political prisoners, the withdrawal of British troops from anti-Unionist areas, a bill of rights for Northern Ireland, the suspension of the current Stormont administration, and immediate talks on these matters by representatives of the London and Dublin governments and of political parties and other organizations in Northern Ireland (*Information Bulletin*, no. 21-22; *Morning Star*, daily organ of the Communist Party of Great Britain, London, 18 October). The program had been stated in essentially the same language by party leaders in February and again in April in a joint statement issued following a London meeting between the CPI and the Communist Party of Great Britain (Budapest radio, 15 February; *Morning Star*, 15 April). On the basis of this program the party has attempted to develop a united anti-Unionist movement, under the leadership of the CRA, that would elect "democratic people's administrations" at the local level which could then form the basis for a new more representative assembly for Northern Ireland.

The CPI position on one of the most heated debates, regarding the presence of British troops in Northern Ireland, was explained in the February statement:

> The critical situation ... is the direct consequence of British colonial policy, and the immediate cause of the recent bloody occurrences is that the British Military Command, with brutally executed house searches, has carried out premeditated provocation against the peaceful population of national sentiment. The British Military Command and the Conservative-Unionist Government of Belfast have tried [to] isolate the progressive forces of the Left from the masses.... The Communist Party of Ireland demands that British troops be withdrawn into barracks and that troops should be used for patrol duties at the most, but even then not with loaded weapons. At present the Party does not consider it right to withdraw the troops completely without a simultaneous political settlement, because in this case reactionary forces would launch a pogrom against the ghettos of the population of Irish nationalistic attachment.

The communists' relationship with the illegal IRA underwent a serious transformation in 1970. While in that year the two Irish parties merged to form the CPI, the then united IRA divided when a large faction (which afterward became known as the "Provisional IRA") accused the organization's leadership of becoming Marxist and walked out. The Provisional IRA—known also as the "green" or "Brady" IRA (after its leader, Rory O'Brady)—is strongest in Northern Ireland, seeks the unification of Ireland at all costs, allies itself solely with Catholics, advocates urban guerrilla warfare, and is strongly anti-communist, though it claims to derive its basic army discipline from communist guerrilla sources (see *New York Times*, 7 December 1971, and *This Week*, Dublin, 12 March 1971).

The original IRA—generally referred to since the split as the "Official" IRA, but known also as the "red" or "Goulding" IRA (after its leader, Cathal Goulding)—is larger in the Republic of Ireland. The CPI supports the Official IRA, over which it has considerable influence and with which it exhibits a close identity of views, notably on the need for the formation of a "national liberation movement" for the creation of a "united socialist republic." Both IRA's have retained a political branch called Sinn Féin ("Ourselves"). The political ambitions of the "Official" Sinn Féin were disclosed in 1971 at its annual conference when it decided to contest future elections to the parliaments at London, Belfast, and Dublin.

The CPI and the Official IRA denounce the guerrilla activities launched by the Provisionals against the British Army troops and civilians (mostly the pro-Unionist Protestants). Party leaders reportedly declared: "The Irish Communists resolutely condemn the methods of individual terror and physical coercion which are applied by the so-called Provisionals....These things only help the anti-democratic policy of the authorities, diverting attention from the real tasks and correct methods of political struggle." (Budapest radio, 15 February.) Both the party and the Official IRA seek to win the support of the British working class in Northern Ireland and, unlike the Provisional IRA, to avoid splitting "Irish and British workers along barren nationalistic lines"(*Morning Star*, 17 August).

International Views and Positions. The anti-Unionist movement was given cosiderable treatment by the Soviet press, but much of this presentation was concerned with the aspects of "class struggle" and "British imperialism," rather than with the activities and positions of the CPI and the two IRA's. Catholic areas were described as "working-class ghettoes" and the hostilities between the two religious communities dismissed. An exception was an article in the Moscow *New Times* (no. 32, August) which gave some attention to the religious aspect and to the views of the CPI.

The CPI made numerous contacts with foreign communist parties at its Fifteenth Congress. Attending were representatives from communist parties of Bulgaria, Cyprus, Czechoslovakia, Denmark, France, Great Britain, Hungary, Romania, the Soviet Union, and the United States.

Publications. The CPI publishes a theoretical journal, *The Irish Socialist Review*. *United Irishman* is the newspaper of the Official IRA's Sinn Féin.

Eric Stromquist

Italy

The Italian Communist Party (Partito Comunista Italiano; PCI) was founded in 1921. In recent years the PCI has been confronted with marginal competition from a number of small parties and groups adhering to Marxism-Leninism of differing shades of interpretation. During 1971, while small groups of Maoist orientation continued to proliferate, the main challenge to the PCI's leadership within the extreme left appeared to originate from the Manifesto group (see below).

The PCI is the largest nonruling communist party in the world. On the last day of 1971 the PCI newspaper *L'Unità* announced that the party had 1,520,974 members: a net increase of 13,927 over 1970. At the same time the Italian Communist Youth Federation (Federazione Giovanile Comunista Italiana; FGCI), was reported to have 85,826 members: an increase of 19,375 over 1970. The population of Italy is 55,000,00 (estimated 1971).

In the May 1968 elections for the Chamber of Deputies and the Senate, the PCI obtained 8,555,131 votes (26.9 per cent) and won 177 (out of 630) seats in the Chamber. It made an electoral alliance with the Italian Socialist Party of Proletarian Unity (Partito Socialista Italiano di Unità Proletaria; PSIUP) for the Senate elections; the combined votes totaled 8,580,813 (30 per cent), and secured 87 seats for the PCI and 14 for the PSIUP. By the end of 1970 five former PCI deputies, having aligned themselves with the views of the aforementioned Manifesto group, had joined the "mixed group" in the Chamber, formed primarily of Alto-Adige independents and Autonomous Socialists.

The PCI and the PSIUP were the two major left-wing opposition parties to the center-left government coalition that has been ruling Italy since 1963 and which in 1971 comprised the Christian Democrat party (Democrazia Cristiana; DC) with 266 deputies and 135 senators; the Italian Socialist Party (Partito Socialista Italiano; PSI) with 62 deputies and 36 senators; the Unitarian Socialist Party (Partito Socialista Unitario; PSU—better known as the Italian Social-Democratic Party (Partito Socialdemocratico Italiano; PSDI)—with 29 deputies and 10 senators; and the Italian Republican Party (Partito Repubblicano Italiano; PRI) with 9 deputies and 2 senators.

On 26 February 1971 the PRI formally announced that it was withdrawing its representatives from the center-left government of Premier Emilio Colombo, indicating that the Republicans wanted to maintain the coalition but to dissociate themselves from its failures. The government crisis which ensued was resolved when the Colombo cabinet obtained a vote of confidence from the parliament.

On 13-14 June, local elections were held in some parts of Italy. The most striking result was the gain for the neo-fascist Italian Social Movement (Movimento Sociale Italiano; MSI), at the expense of other right-wing groups and the DC. The MSI obtained 759,341 votes (13.9 per cent) compared with 457,385 (8.4 per cent) obtained in the same areas in regional elections in 1970, with its biggest advance in Sicily (16.3 per cent). The PCI and the PSIUP registered a small loss, getting 25.4 per cent (27.6 per cent in 1970). The principal loser, the DC, bitterly attacked during the campaign from both left and right, dropped to 31.7 per cent (35.1 per cent in 1970).

With only one-fifth of the electorate involved, mainly in Southern Italy, the results of these elections were not indicative of the country as a whole.

On 24 December Giovanni Leone, a moderate Christian Democrat, was elected the sixth president of the Italian Republic, on the sixteenth day of a wearisome election that strained the nation's democratic system. Leone was elected in the twenty-third poll, with 518 votes out of 1,008 "Grand Electors" (630 deputies, 320 senators and 58 regional delegates). He obtained the necessary majority with the supporting votes of the MSI.

Organization and Leadership. In 1971 the PCI was structured as follows: 109 federations, 18 regional committees, some 11,000 sections, and about 25,000 cells, together with a large number of youth clubs. The party established also four federations and numerous nuclei abroad. The unpaid or part-paid directive committees of these organs numbered more than 80,000 persons; there were probably more than 1,000 full-time paid officials of the federations and sections, with some 200 to 300 at party headquarters in Rome (not including those engaged in the party press). No changes in the basic structure of the party were noted during the year.

The directive organs of the PCI are elected at the party's congresses, the most recent being the Twelfth Congress, held in February 1969. The leadership elected at that time included the Central Committee (171 members) and the Directorate (31), the latter working largely through two executive committees: the Political Office (9) and the Secretariat (7). All members of the Directorate were also members of the Central Committee. In addition there were the Central Control Commission (41 members) and a small audit board. An innovation in party machinery was the setting up, in April 1969, of five permanent commissions of the Central Committee to function in the intervals between plenum meetings. The first commission (31 members) deals with foreign affairs, including relations with other communist parties; the second (33 members), with the parliament and with regional and local authorities; the third (41 members), with economic and social questions; the fourth (35 members), with press, propaganda, and cultural matters; and the fifth (36 members), with questions of party organization.

Luigi Longo was reelected as secretary-general at the Twelfth Congress; he has held the post since Palmiro Togliatti's death in 1964. Enrico Berlinguer was elected deputy secretary-general (the post had been vacant since Longo left it to move to the top). Other leading members of the party elected at the congress were Giorgio Amendola, Pietro Ingrao, Emanuele Macaluso, Giorgio Napolitano, Agostino Novella, Gian Carlo Pajetta, and Aldo Tortorella (members of the Political Office), and Paolo Bufalini, Armando Cossutta, Fernando Di Giulio, Alessandro Natta, and Ugo Pecchioli (members of the Secretariat). Longo and Berlinguer were members of both the Political Office and the Secretariat, and Longo was chairman of the Central Committee; the chairman of the Central Control Commission was Arturo Colombo. In 1970, a new Foreign Policy Commission (headed by Gian Carlo Pajetta) was established, with the participation of Enrico Berlinguer, Umberto Cardia, Carlo Galluzzi, and Sergio Segre. Aldo Tortorella is the director of *L'Unità*, and Luca Pavolini the co-director. Alessandro Natta is the director of *Rinascita* (the party's weekly political organ). Carlo Galluzzi is the head of the party's press and propaganda section.

The PCI dominates the largest of the three main Italian trade union organizations, the General Confederation of Italian Labor (Confederazione Generale Italiana del Lavoro; CGIL). The CGIL contains sizable minorities of PSI and PSIUP workers, but its cadres are predominantly communist. The secretary-general of the CGIL is Luciano Lama, a member of the PCI. During 1971 the CGIL worked in close collaboration with the DC unions represented in the Confederazione Italiana Sindacati Lavoratori (CISL) and the PSU-PRI unions affiliated with the Unione Italiana del Lavoro (UIL). After almost two years of negotiations aimed at reaching a reunification of the three main unions, on 25 November a joint meeting of the general councils of the CGIL, CISL, and UIL approved a final document in which they established the date (21 September 1972) for holding the respective national congresses for unity. A congress to be held in February 1973 would inaugurate officially the new labor front.

Domestic Views and Policies. The PCI's pronouncements on domestic issues during 1971 reflected the complexity of the Italian political situation, the focal events of which were: the growing social and economic unrest of the country; the striking results of the June local elections, with the heavy losses of the DC going to the MSI; the shift to the right within the DC, and the consequent collapse of the center-left coalition; the election of the president of the republic with the support of the fascist vote; the petition for a referendum to abolish the law on the divorce passed in 1970; and the growing power of the three major trade unions (CGIL, CISL, and UIL) and their planned unification.

Since 1970 the PCI has adopted a cautious position in internal and economic policies, which, in turn, has provoked strong reactions from the groups on its left. In 1971 the party insisted on a reformist line, despite accusations of revisionism. One of the major points of the party's left-wing critics was that by fighting for reforms, the PCI had put itself within the capitalist system and in fact become one of its pillars.

In an interview with the Swedish communist organ *Ny Dag* (24-25 February), asked about the possibility of collaboration between the PCI and the DC, Berlinguer stated: "Within the party there is talk of a new majority, which means a change of view, a collaboration between all radical trends from the present ruling parties to the PCI, as well as the not insignificant PSIUP. This would be a long-range process and would include a through reshuffling of the cards.... The dominant line [in the DC] is ambiguous, immovable, and thus conservative, which rules out the prospect of a joint program or a coalition between the DC and the PCI."

In a post-election commentary, Luigi Longo stated: "The Christian Democratic Party is paying a heavy price in losses to the MSI for having abandoned reforms and led the attack on the unions. These results are also a warning against the dangerous lure of the right and are a cause for deep reflection for the leftist Catholic forces and all the democratic and antifascist forces". (*L'Unità*, 15 June.)

The PCI attributed the Italian economic and social unrest to the misgovernment of the center-left coalition:

> In the present situation, the major danger factor resides in the way in which the country is governed. The economic crisis itself is to a great extent brought about by this fact. The paralyzing conflicts of the center-left, the policy of postponement or of living from day to day, the inability to tackle the most serious problems of the country with an organic view, these only increase the state of confusion and disorder, of insecurity and discontent. To this we must add the fearful inefficiency of the government machine, corruption, the practice of governing behind the scenes, the inability to guarantee respect for the most elementary standards of democratic legality. (Enrico Berlinguer, Report on Preparation for the Thirteenth Congress, *L'Unità*, 12 November.)

Berlinguer focussed his criticism on the DC, laying most of the blame for the crisis on it:

> This party is going through a profound crisis: the outcome of its crisis will influence the entire Italian situation. This crisis is undoubtedly linked to the interclass character of the Christian Democratic party and hence to the reflections of the increasing aggravation of social conflicts within that party; but this crisis also has more immediate political aspects, in addition to the cultural and ideal aspects.

Berlinguer also claimed that "The refusal of the DC to make a choice, to distinguish between the various intermediate forces, in the end led to the sacrificing of everything in the interest of the most backward and parasitary sectors, causing it to discharge the tensions which this produces in the form of anticommunism, in an attack against the working class and, in some of its sectors, producing authoritarian tendencies.'' He also criticized the policy of the DC: ''It has for years slowed down the development of Italian democracy; today it puts it in grave danger. The preoccupation prevailing today in the DC seems to be the concern with recovering or not losing to the Right some hundreds of thousands of votes, even at the cost of forcing a shift of the entire situation toward the Right.... It is necessary to deepen the internal crisis in the DC in order to bring about a shift in its position and, for this purpose, it is necessary to pressure the DC and to force it to make certain choices.'' (*Ibid*.)

Examining the causes of the growing power of the MSI, Berlinguer pointed out that every time in Italy the communists managed to advance and to open up a favorable perspective, a problem of this nature came up. One of the major points of the Thirteenth Congress would be: ''How can the PCI continue to advance on the road opened by the struggles and gains of these past years, avoiding a reaction of such breadth and such depth that the entire situation would swing to the Right, beyond the democratic terrain?'' (*Ibid*).

Pointing out the need for unity of all left-wing forces, Berlinguer declared that the PCI's ''relationship with the PSIUP'' was ''being developed, giving rise to a system of common effort, in the center and along the periphery, such as to make the understanding, collaboration, and rapprochement between the two parties ever more profound.'' He criticized the way in which the PSI conducted its action for reforms—''a method which sometimes seems tied rather to the justification of its own presence in the administration rather than to a general view of national development.'' Berlinguer criticized also the Social Democratic Party for the ''anti-communist tone ... which characterized the PSDI in an almost obsessive manner'' (Ibid).

During the presidential election the DC showed its internal disunity. As the DC leftist factions had blocked Amintore Fanfani's candidature in the first week's polls, so the rightist ones later prevented the candidature of Aldo Moro, who would have been acceptable to the Socialists and the Communists.

While the DC demonstrated its disunity, a new left-wing alignment of PCI, PSIUP, and PSI displayed a solidarity unprecedented in recent years, when they supported first the candidature of Francesco De Martino and then that of Pietro Nenni. The PCI violently attacked the center-right operation performed during the presidential election: ''The leaders of the DC, of the PSDI and PRI are responsible for the center-right operation extended to the Fascists. Needing to make a political choice, they pronounced themselves for a reactionary alliance'' (Aldo Tortorella, *L'Unità*, 27 December).

International Views and Policies. In 1971 the PCI maintained a position of autonomy with regard to the views and policies of other communist parties. The party's stance was reiterated on a number of occasions by Berlinguer. In his aforementioned interview with *Ny Dag* (24-25 February), the PCI deputy secretary-general stated: ''We have total autonomy. First of all it is total when it comes to making decisions about the internal affairs of our country. Our assessments of the international workers' movement and the policies of other countries and parties are also autonomous. Even internationalism is the result of a free choice we made and are constantly renewing.'' At the Twenty-fourth Congress of the Communist Party of the Soviet Union (CPSU), 30 March to 9 April, Berlinguer made clear the PCI position: ''Our international solidarity does not and cannot mean our full identification with the choices which each socialist country and more generally each communist and workers' party has made and is making on its own responsibility, but means a basic solidarity with a country such as [the Soviet Union], with the other socialist countries, with a whole world which through its own existence and victories had already changed the fate of mankind.... Our internationalism is founded on the recognition of the full independence of each country and each party and leaves the way open, as has already happened and as can always happen, to moments and circumstances of dissensions and divergence, without in any way, as a result of this, weakening solidarity and duty in the struggle for the great aims which unite us." (*Pravda*, Moscow, 2 April.)

On the occasion of the death of Nikita Khrushchev the PCI reaffirmed, through a number of articles, its independent position, its rejection of Stalinism, and its right to criticize the domestic, international, and inter-party policies of the Soviet leadership. The Italian communists judged as Khrushchev's most important contribution to Communist history his initiation of the process of "de-Stalinization"; they criticized, however, his policy: "What was lacking in the cultural revolution which Khrushchev tried to lead against the bureaucratized apparatus of his own party was the institutionalization and canalization of the movement in lower levels of the country.... If the de-centralization of authority affected the Soviets and the economic planning bodies, it never became a process of democratization of the political organs of the party from below." (*Rinascita*, 17 September.) They also criticized his policy toward China: "With Khruchshev ... the problem of Sino-Soviet relations entered into crisis and reached the point of a rift.... Khruchshev did not understand that China was something different, not just one more third-world country." (*Ibid.*)

Trade union activity is one area in which the divergence of political interests between West European communist parties and the East European governments is most marked. This was admitted by Mario Didò, a leader of the communist-dominated CGIL, on his return from a study tour of Soviet industrial centers in September: "At Togliattigrad they have adopted ... not only Western machines but also Western systems of organization. To have a minimum of equilibrium, however, such a system presupposes at the very least, the existence of a strong trade union force. But at the present time such a force does not exist, either in the Soviet Union or in the other countries of Eastern Europe." (*L'Espresso*, 26 September.)

In a survey of the Soviet economic situation, the Moscow correspondent of *L'Unità*, Adriano Guerra, stressed the need for modernization through the use of computers and other techniques. This, he remarked, raised the question of the "leading role of the party," and he engaged in indirect polemics with conservative Soviet spokesmen. In particular he turned his critical attention to a representative article in the January issue of *Voprosy istorii*. Guerra stressed the need to develop new relationships between the party and other organizations or institutions. For the PCI, however, it was not only a matter of achieving a greater efficiency; the central question was a political one: "The problem on the agenda clearly cannot be solved merely through the use of mathematics and cybernetics. What space does the computerization of the country's economic life leave for the participation of the workers and the citizens in decision making? It is not just a Soviet problem, it concerns communists of the advanced Western countries, and it concerns Marxism in general, which must give a reply [to] the problems of what has been ... called the 'second industrial revolution.' " (*L'Unità*, 23 March.)

Apart from the CPSU none of the ruling parties of Eastern Europe was invited to the celebration of the fiftieth anniversary of the PCI. This fact can be explained as a gesture of disassociation from the East European governments in general.

Particularly strong was the PCI's reaction to a document on the "lesson drawn from the crisis development in the party and society since the Thirteenth Congress of the Communist Party of Czechoslovakia," published by the Czechoslovak leadership in *Rudé Právo*. An editorial in *L'Unità* (15 January) stated: "[The document] maintains that one should reject an 'abstract' interpretation of sovereignty of a socialist country, allegedly disseminated by 'bourgeois propaganda.' ... We do not admit that there can be any conflict between the sovereignty of a socialist country and its 'class and internationalist' character. Sovereignty is an inalienable right. For us this is not an abstract interpretation but a value which we cannot renounce." The editorial noted that the PCI had not changed its judgment of the Czechoslovak situation, and still held the invasion of 1968 to be unjustifiable.

At the Fourteenth Congress of the Communist Party of Czechoslovakia (25-29 May 1971), the PCI delegate, Sergio Segre, was not permitted to deliver his speech. On 29 May, *L'Unità* published the text of the undelivered message, in which the PCI reconfirmed its position: "We also consider it our duty to confirm on this occasion the political and principled positions assumed by our party in connection with the Czechoslovak events of recent years, events which have been of international importance and which have raised questions which are at the moment under discussion within the international workers' and communist movement.... Our differences with regard to the military intervention of five Warsaw Pact countries in Czechoslovakia also arises partly from this. With the frankness that we believe should always inspire relations between communist parties, we say to you that we do not believe that any elements have emerged meanwhile which could induce us to change our positions. They are based, in addition to our judgment of the development of the events, on the firm belief that the independence and sovereignty of every communist party and of every state are the absolute foundations of internationalism. We believe that the national character and internationalism of a revolutionary force are both essential and inseparable, and that only in this way can the working class acquire ever growing importance, become the predominant class in its own country, and thus make an effective contribution to the struggle of the international proletariat."

No foreign communist party has paid as much critical attention to the crisis which broke out in Poland in December 1970 as the PCI. Since the Politburo statement of 16 December 1970, deploring the fact that such a grave economic situation had been allowed to develop and that arms had been used, the Italian communists have returned to the subject often in articles, statements, and reports. The most impressive of these contributions to critical research into the failings of the Polish government, and the lessons to be drawn from them, was offered by a round-table discussion between six prominent members of the PCI, published in *Rinascita* on 19 February. Although the participants were discussing the Polish crisis, they made it clear that they were dealing with phenomena found also, in varying forms and degrees, in other East European countries. The speakers criticized the erstwhile Gomulka regime for its authoritarian character, hierarchic and bureaucratic power structure, and neglect of the interests of the working masses. On 25 June *Rinascita* published a provocative analysis of the same crisis by a Polish economist, Wlodimierz Brus, who argued that it was the result of a "defective political mechanism" characterized by censorship, bureaucratic repression, and a lack of socialist democracy.

In the last months of 1971 a significant rapprochement took place between the PCI and the new leadership of the Polish United Workers' Party. Talks between Luigi Longo and Edward Gierek were followed by the dispatch of a PCI delegation to Warsaw for more extensive inter-party discussions. One member of the delegation, Adriano Guerra, wrote a series of articles publicizing the "new look" of the Gierek leadership and stressing that its great merit was that it was tackling national problems, through "a new method, that of open dialogue with the workers." (*L'Unità*, 10 October.)

The PCI expressed satisfaction about the development of relations between China and the United States: "This new phase which seems to be opening up ... shows the political realism and flexibility of the Chinese leaders and their freedom from rigid schemes or dogmatic and ideologizing stands of a kind which they often used in the past.... We do not believe today that a Sino-American dialogue must assume an anti-Soviet significance." (*L'Unità*, 16 April.)

Alberto Jacoviello's articles on China, published in *L'Unità* in January—based on a visit in 1970—provoked reactions from some PCI members, who argued that these articles lacked critical analysis and were "too pro-Chinese". Jacoviello was the first Italian communist newspaperman admitted to visit the People's Republic of China in ten years.

In 1971 another newspaperman, Luca Pavolini, visited China. His series of articles, published in *L'Unità* in June, apparently was not criticized by the PCI leadership.

International Party Contacts. In January 1971 a delegation of the League of Communists of Yugoslavia met with a PCI delegation including Enrico Berlinguer, Gian Carlo Pajetta, Sergio Segre, and Rodolfo Mechini, On 30 January, Luigi Longo met in Rome with Dinumkhamed Kunaev, alternate member of the Political Bureau of the Central Committee of CPSU. Mrs. Nguyen Thi Binh, the minister of foreign affairs of the Provisional Revolutionary Government of the Republic of South Vietnam, visited Italy in February at the invitation of the "Italian Committee for Peace and Freedom in Vietnam." She met with a PCI delegation headed by Luigi Longo, and conferred with the leadership of the communist-controlled Italian Women's Union and the secretary-general of the CGIL, Luciano Lama. In March-April a PCI delegation attended the CPSU congress. It included, in addition to Berlinguer, Gian Carlo Pajetta and Sergio Segre. The secretary-general of the Communist Party of Chile, Luis Corvalán, met with Luigi Longo in April. In May a PCI delegation headed by Berlinguer, visited Moscow and met with CPSU leaders. Also in May, Pajetta visited the U.A.R. at the invitation of the Arab Socialist Union. A PCI delegation headed by Agostino Novella visited Algeria on 9-18 May at the invitation of the National Liberation Front. On 25 May Luigi Longo met in Rome with Santiago Carrillo, secretary-general of the Communist Party of Spain. On 25 May a PCI delegation attended the congress of the Communist Party of Czechoslovakia. A PCI delegation, led by Emilio Sereni, visited the Federal Republic of Germany on 26-28 May at the invitation of the German Communist Party. On 26 August a group of leaders of the CPSU arrived in Rome, at the invitation of the PCI. On 3 September, a delegation led by Miyamoto Kenji, chairman of the Central Committee of the Japan Communist Party, met with leaders of the PCI in Rome. In September a PCI delegation let by Pajetta visited Poland and met with Edward Gierek, first secretary of the Polish United Workers' Party.

Publications. The PCI has a great number of publications. The principal ones are *L'Unità*, a daily newspaper, *Rinascita*, a weekly political journal, and *Critica Marxista*, a bimonthly theoretical organ. The party also controls a Rome daily, *Paese Sera*. The CGIL publishes *Rassegna Sindacale*, and the FGCI publishes *Nuova Generazione*, both fortnightly. *Giorni-Vie Nuove* (the former *Vie Nuove*, which changed its name in April 1971) is a popular illustrated weekly published by the PCI.

*   *   *

In recent years a large number of new groups have arisen to oppose the alleged reformism of the PCI. The PCI, in turn, has tended to accuse these groups of "ultra-leftism" and "abstract revolutionism," claiming that they facilitated the resurgence of fascism. In 1971 the three main "ultra-leftist" organizations were the Manifesto, Worker Power (Potere Operaio), and Continuous Struggle (Lotta Continua) groups. The Manifesto group—named after its publication, *Il Manifesto*—was formed in 1969 by former PCI leaders (see *YICA*, 1970, pp. 213-14). In April the group's organ, which had begun as a monthly and became a weekly, turned into a daily newspaper. The Worker Power and Continuous Struggle groups concentrated the greater part of their activities in southern Italy. The Worker Power group discussed this new southern strategy at a convention which it held in Rome on 25-26 September. The Continuous Struggle group was one of the strongest extreme-left formations in 1971. It claimed to have about 30,000 members and 130 local offices headed by a national committee of 50 members and an executive committee of 16; the leader of this group was Adriano Sofri. Continuous Struggle tended to extend its influence to many categories:

it created the "Proletarians in Uniform" (Proletari in Uniforme) organization for the military, the "Damned of the Earth" (I Dannati della terra) for convicts, and Red Assistance Society for intellectuals. In the spring the group started to publish the daily *Lotta Continua*.

In 1971 the splinter tendency of the extremist groups was somewhat reversed. They began to show a marked inclination toward "convergence," and to theorize about the need for a "political-organizational funnel" which in a short time would channel the dispersed forces into a "more united and homogeneous" formation. A group which remained outside this unification plan was Worker Vanguard (Avanguardia Operaia). This group took the path of the traditional pro-Chinese, Marxist-Leninist formations. Its principal exponents in 1971 were Massimo Gorla, Silverio Corvisiers, and Luigi Vinci.

The only Italian pro-Chinese party recognized as such by China is the Communist Party of Italy-Marxist-Leninist (Partito Comunista d'Italia-Marxista-Leninista; PCI-ML), which originated from the Italian Marxist-Leninist Movement in 1966. The PCI-ML is led by Fosco Dinucci, its secretary-general. Two other prominent leaders in 1971 appeared to be Livio Risaliti and Manlio Dinucci. The PCI-ML has headquarters in Rome, where it publishes the weekly *Nuova Unità*. The party operates the Italo-Chinese Friendship Association, headquartered in Milan, and the Italo-Albanian Friendship Association, in Rome; both have branches and hold meetings in many parts of the country.

On domestic issues PCI-ML policy was characterized by continuous polemics both with the PCI and with all other extreme-left groups. On international matters the party adhered to strict Maoist interpretation of issues.

At the end of 1968 the PCI-ML was confronted with a split which resulted in the creation of a second party of the same name. The second PCI-ML, which claimed to be the original one, was led by Dino Dini and Vincenzo Misefari. It is known as the "red line" group to distinguish it from the Dinucci-led PCI-ML, known as the "black line." It did not appear to have any significant support in 1971.

Two other pro-Chinese groups of some influence during 1971 were the Organization of Marxist-Leninist Communists of Italy (Organizzazione dei Comunisti Marxisti-Leninisti d'Italia), led by Osvaldo Pesce, a former leader of the PCI-ML, and the Union of Italian Communists (Marxist-Leninist)—Unione dei Comunisti Italiani (Marxista-Leninista). The latter was founded in October 1968 by former PCI student and intellectual groups in Milan and Rome. Its principal publications are the fortnightly *Servire il Popolo* and the irregular *Guardie Rosse*. The party was led by Aldo Brandirali. All through the year it was engaged in criticism of and polemics with the PCI and with all the extreme-left bodies, including the Manifesto group.

The controversial position taken by China, especially its unexpected support to the governments of Pakistan, Ceylon and Sudan, encouraged a revival of Trotskyist organizations, that had maintained a critical attitude toward Mao. The main Trotskyist group in 1971 was the Revolutionary Communist Groups (Gruppi Comunisti Rivoluzionari; GCR), affiliated with the United Secretariat of the Fourth Internationa and led by Livio Maitan. The GCR published the monthly *Bandiera Rossa*. In a related development the PCI also initiated a tentative re-evaluation of Trotskyism, especially by the PCI's official historian, Spriano. This, in turn, provoked a strong reaction from the pro-Chinese groups, who claimed that Trotskyism was the "bourgeoisie's favorite weapon for threatening the unity of revolutionary forces" (*Servire il popolo*, 20 February 1971).

Milano, Italy   Carla Liverani

Luxembourg

The Communist Party of Luxembourg (Parti Communiste de Luxembourg; PCL) was established in January 1921. It is the only communist movement in Luxembourg and enjoys legal status. Membership figures are not published by the PCL, but Western sources place its strength at 500 to 1,000 persons. The population of Luxembourg is 400,000 (estimated 1970). Pro-Chinese sympathizers are organized in the small Luxembourg-China Society. On several occasions during the year the PCL expressed concern with the disruptive activities of "Trotskyite and Maoist" student organizations (e.g., *Zeitung vum Letzeburger Vollek* [ZVLV], 19 October). The PCL is adamantly pro-Soviet.

Major party strength is concentrated in the urban and mining areas of the industrial south. The notable example of PCL influence is in Esch-sur-Alzette, Luxembourg's second-largest city, where PCL Politburo and Central Committee member Arthur Useldinger is the mayor. He heads a coalition government of the PCL and left-wing members of the Luxembourg Socialist Workers' Party (Parti Ouvrier Socialiste Luxembourgeois; LSAP). The LSAP split in December 1970 as a result of a left and right schism.

The PCL is represented by 6 deputies in the 56-member Luxembourg parliament. Since the latest national elections, in 1968, the PCL considers itself to have become a "notable factor in national life" (*WMR*, March 1971). The PCL seeks an active role in the parliament although it is represented on few committees. It justifies this role by quoting Lenin's conclusion that " 'participation in parliamentary elections and in the struggle on the parliamentary rostrum is *obligatory* on the party of the revolutionary proletariat.' " The PCL views this activity as supplementing the efforts of the party press to achieve socialism since copies of parliamentary debates are mailed to all voters in Luxembourg. From this "rostrum" its representatives "exploit in the interest of the working class the contradictions among the ruling parties." (*Ibid*.).

Leadership and Organization. The PCL continued in 1971 to present a strong image of stability and remained without splits on purges. The party leadership experienced no changes and remained in the hands of the Urbany family. Dominique Urbany, the titular family head, is the party chairman and head of the 3-member Secretariat. The other two members are his son, René Urbany, who is also editor of the party organ, *Zeitung vum Letzeburger Vollek*, and Arthur Useldinger (no relation to the family). There are more than 10 members of the Urbany family in the party organization. Claire Urbany, the wife of Dominique, is president of the "Alliance of Luxembourg Women." The party's agitprop apparatus is directed by René Urbany and his wife, Jacqueline. A member of the third generation, Serge Urbany, directs activities on the high school level.

The 10-member Politburo is elected by the 35-member Central Committee. No changes were announced in either body during 1971. Leading figures in the party include Joseph Freismuth, Joseph Grandgenet, J. Hoffmann, Fernand Huebsch, D. Meis, and Elio Ramberti. PCL members are active in the Awakening of the Resistance (an association of former anti-fascist militants), the National Movement for Peace, the Progressive Youth Association (also known as Luxembourg Democratic Youth) and in the U.S.S.R.-Luxembourg Association.

Domestic Attitudes and Activities. In plenary session in September the PCL Central Committee declared its "prime task" to be "unity of action among the workers." Party chairman Urbany reported on current domestic and international problems and on the tasks ahead. The resolution adopted at that meeting stressed the necessity for "realizing as soon as possible the desired cooperation between communists and socialists already achieved in the trade union and communal areas, [and] also on the Provincial political level" (*ZVLV*, 22 September). Following the split of the LSAP in December 1970 the PCL referred throughout 1971 to the necessity for left-wing LSAP members to cooperate with the communist party and "act jointly against the onslaught on living standards" (*ibid.*, 19 October, and *IB*, no. 5-6).

General criticism of the "capitalist system" was bolstered by attacks against alleged exploitation of railroad and transport workers, craftsmen, and government officials (*ZVLV*, 19 October). The Central Committee resolution of September urged support for the "demands" of the workers, "if necessary with trade union actions." The PCL opposed layoffs, wage freezes, and price and tax increases, and advocated "radical social reforms" (*ibid.*, 22 September), calling for "still greater determination in upholding the interests of the population" in view of the attempt by the United States to solve its "financial crisis" at the "expense" of its own citizens and those of other countries (*IB*, no. 20).

The PCL was equally concerned with the "preservation of peace," the protection of "true democracy," and the establishing of "the necessary conditions for implementing socialist trans-formations" in Luxembourg. Therefore it took stronger positions during the year in the enterprises, trade unions, and other organizations of the "working people". For this reason also the PCL conducted a "consistent struggle against the right-wing and 'left' deviations, against revisionist, nationalist, and other trends", in an effort to contribute toward consolidation of leftist unity on a domestic and international level. (*Pravda*, 2 January 1971.) The PCL was especially concerned over "increasing numbers" of young people "who carry red flags" and call themselves "communists", but have only "contempt" for the communist party. In the view of the PCL this represented the attempt, in the words of Friedrich Engels, "to present impatience as a theoretically convincing basis." The PCL condemned "bourgeois publishing houses" that had placed the works of Proudhon, Bakunin, Sorel, Kropotkin, and Trotsky on the market, but expressed the belief that eventually the "honestly intentioned young 'revolutionaries' " would join the party, ". . . which is alone capable of transforming its ideals into action." (*ZVLV*, 26 May.)

International Views and Positions. The principles of "proletarian internationalism, international solidarity of the working class" and Marxism-Leninism remain "the basis" for the activity of the PCL (TASS, 3 January 1971). The party especially favored the development of "scientific Marxism" in an age in which rapid technological development permits the rapid communication of ideas throughout the world via radio and television, and thereby effects the unity of the communist movement (*WMR*, May). In this respect the PCL condemned those who claimed that the communist party was "no longer a monolithic block" (*ZVLV*, 19 October), and criticized especially the Social Democratic Party in West Germany for asserting "that imperialism and socialism are developing more and more into a 'industrial society' " (*ibid.*, 22 July).

Consistent with its unswerving loyalty to the Soviet Union the PCL emphasized that only "complete solidarity and fraternal unity" with the Communist Party of the Soviet Union (CPSU) would preserve the unity of the communist movement and the PCL's own position as the "vanguard of the working class" in Luxembourg (TASS, 3 January). The PCL condemned "anti-Sovietism" as "anti-communism" (*ZVLV*, 19 October), and supported "bilateral meetings and regional and world conferences" in order to "collectively work out strategy and coordinate action in the fight against imperialism." Such cooperation would achieve two goals: (1) the resolution of "crucial" issues through "common endeavor", (2) "closer unity of different detachments of the revolutionary movement in the course of joint action and cooperation as a more solid base for bringing them into a single powerful revolutionary system." (*WMR*, May.) It was on this basis of "unity" that the "Vietnamese people" would emerge victorious, that the Arab countries would be restored "their legitimate rights," and that the "cause of the patriots of Angola and Mozambique, the democrats of Greece, Spain and Portugal [would] triumph" (*WMR*, May).

The party's position on foreign policy issues in Europe also corresponded to that of the Soviet Union. The PCL condemned the "military NATO bloc" (TASS, 3 January), "U.S. imperialism" (*ZVLV*, 19 June) and the Common Market (*ibid*., 19 October). The Central Committee hailed the peace initiatives of the Soviet Union, which were "aimed at easing tensions and promoting peace and security in Europe," and welcomed the "four-power agreement on West Berlin" as having created the prerequisite for a conference on security and cooperation in Europe (*ZVLV*, 22 September). The party condemned "West German militarism" (*ibid*., 19 June) and the expulsion of 105 Soviet "spies" from Great Britain in September (*ibid*., 19 October).

China was criticized in a Central Committee resolution of September for pursuing policies in opposition to "the Soviet Union, the socialist community and the unity of the international working class." One indication of this, the resolution concluded, was the "rapprochement between Peking and Washington," which made it "more necessary than ever to promote the cohesion of the world communist movement and solidarity with the Soviet Union." China, according to the PCL, had not only abandoned the "principles of Marxism-Leninism," but had committed itself to a "great-power, chauvinist line." (*ibid*., 22 September.)

International Activities and Party Contacts. Observances of the fiftieth anniversary of the PCL, in January 1971, were attended by Soviet journalists (TASS, 3 January), while congratulatory telegrams were received from various communist parties in Europe, including those of Czechoslovakia, East Germany, Romania, Bulgaria, France, Poland, and the Soviet Union. The Czechoslovak party praised the "consistent international stance" of the PCL (CTK, Czechoslovak news agency, 31 December 1970). The Romanian party endorsed the continuance of "friendly relations [on] the basis of the principles of Marxism-Leninism", including, "independence, equality of rights, noninterference in internal affairs, and the right of [the] party to work out its affairs independently" (*Scînteia*, Bucharest, 3 January).

The PCL was represented at the Twenty-fourth Congress of the CPSU, in March. René Urbany attended the Eighth Congress of the East German party in June. In December a delegation of former "resistance fighters and political prisoners" from Luxembourg was received in Moscow by the Soviet Committee of War Veterans. In a joint press release following the meeting the groups endorsed efforts toward easing "international tension" (TASS, 28 December).

Publications. In October the PCL celebrated the twenty-fifth anniversary of the party organ, *Zeitung vum Letzeburger Vollek*. The paper is published daily in the party's publishing house in Esch-sur-Alzette. *Wochenzeitung*, a second party periodical, appears weekly.

Stanford University   Dennis L. Bark

Netherlands

The Communist Party of the Netherlands (Communistische Partij van Nederland; CPN) was founded in 1918 as the Communist Party of Holland, but its establishment is officially dated 1919, when it joined the Comintern. Party members number approximately 10,000. The population of the Netherland is 13,193,900 (estimated June 1971). In recent years the CPN has pursued a policy of autonomy within the international communist movement, although it was originally pro-Soviet. A number of pro-Soviet and pro-Chinese splinter groups were also active during the year.

The CPN enjoys legal status but its influence has always been limited. Because of the abolition of compulsory voting the CPN was able to achieve a higher percentage of the total vote in the general election held in April (1971: 3.9; 1967: 3.6), despite a decline in the number of votes received (1971: 246,299; 1967: 248,330). This victory entitled the CPN to an extra seat in the 150-member Lower Chamber of the Dutch Parliament, where it now holds six seats. Although the CPN publicly stated that the election results were a victory, it also expressed its disappointment: "... the decline of the right wing is not accompanied by a strengthening of the workers movement" (*De Waarheid*, 14 May).

Leadership and Organization. Party activities are administered by a nine-member Executive Committee under the leadership of party Chairman Henk Hoekstra. No changes in this committee or in the 33-member Central Committee were announced in 1971. The eight additional members of the Executive Committee are Roel Walraven (organizational secretary), J. IJsberg (administrative secretary and chief of propaganda activities), Joop F. Wolff (editor of *De Waarheid*), W. Nieuwenhuise and F. Meis (in charge of CPN activity in the industrial sector), Marcus Bakker (speaker of the CPN parliamentary fraction), C. IJmkers and Jaap Wolff (treasurer and editor of *Politiek en Cultuur*). P. de Groot, former General Secretary and Chairman of the CPN (1945-1967) is an honorary member of the Central Committee. He continues to exercise considerable influence in the party.

The most important of the CPN front organizations is the Netherlands General Youth Union (Algemeen Nederlands Juegd Verbond; ANJV). Its membership is small but it is the main source of future party members. The Netherlands Women's Movement (Nederlandse Vrouwen Beweging, NVB), that celebrated its twenty-fifth anniversary on 7 September, occasionally combines its activities with those of the ANJV. The organization of former resistance fighters, United Resistance 1940-1945 (Verenigd Verzet 1940-1945), generally restricts its program to entertaining "mutual ties of friendship" and providing information on "neofascist" activities in the Netherlands and West Germany.

Party Internal Affairs. The CPN conducted an extensive election compaign that included publication of a special election paper of 1,250,000 copies. In addition the CPN spent over 100,000 guilders on "brochures, manifestos and meetings alone" prior to and just following the elections

(*De Waarheid*, 27 August). The party praised the "defeat" of the "right wing", but stressed that "shortcomings" in its own activities must be remedied in order "to deal decisive blows to the reaction." Following the election the CPN therefore urged "large-scale discussion" among its members to end "stagnation ... self-sufficiency or complacency" within the party. (*Ibid.*, 14 May.)

This latter point was an issue to which party Chairman Hoekstra paid particular attention during the year. In May the CPN initiated steps to strengthen party ideology on the basis of the works of Stalin and Mao Tse Tung, and in accordance with the lessons to be learned from "the Russian October Revolution, the Chinese revolution and ... the victory of the Vietnamese people over the American imperialists." (*Ibid.*, 14 May.) Simultanously Hoekstra stressed the need to strenghten the party's internal organization, possibly reflecting his concern with the increasing activities of leftist splinter groups in the Netherlands and "sectarianism" within the party (*ibid.*, 14 September). In this connection he emphasized successful recruitment of new members with a target of 2,000 for 1971 (*ibid.*, 14 May). In August a new drive for financial support was announced with a declared goal of 400,000 guilders (*ibid.*, 27 August).

Few party functionaries were replaced in 1971. But Hoekstra declared in November that "... in the coming period the matter of leadership" within the party would be the "principal" issue prior to the party congress scheduled for 1972. He urged that "experienced people must assume the leadership of the party.... Only if we adopt ... [this] course and do not hesitate to replace people if necessary, can we end the existing stagnation." (*De Waarheid*, 2 December.)

Domestic Attitudes and Activities. Prior to the national election the CPN called for a "concentration of the left" in order to form a "progressive government" (*De Waarheid*, 10 October 1970). In March the CPN Executive Committee declared that "the plans of the right wing" would only be successfully defeated if the CPN joined forces with the Socialist Party" (Partij van de Arbeid; PVDA), in order to obtain "a majority within parliament and elsewhere for a new government with a new program." The election platform emphasized a combination of domestic and international issues. It called for raising the standard of living and the abolition of wage freezes and rent increases. "Anti-strike legislation" was to be repealed and those Common Market regulations contrary to the interests of the farmers were to be ignored. The party also advocated a reduction of NATO expenditures, the elimination of the arms race and the termination of all "government support of the American aggression policy" in Southeast Asia. (*Ibid.*, 19 March.)

Following the election the CPN continued to endorse a policy of "unity" with the PVDA, but on a different basis. The CPN accused the leadership of the PVDA and that of the Socialist Trade Union (Nederlands Verbond van Vakvereinigingen; NVV) of collaborating with the "capitalists" (*ibid.*, 6 October).The CPN therefore urged joint action from below to encompass "... all layers of the working population: the working class, the middle class, farmers, the students and intellectuals" (*ibid.*, 23 June). It was hoped that "a strong unity of the left" would be able to successfully place PVDA leaders in a position in which they could no longer ignore the CPN program (*ibid.*, 24 September).

All layers of the "working population" did not participate in "*joint action from below*." The CPN was unsuccessful in its efforts to organize a "Congress for the Population of Groningen" to protest general economic problems. But in October the CPN successfully influenced the statute governing membership in the Industrial Union (Industriebond) of the Socialist Trade Union (NVV). The NVV's Union Committee ruled at its meeting of 11 November that only militant communists may be excluded from membership in the NVV. Chairman Hoekstra considered this a major achievement and urged that "all workers ... join the unions united in the NVV." By this means, he concluded, the working class could more effectively" ... fight for the protection of their wages and work, and ... [could] take advantage of existing contradictions and general depression." (*Ibid.*, 2 December.)

International Views and Positions. The election program of the CPN, published under the title, "For a New Government—For New Policies", addressed a multitude of issues. It endorsed neutrality for the Netherlands, collective security in Europe, a halt to the "arms race," ratification of the nuclear nonproliferation treaty and peace in the Middle East based on the UN resolution. The program rejected the creation of a European nuclear force and nuclear weapons for West Germany, censured "fascist rule" in Spain, Portugal, Greece and South Africa, condemned "generals' rule" in Indonesia and Dutch "colonial rule" in the Netherlands' Antilles and Surinam and urged diplomatic recognition for North Vietnam and the German Democratic Republic. (*Politiek en Cultuur*, February.) The CPN devoted special attention to condemnation of "multinational corporations" in January. These business ventures were viewed by the party to pose a particular threat since they assume " control of the most developed technology and energy production. Such a development will have far-reaching consequences not only for technical and scientific staff workers who will be hampered in their development and openly exploited, but also for world peace." Therefore the CPN considered "cooperation between communists in the multinational industries" to be essential. (*De Waarheid*, 16 January.)

Consistent with its program on foreign policy issues the CPN formed a "National Committee for Changing the Netherlands' Foreign Policies" in August. This initiative was inspired by the announcement of President Nixon's journey to Peking, which the CPN considered to be "the move of a defeated man." The Committee recommended that the Dutch government "dissociate itself from the fatal American policy of world domination" and reduce NATO expenditures. (*Ibid.*, 28 August.) These points and those contained in the party program were again analyzed by Chairman Hoekstra at the CPN Central Committee meeting on 27 and 28 November. "Capitalism", according to Hoekstra, "finds itself in a severe situation of crisis." The "contradictions within the capitalist world" were not only evident on the economic level, e.g. "increasing unemployment, falling prices at the Stock-Exchange, falling prices of raw materials, over-production and monetary crisis," but were also "clearly visible" within "existing blocs and all alliances." (*Ibid.*, 2 December.)

The CPN endorsed "international solidarity" in an effort to achieve greater unity in the international communist movement, but stressed the autonomy of individual communist parties. This position was underlined in May when the party organ *De Waarheid* quoted an article from the Chinese press written to commemorate the Paris Commune: "It is necessary to draw lessons from international experiences, which must not be copied mechanically ... a proletarian party should develop its own experience in a creative way in the light of the reality of its own country." (*Ibid.*, 14 May.)

In principle the CPN endorses the unity of the international communist movement. But it considers the general use of phrases such as "strenghtening international solidarity in the struggle for direct demands, developing the ideological struggle, and popularizing democratic perspectives" to be inadequate, and more likely to produce "schematic and artificial simplification of complicated situations." The CPN therefore criticised a resolution to this effect proposed by the French Communist Party at the "London Conference of Communist Parties of European Capitalist Nations" held on 11, 12, and 13 January. The party made a careful differentiation between cooperating with socialists who were sympathetic to communist views and those who supported the capitalist system without reservation. The CPN condemned the French endorsement of "broadest unity of action," though perhaps applicable to France, becuase "it leads people to believe that it is possible to replace concrete activity in each separate country by eloquent "international declarations which only too often hide lingering passiveness." (*Ibid.*, 16 January.)

International Activities and Party Contacts. During 1971 the CPN continued to pursue its course of rapprochement with the international communist movembent, begun in 1969. The CPN sent party members Henk Hoekstra and Joop Wolff to attend the "London Conference of Communist Parties of European Capitalist Nations" in January, that was devoted to the struggle of multinational enterprises. The delegation departed, however, before the conference had been completed, for the reason that "... the procedures had nothing to do with the fight against monopolies and the EEC." The CPN concluded nevertheless that it had gained an insight into the situation in which other parties found themselves. (*Ibid.*, 16 January and 28 May.)

The London meeting of January led to a bilateral contact with the Spanish Communist Party early in March at Amsterdam. The consultations were terminated with a brief communiqué in which the CPN declared its solidarity with the Spanish CP in its struggle against Franco. (*Ibid.*, 10 March.) Joop Wolff, member of the CPN Executive Committee, addressed a public meeting organized by the British Communist Party in September in London, and declared his opposition to the entrance of Great Britain into the Common Market (*ibid.*, September 29). Other bilateral contacts continued when a delegation of six from the Korean Workers Party conferred with the CPN from November 30 to December 7. The delegation was headed by Kim Dong Kyon, member of the Politburo. Although the CPN condemned the invasion of Czechoslovakia in 1968 the party has sought to steadily improve its relations with the Soviet Communist Party (CPSU). It did not send an official delegation to the .24th Party Congress of the CPSU held just prior to the national elections in April, but sent a telegram in which the CPN regretted that "the political situation in our country" did not permit attendance (*ibid.*, March 30).

Publications. The CPN daily, *De Waarheid*, published in Amsterdam, is the most important party organ (estimated circulation 16,500). Deficits incurred by CPN publications continue to be partially offset by profits from the CPN's two commercial printing firms, Dijkman and Heierman. Additional income is provided by renting conference rooms in the party-owned building in Amsterdam.

The Dijkman publishing house continued to receive a number of commercial orders in 1971. The Heierman publishing house on the contrary, experienced financial difficulties while continuing to print all party publications, including the monthly journal *Politiek en Cultuur* (estimated circulation 2,500), and the organ of the Netherlands Women's Movement *Vrouwen* (estimated circulation 9,500). Additional publications are printed by the Institute for Politics and Social Research (Instituut voor Politiek en Sociall Onderzoek; IPSO), established by the CPN in 1968. Its publications have dealt with wage policies, multinational organizations and the "class struggle against pollution".

*   *   *

The Netherlands-USSR Friendship Society (Vereniging Nederland-USSR) has become the center of dissident pro-Soviet communists in the Netherlands. The Society publishes a monthly journal entitled *NU*. Its membership is estimated at 4,000. In January the Society concluded a cultural agreement with the Union of Soviet Societies for Friendship and Cultural Relations with Foreign Countries. At the same time a cultural "annual plan" for 1971 was concluded. The Soviet delegation that had travelled to the Netherlands for this purpose was headed by Alexei Surkov, Secretary of the Union of Soviet Writers and member of the Supreme Soviet. In October the Society organized a program entitled "Soviet Contemporaries—the USSR today" in conjunction with a "Week of the Soviet Union". Films and exhibitions were organized in several towns by the Society that included performances by Soviet artists and sportsmen. (*NU*, January.)

There are also several other pro-Soviet dissident groups. The small Society for Cultural Exchanges (Vereniging voor Culturele Uitwisseling; VCU) published its first monthly in December 1971. Pro-Soviet publications of other dissident organizations include *Links-Om* (To the Left) and *Communistische Notities* (Communist Notes).

There are five pro-Chinese political groups in the Netherlands. Their influence is small and disputes with one another caused several rifts in 1971. The League of Dutch Marxist-Leninists (Bond van Nederlandse Marxisten-Leninisten; BNML), under the leadership of Chris Bischot, declined in importance in 1971. The party organ, *De Rode Vlag* (The Red Flag) appeared eight times in 1971 in stenciled form. *De Rode Vlag* publishes articles concerning the theoretical foundations of Marxism-Leninism, in addition to criticism of CPN activities. In December and January three BNML delegates paid a three week visit to China. (*De Rode Vlag*, No. 2-5.)

The aim of the Marxist-Leninist Party of the Netherlands (Marxistisch-Leninistische Partij van Nederland; MLPN) is defined as the "capture of political power" in the class struggle, to which all else is subordinate, "... including the individual interests of all who may be considered to belong to the working classes." The party is under the leadership of Chris Petersen. Its monthly organ is entitled *De Kommunist*. The MLPN also publishes a *Central Paper for Industrial workers* (*Centrale Bedrijfskrant*) and maintains contact with a Maoist youth movement, Red Youth (Rode Jeugd). (See *De Kommunist*, September.)

The Rode Jeugd under the leadership of Henk Wubben, Van der Valk and A. Meurs, maintains "action groups" in Amsterdam, Eindhoven, IJmuiden, The Hague and Kampen that participate in local demonstrations and distribute propaganda leaflets. In the party organs, *Voorwaarts* and *Rode Jeugd*, there was continuing discussion on the use of violence throughout the year. The consequence was a split within the party after the Eindhoven group made attempts on the lives of the Mayor and several police officials. The Amsterdam group, presumably the stronger of the two factions, opposed the use of violence and concentrated its activities on "propaganda and organization of the workers against high finance" (*Rode Jeugd*, August). Both the Rode Jeugd and the BNML groups sent letters of greetings to the Chinese CP on the occasion of its Fiftieth anniversary in July (see *Peking Review*, August 13).

The most active pro-Chinese group was the Marxist-Leninist Communist Unity Movement of the Netherlands (Kommunistiese Eenheidsbeweging Nederland/Marxistisch-Leninistisch; KEN/ML), led by Nico Schrevel. The party publishes a monthly paper, *De Rode Tribune*. The KEN/ML considers the CPN to be "... striving for a conciliation of the classes" and therefore seeks to achieve "a real vanguard movement of the working class" (*Rode Tribune*, No. 8). The KEN/ML also considers the Netherland labor unions to have "betrayed the workers" (*ibid.*, No. 1) and thus advocates the use of the unions as a "school for communism" in order to break their "dependence on capital" (*ibid.*, No. 9).

The KEN/ML has several front organizations. The most significant of these are the Marxist-Leninist Students Union (Marxistisch-Leninistische Studentenbond), the Marxist-Leninist Youth (Marxistisch-Leninistische Jeugd), a trade union named Workers' Power (Arbeidersmacht) and a mass organization called Union of Tenants and Those in Search of Housing (De Bond van Huurders en Woningzoekenden). In the course of 1971 controversies arose within the KEN/ML between the group of "theoreticians" (advocates of propaganda) and the group of "practicians" (advocates of action). The differences of opinion caused a split in October. The group of "theoreticians" retained the name KEN/ML and continued publishing the party organ, *De Rode Tribune*. The "practicians", led by D. Monjé, renamed themselves the Communist Party of the Netherlands/Marxist-Leninist (Kommunistiese Partij Nederland/Marxisties-Leninisties) and named its party organ *Tribune*. In its initial declaration the party Central Committee declared that while it was still "a young party" it would pursue "the course of revolution ... [in] the interests of the working class" (*Tribune*, No. 11, No. 12)

The Hague, Netherlands   H.J.M. Mennes
Stanford University   Dennis L. Bark

Norway

The Communist Party of Norway (Norges Kommunistiske Parti; NKP) was founded on 4 November 1923. It has some 2,700 members, out of a population of 3,893,000 (estimated 1970). Support for the party, which has operated legally at all times except under German occupation during World War II, comes primarily from unionized industrial workers in Oslo and from low-income groups in the economically disadvantaged northernmost province, Finnmark.

The NKP has not been represented in the parliament since 1961, when it lost its one seat to the Socialist People's Party (Socialistisk Folkeparti; SF), formed in that year. The SF lost its two seats in 1969. (See *YICA*, 1971, p. 231.) Both parties claim to offer a socialist alternative to the social-democratic—and allegedly class-collaborationist—policies of the ruling Norwegian Labor Party (Det Norske Arbeiderparti; DNA). The NKP and SF programs espouse the same political goal: a democratic transition to socialism on the basis of Marxism, parliamentarianism, and the multi-party system. Yet ideological and tactical differences continue to preclude an alliance. The NKP leadership seeks to avoid an excessively "communist" image that would invite popular alienation (as in 1968, when the party was generally associated with the Soviet-led invasion of Czechoslovakia, despite its vociferous condemnation of that event) and at the same time to maintain external positions sufficiently removed from those of the SF and DNA to ensure a separate identity.

In the September 1969 parliamentary election, the NKP polled 1.0 per cent of the popular vote (down 0.4 per cent from 1965) and the SF, 3.5 per cent (down 2.5); their combined losses went to the DNA. In the September 1971 municipal elections, the NKP polled 1.3 per cent (up 0.1 per cent from 1967), the SF, 4.8 per cent (down 0.4); and the DNA, 42.4 per cent (down 1.6).

Leadership and Organization. Reidar Larsen, the NKP chairman since 1965, was reelected in 1971 by the party's Thirteenth Congress, held in Oslo on 23-25 April. He heads the Secretariat, which includes Arne Jørgensen, Arne Pettersen, Martin Gunnar Knutsen, Rolf Nettum, Kolbjørn Harbu, Leif Johansen, Leif Hammerstad, and Georg Ovesen. There is a 32-member Central Committee and a 6-member Control Committee. Georg Ovesen heads the small and politically insignificant NKP youth affiliate, Communist Youth (Kommunistisk Ungdom; KU).

Among labor organizations the NKP controls only a small number of local bodies and none of the national unions. A "Baltic Sea Committee," under NKP direction, sends delegations to the "Workers' Conferences of Baltic Nations, Norway, and Iceland," held annually by trade unionists in Rostock, East Germany.

Party Internal Affairs. Having survived—at substantial supporter expense—intraparty challenges from pro-Soviet and, more recently, pro-Chinese factions, Reidar Larsen continued in 1971 his self-proclaimed nationalist, left-socialist course. The pro-Soviet opposition reached a peak in 1967, but three of the Muscovites remaining in the NKP leadership announced their retirement in 1971 and this faction apparently no longer poses a threat to Larsen and his followers. On the extreme left flank, current party policy is aimed at minimizing the possible political significance of the generally younger pro-Chinese faction by publicly ignoring it and discouraging intraparty debate. Only nominal, perfunctory exceptions occurred during the year, and the party newspaper made little acknowledgment of any ideological strains. In his speech to the NKP congress Larsen discounted the threat from the left, maintaining that while initially the "verbal revolutionaries" had been successful in making inroads, especially among students and in slowing recruitment of young people to the NKP, this problem (a serious one, inasmuch as the average age of NKP members is close to fifty years) had largely been overcome. Repeating the NKP's frequent contention that the pro-Chinese revolutionaries appealed to intellectuals and students to the exclusion of blue-collar workers, Larsen termed universities a "hopelessly weak base on which to establish a political party, especially a communist party." (*Friheten*, 1-7 May.) The party has admitted the loss of pro-Chinese members of the KU, but claims that the defection of "undesirables" has left a more consolidated and loyal core.

Domestic Attitudes and Activities. The NKP's united front policy made no apparent headway in 1971, and the return to power in March of a labor government had the effect of accentuating further the political isolation of the communists. Arne Jørgensen noted that the event signified no "new socialist era" in the country's history. This was not because of the DNA's lack of a clear majority in the parliament, but because DNA policies were directed at "patching" the existing system rather than advancing a social transformation. (*Friheten*, 24-30 April.) The NKP noted with satisfaction what it viewed as the move of the DNA youth affiliate, the League of Worker Youth (Arbeidernes Ungdomsfylking; AUF) toward a "socialist-oriented ideology" and a break with the "reformist, class-collaborationist" policy of the parent party. Such ideological and political transformation within the AUF, in this view, could ultimately force a reassessment of policies within both the DNA and the National Trade Union Federation. (*Ibid.*, 29 February-3 March.)

Following indications, late in 1970, that the SF might be amenable to cooperation with the NKP in the September 1971 municipal elections, it was a severe blow to the NKP when, in March, the SF announced its refusal to enter into any nationwide agreement on joint slates. Instead, individual district committees would determine whether to enter SF or cooperative lists. The NKP responded that "socialist unity" was not limited to the NKP and SF, and that it would, therefore, establish as many slates as possible under this designation. Having warned the NKP of "serious consequences," the SF announced its campaign platform: it would run as a pacifist "third alternative," depicting the DNA as an ally of "the capitalist/imperialist power bloc led by the United States" and the NKP as an ally of the rival Soviet military bloc and its "questionable socialist banner." The SF alternative, thus, would represent a protest against "repression" in both West and East. (SF congress proceedings, quoted in *Friheten*, 13-19 March.) This situation prompted Knut Løfsnes, a co-founder of the SF and its chairman for eight of the ten years of its existence, and Sigbjørn Hølmebakk, another co-founder, to resign from the party on the basis that "narrow party-political interests" had hampered efforts for a broad leftist front (*ibid.*). The two then became closely identified with NKP electoral efforts.

Despite the breakdown in NKP-SF cooperation at the central level, the NKP did eventually participate with the SF in several individual electorates. Represented in a total of 94 of Norway's 444 electorates, the NKP ran alone in 31, with the SF and independent socialists in 44, and with independent socialists in 19. (*Friheten*, 20-25 September.) The NKP platform, presenting no new positions, reiterated calls for permanent measures to counter rising prices and create economic stability, the easing of tax pressure upon ordinary wage earners and social security recipients, the removal of the added-value tax on foods, a social housing policy with lower loan interest rates; a ceiling on real estate prices, guaranteed employment, and increases in retirement pensions to two-thirds of the average industrial wage (*ibid.*, 1-7 May).

In an interview with the Danish communist daily, *Land og Folk*, on 10 November, Reidar Larsen expressed satisfaction with his party's (0.1 per cent) gain as "the very limit of what we had regarded as possible in this election." An "important victory" had been achieved in the setting up of joint lists of candidates, although the straight NKP and socialist unity slates had produced better results than those with the SF. The NKP Central Committee, he indicated, unanimously favored "a full effort to advance leftist cooperation," the conditions for which were "better than ever before, although within the SF there is a strong faction that resists cooperation." The NKP, finally, would attempt to establish a "central cooperation committee" with the SF with a view to an alliance in the 1973 parliamentary election.

International Views and Positions. Opposition to Norwegian negotiations for membership in the European Economic Community was strongly expressed by the NKP in 1971. The party claimed that membership in the EEC would involve a constantly increasing and irrevocable renunciation of the national right to self-determination, and that any special concessions that Norway might gain would prove to be only temporary and of limited importance (*Friheten*, 1-7 May).

The EEC question, in the NKP view, was the most crucial issue in recent Norwegian history. A Central Committee declaration of 10 January stressed the need to break up "established party fronts" and win over the hundreds of thousands who, allegedly, opposed affiliation with the EEC but continued to vote for the parties favoring it (*ibid.*, 11-16 January). Likening the situation to that in which Norwegian patriots gave their lives under the German occupation of World War II, an NKP editorial recalled that the underground resistance had not been content with a passive role, but had actively opposed Hitler's attempt to force Norway into a general European alliance (*ibid.*, 24-30 April). There could be only two schools of thought with regard to the EEC, NATO, or bloc policy "in all its manifestations" (an aside presumably meant to include the East bloc): any professed third alternative was seen as an impossibility and merely a "camouflage for actual positions" (*ibid.*, 13-16 April).

The NKP was represented by Arne Pettersen at the conference of communist parties of European capitalist countries which met in London on 11-13 January. Pettersen stressed the need to raise the struggle against "international, predominantly American-rooted, monopolies" from the ideological to the political-economic level, and from propaganda to agitation and action—both within and beyond the trade unions. Social democratic forces in Europe, he said, were "well aware of the dangers inherent in the spread of international monopoly concerns," but the posture they had adopted toward this internationalization of production was creating confusion in the working class and weakening its positions. (*Ibid.*, 18-23 January.) Calling upon the DNA to "admit its opposition to EEC affiliation"—the DNA was, in fact, divided over the issue—the NKP charged it with trying to keep the EEC question out of the upcoming municipal election so as to "neutralize the threat of opposition from the left" (*ibid.*, 15-20 February).

The NKP has remained active in the 70,000-strong "Popular Movement Against the EEC." It has been unable to gain control of the organization, but one of the ten leadership positions is held by NKP Secretariat member Leif Johansen. There has emerged a smaller and frequently competitive movement, the "Workers Committee Against the EEC," which agitates against the EEC and against alleged tax and wage injustices. It is supported by the pro-Chinese dissidents. Larsen's address to the NKP congress suggested that the "ultra-radicals" detracted from the effectiveness of mass movements by their refusal to subordinate ideology to a common denominator of political goals. A vital precondition to a united front on opposition to the EEC—and on other issues, such as the Vietnam war, where a similar situation has arisen within the Norwegian antiwar movement—was "strict respect for the minimum and maximum base on which mass movements were founded." (*Ibid.*, 1-7 May.)

The NKP and the International Communist Movement. The Thirteenth Congress of the NKP reaffirmed the party's neutral stand in the Sino-Soviet conflict and demonstrated its continuing efforts to disassociate itself from those features of the socialist regimes that were unpopular with the Norwegian electorate. Reidar Larsen referred to the December 1970 riots in Poland as an instance of negative developments in the socialist world. The Polish crisis, he said, showed that there had been "a dangerous gap between the government and the working people"; moreover, the ruling communist party was chiefly responsible for the bureaucratic degeneration and lack of democracy in Poland. Such conditions, however, did not derive from the socialist system, but from a violation of socialist principles. (*Friheten*, 1-7 May.)

Larsen refrained from direct criticism of the Soviet Union, making only an allusion to the Soviet-led 1968 invasion of Czechoslovakia, of which the NKP had vigorously disapproved. The NKP, he said, would continue to react against and criticize shortcomings in socialist rule, although this practice would not alter its friendship and solidarity with any country building socialism. Implicitly serving notice on both Chinese and Soviet parties of the NKP's rejection of factionalist intervention within the international communist movement, Larsen warned that his party would not give its support to those who failed to demonstrate a desire to establish a common anti-imperialist front or who engaged in activities tending to split communist parties in other countries. (*Ibid.*)

Publications. The central organ of the NKP is *Friheten* (Freedom), issued weekly in Oslo. The KU publishes a bulletin, *Fremad* (Forward).

*   *   *

Splinter Groups. The pro-Chinese challenge derives from (a) NKP and KU secessionists; (b) the similarly radical Socialist Youth League (Marxist-Leninist)—Socialistisk Ungdomsforbund (Marxist-Leninist), or SUF(ml), which seceded from the SF in 1969; (c) the Marxist-Leninist Groups (MLG); and (d) formerly unaffiliated radicals. The NKP secessionists, originally numbering 29, formed in June 1970 the "Marxist-Leninist Front in the NKP" (MLF) following their suspension from the NKP for supporting SUF(ml) activities. During the 1971 NKP congress, 32 dissidents walked out and announced their intention of joining the MLF. The SUF(ml), MLG, and MLF are headed, respectively, by Pål Steigan, Sigurd Allern, and Kjell Hovden.

These Maoists are recognized collectively by Communist China as representing Norwegian Marxist-Leninists. Though their combined numbers are small—membership may be fewer than 500—the groups constitute an active and concerted force which has succeeded in attracting the extreme-left elements of the NKP, KU, and SF. In 1971 the Maoists incited a number of small wildcat strikes among workers and sit-down strikes among university and high school students. They also scored some successes in stimulating popular resistance to military conscription and to regulations and discipline in the Armed Forces. (The NKP has largely withdrawn from the movement against military conscription, owing to its domination by Maoist "sectarianism.")

The poor showing of Sweden's counterpart Communist League (Marxist-Leninist) in its first election effort, in September 1970 (0.4 per cent of the vote), is thought to have slowed down plans for a formal pro-Chinese party in Norway. The Norwegian Marxist-Leninists, Steigan stated in an interview (*Klassekampen*, no. 5, 1971), were prepared for a "patient and lengthy struggle."

Publications. The SUF(ml) issues two monthly bulletins, *Klassekampen* (Class Struggle) and *Røde Garde* (Red Guard). The MLF publication is *Røde Fane* (Red Banner).

Valerie Bloom

Portugal

The Portuguese Communist Party (Partido Comunista Português; PCP) was founded in March 1921 and has been illegal since 1926. Under vigorous repression by the Portuguese government, the party clandestinely maintains a tight organization and continues to operate both at home and abroad, mainly in Romania.

Within Portugal, PCP members worked until 1970 through the underground Patriotic Front of National Liberation (Frente Patriotica de Libertação Nacional; FPLN), established in December 1962. The front, which has its coordinating center in Algiers, also attempts to rally socialists, liberals, republicans, Catholics, and liberal monarchists. In 1970 the PCP was excluded from the FPLN, which announced that the front would pursue a policy of armed struggle.

The PCP's members comprise mainly urban workers concentrated in Lisbon and Oporto, and to a lesser degree middle-class elements including intellectuals. Farm laborers are barely represented, although a few have been enlisted, primarily in the upper Alentejo area. Considerable support reportedly comes from among university students. Western sources estimate PCP membership at 2,000. The population of Portugal was 8,668,000 (official census, 1970).

In addition to the PCP, which has a decidedly pro-Soviet orientation, there appear to exist two small pro-Chinese groups: the Popular Action Front (Frente de Ação Popular) and the United League of Revolutionary Action (Liga Unida de Ação Revolucionaria).

In Portugal, a country that has been led by an authoritarian government since 1926, communism has played only an insignificant role.

Leadership and Organization. The PCP maintains a closely knit apparatus and keeps its leadership within Portugal anonymous. Among the known leaders in exile are the secretary-general, Alvaro Cunhal, Secretariat members Sergio Vilarigues and José Vitoriano, and Central Committee members Francisco Miguel, Manuel Rodrigues de Silva, and Jorge Vieira. According to Cunhal, two-thirds of the Central Committee members are workers (*WMR*, June).

The party claims to be influential in various labor unions through the illegal "Unity Committees." It also claims to be engaged in "anti-fascist" political activity through the various branches of the Democratic Electoral Commission, a united front formed in 1969 to participate in elections to the National Assembly (see *YICA*, 1970, p. 244).

Domestic Attitudes and Activities. The PCP seeks to overthrow the present Portuguese government, which it describes as a "fascist dictatorship," and to "reestablish democratic freedoms" ("Radio Free Portugal," 3 February). In an article written on occasion of the party's fiftieth anniversary, Cunhal reiterated that the PCP emphasized "legal and semi-legal forms of organization and activity," such as participation in elections and government controlled unions and students' associations. Cunhal mentioned that "pseudo-revolutionaries" did not agree with these tactics and advocated instead "higher" forms of tactics, but he argued that, "there is still no revolutionary situation in the country and armed struggle is not the focus of the movement. Our main activity today is mass action for specific immediate objectives" (*WMR*, June).

A policy statement made in December 1970 by the president of Portugal proposed some democratization measures and, particularly, a constitutional change calling for greater administrative and political autonomy for the overseas provinces. This statement elicited extensive PCP analysis. In a broadcast early in 1971 ("Radio Free Portugal," 5 and 8 January) on the subject of "Unity in Action for the Attainment of Freedom and for the Immediate End of the Colonial War," the PCP Central Committee urged the rejection of "any illusions that [the president] proposes to carry out a real process of liberalization, democratization, and decolonization." The broadcast was especially critical of military actions carried out by the government in Angola, Guinea (Bissau), and Mozambique, saying in part:

> The colonial war is a crime against the African peoples. The massacres cause just indignation throughout the world. The policy of plunder, exploitation, and colonial wars is contrary to the interests of the Portuguese people and nation.... The entire national life suffers [from] the war spending.

The "complete independence" of Angola, Guinea, and Mozambique was described as a "national and patriotic task," on the grounds that the people of Portugal could "never be free and independent" so long as the peoples of the colonies were not. In this regard, the broadcast cited the government's action against the Republic of Guinea (condemned as aggression by the United Nations) as evidence of an "adventurist policy."

During the year, the PCP continued to attack the FPLN and accused it of representing "pseudo-revolutionary talkers." The FPLN was said to be calling for "spontaneous terrorist actions which can only disorient the masses and estrange them from the democratic movement and its present tasks" (*ibid.*, 24 May). Scorn for the front was also expressed: "In the past year they have not carried a single concrete action or obtained any valid support among the political forces of the opposition" (*ibid.*, 17 August).

Although the PCP condemned the FPLN for advocating violent means, it offered verbal support for a group called the Armed Revolutionary Action (ARA), which emerged in 1970 and has since carried out various terrorist actions. Thus, a Central Committee statement on 3 February hailed the Armed Revolutionary Action as "a new and positive element" (*ibid.*). The party described it as a "real revolutionary organization, which modestly contributes with its actions to the general struggle of the Portuguese people," and claimed that the ARA recognized the PCP as the "most firm, consequential, and outstanding revolutionary force in the present spectrum of the Portuguese political forces" (*ibid.*, 27 March).

The ARA, whose political composition is not very clear, is believed to include communist militants (*New York Times*, 18 April). It executed significant actions on 8 March, when it destroyed 14 helicopters and three training aircraft at the Trancos Airbase to protest the "shameful colonial war ... against the peoples of Angola, Guinea, and Mozambique who are fighting for their independence," and later when it cut radio, telegraph, and telephone communications for several hours in Lisbon to protest a NATO meeting held there on 3 June. Subsequent to these actions, the PCC issued a statement on October 1971, which included support for the ARA, stressing that its activities had "nothing in common with acts of terror" because they had produced no loss of life. Indicating that this PCP endorsement of the ARA had been carefully examined, the same statement noted that the PCP had "always opposed acts of terror carried out by irresponsible adventurists." (*IB*, nos 1-2, 1972.)

The FPLN did not show much activity during 1971. Its alleged leader, Fernando Piteira Santos, is a former PCP member who was expelled from the party in the 1950's. Broadcasting from its radio station ("Voice of Freedom," 4 July), the FPLN declared that it was composed of dissident communist leaders, Marxist militants without party affiliation, and Christian revolutionaries who wanted to form a "new revolutionary alliance" and not a "classical front." The FPLN apparently suffered from some instability, because it also stated that "not all difficulties [had] been overcome" in the reorganization of the front (*ibid.*, 18 July).

International Views and Positions. The PCP's strongly pro-Soviet orientation was reaffirmed in 1971 by Cunhal (*WMR*, June) in an assertion that the Portuguese communists had an "indestructible friendship with the Soviet Union." The PCP secretary-general also reiterated his party's willingness to combat "all manifestations of anti-Sovietism."

Cunhal attended the Fourteenth Congress of the Communist Party of Czechoslovakia and stated at that time: "Internationalism means struggle against nationalism and anti-Sovietism." The "new models" of socialism, he said, were accompanied by "systematic criticism of relations with the Soviet Union and other socialist countries" and would lead eventually "to the undermining of the confidence of the working people in the socialist revolution." (Prague radio broadcast, 26 May.)

The PCP commented on the fiftieth anniversary of the Chinese Communist Party, "regretting with grief and concern the grave harm to the cause of communism and socialism ... brought about by the anti-Soviet, nationalist and leftwing revisionist line" adopted by the Chinese leadership ("Radio Free Portugal," 2 July). Other PCP views on international issues included "friendship and solidarity with the peoples of Vietnam, Laos, Cambodia, Arab peoples, and all who are fighting against imperialism" (*WMR*, June).

The international position of the FPLN regarding the Sino-Soviet dispute was neutral during 1970. No statements appear to have been made on this issue in 1971. Regarding the independence struggle in the Portuguese territories in Africa, the FPLN expressed, at least verbally, a greater willingness than the PCP for cooperation with guerrilla forces in those areas. It held that the fight against the "Portuguese capitalist state" made imperative an alliance with the liberation movement in Angola, Guinea (Bissau), and Mozambique, and that the "materialization of this alliance [could] only mean opening a fourth front in Portugal" ("Voice of Freedom," 4 July).

International Party Contacts. As noted above, Cunhal represented the PCP at the Fourteenth Congress of the Communist Party of Czechoslovakia. In addition, he met with leaders of the Hungarian Socialist Workers' Party, including Central Committee members György Aczél and Andras Gyenes, on 22 August.

Publications. The PCP official organ is the clandestine monthly *Avante*, founded in 1931. The party claims that it is published inside the country. In addition, the PCP broadcasts to Portugal over "Radio Free Portugal," which is believed to be based in Romania. The FPLN's "Voice of Freedom" radio station is in Algeria.

*   *   *

The two pro-Chinese groups in Portugal are small and apparently isolated internationally. The Popular Action Front (FAP) was founded in 1964 by former PCP Executive Committee member Francisco Rodrigues Campos, who has been imprisoned since 1967. As in previous years, no FAP activities came to notice during 1971.

The other pro-Chinese group, the United League of Revolutionary Action (LUAR), was founded by a group of Portuguese officials and military men in 1966. Its leader, Hermino da Palma Inácio, was last reported to be in England. No LUAR activities came to notice during 1971.

Nelly Stromquist

San Marino

The Communist Party of San Marino (Partito Comunista di San Marino; PCS) was founded originally in 1922, then eclipsed by fascism, and refounded in 1940. Although nominally independent (and represented as such at Italian party meetings and international communist party conferences), it is in reality an offshoot of the Italian Communist Party (Partito Comunista Italiano; PCI). The party has an estimated 1,000 members. The population of San Marino is a little over 19,000 (estimated 1971).

Elections were held on 7 September 1969 for San Marino's 60-member legislative body, the Grand Council. Under San Marino law, eligibility to vote extends to anyone born in that country, although by a law passed in 1966 absentee ballots are limited to residents of Europe. Of the 16,720 registered voters in September 1969, 7,419 lived abroad. The PCS lost a few votes in comparison with the 1964 elections, but continued to hold 14 seats, regaining the seat lost earlier to a PCS dissident who set up his own pro-Chinese Marxist-Leninist Movement (Movimento Marxista-Leninista). The PCS received 22.76 per cent of the vote; the pro-Chinese group, with 1.24 per cent, lost its one seat.

The PCS is the second strongest party in the republic. With the Socialist Party (7 seats, 11.90 per cent of the vote), it stands in opposition to the coalition government of Christian Democrats (27 seats, 44.03 per cent) and Social Democrats (11 seats, 17.94 per cent). The other remaining seat is held by the Movement of Statutory Liberty (2.10 per cent).

Organization and Leadership. The Seventh Congress of the PCS, in April 1968, elected the current Central Committee and 10-member Directorate. Ermenegildo Gasperoni has been secretary-general since 1940.

Party Policy. PCS domestic and foreign policies closely follow those of the PCI, but local issues naturally play a considerable part. The PCS campaigns against the "fascist chains" that (by a 1939 agreement) bind the republic to the Italian state and make it a "mere folklore tourist attraction."

At the Eighth Congress of the Socialist Unity Party of (East) Germany, 15-19 June, Giuseppe Renzi of the PCS Central Committee stated: "The PCS, together with all left-wing forces carries on its struggle for democratic progress and for economic and social rejuvenation of our republic with a prospective toward socialism" (*Neues Deutschland*, Berlin, 21 June). He added: "Recently there have been two big strikes in San Marino in which a considerable portion of the working class participated and which managed to get a commitment from the bourgeoisie, which holds the economic power in its hands, for higher wages and the maintenance of norms which will ensure better living and working conditions."

On international issues, Renzi claimed that "the San Marino government under the pressure of the PCS recognized the People's Republic of China as the only Chinese nation." He promised that the PCS would "use every possible opportunity to advocate the recognition of the German Democratic Republic by the government of San Marino." (*Ibid.*).

Umberto Barulli, deputy secretary-general, represented the PCS at the Twenty-fourth Congress of the Communist Party of the Soviet Union.

Publication. The PCS publishes an irregular newspaper, *La Scintilla*.

Milano, Italy   Carla Liverani

Spain

The Communist Party of Spain (Partido Comunista de España; PCE) was founded on 15 April 1920. It has been illegal since 1939. Despite vigorous government enforcement of the ban and periodic arrest and imprisonment of militants, the PCE maintains an active apparatus and is considered one of the strongest opposition forces.

From a claimed peak membership of 300,000 in 1937 the PCE has diminished to its current level, estimated by non-party observers at between 5,000 and 20,000. In 1969, according to its secretary-general, Santiago Carrillo, the PCE had 22,000 members abroad and "two or three times" that number within Spain. The population of Spain is 32,411,000 (estimated 1970). The bulk of the PCE membership is drawn from among urban intellectuals and workers in Madrid, Barcelona, and Bilbao, and farm and industrial workers in and around Seville, Cádiz, Córdoba, and Málaga. The party also derives support from exiles living in France, mainly in Paris and Toulouse.

Dissidence within the PCE since 1969 over international issues, particularly the role of the Soviet Union in the communist movement, culminated in 1971 in the formation of another party using the same name (here identified as the "rival PCE"). There is also a small splinter group, the Communist Party of Spain, Marxist-Leninist (Partido Comunista de España Marxista-Leninista, PCE-ML), which appears to be divided into two main factions, both of which are pro-Chinese.

Organization and Leadership. The PCE is organized in all of Spain's 50 administrative provinces. At the national level are its Executive Committee and Central Committee, below which are provincial and intermediate-level committees and, finally, the party cells. The Central Committee has 111 members, 90 of whom are said to be in Spain (*Le Monde*, Paris, 4 November 1970).

Little is known about the PCE leadership within Spain. The exile PCE leadership is dispersed mainly in France and the Soviet Union, but also in Czechoslovakia, Romania, and Belgium. The PCE chairman is seventy-six-year-old Dolores Ibárruri ("La Pasionaria" of civil war days), who lives in Moscow. She held the position of secretary-general from 1942 to January 1960, when because of age she accepted the honorary position of party chairman. The secretary-general and actual leader of the party is Santiago Carrillo, who now lives in Switzerland. Besides Ibárruri and Carrillo, the Executive Committee includes Gregorio López Raimundo, Horacio Fernández Inguanzo (in prison since 1969), Ramón Mendezona, Juan Gómez, José Moix, Ignacio Gallego, Santiago Alvarez, Francisco Gutiérrez, Esther Blanco, Juan Calanda, Manuel Delicado, José María González Jérez, V. Martín García, Ricardo Orueta, and Ruy Xordo.

The PCE advocates strong support of rights of self-determination for Spain's three main nationalities, and therefore maintains branches (said to enjoy autonomy in adapting PCE policy to local conditions) in Catalonia, Galicia, and the Basque regions (Euzkadi). Gregorio López is secretary-general of the Unified Socialist Party of Catalonia (Partido Socialista Unificado de Cataluña); Santiago Alvarez has the same post for the Communist Party of Galicia. Since July 1969 the

PCE has cooperated with a faction of the Basque independence movement—Basque Nation and Liberty (Euzkadi ta Askatasuna; ETA)[1]—and the Movement of Basque Priests in a common anti-government front.

The party's youth organization, the Communist Youth League (Liga Juvenil Comunista; LJC) formed in October 1961, is active in the anti-government Democratic Students' Union (Sindicato Democrático Estudiantil; SDE) and in the illegal labor unions called Workers' Commissions (Comisiones Obreras, or "CC OO"). The SDE operates at the university level; it maintains centers in Madrid, Barcelona, Valencia, Seville, Saragossa, and Santiago de Compostela. The communist youth movement as a whole is not considered very strong.

Within the labor movement, the communists occupy influential positions in the Workers' Commissions. Once a faction within the legal, state-controlled trade union movement, the CC OO have become an independent and powerful center of anti-Franco forces that includes "progressive" Catholics (from the Acción Sindicalista de Trabajadores) and socialists (from the Unión Sindical Obrera) as well as communists.[2]

Domestic Attitudes and Activities. The domestic policy of the PCE has been based (since 1965 according to party claims) on specifically Spanish considerations. The party seeks to overthrow the Franco government and establish an "antifeudal and antimonopolistic" democracy which would lead to socialism. To this end, the PCE maintains that an "alliance of labor and culture" is necessary and that a plan of action called the "Pact for Freedom" must be agreed upon by all anti-government forces. A Central being based on a four-point program: a broad provisional coalition government, total amnesty for political prisoners and exiles, political freedoms without discrimination, and free elections to a constituent assembly which would determine Spain's future political system (*IB*, nos. 18-19).

As in previous years, no positive response was forthcoming to the communist proposal for a united front, although communist sources reported that the relations between the PCE and the Socialist Party had improved "despite the still remaining differences."

Since December 1970, when the government yielded to demonstrations and international appeals, and commuted the death sentences of six Basque militants to thirty-year prison terms, the PCE has taken the position that Franco's dominance of the government is "potentially finished" but that the "threat of neo-Francoism" remains. Thus, the PCE continued its opposition to the designated successor to Franco, Prince Juan Carlos, declaring: "The monarchy will be a continuation of the Franco dictatorship with all its vices, only accentuated by the degradation of the present-day system of power," (*Ibid.*)

One of the most important events for the PCE during 1971 was doubtlessly a mass meeting which took place in Paris on 20 June, under the auspices of the French Communist Party. This "meeting of solidarity" (with the policies of Carrillo and Ibárruri) was said to have attracted between 30,000 to 50,000 people and had Ibárruri and Carrillo as the main speakers.

The fact that this meeting took place shortly after pro-Soviet dissidents created a new PCE (see below), seemed to indicate that it was staged mainly as a show of strength. Both Carrillo and Ibárruri spoke at length of the party's struggle in Spain and repeated their appeal for a "Pact

[1]ETA is divided into three known groups. The most militant faction advocates armed struggle and is believed to contain Maoists. The second faction, allied to the PCE, is considered small and uninfluential. The largest group, composed mostly of older Basques, is moderate.

[2]The *Wall Street Journal* (New York, 21 January 1969) estimated that the CC OO provide leadership for 500,000 to a million of Spain's ten million workers. The Soviet publication *International Affairs* (April 1971) maintains that there are CC OO at 2,700 big and medium enterprises, which employ a total of about five million workers.

for Freedom,'' but avoided any reference to the dissidents' actions. Subsequently, apparently due to a protest by the Spanish government, French authorities expelled Carrillo from France; he has been living in Switzerland since then.

The Rival PCE. PCE dissidents, led by expelled PCE Executive Committee member Enrique Líster and Central Committee members Eduardo García, and Agustín Gómez (see *YICA*, 1971, pp. 246-47), held what they called the "Eighth Congress" of the PCE in mid-May 1971 in Paris. At that time the group elected a Central Committee of 21 members and passed resolutions which declared void all decisions made by "Carrillo's group" regarding the 1968 invasion of Czechoslovakia, acknowledged the Soviet Union as the "main criterion of proletarian internationalism," and supported the establishment of economic, consular, and cultural relations between Spain and all socialist countries. This rival PCE is believed to have the following of only a very small number of communists within Spain, but it is said to have a following of some 2,000 to 3,000 Spanish exiles, mostly those living in Eastern Europe (*NYT*, 27 December). In addition, it reportedly counts on covert Soviet financial and moral support.

A confrontation between both PCE factions was created at a meeting of the Soviet-organized front, the World Peace Council (WPC), held in Budapest on 13-16 May, when two rival PCE delegations showed up. The Carrillo group demanded that Líster—who was representing Spain at the meeting—be expelled from the WPC Presidential Committee and that his delegation at the meeting be replaced by an "authentic PCE representation." After much discussion, the Carrillo group walked out of the conference, but the WPC posts for Spain were left vacant, thus indicating some amount of confusion among communist parties in general regarding the developments within the PCE.

The Workers Commissions. The illegal labor unions known as the CC OO, which include not only communists but also socialists and "progressive" Catholics, continued in 1971 to receive special attention from the PCE. Under the harsh repression of the authorities, the CC OO offer the communists the most effective means to oppose the government through the mobilization of workers demanding both labor union and political rights. A PCE statement in August emphasized that the CC OO were not seen by the communists as a duplicate of the party and stated: "These movements must freely decide their own line of action, and, in them, we communists must act with the same duties and rights as the other members" ("Radio España Independiente," 16 August).

When a new law on trade unions[3] was enacted on 16 February, the CC OO as well as the PCE promptly repudiated it. Both, however, announced their intention to participate in the May-June labor union elections provided by the new law. A PCE appeal to workers before the elections asserted that participation was necessary "to conquer positions which permit us to propel the whole workers' struggle, and destroy the unbroken structure of the vertical syndicates [the official trade unions] by attacking them from within and without, using legal and extra-legal forms" (*ibid.*, 14 April).

Communist sources claimed a strong victory by the CC OO in the May-June elections to appoint worker delegates. Reportedly, CC OO candidates defeated the nominees of the official trade unions by an overwhelming majority in big iron and steel factories, in the textile industries, and in printing, and won lesser victories among railroad, construction, and chemical workers and white-collar employees (*WMR*, September). The PCE assertion that 80 to 90 per cent of the workers had

---

[3]Under this law the government retains power to dissolve the labor unions, but the workers have the rights to hold meetings at their place of work and to appeal to the courts any measure passed by the government setting aside the decision of the elected labor union leaders. The new law does not legalize strikes.

participated in the elections (*España Republicana*, 15 June) was contradicted by Trotskyist sources, which maintained that many workers had boycotted the elections and that in the industrial area of the Basque region and at the two biggest factories in Madrid abstentions had been as high as 50 per cent (*Intercontinental Press*, New York, 13 September).

In contrast with their activities in 1970, the CC OO staged no large strikes during 1971, except for one in Madrid in mid-September which involved about 100,000 construction workers. The strikers demanded a new labor contract and the rights to strike, to hold peaceful meetings, and to have other political freedoms. The rural counterpart of the CC OO, the Farm Workers' Commissions (Comisiones de Obreros Agrarios y Campesinos) appeared not to engage in any major efforts during 1971.

International Views and Positions. Long a supporter of Soviet policies in international affairs, the PCE has adopted, since the 1968 Warsaw Pact invasion of Czechoslovakia, an independent position on international issues. During 1971, relations between the PCE and the Communist Party of the Soviet Union (CPSU) continued to be friendly despite the Soviet support for the Líster faction. In April, Ibárruri, Carrillo, and López Raimundo represented the PCE at the Twenty-fourth Congress of the CPSU and approved unanimously its resolutions. At the solidarity meeting held in Paris in June, Ibárruri asserted: "There is no human or divine force capable of separating us [the PCE] from our course or from our friendship with the Soviet Union ... a friendship that we extend and maintain with all countries in the socialist camp" (*España Republicana*, 15 July).

Nevertheless, PCE criticism of the CPSU and pro-Soviet ruling communist parties continued. Thus, a *Mundo Obrero* article (second fortnight of May) stated:

> For many years our party followed and applauded the opinions and decisions of the CPSU on the great problems of the communist movement, regarding them as articles of faith. This hindered the theoretical and political development of the party and made us commit errors such as [our acceptance of] the Stalin cult, our misunderstanding for a time of the real significance of the Chinese Cultural Revolution, and so forth.

Although the PCE has not explicitly criticized the Soviet support given to the Líster faction, a joint communiqué signed by the PCE and the Japan Communist Party (see below), stated that "no intervention into other parties in any form, including raising anti-party factions and supporting them, can be tolerated" (Tokyo radio, 6 September).

Furthermore, the PCE continued to criticize the 1968 intervention in Czechoslovakia. An article in *Realidad* (May) by its editor Manuel Azcárate commented extensively on a document approved by the Thirteenth Congress of the Communist Party of Czechoslovakia (held in May 1971 but not attended by the PCE), which justified the Soviet-led intervention in that country. In Azcárate's view, the document attempted to set up a "theoretical and historical foundation to the official thesis of the military invasion of Czechoslovakia of August 1968" but lacked "facts and proof" to show that the military forces in fact "dismantled a counterrevolution." He held that the choice made by the Czechoslovak party in January-August 1968 had not been between capitalism and socialism but "between two forms or models of socialism."

Likewise, the PCE continued its criticism of the communist regime in Poland. An Executive Committee statement ("Radio España Independiente," 19 February) termed the riots of December 1970 in that country the "product of certain bureaucratic distortions in the building of socialism."

Giving further indication of growing difference with the CPSU and the pro-Soviet European parties, the PCE Executive Committee issued a statement on 19 February expressing the party's "disagreement with the intensification of relations between socialist countries and the ruling regime in Spain." In the past four years Spain has established relations with Romania, Poland, Hungary, Czechoslovakia, and Bulgaria. Spain signed its first trade agreement with the Soviet Union since

1939 in March 1971. In addition, it was reported that the Soviet Union was interested in establishing diplomatic relations with Spain, while the latter sought only commercial exchanges (*Le Monde*, Paris, 27 February).

A salient event during the year was the reestablishment of bilateral party relations between the PCE and the Chinese Communist Party (CCP). Spanish communist sources indicated in August that "démarches made by the PCE" for establishing relations with the CCP had been "positive." Contacts with the CCP, carried on mostly through the Chinese Embassy in Paris, culminated in a PCE visit to China in October-November. The Chinese press reported that the five-man delegation, led by Carrillo, held talks in Peking with CCP leaders, including Keng Piao, director of the CCP Central Committee department in charge of relations with foreign communist parties (NCNA, 17 November).

Reporting on the meeting between Spanish and Chinese communists, Carrillo indicated that their unity was based on a "unity of diversity of the communist movement," according to which each party must act independently and autonomously. Carrillo also said:

> We agreed to shelve our differences until time and revolutionary struggle tells us who is right and to cooperate in all spheres where we are united. The Chinese comrades regard the Spanish Communist Party as a revolutionary party. ("Radio España Independiente, 11 December.)

Other PCE international views were provided by a joint communiqué following an exchange of views between the PCE and the Japan Communist Party at the end of August. It mentioned as an urgent task the elimination of "U.S. imperialist troops and military bases in Japan and Spain." It also expressed "solidarity with the Indochinese people" and support for the Provisional Revolutionary Government of South Vietnam. Maintaining that "the present international communist movement does not require any center," the parties called for strict adherence to the "principles of independence, equality, and mutual noninterference in internal questions." (Tokyo radio, 6 September.)

International Party Contacts. The PCE's numerous contacts with other communist parties during 1971 were mostly with those considered "independent."

PCE delegations met with communist party leaders of Romania in Bucharest in March and on 1-7 July. Carrillo and Ibárruri visited Yugoslavia and held talks with leaders of the League of Communists of Yugoslavia in May and again in early September.

In August, Carrillo held talks with Antonio Brillakis, a leader of a dissident faction of the Communist Party of Greece and Miyamoto Kenji of the Japan Communist Party. Both meetings took place in Bucharest.

A PCE delegation led by Pablo Azcárate attended the conference of Western European communist parties held in London on 11-13 January, which discussed the "struggle of the working class of the capitalist countries of Europe in face of the development of international firms." Manuel Delicado represented the PCE at the Eighth Congress of the Socialist Unity Party of (East) Germany held in June. Other contacts included meetings with the French Communist Party in January, the Communist Party of the Netherlands early in March, the Left Party Communists of Sweden on 10-16 March, and the Italian Communist Party in May.

Publications. The official organ of the PCE is *Mundo Obrero*, published semimonthly. *Nuestra Bandera* is the party's quarterly theoretical journal. Party sources claim a circulation of 60,000 to 70,000 for *Mundo Obrero* and 205,000 for *Nuestra Bandera*. Both are published abroad and distributed clandestinely in Spain. Other major PCE publications include the semimonthly *España Republicana*, published in Havana by the Cuba-Spanish Friendship Society, and *Realidad*, a monthly journal published in Rome. According to party sources, there are 32 PCE publications. In addition, the party directs radio programs to Spain through its station "Radio España Independiente," which broadcasts from Bucharest.

*   *   *

The two pro-Chinese groups in Spain are organized under the name of the Communist Party of Spain, Marxist-Leninist. The original group, which publishes *Vanguardia Obrera*, was formed in 1964. It is believed to be the stronger and is recognized by Communist China. The other group, which publishes *Mundo Obrero Revolucionario*, was formed in 1965. It is small and seems isolated internationally. Very little is known about the leadership and organization of either group, although Albanian sources in 1971 identified Raúl Marko as Secretariat member of the PCE-ML Central Committee. Pro-Chinese cells are known to exist in Madrid, Asturias, Catalonia, Aragon, the Basque region, and the Canary Islands.

An Albanian radio broadcast on 9 February 1971 stated that the PCE-ML (presumably the *Vanguardia Obrera* faction) had decided to form a "revolutionary national democratic front." The objectives of such a front were described as "deposing and liquidating the Opus Dei-Francoite oligarchy presently in power, driving American imperialists from Spain, and establishing a national and democratic regime within the frameowrk of a federal republic."

At the time of the PCE delegation's visit to China, a PCE-ML delegation was attending the Sixth Congress of the Albanian Party of Labor. Marko, acting as the PCE-ML spokesman at the congress, harshly attacked the PCE and, particularly, Carrillo, about whom he said:

> Touring from one country to another [he is] seeking to find bombastic declarations from different organizations and personalities. But they must know that this only serves to make them ridiculous before the Spanish people, who see in Carrillo only an agent of the oligarchy. (Radio Tirana broadcast, 7 November.)

The PCE-ML marked the fiftieth anniversary of the CCP by sending a message to Mao Tse-tung which stated in part: "The unique experience and rich teachings which the history of your party has provided to our Spanish Marxist-Leninists constitutes an immeasurable assistance and support for us in our efforts for the construction and development of our party" (*Peking Review*, 13 August). The message, as printed by the Chinese, did not contain the customary PCE-ML attacks on Carrillo or Ibárruri.

Nelly Stromquist

Sweden

The Communist Party of Sweden (Sveriges Kommunistiska Parti; SKP) was founded in 1921 and renamed the Left Party Communists (Vänsterpartiet Kommunisterna; VPK) in 1967. It has been legal at all times. Drawing support mainly among organized workers in the urban industrial areas of Stockholm, Gävleborg, and Göteborg, and in mining communities in the northernmost province of Norrbotten, the VPK has probably some 16,000 to 18,000 members. The population of Sweden is 8,093,000 (estimated 1970).

Despite its numerical weakness, the VPK has frequently played a role in the balance of power. It currently holds 17 of the 350 seats in the unicameral Parliament, having polled 4.8 per cent (up 1.8 from 1968) in the September 1970 general election. The ruling Social Democratic Party (Socialdemokratiska Arbetarparti; SAP) received 45.3 per cent, for 163 seats to the non-socialist opposition's 170, and was again forced to look to communist support (the SAP's 50.1 per cent majority in 1968 having temporarily freed the SAP from reliance on the communists). The VPK gained representation on 11 of the 16 permanent committees in the new Parliament, as well as its first seat on the inter-Scandinavian Nordic Council.

To the left of the VPK are a number of small splinter organizations formed since the Sino-Soviet rift. Mostly Maoist, these organizations appear to have a greater attraction for intellectuals and students than has the VPK. Currently the largest (with an estimated 850-900 members) and most active is the Communist League (Marxist-Leninist)—Kommunistiska Förbundet (Marxist-Leninist), or KFML—founded in 1967 by VPK secessionists together with existing Maoist groups. The KFML entered its first national election in 1970, but polled only 0.4 per cent, thus failing to qualify for representation in Parliament (see also below).

The VKP. Leadership and Organization. Carl-Henrik Hermansson, VPK chairman since 1964, was reelected by the party's Twenty-second Congress, in September 1969. Lars Werner is vice-chairman, and Tore Forsberg party secretary. The Working Committee (Politburo) consists of Hermansson, Werner, Forsberg, Gösta Johansson, Eivor Marklund, Nils Berndtsson, Rune Pettersson, and Gunvor Ryding. The Party Executive (Central Committee) has 35 members.

The VPK-affiliated Leftist Youth League (Vänsterns Ungdomsförbund; VUF) was almost totally inactive in 1971, following a major secession the year before by pro-Chinese elements who formed the Marxist-Leninist Struggle League (Marxist-Leninistiska Kampförbundet; MLK). The MLK has declared its support for the KFML, but maintains an independent organization. VUF cadres remaining loyal to VUF chairman Anders Carlberg and to the VPK leadership are attempting to reorganize local cells.

The VPK influences no national trade unions, and controls only about 80 of the approximately 9,000 union locals, largely in building and construction, forestry, and mining. Friendship organizations influenced by the VPK include the Sweden-Soviet Union Association and the Swedish-East German Society.

Domestic Attitudes and Activities. The VPK leadership continued in 1971 to steer a left-socialist course, dissociating itself both from restrictive anti-inflationary measures taken by the government with the frequent support of non-socialist parties, and from the SAP's alleged collaboration with "big business," which, in the communist view, was to blame for the inflationary spiral. The VPK charged the SAP with perpetuating an incomes gap, and with "playing" at class struggle through its ostensible "equalization" policies. Developments during the year on the labor front, where pay demands by unionized civil servants and professionals led to a series of strikes and lockouts, posed tactical problems for the VPK. Confronted with the novel phenomenon of strike action by bodies which included highly paid government officers and others of the academic "elite," the VPK vacillated before deeming it appropriate for the communist party to adopt what amounted to a dual stance. It would support the demands of those white-collar workers with low and medium incomes, but pay increases to top functionaries within the Swedish state apparatus—who had traditionally "stood on the capitalists' side in the class struggle"—would mean further widening the incomes gap. In the VPK view, therefore, white-collar union demands for across-the-board percentage raises or increases based on income after taxes were "unacceptable." (*Ny Dag*, 3-4 and 10-11 March.) The subsequent parliamentary adoption of emergency legislation imposing a return to work and banning strikes and lockouts in the public sector was said by the VPK (the only party to oppose the measure) to constitute a "step in the direction of a state-dictated authoritarian and anti-democratic bargaining system," inasmuch as negotiation possibilities, allegedly, had not yet been exhausted (*ibid.*, 17-18 March).

The party continued to call for abolition of the 17.6 per cent added-value sales tax on goods and services, frequently singling out the levy on foodstuffs—which allegedly discriminated against those with lower incomes—and demanding its replacement by a heavier taxation of industrial profits, large personal fortunes, and legacies. Other prominent communist demands focused on housing, including: a freeze on rents; official measures to halt the rise in prices of new homes and to combat real estate speculation; nationalization of the building materials industry; and establishment of a state housing bank with permanent interest rates for (non-commercial) housing construction. (*Ibid.*, 5-9 February.)

A step-by-step reduction in military expenditures, according to the communists, would not only liberate economic resources for social and other domestic needs, but would also serve to reduce monopoly capital's "direct political influence" in the military hierarchy. The VPK favored gradual global disarmament through various restrictive measures, including "effective" nuclear test ban agreements, disarmed zones, neutrality unions, and eventual dissolution of all military blocs. Military defense, in the communist view, was a strictly national concern, each country possessing the unconditional right to self-determination and to defend that right. (*Ibid.*, 26-27 May.)

International Views and Positions. As Denmark and Norway negotiated for membership in the European Economic Community, the VPK charged that the Swedish government and bourgeois parties were prepared to sell national independence via affiliation with the EEC even though affiliation would mean, allegedly, subordination of the labor market and of tax and social policies to the EEC bureaucracy. In February 1971 Hermansson addressed an anti-EEC seminar in Göteborg attended by nine socialist and communist parties from the Nordic countries, telling delegates that eventual Danish and Norwegian membership would be "devastating for the concept of Nordic cooperation" (*Ny Dag*, 24-25 February). When the government declared, in March, that full membership in the EEC was incompatible with Swedish neutrality, the VPK charged that, though this was a favorable development, it in no way altered the government's fundamental position toward the common market as the government was still prepared to participate in expansion of the EEC in specific important areas such as industry and agriculture. The announcement thus was seen as a tactical move on the part of the government, allegedly made only under pressure from a growing opposition to Swedish EEC affiliation which included elements of the SAP itself. Rejecting the bourgeois contention that opposition to the EEC denoted isolationism, the VPK countered that of far greater benefit both from an internationalist viewpoint and also with regard to Swedish national interests would be a new international trade policy based on increased trade with developing nations and with East Europe. (*Ibid.*, 7-13 April.)

In his maiden speech to the Nordic Council, at its Copenhagen meeting in February, Hermansson linked the questions of "the necessity of rejecting EEC affiliation so as to preserve the Nordic peoples' national right to self-determination" with "co-ordinated Nordic efforts in support of the Indochinese people in their liberation struggle against the American aggressors." He proposed that the council condemn U.S. actions in Laos, Cambodia, and Vietnam; recognize the Provisional Revolutionary Government of South Vietnam (PRGSV); break relations with the Saigon "puppet regime"; and, on the basis of "people's internationalism," provide political and economic support to the PRGSV, the Laotion Pathet Lao, and the Cambodian "National United Front of Kampuchea." There were no contradictions, he said, between such "internationalism" and a "healthy patriotism." Capitalist "internationalism" as represented in the EEC, on the other hand, was detrimental to national independence in that its aim was to guarantee capitalism free movement within EEC areas. The correct corollary solution, therefore, would be for the Nordic countries to work together to find "practical and concrete" forms of economic cooperation beyond the EEC. (*Ibid.*, 19-23 February.)

VPK agitation with regard to the Vietnam war continued to be directed against U.S. involvement in the conflict rather than against government attitudes. Sweden's position as the first Western nation to establish full diplomatic relations with North Vietnam (in 1969) and its subsequent promises of aid to the Vietnamese communists have left the VPK little room to agitate against official Swedish policy. The VPK has been criticized by other extreme left political elements—notably the Maoists—for its alleged "apathy" in antiwar activities. It has maintained, however, that it is prepared to cooperate with all organizations and individuals for such goals as recognition of the PRGSV and unconditional aid to North Vietnam, but that it would not restrict its support to any one organization supporting these goals to the exclusion of others (such as "humanitarian" aid to South Vietnam), nor endorse the restriction of support to socialist organizations. (*Ny Dag*, 5-9 February.) Such charges and implied countercharges resulted from the Maoists' efforts in the 1970 election to attract voters through presenting themselves as supporting a nonpartisan antiwar movement (see below).

International Communist Movement. The VPK continued in 1971 to remain aloof from schisms within the international communist movement and to uphold the independence of each party. Representing the VPK at the congress of the Communist Party of the Soviet Union (CPSU), in April, Tore Forsberg presented his address not at the congress but during a visit to a Soviet factory. He hailed the "great significance" of the Soviet Union and the CPSU for world development as a whole and for the common struggle of workers against "imperialist" forces. Forsberg avoided any direct reference to difficulties within the international communist movement. As for interparty cooperation, he emphasized, it was the VPK's "determined concept" that this be developed on the basis of "proletarian internationalism" and "respect for all nations' and all parties' sovereignty and right to self-determination." (*Ny Dag*, 21-22 April.)

The VPK was represented by Party Executive member Urban Karlsson at the May congress of the Communist Party of Czechoslovakia. Other than a report by him on the proceedings (*ibid.*, 11-15 June), no comment was made by the VPK with regard either to the congress or to Czechoslovak developments in general. In his address to the congress Karlsson touched only peripherally on the Soviet-led invasion of 1968, merely expressing his party's hopes that "now that the difficulties have been partially overcome, Czechoslovak communists will be better able to make use of the rich opportunities of socialism." This reference, Karlsson stated afterward in his report, implied no change in the critical stand taken by the VPK at the time of the invasion.

In one of several apparent moves to pursue a policy of accommodation with party conservatives in the north, the VPK leadership designated Alf Lövenborg, editor of the conservatives' daily *Norrskensflamman* to head a delegation that visited Poland on 11-17 October. In a joint communiqué the VPK and the Polish United Workers' Party expressed unanimity of views and called for speedy ratification of the treaties between the Federal Republic of Germany and the U.S.S.R. and Poland, recognition of the German Democratic Republic by all West European countries, convocation of a conference on European security, and Israeli withdrawal from all Arab territories occupied since the June 1967 war (*Trybuna Ludu*, Warsaw, 18 October).

Main Party Publications. The central organ of the VPK, *Ny Dag* (New Day), edited by Per Francke, is issued twice weekly in Stockholm. In Göteborg and western Sweden the same paper is published under the name *Arbetar-Tidningen* (Worker News). The voice of the VPK in Norrbotten is *Norrskensflamman* (Blaze of Northern Lights), the party's sole remaining daily. *Socialistisk Debatt* (Socialist Debate), a theorectical quarterly journal launched by the VPK in 1967 and subsequently relegated to the middle section of *Ny Dag*, resumed formal publication in May 1971.

*　　*　　*

The Communist League (Marxist-Leninist). The KFML has its main strength in the Stockholm, Göteborg, and Uppsala areas, and has also drawn some support from the VPK in the north. Leading KFML figures are: Gunnar Bylin (chairman); Bo Gustafsson, editor of the KFML monthly theoretical journal *Marxistisk Forum*, published in Uppsala; Per Axelsson, who in 1971 replaced Nils Holmberg (one of few veteran communists in the KFML leadership) as editor of *Gnistan* (Spark), the KFML monthly newsletter issued in Göteborg; and Kurt Lundgren, secretary. The Swedish Clarity League (Svenska Clartéförbundet; Clarté), a student organization originally founded in 1924 and currently headed by Peter Emsheimer, has developed close ties with the KFML. Clarté issues eight times a year a journal by the same name; its affiliated "school clubs" also issue a journal, *Skoltidning* (School Journal).

Former KFML vice-chairman Frank Baude, expelled from the KFML in 1970 for splitting activities, leftist opportunism, and misappropriation of funds, joined with a large proportion of the Göteborg membership expelled with him to form a rival group called KFML(r)—the "r" for "revolutionary." The KFML(r) issues a bulletin called *Klasskampen* (Class Struggle), which accuses the KFML of having succumbed to "right deviationism." For some months after the split, there appeared to be clearly drawn social lines between KFML and KFML(r) forces, the former representing intellectuals and students, and the latter being more representative of militant workers. With the efforts of the KFML to appeal to workers, both in its publications and in its active support of their demands, and with the defection of some students from the KFML to the KFML(r)—including the formation of a splinter "Clarté(m-1)" group—the division has become less marked.

KFML and KFML(r) Activities in 1971. The Maoists' most active area of activity and influence continued to be within the United National Liberation Front Groups (De Förenade FNL-grupperna; DFFG), a generally pro-socialist mass movement whose some 120 local "NLF groups" have sponsored campaigns and demonstrations protesting the U.S. role in Vietnam and dispatched financial aid to North Vietnam and the National Liberation Front of South Vietnam. The KFML schism penetrated the DFFG, however, resulting in the expulsion, in January 1971, of 18 NLF groups won over by the Baude camp and alleged to have attempted to persuade other DFFG affiliates to adopt the KFML(r) political line. The KFML(r) has since formed the "Solidarity Front for the People of Indochina," while new NLF groups have been organized to replace those disbanded by the DFFG.

The year's strikes by white-collar unions evoked considerable differences between the KFML and VPK. On the basis that the demands of lower-paid civil servants for improved wage and work conditions could be secured only by the united victory of their representative unions, the KFML, in contrast to the VPK, gave its unconditional support to the strikes. It was noted by the VPK that in so doing, the purportedly revolutionary KFML had aligned itself with bourgeois forces widely represented in the white-collar unions. To this the KFML countered that the VPK tactic of supporting only the lower paid, while refusing to support the unions as a whole, constituted "an attempt to split an organization united in its struggle and thereby weaken that struggle." The VPK position, in this view, had the effect of "serving monopoly capitalism" in its bid to break the demands of the unions. (*Gnistan*, no. 3.)

Communist China currently recognizes both the KFML and Clarté as representing Marxist-Leninists in Sweden, and their delegations to Peking are received by high-ranking officials. No public acknowledgment of the split within the KFML has thus far been made by the Chinese.

*   *   *

Other Communist Splinter Groups. The oldest Maoist organization, the Communist Workers' League of Sweden (Sveriges Kommunistiska Arbetarförbund), formed in 1953 following a VPK purge, has never participated in a local or national election, and remains isolated and unimportant. It publishes a bulletin, *Revolt*. There are also two newer Trotskyist organizations: Revolutionary Marxists (Revolutionära Marxister), which issues five times a year a journal called *Fjärde Internationalen* (Fourth International), and the Bolshevik Group (Bolsjevikgruppen), which publishes the Bolsjevik (Bolshevik) bulletin.

Valerie Bloom

Switzerland

The Swiss Party of Labor (Parti Suisse du Travail; PST/Partei der Arbeit; PdA), pro-Soviet in orientation, operates legally. The party was founded in 1921 and celebrated its fiftieth anniversary in April. During 1971 the PdA received minor competition on the left from the Organization of Swiss Communists/Marxist-Leninist (Organisation des Communistes de Suisse/Marxiste-Leniniste; OCS/ML) and from the Revolutionary Marxist League (Ligue Marxiste Révolutionaire; LMR).

Total membership of the PdA is estimated to be between 4,500 and 5,000. The population of Switzerland is 6,300,000 (estimated 1970). In the October national elections the party polled 2.7 per cent of the vote and thus retained its five seats in the 200-member lower house, the National Council. The party is without representation on legislative committees because it is not large enough to be accorded "fraction" status.

In the cantons of Geneva and Vaud the PdA conducted a joint campaign with the Socialist Party (Parti socialiste; PS), although the two parties presented a separate list of candidates to the voters. Three PdA members from Geneva, Jean Vincent, Roger Dafflon and Nelly Wicky, were elected to the National Council. (*Voix Ouvrière*, 2 and 3 November). The party's fourth and fifth representatives in the National Council were elected in the canton of Vaud. The party is strongest in the cantons of Geneva, Vaud and Neuchâtel in western Switzerland. The PdA has little significant strength in the German-speaking industrial centers, such as Basel or Zürich.

Leadership and Organization. On June 12 and 13 the PdA held its Tenth Congress in Lausanne in the canton of Vaud. At that time no changes in the party's leadership were reported by the party organs. Jean Vincent, a practicing attorney in Geneva, continues as party spokesman in the three-member Secretariat, whose other two members are Jakob Lechleiter (Zürich) and André Muret (Lausanne). The Executive Committee includes the three Secretariat members and eleven additional members: Frédéric Blaser, Ernest Décosterd, Roger Dafflon, Franz Dübi, Etienne Lentillon, Armand Magnin, Pietro Monetti, Karl Odermatt, Louis Sidler, Hans Stebler, Eugénie Tüscher. No replacement was announced for Executive Committee member Henri Trüb, who died early in the year. The 50-member Central Committee did not undergo substantial alteration, although seven new members were elected to that body to replace members who had resigned or who were no longer able to serve for "diverse reasons." Four of the seven newly elected members were between the ages of twenty-five and thirty, reflecting the party's emphasis on participation by younger members. (*Voix Ouvrière*, 14 June.)

The party organization is based on the principle of "democratic centralism," and is entirely "independent in the determination of its policy and its action." Chapter Four on "The Party and its Organization," included in the series of resolutions approved by the Tenth Congress, laid particular emphasis on three points. (1) The principle of "democratic centralism" must insure permanent liaison between the ruling bodies and the party's members. (2) There must exist freedom

231

of discussion and the right of criticism. All members, however, are bound by a decision once taken. (3) All ruling bodies are to be elected from "below" and they, in turn, must submit periodic reports to the party members. Groups or factions, such as "leftist deformations," that practice "anti-Sovietism" or isolate the "worker movement" by their actions, are opposed by the party. (*Voix Ouvrière*, 26 June.)

Numerous organizations within the PdA are designed to appeal to a variety of interests among the population at large: Free Youth of Switzerland, Swiss Peace Movement, Switzerland-DPRK Society (DPRK: Democratic People's Republic of Korea), Swiss-Soviet Friendship Society, Swiss Committee for Aid to Vietnam, Swiss League of Women for Peace and Progress, and Society for the Defense of Tenants. A significant amount of autonomy is permitted these groups in matters of domestic concern. This applies equally to local party leadership committees in Switzerland's cantons. Within the party itself there are cantonal divisions that have French, German and Italian designations.

Party Internal Affairs. PdA attention was focused on two issues of internal concern throughout most of the year: (1) the Tenth Party Congress held in June, and (2) the activities of leftist youth groups in Switzerland.

The Tenth Party Congress was attended by 101 delegates. Prior to its convention 55 program resolutions had been discussed within the party at large (*Voix Ouvrière*, 7 May). In accordance with the mandate approved during the Ninth Congress in 1968 (see *YICA*, 1970, p. 270) the Tenth Congress passed 59 program resolutions in one ballot by a majority vote of 89 with six abstentions. The resolutions, entitled "What does the Labor Party Want?", were divided into four chapters: 1. Socialism and Capitalism. 2. The Situation in Switzerland. 3. Strategy and Tactics. 4. The Party and its Organization. These resolutions were intended to provide specific guidelines for future party activities. They were also to be used as a party platform in the elections for the National Council in October (*ibid.*, 26 June).

The principle position expressed in the introduction to this program stressed the defense of the "... moral and material interests of the Swiss people." Advancement of the struggle "... for the complete political and economic liberation of the workers through the abolition of capitalism and the adoption of a socialist, and then a communist, society" was declared the party's goal. Party action was to be based on the teachings of "scientific socialism—Marxism-Leninism." (*Ibid.*, 26 June.)

In the fourth chapter of the resolutions attention was drawn to the problems of the younger generation. These recommendations were intended primarily for domestic consumption and reflected the concern of the PdA leadership with the leftist activities of various non-party radical groups, composed essentially of students. In March *Voix Ouvrière* condemned such disruptive activities as sit-ins and demonstrations, as inconsistent with the teachings of Karl Marx. Although no groups were specifically identified, such activities were declared contradictory to the "class struggle," and consistent with "the Stalinist distortion of socialism." (*Ibid.*, 2 March.)

Voix Ouvrière was especially concerned with the publication of *The Little Red Book for Students and Pupils*. While acknowledging that *The Little Red Book* had some "very positive sides, in particular the chapters on sexuality and drugs," the PdA attacked the attempt of the author to widen the generation gap. To make a distinction between generations was "... to deny the continuity factor that exists in every dialectic process; it is to claim, in a thoughtless fashion that everything that belongs to the past is without value, for the sole reason that it belongs to the past." (*Ibid.*)

Domestic Attitudes and Activities. The party's policies and proposals were essentially a repetition of those endorsed during 1970. To achieve "socialism, then communism," the PdA leaders continued to call for "unity" and "common action" among all concerned groups. In Switzerland problems such as the cost of living, housing shortages and the absence of "true social security" had produced a "Swiss uneasiness," according to Jean Vincent. (*Voix Ouvrière*, 30 April/1 May.) These issues were defined in greater detail in the resolutions of the party Congress, and were given consistent attention prior to the national elections. The PdA supported price and profit control measures, tax reform, reduction in arms expenditures, a limitation on interest rates, reform of the charter of the National Bank, anti-inflationary policies, protection of tenants, pensions for all by taxing "the profits of big capital," consumer protection, equal pay for men and women, protection of the environment and a more stable fiscal policy. (*Ibid.*, 5 and 26 June, 5 and 23 October.) The world monetary crisis was singled out as proof of Swiss ties to "international capitalism," for which "local capitalism ... [paid] the price of this dependence while rescuing the dollar in crisis" (*ibid.*, 18 June).

The PdA maintained that the establishment of socialism was "a step by step process," only to be achieved "... with the agreement and action of ... the Swiss people." To successfully "rally" the proletariat additional groups of workers and employees, intellectuals and technicians, farmers, artisans and small businessmen, as well as tenants, consumers and the elderly, must join in common action regardless of "political leanings." Swiss workers and foreign laborers were also urged to participate in order to successfully change the government policy of "labor peace" in Switzerland. The PdA also stressed participation by "the younger generation" in the formation of commercial and educational policy in order to ensure the "renewal and transformation of society." (*Ibid.*)

Consistent with its position that the Swiss people could only be "... won over to socialism ... [with] their full consent" (*ibid.*, 30 April/1 May) the PdA supported as much party participation as possible in parliamentary life on a national level and in the cantons (*ibid.*, 26 June). It was in this context that the PdA participated in the elections at the end of October for the 200-member National Council (the lower house). As already noted the PdA retained the same number of seats (5) that it had won in the previous election in 1967. The party is not, however, represented in the 44-member Council of States (the upper house).

The campaign slogan was "On the Offensive through Unity." The PdA criticised the policies of the Swiss government which, the PdA alleged, had produced greater monopolistic concentration at the expense of the working class. Karl Odermatt, a member of the party's Executive Committee, stressed that "...ideological differences of opinion between Communists and Social Democrats should not hinder the force of the entire left from becoming concentrated on the common enemy" (*Vorwaerts*, 7 October). *Vorwaerts* concluded therefore, that a "leftist front" was being formed to oppose the "shameless demands of the administration" (*ibid.*, 30 September). In Geneva and Vaud the Socialists and the PdA combined their election slates. In the canton of Basel City the PdA supported a joint ticket with the "Progressive Organizations of Basel."

The PdA was disappointed with the election results. It had expected to win a greater number of seats. Its failure to do so was attributed to the efforts of "the right" to exploit "the justified fears of the worker class for the security of their jobs." (*Voix Ouvrière*, 3 November.) Of the five party members in the National Council, Nelly Wicky from Geneva took her seat in the Council for the first time. Jean Vincent and Roger Dafflon from Geneva, and Armand Forel and André Muret from Nyon and Lausanne were all re-elected. (*Ibid.*, 2 and 3 November; *Neue Zürcher Zeitung*, 6 November.)

International Views and Positions. The major foreign policy objective presented at the Tenth Party Congress was defined as "the defense of peace" through the establishment of "world security and general détente." Diplomatic recognition was demanded for the German Democratic Republic (GDR), North Korea and North Vietnam. The PdA endorsed Switzerland's entrance to the United

Nations if it would serve to promote "peaceful coexistence and détente" and not violate the country's neutrality. (*Voix Ouvcière*, 26 June.) China's admission to the United Nations was welcomed by the PdA, not in the least because of the "tremendous loss of prestige" sustained by "American imperialism" (*ibid.*, 27 October). "American imperialism" was also criticized for continued U.S. involvement in Southeast Asia. Jean Vincent urged an end to the war in Indochina and called for "freedom and sovereignty" for Cambodia and Laos. In addition he supported the reestablishment of peace in the Near East ". . . by freeing the territory occupied by Israel." He warned that Cuba was still threatened and that Chile was ". . . fighting to get out from under the grasp of the monopolies." (*Ibid.*, 30 April/1 May.)

The Common Market was viewed as "a closed bloc of capitalist powers" and the PdA therefore opposed Swiss participation. Jean Vincent recommended, however, that following "adequate . . . discussion throughout the country" the establishment of "special relations" with the EEC would be in Switzerland's interest, since ". . . it cannot cut itself off from its neighbors." (*Vorwaerts*, 16 September.)

The conclusion of the Berlin agreement also received the support of the PdA. Karl Odermatt welcomed the agreement as (1) a step toward recognition of the GDR, (2) the "prerequisite" for West German ratification of its treaties with Poland and the USSR, (3) a step toward "a general European security conference and negotiations on the reduction of armed forces and armaments." (*Ibid.*, 2 September.)

The necessity for "peaceful coexistence" received considerable attention, particularly in an effort to support Soviet foreign policy and "unity" in the international communist movement. In the resolutions of the Tenth Party Congress "anti-Sovietism" was declared a basic weapon in the hands of the bourgeosie. It was pointed out repeatedly during the year that the PdA was "united in friendship with the Soviet Union and other socialist countries." (*Vorwaerts*, 22 April and *Voix Ouvrière*, 29 October.)

The PdA did emphasize that because of the "diversity of history, origins, and conditions" of the socialist world there must be diversity of forms in the path to socialism (*Voix Ouvrière*, 26 June). To illustrate this point the PdA devoted considerable care to its analysis of the events in Poland of December 1970. The riots were ". . . not directed against socialism; their aim was to effect positive changes . . . so that the forward march of socialism could take place." The PdA defined the path to socialism as ". . . a search for mechanisms that will allow" the discussion of contradictions. (*Ibid.*, 23 February.)

The paper published an equally careful evaluation of the Fourteenth Party Congress of the Czechoslovakian CP in May. The PdA had criticized the Soviet invasion of Czechoslovakia in 1968 and continued to make references to this action during 1969 and 1970. *Vorwaerts* concluded in June, 1971, that the invasion had indeed ". . . evoked an open split in the international communist movement," as was evident in the paper of the Italian delegate to the Congress. *Vorwaerts* did express symputhy with Gustáv Husák's conclusion, however, that the invasion was in the "interests of the Czechoslovakian working class"; Novotńy ". . . had not equipped the party against those methods of ideological diversion, which the imperialists were beginning to apply as the main weapon against the socialist countries." (*Vorwaerts*, 3 June.)

International Activities and Party Contacts. On the occasion of its fiftieth anniversary in March the PdA received congratulatory messages from communist parties on the continent as well as from abroad, including those from the Workers Party of Korea and the Mongolian Communist Party.

Throughout the year the PdA sent delegates to the various party congresses held on the European continent. The most important of these was the Twenty-fourth Congress of the Soviet Communist

Party that opened in Moscow on March 30. The PdA was represented by Jean Vincent and Franz Dübi. As Dübi emphasized following the congress, the PdA considered itself "... united in friendship with the Soviet Union and other socialist countries." PdA delegates attended the congress to demonstrate "solidarity ... in the anti-imperialist struggle." (*Vorwaerts*, 22 April.)

On the twenty-fifth anniversary of the East German Communist Party the PdA sent its congratulations praising "the moral and political unity of the people in the GDR" (*ibid.*, 22 April). Central Committee member Etienne Lentillon addressed the Tenth Party Congress of the Bulgarian Communist Party in Sophia at the end of April, stressing the need for "unity in the international communist labor movement" (*Voix Ouvrière*, 30 April/1 May). The PdA was also represented at the Rumanian Youth Congress held from February 18 to 22 in Budapest (*ibid.*, 26 February).

In July Frédéric Blaser, member of the PdA's Executive Committee met in Rumania with Paul Niculescu-Mizil, Secretary of the Central Committee of the Rumanian Communist Party (*Scînteia*, Bucharest, 27 July). A delegation of the Italian Communist Party met with representatives of the PdA in Switzerland on March 26 (*Voix Ouvrière*, 30 March). In November PdA delegates attended the Second Congress of the West German Communist Party and were also present at a conference on European problems sponsored by the Italian Communist Party (*Voix Ouvrière*, 30 November). Of particular interest was Jean Vincent's praise of the party program of the French Communist Party (PCF) in October. He emphasized that the PdA program resolutions adopted at the Tenth Party Congress in June were "analogous" to the program of the PCF, and moreover that this was not coincidental, for "the same problems arise" in neighboring industrial countries. (*Ibid.*, 15 October.)

Publications. Official organs are published by the PdA in three languages. *Voix Ouvrière* is published daily in Geneva. *Vorwaerts* and *Il Lavoratore* are published weekly in Basel and in Locarno respectively.

Henri Trüb, the Editor-in-Chief of *Voix Ouvrière* and a member of the PdA Executive Committee, died in early 1971. He was replaced as Editor-in-Chief in March by Executive Committee member Armand Magnin. Although *Voix Ouvrière* enjoys the largest circulation of the three newspapers, the Board of Directors of the Voix Ouvrière Publishing Company issued a special appeal in March for new subscriptions "... in order to insure the future appearance of the newspaper" (*Voix Ouvrière*, 16 March).

*   *

Two major communist splinter groups were particularly active during 1971, the Revolutionary Marxist League (LMR) and the Organization of Swiss Communists (OCS). Since the LMR was formed following a split in the Tendance de Gauche 1969 its activities have been limited primarily to the French-speaking part of Switzerland. Thus far it appears to have little influence. During 1971, however, it expanded its activities to the German-speaking areas. In early April the LMR held its first congress, attended by 150 delegates representing Lausanne, Vevey, Nyon, Neuchâtel and Bern-Jura. Observers were in attendance from Zürich and Fribourg. The party organ *La Brèche* reported in May that the dominant theme at the congress was that of "centralization." The purpose of the congress was "... to achieve the concrete political and organizational conditions necessary for creating a real nationwide organization" (*La Brèche*, May).

Two main tasks were approved by the congress delegates: (1) confrontation with the "spontanéist" tendencies favored by existing political conditions, and (2) the achievement of a base in the working class. Efforts toward building the basis of a revolutionary party were to be concentrated initially in the area of education on the university and high school levels. The LMR emphasized the struggle "against all forms of class oppression on the campus (restrictive admissions, bourgeois ideological indoctrination ...)" and devoted special attention to "responding correctly to multiple attempts at 'university reform.' " Discussion also focused on the creation of a revolutionary youth organization and on formulating a strategy to be employed in the trade schools. (*La Brèche*, May.)

The decision of the Swiss government to forbid the Marxist economist, Ernest Mandel, from entering the country, and therefore from teaching at Swiss universities, generated considerable indignation on behalf of the LMR. The party's reaction was to announce a "campaign for democratic liberties." It therefore urged the transformation of the affair "into a basic struggle for freedom of speech and information," to proceed "hand in hand with the strengthening of the revolutionary organization." (*La Brèche*, August.)

The OCS, though its membership is small, is the more closely organized of the two parties and publishes its party organ in Italian, French and German. Its position on foreign policy issues is pro-Chinese (see YICA, 1971, p. 265). Although the party views "the rise of the socialist camp" as representing the "greatest challenge to American imperialism," it also condemns the "revisionism" of the Soviet Communist Party. In February the OCS urged the formulation of "new tactics and new strategy" to confront "American-Soviet cooperation." (*Oktober*, February/March.)

On the domestic level new tactics were to include more strikes and the formation of tenants' committees to oppose rent increases. Though the OCS considered these movements still to be isolated and lacking in "clear political perspectives," they were an indication of "increasing popular discontent, [and] a renewal of the class struggle." The major goal of the party is to replace the bourgeois dictatorship with "the dictatorship of the proletariat" (*Octobre*, June). In October the OCS called for the formation of a revolutionary labor union in addition to establishing "cells in businesses." The party therefore stressed the necessity of connecting "the economic struggle ... with the political struggle," to work initially within the Swiss Syndical Union (USS), to seek its destruction and the formation of unions that will pursue the "revolutionary path." (*Octobre*, October.)

Stanford University   Dennis L. Bark

Turkey

The Communist Party of Turkey (Türkiye Komünist Partisi; TKP) was founded in 1920 in Istanbul. Remnants of two other early Turkish communist organizations, one formed in Anatolia, the other among émigrés in Soviet Azerbaijan, were absorbed soon thereafter. Illegal since 1925 and severely repressed within Turkey, the TKP has never been able to create a strong organization and is an insignificant political force in the country. The party is estimated to have between 1,200 and 2,000 members and 10,000 to 15,000 sympathizers. The population of Turkey is 35,600,000 (estimated 1970).

There exist a number of Turkish leftist organizations in Europe which the TKP supports and appears to have infiltrated, including the Federation of Turkish Socialists, the Association for Vigilant Turks, and the Front for a Democratic and Free Turkey. Within Turkey, the TKP supports various leftist trade-union, teacher, student, and youth groups, including the Union of Progressive Forces, the Confederation of Reformist Trade Unions (DISK), the Federation of Idea Clubs (FKF), the Turkish Teachers' Union (TOS), and the 27 May Clubs.

The TKP has to some extent infiltrated the Turkish Labor Party (TLP), whose policies on many counts parallel those of the communists. The TLP, however, has shown wariness of identification with the outlawed communist party, and most of its members claim to be either "national communists" or "national socialists" with no interest in the international communist movement. Even so, TLP delegations frequently participate in communist-oriented international meetings. In the 1969 parliamentary elections, the TLP secured 2.7 per cent of the vote and 2 of 450 seats—down from 3.0 per cent and 15 seats in 1965. Under a 1969 electoral amendment stipulating a minimum of 25,000 votes in a constituency to qualify a party for mandate distribution, the TLP that year lost any possibility of influencing national policy by parliamentary means. The 1971 outlawing of the TLP, along with many other leftist groups, was an indirect result of terrorist activities opposed by the TLP majority.

Leadership and Organization. Overt TKP activity is directed from abroad. Zeki Bastimar, who goes under the alias Yakub Demir, is the party's secretary-general. Most, if not all, of its thirteen Central Committee members live in and operate from Moscow.

Domestic Attitudes and Activities. Early in 1971 the TKP's "main current task" was described by Yakub Demir in an interview with the East German *Neues Deutschland* (19 January) as the "struggle against imperialism, led by Washington" and its "reactionary agents" within Turkey. A socialist system, the ultimate goal of the party, could only be realized after "completion of the bourgeois-democratic revolution" under the leadership of the Turkish workers' class, which he said was now "far stronger and far more experienced than in the days of Ataturk." Once having overthrown the government and established "a truly democratic rule, "the Turkish people, still led by their workers' class, would "pave the way to socialism." Thus, according to a subsequent party broadcast, "the struggle for democracy must develop hand-in-hand with the struggle against imperialism." Reasoning that anti-communism was imperialism's "most effective weapon against the struggle for national and social liberation," the party termed anti-communism tantamount to "assisting imperialism." Those who professed to be opposed to both imperialism and communism were thus acting as an obstacle to national and social reform—which could only be achieved through the unity of all "reformist, anti-imperialist, and patriotic forces." ("Our Radio," 31 January.)

TKP elements play a small, uninfluential role in the terrorist Turkish Peoples' Liberation Army (TPLA) and in the originally more moderate anti-U.S. and pro-Arab Turkish Revolutionary Youth Federation (Dev-Genc), from which the TPLA emerged in early 1971. (The TPLA and Dev-Genc also contain TLP elements.) The TPLA, pledged to armed struggle to "liberate Turkey from the Americans and all its enemies," was responsible during the year for a number of bomb attacks, bank robberies, and kidnapings. These actions reached a high point with the abduction of the Israeli consul general in Istanbul, Ephraim Elrom, on 17 May and his murder four days later when the Turkish government refused to accede to the TPLA's demand for the release of all imprisoned "revolutionaries." Elrom was reported by the West German *Der Spiegel* (31 May) to have been chosen because he provided the Turkish government with the names of Turks who conspired with the Palestinian guerrillas, leading to some 300 arrests. Although TPLA cadres are known to have received training with Palestinian "liberation" groups in Syria and Jordan (including al-Fatah and the Popular Front for the Liberation of Palestine—both of which denied complicity in the Elrom case), their tactics appear to be inspired also by Latin American urban guerrilla groups—notably the Uruguyan Tupamaros. The TPLA has, by its tactics, split the Turkish Marxist left; particularly, leftist intellectuals blame the TPLA for providing the authorities with a "pretext" to intervene in university affairs. In the meantime, the TPLA was reported to be establishing training camps in remote areas and preparing to conduct rural guerrilla tactics. They have apparently won over small numbers of Turkish security forces.

While TKP disapproval of TPLA tactics was evident, the party displayed a reluctance to condemn the guerrillas openly, inasmuch as their cause—anti-imperialism in general and anti-Americanism in particular—was synonomous with its own. The TKP charged, rather, that the incidents of violence were "planned" by the government as "justification" for repressive measures against "reformists." In purported evidence of this charge, it noted that various incidents coincided with the introduction by the government of "fascist" anti-extremist bills in parliament. ("Our Radio," 17 February.) The government's "campaign of terror" was said, in turn, to be the design of "agents of the U.S. Central Intelligence Agency and Federal Bureau of Investigation" whose mission was "to study the causes of the constantly strengthening anti-imperialist struggle and to direct the [Turkish] government on measures to be taken to thwart it." The party appealed to "patriotic men and officers" in the armed forces "not to remain indifferent," but, as "children of impoverished Anatolians," to "take the side of the workers and all democratic forces in the struggle for national and social independence. (*Ibid.*, 11 March.)

Such "democratic forces," according to the TKP, included, not least, the Kurdish minority in eastern Turkey, whose "liberation struggle" the TKP and TLP have both upheld against alleged government efforts to "crush" the Kurds and "reduce them to slaves" (*ibid.*, 28 April). Both the TKP ar TLP maintained, however, that the Kurdish problem could be solved only within the frameowrk of the "working-class fight for socialism." The more militant within the Dev-Genc asserted that the Kurdish people could obtain "equal rights" only through armed struggle. It is likely that the TKP, TLP, and Dev-Genc were all involved in the establishment of "revolutionary centers" in Kurdish areas in the past two years. The government has attempted to neutralize such centers by sending in paramilitary police units.

On 12 March, twenty-three leading members of the TLP were charged by the government with "disseminating communist and Kurdish nationalist propaganda." A case was also filed against Dev-Genc for "violation of the associations law by engaging in political activity." (Ankara radio, 12 March.) Upon the fall of Süleyman Demirel's government, a day later, the TKP called for amendment of the electoral laws (to legalize the TKP) and the holding of new parliamentary elections. The national crisis, it said, could only be solved by a coalition government representing the "reformist" section of the working class, "patriotic" young people, intellectuals, and "Ataturkist" officers. (Our Radio, 16 March.) The new government headed by Nihat Erim was said by the party to be "the representative of the most reactionary elements," and thus "incapable of carrying out even the minimal reforms envisaged by the 1961 constitution. (*Ibid.*, 20 March.) The new government's program was subsequently described by the TKP as an "affirmation of loyalty to the U.S., NATO, CENTO, the World Bank and the EEC monopolies" and as containing "not a single concrete proposal ... that would benefit the people" (*ibid.*, 4 April).

The imposition of martial law on 26 April in 11 of Turkey's 67 provinces was described by the TKP as a "de facto amendment of the constitution" and as evidence that the government was "prepared to do everything to preserve the U.S. overlordship in Turkey, including changing of the constitution" (*ibid.*, 28 April). Subsequently the TKP Central Committee charged that the government and the military commanders whom it brought to power had, "by disguising themselves and exploiting the desire of the people for democratic and radical reforms," "unmasked their attachment to NATO and CENTO with their very first acts—imposition of martial law, banning of labor movements and strikes, and arrests of trade union officials" (*ibid.*, 22 May). As to tactics during the martial clampdown, the TKP appealed for various forms of resistance, including labor strikes and slowdowns, agitation by Turkish workers at NATO and U.S. establishments, and, in rural areas, protest meetings and rallies against landowners and merchants to "enlighten the public," and the setting up by "patriotic youth and teachers" of village "resistance committees" (*ibid.*, 17 May).

In June, a TKP broadcast entitled "Revolutionary Struggle Strategy and Tactics Must Suit Conditions in Turkey" emphasized that no "national liberation revolution and transformation to a socialist revolution" had ever been achieved without reliance on the masses and their participation and solidarity. Urban and rural guerrillas known as "guerrilleros" or tupamaros, who operated in Latin America and were "mostly groups that broke away from the socialist movement," had "not secured anything beyond the release of a few political detainees in Brazil." Failing to achieve any political success, they had drifted into isolation, and in turn to such "deviations" as "anarchism and personal terrorism," allowing imperialist agents to infiltrate their ranks and making it possible for their anarchist acts to be used against the socialist movement. The terrorist movement in Turkey, which was said to have developed outside the socialist movement, was "roughly at this stage," having broken away from the masses, from the socialist movement leading the masses, and from the liberation struggle against imperialism and the collaborating bourgeoisie." This isolation had led "some youths engaged in revolutionary activities in good faith into ever-increasing anarchism and irresponsibility, giving imperialism the chance to play the same tricks in Turkey it played in Latin America and even such countries as France, West Germany, Britain, the United States, and Italy." The "trick" was based on "infiltrating agents among the youth groups in order to speed up the process toward anarchism." Presumably referring to the Dev-Genc, the TKP broadcast expressed approval of the "initial activities of the youth movement, when it began in the late 1960s to carry revolutionary ideas to rural laborers, and to establish close links with the labor movement, extending moral and financial support to workers on strike, and trying to establish firm ties with the working class and socialist movement." Failing to comprehend that "patience is part of being a revolutionary," however, some youths had "fallen into the traps of provocateurs, anarchists, Maoists, and Trotskyites, and were paying for their mistakes with their lives and harming the socialist movement and working class." Though to be respected for their bravery, these youths must be "shown the correct course for revolution." (*Ibid.*, 5 June.)

In an article on "Problems of Left Unity in Turkey" (*WMR*, July), TKP leader Demir attempted to convey the "disastrous" effect on the Turkish economy of U.S. and other "imperialist" aid, which, in his view, gave foreign "imperialist monopolies" full control of key Turkish industries, undercut the nation's own industry, undermined its scientific and educational achievements, and prevented advances in the general standard of living through "adaptation to the needs of the foreign and national monopolies bossing the country." The party's current programmatic orientation, described in Demir's article, calls for a common platform of "national rebirth" for all "anti-imperialists, patriots, democratic organizations, and progressive groups," whose ultimate goals would be: regaining national sovereignty by annulling all agreements with imperialist powers that curtailed national independence, dismantling the foreign military bases on Turkish soil and securing the withdrawal of foreign military personnel, establishing and abiding by strict neutrality, and following a policy of cooperation and peace with all nations. All foreign enterprises and assets would be nationalized, relieving national industry and agriculture of the burden of unequal competition with foreign capital in their own country, and requiring the U.S., West German, British, French, and Italian "imperialists" to "make good the losses they have inflicted by plundering the [Turkish] people and robbing them of their national resources for years." Domestically, the TKP called for nationalization of all private banks and insurance companies, and abolition of "big landed estates and all semi-feudal forms of peasant exploitation."

The TLP was officially banned on 20 July, and its property taken over by the government. The TKP promptly protested the ban, claiming that more than 500,000 Turkish workers, students, and intellectuals in West Europe, and the "democratic organizations" set up by them, condemned the action ("Our Radio," 23 July). The Dev-Genc was, by this time, also outlawed, and the TKP appealed to leftist youth "not to heed the appeal of the martial law administration to surrender," "not to seek personal heroism, but to work collectively," and, if apprehended, "not to act in a way that would damage [their] revolutionary honor," but to "let the courtroom be a platform for accusations." Under a new slogan, "Fewer Words and More Deeds," they were urged to agitate for university autonomy, a general labor strike, and the organization of a mass resistance movement among rural peasants. (*Ibid.*, 10 August.) A number of constitutional amendments, ratified by the National Assembly on 6 September, gave the government stricter control over universities, youth organizations, labor unions, and the communications media, and provided for the curtailment of civil liberties when national security was at stake. The premier declared that no basic constitutional rights and freedoms would be affected by the amendments; "Only extremist movements leading to Marxism, Leninism, or Maoism have been banned." (Ankara radio, 6 September.)

Neither the government nor the TKP offered any figures on the number of TKP members included among those arrested during the year, but there were probably enough to disrupt the party's domestic organization. What may have been the most serious blow to the party for some time came in October, when security authorities announced the discovery of a 26-member "clandestine Turkish Communist Party organization" which included university teachers, journalists, writers, student leaders, and artists. Demir himself was one of several journalists against whom legal proceedings were initiated in May on charges of intent to "overthrow the economic and social foundations" in Turkey and to "establish the domination of one social class over other social classes." Demir was charged in absentia. (Ankara radio, 12 May.) There was an uncorroborated report, in *Hurriyet* (12 June) that Demir had entered Turkey in March by boat from the Black Sea and stayed briefly.

International Views and Positions. Almost completely dependent upon the U.S.S.R. for its continued existence, the TKP has followed an unswervingly pro-Soviet line. The main thrust of TKP propaganda continued in 1971 to be toward undermining Turkish-U.S. relations with a view to the abrogation of bilateral agreements and the liquidation of U.S. military installations in Turkey. The United States was presented as seeking to "break up the national liberation struggles in the Middle East and the Mediterranean, establish puppet government in these countries, extend greater help to the Israeli militants, and organize the oil areas in these countries on a stronger basis" ("Our Radio," 6 March.) Demir told delegates to the congress of the (East) German Socialist Unity Party in June of "imperialist" efforts to "turn Turkey into an unwitting tool of the NATO war policy and drag Turkey into economic destruction and a national catastrophe." According to this contention, Turkey had concluded an agreement with West Germany under which weapons of mass extermination would be stored in the eastern provinces of Turkey "in compliance with the wishes of West German and American imperialists." The alleged agreement was said to constitute an obstacle to the efforts of the Soviet Union and other socialist countries to have strategic, biological, and chemical weapons destroyed, and to be "proof that Turkey is the lackey of dominant fascist circles." (Our Radio, 25 and 29 June.)

Similarly, the TKP charged in July that Greece and Turkey had reached an accord on Cyprus which would "turn the island into an American and NATO base" for "provocation against the Soviet Union and other socialist countries" and "attack against the Arab states." The Soviets' "gigantic peace force" in the Mediterranean was, however, in the TKP view, "ready to stand up to the imperialist attacks and to oppose policies designed to undermine the independence of the peoples." (*Ibid.*, 18 July.) The Turkish communists continued, paradoxically, to show strong support for the Makarious government and for AKEL, the communist party on Cyprus, which is almost completely Greek in composition. The TKP professes to view the Cyprus problem as one not of a fundamentally internal origin but something engendered and perpetuated by "U.S.-Nato maneuvers." When the problem was referred to the United Nations in September because of a deadlock in the inter-Cypriot talks, the TKP charged that Turkey, as a U.S. "stooge," had "secured" the deadlock so as to advance the partition of Cyprus between Turkey and Greece. The governmental "junta" in Greece, for its part, was said to have "sent [U.S.] Central Intelligence Agency agent Grivas"—the former commander of the Greek Cypriot National Guard who was recalled to Athens in 1967—to "start clashes between the Turkish and Greek communities on the island for this purpose." (*Ibid.*, 22 September.)

The visit to Turkey, in October, of U.S. Vice-President Agnew was said by the TKP to have resulted in a new bilateral agreement providing for the "free" entry of the U.S. Sixth Fleet into Turkish ports. "Dictated" by the United States, the agreement had "encountered no opposition or resistance from either the government or NATO's and CENTO's local collaborators, the army." (*Ibid.*, 14 October.) The party called for an "independent foreign policy free from pacts" as opposed to the existing one "controlled by generals" and "established to serve imperialism's global strategy" (*ibid.*, 30 November). Turkey's support for Pakistan in the war with India was said by the TKP to have "again demonstrated" the government's willingness to "turn foreign policy into an instrument serving imperialist provocations." In its view, the war was the result of imperialist efforts to undermine the "relaxation" that had taken place in Europe and in the world at large by creating new tensions, and to divert the attention of world public opinion from the war in Indochina. (*Ibid.*)

Main Party Media. The most effective medium for the dissemination of TKP propaganda is a clandestine radio station, Bizim Tadvo (Our Radio), which transmits from East Germany to Turkey and to the several thousand Turkish workers in West Germany and other western European countries. TKP delcarations and documents appear in special supplements to *Yeni Cag* (New Age), the Turkish-language edition of the *World Marxist Review*. The party occasionally issues pamphlets which are circulated clandestinely in Turkey.

Valerie Bloom

MIDDLE EAST
AND AFRICA

Algeria

In 1920 when the Algerian Communist Party (Parti Communiste Algérien) was founded, it formed part of the French Communist Party (PCF). After October 1936 it existed independently. In December 1962, five months after the declaration of Algerian independence, the party was banned by the Algerian government under President Ahmed Ben Bella. In 1964, party members were instructed by the PCA leadership to join the ruling Algerian party, the National Liberation Front (Front de Libération Nationale; FLN), and the PCA seemingly disappeared as an autonomous organization. After the June 1965 coup which brought Houari Boumedienne to power, dissident left-wing FLN elements joined with some communist militants to create an illegal opposition group, the Popular Resistance Organization (Organisation de la Résistance Populaire; ORP). On 26 January 1966, the ORP became the Socialist Vanguard Party (Parti de l'Avant-Garde Socialiste; PAGS) which, according to Henri Alleg, one of its leading spokesmen consisted of "communists, and former militants of the FLN who were drawn to Marxism-Leninism" (*Daily World*, New York, 16 January 1969.)

During 1969 and 1970 party strength was estimated at about 750 members. Because of restrictive government policies towards the PAGS, it is unlikely that membership increased in 1971. Support for the PAGS mainly comes from the PCF and among expatriate Algerians. The population of Algeria is 13,000,000 (estimated 1971).

Party Affairs and Leadership. As a banned party, the PAGS has had limited influence on Algerian affairs. In the past it operated clandestinely through the General Union of Algerian Workers (Union Générale des Travailleurs Algériens; UGTA) and the National Union of Algerian Students (Union Nationale des Etudiants Algériens; UNEA). However, in 1968, the former came under government control, and on 15 January 1971 the latter was dissolved by the Interior Ministry on grounds that it had "served as a cover for a counter-revolutionary movement" (*Arab Report and Record*, 1-15 January).

The struggle with the UNEA was a bitter one, involving student demonstrations, a strike by most of the 13,000 students at the University of Algiers, and at least eight student arrests. Although student unrest had been endemic throughout 1970, decisive government action was postponed until student complicity with a Marxist-Leninist group had been "proven," and after a UNEA statement dated 18 December 1970 had condemned the government and called for "elimination of elements hostile to progressive action [which were hindering] the four year plan [1969-73], agrarian and educational reforms, and arabization." Moreover student militants accused the government of being "anti-democratic and provocative," and of stifling mass initiative. (*L'Humanité*, Paris, 6 January 1971). Approximately a month later, the government moved against the student body.

By 23 September the students had been released, and Algeria's three universities "now seemed free of the student unrest to which they had been subject during the past year" (*Le Monde*, Paris,

23 September). Dissolution of the UNEA marked the end of clandestine interference in Algerian domestic affairs by the PAGS.

Consequently, little is known about the present PAGS leadership or organization. In 1969, three known party leaders—Bachir Hadj Ali (a former secretary of the PCA), Hocine Zahouane, and Mohammed Harbi, who were leading left-wingers before Boumedienne's advent to power—were transferred from prison to house arrest. On 1 November 1970, along with about 100 prisoners granted amnesty on Algeria's National Day, these militants regained their freedom. Also granted amnesty in 1970 but barred from the cities of Algiers, Oran, Constantine, and Annaba, were Paul Caballero (former secretary of the PCA in Oran), Brouzid Bouallak, and Jacques Salort; the last two had been associated with the now defunct PCA daily *Alger Républicain* (*ibid.*, 6 March 1970). Since their release, little is known of activities by the party leadership, which also included expatriate Larbi Boukhali (former PCA secretary-general, who as late as 1970 was the PAGS main spokesman.)

Domestic Views and Activities. Largely due to restrictive government policies, PAGS domestic activities have decreased, but during 1971 the party continued to criticize the government's "repressive policies." Voicing their criticisms through *Al-Akhbar*, the Lebanese Communist Party paper, the PAGS railed against the Algerian government for its "arbitrary police actions" and cited "the April persecution of Comrade 'Abd al-Hamid as Zayn," one of the PAGS leaders, as a case in point. The communiqué concluded with an appeal to "Algerian workers and everyone opposed to imperialism to thwart the acts of injustice and repression against democracy [and] to step up vigilance in the face of imperialist and reactionary attempts." (*Al-Akhbar*, Beirut, 23 May.)

Yet two months prior to this attack, the PAGS had voiced approval of the government's seizure, in February, of over 51 percent interest in two French oil companies operating in Algeria and its nationalizing of the companies' interests in natural gas resources and in oil and gas pipelines. The PAGS claimed that the government "had exercised its legitimate and sovereign rights," and urged "militants, sympathizers, and anti-imperialists and progressivists ... to support the government." By arguing that "the best form of attack against imperialist enterprises ... is unity of action" and not persecution of "militants, anti-imperialists, and socialists," the PAGS may have been trying to establish a rapprochement with the government, perhaps even hoping for recognition. (*L'Humanité*, 26 March.).

The ambivalence of the PAGS situation has been further complicated by the government's improved relations with China (NCNA, 30 October) and Cuba (*Bohemia*, Havana, 29 October), together with Soviet Premier Kosygin's visit to Algeria (4-8 October), which tangibly strengthened Algerian-Soviet relations (*Arab Report and Record*, 1-15 October). Moreover, since the Soviet Union is apparently prepared to overlook the non-communist nature of the FLN (which, although socialist, owes more to Islam than to Marxism), provided that it operates in favor of Soviet policies, the pro-Soviet PAGS may have no option but to follow the Soviet line. Thus the government through restrictive measures, on the one hand, has limited PAGS activities, and through its more "militant" posture (oil nationalization) and overtures to leading communist-ruled governments, on the other, has encroached on PAGS policies.

International Views and Party Activities. On the international front, the PAGS apparently had a quiet year in 1971. Contrary to previous practice, there was no Algerian delegation at the Twenty-fourth Congress of the Communist Party of the Soviet Union, in March-April. Neither were PAGS members present at the congress of the Socialist Unity Party of (East) Germany, in June. Through the Beirut communist newspaper, however, they reiterated their distaste for "imperialism," "Zionism," "reactionary fascists," and "the Hashimite army [which] was using American tanks to kill Palestinian people," and reaffirmed their attachment to Arab unity.

The PAGS denounced Libya's role in the abortive Sudanese coup (19-22 July), and the execution of a number of Sudanese communists by the Numairi government. Claiming that "the executed Sudanese officers were among the most sincere [and] devoted to their country's national interests, [and] to the Arab cause in general," they declared that the sacrifices of their "Sudanese brothers" were not in vain. (*Al-Akhbar*, 4 September.)

On the European front the PAGS reaffirmed its amity with its staunchest supporters, the French Communist Party (PCF), in a joint statement issued 24 March. In the communiqué, the two parties exchanged fraternal sentiments based on "mutual respect," "equal rights, noninterference, and mutual interest." They moreover agreed to intensify their attempts to consolidate "the combat alliance between the French working class and Algerian democratic forces." The PAGS expressed appreciation for the PCF's support against the "capitalist petroleum companies" and its defense of the material and moral interests of Algerian immigrant workers in France ... against capitalist exploitation, discrimination, and racialist campaigns.

For its part, the PCF endorsed the PAGS' efforts to create a "broad democratic and popular front of all the progressive and anti-imperialist forces" and its support of the Algerian government's oil takeover, relating this to Algeria's growing economic independence. The PCF similarly encouraged the PAGS to continue agitation for success of the four-year plan, agrarian reforms, and the raising of mass urban and rural living standards. (*L'Humanité*, 24 March.)

Publications. The official organ of the PAGS is a clandestine, irregular newspaper *La Voix du Peuple*; its Arabic version is *Saout Ech-Chaâb*.

University of Maryland   B. Marie Perinbam

Iran

Organized communist activity in Iran dates back to 1920, the year of the founding of the Communist Party of Iran. The present communist party, called the Party of the Masses of Iran (Hizb-e Tudeh Iran), or more popularly the Tudeh Party, was founded in October 1941, after an interval of ten years during which no organized communist party existed in the country. The Tudeh Party was banned by the government in 1949, following an assassination attempt on the Shah's life. Nevertheless, overt activities continued until the fall of Premier Mohammed Mosadeq in August 1953. In 1954 suppression of communist activities was ordered, and thousands of Tudeh Party members and collaborators were arrested. Some leaders escaped into exile in Eastern Europe, managed to regroup, and assumed direction of party affairs from headquarters in East Germany. A pro-Chinese faction split off from the pro-Soviet exiled party in 1965 and called itself the Revolutionary Organization of the Tudeh Party. Additional splintering has occurred since.

Illegal, suppressed, and with most of its members in exile, the Tudeh Party has negligible political significance in Iran. Estimates of its total membership have dropped to approximately 500. The population of Iran is 28,662,000 (estimated 1970).

Leadership and Organization. In 1971 Reza Radmanesh was relieved of his duties as chairman of the Tudeh Party. His ouster was confirmed by the fourteenth plenum of the Central Committee early in the year. Evaluating the findings from a previously ordered investigation of the party's organization, the Committee found serious "shortcomings and deficiencies" and voted for various changes. These included the promotion of Iradj Eskanderi to first secretary and 'Abd al-Samad Kambakhsh to second secretary; both men had previously held important party offices. At the end of the year no announcement had been made of a successor to Kambakhsh, who died of a heart attack in November.

Party Internal Affairs. The Central Committee report on the fourteenth plenum claimed that the meeting was held with "high principles prevailing" and that it was "able to solve problems with decisiveness and unanimity of views" (Radio "Iran Courier," 12 February 1971). The report, however, revealed serious ideological dissension within the party. This had become increasingly apparent the previous year, when fears were expressed for party survival, and "sectarianism," "emotionalism," and "false revolutionism" among its members were blamed for many problems.

The report referred to "adventurist methods" and "evidence of infiltration" by agents of the government security organizations (SAVAK), and to party members' "lack of political awareness and underestimation of the danger posed by the enemy." Reza Radmanesh was charged with "unjustifiable complacency" which had permitted a man called Eslami to engage in unauthorized activities, detrimental to the party. According to the report, Eslami had incorrectly appraised the country as ready for revolution and had secretly collaborated with General Taimur Bakhtiar, the former head of SAVAK. (See *YICA*, 1971, p. 280.)

The plenum report was not the last word on the subject. A few days later, the Central Committee in an open letter to "all democratic parties and organizations and all the democrats of the world" declared: "The Iranian Tudeh Party Central Committee is certain that no member of the Iranian Tudeh Party could have taken part in adventurist activities contrary to the party's political policy, unless that member himself was a provocateur element" (Radio "Iran Courier," 17 February). Eskanderi in a radio interview denied that Tudeh officials, including Reza Radmanesh, had ever collaborated with Bakhtiar (*ibid.*, 3 May).

The party tried to ignore the case of Mahmud Panahian, whose expulsion was announced by the Secretariat on 29 January. He was charged with engaging in "political activities on his own initiative" (*ibid.*, 13 February). No further details were given by the communists, but SAVAK provided its version a few weeks later. It claimed to have proof that both Radmanesh and Panahian had been victimized by their own party for failure to implement collaboration with Bakhtiar, after cooperation had been authorized by a full meeting of the Central Committee at Leipzig, East Germany, a few months earlier (*Kayhan*, Teheran, 4 April).

The fourteenth plenum declared that it was the urgent and foremost duty of the party to determine a "correct policy free from leftism and sectarianism and adventurism on the one hand, and rightism and submissiveness on the other." It demanded that the party leadership establish discipline and united uctivity, remove from its ranks "undisciplined, hesitant, and unfit members," and adopt methods of criticism and self-criticism and review of decisions. (Radio "Iran Courier," 12 February.)

On various occasions the Tudeh Party proclaimed a "struggle for democratic freedoms" as the universal demand of all working classes and promised leadership in this struggle "no matter what the cost." It advocated mass organization as the best road to revolution (*ibid.*, 24 May) and warned against confusing democracy with anarchy, which "puts society on a retrogressive path" (*ibid.*, 18 March); it nevertheless urged readiness to implement revolutionary change "when the masses no longer wish to continue the previous way of life" (*ibid.*, 29 August).

Domestic Attitudes and Activities. The Tudeh Party continued in 1971 to be critical of almost every major governmental development or plan, and charged that all were meant to strengthen the Shah's "despotic powers" and to "defend the throne at any cost and draw blood of those who rise against it" (Radio "Iran Courier," 8 February). When the Shah gave a major speech to inaugurate a new session of the Majlis (parliament), the clandestine radio reported that the "ceremonies were planned so that the position of the Majlis representatives would be lowered to the level of humble workers and the Shah's position would be raised to God's, so that every creature in the nution would know that only one individual's determination rules the country" (*ibid.*, 1 September). The speech itself was scorned for remaining "almost silent" on three major domestic issues—the army, the security organization, and the government's propaganda apparatus (*ibid.*, 3 September).

The communists have long called high expenditures for arms an obstacle to Iran's progress. After the inaugural speech they charged that the Shah had apparently forgotten to mention the figure of 250 billion rials, approved for strengthening the armed forces over the next four years, and contrasted this outlay with 86 billion rials to expand mining and industry (*ibid.*).

The communists similarly accused the Shah of forgetting to mention the activities of SAVAK and charged him with heavy responsibility for the "crimes committed by this murderous organization." They alleged that he had tried to divert the people's attention from the government's "anti-democratic measures" by engaging in intense propaganda campaigns against such enemies as the Tudeh Party and by repeating his "notorious lies that every form of freedom exists except the freedom to commit treason." (*Ibid.*) At the end of the year the Tudeh Central Committee in a special statement denounced the government's "policy of terror and the illegal activities of SAVAK" and cited "unlawful detentions, secret trials, executions, and other oppressive treatment" (*ibid.*, 3 December).

Representing itself as "the persistent defender of the hardworking farmers' rights," the Tudeh Party found the government's extensive land reform program wanting and "undemocratic" and demanded that all land still owned by big landlords, the royal family, the government, or religious institutions be distributed to the peasants debt-free (*ibid.*, 21 November).

Throughout the year, the communists criticized the government for many other economic policies. They likened optimistic official pronouncements to "commercial advertisements," and emphasized that even the major Teheran papers managed to convey the opinion that Iran's economy was not based on a healthy foundation (*ibid.*, 14 September). Calling the increasing dependence on income from "imperialist oil monopolies" extremely dangerous, they demanded that the oil nationalization law be implemented and the National Iranian Oil Company enter world markets independently. At the time of the U.S. dollar crisis, they urged that Iran's economic destiny be separated from the fate of foreign exchange and the dollar, and that the country strive to expand relations with the communist-ruled states, whose economies had "never known crises." (*Ibid.*, 21 August). In general the Tudeh Party called for cuts in the military budget, a decrease in imports, and elimination of "unproductive government expenses."

The communists alleged that the July parliamentary elections had created "rage among the majority of the population" because legitimate democratic rights were being trampled by meaningless "theatrics." The clandestine radio, declaring "the elections behind the people's back and against the people have ended before even starting" (*ibid.*, 22 June) claimed that the results were published before the voting. When a government reorganization occurred in September, the communists referred to "a new cabinet with an old policy" (*ibid.*, 14 September).

The lavish preparations for the 2,500th anniversary of the Persian monarchy in October aroused strong Tudeh opposition against the extravagance and costs of the seven-day affair. They were cited as the immediate cause of a strike at Teheran University, which eventually resulted in battles with the police and the deaths of four persons (*Intercontinental Press*, New York, 14 June).

Government security measures for the celebrations were described by the newspaper *Le Monde* (Paris, 12 October): "Hundreds—some say thousands—of people have been arrested or placed under house arrest for the celebration period. Universities and secondary schools have been closed to foil the strike appeals launched by anonymous groups ... Parents of young militants who are in hiding or who have joined the underground are being held as hostages."

International Views and Activities. the Tudeh Party attributed many of Iran's problems to the "aggressive aims of the imperialists" and stressed the need for a "unified anti-imperialist struggle." (Radio "Iran Courier," 10 August). It asked what enemy Iran might face to require hundreds of tanks from Great Britain, jet airplanes from the United States, and helicopters from Italy. "The clear fact that no danger threatens Iran's borders is known to everybody; they have never been more quiet, and if the Iranian government itself does not create intrigues, the situation could be improved even more." (*Ibid.*, 11 August.)

The party proposed that improvement begin with Iran's withdrawal from the Central Treaty Organization and the expulsion of the British from the Persian Gulf. It described CENTO as an "imperialist, colonialist alliance created by Britain and the United States to impose colonial domination, in the guise of countering the bogey of a communist threat." Accusing Britain of converting its "ostensible withdrawal" from the Gulf into continued domination of the area both economically and militarily, the communists in the summer demanded an "end to British intervention in the domestic affairs of all the nations and amirates of the Persian Gulf," thus granting those states the right to self-determination. On the other hand the Tudeh supported the Shah's claim to the Gulf islands of Abu Musa and the Greater and Lesser Tunbs and called for their return to Iran as a "British duty," in spite of the claim to sovereignty over the disputed lands by two small sheikdoms. When Iranian armed forces seized the islands on 30 November, Tudeh reaction was ambiguous, but inclined to be critical of the move: "By embarking on this adventure, Iran gives up a great many fundamental things which it needs for its economic and social growth, that is, security, tranquillity and capital, without receiving anything important in return." (*Ibid.*, 17 July and 1 December.)

U.S. motives in the Persian Gulf area were also severely criticized by Iran's communists, who reported the application of a "quasi-Nixon doctrine aimed at throwing the Asians at each other's throats, for the benefit of the colonial intentions of the USA," in order to sow discord or even to create military clashes for the benefit of British colonial policy and imperialism in the area (*ibid.*, 2 July).

On 7 July, Radio "Iran Courier," in citing foreign press reports about the visits to Israel, Turkey, and Iran by Richard Helms, director of the U.S. Central Intelligence Agency, denounced the CIA as the "direct supervisor of the Iranian security organization" and alleged that U.S. spies were being sent by the CIA in the guise of "advisers" to "teach their Iranian colleagues how to create an atmosphere of oppression, persecute patriots, use brutal torture to obtain confessions, and employ various methods of committing murder." When the "Pentagon Papers" were published, the clandestine radio commented: "There is no guarantee whatsoever that the U.S. imperialists might not create an incident similar to that of the Tonkin Gulf in the Persian Gulf, if they saw their interests threatened" (*ibid.*, 21 June).

After the announcement of President Nixon's proposed visit to mainland China, the Tudeh Party stated that secret relations between the U.S. government and Mao Tse-tung had existed since the mid 1950s and suvgested that there was connivance to "draw China away from the Soviet Union" (*ibid.*, 7 July). Mao Tse-tung's role was denounced by the Tudeh Party also on occasion of the fiftieth anniversary of the Chinese Communist Party: "It is the duty of every true communist and every Marxist-Leninist party to take an active part in the struggle against the Maoist group's pseudo-revolutionary petty-bourgeois views" (*ibid.*, 1 July). However, on occasion of the visit to China by Princess Ashraf, the twin sister of the Shah, the Tudeh Party came out in favor of diplomatic and trade relations with China, and stressed that it had frequently advocated such a move in the past (*ibid.*, 13, 24, and 27 April). When recognition materialized in August, the party commented that "the People's Republic of China had to be recognized," but expressed "uneasiness" because of the "recent vast international activity regarding China" (*ibid.*, 17 August).

The Tudeh Party also favored recognition of the German Democratic Republic, and objected to the Shah's reasons for withholding recognition, which he expressed in a West German television interview (reported by Radio Teheran, 7 June). The Shah objected to the location of the communist party's headquarters and clandestine radio transmitter in East Germany and to East Germany's "inappropriate position" regarding the Arvand Rud (Shatt al-'Arab)—the contested waterway which is part of the border between Iran and Iraq.

Iranian communists denounced the "slaughter" of communists in Sudan which followed the July coup and countercoup in that country. They were elated with Bahrain's declaration of independence in August, but opposed Iran's support for President Yahya Khan of Pakistan, whom they held guilty of crimes against East Pakistan. (Radio "Iran Courier," 16 September).

Publications. Tudeh publications are illegal in Iran and are printed in Eastern Europe. On 8 February 1971, the party Secretariat issued a special statement to the effect that all official announcements and documents would be published exclusively in the organ *Mardom* (People) or the magazine *Donya* (World) or broadcast by Radio "Iran Courier." It warned that "any document issued in the name of the Central Committee of the Iranian Tudeh Party, which is not referred to in the press or propaganda organs of the party, has no connection with the Iranian Tudeh Party.'' (Radio "Iran Courier," 18 February.)

* * *

In 1971 political opposition groups in Iran apparently were loosely labeled by the government as communist or communist-inspired. They were suppressed under a law providing punishment for ''acts against the state security or the country's independence.''

Early in the year the Confederation of Iranian Students Abroad—directed from Eastern Europe and long an irritant to the Shah—was declared illegal; anyone remaining a member of any affiliate after 21 March was declared subject to arrest and prosecution upon return to Iran (Radio Teheran, 18 January). Promulgation of the formal ban followed a charge by the Science Ministry that confederation leaders in England, Germany, the United States, Turkey, Italy, France, and Austria were engaged in "anti-Iranian propaganda, spreading lies, and creating agitation and confusion among the students" (*Ayandegan*, Teheran, 4 January). The government also claimed to have proof as to the political adherence of various components of the confederation to one or another of the following: the Tudeh Purty Central Committee, the Revolutionary Organization of the Tudeh Party, the Marxist-Leninist ''Tufan'' group, and the ''National Front,'' characterized as ''imperialist.''

Thirteen political prisoners were executed by a firing squad on 17 March after a secret trial by a military tribunal. According to the government, the accused had worked for a ''subversive network with the aim of overthrowing the political regime in Iran.'' (*Intercontinental Press*, 5 April.) Other sources reported that the thirteen had participated in a guerrilla attack on a police station on 8 February in the village of Siakhal, Gilan Province. According to a French source, the executed men were believed to have belonged to a ''group of 150 pro-Chinese communists who were operating in the mountains'' (*Le Monde*, Paris, 19 and 21-22 March). When General Ziaddin Farsiu, head of the military tribunal, died from wounds suffered in an assassination attempt in April, officials attributed his death to ''remnants of a communist guerrilla gang.''

Some of the groups listed by the government as part of the subversive network, came forth with their own comments. Tufan (Storm), the pro-Chinese Marxist-Leninist Organization of Iran, for instance, issued a joint declaration with its Belgian counterpart after a meeting in Brussels. It criticized the Iranian Tudeh Party for having ''sunk progressively deeper into the morass of revisionism and opportunism,'' and for having abandoned its contact with the masses and direction of their actions in favor of playing the role of ''His Majesty's opposition.'' The statement praised the Chinese Communist Party as an ''invincible bastion of socialism'' and Mao Tse-tung as ''the great educator of the proletariat.'' (*Clarté*, Brussels, 19 March.)

The Revolutionary Organization of the Tudeh Party (ROTP) publishes a monthly organ, *Setare-Sorkh* (Red Star), in Rome. According to the Trotskyist *Intercontinental Press* (26 July), the ROTP found itself wrestling with contradictions concerning Maoism. The April issue of the party organ, noting that many Iranians were puzzled by Peking's invitation to Princess Ashraf, explained that the ''imperialists and their stooges'' were being forced by the revolutionary masses of the world to recognize the Chinese government. Predicting that the Shah would try to sabotage this development, the ROTP implied that it was the duty of Iranian revolutionists to pressure the Shah to draw ever closer to China. This position was justified by the claim that the Chinese government had never subordinated the interests of revolution in any country to its diplomatic needs.

Information about a group called the ''Council for Revolution in Iran'' comes mostly from non-communist sources. Referring to this group, a spokesman for SAVAK stated that certain ''enemies of the White Revolution'' had fled the country and been granted asylum in Iraq, where from the safety of exile they planned to stage ''terrorist activities and sabotage'' along the western borders of Iran. He identified the group's leader as Mahmud Panahian and the key men in the organization as Ali Mohammadi, Mahmud Baik Haidari, Issa Zabihi, and Hamad Kalashi. (*Kayhan*, 25 April).

Edith Wyden

Iraq

The Iraqi Communist Party (al-Hizb al Shuyu'i al-'Iraqi; CI) was founded in 1934. It has never enjoyed legal status, although periods of severe repression by authorities have alternated with periods when communism was tolerated or even encouraged. In 1971 the regime of Major General Ahmad Hasan al-Bakr continued the vacillating attitude toward the communists that it has displayed since assuming power after a military coup in July 1968. However, late in the year the fate of al-Bakr himself seemed uncertain, as the civilian faction of the Ba'th Party under Saddam Husain al-Takriti, vice-chairman of the Regional Command Council (which exercises both legislative and executive function) and assistant secretary-general of the Ba'th, appeared to have gained the upper hand in a power struggle.

The ICP is believed to have about 2,000 members. There are an additional 10,000 to 20,000 supporters or sympathizers, who are selective about the communist causes they espouse, but over the years have backed enough of them to have made the ICP one of the more influential of the Arab communist parties. The population of Iraq is 9,400,00 (estimated 1970.

Leadership and Party Internal Affairs. The ICP held its Second Congress in September 1970 and reelected 'Aziz Muhammad—also known as Nazim 'Ali—as first secretary. The outcome of other elections was not announced. Presumably Rahim 'Ajinah, 'Abd al-Razzaq al-Safi, Zaki Khayri, and Makram al-Talabani, known as key members of the Central Committee in 1970, were able to maintain their posts.

Problems of internal dissension—a preoccupation of the ICP since the fall of 1967, when the party split in a violent upheaval into hostile "Central Committee" and "Central Command" factions—were downgraded in significance in 1971 as Iraqui communists tried to cope with external difficulties. 'Aziz al-Hajj, the originator of the schism and subsequent leader of the "Central Command" wing, surfaced only briefly to discuss the basis of the dispute. In a letter to the Tunisian weekly *Jeune Afrique* (9 February), al-Hajj accused the leadership of the Central Committee of "haughty indifference towards the masses," "having no serious revolutionary theory," and "playing the game of the Soviet communist party, accepting all its analyses and all its positions in order to disguise its own failure to set up and apply a coherent revolutionary policy." He denied that his Central Command was "pro-Chinese" and described its position as being closer to that of the Korean or Vietnamese communists and supporting both of the "two great fraternal parties." Although he had been imprisoned in 1969, al-Hajj dealt gently with the Ba'th Party and credited it with "important changes" and improvements since 1968.

The clearly dominant ICP faction under Muhammad was less interested in engaging in dialogue with al-Hajj than in publicizing the government's "terrorist campaign" against members of the communist party and use of "various methods of psychological and physical torture which contravene human and legal principles." Specifically, the ICP cited the fate of two prominent communists,

'Aziz Hamid and Kazim al-Jasim, who allegedly had been arrested and tortured to death. (*al-Nida*, Beirut, 21 January.) A few months later, "atrocities" over a widening number of cities and rural areas were reported; in the town of al-Najaf alone, 162 political arrests were said to have taken place during a short period of time (*ibid.*, 21 April). A real cause celèbre was the case of Thabit Habib al-'Ani, a member of the ICP Central Committee, who allegedly was kidnaped by "Ba'thist security men" in the streets of Baghdad without any indication of his fate or whereabouts thereafter (*ibid.*, 14 May). Confusion—a fundamental characteristic of relations between communists and the government in 1971—was heightened by a report in the Lebanese daily *Beirut* (2 June) that the "missing man had been appointed to an important post in the government department of sequestered funds and property." The facts in the "kidnaping" case or the role played in it by Iraq's pro-communist minister of justice, 'Aziz Sharif, remained elusive, but conceivably this was n example of the government strategy of mixing conciliatory gestures toward the communists with actions formulated to keep the movement from gaining power.

The communists tried to enlist the support of foreign communist parties in protesting the persecution of their comrades and other "progressives." The communist parties of the Soviet Union, Italy, and Great Britain were among those that responded positively, but their efforts of assistance boomeranged when the Ba'th Party issued a statement advising the ICP to refrain from the use of "dubious methods" and instead to be "frank and clear," because the government of Iraq would not permit pressure or infringement of its sovereignty by any foreign power or communist party (*al-Kifah*, Baghdad, 12 March). In spite of the warning, the communist parties of Syria, Lebanon, and Jordan issued a joint denunciation in May of the "kidnaping" of al-'Ani. Later the French Communist weekly *France Nouvelle* (Paris, 8-14 June) published an interview with a leading ICP member, Kamal Bikri, who accused the Ba'th Party of attempting to monopolize all the organs of the administration and of crushing opposition. In addition, the French party newspaper *L'Humanité* (Paris, 15 June) printed the text of an ICP Central Committee statement on the alleged repression of communists and progressives including a list of those "tortured to death" and those whose fate after arrest was unknown.

Domestic Attitudes and Activities. For approximatly two years the ruling Ba'th Party and the communists have negotiated on their possible cooperation in a "national front" government. By 1971 it had become clear that such cooperation would hinge on the resolution of apparently irreconcilable differences. Although the communists had long clamored for a national front government of "progressive" forces, their insistence on equality clashed with the government's condition that all participants recognize the leadership role of the Ba'th Party. Particular controversy swirled around the proposals for a 100-member "national council," the first parliamentary body to be envisioned since the monarchy was ended in 1958. When communist demands for general elections were rejected, the clandestine ICP newspaper *Tariq al-Sha'b* (quoted in *al-Nida*, 21 February) charged that "the way the national council is to be formed has come as a big shock to the Iraqi people"; that it would be "nothing more than a consultative body to the Regional Command Council" and hence could "never be a substitute for an elected parliament."

As the year went on, the ICP appeared to grow more anxious to place the blame for failure to form a national front on the Ba'th Party. 'Aziz Muhammad, in an interview published in *al-Akhbar* (Beirut, 24 July), asserted that his party had not closed the door on cooperation with the Ba'thists and that it had "never backed political activities that could jeopardize the formation of a national front." An agreement could have been achieved, he asserted, "if the Ba'thists had not engaged in continuous unpublicized and unjustified campaigns of repression." The Ba'th Party, somewhat later in the year, took a new approach, intimating that a national front had become a necessity to foil "plots." Its party organ, *al-Thawrah* (Baghdad, 11 October), declared that "colonialist and reactionary forces" would not give up their "conspiracies against the revolution" unless they were "finally defeated by a progressive national unity front" under Ba'th leadership.

After months of charges and countercharges, the political climate improved in November when the government announced its National Action Charter. Meant to provide a basis for the establishment of a national front, the draft charter contained the promise of "democratic freedoms for the people and their patriotic and progressive forces, including the freedom of political parties" (Radio Baghdad, 15 November). ICP reaction was contained in a special statement (dated 27 November and published in *al-Nida*, 8 December), which referred to the proposed charter as "a good basis for national cooperation" and indicated communist willingness to enter into "direct and serious" discussions. The ICP praised the charter's "anti-imperialist character," its "progressive program for economic and social transformation," its "complete alignment with the socialist countries," and its "affirmation of a peaceful and democratic solution of the Kurdish problem based on the 11 March [1970] declaration" (see below). The statement also contained demands for an end to "all forms of political oppression" or "restrictions on democratic freedoms" as prerequisite to communist negotiations with the government.

At its congress in September 1970 the ICP had pointed out a number of positive aspects of governmental policies and had stressed its own fairness in granting all credit due. In 1971, however, the communists observed a "general deterioration of the regime's policies." The French communist newspaper *L'Humanité* (15 June) detailed the following adverse developments, excerpted from a statement forwarded by the ICP: "Continuation and justification of repression; concentration of power in the hands of a small group of Ba'th leaders; the nature of the alliance with the Kurdish democrats; the government's attitude towards the Palestinian resistance when it was attacked by the Jordanian regime in September 1970; the signing of an agreement with the petroleum monopolies which ties Iraq's hands for five years; the weakening of ties with the Soviet Union; the growing poverty of the working classes; and increasing taxes and unemployment."

Dealing with the purely domestic issues on the list of complaints, the ICP considered "equity among cooperating partners" a prerequisite to all major decisions and demanded that the government grant the "right of organizational existence, ideological independence, and freedom of political action" to all nationalist forces (*al-Akhbar*, 25 July). The advocacy of "equity"—besides recalling the cause of the breakdown of the dialogue with the Ba'th Party concerning the national front—seemed to imply a certain amount of animosity toward the Kurds. This was a strange development since the communists were instrumental in negotiating the agreement of 11 March 1970 which ended the civil war in the north by its promise of Kurdish autonomy. They acknowledged that the Kurds had scored "partial gains" since then, but they appeared to be alarmed by the growing collaboration between the Ba'th Party and the Kurdish Democratic Party in the early part of the year. The communists thus seemed to be subtly reproaching the Kurds for indifference toward the communist cause when they claimed that "democracy" in Iraq was "indivisible" and basic to a proper solution of the Kurdish problem (*ibid.*, 23 May). Later in the year, after an assassination attempt on the life of Kurd leader Mulla Mustafa Barazani created suspicion between the Kurds and the Iraqi ernment, and some military clashes occurred in the north, the communists stopped questioning Kurdish motives.

International Views and Contacts. In March 1971 a plenary meeting of the ICP Central Committee discussed developments in the Arab world and international issues. The decisions were published in the April issue of *Tariq al-Sha'b* and revolved mainly around the Arab-Israeli conflict. The ICP called on all Arabs to "liquidate Israeli aggression" by forcing implementation of the U.N. Security Council resolution of 1967, stipulating Israel's withdrawal from all occupied territories.

The party further advocated formation of a united Arab front in support of the "just national aspirations of the Palestinian people, including their right to self-determination.

The plenum considered the Arab situation in the Middle East to be "once again deteriorating" due to U.S. encouragement of Israeli noncompliance with the U.N. resolution and to U.S.-Israeli insistence on "unacceptable conditions intended to foil peaceful efforts" under the pretext of the non-negotiability of "secure borders." Iraq's government was held responsible for the "serious situation created by the withdrawal of Iraqi forces from positions confronting the Israeli aggression and for driving the Palestinian resistance into an unequal battle with the Jordanian authorities." The plenum approved the proposed federation of Egypt, Sudan, Libya, and Syria (later reduced to a tripartite federation without Sudan) and suggested an expansion of the federation to "include all the liberated Arab states, on a democratic basis." (*Ibid.*)

Several joint documents were issued in 1971 by the communist parties of Iraq, Syria, Lebanon, and Jordan. One document protested the moves by the "reactionary element in Jordan to liquidate the Palestine liberation movement" and its resort to "outright brutality" to crush the guerrillas, adding: "It should be perfectly clear that the Jordanian authorities' pledge to abide by the Cairo and Amman agreements is only a dodge to mislead public opinion." Efforts to suppress the resistance movement were said to be part of an "imperialist" strategy to split the Arab progressive forces and thus "hamper the formation of an Eastern Front," "weaken Egypt," and prevent Egypt from "eliminating the consequences of [Israeli] aggression." (*WMR*, March.) In 1970, coordinated efforts by the four parties had resulted in the formation of their own commando organization, Ansar al-Silm (see *Jordan*).

Leaders of the four parties reportedly met secretly at Beirut in late July to discuss the situation in Sudan and to express their horror at the "massacre" of Sudanese communists after a countercoup ended their brief assumption of power. Unable to do more than register a protest with the Sudanese government, the Arab communist parties were said to have decided to send consultative delegations to Moscow and Sofia (*Arab World Weekly*, Beirut, 31 July). The ICP had no quarrel with the Ba'th Party over the Sudan events, since the government had been quick in extending support and recognition to the short-lived communist regime (Baghdad radio, 19 July).

The ICP sought Soviet help against persecution of party members with mixed results, because Iraq and the Soviet Union were more intent on improving relations and economic cooperation than in controversy over the status of the Iraqi communists. In an article, "Iraq on the Path of Changes," (*Pravda*, 14 July) praised progress under Ba'th leadership and concluded: "On the whole an understanding of the importance of establishing an atmosphere of genuine trust and cooperation between all the progressive forces is growing in leading Iraqi circles every year." The Soviet newspaper acknowledged the existence of "vestiges of anticommunism" in Iraq, but found them counteracted by communist efforts to "eliminate the negative stratifications of the past by striving for mutual understanding between the revolutionary detachments of the Iraqi people" in the present.

Some observers have interpreted the *Pravda* article as evidence that the Soviets found themselves in an incongruous position following the Twenty-fourth Congress of the Communist Party of the Soviet Union (CPSU). In a speech at the congress, the ICP first secretary had referred to his party's "struggle full of dangers and victims" and declared: "The arrogation of power by any one single force [and the] disenfranchisement of the popular masses and the oppression of the patriotic parties ... can only hamper the use of the enormous assets of our country in the interest of its people" (*Pravda*, 9 April).

No less than three Iraqi delegations—from the ICP, the Ba'th Party, and the Kurdish Democratic Party—were invited to the CPSU congress. This fact, together with the public denunciation by the ICP leader and the further fact that the leader of the Ba'th group failed to deliver his speech, either by choice or coercion, caused understandable unhappiness in the Iraqi government over the developments in Moscow. Retaliation against the ICP at home may have been the cause for a precipitous return trip to Moscow by 'Aziz Muhammad three weeks after the conclusion of the congress. Subjected to backlash at home, the ICP first secretary probably hoped that a bilateral meeting with CPSU representatives and Soviet expressions of solidarity in the Arabs' "struggle against reaction" might alleviate the situation (*ibid.*, 7 May).

Publications. the ICP Central Committee publishes a monthly organ, *Tariq al-Sha'b* (The People's Road), which is distributed clandestinely in Iraq. ICP information is also regularly disseminated by the Lebanese communist publications *al-Nida* and *al-Akhbar*.

Edith Wyden

Israel

The first communist party in Palestine was the Socialist Workers' Party, organized in 1919 and renamed the Palestine Communist Party two years later. In 1948, after Israel became an independent state, the party changed its name to the Communist Party of Israel (Miflago Komunistit Yisraelit; MAKI). In 1965, conflict between Arab and Israeli nationalist elements resulted in a split, with each of the two resulting parties claiming to be "the" communist party of Israel. The basically Jewish and nationalist group retained the party name. The predominantly Arab group called itself the New Communist List (Reshima Komunistit Hadasha; RAKAH), in reference to its separate "list" of candidates for election to Israel's legislative assembly, the Knesset.

The Soviet Union maintained an attitude of fraternal neutrality toward the disputing groups up to the time of the Arab-Israeli war of 1967. When the MAKI supported Israel's official course of action, Soviet leaders announced that the RAKAH alone was truly internationalist and hence the only proper representative of the Israeli working class. All the countries of the Soviet bloc, with the exception of Romania, followed the Soviet lead in severing relations with the MAKI.

Both Israeli communist parties are small. Each has a membership of about 1,000. The population of Israel is 2,900,000 (estimated 1970). The two parties enjoy legal status, but play a marginal role in the politics of the country. In the national elections of October 1969, the MAKI received 15,712 votes (1.15 per cent of the total cast) and kept its one seat in the 120-member Knesset; the RAKAH received 38,827 votes (2.84 per cent) and kept its three seats. The RAKAH has also had some success in placing representatives on a number of municipal councils in recent years; in Nazareth it polled almost 40 per cent of the vote in municipal elections held in 1970

Leadership and Organization. The MAKI held its most recent congress, known as the Sixteenth Convention, late in 1968. Moshe Sneh was elected party chairman and Shmuel Mikunis secretary-general. The eleven-member Politburo—consisting of Sneh, Mikunis, Berl Balti, Eliyahu Drukman, Eliezer Failer, Shmuel Litvak, Ya'akov Zilber, Raoul Teitelbaum, Pinhas Tubin, Esther Vilenska, and Yair Tzeven— was also chose.

The RAKAH's Sixteenth Convention was held early in 1969. Meir Vilner, a Jew, was reelected secretary-general and anmed to the nine-member mixed Arab-Jewish Politburo along with Tawfiq Tubi, Wolf Ehrlich, Uzi Burstein, Emile Habibi, David Khenin, Saliba Khamis, Emile Tuma, and Ruth Lubitsh. Tawfiq Tubi was chosen to head the seven-man Secretariat.

Both parties have made serious efforts to recruit young people. The Young Communist League of Israel, known as BANKI, was the party youth auxiliary before the split, but now is RAKAH-controlled. It appears to be more active than the MAKI's "Young Generation." Both parties also seek to increase their influence over what they term the "democratic organizations" in Israel, but reserve their most determined efforts for strengthening their position within the powerful Israeli labor federation, Histadrut.

259

The MAKI has never quietly accepted its role as an outcast in the international communist movement or its negligible political role within Israel. Shmuel Mikunis expressed MAKI sentiments regarding its status in an address to the Fifteenth Plenum of the Central Committee of his party early in 1971:

> The active support of MAKI, in our country and in the communist movement alike, is still *out of all proportion* to the innovating, patriotic and internationalist role that our Communist Party fulfills on the Israeli soil as well as in the movement of renovation that is expanding among several Communist parties. We have still to be content with a "meritorious deed that yields no profit," because the closure of the gap between overt sympathy and active support of MAKI is an inevitable, but perhaps long process.

Mikunis rejected the suggestion that the MAKI had grown "repentant" and explained that his party simply sought change and freedom "from the pressure of Arab chauvinism and Jewish national nihilism and from subordination to any hegemonist center." (MAKI *Information Bulletin*, no. 4, April.)

Within MAKI ranks, unanimity was sometimes lacking on important issues. Opposition to Sneh's liberal-Zionist attitudes developed under the leadership of Esther Vilenska, who was generally known as the party's most outspoken hard-line communist. In the *Jerusalem Post* (19 July), Dr. Sneh confirmed rumors that the Soviet Union had initiated noncommittal approaches to MAKI representatives and had asked "How could relations be improved?" The newspaper named Mrs. Vilenska as one of two contacts, calling the choice "not a chance one" and adding: "It is understood that the Soviet officials sought to undermine Dr. Sneh's position inside MAKI, but on this matter he was not ready to be drawn." Sneh was quoted as saying that the Soviets were "only going through the motions of rapprochement and perhaps were trying to create for themselves an "international public relations image" to "counter the argument that they cannot mediate like the Americans because they are not on speaking terms with the Israelis, while the United States has the leverage of talking with both sides."

The RAKAH expressed bitterness about MAKI policies and described the "devoted disciples of Moshe Sneh" as "progressing to the right with giant steps" and being "engaged in the service of the reactionary government war policy" (*Zo Ha'derekh*, 7 April). As for its own position within Israel, the RAKAH noticed an improvement over the past when "no one even wanted to talk with the communists" (*L'Humanité*, Paris, 13 April; interview with Meir Vilner). Although the party's "public isolation [was] no longer absolute," spokesmen acknowledged the difficulties of carrying on political activity. On a visit to Bulgaria, for instance, Politburo member Wolf Ehrlich told the Sofia newspaper *Rabotnichesko Delo* (2 May) that many RAKAH members could not get work in large industrial enterprises and were severely handicapped by restrictions on movement and travel. Regulations left over from the time of British rule, Ehrlich asserted, permitted authorities to detain suspects indefinitely without bringing charges or arranging for trials.

Arab-Israeli Conflict. The Arab-Israeli conflict remained the most divisive and urgent issue confronting the two Israeli communist parties. Early in 1971 an article by Moshe Sneh in the Tel Aviv newspaper *Haaretz* (26 February) outlined "Four Bases for Peace" which would seek a political settlement, allow for a reduction of suspicions between Arabs and Israelis, and take into account the international aspect of the Middle East crisis. The MAKI leader listed these prerequisites: (1) a peace treaty between the Arab countries and Israel, (2) self-determination for the Palestinian Arabs, (3) a joint Israeli-Arab development plan, (4) removing the area from the Cold War and the international arms race between the great powers.

The Seventeenth Plenum of the MAKI Central Committee, held on 17 July, adopted a number of resolutions detailing the principles for peace outlined by Sneh. In substance they demanded the signing of a peace treaty on the basis of mutual recognition of the legitimate national rights of all people concerned; determination of safe recognized borders by mutual agreement resulting from free negotiations without any preliminary conditions; recognition by Israel of the right of the Palestinian Arabs to self-determination and non-interference in the relations between the Palestinians and Jordan, "whether they shall live in one joint state or in two separate states"; demilitarization of occupied territories after Israeli withdrawal; a regional development plan for the resettlement of refugees and for reconstruction of the entire area to be proposed to neighboring countries; international freedom of navigation in the Suez Canal and the Red Sea; and firm international guarantees of the agreements to be reached by the Arab states and Israel. (MAKI *Information Bulletin*, no. 8, August.)

The RAKAH sought a solution to the Arab-Israeli conflict through Israeli cooperation with the Arabs and the Soviet Union. The basic views were contained in a statement marking the fourth anniversary of the outbreak of war in June 1967. Revolving around the slogan "Down with the Policy of War and Annexations!" it called upon "all champions of peace in Israel to act jointly and persistently as long as there is still time" so as to end the government's "adventurist and disastrous policy," to require that Israel "give a positive reply to the peace proposals of the UNO envoy Dr. Gunnar Jarring [and] Egypt President Anwar al-Sadat" and to implement the U.S. Security Council resolution of November 22, 1967," in all its parts" (RAKAH *Information Bulletin*, no. 6). In marked contrast to the MAKI, the RAKAH did not ask for a deferral of withdrawal from occupied areas until secure and recognized Israeli borders could be negotiated. Instead the RAKAH expressed the opinion that the "occupation is illegal and contrary to international law and the interests of peace and security of Israel" (*Zo Ha'derehk*, 8 December).

The RAKAH charged that the Israeli government lacked the power of major decision making and was "politically, economically and militarily dependent more than ever before on the USA" and could continue its "peace-preventing policy only as long as Washington permits it" (*ibid.*). According to a Knesset speech by Meir Vilner (on 9 June), this did not signify U.S. identification with Israeli needs, but merely pursuit of their own interests by the "American imperialists," using Israel as an instrument for carrying out their own global policy: "The intention is to overthrow the progressive regimes in the Arab countries, and in the first place, in the UAR and Syria; to hit the anti-imperialist Arab national movement" (*ibid.*). When the Israeli government proposed to grant NATO the right to use airfields on the occupied Sinai Peninsula, a RAKAH Politburo statement (dated 14 July) censured the proposal as an effort to perpetuate the occupation and to achieve "complicity in the dangerous, adventurist plans of American imperialism" (*IB*, no. 16-17). Thereafter the RAKAH warned of the dangers of renewed hostilities due to Israeli policies and despite the country's "isolation in the international political arena and the weakening position of the United States on which [Israel] depends." (*Haaretz*, Tel Aviv, 15 October).

Domestic Attitudes and Activities. On purely domestic issues the MAKI and RAKAH were almost equally critical of government policies. A MAKI leaflet urged participation in May Day demonstrations with slogans demanding an end to poverty or substandard living wages, communal discrimination in housing and education, inequality of the rights of children, and curbs on the freedom of trade unions in the country (MAKI *Information Bulletin*, no. 5).

While the RAKAH exposed similar economic and social causes, it alone accused the authorities of permitting "violence against those opposed to the policy of war, occupation, and oppression," and charged that "hoodlum groups composed of thugs and members of the militant fascist organizations" were able to publish inciting material without obstruction by the police and to threaten physical harm even to members of the Knesset who opposed their views (*al-Ittihad*, 26 February). In the Knesset, Tawfiq Tubi called the government "guilty of corruption" and the cause of "economic and political scandals" (*Zo Ha'derekh*, 15 December).

Both communist parties objected to the government's handling of strikes and efforts to enforce emergency laws against participants. The MAKI party organ *Kol Ha'am* (24 June) proclaimed that "Restraining Orders Did Not and Will Not Deter!" and that work stoppages were due to labor's decreasing share in the economy while output and profitability were rising at an unprecedented rate. The RAKAH attributed the "swelling wave of strikes" to a general disenchantment of the people with government policies and "security-oriented demagoguery." It claimed that the "package deal"—based on a complicated formula providing for wage-price-tax increases negotiated between the government and Histadrut early in 1970—had proved to be a "dishonest deal," was working to the detriment of the workers, enhancing social polarization, and leading to increased "suffering of the impoverished and disadvantaged segments." (*Zo Ha'derekh*, 23 June.) The Twenty-second Plenum of the RAKAH Central Committee late in November passed a resolution proposing fundamental changes in labor contracts to be negotiated early in 1972 upon expiration of the existing contracts (*ibid.*, 1 December).

The RAKAH Politburo deplored the "intensification of the aggressive annexationist policy" of the government and specifically any plans to turn Israeli administration of occupied territories into a "permanent government." It also condemned what it called the "wholesale destruction of houses in the refugee camps," the "massive expulsion of residents," and the "growing terror" against the population of the captured territories as "criminal acts against humanity according to international law." It described the devaluation of the Israeli pound as having the effect of "robbing the working masses" and increasing the profits of "foreign and local big capitalists and all those who invest in dollars." Inflation was called the inevitable result of "huge military expenditures, a foreign debt exceeding 3 billion dollars, and an unfavorable balance of payments approaching 1.5 billion dollars." (*Ibid.*, 1 September.)

International Views and Activities. In 1970 the MAKI had been highly critical of the Soviet Union's "bankrupt line of identification with the warring Arabs," its "official anti-Semitism," and "poisonous anti-Israeli campaign," while at the same time objecting to what it considered "hysterical anti-Sovietism" in Israel. In 1971, in the wake of rumors about impending Israeli-Soviet contacts, Secretary-General Shmuel Mikunis expressed different views in an article entitled "An Israel-Soviet Dialogue is Possible and Necessary":

> We must continue establishing contacts with representatives of the Soviet Union, even though not we, but they have severed the relations with us. We have something to "sell" Moscow—Moscow has something to "sell" us. Neither the repeated anti-Israeli curses from Moscow nor ideological differences must prevent this. (*Ma'ariv*, Tel Aviv, 25 June.)

In accord with these ideas the MAKI Politburo a few weeks later called upon the government to "work for a dialogue and the resumption of diplomatic relations with the Soviet Union" (*Davar*, Tel Aviv, 2 August).

MAKI Chairman Sneh, commenting on the Soviet-Egyptian treaty of friendship and cooperation that was signed on 27 May, warned against exaggerating its implications: "There was an alliance before, but there was no treaty; now there is a treaty, but it is very doubtful whether there is a full alliance." According to Sneh, Egypt had "ceased to be an arena of exclusive Soviet influence," and it was unlikely that Egypt President al-Sadat—after discovery of a plot against him—would have "removed all the trustees of Moscow ... so that he himself coult become the man who does what Moscow says." Instead Sneh saw the Soviet Union's polition in Egypt as having been transformed into a "position of partnership" with the United States, although the Soviet Union was "still the first partner" (interview, Jerusalem radiom, 28 May).

Consistently loyal to the Soviet Union, the RAKAH supported all Soviet international moves and views and held that improved relations with the Soviet Union and opposition to anti-Soviet propaganda were "an essential national interest of Israel." Soviet foreign policy, the RAKAH asserted, "consistently supports all peace-loving nations and all peoples struggling against aggression and enslavement." In accord with the general view, the party looked upon the Soviet-Egyptian treaty as having "increased the chances for peace in and out of the area by defeating the American imperialist plot to replace the anti-imperialist rulers of Egypt and other Arab countries, and by strengthening the unity of the socialist and national liberation forces." (*Zo Ha'derekh*, 23 June).

The RAKAH looked upon the Brussels International Jewish Conference on Soviet Jewry, held in February, as an attempt to "mount a broad anti-Soviet slander campaign with the support of U.S. imperialism" while "pretending concern" for Soviet Jews. "The Jews in the USSR," a RAKAH Central Committee decision declared, "live a free and happy life in their socialist motherland" (*IB*, no. 5-6), and Meir Vilner stated that "all this inciting nonsense about discrimination and oppression of Jews in the Soviet Union is both ugly and ridiculous" (*Zo Ha'derekh*, 2 March). The MAKI was considerably less critical of the Brussels conference, expressing regret that it was "not representative" but a "result of improvisation" and had failed to "adopt a clear, unequivocal stand in support of the just rights of the Soviet Jews," instead of letting the "provocative violent methods of the extreme right" set the tone. (*Kol Ha'am*, 4 March.)

The U.S. role in Southeast Asia was criticized by both parties. The MAKI warned against the "heavy hand" of the U.S. "friend" and urged continued awareness because "American imperialism shows its 'teeth' not only in the cruel, murderous offensive in Vietnam, Cambodia, and most recently in Laos, but also in the Middle East crisis" (MAKI *Information Bulletin*, no 4, April). The RAKAH, proclaiming that it sided with the Soviet Union and other socialist countries and "all anti-imperialist forces of the world, as well as broad segments of the public in the United States itself" (TASS, 18 February) repeatedly denounced U.S. actions in the area.

The RAKAH condemned the "bloody terror" in Sudan and expressed solidarity with communist victims after a coup and countercoup led to mass arrests and executions of party members. "The anti-communist campaign causes grave damage to the national interests of the Sudanese people, to the national, anti-imperialist freedom movement of the Arabs and helps the imperialists, the enemies of freedom and progress." (*Zo Ha'derekh*, 11 August.)

International Communist Movement and Party Contacts. In the role of outcast, the MAKI reacted by freely expressing dissident views of the communist world, in which it found neither "Soviet hegemonism" nor the Chinese call for the "renewal of the revolutionary line" an acceptable alternative. The boldest views and conclusions were expressed by Politburo member Ya'akov Zilber in an address on "The Situation in the Communist Movement and the Chances of MAKI" to the party's Central Committee on 2 February. Zilber saw the international communist movement as so fragmented "that it is difficult to speak today of one 'movement,' just as one almost does not speak any more of a 'camp' of socialist states." He attributed this fragmentation largely to Soviet efforts to "bring about a Soviet-American world 'condominium' " and hence a "fading of exaggerated hopes for the superiority of the socialist world system" which made the "spread of revolutions a remote prospect."

Zilber further asserted that although many foreign communist parties were at times severely critical of the policies of the Communist Party of the Soviet Union (CPSU), self-interest on both sides normally allowed reciprocal relations to continue. His analysis of interparty relations came to the conclusion that the communist movement was passing through a period of transition and expressed hopes for the evolution of a system in which divergent views and greater independence would be tolerated and the MAKI reinstated as an equal member: "We are entitled to hope for such an advance still in the year 1971." (*Ibid*.)

The MAKI was not invited to the Twenty-fourth Congress of the CPSU, but managed to maintain ties with a few communist parties abroad. Late in August, Secretary-General Mikunis left for Romania on a visit described as a vacation at the invitation of the Central Committee of the Romanian Communist Party. There were rumors that while in Bucharest Mikunis would be in contact with representatives of the Chinese Communist Party. Earlier in the year the MAKI publicized its esteem for the Romanian party on the occasion of its fiftieth anniversary and praised Romania as a kind of "Switzerland" among the community of socialist countries. (*Kol Ha'am*, 13 May.). The MAKI also tried to maintain contacts with the Communist Party of Australia and lauded the "positive resonance in Australia of the conception of MAKI."

Meir Vilner and Emile Habibi represented the RAKAH at the congress of the CPSU and reported from Moscow that the Soviet Union would be prepared to establish normal relations with Israel if and when peace were established on the basis of the U.N. Security Council Resolution (Jerusalem radio, 31 March). Other members of the party traveled to the socialist countries of Eastern Europe. Most importantly perhaps, a member of the RAKAH Politburo, Ruth Lubitsh, was among six Israelis described by TASS as a "group of progressive public figures" who toured the Soviet Union at the invitation of the Soviet Committee for the Defense of Peace. The *Christian Science Monitor* (10 September) headlined its story of the visit as "Kremlin eases anti-Israeli line-rapprochement talk heard" and pointed out that this was the first time since the Arab-Israeli war in 1967 that an Israeli delegation to the Soviet Union was not comprised entirely of communists. The RAKAH stated that the "invitation of Israeli public personalities of different political and ideological views to visit the Soviet Union evoked feelings of appreciation and also joy among many circles of persons of good will in Israel." (RAKAH *Information Bulletin*, no. 9, September.)

Publications. The MAKI central organ *Kol Ha'am* (Voice of the People) is published weekly. The party's Information Bulletin has monthly English and French and occasional Spanish and Italian editions. There are also MAKI publications in Hebrew, Yiddish, Romanian, Hungarian, Bulgarian, and Polish, but financial difficulties have dictated considerable cutbacks in recent years.

RAKAH publications include the Hebrew weekly *Zo Ha'derekh* (This Is the Way), the Yiddish *Der Veg* (The Way), the Arabic *al-Ittihad* (Unity), and the theoretical journals *Arakhim* (Values) and *Ad-Darb* (The Way) in Hebrew and Arabic respectively, as well as the party's monthly *Information Bulletin*.

Edith Wyden

Jordan

The founding year of the Communist Party of Jordan (al Hizb al-Shuyu'i al Urdunni; CPJ) is commonly given by non-communist sources as 1951. Communist activity in Jordan territory on the west bank of the Jordan River can be traced back to 1943, however, and in November 1968 the CPJ received congratulatory messages on its twenty-fifth anniversary. The discrepancy is due to the fact that the territory of Jordan was limited to the east bank of the river when the country emerged as an independent entity; land on the west bank was acquired only after Israel became a nation in 1948, and was not until 1951 that a communist party for the whole of Jordan was established.

The CPJ and all other political parties in Jordan were outlawed by royal decree in 1957, after an abortive attempt was made to topple the constitutional monarchy. The CPJ has been illegal ever since, although the normally severe repressive measures have occasionally been relaxed. Under a political amnesty granted at the outbreak of war with Israel in 1967, communists were released from Jordanian jails and a period of tacit tolerance of communist activity began. The change was also due both to communist efforts to gain greater respectability and avoid provoking the government, and to the fact that the political significance of the CPJ was so slight as to cause no worry to the authorities. Party members are believed to number fewer than 1,000 and sympathizers around 5,000. The population of Jordan is 2,418,000 (government figures, 1971).

Leadership and Party Affairs. There has never been much information available about the CPJ's hierarchy. In the past, activities seemed to be firmly controlled by Fuad Nassar, first secretary since the party's inception. In addition, Fahmi Salfiti and Rushdi Shahin were known to have held positions of influence in 1970, but in 1971 both were expelled by unanimous decision of the Central Committee for their "insistence on following the disgraceful road of secession and sabotage." (*al-Akhbar*, Beirut, 16 May).

Late in 1970 serious internal dissent within the CPJ had become clearly apparent. Trouble was confirmed on 9 January 1971, when the Lebanese communist daily *al-Nida* (Beirut) carried the text of two statements by the CPJ, one issued by the Politburo (dated 1 January) and the other by the Central Committee (dated 3 January). The Politburo announced that a dissident group, calling itself the "Leninist Cadre," had split away from the party and established its own "Provisional Central Committee." Appealing to the secessionists — whose leaders eventually were identified as Salfiti and Shahin — to return to the party ranks, the statement declared: "there is no problem, complaint, or dispute that cannot be solved within the framework of party unity and organization."

The more strongly worded Central Committee statement condemned the dissidents for attempting to split the party at "a time when all the united resouces of the national, progressive and commando forces" were needed to to "combat the conspiracies of imperialism and reaction against the [Jordanian] people and to resist the aggression and occupation of the land by Zionists." Like the Politburo, the Central Committee urged complete adherence to the resolutions of the party conference of April 1970, and recalled that many of those defying the party in 1971 had participated in that meeting and "voted in support of its resolutions without reservations."

The Beirut newspaper *al-Hayat* reported on 7 January that the conflict within the CPJ revolved around the commando organization Ansar al-Silm (Partisans of Peace), established by the communist parties of Jordan, Lebanon, Syria, and Iraq in 1970. According to this report, Ansar had encountered difficulties from the beginning of its existence, because action on its application for admission to the umbrella organization of the commandos, the Palestine Liberation Organization, had been deferred until the Partisans could meet two requirements — prove themselves in battle and renounce their support for a political settlement in the Middle East. Some members of al-Ansar did indeed join the fighting against the government during the Jordanian civil war in September 1970, but when the communist commandos early in 1971 tried to meet the second requirement by issuing a stirring statement in support of armed struggle against Israel, Salfiti and an undisclosed number of other CPJ members, refused to go along with the plans for Ansar or the decisions of the CPJ on Arab questions. Salfiti, in fact, had previously been known to be opposed to terrorist activities against Israel and to favor a political solution to the Arab-Israeli conflict. (*Arab World Weekly*, Beirut, 6 February.)

Not only did Salfiti and Shahin openly break with the CPJ and organize the Leninist Cadre, but there were rumors of further dissension in the party. According to these rumors, Fuad Nassar could count on the loyalty of such communist leaders as 'Isa Madanat and Taysir Barghuti, but encountered opposition of a group formed around Fa'iq-Warrad and Dr. Ya'qub Ziyadin, who advocated giving priority to national issues. In spite of its discontent, this faction was said to have been persuaded to remain within the party (*ibid.*). In February, Fa'iq-Warrad caused a sensation when he spoke on behalf of Ansar and the CPJ at a Central Committee meeting of the Palestine Liberation Organization, stating: "We do not hesitate to declare that we are for the liberation of the whole of Palestine and the establishment of a democratic state there. But this is a long-term strategy. There must be some tactical and phased solutions." Warrad went on to say that the CPJ believed that the Palestinian resistance movement should call for implementation of the U.N. resolution on Palestine; once this was accomplished, the movement would be able to "pursue efforts for the achievement of [its] strategic goal and if they were unsuccessful nothing would have been lost." (*Ibid.*, 15 February.)

Persuasion may have succeeded with one discontended faction of communists, but it obviously failed as far as the Leninist Cadre group was concerned. On 16 May the Lebanese communist weekly *al-Akhbar* reported that the CPJ Central Committee had voted to expel Salfiti and Shahin from the party, along with Emile Naffa', Amal Naffa', Khalid Hamshawi, and Fu'ad Qassis, after "reviewing the sabotage activities of the secessionist clique and its refusal to take advantage of the opportunity provided by the Politburo on 1 January and the Central Committee of the CPJ on 3 January."

Domestic Attitudes. As in previous years, the CPJ continued to place heavy emphasis on the formation in Jordan of a "broad national patriotic front of the working class, the peasantry, [and] the national bourgeoisie, primarily the small and middle sections" (Fu'ad Nassar in *New Times*, Moscow, 14 April 1971). Such a national front, according to communist hopes, would be the forerunner of a "national unity government" in which, "all the patriotic, sincere, and honest elements" would be represented and which would be able to "safeguard the people's freedom and create an atmosphere of stability throughout the country" (CPJ statement, *al-Nida*, 7 April.

Jordan's communists denounced the government for the "state of continuous and dreadful agony" to which the population was subjected, and the frequeft bloody clashes between the army and guerrilla groups at a time when adherence to the Cairo and Amman agreements controlling relations between the government and the Palestine Liberation Organization should have prevented the bloodshed (*ibid.*).

Later in the year, Fuad Nassar in an interview with the Bulgarian newspaper *Narodna Armiya* (Sofia, 10 August) declared: "The Jordanian reaction is afraid of new Israeli aggression, but it is even more afraid of the people, the resistance movement, the Communist Party, and the progressive forces." Consequently, the CPJ leader concluded, the Jordanian authorities looked for a settlement of the Middle Eastern conflict to "emerge under pressure from the United States and the other imperialist states, through agreement between the Jordanian monarchy and the aggressors, and as a result of a compromise benefiting imperialism and reaction." The communists did acknowledge, however, that the Palestinian resistance movement itself had committed "no few errors of judgment" and had advanced some "unrealistic views" that played into the hands of its opponents, especially at a time when King Husain of Jordan was successful in weakening the movement by dealing with it in a "barbarian way" (Fuad Nassar in *New Times*, 14 April).

The assassination on 28 November of Jordanian Premier Wasfi al-Tall had an adverse effect on all political opponents of the government, although by the end of the year it remained unclear who had arranged the premier's death on a visit to Cairo. The *New York Times* (29 November) reported that the Marxist-oriented commando organization Popular Front for the Liberation of Palestine had claimed responsibility.

International View and Activities. On several occasions during 1971 the CPJ expressed its "deep gratitude" to the Soviet Union for "tremendous all-around assistance to the Arabs" and for "unceasing efforts to achieve a just political settlement in the Middle East." In contrast, blame was heaped on "U.S. imperialism," which was accused of striving to destroy pan-Arab unity throughout the Middle East and in each country individually, and of trying to enhance its own position by driving a wedge between the Arabs and the Soviet Union and other socialist states (e.g., *Narodna Armiya*, 10 August).

The CPJ generally shared the views on foreign affairs of the communist parties of Syria, Lebanon, and Iraq. In mid-January, the four parties held a meeting to survey the most important current problems around the world, with the focus mainly on Arab progress or problems. A listing of "notable successes" hailed the completion of the Aswan Dam and the improvement of defensive and offensive capability in Egypt; "the victory of the Sudanese revolution," the overthrow of the monarchical regime in Libya, and the progressive developments in southern Yemen; and the proclamation of the four-state union of Egypt, Sudan, Libya, and Syria" (which later became a tripartite federation without Sudan). Ranging outside of the Arab world, the conferences expressed satisfaction concerning the treaties on the renunciation of force signed by West Germany with the Soviet Union and with Poland and viewed them as an aid to the relaxation of tensions in Europe and to the promotion of an all-European security conference. The parties approved the recognition of the German Democratic Republic by some Arab states and called for firmer ties of friendship and cooperation with East Germany by the entire Arab world. (*al-Akhbar*, 24 January.)

The four communist parties jointly denounced the government of Iraq for the "use of tactics totally contradictory to the most basic principles of democracy and human rights," evidenced by "blatant crimes ugainst members of the Iraqi Communist Party and other democrats and progressives" (*ibid.*). Intense alarm was expressed over the anti-communist campaign in Sudan which was initiated by the government of Ja'far Muhammad al-Numairi in February and, following a shortlived leftist coup and a sucessful countercoup in July, ended with the arrest or execution of scores of communists. The communist parties of Jordan, Lebabon, Syria, and Iraq met secretly in Beirut and reportedly sent a message to the Sudanese government calling the execution of the secretary-general of the Sudanese Communist Party, 'Abd al-Khaliq Mahjub, a "brutal crime ... which all the honest people in the world will not forgive" and condemning the "bloody executions" as "barbarianism" that would remain a blot on the conscience of all Arab people. Moreover, the communist parties alleged that "hoisting the banner of antagonism against communism could only aid Israel, imperialism, and all the enemies of Arab liberation." (*Arab World Weekly*, 31 July.)

It is not known whether the other communist parties of the Middle East shared the sentiment expressed by the Jordanian Communist Party on the Israeli-occupied West Bank; this faction for the first time attacked Egyptian views and actions, when it reproached President Anwar al-Sadat for his intervention to suppress the progressive democratic movement in Sudan and for the "offensive he launched against Egyptian forces which oppose the dialogue with the United States."

Publications, In January 1970 the CPJ announced that it was changing the name of its monthly organ from *al-Taqaddum* (Progress) to *al-Jamahir* (The Masses). Despite the publicity given to the name change, in 1971 the CPJ seemed to publicize its activities mainly through the Lebanese communist newspapers *al-Akhbar* and *al-Nida*.

Edith Wyden

Lebanon

The Lebanese Communist Party (al-Hizb al-Shuyu'i al-Lubnani; LCP) was established in 1924 as the Lebanese People's Party (Hizb al-Sha'b al-Lubnani). It was reconstituted in 1930 as the Lebanese Communist Party, which accepted members from both Lebanon and Syria during the period of the French mandate. In 1944, after the two countries gained national independence, the First Congress of the LCP decided to establish separate Lebanese and Syrian communist parties.

The LCP was banned until 13 August 1970, when it was granted recognition by Lebanon's interior minister and became the only communist party in the Arab countries of the Middle East to gain legal status thus fur. In 1971 it was not yet clear whether legalization had affected the size of the party, which previously was estimated to have about 2,000 members and 4,000 sympathizers. The population of Lebanon is 2,800,000 (estimated 1970).

Leadership and Organization. The LCP request for recognition was signed by Nicola Shawi, Artine Madoyan, Yusuf Khattar al-Halu, and Mustafa Muhammed al-'Aris—all described as "founders of the society." Shawi has been secretary-general of the purty for more than thirty years; al-Halu is editor of the Beirut communist weekly *al-Akhbar*; al-'Aris is believed to be in charge of trade union activity for the party; and Madoyan headed the Armenian communists in Lebanon before their group merged with the LCP. Others known to have held important party posts at the time of the LCP's Second Congress, in 1968, ure Georges Batal, Khalil Dibs, 'Abd al-Karim Muruwwah, Khalil Na'us, and Nadim 'Abd al-Samad. Georges Hawi, who in 1967 lost the editorship of the party newspaper *al-Nida* and left for Eastern Europe after leading an opposition group within the party, by 1971 had regained an eminent position in the LCP. New elections are on the agenda for the Third Congress, scheduled to open in Beirut on 7 January 1972 (see below).

Party Internal Affairs. Although the constitution of the LCP stipulates that a congress is to be held every three years, the party has so far held only two congresses. In June 1971 a Central Committee plenum approved plans and an agenda for the Third Congress to be held later in the year. The Central Committee attached particular importance to the timing, explaining that the congress would take place "while the conflict between the Arab liberation movement and its allies on one side and imperialism, Zionism, and reaction on the other is being intensified" (*ul-Nida*, Beirut, 20 June). The reason why the plans could not be implemented during the calendar year and the congress had to be postponed until early in 1972 became clear in November when the LCP issued an appeal for funds to finance the congress and help with the party's "monetary burdens resulting from the expansion of its fields of activity and the new condistions of its work" (*al-Akhbar*, 20 November).

The Central Committee's June communiqué on convening the congress also threw some light on the internal problems of the LCP. Announcing its "sympathy with all sincere self-criticism," the party used the occasion to "offer an opportunity to all communists who have left the party for any reason, or those who would agree to the political program and desire to rejoin the party to struggle within its ranks while adhering to its bylaws," to submit their applications. Calling itself the party of "honest workers, peasants, intelligentsia, and various popular circles," the LCP assured all those willing to pick up the proffered option of their right to "participate in drawing up the party's policy and in expressing their views regarding its function and course." (al-Nida, 20 June.)

It is not known whether the invitation to return to the fold included the "left isolationist" and "right deviationist" factions, which had been acknowledged as a threat to LCP effectiveness in 1970. From vague statements, however, it would appear that internal dangers to the party persisted in 1971: "The rightist trend, calling for 'nationalization of the battle' denies the social, progressive, and anit-imperialist character of the battle and consequently places Arab reaction within the progressive forces' ranks....The adventurist leftist trend calls for the downfall of progressive regimes and the small bourgeoisie and sets the task of removing them [while assigning to the working class] the immediate task of taking over leadership regardless of the availability of opportunities." (Ibid.)

In 1971 the party also referred to the existence of major organizational problems which—although not further identified—were big enough to keep the LCP from reaching its "proper level of political and mass influence." Although the 1968 congress was held under the slogan "For a Militant and Mass Communist Party in Lebanon," the party was unable to bring about the desired transformation, and acknowledged in 1971 that to "take bigger steps along this course" remained an urgent task. (Ibid.) One of the consequent initiatives was the invitation issued by the LCP for "participation of broad sections of the people in preparing the Third Congress," with the aim of "working for the unity of the progressive forces in the Lebanon and for a common program" (IB, no. 18-19). A more specific request for cooperation in a united progressive front went to the Progressive Socialist Party, led by Kamal Jumblatt (Minister of the Interior in 1970 and responsible for the legalization of the communist party and other parties previously banned), the Syrian Social Nationalist Party (Partie Populaire Syrien—best known as the PPS), and even the ruling Ba'th Party.

While the LCP was trying to gain support among the masses and working for unity of "progressive forces," the leader of the right-wing Phalangist Party challenged the 1970 decision to lift the ban on previously illegal political groups. Early in March the Phalangist organ al-'Amal demanded that the government review the year-old decision by the Minister of the Interior and that it "reorganize partisan life in Lebanon under sound and objective principles" (Arab World, Beirut, 8 March). The paper asserted that since the original ban was imposed by a court ruling, a minister's decision would be insufficient to remove it and in fact constituted defiance of the authority of the judicial arm of the government. The protest brought no official reaction. At the end of the year there were rumors that the Lebanese premier was considering an LCP invitation to attend the party congress early in January 1972.

A disconcerting development for Lebanon's communists in 1971 was the arrest of Georges Hawi on 3 July. Hawi was charged with slandering the army and making insinuations against the government in a speech at Nabatiya in southern Lebanon. Both he and the LCP denied the charges and accused authorities of justifying the arrest on the basis of a 1969 warrant issued for his part in a Beirut demonstration which had resulted in armed clashes with police. Hawi's detention aroused serious fear in communist ranks that it might foreshadow reimposition of the party ban; concern reached a high when Lebanon radio on 4 July attacked the communist party as "subversive"—a term regularly used when the LCP was illegal. Hawi was released after three days, however, and the Central Committee claimed a "victory for democratic liberties" and gave special credit to the PPS and the Interior Minister for effecting his freedom.

The Lebanese president president held a meeting a few weeks later with Shawi, Hawi, and Central Committee member Muhammad al-Wawi, during which he warned the LCP leaders against the use of "provocative empty slogans" and urged them instead to "face responsibilities which would bear positive results." In the course of the discussion he asked to be shown "where imperialist colonial influence can be found in Lebanon" and to be allowed participation in eliminating it, if and wherever it existed. (*Lisan al-Hal*, Beirut, 16 September.)

About the time of Hawi's arrest the government showed great concern over commando activities in southern Lebanon which had led to retaliatory strikes against Lebanese villages by Israel. At the same time there were leftist claims that the government was "doing nothing to protect the villages against Israeli incursions" and demands for a more active defense policy. Rightly or wrongly, officials may have suspected that the communists were promoting the commando actions, especially since elements of Ansar al-Silm (Partisans of Peace)—the commando organization set up in 1970 by the communist parties of Iraq, Lebanon, and Jordan (see *Jordan*)—were known to be in that part of the country. At the beginning of July Ansar claimed to have carried out their first operation inside Israeli territory just across from the Lebanese border. Past communiqués had indicated that their contacts with Israeli troops were on Lebanese territory. (*al-Nida*, 3 July.)

Domestic Views and Activities. A plenary meeting of the LCP Central Committee early in February 1971 discussed the domestic situation and concluded by "defining the future political and organizational tasks of the communists" as follows: to expose U.S. pressures, including those in the form of financial and military aid; to expose the attitude of domestic reactionaries (said to be in full harmony with the "imperialist-Zionist" plans in the area); to defend democratic liberties and struggle to bolster them and to prevent reactionary forces from attaining positions of control; to amend the election law on a democratic and proportional basis to provide a "minimum degree of democracy" and to give the working class and popular forces the opportunity to place representatives in parliament; to escalate the fight to preserve the achievements of the working class, the peasants, and the students, to add to those gains, and to avoid losses and suicidal battles for them; and "to protect all the progressive forces from the reactionary and imperialist plots aimed at their liquidation." (*al-Akhbar*, 14 February).

Similar ideas were expressed in the LCP Action Program, prepared for discussion by the Third Congress. Sections on the domestic situation in Lebanon considered the "crisis of the free economy and its political complications; the unity of the progressive, nationalist and democratic forces in the struggle for safeguarding the vital interest of the working class and the peasants and of democracy and independence; and ways of attaining the nationalist democratic rule that would allow for a transition to socialism" (*Arab World*, 13 October). Although the communist desire for major domestic changes was implied, the LCP refrained from attacks on the ruling Ba'th Party, with which it hoped to join in a united front of "progressive patriotic forces" (*Daily Star*, Beirut, 9 July).

The LCP and the Arab World. The LCP Politburo report to the Central committee in June summarized the party's views on the Arab liberation movement and the problems of the Middle East, and listed the following main tasks: "Eliminating the effects of the imperialist-Zionist aggression, supporting the Palestinian people's struggle for their right to self-determination, safeguarding national independence, und achieving the lawful national aspirations of the Arab people" (*al-Nida*, 20 June).

The LCP continued to consider the U.N. Security Council resolution of November 1967 on the Arab-Israeli conflict as "positive," but held that a political solution of the conflict and the implementation of the resolution would be dependent on the "availability of material capabilities" to assure compliance by Israel. The LCP asserted that this meant strengthening the combat capability of the Arab states and "minimum political and military cooperation between them," whereas in actuality "gaps and shortcomings ... and contradictions" have appeared within the Arab liberation movement (*ibid.*). Shawi, writing in *World Marxist Review* (September), explained that the situation was due to pack of a "program defining the nature of the struggle now being fought on various fronts" and the inability by some elements of the liberation movement to "distinguish between friend and foe, both in the Arab East and the larger world."

The LCP declared that it had given support to the Palestinian resistance movement with all political, moral, material, and human means at its disposal, "including direct participation in armed operations," and had tried to protect the movement against "reactionury conspiracies and liquidation attempts," especially in Jordan and Lebanon (*Arab World Weekly*, 3 July). The role of the United States was discussed in the party's Action Program and was criticized not only for "absolute support of Israel," but also for conducting "political maneuvers aimed at strengthening its positions and the positions of its lackeys in the region, deceiving Arab and world public opinion and pretending that it seeks a solution to the Middle East crisis." In particular, the LCP opposed the Rogers plan (of the U.S. secretary of state, William Rogers)—although it mude a big issue of not participating in mass demonstrations organized at the time of Rogers's visit to Lebanon—claiming that its real objective was to strengthen Israel's position and "draw the Arabs into flagrant bargains that would lead to successive concessions," while in the process hurting Arab-Soviet friendship. (*Ibid.*, 16 October.) In reviewing its attitude toward Egypt, the LCP recalled its own support for Egyptian "political initiatives" to "isolate Israel internationally and expose its aggressive, expansionist nature." The communists, on the other hand, were critical of Egypt because its "elastic political position was not always accompanied by a comprehensive political plan, capable of activating and mobilizing the popular struggle against imperialism and reaction in the region," and because rightist factions in the war and elsewhere within the Arab Liberation movement were lured by the idea of "neutralizing" the United States and unaware that this would "aid Arab reaction in the process." (*Ibid.*) A story in the LCP organ *al-Nida* (7 March) even made a direct attack on Muhammad Hasanain Haikal, editor of Cairo's daily newspaper *al-Ahram*, although he usually expresses official government views and wields great influence in Egyptian culing circles. Haikal was accused of serving U.S. imperialist designs in an article which implied "Israel is our enemy, but the United States is not." Only the Soviet Union received unmitigated praise for its actions in the Middle East. According to the LCP, the "comprehensive assistance given by the Soviet Union" had "constituted a basic element in the Arabs' steadfastness against the aggression that has prevented it from achieving its objective" (*al-Nida*, 20 June).

The Arab national liberation movement, in the LCP view, was split to such an extent that it had lost sight of the need to fight "imperialism" and instead had accented "internal differences, culminating in armed conflicts that further aggravate divisions." As an instance the party cited the "anti-communist campaign" started in some Arab countries following the briefly successful communist coup in Sudan in July and a quick countercoup, which involved "mass arrests and murder of consistent and staunch Arab patriots" (*WMR*, September). It also considered the rulers of some Arab countries guilty of "subversion" through interference in the "interests of reaction" in the Persian Gulf area and by support of the monarchists in Northern Yemen. It accused Saudi Arabia of trying to exert economic pressure on Lebanon, to pave the way for the creation of a new bloc linking the two countries with Jordan, and to have the resulting "power axis" safeguarded by the United States (*ibid.*; *al-Nida*, 9 May).

The Lebanese communists made a generally "positive evaluation" of the tripartite federation of Egypt, Syria, and Libya even though its establishment in 1971 had been accompanied by some "negative phenomena" which threatened to "fetter the federation and circumscribe it within narrow 'nationalist' and reactionary, chauvinist contexts." Libya was considered by the communists as the weakest of the federation partners and its rulers were accused of "fanning enmity toward communism, progressiveness, the Soviet Union, and the true socialist ideas in general," while simultaneously trying to "consolidate ties with such Western imperialist states as West Germany." (*al-Nida*, 2 September; *Arab World Weekly*, 16 October.)

Other International Views and Contacts. Much of the LCP's energy in 1971 seemed to be spent promoting Soviet views and criticizing anti-Sovietism wherever it cropped up. Party leaders Shawi and Hawi attended the Twenty-fourth Congress of the Communist Party of the Soviet Union and lauded the event over Soviet radio as a "remarkable international manifestation" in support of the international communist movement. When an international conference was convened in Brussels in February to discuss the plight of Soviet Jews, an LCP editorial (*al-Nida*, 24 February) disparaged the meeting as a "Zionist attempt, backed by U.S. imperialism to undermine the prestige of the Soviet Union," and as a "hysterical campaign" waged by Zionism because of Soviet and East European support for the Arab cause.

The LCP Politburo issued a special statement on 28 May hailing the conclusion of the Egyptian-Soviet treaty of friendship and cooperation as a sign that "Arab-Soviet friendship is as solid as a high mountain" and that "imperialist and reactionary circles" had lost their bets that the relationship would flounder or could be undermined (*ul-Akhbar*, 30 May). The LCP was also elated when Lebanon and the Soviet Union reached agreement on a program of cultural cooperation between the two countries (*al-Nida*, 12 August) which even provided for the celebration of important Soviet events in Lebanon. To "share Russia's celebrations amid the victories it has scored," the LCP a few weeks later organized a rally at a Beirut theater on the occasion of the fifty-fourth anniversary of the October Revolution (*al-Muharrir*, Beirut, 15 November).

When Malta's prime minister ordered NATO forces to leave the island, the Lebanese communists gave credit for this move to the Soviet fleet's presence in the Mediterranean and claimed that the Soviet Union was providing "national forces" with confidence to "break the shackles and chains" that had "hitherto curbed their movements and suppressed their cries" (*al-Nida*, 29 June). In December the communist organ rapped critics of Soviet policies in the India-Pakistan conflict for "viciousness" in comparing Soviet views on India's fight "on behalf of self-determination and freedom from oppression" with Soviet attitudes toward similar problems of the Arabs (*al-Nida*, 9 December). In particular, the anti-Soviet campaign in the Libyan press alarmed the Lebanese communists, who questioned the logic of Libyan leaders in trying to present Pakistan as a "model of neutralism" and simultaneously discrediting India and Soviet-Indian cooperation (TASS, 21 December).

In stark contrast with the LCP's unstinting endorsement of Soviet activities around the world was its frequent criticism of the leaders of the People's Republic of China for their "fundamental deviation from the Marxist-Leninist line." Beirut's *An-Nahar* (20 December) predicted that the upcoming LCP congress would be the "first public occasion used by an Arab communist party to launch a violent and concentrated attack against China and accuse 'Mao Tse-tung's clique' of allying itself with the United States and imperialist forces in order to strike at the communist movement and world liberation forces." A prelude also was provided by a Shawi interview with the French-language newspaper *L'Orient-Le Jour* (Beirut, 1 January 1972) just a week prior to the opening of the congress; the Lebanese party leader described the Chinese Cultural Revolution as marked by infantile radicalism and such frightening manifestations as turning Chairman Mao into an idol.

Several times during the year the LCP denounced the government of Iraq for its "reign of terror" as evidenced by a stepped-up persecution of communists, and even warned that the Iraq government might fall unless it abandoned the "bloody course" of fighting the "national forces and parties'' and against the people's liberties and democratic rights (*al-Akhbar*, 14 February). In May the party made a special appeal to the president of Iraq for the release of Thabit Habib al-'Ani, a member of the Iraqi Communist Party's Central committee, who allegedly was ''kidnapped'' in the streets of Baghdad without explanation as to his fate and whereabouts (*al-Nida*, 12 May). It also participated in a joint appeal on his behalf with the communist parties of Jordan and Syria in which the Iraqi government was generally denounced for ''flagrant violation of its own slogans about struggle against imperialism and for social progress'' (*ibid.*, 14 May).

Alone or jointly with other communist parties of the Middle East, the LCP attacked ''hysterical anti-communism'' in Sudan and ''Khartoum ravings'' following the executions of communist party leaders in that country in July, and concluded that the aim of the executions was not only to strike at the Sudanese Communist Party, but to strike at Arab-Soviet friendship in exchange for ''god conduct certificates'' from ''reactionary Arab rulers and Western imperialist leaders'' (*al-Akhbar*, 15 August).

Publications. The Principal publications of the LCP are the daily *al-Nida* (The Call) and the weekly *al-Akhbar* (The News). Both have been distributed openly for a number of years, even before the party gained leval status. Both organs also serve as general information media for the illegal communist parties of the Middle East.

*   *   *

Fragmentation and reorganization have been characteristic of Lebanese communism for many years. The year 1971 was different only because changes were better publicized than in the past. On 5 july the Beirut weekly *al-Hurriyah*—organ of the Marxist-Leninist ''Organization of Lebanese Socialists'' (OLS) and its Palestinian commando arm, the ''Popular Democratic Front for the Liberation of Palestine'' (PDFLP)—announced the establishment of the ''Organization of Communist Action in Lebanon'' (OCAL). The OCAL was said to be the result of a merger of the OLS and the smaller ''Organization of Socialist Lebanon'' (OSL). The identity of the leaders of the OCAL was not revealed, but the most prominent members of the OLS had been Muhsin Ibrahim and Muhammad Kashli; the best-known members of the OSL were Fawwaz Tarabulsi and Mahmud Suwayd.

Al-Hurriyah, serving as the party organ of the new group, indicated that the merger had been arranged a year ago, but that announcement had been deferred to allow for a ''substantial period of united action'' und a constituent conference in May 1971. The paper also characterized the OCAL as a ''revolutionary organization ... working for the application of Marxism-Leninism in order to understand and change reality,'' and as being opposed to the ''infiltration of bourgeois ideologies.''

Basically the OCAL is strongly critical of the Soviet Union and its stand in the Middle East conflict and similarly disapproves of the LCP, without wishing to be labeled a Maoist group. The conflict between the LCP and the OLS became evident earlier in the year in physical confrontations on the campus of Beirut's Lebanese University. Fist fights broke out when the OLS posted notices calling for rise of a new communist party and charging that the existing party had grown rigid and was not truly Marxist (*Arab World Weekly*, 15 May). This was the climax to the exchange of verbal attacks in LCP and OLS publications.

Only three months after OCAL's birth was announced, stories of a serious rift within the group began to circulate, with Ibrahim and Kashli reportedly at odds. *Al-Muhurrir* (Beirut, 7 October) predicted that Kashli and his supporters would leave the organization and regroup on their own. In November the impasse reached a point where the OCAL organ announced its temporary suspension (*al-Hurriyah*, 22 November), as disagreement seemed to revolve around China, the Soviet Union, the DPFLP, and the attitude toward the working class in Lebanon.

Edith Wyden

Lesotho

The Communist Party of Lesotho (CPL) was founded in 1961, in close cooperation with South African communists. An inaugural congress took place the following year. Banned in February 1970, the CPL has since sought to work clandestinely. Its membership remains insignificant, and influential supporters are in prison.

Leadership and Organization. According to Soviet sources, the CPL chairman is R. Matji and the secretary-general is J. M. Kena. The party numbers no more than "a few hundred persons." Its social base derives from migrant workers employed in South Africa, where many became members of various organizations, including the African National Congress and the South African Communist Party (*Political Parties of Africa: A Soviet Study*, Joint Publications Research Service, Arlington, Virginia, 1971, p. 191).

Party Internal Affaics, Domestic Attitudes and Activities. CPL policy was laid down in a draft program, "The Lesotho Road to National Democracy," at the party congress in October 1969. CPL views also found expression in a statement presented at the Moscow International Meeting of Communist and Workers' Parties in 1969. The CPL aims at achieving a united front of all "progressive" forces. This united front is intended to bring about a "national democratic revolution," resulting in a socialist republic. The party looks to a social transformation which would put down the "fascist" regime of South Africa, the "pro-fascist leadership" exercised by Leabua Jonathan in Lesotho, and the machinations of U.S., British, and West German "imperialists." The CLP calls for land reform, encouragement of cooperative farming, mechanization of agriculture, and promotion of industries. It also demands the return to Lesotho of territory now occupied by South Africa. The party stresses that, while migrant workers participate in what it calls the "South African freedom struggle," the conditions of Lesotho and South Africa are different. Hence, progress can be achieved in a Lesotho independent of South Africa.

International Views and Positions. The CLP follows a pro-Soviet course. It condemns what it considers the erroneous theoretical views and factional activities of the Chinese Communist Party. CPL instead supports solidarity of the international communist movement, as proposed by the CPSU. The CPL maintains close links with the South African Communist Party.

Lewis H. Gann

Morocco

The Moroccan Communist Party (Parti Communiste Marocain; PCM) was founded in 1943 by former members of the "Moroccan region" of the French Communist Party. Although suspended by the Moroccan government in 1959 and banned in 1960 for its incompatibility with Islam, the PCM continued to operate more or less openly, although several appeals to lift the ban were denied by the government. In 1968, the long-time secretary-general of the party, Ali Yata, announced formation of the Party of Liberation and Socialism (Parti de la Libération et du Socialisme; PLS) and declared himself head of the new group. By presenting itself as a "national" political party, "strongly attached to the revolutionary traditions of the Moroccan people, the inheritance of Arab thought, and the liberal content of Islam," the PLS was able to register with the government as a legal party. Moroccan authorities soon realized, however, that the dogma and ideology of the PLS were identical with those of the PCM. In August 1969, Ali Yata was arrested, and in September he was tried and sentenced to ten months in prison for reviving an illegal political party under a new name. The PLS and its newspaper, *al-Kifah al-Watani*, were banned.

PLS membership in 1971 probably fell below the 400 estimate for the previous year. The population of Morocco is 15,700,000 (estimated 1970). Even during the period of its legal status, the party's influence was negligible and largely dependent on the prominence of a few of its members. Ali Yata has tried to cope with this handicap by constantly attempting to modify the party's program and by soliciting support of the major opposition groups, such as the Istiqlal party, the National Union of Popular Forces (Union Nationale des Forces Populaires; UNFP), the General Union of Moroccan Students (Union Générale des Etudiants Marocains; UGEM), the National Union of Moroccan Students (Union Nationale des Etudiants Marocains; UNEM), the two main trade unions, the Moroccan Labor Union (Union Marocain du Travail; UMT) and the General Union of Moroccan Workers (Union Générale des Travailleurs Marocains; UGTM), the Democratic Constitutional Party (Parti Démocratique Constitutionnel; PDC), the Popular Democratic Movement (Mouvement Populaire Démocratique; MPD), and even the Popular Movement (Mouvement Populaire; MP), the weakest among the government opposition groups.

Ali Yata had urged for years formation of a united front of all opposition forces in the country, but had attained only limited support from the UNFP, while the strongly nationalistic Istiqlal Party openly expressed strong criticism of the communists. In July 1970 the UNFP and the Istiqlal, which the PLS had sought as partners in cooperation, announced establishment of a United National Front for the purpose of enabling "national aspirations to triumph" (see below), with a joint leadership, but they did not include the PLS in their unity plans. Ali Yata quickly expressed approval of and pledged his support to the union, calling for "creation of a real nationul front of all progressive and patriotic forces, without excluding anyone." He asserted that "this front must be openly negotiated between equal partners, with the support of the militants and the masses, and be created on the basis of an anti-imperialist and democratic program with respect for the autonomy of each of the member forces.''

Leadership and Party Affairs. Ali Yata headed the PCM as its secretary-general from 1945 until 1968, when he assumed leadership of the PLS. Among other well-known Moroccan communists are Abdallah Hocine Layachi, Abdessalam Bourkia, Abdelaziz Belal, Simon Levy, and Hadi Messouak. Muhammad Chouaib Rifi, co-signer with Ali Yata of the statuses of the PLS, was also arrested in August 1969 and sentenced to prison. Both men were released in 1970.

The difficulties of the political opposition in Morocco were highlighted by King Hassan's announcement on 8 July 1970 that the country would return to constitutionap rule (abrogated in 1965 when the king proclaimed a state of emergency and assumed legislative and executive power). A referendum on a new constitution, held 24 July, resulted in approval by 98.7 per cent of the voters. The UNFP and the Istiqlal had challenged ceferendum methods, and the PLS had condemned the ''complete secrecy'' under which the constitution had been formulated. After the referendum, the communists and the United National Front called for a boycott of the elections for a legislature in August. In July 1971, following the unsuccessful Royal Moroccan Army mutiny attempt to overthrow him, King Hassan, immediately took steps (similar to those in 1965) to tighten his grip on the country. The ten ringleaders in the mutiny were executed, immediately after questioning. Another 193 opponents, most of them leaders of the supposedly legal NUPF, were charged with ''elaborate plotting to overthrow the government by military means.'' On 17 September, the verdict was announced in the trial at Marrakesh. Five of the accused were condemned to death (the prosecutor had asked for 48 death penalties) and 6 were sentenced to life imprisonment (the prosecutor had asked this for 122), while 2 were given thirty years in jail; 5, twenty years; 24, ten years; 7, five years; and 84, six months to two years. After the verdict had been read, the defendants rose and said in unison, ''We are all with the NUPF and we will never renounce our party.'' (*Le Monde*, Paris, 19 February.)

Among frustrations suffered by the PLS during the year were the closure for one month, beginning 15 February, and repeated seizure of Istiqlal newspapers *al-'Alam* and *l'Opinion* by order of the government. This was coupled with continued absence of the PCM weekly *al-Kifah al-Watani*, suspended since the party was banned in September 1969. The founding of the U.S.S.R.-Morocco Friendship Society on 19 February, Soviet Premier Kosygin's visit to Morocco, and increased economic, trade, and technical relations between the Soviet and Moroccan governments all contributed greatly to the obstacles that stood in the way of political activity on the part of the PLS throughout 1971.

Mounting restrictions by the government against all leftist opposition groups in the country made them feel the weight of suppression and share an apprehension of common danger, even though a firm political union had not been effected. This was revealed in statements of UNFP member Mehdi Alaoui, Ali Yata, and several others when they referred to ''the latest wave of repression [in Morocco], which began with the kidnapping and death of our valorous comrade Mehdi Ben Barka, continued with the arrest of Mahjoub Ben Seddik and Aouab, leaders of the Moroccan working class, and the arbitrary arrest and condemnation of Ali Yata and Rifi and the dissolution of their party, the PLS, and which has resulted in the kidnapping of a number of UNFP leaders and left-wing activists'' (*L'Humanité*, Paris, 7 February). After interdiction of the PLS and condemnation of its leadership, a hardening of the government attitude toward the UNFP and the progressive UNEM as well as all opposition became clear.

Domestic Attitudes and Activities. Opposition leaders, led by Ali Yata, seized every opportunity to comment on Morocco's ''state of crisis'' — economic, social and political—which they attributed to "rigid conservatism" and the country's "alliance with neo-colonialism." In the economic sector, they strongly criticized the "abandonment of the national options of independence," absence of agrarian reform, dependence of exports on "Western imperialist partners," and negligence of priority attention to industrialization. In the social sector, they alleged a lack of any kind of progress, as indicated by the wage freeze, increased cost of living, higher unemployment, and "aggravation of the material and moral poverty of the people." Stagnation of cultural life, they asserted, was a reflection of the low standards of education in the country.

Severe government opposition to national parties, they contended, was the underlying cause for the crisis in political affairs. They continued their criticism of the constitution, claiming that it had been imposed on the people through "falsification and fraudulence" and was "authoritarian and backward" even in comparison to the previous constitution. Abderrahim Bouabid, well-known opposition figure and NUPF leader, stated that he was very pessimistic about the country's future. He said that there was crisis in the army, in the political parties, and in all social classes. Bouabid showed his deepest concern and scepticism regarding any prospects of the new government. He criticized the cabinet as not being a national coalition government and as being weak and lacking popular support to cope with the prevailing conditions. He reaffirmed that a real constitutional and parliamentary monarchy was needed (Agence France Presse, 13 August).

Despite veiled royal threats, there was speculation that the king had been making direct overtures to opposition leaders. Neither Abderrahim Bouabid nor Allal el Fassi, spokesman for the Istiqlal party, seemed to rule out the possibility of such dialogue. Reportedly, however, they insisted on certain conditions before discussions could begin: " well-defined programme, and the establishment of democratic structures which would permit the intellectual and professional elite to have a hand in defining the country's major options" (*Guardian*, London, and *Le Monde*, Paris, 7 August). All previous attempts to start a dialogue with the opposition have ended in failure. The Moroccan communists have always looked upon their government's power structure as little short of absolutism.

International Views and Positions. The ban imposed on the PLS and the UNFP-Istiqlal front has placed all opposition in Morocco in a defensive mood. The communists might well have opted to direct their fight for survival toward closer ties with the international communist movement, but during 1971 there were no new or important pronouncements forthcoming from them. Token repetitive slogan-promises by Ali Yata and other opposition spokesmen to "go on fighting imperialism and anti-Sovietism, whatever its form or origin," and to "strengthen international links with all the fraternal parties without exception," were heard throughout the year.

Ali Yata repeated his own self-styled description of himself as "an Arab Communist" with an "internationalist duty."

The PLS like other communist movements in the Maghreb, sisters, was absent from the Twenty-fourth Congress of the Communist Party of the Soviet Union, held in Moscow, in March-April. Despite the fact that the Soviet Union strengthened its relations during the year with all the Maghreb countries, where communism is severely suppressed by local governments, Moroccan communists continued their allegiance to Moscow. They remained ambiguous in their acceptance of Soviet foreign policies, especially in view of the U.S.S.R.'s willingness to maintain good political and economic relations with governments that practice anti-communism at home.

Moroccan communists expressed their support for the Palestine resistance movement and all "liberation movements" in the Middle East. They continued their close fraternal relations with the French Communist Party, which has been a model and champion of the Moroccan communists. Like the French party, they expressed serious concern over the strengthening of U.S., British, and NATO naval positions in the Mediterranean, calling them bases of aggression against socialism in the region.

Publications. Until the party was banned in September 1969, the PLS published a weekly, *al-Kifah al-Watani* (The Patriotic Struggle). Efforts to revive the paper in 1971 met with failure.

Michel G. Nabti

Nigeria

The Nigerian communist party is known as the Socialist Workers' and Farmers' Party (SWAFP), founded in 1963. Although all political parties were banned in 1966, the SWAFP has continued to operate through various subsidiary organizations and its trade union connections. The party's membership is small and consists mainly of intellectuals and white-collar workers, especially in the southern part of the country.

Organization and Leadership. The party abstains from publishing current lists of officials. According to past published accounts, Dr. Tunji Otegbeye has served as secretary-general.

The party is linked to the Nigerian Trade Union Congress (NTUC), one of the largest trade union organizations within the country's divided labor movement. The NTUC claims a membership of some 80,000 persons (previous party estimates were much higher) and some 350 affiliated bodies. It belongs to the All-African Trade Union Federation and the Soviet-dominated World Federation of Trade Unions.

Wahab O. Goodluck is the NTUC president. S U. Bassey is secretary general; he is also a vice-president and Executive Committee member of the All-African Trade Union Federation. Hudson Momodu is the NTUC deputy president. M. O. King is assistant secretary. (*Advance*, Lagos, 12-18 April.) Goodluck and Bassey also occupy key positions in the United Committee of Central Labour Organisations. During 1971 there was a good deal of labor unrest, but these industrial disputes apparently did not constitute a serious threat to the Nigerian military regime (*Economist*, 27 March, p. 41). The government nevertheless decided to arrest a number of leading Marxist-Leninists including Otegbeye, Goodluck and Bassey.

Nigerian communists participate in a number of friendship societies. One of the most active is the Nigerian-German Democratic Friendship Society, founded in 1963, which has branches in Kaduna, Kano, Onitsha, Warri, and in the South-East State. Others include the Nigerian-Polish Friendship Society, the Nigerian-Hungarian Friendship Society, the Association of Nigerian-Soviet Friendship, and the Youth Thinkers Club.

SWAFP stands for an orthodox Marxist-Leninist program. It seeks to effect a "national democratic revolution" through a united front with all "progressive" elements. The revolution in turn is intended to bring about socialism. The party gives qualified support to the federal government, which maintains cordial relations with the Soviet Union. The party has, however, backed militant students at Ibadan University, where disturbances in 1971 led to the death of a student. Pro-communist political and trade union leaders exploited the riots to conduct protest demonstrations against university authorities and, by implication, against the government.

The NTUC has called for a decree to make "excessive and scandalous" profiteering punishable by death. Price control regulations, it argues, should be more adequately enforced (*Advance*, 1-7 March). In addition, NTUC calls for "struggle against Western monopolies," which allegedly exploit the working masses. Its program includes nationalization of oil, timber, cigarette, and beer plants, and holds that increasing unemployment should be alleviated by government-sponsored industries. It calls on workers to support the federal military government's efforts to stamp out corruption. (*Ibid*., 18-24 January.)

International Views and Activities. Nigerian communists have consistently denounced what they call imperialist machinations of the United States, Great Britain, the Federal Republic of Germany, and other NATO members. They oppose the so-called unholy alliance of South Africa, Portugal, and Rhodesia. *Advance*, the leading pro-communist newspaper, rejects any form of dialogue with South Africa. It condemns alleged aggression by Israel against Arab states, by Portugal against Guinea, Mozambique and Angola, and by the United States against Vietnam; it associates itself with the "heroic struggle of the American negroes" and with U.S. communist Angela Davis. *Advance* likewise has called for nationalization of all British property in Africa without compensation, Nigeria's withdrawal from the Commonwealth, and sanctions against the United States, West Germany, France and other "imperialist" states engaged in selling arms to South Africa (issue of 18-24 January 1971). At the same time, it has praise for the "courageous and progressive" decision of the federal military government in recognizing the People's Republic of China (15-21 February).

Publications. SWAFP views are expressed in *Advance*, a fortnightly published at Lagos, which acts as NTUC organ. The editor, Jimmy Chijokwe, was briefly inprisoned at Lagos.

There is no recognized Maoist party in Nigeria, but the Nigeria-China Friendship Association, founded at Kaduna in 1962, articulates pro-Chinese views. After establishment of diplomatic relations between China and Nigeria, two new rival societies were set up. One is the Nigerian-China Cultural and Friendship Society, with headquarters at Kaduna. The second is the Nigerian Chinese People's Friendship Association, which during the year held a photographic exhibition at Lagos.

Lewis H. Gann

Réunion

The Réunion Communist Party (Parti Communiste Réunionnais; PCR) was founded in 1959 by the transformation of the Réunion Federation of the French Communist Party into an autonomous organization.

The PCR is legal. In 1967 the party claimed to have 3,500 members; a recent Western estimate put the active membership at 500 (*World Strength of the Communist Party Organizations*, Washington, D.C., 1971). The population of Réunion is 450,000 (estimated 1970). In 1968 the PCR secretary-general, Paul Vergès, stated that the party was limiting its numbers in favor of improving the members' ideological quality (*Tricontinental*, Havana, March-April 1969). This emphasis appeared to continue into 1971.

Although its membership is small, the PCR succeeds in mobilizing considerable electoral support, particularly among the island's sugar workers and in certain towns. It is the island's only party with a local organization; electoral candidates of other parties are normally Frenchmen without permanent organizations in Réunion. The PCR, however, has no representatives in the French Assembly or Senate.[1] On the 36-member General Council, it is represented by party members Vergès, Elie Hoarau, Evenor Lucas, Bruny Payet, and Jean-Baptiste Ponama. In local elections in March 1971 the PCR, which until that time had little influence in Réunion's municipal government, gained control in three towns (see below).

The PCR controls the island's largest trade union, the General Confederation of Labor of Réunion (Confédération Générale du Tavail de la Réunion; CGTR). The organization's secretary-general is Bruny Payet. The party is also influential within the Réunion Front of Autonomous Youth (Front de la Jeunesse Autonomiste de la Réunion; FJAR), whose secretary-general is André Hoareau, and in the Union of Réunion Women (Union des Femmes de la Réunion; UFR), whose secretary-general is Isnelle Amelin.

Domestic Views and Policies. During 1971 the PCR continued to advocate autonomy for Réunion within a framework of cooperation with France. The political structure of such autonomy, as proposed in resolutions of the party's 1967 congress, would place the island's legislative and executive functions under local control, leaving affairs with France to be handled through a special body (see *YICA*, 1968, p. 506). At a press conference in Paris on 27 April, Vergès stated that France should either renounce the use of "repression" to preserve the colonial government, or accept the right to self-determination of the people of Réunion. The latter solution, sought by the PCR, would create "new and more solid relations with France." (*Témoignages*, 12 June.)

---

[1] Réunion is one of France's Overseas Departments and thus an integral part of the French Republic, administered by a prefect, with an elected General Council and with elected representatives in the French National Assembly and Senate in Paris.

The main domestic preoccupation of the PCR during 1971 was the elections for Réunion's 24 municipalities on 14 March (with runoffs on 21 March). Campaigning as the leading member of a coalition called the Democratic Union, the party gained control in Le Port, Possession, and Saint-Louis, on slates headed respectively by Vergès, Roland Robert, and Christian Dambreville (who, though not a party member, headed a largely communist list).[2] Vergès's list obtained 3,172 votes in the runoffs (52 per cent), Robert's, 1,261 (51 per cent), and Dambreville's, 4,989 (57 per cent). The PCR boasted near victories in Saint-Pierre and Saint-Benoit, where party members Elie Hoarau and Bruny Payet led lists that won 44 per cent of the vote (5,803 and 2,499 votes, respectively). (*Témoignages*, 1 April.) The party claimed also that there was a noticeable rise of leftist forces in Saint-Leu, Saint-Paul, and Saint-André.

International Views and Policies. In international communist affairs the PCR has shown a tendency to adopt independent stands on various issues—divorcing itself from an earlier alignment with the Communist Party of the Soviet Union (CPSU) and the French Communist Party. This tendency was particularly evident in 1968 and was dramatized at the International Meeting of Communist and Workers' Parties at Moscow in June 1969 (see *YICA*, 1970, p. 317). While continuing their relatively independent stance, PCR members traveled widely in 1971, as in previous years, maintaining contacts with other communist parties. Secretary-General Vergès was out of Réunion the entire month of April, during which time he attended the Twenty-fourth Congress of the CPSU and the Tenth Congress of the Bulgarian Communist Party, (besides meeting with communist leaders from Guadeloupe and Martinique in Paris on 14 April (*ibid.*, 3 May). On 27 April, Vergès, Aimé Césaire (leader of the Martinique Progressive Party), and Guy Daninthe (secretary-general of the Guadeloupe Communist Party) met with the press in Paris to talk mainly of the autonomy movement. The interview was reproduced in daily installments in the PCR newspaper *Témoignages* (26 May-12 June). The paper gave much publicity to Césaire, whose party is a strong rival of the Martinique Communist Party, on this occasion and also during the March elections. Held simultaneously in all French overseas departments, the elections were said to have demonstrated the growing strength of the forces favoring autonomy. The "irreversible rise of the popular forces, supported by the great majority of young persons," was seen as reflecting a "fundamental change of the colonial structures" in these departments (*ibid.*, 3 April). A significant effort toward coordinating the autonomy movement was the convening of the communist parties of Réunion, Martinique, and Guadeloupe in Martinique on 16-18 August and the resulting declaration, which called for the preparation of a joint program for autonomy (see *Martinique*). The PCR was represented by Vergès, Elie Hoarau (for the FJAR), and Bruny Payet (for the CGTR). (*Témoignages*, 21 August.)

On 13-16 May Bruny Payet visited Budapest to attend a meeting of the World Peace Council and on 14-19 June Jean-Baptiste Ponama attended the Eighth Congress of the Socialist Unity Party of (East) Germany.

Publications. The daily organ of the PCR is *Témoignages*, edited by Bruny Payet. It claims 6,000 subscriptions. *Jeune Réunion* is the weekly publication of the FJAR.

Eric Stromquist

---

[2]Under the French election system, those persons who represent a party or coalition on a successful list are given authority to elect a municipal council which in turn selects a mayor.

Senegal

The Communist Party of Senegal, designated officially Parti Africain de l'Indépendance (PAI), was founded in 1957. The party was banned in 1960 and many supporters later were jailed. The PAI inaugural congress in 1962 assembled outside the country. PAI membership remains small and appears confined mainly to intellectuals. Exact figures are unavailable. In addition to the PAI, the government banned a number of student and youth organizations, and also the General Union of the Working People of Black Africa (*WMR*, August 1971, p. 86).

Organization and Leadership. The PAI has been careful not to publish current lists of leading officials. According to earlier sources, the secretary-general was Majhemout Diop. In August 1971 the Central Committee reportedly met at Dakar (*IB*, no. 21-22, 1971, pp. 70-71).

Party Policy. The PAI supports an orthodox Marxist-Leninist program. It aims at a "national-democratic revolution," to be achieved through a national unity front. The party opposes "erroneous tendencies that idealize the process of struggle, separating it from the antagonistic class relations." According to PAI interpretation, "American imperialism ... stands at the head of international reaction" and, as these forces weaken, they become more aggressive. ("Declaration of the CC African Independence Party of Senegal," *IB*, no. 21-22, 1971). The party claims that Senegal must achieve "complete political independence." At the moment, political power in Senegal is exercised by the pro-Western section of the African elite. Eighty-five per cent of the modern economic sector (industry, commerce, and transport) is controlled by "foreign monopolies." The French military presence in Senegal, the PAI argues, further curtails Senegalese sovereignty. (*WMR*, August, pp. 85-86).

The party has met with some competition from what it calls "pro-Chinese factionalists," including Malik Kamara, Babakar Niang, and Sall Halil. They seceded from the PAI in 1965 and have carried on active work at lower party levels (*Political Parties of Africa: A Soviet Study*, Joint Publications Research Service, Arlington, Va., 1971, pp. 200-201).

Militant left-wing student activism centers on two groups, the Union Démocratique des Etudiants Sénégalais and the Union des Etudiants de Dakar. In February 1971 both organizations were outlawed. The party also has sympathizers within the Union Générale des Travailleurs Sénégalais en France.

International Views and Positions. The party follows a rigidly pro-Soviet policy. In 1971 it was represented by a "delegation of Marxists" at the congress of the Communist Party of Czechoslovakia (*WMR*, August, p. 86).

Lewis H. Gann

South Africa

The communist party of South Africa, founded in 1921 but officially banned in 1950, reconstituted itself as the South African Communist Party (SACP) in 1953. It was the first such movement to be established on the African continent and the first multi-racial party in South Africa. For considerable time, the SACP has been in a state of disarray. Many leaders and supporters are in prison. More live abroad, especially in Great Britain and Tanzania.

Leadership and Organization. The SACP is now mainly a movement of exiled intellectuals. The only prominent Afrikaner is Abraham (Bram) Fischer, formerly acting chairman of the Central Committee, who was sentenced to life imprisonment in 1966. John B. Marks holds the chairmanship; Moses M. Kotane is general secretary.

In 1970 an augmented meeting of the Central Committee determined that the SACP should be restructured as an organization of professional revolutionaries, close to workers and peasants (*African Communist*, no. 43, p. 54). The party then appointed a new Central Committee but did not publish the names. According to Soviet sources, Brian P. Bunting and Michael A. Harmel are members. Mrs. Hilda Lilian Bernstein, active in the World Peace Council, has been described as belonging to both the Central Committee and Secretariat. Prominent exiles include Ruth Slovo (who publishes under her maiden name, Ruth First), and Percy John (Jack) Hodgson.

The party is closely linked to the African National Congress (ANC), outlawed in 1960. ANC headquarters are in Tanzania. The SACP looks on the ANC as a mass organization dedicated to the struggle for a national democratic revolution. ANC policies correspond in every significant respect to those of the SACP. Oliver Tambo is the ANC chairman, Alfred Nzo, the general secretary.

Early in 1971 the ANC agreed to hold talks in Moshi, Tanzania, for creating a united front with the Pan-Africanist Congress (PAC) of Azania (*Agence France Press*, 23 January). The PAC—a militant African nationalist and non-communist organization—is an offshoot from the ANC, headed abroad by acting president Potlako Leballo. An effective unity movement, however, has yet to be achieved. The SACP, ANC and PAC have been unable to rebuild efficient underground organizations in South Africa. Reportedly, the ANC suffers from internal dissension between Tambo and other leaders such as Duma Nokwe, Tenkyson Makewane, and Reginald September (*Sunday Times*, Johannesburg, 11 April).

Domestic Attitudes and Activities. The SACP program issued in 1962 as *The Road to South African Freedom* (Aldenham, England, Farleigh Press) was developed further by a 1968 meeting of the Central Committee. Its main points were reiterated the following year by J. Marks at the International Meeting of Communist and Workers' Parties in Moscow.

The SACP considers that South Africa differs in many ways from other states. "On the one hand, there is a White South Africa with all the characteristic features of monopoly capitalism. On the other, there is a Non-White South Africa with all the characteristic features of a colony." (John Marks in *WMR*, December 1971). South African monopolists allegedly run the state in collaboration with foreign capitalists—especially British, American, West German and Japanese. This partnership, according to SACP, uses apartheid as a political tool and has created a new form of Nazi dictatorship. All whites enjoy privileges, but the system is reportedly subject to internal contradictions of an irreconcileable nature. In the SACP view, creation of a socialist South Africa must be preceded by a national-democratic revolution, to be attained by forming a united front of all progressive forces.

Under conditions in South Africa, the SACP argues, emancipation cannot be achieved without armed struggle. The party thus rejects the assumption that violent activities should only be initiated when complete political mobilization and nationwide organization have been achieved. On the other hand, it also rejects the concept that localized operations by full-time guerrillas alone can generate revolution. (*African Communist*, no. 43, p. 60)

The SACP and ANC work in alliance with other African organizations such as the Zimbabwe African People's Union (ZAPU), an organization composed of Rhodesian Africans in exile; South-West African People's Organization (SWAPO)' Frente de Libertação de Moçambique (FRELIMO); Movimento Popular de Libertação de Angola (MPLA); and Partido Africano de Independência da Guiné e Cabo Verde (PAIGC). Attempts to send armed guerrillas into Rhodesia and South Africa have met with little success. Guerrillas have not been able to set up bases in Rhodesia, South-West Africa (Namibia), or in South Africa itself. According to government sources, the new revolutionary policy aims at infiltrating unarmed underground fighters with forged passports into Southern Africa. In addition, the ANC intends to intensify underground propaganda, especially among students (*Sunday Times*, 11 April).

The SACP admits that the guerrilla campaign waged in Rhodesia during the 1960's led to "negative experiences" because of "the need to operate in unfamiliar geographic, cultural and social surroundings." (Sol Dubula in *African Communist*, no. 47, pp. 22-38). The Party members argue therefore that "without internal organisation, mass mobilisation and mass support, armed activity becomes strangulated." The resistance forces must initially reply upon "organised full-time guerrilla groups with firepower" and be able to draw on the aid of armed auxiliaries as well as civilian defense groups. The struggle must begin in the countryside, though urban partisan groups should operate in an ancillary capacity. The initial emphasis on waging guerrilla warfare in the countryside "does not of course imply that the rural population (whose support must be won if victory is not to evade us) is the most significant revolutionary force." The armed forces must at all stages remain subordinate to the political leadership. The guerrillas should avoid the "domino theory" according to which the armed struggle in South Africa should be delayed until Portuguese rule has collapsed. On the contrary, ANC, ZAPU, SWAPU, MPLA and FRELIMO can only win by coordinating their operations. (*Ibid*.)

During 1971 South African authorities carried out various arrests under "Suppression of Communism" and "Terrorism" laws. Persons jailed include the Very Reverend Gonville ffrench-Beytagh, Anglican Dean of Johannesburg, who was charged with working for ANC and FRELIMO and was sentenced to five years imprisonment.

International Views and Positions. The party follows a pro-Soviet course. Marks, Tambo, and Nzo attended the Twenty-fourth Congress of the Communist Party of the Soviet Union. In an official message, Marks argued that the growing strength of the Soviet Union would strengthen all working class, revolutionary, democratic and national liberation forces throughout the world (*African Communist*, no. 46, pp. 77-78). Declaring that the congress "bore full testimony to the monolithic unity of the Party of Lenin," he proclaimed undeviating SACP support for Southeast Asian and Arab liberation movements, condemned U.S. and Israeli "aggression," and stressed the party's solidarity with all struggling against "the fascist white minority of the South African Republic, Smith's illegal regime in Zimbabwe [Rhodesia], and the fascist Portuguese colonial regimes." (*WMR*, June, pp. 30-31.) In a joint statement with communist parties in Australia, Canada, Ceylon, Great Britain, Guyana, India, New Zealand, the United States, and Ireland, the SACP condemned British arms sales to South Africa (*African Communist*, no. 46, pp. 79-80). The ANC was represented at the Eighth Congress of the (East German) Socialist Unity Party by Josiah K. Jele.

Publications. The SACP publishes the *African Communist*, a quarterly issued in London, as "a forum for Marxist-Leninists" throughout Africa. In 1971 the party began to publish *Inkululeko* (Freedom), an underground sheet. The ANC publishes *Sechaba*, a monthly, in Dar-es-Salaam. The *Sechaba* office in London also circulates other political publications.

Lewis H. Gann

Sudan

The Sudanese Communist Party (SCP) traces its origins to 1944. Two years later, it first appeared as a properly constituted body under the name Sudanese Movement for National Liberation. Between 1958 and 1964, it was forced to operate clandestinely. Temporarily legal, it was once more banned within a year. The communists nevertheless continued to operate almost openly, and in 1967 the SCP held its Fourth Congress at Khartoum. In May 1969 all Sudanese political parties, including the SCP, were banned, following a coup détat led by Ja'far Muhammad al-Numairi. At the same time, several communists and pro-communists joined the government. They included left-wing officers such as Lieutenant Colonel Ba Bakr al-Nur, Major 'Uthman Hamd Allah, and Major Hashim al-Attah who became members of the Revolutionary Council. Two reputed members of the SCP Politburo Joseph Garang (a southerner) and Faruq Abu 'Isa, were admitted to the cabinet. But relations between the SCP and the government soon deteriorated. In November 1970, party secretary-general 'Abd al-Khaliq Mahjub was placed in detention together with Dr. 'Izz al-Din 'Amir, one of Mahjub's leading communist supporters. Ba Bakr al-Nur, Hashim al-'Attah, and Faruq 'Uthman Hamd Allah, were dismissed from their government positions. In 1971 these officers carried out a short lived coup. Numairi, however, turned against his opponents, including the SCP, and executed many of the party's leaders (including Mahjub and supporters. (See below.)

There are no reliable figures concerning SCP membership. Most estimates ranged from 5,000 to 10,000 before Numairi's liquidation campaign. The total losses suffered by the party are hard to gauge, as opinions differ widely on the total number put to death. Clearly, the party has been thrown into a temporary state of disarray. But the SCP had been the largest communist party in Africa. It had numerous supporters among intellectuals (including teachers, doctors, government officials, and army officers), tenant farmers, railroad workers, and urban workers. The party also had extensive experience with underground organization. A good many of its leaders escaped the purge and they will certainly try to rebuild the cadres.

Leadership and Organization. Before the Sudanese government set out to destroy the SCP, the party had been structured on what was styled "territorial-production" lines. It claimed to be a party of laborers in factories, fields, and offices. At the same time it considered the working class as the most organized element in society, since it was most closely connected with modern methods of production. The primary organizations centered both on the members' work location and their place of residence. The primary organizations were run by zonal committees, organized on a "place of production" basis. The three southern provinces comprised one zone (this zone posed special problems for the party owing to the backward nature of the region, its ethnic and cultural composition, and local guerrilla warfare waged by militant African separatists).

According to the rules adopted at the Fourth Congress, zonal committees call annual conferences. The highest organ was the party congress, which assembled every two years. Between congresses, the party was governed by the Central Committee, which elected the Politburo responsible for party work between plenums of the Central Committee. (*Political Parties of Africa: A Soviet Study*, Joint Publications Research Service, Arlington, Virginia, 1971. pp 219-20.)

The party has exercised considerable influence within labor unions, especially the Federation of Farmers' Unions and the Sudan Workers' Trade Union Federation, both affiliates of the All-African Federation of Trade Unions. (Al-Shafi Ahmad al-Shaikh, a Lenin Peace Prize laureate who served as secretary-general of the Sudan Workers' Trade Union Federation was executed in the wake of the coup.) The communists ran the so-called Democratic Front, a student organization financed by the SCP. (Salah al-Din al-Zain al-Tayyib, *The Students' Movement in the Sudan* 1940-1970, Khartoum University Press, 1971, pp. 43-43). The party had electoral support especially in Omdurman, where Mahjub was elected to the legislature in 1969 as an "undeclared candidate."

After Mahjub's execution, Muhammad Ibrahim Naqud was elected secretary-general. Naqud has been an SCP member since 1950, the party's leading ideologue, and, since 1960 a Central Committee member (*Arab World*, Beirut, 12 August 1971). Other leaders are Dr. 'Izz al-Din Ali Amir and Mahjub 'Uthman, both living in London which at present is the main opposition center, followed in importance by Cairo (*An-Nahar Arab Report*, Beirut, 11 October.) Other communists said to have escaped from the purge include Tijani al-Tayyib, reputedly head of the party secret apparatus, and Jazul al-Sayyid and Sulaiman Hamid, member of the Politburo (*Arab World*, 12 August).

In October 1971 Sudanese communists in London circulated a statement signed by the "provisional General Secretariat of the Sudanese Popular Resistance Front." It claimed to represent the SCP, the Federal Democratic Party, the Umma Party, the Sudanese Federation of Trade Unions, the Federation of Youth, and the Federation of Students. These exiles announced a conference, to be held in the first week of October, for the purpose of reorganizing the SCP. The conference sought to mobilize support among Sudanese students in Eastern and Western Europe. It also proposed to re-evaluate the purge and make plans to overthrow Numairi. (*An-Nahar Arab Report*, 11 October.)

Domestic Views and Policies. At its 1967 congress the SCP declared its goal to be a national-democratic revolution through a bloc of democratic forces, including workers, farmers, revolutionary intellectuals, and anti-imperialist members of the national bourgeoisie. According to the SCP, the main danger facing Sudan was neo-colonialism, while indigenous Sudanese capitalists were not necessarily regarded as members of a comprador-bourgeosie. Private capital was seen as having a constructive role, provided its operations corresponded to the national interest. The SCP looked to agrarian reform to eliminate foreign capital from the agricultural sector, and put an end to semi-feudal relations and the power of large landowners. The party also called for industrialization as an essential step on the way to socialism, in which basic enterprises would become part of the state sector. The SCP strongly opposed the secessionist movement in the southern provinces which had led to prolonged fighting there. Southern secessionism was held to be a legacy of "Arab feudal lords" and "British colonialists." Hence the southern problem would hinge on the struggle against backwardness. Success, however, could only come through a democratic victory in the Sudan as a whole. (See *WMR*, July 1968; *African Communist*, London, no. 37, 1969).

The SCP meanwhile suffered from disagreements concerning tactics. A "left" faction apparently accused Mahjub of wishing to liquidate the SCP as a party, and to substitute "the ideas of the Socialist Democrats" for Marxist theory. According to these dissidents, the party leadership had failed in developing a revolutionary policy toward southern Sudan. The party leadership, moreover, had remained silent regarding official Sudanese state visits to the People's Republic of China and the Democratic People's Republic of Korea. (*An-Nahar Arab Report*, 3 May 1971). Mahjub himself held to a pro-Soviet line. He gave qualified support to the government, but refused to merge the

SCP with Numairi's other supporters, and apparently he disagreed with various SCP members who had joined Numairi's administration. This latter group included prominent party members, such as Abu 'Isa, Ahmad Sulaiman, Mu'awiyah Ibrahim, and Joseph Garang. (*Ibid.*, 19 April.) The Central Committee was said to have split over the question, while the Politburo apparently remained unaffected directly, as most of its members supported Mahjub (*Ibid.*, 5 April). The division between those who were willing to accept a single national party, comparable to Nasser's Arab Socialist Union in Egypt, and those who wanted to maintain the SCP as a separate organization, was made more bitter by disputes over Arab-Sudanese relations. Militant nationalists desired a federation of Egypt, Libya, and Sudan. Mahjub and his adherents considered such a project premature, because it would have further diminished SCP influence within the Sudan.

The SCP thus became weakened by internal disagreements. In late 1970 and early 1971 Numairi embarked on a selective purge of communists and communist sympathizers from his administration. Ba Bakr al-Nur, Faruq 'Uthman Hamd Allah, and Hashim al-Attah were forced to retire from their official posts. Mahjub was arrested, and Numairi quietly tried to restore confidence in the private sector at a time when the country faced serious economic difficulties. In February 1971, in a nationwide broadcast, Numairi accused communists of plotting against his government and called on the people to "destroy" the party (*New York Times*, 13 February). This move was linked to an anti-left campaign pursued by the Libyan government, which had begun to deport leftist Palestinians and other opponents of the regime (*Arab World Weekly*, Beirut, 20 February). In June, Numairi carried out further arrests, including nearly all members of the Central Committee; another 130 were placed under surveillance. (*Foreign Report*, Washington, 17 June).

The left-wing officers referred to above then embarked on their ill-fated coup. An authoritative account remains to be written, but it is clear that on 19 July army units commanded by Hashim al-'Attah occupied all important public buildings in Omdurman and arrested al-Numairi. The next day a new Revolutionary Council took office, headed by Ba Bakr al-Nur, with Hashim al-'Attah as his deputy and Hamd Allah as a member. Omdurman radio proclaimed that the new government would establish a national-democratic alliance composed of toilers, intellectuals, "free officers," soldiers and national capitalists. Sudan would take a "non-capitalist course" and collaborate with the "anti-imperialist camp of the world." Enemies of the revolution would be jailed or executed. (*Arab World Weekly*, 24 July).

According to the SCP account, the party had been unabiguously against a "strategy of conspiratorial military *coups d'état*, as opposed to or detached from patient mass upheaval." Yet, when the Free Officers' Organisation staged the coup, "the Communist Party felt that it could not betray its allies ... The Communist Party mobilised its members and rallied the progressive masses in support of the new regime." (al-Mahdawi, "Dark Days in the Sudan," *African Communist*, no. 47.) Certainly, the party backed the left-wing officers, once they had assumed power. On 21 July the Sudanese trade unions called for a mass demonstration of solidarity with the new authorities. On the following day, Ba Bakr al-Nur and Hamd Allah flew from London to Sudan in order to assume their seats on the Revolutionary Council. The aircraft was forced to land in Libya, where both men were arrested by Libyan policy.

The insurgents appear to have made a serious mistake in their assessment of the army's political loyalties. Troops loyal to Numairi struck back. They were reinforced by Sudanese soldiers flown back in Egyptian planes from their stations along the Suez Canal Zone. In the last hours of the coup, the insurgents decided to execute all pro-Numairi officers held in detention. Thirty-eight were reportedly shot, but the killing only further embarrassed the communists and their supporters. Numairi returned to power and decided to exterminate the opposition. (Colin Legum, "Sudan's Three Day Revolution," *Africa Report*, Washington, October, pp. 12-15; "Sudan: Chronik eines Putsches," *Internationales Afrika Forum*, Munich, September-October, pp. 501-10.)

Leaders of the coup were executed, including Hamd Allah, Ba Bakr al-Nur and Hashim al-'Attah. Also killed were Mahjub, Shafi Ahmad al-Shaikh, head of the Trade Union Federation, and Joseph Garang, Minister of State for Southern Affairs. (*Economist*, 31 July.) Soviet sources complained of the "continued reign of terror," and Nikolai Podgorny, the Soviet head of state, appealed personally to the Sudanese government to abstain from further "harsh sentences" (TASS, 31 July). Published figures on persons imprisoned or put to death differ. The Sudanese Information Minister stated that more than 1,000 persons would face possible prosecution for complicity in the coup (*New York Times*, 29 July). In another statement Muhammad Idris, Minister of the Economy, stated that "some 20,000 to 30,000" communists would be rounded up (*Le Monde*, Paris, 29 July). Another source reported that 2,000 communists had been arrested immediately after the coup and that another 700 were jailed early in August (*New York Times*, 15 August).

Communist-controlled mass organizations were broken up and their leaders jailed, including activists such as the head of the women's organization, Mrs. Fatimah Ibrahim (*Le Monde*, 29 July).

International Views and Positions. The SCP follows essentially a pro-Soviet course, though some members appear to have taken a more independent line. At the International Meeting of Communist and Workers' Parties in 1969 at Moscow, Mahjub congratulated the Soviets "on the result of measures taken in August to safeguard socialism in Czechoslovakia." The SCP condemns consistently what it describes as the machinations of "American imperialists" and of their various "allies," especially the Zionists. The party, however, is by no means united on international questions, as some communists are apt to place more stress on Arab nationalism than on international "socialist solidarity." Soviet attitudes themselves are by no means clear cut. At the Twenty-fourth Congress of the Communist Party of the Soviet Union (CPSU), the official Sudanese delegation was headed by Interior Minister Major 'Abdal-Quasim Muhammad Ibrahim, and included the very man in charge of national security and engaged in repressing the SCP, Major Ma'mun 'Awad Abu Zaid. (*Arab World*, 29 March.) The Sudanese delegation supposedly included also two members of the SCP whose names were kept secret (*An-Nahar Arab Report*, 5 April). Published reports do not permit an exact assessment of relations between the CPSU and the SCP, but apparently the Soviet Union endeavored to mediate between the SCP and the Numairi regime before the left-wing coup was launched. A point of dispute is whether and, if so, to what extent the Soviet Union was involved in the attempt to seize power. Certainly the abortive coup, for the time being, had a negative effect on relations between the two countries.

The coup also involved the broader question of inter-Arab relations. For example, the Ba'thists in Iraq defended the Sudanese communists (*Arab World*, 27 July). Libya and Egypt, on the other hand, backed the Numairi government.

According to a public statement attributed to Dr. 'Ali 'Amir, the failure of the coup was made possible only by concerted action of Egypt, Libya, and the Numairi government. The "counterrevolutionaries" were able to make use of Egyptian army radio transmission facilities and military aircraft. 'Ali 'Amir expressed fears that Egypt, Syria, and Libya together might act as "gendarmes" against the Arab peoples and, thereby, aid the colonialist cause.

According to published reports, the Chinese gave implied support to Numairi during the coup and, unlike the Soviet Union, made no public protest against the persecution of Sudanese communists. In October, the People's Republic of China officially congratulated Numairi on being elected president of Sudan.

Publications. Before its suppression, the SCP published an illegal daily, *al-Maidan* (The Arena). The party reportedly once again is attempting to create facilities for underground propaganda.

Lewis H. Gann

Syria

The Syrian Communist Party (al-Hizb al-Shuyu'i al-Suri; SCP) is an offshoot of the Lebanese Communist Party (LCP). During the French mandate over Syria and Lebanon, membership in the LCP was open to communists from both states. Under the guidance of Khalid Bakdash, a dynamic Syrian Kurd who became first secretary of the party in 1932, Syrian elements attained dominance. When national independence was granted to Syria and Lebanon in 1943, party independence was a logical consequence and Bakdash assumed the leadership of the newly formed SCP. Separation occurred under amicable conditions, and the strong initial ties between the Lebanese and Syrian communist parties have weakened only gradually over the years. The SCP is firmly pro-Soviet in orientation.

French authorities proscribed all communist activity in 1939, and this ban continued after Syria's independence. Despite illegality, the SCP has enjoyed several periods of considerable political freedom. The last began in 1966 when a communist was named to a cabinet post for the first time by the extreme left-wing faction of the Ba'th (Arab Socialist) Party that had just assumed power after a successful intra-party coup. The new rulers were willing to grant a certain measure of tolerance for SCP activities in exchange for communist cooperation—an arrangement of convenience that has continued. In fact, the communist position improved further after a bloodless coup in November 1970 gave control of both the Ba'th Party and the government to Lieutenant General Hafiz al-Asad, previously the defense minister and head of the "military" faction of his party. As a result of changes brought about by al-Asad, two communists held cabinet posts in 1971 and eight were members of the People's Council, the newly established 173-seat Syrian legislature.

Leadership and Organization. Membership in the SCP is believed to range between 3,000 and 4,000. The population of Syria is 6,294,000 (estimated 1970). The party is headed by Khalid Bakdash, who is generally considered the most important communist in the Arab world. He has held the post of first secretary—with a brief interval in 1968—since the party was established. Bakdash was reelected to lead his party in June 1969, when the SCP held its Third Congress. The Politburo chosen at the same time was composed of Bakdash, Ibrahim Bakri, Riyad al-Turk, 'Umar Qashshash, Yusuf Faisal, Daniel Ni'mah, and Zuhair 'Abd al-Samad. The last three and Murad Yusuf were named party secretaries.

Politburo member Yusuf Faisal is the minister of state in the Syrian cabinet, and 'Umar Siba'i, a member of the Central Committee and chairman of the SCP Control Commission, is communications minister. The communists on the People's Council are Ibrahim Bakri, Maurice Salibi (who briefly headed the SCP in 1968 while Bakdash was out of the country, reportedly recuperating from a heart attack), Khalid Hammami, Muhammad al-Habal, Samih 'Atiyah (a predecessor of 'Umar Siba'i in the communications ministry), Hazim Mahmud Hazim, 'Isam 'Abd al-Rahman, and 'Uthman Ibrahim.

Party Internal Affairs. The Beirut daily newspaper *al-Hayat* on 25 November reported that Khalid Bakdash had been removed as leader of the SCP and that Daniel Ni'mah was expected to succeed to the top party post. The paper described a "coup" within the SCP against "the Stalin of Damascus" and cited divergent views on Syrian participation in the tripartite federation of Arab states (see below) as the immediate cause of the conflict. The SCP promptly issued a denial in a statement carrying the signatures of Bakdash and the members of the Politburo. *Al-Hayat* (4 December), nevertheless, followed up with a story that the SCP had set up a "General National Council" and alleged that this proved party adoption of collective leadership and the demotion of Bakdash after thirty years of party service. At the end of the year the facts remained to be ascertained.

Domestic Attitudes and Activities. Anti-communist campaigns that threatened the life and freedom of SCP members in 1970 and caused marked hostility between the Ba'th government and the communists did not recur in 1971. Instead, communists enjoyed unprecedented recognition and freedom. In turn, they showed their appreciation by fully backing al-Asad's nomination for the presidency and urging SCP members to vote for him in the popular referendum held in March. In a speech before the People's Council, Ibrahim Bakri praised the "positive achievements" under al-Asad, especially noting his intention to draft a permanent constitution for the country that would include provision for parliamentary elections by direct vote of the populace. Bakri also paid special tribute to al-Asad's government for having introduced family allowances, cuts in some essential commodity prices, and additional freedom of movement and travel. He considered all these innovations as benefiting the popular masses as a whole. (*al-Nida*, Beirut, 9 March.)

Syria's communists have for several years advocated the "unity of all the devout and noble forces in a single progressive front." In 1971 they expressed willingness to cooperate with the Ba'th leaders, who themselves were hoping to set up a permanent "national front" to be composed of the various groups participating in al-Asad's coalition government. When a special 13-member committee was appointed on 22 May to lay the groundwork for the eventual implementation of such a national front, the SCP was represented by Yusuf Faisal. Most committee members belonged to the Ba'th Party, but in addition to the SCP the group included representatives of the Nasserite faction of the Arab Socialist Union in Syria, the Socialist Unionists, and the Syrian Socialist Party (*Arab World Weekly*, Beirut, 29 May).

Before the referendum in March, al-Asad indicated that he foresaw the eventual transformation of the proposed national front into a single political party. The communists withheld comment, and it remains questionable whether they would agree to dissolution of their party. Arab communists undoubtedly are mindful of the fate of Sudan's communists in 1971, subsequent to the request by the government of Ja'far Muhammad al-Numairi that the Sudanese communist party disband and join a proposed Sudanese state-controlled political organization patterned after the Egyptian model.

In this frame of reference the reaction of the SCP to the establishment of the tripartite Federation of Arab Republics by the United Arab Republic, Syria, and Libya is important. After the agreement was signed in April the Politburo of the SCP in a special communiqué (published in *al-Nida*, 24 April) announced "support for this step" and called on party organizations and members to "work for its success and realization." The pillars of the federation, the statement declared, "are in content democratic, progressive, anti-imperialist, and anti-Zionist." The principles of the federation were described as "realistic and consistent" and in accord with the conclusion of the party's Third Congress that "Arab unity, when achieved, must only be progressive Arab unity." Later the SCP reaffirmed its "approval of the basic provisions of the Federation" before Syrian citizens were to cast their votes in a referendum in September. "May the referendum be a great manifestation against imperialism, Zionism, and reaction, and for friendship with the Soviet Union," the Politburo declared in a statement issued in Damascus on 16 August (*al-Nida*, 18 August).

These lukewarm phrases produced a feeling of scepticism in non-communist circles. The *Arab World Weekly* (August 19), for instance, cited the opinion expressed by some independent or right-wing observers, who attributed the SCP endorsement of the federation to the party's desire to "play a greater nationalist and internationalist role," and held that the sole communist alternative to approval was to return to "their cells underground" and withdraw from participation in the government. In any case, there was reason for communist apprehension about the federation and the influence exerted within it by Egypt and Libya, neither of which tolerates communist parties at home.

International Views and Activities. The SCP's international views revolved around its opposition to "imperialism, Israel, world Zionism, and the lag in building a unified Arab socialist society" and its efforts to gain greater solidarity with the socialist states and especially with the Soviet Union (*al-Nida*, 18 May). The SCP frequently stressed the interrelationship of various forces: "To fight Israel, it is necessary to oppose the plans of U.S. imperialism—the plans that prompted [Secretary of State] Rogers's visit to several Arab states, Turkey, England, and Israel ... particularly for the purpose of preserving oil concessions and to impose solutions of capitulation on the Arab countries." All such moves, the SCP alleged, were meant to advance the imperialist objectives of the United States—to expand Israeli territory, to liquidate the progressive regimes in Egypt, Syria, and other Arab states; to strike a fatal blow at the Arab liberation movement; and to break up Arab-Soviet friendship. (*Ibid.*)

The communist parties of Syria, Iraq, Lebanon, and Jordan issued a number of joint documents relating to the Arab-Israeli conflict or the problems of the Arab world. At the conclusion of a conference held early in the year to discuss the most urgent current events, the four parties commented on some "internal difficulties and hindrances obstructing the course of the Arab national liberation movement," but also recorded these "notable successes": (1) "Preservation of the progressive regimes in Egypt and Syria and their great economic and social achievements. New gains, especially completion of the Aswan Dam and work on the Euphrates Dam." (2) The "victory of the Sudanese revolution, the overthrow of the monarchical regime in Libya, and the progressive developments in southern Yemen." (3) The "introduction of great changes in the armed forces of Egypt and their defensive and offensive capabilities ... all with the effective and unlimited aid of the Soviet Union." (*al-Akhbar*, Beirut, 24 January.)

The joint party statement balanced confidence with suggestions for greater achievements and warnings of the "danger to peace" caused by Israel's "aggressive expansionist policy." It focused on the need to strengthen the combat ability of the Egyptian and Syrian armies and to make Iraq a more reliable partner on the eastern front. Iraqi effectiveness, it was argued, would have to be preceded by the government's solution of domestic problems, "especially the questions of democracy and the implementation of the 11 March [1970] agreement with the Kurds." Early in the year the Palestinian resistance was urged to escalate operations inside the occupied territories. Most importantly, and throughout the year, all Arab countries were reminded that the elimination of all manifestations of anti-democratism and anti-communism was basic to the adoption of united positions on all major issues.

The four communist parties jointly protested against the "moves by the reactionary element in Jordan to liquidate the Palestine liberation movement," and against its "criminal campaign," with its "outright brutality" and "massacres." At the same time they suggested adherence to the action program which the communist commando organization Ansar al-Silm (Partisans of

Peace) had submitted to the Palestine Liberation Organization. Included in the program were proposals for safeguarding the rights of guerrillas, opposing trends towards isolation and adventurism, and forming a united front with the Jordanian national forces. (*WMR*, March.)

On 13 May the communist parties of Syria, Lebanon, and Jordan denounced the Iraqi government for "measures of suppression and terrorization" against the Iraqi Communist Party. In particular they protested the disappearance of Central Committee member Thabit Habib al-'Ani after an alleged kidnaping in the streets of Baghdad (*al-Nida*, 14 May). The most "wrathful condemnation," however, followed the reprisals against the communists in Sudan, subsequent to their brief assumption of power after a coup in July (see *Sudan*). The execution of the secretary-general of the Sudanese Communist Party, 'Abd al-Khaliq Mahjub, and dozens of other party leaders and members was characterized as a "crime" and "savagery" and the deaths as a "shameful stain" on the Sudanese authorities. The terror, according to a joint document (TASS, 30 July) played only into the hands of imperialist and reactionary circles by undermining Arab cooperation. The document further called upon the progressive forces of the world to stop the "massacre" and to encourage the Sudanese Communist Party to "rally its ranks" and continue its "historic mission." More importantly perhaps, the SCP Politburo appealed to the Syrian Ba'th Party on 25 July to "use its influence and power in a way it deemed fit, to stop the blood bath and executions in the Sudan." (*An-Nahar Arab Report*, Beirut, 9 August).

The Syrian communists looked to the Soviet Union for moral support or assistance with serious problems. This is hardly surprising since Khalid Bakdash is known as one of the most loyal boosters of the Communist Party of the Soviet Union (CPSU) and as a propagandist for the "harmfulness" of anti-Sovietism. In 1971 Bakdash had an opportunity to heap praise on the Soviet Union in his address to the Twenty-fourth Congress of the CPSU in Moscow early in April: "The interests of the USSR are inseparable from those of the world Communist movement and of all the peoples. There are no contradictions between their genuine national interests and those of the great socialist state, the USSR. That, indeed, is the objective foundation of true internationalism, and we are confident that harmony and identity of genuine patriotic and international interests is fully possible." (*WMR*, June.)

Some mystery surrounds the return of Bakdash and an SCP delegation to Moscow three weeks after his departure at the conclusion of the congress. A communiqué covering bilateral talks with the Soviet Union early in May merely referred to an "exchange of views on the situation in the Middle East," but it is probable that intervening developments alarmed Syria's communists to such an extent that they dispatched a delegation to seek Soviet advice. The new meeting may have been related to any or all of the events that had occurred in the meantime in the Arab world—U.S. Secretary of State William Rogers's visit to Cairo for discussions with Egyptian President Sadat; the signing of the tripartite agreement setting up the Federation of Arab Republics; and the extensive political purges in Egypt, where many men considered sympathetic to the Soviet Union had been ousted from sensitive posts.

An SCP party statement issued early in May specifically criticized Rogers's travels: "Before coming to the Middle East, Rogers visited London where he met with British and NATO officials and obtained their support for U.S. imperialist policy in the area—a policy hostile to the Arab liberation movement, the U.S.S.R. and the other socialist bloc countries." Rogers was said to have gone on from Europe to the Middle East in order to forge a "new link in the chain of imperialist conspiracies to entrench Israeli occupation of Arab territory, gain time, and weaken and liquidate the progressive Arab regimes, particularly those of Syria and Egypt." (*al-Nida*, 6 May.) A few weeks later the SCP welcomed the signing of the Soviet-Egyptian treaty of friendship and cooperation, which it called a "serious blow" to the United States and Israel (TASS, 3 June).

Publications. The SCP party organ, *Nidal al-Sha'b* (People's Struggle), is printed in Lebanon. The party, however, disseminates most of its news through the two legal Lebanese publications, *al-Nida* and *al-Akhbar*.

*　　*　　*

In 1970 a small pro-Chinese splinter group, calling itself the Arab Communist Marxist-Leninist Party, was reportedly gaining strength. In 1971 no new information became available about this Maoist group, which had been most vocal at the time of the Jordanian civil war in September 1970.

Edith Wyden

Tunisia

The Tunisian Communist Party (Parti Communiste Tunisien; PCT) was founded in 1920 as a part of the French Communist Party. It became independent in 1934. Banned since 1963, the party has continued to operate in a clandestine fashion, but its membership remains insignificant. Its main appeal seems to be confined to students and intellectuals, including Tunisian residents abroad, especially in France.

Leadership and Organization. Mohammed en-Nafaa is secretary-general of the PCT. In January 1971 he officially asked President Bourgiba to lift the ban against the PCT, in accordance with the "liberalization and democratization" advocated by the government (*Jeune Afrique*, Paris, 19 January). The PCT, however, has not as yet succeeded in its endeavor to reform the party on a basis of legality.

Domestic Views and Activities. In a published statement, en-Nafaa argued that the party should take a positive view of President Bourgiba's views concerning a "socialist option." Nevertheless these views would have to be translated into practice. For instance, Ahmed ben Salah (formerly head of the Union Générale des Travailleurs Tunisiens, UGTT, and a cabinet minister), who had been imprisoned as a result of a "political trial" in Tunisia, should be released. Tunisian democracy, en-Nafaa continued, could only be assured by protecting the workers against "the egoism of certain employers," and against the effects of inflation. Farmers must be safeguarded against the encroachment of speculators; landless peasants should be enabled to own land. Young people should be able to exercise their right to better education and better jobs. "All democrats, all progressives and supporters of socialism should be free to express and uphold their views." (*IB*, 21 February 1972, p. 60-61.)

Communists have some influence among Tunisian students. The Tunisian university students comprise Arab nationalists, Destourians, Maoists, and Trotskyists. Toward the end of the year students assembled in the courtyard of the Faculty of Law at Tunis attacked the officially sponsored Union Générale des Etudiants Tunisiens (UGET) on the grounds that the union was unrepresentative of students and subject to government control. The communist students took a more conciliatory line; they censured the UGET Executive Bureau but spared the "orthodox" Destourians. According to published reports, the communists hope to share control of the UGET with the Destourians. (*Jeune Afrique*, December 1971.)

International Positions. The PCT follows a pro-Soviet and anti-Maoist line. Its views received authoritative expression in 1969 when, at the International Meeting of Communist and Workers' Parties held in Moscow, Mohammed Harmel, secretary of the Central Committee, expressed his party's complete agreement with the policy of the Communist Party of the Soviet Union (CPSU) and the proceedings of the conference. Harmel criticized the foreign policy pursued by the Tunisian government on the grounds that it did not follow an "anti-imperialist" course (*IMCWP*, p. 185-90). In 1971 the PCT was represented, again by Harmel, at the congress of the CPSU (*Internationales Afrikaforum*, Munich, June, p. 356).

Publications. In January 1971 the PCT requested the Minister of the Interior to permit the publication of a periodical to be entitled *Dialog* (*Jeune Afrique*, 19 April). This application does not as yet appear to have succeeded. Earlier publications have included *al-Tariq* (The Way, in Arabic) and *Espoir* (Hope, in French).

United Arab Republic (Egypt)

A communist party existed in Egypt from 1923 to 1965, but never enjoyed legal status or more than negligible political influence. Fragmented and subject to internal dissension, the Communist Party of Egypt (CPE)—reportedly with the blessing of the Soviet Union—decided to dissolve itself in April 1965. It urged its estimated 800 to 1,000 members to affiliate on an individual basis with the Arab Socialist Union (ASU), the mass political organization established by the regime of Gamal Abdel Nasser in 1962 as the only legal political group in the country. Rationalized as a step consistent with the Soviet policy of "progressive" single-party rule, the dissolution of the CPE resulted in lessening of friction between Egypt and the Soviet Union.

The influence of individual Egyptian communists was hardly diminished when the CPE ceased to exist. In fact, the new conditions permitted some party members to melt into the mainstream of Egyptian political life by becoming active in the ASU, while others continued to hold on to powerful positions in the government-controlled press. Some became, or remained, active in international communist front organizations, notably the Egypt branch of the World Peace Council (WPC) and the Cairo-based Afro-Asian Peoples' Solidarity Organization (AAPSO). From these various vantage points, dedicated communists could advocate close ties with the Soviet Union and emphasize "socialist construction" at home.

After 1965, the best-known Egyptian communist was Khalid Muhyi al-Din, (the "Red Major"), a Marxist politician of long standing, who served as secretary-general of the Egypt National Peace Council and a member of the Presidential Committee of the WPC. In spite of his outspoken views, Muhyi al-Din became a member of the ASU Central Committee in 1968, and in 1969 was elected to the National Assembly, the legislative body of Egypt. It is significant that he assumed these offices even though early in 1968 he had used the pages of a French communist publication (*Démocratie Nouvelle*, Paris, February 1968) to advocate the formation of a "revolutionary vanguard party" that would "constitute the nervous system of the ASU and work inside it to direct the masses."

In 1971, the year of political upheaval and "plots" and "purges" in the U.A.R., both Muhyi al-Din and a "vanguard" organization within the ASU figured prominently in the news. Early in May, when President Anwar al-Sadat ousted the "pillars of the Nasserite regime" (including a vice-president, several cabinet ministers, leaders of the ASU, and the commander of the army) and accused them of masterminding planning for the overthrow of the existing government, attention focused on the semi-secret "Socialist Vanguard" organization within the ASU as the nucleus of the conspiracy. The group was suspended by Sadat on 14 May because of "deviation by certain leaders." There remained an aura of mystery, but also the growing impression that the "special organization" was identical with the "vanguard party" within the ASU, which Soviet commentators had hailed for several years as "recognizing the leading role of the working class and the principles of scientific socialism.'' The *New York Times* (18 and 21 May) called the faction ''Communist-oriented,'' and said that it was believed to comprise 500 to 800 persons, ''some acknowledged Communists and other opportunists or fellow-travelers,'' and that members had infiltrated key areas of the Egyptian administration during the past several years. Other connotations used in the foreign press for the group were the ''Nasserite left,'' ''pro-Communist,'' or the ''pro-Soviet wing of the ASU'' (*Intercontinental Press*, New York, 31 May).

Khalid Muhyi al-Din escaped arrest at the time of the major roundup of leftists and ''plotters'' in May, when President Anwar al-Sadat ousted the ''pillars of the Nasserite regime'' (including policy maker—what the Communist Party is in the Soviet Union.'' This view was reportedly shared by then Vice-President 'Ali Sabri and other Egyptian officials subsequently arrested and brought to trial for conspiracy later in the year; it was also said to be enjoying the backing of the Soviet Union and to be suspect because it was impinging on the authority of Egypt president himself.

In spite of this background, Muhyi al-Din, as head of the Egyptian Peace Council, was quick to announce support for Sadat after the May purges. He declared that Egyptian Marxists had but a single ''mission''—to assure that Sadat's promises of public freedom and democracy would be realized (*Arab World*, Beirut, 31 May). Questioned as to whether Marxism seemed suitable to Egyptian needs, Muhyi al-Din acknowledged that he supported Marxism politically, but that in Egypt it was necessary to ''find special methods and ways'' to apply it ''in the light of existing realities, socioeconomic conditions and the degree of intellectual development.'' He explained by adding: ''We cannot ignore religion.'' (*Arab World Weekly*, Beirut, 5 June).

On 6 August the Beirut newspaper *al-Nahar* reported that Muhyi al-Din had been placed under house arrest and that the timing coincided with the recess of the National Assembly, because as a member he had enjoyed immunity while the assembly was in session. Simultaneously the imprisonment of Dr. Ibrahim Sa'd al-Din, director of the Socialist [Studies] Institute in Cairo was announced. Both men were held responsible for a statement by the Executive Council of the Egyptian Trade Union Confederation (issued on 1 August) expressing shock at the bloody persecution of communists in Sudan following their abortive coup. The statement embarrassed the Egyptian government, which officially supported Sudanese President Ja'far Muhammad al-Numairi. The less punitive treatment accorded Muhyi al-Din may have been due to his status as a member of parliament, but it was also rumored that the Soviet Union had requested ''clarification'' on his arrest and had threatened to hold up deliveries of arms. It is likely that the Soviet Union, which had awarded Muhyi al-Din a Lenin Peace Prize in 1970, was alarmed at his detention and may have been instrumental in arranging for his release on 22 August for ''special reasons'' that the public prosecutor refused to divulge.

By no means all Egyptian Marxists—they prefer that connotation rather than ''communists''—were in serious trouble with authorities in 1971. Two of them, Dr. Fu'ad Mursi and Dr. Isma'il Sabri 'Abd Allah, were appointed to high-level governmental positions after the purge, even though both had been leaders in the Communist Party of Egypt before its dissolution. Mursi was named to the nine-member interim secretariat of the ASU, which was charged with reorganizing the organization. He expressed his loyalty to Sadat and pointed out that for the first time a prominent Marxist had been appointed to an important ASU committee. He noted that ousted leaders like former Vice-President 'Ali Sabri had tried to identify themselves with Marxists, ''but they never allowed us to be members in leadership units'' (*Arab World Weekly*, 29 May). He also implied that Marxists would not try to reestablish the communist party, because they considered the ASU ''the best formula for progressive forces, within which to operate'' (*Arab World*, 31 May).

Dr. Isma'il Sabri 'Abd Allah, appointed the new deputy minister of planning late in May, was reportedly reluctant to accept the post, but took the oath of office a few days after the signing of the fifteen-year Soviet-Egyptian Treaty of Friendship and Cooperation on 27 May (*ibid.*, 4 June).

The treaty was probably of some benefit to the interest of Egypt's communists, although a few days after its signing events in Sudan induced Egypt president to rebuff the Soviet Union by his unequivocal declaration that Egypt would continue to resist communism in the Arab world and would never be communist herself or recognize an Arab communist government (*New York Times*, 8 June). This attitude was slightly tempered in October when a joint communiqué issued at the conclusion of President Sadat's visit to the U.S.S.R. included a strong condemnation of "anti-Communism and anti-Sovietism" in the Arab world (*ibid.*, 17 October). The non-communist Lebanese newspaper *al-Hayat* (Beirut, 4 October) expressed the belief that the Soviet Union may have had to make some concessions of its own, and that President Sadat traveled to Moscow to submit some of his country's demands, including the following: "[That the Soviet Union] instruct the communist parties in the Arab world to suspend their activities against the Arab regimes which support Egypt in its struggle against Israel, to shelve for the time being the question of local communists, and not to include them in [Soviet] political strategy for the area."

In 1971 Egyptian political ideology and communism continued to be as far apart as in the past. Nevertheless, Soviet ideologists refused to acknowledge that Arab forms of socialism were based on local conditions and preferred to regard them as steps on the road to "scientific socialism." A commentator on Moscow radio (18 October) attributed Egyptian progress to its "socialist orientation" and close links with the Soviet model, and concluded that Egypt would "strive to exploit the rich experience of the Soviet Union and other socialist countries." Soviet scholar Rostislav Ulyanovsky, writing in *World Marxist Review* (September) on "Marxist and non-Marxist Socialism," stated that "left wing groups, can, after starting from non-Marxist national socialism, advance toward scientific socialism," and that this possibility "should never be underestimated."

Soviet claims appear to run counter to the late President Nasser's warnings against the dangers of "accepting ready-made theories and dispensing with national experiences" because the "real solutions of any people cannot be adopted from the experiences of other peoples." As late as May 1970 Nasser also tried to distinguish between Egyptian and Soviet systems with the comment: "The Soviet Union is a communist state, while we are trying to be a socialist state." Throughout the years of his rule, he rejected force and violence associated with communist social change, disavowed a dictatorship of the proletariat or one-class government of any kind, and termed freedom of religion "a sacred thing."

There was no sign in 1971 that Nasser's views had been repudiated. In fact, the new constitution of the Arab Republic of Egypt—the country is renamed in the document promulgated and approved by plebiscite in September—contains nothing to give new hope to communists at home or abroad.

Edith Wyden

WESTERN HEMISPHERE

Argentina

The Communist Party of Argentina (Partido Comunista de Argentina; PCA) originated from the International Socialist Party (Partido Socialista Internacional), founded in 1918. Its present name was adopted in 1920.

The PCA claims to have "over 100,000 members" (*WMR*, April 1971), and thus to be the second largest communist party in Latin America, outside of Cuba. Non-communist sources, however, put PCA membership at between 30,000 and 60,000. The population of Argentina is 23,800,000 (estimated 1970).

PCA membership, two-thirds of which is concentrated in Buenos Aires Province, is drawn mainly from the middle and lower urban classes. The social composition of the party was reflected in the class distribution of delegates at its Thirteenth Congress, held in March 1969: 72 workers, 10 persons in the "liberal professions," 6 teachers, 5 writers and journalists, 4 peasants, 2 housewives, and one student. The PCA is believed to be financially wealthy, mainly because of its indirect participation in various commercial and banking enterprises.

On 1 July 1971 the military government allowed the functioning of political parties, which had been banned since 1966. The PCA continued to be an illegal party due to various anti-communist laws still in effect (see *YICA*, 1971, p. 363). The government reportedly was willing to grant legal status to the PCA, which was considered different from the leftist groups that advocate violence, but this did not materialize. Meanwhile the PCA operated more or less openly, and its participation in the National Assembly of Argentines (see below) was not hindered.

In addition to the PCA, which follows a pro-Soviet line, other communist parties in Argentina include the Revolutionary Communist Party (Partido Comunista Revolucionario; PCR), the pro-Chinese Communist Vanguard (Vanguardia Comunista; VC), and a Trotskyist movement, split into several factions.

In recent years other small leftist groups (composed of Castroite or Peronist radicals, or both) have emerged. While not all of these espouse communist ideologies, they share a strategy of armed struggle to seize power. Their total membership, distributed in about 15 organizations, is estimated at between 6,000 and 7,500 (*Latinamerica Press*, Lima, 17 March 1970).

The military regime which has governed Argentina since 1966 has been unable to resolve the nation's economic difficulties, and has faced increasing labor pressures and disturbances, but these have come mostly from pro-Peronist sectors; communist influence on national affairs has been negligible thus far. The numerous subversive actions carried out by the small leftist groups have forced the government to adopt harsh measures against terrorism.

The PCA. Leadership and Organization. The PCA is led by Secretary-General Gerónimo Arnedo Alvarez. Important members of the Central Committee, elected in March 1969, include

Rodolfo Ghioldi, Orestes Ghioldi, Vicente Marischi, Alcira de la Peña, Fernando Nadra, Héctor Agosti, Pedro Tadioli, Rubens Iscaro, Benito Marianetti, Oscar Arévalo, and Julio Laborde.

The PCA is organized pyramidally from cells, neighborhood committees, and local committees on up to provincial committees and the Central Committee. The Central Committee is composed of 21 full and eight alternate members. In addition there is the Executive Committee, with 11 members, and the Secretariat, with five.

The PCA youth movement, the Communist Youth Federation (Federación Juvenil Comunista; FJC) is organized along the same lines as the party. It claimed to have 35,000 card-carrying members in 1967; however, defections during 1967 and 1968 affected its strength considerably. Admitting weakness in factories and rural areas, the FJC reported to have at present 30,000 members (*Nueva Era*, April 1971). The FJC also claims to control the University Federation of Buenos Aires, which consists of 40 per cent of all Argentine university students. The FJC's Ninth Congress, held on 19-22 February 1971, approved documents reflecting the PCA political line. Héctor Santarén is the FJC secretary-general.

The PCA is weak within the labor movement despite the presence of party branches at working centers in the oil and timber industries and in sugar refineries, mines, and steel plants. The major trade union body, the General Workers' Confederation (Confederación General de Trabajadores; CGT) is controlled by Peronists, who are very powerful and reject communist support. The PCA influences the Movement for Trade-Union Unity and Coordination (Movimiento por la Unidad y Coordinación Sindical; MUCS), which represents small regional unions, mostly those centered in Córdoba Province. PCA Central Committee member Rubens Iscaro is its secretary-general. The MUCS was expelled in 1970 from the "Opposition CGT"[1] and since then has been unable to work with a nationwide labor confederation.

Although peasant organizations are mostly grouped under the non-communist Argentine Agrarian Federation, the PCA claims to be an active participant in the "Union of Agrarian Producers of Argentina" (UPARA), which was formed in 1969. UPARA is composed of small and medium-sized farmers and is said to have 60,000 members (*ibid.*, March).

Most PCA fronts, such as the Argentine League for the Rights of Men, the Union of Argentine Women (UMA), and the Argentine Peace Council, are illegal. There is, however, communist participation in the Argentine's Women League, in MODENA (a group composed of civilian and military men seeking to protect national resources), and in MAVIET, the "Argentine Movement of Help to Vietnam."

Domestic Attitudes and Activities. The PCA subscribes to the policy of creating a "broad democratic front" to overthrow the present military government. In this context, the most significant PCA activity during 1971 was the apparent consolidation of the National Assembly of Argentines (Encuentro Nacional de los Argentinos; ENA), a coalition formed on 20 November 1970. PCA Executive Committee member Rodolfo Ghioldi is a member of the central governing board of the ENA. Along with communists, the coalition appears to include large numbers of dissidents from the People's Radical Civic Union and the Christian Democratic, Argentine Socialist, Popular Union, and Progressive Democratic parties.

On 26 April 1971 the ENA held an open meeting in Buenos Aires that was attended by some 25,000 persons. At that time its leadership signed a statement calling for the construction of a

---

[1]The "Opposition CGT," also known as the "Rebel CGT," is a radical labor union advocating "national and social liberation," meaning the expulsion of the monopolies, destruction of the oligarchy, and the implantation of socialism. It is considered to represent about 10 per cent of the organized workers.

new Argentina to be accomplished through the "eradication of two evils": the "imperialist domination" of the economy and the "anachronistic" system of ownership and use of the land (*Propósitos*, Buenos Aires, 22 April). The same document declared that the ENA sought a "complete electoral solution" to the political situation but held that the prerequisite to "genuine elections" was the establishment of a provisional government composed of representatives of all civilian and military sectors opposed to the existing regime. The program approved by the ENA, as described in the document, called for the elimination of foreign monopolies, nationalization of foreign trade and banks, agrarian reform, higher wages and pensions, new policies on housing and health, and an "independent" foreign policy (*ibid.*). During the year, the ENA held anti-government rallies in several large cities and claimed to have won the adherence of various small political groups and labor unions.

The PCA also issued appeals for the formation of a provisional government. On 16 July the Central Committee delivered a statement to the press media, in which it described President Alejandro Agustin Lanusse (who seized power on 23 March) as "a typical representative of the oligarchy and the Pentagon's man." The PCA reportedly printed more than a million copies of a pamphlet describing Lanusse's proposal to hold elections on 25 March 1973 and to return the country to civilian rule as a "great alliance between the dictatorship and the right wing of the political parties." Subsequently the PCA seemed to modify its appraisal of Lanusse. According to *La Opinión* (Buenos Aires, 29 September), the PCA Executive Committee had decided not to use the word "dictatorship" to describe his government and intended to support his political plans, including the 1973 elections. A September issue of *Nuestra Palabra*, the party's official organ, praised Lanusse's closer ties with Chile, his visit to Peru, the establishment of relations with Mongolia, and the announcement of future recognition of the People's Republic of China which took place in February 1972). Furthermore, when there was an attempted coup against Lanusse on 8 October by two army regiments, the PCA immediately released a statement calling upon the people to "rebuff" the attempt to overthrow the government. The statement referred to the rebel army officers as "extreme rightists" and accused the U.S. Central Intelligence Agency of conspiring with them to establish a "Brazilian-type fascist dictatorship" in Argentina (*IB*, no. 20).

The PCA continued to seek increased participation with workers. Acknowledging the predominance of Peronist-oriented workers in labor unions, the party differentiates between a "rightist" Peronist leadership, which is said to "gravitate toward fascist corporatism," and the masses, who are "under the spell of Peronist ideology" but hold "anti-imperialist and anti-oligarchic" positions (*WMR*, July). The PCA was able to participate through the MUCS and a smaller group, the National Inter-Union Commission, in a "Plenary of Combative Unions" held at Córdoba in June and attended by representatives of 124 unions and 17 federations. This meeting—which included participation of orthodox Peronists (from the "62 Organizations") and independent workers from the Fiat-Concord automotive complex in Córdoba—approved a program calling for a "classist labor movement" to achieve nationalization of foreign trade, banking, and insurance, expropriation of all strategic industrial monopolies, government appropriation of national resources uncompensated expropriation of landholdings, and total planning of the economy (*Cristianismo y Revolución*, Buenos Aires, June).

Other PCA activities during the year included the holding on 8-9 May of a "National Conference of Communist Women," one of whose objectives was the attainment of a 30 per cent female membership in the party.

International Views and Positions. In 1971 the PCA continued its pro-Soviet orientation. On 24 April its Executive Committee passed a resolution praising the Twenty-fourth Congress of the Communist Party of the Soviet Union (CPSU), which it described as "a substantial and most important contribution to the cause of communism and socialism, anti-imperialist liberation, peace, and democracy'' (*Nueva Era*, May). The party reaffirmed its appraisal of the CPSU as the "vanguard of the world revolutionary movement" and affirmed that "close and unbreakable friendship with the CPSU" was the "fundamental element of the PCA's political line." The same resolution referred to "crude and mendacious attacks" against the Soviet Union and its party by the Chinese communist leaders, whom it condemned for attempting to split the communist movement in many countries (*ibid.*).

The PCA gave considerable attention to political developments in Chile, Peru, and Bolivia (under the government of General Juan José Torres). These events, it declared, had "shaken U.S. imperialism and the Rightists" (*WMR*, April). Fernando Nadra, in a speech at the Fourth Congress of the Communist Party of Venezuela declared that the victory of Popular Unity in Chile had opened new prospects for the revolutionary forces in Latin America (*Tribuna Popular*, Caracas, 11-17 February). A plenary meeting of the PCA Central Committee on 7-8 August commented on the Salta Declaration by the presidents of Argentina and Chile (expressing the mutual desire to respect each other's sovereignty and to maintain friendly relations) signed on 24 July, and asserted that the declaration had "struck a blow at the policy of aggression pursued by the U.S. imperialists, who wanted to isolate Chile from the rest of Latin America" (*IB*. nos. 18-19).

The PCA expressed solidarity with the peoples of Vietnam and the Arab countries in their struggle against "imperialist" and "Zionist" aggression, respectively. As in previous years, the PCA donated 5 per cent of the proceeds from its annual fund-raising campaign to North Vietnam. This gift in 1971 amounted to about $26,700.

The jailing, in the United States, of the black communist Angela Davis, aroused the interest of the PCA, which called for international expressions of support for her. Davis was said to personify the "revolt of the blacks and impoverished classes." (*Nuestra Palabra*, 19 October.)

International Party Contacts. The PCA was represented at the Twenty-fourth Congress of the CPSU by Rodolfo Ghioldi, Athos Fava, and Alcira de la Peña.

Other PCA contacts included the attendance of Fernando Nadra at the Fourth Congress of the Communist Party of Venezuela (January), Pedro Tadioli at the Eighth Congress of the Socialist Unity Party of (East) Germany (June), and Eduardo Yañez at the Third Congress of the Communist Party of Bolivia (June). Repeating relations initiated in 1970 when a PCA delegation visited Cuba on 24 December 1970-19 January 1971, Secretary-General Arnedo Alvarez visited Cuba on 27 October-12 November at the invitation of the Communist Party of Cuba. He met with Fidel Castro and other party and government leaders. The PCA also attended a meeting of seven South American communist parties held in September at an undisclosed location.

An ENA delegation attended a meeting of the Uruguayan Broad Front in Montevideo on 8 October.

Publications. The PCA weekly, *Nuestra Palabra*, claims a clandestine circulation of 30,000 copies. The PCA also publishes *Nueva Era*, a monthly theoretical journal, and the bimonthly *Cuadernos de Cultura*, catering mainly to intellectuals. Since August 1970 the party has published the *Boletín de Informaciones Latinoamericanas*, a fortnightly report on communist activities and revolutionary events in Latin American countries. The Communist Youth Federation prints a fortnightly paper, *Juventud*.

*   *   *

The PCR. The Revolutionary Communist Party, formed originally as the Communist Party of Revolutionary Recovery, was created on 6 January 1968 by dissidents from the PCA and especially its Communist Youth Federation, who rejected the PCA's attempt to create a "broad democratic front" as an attempt at "class conciliation" and "conciliation with imperialism."

The PCR leadership includes César Otto Vargas (as secretary-general), Carlos Echagüe, Jorge Rocha, Miguel Rubinich, Sergio Rodríguez, Manuel Campos, Fanny Echagüea, and Lucila Irene Edelman, all of whom held important positions within the FJC before their expulsion from the PCA in 1967.

The PCR advocates armed struggle to gain power, but believes that the leadership in the revolutionary movement must be held by the party. The PCR favors only urban guerrilla struggle, contending that the "wide plains" of Argentina's interior and the "highly developed agriculture on the coast" would not permit successful operations by peasant guerrillas (*Punto Final*, Santiago, Chile, 17 June 1969).

The PCR apparently engaged in no major activities during 1971, except for its participation in the elections held on 27-30 November by the Argentine University Federation (Federación Universitaria Argentina; FUA), in which its candidates were defeated.[2]

Publications. The PCR publishes the clandestine *Nueva Hora*.

*   *   *

The VC. The Communist Vanguard was founded by Elías Seman, probably in 1964. Although this pro-Chinese movement is said to have some influence among student and worker groups, it has few militants and did not seem to be active during 1971.

*   *   *

Trotskyism in Argentina is represented by two groups, the Revolutionary Workers' Party (Partido Revolucionario de los Trabajadores; PRT), aligned with the United Secretariat of the Fourth International, and Política Obrera, which is apparently an independent Trotskyist group. Several PRT factions and Política Obrera endorse Castroite principles and the Latin American Solidarity Organization, based in Havana.

The PRT. In 1968 the PRT divided when two-thirds of its members espoused the concept of armed struggle. The views of the majority faction are expressed in its organ, *El Combatiente*, and those of the minority in *La Verdad*.

The "armed branch" of the "majority" PRT, the People's Revolutionary Army (Ejército Revolucionario Popular; ERP), has been in existence since August 1970. The ERP is believed to be strong in Córdoba and Rosario, and to a lesser degree in Tucumán and Buenos Aires. It is reportedly led by Robi Santucho, although it follows a cellular type of organization, with a political commissar in each cell appointed by the PRT.

During 1971 the ERP carried out numerous actions, involving mostly money robberies. Many of the ERP activities, which paralleled those of the Tupamaros in Uruguay, followed "armed propaganda" tactics; that is, they were executed with the purpose of "linking the masses to the revolutionary forces." Thus the ERP undertook numerous actions involving the distribution of food and clothing in poor neighborhoods.

---

[2]There appear to be two FUA groups. One, centered in Buenos Aires and led by Hugo Varsky, is said to be under the control of pro-Soviet students. The other FUA, apparently the larger group, was previously under the leadership of the PCR but is now in hands of relatively moderate leftist students.

On 23 May the ERP kidnaped the British consul in Rosario, who was also the manager of the U.S.-owned Swift meat packing plant, and subsequently released him in exchange for Swift's distribution in ten slums of foodstuffs, blankets, shoes, and other supplies valued at $57,000. The ERP staged one of the largest thefts in Argentina's history on 12 February, when it obtained $302,500 from an armored truck in Córdoba. Another large robbery was carried on 1 September, when the ERP "expropriated" some $64,000 from the Tucumán telephone company payroll.

The ERP program (quoted in *Cristianismo y Revolución*, Buenos Aires, April) called for an end to political and military pacts with the United States, the establishment of a revolutionary people's government led by the working class, expropriation without payment of enterprises connected with "imperialist" capital, agrarian reform, and termination of agreements with the International Monetary Fund and other organizations "dominated by imperialist capital."

In an interview given to *Indoamérica* (Santiago, October), ERP leaders stated that the party believed in "revolutionary civil war" to attain power. At the same time they declared a willingness to participate in the proposed 1973 elections if this "suited" ERP purposes. They were careful to specify that such a participation would be independent of the ENA or the "Hour of the People,"[3] both of which were said to be "closely identified with the government's farce."

Statements by the ERP on international issues referred to the "recognized leadership" of the Communist Party of Cuba in the revolutionary movement in Latin America. Regarding Chile, the ERP held that the "hour of armed confrontation" was coming closer because the Chilean bourgeoisie would not give up its privileges easily. Further, the "correct line and action to bring about the success of the revolution in Chile" was that being advocated by the Movement of the Revolutionary Left (see *Chile*).

The police arrested several ERP militants in April in Rosario and particularly on 12 December in Córdoba, where about 30 members were arrested and weapons and documents were seized.

A third PRT faction, formed in 1970 under the name of Milicia Obrera, apparently was inactive during 1971.

*   *   *

Castroite groups in Argentina are small and tend to have a brief existence. Among these, the Argentine Liberation Front (Frente Argentino de Liberación; FAL) and the Revolutionary Armed Front (Frente Armado Revolucionario; FAR) continued to be the most prominent.

The FAL. The Argentine Liberation Front, a Marxist-Leninist group advocating Castroite tactics, was formed in 1962. Its membership is believed to include many students and persons in professions.

An FAL communiqué early in the year called for mass actions to end the "exploitation of the working class" and the people in general. It concluded with the slogan: "Neither Coup nor Election—Revolution for Liberation and Socialism!"

The FAL was involved in various bombings and assaults during 1971, including the setting off 11 bombs in business firms in Córdoba on 30 March. A FAL group of some 15 members was arrested by police in the city of La Plata in July.

The FAL reportedly has established contacts with the ERP, with the objective of signing an agreement. The two groups are known to have staged minor joint actions.

---

[3]The "Hour of the People," formed in December 1970 in response to the emergence of the ENA, is composed of the National Justicialist Movement, the People's Radical Civic Union, the Popular Conservative Party, and moderate sectors of the Progressive Democratic and Argentine Socialist parties. It was believed to be almost dissolved by the end of 1971.

The FAR. The Revolutionary Armed Front, which began to operate in July 1970, has been described as a "conglomeration of ultra-left Marxist groups with sectors of revolutionary Peronism" (*Análisis*, Buenos Aires, 4-10 August 1970). The FAR advocates Guevarist tactics, holding that "it is not possible to wait for all conditions to exist; they will never exist all at the same time if revolutionary action is not begun" (*Cristianismo y Revolución*, April 1971). At the same time, the FAR considers itself Peronist because it shares the objectives of "social justice, economic independence, and political sovereignty" with other Peronist groups.

Toward the end of May, the FAR, the Peronist Armed Forces, and another Peronist group called the Montoneros formed an alliance as the "Peronist Army." Spokesmen for these three groups declared that they were not divided by basic political issues and that they were united by "three key factors: the method, the energy, and the final goal" (*Guardian*, New York, 25 August).

FAR actions during 1971 included stealing ammunition from army trucks and police stations. It was credited with bombing a country club at Córdoba in October and stealing drugs and surgical equipment valued at $8,000 from a Buenos Aires clinic in December.

Nelly Stromquist

Bolivia

The Communist Party of Bolivia (Partido Comunista de Bolivia; PCB) was founded in 1950. It is pro-Soviet in alignment. A pro-Chinese splinter of the PCB became the Communist Party of Bolivia, Marxist-Leninist (Partido Comunista de Bolivia, Marxista-Leninista; PCB-ML) in 1965. A Trotskyist group, the Revolutionary Workers' Party (Partido Obrero Revolucionario; POR), is currently split into three factions. A Castroite guerrilla organization, the National Liberation Army (Ejército de Liberación Nacional; ELN) has existed since 1966.

The various party memberships are estimated as follows: PCB, 3,000; PCB-ML, 1,000; the three factions of the POR, a total of 1,000; and the ELN, between 80 to 100 members. The population of Bolivia is 4,600,000 (estimated 1970).

All of these groups continued to be technically illegal during 1971, but were allowed to engage in political activities under the leftist government of General Juan José Torres (7 October 1970 to 22 August 1971). In fact, the alliance of leftist and communist forces that was instrumental in helping Torres attain power organized itself early in 1971 into a "People's Assembly," which was granted recognition by the government (see below). Following the rightist military coup led by Colonel Hugo Bánzer, the communist movement was driven underground and many of its leaders were forced to flee to Chile. Since November 1971, the PCB, PCB-ML, two factions of the POR, and a new Marxist-Leninist group, the Revolutionary Left Movement, have joined forces with the Revolutionary Party of the Nationalist Left (Partido Revolucionaria de Izquierda Nacionalista; PRIN), the Revolutionary Armed Forces, and General Torres to form the Anti-Imperialist Revolutionary Front (Frente Revolucionario Anti-imperialista; FRA), which seeks to overthrow Bánzer.

The PCB. Leadership and Organization. The first secretary of the PCB is Jorge Kolle Cueto. Other prominent party members are Mario Monje Molina, a former first secretary, and Central Committee members Simón Reyes, Aldo Flores, and Luis Padilla.

The PCB's youth organization is the Communist Youth of Bolivia (Juventud Comunista de Bolivia; JCB). It is illegal and is operated clandestinely by its Executive Committee. Spokesmen for the group include Jorge Escalera and Carlos Soria Galvarro. At the university level the PCB influences the University Front of National Liberation (Frente Universitario de Liberación Nacional; FULN).

Despite party claims to represent the "largest and best organized labor movement" in Bolivia, the PCB appears to influence only marginally the powerful Bolivian Workers' Center and the Minerworkers' Federation of Bolivia, both of which are led by Juan Lechín Oquendo, who is also a leader of the PRIN. PCB Central Committee member Simón Reyes occupies a leadership position within the Minerworkers' Federation. Little or no influence in the countryside is attributed to the PCB.

Domestic Attitudes and Activities. The PCB seeks to unite all revolutionary forces in order to create a "people's government" to carry out an anti-imperialist revolution and establish a socialist system. As a pro-Soviet party, the PCB emphasizes mass struggle as the means to power and pays only lip service to the concept of armed struggle. It maintains that under Bolivia's social, economic, and political conditions the leadership of the revolution can belong "only to the working class" (Central Committee report, *El Diario*, La Paz, 20 June).

Most important among the PCB's activities during the year was the holding of its Third Congress, on 11-12 June. Held seven years after the previous congress, the Third Congress addressed itself mainly to the changes in the domestic scene brought up by the Torres government—which, as noted above, permitted the left to function openly—and to the guerrilla actions of 1967.

In response to charges that have been made by various revolutionary communist groups both in Bolivia and in the rest of Latin America who accuse the PCB of having "betrayed" Che Guevara, the Third Congress devoted extensive coverage to the guerrilla actions undertaken in Bolivia by the ELN in 1967. A report presented by Secretary-General Kolle stated that the PCB had not learned of the ELN plans until January 1967 and that the decision on whether or not to support Guevara, who had asked for military command over political leadership, had been taken in the "course of one single session" and that the "absolute majority" determined at that time that the situation was unfavorable to develop armed struggle. Kolle stated that according to the ELN plan Bolivia would be the last country to be liberated, probably following a long struggle lasting 10 to 20 years, and that it was going to serve mainly as a "disseminator of armed struggle." Che Guevara's failure was attributed to "the manner in which the guerrilla group was organized" and to "the political and social conditions surrounding its development." Furthermore, Kolle argued:

> Even if true military and paramilitary support had been put in practice by the party, the final course of the guerrilla movement would not have changed. There probably would have been more fighters and, consequently, more revolutionary heroes, but there is no valid reason for maintaining, a posteriori, that things would have changed radically. (*Ibid.*)

The Third Congress made reference to the Torres government as the "expression of a break in the political unity of the Armed Forces, placing a patriotic, progressive sector, a democratic group in open confrontation with a counterrevolutionary, Pentagon-controlled group." The PCB expressed support for the "anti-imperialist features" of the Torres administration but held that the "best ensurance of a consistent course for the anti-imperialist offensive" was to be found in the newly formed People's Assembly, which in the party's opinion was to become "an instrument of apprenticeship in political and government activity for worker leadership and for leaders of the people." The report presented by Kolle read in part:

> The People's Assembly is and can be objectively the great unifier, the organized force of the masses, their instrument to which is allied the military team that is aware of the needs of the Bolivian people. Only imperialism, the reactionaries, and those who feel jealous of its activity because they place personal interest above the interests of the people can fear it. (*Ibid.*)

The fall of Torres in August was attributed in part to the failure of the People's Assembly to unite and mobilize the "anti-imperialist forces." In an article published in *World Marxist Review* (November), Central Committee member Luis Padilla asserted that the poor performance of the People's Assembly was, in turn, the result of the "negative, misleading role of the ultra-leftists," who, instead of strengthening the People's Assembly by neutralizing the "bourgeois and petty-bourgeois groups" in it, wanted to convert the assembly into a parallel government—that is, they considered it a "dual power." Padilla also held that the coup led by Colonel Bánzer had been directed by the U.S. Central Intelligency Agency, which sought to "check the liberation movement, restore the U.S. monopolies to their lost position, and 'rehabilitate' the capitalist way of development."

During 1971, the PCB continued its condemnation of the more revolutionary communist groups, which advocate armed guerrilla struggle. At a party meeting on 18 June, Kolle stated that "no one in Latin America or in our country has inflicted such great harm on the communist movement as the ideological deserters who call themselves 'leaders' and 'heroes.' A war must be proclaimed against the theory of 'foci' within our ranks and especially among the youth." The Third Congress, on the other hand, specifically attacked the ELN for having "facilitated the enemy's work of disorganizing the revolutionary forces," and thus "delayed the goals for which it said it was fighting." The congress also accused the pro-Chinese and "ultra-leftist" groups of "destroying the political possibilities of the urban middle groups" and of "frightening" the progressive sectors of the bourgeoisie.

The PCB did not engage in any significant domestic action following Bánzer's takeover in August. As noted before, the PCB leadership exiled in Chile formed a united front with other Bolivian communist and leftist forces with the objective of overthrowing Bánzer and establishing "a government of Bolivians under the leadership of the proletariat" (*El Siglo*, organ of the Communist Party of Chile, Santiago, 14 November).

The People's Assembly. This body, officially organized on 11 April 1971, had its origins in the alliance of leftist forces in October 1970, which threw its support behind General Torres and enabled him to seize power. Although the People's Assembly came into being primarily through the efforts of the non-communist Bolivian Workers' Center, which sought to have "its own political instrument," it became very important in the Bolivian political scene because it brought together labor unions and several leftist parties in an organized form for the first time in the nation's history.

The People's Assembly was composed of some 218 members, with labor unions accounting for 60 per cent of its membership, the middle class sectors 25 per cent, peasants 10 per cent, and left-wing parties 5 per cent. Seats among these parties were distributed as follows: PRIN, 2 seats; PCB, 2 seats; PCB-ML, 2 seats; POR (Lora faction), 2 seats; Revolutionary Christian Democratic Party, 2 seats; and MIR, 1 seat.

The assembly did not achieve legal status, but it was recognized by Torres, who saw in it a significant and very much needed source of support. For its part, the People's Assembly, led by Juan Lechín Oquendo, purported to keep a "check" on the Torres government to prevent it from making concessions to the right and to impose laws designed to "deepen the anti-imperialist struggle going on."

The People's Assembly installed itself in the Bolivian Congress building (left vacant since 1969) and held several meetings between June and July, during which time personal conflicts and a lack of political agreement were observed. Among the measures passed by the Assembly were the participation of miners in the administration of the Mining Corporation of Bolivia; an investigation of "criminal acts committed against workers, students, and revolutionaries during prior administrations"; and the establishment of diplomatic relations with Cuba. Despite rumors of plotting by rightist army officers, the assembly adjourned in July for two months. It was expected that after reconvening the assembly would discuss the formation of a people's militia, which was being strongly advocated by the labor unions.

Although the People's Assembly had threatened to call for a general strike in case of a "fascist coup," such action did not materialize. The military forces under Bánzer repressed with violent means the physical opposition of several hundreds of workers and students, and after defeating them proceeded to dissolve the People's Assembly.

International Views and Positions. The PCB continued to be closely aligned with the Soviet Union, a position which was reaffirmed at its Third Congress.

The PCB congress also made reference to the "patriotic, progressive position of the military government of Peru" and to the changes brought forth by the Allende government in Chile. The congress maintained that Bolivia, Peru, and Chile had formed the "Triangle of the Pacific," which was said to represent "a common process [of liberation], although on different levels and also with different possibilities. (*El Diario*, 20 June.)

A Soviet broadcast in Mandarin to China (21 May) referred to a PCB Central Committee plenum held on 8-9 May, during which the Bolivian party praised Soviet efforts to "defend the pureness of Marxism-Leninism" and attacked the Chinese "anti-imperialist struggle program," which was said to be directed toward "opposing the unity of the revolutionary forces and the communist parties of various countries" and to have "nothing to do with anti-imperialism."

Party Contacts. The PCB attended a meeting of seven Latin American communist parties held in September, possibly in Argentina, to exchange information and opinions on problems common to the Latin American countries.

Publications. The PCB organ is *Unidad*. The JCB publishes *Temple*.

*   *   *

The PCB-ML. Although the Communist Party of Bolivia, Marxist-Leninist was formally established in April 1965, for several years previously pro-Chinese tendencies and even organizations existed among Bolivian communists. The secretary-general of the PCB-ML is Oscar Zamora Medinacelli, who is also the primary spokesman for the party.

A rival PCB-ML was apparently set up early in 1971. In a letter published in *El Diario* (9 February), Jorge Echazú Alvarado accused Zamora of betraying the party to further his own personal ambitions. He said that Zamora and his group had "degenerated into a group of friends who methodically practice slander, blackmail, and the most barefaced demagogy," and called for their expulsion from the party.

The youth group of the PCB-ML bears the same name as its pro-Soviet counterpart, the JCB. Among its leaders are Roberto Sánchez, Raúl González, and Jorge Rodríguez. The group plays an active role in university affairs and influences the Anti-Imperialist University Front (Frente Universitario Anti-imperialista; FUA). Oscar Paz, a leading FUA member, was reportedly shot to death by pro-Bánzer forces on 20 August.

The PCB-ML seems to have developed a peasant base. Its secretary-general, Zamora, was said to lead the Union of Poor Peasants (Union de Campesinos Pobres; UCAPO), which seeks agrarian reform through armed struggle.

Domestic Attitudes and Activities. The most significant event by the PCB-ML was doubtless its participation in rural guerrilla actions, together with various undetermined peasant groups. Early in February the Bolivian armed forces discovered a pro-Chinese guerrilla camp near Santa Cruz Department and seized arms, uniforms, and several guerrilla members, including PCB-ML Secretary-General Zamora. Because of student pressure, the Torres government was lenient with the guerrillas and exiled them to Chile on 14 February. It was later reported that Zamora had secretly returned to Bolivia in June.

Zamora, known as "Commander Rolando," was active encouraging peasants in Santa Cruz Department to seize private lands. UCAPO actions were reported also in the departments of Beni, Cochabamba, and Potosí. On 24 August the UCAPO joined forces with the ELN in an attempt to fight Bánzer's government. Subsequently, army clashes with guerrilla groups were reported in Santa Cruz and Cochabamba.

The PCB-ML took part in the People's Assembly. Its delegation introduced a motion calling for the adoption of the policy of armed struggle to achieve power. This motion, which received the support of university student and peasant delegates, was rejected by labor leaders in the People's Assembly, some of whom refusted to debate the motion and staged a walkout.

Publications. The organ of the PCB-ML Central Committee is *Liberación*. Party statements are also found in the *Peking Review*.

*   *   *

The ELN. The National Liberation Army, formed late in 1966, came into wide notice during 1967 under the leadership of Che Guevara. In October of that year Guevara and all but five members of the group were killed by Bolivian military forces. Present leaders of the reorganized ELN are Osvaldo "Chato" Peredo, Jorge Gustavo Ruíz Paz (alias Omar), and Moisés Suárez Moreno.

The ELN subscribes to the "foco" theory of armed struggle and is avowedly an international organization, incorporating within its ranks guerrillas from Bolivia, Brazil, Argentina, Colombia, Peru, Chile, and perhaps other countries. A party publication issued in July 1971 maintained that the ELN "has not and will not back down on the necessity to form a revolutionary guerrilla army with the support of a military and political leadership capable of encouraging armed actions in every possible area, such as in mines and farming areas."

During 1971 the ELN published a document entitled *Teoponte, Our Guerrilla Experience*, in which it revealed details about the guerrilla actions of July-October 1970. This document asserted that the failure of the Teoponte actions had demonstrated the necessity to "be able to depend on a solid base of clandestine urban and rural organization" and that, therefore, the ELN would attempt to create a "physical-military apparatus" for that purpose.

Actions by the ELN during 1971 included the kidnaping of a businessman, Johnny von Berger, in La Paz on 3 May. He was released two days later after payment of a $50,000 ransom. Another ELN action was the assassination in Hamburg of Colonel Roberto Quintanilla, a former chief of the Bolivian Department of Intelligence. The ELN called his death "an act of revolutionary justice" because of his participation in the deaths of Che Guevara and "Inti" Peredo (the latter killed in 1969).

ELN reactions toward the government of General Torres seemed mixed. A party bulletin issued on 24 March stated that there were anti-imperialist men in the government and that Torres was one of them, but argued that they were few in number and that, as long as the army was the basis of support, the Torres government would not be able to carry out a real revolution. Another ELN bulletin, in May, called upon the "honest military men" who had been "deceived and confused by imperialism" to form another army "led by military patriots and revolutionaries, which will serve the people with their weapons."

The ELN did not participate in the People's Assembly; a party statement regarding the Assembly argued that it should become not "a financial instrument of government work, much less a parliamentary group that elaborates suggestions," but "a real structure of political and military organization of the masses, capable of taking the offensive through direct action" (*El Diario*, 1 July).

In the midst of the coup against Torres, the ELN issued a communiqué on 21 August announcing that it was joining the forces of General Torres to fight against the rebel army groups. It was later reported that following Bánzer's coup, "Chato" Peredo and other guerrillas in exile in Chile had returned to Bolivia. The ELN claimed responsibility for several explosions in the Santa Cruz airbase on 23 September.

In March 1971 the ELN began to publish *Inti*, allegedly a regular monthly bulletin.

*   *   *

The POR. The Revolutionary Workers' Party, which has some influence among miners and students, is divided into three factions. The first, under Hugo González Moscoso, is aligned with the Trotskyist Fourth International-United Secretariat. The second faction, headed by a well-known political figure and historian of the Bolivian labor movement, Guillermo Lora, has contacts with the Fourth International-International Committee. The third faction, the POR-Trotskyista (PORT), is the smallest. It is aligned with the Fourth International-International Secretariat (Posadas branch) and is led by Amadeo Vargas.

The Lora faction, as noted above, took part in the People's Assembly, where it was represented by two delegates. In May, the Lora faction, as well as the PCB-ML and the revolutionary wing of the Christian Democratic Party, was accused by government officials of causing social unrest by occupying farms and public buildings with the purpose of turning them into schools and colleges. Lora was forced to seek asylum in the Mexican Embassy in September, following the overthrow of President Torres.

The González faction did not participate in the People's Assembly. Apparently it felt that the People's Assembly could "have no role except as an organ of dual power." The González faction's publication (*Combate*, 1-15 May) maintained that the assembly "must not simply debate and watch over government functions; it must—as the expression of the power of the great masses of our people—decide the basic questions facing the workers and the masses." In an interview with *Bandiera Rossa* (Rome, September), González stated that his group had "good relations" with the pro-Chinese and that "it was capable of coordinating actions with them." He also declared that his party's relations with the ELN were "marked by sympathy" despite disagreements on the concept of armed struggle, since González group advocates guerrilla war "tied to the masses, developed in the most important cities, in the mining regions where the most radicalized and aware sectors of the proletariat can be found, and in the rural areas, side-by-side with the peasant masses."

The González group claims to influence the Independent Confederation of Bolivian Peasants, whose leadership it shares with the PCB-ML and the newly formed Marxist-Leninist group MIR. This peasant confederation is strong both in La Paz and Santa Cruz.

Publications. The organ of the Lara faction is *Masas*. The González faction publishes *Combate*. Both are monthlies.

Nelly Stromquist

Brazil

The original Communist Party of Brazil (Partido Comunista do Brasil) was founded in March 1922. In 1960, in an effort to give the party a more national character, the name was changed to the Brazilian Communist Party (Partido Comunista Brasileiro; PCB). In 1961 a pro-Chinese faction broke away from the traditionally pro-Soviet PCB, forming a new party in February 1962, the Communist Party of Brazil (Partido Comunista do Brasil; PCdoB). Dissidence within the PCB ranks between 1967 and 1969 led to the formation of several splinter groups, predominantly of Castroite tendency, that strongly advocate subversive activities. Important among these groups are: the Revolutionary Vanguard Party (Vanguarda Popular Revolucionária; VPR), the National Liberation Action (Ação Libertadora Nacional; ALN), the Revolutionary Brazilian Communist Party (Partido Comunista Brasileiro Revolucionário; PCBR), and the Tiradentes Revolutionary Movement (Movimento Revolucionário Tiradentes; MRT).

The communist movement has been illegal in Brazil throughout most of its existence. Although outlawed in 1947, the PCB was allowed to function and its members ran in elections under the label of other parties. During the presidency of João Goulart (1961-64) the PCB succeeded in infiltrating and controlling important labor, student, political, and bureaucratic groups. The military regime which came into power after the March 1964 coup d'état drove the party underground and banned the existing communist-influenced organizations. In September 1969, in an attempt to curb terrorist activities, the government issued laws providing the death penalty for subversive acts.

Estimates of recent PCB membership have dropped from 40,000 in 1964 to between 15,000 and 20,000 in 1970. Members of the PCdoB are believed to number about 750. The Castroite and other groups are estimated to have a total membership of 1,000 to 5,000. The population of Brazil is 93,305,000 (estimated 1970).

The PCB. Organization and Leadership. The PCB apparatus includes a 21-member Executive Commission (whose existence was first revealed in *Rabotnichesko Delo*, Sofia, 4 May) a Central Committee, various state committees, and local cells. The Sixth Congress of the PCB, its latest, took place in December 1967.

The PCB secretary-general is Luís Carlos Prestes. Other prominent leaders are Oto José Santos, Armando Ziller, Giocondo Días, Lucas Romão, Alfredo Castro, J. B. Tavares de Sá, Augusto Bento, Iracama Ribeiro, Olga Maranhão, Jorge Villa, Sabino Bahia, Felipe Rodrígues, María Segovia, Abel Chermont, Luís Tenório de Lima, Gentil Correa, Firmino de Lima, Marcel Braz, Luís Menesse, Valerio Konder, and Gregorio Bezerra.

The PCB formerly derived considerable support from the National Union of Students (União Nacional dos Estudantes; UNE) and the Workers' General Command (Comando Geral dos Trabalhadores; CGT), both of which were abolished after 1964. The UNE, one of the few remaining sources of unqualified support of the PCB until 1967, was disbanded by the government in October 1968 when its most important leaders were arrested during the organization's clandestinely convened Thirtieth National Conference.

According to Secretary-General Prestes, the PCB participates at present, together with Catholic elements, in some 1,000 unions of agricultural peasants, representing a total of "not less than 10 million peasants" affiliated with the National Confederation of Agricultural Workers (*Kooperativno Selo*, Sofia, 29 April).

Domestic Attitudes and Activities. The PCB is an orthodox pro-Soviet party which upholds the role of the masses in obtaining power and opposes many of the subversive activities advocated by Castroite elements.

Under the present conditions of Brazil, whose government is in the hands of the military, the party follows a line that maintains that "the dictatorship can be isolated and overthrown only through large-scale, organized, joint mass actions," holding that the "main task is to mobilize, organize, and rally the worker class and other patriotic and democratic strata . . . against the dictatorship and for the establishment of a government of antidictatorial forces" (Prestes's statement, *Rabotnichesko Delo*, 4 May).

PCB activities during 1971 were very limited. The party organ (*Voz Operária*, February) indicated that special attention was being given to the "task of building the party within large companies," especially in São Paulo. The paper noted that the PCB had encountered two problems in their attempt to indoctrinate workers: the underestimation of the educational effort by several members who considered education "just one task among many others," with the result that workers were still seeking an "economic battle" rather than the "political battle" of the working class; and the belief that education would organize the party "all by itself." No further indications were given about the PCB performance in the labor movement.

A Central Committee plenum held toward the end of the year stated that the PCB would seek to mobilize the "masses in a united front" in the 1972 municipal elections because these "could facilitate the consolidation of forces opposing the dictatorship, above all by drafting a common platform." Also, the plenum resolved that it would "step up its activities in support of direct elections or governors and the President and for democratization of the 1974 parliamentary elections." (*IB*, nos. 23-24.)

As in previous years, the PCB continued to attack the extreme left-wing groups in Brazil. Arguing that the present military government could be defeated only through mass actions, the party condemned terrorist groups, whose activities were said to have become "ends in themselves" (*Voz Operária*, January). An article by Assis Tavares (*WMR*, April) declared that the PCB favored the creation of "self-defense" groups as a means to organize mass actions, but held that these groups had "nothing to do with Leftist ideas reducing the fight against the dictatorship to isolated actions by small groups." Emphasizing to a greater degree the PCB's rejection of violent tactics, Prestes declared: "The petty bourgeoisie groups which attack banks, kidnap diplomats, and hijack airplanes, actually struggle against our party." He added that those groups "hold anti-Soviet feelings and struggle for dissidence within the party." (*Rabotnichesko Delo*, Sofia, 4 May.)

Revealing further differences within the communist movement in Brazil, Jaime Paiva, an alternate Central Committee member who represented the PCB at a regional conference of communist parties held in Santiago, Chile, attacked the pro-Chinese communists for having done "much damage to the communist movement in Brazil." Paiva also attacked those extremists whose "one-sided interpretation" of the Cuban Revolution had led them to imitating the revolution while completely disregarding the "real situation of strength, and the objective and subjective conditions" within Brazil. (*WMR*, July.)

International Views and Positions. The PCB's strongly pro-Soviet position was reaffirmed in 1971. Secretary-General Prestes, speaking at the Twenty-fourth Congress of the Communist Party of the Soviet Union (CPSU), praised Brezhnev's report to the congress and the Soviet support of "liberation movements" in Indochina and the Middle East. Prestes was critical of the People's Republic of China, stating that in Brazil the PCB's efforts against "right opportunism and left adventurism" had been rendered difficult by the "stand taken by the leadership of the Chinese Communist Party," which was trying to "introduce to the Brazilian people things that are not in their interest" (Moscow radio, broadcast to China in Mandarin, 10 April).

The PCB expressed satisfaction with what it interpreted as increased activity "against imperialist oppression and for national liberation" in Latin America. Speaking at the Fourteenth Congress of the Communist Party of Czechoslovakia, Prestes noted that, in addition to Cuba, Chile had an "anti-imperialist government," and that the military governments of Bolivia (under General Juan José Torres) and Peru were "expropriating the enterprises of North American monopolies" (Prague radio, 27 May). A PCB Central Committee statement in March asserted that "North American imperialism" was being defeated in Latin America, citing "nationalist victories" in Peru, Bolivia, and Panama, and hailing the election victory of the Popular Unity bloc in Chile as an "event of tremendous significance" not only for the people of that country, but for "all peoples of Latin America" (*IB*, no. 9).

Further reflecting the endorsement of a broad front as a means to attain power, a PCB message to the Communist Party of Venezuela on occasion of its Fourth Congress hailed the legal status now enjoyed by that party and its participation in parliamentary elections as "events of importance for our whole continent" (*Tribuna Popular*, Caracas, 1 April).

Other PCB international positions included condemnation of Israel's conditions for peace in the Middle East, and appeals for the release of jailed U.S. communist Angela Davis (charged with murder, kidnaping, and conspiracy), whose life was said to have been threatened by "the racists that govern the state of California." The PCB reported the emergence of a "National Movement against Violence" in Guatemala, which it termed a "national front against government repression and organized violence by anti-communists." (*Voz Operária*, January.)

International Party Contacts. Besides the congresses of the CPSU and Czechoslovak party, the PCB was represented at the congresses of the Bulgarian Communist Party, in April, and the Socialist Unity Party of (East) Germany, in June.

PCB Central Committee members José Castro de Souza and Ernesto Ferreura visited Bucharest on 18 July-27 August at the invitation of the Romanian Communist Party. In July, alternate member Jaime Paiva represented the PCB at a round table conference in Chile, organized by the *World Marxist Review* and attended by delegates of five other Latin American communist parties. The PCB was also present at a meeting of seven South American communist parties held in September at an undisclosed location.

Publications. The PCB's irregular clandestine newspaper, *A Voz Operária*, is circulated primarily among party members. Since December 1970 the party has issued a theoretical quarterly, *Estudos*. To reach wider audiences for important statements and appeals, the party distributes clandestine leaflets.

*　　*　　*

The PCdoB. Organization and Leadership. Little is known of the organizational structure of the pro-Chinese Communist Party of Brazil. Leading figures are believed to be founding members

Mauricio Grabois and João Amazonas. Other important leaders include Benedito de Carvalho, Guido Enders, Manoel Ferreira, Calil Chade, Walter Martins, Lincoln Oeste, Alcira Grabois, Ari Gonçalves, and Tarzan de Castro (arrested by police in February 1971).

Domestic Attitudes and Activities. The PCdoB holds that the "only road for the liberation of the Brazilian people is the road of a people's war," to be taken primarily "in the countryside with the broad masses of peasants as its mainstay." Various other efforts would be implemented in the cities, with the participation of workers, students, and other forces, but "in close combination with the armed action in the interior." (Central Committee statement, reported by NCNA, 1 March 1970.) The party did not engage in significant activities during 1971.

International Views and Positions. The PCdoB, in a message of congratulations to the Chinese Communist Party on its fiftieth anniversary, hailed the "victory and examples of the Chinese communists" as a "great encouragement to those who are fighting [in Brazil] for the strengthening of the Marxist-Leninist party of the proletariat" (*Peking Review*, 30 July 1971).

Another PCdoB statement (publicized by NCNA, 23 August) demanded the immediate withdrawal of U.S. troops from Indochina, claiming that "increasingly broader sections of the American people" had realized that it was necessary to fight against the "capitalist system with U.S. imperialism as its most salient expression."

Publications. The PCdoB publishes an irregular clandestine newspaper, *A Classe Operária*.

*   *   *

Castroite Organizations. Like some other Latin American countries, Brazil has seen the emergence of various small subversive groups which hold communist and nationalistic views and advocate "armed struggle" tactics as a means to establish a socialist system. Important among these groups are the VPR, ALN, the PCBR, and the MRT.

These predominantly Castroite groups function at regional and local levels, since they are not organized on a national basis. Support is drawn mainly from students, workers, former soldiers, and, to a much lesser degree, elements of the Catholic church. According to government sources, the proportion of students involved in subversive activities is high (estimates range from 35 to 56 per cent of the memberships) and the average militant's age is twenty-three years. These revolutionary groups receive verbal and possibly material support from Cuba, where reportedly there is a coordination center for Brazilian revolutionaries.

In addition to the deaths of Carlos Marighella in 1969 and Joaquim Camara Ferreira in 1970, the extremist movement lost its third major leader, Carlos Lamarca, a former army captain, in 1971 (see below). Harsh police and army measures undertaken against the subversives have proven successful and as a result the movement has been weakened considerably. Important defections also seem to have occurred.

The VPR. Considered the largest and most active group, the Revolutionary Vanguard Party is said to derive from a small left-wing organization of former army officers (the National Revolutionary Movement) and from PCB and PCdoB dissidents.

The VPR, which operates in all the major states of Brazil, particularly in São Paulo, Rio de Janeiro, and Bahia, was led by Carlos Lamarca. According to various sources, Lamarca left the VPR early in 1971, possibly in March, allegedly due to disagreements on tactics. A letter apparently written by Lamarca to the Brazilian revolutionaries in Chile (those released in exchange for the Swiss ambassador kidnaped on 7 December 1970) and found on an arrested VPR leader asked the physically able revolutionaries to go to Cuba for training and to place themselves under the central coordination group there. The letter also told the militants staying in Chile to establish contact with the Movement of the Revolutionary Left there (see *Chile*) and to set up communication channels with Brazil, Cuba, and Algeria.

Lamarca was killed by police forces on 17 September in the small city of Pintada, in the state of Bahia. Following his death, the VPR, and ALN, and the Revolutionary Movement-8 (see *YICA*, 1971, p. 386) released a communiqué from Havana accusing Brazilian authorities of having tortured and murdered Lamarca. The communiqué stated that his death was a severe blow to the revolutionary movement but that it did not "represent its termination."

A VPR statement (reproduced in *Les Temps Modernes*, Paris, March) indicated that VPR cadres were actively engaged in political work in the "most representative plants and economic sectors: faculties, suburbs, and 'favelas.' " The same statement said that the process of revolution would involve a "long war of attrition demanding the establishment of sound political bases." The VPR does not seem to have engaged in significant activities during 1971. The "Brazilian Revolutionary Information Front" (operating in Algiers), however, reported that the various revolutionary organizations in Brazil carried out 36 armed operations during the last six months of 1971.

The ALN. The National Liberation Action is the second-largest Castroite group. It was founded, possibly in February 1968, by dissident PCB members who became disappointed with the nonviolent "conventional models and methods" of the pro-Soviet party and decided to adopt the tactics of urban and rural guerrilla warfare associated with Castroism.

The ALN believes that "the supreme duty of every revolutionary is to make the revolution." It regards the proletariat as "conformist" and "conciliatory" hence it advocates the fusion of military and political concepts to create a "revolutionary organization." Unlike the VPR, the ALN gives priority to urban guerrilla warfare, although it regards rural guerrillas as the basic forces for an army of national liberation.

The group has suffered from the loss of its leaders, Carlos Marighella and Joaquim Camara Ferreira, and seems to have had little activity during 1971.

The PCBR. The Revolutionary Brazilian Communist Party was founded in April 1968 by Mário Alves de Souza Vieira, Jacobo Gorender, and Apolonio Pinto de Carvalho, all of whom were expelled from the PCB in 1967. It seems to be based in Pernambuco. No PCBR activities were reported during 1971.

The MRT. The Tiradentes Revolutionary Movement was founded in 1969 by dissident members of the PCdoB. Its leader, Devanir José de Carvalho, was killed on 5 April 1971 by police forces. In retaliation the MRT killed a Brazilian industrialist, Henning Albert Boilesen, on 15 April. An MRT statement following his assassination asserted that Boilesen had not been chosen "at random" or because he was a "bourgeois," but because he was "one of the most prominent representatives of the U.S. imperialist monopoly and hence one of the men responsible for the military dictatorship and the conditions of terror, hunger, and suffering currently existing in the country" (*Ultima Hora*, Santiago, Chile, 19 April).

Nelly Stromquist

Canada

The Communist Party of Canada was founded in 1921. It functions legally and has a membership estimated at 2,000 to 3,000. The population of Canada is 21,681,000 (estimated 1971).

Most CPC members are no longer young. Old-age pensioners, manual workers, and white-collar employees concentrated in the urban areas of Ontario, British Columbia and the prairies comprise the bulk of the membership.

The CPC is not represented in the Federal Parliament or the provincial legislatures. In 1971 it put up a token number of candidates in the provincial elections in Alberta, Ontario, and Saskatchewan. Their electoral performance confirmed the limited appeal of the CPC and indicated, according to the leader of the party in Ontario, "the degree of social reformist and bourgeois illusions and influence still present in the working class movement (*Communist Viewpoint*, September-October).

At the municipal level the CPC won again a seat in Winnipeg, and party members and sympathizers who had the backing of pro-communist labor bodies were successful in several other localities.

Party members were active in the trade unions, in particular in the United Fishermen and Allied Workers Union, the United Electrical, Radio and Allied Workers Union, and the Marine and Boilermakers Union.

Others played a leading role in ethnic organizations that the CPC sponsored and still controls. Among the twelve organizations in the Canadian Council of National Groups, the most important are the Association of United Ukrainian Canadians and the Federation of Russian Canadians. The communists are also prominent in the Benevolent Association of Canada and the United Jewish People's Order. They were sufficiently strong to call for and obtain the resignation of the Reverend James G. Endicott barely nine months after this veteran of the peace movement and member of the executive of the World Peace Council had been reelected chairman of the Canadian Peace Congress. He aroused the ire of the CPC by questioning the Soviet approach to China, where he had spent twenty-two years prior to his return to Canada in 1947, and by objecting to Soviet support of India at the time of the India-Pakistan war (*The Globe and Mail*, Toronto, 23 December 1971 and 12 January 1972).

The Young Communist League (YCL) of Canada continued to compete with the stronger Maoist and Trotskyist youth groups. The Ligue des jeunesses communistes du Quebec, which enjoys a certain autonomy within the YCL, held its second convention in February 1971 and reelected Claude Demers as president.

Leadership and Organization. The CPC held its Twenty-first Convention in Toronto on 27-29 November 1971. The delegates, 113 men and 34 women, were addressed by representatives of the communist parties of France (Marius Berton), Italy (Vicenzo Corghi) and the United States (Helen Winter). As on previous occasions, the Canadian government refused to grant visas to the representatives of communist parties in power—a move that the CPC denounced as an example of "cold war attitude and lack of courage." Some thirty "fraternal parties" sent greetings to the convention. Among them were the communist parties of the Soviet Union, Cuba, Israel, and Malta, the People's Progressive Party of Guyana, the Vietnam Workers' Party, the National Liberation Front of South Vietnam, and the League of Communists of Yugoslavia, but not the parties of China and North Korea.

The convention reelected William Kashtan as secretary-general of the CPC, and Tim Buck as chairman of the Central Committee, which consists of 55 members and 11 alternates. Prominent members of the committee in 1971 were Alfred Dewhurst (executive secretary of the CPC), Norman Freed (in charge of ideological work), Bruce Magnuson (labor secretary), and the leaders of the provincial party organizations: Nigel Morgan (British Columbia), William Tuomi (Alberta), William Beeching (Saskatchewan), William Ross (Manitoba), William Stewart (Ontario), and Sam Walsh, chairman of the Parti Communiste de Quebec (PCQ), which enjoys a certain organizational autonomy within the CPC.

Professor S. B. Ryerson, a leading member of the Political Bureau during the cold war, informed his colleagues that "he had decided to withdraw from the Party" (*Canadian Tribune*, 10 March). His departure followed growing disenchantment with CPC policies, some of which he criticized in the party press before the twentieth convention of the CPC in 1969.

Domestic Attitudes and Activities. During 1971 the CPC concentrated on the struggle against various manifestations of "monopoly capitalism." The federal and provincial governments were attacked for their failure to solve economic and other problems facing Canada. In addition, the CPC put forward proposals that were incorporated in the redraft of the party program, *The Road to Socialism in Canada*. This document was the subject of discussions at the meeting of the Central Committee in April and later at the party convention, which approved it with amendments. The convention also passed the "Main Policy Resolution" which set out the policies to be "pursued in the immediate period ahead."

The CPC called for a "long term and balanced all-Canada industrial development program;" for the "restructuring of Canada's trade policies to make possible the extension of trade with the socialist and newly liberated countries;" for "economic and social policies directed to achieve full employment, rising standards, adequate income, decent health, housing and education as a right for all Canadians;" for "a Bill of Rights which guarantees the rights of labor" and "No wage freeze or incomes policy."

The unity of "all patriotic, democratic and progressive forces" was considered a necessary prerequisite for success in the campaign for "a genuine Canadian independence from U.S. imperialism and liberation from the rule of Canadian monopoly capital." As in previous years, the CPC came out in favor of collaboration with the much more numerous democratic socialists organized in the New Democratic Party (NDP), and welcomed the existence of the left-wing "Waffle" group within that party.

The problems of French Canada attracted the attention of communist spokesmen in and out of Quebec. The CPC and PCQ condemned individual terrorism and advocated mass action instead. The communists welcomed the decision of Charles Gagnon, one of the best-known members of the Front de Liberation de Quebec, to abandon terrorism and his call for a political organization to "regroup the largest possible number of workers" and for a "Marxist-Leninist revolutionary society" (*ibid.*, 27 October).

Editorials in party newspapers and CPC briefs submitted to legislative bodies urged that Quebec be allowed to "adopt its own constitution establishing control over matters affecting their national interest. Then Quebec can negotiate freely with English-speaking Canada what aspects of foreign relations, defense, customs, immigration, money, postal matters, etc., should be handed over." (*Ibid.*, 2 June.) The call for a voluntary union between the French and English-speaking parts of Canada was coupled with statements insisting on the necessity for the right of self-determination although Jeannette Walsh, a party organizer in Quebec, stated: "We do not believe that separatism is necessary or useful for the workers of Quebec" (*ibid.*, 17 March).

International Views and Positions. The Twenty-first Convention of the CPC came out in favor of a "fully independent" Canadian foreign policy:

> This must find expression in withdrawal from NATO and NORAD, cancelling the Canada-U.S. defense sharing agreement which makes Canada an accessory to the war in Indochina, declaring Canada a nuclear free zone, demanding U.S. withdrawal from Indochina, for a political settlement in the Middle East based on the 1967 U.N. Security Council resolution, in support of a European Security Conference, recognition of the G.D.R. [German Democratic Republic], the [Democratic] People's Republic of Korea, the Democratic Republic of Vietnam and the [Provisional] Revolutionary Government of South Vietnam, for the banning of bacteriological and chemical weapons and their destruction, the banning and destruction of all nuclear weapons, and an end to the arms race.

This program was coupled with opposition to "Canadian imperialist economic penetration and exploitation of other countries and peoples, particularly in the Caribbean and Latin America" and an invitation to "give unstinting increasing support to the peoples of South Africa, Rhodesia, Portugal, Greece, Spain and other countries striving for national and social liberation."

Denunciations of U.S. and Canadian defense, foreign, and economic policies were accompanied by expressions of approval for agreements and communiqués issued on occasion of Soviet Premier Kosygin's visit to Canada. While welcoming the establishment of diplomatic relations between Canada and the People's Republic of China, and the seating of the latter in the U.N., the CPC condemned the "splitting and divisive policies" of the "present Chinese leaders" who "are doing great harm to the cause of peace, democracy, independence and socialism." The CPC promised to work for "unity of action against the common enemy—imperialism—on the basis of Marxism-Leninism and proletarian internationalism."

International Party Contacts. During 1971, Canadian communist leaders attended a number of party congresses abroad. William Kashtan addressed the Twenty-fourth Congress of the Communist Party of the Soviet Union. William Stewart represented the CPC at the congress of the Bulgarian Communist Party, John Weir at the congress of the Mongolian People's Revolutionary Party, and William Ross at the congress of the Socialist Unity Party of (East) Germany.

A CPC delegation led by Kashtan called on Kosygin at the Soviet Embassy in Ottawa during his visit to Canada.

Observers from the YCL were at the Tenth Congress of the International Union of Students, in Bratislava in February. John Bizzell, chairman of the YCL, attended the World Federation of Democratic Youth conference in Chile in December.

Publications. The weekly *Canadian Tribune*, published in Toronto, is the official organ of the CPC. Mel Doig replaced Bill Beeching as its editor early in 1971. The West Coast edition of the *Canadian Tribune*, called *Pacific Tribune*, appears in Vancouver under the editorship of Maurice Rush. The theoretical journal *Communist Viewpoint* is published six times yearly and is edited by Norman Freed. The fortnightly *Combat*, edited by Claude Demers, is the organ of the PCQ. The Young Communist League of Canada publishes the *Young Worker* in Toronto; the Ligue des jeunesses communistes de Quebec publishes *Le Révolutionnaire* in Montreal.

The North American edition of the Prague-based monthly *Problems of Peace and Socialism* is printed in Toronto as the *World Marxist Review*. The monthly *Information Bulletin* is its companion publication.

*   *   *

The Communist Party of Canada (Marxist-Leninist). The Progressive Workers' Movement, the first pro-Maoist organization in Canada, which has been in the doldrums for several years, showed no signs of activity in 1971. The strongest Maoist group is the Communist Party of Canada (Marxist-Leninist), or CPC(M-L). It was formed in March 1970. It is an offshoot from the Internationalists, a discussion circle founded by students in Vancouver in the early 1960s.

The Maoists engaged in confrontations with the authorities, civil as well as university, attempted to organize strikes, boycotted the provincial elections, and sponsored the formation of auxiliary organizations for workers and students. They also launched a number of bulletins, all of which appeared irregularly with the exception of the *People's Canada Daily News Release*, which published extensive material from the People's Republic of China.

The leaders of the CPC(M-L) include Hardial Bains (national secretary), David Orton (vice-president), Arthur Vachon—chairman of the Communist Party of Quebec(M-L), Georgina Olivere (chairman of the Canadian Revolutionary Youth), and B. Carlson, chairman of the Canadian Student Movement. One of the veterans of the Maoist movement, Robert A. Cruse, was demoted with a reprimand for the "erroneous" view that "under certain conditions, formal party leadership is not necessary" (*People's Canada Daily News Release*, 23 December).

*   *   *

The League for Socialist Action. The League for Socialist Action (LSA), whose executive secretary is Ross Dawson, remained in 1971 the most important Trotskyist organization in Canada. Affiliated to the United Secretariat of the Fourth International in Paris, the LSA was the object of attacks in CPC publications. Members of the LSA were active in the peace, student, and women's movements, and agitated within the NDP and those French Canadian circles that are opposed to the status quo.

The fortnightly *Labor Challenge* is the organ of the LSA in Toronto. In Montreal the Ligue socialiste ouvrière publishes the monthly *Libération*. The mouthpiece of the youth organization of the LSA, the Young Socialists, is the monthly *Young Socialist*.

University of British Columbia   Ivan Avakumovic

Chile

The Communist Party of Chile (Partido Comunista de Chile; PCCh) was first established as the Socialist Workers' Party (Partido Obrero Socialista) in 1912 by Luis Emilio Recabarren. The name Communist Party of Chile was adopted in January 1922, following the party's decision in 1921 to join the Communist International. The PCCh was illegal from 1949 to 1958. It is firmly pro-Soviet in its international policies.

A pro-Chinese party, the Revolutionary Communist Party of Chile (Partido Comunista Revolucionario de Chile; PCRCh) was established in May 1966 primarily from members of the "Spartacus" group of communists which the PCCh expelled in late 1963. The Movement of the Revolutionary Left (Movimiento de Izquierda Revolucionaria; MIR) brought together several leftist groups in 1965.

PCCh membership at the time of the party's Fourteenth Congress, in November 1969, was said to be about 60,000. In May 1971 Mario Zamorano claimed that membership had risen to 117,000 and at the end of the year Luis Corvalán reported a membership of 150,000 (*WMR*, September 1971; *Pravda*, 2 January 1972). In May 1971 Zamorano claimed that workers comprised 65.3 per cent of the membership, peasants 13.6 per cent, white-collar workers 8.9 per cent, intellectuals and persons of middle-class background 8.1 per cent, and artisans 4.1 per cent. Some 30 per cent of the party members were women. According to Zamorano 30.6 per cent of the members were under thirty years of age, 29.1 per cent between thirty and forty, 20.7 per cent between forty and fifty, and 19.6 per cent over fifty. (*WMR*, September.) The population of Chile is 10,000,000 (estimated 1971).

The PCCh holds 6 (out of 50) seats in the national senate and 22 (out of 150) in the Chamber of Deputies. In the 4 April municipal elections (see below) the PCCh won 17.36 per cent of the total vote.

The Popular Unity Alliance. Between 1956 and 1969 the PCCh allied itself for electoral purposes with the Socialist Party (Partido Socialista de Chile; PSCh) in the Popular Action Front (Frente de Acción Popular; FRAP). On numerous occasions in 1969 PCCh leaders argued that leftist unity was necessary in order to transform Chile into a socialist state, but concluded that present conditions required an alliance more broadly based than the FRAP. Thus the PCCh played a leading role in founding the Popular Unity (Unidad Popular; UP) coalition at the end of 1969. The UP coalition was made up of the PCCh, the PSCh, the Radical Party (Partido Radical; PR), the Social Democratic Party (Partido Social Demócrata; PSD), the Unitary Popular Action Movement (Movimiento de Acción Popular Unitaria; MAPU), a group of dissidents from the ruling Christian Democratic Party (Partido Demócrata Cristiano; PDC) of then President Eduardo Frei, and the Independent Popular Alliance (Alianza Popular Independiente; API). The PCCh was the largest, best organized, and most disciplined participant. During 1971 two UP members, the PR and MAPU, become so dominated by their left wings that center and right-wing members broke away to form separate organizations. The PR splinter established itself as the Radical Movement of the Independent Left (Movimiento Radical de Izquierda Independiente), and the MAPU dissidents joined forces with new dissidents from the PDC to form the Movement of the Christian Left (Movimiento de Izquierda Cristiana). Both splinters reaffirmed their support for the UP program.

On 4 September 1970 Salvador Allende narrowly defeated National Party (Partido Nacional; PN) candidate Jorge Alessandri and PDC candidate Radomiro Tomic, falling considerably below the absolute majority required for direct election to the presidency. Consequently, in accordance with the Chilean constitution, the final decision was made between the two leading candidates by the Congress. After extensive discussion between UP and PDC legislators, Allende's agreement to support a constitutional amendment designed to guarantee the continuation of a free society in Chile, and Alessandri's withdrawal of his candidacy, the Congress voted for Allende on 24 October by a margin of 153 to 35 (with 12 abstentions and blank votes cast). Allende was inaugurated on 3 November. The UP won 50.86 per cent of the votes in the April 1971 municipal elections. In the July congressional by-election in Valparaíso, however, the PDC-PN candidate narrowly defeated UP candidate Hernán del Canto, secretary general of the Single Center of Chilean Workers (see below). At the end of the year tensions increased as two by-elections scheduled for mid-January 1972 approached.[1]

The "Basic Program of Popular Unity" was signed on 17 December 1969, after a meeting of the six participating organizations, and was published promptly in the PCCh organ, *El Siglo* (23 December; reprinted in *Tricontinental*, Havana, March-April 1971). This program, which the PCCh adopted as its own immediate program, rejected the "reformism" of the Frei government, pledged to rid the country of the influences of "monopolistic capitalism" and "imperialist exploitation," and promised to "begin the construction of socialism in Chile." It called for a "people's assembly" to replace the existing two houses of Congress and for "democratization" of the political process on all levels. Other objectives included: nationalization of basic resources controlled by foreign capital and domestic monopolies, while leaving the vast majority of enterprises entirely or partly under private ownership; acceleration of agrarian reform, with special emphasis on the development of peasant cooperatives; and greatly increased state control of social, cultural, and educational programs. The Basic Program stated that the "popular government" would be "multi-partied" and include all "revolutionary" parties, movements, and trends; it would "respect the rights of opposition ... exercised within legal bounds."

The foreign policy objectives outlined in the Basic Program include: complete political and economic independence of Chile; maintenance of relations with all countries irrespective of their ideological and political positions; friendship and solidarity with independent or colonial peoples, "especially those developing their struggles for liberation and independence"; and promotion of "strong Latin American and anti-imperialist feelings by means of a people's international policy." The program described Cuba as the "advanced post of the revolution and the construction of socialism on the Latin American continent."

The UP has been quite successful in implementing major portions of its domestic program, occasionally with, but generally without, the support of the opposition parties. It nationalized the mainstays of the copper industry, the Anaconda, Kennecott, and Cerro Companies. The state bought controlling interest in Chile's private banks and took over major productive sectors by "requisitioning" appliance factories, automobile and textile plants, and other private enterprises allegedly engaged in illegal practices in production and labor relations. More land was expropriated in 1971 than

---

[1]PDC-PN supported candidates decisively defeated UP candidates in both elections.

during the previous six years. Some objectives were postponed, such as the establishment of "people's courts" and the replacement of the existing legislature with a "people's assembly."

In pursuance of its foreign policy objectives the UP government established diplomatic relations in 1970 with Cuba and in 1971 with the People's Republic of China, Albania, Hungary, East Germany, Mongolia, and Tanzania. In November President Allende reported that the Soviet Union and Eastern European countries had agreed to give Chile credits valued at $380 million. Allende tried to maintain good relations with neighboring Latin American countries of various political orientations, personally visiting Argentina, Colombia, Ecuador, and Peru. Cuban Prime Minister Fidel Castro paid a 25-day visit to Chile in November and December. Chilean relations with the United States were more strained than during the Frei administration, due, among other causes, to Chilean nationalization of privately owned U.S. businesses without what the U.S. regarded as adequate compensation.

The UP encountered active resistance during 1971 from the PDC and the National Party, the two at times forming a bloc after mid-year. Their opposition was most vigorous at the end of the year in reaction to increasing food shortages and the inability or unwillingness of the government (particularly Interior Minister José Tohá) to stop the continual land seizures in city and countryside led by the MIR. "Ultra-leftist" activities, such as the MIR land seizures and the assassination of Edmundo Pérez Zujovik, interior minister during the Frei government, carried out by the People's Organized Vanguard (Vanguardia Organizada del Pueblo; VOP), a splinter of the MIR, were an important source of dissension within UP ranks.

Three important PCCh leaders were ministers in President Allende's cabinet, in the top economic positions: Américo Zorrilla (finance), Pascual Barraza (public works), and José Oyarce (labor). PCCh spokesman Waldo Atias was director of the Cultural Department of the Presidency.

The PCCh. Organization and Leadership. The party's secretary-general is Luis Corvalán. The Political Commission includes Corvalán, Oscar Astudillo (died, September 1971), Víctor Díaz, Orlando Millas, José Oyarce, Gladys Marín, Mario Zamorano, Manuel Cantero, Rodrigo Rojas, Carlos Jorquera, Volodia Teitelboim, Jorge Insunza, Bernardo Araya, Julieta Campusano, José Cademártori, and Américo Zorrilla. The Central Committee has 75 members.

The PCCh-affiliated youth movement, established in September 1932, is the Communist Youth of Chile (Juventudes Comunistas de Chile; JCCh). During 1971 the most important JCCh members were Gladys Marín (secretary-general), Omar Córdova (killed in a traffic accident on 31 August), José Weibel, Carlos Cerda, and Alejandro Rojas. The JCCh had 20,000 members in mid-1970. According to the party's organizational secretary, membership had risen to 40,000 in May 1971 (WMR, September); at the end of the year Luis Corvalán claimed 50,000 members (Pravda, 2 January 1972).

JCCh members, working in large part through the Ramona Parra Brigades (Brigadas Ramona Parra), have been among the most loyal and enthusiastic supporters of the Allende government. Indeed, the primary task of the JCCh in 1971, according to Gladys Marín at the JCCh convention in June, was to support actively the policies of the UP government (El Siglo, 19 June). The JCCh took strong stands against "rightist sedition" (ibid., 13 September) and against the "ultra-leftist" policies of the MIR. Tensions between the JCCh and the MIR reached a peak in December 1970, subsided in early 1971, and began to increase again by mid-year.

In recent years the JCCh has become increasingly important in Chilean student affairs. In university elections since 1970 the JCCh has joined with other UP youth groups to oppose slates of non-UP groups, whether of the "right" or the "ultra-left." UP slates were dominant in seven universities in 1970, JCCh members being elected president of the university student federations in four universities, including the University of Chile in Santiago. Although UP strength in student federations decreased somewhat during 1971 the alliance maintained its leading position in the University of Chile and in most other schools it controlled in 1970. (The most important university student federation under opposition control was at the Catholic University in Santiago.) The JCCh claims to direct the activities of the youth departments of the CUTCh and Ranquil organizations (*WMR*, September; see below).

The Single Center of Chilean Workers (Central Unica de Trabajadores de Chile; CUTCh), the largest confederation of unions in a country where about 40 per cent of the labor force has been unionized, is largely controlled by the PCCh. The CUTCh held its Sixth Congress in mid-December 1971. New officers were not elected at the congress, but it was stated that elections would be held within 120 days. Thus Luis Figueroa, a member of the PCCh Central Committee, and Hernán del Canto, a member of the PSCh Central Committee, remained president and secretary-general respectively, positions to which they had been elected at the CUTCh Fifth Congress in November 1968. The 27-member Leadership Council (Consejo Directivo) continued to be dominated by 14 PCCh and 7 PSCh members, with Víctor Díaz, of the PCCh Political Commission, as the head. Membership jumped from about 750,000 to some 900,000 early in the year when PDC unions agreed to collaborate with CUTCh. Early in December CUTCh claimed 1,000,000 members. The PDC delegates all walked out of the Sixth Congress, however, charging that no views were tolerated aside from those of the UP delegates.

In accordance with an agreement signed at the end of 1970 (see *La Nacion*, Santiago, 8 December), the CUTCh has cooperated with the government in the formation and implementation of labor policy. On 12 May 1971 the CUTCh was granted legal status, without which it had nevertheless operated with complete freedom in years past. In an article in the monthly organ of the World Federation of Trade Unions (*World Trade Union Movement*, London, September) a CUTCh official stated that the "main line" of CUTCh policy was "consistent defence of the economic and social demands of the workers, linking them to the national struggle of the Chilean people for the economic and social transformation of the country."

The Ranquil Peasant Confederation is controlled by the PCCh. According to Ranquil President Enrique Avendano, there were some 90,000 members in May 1971. Ranquil opposes extra-legal, "anarchistic" land seizures which "embarrass the popular government and sow distrust in it." (*WMR*, September.)

Party Internal Affairs. The PCCh held plenary sessions of its Central Committee on 3-5 March and 24-26 June. The party's National Conference was held on 30 September-3 October. Considerable attention was given to the PCCh's forthcoming fiftieth-anniversary celebration (which took place during the first week of 1972). All meetings discussed forms of PCCh support for and participation in the UP government, the need to make the reforms of the government "irreversible," and alleged plots against the government by "counterrevolutionaries" and "fascists."

PCCh membership has increased rapidly in the past year, as noted above. Mario Zamorano stated: "We have started a number of regional and local committees and we intend to start intermediate links, sector and factory committees, to assure better contact with primary units, the Party branches" (*WMR*, September; see *Principios*, May-June).

Domestic Attitudes and Activities. The PCCh regards the "Basic Program of Popular Unity," signed on 17 December 1969, as its own immediate program. In an "Appeal to All Chileans," published in *El Siglo* on 4 October 1971 the PCCh National Conference directed particular praise to the nationalization of the large-scale copper mining industry and the telephone company, the "abolition of textile monopolies," the "institution of state control of the banks," and the accelerated agrarian reform (*IB*, no. 21-22; also see *El Siglo*, 4 September). The outstanding feature of these reforms, according to Luis Corvalán, was that they were being implemented "in accordance with the constitution and on the basis of the principles of law and order which have been formed in the course of Chile's history." "Much that has been achieved is irreversible," Corvalán continued; the remaining task was to make "the whole process of the country's development irreversible, of consolidating it, and taking it further." (*Pravda*, 2 January 1972.)

Addressing the June plenum of the Central Committee, Volodia Teitelboim gave PCCh backing to President Allende's May Day call: "The great battle for Chile, now and henceforward, is production" (*El Siglo*, 25 June). In the "Appeal to All Chileans" the PCCh called for a number of specific activities in the immediate future:

(1) greater output at enterprises, mines, in agriculture and improvement of the services;

(2) immediately rendering effective participation of the working people in management of all enterprises in the state and mixed sectors, economy, public services and government offices;

(3) organization of supply commissions in which housewives, trade unions, maternal centers, block committees and shop keepers from every village and block would fight speculators and ensure regular supply of the prime necessities;

(4) the creation of centers for implementation of the agrarian reform on all confiscated estates to give effect to the transfer of land to the peasants;

(5) preparation for the Sixth Congress of the United Trade Union Center of the Working People of Chile [CUTCh] as a true expression of the unitarian will of the working people;

(6) increased vigilance of the masses and committees for the protection of enterprises and public service offices;

(7) abolition of bureaucracy and achieving effective and true solutions of every concrete problem." (*IB*, no. 21-22.)

Throughout the year, particularly from the time of the National Conference, PCCh leaders charged that opposition groups and individuals (including former President Eduardo Frei) were guilty of sedition. With increasing frequency the "seditious" forces were said to be in league with foreign interests, particularly the U.S. Central Intelligence Agency. (E.g. see Corvalán in *El Siglo*, 13 March and 6 September, and *Pravda*, 2 January 1972.) The "Appeal to All Chileans" stated: "All attempts to oppose the Popular government will be crushed by the full force of the law, through the unanimous and militant mobilization of the masses" (*IB*, no. 21-22).

The PCCh also directed much attention to what it regarded as threats from the "ultra-left." Addressing the June plenum, Volodia Teitelboim said that Marx and Lenin, in their times, had "analyzed, fought, and unmasked" the ultra-left, "whose schizophrenia is mixed with crime and extremism." According to Teitelboim "their adventurous and suicidal action is removed from all reality and helps to orchestrate the campaigns of right-wing sedition." (*El Siglo*, 26 June.) The PCCh attack on "ultra-leftist adventurism" was continued in El Siglo editor Eduardo Labarca's *Chile al rojo* (Santiago, 1971), a book which drew particular concemnation from the MIR and the MIR-oriented members of the PSCh.

International Views and Positions. The PCCh is one of the most firmly pro-Soviet communist parties in Latin America. Contacts with the Communist Party of the Soviet Union (CPSU), which have always been close, were particularly cordial in 1971.

PCCh leaders have repeatedly denied that the electoral victory of the UP in Chile can serve as a "model" for other countries to follow. In a press conference in Rome on 26 April Luis Corvalán said that some Latin American countries would have to follow the path of armed struggle while others would find "intermediate variants" between the armed Cuban and non-armed Chilean roads to power (*L'Unitá*, Rome, 27 April). Corvalán frequently acknowledged, however, that many other countries were intensely interested in the Chilean experience. Europeans, particularly the French and the Italians, had shown growing interest (*Plan*, Santiago, May 1971). Early in the year, in Santiago, Orlando Millas told a meeting of officials from the communist parties of Venezuela, Peru, Brazil, Argentina, and Colombia that some features of the Chilean experience should be "taken into account regardless of the distinctive characteristics of the revolutionary movement in each particular country." These features, as summarized from Millas comments by the *World Marxist Review* (July), included

> the guiding political role of the Communist Party, the Communist-Socialist alliance, the unification of the working class in one trade union center, the mobilization of the peasantry to win a radical agrarian reform, the formation of a broad democratic, national revolutionary coalition on the basis of an anti-imperialist and anti-oligarchic program, the consolidation of mass organizations of the population (such as house committees) uniting various segments of the people in the fight for pressing demands, and the campaign for an educational reform.

PCCh relations with Cuba were generally friendly during the year with Volodia Teitelboim, who was in Havana as a special guest of the Cuban government for the tenth-anniversary observances of the Bay of Pigs invasion, acting as the primary contact. A generally favorable attitude was maintained toward the government of Juan Velasco in Peru.

Throughout the year the PCCh condemned alleged U.S. support for "sedition" in Chile and other Latin American countries. The party repeatedly confirmed its belief in the need for "proletarian internationalism" and took positions on international issues parallel to those of the CPSU.

International Meetings and Contacts. In April the *World Marxist Review* Editorial Board sponsored a round table conference in Santiago which included: Orlando Millas (Chile), Pedro Ortega Díaz (Venezuela), Félix Arias Schreiber (Peru), Jaime Paiva (Brazil), Alberto Cohen (Argentina), and Edgardo Caicedo (Colombia). In September representatives of seven Latin American communist parties (Argentina, Bolivia, Brazil, Chile, Paraguay, Peru, and Uruguay) met at an undisclosed place, probably in Chile.

Two Soviet front organizations, the World Federation of Democratic Youth (WFDY) and the International Union of Students (IUS), sponsored a North American and Latin American youth and student meeting in solidarity with Vietnam, Laos, and Cambodia on 31 August-3 September in Santiago. The more than 300 delegates from 58 countries were addressed by JCCh leader Gladys Marín (see *El Siglo*, 2 September) and the Chilean minister of the interior, José Tohá. The Executive Committee of the WFDY met in Valparaíso on 6-8 September, its first meeting outside Eastern Europe in five years. The Presidium of the World Peace Council has scheduled its first meeting ever in Latin America for Santiago in September 1972.

PCCh visitors to the Soviet Union during 1971 included Luis Corvalán and Samuel Riquelme, to the CPSU congress in March-April, and Orlando Millas and José Cademártori, to the celebration of the October Revolution, in November. Alejandro Rojas attended the IUS congress in Czechoslovakia, in January-February. Samuel Riquelme attended the Tenth Congress of the Bulgarian Communist Party, in April. Julieta Campusano went to the Sixth Congress of the Polish United Workers' Party, in December.

PCCh visitors in Latin America included: Volodia Teitelboim and Carlos Cerda to the Fourth Congress of the Communist Party of Venezuela, in January; Teitelboim to Cuba for the anniversary of the Bay of Pigs invasion, in April; Víctor Díaz to the Third Congress of the National Convention of Workers in Uruguay, in June; and Luis Corvalán to the Eleventh Congress of the Communist Party of Colombia, in December.

Fidel Castro visited Chile as a guest of President Allende on 10 November-4 December.

Publications. The most important of the PCCh publications are *El Siglo*, the daily official organ of the party, and the theoretical journal *Principios*. The PCCh also controls the daily paper *Puro Chile*. All are published in Santiago.

*   *   *

The PCRCh. The PCRCh is a small party whose influence is primarily among students in Santiago. In the June 1971 election for the Higher Administrative Council at the University of Chile the pro-Chinese Marxist-Leninist Unity Front elected no representatives (*Ultima Hora*, Santiago, 29 June).

The PCRCh considered the 1970 election a "circus," an infamous form of deception serving merely as an "escape valve utilized periodically by reaction in order to prevent a direct confrontation between exploiters and exploited" (*Causa Marxista-Leninista*, Santiago, August-September 1970). Salvador Allende, according to the PCRCh, represented the interests of the bourgeoisie, the petty bourgeoisie, and the labor aristocracy (*ibid.*, February-March 1970). During 1971 the party continued to consider the UP government "revisionist," charging that it hampered the mass struggle, exploited the working class, and concentrated merely on winning the "battle of production" (see *The Guardian*, London, 29 January 1972).

The PCRCh condemns the "modern revisionism" of the CPSU, and praises the Chinese communists, who have "led the world struggle against revisionism, a struggle which finds expression in the victorious Proletarian Cultural Revolution." The party hails the international importance of the "invincible weapon of Marxism-Leninism-Mao Tsetung Thought." (*Peking Review*, 13 August 1971.)

*   *   *

The MIR. The Movement of the Revolutionary Left is generally said to have been formed in 1965. In December 1967 the organization adopted a more activist line than previously, becoming avowedly "Castroite" and advocating the armed road to power enunciated at the Latin American Solidarity Organization (OLAS) conference held in Havana in August of that year. Early in 1969 the MIR went "underground" and did not surface again until after Salvador Allende's inauguration as president of Chile in November 1970.

MIR leaders include Miguel Enríquez (secretary-general), Sergio Zorrilla, Nelson Gutiérrez, Jorge Fuentes, and Luciano Cruz (who died in August 1971). The MIR dominates two leftist university fronts: the University Movement of the Left (Movimiento Universitario de Izquierda; MUI) at the University of Concepción, where the MIR has controlled the student federation in recent years, and the Revolutionary Students' Front (Frente de Estudiantes Revolucionarios; FER) at the University of Chile in Santiago, where MIR influence in the university as a whole has been overshadowed by that of the Christian Democrats and the more traditional left. MIR influence is strong in the Revolutionary Peasant Movement (Movimiento Campesino Revolucionario; MCR) and in the Revolutionary Workers' Front (Frente de Trabajadores Revolucionarios; FTR), the latter formed in late 1971.

In the past few years several splinter groups have broken away from the MIR: the "Manuel Rodríguez Revolutionary Movement (Movimiento Revolucionario "Manuel Rodriguez"; MR-2), which decided at its first National Congress in September 1971 to rejoin the MIR (*Punto Final*, Santiago, 28 September); People's Organized Vanguard, whose assassination of the former PDC interior minister, Edmundo Pérez Zujovic, in June was immediately denounced by the MIR (*ibid.*, 22 June).

The MIR's frequently stated objectives are the uprooting of the Chilean state and social structure—which it charges with serving only the interests of capitalists and "imperialists"—and its replacement by a socialist state which serves the workers. The controversial position of the MIR within the Chilean left does not derive from this long-term goal, however, but from its concept of the proper road to its achievement.

The MIR did not support Allende's campaign for the presidency in 1970 but pledged to defend the UP after it was elected from any threats originating on the right. In a document released by its National Secretariat in October 1970, the MIR warned that once the "euphoria of the triumph" had passed, the UP would have to "satisfy the desires of the masses concretely and in a short time," for the strategy of the bourgeoisie and "imperialism" would be to discredit the UP by keeping it from carrying out its programs, thus opening the way for a reactionary takeover with some degree of popular support (*ibid.*, 13 October 1970, supplement). After violent clashes between the MIR and the JCCh during late 1970 led to the death of one MIR militant, a truce was reached with the UP generally which lasted through the April 1971 municipal elections, which the MIR supported. By mid-1971 the MIR was again charging that the UP was failing to make a revolution in Chile (see the exchange between Nelson Gutiérrez and Salvador Allende, *ibid.*, 8 June 1971). On 1 November Miguel Enríquez accused the UP of moving too slowly in its agrarian and other programs, of neglecting—and at times even thwarting—the mobilization of the masses, and of losing strength and support while the opposition groups were "confusing some sectors of the popular masses" and generally consolidating their forces (*Intercontinental Press*, New York, 10 January 1972).[2] During his visit to Chile in November-December Fidel Castro repeatedly urged the MIR and other leftists to support the Allende government. Some efforts to reach agreements with the UP in December were unsuccessful, however, and tensions merely increased after the UP electoral defeats in the two January 1972 by-elections.

The MIR carried out a variety of activities during the year in its effort to "mobilize" the Chilean masses. Among them were illegal seizures of public and private lands by MIR-led peasants, workers, Indians, and unemployed persons, particularly in the southern provinces. The MIR continued to assist in the establishment of self-governing squatter settlements and participated in a form of agitational campaigning for the January 1972 by-elections, particularly in Linares Province.

William E. Ratliff

[2]The Political Committee of the UP immediately issued a statement accusing the MIR of "opportunism," of presenting an "infantile" program, and of moving toward a "counterrevolutionary" role in the Chilean revolutionary process (*El Siglo*, 4 November).

Colombia

The communist movement in Colombia began within the ranks of the Socialist Revolutionary Party (Partido Socialista Revolucionario; PSR) shortly after the party's formation in December 1926. Contacts between the PSR and the Communist International during 1929 and 1930 inspired a group of PSR members to proclaim publicly the creation of the Communist Party of Colombia (Partido Comunista de Colombia; PCC) on 17 July 1930. The party has retained this designation ever since except for a short period (1944-47) during which it was called the Social Democratic Party (Partido Social Democrático). In July 1965 a schism within the PCC between pro-Soviet and pro-Chinese factions resulted in the latter's becoming the Communist Party of Colombia, Marxist-Leninist (Partido Comunista de Colombia, Marxista-Leninista; PCC-ML). Only the PCC has legal status.

Indicative of the degree of PCC strength were the results obtained in the 1970 elections to departmental assemblies and municipal councils. PCC candidates, who ran under the banner of the Liberal Revolutionary Party, received less than 0.5 per cent of the total vote, although PCC deputies were elected in six departments (*IB*, no. 20, 1970). The PCC is estimated to have 8,000 to 10,000 members. Both the pro-Soviet and the pro-Chinese parties maintain guerrilla organizations. The PCC-controlled Revolutionary Armed Forces of Colombia (FARC) is believed to be the largest. A recent estimate put its membership at 400 (*New York Times*, 24 January 1971). The pro-Chinese direct the People's Liberation Army (EPL), which probably has some 150 members.

In addition to the PCC and PCC-ML, there is a Castroite group, the National Liberation Army (Ejército de Liberación Nacional; ELN), with an estimated membership ranging between 80 and 250 members.

The population of Colombia is 21,116,000 (estimated 1970).

Communist influence in national affairs is quite limited. Guerrilla warfare, although not a serious threat to the government, has been a feature of Colombian life since the late 1940's, the current wave beginning in 1964. During 1971, guerrilla actions, particularly by the FARC, were on the increase and several small clashes with government armed forces took place.

The PCC. Leadership and Organization. The PCC is headed by its 12-member Executive Committee and 45-member Central Committee. The leadership, elected in 1971 at the party's Eleventh Congress, includes the secretary-general, Gilberto Vieira, and the following Central Committee members (most of whom also are on the Executive Committee): Alvaro Vásquez, Jésus Villegas, Hernando Hurtado, Julio Posada, Roso Osorio, Gilberto Castro, José Carmona, Alberto López, Orlando Nuñez, Carlos Romero, José Arizala, Aristóbulo Marciales, Teófilo Forero, Victor Herrera, Manuel Cepeda Vargas, Ramón Tovar, Joaquín Moreno, and Miguel Rueda.

The PCC controls the Trade Union Confederation of Workers of Colombia (Confederación Sindical de Trabajadores de Colombia; CSTC), which has approximately 150,000 members and is the second-largest labor organization in the country. The CSTC president is Pastor Pérez, a member of the PCC Executive Committee. The CSTC and the largest labor organization, the Union of Workers of Colombia (Unión de Trabajadores de Colombia; UTC) called a 24-hour strike on 8 March to protest the high cost of living. The strike, which was opposed by the smaller Confederation of Workers of Colombia, involved an estimated 10 per cent of Colombian workers.

Pro-Soviet communist influence is also present within the 900,000-member National Peasant Association of Land Users (Associación Nacional de Usuarios Campesinos; ANUC). Although founded by the government to encourage peasant purticipation in the development and implementation of agrarian reform, the ANUC has become very independent. In September 1971 it formulated its own revolutionury program of land distribution. In addition, it has been quite active organizing land seizures by peasants. PCC sources estimate that the ANUC directed the seizure of 473 estates in 22 provinces during 1971 (WMR, February 1972). The current ANUC president, Jaime Vásquez, is reportedly a PCA member.

The PCC's youth organization, the Communist Youth of Colombia (Juventud Comunista de Colombia, JCC), has its own National Directorate, Executive Committee, and Central Committee. The secretary-general is Carlos Romero. Other JCC leaders include José Miller Chacón, Jaime Caicedo, Alejandro Gómez, and Eduardo Martínez. At a plenum held on 1-2 May to evaluate JCC performance, it was mentioned that one important fault was the "lack of firmness" of many cadres and activities in defending the PCC position in the face of extremist leftist opinions (Voz Proletaria, 13 May).

The PCC controls a peasant guerrilla group, the FARC, formed in 1966. This group operates mainly in the south-west region of the country and is led by Manuel Marulanda Vélez (alias "Tiro Fijo"). During 1971 FARC actions were numerous and consisted of stealing cattle and having brief encounters with government forces, especially in the departments of Tolima, Huila, and Cundinamarca. In February the FARC kidnaped a rancher in Huila and released him subsequently in exchange for $68,000.

The Cuban Tricontinental Bulletin (December 1971) reported that the FARC attended a fourth "general guerrilla conference" in Colombia, presumably also attended by ELN and EPL representatives, held in April. The same source stated that the guerrillas had decided on a strategy that called for "attacks on the fundamental supports of the regime, such as the economy, transportation, communications, and the Armed Forces," although they indicated a desire for cooperation with "democratic and progressive sectors of the Armed Forces."

A clandestine communiqué released in Bogota on 8 April announced the formation of the United Front of Guerrilla Action (FUAG), whose objective was said to be the coordination of urban center support for the three guerrilla movements of Colombia. However, the report presented by Secretary-General Vieira at the PCC congress indicated that while the FARC had appealed for unity of action, there had been "no positive reply so far, probably because some of their leaders persist in their negative, anti-unitarian, and anti-party positions" (Voz Proletaria, 16 December).

Domestic Attitudes and Activities. According to the PCC resolutions passed at its Eleventh Congress, the party continues to emphasize the "mobilization and action of the masses" as the "basic form of struggle." The party centers its efforts on legal and peaceful methods, and considers the creation of a united front movement the "most important task." Resolutions passed at the congress praised the FARC and described it as representing a "form of struggle [which] is in keeping with the reality of the country's political and social conditions" because its actions facilitated the "maturing of a revolutionary situation." At the same time, however, the congress stressed that armed action was to be taken as a "reserve" and that the main forms of struggle were "broad mobilization of the masses and joint actions." (Ibid.)

Continuing the appeals made in 1970 for the formation of an "opposition front," the PCC reiterated its willingness to form an alliance with ANAPO, a party that counts on increasing popular support and is led by former dictator Rojas Pinilla. On 24 February 1971 the PCC issued a communiqué proposing the union of various opposition groups in order to achieve a minimal joint program of "combative unity." Reportedly, it sent copies of this program to ANAPO, the followers of Belisario Betancur (a dissident group from the Conservative Party), and "rebel priests and patriotic soldiers." Although PCC leaders claimed increased cooperation with ANAPO members, there were indications that this may not be true. Senator Ignacio Vives Echeverria, leader of the left-wing of ANAPO (said to have been infiltrated by the PCC) was expelled from his party early in January 1971, thus rendering difficult the possibility of a formal PCC-ANAPO alliance. Furthermore, toward the end of the year there were reports that the followers of Betancur were in the process of establishing an opposition electoral alliance with ANAPO and some independent liberals. No mention was made of the PCC.

The main domestic affair of the PCC during 1971 was the holding of its Eleventh Congress on 6-10 December. The meeting was held in Bogota, with government consent, and took place five years after the Tenth Congress. Delegates from 15 foreign communist parties attended, including representatives of the communist parties of the Soviet Union and Czechoslovakia. There were 200 Colombian delegates, of whom 54 were said to be workers, 65 professionals, and 27 leaders of mass organizations. According to PCC sources, 88 per cent of those present had been party members for ten to thirty years.

The congress devoted special attention to the question of national unity. A resolution passed on this subject indicated that a democratic opposition front should seek the following objectives: nationalization of the petroleum industry; surrender of land to the peasants by the latifundists; general upgrading of wages and salaries; legal power to safeguard civil liberties and the right to strike; university reform along democratic and anti-imperialist lines. (*Vox Proletaria*, 16 December.)

The PCC also stated that it sought the creation of a front only for the 1974 presidential elections, as it intended to participate in the 1972 municipal and departmental elections on its own list. In a subsequent statement, however, Secretary-General Vieira expressed contradictory intentions. *El Popular* (Montevideo, 23 December) quoted him as having said that the PCC was forming an opposition front with ANAPO and the Betancur group and that this front would participate in the 1972 elections. Vieira also predicted that this front would probably win in 17 of the 23 departmental assemblies and that it would obtain a majority in the municipal councils.

The renewed encouragement of guerrilla actions, given cautious endorsement at the Eleventh Congress, was apparently not due to an emphasis on armed struggle as such but rather was the consequence of a policy that sought to give more attention to peasant issues and the need for land distribution. Vieira declared in the *World Marxist Review* (June): "The agrarian reform in Colombia will be accomplished exclusively through revolutionary struggle by the peasants in alliance with the working class and the advanced sectors of the petty bourgeoisie, with part of the national bourgeoisie also possibly involved in the struggle." During 1971 land occupations were frequent, particularly in Córdoba, Tolima, and Sucre. Most of these were organized by the ANUC (see above), which is influenced to a significant degree by pro-Soviet members. Government officials attributed ANUC's policy of land seizing to a definite communist leadership within this organization.

The labor situation in Colombia was said by the PCC to have undergone "a major negative development," caused by the "division and disarray of the trade union movement." Responsible for this condition were the "revolutionaries" (presumably pro-Chinese activists), who advocated that "any action in support of vital demands must immediately grow over into a struggle for power." (*WMR*, Februury 1972.)

International Views and Positions. The PCC continues to be a firm supporter of Soviet views. At the Twenty-fourth Congress of the Communist Party of the Soviet Union (CPSU), the PCC was represented by Vieira and Teodosio Varela. Reporting on the congress, Vieira stated that it had been "an event of world-wide historical scope" because of the "realism and magnitude" of the ninth five-year plan proposed at that time and the "Leninist policy of peace" expounded by the Soviet party. The attendence of delegations from numerous "national democratic parties" of Africa and Asia and from the leftist socialist parties of Chile, Japan, and Italy, he said, reflected "current progress toward the creation of the world's anti-imperialist front." (*Voz Proletaria*, 27 May.)

The apparently impending border conflict between Colombia and Venezuela received frequent coverage in the PCC's organ, *Voz Proletaria*, and also was mentioned by Vieira at the CPSU congress, where he accused "imperialist interests" of abetting the conflict in order to benefit the "oil monopolies and the arms sellers" (*ibid.*).

Party statements described the present situation in Czechoslovakia as normal and held that "those who wanted to restore cupitalism behind the mask of 'humanized' socialism" had been completely defeated (*ibid.*).

Expressing the PCC's continuing support for Cuba, at a plenary session in August Vieira said that the Cuban Revolution had given impetus to the "anti-imperialist movement" in Latin America. As evidence of this, he cited the Popular Unity victory in Chile and changes taking place in Peru and Bolivia.

An article by Vieira (*Za Rubeshom*, Moscow, 19 January 1972) referred to the admission of the People's Republic of China into the United Nations as constituting "an important shift in the relations in the world." China's presence at the United Nations, Vieira added, would "permit the world to see for themselves how great the gulf is between the Maoist leaders' words and deeds."

Party Contacts. At the CPSU congress Vieira and Varela held meetings with delegations from North Vietnam, Cuba, Chile, Poland, Argentina, Brazil, and North Korea.

A PCC delegation led by Manuel Cepeda Vargas, Executive Committee member and editor of *Voz Proletaria*, visited North Korea on 28 August-2 September and held talks with Central Committee members of the Korean Workers' Party. Jesús Villegas represented the PCC at the Eighth Congress of the Socialist Unity Party of (East) Germany, held in June.

Publications. The PCC publishes a weekly newspaper, *Voz Proletaria*, under government censorship since October 1971. It also has a theoretical journal, *Documentos Políticos*, and a news sheet, *Noticias de Colombia*. The FARC publishes a clandestine bulletin, *Resistencia*.

*　　　*　　　*

The PCC-ML. The Communist Party of Colombia, Marxist-Leninist is firmly pro-Chinese. Its leadership hierarchy is not clearly known, but important positions have been held in recent years by Francisco Gárnica, Pedro Vásquez, Luis Carlos Miranda, Carlos Arias, Jorge Restrepo, Daniel Díaz, Humberto Salamanca Alba, Napoleón Martínez, Alejandro Soto, Víctor Julio Ramos, Pedro Lupo León Arboleda, Guillermo Ciro, and Antonio Osorio.

The party's youth group, the Colombian Communist Youth (Juventud Comunista de Colombia), was formed in February 1964. It reportedly has some influence within the universities. Within the labor movement, the PCC-ML controls the Bloque Independiente, a small trade union organization with an estimated membership of 20,000. During 1971 another labor union, the Independent Revolutionary Workers' Movement (MOIR), emerged; this group was described as being pro-Chinese.

The PCC-ML's "armed branch," the EPL, established in 1967, is the first pro-Chinese rural guerrilla force to be active in Latin America. The EPL operates mainly in the central range of the Colombian Andes and apparently is strongest in Apto Sinú. It undertook several small actions, mostly clashes with government forces, during 1971. Two of its highest leaders, Gonzalo González and Libardo Mora Toro, were reported to have died in a skirmish in the Córdoba Department, in northern Colombia, in December 1971.

Considerable student unrest, produced mainly by demands for more student participation in academic and administrative affairs, troubled Colombian universities during most of the year. Serious student riots in Cali and Medellín were declared by police authorities to have been inspired by the pro-Chinese MOIR labor group, which reportedly participated with students in the violent demonstrations. Despite communist (particularly pro-Chinese) activity in the universities, elections held at the National University on 16 November resulted in a defeat for communist candidates.

Publications. The organ of the PCC-ML is *Revolución*. PCC-ML statements are sometimes found in Chinese Communist publications and those of pro-Chinese parties in Europe and Latin America, particularly *Causa Marxista-Leninista*, Santiago, Chile.

*　　*　　*

The ELN. The National Liberation Army was formed in Santander, northeast Colombia, in 1964, by young former members of the PCC who were deeply influenced by the Cuban Revolution. It mounted its first military action in January 1965. Because of strategic and, especially, personal differences, the ELN finds itself divided into four groups at present. The main group, active in Antioquia and Santander, is led by Fabio Vásquez Castaño and is said to favor sporadic raids. A second group, operating mostly in Antioquia, is led by Ricardo Lara Parada and allegedly favors continuous assaults of military patrols. A third group, led by Vásquez's brother, Manuel, also operates in Antioquia, in the regions of Yondo and Boyacá. A fourth group, led by Juan de Dios Aguilera, is said to oppose Fabio Vásquez but to support Lara.

In contrast to the pro-Chinese EPL and the pro-Soviet FARC, the ELN is considered to have very few peasants and to consist mainly of professional people, although Cuban sources claim that it is "made up chiefly of peasants." Much of its present weakness is also attributed to its severe disciplinary punishments, which apparently include the death penalty.

The Lara group kidnaped seven persons (including four German engineers) on 26 March in the Santander Department. The following day, after a brief clash with the guerrillas, a Colombian army force rescued those kidnaped. In July and August the same ELN group kidnaped two ranchers and released them following payment of a $34,000 ransom for each.

A former ELN member, Jaime Arenas, published a book about the ELN entitled *Inside the Guerrilla Movement (La Guerrilla por Dentro)*. His book, which appeared in February 1971, was sharply critical of the Fabio Vásquez leadership. According to Arenas, the ELN had failed in its 1965-67 activities because of its failure to develop links with other political parties and its heavy emphasis on the "foco" theory. Also, Arenas contended that the ELN, instead of trying to become self-sufficient, had relied "excessively on Cuban help." Arenas was killed by ELN forces on 28 March in Bogotá.

Perhaps trying to emulate Father Camilo Torres, two Spanish priests were said to have joined the ELN during 1971. (Torres joined the ELN guerrillas in January 1965. He was killed forty days later in a clash with the army.) Another priest, who joined the guerrillas in 1970, was shot in 1971 by the Fabio Vásquez group, allegedly because he had questioned food privileges enjoyed by guerrilla leaders. A spanish priest, Domingo Laín, was reported in March to have been promoted to the rank of ELN major. Although police sources announced that he was arrested and expelled from Colombia on 23 September, reports on the seizure of a northern town, San Pablo, on 7 January 1972 by some 200 ELN guerrillas indicated that the leaders of the group were Ricardo Lara Parada and Domingo Laín (Radio Cadena Nacional, Bogotá, 7 January).

The ELN organ is the irregular *Venceremos*.

Nelly Stromquist

Costa Rica

The Communist Party of Costa Rica (Partido Comunista de Costa Rica) was founded in 1931 and accepted as a full member of the Comintern in 1935. In 1943, following the wartime policy of many Latin American parties, the Costa Rican communists reorganized under a new name, the Popular Vanguard Party (Partido Vanguardia Popular; PVP).

The Authentic Revolutionary Movement (Movimiento Revolutionaria Auténtico; MRA) is a small guerrilla group.

The PVP was outlawed in 1948 and legalized again in 1970. The party continues a rather ineffectual existence and occasionally uses front parties in an attempt to establish itself as a political force. In 1970 two PVP members, including Secretary-General Manuel Mora, were elected to the 58-member Legislative Assembly as candidates of the Socialist Action Party (Partido de Acción Socialista; PASO).

The membership of the PVP, which reached a peak of about 3,000 in 1948, was estimated to number only about 600 in 1969. According to a report on the PVP Eleventh Congress, held in 1971, membership had increased fourfold over the past two years (*WMR*, November 1971). The population of Costa Rica is 1,800,000 (estimated 1970).

Organization and Leadership. Manuel Mora Valverde, founder of the PVP, has been secretary-general of the party from its beginning. The assistant secretary-general is his brother, Eduardo Mora Valverde. The organizational secretary is Arnoldo Ferreto Segura ("Oscar Vargas"). In the new Party Rules adopted by the 1971 congress, the Central Committee was enlarged to thirty full and fifteen alternate members and the Central Committee Political Commission was increased to eleven members.

The PVP controls the General Confederation of Costa Rican Workers (Confederación General de Trabajadores Costarricenses; CGTC) which includes about 2,500 of Costa Rica's 24,000 unionized workers. The secretary-general of the CGTC is Alvaro Montero Vega. On 1 May 1971, speaking at the celebration of International Labor Day in San José, he declared that in order for the Costa Rican labor movement to "play the revolutionary role that it should, it must be classist and it should maintain its total independence from governments and from employers." He also expressed CGTC support for the people of Chile, Bolivia, Peru, and Cuba and sympathy for all workers who live under "colonialist, neocolonialist-capitalist, and imperialist systems." (*Libertad*, 8 May.)

The PVP sponsors the "United Agricultural Workers' and Peasants' Federation" (FUNTAC). Its secretary-general is Gonzalo Sierra Cantillo and its main goal is agrarian reform through legislative channels.

The University Action Front (Frente de Acción Universitaria; FAU) is a PVP-affiliated student organization. The secretary-general is Oscar Madrigal Jiménez. The FAU publishes a weekly organ, *Unidad*. Although its membership reportedly is small, the FAU was able to elect three representatives to the directorate of the Federation of University Students of Costa Rica (Federación de Estudiantes Universitarios de Costa Rica; FEUCR) in elections held in May. (The FAU received 1,419 votes out of a total of 6,036). Although it cannot control the FEUCR, the FAU appears to have sufficient support to influence the policy and programs of the university organization.

The official youth group of the PVP is the Vanguard Youth of Costa Rica (Juventud Vanguardia de Costa Rica; JVCR). Its secretary-general is Luis Orlando Corrales. In commemoration of the PVP's fortieth anniversary, the JVCR launched a recruitment campaign with the aim of enlisting 1,500 young workers and students as new members.

Party Internal Affairs. The PVP has traditionally been and currently remains a supporter of the Soviet Union. There are no apparent splits within the party.

The PVP's Eleventh Congress, held on 14-18 May 1971, passed resolutions stressing the need to "fight resolutely all forms of anti-communism and anti-Sovietism directed at weakening and dividing the world revolutionary movement," and to "defend Marxist-Leninist theory and spread it among the masses." The congress also elected the Central Committee and returned Manuel Mora Valverde and Eduardo Mora Valverde to their leading offices. Among the foreign delegations at the congress were those of the communist parties of the Soviet Union, Chile, and Venezuela. (*IB.*, no. 10-11.)

The PVP claimed that its party-building campaign, due to the "rising interest among the people," had doubled the membership in recent years, and reported that 45 per cent of the new members were factory and farm workers. The PVP hoped to conduct "systematic ideological work" among new members and opened a party school which gives a course in the fundamentals of Marxism-Leninism. (*WMR*, February.) Delegates at the congress approved the political line of a "non-violent path" for the "revolution" (*ibid.*, November).

Domestic Views and Activities. In the party program adopted at the Eleventh Congress, the PVP described Costa Rica as an underdeveloped country controlled economically by "foreign imperialists" and dominated politically by the United States. Socialist revolution in Costa Rica was seen as requiring, in its first stage a "basically democratic, popular, anti-imperialist, and agrarian" movement which would achieve "full economic and political independence" for the country and would "pave the way toward socialism." Among the specific policies proposed for the first stage were the nationalization of lands owned or controlled by foreigners, the abrogation of concessions and treaties which "violated national sovereignty," and the establishment of an "independent foreign policy." Particular attention was devoted in the program to the need for agrarian reform, "democracy and the social rights of workers," national economic development, tax reform, and educational reform. (*Libertad*, 22 May.)

The PVP argued that peaceful revolutionary development was possible in Costa Rica for various reasons: the country's "deep-rooted democratic feelings" and lack of a military caste or powerful army, the favorable current international balance of forces, and the "humanitarian feelings of the communists." The party acknowledged that the successful "transfer of power into the hands of the people" would depend on the "extent of unity achieved by the popular forces." Unity in the first stage of revolution, according to the PVP, meant a "broad coalition of forces with the worker-peasant alliance as its base, and including the urban petty and middle bourgeoisie, the intellectuals, and the students." The leading role of the PVP would be won in the course of the struggle. The success and character of the next stage—the transition to socialism—was said to "depend basically on the role played by the workers' class and its ability to organize and direct the other forces participating in the revolutionary process." (*Ibid*.)

On 1 May an article in the PVP newspaper, *Libertad*, declared that a "wave of repression" had been unleashed on the country in spite of public declarations made by the president and his state secretaries about strict adherence to constitutional rights. The article concluded that the "police have more power than the ministers and more than the President of the Republic himself."

International Positions and Policies. The PVP regards the Communist Party of the Soviet Union (CPSU) as the "bulwark of the socialist sector and the revolutionary movement of the world." Despite the "criminal attacks" of the "imperialists" on the people of Cuba, Indochina, and the Middle East, the PVP party program considered that in 1971 the general balance of forces in Latin America and the world as a whole was favorable to the forces "struggling for democracy, national liberation, and socialism." The PVP proclaimed itself a "detachment of the international communist movement" and declared that proletarian internationalism (which did not deny the "national nature of the party") was "one of the foundations of its activities." (*Libertad*, 22 May.)

Reporting on his visit to the Soviet Union to attend the Twenty-fourth Congress of the CPSU, Eduardo Mora condemned the leaders of the Chinese Communist Party for "playing a foul and shameful part in pushing anti-Sovietism" and called them the perpetrators of "terrible misdeeds against the CPSU" (*ibid*., 12 June).

The PVP position on the Central American Common Market was also discussed by Eduardo Mora. The Common Market, he said, was "faulty from its inception" and had been "conceived by technicians from the Economic Commission for Latin America and the United Nations as a plan to benefit the interests of the monopolistic imperialists." The PVP, he continued, believed that the process of integration of Central America must be developed "within the framework of a revolutionary process." (*Ibid*., 26 June.)

On 6 June the communist parties of Central America, Mexico, and Panama held their eighth annual conference at an undisclosed location in Central America. The final communiqué included pledges of solidarity with the Cuban Revolution, denunciation of crimes of the governments against the peoples of Guatamala and Nicaragua, an enthusiastic salute to the electoral victory of the "Popular Unity" alliance in Chile, and a call for the defense of jailed U.S. communist Angela Davis. The communiqué charged that "American imperialism and its Latin American servitors" were preparing a "new military act of agression" against Cuba, and reiterated support for the "peoples of Vietnam, Laos, and Cambodia" and the CPSU. The Soviet party was said to be the "main target of attack by the forces of reaction and imperialism." (*Ibid*., 12 June.)

International Contacts. During 1971, Secretary-General Manuel Mora and Central Committee member Adan Guevara attended the congress of the CPSU, at Moscow in March-April, and the Congress of the Bulgarian Communist Party, in April. In June Manuel Mora, on behalf of the Costa Rican government, again traveled to Moscow to assist in trade negotiations between the Soviet Union and Costa Rica.

Publications. The PVP publishes a weekly newspaper, *Libertad*, which circulates openly, and a theoretical journal, *Trabajo*.Enrique Mora Valverde is the TASS correspondent in Costa Rica.

*   *   *

The MRA. The Authentic Revolutionary Movement is a small Castroite group which advocates armed struggle in the ''present stage of revolution'' in Costa Rica. In recent years the MRA has been active in small-scale guerrilla activities and is believed to have close connections with the FSLN of Nicaragua. No reports of MRA activities were available in 1971.

Lynn Ratliff

Cuba

The Communist Party of Cuba (Partido Comunista de Cuba; PCC) was founded in August 1925. In 1944 it became the People's Socialist Party (Partido Socialista Popular; PSP), which it remained until its merger in July 1961 with Fidel Castro's 26 July Movement and the small Revolutionary Directorate (Directoria Revolucionaria) to form the Integrated Revolutionary Organizations (Organizaciones Revolucionarias Integradas). This was transformed into the United Party of the Socialist Revolution (Partido Unido de la Revolución Socialista) in 1963. In October 1965 that party was reconstituted along more orthodox communist lines and again took the name PCC.

Although the PCC has not published membership figures, it is generally thought to be the most elitist of all ruling communist parties, including within its ranks less than 1.5 per cent of the country's population. Recent membership figures found in Western communist party publications, usually quoting PCC members, are: about 55,000 in 1969 (Blas Roca, in Gil Green, *Revolution Cuban Style*, New York, 1970); about 70,000 in 1969 (*Trybuna Ludu*, Warsaw, 16 April 1969); more than 100,000 in 1970 (Fabio Grobart, in *Népszabadság*, Budapest, 5 December 1970); and approximately 60,000 between 1965 and early 1971 (Carlos Rafael Rodríguez, in *Land og Folk*, Copenhagen, 18-19 April 1971). The U.S. State Department estimated party membership at about 120,000 in mid-1970 (*World Strength of Communist Party Organizations*, Washington, D. C., 1970). The population of Cuba was 8,553,395 at the time of the September 1970 census.

Organization and Leadership. Political power in Cuba in 1971 continued to be primarily in the hands of Fidel Castro Ruz and was exercised through his positions as prime minister, commander in chief of the armed forces, and first secretary of the PCC. Persons wielding varying amounts of secondary but not insignificant power are found in the party's eight-member Political Bureau, seven-member Secretariat, and 100-member Central Committee. The Political Bureau is headed by Fidel Castro; the other members are Major Raúl Castro Ruz (deputy prime minister and armed forces minister), Osvaldo Dorticós Torrado (president of Cuba), Major Sergio del Valle Jiménez (interior minister), Armando Hart Dávalos (organizing secretary) and Majors Juan Almeida Bosque, Ramiro Valdés Menéndez, and Guillermo García Frias. The Secretariat is also headed by Fidel Castro; the other members are Raúl Castro, Osvaldo Dorticós, Armondo Hart, Faure Chomón Mediavilla (former Revolutionary Directorate leader, who was removed from the position of transportation minister in December 1970), Blas Roca Calderio, and Carlos Rafael Rodríguez (the last two are former PSP leaders). Among the Central Committee members are the following ministers: Alfredo Yabur Maluf (justice), Major Belarmino Castilla Mas (education), Raúl Roa García (foreign relations), Captain Jorge Risquet Valdés (labor), and Marcelo Fernández Font (foreign trade), along with Captain José Abrahantes Fernández (deputy interior minister and head of the State Security Department), Major Manuel Piñeiro Losada (head of the General Directorate of Intelligence), Celia Sánchez Manduley (presidential secretary), and Vilma Espín Villoy (wife of Raúl Castro).

Approximately two-thirds of the Central Committee members are officers in the Revolutionary Armed Forces (Fuerzas Armadas Revolucionarias; FAR)—the designation of the Cuban military.

Mass Organizations. The Cuban mass organizations during 1971 were: the Central Organization of Cuban Workers (Central de Trabajadores de Cuba; CTC), the National Association of Small Farmers (Asociación Nacional de Agricultores Pequeños; ANAP), the Committees for the Defense of the Revolution (Comités de Defensa de la Revolución; CDR), the Federation of Cuban Women (Federación de Mujeres Cubanas; FMC), and the Union of Cuban Pioneers (Unión de Pioneros de Cuba; UPC). The Union of Young Communists (Unión de Jóvenes Comunistas; UJC), the University Student Federation (Federación Estudiantil Universitaria; FEU), and the Federation of Students of Intermediate Education (Federación de Estudiantes de la Enseñanza Media; FEEM) were sometimes regarded as mass organizations. In the words of Fidel Castro on 18 November, these organizations are "the instruments of the Revolution" (*Granma*, English, 28 November).

The mass organizations received unusually great attention during the year amid increasing discussion of political democratization and popular participation in the affairs of the country. According to Fidel Castro on 7 December 1970, this effort to "revitalize" the mass organizations, which had begun several months earlier in response to the economic setbacks of 1970, was to form the basis of a "really advanced, non-bureaucratic form of social and political life" (*ibid.*, 20 December).

Central Organization of Cuban Workers. The CTC is headed by its National Committee, under Héctor Ramos Latour as first secretary. In mid-1970 its membership, including both state-farm laborers and urban workers, was reportedly 1.4 million (*WMR*, August, supplement), though workers said to be voting in local union elections were numbered at two million (*Granma*, 11 November).

Early in 1971 Lionel Martín wrote that in recent years the Cuban union movement had "almost reached the point of complete dissolution," asserting that "a vanguard movement among the workers was beginning to replace a movement which included all the workers" (*Cuba Internacional*, April). Hence efforts to democratize the mass organizations had begun at the end of 1970 with elections of local officials in the CTC. Addressing the closing session of the Sixth National Council of the CTC on 11 October 1971, Jorge Risquet stated that the "merits and qualities" of more than 300,000 workers had been discussed prior to the "direct, secret ballot" which resulted in the election of almost 163,000 workers for one-year terms as leaders of some 35,000 trade union locals. A few of these leaders lacked "sufficient merits," Risquet continued, their election pointing up those areas where the "political work" of the Revolution had failed. (*Granma*, English, 24 October.)

On 25 November 1970 the CTC National Committee appointed a committee to arrange for the renewal or creation of national unions in the various industries. By mid-October 1971 eleven national trade unions had been formed, covering basic industry, light industry, the food industry, mining, oil, transportation, merchant marine and ports, the sugar industry, communications, civilian workers of the FAR, and education and culture. On 1 May Castro said it was "quite likely" that all national trade unions would be formed by May Day 1972 and that a "national congress of workers" could be held in the last half of that year (*ibid.*, 16 May 1971).

At a trade union conference on 19 September, Raúl Castro outlined the functions of the unions under socialism, namely, "to serve as a vehicle for the orientations, directives, and goals which the revolutionary power—the power of the working class—must convey to the working masses." Emphasizing that "the Party is the vanguard," he added that the trade unions "should be the workers' avenue to convey to the Party their concerns and ideas." (*Ibid.*, 26 September.) On May Day Fidel Castro had announced that "work productivity must from now on be the number one objective of the labor movement" (*ibid.*, 16 May; also see Jorge Risquet, *ibid.*, 24 October).

National Association of Small Farmers. The ANAP is headed by PCC Central Committee member José ("Pepe") Ramírez Cruz. It regulates the small farmers who retain, under what is called private ownership, 32 per cent of the Cuban farmland. This land, in plots of 67 hectares or less, can be sold only to the state and some of it is under rental to the state. The ANAP has 225,000 members, drawn from some 180,000 small farm families. Most farmers are told what they must grow and all are expected to sell their crops to the state at fixed prices. The ANAP held a national plenary meeting on 16-17 May and its Fourth Congress on 25-31 December, both of which were closed with a long address by Fidel Castro. At the time of the congress it was reported that small farms produced 23 per cent of the sugar cane, 85 per cent of the coffee, 90 per cent of the tobacco, almost all of the cocoa, and high percentages of the bananas, greens, and citrus fruits.

Committees for the Defense of the Revolution. The CDR's were first formed on 28 September 1960. The CDR national coordinator, Luis González Maturelos, heads the 13-member National Bureau, which is directly responsible to the PCC Central Committee and whose central office in Havana controls a substructure of provincial, district, sectional, zonal, and block committees. In September 1971 Fidel Castro announced its membership at some 3.5 million. On the eleventh anniversary of the CDR, Fidel Castro reminded the Cuban people that the "essential objective" of the committees was "the struggle against the enemies, the struggle against the agents of imperialism and the struggle against saboteurs and counterrevolutionary elements." (*Ibid.*, 10 October.) The CDR also participated in a wide variety of other activities, including the mobilizing of workers and the administering of programs related to public health, education, recreation, local government, and law enforcement.

Federation of Cuban Women. During 1971 the FMC remained under the control of its president, PCC Central Committee member Vilma Espín. On its eleventh anniversary, in August, the FMC announced that it had 1,401,348 members, comprising roughly 55 per cent of Cuban women over the age of fourteen. The FMC undertakes to mobilize women for agricultural and other work, manage child-care centers, provide general education and technical training, and organize ideological study groups. It places particular emphasis on getting volunteer labor. In a *Granma* editorial of 23 August the FMC was described as a "powerful, enthusiastic and disciplined force" and one of the most effective mass organizations in the country (*ibid.*, 29 August).

Union of Cuban Pioneers. The UPC, founded in April 1961, was officially recognized as a children's mass organization on 17 February 1971. It includes some 1.2 million school children from kindergarten to the sixth grade in 12,445 schools. Although now regarded as an autonomous organization, it remains under the leadership of the UJC. UPC president Juan Mok is a member of the UJC National Committee. It objectives, according to a *Granma* editorial of 22 February, are to promote interest in studying, strengthen discipline, organize leisure time, imbue the "highest revolutionary virtues," and "develop, through concrete activities, a love of our Revolutionary Armed Forces and the Ministry of the Interior." The activities of the UPC were seen as becoming a "decisive, far-reaching support to the Revolution's great battle for the formation of a new man." (*Ibid.*, 28 February.)

Union of Young Communists. The UJC was described by Fidel Castro on 18 November 1971 as a "school for training future Party members" (*ibid.*, 28 November). Jaime Crombet was renamed first secretary, and the new 52-member National Committee was presented, at the Sixth National Plenum of the UJC, in late January (*Juventud Rebelde*, 25 January). On 30 September it was announced that the UJC would hold its Second National Congress on 29 March-4 April 1972. The UJC is believed to have approximately 200,000 members. This organization is responsible for carrying out or overseeing the tasks of the Cuban leaders among young persons. Its principal task for 1972, discussed at the January plenum, was "the battle for the increase of productivity" (*Granma*, 23 January). It is active in all of the youth mass organizations (see below) and in the Centennial Youth Column (Columna Juvenil del Centenario; CJC), first organized along military lines in 1968 to harvest sugar in underpopulated Camagüey Province, made up to approximately 40,000 members in 1971, the Ocean Youth Column (Columna Juvenil del Mar), which trains young persons for the fishing industry; and the Textile Youth Column (Columna Juvenil Textil), to train young girls for the textile industry.

University Student Federation. The FEU, which was merged with the UJC in November 1967, was reconstituted as an independent organization in early 1971. The First National Council of the FEU was held on 22-23 May under the guidance of the UJC and the PCC. The universities of Havana, Oriente, and Las Villas, and the University Center of Camagüey, elected Néstor del Prado, of the University of Havana, and Miguel Mancheco, as president and vice-president respectively. According to the "Declaration" of the council, published in *Granma* on 24 May, Cuban universities are

> first of all, places for forging revolutionaries.... Admittance of young people into our universities and their stay in them must result from political and moral as well as educational factors. In our educational centers not only is there no room for the antisocial and counterrevolutionary elements but also for the so-called 'neutrals' and 'apathetics' who are in effect taking sides with the enemy. (*Ibid.*, English, 30 May.)

Throughout, the Declaration reflected the resolutions of the recently concluded First National Congress on Education and Culture (see below).

Federation of Students of Intermediate Education. The first National Congress of the FEEM, an organization comprising students from technical, secondary, pre-university, and other equivalent institutions, was held on 27-28 January. The 41-member National Council was announced and Jorge Aldereguía Henríquez was elected president. The "Final Statement" of the congress pointed out Che Guevara as "the best example of the new man which our society hopes to form," declared that "study, work, and defense are the duties of all revolutionary young people," and called for the development of "strength of character, austerity, and collectivism" (*ibid.*, 7 February).

Revolutionary Armed Forces. The FAR is estimated to enroll some 250,000 persons (Eleazar Díaz Rangel, in *Momento*, Caracas, 11 April), approximately 50,000 of whom cut 17 per cent of the sugar cane harvested in 1971. Militia membership is estimated at an additional 200,000 to 250,000. On 2 December Fidel Castro stated: "We can have 600,000 men in arms within 24 hours" (*Granma*, English, 19 December). Cuba devotes a significant part of its budget to the military, some $500 million per year (according to *Clarin*, Santiago, Chile, 12 July). This figure does not includ foreign military aid, which Fidel Castro valued at $1.5 billion from the Soviet Union alone between 1959 and April 1970 (*Granma*, English, 3 May). Raúl Castro, armed forces minister, stated on 17 April that "practically all" command officers and 75 per cent of FAR officers in general are members of the PCC or UJC (*ibid.*, 25 April). Almost all top officers are former members of Castro's 26 July Movement. In recent years the discipline and organization of the FAR have spread into most sectors of Cuban society and by the end of 1971 FAR personnel had taken over the majority of decisive leadership positions on the national level.

Party Internal Affairs. Fidel Castro created the PCC in 1965 and appointed the members of the Political Bureau, Secretariat, and Central Committee. The party, which has still not held its first, "founding," congress, is controlled by its creator. The institutional structure of the PCC is undeveloped and does not provide either mechanisms for internal debate or guarantees against abuses by superiors. Carlos Rafael Rodríguez commented early in 1971 that the PCC was being reorganized somewhat so that members could devote more time to political, and less time to administrative, work. He noted, however, that Cuba did not have enough experts to move ahead smoothly on all fronts. (*Land og Folk*, 18-19 April.) During the year the Cubans increasingly sought expert advice from Communist parties in Europe. For example, a PCC delegation visited Czechoslovakia in July to study party structure, and Orlando Fundora, head of the PCC Central Committee's Commission of Revolutionary Orientation (Comisión de Orientación Revolucionaria; COR), led a delegation to Eastern Europe in September. On 2 November Moscow radio commented that the Soviet Union was giving Cuba moral and political, as well as military and economic, aid. There is still no indication, however, as to when the first congress of the PCC will be held.

Domestic Attitudes and Activities. Officially proclaimed the "Year of Productivity," 1971 might more accurately have been called the "Year of the Mass Line." "Workers' democracy" and the "mass line"—that is, popular participation in the governing of the country—have been widely discussed since Fidel Castro acknowledged the domestic setbacks of 1970 (see *YICA*, 1971, pp. 412-15). Implementation of the mass line occurred in the mass organizations (see above) and in such fields as justice, education, culture, and labor legislation (see below).

The need for 'democracy' in the development of socialism has been discussed much more frequently since mid-1970 than it was during most of the 1960's. In the early years of what is called the Revolutionary Government, Cuban leaders argued that democracy was found in public rallies and in personal contacts with the people. Since mid-1970, however, Cuban leaders have often appeared to discount the effectiveness of Cuban democracy during the 1960's. For example, on 23 August 1970 Fidel Castro called for the development of "a new society and of genuinely democratic principles." The government, he continued, had just begun to "substitute democratic methods for the administrative methods that run the risk of becoming bureaucratic methods." (*Granma*, English, 30 August.) On 29 November 1971, during his visit to Chile, Castro declared:

> In our country, the Revolutionary Government began by governing by decree. But, by now [i.e., since late 1970; see below], every important law that has to do with main interests of the people is discussed by millions of people through our work centers, our mass organizations and our military units.... In Cuba we all belong to the Parliament, we are all lawmakers, day in and day out!" (*Ibid.*, 12 December.)

It is apparent from PCC attitudes toward elected labor leaders who lacked "sufficient merits" (see above), from the FEU position on "neutral" students (see above), from the declarations of the First National Congress on Education and Culture (see below), and from other nationally accepted policies, that the "new proletarian democracy" which Castro says the government seeks but has not yet achieved (*ibid.*) is not intended to guarantee a voice to all Cuban citizens. Fidel Castro made this clear in December 1970 when he said: "We're talking about workers' democracy, not liberal or bourgeois democracy. Liberals and the bourgeoisie have no rights, except to disappear as a class" (*ibid.*, 20 December). On a number of occasions during 1971 Castro condemned foreign "bourgeois liberals" and even socialists who called for freedoms which the Cubans held to be incompatible with socialism and workers' democracy (e.g., on 30 April and 6 June; see below).

The restructuring of the judicial system was also undertaken with the stated objectives of increasing popular participation in the governing of the country and of creating a unified judicial system which in all details conformed to the program for Cuban socialism. According to an article in *Granma* (English, 5 September), Cubans recognized the separation of powers in government as one of the "myths of the past." The Cuban courts would be subordinated to the Council of Ministers, which has "executive, legislative and constitutional functions, all in one." The structure of the new system, discussed in detail in *Verde Olivo* (4 April) would be: (1) People's Tribunals, which would try minor criminal and civil cases; (2) Regional Tribunals, for criminal and civil cases of a certain degree of importance; (3) Provincial Tribunals, for more serious crimes and counterrevolutionary activities; (4) the Supreme People's Tribunal; and (5) military tribunals and courts. According to *Granma* (English, 5 September), "the courts on all levels will have both professional [lawyers] and nonprofessional judges. Both will be elected by delegates of the people selected by different organizations."

The First National Congress on Education and Culture convened in Havana on 23-30 April with some 1,800 delegates in attendance, representing teachers, educational, scientific, and cultural agencies, the PCC, the UJC, and the mass organizations. In a speech at the closing session, Fidel Castro said that the congress had reflected the "mass line of the Revolution" since it had been preceded and influenced by "hundreds of meetings" at the "grass roots level" (*ibid.*, 9 May). The "mass line" orientation of the congress was emphasized by Belarmino Castilla Mas, the education minister, in his opening address: "The Revolution does not seek an art of the elite or an exclusive culture, but rather an art which comes from the very heart of the people and is a tool for their most noble and greatest expressions" (*ibid.*).The General Declaration contained sections on teachers, education in all its aspects, fashion, religion, juvenile delinquency, sex, extracurricular activities, the mass media, the arts, and foreign criticism of the revolutionary regime. It asserted repeatedly that education and culture could not be apolitical and impartial. Indeed, Fidel Castro insisted that the "themes that aroused the most ardor, the most passion and unanimity," were "precisely those dealing with ideological, political, and revolutionary matters"; on these "there was only one attitude: a firm, solid, unanimous, monolithic attitude" (*ibid.*). According to an article appearing at the same time, the congress "set the guidelines for a new, higher stage of revolutionary action in the fields of teaching, science, and culture" (*ibid.*). The Cuban novelist Edmundo Desnoes later compared the "ideological revolution" under way in Cuba to the Cultural Revolution in China (interview, *Guardian*, New York, 17 November).

The effort to enforce a "mass line" in the arts was most apparent in the "Padilla affair."[1] Heberto Padilla, a well-known young Cuban poet who had previously been in official disfavor, was arrested on 20 March on orders from Fidel Castro (*Le Monde*, Paris, 29 April). He was not released from prison until 27 April, several weeks after he had signed a 4,000-word "confession" repudiating his "insults and defamations to the Revolution" over the past five years. (The official "synthesis" of Padilla's confession was published in *Direct From Cuba*, Havana, 30 April, and reprinted in *Intercontinental Press*, 24 May.) According to Prensa Latina, a number of other Cuban writers, all named in Padilla's confession, criticized their own works before Padilla and a meeting of the National Union of Writers and Artists of Cuba (UNEAC) on 27 April (*Le Monde*, 30 April). The affair was not reported directly in the Cuban domestic press, though it caused international repercussions of some importance (see below). On 30 April, in response to foreign criticism Castro declared that the whole affair was "too unimportant, too much rubbish to appear in our newspapers or concern our workers" (*Granma*, English, 9 May).

Other evidence of the stricter cultural line occurred during and immediately after the Congress on Education and Culture. On 29 April *Granma* announced that Angel Guerra Cabrera, editor of the UJC daily, *Juventud Rebelde*, had replaced Enrique de la Osa, who had incurred official displeasure several times since 1969, as editor of the weekly Bohemia. One week after the congress it was announced that Luis Pavón, formerly editor of *Verde Olivo*, the armed forces journal, which had launched a campaign against Padilla in late 1968, had been made the new director of the National Council of Culture.

On 26 July 1968 Fidel Castro declared that the "great task of the Revolution" was "basically the task of forming the new man"—"the man of a truly revolutionary conscience, the man of a truly socialist conscience, the man of a truly communist conscience" (*Granma*, English, 28

---

[1]On Padilla see *Le Monde*, Paris, 9, 23, 28, 29, and 30 April, and *Intercontinental Press*, New York, 17 and 24 May.

July). Che Guevara has been the model of the new man since his death in Bolivia in October 1967. In recent years this objective was reportedly sought in a variety of ways: education programs, mass participation in production, popular participation in the administration and solution of community problems, and the development of a "sense of revolutionary honor and social responsibility" (*Granma* editorial, 17 September 1967). Moral incentives were stressed during the late 1960's. Beginning in late 1970, however, Cuban leaders themselves often questioned the effectiveness of their past policies, and important shifts have recently been announced and in some cases implemented: education and cultural reform has been extensive (see above); Fidel Castro noted, in speeches on 23 August and 28 September 1970, that the ANAP and the workers' movement in general were neglected in recent years because of an overemphasis on "vanguard workers," and the "democratization" of the movement has been stressed ever since (see above); setbacks in the development of conscience have been acknowledged (e.g., by Fidel Castro on 1 May 1971) and laws have been passed to fight the chronic problems of absenteeism, loafing, and inefficiency (see below); worker productivity has been given higher priority than the development of conscience in the workers' movement (Castro's speech of 1 May 1971), and material incentives have been increasingly employed (see below).

The related problems of absenteeism, loafing, and worker inefficiency, which have held back production in Cuba in recent years, have been raised time and again since mid-1970 by Cuban leaders. One effort to alter the situation was introduced in August 1969 in the form of Law 1225 (text in *Granma*, 18 September), which required the keeping of labor dossiers to record the merits and demerits of each worker. The law was not implemented, however, until the "Resolution No. 425 on Labor Merit" was signed by Jorge Risquet on 15 October 1970 (*Granma*, English, 25 October).

The Labor Merit law was followed in early 1971 by Law No. 1231, the Law on Loafing. Some 115,000 local assemblies, attended by more than 3,000,000 persons, are said to have been held to discuss the provisions of the law between its publication in draft form on 11 January and its enactment, significantly modified, on 16 March (final text in *Granma*, English, 28 March). The law states that all men from seventeen through sixty years of age, and all women from seventeen through fifty-five, who are "physically and mentally fit have the social duty of contributing to the community with their work." The law describes the "precriminal state of loafing" and the "crime of loafing," the former punishable by up to a year's internment in a "rehabilitation center" doing "productive work," and the latter by imprisonment of up to two years in a "rehabilitation center." In a speech on 11 January 1972, at the National Plenary Meeting on Labor Justice, Major Jesús Montane explained that Law No. 1231 was "a labor law made by a society of workers, to protect this society from the negative effects of old bourgeois hangovers such as absenteeism, loafing and lack of work discipline" (*ibid.*, 23 January 1972). On May Day 1971 Fidel Castro stated: "The Law on Loafing lays the foundation of discipline, the foundation for solving our material problems" (*ibid.*, 16 May).

The January 1972 National Plenary Meeting on Labor Justice, called to determine the effectiveness of the law on loafing, concluded that it had been successful politically, economically, socially, and, above all, ideologically. According to Jesús Montane, more than 100,000 persons not working had signed up for jobs at the regional offices of the Interior Ministry during the grace period before the law went into effect (*ibid.*, 23 January). Serious problems remained, however. Elaborating on a charge made by Fidel Castro on 28 June 1971, Jorge Risquet reported to the National Council of the CTC on 11 October that many factory managers were not demanding enough from their workers and were failing to report "habitual absenteeism or unjustified absences" of more than fifteen days. Further, Risquet reported that there was a "small but not unimportant group of absentee workers who do not fulfill their goals, who waste materials, fuel, water and light in an indolent manner and irresponsibly damage equipment. (*Ibid.*, 24 October.) In August Cecilio Sánchez reported that in the important sugar-producing Oriente Province experienced workers were retiring and young replacements were undisciplined and had low political and ideological understanding (*Sierra Maestra*, 11 August).

Cuban leaders, who have for years shown a decided preferance for moral over material incentives, acknowledged the value of the latter more openly in 1971 than they have in recent years. At the beginning of the year the Internal Trade Ministry announced a plan for the distribution of such scarce items as household electrical goods, bicycles, pressure cookers, and watches only through work centers, and only to workers who "fulfill their social duties" (*Granma*, 2 January). According to Fidel Castro on 28 September, the same criteria would be used to determine which workers get new houses as they are built. On 1 May Castro even stated that "at the present stage of the Revolution," it was understandable that a worker would not go to the extra trouble of improving his education and work skills if he were not assured that a more skilled and responsible job would draw a better wage. Cuban leaders have had to recognize, however, that cash incentives may not always be effective, since there is more money now in Cuban pockets than there is merchandize in Cuban stores. On 1 May Fidel Castro stated that some money should be withdrawn from circulation since "we must avoid having more money in circulation than available goods and services, because this results in vice, corruption and commercialism, in short, in setbacks for consciousness" (*Granma*, English, 16 May). The problem faced by the government, according to Jorge Risquet on 11 October, was to make the people appreciate "the contradiction between the desire to obtain an ever better standard of living and the reality of our limited natural, material and human resources; and that these contradictions can only be solved through effort, work, organization and productivity" (*ibid.*, 24 October).

Sugar. The 1970 harvest produced a record 8,535,281 metric tons of sugar.[2] This record, however, was far short of the target of 10 million tons, and was achieved at the expense of the 1969 and 1971 harvests and of other Cuban economic programs. (See *YICA*, 1971, pp. 412-14.) The target for the 1971 harvest was first set at 7,000,000 tons. When this target was lowered to 6,650,000 tons on 1 May, it was accompanied by a warning from Fidel Castro: "Less than that amount would adversely affect our foreign exchange receipts" (*Granma*, English, 16 May). The actual harvest was 5,924,335 tons (*Granma*, 21 July).

On 26 July, after the completion of the 1971 harvest, Fidel Castro declared: "In many ways the problems of 1970 were still making themselves felt this year." These included too little cane ready to harvest, delays in mill repairs, insufficient weed killer, and bad weather. Full recovery, according to Castro, would not come until the 1973 harvest. The problem of manpower was reduced—the number of cane cutters during the peak of the season dropped from approximately 360,000 in 1970 to 230,000 in 1971—by the adoption of the "Australian method" of burning off the cane fields. (*Granma*, English, 1 August.) This method, which makes the cane easier to cut by machine or by hand, requires greater coordination of burning, cutting, transporting, and milling since the cane must be ground within 48 hours after it is burned. Furthermore, it necessitates more weeding, additional fertilizer, and produces less bagasse to be used for fuel in the mills or for animal fodder.

---

[2]Statistics available from Cuba are of varying reliability. Some, such as those relating to foreign trade, are essentially accurate; most, including those dealing with social services, labor, industry, and agriculture, must be used with care. Cuban statistics are often incomplete, usually inadequate for cross-checking, and at times contradictory; they are sometimes deliberately misleading, in particular when an effort is being made to compare Cuba after the revolution with pre-Castro Cuba. Recent indices of agricultural output, for example, often reflect great increases because they are based on 1962-63, in most respects one of the worst years since Castro's rise to power, when the momentum of pre-Castro production had been lost. These difficulties are discussed at length by Carmelo Mesa-Lago in "Availability and Reliability of Statistics in Socialist Cuba," *Latin American Research Review*, Spring 1969, pp. 53-91, and Summer 1969, pp. 47-81.

On 30 August Fidel Castro announced the formation of the Sugar Harvest Sector, an agency for managing the sugar harvest, headed by Major Diocles Torralba, formerly chief of staff of the FAR. Efforts to mechanize the harvest, with increasing assistance from the Soviet Union (see Soviet-Cuban protocol, *ibid.*, 19 September), are continuing though they have thus far been generally unsuccessful. The 1972 harvest began on 3 November and was scheduled to end in May.

Social Services. Of all the "basic social services" in Cuba, education is considered the most important. This importance was reflected in the First National Congress of Education and Culture (see above), in frequent comments on the subject by Fidel Castro (e.g., speeches of 30 April, 15 September, 12 November), and in various educational developments. The principles governing the Cuban education system were summarized by *Granma* (English, 17 October) in the following propositions:

> Channeling education toward concrete objectives
> Establishing close links between the school and life
> Training the new generations for work and in work
> Educating for the collectivity
> Combining conscious but firm discipline with the most strict respect for the personality of the student

These principles were declared the basis of the recent widely publicized "School in the Countryside" system, an outgrowth of the "School Goes to the Countryside" system which dates from 1966 (see *ibid.*). Major Belarmino Castilla, minister of education, reported in late April that there were 2,262,587 students in Cuba: 1,652,700 in the primary level, 185,511 in the junior high school to university level, 327,521 in adult education, and some 100,000 in technical and professional training, teachers' training, special training, and advanced education. He also reported that some 300,000 children in the age group from six through sixteen years were out of school and that academically speaking many of the schools were "not so good." According to Major Castilla, the most serious problem the education system faces is the lack of teachers. (*Ibid.*, 9 May.) A high percentage of Cuban students are taught by unqualified teachers.

The Cuban government has devoted considerable attention to national health programs. New hospitals and dispensaries, which offer free services, have been established, especially in rural areas. At the same time the overall quality of existing health services seems to have declined, largely because almost half of the trained doctors in Cuba before 1959, when health conditions were high by Latin American standards, have gone into exile; their replacements, though more numerous, have not been as well trained.

Inadequate housing has become an increasingly serious problem, a "supercritical" problem according to Fidel Castro on 3 September 1970 (*ibid.*, 20 September). On 6 January 1969 Castro stated: "In the years of the Revolution we have not built more than 10,000 dwellings per year, whereas we need to build approximately 100,000 per year" (*ibid.*, 14 January). On 1 May 1971 he estimated that in 1972 it would be possible to build some 30,000 dwellings. Castro later acknowledged that there had been "very little" new construction of houses during 1971 and suggested that in the future "minibrigades of industrial workers" could build houses in their spare time, the houses to go to the most needy and deserving workers in the area (*ibid.*, 10 October).

Refugees. Approximately 650,000 persons voluntarily left Cuba between 1959 and the end of 1971, about a quarter of a million on the refugee flights which have taken place twice each week day since 1965 between Cuba and Miami. The U.S. State Department reported on 31 August that Cuba had announced its intention to suspend the flights by the end of the year when the persons on the present waiting list—all of whom signed up before May 1966, when applications to leave were closed—had left Cuba.

International Views and Activities. Inasmuch as the PCC has only once issued anything approaching an overall statement on foreign policy (the Central Committee statement of 18 May 1967), Cuban international views and positions must be sought in the speeches of Fidel Castro and other top officials.[3]

Revolution in Latin America. At a press conference in Chile on 3 December 1971 Fidel Castro said: "This hemisphere carries a child in its womb that is known as Revolution, that is on its way and that, inexorably, ... will be born" (*Granma*, English, 19 December). Ever since the overthrow of Fulgencio Batista in 1959, Fidel Castro has called upon revolutionaries in Latin America to seize power in their countries by armed struggle, generally by rural guerrilla warfare. The urgency of this call, however, and the breadth of its applicability, has varied from one period to another.[4] During 1971 it was relatively low-keyed. While Cuban leaders still professed to believe that revolution would come to the vast majority of countries only through armed struggle (e.g., see comments by Castro and Carlos Rafael Rodríguez in *Punto Final*, Santiago, Chile, 2 February, supplement), they recognized that this would not be in the immediate future. On 3 December, commenting on Cuban disputes with other members of the socialist camp in years past, Castro made what was almost certainly a reference to his own single-minded advocacy of guerrilla warfare several years before: "On occasions, the contradictions [with other socialist countries] were due to a certain idealism—and I say this in all frankness—because, on occasion, we expect things to develop the way our imagination pictures them" (*Granma*, English, 19 December).

Cuban leaders acknowledged during 1971 that the most revolutionary policies being implemented in South America were those of governments which had achieved power without the use of armed struggle. On 27 August Castro declared that the "tremendous anti-imperialist revolutionary upsurge" in Latin America was most apparent in Chile, under the elected government of Salvador Allende; in Peru, under the military government of Juan Velasco; and in Uruguay, where the leftist Broad Front had "great possibilities of defeating the oligarchy" in the November election (*ibid.*, 5 September).In the months just before the right-wing military coup in Bolivia in August, Castro had even begun praising the "revolutionary process" taking place in that country (e.g., speech of 26 July, *ibid.*, 1 August). Castro showed particular interest in the policies of the Chilean Popular Unity government, arguing, on 25 November, that it was the first in history to seek "social change through elections, that is through peaceful means" (*ibid.*, 19 December). While visiting Chile in November and December, Castro repeatedly urged the Chilean left to unite in support of the Allende government against the threat from the "reactionaries," "fascists," and "imperialists." On 2 December, in his farewell speech in the National Stadium in Santiago, and in a press conference on 3 December, he commented that the Popular Unity forces had apparently failed to unite and consolidate as effectively as the opposition.

Cuban relations with the communist parties of Latin America have fluctuated in recent years, reaching their lowest point in 1967. Early in 1971 Carlos Rafael Rodríguez indicated that current Cuban relations with most of these parties were good, though not with those in Bolivia and Venezuela (interview, *Land og Folk*, 18-19 April). Cuba has no relations with, and apparently pays no attention whatsoever to, the pro-Chinese communist parties in Latin America. Relations with the so-called "Castroite" groups in some countries (e.g., Colombia and Venezuela) have become strained or even broken in recent years due to the apparent withdrawal of Cuban material and moral support. Cuban publications give considerable publicity to guerrilla groups in Argentina, Bolivia, Brazil, and Uruguay, however, and Fidel Castro himself has expressed admiration for the National Liberation

[3]Cuban positions on most international issues are summarized in the yearly speeches of Ricardo Alarcón to the United Nations General Assembly. For his report of 12 October 1971 see *Granma* (English, 24 October).
[4]See *Yearbook on Latin American Communist Affairs, 1971* (Stanford, 1971, pp. 8-10).

Army in Bolivia and the Tupamaros in Uruguay. On 27 August, after the coup in Bolivia, Castro promised "moral and material support to the Bolivian revolutionaries who are fighting for liberation" (*Granma*, English, 5 September).

Soviet Union. According to Fidel Castro on 3 December, Soviet-Cuban relations were "very good" during 1971 (*ibid.*, 19 December). During the year a number of top-level contacts took place (see below), one of the most important of which was during the visit of Soviet Premier Alexsei Kosygin to Cuba in late October. The "Joint Soviet-Cuban Communiqué" issued on 30 October demonstrated a considerable degree of agreement between the two governments on international issues, ranging from support for the Popular Unity government in Chile to the desirability of a world disarmament conference. Fidel Castro accepted an invitation to make his third trip to the Soviet Union (having visited there previously in 1963 and 1964) at an unspecified date in the future. (See text of communiqué, *ibid.*, 7 November).

Soviet economic aid to Cuba during 1971 is estimated at roughly $500 million (*New York Times*, 21 October). Cuban indebtedness to the Soviet Union at the beginning of the year, including trade deficits but not military assistance, was estimated at approximately $3 billion (*ibid.*, 28 February). After Kosygin's visit to Cuba in October, East European sources in Havana were quoted as saying that Soviet aid to Cuba would be increased by about $1 billion during the next five years (to about $700 million annually). A Prensa Latina release at the end of December, reporting on the outcome of Osvaldo Dorticós's trip to the Soviet Union (21-28 December), indicated that both countries were willing to increase the levels of trade in the future. A far-reaching protocol on economic, scientific, and technical collaboration was signed by V. N. Novikov, deputy chairman of the Council of Ministers of the U.S.S.R., and Carlos Rafael Rodríguez, minister without portfolio, on 8 September (see *ibid.*, 19 September).

Cuban relations with the socialist camp generally were described as good by Fidel Castro on 3 December. Top-level contacts between Cuban and Eastern European officials increased during the year.

Communist China. Cuban relations with the government of the People's Republic of China (PRC) continued to improve slowly during 1971. Diplomatic relations at the ambassadorial level, which had been broken for almost four years, were reestablished at the end of 1970: credentials were presented by the Chinese ambassador in Havana on 15 December and by the Cuban ambassador in Peking on 6 June 1971. Cuban leaders expressed their pleasure over the admission of the PRC to the United Nations, which they had long supported. Although the volume of Sino-Cuban trade was reduced somewhat in 1966, when political disputes between the two governments and parties came into the open, commercial links remained fairly steady between 1967 and 1971. Cuba receives rice, soya beans, and cotton cloth from China, and the Chinese continue to be Cuba's second largest market for sugar.

Cuban leaders showed decreased interest in other Asian affairs during 1971, though they reiterated their support for all Indochinese people who resisted "U. S. imperialism."

Latin America. In accordance with a decision reached in 1964 by the Organization of American States (OAS), all Latin American countries (except Mexico, which refused to comply) broke diplomatic relations with Cuba in that year. Since 1969 a number of Latin American countries have at various times shown interest in reestablishing diplomatic relations. Chile, in November 1970, after the inauguration of Salvador Allende, resumed relations. On 12 August 1971 the Cuban Ministry of Foreign Relations issued a statement saying: "The Cuban Government ... is willing to maintain relations with all Latin-American governments which ... are outside the sphere of influence of Yankee imperialism and have enough backbone not to servilely carry out its orders" (*ibid.*, 22 August). On 3 December Fidel Castro emphasized that these governments did not have to be socialist, or as independent as the Cuban government, but merely independent in their foreign policy (*ibid.*, 19 December). He made it clear on many occasions, however, that his government would not under any conditions reenter the OAS (which excluded Cuba in 1962). On 27 August he described the OAS as "that filth, that trash, that rotting corpse" (*ibid.*, 5 September).

United States. Cuba continues to call the United States the bulwark of exploitation and oppression throughout the world. The subject of Cuban-U.S. relations arose repeatedly during 1971. According to Castro on 19 April, the United States was "almost longing for a gesture from Cuba" which would make improved relations possible (*ibid.*, 2 May). The Cubans would not make any gestures of good will, however, or open talks with the United States. In Castro's words on 27 August, Cuba had "nothing to negotiate": "Any day they [the U.S. "imperialists"] decide to lift their blockade against Cuba and stop all their measures against Cuba they must do so unconditionally and without discussing one single thing with us" (*ibid.*, 5 September). On 3 December Castro said Cuba would recognize the United States only when the latter stopped playing "the role of world gendarme" (*ibid.*, 19 December). In December the Cuban government published a long "record of U.S. aggression against Cuba," with 128 entries for the 1959-71 period (*ibid.*, 26 December). The problem of increasing Soviet military influence and presence in Cuba, particularly the periodic visits of Soviet submarines to the port of Cienfuegos, has been a major factor in continuing bad relations between the United States and Cuba.[5]

Cultural Colonialism. The stricter cultural line which became evident in Cuba in early 1971 (see above) attracted international attention because of the "Padilla affair" (see above). News of Padilla's arrest prompted a letter expressing deep concern from thirty-three leftist writers living in Western Europe who had long been sympathetic toward the Cuban Revolution, including a number of Latin Americans (among them Julio Cortazar, Octavio Paz, Carlos Fuentes, Mario Vargas Llosa, and Carlos Franqui) and Europeans (including Jean-Paul Sartre, Simone de Beauvoir, Alberto Moravia, and Rossana Rossanda). The release of Padilla's "confession," and the "self-criticisms" of his literary colleagues, drew a statement signed by sixty intellectuals (including most of those who signed the first letter) which said that the affair recalled "the most sordid moments of the era of Stalinism, with its prefabricated verdicts and its witch-hunts" (text in *New York Times*, 22 May). In response, the "Declaration" of the First National Congress of Education and Culture condemned the "Mafia of pseudo leftist bourgeois intellectuals" abroad who wanted to become the "critical conscience of [Cuban] society" (*Granma*, English, 9 May). On 30 April, Fidel Castro branded the signatories "two-bit agents of cultural colonialism," and "bourgeois libelants, agents of the [U.S.] Central Intelligence Agency and intelligence services of imperialism." None of them, he concluded, would ever be permitted to enter Cuba again. (*Ibid.*) The attacks on the signatories, and on other European leftists who had written books critical of the revolutionary regime in Cuba,[6] continued. On 6 June, Castro said that "bourgeois" criticism of Cuba was so discredited that "the style now is to attack the Revolution from communist positions, from socialist positions, from Marxist positions and from leftist positions" (*ibid.*, 13 June).

International Contacts. Cuban visitors to the Soviet Union included Osvaldo Dorticós, Ramiro Valdés, and Jesús Montané, to the Twenty-fourth Congress of the Communist Party of the Soviet Union (CPSU), in March-April; Raúl Roa, in June; Antonio Nuñez Jiménez, in November; and Dorticós, in December. Among the Cuban visitors to Eastern Europe were Armando Hart, to Bulgaria in April for the Tenth Congress of the Bulgarian Communist Party; Blas Roca, to Czechos-

---

[5]The submarine issue is discussed in detail in *Washington Post* (15 February).
[6]E.g., René Dumont, *Cuba est-il socialiste?* (Paris, 1970, and K. S. Karol, *Guerrillas in Power* (New York, 1970).

lovakia in May for the Fourteenth Congress of the Communist Party of Czechoslovakia; Carlos Rafael Rodríguez to the German Democratic Republic in June for the Eighth Congress of the Socialist Unity Party of Germany; and Raúl Roa to Poland and Czechoslovakia in June, and the German Democratic Republic in June-July.

Cuban visitors to Latin America included Ricardo Alarcón, to Chile in June; Raúl Roa, to Chile in August; Vilma Espín, to Chile in September-October; Raúl Roa to Peru in November; Fidel Castro, on his first trip to South America in a decade, to Chile on 10 November-4 December for traveling and talking with President Allende and other government officials; Castro, on his return to Cuba from Chile, to Lima for talks with Peruvian President Juan Velasco Alvarado, and to Quito to meet Ecuadorian President José María Velasco Ibarra; and Jorge Risquet, to Chile for the fiftieth anniversary of the Communist Communist Party of Chile in December 1971-January 1972.

In July Raúl Roa visited Algeria and Blas Roca visited Mongolia.

Soviet visitors to Cuba included Nikolai K. Baibakov, vice-president of the Council of Ministers of the U.S.S.R., in April-May; Premier Kosygin in October; and Andrei Kirilenko, a member of the CPSU Political Bureau, in December. Among visitors from Eastern Europe were Stephan Vasilev, Bulgarian minister of education, in February; General Heinz Hoffman, minister of national defense of the German Democratic Republic, in April Gheorghe Rădulescu, vice-president of the Romanian Council of Ministers, and Edward Babiuch, a member of the Political Bureau of the Polish United Workers' Party, in May; and Miklós Ajtai, deputy premier of Hungary, in November.

The International Organization of Journalists held its Seventh Congress in Havana on January 4-11 (see *International Organization of Journalists*), and the International Medical Association held its Fifth Congress there on 6-9 April. Romesh Chandra, secretary-general of the World Peace Council, visited Cuba in February and Hertta Kuusinen, president of the Women's International Democratic Federation, in April.

Latin American visitors in Cuba included: Gerónimo Arnedo Alvarez, secretary-general of the Communist Party of Argentina, in December 1970-January 1971 and October-November 1971; Volodia Teitelboim, a member of the Political Commission of the Communist Party of Chile, in April; Carlos Altamirano, general secretary of the Socialist Party of Chile, in May; Jaime Pérez, a member of the Secretariat, and Leopoldo Bruera, a member of the Executive Committee, of the Communist Party of Uruguay, in June; Wladímir Turiansky and Félix Díaz, members of the Executive Committee of the Communist Party of Uruguay, in July; Alfredo Llanos, a member of the Presidium of the Bolivian People's Assembly, in July-Agust; and Clodomiro Almeyda, Chilean minister of foreign relations, in July-August.

Other visitors to Cuba included: Régis Debray, the French Marxist author of *Revolution in the Revolution?*, for several months beginning in February; André Vieuguet, member of the Political Bureau of the French Communist Party, in February; Lieutenant Ange Diawara, member of the Political Bureau of the Congolese Workers' Party, in February-March; P. Sundarayya, secretary-general, and H. Singh Surjeet, member of the Politburo, of the Communist Party of India (Marxist), in October; and Abdelaziz Bouteflika, Algerian foreign minister, in November.

Publications. *Granma*, under the direction of Jorge Enrique Mendoza, is the daily organ of the PCC; it appears also in weekly editions in Spanish, English, and French. *Juventud Revelde*, edited by Angel Guerra Cabrera until April, and by Jorge López thereafter, is the daily organ of the UJC. Both are ciruclated nationally. Provincial papers are: *Sierra Maestra* (Oriente), *Adelante* (Camagüey), *Vanguardia* (Las Villas), *Girón* (Matanzas), and *El Guerrillero* (Pinar del Rio). *Verde Olivo*, under the directorship of Luis Pavón until May, and Eduardo Yasells Ferrer thereafter, is the weekly organ of the FAR and often an indicator of PCC positions. Two publications of the Cuba-based Afro-Asian-Latin American Peoples' Solidarity Organization are *Tricontinental* (in Spanish, English, French, and Italian), which appears six times a year, and the monthly *Tricontinental Bulletin* (in Spanish, English, and French).[7]

Prensa Latina is the only Cuban news agency.

William E. Ratliff

---

[7]Information on more than 100 periodicals published in Cuba during the period 1959-1971 is found in *Cuban Studies Newsletter*, vol. 1, no. 2 (May 1971), published by the Center for Latin American Studies at the University of Pittsburgh.

Dominican Republic

Intense disagreement over leadership and policy questions, especially since 1965, has led to the fragmentation of the communist movement in the Dominican Republic. There are three principal organizations: the Dominican Communist Party (Partido Comunista Dominicano; PCD), which, although given recognition by the Soviet Union, has adopted an "independent" line on domestic and foreign issues; the Dominican People's Movement (Movimiento Popular Dominicano; MPD), which is pro-Chinese; and the Revolutionary Movement of 14 June (Movimiento Revolucionario 14 de Junio; MR-1J4), which is pro-Chinese and at the same time sympathetic toward the Castroites. Splits within these groups have created several new factions and parties, including the People's Socialist Party (Partido Socialista Popular; PSP), the Communist Party of the Dominican Republic (Partido Comunista de la República Dominicana; PCRD or PACOREDO), and the Red Line (Línea Roja) of the MR-1J4. Only the PCD appears to enjoy recognition within the international communist movement.

Communism in the Dominican Republic is proscribed under National Laws 6, 70, and 71, which refer to propaganda and subversive activities. The present government under President Joaquín Balaguer, while allowing communist parties to issue statements in the mass media and permitting communist student groups to operate more or less uninhibitedly, maintains strict control over communist activities. Politically motivated murders of leftists (estimated to have totaled more than 150 in 1971) seem to be an established feature of the Dominican scene. These killings have been attributed both to feuds between communist groups and to actions by paramilitary groups reportedly organized by the army and police.

The total membership of communist groups in the Dominican Republic has been estimated at about 1,100 persons, with the following breakdown: PCD, 250; MPD, 250; MR-1J4, 400; PSP, 50; PCRD, 100 (*World Strength of the Communist Party Organizations*, Washington, D.C., 1970). Another source estimates that the MPD has the largest following, which allegedly amounts to "several thousand." The population of the Dominican Republic is 4,300,000 (estimated 1970).

Sources of support for the communists, which include universities, secondary schools, and labor unions, reflect the fragmentation of the movement. At the university level, the student movement has divided into the following organizations: "Fragua," led by the Red Line of the MR-1J4; Juventud Comunista, headed by PCRD members; the Comité Universitario "Julio Antonio Mella," led by PCD members; and the Comité "Flavio Suero," led by MPD members. The powerful Federation of Dominican Students (Federación de Estudiantes Dominicanos; FED), which is said to enroll about 200,000 university and secondary school students, has been since 1969 in the hands of non-communist but left-wing students belonging to the Dominican Revolutionary Party (Partido Revolucionario Dominicano; PRD). The communist movement at the secondary school level is represented by the Union of Revolutionary Students (Unión de Estudiantes Revolucionarios; UER).

Within the labor movement, communist support is more limited. The leadership of the "Foupsa-Cesitrado" labor confederation is reportedly in hands of MPD members. The powerful "Unachosin" drivers' union includes communist party members, mostly of the MPD.[1]

The PCD. The PCD was founded clandestinely in 1942. It was reestablished openly as the Dominican People's Socialist Party in 1946. During the military-civilian revolt in April 1965 the party identified itself once again as the Dominican Communist Party and has used this name since then. In August 1967 it adopted (verbally but not in practice) a Castroite line advocating the concept of armed struggle in most Latin American countries—a position that did not affect its relations with the Communist Party of the Soviet Union (CPSU).

Leadership and Organization. PCD leaders include Narciso Isa Conde (secretary-general), José Cuello, Antonio Isa Conde, Fabio Ulises García, Manuel Sánchez, Luis Gómez, Asdrúbel Domínguez, Mario Sánchez Córdoba, Carlos Doré, and Alfonso Sandoval.

The PCD claims to be organized on a national scale, with cells in almost every city and in many regions of the countryside. The party has also a committee operating in New York City, where some 250,000 persons of Dominican origin reside.

Domestic Attitudes and Activities. The PCD rejects any "illusions about the electoral path" and holds that the political and economic structures of the Dominican Republic can be changed only by revolutionary means. Declarations made by Secretary-General Isa Conde stated that the PCD sought a "revolutionary transformation of the backward and dependent capitalist structure" in the Dominican Republic and the "establishment of an anti-oligarchic and anti-imperialist system which would be a transitional stage toward the building of socialism" (speech made at the CPSU congress, *Pravda*, 6 April).

During 1971, as in the two previous years, the PCD continued to express support for the "dictatorship with popular support"—the thesis propounded by Juan Bosch, leader of the influential PRD. This was reiterated by Isa Conde, who stated that the PCD supported Bosch's thesis because it would fulfill the "immediate revolutionary tasks" set by the PCD; and also by Alfonso Sandoval, who declared that the "dictatorship with popular support" was endorsed because it "has a program and a proposal for a front that coincides on essential matters with the minimum program and the front" proposed by the PCD (*Tribuna Popular*, Caracas, 15 April). But, as before, Bosch has ignored such implicit appeals for joint action between his party and the PCD.

The PCD was not involved in significant domestic activities during 1971. It did, however, express concern over the existing political violence. Thus, the PCD sent a letter to the Communist Party of Venezuela asking this party to make statements protesting against the "crimes, repression, and terrorist acts that take place under Balaguer." The same letter held the government and terrorist groups of the right responsible for these actions, and maintained that the U.S. Central Intelligence Agency had been "directing" them.

International Views and Positions. Most significant, especially in view of its refusal to sign the Main Document of the International Meeting of Communist and Workers' Parties held in Moscow in 1969, was the PCD's attendance in 1971 at the Twenty-fourth Congress of the CPSU. Isa Conde, who represented his party at the congress, expressed wishes that the meeting would "further

---

[1] "Foupsa-Cesitrado" is an abbreviation for United Worker Front in Support of Autonomous Trade Unions and Trade Union Central of Dominican Workers. "Unachosin" stands for National Union of Independent Drivers.

the improvement of the socialist system and the Soviet Union and the raising of the role of the CPSU and the Soviet state in the struggle against international imperialism headed by the United States.''

Referring to the international situation, Isa Conde declared that there existed "positive aspects" at present, but that this "does not mean that the forces supporting revolution and socialism do not come up against problems, contradictions, and greater or lesser difficulties." His speech specifically noted "the decisive exposure, in Comrade Leonid Brezhnev's report, on the aggressive nature of imperialism" and "the statement that the CPSU will continue to support the national liberation revolutionary movements throughout the world." (*Pravda*, 6 April.)

Other PCD statements on international issues, also expressed by Isa Conde at the Soviet Congress, included support for the "peoples of the Indochinese Peninsula" in their fight against the United States. The PCD also expressed support for Cuba and for the "anti-imperialist" processes taking place in Chile under Allende and in Bolivia, Peru, and Panama through the armed forces, declaring that these latter events showed that Latin America was "entering the second stage of the liberation process."

Party Contacts. In addition to attending the CPSU congress in March-April, Secretary-General Isa Conde represented his party at the congress of the Communist Party of Czechoslovakia, held in May.

In February Isa Conde and Alfonso Sandoval visited Romania at the invitation of the Central Committee of the Romanian Communist Party. Isa Conde visited Hungary on 2-14 July. Visiting Cuba in July and August, he attended the eighteenth anniversary observances of the Cuban Revolution.

Publications. The PCD publishes a clandestine weekly, *El Popular*. Its declarations also appear as paid announcements or as letters to the editor in the independent daily *El Nacional de Ahora*, Santo Domingo, which also publishes letters from other communist groups.

*   *   *

The PSP. The adoption by the PCD of Castroite views and tactics in both domestic and international policies, although mostly limited to verbal declarations, created a split within the party in 1967. The less militant members, proclaiming their support for Moscow and "peaceful coexistence," formed then a new party using the PCD's former name, the Popular Socialist Party. Despite its pro-Soviet stance, however, the PSP has not been recognized by the Soviet Union.

The PSP is led by Tulio H. Arvello, Félix Servio Doucoudray, and José Espaillat. PCD leader Alfonso Sandoval has described the PSP as "a small group that is dedicated exclusively to fighting the PCD internationally." Unlike the PCD, the PSP does not support Bosch's thesis of the "dictatorship with popular support," considering it "ultra-leftist." (*Tribuna Popular*, 15 April.)

*   *   *

The MPD. Formed in Havana in 1956 (by a militant wing of what was then called the Dominican People's Socialist Party) to fight "revisionist tendencies," the MPD became a formal party only in August 1965. It is pro-Chinese and is considered to be one of the most active and violent leftist groups. It is said to draw considerable support from among students and slum dwellers.

Leadership and Organization. MPD leaders include Julio de Pena Valdés (secretary-general of "Foupsa-Cesitrado"), Agustín Moisés Blanco, David Onelio Espaillat, Edgar Erickson, Rafael

Báez Pérez, and Luis Elpidio Sosa Rodríguez, all of whom have been in prison since 13 January 1971, accused of illegal possession of arms and planning the assassination of government officials, army and police officers, and foreign diplomats. (The six were sentenced to ten-year prison terms on 10 February 1972.) Other leaders are Jorge Puello, Fernando de la Rosa, and Rafael "Fafa" Taveras, the latter in prison since 1970.

Maximiliano Gómez, the secretary-general of the MPD—who reportedly had been in exile in Paris since 1964—was found dead in Brussels on 23 May 1971. His death, originally attributed to an accicent in the gas heating system, was later said to have been caused by poisoning. Miriam Pineda, the widow of Otto Morales—an MPD leader killed in Santo Domingo in 1970—was found murdered on 12 December 1971, also in Belgium.

Domestic Attitudes and Activities. The MPD seeks to seize power by the proletariat, peasantry, and other "progressive" forces to install a "people's democratic dictatorship." It maintains that the "only road to a Dominican solution is armed violence," but also argues that the present conditions call for the overthrow of the Balaguer government and that this can "only come about through a putschist coordination with malcontent militarists and with the civilian right" (*Tricontinental Bulletin*, Havana, August). The MPD's willingness to cooperate with rightist groups, an attitude that has evoked no response from right-wing parties, has given it a reputation as an "opportunist" party.

Most activities of the MPD during 1971 centered on its continued and bloody feud with another pro-Chinese group, the PCRD. On 6 January the MPD together with four other communist groups—the Red Line of the MR-1J4, and the smaller factions called "Voice of the Proletariat," "Red Flag," and the "24 April Movement—released a joint communiqué stating their agreement to fight together against the "criminal aggressions and provocation by words and arms" carried out by the PCRD primarily against members of the MPD and other revolutionary groups. The communiqué accused the PCRD of a "coldly calculated series of murders of MPD members" and declared that the PCRD would have to "pay its debt to society." The communiqué also made an appeal for general mobilization to

> intensify the fight against official terrorism, for amnesty of political prisoners and prison reform, for an increase in the education budget and for a budget per student for secondary school and university students, for the basic demands of the workers, peasants, professionals, and other popular sectors, and for an intensification of the struggle for the ousting of the Yankee-Balaguer dictatorship. (*El Nacional de Ahora*, 6 January.)

Subsequently, on 25 May, the MPD and the same four communist groups issued another joint communiqué to examine the country's political situation, which was found "worsened by bands of delinquents and disrespect for court orders." This communiqué, which was quoted in part by the New China News Agency a month later (26 June), also accused "U.S. imperialism and its lackeys" of a policy of "savage economic exploitation and cruel political repression" in the Dominican Republic.

On university affairs, a coalition formed by the Red Line of the MR-1J4 and the MPD students —"Fragua" and the Comité "Flavio Suero," respectively—won elections held on 24 November to choose student representatives to the co-government of the Autonomous University of Santo Domingo.

The feud between the MPD and the PCRD, which is attributed mostly to personal differences, seemed to have spread to the university during 1971. Although no physical confrontation took place between students of these two groups, the Comité "Flavio Suero" and the "Voice of the

Proletariat" group asked the university community to condemn and isolate the PCRD student group, Juventud Comunista.

Publications. The MPD publishes an irregular clandestine weekly, *Libertad*.

*   *   *

The PCRD. The Communist Party of the Dominican Republic was formed by dissidents of the MPD after the 1965 uprising. It defines itself as a Marxist-Leninist party, "created in conformity with the thoughts of Mao Tse-tung." The party's main objective is to install socialism and later communism; its immediate program attempts to "defeat Yankee imperialism and all its Creole lackeys" through a democratic revolution. (Statements made by Luis "Pin" Montás, Radio Continental, Santo Domingo, 17 January 1971.)

The PCRD is considered a very extreme party. Its membership is limited mostly to the city of Santo Domingo.

Its leaders include "Pin" Montás (secretary-general), Jorge Mora Cepeda, Héctor René Montás, Amado Robles, and Miguel Angel Duval Ferrer.

Most PCRD activities during 1971 seemed devoted to attacking its rival party, the MPD. The feud between the MPD and the PCRD is believed to have been caused mostly by personal differences, although also important has been the MPD's tendency to take a somewhat "opportunist" attitude. Duval Ferrer, speaking on behalf of the PCRD, reiterated criticism against the MPD, charging that its program violated Marxist-Leninist principles since "in no way reflected the interests of the popular masses but only those of that sector of the oligarchy now in opposition" (*El Nacional de Ahora*, 9 January).

On 7 January, following the joint communiqué by the MPD and four other communist groups, the PCRD stated that such a communiqué was "threatening and provocative." The PCRD also stated that it was still interested in a pact with the MPD for a policy of nonaggression and mutual respect (proposed by the PCRD since 1970) and that it was willing to hold talks with the MPD provided that there were "democratic mediators" and the MPD accepted "publications of the talks." (*Ibid.*, 9 January.)

Statements by "Pin" Montás (*ibid.*, 17 January) accused the MPD of creating "individual terrorism which disorganizes, stagnates, and harms the popular forces while it benefits the enemy." Montás also accused the MPD of being an "instrument of Yankee imperialism," a charge that had been made by the MPD against the PCRD.

There apparently were no PCRD statements on international issues in 1971.

Publications. The PCRD's official organ is *El Comunista*, an irregular clandestine weekly.

*   *   *

The MR-1J4. The Revolutionary Movement of 14 June derives its name from an unsuccessful attempt to overthrow the former dictator Trujillo on that date in 1959.

The MR-1J4 apparently remained inactive during 1971. Its Red Line faction, as noted above, joined forces with the MPD and other smaller revolutionary groups in order to present a common front against the PCRD "aggressive actions." It does not, however, seem to have developed any subsequent activities.

Nelly Stromquist

Ecuador

The communist movement in Ecuador began in 1926 with the founding of the Socialist Party of Ecuador (Partido Socialista Ecuatoriano; PSE). In 1928 the party became a member of the Comintern, and in 1931 it changed its name to the Communist Party of Ecuador (Partido Comunista del Ecuador; PCE). A pro-Chinese splinter party, the Communist Party of Ecuador, Marxist-Leninist (Partido Comunista del Ecuador, Marxista-Leninista; PCE-ML) dates from 1963.

PCE members are estimated to number between 700 and 800. Most are students and workers; a few are peasants. The PCE-ML is believed to have between 300 und 400 members, mostly students, with some workers included.

The Socialist Revolutionary Party of Ecuador (Partido Socialista Revolucionario del Ecuador; PSRE) is a Castroite organization of 500 to 600 members. The Revolutionary Workers' Party-Trotskyist (Partido Obrero Revolucionario, Trotskista; PORT) is of unknown size.

The population of Ecuador is 6,100,000 (estimated 1970).

The military junta that assumed power in July 1963 declared the PCE illegal, but the party was able to remain intact through clandestine activities and its representation in various mass organizations. Since 1966, when the government returned to civilian control, the party has been able to function openly, although the 1963 anti-subversion laws have not been rescinded. In order to participate legally in the electoral process of 1968, the PCE formed the Popular Democratic Union as a front organization for its candidates, who received two per cent of the vote. It sought to participate in the promised 1972 elections through the newly formed Popular Unity bloc (see below).

Organization and Leadership. The PCE has a 10-member Executive Council and a 21-member Central Committee. At lower levels are provincial, zonal, and cell divisions. The secretary-general is Pedro Saad Niyaim. Executive Council members include Elías Muñoz, Miltón Jijón, Alejandro Idrovo, Alba Calderón, Efraín Alvarez, Enrique Gil, and René Mauge.

The party's youth organization is the Communist Youth of Ecuador (Juventud Comunista Ecuatoriana; JCE), headed by Solón Guerrero as secretary-general. Early in 1971, articles appeared in the Ecuadorean press belittling the training of Ecuadoreans in Moscow at the Patrice Lumumba People's Friendship University, and the JCE replied with a statement condemning their publication as "pseudo-police tactics against the PCE and the JCE" (*El Pueblo*, Guayaquil, 17 April).

The most active student organization at the university level, the Federation of University Students of Ecuador (Federación de Estudiantes Universitarios del Ecuador; FEUE), is in the hands of leftist students, but PCE influence seems to have declined since 1969, while that of pro-Chinese students has increased. FEUE leaders associated with the PCE include Edison Fonseca and Jorge Rodríguez. Many FEUE activities during 1971 were directed against the education law issued early in the year, which contained provisions for eliminating university autonomy and co-government (student participation in university government). The universities of Quito, Guayas, Cuenca, and

Loja, which had been closed down in June 1970 because of student unrest, were reopened in January 1971, but student demonstrations against the government continued.

The Ecuadorian Federation of Secondary Students (Federación de Estudiantes Secundarios del Ecuador; FESE), an active organization for younger students, has traditionally been considered under the primary influence of the PCE. Since 1970, however, it seems to have split into pro-Soviet and pro-Chinese factions.

The most important PCE-dominated organization is the Confederation of Ecuadorean Workers (Confederación de Trabajadores Ecuatorianos; CTE), formed in 1944. It claims a membership of 60,000. Its secretary-general is Leonidas Córdova and its organization secretary is Dr. Bolívar Bolaños. During 1971 the CET carried out joint actions both with students and with other worker groups. In March, the CTE and the FEUE stated their decision to struggle to obtain "absolute autonomy, co-government, and basic democratic principles" in the universities. On 25 June it was announced that the CTE, FEUE, and FESE would form a "national united front" and call for a national strike (see below). In mid-June, the CTE and various worker groups (including the Ecuadorian Confederation of Catholic Workers, the Ecuadorean Federation of Free Union Organizations, and the Ecuadorean Confederation of Semipublic Entities and Bank Employees) formed the United Workers' Front (Frente Unido de Trabajadores; FUT), with the objective of installing "a regime of social justice within a genuinely popular judicial-political structure" (*El Universo*, Guayaquil, 15 June).

The FUT called for a 48-hour national stcike on 28-29 July to press demands for a general wage raise, a "democratic and radical" agrarian reform (including free land for peasants), fixed staple food prices, and a total reorganization of the government's Agrarian Reform and Colonization Institute (Quito radio, 27 July). Harsh measures taken by the government (such as authorizing employers to dismiss workers and administrators to dismiss teachers and expel students joining the strike) contributed in good measure to the failure of the national strike. A few weeks before, the government had expelled the first secretary and a counsellor of the Soviet Embassy. Semi-official sources reported that both men had been charged with subversion and, more specifically, with financing activities of left-wing groups, such as the CTE (*El Universo*, 7 July).

The CTE has two small peasant affiliates, the Coastal Farm Workers' Federation (Federación de Trabajadores Agrícolas del Litoral; FTAL) and the Ecuadorean Federation of Indians (Federación Ecuatoriana de Indios; FEI). Both are considered ineffectual; they did not register major activities during 1971. Luis Castro Villamar, a PCE Central Committee member, is president of the FTAL, and Bolívar Bolaños is president of the FEI.

Party Internal Affairs. Party statements in March and April 1971 regarding "certain weaknesses in organized party action" and the existence of "non-proletarian, sectarian, liberal, literary, and anarchist positions" within the party culminated in disciplinary measures against four Central Committee members on 12 September. Francisco Guzmán and Patricio Paredes were "excluded" from the Central Committee on charges of pursuing "local, opportunist, and profit-making" activities; Santiago Santillán was excluded and Enrique Bazante was suspended without reasons being given. A month later, an article in *El Pueblo* (16 October) indicated that Guzmán, Paredes, and another Central Committee member, Eduardo Nieto, had been maintaining "a splittist attitude liable to liquidate the authority and the relations the party maintains with the mass organizations." The same article accused Paredes and Guido Ribadeneira, a JCE leader, of having taken over a piece of property belonging to the FEI.

Domestic Attitudes and Activities. A plenary session held by the PCE on 10 July 1971 reaffirmed that the party's objective under the present conditions was the "replacement of the current dictatorship by a popular, democratic, and patriotic government" that would rid Ecuador of "imperialist en-slavement," execute a genuine and radical agrarian reform, stimulate the country's industrialization, improve the living conditions of the masses, and maintain an independent foreign policy (*El Pueblo*, 18 September).

Early in the year the PCE made intense appeals for the creation of a "broad unity" to be composed not only of workers, peasants, and students but also of "all those sectors which desire or are ready to struggle for radical changes in the country" (*ibid.*, 10 April). On 3 June the Soviet news agency TASS reported that the PCE and three other small parties—the National Union of the Revolutionary Left, the Popular Democratic Union, and a faction of the Socialist Party—had formed a bloc called Popular Unity, whose main objectives were a radical agrarian reform and the nationalization of Ecuador's natural wealth. The PCE, however, did not announce the formation of the bloc until 29 September. The announcement stated that it was imperative that the people take over the government, but left unclear whether the seizure of power was going to be through elections (promised by the Velasco government for 1972) or by violent means. Although no significant activities appear to have been carried out by Popular Unity during the year, the bloc reportedly was endorsed by the CTE.

The PCE continued to express its opposition to the plebiscite proposed by President Velasco Ibarra. The plebiscite, which seeks a return to the 1946 constitution (characterized by a strong executive power), was described by PCE Executive Council member René Mauge as "tantamount to clothing the dictatorship in the mantle of legality" (*Tribuna Popular*, Caracas, 28 January-3 February 1971). PCE Secretary-General Saad stated that the plebiscite was a "maneuver on the part of the reactionaries, which should be soundly rejected" (*Vistazo*, Guayaquil, January 1971).

The PCE has defended the government's claim to a 200-mile limit for territorial waters, but has carefully avoided any mention of the fact that the Soviet Union shares the U.S. position of recognizing a limit of only twelve miles.

The party's constant criticism of the government, which it characterized us a "military dictatorship" because of the alleged domination by the armed forces over the executive, was momentarily suspended on 2 February, when a Central Committee statement "applauded" the government's decision to ask for the withdrawal of U.S. military missions in Ecuador. The statement read in part: "The expulsion of the Yankee missions is part of the struggle for our independence from the yoke of imperialism and should be broadened and deepened through further measures such as the defense of 200 miles of territorial waters, the confiscation of pirate fishing boats, the creation of state fishing and canning enterprises, and the nationalization of the foreign oil com-panies" (*El Pueblo*, 6 February).

International Views and Positions. The PCE has long maintained a strong pro-Soviet orien-tation. In April 1971 the report presented by Leonid Brezhnev at the Twenty-fourth Congress of the Communist Party of the Soviet Union (CPSU) was given high praise and full approval by the PCE. Secretary-General Saad hailed it as a "document of extraordinary importance for theoretical, political, and practical viewpoints" and declared that it would "make a great contribution to the political and ideological education of the PCE" (Moscow radio, 31 March).

A Central Committee statement in March held that there had emerged "in the world as a whole a general picture of resistance to imperialism." The statement condemned the "imperialist aggression" in Southeast Asia and affirmed that the "national liberation struggle" in Latin America was also growing, as evinced by the electoral victory of Popular Unity in Chile, the "building of socialism" in Cuba, "radical social conquests" in Peru, and the strong "anti-imperialist stand" of General Juan José Torres's government in Bolivia. (*El Pueblo*, 27 March.)

The visit to Ecuador of the president of Chile, Salvador Allende, on 24-28 August was noted as "one more opportunity for our people to reaffirm their decision to progress along the path of profound revolutionary changes" (Saad's declaration in an interview with East German newspaper *Nueues Deutschland*, 30 September). Saad also said that the Popular Unity victory in Chile, like the earlier triumph of the Cuban Revolution, "exerted a far-reaching influence on the development of political and class forces in Ecuador."

The announcement of U.S. President Nixon's projected visit to the People's Republic of China was seen by the PCE as a "disgraceful event" which represented the "consolidation" of the "anti-communist and anti-Soviet policy" of the Chinese. The PCE expressed condemnation of the Chinese leaders, who were said to have "replaced Marxism-Leninism and proletarian internationalism with the 'thought of Mao,' which has a petty-bourgeois content and a nationalistic and chauvinistic nature, and contains much boasting" (*El Pueblo*, 31 July). Later the Central Committee unanimously condemned the actions of the "leaders of the People's Republic of China and the Chinese Communist Party." At that time, the PCE attacked the Chinese thesis of "two superpowers" as "false" and as being "aimed at undermining the scientific conclusion that the basic contradiction of our epoch is that between the socialist camp and the camp of imperialism, [and] between the working class and the capitalist class." The party also condemned China's actions in the United Nations in voting "against U.S.S.R. proposals" and "in solidarity with the U.S.A." Regarding events in East Pakistan, the PCE characterized the Chinese position as one "hostile to the interests of the Bengali patriots" and affirmed that this attitude "clearly showed the inconsistency of the Maoists' demagogic claims to the role of a leader of the peoples fighting against imperialism, for their national independence and social progress." (TASS, 29 December.)

International Party Contacts. Besides the CPSU congress, PCE delegations attended the congresses of the Socialist Unity Party of (East) Germany, the Communist Party of Czechoslovakia, the Bulgarian Communist Party, the Mongolian People's Revolutionary Party, the Communist Party of Venezuela, and the Communist Party of Bolivia.

Publications. The official organ of the PCE is *El Pueblo*, published semi-weekly in Guayaquil. Since May 1966 it has been openly distributed.

*   *   *

The PCE-ML. The Communist Party of Ecuador, Marxist-Leninist is an outgrowth of the split within the PCE which became evident in 1963. At that time a number of dissident party members led by Rafael Echeverría Flores, and including José María Roura Cevallos and César Muñoz Mantilla (both members of the Central Committee), Carlos Rodríguez, and Jorge Arellano, attempted to take over the leadership. Expelled from the PCE, they formed the pro-Chinese PCE-ML, which has claimed to be the legitimate communist party of Ecuador. As a result of constant ideological disputes and personal rivalries, the PCE-ML had split by 1968 into three factions, led respectively by Jorge Arellano, Rafael Echeverría, and Pedro Sorroza. Since 1966 Echeverría has been recognized by the Chinese communists as the spokesman for the PCE-ML.

The PCE-ML seems to have been involved in the student demonstrations and activities against the government during 1971, but the party did not claim credit for these actions.

The PCE-ML organ *En Marcha* (quoted by NCNA on 19 May) held that the "world people's united front" against "U.S. imperialism" was becoming increasingly stronger, especially in Latin America. Bringing the Soviet Union also under attack, the article stated: "It is not the people of the world who fear U.S. imperialism and Soviet social-imperialism. It is U.S. imperialism and Soviet social-imperialism who fear the world people."

On occasion of the fiftieth anniversary of the Chinese Communist Party, the PCE-ML sent a message of congratulations. The message revealed that party meeting in April had decided that the central task of the PCE-ML was to "build up the movement of the revolutionary masses and to obtain the ideological, political, and organizational consolidation of the party" (NCNA, 6 July).

A delegation of the PCE-ML, in what was apparently the party's first contact with pro-Chinese communists abroad, visited Albania in August. The delegation, led by Politburo member Camilo Almeida, met with members of the Politburo and Central Committee of the Albanian Party of Labor.

Publications. The PCE-ML publishes a weekly organ, *En Marcha*, and an irregular weekly, *Espártaco*, both in Quito. In Guayaquil the PCE-ML publishes some materials through the Ediciones Liberación firm. Its views also appear in the *Peking Review*.

*   *   *

The PSRE. The Socialist Revolutionary Party of Ecuador adheres to a Castroite ideology but has not been very militant. The PSRE worked in the past quite closely with the PCE, but since 1966 it has "frozen" its relations with the pro-Soviet party. Its secretary-general is believed to be Jorge Reynolds. Statements made by Luis Terán, possibly another PSRE leader, declared that the party maintained two fronts: "one legal, where the political line is developed and where its ideological stand can be seen by all sectors of the population; the other, of deeper implications, is seriously involved in the problem of fomenting armed insurgency in Ecuador" (*El Oriental*, Montevideo, 5 February). Despite these assertions, no PSRE actions seemed to have been carried out during 1971.

*   *   *

The PORT. The Trotskyist Revolutionary Workers' Party is a part of the Posadas branch of the Fourth International. Besides the assumption of power, the PORT is dedicated to the establishment of a "Federation of Soviet Socialist Republics of Latin America." The PORT seemed to be inactive during 1971.

*   *   *

There are a number of very small terrorist-inclined groups in Ecuador which are unstable and frequently shifting in membership. These included, during 1971, the Victory or Death (Vencer o Morir) group, and the Movement of the Revolutionary Left (Movimiento de Izquierda Revolucionaria; MIR), which is Castroite. Both groups seem composed of young students, especially high school students in the case of Vencer o Morir. On occasion of the 28-29 July strike organized by the FUT (see above), the MIR issued a statement contending that the revolutionary struggle could not be left to the "revisionist, opportunist, mass oriented sectors"—possibly a reference to the PCE—and that "armed struggle" was the "valid basic tactic for Ecuador" (*Ecuador 71*, Quito, June).

Nelly Stromquist

El Salvador

The Communist Party of El Salvador (Partido Comunista de El Salvador; PCES) was organized in 1925 by communists from Mexico and Guatemala as part of a plan to establish a "Communist Party of Central America." By 1930 the regional concept had been discarded and the PCES was operating as a national body.

The Salvadoran Revolutionary Action (Acción Revolucionaria Salvadoreña; ARS) and the Salvadoran Revolutionary Party (Partido Revolucionaria Salvadoreña; ARS) are small Castroite guerrilla groups.

Since the early 1930's the PCES has been illegal and has functioned clandestinely. Its influence on the political situation in El Salvador is negligible due to the party's weak organization and the government's increasingly successful programs in such areas as education and agrarian reform.

The PCES is believed to have about 200 members. The population of El Salvador is 3,541,000 (census report of July 1970).

Leadership and Organization. The secretary-general of the PCES since 1969 is believed to be Salvador Cayetano Carpio. Important identifiable members of the leadership include Antonio Pineda, secretary of the Executive Committee, and Schafik Jorge Handel, a member of the Political Bureau and the Secretariat who has been in exile for the past nine years. The poet Roque Dalton is a prominent spokesman for the party.

The PCES controls the United Federation of Salvadoran Trade Unions (Federación Unido de Sindicatos Salvadoreños; FUSS). According to the World Federation of Trade Union publication *World Trade Union Movement*, (London, April 1971), there are 12,000 workers grouped in twenty-one national unions which are affiliated to FUSS. FUSS objectives include: formation of a communist-controlled central union; trade and diplomatic relations with all countries, especially communist ones; nonintervention in the affairs of other states.

The PCES is believed to control two small youth organizations: the Revolutionary University Students' Federation (Federación de Estudiantes Universitarios Revolucionarios) and the Vanguard of Salvadoran Youth (Vanguárdia de las Juventudes Salvadoreños). Little is known about these groups which appear to have only minimal support among students.

Party Internal Affairs. The PCES has traditionally been pro-Soviet, but in recent years some divisions reportedly have arisen among party members over the question of armed struggle. It is believed that Roque Dalton leads a faction which advocates armed struggle.

In February 1971 an article in the PCES organ *La Verdad* explained that the party was emerging from its underground status after thirty-eight years of clandestine operation. The change was termed not an "adventurist act but a carefully thought-out step based on a correct appraisal of the present historical stage in the life of the country." (Reprinted in *IB.*, no. 5-6.)

In July Schafik Handel stated that the fundamental concern of the PCES was the "strengthening and development" of the party, which had been "weakened by years of great repression," but nevertheless was "strongly entrenched among the masses." The PCES, he added, had designated the unification of the working class as a fundamental task. (*Unidad*, Lima, 8 July 1971.)

Domestic Views. In the above-mentioned 1971 interview Schafik Handel described El Salvador as an essentially agricultural country whose arable land was "monopolized by no more than fourteen families." The country has had forty years of military dictatorship, according to Handel, and "belongs to Bond and Share of New York and the El Salvador Mining Company." He described the current president as a "typical representative of oligarchical, pro-imperialist government" who had "already shown his true colors, despite the fact that some reform elements joined his first cabinet, and notwithstanding his statements full of cheap demagogy." This situation, Handel declared, had intensified "mass struggle" and caused the "forces of democracy" to consolidate. Hence in the 1972 elections the PCES hoped to present a "very broad alliance" of anti-imperialist and anti-oligarchical forces.

In March the PCES issued a manifesto claiming that "reactionary circles" in El Salvador had conspired with the U.S. Central Intelligence Agency to create a dictatorship and prevent the unification of the country's "democratic forces."

International Positions. In the main, the PCES supports the policies and activities of the Soviet Union. It charges the Chinese Communist Party with obstructing unity in the international communist movement and among other "progressive" forces.

Schafik Handel, in his 1971 interview, declared that the El Salvadoran people approve Peru's "anti-oligarchical, anti-imperialist process" and that many believe it would be a good example for El Salvador to imitate. The Central American Common Market, he said, was dominated by the North American "imperialists" and regional "bourgeoisie." (*Unidad*, 8 July.)

The PCES sent a representative to the Eighth Conference of Communist Parties of Central America, Mexico, and Panama in June (see *Costa Rica*).

Publications. The PCES issues a semiweekly clandestine newspaper, *La Verdad*.

Lynn Ratliff

Guadeloupe

The Guadeloupe Communist Party (Parti Communiste Guadeloupéen; PCG) originated in 1944 as the Guadeloupe Federation of the French Communist Party, which in March 1958 transformed itself into the present autonomous party. In recent years the PCG has been plagued by conflict and expulsions, and the communist left in Guadeloupe is now represented by several diffuse groups in addition to the PCG, of which the most prominent is the Guadeloupe National Organization Group (GONG).

The PCG is legal. It was estimated in 1970 to have some 1,500 members. The population of Guadeloupe is 335,000 (estimated 1970). The PCG is an active participant in Guadeloupe's political life, on both departmental and local levels.[1] The party controls several municipal governments. In municipal elections held on 14 March 1971, communist candidates won in seven of the 34 municipalities of Guadeloupe, including Pointe-a-Pitre, the largest city. The PCG also participates in Guadeloupe's 36-member General Council, where it is represented by Gerty Archimède, Hermann Songeons, Daniel Géniès, Paul Lacavé, Charles Edwige, Henri Bangou, Maximilien Vrécord, Jérome Clery, and Félix Flémin. The PCG also has participation at the national level. Paul Lacavé, a PCG Politburo member, has been a member of the French National Assembly since 1968; within the French Senate, the PCG is indirectly represented by Marcel Gargar, a "progressive ally" elected in 1968 with communist support.

Leadership and Organization. The PCG leadership, as identified in the party's press, includes First Secretary Guy Daninthe and Politburo members René Georges, Bernard Alexis, Henri Bangou, Hégésippe Ibéné, Paul Lacavé, R. Baron, Daniel Géniès, Serge Pierre-Justin, Hermann Songeons, and Pierre Tarer.

The party held its Fourth Congress on 13-14 April 1968. Announced plans for a fifth congress to be held in December 1971 did not materialize.

The PCG has strong influence in Guadeloupe's largest trade union, the General Confederation of Labor of Guadeloupe (Confédération Général du Tavail de la Guadeloupe; CGTG), which has some 5,000 members. PCG Politburo member Hermann Songeons continued in 1971 to be its secretary-general.

The party has also a youth front, the Union of Communist Youth of Guadeloupe (Union de la Jeunesse Communiste de la Guadeloupe; UJCG), established in 1967. It is led by Claudy Chipotal, its secretary-general. The party's influence among young people, however, appears to be limited. The UJCG held a department-level meeting early in the year, reportedly attended by some 200

---

[1]Guadeloupe is one of France's Overseas Departments and thus an integral part of the French Republic, administered by a prefect, with an elected General Council and with elected representatives in the French National Assembly and Senate in Paris.

delegates. The two main topics discussed, which received little press coverage, were Guadeloupe's economic difficulties, the question of autonomy from France, and the problem of extreme leftism in Guadeloupe.

The PCG attitude toward the extreme left was exemplified in 1971 by the party's criticism of "leftist" students at the polytechnic school of Baimbridge, who called (unsuccessfully) for an indefinite strike in April in "solidarity" with a strike by construction workers. The PCG and the CGTG also supported the construction workers' strike, but unlike the "leftists" they expressed satisfaction with the compromise resolution of the workers' grievances reached in mid-June.

The party seems to have influence within the Union of Guadeloupe Women (Union des Femmes Guadeloupéennes; UFG). Prominent party members within the UFG include Gerty Archimède, Huguette Daninthe, Georgette Pierre-Justin, and George Tarer. The UFG is affiliated to the Soviet-controlled Women's International Democratic Federation.

Party Internal Affairs. Dissension within the PCG apparently continued during 1971, although less overtly than in previous years. *L'Etincelle*, the PCG's weekly organ, reported that a Central Committee meeting was held on 25 July to deal exclusively with organization and leadership problems. The committee reportedly approved various measures "with a view to improve party functioning," but no details were given.

Domestic Views and Policies. The PCG seeks autonomy for Guadeloupe within the framework of an alliance with France. Politically such an alliance would involve a local legislative assembly, an executive Guadeloupe organ responsible to that assembly, and a body to determine the details of cooperation with France; economically, it would require an agrarian reform, whose leadership would be in the hands of workers and employees now engaged in sugar production and marketing.

Related to the question of autonomy, an important event for the PCG was the Martinique convention (see below), which resulted in a declaration demanding autonomy for the four overseas departments of France, Martinique, Guadeloupe, French Guiana, and Réunion. *L'Etincelle* reported on 20 November that the declaration had been widely publicized to "thousands" of the island's inhabitants through lectures, door-to-door campaigns, and informal discussions, and that local action committees to implement the declaration's objectives had been set up in several municipalities.

Another significant event was the victory of communist and communist-supported candidates at the municipal elections held on 14 March. Of the 34 municipalities, seven were won by PCG lists, led by Henri Bangou (Point-à-Pitre), Hégésippe Ibéné (Sainte-Anne), Paul Lacavé (Capesterre-de-Guadeloupe), Charles Edwige (Port-Louis), Félix Flémin (Deshaies), Dr. Jérome Clery (Basse Terre), and Maximilien Vrécord (Petit Canal). Another municipality (Baillif) was led by a non-communist, Albert Michel, but included many PCG members. Four others (Goyave, Pointe Noire, Baie-Mahault, and Saint-Louis) were won by "progressive lists," that had PCG support.

The election outcome was described by the party press as a "brilliant victory of the forces of progress and democracy over the forces of reaction, colonialism, and its agents," noting that all municipal governments led by communists had been reelected and that two new municipalities (Basse Terre and Sainte-Anne) were now under communist administration.

International Views and Positions. The PCG remained in 1971 a strong supporter of both the Communist Party of the Soviet Union (CPSU) and the French Communist Party. Guy Daninthe, who attended the Twenty-fourth Congress of the CPSU, and subsequently recorded his impressions in *L'Etincelle*, specifically praised the Soviet party for placing "on the foreground not the divergences that may exist with other parties, but the realization of unity of action by communist and all anti-imperialist forces in order to answer with increasing efficiency the imperialist acts of aggression, especially in Indochina and the Middle East."

The PCG, together with the CGTG and the UFG, participated in the Morne-Rouge "convention on autonomy" held on 16-18 August in Martinique. This convention drafted a declaration committing various parties from the four French overseas departments to achieve an autonomous status vis-à-vis France through the use of electoral means (see also *Martinique*).

The admission of the People's Republic of China to the United Nations was welcomed by the PCG, which stated that it was now up to the Chinese to "utilize this new springboard in the interest of peace, socialist progress, and the national independence of the people" (*L'Etincelle*, 30 October).

Party articles also gave wide coverage to the execution of communist leaders in Sudan. The party condemned the "savage repression" by the Sudanese government and demanded an "immediate stop to the persecution of Sudanese communists and democrats" (*ibid.*, 31 July). Also receiving considerable attention was the arrest and imprisonment of U.S. communist Angela Davis, whose immediate release was frequently demanded by both the PCG and the UJCG in articles appearing in *L'Etincelle*.

International Party Contacts. In addition to being represented at the Twenty-Fourth CPSU Congress, the PCG sent delegates to the Tenth Congress of the Communist Party of Bulgaria (Guy Daninthe), and the Fourteenth Congress of the Communist Party of Czechoslovakia (Lacavé).

Daninthe, together with Armand Nicolas, and Paul Vérgès, secretaries-general of the communist parties of Martinique and Réunion, respectively, met with leaders of the French Communist Party on 14 April in Paris. Jacques Duclos, Politburo member of the French party, had been scheduled to visit Guadeloupe on 13-21 January 1971, but his visit was canceled because of poor health.

A PCG delegation led by Gerty Archimède visited Romania in September at the invitation of the Central Committee of the Romanian Communist Party.

Publication. The PCG publishes a regular weekly newspaper, *L'Etincelle*, with a claimed circulation of 5,000.

*   *   *

The GONG. Many of the expelled members of the PCG (and apparently also some members of the party) have associated themselves with a small militant group, the Guadeloupe National Organization Group (Groupe d'Organisation Nationale de la Guadeloupe; GONG), created in 1963 and based in Paris. In 1964 the group espoused a pro-Chinese stand, accusing the PCG of "revisionism." It calls for independence for Guadeloupe by means of armed struggle.

There is very little reliable information on the leadership or organizational structure of the GONG, which, while still believed to be headquartered in Paris, has a number of activists in Guadeloupe.

The main publication of the group is the monthly *GONG*. PCG sources made reference in 1971 to a pro-Chinese publication, *Verité et Progrès Social* (Truth and Social Progress), which may or may not be associated with the GONG. It was said to devote itself mainly to attacking the PCG and its leadership, while failing to criticize and condemn "capitalism and colonialism."

Eric Stromquist

Guatemala

The communist party in Guatemala, which since 1952 has been called the Guatemalan Party of Labor (Partido Guatemalteco del Trabajo; PGT), originated in the predominantly communist-controlled Socialist Labor Unification (Unificación Obrera Socialista), founded in 1921. This group became the Communist Party of Guatemala (Partido Comunista de Guatemala; PCG) in 1923 and joined the Communist International in 1924. Increasing communist activities among workers during the mid-1920s were cut off by the end of the decade and were kept at a minimum throughout the dictatorship of Jorge Ubico (1931-44). In 1947, during the presidency of Juan José Arévalo, the communists as an organized group reappeared in the clandestine Democratic Vanguard (Vanguardia Democrática). In 1949 this group took the name PCG. Communist labor leader Víctor Manuel Gutiérrez founded a second and parallel communist party in 1950, called the Revolutionary Workers' Party of Guatemala (Partido Revolucionario Obrero de Guatemala). The two groups merged in 1951 when Gutiérrez, after a trip to Moscow, dissolved his party and joined the PCG. During 1952 the PCG adopted the name PGT, which it has continued to use. The PGT was legal between 1952 and 1954 and played an active role in the administration of President Jacobo Arbenz. It has been illegal since the overthrow of Arbenz in 1954.

There are three known guerrilla groups in Guatemala. The Revolutionary Armed Forces (Fuerzas Armadas Revolucionarias; FAR) is the military arm of the PGT. The largest and most active group during 1971 was the Rebel Armed Forces (Fuerzas Armadas Rebeldes; FAR) (see below). A third guerrilla organization is the 13 November Revolutionary Movement (Movimiento Revolucionario 13 de Noviembre; MR-13) (see below).

The PGT is estimated to have 750 members. The FAR and MR-13 are believed to have only 50 to 100 members each and several hundred sympathizers. The population of Guatemala is 5,100,000 (estimated 1970).

The terrorism that has been a serious problem in Guatemala for several years continued throughout 1971. Hundreds of incidents occurred, including kidnapings, assassinations, robberies, and other acts of violence. During the first half of the year this activity was intensified both by the left-wing guerrilla groups and by right-wing groups such as the Organized National Anti-Communist Movement (Movimiento Anticomunista Nacional Organizado; MANO) and the "Eye for an Eye" (Ojo por Ojo). The second half saw some decline, due partly to the government's increased severity in dealing with the terrorists, especially those of the left, and partly to the fatigued and depleted guerrilla forces' need for a period in which to regroup and reorganize. Many guerrilla leaders had been killed or arrested. On 23 November President Arana lifted the year-old state of seige but there was considerable expectation among observers that the country would experience a stepped-up level of terrorism in 1972.

Leadership and Organization. Little information is available on the leadership and organization of the PGT. The party is headed by its secretary-general, Bernardo Alvarado Monzón. Others prominent in the party include Central Committee members Mario Silva Jonama, José Manuel Fortuny, Julio López, Miguel Rodríguez, Huberto Alvarado, and Antonio Carrillo Giles.

The Patriotic Youth of Labor (Juventud Patriotica del Trabajo; JPT) is an auxiliary of the PGT. According to Mario Silva Jonama, "leftist views practically dominated" the JPT during the late 1960's, resulting in "subjectivist and voluntarist positions" and "petty-bourgeois 'revolutionism' " (*WMR*, March 1969). When the FAR broke with the PGT in 1968 a high percentage of JPT members allied themselves with the guerrillas. In December 1969 the PGT set up a special commission to supervise the work of the JPT, but there has been little evidence of a revitalization of the group.

The PGT has little influence among Guatemalan workers. It controls the clandestine Guatemalan Autonomous Socialist Federation (Federación Autónoma Socialista Guatemalteca), a small and relatively unimportant labor organization.

The PGT's small guerrilla arm, the Revolutionary Armed Forces, is believed to be quite ineffectual and during 1971 was probably inactive.

Party Internal Affairs. The most recent congress of the PGT was held clandestinely in December 1969. Reviewing the party's development since that time, Central Committee member Huberto Alvarado wrote that the PGT was "passing through a particularly trying period" when it had to deal with the problems of "armed struggle and those of fighting splitters and liquidators." The PGT has continued its rivalry with the FAR, which it has called "a leftist, militarist and sectarian trend rooted in ideological immaturity." The PGT, however, has for some time approved the use of violent tactics, as evidenced by the establishment of its own guerrilla branch. Alvarado discussed the current weakness of the party, giving a number of factors as causes for its admitted lack of success. First, there were the divisions and desertions from the leadership which he attributed to "conservative, Right-opportunist, Leftist and adventurist trends" stemming from inadequate ideological training and from a "dogmatic study of Marxism-Leninism." Second, the "revolutionary potentialities of the peasants" had been overestimated—the Indians, Alvarado declared, were not the "vanguard of the revolution" and a "revolutionary race" as some Leftists claimed, although they were involved in the revolutionary process. Third, "theoretical and practical preparation for armed action" had been frustrated by "conservatives" within the party, causing the loss of some of its "best leaders, cadre members and activists." And finally, Alvarado admitted that the PGT was unable to attract sympathizers because of the government's own social reform program, which "through limited reforms meeting some material needs" had induced "political neutrality in a section of the population." (*WMR*, December, 1970.)

Domestic Attitudes and Activities. A communiqué issued by the Central Committee in January 1970, shortly after the party's Fourth Congress, stated that the PGT expected an "agrarian, anti-imperialist and popular" stage of revolution to precede the "building of socialism and communism" in Guatemala. At the end of 1970 the party reported that, although it had recently been "active in economic, political, and armed struggles," the "alignment of forces [was] still unfavorable to the revolution" (*WMR*, December).

The PGT's "Program of People's Revolution" reaffirmed its position that "armed struggle in the form of a people's revolutionary war is the only correct path of the Guatemalan revolution." At the same time, the program stated: "The people will have to use every form of economic, social and ideological struggle ... for the simple reason that *a correct combination of armed and political action* is an indispensable factor of victory." (*WMR*, October 1970, emphasis in original.) Thus the Central Committee communiqué in January had called for a "revolutionary patriotic front capable of rallying all forces" and based on a "firm alliance of the working class and the bulk of the peasantry." In order to "unite, organize and mobilize the people for advance to higher objectives," the PGT program stressed the need to "fight in united and organized fashion for [the people's] immediate economic, political and social demands and at the same time for power" (*IB*, no. 15-16, 1970).

In April 1971, speaking at the Twenty-fourth Congress of the Communist Party of the Soviet Union (CPSU), PGT Central Committee member Miguel Rodríguez declared: "The economic, social and political crisis in Guatemala is becoming acute; imperialism and oligarchy are resorting ever more frequently to bestial methods of oppression and exploitation." The PGT, he said, "was obliged to reply to reactionary terrorism with revolutionary violence." He alluded also to the party's "tremendous sacrifices in the decisive struggle for democracy and national independence, the struggle to open up the road to revolutionary changes which would enable our people to finish with the American dominance which engenders poverty and ignorance." (*Pravda*, 9 April.)

International Views. In recent years the PGT has had only limited interest in international affairs. In 1971 it sent a representative to the congress of the CPSU. In his speech to the congress Miguel Rodríguez praised the economic, social, and political achievements of the Soviet Union which "stimulate the working class and people's struggle for their liberation, strengthen the international communist movement, guarantee peace throughout the world and provide increasing aid to the "peoples' struggle against imperialism." Rodriguez supported the unity of the international communist movement, which he said was essential for support of the struggle of the "heroic peoples of Vietnam, Laos and Cambodia and the Arab and other countries struggling against imperialist aggression." (*Pravda*, 9 April.)

The PGT sent a representative to the Eighth Conference of Communist Parties of Central America and Mexico, held in June (see *Costa Rica*).

Publications. The PGT's national organization and its Southern Regional Committee issue the clandestine newspapers *La Verdad* and *Grito Popular*, respectively. The JPT organ is *Juventud*; that of the PGT's Revolutionary Armed Forces is the clandestine *FAR* (not to be confused with Rebel Armed Forces having the same initials.)

*   *   *

The FAR. In December 1962 the Rebel Armed Forces was formed by members of three existing guerrilla organizations and after a series of shifts and reorganizations became an independent group. The most important early leaders of the FAR were Marco Antonio Yon Sosa and Luis Augusto Turcios Lima, former Guatemalan military officers trained in the United States.

For several years the FAR has emphasized urban activities, the most important of which were political assassinations and the kidnaping of businessmen and politicians—whose safe return was guaranteed only in exchange for the release of "political prisoners" held by the government or the payment of large ransoms, or both. During 1971 the FAR continued its program of urban guerrilla activities, although a spokesman indicated kidnapings and bank robberies were being deemphasized, because under present circumstances they were difficult and costly to execute, and were being replaced by "voluntary contributions and various kinds of taxation." The FAR, he said, nevertheless was seeking to "bring to justice those who are mainly responsible for the white terror"—a reference to the extreme right-wing forces which, like the FAR, have been responsible for a large number of murders and other forms of violence in Guatemala in the recent past. He added: "[Nothing is] more alien to us than violence. However, the Guatemalan people are subjected to violence in the form of disease, hunger, isolation, and oppression, [and] we have no choice but to fight violence with violence." (Interview with an unidentified FAR member, *L'Espresso*, Rome, 21 February.)

It appeared that the level of activity of the FAR was noticeably declining by the end of 1971, and it had been acknowledged earlier by the FAR that the "movement is doubtless at an ebb" (*ibid.*). The recent history of Guatemalan politics suggests, however, that the guerrilla forces will reemerge in some form in the near future.

The official organ of the FAR is *Guerrillero*.

The MR-13. The 13 November Revolutionary Movement was formed by Marco Antonio Yon Sosa and other young military officers after an abortive uprising against the government of Miguel Ydígoras Fuentes on 13 November 1960. Yon Sosa commanded the organization until he was killed on 18 May 1970 in an encounter with Mexican troops on the Mexican-Guatemalan border. The status of the organization since his death has been uncertain. It is believed that during 1971 the group was inactive.

During its period of greatest activity (1964-66) the MR-13 was influenced by Trotskyist ideas and Communist Chinese ideology. It differed from the FAR primarily in its steady advocacy of a socialist revolution, its greater emphasis on political and social (in addition to military) activities, and its concentration on developing a single, secure base area in the Sierra de las Minas region (rather than maintaining a national and highly mobile guerrilla force). Unlike the FAR, the MR-13 under Yon Sosa has not participated in spectacular terrorist activities or kidnapings.

The official organ of the MR-13 is *Revolución Socialista*.

Lynn Ratliff

Guyana

The People's Progressive Party (PPP) of Guyana was founded in 1950. At its first congress, in 1951, it declared itself a nationalist party, committed to socialism, national independence, and Caribbean unity. During the nearly two decades following, the leadership of the PPP claimed to be Marxist-Leninist, but the party was not officially affiliated with the international communist movement. During 1969 the leadership, in particular its head, Dr. Cheddi Jagan, made an unequivocal move to align the party with the Soviet Union. In turn, the PPP was recognized by Soviet leaders as a bona-fide communist party.

The Working People's Vanguard Party (WPVP) is a small pro-Chinese party (see below).

The PPP is a legal party. From 1957 to 1964 it was the ruling party in British Guiana (which became independent and took the name Guyana in 1966). In the most recent national elections, held in December 1968, the People's National Congress (PNC) led by Forbes Burnham won a clear majority and since then the PPP has been an opposition party. The PPP abstained from running candidates in the local elections of December 1970, charging the PNC with fraud and violence. It is in the nature of politics in Guyana that support for the two principal parties, the PPP and the PNC, is based to a great extent on race. The PNC is supported by the Negro population. The PPP is supported primarily by the East Indian population, representing about 50 percent of the total, and has a membership of some 20,000. Many non-member East Indians support the PPP in elections. It is estimated, however, that there are only about 100 hard-core communists within the PPP at the present time. The population of Guyana is 721,000 (estimated 1970).

The process of national unification and economic development which had promising beginnings in Guyana at the time of its independence has continued to falter due to racial antagonisms, divergent sectional and economic interests, border disputes, election frauds, and the influence of U.S. and British foreign policy. The PPP, in particular, has lost significant support and influence in recent years. According to Ricky Singh, a writer for an independent Guyanese paper, it is so "demoralized that it offers little hope as the movement through which any serious non-conventional struggle can possibly be waged" (*Sunday Graphic*, Georgetown, 10 January 1971). Although this is partly due to underdevelopment of the region and the strength of the PNC, much of the PPP's weakness is due to increased ideological conflicts within the party and the defection of many supporters (see below).

The PPP. Leadership and Organization. In 1970 the PPP was reorganized on the pattern of the Soviet and East European communist parties (see *YICA*, 1971, pp. 446-47), and its congress that year elected the party's founder and leader, Cheddi Jagan, as first secretary. Other important figures in the party include Janet Jagan (wife of Cheddi Jagan), Ranji Chandisingh (secretary for education), Derek Jagan, Vincent Teekah, Philomena Sahoye, Harry Lall, E. M. G. Wilson (secretary for mass organizations and civil liberties) and Charles Jacob (secretary for economic affairs). The

Ideological Committee, headed by Jagan, his wife, and other leaders trained in Moscow, was established in 1970 to ensure the conformity of PPP policies to Marxist-Leninist teaching.

The Progressive Youth Organization (PYO) is the PPP youth group and is believed to be a primary source of support for the party and for Cheddi Jagan personally. During the past year the PYO held some demonstrations and issued a statement addressed to U.S. President Nixon ordering the release of Angela Davis (see *United States of America*).

The PPP controls the Guyana Agricultural Workers' Union (GAWU), which is made up primarily of workers in the sugar industry and is headed by Harry Lall as president and Philomena Sahoye as vice-president. For the past twenty years the GAWU has tried to gain recognition as the bargaining agent for the nation's sugar workers. During 1970 it succeeded in bringing the sugar industry to a standstill by strikes. Although the PNC had consistently refused to allow a poll among the workers to determine whether they wished to be represented by the GAWU or the PNC-controlled Man Power Citizens' Association, it was reported in early 1971 that the government had agreed to permit such an enquiry. The precise time and conditions have not as yet been announced.

For many years the PPP has maintained a highly profitable trading arm known as GIMPEX, which enjoyed a privileged position in communist-bloc trade with Guyana. Since the government took over control of such trade through its own External Trade Bureau, established in 1970, the role of GIMPEX has been seriously undermined.

The PPP maintains a women's group, the Women's Progressive Organization.

Party Internal Affairs. The PPP congress that met on 5-8 September 1970 was said by Cheddi Jagan to have ended on a "high note of unity and determination" (*WMR*, December 1970). It has become increasingly clear, however, that defection and dissension have seriously affected the party's solidarity and influence. According to the aforementioned article by Ricky Singh, the "penchant of the PPP leadership for reflecting the 'Moscow' line, bad judgment on important questions, and the impression of a strong 'family group' within the party that often stifles initiative for a more pragmatic approach to local problems, have also contributed to the present dilema of the movement" (*Sunday Graphic*, 10 January 1971). Singh interviewed H. J. B. Hubbard, one of the founders of the PPP, who was ignominiously dropped from the party leadership in 1970. Hubbard stated that the "influence of the PPP has been great, but the Jagans have been unable to adapt to the new conditions of independence.... They are still looking outside for the influence that is to give them strength here." Hubbard also noted the large number of comrades the party had dropped over the years, which reflected the "inability of the Jagans to hold loyalty." (*Ibid.*) Singh talked to founding member, Ashton Chase, who recently stepped down from a leading role in the PPP. Chase declared that the party had made "significant strides, particularly in the field of political awakening of the country and the struggle for independence," but had been deflected along the way by "Marxist ideology and the question of race," to the benefit of the main enemy, "imperialism." The struggle, he added, must now fall to the young, who must "work within the party for the conquest of imperialism and the elimination of racial bugbears." (*Ibid.*)

Commenting on these criticisms, Cheddi Jagan replied that the PPP would continue to be the "vanguard, exposing pitfalls and traps and pointing the way forward for complete emancipation and the building of a new Guyana" (*ibid.*). The "loose, mass party," Jagan said earlier in defense of his reorganization of the PPP, "has served its purpose," and the "conditions of the struggle today and in the future demand a more effective vanguard such as can be provided only by a Marxist-Leninist party" (*WMR*, December 1970).

On 1 January 1971 the PPP observed its twenty-first anniversary. It was reported that party researchers were preparing a new publication which would record the activities of the party since its inception.

Domestic Attitudes and Activities. The PPP maintains a continual barrage of criticism of the ruling PNC. In an article for the monthly organ of the International Union of Students, its leader, Cheddi Jagan, described Guyana as passing through a period of "mounting social, political and economic crisis." The PNC government, he continued, attained power by a "blatant rigging of the 1968 elections" and carried out even greater "fraud" in the 1970 local elections. Charging that the PNC had "reduced the National Assembly to a farce," he declared: "Parliamentary processes are being flouted, the oppositions's questions and motions are being ignored and bills are being railroaded through the National Assembly." Jagan also claimed that the PNC was continuing to "deepen and intensify the cleavage between the two major racial groups" and permitting "bribery, corruption and nepotism" to spread. (*World Student News*, V. 25, no. 3, 1971.)

In the economic sphere, Jagan declared that the PNC Seven Year Development Plan (for 1966-1972) had "ground to a halt," while the cost of living continued to rise, unemployment idled 20 to 30 per cent of the labor force, schools were overcrowded and foreign debts had accumulated to the extent that 20 per cent of expenditures were for paying off foreign loans. (*Ibid.*)

According to Janet Jagan, the "repressive action" of the PNC had increased during the year and PPP activists were "constantly being molested;" under the National Security Law, she declared, citizens can be restricted or detained, the right of habeas corpus can be suspended and passports can be denied. To draw attention to the kind of repression the PPP was concerned with, it organized a world-wide drive for the release of PPP member Balchand Persaud, who the party claims had been falsely convicted of murder through the government's "abusive violation of the judicial system." Mrs. Jagan further claimed that workers' rights were being violated and that the government would soon promulgate a law prohibiting strikes. (Address to the Fourth Congress of the Venezuelan Communist Party, *Tribuna Popular*, Caracas, 28 January-3 February, 1972.)

The program of the PPP, adopted by the party's Fourteenth Congress in 1970, announced a primary decision to "utilize all means possible to unite all opposition forces in a broadly-based anti-imperialist alliance for democracy and national independence." The congress also called for a new strategy of economic planning and development which would include:

> Nationalization of the pillars of the economy—foreign and local comprador capitalist-owned and controlled factories, mines, plantations, banks, insurance companies and foreign trade.
> A strict system of foreign exchange control.
> Emphasis on simultaneous industrial and agricultural development, mainly in the public and cooperative sectors.
> Effective rent and price controls.
> Land reform.
> Trade with and aid from countries in both the East and the West.
> Full democracy and workers' participation and control at all levels. (*World Student News*, V. 25, no. 3.)

Perhaps the most important domestic question for the country during 1971 was the nationalization of the Canadian-owned Demerara Bauxite Company, which had been extracting bauxite in Guyana since 1917. By means of a constitutional amendment the government nationalized the company's assets in return for what was termed "reasonable compensation." Reportedly, in return for the PPP's formal approval of this action the government made concessions to the party which would allow it more influence in making political decisions. Cheddi Jagan said in a statement on 25 February that the PPP gave its approval not because this action by the government was a "step towards socialism" but because it would "firstly intensify the contradictions of and competition between imperialism, and secondly sharpen the liberation and class struggle in Guyana for genuine independence and socialism."

International Views. In 1971 Cheddi Jagan represented the PPP at the Twenty-fourth Congress of the Communist Party of the Soviet Union. While in Moscow, Jagan wrote: "The peoples of capitalist countries are being convinced of the advantages of socialism by the example of the successes of the land of Soviets. On the other hand, the constantly worsening material situation of the working people in the capitalist countries is leading them to the conclusion that capitalist society is bankrupt and that struggle for profound social change is essential." (*Trud*, Moscow, 15 April.) Regarding the Chinese Communist Party, Janet Jagan stated unequivocally that the PPP does not have relations with the Chinese communists and "does not like" them (*Ultimas Noticias*, 26 January 1972).

In an interview in Moscow, Cheddi Jagan criticized the government of Guyana for failing to arrange "close political, cultural, and economic links with the socialist world and particularly with the Soviet Union" and for "spreading anti-communism and anti-Sovietism." Instead of developing trade relations with the socialist countries, he added, the government had imposed a "special, discriminatory 10 per cent tariff on commodities exported from socialist countries." Jagan concluded by declaring: "Taking into account the external and internal changes in the balance of power, the position in Cuba and also the anti-imperialist development in Chile, Peru and Bolivia, the defeat of the American war machine in Vietnam, the strengthening peace movement in the United States, and the growing power of the socialist world and in particular of the Soviet Union, one can confidently say that the imperialists and their puppets will suffer defeat in Guyana." (*Pravda*, 23 April 1971.)

While attending the Congress of the Communist Party of Venezuela, Janet Jagan condemned the negotiations of the PNC government with Venezuela over the contested Esequibo region, saying that the region belonged to Guyana and that the border dispute over it was "invented as a strategem by interested international parties." She also declared her party's support for the Allende government in Chile and the governments of Bolivia, Peru, and Cuba. (*Ultimas Noticias*, 26 January 1972.)

The PPP views the Organization of American States as a "puppet of the United States" but would nonetheless like Guyana to follow Canada's policy of entering the OAS as an observer.

The PPP urged support for India in its conflict with Pakistan in order to "restrain the adventurers in West Pakistan and the backers in Washington" (Windward Islands radio, 20 September 1971).

Publications. The PPP publishes a quarterly journal, *Thunder*, edited by Charles Jacob, Jr., and a daily newspaper, the *Mirror*, edited by Janet Jagan.

*   *   *

The WPVP. The Working People's Vanguard Party (Marxist-Leninist) was founded in January 1969 by Brindley Benn, a former PPP member and associate of Cheddi Jagan. Benn questioned Jagan's form of Marxism and held that the PPP was following the path of "opportunism and revisionism." The WPVP is opposed to participation in elections, on the grounds that both the PNC and PPP are "racist" and thus are impeding the unification of workers in the socialist cause. Unequivocally giving his allegiance to Mao Tse-tung, Benn has applauded the Cultural Revolution and criticized the Soviet Union as a class-dominated society. The PPP's alignment with the Soviet Union was branded by Benn as "betrayal" of Guyanese and others fighting for national liberation.

On 9 October the WPVP issued a statement commemorating the anniversary of the suspension of the then British Guiana Constitution and landing of British troops in Guyana eighteen years earlier and called on all sections of the Guyanese population to mobilize to liberate Guyana from "neo-colonialist bondage." (Barbados radio, 10 October.)

The WPVP publishes a newsheet entitled *Creole*.

Lynn Ratliff

Haiti

The Communist Party of Haiti (Parti Communiste d'Haïti) was founded in 1930. It disintegrated the following year when its leaders were forced to flee the country. The year 1946 saw the founding of the Popular Socialist Party (Parti Socialist Populaire; PSP), which was recognized by the international communist movement, and the formation of a second Communist Party of Haiti; but by 1947 both had collapsed.

In November 1954 a new communist movement, the People's National Liberation Party (Parti Populaire de Libération Nationale; PPLN), was formed. The PPLN broke up in July 1965, but reappeared the following year as the Party of the Union of Haitian Democrats (Parti d'Union de Démocrates Haïtiens; PUDH or PUDHA—or in Creole, Pati Union Demokrat Ayisiin, PUDA), a Castroite group that placed strong emphasis on guerrilla tactics. A pro-Soviet movement, the People's Entente Party (Parti d'Entente Populaire; PEP) was formed in 1959. Although the PUDHA and the PEP based their activities on divergent strategic and tactical concepts, they cooperated from 1964 to 1968 in the "anti-imperialist" and "anti-feudal" United Democratic Front of National Liberation. In January 1969 the PUDHA and the PEP merged to form the United Party of Haitian Communists (Parti Unifié des Communistes Haïtiens; PUCH). The combined PUCH is believed to have about 500 members and presumably derives support from elements in and around the capital, Port-au-Prince, and from a very small rural following (although before the merger the PUDHA claimed to be organized in eight of Haiti's nine provinces). The population of Haiti is 5,200,000 (estimated 1970).

All political parties in Haiti have been proscribed since 1949. In April 1969 a law was passed declaring all forms of communist activity crimes against the state, the penalty for which would be both confiscation of property and death. François Duvalier, who had been president since 1957, died on 21 April 1971 and was succeeded by his son Jean-Claude, who was expected to continue the harsh repression of communists and other anti-Duvalier groups. Most PUCH activity has necessarily been carried on outside Haiti among exiles in Europe (especially the Soviet Union), Cuba, and, to a much smaller degree, the United States.

Leadership and Organization. The PUCH is headed by Secretary-General Joseph Roney, Deputy Secretary Arnold Devilme, and Secretary Miklimbourg. Known Central Committee members are Jacques Dorsilien (or Dorcilier), Jean Pierre, Robert Cherelus, Florient Marrat, Gerard Remy, Jacques Tinois, Ernest le Grand, Francois Matthieu, and Jean Gerard, most of whom reside either in Moscow or Havana.

There is a youth group, possibly affiliated with the PUCH, which calls itself the Union of United Communist Youth of Haiti. It appears to be based outside Haiti.

Little is known about the party's organization within Haiti. Party broadcasts from abroad during

1971 claimed a strong PUCH leadership in "peasant leagues for agrarian reform," which were said to be active in the northwestern part of the country (see below).

Domestic Attitudes and Activities. Although the PUCH "Charter of Unity" (signed by the PUDHA and the PEP upon merging in 1969) stated that the formation of urban and rural guerrilla units was the "chief task" of the party, no PUCH statements or actions during 1971 seemed to indicate that this policy was being upheld.

Party declarations advocated, instead, armed struggle by means of mass actions. A broadcast ("Radio Peace and Progress," Moscow, 1 July) asked the people to use "revolutionary violence" but added that, "faithful to Marxist-Leninist principles, the PUCH thinks that the people must not take up arms before they are well prepared." Another broadcast (*ibid.*, 30 September) called for the "formation of a great mass, a broad popular front with all progressive forces in the country," to overthrow the Duvalier government. According to Politburo member Jacques Dorsilien (interview, *Rabotnichesko Delo*, Sofia, 26 October), the PUCH was trying to create an "anti-dictatorial, anti-imperialist, and anti-feudal movement" and to work together with other anti-dictatorial groups, including a small sector of the Catholic church that favors a "socialist solution to socioeconomic problems but not to ideological problems."

The death of François Duvalier and the immediate ascent to power of Jean-Claude Duvalier produced strong PUCH appeals to the Haitian people, asking them to take up arms and create a "people's government." These appeals also stated that the time had come for the Haitian people to "take the intiative, stand up for their rights, and take full advantage of the contradictions within the semi-colonial state apparatus and throughout the Haitian oligarchy" (Havana radio, 23 April). Apparently, however, the PUCH leadership within Haiti did not organize any resistance against the new government, although this was considered to be essentially a continuation of the autocratic rule that has prevailed in Haiti since 1957. The party rejected as "demagogic" the proposal in May by Jean-Claude Duvalier of an amnesty (applicable to exiles but not specifically to communists) and described as "deceptive" the dissolution of the feared Tontons Macoutes (François Duvalier's personal militia) since this force would be replaced by a special army corps called the "Leopards." In July the PUCH expressed belief that the government might fall, declaring in a broadcast that the disappearance of the Tontons Macoutes had "destroyed the guarantees of survival for the Jean-Claude Duvalier's government and that a military coup was quite possible ("Radio Peace and Progress," 7 July).

Most PUCH broadcasts during 1971 were addressed to the peasantry. Early in the year agrarian reform was proclaimed as one of the main objectives of the Haitian communists and the PUCH was said to be actively organizing "peasant leagues for agrarian reform" composed of landless peasants and agricultural workers (*ibid.*, 8 January). Another broadcast reported that peasants had set fire to sugar cane plantations of the "Yankee monopolies" in Cul-de-Sac, Croix-des-Missions, and Drouillard (*ibid.*, 12 January). In September a party statement asserted that the peasant movement was increasing and that "thousands of workers who had no land" were supporting the PUCH program by participating in the peasant leagues for agrarian reform (*ibid.*, 7 September).

International Views and Positions. The PUCH maintains a strong pro-Soviet position and, at the same time, apparently refrains from attacking Chinese communist policies.

A Central Committee statement in April 1971, delivered to the Twenty-fourth Congress of the Communist Party of the Soviet Union (CPSU), stated that this meeting was a "proof of the growing successes" and that it confirmed the "exceptional role that the Soviet Union is playing in the struggle for national liberation, for socialism, and for communism—a struggle which is gradually enveloping the whole world" (*Pravda*, 12 April). The same statement expressed the PUCH's solidarity with the "peoples of Indochina and the Middle East" in their fight against "imperialism" and "neo-colonialism," and with the "peoples of Cuba, Chile, and other Latin American nations fighting for their liberation." It added: "We stand firmly with the Negro movement and all progressive people in the United States—people whose conscience, courage, and will to oppose have found live personification in the form of Angela Davis."

International Party Contacts. The PUCH delegation at the CPSU congress in April 1971 was led by Jean Gerard. Jacques Dorsilien represented the PUCH at the congress of the Bulgarian Communist Party in April.

Publications. Since 1969 the PUCH has published a clandestine newspaper, *Boukan* (Torch). In addition, the party relies on radio broadcasts from abroad. Havana radio transmits fourteen hours weekly to Haiti (eleven broadcasts in Creole and three in French). Moscow's "Radio Peace and Progress" broadcasts daily thirty-minute programs in Creole.

Nelly Stromquist

Honduras

The Communist Party of Honduras (Partido Comunista de Honduras; PCH) was organized in 1927, disbanded in 1932, and reorganized in 1954 (now considered its official founding date). In 1961 a small group claiming to be "scientifically Marxist" split from the PCH to become the Hunduran Revolutionary Party (Partido Revolucionario Hondureño; PRH) and is believed to have become primarily Castroite.

In 1967 a major dispute over tactics and strategy split the PCH. One faction retained the PCH name. The other, a pro-Chinese group, became the Communist Party of Honduras/Marxist-Leninist (Partido Comunista de Honduras/Marxista-Leninista; PCH/ML).

The Francisco Morazán Movement (Movimiento Francisco Morazán) is another Castroite group. A guerrilla force called the "Ernesto Che Guevara Revolutionary Front" was reported as operating in Honduras in 1970. Both are thought to be very small; no activities of either were reported in 1971.

Although not formally outlawed, communist and other left-wing groups are implicitly proscribed under the 1957 Honduras constitution.

On 28 March 1971 elections were held to choose a successor to General Oswaldo López Arellano, president since 1965. By a narrow margin the ruling Nationalist Party candidate was elected. Various left-wing elements formed the opposition Frente de Unidad Popular (FUP) before the election. When it was not permitted to register as a political party or enter a candidate, the FUP called for a protest against the elction and this apparently contributed to the high abstention rate among the electorate. The PCH tried to join the FUP, but failed to do so and played no significant part in the elections. In general, the PCH has little influence in Honduran political affairs due to its small, weak organization and the traditionally severe restrictions maintained by the government on leftist activities.

Estimates of the membership of all factions of the PCH range from 500 to 1,500. The population of Honduras is 2,700,000 (estimated 1970).

Leadership and Organization. Due to its clandestine existence, little is known about the structure or leadership of the PCH. Its first secretary for many years has been Mario Morales. Longino Becerra and José Pérez are among the known PCH leaders.

PCH-affiliated mass organizations are extremely small, both in size and influence. The Communist Youth of Honduras (Juventud Comunista de Honduras; JCH) is believed to be under the control of the PCH/ML. The University Reform Front (Frente de Reforma Universitaria) is a communist-oriented student organization. The vast majority of students belong to the Honduras University Students' Federation, which is controlled by non-communists. There is a small PCH-affiliated group called Socialist Youth (Juventud Socialista).

Most Honduran trade unions are organized under the influence of predominantly American-owned fruit companies. The Committee of Revolutionary Workers (Comité de Trabajadores Revolucionarios) is believed to be influenced by the PCH.

Internal Affairs. Since the dispute of 1967 (see above) the PCH has remained pro-Soviet and no further dissension has been evident. In June 1971 the PCH clandestinely held its Second Congress.

Domestic Views. Early in 1971 the PCH Central Committee issued a "Statement on the Present Political Situation in Honduras." As a result of the recent war with El Salvador, it said, a "distinct nationalistic tendency" had arisen among the people, finding expression in the "subsequent anti-imperialist struggle of the most advanced sections of the working class and progressive intellectuals and genuine patriotism displayed by the country's armed forces." The party believed these tendencies would be developed further by the increasing "economic and political pressure of the Central American oligarchical groups, the monopolies supporting integration, and the U.S. State Department [which was] striving to restore the broken-down mechanism of the Central American 'common market.' " The Honduran bourgeoisie, the statement continued, was "conciliatory" in nature, having negotiated openly with "North American neocolonialist bodies"; being "connected with local and foreign latifundists," it considered the "growing militancy of the working class and the awakened peasants to be a threat to its class interests." (*Trabajo*, quoted in *IB*, no. 1, 1971.)

According to the PCH, the "greatest danger" and "topmost problem" for Honduras was its "backwardness in all fields." The PCH statement declared that a "socialist society" must be constructed through a "democratic, agrarian and anti-imperialist revolution" in order to solve the country's problems and supply the "material and moral requirements" of the people. However, since such a solution demanded a "level of organization and of popular awareness which [did] not exist at present," the immediate task would be the unification of all forces interested in democratization of the country, regardless of "ideological, religious and social differences." These forces would demand a new electoral law which would legalize new parties and independent candidates and would force the "ruling classes to reject their anti-popular plans." (*Ibid.*)

The government's agrarian policy, the document declared, was "reformist" in concept, attempting to modernize farming by turning "large, semi-feudal estates into capitalist-type estates and to create large production units under the guidance of the National Agrarian Institute." This "reformism," the PCH said, infringed the rights of the peasants and failed to expropriate the large holdings of the latifundists or to return to the country the unused land owned by the fruit companies. (*Ibid.*)

By the end of 1971 the PCH was even more dissatisfied with the newly elected government and in December issued a statement condemning it as more autocratic in its land policy than its predecessor and more violently repressive. The country, according to the PCH, was in a state of crisis created by the "paralyzation of the agrarian reform, growing unemployment, a rising cost of living, hunger and malnutrition, a price policy that helps only the bourgeoisie, freezing and even reducing the working class wages, speedier decapitalization of the country and impoverishment of the working masses by the Yankee monopolies."

International Positions and Contacts. First Secretary Mario Morales attended the Twenty-fourth Congress of the Communist Party of the Soviet Union, where he expressed his party's admiration for the Soviet Union and its revolutionary activity throughout the world. Alluding to Soviet support of revolutionary movements in Vietnam, Laos, Cambodia, and the Middle East, Morales asserted that, in contrast, the majority of the Latin American countries were still under the "yoke of imperialism," which "with all the means of force at its disposal" was trying to "perpetuate existing regimes and suppress the peoples' legal aspiration to a better life." (*Pravda*, 9 April 1971.)

The PCH sent a representative to the Eighth Conference of Communist Parties of Central America, Mexico, and Panama in June (see *Costa Rica*).

Publications. The organ of the Central Committee of the PCH is *Trabajo*, which appears irregularly and clandestinely. The party's information sheet, *Voz Popular*, is supposed to be issued weekly and is also circulated clandestinely.

*   *   *

The PCH/ML. The PCH/ML is pro-Chinese in orientation and, unlike the PCH, advocates armed struggle as the road to power in Honduras.

The first secretary of the PCH/ML is Dionisio Ramos Bejarano. Although very little is known of the groups' organizational apparatus, it is believed that its primary base of support comes from the JCH (see above) and from university students who are not necessarily members of any communist organization.

Domestic Views. The PCH/ML has outlined its objectives as the destruction of the existing government through mass movements and armed struggle and the establishment of a revolutionary government which would carry out agrarian reform, recover the national wealth, give state power to the people, establish economic independence for the country, carry out a cultural revolution, and establish full popular rights. The party condemns the PCH as being "rightist opportunist" and for betraying the fundamental principles of Marxism and the interests of the Honduran people.

International Positions. In July 1971 the PCH/ML Central Committee sent a message to the Chinese Communist Party on the occasion of its fiftieth anniversary. Praising the Chinese party as the "bulwark of the world revolutionary movement in the struggle against imperialism, modern revisionism and all reactionaries," the message reaffirmed the PCH/ML's commitment to armed struggle and hailed the Chinese defense of Marxism-Leninism against the Soviets' "deviations of modern revisionism." (*Peking Review*, no. 31.)

Publications. The PCH/ML publishes a clandestine propaganda organ, *Unidad*, and reportedly has launched a journal entitled *Abril*.

Lynn Ratliff

Martinique

The Martinique Communist Party (Parti Communiste Martiniquais; PCM) traces its founding to July 1921, when a socialist group, the "Friends of Jean Jaurès," adopted a communist ideology. In 1935 this and another Marxist group, the "Common Front," merged, and the new organization affiliated with the French Communist Party the following year. The party was disbanded while Martinique was under the control of the Vichy government in France (1940-43). In 1944 it reorganized as the Martinique Federation of the French Communist Party, and in September 1957 it became the autonomous PCM. The party is legal.

The PCM is estimated to have from 700 to 1,300 members. The population of Martinique is 335,000 (estimated 1970).

The PCM is an active participant in Martinique's political life, on both departmental and local levels.[1] Its following, however, has generally been declining over the past fifteen years, partly because one of its leaders, Aimé Césaire, withdrew from the party with his supporters in 1956 to create the left-wing non-communist Martinique Progressive Party (Parti Progressiste Martiniquais; PPM), and partly as a consequence of the PCM's policy of autonomy for Martinique (see below), which does not have mass support. In contests for the three seats allocated to Martinique in the French National Assembly, the party won 62.5 per cent of the votes cast in the 1956 elections (before the PCM-PPM split). In 1968, running separately, the PCM won about 17 per cent; the PPM, about 20 per cent; and the governing Gaullist party, the Union of Democrats for the Republic (UDR), some 58 per cent.

The PCM controls four municipal (or commune) governments in Martinique. The mayors of Lamentin, Saint-Esprit, Morne-Rouge, and Macouba are PCM members. All four were reelected to their posts in March 1971 (see below). Within Martinique's 36-member General Council the party was represented in 1971 by Georges Charles-Alfred, Georges Fitte-Duval, Georges Gratiant, and Victor Lamon.

Leadership and Organization. The PCM is led by its Politburo and Secretariat, which are elected by the Central Committee, following the latter's election by the party congress. The PCM's Fourth Congress was held in December 1968. On 8 January 1969 the following were elected to the party's leadership: Armand Nicolas, secretary-general; Politburo—Dolor Banidol, Philipbert Duféal, Georges Fitte-Duval, Mathurin Gottin, Georges Gratiant, Walter Guitteaud, Victor Lamon, Georges Mauvois, René Ménil, and Armand Nicolas; Secretariat—Philipbert Duféal (party

---

[1] Martinique is one of France's Overseas Departments and thus an integral part of the French Republic, administered by a prefect, with an elected General Council and with elected representatives in the French National Assembly and Senate in Paris.

organization), Mathurin Gottin (finances), Georges Mauvois (propaganda), Armand Nicolas (secretary-general), and Albert Platon (workers' and peasants' organizations). Banidol died late in 1969, and Edgard Nestoret apparently has taken his place in the Politburo. In October 1970 Guitteaud was elected to the Secretariat and put in charge of party organization, and Duféal assumed the duties of propaganda secretary; there was no report of any new responsibilities for the former secretary of propaganda, Mauvois.

The PCM obtains its primary support from the communist-controlled General Confederation of Labor of Martinique (Confédération Générale du Travail de la Martinique; CGTM), whose secretary-general is PCM Politburo member Victor Lamon. The CGTM, with some 4,000 members, is the largest trade union in Martinique.

The PCM has a youth organization, the Union of Communist Youth of Martinique (Union de la Jeunesse Communiste de la Martinique; UJCM). In 1969 the UJCM Central Committee was disbanded and a "Provisional Committee" was fomed to reorganize local groups and prepare for a congress to elect a new UJCM leadership. No further reference to the youth organization was made in the PCM press until mid-1971, and then comment was limited primarily to UJCM activities marking the party's fiftieth anniversary. Gabriel Lordinot, a member of the PCM Central Committee, was identified at that time as both secretary-general and president of the UJCM. Until recently, the PCM could count on considerable support from the General Association of Martinique Students (Association Générale des Etudiants Martiniquais), a member of the communist-controlled International Union of Students, but in 1970 controversy between the party and the more radical student organization attained such proportions that cooperation between the two was impossible. Somewhat less support had been derived from the Organization of Anti-colonialist Youth of Martinique (Organisation de la Jeunesse Anticolonialiste de la Martinique), whose relations with the PCM also appeared to suffer in 1970. The two student groups received only slight mention in the PCM press in 1971.

Domestic Views and Policies. While attacking such domestic problems and institutions as industrial unemployment, racial discrimination, the educational system, and the influence of the church, the PCM in 1971 continued to put emphasis on a drive to achieve autonomy for Martinique—an autonomy that would give the island control over its own legislative and executive functions, although cooperation with France would be maintained through a body comprising equal representation from Martinique and France. Throughout the year the CPM newspaper, *Justice*, elaborated on the party's proposal, on the one hand insisting that such an autonomy would not mean a rupture with France, and on the other ridiculing the "mother country" attitude promoted by the "*békés*" (colonialists) and members of the majority UDR. Although *Justice* stated that relations should be established on a "mutually advantageous base," the advantages in the proposal appeared to be weighted in favor of Martinique. For example, France would be allowed to maintain "many interests" on the island, but would be obligated to provide substantial technical and financial aid as "just compensation for the exploitation of Martinique during more than three centuries of French colonialism" (*Justice*, 10 June). Autonomy was not a "magic virtue," the party stressed: autonomy could become either "reactionary" or "progressive," but it would "march toward progress" if the popular forces could "carry the mass struggle to impose a democratic autonomous leadership" (*ibid.*, 12 August).

To strengthen its weakened political position, the PCM has periodically sought to unite Martinique's "democratic forces." These efforts, directed mainly toward the PPM, the only other leftist party of consequence, are for the most part limited to election campaign periods and have as their goal the undermining of the UDR. From the beginning of the year, the PCM sought to form electoral agreements with the PPM in a number of important municipalities—particularly the capital, Fort-de-France—in preparation for the municipal elections of 14 and 21 March. The result of a February meeting between the two parties was not favorable to the PCM. The views of the PPM, expressed in a joint communiqué (carried in *Justice*, 18 February), were that "serious ideological divergences" existed between the two parties, that conditions promoting unity did not prevail, and that the PPM would be deceiving itself and the electorate if a "premature unity" were achieved. The PCM countered that ideological differences between parties were only normal. The refusal of the PPM to include PCM candidates on its list for Fort-de-France prompted the PCM to charge in the communiqué that the PPM sought the "fading out" of the communist party in the capital city, and to state that, therefore, the PCM would present its own list. (Under the French electoral system those persons who represent a party or coalition on a successful list are given authority to elect a municipal council which in turn selects a mayor.)

The PCM presented lists of its own in ten of Martinique's 33 municipalities and participated with "democratic forces" in another three. The elections did not produce any significant changes for the PCM. It retained control of the four municipalities where party members were mayors before the elections, returning Gratiant to that post in Lamentin, Fitte-Duval in Saint-Esprit, Nestoret in Morne-Rouge, and Sévère Cerland in Macouba. In François a coalition of communists and "democrats" won, and in Ducos a list supported by the PCM won. In Fort-de-France the PCM received 859 votes, as compared with 21,349 for the successful PPM slate which reinstated Aimé Césaire as mayor.

The PCM expressed satisfaction with the results. The elections, according to a Central Committee statement, showed that the party had consolidated its positions in its four incumbent municipalities and gained substantially in François. Further, "democratic forces" had gained positions from the UDR in Rivière-Pilote, Rivière-Salée, and Trinité and made progress in Schoelcher, Lorrain, Sainte-Marie, and Sainte-Anne. The masses—particularly young persons—were said to have played a dynamic role in supporting the left. (*Ibid.*, 29 April.)

The Central Committee outlined the new tasks of the party in the same statement. These were: (1) to broaden the unity of "democratic forces" by including all those opposed to the UDR; (2) to organize "concrete actions" to further the autonomy movement, and to seek unity with the PPM in this regard; and (3) to coordinate the anti-colonial struggles in the four overseas departments of Martinique, Guadeloupe, Guiana, and Réunion.

International Views and Policies. In the spring of 1971, PCM Secretary-General Nicolas and Central Committee member Luc Bourgeois visited Moscow to attend the Twenty-fourth Congress of the Communist Party of the Soviet Union. The PCM hailed the congress as accelerating "humanity's march toward socialism" (*Justice*, 22 April) and in its pronouncements on international situations—including Poland (the December 1970 unrest), Chile (the progress of the Marxist government), Indochina (the war), Pakistan (the East Pakistan secessionist movement), Sudan (the execution of communists), and China (its admission to the U.N.)—it closely followed the Soviet line.

Most PCM statements on international affairs were related to the party's campaign for Martinique's autonomy and hence involved France and the other overseas French departments. During the year solidarity within the autonomy movement in these areas was expressed by strikes and conferences coordinated among their pro-autonomy groups. The general confederations of labor and national education federations of Martinique and Guadeloupe, and the Guiana Workers' Union in French Guiana jointly called one-day general strikes on 10 February to protest alleged grievances in employment conditions for workers and teachers.

Secretary-General Nicolas represented the PCM at a Paris meeting of the communist parties of Martinique, Guadeloupe, and Réunion on 14 April to discuss the results of the March elections (held simultaneously in the three departments (*ibid.*). On 16-18 August a "convention on autonomy" in Martinique was attended by the same three parties and 13 other organizations, including the "Marxist Circle" from French Guiana and the PPM. According to the PCM, this was the first time that the "anti-colonial" forces of the French overseas departments had assembled to prepare a program for autonomy. A joint declaration expressed agreement that autonomy should include control by the overseas departments of their own development plans, foreign and domestic trade, credit and savings banks, fiscal and customs systems, industry ownership, education, police, and local administration. (*Ibid.*, 19 August.)

Publications. The PCM publishes a weekly newspaper, *Justice*, and an irregular theoretical journal, *Action*.

Eric Stromquist

Mexico

The Mexican Communist Party (Partido Comunista Mexicano; PCM) was founded in September 1919 with the assistance of a number of foreigners, including M. N. Roy and Mikhail Borodin. The PCM sent a delegation to the 1920 congress of the Communist International in Moscow and has on most occasions been a supporter of the Soviet Union since that time.

There are numerous left-wing parties and groups in Mexico, many of which have shifting or temporary organizational structures and memberships. In the pro-Chinese category among those reportedly active in 1971 were the Mexican Movement of Marxist-Leninist Anti-revisionist Unification (Movimiento de Unificación Marxista y Leninista Antirrevisionista; MUMAM), the Mexican Bolshevik Communist Party (Partido Comunista Bolchevique Mexicano; PCBM), and the Communist Spartacus League (Liga Comunista Espártaco; LCE). There are two Trotskyist groups: the International Communist Group (Grupo Comunista Internacionalista; GCI), associated with the Fourth International, and the Trotskyist Revolutionary Workers' Party (Obrera Revolucionario Trotskista; PORT), associated with the Posadas Branch of the Third International, the International Secretariat. An extreme left-wing guerrilla group called the Revolutionary Action Movement (Movimiento de Acción Revolucionaria; MAR), attracted international attention during the year (see below). The National Civic Revolutionary Association (Asociación Civica Nacional Revolucionaria; ACNR), led by a well-known rural figure named Genaro Vásquez Rojas and operating primarily in the mountains of South West Mexico, received some notice in the Cuban press during 1971.[1] Within all these organizations may be found various splinters and subgroupings. There are also some guerrilla-like groups operating in rural areas which are made up of bandits rather than political activists. The Socialist People's Party (Partido Popular Socialista; PPS) is the largest left-wing organization in Mexico (see below).

In 1971 a group of prominent leftists, including writers Octavio Paz and Carlos Fuentes and student leader Heberto Castilla, announced the formation of the "Movement of Popular Consultation" as the initial stage of a new "democratic socialist party" as yet unnamed and unstructured. Seeking to challenge the ruling Party of Revolutionary Institutions (PRI), which has dominated Mexican politics since 1929, the leaders of the new movement hoped to unite forces of the left and raise the political consciousness of the people without either violence or guerrilla activities. (See *New York Times*, 23 September 1971.)

All political parties in Mexico are legal, but in order to enter candidates in national elections a membership registration of 75,000 is required. Among the myriad of left parties only the PPS, with over 75,000 members, has ever fully participated in the electoral system. The latest estimate of PCM membership is 5,000. The membership of the remaining groups mentioned above is very

---

[1]Genaro Vásquez Rojas was killed in February 1972.

small, some being hardly more than bands, but no precise figures are available. The population of Mexico is 50,700,000 (estimated 1970).

During 1971 the newly elected (1970) government of Luis Echeverría Alvarez took increasingly liberal positions on such issues as student unrest and social and economic reform, causing some concern in the right wing of the PRI, which feared the possible loss of its traditional economic and political privileges. The left wing parties were also concerned since such liberalized politics and social reform could win the president great popular support. Following the crisis of 10 June in Mexico City, in which a student demonstration was turned into a riot by extreme right-wing gangs (see below), Echeverría emerged with his authority strengthened and his position in the eyes of the student left improved. Although his government has continued to release or deport political prisoners and students are still in jail because of their parts in the 1968 disorders, Echeverría has also mounted a severe campaign to rid the country of urban and rural guerrillas. Within this political climate the weak and divided PCM is almost completely ineffectual and its program appears to have little popular appeal.

Leadership and Organization. The Secretary-general of the PCM is Arnoldo Martínez Verdugo, a leader in the party since the 1940's.

The Communist Youth of Mexico (Juventud Comunista de México; JCM) is an auxiliary organization of the PCM. The JCM secretary-general is believed to be Celso Garza Guajardo. After the 1968 student disorders the JCM began to split into a number of contending factions, and after its 1970 congress was reportedly in almost hopeless disarray. In 1971 the "Coordinating Committee for the Struggle Committees" of all the major Mexican universities indicated at a press conference on 30 April that it was organizing a congress of Mexican students in hopes of creating a national student organization. At the conference, members of the JCM were highly criticized and it was clear that JCM views were not shared by the majority. During the year some members of the JCM who had been imprisoned in 1968 were released into exile.

Party Internal Affairs. For well over a decade the PCM has been torn by internal disputes and serious conflicts within its organization, resulting in the expulsion of many members, the overshadowing of some former leaders, and a decline in the party's national influence and internal strength. Late in 1970 the party tried to deal with these problems by publishing a "Thesis on Problems in the Development of the Mexican Communist Party" (*Tesis sobre los problemas del desarrollo del Partido Comunista Mexicana*) which presented four historical reasons for the party's weakness: (1) the "reformist conceptions" which have predominated in the workers' movement; (2) the "caudillismo [strong man-ism] and paternalism of the bourgeoisie and the low cultural level of a large section of the workers"; (3) the "reformist and bourgeois nationalist currents" which "spread bourgeois ideology among the worker masses" during the period 1940-60, coincidental with the period of crisis within the party; (4) the "dogmatic conceptions that left a profound imprint on all the party's activity," resulting in failure to understand the "need for developing a revolutionary theory based on Marxism-Leninism but suited to the particularities of the country and rooted in the tradition of the struggles of the Mexican people." (For excerpts from the "Tesis" and other documents on PCM internal affairs, see the article by Ricardo Ochoa in *Intercontinental Press*, 5 July 1971.)

The PCM thesis declared that the Party's most important theoretical task was to apply the "general principles of Marxism-Leninism to the concrete reality of Mexico" and that the "development of the party itself [was] dependent on fulfilling this task." (*Ibid.*)

During the past few years discontent among some factions of the PCM increased, not only over disagreement about the party's explanations of its problems, but also because of the dominant faction's growing dispute with the Soviet Union. Since 1968, when the PCM protested the Soviet-led invasion of Czechoslovakia, Martínez Verdugo has aligned the party with expelled French communist Roger Garaudy (who attended a Central Committee meeting in 1971 at the invitation of Martínez), communist dissident Teodoro Petkoff of the Venezuelan "Movement Toward Socialism," and Santiago Carrillo, secretary-general of the Communist Party of Spain. On 1 July the PCM issued a statement announcing the expulsion of the well-known painter and pro-Soviet communist leader David Alfaro Siqueiros for "activities contrary to the party's political line and his violation of internal discipline." Siqueiros had openly quarreled with the party leadership for some time and on 30 January had issued an "Appeal to Communists" (*Llamado a los comunistas*) in which he attacked the PCM for lacking tolerance and democracy, "losing sight of the Leninist norms in the party," "abandoning the historic tasks of a communist party," "bureaucratizing its methods of work," and "moving away from the masses." (See *Intercontinental Press*, 5 July.) The two immediate points of the controversy were (1) Siqueiros's opposition to the party position in condemning the Soviet-led invasion of Czechoslovakia in 1968, and (2) his continued public support for the Echeverría government, which he believed was embarked on changes that showed an opening toward greater democracy and reform in Mexico. The PCM leadership countered his criticisms by accusing him of throwing a smokescreen over the party's efforts to "root out the decrepit habits and methods which Stalinism passed on to the immense majority of communist parties." (*Ibid.*)

Although the internal dispute within the PCM is probably far from over, it does not appear that as yet the pro-Soviet faction has enough support to form any organized resistance to the leadership.

Domestic Attitudes and Activities. Unnamed PCM delegates to the Eleventh Congress of the Communist Party of Costa Rica held in San José in June, gave an address in which they described the situation in Mexico in 1971 as "complex and difficult," with the Echeverría government favoring the "interests of the country's monopolies and financial oligarchy." The government was said to be intervening in the internal affairs of labor unions by using the army to accupy labor union buildings, intervening in a "paternalistic manner" in peasant organizations, and failing to respect the country's constitutional freedoms. According to the delegates, 100 political prisoners were unconstitutionally held in jail, "military brutalities and persecution" in the countryside were frequent, rural hunger and unemployment were worsening, and the government was "constantly violating university autonomy and favoring a so-called educational-technocratic reform that tends to create skilled labor for the capitalists." The party further criticized the government for failing to free the economy from dependency on "imperialism," which tied the "fate of the bourgeoisie" to "Yankee monopolies." The PCM called for the unity of all leftist forces to fight against the government's "reactionary and anti-popular policy" and for the freeing of all political prisoners through an amnesty, and declared that there was need for a "revolution that, given its socioeconomic content and the conditions of today's Mexico, will be popular, democratic, and anti-imperialist, as the first stage of a revolutionary process toward communist reorganization of Mexican society." (*Libertad*, San José, Costa Rica, 19 June.)

While attending the Fiftieth Anniversary celebration of the Communist Party of Chile in January 1972, PCM Central Committee member Valentín Campa described the domestic situation to *El Siglo* correspondents as "extremely critical." Reiterating the view of a PCM statement issued in Mexico during the summer of 1971, Campa noted the country's "advanced capitalist development," and high population growth rate which had produced a "powerful bourgeoisie" that controlled the "economic and political power." The system in Mexico, he continued, is chiefly characterized by "repression resulting in more frequent "outbursts of indignation" by students and workers; there has been an "increase in the working class conscience for struggling against the great bourgeoisie that is allied with capitalism." (*El Siglo*, Santiago, Chile, 9 January 1972.)

In March, following the arrest of 19 members of the MAR (see below), the government expelled five members of the Soviet Embassy on the charges of organizing strikes and engaging in subversive activities in collusion with the MAR. The PCM, although not directly involved and in spite of its recent differences with the Soviet Union, expressed indignation at the incident, claiming there was no justification for such a hostile action which it said was taken to "distract our people's attention in order to make them believe that the main thing is to defend our fatherland from alleged Soviet intervention in Mexican affairs" (*Libertad*, 19 June).

On 10 June a student demonstration became a government crisis when street-fighting broke out, between the students and armed right-wing bands, causing at least 10 deaths and many injuries. The PCM responded to this event by issuing a 10-page manifesto calling for the "overthrow of the oligarchy" and stating that "once again the reactionary and dictatorial nature of the haute bourgeoisie's governing methods [had] been laid bare." The government itself, the manifesto commented, had admitted the existence of a "fascist-type paramilitary organization" and was therefore itself to blame for the casualties.

International Views. The animosity which developed between the traditionally pro-Soviet PCM and the Soviet Union over the 1968 invasion of Czechoslovakia has persisted and in 1971 became even more pronounced. In March the PCM published an article, reiterating its denunciation of the "lamentable events" of 1968 and declaring its intention to stand firm on its position (*Oposición*, 1 March). Earlier the party defied the Soviet Union in a statement on the split in the Communist Party of Venezuela by declaring that "in compliance with its line of respect and noninterference in the internal affairs of fraternal parties" it would maintain friendly relations with both factions in spite of Soviet condemnation of the splinter faction (*ibid.*, 15 February).

Nevertheless, PLM Secretary-General Martínez Verdugo attended the Twenty-fourth Congress of the Communist Party of the Soviet Union, in April, and delivered an address in which he declared: "Old and close ties of friendship, solidarity and comradeship link us with the members of Lenin's party, thanks to whose revolutionary activity the international communist movement has today become a decisive and invincible force." He added, however, that the struggle for unity in the international communist movement "presupposes the sovereignty of each state and the independence of each party in elaborating its own strategy and tactics and noninterference in the domestic affairs of other fraternal parties." (*Pravda*, 9 April.)

In Latin America, Martínez declared, "advanced forces" were "changing the political panorama." In particular, he commented: "The victory of the Popular Unity Front in Chile and the anti-imperialist processes taking place in Peru and Bolivia are continuing in new forms the revolutionary development that was begun in Latin America by the victory of the Cuban revolution." (*Ibid.*)

The PCM sent a representative to the Eighth Conference of Communist Parties of Central America and Mexico, in June (see *Costa Rica*).

On 6-7 June the PCM met with members of the Communist Party, USA in Mexico City. The PCM expressed support for the struggle of the "North American people for withdrawal of troops from Vietnam," the "civil rights movement of Black and Chicano peoples," and for "solidarity with the movement to free political prisoners, especially Angela Davis." (*IB.*, no. 16-17.)

Publications. The official organ of the PCM is the weekly newspaper *La Voz de México*. In 1971 a journal entitled *Oposición* was being issued by the PCM.

*   *   *

The PPS. The Socialist People's Party, which resulted from a split in the PCM in 1948, was founded and led by Vicente Lombardo Toledano until his death in November 1968. It is one of the largest pro-communist parties in Latin America. Some PPS leaders are communists (Lombardo Toledano considered himself an independent Marxist), but the overall membership is not. During Lombardo's leadership of the PPS there were periodic rapprochements with the PCM but no permanent alliance. Since his death the PPS has been weakened by internal leadership struggles.

The MAR. The existence of the Revolutionary Action Movement was revealed in March 1971 when the Mexican government arrested 19 of its members on charges of subversive activities and expelled five members of the Soviet Embassy for alleged collusion with them. The MAR members disclosed that they had been trained in North Korea in terrorism, sabotage, weapons training, and expropriations, their objective being the imposition of a "Marxist-Leninist" regime in Mexico.

During the year the MAR carried out numerous small raids on banks and businesses and in September kidnaped the director of Civil Aviation Services, Julio Hirschfeld. After his release the government began a campaign to suppress the MAR. By the end of the year virtually all its active members were believed to have been arrested or driven underground.

Lynn Ratliff

Nicaragua

The Socialist Party of Nicaragua (Partido Socialista de Nicaragua; PSN) was formed in 1937 as the result of a split in the Party of Nicaraguan Workers, within which the communists had operated. In 1944 the government of Nicaragua permitted communists to hold a national congress, and the PSN regards that year as the date of its official founding. The party was outlawed in 1945 and has been illegal during most of its subsequent existence. Although it has occasionally attempted to influence the political situation through front organizations, the PSN at present is almost totally ineffective, owing both to its small size and weak organization, and to the government's suppression of left-wing groups. The PSN is pro-Soviet.

The Sandinist National Liberation Front (Frente Sandinista de Liberación Nacional; FSLN) is a small Castroite organization (see below).

The PSN is estimated to have about 200 members, the FSLN about 100. The population of Nicaragua is 2,000,000 (estimated 1970).

The PSN. Leadership and Organization. For several years little information about the PSN and its structure has come to light. It is believed that many of its leaders are in prison or exile. The first secretary was reported in 1968 to be Alvaro Ramírez Gonzáles. The latest party congress was held in 1966. Plenary meetings were held in 1967 and 1969.

The PSN is believed to control only the extreme left-wing faction of the General Confederation of Labor (Confederación General de Trabajo), which itself represents only a small portion of the country's workers. In 1971, speaking at the Twenty-fourth Congress of the Communist Party of the Soviet Union (CPSU), PSN Central Committee member Favio River declared that the "revolutionary trade union movement and parties of the middle strata and bourgeoisie [had] begun the struggle for the overthrow of the militarist dictatorship oppressing the Nicaraguan people" (*Pravda*, 9 April). There is, in fact, no evidence of such activity at present in Nicaragua.

The "Confederation of Peasants and Agricultural Laborers" was founded by the PSN in 1967. To date, little is known of its program or activities (see *YICA*, 1970, pp. 449-50).

The PSN has attempted to maintain front groups among students and other young persons, but over the past four or five years its influence has been minimal. The continuing student unrest and violence in Nicaragua is probably carried out almost entirely by members of guerrilla-oriented Castroite groups. The PSN reportedly maintains a small youth front called the Nicaraguan Socialist Youth (Juventud Socialista Nicaraguense).

Party Internal Affairs and Domestic Views. According to Favio River, the PSN has been "forced to operate by underground or semi-underground methods and under conditions of cruel police repression," but he added that it nevertheless "exists and operates," guided by the "wise doctrine of Lenin" (*ibid.*).

In his speech at the CPSU congress, River described Nicaragua as "deprived of its freedom" and "economically and politically dependent on American imperialism because bourgeois governments have sold out their country," adding that poverty "prevails everywhere," "65 per cent of the population are illiterate," and "civil liberties are completely lacking" under the "military dynasty" of Anastasio Somoza that has controlled Nicaragua for 40 years. He declared, however, that the struggle for the "overthrow of the militarist dictatorship" had begun and that the "dawn of better days" was "glimmering on the horizon." (*Ibid.*)

International Views and Activities. In 1971 the PSN reiterated its pro-Soviet position and praised the Soviet Union for its "vanguard role" in the socialist camp, its "struggle against the imperialist aggressor," its policy of "peaceful coexistence and nuclear disarmament," and its "proletarian internationalism" which "raises still higher the authority of the great motherland of working people throughout the world" (*ibid.*).

The Eighth Conference of Communist Parties of Central American Countries, Mexico and Panama was held in Costa Rica in June 1971. Traditionally the PSN has attended these conferences. Although its representative was unable to attend the 1971 meeting, presumably the party would have supported the conference statement (see *Costa Rica*).

As already noted, the PSN was represented at the CPSU congress in Moscow during April 1971.

Publications. The long-standing PSN organ, *Orientación Popular*, was suppressed in 1967. Its successor, *Tribuna*, met the same fate in 1968. Apparently no publication is currently being issued by the PSN on any regular basis.

*   *   *

The FSLN. The Sandinist National Liberation Front is a small but active Castroite guerrilla organization founded in 1961 by Carlos Fonseca Amador and still led by him (see *YICA*, 1971, pp. 467-68).

In an interview with *Punto Final* correspondents (Santiago, Chile, 27 April 1971), the FSLN leader maintained that armed struggle, though it "involves the most difficult course," is the "only sure one." At the same time the Sandinist Front "takes up the guerrilla rifle, it inculcates a class consciousness. For the peasants in the mountains, for the poor in the suburbs, for the students in remote towns, the revolutionaries, the rebels, the communists, are the members of the Sandinist Front, although that legitimate quality is not recognized in us, against all reason, in some international meetings overseas."

Domestic Views. According to Fonseca, "United States imperialism is renewing its century-old covetousness of Nicaragua," and continuing its "traditional utilization" of Nicaraguan territory as a base for "acts of aggression against other countries in the area" (*Punto Final*, 27 April 1971).

The FSLN characterizes the "despotic [Somoza] family" of Nicaragua by its "bloodthirsty covetousness and its passion for possessing all of Nicaragua's riches." According to some party members, who were interviewed in Chile, Anastasio Somoza does nothing for Nicaragua except inflict a "repressive policy on the people;" his "anti-communism is grotesque [and] without mercy." (*Ibid.*, 13 April.) In spite of this situation, two factors were said to be casting a "shadow over Somoza's tyrannical dreams: the development of the FSLN and the course of the Cuban revolution" (*ibid.*)

International Positions. Since its inception the FSLN has been a self-proclaimed Castroite organization and has had at least moral support from Cuba. In 1971 Carlos Fonseca sent a message to the CPSU congress stating: "The ideals of the immortal Lenin, founder of the CPSU, are a guiding star in the struggle which the revolutionaries of our country are waging with the aim of overthrowing the reactionary regime." The FSLN, he continued, was proud to be bringing to the "popular masses of [Nicaragua]—workers, peasants, and all oppressed and exploited peoples—socialist ideals which were victoriously implemented for the first time in history in the great Soviet Union." "With complete justification," he concluded, the Sandinist Front considers itself the "successor of the Bolshevist October Revolution."

The FSLN applauded the 1970 election of Salvador Allende as president of Chile, as an "important victory for the revolutionary movement in Latin America," but expressed the conviction that the "hardest battles are reserved for the future in Chile." The Chilean proletariat, according to the FSLN, cannot fight and "win definitely if they do not have their own armed detachment." (*Punto Final*, 27 April.)

Publications. The FSLN has a publication entitled *Trinchera*, whose frequency and extent of distribution are unknown.

Lynn Ratliff

Panama

The Communist Party of Panama (Partido Comunista de Panamá) was founded in 1930. During World War II the name was changed to People's Party of Panama (Partido del Pueblo de Panamá; PDP).

Other left-wing groups in Panama include the Revolutionary Unity Movement (Movimiento de Unidad Revolucionario; MUR), the National Action Vanguard (Vanguardia de Acción Nacional; VAN), the Panamanian Revolutionary Union (Unión Revolucionaria Panameña; URP) and the National Liberation Movement of 29 November (MLN-29-11) (see below).

The PDP has been illegal since 1953. When the government of General Omar Torrijos Herrera took power through a coup in October 1968 all political parties were dissolved. After a period of intensified suppression of communist and left-wing groups, civil liberties were officially restored in November 1969. In August 1970 Torrijos declared a general amnesty whereby many jailed leftist leaders were released. In March 1971 he pardoned a number of prisoners convicted of terrorism, reminding them that "terrorism does not pay in Panama." Many members of leftist revolutionary groups were pardoned but sent into exile. The political atmosphere in Panama continued to become increasingly less restrictive during 1971 although the ban on the communist party and any organized revolutionary leftist groups was continued. Nevertheless some communists reportedly hold positions of influence in the Ministries of Trade and Industry, Agriculture, and Education. While the mixture of left-wing agitation and national feeling over the perennial issue of the U.S. presence in the Canal Zone and the renegotiation of the Canal treaty continued to increase in 1971, the role of the PDP was probably more that of a joiner than an instigator of mass activities.

PDP members are estimated to number about 250. The population of Panama is 1,500,000 (estimated 1970).

Leadership and Organization. Since 1951 the secretary-general of the PDP has been Rubén Darío Sousa. Other leading figures in the party include Hugo Víctor (chairman of the Central Committee), Professor César A. de León, the poet Carlos Francisco Changmarín, and Simón Vargas. All those named are in exile, probably in Chile. In June 1971 the Panamanian Immigration Office was instructed to prohibit Hugo Víctor from accomplishing his announced return, thus reaffirming the government's intention to keep the PDP from regrouping within Panama.

The University Reform Front (Frente Reformista Universitaria; FRU) is a student affiliate of the PDP. The PDP, among other leftist groups, exerts some influence within the large Federation of Students of Panama (Federación de Estudiantes de Panamá; FEP) which is a member of the communist-front International Union of Students. Although student organizations were dissolved following Torrijos's takeover in 1968, they have begun to reemerge as restrictions on mass organizations have been lessened. In July 1971 an FEP communiqué stated that the National Guard, previously a "loyal watchguard of the interests of the oligarchy and imperialism," was now taking "patriotic sides with the popular movement." In mid-December the FEP and some 50 other high school and university groups held an Anti-Imperialist Week featuring speeches by student and government leaders, including General Torrijos himself. The theme of the event was the present discussions on renegotiation of the Canal Zone treaty and the removal of U.S. control over the Canal. In his speech at the closing ceremony, Torrijos reiterated his promise to gain a satisfactory treaty from the U.S. or else lead the National Guard in the inevitable "patriotic rebellion" that would erupt in Panama.

The FRU issued a statement on 6 August "resolutely supporting the sectors which in the current government and outside it, have publicly committed themselves to struggling to liquidate the colonial enclave in our country" and appealing for unity among the "patriotic and people's sector, including the military."

The Trade Union Federation of the Workers of the Republic of Panama (Federación Sindical de Trabajadores de la República de Panamá; FST) is an affiliate of the PDP. It is of very minor influence and small size and its leader, Angel Gómez, is believed to be still in prison. The FST offices were closed by the government in 1968 and there has since been no indication that they would be allowed to reopen.

Party Internal Affairs. In September 1971 an enlarged plenary session of the PDP Politburo discussed three main questions: (1) the political situation in Panama, (2) relations with the world revolutionary movement, and (3) measures for reorganizing the party's leadership in accordance with the directives of its Fifth Congress. The plenum communiqué emphasized the importance of ideological struggle against the tendency to minimize the party's role and called for "strict revolutionary vigilance based on the defense of Marxist-Leninist principles." (*IB.*, no. 23-24.)

Early in the year, the above-mentioned leaders of the PDP published a book in Chile entitled *Panamá, 1903-1970* in which they called on all the "anti-imperialist and democratic forces in Panama, including sectors of the national bourgeoisie and the military that are not contaminated with proimperialist perfidy, to form a popular, democratic, and national liberation alliance of the people which will immediately make impossible the return of the oligarchy to power" (quoted in *Punto Final*, Santiago, 13 April).

Domestic Views. Early in 1971 the PDP assessed the situation in Panama and issued a lengthy statement in which Secretary-General Darío Sousa observed that "repressive measures" had been halted, "political prisoners" had been released (including some communists), student groups had been allowed to reorganize, and negotiations had been started for a "democratic education reform." These improvements were attributed to the "abortive 1969 coup" (against Torrijos) which, according to Sousa, had "revealed the deepening contradiction between the oligarchy and imperialism" and the "military government." (*WMR*, February 1971.)

Panama, according to the PDP leader, was in a new stage of "political transition" in which the "subjective prerequisites for accomplishing the tasks of the democratic and anti-imperialist revolution [were] building up." Imperialism, he declared, could no longer "use the oligarchy to suppress the people's effort for freedom," because the oligarchy had been "swept from power." The trend of the 1968 military coup led by Torrijos "coincided with that of the people's struggle" and was directed against the "big bourgeoisie" and "imperialist plunder and oppression." The main task of the PDP in the current situation, Sousa explained, was to "heighten the revolutionary awareness of the masses and unify the forces seeking change." Although the majority of the people realized that there must be no return to the past, their political consciousness was "still too low for them to have a clear idea of the subsequent course of events." Hence the PDP, he explained, must (1) make clear to the people that "capitalist development" would not solve their problems,

(2) draw up a program "reflecting the interests of the people and serving as a basis for their unity and a guide to exercising power." Further, the party must "expose the false contention that economic and social progress is possible without a genuinely revolutionary government" and refute the "harmful allegation that the working class cannot play the role of vanguard because of the democratic character of the Panamanian revolution and also because at this stage the petty bourgeoisie has allegedly assumed this role." (*Ibid.*)

The PDP leader warned that "U.S. imperialists' sophisticated ideological subversion" posed a "great menace" by keeping the "increasingly mature working class from bringing revolutionary consciousness into the struggle of the people," forming an alliance with the peasants, or winning the support of the military and civil servants. Therefore, he added, the "Marxist-Leninist party of the working class"—the PDP—was the "ideological and political force which U.S. imperialism [would] have to face first and foremost." The party's analysis of the changes taking place in Panama and its "theoretical substantiation of the unfolding of the popular movement" would help "foil the maneuvers of imperialism and its allies who [were] trying to stave off change." (*Ibid.*)

The economy of Panama was described by Darío Sousa as being dominated by "U.S. monopolies" which controlled, in addition to the Panama Canal, the banks, the electric power companies, the banana plantations, and a sizable part of trade. The oligarchy, he said, had used its "political power to further its economic interests" and had "consistently channeled industrial development into an anti-national course," intensifying the "harsh exploitation of the people." Although the 1968 coup had not changed the economic structure, the communists believed that the Torrijos government intended to "reform taxation, agrarian relations, education, labor-employer relations, and also limit monopoly profits," thus "stimulating the popular movement." (*Ibid.*)

The PDP supported the government's decision to allow "democratic trade unions" and its promise to "respect trade union rights and the existence of differing trends in the labor movement." The outlook for the peasant movement was also held to have improved: the government's policy was affording "opportunities for organizing the peasants to fight for a consistent solution of the agrarian problem," and the situation of the peasants was being normalized by "legalizing peasant ownership of the land with no compensation to estate owners." (*Ibid.*)

Later in the year, the aforementioned PDP Politburo communiqué called for "radicalization of Panamanian nationalism" and emphasized that the "main political issue in Panama" concerned the "restoration of the country's sovereign and jurisdictional rights over the Canal Zone, which would constitute culmination of the process of forming a national and independent state." The PDP called on international public opinion to support the liquidation of "U.S. colonialism in the Canal Zone." It also urged "democratic forces" to support abolition of deportation measures being used against members of the PDP. (*IB.*, no. 23-24.)

International Positions. Traditionally pro-Soviet, the PDP was represented by Secretary-General Darío Sousa at the Twenty-fourth Congress of the Communist Party of the Soviet Union (CPSU) in April 1971. In his speech to the congress Sousa praised the CPSU for its "profoundly international spirit and its loyalty to Marxist-Leninist principle" and for its role in the struggle for "freedom, peace, and socialism." The PDP, he said, shared the view of fraternal parties that anti-Sovietism was a "crime against the working class and all who fight against exploitation and oppression." (*Pravda*, 8 April.)

Concerning Latin America, the PDP stressed the party's need for increased solidarity with the people of Cuba, Chile, and Peru, who were "engaged in struggle against the U.S. imperialist offensive" and for expansion of relations between the Panamanian, Cuban, and Chilean communist parties. The PDP also urged the coordination of the revolutionary movement in Latin America, while acknowledging the particular conditions of the struggle in each country in order to face the "U.S. imperialist onslaught." (*IB.*, no. 23-24.)

The PDP sent a representative to the Eighth Conference of Communist Parties of Central America, Mexico, and Panama in June (see *Costa Rica*).

Publications. The organ of the PDP is *El Mazo*, published irregularly and clandestinely.

*   *   *

The MUR and Other Castroite Organizations. The MUR, an organization particularly active during the 1960's, was founded and led by Floyd Britton, who died in prison in Panama in 1969 (see *YICA*, 1970, p. 457). During 1971 it became known that the MUR and the VAN, a Castroite group led by Jorge Turner, had joined with some dissidents from the PDP to form the National Liberation Movement of 29 November. (The date commemorated the death of Floyd Britton.) The MLN-29-11 is committed to the armed road to gaining power and has engaged in guerrilla activities, bank robberies, and the forcible takeover of businesses. The leaders of the MLN-29-11—Freddy Britton, Bolívar Crespo, and Evariso González—were deported in March 1971. This brought the activities of the group to an end, at least for the present.

Lynn Ratliff

Paraguay

The Paraguayan Communist Party (Partido Comunista Paraguayo; PCP) was founded in 1928. In mid-1963 a small group split from the PCP and formed the pro-Chinese Paraguayan Leninist Communist Party (Partido Leninista Comunista Paraguayo; PLCP). By 1969, however, the PLCP had rejoined the PCP. Another, more serious split within the PCP occurred in 1965 when the Soviet Union backed the organization of a commission which expelled Secretary-General Oscar Creydt from his long-held position in the party. The National Committee for the Defense and Reorganization of the Paraguayan Communist Party (Comité Nacional de Defensa y Reorganización del Partido Comunista Paraguayo)—the name the commission assumed in 1966—accused Creydt of being too lenient with dissident pro-Chinese members of the party and of acting in a high-handed, dictatorial manner in the conduct of party affairs. Creydt, followed by many of his colleagues, then established what he claimed was the legitimate PCP. The original party remained securely under the control of the pro-Soviet leaders of the National Committee.

The communist party and all left-wing groups have been illegal in Paraguay since October 1936. Under the government of General Alfredo Stroessner, who has been president since 1954, enforcement of the anti-subversion laws has been strict and all opposition groups have been suppressed. The PCP operates from exile in Argentina, Brazil, and Uruguay. It is believed that fewer than ten per cent of its members actually live in Paraguay. Domestic support for the party is insignificant.

The membership of the PCP, including all factions, is estimated to be between 4,500 and 5,000. The population of Paraguay is 2,400,000 (estimated 1970).

Leadership and Organization. Since 1967 the PCP has been under the leadership of Miguel Angel Soler and Obdulio Barthe. Other prominent figures include Hugo Maciel Campos, Gustavo Colman, and Augusto Canete. It is believed that most PCP leaders live in Buenos Aires.

Party Internal Affairs. The Third Congress of the PCP was held secretly in April 1971 after many postponements. It had been twenty-one years since the Second Congress and four years since the party was reorganized and a congress promised. The 26 delegates approved the basic report of the Central Committee, which was concerned primarily with the party's position and the domestic political situation in Paraguay. The Program and Rules and political theses were also adopted and a new Central Committee of 24 members and 14 alternates was elected.

Other business of the congress included adoption of resolutions concerning the need to defend Marxism-Leninism "against all manifestations of right or left-wing opportunism" (*Adelante*, May 1971). A message from the Communist Party of the Soviet Union (CPSU) praised the PCP for its consistent struggle on behalf of the unity of the international communist movement, but referred also to the party's need for better organization and greater ideological strength.

Congress delegates reported PCP achievements in recent years as including the establishment of modest but important ties with the masses, advancement in relations with its allies and reorganization of the partisan forces, increased distribution of Party propaganda, and an expanded organization within the country. The newly elected Central Committee was characterized by Central Committee member Hugo Campos as representing greater unity and consistent Marxist-Leninist ideology; its members included a nucleus of faithful "old cadres" and "determined young cadres who [had] received higher training" (report by Hugo Campos in *El Siglo*, Santiago, Chile, 12 May). It was also reported that since 1967 the membership of the PCP had doubled and its prestige had increased considerably.

Domestic Views and Programs. The PCP program as approved by the Third Congress described Paraguay as a "dependent and backward capitalist country where the development of productive forces is hindered by the landowning system of agrarian property" and by "imperialist exploitation." U.S. "imperialism" was said to be "turning the country into a strategic communications center, training base, and bastion to crush the national liberation movements in Latin America." In a speech to the Twentieth Congress of the Uruguayan Communist Party, the PCP delegate reported that the "military-police dictatorship regime" of General Stroessner was continuing to "unleash violence and terror furiously against the communists and other patriots," conduct elections which were "farces," and make "deceitful promises of democratization." The "Yankee-Stroessner dictatorship" had adopted new measures to "silence all manifestations of criticism or protest," such as a law prohibiting publication of anything dealing with "internal disturbance" and a "law for the peace and freedom of persons" which provided up to twelve years' imprisonment for "criticizing the corrupt prevailing military system." (*El Popular*, Montevideo, 16 December 1970.)

The party program claimed that conditions in Paraguay were ripe for a "democratic revolution of national and social liberation" led by the "working class, the peasantry, and the urban middle classes." The role of the PCP was to remove the present regime and to form a government capable of ensuring the country's democratization. The need for widespread mass action and unification of the working classes was emphasized. In particular the PCP sought repeal of repressive laws and a general amnesty, development of a worker-campesino alliance, cancelation of all economic and military treaties, and an independent foreign policy for Paraguay.

During 1971 the PCP continued its movement for the release of political prisoners in Paraguay. The party issued an appeal on 9 March for the release of party members Antonio Maidana, Julio Rojas, and Alfredo Alcorta, who had been imprisoned for twelve years. The appeal declared that the movement, once supported only by communists and a few democrats, was now supported by almost all political parties, the Catholic church, the Paraguayan University Federation, and many other popular organizations. Although the support for release of political prisoners has widened, there is as yet no indication that it is sufficient to affect the policy of the Stroessner government in this regard.

International Views and Activities. Traditionally a loyal supporter of the Soviet Union, the PCP sent a congratulatory message to the CPSU's Twenty-fourth Congress in May 1971. The message stressed the historic significance of the Soviet Union's successes in the economic, political and social spheres and praised the congress for its "development of Marxist-Leninist science" and the strengthening of "friendship, unity, and cohesion" among the world communist and workers' movements.

In the same message the PCP condemned the "splitting activities" of the leadership of the Chinese Communist Party and its "campaign of slander and lies" directed against the Soviet Union and the CPSU. (*IB.*, no 10-11, 1971.)

In his address to the Uruguayan Communist Party congress the PCP delegate stressed the importance of international solidarity to the "struggle of the Paraguayan people." Contrary to "reactionary propaganda," he said, "the event which moved our people most profoundly was the triumph of popular unity in Chile." The Paraguayan people were "making the victory of the Chilean workers and entire people their own victory." (*El Popular*, 16 December 1970.)

In September 1971 the PCP participated with the communist parties of Argentina, Bolivia, Brazil, Chile, Peru, and Uruguay in a series of meetings to exchange views and discuss common problems. A joint statement was issued in the Chilean party organ, *El Siglo*, on 11 October which said that "a pronounced leftward swing among the popular masses" was taking place in Latin America and that the working class, "which shows increasing proof of maturity," was being joined by new "patriotic sectors." It stressed the importance of united front tactics and saw the start of a new stage in the revolutionary struggle in the victory of the Popular Unity coalition in Chile.

Publications. The PCP issues a monthly magazine, *Adelante*, which is published abroad and distributed clandestinely in Paraguay. The party also makes its views known through articles and reports in the *World Marxist Review* and over radio broadcasts from Moscow.

*   *   *

The PCP-Creydt. Oscar Creydt, the long-time leader of the Paraguayan communists, has been the secretary-general of what he claims is the legitimate PCP since the split of the party in 1965 (see above). In the late 1960's Creydt was openly critical of the Soviet Union and adopted pro-Chinese and pro-Castro positions, perhaps partly as a reaction to the increasing strength of the pro-Soviet PCP faction and partly in an attempt to appeal to the more radical elements in the Paraguayan left wing.

Aside from Creydt's preeminent position, little is known of the leadership of his faction. The second secretary is nominally Antonio Maidana, who has been in prison for twelve years in Paraguay. Most members of the PCP-Creydt are believed to live in Montevideo, but its size is undetermined. The Creydt party has apparently retained greater strength than the pro-Soviet faction would have predicted at the time of the split, and it is believed to have the support of a majority in the Communist Youth, the youth movement of the PCP.

Domestic Views. The PCP-Creydt has regularly characterized the government of Paraguay as an "anti-national military dictatorship" dominated by "North Americans" and "big landholders, traders, and speculators." Manuel Julio Mandelik, a PCP member who was arrested in 1970 by Argentine authorities, was released in 1971 and was granted asylum in Chile where he was interviewed by *Punto Final* (Santiago, 25 May 1971). According to Mandelik, the country was under the control of the army, which had established a "terrorist, murderous regime, with constant martial law, trade unions under police intervention, and arrests of both political and union representatives." He stated that the PCP-Creydt was making a "serious effort to coordinate its action with all sectors" which were willing to "fight for the overthrow of the regime" and to form a "democratic National Liberation Front." He added that although the people must be organized to fight in "every possible way against the regime for the purpose of overthrowing it—with or without weapons, and in semi-legal or clandestine ways," the chief method was "armed struggle, especially guerrilla warfare."

Mandelik went on to express the view of the Creydt faction in its continuing bitter feud with the pro-Soviet PCP, condemning that faction as a "phony," "revisionist," and "opportunistic" communist party whose leaders were failing to oppose the Stroessner regime in hopes of achieving legal status (*ibid.*). On the issue of political prisoners, the PCP-Creydt believed their release could be obtained only "in the course of the popular struggles to overthrow the regime," not through "overt legal channels" as it charged the Soler-led party favors (*ibid.*).

International Views. In the aforementioned interview, Manuel Mandelik declared that the PCP-Creydt is of the opinion that the "vanguard of the international revolutionary movement lies in Vietnam, and identifies itself completely with the Marxist-Leninist line of the Vietnamese Workers' Party. It is aligned with all the communist parties which are in the revolutionary current of the international communist movement, such as the communist parties of Cuba, China and Korea." (*Punto Final*, 25 May.)

Lynn Ratliff

Peru

The Peruvian Communist Party (Partido Comunista Peruano; PCP) had its origins in the Peruvian Socialist Party, founded in 1928 by José Carlos Mariátegui. The present name dates from 1930. Since 1964 the communist movement has been divided into a pro-Soviet and a pro-Chinese group, each calling itself the PCP

There exist in Peru also various leftist organizations more revolutionary in spirit, with Trotskyist and Castroite sympathies, such as the Movement of the Revolutionary Left (Movimiento de Izquierda Revolucionaria; MIR), the Army of National Liberation (Ejército de Liberación Nacional; ELN), the Revolutionary Leftist Front (Frente Izquierdista Revolucionario; FIR), and the Revolutionary Vanguard (Vanguardia Revolucionaria; VR).

The pro-Soviet and pro-Chinese groups have memberships estimated at 2,000 and 3,000 respectively (*World Strength of the Communist Party Organizations*, Washington, D.C., 1970). The pro-Soviet PCP claims that its members and affiliates (those not assigned to a cell) together number 35,000. The other communist and leftist groups are considered small, the MIR and the VR having perhaps the largest membership. The population of Peru is 13,600,000 (estimated 1970).

Communist membership is predominantly urban, mainly drawn from workers, students, and professional groups. The pro-Chinese PCP seems to have the stronger hold in the universities. Communist influence within the trade union movement is exercised mainly by the pro-Soviet PCP, which influences the General Confederation of Workers of Peru (Confederación General de Trabajadores del Perú; CGTP).

A constitutional provision prohibits communist parties from participating in Peruvian elections, but they have been allowed to operate under various degrees of police surveillance and harassment. The present military government, led by President Juan Velasco Alvarado, has permitted the pro-Soviet PCP to function freely, but it has kept some control over other leftist groups by deporting several pro-Chinese and Trotskyist leaders. On 1 December 1971 the government passed a law providing for the death penalty and twenty-five-year prison terms in cases of terrorist attacks causing death, serious injury, or property destruction.

*   *   *

The Pro-Soviet PCP. Leadership and Organization. The highest organ of the pro-Soviet PCP is the national congress, which is supposed to meet every three years. The fifth such gathering was held in March 1969. The principal party leaders include Jorge del Prado Chávez, secretary-general; Raúl Acosta Salas, undersecretary-general; and Central Committee members Félix Arias Schreiber, Jorge Béjar, Alfredo Abarca, Segundo Collazos, Andrés Paredes, José Reccio Gutiérrez, Pompeyo Mares, Magno Falcón, Mario Ugarte Hurtado, and Juan Cáceres.

The pro-Soviet party is organized from cells through local and regional committees, to the Central Committee. Known regional committees exist in the cities of Lima, Callao, Arequipa, Oroya, Cerro de Pasco, Cuzco, Huancayo, Huánuco, Chiclayo, Chimbote, Andahuaylas, Tarma, Huancavelica, Abancay, Tacna, Cajamarca, Piura, Trujillo, Ica, Ayacucho, and Puno. Lima has the largest number of local committees, concentrated in low-income neighborhoods and in the slum areas which the government now refers to as "new towns" (*pueblos jóvenes*).

The pro-Soviet youth group, the Peruvian Communist Youth (Juventud Comunista Peruana; JCP), appears to be small and operates mainly at the university level. Jorge Tapia continues to be the JCP secretary-general. The JCP, according to Tapia, has the following composition: university students, 45 per cent; high school students, 35 per cent; workers and employees, 16 per cent; and peasants, 4 per cent (*Unidad*, 21 January 1971). The JCP held its First Congress on 29 August, which was attended by delegates from the Soviet Union, Chile, Venezuela, and Costa Rica. The congress acclaimed the agrarian reform being implemented by the government and demanded nationalization of the copper mines. It also decided that it would seek to organize "youth participation in the revolutionary process" taking place in Peru.

The most influential pro-Soviet PCP front, the CGTP, was officially recognized by the government on 29 January 1971. It now claims to represent 350,000 workers (*Caretas*, Lima, 3-12 March). The CGTP, while reflecting the domestic positions of the PCP—which includes support for the military government, actively supported numerous strikes within the mining sector (see below, CGTP).

Party Internal Affairs. Although no significant conflict seemed to exist within the party, the PCP organ (*Unidad*, 9 January) reported that a Central Committee plenum held at the end of 1970 had expelled Guevara Gálvez, possibly a Central Committee member, because of his "factional activities and attempts to create a new opportunistic, ultra-left, neo-Trotskyite political organization."

Domestic Attitudes and Activities. The pro-Soviet PCP seeks the establishment of a communist society through a "democratic, agrarian, and anti-imperialist revolution." According to the party statutes (issued in March 1969), the party wants to "free Peru from imperialist domination, mainly by the United States; to eliminate all feudal remnants; to end racial and national discriminations; and to liquidate the economic and political power of the large landholders and capitalists."

Given the present Peruvian situation, in which a military government has been undertaking various measures to effect social and economic changes to the benefit of the country's lower and middle sectors, the pro-Soviet PCP has adopted and maintained a policy of almost total support for the government. During 1971, this position was repeatedly emphasized by the party. Secretary-General del Prado stated in an interview (*Népszabadság*, Budapest, 27 April), that the party considered as the two most important measures taken by the government thus far the nationalization of petroleum and the radical agrarian reform. He also said:

> Although subsequent measures have not been as significant—the trend of development is not consistent, but often contradictory—we are advancing toward economic independence and social progress. We feel that our revolution is in the initial phase of an anti-imperialist, agricultural democratic, and national liberation revolution. It goes without saying that socialism and communist are our ultimate goals, the goal of the Peruvian communists.

Del Prado also stated that the party's main task in the present political situation was to "win over the rapidly growing front of anti-imperialist and anti-oligarchic civilian and military forces."

The PCP welcomed the creation of the National System of Support for Social Mobilization (Sistema Nacional de Apoyo a la Mobilización Social; SINAMOS), decreed by the government on 23 June with the purpose of introducing popular participation in the revolutionary process. SINAMOS—whose functions would include that of supervising and helping in the formation of cooperative enterprises resulting from the government laws on land tenure, industry, fishing, and mining—was placed under the direction of a military man, thus minimizing the likelihood of communist infiltration.

A PCP Central Committee plenum on 3-4 July maintained that the "revolutionary process" in Peru was undergoing the "most dangerous period of its entire development," asserting that "imperialism and the local oligarchy" were attempting to weaken the government indirectly by attacking the CGTP. In view of this appraisal, the PCP concluded that the military government, "as a way out of the grave situation," should accelerate the nationalization of large mines, enterprises, and banks; complete the agrarian reform; reduce the exports of "foreign monopoly" profits; and, "if necessary," stop payment of foreign debts. (*Unidad*, 8 July.) The same plenum also stated that the PCP "in spite of differences with the government will not waver a second in offering its aid, including mobilization of its people if the situation comes to the point of a civil war" (*ibid.*).

The PCP devoted some attention during the year to the threat to the Peruvian revolution posed by the "ultra-left." This term was employed by the government to refer to communist and radical groups, but the PCP itself used it to refer mainly to the pro-Chinese PCP and Trotskyist groups. An article in *Unidad* (22 April) accused Maoist and Trotkyist militants, particularly those belonging to the Revolutionary Vanguard, of working to "discredit the revolutionary struggles of the Peruvian people and workers." It charged that these elements had been calling for provocative meetings, marches, and ceremonies in order to create a confrontation between the government and the workers. *Unidad* also suggested that these activities were maneuvers "financed and directed by the U.S. Central Intelligence Agency, the Aprista Party, the oligarchy, and the large Yankee imperialist companies."

The CGTP. The communist-influenced General Confederation of Workers of Peru was formed in 1968, mainly by pro-Soviet PCP efforts, as a rival to the Confederation of Workers of Peru, which claims to represent more than 70 per cent of the organized workers of the country and is dominated by the non-communist Aprista Party. Its main leaders are Isidoro Gamarra, president; Gustavo Espinoza, secretary-general; and Claudio Santa Cruz, organization secretary.

The CGTP held its Second National Congress on 1-5 December, which was allegedly attended by some 50 national labor federations and some 170 departmental labor unions (*Unidad*, 9 December).

During 1971 the CGTP, through its National Federation of Mine and Metal Workers, organized numerous strikes within the mining sector. Miners went on strike demanding higher wages, better working conditions, and increased fringe benefits. The demands also included nationalization of the large mining enterprises.

Following the enactment of a general law on mining promulgated by the military government on 8 June, a CGTP delegation led by Isidoro Gamarra visited the Minister of Energy and Mines to express the CGTP's support. In addition, the confederation issued a statement indicating its firm decision to "make the mineworkers of the republic understand and support the law," which was said to "coincide basically" with the demands of the CGTP and its strong affiliate, the National Federation of Mine and Metal Workers. The new law on mining gave the government the right to determine which areas and minerals it may reserve for exclusive state exploitation and established miners' participation in the sharing of profits.

Mining strikes, however, continued after the passing of the law on mining. CGTP Secretary-General Espinoza attributed the unrelented strikes to both a new awareness in the miners, said to have been produced by the atmosphere of change of the Peruvian revolution, and the "policy of endless provocations by national and foreign mining enterprises,'' which refused to deal with the workers' complaints (*Unidad*, 2 July). Likewise, a communiqué issued by the National Federation of Mine and Metal Workers accused national and foreign mining companies of pursuing an "intense campaign of provocation'' with the purpose of causing the failure of the new law on mining.

International Views and Positions. The PCP continued in 1971 to maintain a very close pro-Soviet alignment. Secretary-General del Prado attended the Twenty-Fourth Congress of the Communist Party of the Soviet Union (CPSU). He praised the resolutions passed at the congress and described it as "a new stage in human progress."

A Central Committee meeting held on 3-4 July approved a resolution expressing solidarity with the Cuban people and communist party in their "struggle to build socialism." The resolution rejected the "anti-Cuban and anti-socialist campaign carried out by the U.S. CIA, along with the Peruvian oligarchy and Trotskyism,'' regarding the case of writer Heberto Padilla. Another resolution passed at the Central Committee meeting manifested support for the policies of Popular Unity and the Communist Party of Chile in their "struggle against internal and foreign counter-revolution.'' The constitutional amendment passed by the Chilean Congress to nationalize all copper mines was highly praised by *Unidad*, which hailed this event as the "beginning of the end of a gigantic plundering."

Unidad (29 April) noted Fidel Castro's speech on occasion of the Playa Girón anniversary, in which Castro stated that the process taking place in Peru "is not a Marxist-Leninist revolution, but is undoubtedly a revolutionary process from the Marxist-Leninist point of view.'' The PCP organ expressed that Castro's statements should help the "self-styled revolutionaries understand that what is developing in Peru is an authentic revolutionary process with its own characteristics, and that it must be supported."

International Party Contacts. During 1971, in addition to attending the CPSU congress, the PCP was represented at the congresses of the Bulgarian Communist Party by del Prado and Andrés Paredes), the Communist Party of Czechoslovakia, and the Mongolian People's Revolutionary Party (both by José Reccio).

Early in February, del Prado met in Lima with Konstantin Telalov, Central Committee member of the Bulgarian Communist Party. In May, del Prado and Mario Ugarte met in Budapest with János Kádár and other leaders of the Hungarian Socialist Workers' Party. In September the PCP (represented by Reccio) participated in a conference of Latin American communist parties which included parties from Argentina, Bolivia, Brazil, Chile, Paraguay, and Uruguay. In October, del Prado met in Moscow with B. N. Ponomarev and Ye. I. Koskov, Central Committee members of the CPSU.

A PCP and CGTP delegation visited Cuba on occasion of the 26 July celebrations. Earlier, on 12-22 April, a CGTP delegation visited Cuba.

Publications. The pro-Soviet PCP official organ is a weekly newspaper, *Unidad*. It claims a circulation of 14,000 to 15,000. The party also publishes *Ensayos*, a bimonthly theoretical journal, and *Joven Guardia*, the communist youth organ.

* * *

The Pro-Chinese PCP. Leadership and Organization. The leadership of the pro-Chinese Peruvian Communist Party is not well known. Saturnino Paredes Macedo heads the group which is recognized by the People's Republic of China. Gotardo Hernán Rojas and José Carlos Vertiz head the "Patria Roja" faction, which apparently consists mostly of university students but seems to be larger than the Paredes group. The pro-Chinese PCP reportedly has some influence among a small number of unions, including some in the mining and fishing sectors.

As in previous years, pro-Chinese students continued to control university student federations. Elections to the San Marcos University Student Federation, held in March (despite a law prohibiting such elections, but with a small student participation), gave 4,914 votes to the pro-Chinese Revolutionary Student Front (Frente Estudiantil Revolucionario; FER). José Ñique de la Puente (a nephew of the former guerrilla and founder of the MIR, Luis de la Puente Uceda) was elected president. The FER's platform sought the abrogation of the university law passed by the military government in 1969 and the creation of a joint administration composed of students, faculty, and staff to control the university. To achieve these demands the FER called for an indefinite strike at San Marcos on 20 April, whereupon the administration decided to end the semester.

Toward the end of the year, the military government released a new education law, to be enacted in the immediate future, which would provide for the reestablishment of student representation in the university at all administrative and academic levels. On 27 December, however, the Peruvian Student Federation—a body that has been inactive since 1963 and now is apparently in the process of reorganization—issued a communiqué criticizing several aspects of the proposed educational reform and asking for authentic university autonomy, "without the supervision of supra-university organizations." The same communiqué demanded the release from prison of student leader Ñique de la Puente and the return to Peru of Rolando Breña Pantoja, a former president of the San Marcos University Student Federation, expelled from the country by the military government on 15 September.

The only known pro-Chinese PCP statement on international issues was provided by a letter of greetings signed by Saturnino Paredes on behalf of the Central Committee and sent to the Chinese Communist Party on its fiftieth anniversary. The letter stated that this occasion signified the "triumph of the proletariat in the most populous country of the world" and that Mao Tse-tung's thought belonged "not only to the Chinese people, but also to the revolutionary peoples of the world." (*Peking Review*, 13 August.)

Publications. The Paredes group of the pro-Chinese PCP publishes *Bandera Roja*. The "Patria Roja" faction publishes *Patria Roja*. Both newspapers appear irregularly. The FER publishes *El Amauta*.

*   *   *

In addition to the above-mentioned communist parties, there exist among Peru's extreme left various groups of Castroite and Trotskyist orientation, which although small in membership maintain some ideological influence among young people.

The MIR. The Movement of the Revolutionary Left, originally an Aprista Party splinter group heavily influenced by the Cuban Revolution, was founded by Luis de la Puente Uceda. It reached national prominence through an active peasant guerrilla movement (during 1965) that ended with most leaders either killed in action or imprisoned.

The extent of the MIR membership is not known, but apparently the movement has some influence in the universities. Ricardo Gadea is the principal MIR leader. Elio Portocarrero Ríos is another important figure. Both men were released from prison on 22 December 1970 following a political amnesty.

The MIR continued in 1971 to maintain a critical attitude toward the military government. It issued a communiqué in January listing a six-point minimum program to achieve the integration of the "revolutionary left." Such program called for the expulsion of all "imperialist enterprises," especially those in mining; free land to the farmers; basic family wages for all workers; social security for the unemployed; suspension of housing rents and the turning over of housing property to the people; and diplomatic and trade relations with all socialist countries. The same communiqué asserted that the "only revolutionary alternative possible" for Peru was socialism and that the "conciliation of classes advocated by the junta is nothing but a way to break the revolutionary mobilization of the masses."

There were reports in mid-June that the MIR, together with the FIR and the VR, had organized a guerrilla group in Oxapampa, Pasco Department. But a communiqué issued by the MIR on 18 July denied such reports and labeled them "provocative maneuvers" by the Aprista Party and the U.S. mining enterprises designed to justify repression against the "workers and socialist and anti-imperialist movements."

The organ of the MIR is a clandestine newspaper, *Voz Rebelde.*

The ELN. The Army of National Liberation, founded in 1962 by former members of the PCP, participated also in the peasant guerrilla movement of 1965 (although its activities were not coordinated with those of the MIR). Its main leader, Héctor Béjar Rivera, was released from prison on 22 December 1970 in the government's general political amnesty.

Although in previous years Béjar had assumed a critical attitude toward the military government, holding that there could be no revolution "from above," he evinced a change of mind during 1971. In declarations to the Cuban news agency Prensa Latina (11 April), Béjar stated the armed forces had indeed assumed a revolutionary role and that this was possible because of the "absence of a Marxist political vanguard backed by the masses, the decline of the oligarchy, and the weakening of organizations representing the masses." He also called upon the left groups to "support the construction of a new society" because "a revolution can begin without the people but cannot fully succeed without them."

Béjar is working with the government at present, serving as an official in the social mobilization agency SINAMOS.

The VR. The Revolutionary Vanguard is a Marxist-Leninist party founded by former Aprista Party members in 1965. It advocates armed confrontation as a means of achieving socialism, but holds that its members should have theoretical and practical training before engaging in actual struggle.

The VR is composed primarily of intellectuals; it includes some workers as members but apparently no peasants. It is considered to have a significant following among university students.

Apparently, the VR split on 19 April when a new party, the Marxist Workers Party (Partido Obrero Marxista) was formed by Ricardo Napurí. This new group declared that the VR had failed to assume a "coherent ideological position" vis-à-vis the government and that personal disagreements existed with Ricardo Letts Colmenares, the leader of the VR.

In the March elections to choose representatives to the San Marcos University Student Federation, the VR candidates obtained 1,914 votes, a gain of 655 over 1970.

The FIR. The Revolutionary Leftist Front is a Trotskyist party associated with the United Secretariat faction of the Fourth International. It is led by Hugo Blanco, who in 1962 sought to radicalize peasant unions in the department of Cuzco, believing that political agitation from within would encourage peasants to claim land and would lead eventually to the larger goal of armed struggle. Blanco was released from prison in December 1970 under the political amnesty. Because of his active involvement in public meetings and his expressed opposition to the government, Blanco was deported to Mexico on 15 September.

Blanco showed a very critical attitude. In declaration on 20 January (*Gente*, Lima), he stated that all changes in Peru were only to the "benefit of the industrial bourgeoisie" and not the masses. In another interview (see *Intercontinental Press*, New York, 18 October), he said that the reforms implemented by the government were "confined within the capitalist system" and that they would "lead toward industrial development of the nation without severing its ties to imperialism."

Although closely watched by the government, Blanco became politically active. He participated in the "First Anti-Imperialist Congress," held in Lima in June and attended by various unidentified leftists. In a press conference following the congress, Blanco affirmed that an anti-imperialist campaign would be initiated in July and that it would seek the nationalization of all large mines and the expulsion from Peru of several U.S. mining enterprises. It was also indicated that part of this campaign would involve support for the "miners' struggle for the nationalization of mines."

Blanco expressed disagreement with Fidel Castro's endorsement of the military government. He termed Castro's approval of the junta "an unfortunate capitulation to the pressure of the Soviet bureaucracy."

The FIR has a monthly publication, *Revolución Peruana*.

Nelly Stromquist

Puerto Rico

Up to 1971, communism in Puerto Rico was represented by the miniscule Puerto Rican Communist Party (Partido Comunista Puertorriqueño; PCP) under the leadership of Félix Ojedo Ruiz and the similarly small and isolated Puerto Rican Socialist League (Liga Socialista Puertorriqueña; LSP) under Juan Antonio Corretjer. The PCP has close links with the Communist Party, USA (CPUSA) and shares its pro-Soviet orientation. The LSP is identified with the Progressive Labor Party (PLP) of the United States; up to the end of 1971 the PLP supported Mao and the Chinese Communist Party. Together the PCP and LSP probably have fewer than 100 members.

A party that far overshadows the PCP and LSP is the Movimiento pro Independencia (MPI), under Juan Mari Bras. The MPI has been in existence for fifteen years and is believed to have 750 to 1,500 members and up to 5,000 supporters. The MPI in the past has primarily attracted Puerto Ricans dedicated to achieving national independence. It differed from the Puerto Rican Independence Party (PIP) by rejecting reformist and constitutional methods. The MPI has strong nationalist origins and reveres the traditions of the old Nationalist Party (Partido Nacionalista). It continues the annual pilgrimages initiated in 1930 by Pedro Albizu to commemorate the "Grito de Lares"—the uprising of 23 September 1868 against Spain led by Ramón Betances. Where formerly the pilgrimage was small and the largest turnout was 1,000 persons, it has been renewed by the MPI with spectacular results. Participants reportedly numbered 25,000 in 1968 and increased to about 100,000 in 1971 (*America*, 24 July 1971).

Main MPI support has come from students in the universities and high schools. Recently this has been extended to include factory workers and peasants as a result of emphasis on economic and social issues—in contrast to the conservative PIP program. During 1971 the MPI moved to transform itself into a political party that would combine nationalism and socialism based on the principles of Marxism-Leninism. Its Eighth National Assembly was held on 19-21 November in San Juan as the founding convention of the Puerto Rican Socialist Party (PSP), with some 500 delegates, visitors, and guests in attendance. More than half of the delegates were factory workers, with the next largest group comprising high school and university students. Jenaro Rentas, the organizational secretary of the MPI, reported that the movement had members working in 100 factories, 43 neighborhoods, 33 high schools, and 8 universities, and that its publication *Claridad*, had reached a weekly circulation of 40,000. Rentas added that MPI had 53 full-time organizers, 1,500 active cadres, and a total of about 6,000 members. Both the Federation of University Students (FUPI) and the Federation of High School Students (FEPI) are active supporters. Over 1,000 workers have been organized into the new National Union of Workers, sponsored by the MPI.

According to a report on the MPI assembly, when it completed its sessions on late afternoon of 21 November "a new party had come into being; a new flag, red with a single white star; a new central committee and a political commission under the leadership of Juan Mari Bras as general secretary; and a new ambitious program for advancing the struggle for independence and socialism'' (*The Guardian*, New York, 1 December). The following week a mass rally was held in Bayamon to commemorate the formation of the new party. About 5,000 ''militantes'' gathered at an indoor sports arena, under hugh portraits of Che Guevara, Ramon Betances, Pedro Albizu Campos, and V. I. Lenin—the symbolic figures of the new movement, to hear the main address by Juan Mari Bras, who declared:

> We believe in the inalienable right of our country to independence and total sovereignty; in the right of the Puerto Rican people to recover completely their patrimony from those persons, corporations, governments or foreign forces who have taken it from them; the right to the progressive socialization of all means of production, taking them out of the hands of both strangers and nationals; and the construction of a socialist society where there will be neither exploited nor exploiters. He went on to proclaim ''the right of the patriotic people to utilize all forms of struggle available to them, including revolutionary violence against the repressive violence of the system, in order to exercise the above rights.'' (*Ibid.*, 8 December.)

Bras outlined the eleven fundamental principles of the PSP:

1. The construction of a socialist Puerto Rico based upon the dictatorship of the proletariat.
2. Complete political independence of the Puerto Rican nation.
3. The PSP bases itself on the science of Marxism-Leninism.
4. A pledge to guarantee the democratic rights of the Puerto Rican working class in a socialist society, based upon full worker participation in free elections, an open press and a secret ballot.
5. A pledge to use revolutionary power to suppress counter-revolutionary resistance within the framework of protecting the democratic rights of the working class combined with an intensive educational campaign to eliminate the remnants of petty bourgeois ideology.
6. Workers' control, in a socialist Puerto Rico, over the direction of the economy, politics and education, along with a people's militia to defend the revolution.
7. Guaranteeing the rights of youth.
8. A guarantee of religious freedom.
9. Equal rights for women.
10. Recognizing ''overseas'' Puerto Ricans—that is, those in North America—as part of the Puerto Rican nation.
11. Affirmation of the principles of proletarian internationalism based upon a recognition of diverse forms of struggle in different countries; independent strategy, tactics, organization and ideology in the various countries of the anti-imperialist camp; and the rejection of any concept of a center of leadership in the world revolutionary movement. Specifically, the PSP deplored the divisions within the socialist camp while refusing to take sides in the Sino-Soviet ideological dispute.

Linda Jenness, presidential candidate of the Socialist Workers' Party in the United States, attended the rally at Bayamon to present the greetings of her party. In turn, the convention saluted its revolutionary allies in the United States with a militant declaration on the Vietnam war, freedom for U. S. communist Angela Davis, and the like. Luis A. Ferré, governor of Puerto Rico, was described as an ''ally of the most Neanderthal sectors of the United States.'' (*The Militant*, 10 December.)

The Puerto Rican Communist Party in 1970 rejected an appeal by its former general secretary, Juan Santos Rivera, that it merge with the MPI. Gus Hall, of the CPUSA, on his visit to Puerto Rico in January 1971, urged a policy of cooperation. The PCP decided to maintain its own identity, although members were permitted to participate in MPI affairs. Later the MPI's formation of a new party—the PSP—left the PCP in an isolated position in the political life of Puerto Rico and faced with the problem created by the neutral attitude of the PSP on the Sino-Soviet conflict. The Puerto Rican Socialist League, consistent with its opposition (corresponding with that of the PLP in the United States) to all national independence movements, is critical of and opposed to the PSP.

The forming of the PSP led to a dramatic reversal of the traditional opposition of its predecessor—the MPI—to electoral participation. The MPI in the past pursued a strict policy of boycotting the polls. Its refusal to vote in the plebiscite of 1967 and the regular elections of 1968 was based on its view that the electoral process had been corrupted by the "colonialist" government. The MPI relied primarily on the militant actions of its supporters to advance its program. The formation of the PSP was accompanied by a shift in strategy in favor of elections. At its founding convention and at the rally in Bayamon, the PSP announced its willingness to enter into a united front agreement with the Independendistas (PIP). Five members of the PIP Central Committee, including its president, Rubin Berrios Martínez, attended the rally and were given honored seats on the dais. When Berrios and Bras embraced on the platform, the audience cheered and clamored for unity. Berrios greeted the assembly warmly but avoided any specific commitments. In an interview, Bras declared:

> There has been a dramatic increase in the backing of independence by the Puerto Rican people. If the independence party and the Socialist party join to form a united front, we can very rapidly organize, in a few months, not less than 1,000 committees of a united front in all neighborhoods, communities, public housing projects, towns, barrios, throughout the island. And that would put the independent forces in a position to make a good utilization of the electoral process next year. A good utilization would mean to be in the center of the political debate in Puerto Rico.

Bras predicted that a coalition could win 20 to 22 percent of the vote in 1972. (*Guardian*, 8 December).

*   *   *

Independent of the MPI and its revolutionary appeal, an organization known as the "Armed Liberation Commandos" (CAL) came into being in 1967. It is a clandestine, terrorist movement, reportedly led by Alfonso Beal. It claimed credit for 100 bombings during 1971 in the hotel section of San Juan. Juan Angel Silén in his book *Hacia una vision positiva del Puertorriqueño* (Toward a Positive Vision for the Puerto Rican), published in 1970 at Bilbao, Spain, speaks of the CAL as the "armed power of the independence struggle." Its objective, he says, is to undermine the economic base of "imperialism" and provoke a crisis in the "colonial system" in the country. Its "military" targets are firms such as Woolworth's, Pueblo, Kresge, Sears, and "other U.S. enterprises." El Candado, the hotel section in San Juan, is considered the "war zone" that must be destroyed as the symbol of colonialism. As to military service, Silén reports that CAL has issued a warning: "For each Puerto Rican youth jailed for refusing service in the armed forces of the United States, we will execute a Yankee." He thus concludes that no North American can feel safe in Puerto Rico. (Pp. 21, 215.) Neither the MPI nor the PSP has endorsed the terrorist acts of the CAL. Nevertheless, the MPI has supported closing the hotels in San Juan, and it endorsed the action that led to destruction of the ROTC building at the university in Rio Piedras.

*   *   *

The formation of the PSP sheds a new light on the question of the political future of Puerto Rico. In past years, the issue appeared to be between commonwealth and statehood. Popular support for independence seemed to be negligible or moribund. But plebiscites of the past are not a reliable guide to the future. The view expressed by former Governor Rexford G. Tugwell in 1953 that Puerto Rico is "likely to become a State because no proud and achieving people can go on being excluded from the highest political process of the nation of which it is a part" is now under serious challenge.

The present governor, Luis A. Ferré, proposes a "jibaro state" that would preserve the ethnic and cultural traditions of the people. The proposal itself reveals the dilemma. The problems of the "bootstrap" economy, widespread unemployment, the poverty of the barrios on the mainland, the split in the Popular Democratic Party, and pressures of the "Third World" have all contributed to a surge toward independence. The elections of 1972 may clarify the road ahead.

*   *   *

Publications. The LSP publishes irregularly *Pabellón*, *El Socialista*, and *Correo de la Quincena*. LSP statements and reports also appear in the fortnightly organ of the Progressive Labor Party, *Challenge/Desafío*, New York. The PCP publishes a newspaper, *Pueblo*, and an information bulletin, *El Proletario*. Both appear irregularly. The MPI publishes the weeklies *Claridad* and *Carta Semanal*. Reportage also appears in *The Guardian*, New York.

New York City   George Charney

United States of America

The communist movement in the United States includes a number of rival parties, with estimated memberships ranging from fewer than 10 persons to some 15,000 and offering a broad variety of views in domestic and foreign policies. In addition to these "orthodox" movements, there are numerous groups (primarily among young persons and the country's ethnic minorities) that in varying degrees accept Marxism-Leninism as a guiding ideology. Mercurial in their political views and often heterogeneous organizationally, these latter groups, such as Weatherman and the Black Panther Party, continued in 1971 to represent a challenge to traditional communist parties (see below).

THE CPUSA. The oldest and largest among orthodox movements in the United States is the Communist Party, USA (CPUSA), founded in 1919. The party became legal in 1967, following a decision by the U.S. Court of Appeals for the District of Columbia (see *YICA*, 1968, p. 834), but electoral restrictions work against it in certain states.

In February 1971, CPUSA General Secretary Gus Hall reportedly claimed a party membership of approximately 15,000. This represented an increase of some 2,000 to 3,000 over the last figure, publicized in 1969 (see *YICA*, 1970, p. 479). The party's youth movement, the Young Workers' Liberation League (YWLL), founded in 1970, reported in June that its membership had increased from an original 600 to 1,000 (*Daily World*, 16 June).

The CPUSA is not represented politically at either national or local levels. The party's most recent major bid for elective office was made in 1968, when it sponsored the candidacies of Charlene Mitchell and Michael Zagarell for President and Vice-President of the United States, respectively. This was the first time that the CPUSA had contested a Presidential election since 1940, when then General Secretary Earl Browder received 48,579 votes, with the party on the ballot in 32 states. In 1968 the CPUSA was on the ballot in the states of Minnesota and Washington, and received 1,075 votes out of a total of some 73 million. On 25 August 1971 the CPUSA announced that Gus Hall and Jarvis Tyner, chairman of the YWLL, would be candidates in the 1972 elections for President and Vice-President, respectively (*Daily World*, 26 August).

Organization and Leadership. The party's Nineteenth National Convention, held in 1969, reelected Gus Hall as general secretary and Henry Winston as chairman. It also chose an 83-member National Committee. This committee, in turn, elected the National Executive Board (or National Political Committee, as later called). In 1971 this latter group was believed to comprise the following persons: Gus Hall, Matthew Hallinan, James Jackson, Arnold Johnson, Claude Lightfoot, Hyman Lumer, George Meyers, Charlene Mitchell, William Patterson, John Pittman, Irving Potash, Roscoe Proctor, Jose Ristorucci, Daniel Rubin, Rasheed Storey, Jarvis Tyner, William Weinstone, Henry Winston, Carl Winter, Helen Winter, and Michael Zagarell. Most Political Committee members are also party officials. In addition to the aforementioned posts held by Hall and Winston, the following were officials in 1971: Hallinan (education director); Jackson (international affairs secretary); Johnson (public relations director and secretary, Peace Commission; formerly chairman of the latter, he was replaced at the beginning of the year by Gil Green); Lightfoot (co-chairman, Black Liberation Commission); Lumer (editor, *Political Affairs*); Meyers (co-chairman, Labor Commission); Mitchell (secretary, Black Liberation Commission); Patterson (co-chairman, Black Liberation Commission); Pitman (co-editor, *Daily World*); Proctor (co-chairman, Labor Commission); Rubin (national organizational secretary); Carl Winter (co-editor, *Daily World*); and Zargarell (national youth director).

Apart from its party structure, the CPUSA in 1971 had no official auxiliary bodies (such as organizations for young persons and women.) Nonetheless, the party was active in a number of organizations which, though professing independence of the CPUSA, followed party policy and directives and whose leaderships were composed primarily of party members. The most significant of these is the above mentioned YWLL. Despite investigations during the year by the Subversive Activities Control Board to determine whether the YWLL was a CPUSA front, the youth organization openly proclaimed its "fraternal ties" with the party. At the end of the year one of the CPUSA draft these for its 1972-scheduled Twentieth Convention noted under pary "achievements" since the last convention, "launching of the YWLL" (*ibid.*, 22 December). During 1971 the leadership of the YWLL included: Jarvis Tyner, chairman; Matty Berkelhammer, organizational secretary; Carolyn Black, black liberation secretary; Judy Edelman, labor secretary; Roque Ristorucci, publications director; and Michael Zagarell, education director.

The CPUSA continued to be active in a number of organizations opposing U.S. policy in Vietnam. Although the party appeared to have considerable influence in a number of local groups, it did not control any of the major national movements. The most prominent of the latter included the National Peace Action Coalition (NPAC)—controlled by the Trotskyist Socialist Workers' Party (SWP)—and the National Coalition Against War, Racism and Repression, which early in the year, changed its name to People's Coalition for Peace and Justice (PCPJ).[1] The CPUSA aligned itself with the PCPJ, an "umbrella" organization comprising groups of a broad variety of political and tactical persuasions, and repeatedly attacked the views and policies of the NPAC (see below).

The CPUSA derives its principal support from states on the east and west coasts, primarily New York and California. Within organized labor the party's influence continued to be minimal despite a concerted effort to extend its role, particularly among the rank-and-file. At a party "industrial conference," held 11—12 December in Chicago, Gus Hall claimed that there had been a "sharp improvement" in CPUSA "industrial work" since the last such meeting, almost years ago, but added that this comparison was "inadequate." He stated: "We must compare the work of today with the reality of today. In that sense, it doesn't quite match up." (*Ibid.*, 16 December.) As its vehicle for work within the trade unions, the party used the National Coordinating Committee for Trade Union Action and Democracy, a body formed in June 1970 (see *YICA*, 1971, pp. 345-46; James West, "The Rank and File Movements," in *Political Affairs*, May, pp. 23-39, and *ibid.*, November, special issue on "The Class Struggle and the Trade Union Movement in the U.S.").

---

[1]The PCPJ claims to have developed "close relations" with a number of groups including the Fellowship of Reconciliation, War Resisters League, Women Strike for Peace, Women's International League for Peace and Freedom, Clergy and Laymen Concerned, the Mayday Collectives, National Welfare Rights Organization, Southern Christian Leadership Conference, the Vietnam Veterans Against the War, the Welfare Rights Organization, and the Chicano movement in California (*Daily World*, 3 April and 4 December).

The PCPJ criticized the single issue ("Out of Vietnam Now") approach of the NPAC, favoring a multi issue program combining domestic issues with opposition to the war. Among other things, the PCPJ condemned the NPAC for not signing "The People's Peace Treaty," and for its unwillingness to set a date to end the war. (*Ibid.*, 7 August and 4 December.)

Party Internal Affairs. There were indications during 1971 of ethnic friction within the party. A report on the 12-14 March conference noted that "the most prolonged discussion during the national committee meeting was held around Gus Hall's report on the influence of white chauvinism on the people's movement and its 'seepage' into the Left and into the Communist Party" (*Daily World*, 23 March). Hall claimed that white chauvinism was the "most important danger" confronting the "unity of the working class." He noted that progress in combating it within the party had been "inadequate." Portions of Hall's report were reprinted in the newspaper's weekly magazine section for 3 April, and the full text was published in early summer as a pamphlet, *Racism: The Nation's Most Dangerous Pollutant* (New York, New Outlook Publishers, 1971, 40 pp.). Although the party placed "the fight against white chauvinism in the forefront of its responsibility," by the end of the year it was still, according to the aforementioned pre-convention draft theses, "plagued by routinism and a lack of self-critical examination on the part of white comrades" (*Daily World*, 22 December).

These draft theses included other elements of self-evaluation during the period since the Nineteenth Convention of 1969. It was claimed that the CPUSA had made "substantial headway" in becoming "more decisively" a working class political party; the *Daily World*'s circulation had doubled; the party's "influence within the Left" had "considerably increased, particularly among the youth," and it had "become a significant force in the trade union rank and file movement." The theses also claimed improvements in party structure, standards of organization, participation in ideological struggle and a drive which had "tripled prior recruiting ... especially among Black workers and Black youth as well as among youth generally." On the negative side, the theses focused primarily on the party's clubs, which reportedly suffered from "a lack of initiative and dynamic inner life, from routinism and conservatism." It was also stated that there was a "serious gap in communications between the party leadership on all levels and the club." Noting that the "fight to improve the work and life of the party clubs" was "a cardinal task," the theses proposed the restoration of "membership books and dues stamps as a much-needed basis for a turn to ending the organizational looseness." Finally, the theses noted that "looseness and permissiveness on ideological questions allowed on the grounds of tactical necessity [had] weakened the firmness and unity of the party in the mass ideological struggle." (*Ibid.*)

About 100 delegates attended the already mentioned two day industrial conference of the CPUSA during December in Chicago. Gus Hall lauded young black and white workers for their enthusiasm while stressing the necessity for "ideological clarity" in the working class—an advance that can only come about under direction of the Communist Party. The central theme of the conference was to discuss ways to advance the Party in the ranks of the working class. (*Ibid.*, 16 December.)

Domestic Views and Policies. Jarvis Tyner, national chairman of the YWLL, admonished the Weatherman (a violent splinter group of SDS) for not making mobilization of the working class and black people the primary revolutionary objective. The Weatherman had recently admitted failure of its terrorist bombing program and now advocated commune living and the adoption of revolutionary culture for middle-class white youth. It was criticized for "petty-bourgeois fantasies," and Tyner advised the group that it was a long way from achieving working-class consciousness (*ibid.*, 2 January).

Angela Davis, former acting assistant professor at the University of California at Los Angeles who held membership in both the CPUSA and the Black Panther Party (BPP), was brought to trial in 1971 for murder, conspiracy, and kidnaping in connection with an attempted escape from the Marin County, California, courthouse in August 1970. The YWLL announced its "key task" to free Angela Davis. The group encouraged Miss Davis's supporters to recruit young white workers in a drive to obtain her release (*ibid.*, 18 June). At a three-day meeting of the national committee,

National Chairman Henry Winston stated the CPUSA goal for the year as "Freedom for Angela Davis" (*ibid*, 13 July). In a related operation, the PCJP promulgated its intention to organize 100 "Free Angela Davis" teach-ins during 1971 at colleges throughout the country (*ibid*., 3 April).

The CPUSA disagreed with the program of both the Huey Newton and the Eldridge Cleaver factions of the BPP. Early in the year, it denied a charge by BPP Minister of Information Eldridge Cleaver that the CPUSA was participating in a campaign to free Angela Davis at the cost of "concealing the trial of [BPP chairman] Bobby Seale" (*ibid*., 6 February). Henry Winston charged Cleaver with doing a ":distinct disservice" to the fight against "racism" with his charge. According to Winston, Angela Davis personified the plight of "all political prisoners" (*ibid*., 28 January).

Charlene Mitchell, secretary for the CPUSA Commission of Black Liberation, accused Cleaver's faction of using "individualistic, anarchistic, adventuristic, elitist and provocative tactics" because Cleaver insisted a revolutionary situation existed in the United States that justified the use of armed force (*ibid*., 11 February).

The CPUSA contended that neither the "black capitalism" of BPP Defense Minister Huey Newton nor the "ultra-revolutionary rhetoric" of Eldrigde Cleaver provided acceptable guidelines for the Black Liberation movement of the party. The CPUSA criticized both factions for basing their policies on the "Lumpenproletariat"—an offense to the black unemployed who were workers and not Lumpenproletariat. According to Henry Winston, Huey Newton's plan to "wait until the masses are ready to pick up the gun" was in reality an abandonment of the "people's struggle." Winston accused Newton of implying that anything short of armed force in the ultimate sense of revolution was inadequate. (*Political Affairs*, August; *Daily World*, 18 June).

The CPUSA regarded the drive for women's liberation as "one of the most important aspects of the class struggle in the United States today." The party warned that the problem of obtaining equality for women, whether black or white, was possible only in the framework "of the class struggle." CPUSA spokesmen noted that the ideological considerations of the struggle for womens' liberation must be underscored in the future (*Political Affairs*, July).

International Views, Policies,and Contacts. In 1971, the CPUSA continued to support the policies of the Soviet Union and reaffirmed this alignment at the Twenty-fourth Congress of the Commist Party of the Soviet Union (CPSU) in Moscow. General Secretary Gus Hall addressed the gathering and described Soviet party members in the following manner: "You, Soviet Communists, are the advance guard in giving real life a quality, a beauty that till now appeared only in poetry and song" (*Daily World*, 15 April).

The CPUSA joined the Soviet government newspaper *Izvestia* in denying the existence of anti-Semitism in the U.S.S.R., claiming that attempts to illustrate such a state of affairs was a "deliberate distortion" (*ibid*., 21 January).

In a meeting at Prague with Gustav Husák, first secretary of the Communist Party of Czechoslovakia, Hall stated that "both parties confirm their determination to continue their support for the liberation struggle of the nations of Africa, Asia, and Latin America, against imperialism, against all forms of colonialism" (*ibid*., 30 March).

The CPUSA highlighted in its press various cultural, economic and political developments in Cuba. The favorable reporting of these events followed a policy started in 1969 with the Soviet-Cuban rapprochement (see *YICA*, 1970, p. 350). Extensive coverage was provided by the CPUSA for the celebration of Cuba's first national congress on education and culture in Havana during April (*ibid*., 31 July). At the CPSU Congress Gus Hall lauded Cuba by stating that "we glory in socialist Cuba's every advance" (*ibid*., 15 April).

The announced trip by President Nixon to the People's Republic of China (RPC) in 1972 engendered critical comments by the CPUSA against the Chinese communists, whom it accused of "sabotaging the unity of the people" (*ibid.*, 16 April). Nixon's attempt to negotiate a new relationship with the PRC was seen by the CPUSA only as a ploy "to advance the interest of imperialism." When Chinese Premier Chou En-lai used the term "two superpowers" to describe the Soviet Union and the United States, the CPUSA censured him for disregarding the distinctions between socialism and capitalism and for considering an alliance with "United States imperialism directed against the Soviet Union and Japan as common foes" (*ibid.*, 30 and 31 December; *Political Affairs*, September).

Publications. The two principal publications of the CPUSA are *Daily World*, a newspaper published in New York five times a week (Tuesday through Saturday), and the monthly theoretical organ *Political Affairs*. Other publications following the party's line include *People's World*, a weekly San Francisco newspaper; *Freedomways*, a quarterly review addressed to Blacks; *Labor Today*, a bimonthly trade union magazine; *American Dialogue*, a quarterly cultural magazine; and *New World Review*, a quarterly on international issues. In June 1970, the CPUSA initiated publication of *Jewish Affairs*, a bimonthly newsletter.

*   *   *

The SWP. The Socialist Workers Party (SWP) was founded in 1938 and is the oldest and largest among Trotskyist movements in the United States. The Young Socialist Alliance (YSA) operates as the youth arm of the SWP. The three most prominent Trotskyist organizations that have split from the SWP appear to be the Workers' League, the Workers' World Party, and the Spartacist League.

The SWP and the YSA continued in 1971 to have relatively few members, yet their influence, especially on college campuses and within the movement against U.S. involvement in Vietnam, appeared to be at the 1970 level (See *YICA* 1971, p. 352). The activities of SWP and the YSA in the radicalization of high school students seemed to be more intense than previously.

The SWP is a legal party and actively participates in both national and local elections.

Leadership and Organization. The SWP held its Twenty-fourth National Convention 8-12 August in Cleveland. More than 1,100 delegates attended. Regarding anti-war plans, the convention pledged its support for demonstrations on 6 November. In terms of electoral programs, the delegates agreed to campaign actively to elect Linda Jenness and Andrew Pulley for president and vice-president, respectively, on the national SWP ticket. Resolutions were passed by the convention that included "Toward a Mass Feminist Movement" and "The Struggle for Chicano Liberation." The three-pronged program for womens' liberation comprised a demand for free abortions, free community controlled child care centers on a 24-hour basis, and increased pay as well as greater educational and job opportunities for women. The Chicano movement is centered on the concept of community control in order that residents may "control their own lives." Advances by the La Raza Unida party in Texas, Colorado, and California were noted at the convention.

The rapid SWP growth was emphasized by convention officials and underscored by the number of delegates (660) who attended the convention, almost twice the number that participated in the 1969 SWP convention. Some minority positions were put forward against certain resolutions proposed by outgoing committees (*The Militant*, 3 September; *International Socialist Review*, November).

In July, the YSA held the largest national committee plenum in its history. More than 85 YSA leaders present reelected Frank Boehm as national chairman, Cindy Jaquith as national secretary, and Norman Oliver as national organizational secretary. The YSA planned a recruitment drive that began in the fall and will continue through the 1972 election campaign. It hopes to exceed gains made during the 1968 SWP election campaign, when the YSA doubled its membership. Ruth Robinett delivered the womens' liberation report and stressed the national campaign to repeal all abortion laws. Norman Oliver, national Black Liberation director, noted gains in the building of a black anti-war movement. The general anti-war report presented by Dave Frankel emphasized the importance of establishing chapters of the Student Mobilization Committee on college and high school campuses throughout the country. Mirta Vida, the YSA Chicano and Latino Liberation director gave a report that elaborated on the rise of La Raza Unida parties in the Southwest and the enlargement of the Chicano anti-war movement. Cindy Jaquith contended that high school students were becoming more radicalized and that the YSA was leading the fight for "democratic rights of high school students to organize against the war and for national liberation, women's liberation, gay liberation and other struggles" (*The Militant*, 23 July).

Domestic Views and Policies. Organizing mass demonstrations in opposition to U.S. policy in Southeast Asia remained of central concern to the SWP. In February some 2,000 activists attended a national student anti-war conference at the Catholic University of America, sponsored by the Student Mobilization Committee (SMC) to End the War in Vietnam. SMC national officers Don Gurewitz and Debby Bustin proposed an all-out effort to support the mass antiwar marches planned for 24 April in Washington, D.C., and San Francisco. This action, organized by the NPAC, received overwhelming acceptance. At a Third World workshop of the conference, Chicano delegates agreed that a wholehearted effort against the war on 24 April would be the best way to help the Chicano people determine their own future. (*Ibid.*, 5 March.)

The People's Coalition for Peace and Justice (allied with the CPUSA) subsequently decided to cosponsor with the NPAC the 24 April march on Washington. Subsequently the NPAC, in conjunction with the SWP, criticized the People's Coalition for Peace and Justice because of its opposition to "democratic decision-making"; the PCPJ, on the other hand, criticized the NPAC for "manipulation." The SWP supported National Peace Action Coalition also claimed that the PCPJ's multi-issue approach, combining opposition to the war with domestic social issues, had not succeeded because "all of the programs it has projected so far have been absolute failures." (*Ibid.*, 2 April.) The SWP criticism of the CPUSA continued after the 24 April for agreeing to cooperate and supporting "liberal capitalist politicians and the Democratic Party in particular" (*ibid.*, 4 June).

The SWP also admonished the "Mayday Tribe," a small cluster of young anti-war protestors, which had announced that it would "close down the government" in confrontation-type demonstrations at Washington, D.C. during May. According to the SWP, political protests that verge on disruption and engage in civil disobedience are inimical to the building of a mass movement involving great numbers of American citizens (*ibid.*, 14 and 21 May).

Over 1,400 participants gathered at the national anti-war convention sponsored by the NPAC at Cleveland. The convention approved plans for mass demonstrations against the Vietnam war on 22 April. New national NPAC coordinators were elected: Debby Bustin, Stephanie Coontz, and Katherine Sojourner (*ibid.*, 17 December).

The SWP joined the CPUSA in denouncing the Black Panther Party for deviation from accepted ideology and programs. The SWP claimed that the Panther contention that states and nations no longer existed was false. Both factions were included in the SWP rebuke which asserted that "neither faction provides anything resembling a program that can advance the Black liberation movement." Specifically, the SWP reprimanded the Panther Party for failing to mobilize the black community around nationalistic demands, failing to engage in united-front actions, and building a cult of hero-worship around Huey Newton and Eldridge Cleaver (*ibid.*, 2 April).

As far as implementing the SWP women's liberation program is concerned, a national conference on abortion was held in July. It was estimated that "at least half of the 1,025 delegates were members of either the SWP or YSA." (*Daily Worker*, 20 July.) The conference initiated and took steps to organize a drive to repeal all abortion laws.

International Views and Policies. Conforming to its ideological alignment with the United Secretariat of the Fourth International, the SWP criticized policies of both the Soviet Union and Communist China. For example, the SWP revealed opposition to "repressive uses of psychiatric techniques" in Soviet hospitals. The criticism described the U.S.S.R. practice of confining individuals opposed to certain government policies in mental hospitals for "examination and treatment." (*The Militant*, 10 December.)

At its Twenty-fourth Convention the SWP took the People's Republic of China to task for following a restricted nationalist concept of "building socialism in one country," a policy that allegedly relegates the world revolution to the interests of the Chinese Communists (*ibid.*, 3 September). The SWP defended the Chinese government from extreme attacks by the Progressive Labor Party, which had labeled mainland China "a capitalist state" (*ibid.*, 24 September).

The SWP also accused the Cuban leadership, supported by the Soviet Union, of retreating from "socialist democracy." The Communist Party of Cuba was condemned for imprisoning a "distinguished revolutionary poet, Heberto Padillo, because he had expressed critical views of the regime, and then releasing him only after he admitted his guilt and agreed to name other writers who had been similarly critical of Cuban party policies (*ibid.*, 3 September).

Publications. During 1971 the two major publications of the SWP were a weekly newspaper, *The Militant*, and a monthly journal, *International Socialist Review*. The YSA published a fortnightly newspaper, *The Young Socialist Organizer*. Similarly, the United Secretariat of the Fourth International continued to publish the weekly *Intercontinental Press*.

*   *   *

The PLP. The Progressive Labor Party (PLP) originated in 1962, after expulsion of Milton Rosen and Mortimer Scheer from the CPUSA the year before. The PLP initially had been known as the Progressive Labor Movement. Its present name was adopted by a founding convention held at New York in April 1965. Until 1971, the PSP followed a pro-Chinese Communist line and was described as Maoist. The PLP does not publish details about its organizational structure.

Domestic Views and Policies. In June, almost 150 faculty members and students met in Boston to attend the first eastern regional conference of the University Action Group (UAG). According to PLP, many of the graduate students and college teachers assembled at Boston had left the New University Conference, a radicals in the professions group, to form UAG because of the "anti-communist practice" of the New University Conference. The UAG meeting decided to launch a national program of building a worker-student-faculty alliance. The alliance was designed to foster a "pro-working class organization of intellectuals on the nation's campuses." (*Challenge*, 10 July.)

In general, the PLP felt that by promoting a vigorous worker-student alliance, many students would be given an opportunity to adopt a perspective for "the class hatred" they possess. The PLP claimed that such a perspective would provide the framework for an anti-imperialist movement focusing on "racist unemployment" and not the Vietnam war.

The PLP admitted that it had not succeeded in persuading the majority of students who had joined the anti-war movement to adopt an anti-imperialist point of view. However, it took credit for the fact that many activists involved in the peace movement did adopt the platform demanding immediate U.S. withdrawal from Vietnam and without recourse to negotiations (*Progressive Labor*, August).

The PLP confessed that in 1970 it had been unable to develop real unity with minority students on college campuses. It contended that improvements were made in 1971 because of a change of approach by the PLP which accentuated commingling of white and minority students and abandonment of policies that encouraged the separation of the races in any way (*ibid.*).

Although the PLP agreed that Angela Davis "should be freed," it took the opportunity to state its opposition to the CPUSA for promoting nationalism and nonviolence (*ibid.*, February).

International Views and Policies. The most difficult problem faced by the PLP in 1971 was how to deal with the emerging policy of coexistence between the United States and the PRC. It dealt with the situation by renouncing the pro-Chinese ideological and programmatic guidelines it had followed since emergence in 1962. In an analysis, the PLP maintained that the "Great Proletarian Cultural Revolution" in China had been started to mask early opportunist policies of the Chinese Communist Party (CCP). This opportunism allegedly reached its zenith with the invitation to President Nixon to visit China in 1972. (*Challenge*, 21 August.) The PLP concluded that, by contemplating a rapprochement with the United States, the CCP had "betrayed the revolution." It then denounced the idea of a "united front with revisionists" and accused Mao Tse-tung of pursuing right-wing policies and thwarting the revolutionary process in China, with the result that China was "back on the path of capitalism." (*Progressive Labor*, November.) Instead of future reliance on Mao and the PRC, the PLP reemphasized its dependence on the workers, "not only the workers in the United States but all over the world." (*Ibid.*)

Publications. During 1971 the PLP issued two publications: *Challenge Desafio*, a monthly English-Spanish newspaper, and *Progressive Labor*, a bimonthly journal (in 1971, only three issues of the latter were published).

Edward J. Bacciocco, Jr.

Uruguay

The Communist Party of Uruguay (Partido Comunista del Uruguay; PCU) dates its formation from September 1920, when the congress of the Socialist Party voted in favor of joining the Communist International. The present name was adopted in April 1921. The party has always been legal. It is firmly pro-Soviet.

The Movement of the Revolutionary Left (Movimiento de Izquierda Revolucionaria; MIR) was founded in 1963 and is pro-Chinese. The Revolutionary Workers' Party (Partido Obrero Revolucionario; POR), originally founded in 1944 as the Revolutionary Workers' League, is Trotskyist and is aligned with the International Secretariat (Posadas faction) of the Fourth International. The Revolutionary Party of the Workers (Partido Revolucionario de los Trabajadores; PRT), also Trotskyist, is aligned with the United Secretariat of the Fourth International. Numerous other leftist organizations operate in Uruguay and display Soviet, Chinese, Cuban, or nationalist leanings or combinations thereof. Among the most important are the Uruguayan Revolutionary Movement (Movimiento Revolucionario Oriental; MRO), the Socialist Party of Uruguay (Partido Socialista del Uruguay; PSU), the Uruguayan Revolutionary Armed Forces (Fuerzas Armadas Revolucionarias Orientales; FARO), and the National Liberation Movement (Movimiento de Liberación Nacional; MLN)—better known as the Tupamaros.

The PCU and most of the other left-wing parties are legal in Uruguay. Only the FARO and the MLN remain illegal on the grounds that they advocate the overthrow of the existing government.

Except for the PCU all these organizations are apparently small though no precise membership figures are known. The PCU is estimated to have 30,000 to 35,000 members, with workers accounting for about 73 per cent of the total. The population of Uruguay is 2,900,000 (estimated 1970).

The electoral strength of the PCU long resided in the Leftist Liberation Front (Frente Izquierda de Liberación; FIDEL), founded by the PCU in 1962 and composed of some ten small political and cultural groups. Luis Pedro Bonavita is president. According to the General Resolution of the Twentieth Congress of the PCU (December 1970), FIDEL represented an "advanced sector of the anti-imperialist and revolutionary forces which are growing in the republic, the fundamental part of the national left." In an electoral system that discourages voting for candidates on minority party tickets, FIDEL has had only limited success. In the 1966 election FIDEL received less than 6 per cent of the vote. In the 1971 election, held on 28 Novemeber, FIDEL was a member of the Broad Front (see below).

THE BROAD FRONT. According to Rodney Arismendi, first secretary of the PCU, the PCU had for some fifteen years tried to achieve a united left but other leftist parties in Uruguay were hesitant about forming an alliance with the communists. The idea of a leftist front received a significant boost from the formation of the Popular Unity in Chile at the end of 1969, and after the Popular Unity victory in 1970 the situation in Uruguay changed rapidly. Contacts between the Christian Democratic Party (Partido Demócrata Cristiano; PDC) and FIDEL quickly led to an agreement on a front, and by the end of the year the Broad Front (Frente Amplio; FA), as it came to be called, was a reality. By January 1971 it included the PCU, FIDEL, PDC, PSU, POR, a faction of the Colorado Party led by Senator Zelmar Michelini, a faction of the National Party led by Senator Francisco Rodríguez Camusso, a group of independent citizens led by Carlos Quijano (the publisher of the weekly newspaper *Marcha*), and several other small leftist groups. The recently formed 26th of March Movement (Movimiento 26 de Marzo), which joined the FA, is believed to be a front for the MLN (Tupamaros). Although ideological and tactical differences existed among the total of 17 member groups, it was the most far-reaching coalition in Uruguayan history.

The FA was formally launched on 5 February and in March announced its three principal candidates. They were: retired General Liber Seregni Mosquera (formerly a member of the left wing of the Colorado Party) for president; Juan José Crottogini, a professor at the University of Montevideo, for vice-president; and Dr. Hugo Villar, head of Uruguay's largest hospital, for mayor of Montevideo. In late April the FA began its election campaign with tours of the provinces, mass rallies in the large cities, and the establishment of hundreds of base committees (Comités de Base).

The FA program, issued on 17 February and published in *El Popular* (18 February; reprinted in *Tricontinental*, Havana, no. 62, 1971) called for (1) lifting of government security measures against the Tupamaro guerrillas, 2) full autonomy for all educational establishments, (3) agrarian reform, (4) nationalization of banks and foreign trade, (5) termination of dealings with the International Monetary Fund, (6) establishment of commercial and diplomatic relations with all countries, (7) an end to prices and income control, and (8) return of the police force to its "civilian" function, among other items. On 25 August, General Seregni announced the first 30 measures the FA would enact upon election. He outlined four basic measures for the process of change in Uruguay: agrarian reform, nationalization of private banks, nationalization of the main areas of trade, and vigorous industrial activity by the government, including nationalization of the meat-packing industry. (For text of the 30 measures see *El Popular*, 26 August.) FA candidate Seregni stated during the campaign that the front's program was not Socialist or Marxist but a "sort of very advanced democracy."

At the beginning of the year a survey by the University of Uruguay showed that between 25 and 30 per cent of the electorate contemplated voting for the FA. During the summer, support drifted from the FA to the traditional parties and in the election on 28 November the FA polled about a fifth of the vote. By a narrow margin the Colorado Party candidate, Juan M. Bordaberry, won the presidency, but no party or faction gained a majority in the new congress. The results for deputies were: Colorados, 41; Nationals, 40; and FA, 18. For senators: Colorados, 14; Nationals, 12; and FA, 5. Although the FA did not declare its immediate post-election plans, there seems little doubt that it will continue to have an active role in the politics of Uruguay.

Uruguay has long been known among Latin American countries for its democratic form of government and its far-reaching system of public welfare. By the mid-1960s a state of near national economic collapse had been created by years of excessive spending, labor demands, and bureaucratization, increasingly aggravated by government inefficiency and corruption. In June 1968 the government promulgated "urgent security measures" and froze wages and prices of all goods and services. The PCU, with its strong position among unionized workers and students, played a leading role in opposing government efforts to stabilize the economy. The Tupamaros, with their well-known guerrilla exploits (see below), created increased national tensions in spite of the government's continued "state-of-siege" tactics. In this setting, Uruguay anticipated the 1971 elections with some uneasiness. However, the elections were carried out without incident. It is anticipated that the position of the FA will cause increased pressure on minority President Bordaberry and that the Tupamaros are likely to renew their guerrilla activities in the coming year.

The PCU. Leadership and Organization. The PCU has national and departmental structures, the latter corresponding to the country's 19 departments. At the party's Twentieth Congress, held in December 1970 (see *YICA*, 1971), the Central Committee membership was raised to 48 regular members and 27 alternates. The Secretariat was reduced to five members—Rodney Arismendi, Enrique Pastorino, Jaime Pérez, Enrique Rodríguez, and Alberto Suárez. The Executive Committee was reduced to fifteen, consisting of the five Secretariat members and Alberto Altesor, Leopoldo Bruera, Félix Días, José L. Massera, Rosario Pietrarroia, César Reyes Daglio, Gerardo Cuesta, Jorge Mazzarovich, Wladímir Turiansky and Eduardo Viera. Rodney Arismendi was confirmed again as first secretary.

The party's youth organization, the Union of Communist Youth (Unión de la Juventud Comunista; UJC), was founded in 1955. At the beginning of 1971 its membership was reportedly 20,000 (*WMR*, March). The first secretary of the UJC is Jorge Mazzarovich.

In May the UJC held a national convention, attended by delegations from all over Uruguay and by foreign observers from the World Federation of Democratic Youth and communist youth groups of Argentina and Chile. The convention was dedicated to a report presented by First Secretary Mazzarovich which was primarily ideological and political in content. The report analyzed the tasks of Uruguayan youth which were summarized in the slogan displayed at the convention: "Youth with Frente Amplio in Conquest of Power." Mazzarovich declared: "The essential task of this period is to win the election, guaranteeing the victory of Frente Amplio, freeing the large masses of Uruguayan youth into the Frente Amplio." (*El Popular*, 22 May.)

At the end of the year it was reported that the UJC had "wholeheartedly joined base committees, participated in Broad Front activities, days of campaigning and diverse confrontations," in addition to striving to meet a goal of 6,000 new members. By November the recruitment campaign had brought 3,250 new members to the UJC, approximately 28 per cent of whom came from the interior, where "employment conditions are especially difficult, where acts of terrorism and anti-communist calumnies effortlessly transpire" (*El Popular*, 3 December).

In recent years the UJC has played an important, and sometimes dominant, part in the Federation of University Students of Uruguay (Federación de Estudiantes Universitarios del Uruguay; FEUU), an affiliate of the Soviet-front International Union of Students.

The National Convention of Workers (Convención Nacional de Trabajadores; CNT) was established in 1966. Individual unions in the CNT are largely non-communist, and some non-communists hold high positions in them. The decision-making offices, however, are dominted by officials of the PCU, including Enrique Pastorino, Félix Díaz, Wladímir Turiansky, and Antonio Tamayo. According to the credentials committee of the CNT, the organization now has 500,000 members. The Soviet Union has retained particular interest in the CNT, and Soviet activities in connection with labor strikes and demonstrations have led to expulsion of their embassy officials in the past. In 1969 CNT Secretary Enrique Pastorino was made president of the Soviet-front World Federation of Trade Unions (WFTU), the first Latin American to hold this high position.

The Second Congress of the CNT was held on 23-27 June, 1971. It was attended by 78 affiliated organizations and foreign visitors from the WFTU, the Latin American Confederation of Christian Workers, and the Single Center of Chilean Workers, among others. Invited delegates from the Soviet Union and Eastern Europe did not attend because the Uruguayan government refused them visas. The congress approved a general resolution which stated, in part, that a new Uruguay was being born in which "a new consciousness is appearing which is the fruit of qualitative changes that have taken place in the social relationahip of forces in the Republic and which offers the working class and the people, on the political level, a real opportunity of coming to power" (*World Trade Union Movement*, London, October). The congress pledged the support of the workers for the Broad Front.

The tasks for the trade union movement were set out in the general resolution and included: abrogation of the emergency security measures, reestablishment of constitutional liberties, freeing of political and trade union prisoners, reemployment of dismissed workers, abolition of COPRIN (the government body in charge of wage and price controls), increased wages, salaries, and pensions, solution of the housing problem, improved education and work opportunities, increased credits for small and medium industry, establishment of just prices for agricultural products and a solution to the urban transport problem. The congress further ratified the CNT program, which called for the breaking off of relations with the International Monetary Fund and a moratorium on external debts, the nationalization of banking, foreign trade, and the freezing industry, defence of nationalized companies and revival of national industries, co-ordination of transport, and agrarian reform.

The congress expressed fraternal solidarity with workers of Cuba, Chile, and other Latin American countries, and those of Africa, Asia, and Europe, in their fight against "capitalist exploitation." Finally, the delegates supported the initiative of the WFTU for an international round table trade union conference.

During 1971, as in years past, one of the primary activities of the CNT was the organization of strikes and demonstrations. On 1 April a 24-hour strike shut down Montevideo completely in protest against the government's wage freeze, "repression of the people," and ties with the International Monetary Fund. On 1 May a large rally and demonstration was held to commemorate the "first anniversary of the great workers' counter-offensive, the culmination of a year of hard combat." (*El Popular*, 2 May).

Party Internal Affairs. The PCU congress in December 1970 particularly stressed its membership growth, a primary objective of the PCU in recent years. Between its 1966 and 1970 congresses, the party took in 26,087 new members: a major percentage were workers, about 75 per cent were under forty-five years, and some 30 per cent were women. These figures, according to the PCU, reflected the "political and ideological cohesion of the party" and the extent of its "inner-party democracy (*WMR*, March 1971). According to First Secretary Arismendi, the 1970 congress was in "complete agreement in the assessment of the past road and future prospects." This unity, he said, was "confirmed by the unanimous election of the new Central Committee." (*Neues Deutschland*, Berlin, 22 January.)

The Central Committee of the PCU held a plenary meeting on 6-7 February. The formation of a broad front of progressive forces was the main topic.

On 7-8 May the PCU held a national conference, attended by 500 delegates, for the purpose of discussing problems in regard to strengthening the party organizationally. The desire for unity among the masses was pointed out and the need for strengthening the organizational, political, and ideological aspects of the party was stressed. Arismendi urged "extention of the anti-imperialist movement" and the setting up of "thousands of new Broad Front committees." (*WMR*, July.)

At a meeting in September the PCU announced that in the first eight months of 1971 the party had won 6,718 new members. At the traditional end-of-year meeting Arismendi hailed the progress of the "people's struggle" in "advancing along its path toward power" in spite of the Broad Front's numerical loss in the election. The communists, he said, had given their all for the Broad Front and "worker-Popular unity," adding: "We have done this without sectarianism, without petty politicking, aware of the historic nature of the battle undertaken, and we feel profound satisfaction with it." (*El Popular*, 2 January 1972.)

Domestic Attitudes and Activities. The domestic situation in Uruguay was described by Rodney Arismendi in an interview with *L'Unità* (Rome, 16 April 1971). Uruguay, he said, was shaken by a "profound crisis." He then stated that the ruling class "represented by the old Blanco and Colorado bourgeois parties is no longer capable of governing," the country is "burdened by debts contracted with North American banks," industrial and agrarian production has been reduced after "years of falling growth rates and stagnation," and there was a "tremendous inflation" and devaluation of the peso. In order to resolve the crisis the president had initiated a "stabilization plan" in 1968 which devalued the currency, froze wages, salaries and pensions, restricted credits to various sectors of the economy, and tried to prevent price increases. Arismendi declared that the plan was imposed by restricted freedom of the press, suspended constitutional guarantees, military supervision of many workers, and the arrests of "thousands of students, intellectuals, and workers." During the following years, the working class "replied with a powerful counter offensive" which included strikes, demonstrations, and marches. According to Arismendi, the "repression" failed, while the "working class extended its alliances among the middle classes, and a new political consciousness emerged in the country," culminating in 1971 with the formation of the Broad Front.

By the time of the PCU congress Arismendi declared that it was "becoming really possible to achieve decisive victories that may lead to a new political reality." In the coming period, he said, the main object must be the "forming of a government which could carry out a program of democratic change and restore national sovereignty." (*WMR*, March.)

Most PCU activities during the year had to do with the campaign of the Broad Front in the national election. Although the front did not win the election (see above), Arismendi said that it did "triumph in history, in advancing along its path toward power." He added that it was not possible to turn back and that therefore the "unity of the Front will become greater in its popular setting, within the parties, within the base committees." (*El Popular*, 2 January 1972.)

In December, following the elections, Arismendi declared that the government was becoming even more "repressive" with the closing of some newspapers and promulgation of new decrees that threatened "all leftist and democratic forces" by proscribing "all theoretical-political and even journalistic material that deals with the struggle of the world's people, with Marxism-Leninism, with the anti-imperialist and liberationist movement. (*Ibid.*, 17 December 1971.)

In consistently pursuing the electoral road to power the PCU has come into conflict with some of the more radical groups in Uruguay. In April, however, Arismendi stated that while the PCU considered the Tupamaros to be "sincere, honest and brave revolutionaries" and had defended them whenever necessary," the parties believed that "their tactics do not correspond with Uruguay's needs" (*L'Unità*, 16 April).

International Views and Positions. The PCU has traditionally been firmly allied with the foreign policy positions of the Soviet Union. In April 1971, First Secretary Arismendi attended the Twenty-fourth Congress of the Communist Party of the Societ Union (CPSU). In preparation for the congress he wrote that in the "complex international situation" the foreign policy line of the CPSU was a "distinct and clear-cut guideline for all who defend the cause of peace and progress on earth." Arismendi reiterated the PCU position that "in the unification of diverse, anti-imperialist movements the basic role falls to the Socialist camp and the international proletariat, against whom Yankee imperialism is directing all its force." The prerequisite for this unification, he added, was the "solidarity of the Socialist camp and the international communist and workers' movement." (Article by R. Arismendi, *Pravda Ukrainy*, Kiev, 20 February.)

According to the resolution of the PCU congress, "changes in Latin American reality are speeding the patriotic, democratic revolutionary liberation process in individual countries," each country with its own "historical characteristics" and an alignment of social and political forces which determine the "ways and means" of gaining power. The resolution stated that "imperialism and Latin American reaction" would in many cases try to prevent the assumption of power by the people by force, thus "predetermining" the "armed path of the revolution." (*WMR*, March.)

While at the CPSU congress, Arismendi noted with pleasure the "exchange of brotherly and warm words between Cuba and the Soviet Union" (interview in Moscow, 3 April). In November he talked with Fidel Castro in Santigo during the latter's Chilean tour. There he said that Cuba signifies a "qualitative change in the reality of the continent." A report of his visit stressed that the ability of Castro to "parade the victorious banner of the Cuban revolution through Latin America," together with the reestablishment of relations between Chile and Cuba, marked the "breakup of the infamous blockade of Cuba" and discredited the Organization of American States, which expelled Cuba. (*El Popular*, 19 November.) The Popular Unity victory in Chile, Arismendi said, had created a "zone of anti-imperialist resistance . . . in the continent" (*ibid.*).

In February, PCU member José Luis Massera attended the congress of the Communist Party of Venezuela where he spoke of the importance of "proletarian internationalism" and "solidarity with the Soviet Union." (*Tribuna Popular*, Caracas, 4-10 February).

The communist parties of Argentina, Bolivia, Brazil, Chile, Paraguay, Peru, and Uruguay held a series of meetings in September. A statement issued by the group noted that "a pronounced leftward swing among the popular masses" was taking place in Latin America, and that the working class, "which shows increasing proof of maturity," was being joined by new "patriotic sectors" (*El Siglo*, 11 October). The parties appealed to all "patriots, irrespective of philosophy and religion, to unite in a resolute effort to ward off the U.S. imperialist menace" (*WMR*, December).

Publications. The most important PCU publications are the daily newspaper *El Popular* and the theoretical journal *Estudios*.

*   *   *

The MIR. The movement of the Revolutionary Left, founded in 1963, is the main pro-Chinese organization in Uruguay. In mid-1970 the MIR organ *Voz Obrera* stated that the seizure of political power in Uruguay required a "Marxist-Leninist revolutionary party," a "people's liberation army led by this party," and a "united front of all revolutionary classes and sections" (quoted in *Peking Review*, 11 September). Nonetheless the MIR was one of the few leftist organizations that did not join the Broad Front, reportedly stating that whereas it was willing to form a bloc with the national bourgeoisie, it would not do so if the bloc included the PCU (*Intercontinental Press*, New York, 1 March 1971).

A pamphlet issued by the MIR—*Tupamaros, ¿Conspiración o Revolución?: Respuesta de los Marxistas-Leninistas del Uruguay* (Montevideo, September 1970)—declared that the Tupamaros were characterized by adventurism, subjectivism, leftist opportunism, and terrorism, and were "the national expression of the focoist doctrine," which was "totally at odds with Marxism."

*   *   *

The MLN (Tupamaros). The idea for the MLN arose among Uruguayan leftists in the early 1960s. The organization carried out its first raid in July 1963. Since 1969 the MLN has carried out a series of dramatic exploits (e.g., kidnapings, robberies, occupations of small towns and radio stations) intended to call into question the ability of the Uruguayan government to protect its own or foreign nationals. The Tupamaros attracted international attention between July 1970 and January 1971 by kidnaping a number of foreign nationals living in Uruguay—most importantly, Brazilian diplomat Aloysio Dias Gomide (on 31 July 1970), U.S. security adviser Dan A. Mitrione (31 July), U.S. agricultural expert Claude Fly (7 August), and British ambassador Geoffrey Jackson (8 January 1971). Mitrione was murdered on 9 August 1970; the others were released in 1971: Dias Gomide on 21 February, Fly on 2 March, and Jackson on 9 September. After the seizure of Jackson the Tupamaros turned to kidnaping prominent Uruguayans between March and May. In the months that followed the MLN concentrated on freeing imprisoned members of their organization: Juan Almiratti and Raúl Bidegain, important MLN leaders, escaped from prison on 26 May and 17 July respectively; 38 women escaped from the women's prison on 30 July; and 106 Tupamaros, including Raúl Sendic, the founder of the organization, escaped from prison on 6 September.

In a "Manifesto to Public Opinion," published in mid-September 1970, the MLN described itself as an "armed political organization of students, workers, employees, rural workers, intellectuals, and unemployed" (*Granma*, Havana, English, 27 September). It believes that revolution can come to Uruguay only by means of armed struggle. In late 1970 an MLN leader identified only as "Urbano" said the Tupamaros carried out three sometimes overlapping kinds of actions. These were: "tactical actions, aimed at obtaining supplies"; "propaganda actions" which "by themselves define the movement's objectives and conduct"; and "actions against the regime," which were "mainly aimed at undermining the foundations of the regime itself." Kidnapings, according to Urbano, were originally intended both to get money or secure the release of imprisoned comrades and to "undermine the foundations of the system." (*Ibid.*, 18 October.)

The Tupamaros have always sought to avoid the conflicts which have divided leftists in Uruguay. In December 1970 they commended the leftist unity achieved in the Broad Front and gave the election coalition their support, while restating their conviction that revolution cannot be achieved through elections. MLN support for the front was given "with the understanding that its principal task must be the mobilization of the working masses and that its labor among these masses does not begin or end with the elections" (*Tricontinental Bulletin*, Havana, May 1971). In a statement issued on 8 September 1971 the Tupamaros denied charges that they were "conspiring against the election." After calling for a number of election "guarantees which are nonexistent today" they concluded: "Our support for the Broad Front includes a positive attitude regarding the elections" (*Granma*, English, 19 September). The MLN was reportedly represented in the Broad Front by the "26 March Movement of Independents" (*Intercontinental* Press, 13 December).

On 20 March the Tupamaros issued their "Program of the MLN Revolutionary Government." This first systematic statement of the policies an MLN government would seek to implement did not mean, according to the program, that the Tupamaros had ceased giving support to "any other transitional program that has the same ends, such as that proposed by the CNT and other people's forces." The MLN program comments specifically, (and very briefly) on agrarian reform, industry, commerce, credit, urban reform, planning, foreign investments, wages, education, public health, old age and disability, justice, and the armed defense of the revolution. (*Granma*, English, 28 March.)

As early as 1968 the MLN stated that one of its chief objectives was to "establish connections with other revolutionary movements of Latin America for continental action" (*Punto Final*, Santiago, 2 July 1968). The MLN has reportedly had contacts with urban and rural querrilla groups in Argentina, Bolivia, Brazil, and other countries.

Lynn Ratliff

Venezuela

The Communist Party of Venezuela (Partido Comunista de Venezuela; PCV) was founded in 1931. In December 1970 the party split, one group maintaining the PCV name and the other calling itself the Movement toward Socialism (Movimiento al Socialismo; MAS).

Although precise membership figures are not available, the PCV in 1970 was estimated as having from 8,000 members (*World Strength of the Communist Party Organizations, 1970*) to several times that number. The number of members who joined with the MAS faction late in 1970 is unknown and each group claims to represent the majority. According to the national secretary of the PCV, Alonso Ojeda Olaechea, 68 per cent of the communists remained with the PCV (*Tribuna Popular*, 14 January 1971). The population of Venezuela is 10,800,000 (estimated 1970).

The PCV was legalized on 26 March 1969 after a period of illegality due to its policy of active armed struggle adopted in 1962. This unsuccessful policy was abandoned in 1967, and the PCV under a front organization called Union for Advancement (Unión para Avanzar; UPA) decided to participate in the 1968 national election. The UPA received 2.8 per cent of the vote and six high-ranking members of the PCV were elected to the legislature. Rafael Caldera, leader of the Social Christian Party (COPEI) was elected president.

The New Force. Early in 1971 an alliance between two left-of-center opposition parties, the People's Electoral Movement (Movimiento Electoral del Pueblo; MEP) and the Democratic Republican Union (Unión Republicana Democrática; URD) was begun in anticipation of the 1973 elections. The PCV joined the alliance, which adopted the name People's Nationalist Front (Frente Nacionalista Popular) but is commonly referred to as the New Force (Nueva Fuerza). The youth groups of the MEP, URD, and PCV simultaneously formed a parallel united front organization. At the end of October the New Force announced its "Essentials for Drawing up the Governmental Program of the Nationalist Popular Front" ("Bases para la Elaboración del Programa de Gobierno del Frente Nacionalista Popular") which described the front's goals as (1) the defeat of imperialism and the oligarchy, (2) national liberation, and (3) the transformation of the economic and social structure as the beginning of the development of a socialist democracy.

The PCV. Organization and Leadership. After a number of delays caused by the internal dissension in the party, the PCV held its Fourth Congress on 23-28 January 1971. The congress elected a new 47-member Central Committee and 16 alternate members (the former Central Committee had 57 members and 24 alternates) (*IB.*, no. 5-6). The May plenum of the Central Committee elected a 13-member Politburo (reduced from 15 members) which included Gustavo Machado, chairman, Jesús Faría, secretary-general, Eduardo Machado, Guillermo García Ponce, Pedro Ortega Díaz, Antonio García Ponce, Eduardo Gallegos Mancera, and Alonso Ojeda Olaechea.

The Venezuelan Communist Youth (Juventud Comunista Venezolana; JCV) had in recent years been the most active and successful auxiliary organization of the PCV. Following the split in the PCV in 1970, the JCV became disorganized and underwent a split into two factions also. It has been admitted by the JCV that most of the leadership and "almost all its old cadres deserted" to form the youth arm of the new MAS (*Tribuna Popular,* 10 June). In January the JCV held a reorganizational meeting at which its National Communist Youth Organizing Commission declared that the JCV previously had been a "petty-bourgeois organization" whose attention had been focused on student activities. The commission pointed out the necessity of having peasants and workers as well as students in the ranks of the youth organization. The new JCV, it declared, will be "more proletarian, more aggressive, and more rooted among the masses." (*Ibid.,* 19-27 January.) The JCV set a goal of 5,000 new members by 1972. Leaders of the JCV during the year were Américo Díaz Nuñez and Noel Sirit. As of March 1971 the JCV began publication of a biweekly journal, *Joven Guardia.*

In order to avoid past mistakes and a recurrence of the 1970 events the JCV stressed the need for ideological training of communist youths under the "efficient, politically organized vigilance" of the PCV (*Joven Guardia,* 1 April). In May the JCV issued a statement urging students to stop their tactics of violence and destruction and to direct their protests towards demands for the resignation of the minister of education, a new educational policy, the reopening of the Central University, and the reinstatement of expelled stedents (*El Nacional,* Caracas, 16 May).

The JCV joined with youth groups of other left-wing parties, including the URD and the MEP, to form the Popular Youth Front as an auxiliary of the New Force (see above).

At the Executive Committee meeting of the World Federation of Democratic Youth (WFDY) in Valparaiso, Chile, on 7 September, the JCV protested the continued presence of Antonio Meza, who had joined the MAS youth group. The WFDY decided to expel Meza as the Venezuelan representative. Américo Díaz Nuñez represented the Federation of University Centers at the congress of the International Union of Students in Czechoslovakia.

The United Workers' Federation of Venezuela (Confederación Unitaria de Trabajadores de Venezuela; CUTV) is the labor affiliate of the PCV. It has been active, although it is small in numerical strength. The split in the PCV was reflected in the CUTV at meetings held in February and March, during which some members of the leadership left to form a new organization under the auspices of the MAS. The PCV claimed it still represented the majority, and held the Fifth Plenum of the General Council of the CUTV in March. The leadership includes Cruz A. Villegas, Américo Chacón and Laureano Torrealba (see *Tribuna Popular,* 25 March).

The PCV described the women's movement in 1970 as having been in a "state of completely unjustified neglect" (*ibid.,* 4 February). In August the women communists held their First National Meeting in Caracas, attended by 105 delegates. The meeting approved messages of solidarity with U. S. communist Angela Davis and the "heroic people of Vietnam," and expressed its allegiance to the newly formed Peoples Nationalist Front. PCV Secretary-General Jesús Faría addressed the group, urging the women to "step up their struggle for the independence of Venezuela." (*IB,* no. 18-19.)

Party Internal Affairs. The PCV held its Fourth Congress on 23-27 January 1971. Delegations from fourteen communist and workers' parties, including the Communist Party of the Soviet Union (CPSU), attended. A report on party activity since the Third Congress (1962) was made by Secretary-General Jesús Faría; the party program, theses, and organizational problems were discussed; and the political declaration and theses on the agrarian question and trade union work were approved. The expulsion from the party of the "Petkoff-Marquez factional anti-party group" was welcomed as a victory of the PCV's "Marxist-Leninist forces over the opportunist and anti-Leninist trend attempting to destroy the party" (*IB.*, no. 3-4). (For a discussion of the dispute between the two factions see *YICA*, 1971, pp. 506 ff.) In summing up the work of the congress, Jesús Faría stated that the party had carried out "fruitful organizing, ideological, and political work," amended its Rules, and made preparations for the next congress, to be held in two years (*WMR*, May). (For texts of Fourth Congress documents see *IB.*, no. 5-6.)

On 5 March the fortieth anniversary of the PCV was celebrated with emphasis placed on party discipline, "fraternity among the old and young comrades," and the "rebirth of the prestige of the name of the communist party" (*Tribuna Popular*, 11 March).

The PCV Politburo meeting on 3 May was devoted primarily to a discussion of the national political situation, the struggle against "left-wing and right-wing revisionism," and preparation for the Third Plenum of the Central Committee (*ibid.*, 6 May).

The Third Plenum was held on 20-22 May. The three main subjects discussed were (1) participation of the PCV in a popular front (see above), (2) the organizational situation and the recovery and strengthening of the party, and (3) a review of the ideological and theoretical situation since the expulsion of the "revisionists" in January (*ibid.*, 27 May).

It was announced in July (*ibid.*, 22 July) that party cards would be distributed to PCV members in August—a practice previously prohibited by the government, a Salary Day for contributions to party finances would be observed, paid circulation of *Tribuna Popular* would be urged, and creation of popular committees for the New Force would be stressed.

Domestic Attitudes and Activities. The PCV program as set forth by the 1971 congress began with a statement reiterating the party's opposition to the Social Christian government of Rafael Caldera and to the government's "concurrences" with the Democratic Action Party which were designed to maintain the "imperialist and oligarchic domination" of the country while blocking the way to a "popular, democratic, nationalist, and patriotic alternative." The program stressed "indefatigable struggle for unity, rapprochement, concurrences, and cohesion among political parties" toward the formation of a "broad democratic and popular front in support of the radical transformations which Venezuelan society requires." (*Tribuna Popular*, 4-10 February.)

Among the many items the party program called for were: expansion and defense of civil liberties, freedom for political prisoners, cessation of "repression and torture," elimination of the anti-guerrilla camps, struggle against the "militarization of ordinary justice," and elimination of "infamous police methods." In the area of labor the party called for "free organization of the toiling and peasant masses, students, professional people, intellectuals, and artists; unity of the workers' and peasant movement; "class renovation" of the workers' organizations; and "free and democratic election and removal" of labor and peasant union leaders. In the area of education the program stressed the "defense of the people's culture" and called for free education at all levels, educational diversification and planning" in the service of the "independent development of the nation on scientific, lay, and nondogmatic bases."

Regarding the economic situation, the PCV program favored nationalization of the oil industry and "extensive promotion of state enterprises" (as opposed to the trend toward association with foreign capital), renunciation of the commercial treaty with the United States, and diversification of foreign trade.

In the fall of 1971 the PCV's National Agrarian Commission circulated a pamphlet containing the "agrarian Program of the Communist Party" which had been approved by the congress in January. The program was based on the premises that (1) peasant and state ownership of the land must replace the latifundistas and monopoly system of ownership, (2) agrarian reform is part of the "overall struggle against imperialism," (3) only a "popular revolutionary government" can achieve reform, (4) a worker-peasant alliance must be developed, (5) the peasantry must share in the leadership, and (6) there must be a new agrarian reform law. (*Ibid.*, 3 October.)

International Views and Positions. The foreign policy section of the PCV program advocated a "sovereign policy of relations with all the countries of the world, based on respect for the free determination of nations, non-interference, and mutual advantage." The party favored "support and solidarity" with all nations struggling against the "colonialist and neo-colonialist yoke of imperialism," diplomatic and commercial relations with socialist countries including Cuba, diplomatic recognition of the People's Republic of China, the Democratic Republic of Vietnam, the Democratic People's Republic of Korea, and the German Democratic Republic, and increased ties with Chile. The PCV denounced the Organization of American States and supported a policy of integration and mutual aid with other Latin American countries. (*Tribuna Popular*, 4-10 February 1971.)

The International Commission of the Fourth Congress reported that problems had arisen among students who had been sent by the party to study in communist countries. Many of the students had behaved "irregularly" in their studies and morals and had returned to Venezuela either opposing or defecting from the party.

In August the PCV held a "Forum on the Cuban Revolution" during which the Cuban revolutionary process and questions regarding economics, education, and living conditions in Cuba and the controversy over intellectual freedom under Fidel Castro were discussed. The forum followed a period of hostile relations between the PCV and Cuba, which reached a peak in 1967, and at its close Jesús Faría revealed that "efforts have continued on a permanent basis at various levels" to renew relations with Cuba, but that "it is not a matter for undue haste." (*Ibid.*, 26 August.)

The PCV sent Guillermo García Ponce and Jesús Faría as its representatives to the Twenty-fourth Congress of the CPSU. Reporting on the congress, García Ponce said that great cultural and material gains were being made by the Soviet people under "socialist organization of the economy" and the "Leninist leadership of the CPSU." He noted that the congress had condemned "opportunism of the left as well as the right and reassured fundamental principles of poletarian internationalism," thus giving support to the recent struggle of the PCV against "revisionism." (*Ibid.*, 12 April.)

In an effort to reaffirm support for the PCV after the split, the party sent representatives to confer with many communist party officials abroad, especially in Europe. Prior to the CPSU congress, Jesús Faría visited leaders of the Communist Party of Czechoslovakia in Prague and the leaders of the German Democratic Republic in Berlin. The PCV foreign relations secretary, Eduardo Gallegos Mancera, made a tour of European countries including Yugoslavia, Romania, France, Spain, and Italy during March. According to Gallegos, the PCV had the "support, confidence, and solidarity" of these parties and its international links had been strengthened (*ibid.*, 1 April).

In April, Jesús Faría led the PCV delegation to the congress of the Bulgarian Communist Party. Eduardo Machado represented the party at the congress of the Socialist Unity Party of (East) Germany.

Publications. The organ of the PCV is *Tribuna Popular*. Previously a biweekly newspaper, it began daily publication on 14 September 1971. The editor-in-chief is Américo Díaz Nuñez.

*   *   *

The MAS. The "Movement toward Socialism" was formed late in 1970 as the result of the split within the PCV. The MAS claims that the split came about as the "result of the internal debate in the party itself" and that its movement is "neither pro- nor anti-Soviet, neither pro- nor anti-Chinese, neither pro- nor anti-Cuban," but is "national" in motivation (*Deslinde*, 9 February.).

Leadership and Organization. The MAS held its first congress on 14-17 January 1971 in Caracas. Pompeyo Márquez (former member of the PCV Politburo) was unanimously elected secretary-general. The Central Committee included: Alexis Adam, Eleazar Díaz Rangel, German Lairet, Augusto León, Freddy Muñoz, Alfredo Padilla, Teodoro Petkoff (one of the leading dissenters from the PCV, described by Le Monde, Paris, as "a Venezuelan Roger Garaudy"), Tirso Pinto, Hector Rodríguez Bauza, and Eloy Torres.

The MAS formed a subsidiary youth organization made up largely of dissident members of the JCV. The new group adopted the name Communist Youth—MAS (Juventud Comunista—MAS; JC—MAS) and elected Alfredo Padilla secretary-general. The JC—MAS held its first conference in Caracas on 17-20 June. A report on the conference, published in the MAS organ Bravo Pueblo (3 July), stated that delegates had agreed to "reformulate their policy, broaden their program of overall criticism of the education system and of the capitalist system, and channel the activities of their student organizations into the struggle against the government." The conference decided that the JC—MAS would put up "militant opposition" to the holding of academic elections at the Central University and would call a national meeting of student leaders from all the country's universities in August or September. Some leaders commented on the low ideological level of the party's "militants." (Ibid.)

The president of the JC—MAS is Alexis Adam (president of the student body at the Central University and formerly a member of the PCV Central Committee). Antonio Meza was the Venezuelan representative to the WFDY until September, when the WFDY expelled him after protests by the JCV.

During the year the JC-MAS was especially active in student protests and demonstrations which disrupted the Central University and drew attention to the group and its parent organization, the MAS.

On 14 March a majority (8 out of 13) of the executive leadership of the CUTV and 41 of the 70 members of the General Council met to resolve the crisis caused by the division of the PCV. At the meeting, the leaders Cruz Villegas, Américo Chacón, Laureano Torrealba, and Frederico Rondon were expelled and the Executive Committee was reorganized. José Marcano was elected secretary-general. The new General Council approved a document on the situation in the Venezuelan trade union movement and approved the convocation of the Sixth Congress of the CUTV for later in the year.

Internal Party Affairs. The first congress of the MAS was held on 14-17 January 1971 (the MAS referred to the congress as its Fourth since it claimed to represent the majority of Venezuelan communists.) In a long analysis of the MAS, Secretary-General Pompeyo Márquez stated that an "authentically revolutionary current has matured in the party," which has "national roots" and whose "theoretical guide is Marxism-Leninism." (Deslinde, 9 February.)

Domestic Attitudes and Activities. The MAS, according to Pompeyo Márquez, conceives of the party as a "force which gives its energy to the construction of a popular, anti-imperialist, and socialist government, based on the confidence and participation of the people, in which the working class and the masses in general will not be spectators, but creators of a new society." Therefore, he added, it is necessary to restore the "effective link between the revolutionary movement" and the "political processes" of the country. (Deslinde, 9 February 1971.)

The MAS declared itself a "resolute opposition force against the Caldera administration," which had demonstrated that it was "incapable of solving the country's fundamental problems." The Caldera government, in the view of the MAS, "represents and essentially serves" the interests of the "U.S. monopolies" and the "bourgeoisie" associated with them. (Ibid.)

The MAS considered its main chance of success to be in the formation of a front representing different sectors of society and cutting across party lines. Pompeyo Márquez expressed the hope that the MAS could join with "anti-imperialists and patriots" in all parties in a grouping that the MAS would lead (*ibid.*, 8 January). In an article in the Caracus newspaper *El Mundo*, (19 January), Teodoro Petkoff emphasized the importance of preparing for the 1973 elections in order to present to the masses a "concrete revolutionary alternative." The MAS was not, Petkoff declared, proposing a "Chilean-type formula." Venezuela, he said, did not have any "revolutionary political organization that could shape a 'popular unity' similar to the Allende-type unity," but the next elections could be an important event in the "long-term reconstruction of a revolutionary alternative." The MAS did not join with the united front organization, "New Force" (see above).

International Views. As was the case for the PCV, the MAS concentrated its attention in the international arena during 1971 on efforts to gain or retain support for itself among other communist parties. In the spring Secretary-General Márquez and Héctor Rodríguez Bauza visited Romania, Yugoslavia, Italy, France, Spain, Chile, and Peru. Upon their return, Pompeyo Márquez stated that the emergence of the MAS was "viewed with hope everywhere, especially in the communist movement" (*Bravo Pueblo*, June).

MAS member Díaz Rangel visited Cuba and Mexico in January as chairman of the Venezuelan Journalists' Association, in connection with the Seventh Congress of the International Organization of Journalists. Representatives of the Cuban Communist Party showed interest in the MAS movement, according to Rangel, and the Mexican Communist Party expressed solidarity with it (see *Deslinde*, 22 January).

Responding to criticism of the MAS by the Soviet Union, Pompeyo Márquez declared: "It will be difficult for the Soviet comrades who shape the opinion of the CPSU on the Venezuelan communist movement to understand or explain what happened inside the PCV. It cannot be done with four cliches and a few epithets [such as treacherous, splittist, or anti-Leninist]." (*Ultimas Noticias*, Caracas, 20 February.)

In his report to the party, Pompeyo Márquez stated that the members of the MAS were "above all Marxist-Leninists, proven revolutionaries, and consistent internationalists." The MAS would try, he said, to "maintain equal relations of mutual solidarity and non-interference in internal affairs with all of the communist and workers' parties." (*Deslinde*, 9 February.)

Publications. In February it was announced that *Deslinde*, the organ of the MAS, would be renamed *Bravo Pueblo*.

*   *   *

Guerrillas. Most of the guerrillas in Venezuela during the 1960s belonged to either the Armed Forces of National Liberation (Fuerzas Armadas de Liberación Nacional; FALN) or the Movement of the Revolutionary Left)Movimiento de Izquierda Revolucionaria; MIR). By the mid-1960s these organizations had begun to disintegrate due to personal rivalries, differing views on forms of armed and peaceful struggle, and varying reactions to the pacification program inaugurated by President Caldera in March 1969.

By January 1971 two of the country's best-known guerrillas, Douglas Bravo and Carlos Betancourt—leaders of the FALN and the Antonio José de Sucre Guerrilla Front (Frente Guerrillero Antonio José de Sucre; FGAJS) respectively—had formed the Committee for Revolutionary Integration (Comité de Integración Revolucionaria; CIR) to try to work out cooperation between the guerrillas. According to Bravo, the combined FALN and FGAJS consisted of three revolutionary fronts or columns and various urban units (*Vea y Lea*, Caracas, 18 January 1971). After a meeting in October 1971 the CIR issued a statement calling for the establishment of a "Single Marxist-Leninist Party" to bring together all Venezuelan revolutionaries (*Punto Negro*, Caracas, 15-30 November). The CIR apparently hoped that such a party could recruit the pro-Chinese Organization of Revolutionaries (Organización de Revolucionarios), whose leader, Julio Escalona, had called for such a united party of revolutionaries early in the year (*Vea y Lea*, 28 May).

Several prominent guerrillas were captured during the year, foremost among them being Francisco Prada, long Douglas Bravo's chief lieutenant.

Lynn Ratliff

ASIA AND
THE PACIFIC

Australia

The Communist Party of Australia (CPA) was founded in October 1920. Membership reached a high of some 20,000 during World War II, but has since declined steadily and is currently estimated at 3,600. The population of Australia is 12,713,000 (estimated 1970). The party's main strength is among organized workers in the major industrial and urban centers. The orientation of the CPA is generally pro-Soviet.

An offshoot of the CPA, the Australian Communist Party (Marxist-Leninist), or ACP(ML), was established in March 1964. It is believed to have about 250 members. The ACP(ML) supports the policies of the People's Republic of China.

Both parties are legal. The CPA participates, though with little success, in all national and some state elections. In the latest national election, in October 1969 (which returned the Liberal-Country Party coalition with a narrow majority over the Australian Labor Party), the CPA's seven candidates together received 0.08 per cent of the vote, down from 0.4 per cent in 1966.

The CPA. Leadership and Organization. The CPA national president is Richard Dixon, who is expected to relinquish his position soon because of ill health. The party's national secretary and most powerful figure is Laurie Aarons. The leading body of the CPA is the 12-member National Executive, consisting of Dixon, Aarons, Laurie Carmichael, N. Docker, Charlie Gifford, Claude Jones, Jim Moss, Joe Palmada, Alec Robertson, Mavis Robertson, John Sendy, and Bernard Taft, all of whom were elected in May 1970 by the 38-member National Committee, which itself was elected by the party's Twenty-second Congress in March 1970.

Some 80 young communists from throughout Australia met on 13-14 February 1971 and established the Young Communist Movement (YCM). Endorsed by the CPA, the YCM is an autonomous body "composed of young workers and students who are members of the CPA and others who support the CPA's general outline for socialism" (*Tribune*, 17 March). It calls for "worker control" and "academic self-management," and opposes "bureaucratic deformations of socialism" (*ibid.*, 6 October). The CPA's National Youth Committee, through which young communists had previously operated, will apparently continue to function. The CPA controls the Union of Australian Women, headed by Freda Brown, a vice-president of the Women's International Democratic Federation.

The CPA continues to play a disproportionately strong role in organized labor despite recent intra-party differences which have resulted in the resignation from the CPA of several leading trade unionists in key industries. CPA leaders still holding important posts include Laurie Carmichael, who is Victoria State and assistant Commonwealth secretary of the Amalgamated Engineering Union, and Jack Mundey, a CPA National Committee member and the party's Sydney district president, who is secretary of the Builders Workers Industrial Union in New South Wales.

Party Internal Affairs and Relations with the Soviets. Since the outbreak of the Sino-Soviet dispute in the early 1960s, there has existed severe factionalism between the "progressive" CPA leadership majority, which is bent on increasing the party's independence of Soviet ties and the development of a national image among the electorate, and a conservative minority, which upholds the leading role of the Soviet Union in the communist camp. Recent developments have produced a measure of victory for the progressives, but have neither quelled the conservative challenge nor enhanced the CPA's national stature. The CPA leadership's assertion of its independence within the international communist movement, however, does appear to have evoked wide respect and empathy among parties of a similar inclination—the Italian Communist Party, for example—which have not generally gone so far in their pronouncements as has the CPA.

The new party program, "Aims, Methods, and Organization," adopted at the CPA's Twenty-second Congress, reasserted the party's right to criticize "existing socialist-based societies," and endorsed both the party leadership's condemnation of the 1968 Soviet-led invasion of Czechoslovakia and its independent stand at the International Meeting of Communist and Workers' Parties in June 1969 (see *YICA*, 1970, p. 517). It was subsequently revealed that the Communist Party of the Soviet Union (CPSU) had intervened directly—without success—to try to curb the CPA's "rebel" stance. The Soviets have manifested firm support for the minority faction of the CPA and endorsed the *Australian Socialist*, a journal first issued in July 1970, which assails CPA policy and seeks the establishment of organizations around the publication. The journal's initiators, Edgar Ross and Alf Watt, were expelled from the CPA in late 1970. Since then, relations between the pro-Soviet opposition and the leadership majority of the CPA and between the latter and the CPSU have deteriorated further. In 1971 the pro-Soviet opposition appeared to be divided on the question of whether to form a new party or to try to bring the CPA back to the "correct" path.

A Soviet attack on the CPA, in an unsigned article in *New Times* (Moscow, 1 January 1971), was reprinted in the party organ (*Tribune*, 27 January) with a comment that it was "extremely unlikely that such an article could have been published except on the initiative of the top leadership of the CPSU." Events within the CPA were said to have "aroused anxiety in those who sympathetically follow the struggle of the working class and all working people of Australia against the ruling circles' domestic and foreign policies, for the socialist future of their country." The "turning point" in the development of the CPA, in the Soviet view, had been its Twenty-first Congress, in 1967, which, "on the new leadership's recommendation," had annulled the existing program. Leading figures of the CPA thereafter "began to make unfriendly and even hostile statements about the [Soviet-bloc] socialist countries and their policy," while, on the other hand, they had "gradually rejected criticism of the splitting and adventurist course of the Peking leaders." Further, they had defended the "right-opportunist 'Dubček line,'" even though it had been "fully exposed and rejected by the Czechoslovak communists."

The Soviet article recalled the CPA delegation's refusal to sign the final document at the 1969 international conference, and charged it with having attempted to "minimize the significance of the conference, to vilify its results, not stopping at downright falsification." Since then there had been a marked increase in the CPA's "tendency toward deviation from views common to the communist movement," as a result of its "inability to withstand the pressure of bourgeois ideology" and the "blackmail" of "anarchist, Trotskyite, and other anti-Marxist groups for whom anti-Sovietism is practically the hallmark of 'revolutionariness.'"

The CPA's new program was criticized by the Soviets for "treating extremely narrowly the principles of proletarian internationalism and the party's international duty." The "necessity to fight for an end to the Vietnam war," for example, was "motivated rather by considerations of abstract humanism than by the desire to rebuff imperialism"; the world-wide struggle for peace was "barely touched upon"; the critical situation in the Middle East, where the Arab peoples had become the "victims of the imperialist conspiracy," had been "passed over in silence." The international horizon of the CPA's activity was limited essentially to support for the national liberation struggle in New Guinea and other Pacific islands, and of the Australian Aborigines. Such "regionalism" was "remote from internationalism in the broad sense as it has always been understood by communists."

The Soviets went on to accuse the CPA of diluting Marxist-Leninist tenets and theories, and of advancing the idea of a "motley" coalition of the left, "with vaguely defined common ideals and objectives counterposed to the Marxist principles of the leading role of the working class." The "liberal leanings" of those Australian communists who preached "tolerance" of views inimical to communism were seen as leading to the eradication of distinctions between the communist party and its "coalition" partners. The CPA leadership had "to all intents and purposes" broken with the communists in the trade unions, and drawn into the party "elements patently hostile to communism," permitting them to utilize the party platform to demand the CPA's complete disassociation from the CPSU. The Soviets, finally, praised the efforts of the CPA minority to "avoid a split" and to work out "a strategic line and tactics acceptable to the entire party."

This was the second *New Times* attack on the CPA. The first, on 9 September 1970, came in its reprinting of an article from the Czechoslovak *Rudé Právo* (Prague, 15 July 1970) denouncing the CPA leaders as "right-wing, opportunist, revisionist elements" who had "abandoned the interests of the working people." When *New Times* refused to print the CPA's denial of the charges, the Australians moved to the forum of the dissident Austrian communist monthly *Wiener Tagebuch* (Vienna, October 1970) to trace their differences with the CPSU. Apparently this move prompted the Soviets to publish their own condemnation of the CPA leadership.

The CPA responded to the second Soviet attack in an open letter (*Tribune*, 3 February 1971), the text of which was also distributed to many communist parties. Charging that the *New Times* article had distorted and misrepresented CPA policies, the letter upheld the party's new, liberal program as being representative of the majority of Australian communists, declared that the alternative draft program drawn up by the pro-Soviet minority had been "rejected overwhelmingly" by the Twenty-second Congress, and explained that Edgar Ross and Alf Watt had been expelled from the CPA not for their political views, but for their establishment of an "exclusive separate group within the party, with its own platform, loyalty, and discipline." To the Soviet criticism of CPA foreign policy, the Australians replied that internationalism meant "first of all to oppose one's 'own' imperialism." Internationalism also required support for all anti-imperialist struggles "without exception, and applying equally to all." The CPA supported the Soviet Union, therefore, against "U.S. imperialism," and opposed U.S. efforts at containment of all socialist countries—"including the People's Republic of China." While internationalism was the "coordination and mutual support of the struggles of all communist parties, for anti-imperialist struggle and world revolution," this could not mean "unconditional support for every action of every socialist country," but, rather, a policy of "independently judging issues." The CPA upheld its demand for recognition of Israel's "right to national existence with equality of Jews and Arabs," and suggested that the Soviets were prejudiced against the prominence of Jews in the CPA leadership. For the Soviets, the letter went on, criticism of policies and discussion of problems in the Soviet Union and other socialist countries were tantamount to a betrayal of internationalism, while the "magic words 'anti-Soviet' " were "used to evade discussion of real problems of socialist development." The CPA gave as examples of such problems the "unsolved" Czechoslovak issue, and the recent crisis in Poland.

The *Tribune* (3 March) announced that 80 per cent of the delegates to the Twenty-second Congress had signed an appeal to *New Times* to publish the CPA's reply to the Soviet charges after the Soviet journal had cabled its refusal of a request by the CPA National Executive for publication of its reply. The delegates asked that *New Times* readers be provided the opportunity to "read the other side" so as to promote "open discussion and debate . . . in the Leninist tradition." The appeal was not acknowledged by the Soviets.

In the meantime, an investigating committee was set up by the CPA to hear a charge against William Brown, a pro-Soviet oppositionist who had failed to gain reelection to the National Committee in 1970, of persistently breaching CPA rules. (The hearings against Brown were deferred at his request until 8 February because he was going to East Europe at the invitation of the International Organization of Journalists.) Brown countered by laying charges against CPA National Secretary Laurie Aarons, of engaging in "private" discussions with "acknowledged Trotskyites and non-party radicals" which had resulted in "far-reaching agreement to change party policy from its original Marxist basis on national and international questions to its present neo-Trotskyite and 'national communist' orientation." (*Tribune*, 13 January.) The CPA leadership clearly welcomed this opportunity to engage in debate with Brown and others opposing CPA policies. At the first session of the hearings against Aarons, on 24 February, Brown attempted to substantiate his charges by alleging that Aarons had "implemented demands" made by Denis Freney, who had returned to Australia in 1968 after a period overseas working with the Trotskyist Fourth International. (Freney, who was expelled from the CPA in the late 1950s, rejoined the party in 1970 and became a member of the *Tribune* editorial board.) Brown also claimed that the CPA had been brought into "international disrepute" by Aarons's "uncommunist, unbalanced approach" on the Czechoslovak question and by his "regional internationalism," which allegedly distorted priorities. (*Ibid.*, 3 March.)

Notwithstanding a petition circulated by the minority to challenge his eligibility, Aarons was elected (together with National Committee member Dave Davies) to represent the CPA at the CPSU congress. Pat Clancy, a prominent trade union official and member of the minority faction, followed the proceedings from a special seat among CPSU delegates. (*Ibid.*, 12 May.) Clancy resigned from the CPA in October and, with William Brown and G. Curthoys, headed a new splinter "Socialist Party of Australia" that was formed in December by a sector of those opposing CPA policies. (*Ibid.*, 8 December.) Aarons's speech at the CPSU congress, although on the surface low-keyed and uncontroversial, contained implied responses to most of the Soviet criticisms. For example, he commented—in an allusion to the Soviet charge that the CPA was concerned only with Australasian affairs—that it was the CPA's duty to oppose primarily "our own" capitalism, and that its "prime international task" was "the struggle against Australia's colonial pressure against the developing national liberation struggle in New Guinea, and support for the demands of the oppressed indigenous population of Australia [the Aborigines]" (*Pravda*, 9 April). Aarons went from Moscow to Bucharest for talks with the Romanian communist party before returning to Australia. A joint communiqué noted that the Australian and Romanian parties "agreed that a decisive role in assuring unity of the international communist movement is played by promotion of relations among parties based upon Marxist-Leninist principles of proletarian internationalism, respect for independence, full equality of rights and non-interference in internal affairs and the right of every party to decide its own domestic and external policy" (*Tribune*, 28 April). In an interview (Melbourne radio, 5 May) Aarons said there was "little sign of the development of a socialist democracy in the U.S.S.R." and that there were "still considerable differences" between the CPA and CPSU. The congress, he said, had been "mainly ritualistic," with little chance for party delegates to influence decisions. He added that he and Davies had declined to join other foreign delegations at the conference in criticizing Communist China.

The CPA leadership appeared bent on keeping alive the Czechoslovak issue—one of its major differences with the Soviets. The CPA journal *Australian Left Review* (March) published a lengthy interview with the exiled Czechoslovak reformer, Jiri Pelikan, who expressed strong opposition to Soviet influence in Czechoslovak affairs. The CPA did not attend the Czechoslovak party congress in 1971, but whether because it was not invited or because it chose not to be associated with the "legitimization" of the new Czechoslovak leadership was not disclosed.

Early in May, Aarons published a rebuttal to Brown's charges. He suggested that Trotskyism was being made a scapegoat, both in Australia and elsewhere, for "everything that is wrong in the revolutionary movement." The whole concept of Trotskyism as a counter-revolutionary conspiracy, he declared, was based upon Stalin's *Short History of the CPSU*, which described as a Trotskyist "fabrication" the "testament" by Lenin praising Trotsky as the most able of all the leaders of the communist party and recommending Stalin's removal from the position of secretary-general. Aarons upheld democratic centralism, however, as opposed to the Trotskyist view that "factionalism is permissible within a revolutionary party." It was, he pointed out, not he but Brown, Ross, Watt, and other pro-Soviets who were advocating and practicing factionalism. (*Tribune*, 5 May.)

The hearings of Brown's charges against Aarons continued until 9 May. Aarons was subsequently cleared of all charges. The expulsion of Brown, recommended by the investigating committee, became effective on 15 June. The National Committee announced that it would launch a discussion on the "character and organizational principles of a revolutionary working class party prior to the membership card reissue in September and October" (*ibid.*, 26 May).

Domestic Views and Activities. As in 1970, the CPA's attention to domestic affairs in 1971 was overshadowed by its preoccupation with intra-party developments. On most major issues for the party—military conscription, wage and price demands, and the alleged domination of the economy by foreign interests—it generally echoed the policy and rhetoric of the Australian Labor Party. The formation, in March, of the McMahon government, and the "tough Establishment line" which the CPA predicted it would adopt, were said to be "signs not of the strength of the Liberal-Country Party coalition, but of its weakness." Behind the Liberal Party crisis—"only temporarily resolved by McMahon's election"—lay "deeper clashes of powerful monopoly interests and their divergent policies." McMahon, in this view, favored an "open door to U.S., Japanese, and other foreign capital," the results of which could be averted only by maintaining and intensifying the "present upsurge of militancy in the Australian union movement." (*Tribune*, 17 March.)

International Views and Positions. Laurie Aarons told the National Anti-War Conference, held in Sydney on 17-21 February 1971, that a new "imperialist" strategic concept was emerging—a U.S.-Japanese alliance to dominate the Pacific and maintain imperialist influence in Asia, in which Australia was to be "integrated economically and militarily." The already close economic ties between Britain, Australia, and South Africa were to be gradually developed into a political-military alliance, using as a pretext the alleged Soviet "penetration" of the Indian Ocean, so as to hold back the national liberation revolutions in Asia, Africa, and the Middle East. Australia's traditional "dependence" had led it toward social militarization, authoritarianism, and repression, and reduced its capacity for independent initiative in foreign policy. In implicit consideration of the winding down of Australia's combat role in the Vietnam war, Aarons appealed for the continuation of the anti-war movement on the grounds that Australia's entry into the war had not been an isolated development, but was a reflection of the basic "racialism, mixed with anti-communism, in government policy," which he described as the "main ideological weapon used by the government," citing such alleged slogans as "Stop China's Southward Thrust" and "Fight Them over There Instead of Fighting Them Here." Preservation of "White Australia" and condemnation of "multi-racialism" would constitute the "trump card" of the Australian imperialists. Therefore, he argued, the anti-war movement must continue to focus on racially toned issues: the Aborigines, New Guinea, and

South African apartheid—the latter "certain to become a key issue in Australian political life." (*Australian Left Review*, March.)

The CPA welcomed the People's Republic of China's recent interest in increased foreign contacts which, it commented, had caused "hasty and undignified shifts in policy" by the McMahon and other "reactionary" governments. The Labor Party, "though more sensitive to the Australian people's readiness to be friendly with the Chinese people," had nevertheless "vacillated on the issue, due to right-wing subservience to American imperialist policies." The CPA praised China for its "modification of some previous policies which we regarded as mistaken or ineffective," but scored the Chinese for their support for Yahya Khan in "crushing the legitimate move for autonomy by the people of East Pakistan." (*Tribune*, 26 May.) The visit to China of a Labor Party delegation in July and the forthcoming visit of U.S. President Nixon were said by the CPA to be "guarantees thut the public debate on relations with China will rise far above the past crude rigidity" (*ibid.*, 14 July). The party hailed the United Nations vote to give China its "rightful" seat, a decision which, according to the CPA, "reveals clearly the decreasing scope for maneuver and international domination by the imperialist forces." It charged that the Australian government was ignoring "the significance of the U.N. decision" and "obstinately" continuing to "exclude the world's biggest nation from Australian foreign relations by maintaining its diplomatic connections with the completely discredited and impotent Chiang Kai-shek remnant in Taiwan." (*Ibid.*, 3 November.)

Publications. The CPA's weekly newspaper *Tribune*, its bimonthly *Australian Left Review*, and its quarterly theoretical journal *Discussion* are published in Sydney.

*   *   *

The ACP(ML). The founder and chairman of the Australian Communist Party (Marxist-Leninist) is Edward Hill, a Melbourne attorney. Vice-chairmen are Clarence O'Shea and N. Gallagher; the secretary is Frank Johnson. The party is estimated to have about 250 members, drawn from among organized workers and some student groups.

The ACP(ML) maintains extensive contacts with Communist China, and its statements faithfully reflect Chinese views. Praise for China's Cultural Revolution and criticism of Soviet policy appear regularly in the party's newspaper, *Vanguard*, and its monthly theoretical journal, *Australian Communist*.

The Chinese, for their part, afford the ACP(ML) recognition far beyond that which would be warranted by its size and importance. During Hill's most recent visit to Peking, from 20 November to 2 December 1971, for example, he met with Chou En-lai and a report of his visit was carried in *Peking Review* (10 December).

Valerie Bloom

Burma

The Burma Communist Party (BCP) was founded on 15 August 1939 under the leadership of Thakin Soe.[1] In 1946, following a dispute over the correct strategy for achieving Burmese independence, Thakin Soe and his followers withdrew from the party and formed the Communist Party of Burma (CPB), known as the "Red Flags," and Thakin Than Tun reorganized the Burma Communist Party which became known as the "White Flags." Considerable confusion exists regarding the names of the two groups. While "Burma Communist Party" is in general used to refer to the White Flags, and "Communist Party of Burma" to identify the Red Flags, the two names are frequently interchanged. For convenience the parties will be identified here as BCP(WF) or White Flag for the party reorganized by Thakin Than Tun, and CPB(RF) or Red Flag for the party founded by Thakin Soe in 1946.

While the Red Flags went underground to initiate armed insurrection against the government, the White Flags placed primary emphasis on legal struggle until 1948, when they, too, went underground and launched armed attacks. Since the military coup led by General Ne Win on 2 March 1962, the only legal political party has been the Burma Socialist Program Party (BSPP), which was established by the Ne Win government.

Effective government security operations in recent years have forced the White Flag insurgents to shift their activities from their traditional stronghold in the Pegu Yoma mountains of central Burma to the northeastern border regions.

Between 1951 and 1963 some coordination of activities existed between the two movements. In July and August of 1963 a group of White Flags who had taken up residence in Communist China returned to Burma to participate in negotiations between General Ne Win's "Revolutionary Government of the Union of Burma" and members of both communist parties. In November, after the negotiations broke down, the China-based group joined Thakin Than Tun's BCP(WF) in an attempt to dominate it. Subsequently, Thakin Soe's CPB(RF) was labeled as Trotskyist by the other communists. While both have continued insurgent activities, the Red Flags appear to have receded into the background. Most pronouncements and terrorist activities originate from the White Flags.

Accurate membership figures for the communist parties in Burma are not available. Although estimates vary, the communist insurgents are generally thought to number altogether about 5,000. Perhaps 4,000 to 4,500 of these follow the White Flag party, with fewer than 500 in the Red Flag party and the remainder in small splinter movements such as the Arakan Communist Party (ACP). The population of Burma is about 27 million (estimated 1970).

---

[1]The name "Thakin" literally means "Master." Traditionally reserved for Europeans during the colonial period, it was adopted by nationalists in the 1930's. While still in use today, it is sometimes omitted. Thus, "Thakin Tin Tun" and "Tin Tun" denote the same individual.

Leadership and Organization. The Burma Communist Party (White Flag) has experienced significant leadership changes during the past few years due to a combination of internal friction and increasingly effective government security operations. Party founder and chaiman Thakin Than Tun was assassinated by fellow party members on 24 September 1968, during the party's "cultural revolution." In the next two years only two Politburo and nine Central Committee members escaped similar executions. General Ne Win's "People's Army" and other government security forces killed or arrested a number of important White Flag leaders in late 1970 and in 1971.[2]

At the end of 1971 the BCP(WF) Central Committee was thought to consist of Thakin Zin (chairman), Thakin Ba Thein Tin (first vice-chairman),Bo Thet Tin (Politburo member), Thakin Chit (Politburo member), Aung Myint, By Myint, Kyaw Mya, Naw Seng, Thakin Pe Tint, Thakin Pu (who may have been captured in 1968), and Than Shwe.

The Communist Party of Burma (Red Flag), which some observers concluded had become little more than a "personality cult" for its founder and party chairman, Thakin Soe, was critically weakened on 8 November 1970 when Thakin Soe and three other Central Committee members were captured by the government. By the end of 1971 eight more Central Committee members had either surrendered or been captured or killed.[3]

White Flag organizational structure reportedly extends from the Politburo, through the Central Committee and district committees, down to the township committees. The BCP(WF) "People's Army" is structured along traditional communist lines with party political cadres superior to military commanders at all levels.

The White Flags—with considerable assistance from China—established the "Northeast Command" in 1968, under the leadership of BCP(WF) Central Committee member Naw Seng, who had fled to China in 1949 after deserting the Burmese army. In late 1967 Naw Seng returned to Burma with perhaps 300 men armed and trained by the Chinese. This group formed the nucleus of the Northeast Command, which reportedly has recruited 2,000 to 3,000 troops, primarily from among the large Kachin communities on both sides of the Sino-Burmese border.

The Red Flags have attempted to unite with ethnic minorities, generally with little success. There were reports in mid-1971 of clashes along the southern portion of the Burma-India border between government forces and bands of the "Tripartite Unity Organization," composed of Indian "bandits" and Red Flag communists (*Botataung*, Rangoon, 31 July).

Party Internal Affairs. The purge of "revisionists," which began in 1967 and was still in progress in mid-1970 (Rangoon Domestic Service, 26 June 1970), exacerbated an already significant split between BCP(WF) elements over the issue of armed versus legal struggle. The loss of the party chairman and much of the central committee during the "cultural revolution" was accompanied by additional casualties inflicted by the government militia. Mass defections, which began in 1970, continued during 1971. On 28 March a ceremony was held in Ingaby township to welcome some

[2]The White Flag party secretary-general, Thakin Tin Tun, was killed on 8 September 1970. During 1971, Maung Aye Tha, an important military and finance officer, was captured on 6 March; Ko Htway, officer in charge of tribute collection, surrendered on 19 May; Salaing Tha U, a district secretary, political officer, and commanding officer of the "People's Army's" Number Two Batallion, was killed on 2 July; Sein Pyu Aung, organizer for Kyauktaw township, was killed by government forces on 15 July; San Win, leader for Letpadan township, was severly wounded on 9 August; Tun Hlaing, township officer, was killed on 15 August; and Soe Naung, district committee member, was captured on 17 August. Bo Kan Nyunt, Minby District leader, was reportedly killed by his own men before their surrnder in late 1971.

[3]Immediately following the capture of Thakin Soe and the others, Central Committee member U Thaw Ka surrendered. Soe Lin surrendered on 14 December 1970. Surrendering during 1971 were Shwe Min on 2 July and Bo Mo and Tin U on 26 August. U Ba Yin was captured 21 January. Soe Thien was killed on 7 June and Kya Gyi on 23 June.

200 White Flag insurgents from three townships who had surrendered (*Botataung*, 5 April). Three insurgents who surrendered on 27 August, after killing their commander, reported "distrust and killings" among the White Flags, whose forces were dwindling because of the government's offensives (*ibid.*, 2 September). At the end of the year the pro-Chinese element of the BCP(WF) appeared to be in full control of an organization confronted by serious leadership problems, shortages of food and supplies, and low morale.

The slight information available about the internal affairs of the CPB(RF) suggests that it is facing even more serious problems. Central Committee members who surrendered to the government reportedly asserted: "Red Flag insurgents in the jungle ... are starving, demoralized, and disunited, and are planning to surrender" (*ibid.*, 27 February). They attributed their defection to "oppression and lack of democracy within the party and occasional shortages of food" (*ibid.*, 25 August).

The small Arakan Communist Party (ACP)—a CPB(RF) splinter group—apparently was experiencing organizational difficulties. Reportedly, the ACP split into two hostile factions in late 1970 (*Working People's Daily*, Rangoon, September 4). In November 1971 an ACP township party chairman and his secretary surrendered with three soldiers because of "lack of faith" in the party's line (*Botataung*, 5 November).

Domestic Attitudes and Activities. The victory of the anti-"revisionist" forces in the Burmese communists' "cultural revolution" was apparent in the emphasis on armed struggle in BCP(WF) statements. On 15 August 1971, in a broadcast commemorating the thirty-second anniversary of the founding of the communist movement in Burma, the party's newly created radio station, the "Voice of the People of Burma" (see below), declared:

> The history of the BCP is basically the history of armed struggle, the history of armed revolution of the Burmese people. The BCP existed as a legal political party for only three years, but it has grown during the remaining twenty-nine years while waging underground and armed struggles.

With indirect reference to the "cultural revolution" of 1967-69, the broadcast announced:

> The glorious BCP ... eliminated false rightist and leftist thoughts within the party. The party successfully fought against the revisionist line.... The whole party was made to march along the road of armed struggle and power seizure.... The policy of armed revolution, military victory, and political seizure is the only policy for Burma.

The broadcast continued:

> The final victory of the Burmese people can only be achieved under the leadership of the BCP and the policy of military victory and power seizure. Only when the policies—(1) concentrate on military affairs; (2) peasant base; (3) form alliance with nationalities; (4) expand the united front; and (5) party construction is the key factor—are materialized in accordance with the policy of military victory and power seizure laid down by Thakin Than Tun can final victory be achieved.

General Ne Win's BSPP has become increasingly Marxist in recent years. Following the First Congress of the BSPP, held in June and July, Ne Win's "Revolutionary Council of the Union of Burma" formed the "Government of the Union of Burma," with Ne Win holding the offices of prime minister and minister of defense. Civilian officials were brought into the government, and the BSPP was transformed from a "cadre party" into a "people's party" (Rangoon radio, 24 August). The new party was intended to serve as the "vanguard of the people" (*Far Eastern Economic Review*, Hong Kong, 27 February). At the congress, the BSPP was described as the party of "workers and peasants"—the "basic classes in waging the socialist social revolution" and the "main force behind the BSPP" (*Botataung*, 12 July). BSPP programs for agricultural collectivization, education, medical services, and the establishment of workers' and peasants' councils, and youth, women's, and other mass organizations have frequently been praised by Soviet and

East European communist states (e.g., "Radio Peace and Progress," Moscow, 4 January; *International Affairs*, Moscow, September 1971, p. 118).

The Marxist orientation of the Ne Win government has forced the BCP(WF) publicly to oppose traditional communist policies such as agricultural collectivization and to endorse capitalistic tenets such as private property:

> Only their military government owns the country's farmland, hence only they will sell, mortgage, and transfer ownership of these lands. According to them, the peasants have only the right to till but not to own land.... The policy of the Communist Party of Burma, however, is to allow the tiller to own the land. ("Voice of the People of Burma," 26 September.)

White Flag leaders were obviously concerned about the appeal of the Ne Win government to the people, and often charged it with deceit:

> The Ne Win military government is cheating and tricking the people with sweet words and attractive phrases. They call seizure of political power by reactionaries a revolution, economic robbery and monopoly by top military officials nationalization, and the party of military officials ... the people's party. They are now shamelessly trying to name their mercenary executioners the people's army. (*Ibid.*, 21 October.)

> Ne Win is trying to use sly tricks to get out of ... difficulties. He is cheating the people with all kinds of tricks, such as, transformation of the cadre party into the people's party, return of power to the people, and visiting the People's Republic of China. (*Ibid.*, 15 August.)

A major theme in White Flag propaganda during 1971 was the importance of unity among minority ethnic groups. On 30 September the clandestine radio station asserted:

> The nationalities fighting the Ne Win military government are gradually becoming united and the unity among the Ma-Da-Nya-Ta [NDUF] forces is also growing. The Communist Party of Burma [White Flag], which is a member of the Ma-Da-Nya-Ta, will continue to aid the further growth of these forces as well as the unity of the nationalities in order to defeat Ne Win's military government.

The White Flags have in the past collaborated with the 5,000-strong Karen National Defense Organization. Although they are not thought to have been very successful in attempts to infiltrate the Kachin Independence Army, on 3 September a government spokesman reportedly stated that the Kachin force had joined the BCP-WF (*Botataung*, 10 September).

On 9 April an inaugural broadcast announced the establishment of the party's radio station:

> The "Voice of the People of Burma" radio station of the Burmese Communist Party Central Committee has been inaugurated. [It will] fight Ne Win's military government [and] will be able to organize [the party's] forces all over Burma more easily and quickly.... Revisionism must be combated. The "Burmese Way to Socialism" [the BSPP program] must be fought....The people's radio will reveal to the country, whenever possible, how Ne Win's military government is acting as a U.S. running dog.... It will strive with great loyalty to uphold Marxism-Leninism-Mao Tse-tung Thought.... It will strive to fight for the BCP's ultimate aim—to establish the communist system in Burma.

The voice of the female announcer was clearly recognized as that of one of Peking radio's Burmese staff, and the transmitter was assumed to be situated in China. The fact that the station began to broadcast during the same month that diplomatic relations were restored between Burma and China gave support to the theory that China might tone down its overt anti-Ne Win propaganda, as an indication of friendliness, while covertly continuing to assist the White Flag insurgents. The Soviet Union charged in mid-year:

> In recent times the Chinese leadership has superficially endeavored to improve relations with Burma. Chinese officials have toned down the statements against Burma. However, the Burmese radio station in China has continued the slanderous campaign against Burma.... These facts show that

the Peking leadership has changed only its political tactics towards independent Burma while its true attitude has remained the same. ("Radio Peace and Progress," 30 June.)

In spite of the resumption of diplomatic relations, in April, White Flag insurgents continued to plague the government, claiming that in northern Burma between February and April they "engaged in 71 battles with Ne Win's troops, killing 96 and wounding 56" ("Voice of the People of Burma," 17 June). Later in the year, the *Christian Science Monitor* (2 October) reported from Rangoon: "The level of Chinese Communist-inspired and backed insurgency in Burma's northern region has not diminished."

The White Flags did not restrict their military activities to attacking Ne Win's "People's Army." There were reports of raids on cooperatives, during which the insurgents ordered villagers not to continue their cooperative work (*Botatung*, 12 January). Schools were another favorite target. Having caused hundreds of schools to be closed during 1970 and 1971, the White Flags boasted:

> The people's armed forces' ... attacks against the half-colonial, half-feudal educational system ... can no longer be concealed [by Ne Win]. These events are just part of the people's armed revolutionary struggle which is spreading all over Burma. ("Voice of the People of Burma," 21 October.)

International Views and Positions. The BCP(WF) is firmly aligned with Communist China, a position readily apparent from party pronouncements. On the occasion of the fiftieth anniversary of the founding of the Chinese Communist Party, a BCP(WF) Central Committee message to its Chinese counterpart declared:

> China has not only become a vanguard of the world proletarian revolution against U.S. imperialism, Soviet revisionism and the reactionaries of all countries, but also a great reliable rear for the world revolution.... The Communist Party of China and the Chinese revolution have made the greatest contribution to the liberation struggle of the world's revolutionary people by bringing them the spiritual atom weapon of inestimable power—Marxism-Leninism-Mao Tse-tung Thought. Mao Tse-tung thought is Marxism-Leninism of our era.... Together with the great Chinese Communist Party as well as the Marxist-Leninist Parties of various other countries, we will fight against revisionism both at home and abroad, against U.S. imperialism, against the revived Japanese militarism and against the reactionaries of all countries until final victory. (*Peking Review*, no. 30, 23 July, pp. 15-16.)

The exchange of ambassadors between Burma and China and the subsequent good-will visit to China by Ne Win did not appear to affect significantly the relationship between the Burmese communists and their Chinese benefactors.

No cordiality is wasted between the BCP(WF) and the Soviet Union. Following a Peking radio broadcast on 3 July of the White Flag message quoted above, Moscow "Radio Peace and Progress" (9 July) stated:

> At the time of the fiftieth anniversary of the Chinese Communist Party, the New China News Agency disseminated vehement attacks by the extreme left-wing White Flags against the Burmese Government.... The NCNA is once again spreading lies and slanders against independent Burma.... Why do the Chinese leaders choose to publish this open appeal for subversion against the legal government of Burma?

In October the Soviet head of state, Nikolai Podgorny, stopped off in Rangoon en route to North Vietnam. The visit was attacked by the White Flags:

> Ne Win's military clique and Podgorny held talks and drew up plans to destroy Burma's revolution.... The Communist Party of Burma, which opposes revisionism, will surely crush Podgorny's sly scheme to destroy Burma's revolution, just as the international communist movement crushed Khrushchev's revisionism. Final victory will not be won by the counterrevolutionary scheme of

Ne Win and Podgorny, but it will be won by the people's democratic revolution led by the Communist Party of Burma. ("Voice of the People of Burma," 21 October.)

The "revisionist countries of Eastern Europe" (*ibid.*, 7 November) also came under attack, as did Japan and most of the non-communist countries of Southeast Asia.

Publications. BCP(WF) statements are primarily publicized by the clandestine "Voice of the People of Burma" radio. After broadcasts began in April, coverage of the party's activities in Chinese media appeared to decrease. In the past the party published irregularly a clandestine organ, *People's Power*, which may have been discontinued.

Robert F. Turner

Cambodia

Communism first came to Cambodia in late 1930, when the Communist International instructed the Vietnam Communist Party to change its name to the Indochinese Communist Party because "the Vietnamese, Cambodian and Laotian proletariat have politically and economically to be closely related in spite of their difference in language, customs and race" (quoted in *Thirty Years of Struggle of the Party*, Hanoi, Foreign Language Publishing House, 1960, p. 27). In November 1945, the party was nominally dissolved, but continued to function covertly (see *Vietnam, Democratic Republic of Vietnam*). In 1951 the movement surfaced—ostensibly there were three new parties, representing the communist movements in Vietnam, Laos, and Cambodia; however, the Vietnamese made it clear in their internal party documents that the distinction was only tactical and that a single party would again be formed when the situation was favorable (see P. J. Honey, *Communism in North Vietnam*, Cambridge, Mass., M.I.T. Press, 1963, p. 25). The Cambodian communist movement founded in 1951 was the People's Revolutionary Party of Cambodia (*Dang Nhan Dan Cach Mang Cao Men*; PRP). Its name and statutes were originally set forth in Vietnamese and later translated into Cambodian. Following the Geneva agreements on Indochina (1954), Cambodian communists sought to escape the label of "Vietnamese puppets" by forming the Khmer People's Party (Pracheachon Party; PP) in 1955. They have continued to operate through this front, although since the arrest of PP leaders in 1962 and the subsequent ban of the party itself, little has been heard of this organization. There have in the past been references to a "Khmer Revolutionary Front," reportedly commanded by South Vietnamese communists and based in South Vietnam near the districts of Svay Teap and Rumduol; however, there was no evidence during 1971 that this organization continued to exist.

The PRP is illegal and is estimated to have as many as 1,000 members. The PP is thought to have some 1,000 members and the support of several thousand sympathizers. The Cambodian communist armed forces, the Khmer Rouge, are thought to number about 3,000. (*Far Eastern Economic Review*, Hong Kong, 4 September 1971.) The large majority of the communist military forces fighting in Cambodia are Vietnamese (see below). Both communist and anti-communist sources in Cambodia agree that about 12,000 Cambodians wear Sihanoukist uniforms, indicating their support for the former chief of state. There are thought to be as many as 18,000 unarmed Cambodians involved in supply efforts for the North Vietnamese (*ibid.*).

On 18 March 1970 the Cambodian National Assembly voted unanimously to depose the chief of state, Prince Norodom Sihanouk, who was at the time in Moscow, trying to obtain the assistance of Soviet leaders in his attempt to force the Vietnamese communists to reduce their activities on the Cambodian side of the Cambodia-Vietnam border. There had been widespread dissatisfaction with Sihanouk over a number of issues, but none was more crucial than the open violation of Cambodian territorial integrity by the Vietnamese communists. The deposed Sihanouk went to Peking, where he received a warm welcome from Premier Chou En-lai and a promise of support in his attempt to return to power. On 23 March 1970 Sihanouk announced the formation of the "National United Front of Kampuchea" (NUFK—sometimes identified as FUNK), which he said "unites Communists, monarchists, followers of Sihanouk, and even socialists who are neither monarchists nor communists" (interview, *L'Espresso*, Rome, 21 November 1971). All significant communist activity in Cambodia during 1971 was under the banner of the NUFK, the "Cambodian National People's Liberation Armed Forces" (CNPLAF), or the "Royal Government of National Union" (RGNU) proclaimed by Sihanouk in May 1970. The population of Cambodia is slightly over seven million (estimated 1971).

Leadership and Organization. Little is known about the leadership of the PRP, the PP, and the Khmer Rouge. Tou Samouth has been identified as "president of the clandestine Khmer communist party," and at times as head of the Khmer Rouge. Other sources have asserted that the PRP is controlled from Hanoi by Son Ngoc Minh. Sihanouk has identified Khieu Samphan, Hou Youn, and Hu Nim as the leaders of the PP.

Khmer Rouge leadership is composed primarily of former members of the Viet Minh, Khmer Viet Minh, and Khmer Issarak (Free Cambodia Organization), most of whom reportedly have been PRP members since 1954. The Khmer Rouge rank-and-file is largely recruited from among dissatisfied peasants and some ethnic Cambodians residing in Vietnam (referred to as Khmer Krom). Khmer Rouge leaders allegedly include Neou Pal, Phieun Hak, Nuon Son, and Phouk Chhay.

Since the creation of the NUFK and RGNU in 1970, the importance of the PRP and PP appears to have decreased. Although NUFK/RGNU pronouncements stress "neutralism," Sihanouk has admitted that the majority of the members of the RGNU are Khmer Rouge leaders, and that the power is in the hands of the Cambodian communist party (*New York Times*, 26 September 1970). The NUFK, which controls the RGNU, appears to be similarly controlled by the communists.

The NUFK Politburo consists of: Penn Nouth (chairman), General Duong Sam Ol, Chau Seng, Chan Youran, Chea San, Hu Nim, Khieu Samphan, Thiounn Mumm, Hou Youn, Hout Sambath, and Sarin Chhak. In 1971 three of these—PP members Hu Nim, Khieu Samphan, and Hou Youn—were allegedly carrying out revolutionary struggle in the "liberated areas" of Cambodia. The others, like Sihanouk, were living in Peking. Keat Chhon and Thiounn Prasith are alternate members of the Politburo.

Norodom Sihanouk is head of state of the RGNU, Penn Nouth is premier, and Khieu Samphan is deputy premier, minister of national defense, and (as of June 1971) commander in chief of the Cambodian National People's Liberation Armed Forces (according to the Cambodian Information Agency, AKI, 3 June). Other heads of ministries are Sarin Chhak (foreign affairs), Chau Seng (special missions—thought to be a member of the French Communist Party), Chun Youran (popular education and youth), Dr. Ngo Hu (public health and religious and social affairs), Thiounn Mumm (economy and finance), General Duong Sam Ol (military equipment and armament), Hu Nim (information and propaganda), Hout Sambath (public works, telecommunications, and reconstruction), Hou Youn (interior, communal reforms, and cooperatives), Chea San (justice and judicial reforms), Keat Chhon (minister delegate to the premier), and Thiounn Peasith (minister in charge of coordination of the effort of struggle for national liberation). It is perhaps worth noting that 13 of the 14 ministers are also NUFK Politburo members or alternate members.

NUFK member organizations include the Peasants' Union, the Association of Democratic Youth, the Association of Patriotic Teachers and Intelligentsia, the Writers' League, "representatives of national minorities and the Buddhist faith," and several student organizations operating "beyond the Cambodian borders" (*Izvestiia*, 7 May 1971). Other groups identified as belonging to the

NUFK are the Cambodian Trade Labor Union, the Cambodian Democratic Women's Union, and the Cambodian People's Movement of United Resistance.

There have been reports of friction between the Khmer Rouge and Sihanouk, who was viewed as an opportunist and therefore unacceptable as the leader of a communist movement (see *YICA*, 1971, p. 531).

Domestic Attitudes and Activities. Since the Cambodian communists declared their support for the NUFK and RGNU, almost all statements on domestic matters have been made in the name of one of these Peking-based organizations. During 1971 primary attention was given to military activities. The Maoist doctrines of armed struggle, self-reliance, and protracted warfare were frequently evident in propaganda broadcasts:

> The Cambodian people are fully aware that the final victory of the Cambodian revolution will be decided on the battlefield by the Cambodian people themselves by relying on revolutionary violence—political struggle and non-political struggle, with armed struggle as the principal form of struggle ... and by following the slogans: independence, sovereignty, relying mainly on their own forces, and conducting a protracted but certainly victorious struggle, whatever the difficulties. (AKI, 10 August 1971.)

Although the Cambodian government of Premier Lon Nol surpassed the expectations of most of his critics and many neutral observers, the communists were able to make significant military progress during 1971. At the end of 1971 the NUFK was claiming control of four-fifths of the territory of Cambodia and five million of the seven-million population (TASS, 10 September). While these claims were clearly inflated—U.S. journalists put the figure at half of the territory (*New York Times*, 19 November)—the communist military threat to Cambodia was serious. On 22 January the communists conducted a surprise raid on Pochentong airport at Phnom Penh and "all but entirely wiped out Cambodia's operational air force" (*Le Monde*, Paris, 3 February). The communists' capture of Snuol was the subject of several propaganda broadcasts in June (AKI, 2 June). The most important government operations during 1971 were "Operation Tchenla Two" along Route Six north of Phnom Penh, and the complementary "Operation Kraham Kor" moving southward from Kompong Thom along Route Six. Both operations began in August, with the objective of opening the important road and cutting communist supply lines. Both operations began with modest successes in recapturing villages and hamlets along the communications route, but in December government forces were forced into a general retreat following "a fierce communist onslaught along the entire line of advance" (Reuter, 10 December). Following a pattern established by Vietnamese communists in South Vietnam during the early years of their insurgency, an increased emphasis was given to terrorism—especially assassination and abduction. The Cambodian government also followed a South Vietnamese precedent and established a "Chieu Hoi" program to encourage Cambodians fighting with the communists to defect or "rally" to the side of the government. The communists made a similar appeal, urging "soldiers, officers, commandos, self-defense forces, and functionaries serving the traitorous Lon Nol-Sirik Matak ... clique" to "join our armed forces and people in the liberated zone":

> Your wives and children are awaiting your return. If you take risks to go back to the Lon Nol-Sirik Matak-Son Ngoc Thanh clique you will never see your kin again.... Do not sacrifice your lives for Lon Nol [etc.,]—they are approaching their doomsday and preparing to take flight abroad.... If you are brave you should turn your guns and cannons against the Lon Nol [clique]. If you want to escape death and desert to the liberated zone, you should kill [your leaders] first, otherwise they will not allow you to come with us. (Voice of the NUFK, 10 December).

During 1970 there were reports that Sihanouk had been denied his request to visit the "liberated zone" of Cambodia by the Chinese and Vietnamese communists (see *YICA*, 1971, p. 538-39). In 1971 he announced that he had intended "to return to the liberated areas of Cambodia to direct the resistance there," but had been dissuaded by army leaders for "security reasons" (Agence France Presse, AFP, 3 August). In the July issue of *Le Bulletin Mensuel de Documentation*, Sihanouk printed a message allegedly written by Khieu Samphan in April, which stated:

> Considering the present conditions of our struggle and interests of our people, it is imperative that Samdech head of state [Sihanouk] and other principal NUFK members reside in Peking.... The presence of [Sihanouk] in our liberated zone will undoubtedly strengthen our struggle. We would like this except for the problem of your security. (AKI, 16 August.)

Sihanouk continued throughout 1971 to issue lengthy "Messages to the Khmer Nation," most of which were broadcast in several parts because of their length. Each message dealt with a different subject, ranging from charges that the South Vietnamese had annexed Cambodian territory with the consent of Lon Nol (21st message, 6th part, NCNA, 18 June), to attacks on the announcement by the Lon Nol government that it would write a new constitution (22d message, NCNA, 27 June). These messages consisted primarily of quotations (always shortened to omit unfavorable references to Sihanouk or to the presence of North Vietnamese soldiers in Cambodia) from Western press sources, spliced together by Sihanouk's commentary.

The proposal of national elections by the Lon Nol government was the subject of bitter attack, often in conjunction with attacks on the proposed constitution:

> How can a deformed monster, half dog and half pig, be transformed into a normal human being? Can this republic of traitors, fascists, and corrupt persons be metamorphosed overnight ... into a popular regime? Can the adoption of a constitution ... change the nature of the bandits and knaves holding sway in Phnom Penh? Can the farce of demagogic, fraudulent, and utterly deceitful elections give a truly representative face to a national assembly composed of hooligans, traffickers, boozers, criminals, and traitors? Can ignominious individuals who would sell their fathers and mothers for a few dollars surreptitiously turn into honest citizens and patriots respectful of national traditions and customs? (AKI, 3 June).

The Buddhist religion plays an extremely important role in Cambodian society, and because of this the communists have attempted to exploit it. During the month of May (the month of Buddha's 2,515th birthday anniversary), the Cambodian Information Agency (AKI) reported details of three separate gatherings of Buddhist monks in various parts of the "liberated zone," and claimed that at each "congress" a resolution condemning the Lon Nol government and praising the NUFK was "unanimously adopted" (see, for example, AKI, 3 June). The monks were told to relay the communist message to the rural population. As had been the case in the past, monks who refused to cooperate were sometimes executed by the communists (*Far Eastern Economic Review*, 22 May).

Interviews with Sihanouk during 1971 gave some indications of his assessment of the future. In June he announced that after the war was over he would retire to France with his family: "I don't want to rule any more." He predicted that after "liberation" Cambodia would become a Marxist state "modeled on Romania," but retaining Buddhism as the state religion. (*Washington Post*, 17 June.) In November he said that "perhaps after the liberation the communists will try to eliminate the others [in the RGNU] from power, as happened in Czechoslovakia with Masaryk." He said that there was "no possibility of negotiating" a settlement, and a coalition government was "absolutely out." Sihanouk stated that if Cheng Heng—currently Cambodian chief of state—were to "come to our side," he could be appointed prime minister "or something on that order" of the RGNU. "Even Lon Nol, if he should come to our side, we would be disposed to accept him." (*L'Espresso*, Rome, 21 November.)

International Views and Positions. Although Cambodian communists have traditionally been most closely aligned with North Vietnam, and the presence of an estimated 60,000 Vietnamese communist troops in Cambodia during 1971 reflected Hanoi's continued involvement, the NUFK and RGNU appear to be more closely attached to the Chinese communists. This appearance may well be the result of an intentional attempt to underplay the North Vietnamese role in the fighting in Cambodia, and to increase the appeal of the Sihanouk "government" to the traditionally anti-Vietnamese Cambodian people. In an interview in December, Sihanouk said:

> China is giving us all kinds of aid, which enables us to exist as a state. We have a national budget, the money for which comes from China as a long-term, no-interest loan.... With China's help, we are going to win this war.... China will always be there to give us whatever we need. I will add that the military aid China is giving us is free. (*Tribune de Genève*, Geneva, 10 December).

In March Sihanouk announced that China was ready to send volunteers to fight in Indochina if necessary:

> I can tell you that the Chinese people are quite ready to aid physically the three Indochinese peoples in any new escalations of the war.... Physically, that means that Chinese volunteers could go to one or the other of our Indochinese countries to help one or the other of our three peoples defeat the American aggressors and their mercenaries. (Reuters, 10 March.)

Sihanouk said that Chinese leaders had assured him that they would send volunteers in response to calls for help.

On the first anniversary of the founding of the NUFK, *Jen-min jih-pao* featured an editorial affirming China's "unshirkable internationalist duty to do everything in our power to support and aid the Cambodian ... peoples in their anti-U.S. struggle" (*Peking Review*, no. 13, 26 March). Chou En-lai sent a message to Penn Nouth on the occasion of the first anniversary of the founding of the RGNU (*ibid.*, no. 20, 14 May).

The announcement that U.S. President Nixon was to visit China during 1972 was apparently viewed with some alarm by Cambodian communists, as a great deal of propaganda coverage was devoted to the subject. In July Sihanouk praised the Chinese invitation as showing "political courage and imagination," and expressed his confidence that Chine would "maintain the solidarity that has permitted Cambodia to survive in the face of imperialism" (Reuter, 24 July). In September he said that Chou En-lai had promised him that "We shall cede nothing to Nixon. We shall never abandon you. We shall support you until final victory." (AFP, 10 September.) Perhaps in an attempt to reverse the psychological pressure, Sihanouk asserted that "President Nixon's upcoming visit to China heralds the abandoning by the United States of the rightist regimes that are in power in Saigon, Phnom Penh and Taipei" (AFP, 2 September).

NUFK/RGNU relations with the Soviet Union, which has refused to grant official recognition to the Sihanouk "government" and still maintains a diplomatic mission in Phnom Penh, ranged from cordial to cold. This was the result of the NUFK's desire to gain Soviet recognition on the one hand, and anger at the Soviet refusal to give it on the other. In March, Chea San (RGNU minister of justice and Sihanouk's envoy to Moscow) stated in Moscow that the RGNU was "very happy" with the Soviet position on Cambodia, in spite of the Soviet failure to recognize the Sihanouk "government" (Reuter, 23 March). On 6 May the U.S.S.R. ended a "week of Soviet people's solidarity with the Cambodian people's struggle against the aggression of American imperialism" (*Izvestiia*, 7 May). From 1 through 10 September an NUFK delegation headed by General Duong Sam Ol was in the Soviet Union on a friendship mission. The visit was in response to an invitation from the Soviet Association of Solidarity with Afro-Asian People, issued earlier in the year, and had as its purpose to "try to strengthen the ties of solidarity between the Soviet and Cambodian peoples [and] to create favorable conditions to obtain the U.S.S.R. government's recognition of RGNU'' (Voice of the NUFK, 2 September). At the conclusion of the visit, General Duong Sam Ol "emphasized that the Cambodian people know well and highly appreciate the support that the Soviet people are rendering to the Cambodians," and expressed his gratitude to the Soviet communist party (TASS, 10 September). The U.S.S.R. stated that it "fully supports the courageous struggle of the Cambodian patriots who have rallied behind the banner of the National Unity Front," and asserted that "the Soviet public supports the political program of the National Unity Front" (TASS, 10 September).

On the other hand, as early as April Sihanouk expressed obvious bitterness about his treatment by the Soviet Union. He remarked at a lunch attended by several journalists: "I tell you we have not got anything, not one thing, from them" (*Washington Post*, 20 April). After the failure of the September friendship delegation to secure Soviet recognition of the RGNU, anti-Soviet statements became commonplace. On 1 December, Chau Seng charged in Paris that the Soviet Union had violated the principles of internationalism by refusing to recognize the Sihanouk government: "The position taken toward us by the U.S.S.R. is not in conformity with the principles of internationalism" (AFP, 1 December). In an interview with a Swiss journalist nine days later, Sihanouk was asked to explain the Soviet attitude toward his "government":

> I think the Russians feel like whites, and they don't want the yellow people to get too strong. It would be hard for the U.S.S.R. not to help North Vietnam, which is in the socialist camp. But I've seen what the Russians are giving Hanoi. The planes, the rockets, the radar—none of it is modern equipment. The Russians haven't given Hanoi a quarter of what they have given Egypt. Why? I'll tell you; it's because the Russians don't want Hanoi to win. They give the Vietnamese just enough so they won't lose the war, but not enough to win it, even though they could do it. The Russians have a complex about the yellow peril [and] they are really aiming at the Chinese. (*Tribune de Genève*, 10 December).

Sihanouk led a friendship delegation to North Vietnam from 26 January to 9 February, where together with that country's president he reaffirmed "strict loyalty to the Joint Declaration of the Indochinese Peoples' Summit Conference" (*Peking Review*, no. 8, 19 February). On the first anniversary of the conference (see *YICA*, 1971, pp. 536-38) Sihanouk exchanged messages of solidarity with the other participants. The RGNU issued a statement supporting the 22 June "peace initiative" of Laotian communist leader Prince Souphanouvong (see *Laos*) (AKI, 7 July). En route back to China from North Vietnam, Sihanouk allegedly held talks with Souphanouvong in the "frontier region of Laos." A joint statement of solidarity was issued on 9 February. (*Peking Review*, no. 8, 19 February.)

Following China and North Vietnam, North Korea and Cuba were the main suppliers of aid to the Sihanouk government (*Washington Post*, 20 April). Albania was listed on one occasion as a supplier of aid (AKI, 10 August).

By the end of 1971 the RGNU claimed to have established diplomatic relations with Albania, Algeria, Central African Republic, the People's Republic of China, Congo (Brazzaville), Cuba, Equatorial Guinea, Republic of Guinea, Iraq, Libya, Mali, Mauritania, North Korea, North Vietnam, Romania, Senegal, Somalia, the Provisional Revolutionary Government of South Vietnam, South Yemen, Sudan, Syria, Tanzania, the U.A.R., Yemen, Yugoslavia, and Zambia.

Sihanouk paid a friendship visit to North Korea from 22 July to 11 August, ut the invitation of Kim Il-Song, and the two exchanged messages of solidarity on several occasions during the year.

The RGNU "foreign minister," Sarin Chhak, made an extensive tour of Asia, Africa, the Middle East, and Eastern Europe during the first six months of 1971. His stops included: Ceylon, North Korea, Mali, Guinea, Mauritania, Ethiopia, Yugoslavia, Albania, Equatorial Guinea, and

Romania. Sihanouk met in Peking with Romanian Communist Party Secretary-General Ceauşescu (*Peking Review*, no. 25, 18 June), and eight days later with Yugoslav Foreign Minister Tepavac (Belgrade radio, 10 June).

Japan and Thailand were subjects of attacks by the Cambodian Information Agency of the NUFK. In December, France and Switzerland were criticized by Sihanouk for continuing to recognize the Lon Nol government instead of the RGNU. South Korea and "the Chinese province of Taiwan" were also denounced.

Publications. The official organ of the PP is *Somleeng Apyiakrut*, a semiweekly publication. The PP puts out three other journals: *Mitt Pheap*, *Ek Peap*, and *L'Observateur*. The official Vietnamese communist organ in Cambodia is a daily newspaper, *Trung Lap* (Neutrality).

The NUFK has its own "Cambodian Information Agency" (AKI), thcough which it releases periodic propaganda statements. The "Voice of the NUFK" radio began broadcasting on 1 August 1970, and is "the sole voice of the Cambodian people" according to Sihanouk (AKI, 1 August 1971). The Voice of the NUFK is thought to be located in southern North Vietnam, or according to some sources in "a hole in the ground in northeastern Kratie Province" (*Far Eastern Economic Review*, 21 August).

Peking, Hanoi, and Moscow radio and the Viet Cong Liberation Radio all broadcast for Cambodian listeners. Major NUFK and RGNU documents and events are recorded in *Peking Review* and are reported by the NCNA.

Robert F. Turner

Ceylon

The first Marxist party in Ceylon was the Ceylon Equal Society Party (Lanka Sama Samaja Pakshaya; LSSP), formed in 1935. Its founders were young Western-educated intellectuals, including N. J. Perera, Colvin R. de Silva, S. A. Wickremasinghe, Philip Gunawardena, and Leslie Goonewardene. In 1939 the LSSP rejected the Stalinist line of the Third International in favor of Trotskyism, and in 1940 expelled a small Stalinist group led by Wickremasinghe. This group immediately formed the United Socialist Party, which in 1943 became the Ceylon Communist Party (Lanka Kommunist Pakshaya; LKP).

The original LSSP, now led by N. M. Perera and Leslie Goonewardene, lost much of its Trotskyist character in 1964 when it was expelled from the Fourth International. A number of small Trotskyist parties have broken from the LSSP, most of them since 1964. One such party, formerly known as the Viplavakari LSSP, is now called the People's United Front (Mahajana Eksath Peramuna; MEP) and is led by Philip Gunawardena. There are also the LSSP-Revolutionary (LSSP-R), headed by P. Bala Tampoe, and its offshoot, the Revolutionary Samasamaja Party (RSP), led by Edmond Samarkoddy. Still another splinter is the Revolutionary Communist League (RCL), formed in 1968 and led by Keerthi Balasuriya.

The predominantly pro-Soviet LKP suffered a split in 1963 when a pro-Chinese faction broke away following the expulsion of its leader, Nagalingam S. Sanmugathasan. In 1964 each LKP group held its own "Seventh Congress of the Ceylon Communist Party," and each has continued to use the LKP name.

At the end of 1969 an apparently new group became active. This was the People's Liberation Front (Janata Vimukthi Peramuna; JVP), popularly called the "Che Guevara movement."

The parties representing the core of the leftist forces in Ceylon are the LSSP, the pro-Soviet LKP, and the socialist Holy Ceylon Freedom Party (Sri Lanka Freedom Party; SLFP), led by Mrs. Sirimavo Bandaranaike. The latter, except for a brief period in 1960, was the island's ruling party from 1956 to 1965, either by itself or as the dominant member of a leftist coalition. All three parties, which had formed a "United Front" in 1968, became partners in a coalition government as a result of national elections held in May 1970.

The population of Ceylon is 12,800,000 (1971 census).

The Pro-Castroite JVP. The People's Liberation Front (Janata Vimukthi Paramuna; JVP) was created secretly in 1966 by 22-year-old Rohan Wijeweere, former medical student from Patrice Lumumba University in Moscow and a second-generation Marxist, his father having been a founding member of the group which became the LKP. Wijeweere apparently followed the Maoist revolutionary line in Moscow because he was refused permission to return to Russia after 1964. He went instead to North Korea for training in subversion and sabotage. On completion of this training he returned to Ceylon and joined the pro-Chinese LKP. Two years later, he broke with that small, highly disciplined group and formed the JVP among disgruntled Sinhalese Buddhist young people in rural areas. Aiming at an armed revolution along the Castro-Guevarist lines, the JVP drew its recruits mainly from among the 14,000 unemployed graduates of Ceylon's universities and high schools. Some of these young people belonged to the Revolutionary Communist Youth (the student organization of the LSSP), the LSSP-Revolutionary, and the All-Ceylon Federation of Communist and Progressive Youth League of the pro-Soviet LKP. The JVP was composed of comparatively well-educated young men and women from middle-class homes, some 75 per cent between 18 and 20 years of age, 15 per cent between 16 and 18, and 10 per cent over 25.

Leadership and Organization. In addition to Wijeweere, the movement's only public figure, leaders mentioned by various sources include Mahinda Wijesekera, Dharmedasa Jayasinghe, Ven Mangala, Themis Silva (editor of the movement's journal), and a schoolgirl named Sumana.

The basic JVP unit is a five-man cell: ideological indoctrination has been conducted through five special lectures given to large and small groups, more or less secretly, throughout the island. The lecturers, sometimes wearing masks or speaking from behind a screen, dialectically covered the following subjects: Ceylon's Economic Crisis, Indian Communalist Expansionism (addressed primarily to anti-Tamil emotions of the Sinhalese majority), The Failure of the Left in Ceylon (emphasizing the generation gap and unfulfilled electoral promises of the United Left Front), and The Need for Revolution. Less trusted recruits were sent away after four lectures and told that the last talk did not concern them. (*Washington Post*, 9 May 1971.)

Domestic Attitudes and Activities. The JVP first received publicity when it was reported that extremists intended to disrupt the 1970 general election campaign. Wijeweere and other former students of Lumumba University were arrested. The government, apparently aware of the growing danger and informed about the production of bombs, cracked down on the JVP. Wijeweere was released after the elections at the insistence of communists serving with the LSSP in the coalition of Mrs. Bandaranaike's moderately socialist SLFP. At an open JVP rally in Colombo, Wijeweere claimed that the JVP had contributed to the electoral success of the coalition by preaching Marxist-Leninist ideology in the villages and agitating against the incumbent capitalist government. Cleavage between the young radicals and the two major Marxist parties in the coalition was bound to occur, in view of the fact that the latter "tended to downgrade the importance of direct action and extra-constitutional struggle in achieving their objectives" and were emphasizing "parliamentary and electoral activities" (R. N. Kearney, *Trade Unions and Politics in Ceylon*, Berkeley, Calif., 1971, p. 63).

At a public rally in Colombo on 27 February 1971 Wijeweere and other JVP speakers alleged that Mrs. Bandaranaike's coalition had failed the working class and that the parliamentary process was futile as a road to real socialism. Calling for a socialist state based on principles of Marxism, Leninism, and Maoism, Wijeweere claimed that he believed only in a Marxist dictatorship secured by revolution, and warned that revolution would start on the day his group was banned.

The Rebellion. On 6 March about 150 youths made a violent assault against the U.S. Embassy in Colombo. It is not clear whether this attack—by a self-styled "Mao Youth Movement" and involving the death of a police inspector—represented a part of the JVP revolutionary program. The attackers left leaflets reading: "American murderers, get out of Vietnam, Cambodia and Laos. Stop immediately your aid to the anti-Che Guevara movement. Peoples of Indo-China, we are with you." Reportedly, five groups were involved in the subsequent March-April uprising—"all supporting Peking's interpretations of Marxist-Leninist theory and strongly pro-Sinhalese Buddhist" and planning to "overthrow Mrs. Bandaranaike's government and install one of their own"—and the JVP "was the prime one" (*Asian Survey*, February 1972).

The government used the assault on the Embassy as grounds for preventive measures against the revolutionaries. Wijeweere was arrested on 13 March and a state of emergency declared three nights later following the accidental explosion of a large bomb cache which killed five youths.

Searches by police and armed services discovered large quantities of explosives, firearms, uniforms, and subversive literature. A young cashier made off with Rs. 57,000 (about $6,000 on the black market) from the Bank of Ceylon, apparently destined for JVP funds; a kidnaping attempt on the Social Service Minister was reported; explosives were found to have been stolen from government depots; sabotage caused power failure in one town; a bomb explosion at Ceylon University brought police to the dormitories and led to the discovery of bombs and large quantities of explosive material. In 22 March a UPI dispatch quoted a government official as saying that there had been 150 arrests since beginning of the emergency. Some of the arrested wore blue jeans and blue shirts resembling the Che Guevarist clothes of Latin American revolutionaries; many had weapons and explosives. Among them were unemployed graduates, village teachers, and teen-age girls trained for guerrilla-type activities. In 23 March Prime Minister Bandaranaike stated:

> Inquiries have revealed [a] widespread plan for a violent attack on public institutions.... Significant material preparations such as the large manufacture of hand-bombs, the collection of explosives and detonators, the careful preparation of maps indicating the position of key installations, police stations, and residences of important government personnel provide ample proof that the instigators of this movement had no intention of confining themselves to social change through democratic processes. Large-scale thefts of guns, corrosive acids, and other dangerous substances in different parts of the island added further proof of the intentions of this movement.

Evidently Mrs. Bandaranaike and her ministers believed that in the circumstances it was necessary to call out not only regular police but all the armed forces to prevent a revolt. According to some interpretations, however, "A witch-hunt campaign against the JVP and similar left-wing groups must seem just what the United Front needs to distract public attention away from the sagging economy" (*Intercontinental Press*, New York, 5 April). That Trotskyite viewpoint was supported by the *Far Eastern Economic Review* (Hong Kong). Emergency measures seem to have prematurely forced the JVP leadership into open rebellion so as to prevent extermination of the movement.

On 5 April insurgents made a concerted attack on at least 25 police stations throughout the island, disarming the men and capturing vast amounts of light weapons and ammunition. The strongholds of the rebellion were in the rubber-producing district of Kegalle and the southern jungle of Sinharaja. The government hit back by imposing curfews and by outlawing the JVP movement on 6 April. Schools and universities were closed; security forces (police, army, air force and navy) totaling 25,000 men took part in counter-insurgency operations; foreign powers regardless of political coloration were approached for assistance. On the other side, about 100,000 Sinhalese gave logistic support to an estimated 20,000 JVP members and a hard-core closer to 3,000 or 5,000.

In her 6 April broadcast, the Prime Minister said that the capture of ammunition and bomb caches at Colombo by security forces had enabled the government to prevent an attack on the capital city and that attackers "using firearms and bombs" had been repulsed. At the military part of the Bandaranaike National Airport some 30 miles north, an attack was prevented by the Ceylonese Air Force. In the city of Polonnaruwa in North Central Province, 29 insurgents were killed when they assaulted a police station. Tanks, helicopters, and fighter aircraft were used in the final operations, which included air raids on jungle strongholds and the machine-gunning of streets in cities to enforce the curfew.

On 9 April Mrs. Bandaranaike broadcast an appeal to the nation to help stamp out the "gang of power-hungry schemers'' who were trying to topple her socialist government. The following day, the government decreed the death penalty for any one aiding insurgents or plotting against any government official, including police and military personnel. A call for volunteers was issued to strengthen the 12,000-man army (only 6,700 well-trained). Some 5,000 civilians took up positions as a defense guard in the capital to help the police patrol streets and protect vulnerable factories or public buildings. Loyal trade union leaders associated with parties of the ruling coalition appealed to plantation workers (mainly stateless Tamils) to defend the tea and rubber estates, allegedly chief targets of the revolt. Indeed due to the communalist (Sinhalese) character of the JVP movement, the rebels were never able to tap the Tamil resources of that potential epicenter for a class revolt in Ceylon. There is evidence that many Sinhalese peasants actively supported the rebellion, while others were afraid to cooperate with the police in remote rural areas. As in most counter-guerrilla operations, innocent bystanders suffered. An official quoted in the *Washington Post* (9 May) said: "For every insurgent killed, 5 or 10 villagers are detained and beaten, maybe killed."

One by one, JVP strongholds were eliminated. The situation had returned to normal by the beginning of June, when schools reopened. Altogether 16,000 suspects were incarcerated and sent to rehabilitation centers to await screening. According to Prime Minister Bandaranaike's official account in parliament, the number killed in action during the April upheaval did not exceed 1,200 police, troops, and rebels. (Other sources give much higher figures.) The damage to public and private property was estimated at some Rs. 400 million ($67 million at the official exchange rate) (*Asian Survey*, February 1972).

Only three major figures known in Ceylonese politics were identified as directly involved in the insurgency: Vasudeva Nanyakkara (an LSSP parliament member, also youth league leader of the party), S. D. Bandaranayake (a former parliament member who started in the SLFP but joined the pro-Peking LKP), and Susil Siriwardena (a senior civil servant affiliated to the LSSP who was tipped for a distinguished future in the administration). (*Far Eastern Economic Review*, 14 August).

Foreign Support. Officially only one country, the Democratic People's Republic of Korea (DPRK) was identified by the Bandaranaike government as fomenting and supporting the rebellion. The North Korean ambassador and his entire staff were expelled on 16 April—only half a year after relations had been established to implement one of Mrs. Bandaranaike's electoral planks, namely to recognize all communist regimes while suspending relations with Israel. The government refrained, however, from severing diplomatic ties with the DPRK. Causes for the expulsion may have been several. For instance, the rebels claimed to have received ideological guidance from the teachings of such prominent communist revolutionary leaders as Mao Tse-tung, Che Guevara, Régis Debray, and Kim Il-sung. Portraits of Kim were discovered at some of the caches, in addition to North Korean pamphlets. The Sinhalese translator in the embassy, T. G. Kalyananda, was found to be a key figure in the conspiracy, and Rohan Wijeweere was apparently trained both in Moscow and in North Korea. It seemed symptomatic that the embassy staff left Ceylon on a Soviet Aeroflot flight after spending some time at the U.S.S.R. Embassy prior to departure.

Although the Soviet Union refrained from giving any open support to the Ceylonese insurgents, there were indications of indirect assistance. The SEATO Bulletin of 1 June found suggestions of "a measure of Soviet complicity in the whole affair, or at least foreknowledge and tacit approval." For its part, TASS on 19 May reminded the Ceylon government that "the people" expected "energetic measures in the implementation of the programme of progressive changes," and said that these measures were meeting "growing resistance from right-wing forces and their allies abroad." Those comments were probably meant to strengthen the LKP stand in the coalition government against its right wing, led by Minister of Home Affairs Felix Dias Bandaranaike, the influential nephew of the Prime Minister's assassinated husband. In reply, the Colombo *Sun* (21 May) denounced the Soviet interpretation as "lopsided, cock-eyed, and prejudicial." Later a Soviet writer tried to put the blame for the JVP rebellion on the U.S. Central Intelligence Agency (*New Times*, Moscow, no. 37, September).

Officially the Soviet Union and the LKP disassociated themselves from the rebellion. Moscow radio, broadcasting to Southeast Asia on 18 April, said that the emergency had arisen from "a plot by ultra-left terrorists and reactionary forces" and that JVP objectives had nothing in common with true socialism. In response to Mrs. Bandaranaike's appeal for assistance the Soviet Union supplied six MIG-17s and two K-26 troop-carrying helicopters which arrived on 19 April together with about 60 Soviet personnel. The planes were to be flown only by Ceylonese pilots, who would be trained by Soviet instructors. This "assistance" enabled the Soviet Union to establish an important foothold at the strategic Katuanayake airport.

The Czechoslovak news agency CTK on 20 April, reported an interview in the Hungarian party organ *Népszabadság* with the chairman of the pro-Soviet LKP, Dr. Sugiswara Abeywardna Wickremasinghe. He alleged that "rightist groups opposing the progressive program and nationalization put forward by the leftist government of Ceylon [were] in the background of the rebellion." The U.A.R. and Yugoslavia reportedly have channeled Soviet arms and ammunition to Ceylon.

Mainland China's first comment on the rebellion came in   a letter to Mrs. Bandaranaike from Premier Chou En-lai, dated 26 April, but released by the Ceylonese government a month later. It reaffirmed China's opposition to "ultra-left and right opportunism" and added: "Thanks to the efforts of your Excellency and the Ceylonese Government, the chaotic situation created by a handful of persons who style themselves 'Guevarists' and into whose ranks foreign spies have sneaked has been brought under control." In the same letter, Chou offered a long-term, interest-free loan of Rs. 150 million (some $25 to $30 million) in convertible foreign exchange. The hard-pressed government expressed its gratitude with a statement from a former Trotskyite, Dr. Hilary A. de Silva Gunasekera, permanent secretary in the Ministry of Planning and Development, who said on 2 June, after the signing of the aid agreement:

> It is a gesture unprecedented as far as Ceylon is concerned and unprecedented in the annals of economic assistance.... The gesture is all the more appreciated because China herself has enormous problems of economic development.... It will help in supporting our ability to pay for imports when the five-year plan of economic development now under preparation will come into effect from 1972. In this way it will help ease our liquidity crisis. (*Ceylon Daily News*, 3 June.)

Nevertheless, China was reproached by the United National Party (UNP) opposition speaker in the Ceylon senate with the charge that the loan was "conscience money," presumably to compensate for stirring up the rebellion or for providing it with material aid. In response to such accusations, the Bandaranaike government declassified "top secret" documents providing further evidence of the lengths to which China had gone in accommodating Ceylon and in backing the government's effort to crush the rebellion. A letter by Ceylon's ambassador on a talk with the Chinese premier said that Chou expressed concern over developments in Ceylon and disapproval of the "Che Guevarist" movement, and was surprised that

> a left government in Ceylon could be attacked by counter revolutionaries. He had also said that China had had good relations with the governments of Mr. and Mrs. Bandaranaike. The Chinese Prime Minister had also expressed regret that China was unable to provide military aid to Ceylon as Chinese ships carrying arms to Tanzania had left Colombo before Ceylon's request was made. Mr. Chou En-lai had said that China could give both financial and military aid to the Ceylon Government. The Chinese Premier in conclusion had promised wholehearted support of the Ceylon

Government, saying, "Whom else can we support in Ceylon except the Government of Mrs. Bandara-naike?" (*Ibid.*, 24 June.)

Despite the fact that the secretary-general of the pro-Chinese LKP had been arrested in mid-April, China obviously decided to counteract Soviet influence by strengthening its political position in the strategic island halfway between the Black Sea and Vladivostok.

The country most interested in suppressing the rebellion was India, which promptly provided six helicopters and pilots, a 150-man infantry unit to guard the airport and its Embassy, and four naval frigates to patrol coastal waters and prevent smuggling of arms to the guerrillas. Pakistan, despite or because of its disputes with India, provided two helicopters. In turn, Ceylon granted permission for Pakistan planes to refuel at Bandanaraike Airport en route to East Pakistan during the months before the outbreak of the December war in that area.

Great Britain supplied small arms and ammunition from its Singapore base and six helicopters, originally purchased from the U.S.A. Spare parts for three U.S.-built helicopters, bought by the previous government of Dudley Senanayake, were delivered from the United States. This speedy military support from countries belonging to rival power blocs helped Prime Minister Bandaranaike to present the results "as a vindication of her policy of non-alignment and neutralism." (*Ibid.*, 1 December.)

*   *   *

Marxist Establishment. While the JVP rebellion made headlines in the late spring of 1971, the two traditional Marxist parties of Ceylon and their leftist splinter groups remained out of the limelight and adjusted their theoretical positions to the situation. The year ended anti-climactically with economic and constitutional reform by the coalition government, to save the country from financial insolvency and implement some of the demands for more socialism by the defeated young radicals. It was, thus, a bad time for the aging Marxist leaders of all persuasions. None of the four Marxist groups could afford to go through any substantial change of leadership or structure. Perhaps their elitist character and ossification called for revolt by the disgruntled younger generation—a revolt which further undermined the political weight of the old-fashioned communists and former Trotskyists vis-à-vis the majority member of the ruling coalition, namely the semi-bourgeois SLFP of Mrs. Bandaranaike.

The LSSP. The Lanka Sama Samajo Party, which celebrated its thirty-fifth anniversary on 18 December 1970, still remains not only the oldest but also the largest of Marxist political movements on the island. All the parties and splinter groups in the fragmented movement, with the possible exception of the JVP, originated from it. By its ideological about-face decision of June 1964 to enter into coalition with the centrist SLFP and the pro-Soviet LKP, the LSSP abandoned its Trotskyism and was subsequently expelled from the Fourth International.

Following an official explanation for this shift from revolutionary rhetoric to parliamentary socialism in the popular front tradition (see *YICA*, 1970, pp. 549-50), the LSSP seemed to concentrate on using its position in the government in support of a steady evolutionary progress toward socialism in Ceylon. To emphasize its dependent position among the coalition partners, particularly the pro-Soviet LKP, the LSSP issued a strong protest against the Prague trial of the Czechoslovak Movement of Revolutionary Youth, a branch of the 1968 reform movement suppressed by the Warsaw Pact intervention in that year. The concluding paragraph of the protest stated:

Not only have the students and youths of Czechoslovakia the inalienable right to fight the bureaucratic regime and the military occupation, a right which the international socialist movement must defend!

> More important is the fact that if the bureaucratic regime succeeds against the student and youth leaders now arraigned in the dock, this will embolden it to similar measures against the recognized leadership of the Czechoslovak people. (*Ceylon Daily News*, 8 March 1971.)

About the same time, LSSP leaders participated in a mass anti-U.S. demonstration in Colombo "to protest against the American invasion of Laos, Cambodia, and Vietnam, the increased freight charges, and the increase of oil prices." They also condemned the establishment of a U.S. military base at Diego Garcia as a threat to countries in the Indian Ocean region.

As a partner of the ruling coalition, the LSSP supported the government's suppression of the JVP rebellion. The secretary-general of the LSSP, Communications Minister Leslie Goonewardene, reportedly stated at a meeting on 18 March that "The Government would not give in to the attempts of misguided youths to use terrorism to destroy the democratic privileges enjoyed by the masses. It would take every possible measure to wipe out such disruptive activities." Goonewardene also said that Mrs. Bandaranaike had "declared a state Emergency with the whole-hearted support of the Cabinet. Under this, the Government gave necessary powers to the armed forces to wipe out disruptive elements and preserve law and order." (*Intercontinental Press*, 19 April.)

Two leaders of the party—Colvin R. de Silva, minister of plantation industries and constitutional affairs, and M. P. for Colombo South Bernard Soysa, parliament member—agreed to serve on the government's special seven-member committee to reestablish civil authority. At the annual general meeting of the Planters' Association, on 29 April, Dr. de Silva claimed that the government's first task would be to repair the willful destruction caused to the country's assets. He stressed that the Planters' Association meeting

> was being held when the country was facing an unusual and unprecedented situation created by a group of narrow-minded people, conspiratorily organized, who had launched an effort by force of arms to displace the duly constituted government of the day in order to replace the entire system of parliamentary democracy by a system of dictatorial rule. Those who led and nurtured that effort imagined they could topple with one blow the people's government of the United Front constituted by the Sri Lanka Freedom Party, the Lanka Sama Samaja Party, and the Communist Party, without countering retaliation. (*Ceylon Daily News*, 30 April.)

Though May Day was not publicly celebrated in Ceylon for the first time since independence, broadcasts by leading personalities reflected a deep analysis of the defeated rebellion. Speaking for his party, Leslie Goonewardene claimed that "one of the major causes for the month-old revolt was the slowness of the United Front government in proceeding with its radical reforms" (*Far Eastern Economic Review*, 8 May). In expressing sympathy for some of the JVP demands, the LSSP spokesman evidently attempted to strengthen his party's position against the right wing of the majority SLFP.

Two important members of the LSSP—Parliament member and youth league leader Vasudeva Nanayakkara and senior civil servant Susil Siriwardena, were arrested on 15 April for complicity in the revolt (see above). This could well indicate some dissatisfaction in party ranks with the course of the coalition government and possible further shrinkage of LSSP membership. The Peradeniya campus of Ceylon University, until 1964 the stronghold of the Trotskyite movement, proved to be the main training ground for insurrection against the Marxist establishment.

Party leaders provide valuable services for the coalition government, giving it intellectual inspiration to meet crises by means of new reform measures. Finance Minister Dr. N. M. Perera, in addition to extensive travel for economic aid from various countries and international institutions, is responsible for budgetary planning. He is particularly concerned with the problems of unemployment and population explosion. Another crisis faced by Perera is the deteriorating foreign exchange situation, aggravated by the need to service foreign debt obligations which absorb over one-third of all export earnings. He explained to the parliament that he would have nationalized foreign-owned banks more rapidly, in keeping with 1970 election pledges, but Ceylon owed these very banks between 700 and 800 million rupees (one rupee equals 17 cents, U.S.) in foreign currency. (*Ceylon Daily News*, 16 December.)

The five-year plan, tabled by the prime minister and parliament on 9 November, was the product of joint effort by two economic experts of the LSSP, N. M. Perera and H. A. de S. Gunasekera. One source describes the plan as

> ...a strange amalgam of the left's program for widening the public sector and drastically curtailing the economic privileges of some 50,000 persons who may be categorized as belonging to the affluent layers of Ceylonese society, while at the same time seeking to provide a climate of investment of Rs. 14,820 million envisaged.... The plan hopes to achieve an annual growth rate of 6%, raise domestic savings from the present level of 12.5% of national income to 17%, and improve the living standards of some 40% of the population who at present earn incomes of less than Rs. 200 a month. Per capita income is expected to rise from Rs. 910 per annum to Rs. 1150 at the end of the plan period (at 1970 prices). (*Asian Survey*, February 1972.)

The proposals for the plan provide for

> (a) a ceiling on landholdings from which, however, foreign and local public limited liability companies are exempt (the land thus acquired with compensation will be made available to the landless and unemployed); (b) government acquisition, with compensation, of shares in plantation companies and the appointment of government directors to the boards of such companies; (c) the appointment of government directors to public and private companies; (d) either nationalization or state acquisition of not less than 51% of any trade or industry where necessary; (e) the overhauling of the wage and salary structure so as to reduce disparities between manual and service or clerical occupations; and (f) a charter of workers' rights. (*Ibid.*)

The finance minister presented a 1971-72 austerity budget which included, among other things,

> a 25-cent [Ceylonese] increase (to one rupee) on the second measure of rice issued on the ration; a 15-cent rise (to 48 cents) on flour; a price boost for bread—from 35 cents to 48 cents—and sugar rationing at 2 lbs. per month for 72 cents per pound. In addition, the Finance Minister introduced a five-cent increase in postal rates and told Ceylonese they would have to pay 25 cents every time they visited at governmental hospitals. (*Far Eastern Economic Review*, 20 November.)

It is paradoxical that abolition of the second measure of free rice, enacted by the leftist government in fewer than two years of tenure, was the very issue which had toppled the previous UNP government of Dudley Senanayake. It was difficult for the ex-Trotskyite economist who had agitated over 35 years of his political life to give the masses a better deal. In view of Ceylon's deteriorating economy, however, it had been necessary to cut down on the numerous welfare state subsidies which the country could no longer afford.

Colvin R. de Silva, first president of the LSSP, in his capacity as constitutional affairs minister proposed a series of far-reaching reforms which would change substantially the nature of the country's political framework. An authority on British colonial government earlier in his life, he now took upon himself the task of abolishing what he and his party considered the evils of an imposed foreign system.

Since the coalition government has the necessary two-thirds majority to change the 1948 constitution (based on the British model), it was decided that the House of Representatives would function as constituent assembly to draft as well as adopt a new supreme law. The decision to cut all links with the British Crown had been taken in June 1970 when Mrs. Bandaranaike convened parliament to discuss the question of republic status and implementation of a social democracy. At that time, she pledged to safeguard fundamental rights and freedoms, but, according to B. H. S. Jayewardene (*Far Eastern Economic Review*, 24 July), "Public suggestions were called for but so far all have been ignored. Even the elected opposition's protests and its pleas to have specific freedoms and rights written into the new constitution have remained voices in the wilderness as the government's 114-man majority has ruled out guarantees of press freedom and private ownership.''

On 17 January 1971 a draft constitution was presented to a committee of the constituent assembly by Dr. de Silva. It provided for establishment of a free, sovereign, and independent republic which would end dominion status within the Commonwealth. The proposed constitution sought ''the development of the collective forms of property as a means of ending exploitation of man by man.'' It would also strip courts of their powers to decide on the constitutional validity of laws enacted by parliament. This would be determined instead by a constitutional court. Judgments of the latter, however, would be sought only on issues referred to it by the speaker of the National Assembly.

The upper house of Ceylon's parliament, the Senate, was abolished on 28 September because of its alleged reactionary composition and obstruction of progressive legislation introduced by the United Front government.

The final draft of the basic law, presented to the constituent assembly on 29 December, in addition to the foregoing measures, provided that

> Buddhism, the religion of the majority of the people, ''will be given its rightful place and accordingly it will be the duty of the state to protect and foster Buddhism,'' according to the draft, while the rights of other religions will be assured.
>
> A national assembly will replace the existing 157-member House of Representatives, as ''the supreme instrument of the state.'' It will exercise legislative and executive powers, and judicial powers through courts and other institutions. Membership in the assembly will be determined following a commission study report in 1972.
>
> The language of the courts will be Sinhalese, the official language of Ceylon, which is spoken by the majority community of Ceylon.
>
> All laws (until now in English) will be drafted in Sinhalese, with a translation in Tamil, the language of the largest minority community.
>
> The person holding the office of prime minister when the constitution is adopted will be the first prime minister of the new republic....
>
> The head of state will be the president of the republic, who will also be chief of the executive and commander in chief of the armed forces. The president will hold office for four years, will be appointed by the prime minister and will act on the advice of the prime minister. (*New York Times*, 30 December.)

The Judicial Committee of the British Privy Council which had served as the highest court of appeal was replaced on 15 November by an indigenous Court of Appeals as the highest judicial tribunal. The government also proposed that it continue in office for up to six years (parliament's new term) after the new constitution had been promulgated in 1972. Another innovation was the establishment in December of some 1,800 ''people's committees,'' with 22,000 members, all under the public administration ministry.

There was little information during 1971 about LSSP-controlled or -oriented trade unions: the Ceylon Federation of Labour, Government Workers' Trade Union Federation, and Public Services League. Presumably, as usual, they followed the party's lead on major political issues.

The LSSP-R. Bala Tampoe's splinter Lanka Sama Samaja Party (Revolutionary) remained throughout 1971 affiliated with the Fourth International, stressing its Trotskyite character. The only official political group openly supporting the JVP revolt, it protested suppression of the uprising. On 6 February the party co-sponsored with the JVP and the Ceylon Mercantile Union (CMU) a mass rally at Colombo:

> The gatering condemned setting up a U.S. imperialist base in the Indian Ocean, called for Ceylon to immediately leave the British Commonwealth, demanded nationalization of the banks, plantations,

and foreign trade, and appealed for defense of the masses' standard of living by an all-out war on unemployment and rising prices. (*Intercontinental Press*, 3 May.)

The LSSP-R general secretary, Tampoe, who is also CMU general secretary, made his views known to Prime Minister Bandaranaike in letters of 30 March and 30 April concerning the state of emergency and the JVP insurrection. He protested police action and "military terrorism against the people." Despite a statement in Paris on 3 January 1970 that "guerrilla war is completely unrealistic in Ceylon" (see *YICA 1971*, p. 551), Tampoe attempted to associate his numerically weak movement with the insurrectionists and, thus, profit politically from the JVP revolt despite the Trotskyite dogma of permanent revolution. For instance, in a June 1971 interview he claimed that 48 CMU officeholders in branch and shop committees had disappeared and presumably had been arrested in connection with the rebellion (*Intercontinental Press*, 13 December). According to one observer,

> The Ceylon Mercantile Union is unquestionably among the most powerful labor organizations in Ceylon, and is generally conceded to be the most successful Ceylonese union in performing the conventional "economic" functions of trade unions through collective bargaining on issues of wages and employment conditions.... CMU membership, which stood at 5,256 in 1955, had climed to 16,867 by 1965 and in 1969 reached 33,031. (Kearney, *op. cit.*, p. 111.)

Tampoe's party also has some influence in the Government Clerical Service Union, and it seems to continue publication of *Samasamajist* as organ of the Trotskyite movement.

The Fourth International also associated itself with JVP rebels in a statement from its United Secretariat dated 19 April (*Intercontinental Press*, 3 May). The same New York organ of the Fourth International carried an article (1 November) describing events that had taken place early in October at five of the detention centers, particularly "the campuses of Vidyodaya and Vidyalankara, which have been transformed from universities into prisons." In most communications about Ceylon, this publication joined Bala Tampoe in expressing contempt for LSSP comrades in Mrs. Bandaranaike's government. A representative of the Ceylonese Trotskyists participated in the second national convention of "German Revolutionary Communist Youth" at Cologne, 30 October-1 November, held under auspices of the Fourth International.

The main shortcoming of the LSSP-R is the fact that it is a one-man operation. Despite Tampoe's experience, political acumen, and faithfulness to the basic concepts of Trotskyism, as a Tamil he apparently lacks rapport with Sinhalese leftists. This may have been the cause of his parting with another militant Trotskyite dialectician, Edmund Samarakkody, who formed the RSP. Nothing came to light during 1971 about activities of the RSP or of the RCL. (See *YICA*, 1971, p. 551.) Theoretically speaking, some potential remains for a genuine Trotskyite movement in Ceylon, and the JVP rebellion may be interpreted as an attempt at a revival.

The Pro-Soviet LKP. The sterility of the communist establishment became particularly evident during the 1971 performance by LKP leaders. The party entrenched itself as the least responsible junior partner of the United Front government, pressing the prime minister to carry out radical reforms which she felt the economy could not yet support. The LKP secretary-general, Pieter Keuneman, retained his cabinet post as housing and reconstruction minister.

With the help of two Marxist colleagues from the majority SLFP—the internal and external trade minister, Tikiri Bandara Ilangaratne, and industries and scientific affairs minister, Tikiri Banda Subasinghe—Keuneman exercised significant influence on Ceylon's foreign policy. This could be seen when the government established diplomatic relations with the communist regimes of East Germany, North Korea, North Vietnam, and the Provisional Revolutionary Government of South Vietnam. Simultaneously relations were suspended with Israel and the operations in Ceylon of the U.S. Peace Corps and the Asia Foundation were closed down. These actions drew praise from a Soviet commentator for "the progressive socio-economic measures of the Ceylonese Government at home and the policy of peace and non-alignment in the international arena." The same commentator quoted approvingly this statement by Mrs. Bandaranaike: "Ceylonese-Soviet relations are very good. We maintain friendly ties, implement broad cooperation. With the economic aid of the Soviet Union large enterprises, including a metallurgical and a tyre plant, have been built in Ceylon." (TASS, 4 February.)

Although fearful of being outflanked on the left, the LKP condemned the JVP rebellion as sponsored by ultra-left adventurist elements. The Central Committee ridiculed the JVP because its "so-called ideology, reduced to five basic lectures, is a hodgepodge of concepts from Maoism and from certain contemporary forms of petty-bourgeois pseudo-radicalism in the West, combined with anti-Sovietism, anti-Communism and masked racism." (*WMR*, January 1972.) Annoyed by the impact of the JVP rebellion on its own rank and file, the LKP referred to JVP resistance to government attacks as "reactionary and potentially counter-revolutionary" (*Intercontinental Press*, 20 September).

Trade unions controlled by the LKP include the Ceylon Federation of Trade Unions, the Public Service Workers' Trade Union Federation, and the Ceylon National Teachers' Union. All are members of the pro-government Joint Committee of Trade Union Organisations which followed an anti-JVP line during the insurrection.

The LKP did not take too well to the imposed censorship. An unsympathetic correspondent reported: "The Party's Sinhalese daily *Aththa* snarls its defiance at the embarrassment of having to conform in the same way as capitalist competitors and continues to demand preferential treatment. Across the blank spaces on its editorial pages runs the racy Sinhalese expression, "Our own dogs have chewed us up." (*Economist*, London, 3 July.)

As soon as the rebellion was under control, the LKP Central Committee tried to capitalize on revolutionary dissatisfaction by demanding that the government work out a program of sweeping socioeconomic reform. It proposed democratization of the administrative system, implementation of a program to eliminate unemployment, and immediate adoption of a new constitution. The statement stressed the need for strengthening the United Front of left-wing and democratic forces as well as greater working class influence within the front. (TASS, 26 August.)

Party Chairman Wickremasinghe attended the Twenty-fourth Congress of the Communist Party of the Soviet Union, and declared:

> The unselfish assistance the Soviet Union renders newly independent states is felt also by the people of Ceylon, who are at present waging a struggle for genuine political and economic independence. That is why the Communist Party of Ceylon stands solidly for closer cooperation with the Soviet Union. We know that this cooperation plays and will continue to play an increasing role in the efforts to build a diversified economy on our island in place of the one-sided, monoculture economy we inherited from the colonialists. (*Pravda*, 9 April.)

Dr. Wickremasinghe, in an article published by the *World Marxist Review*, commented on the proceedings of that Moscow congress with regard to the demilitarization of bordering states and islands of the Indian Ocean:

> The Ceylonese are aware that it was U.S. imperialism which created the danger of militarizing the Indian Ocean, brought its navy there and is planning a naval base in Diego-Garcia. This prompted Ceylon to raise the issue at the Commonwealth Conference in Singapore and then make its proposal to the latest UN General Assembly.

In the same article he praised the Soviet-Indian treaty of August as "an inspiring example for a more comprehensive collective security treaty for Asia."

The party seemed impatient with the slow pace of socialist reform, e.g., nationalization of foreign banks and tea plantations, and urged speedy establishment of peoples' committees to watch over the country. These local "soviets" would possess

> powers "to prevent antisocial, illegal and immoral activities such as smuggling, illicit immigration, profiteering, and the running of brothels." Their task is to turn the peoples' minds to healthy and useful institutions: the co-operative movement, cultural committees, rural development societies, community centres and women's welfare organisations. The bodies will act as ombudsmen, as peacemakers between different sectors of the community—and as their own publicity agents. (*Far Eastern Economic Review*, 3 July.)

The problem arises who will actually control these political watchdogs: the dynamic public administration, local government and home affairs minister, Felix Dias Bandaranaike, considered to be leader of the SLFP right wing majority, or young communists like Dr. W. A. Warnapala who is lecturer in public administration for the department of economics (the Marxist think tank) at the Peradeniya campus of Ceylon University. The latter seems to be one of the theoreticians behind the scheme for social reform, necessary to bridge the gap with the younger leftists in rural Ceylon.

The Pro-Chinese LKP. The main weakness of the pro-Chinese splinter group of the LKP, from the beginning, has been similar to that of the LSSP-R. It is run by one man, Nagalingam S. Sanmugathasan, secretary-general of the party and of the Ceylon Trade Union Federation (CTUF). One asset has been control over the CTUF, which possibly had a membership of about 110,000 in 1971. The president is Watson Fernando, a much less advertised political figure.

Sanmugathasan was arrested on 14 April, probably as a preventive measure, during the JVP rebellion. The pro-Chinese LKP thus suffered a major blow, and their Chinese communist friends did little to save this predominantly Tamil group of loyal followers. In line with its new pragmatic orientation in foreign policy, China apparently decided to court Mrs. Bandaranaike and her SLFP followers rather than support the insignificant group led by Sanmugathasan. The Chinese government sent its foreign trade minister in January to sign a protocol on commodity exchange. Ceylon agreed to provide 41,000 tons of rubber for 200,000 tons of Burmese rice, supplied by China—which at the last minute cut the agreed price of rice to 34.75 per ton, five shillings lower than the world market price. Moreover, the Chinese revived a six-year old prestige project to design and construct the Bandaranaike Memorial International Conference Hall in Colombo. Later they provided Ceylon with a loan valued at approximately 16,571,940 yuan (about 40.1 million rupees), to pay for 100,000 metric tons of Chinese rice. Apparently this was "the second interest-free loan granted by the People's Republic of China for financing supplies of rice. With the present loan the total assistance made available to Ceylon amounts to Rs 445 million. Of this amount Rs 130 million were grants while the balance consists of interest free loans." (*Far Eastern Economic Review*, 23 October).

In view of such help to the government, it is doubtful whether the opposition pro-Chinese LKP with an estimated 500 members or fewer at the beginning of 1971 will survive the double shock of suppression by Mrs. Bandaranaike's coalition and of negligence from its friends in Peking.

Publications. The pro-Soviet LKP publishes a Sinhalese daily paper, *Aththa* (Truth), which has a circulation of 22,000. It also publishes the Sinhalese weeklies *Tarunahanda* (Voice of Youth), *Nava Lokaya* (New World), and *Mawbima* (Motherland). The party's main Tamil publication is *Desabhimani* (Patriot), also a weekly. It has an English weekly, *Forward*. Two publications, *Kommunist Lokaya* (Communist World) and *Nava Sakthi* (New Strength), appear during campaign periods.

The pro-Chinese LKP publishes a weekly in English, *Red Flag*. It also has two "worker" dailies—*Kamkaruwa* in Sinhalese, and its Tamil counterpart, *Tolilali*, with estimated circulations of 3,000 and 2,000 respectively. The party also publishes a Tamil "cultural and general affairs" monthly, *Vasantham*.

The LSSP publishes the weeklies *Samasamajaya, Samadharmam*, and *Samasamajist* in Sinhalese, Tamil, and English respectively. The MEP publishes the weekly *Mahajana Eksath Peramuna*. The RCL has a Sinhalese publication, *Virodhaya*; a Tamil publication, *Ethirppu*; and since 1969 an English publication, *Asian Marxist Bulletin*, the last being dedicated to the rebuilding of the Trotskyist movement in the Indian subcontinent.

University of San Francisco   George J. Lerski

China

The First Congress of the Chinese Communist Party (Chung-kuo kung-ch'an tang; CCP) was held in Shanghai in July 1921. Mao tse-tung, the present party chairman, was one of the twelve delegates known to have attended. The party celebrates its anniversary every 1 July.

The People's Republic of China (PRC) was established 1 October 1949. State organs are in all important respects dominated by the CCP, the sole legal party. The party constitution adopted in 1969 stresses the dominance of party over government in these words: "The organs of state power of the dictatorship of the proletariat ... must all accept the leadership of the party."

The CCP is the largest communist party in the world. No membership figures, however, are available for later than 1961, when *Jen-min jih-pao* (People's Daily) reported on 1 July that there were more than 17 million CCP members. In 1971 the party was still being reconstructed in the wake of the purges during the Great Proletarian Cultural Revolution (1966-68), making membership estimates mere guesswork. The population of mainland China is commonly estimated at 750-800 million.

Organization and Leadership. According to the party constitution, the "highest leading body" of the CCP is the national party congress, which is to be convened every five years; under "special circumstances" the congress may be convened early or postponed. The national congress elects the Central Committee, which in turn elects the Politburo, the Standing Committee of the Politburo, and the chairman and vice-chairman of the Central Committee. The Central Committee elected at the party's Ninth Congress (April 1969) consisted of 170 full members and 109 alternates.

Effective policy-making power within the party rests with the Central Committee and at higher levels, particularly the Standing Committee of the Politburo (though this body appeared to have been abandoned as a result of a purge of a number of Politburo members in September 1971). Except for Mao Tse-tung and Lin Piao, the Politburo elected at the Ninth Congress was identified in Chinese alphabetical order. Subsequent listings in order of rank revealed the relative positions of most of the others. The composition and hierarchial order of the Politburo underwent substantial alteration particularly in the last quarter of 1971, leaving that body with ten active members.

Six of the original 25 full and alternate members were victims of what seemed, despite inconclusive evidence at the end of 1971, to have been a purge of the highest military leaders: Chief of Staff Huang Yung-sheng (who last appeared in public on 10 September), Air Force Commander Wu Fa-hsien (8 September), Naval Political Commissar Li Tso-p'eng (9 September). Lin Piao, minister of national defence, had not been seen since 3 June 1971 (during the visit of a high-level Romanian delegation) and references to him began to diminish in mid-September, the last having been on 8 October; Lin's wife, Yeh Ch'ün, presumably was removed with him. There was speculation outside China that the absence of Ch'iu Hui-tso, director of the People's Liberation Army (PLA) Logistics Department (missing since 24 September), from important year-end events (notably a

POLITBURO
By order of rank existing January 1971

Standing Committee:

Mao Tse-tung, chairman

Lin Piao, vice-chairman

Chou En-lai

K'ang Sheng

Inactive members
(alphabetical order):

Ch'en Hsi-lien

Ch'en Po-ta (purged)

Chu Teh

Hsieh Fu-chih

Hsü Shih-yu

Li Hsüeh-feng (alternate)

Liu Po-ch'eng

Tung Pi-wu

Other full members:

Huang Yung-sheng

Chiang Ch'ing

Chang Ch'un-ch'iao

Yao Wen-yüan

Yeh Ch'ün

Li Hsien-nien

Yeh Chien-ying

Wu Fa-hsien

Li Tso-p'eng

Ch'iu Hui-tso

Alternate members:

Li Te-sheng

Chi Teng-k'uei

Wang Tung-hsing

Active members by order of rank, December 1971

Full members:

Mao Tse-tung

Chou En-lai

Chiang Ch'ing

Yeh Chien-ying

Chang Ch'un-ch'iao

Yao Wen-yüan

Li Hsien-nien

Alternate members:

Li Te-sheng

Chi Teng-k'uei

Wang Tung-hsing

rally on 8 November) suggested that he too may have been associated with the purged military group. Two regional military leaders, Hsü Shih-yu and Ch'en Hsi-lien, were also missing at the end of the year. (Hsü, who had not been seen since 6 June, reappeared on 1 February 1972 with all his previous titles.) There was no immediate explanation for Ch'en's absence since 6 June 1971. More certainty was attached to the significance of the absences of Li Hsüeh-feng (an alternate) and particularly Ch'en Po-ta (missing since October and August, respectively, 1970), whom through oblique statements the Chinese press criticized as exhibiting "leftist deviations."

Other Politburo members missing from public view at the end of 1971, but who for a variety of reasons are not often seen, were K'ang Sheng (who last appeared on 3 June, but was listed among those who sent wreaths to the funeral of former Foreign Minister Ch'en Yi, who died 6 January 1972), Hsieh Fu-chih (who last appeared also on 3 June 1971, and before that on 19 March 1970, although he was elected first secretary of Peking's new Party Committee in March 1971, apparently in his absence), Chu Teh (last seen on 1 August 1971, but sent a wreath to Ch'en Yi's funeral), and Liu Po-ch'eng (last seen 1 October 1970). The 86-year-old Vice-President Tung Pi-wu is still active, but limited to the ceremonial duties of receiving the credentials of incoming ambassadors.

Below the Central Committee there is a network of party committees at the provincial, special district, county, and municipal levels. There is a similar network of party committees within the PLA, from the level of the military region down to that of the regiment. The primary level of party organization is the branch; the party constitution says that branches are formed "in factories, mines, and other enterprises, people's communes, offices, schools, shops, neighborhoods, companies of the PLA, and other primary units.''

This hierarchy of party committees which, excepting that of the PLA, disintegrated during the Cultural revolution, began to reconstruct itself in late 1969. By mid-August 1971 the last committee at the provincial level was formed, although many at the lower and intermediate levels had yet to be reestablished. The ''revolutionary committees,'' created at all levels during the Cultural Revolution to fill the void left by the destruction of party and government organizations, survived as apparently permanent structures. Where parallel party committees were reestablished, the revolutionary committees took on exclusively executive functions under the guidance of the former (usually with identical leadership in both bodies); where party committees had not been formed, party control was exercized through ''core groups'' within the revolutionary committees.

Party Internal Affairs. Party leadership appeared relatively stable during the first three-quarters of 1971, though a campaign against left and right extremism continued from the previous year. The unexplained protracted absences of some—notably K'ang Sheng who, it was suggested, had been purged as a victim of the anti-radical campaign—were later apparently resolved by public appearances or by references to them in China's news media.

The party rebuilding campaign, though perhaps not proceeding so fast as had been expected, did nevertheless succeed in completing the reestablishment of party committees at the province level by August, two months after the party's fiftieth anniversary, which had seemed to be the original target date. Party reconstruction was made possible largely by the stabilizing influence of the PLA; but the following month (September) a number of top-ranking military leaders disappeared, suggesting, among other things, that the PLA, whose power grew rapidly as a result of the Cultural Revolution, had achieved a dominant position that was no longer necessary once the party had regained its authority.

The CCP Fiftieth Anniversary and the Campaign against Extremism. On 1 July 1971 the three major party publications—*Jen-min jih-pao*, *Hung ch'i* (Red Flag), and *Chieh-fang chün-pao* (Liberation Army Daily)—jointly published a 20,000-word editorial to mark the CCP's fiftieth anniversary. The article, which traced the party's history from its founding to the present, concentrated on attacking those who had led it on erroneous paths. Ironically relating Lin Piao's condemnation of the same persons at the Ninth Congress, the editorial identified them as Ch'en Tu-hsiu (''right opportunist''); Ch'ü Ch'iu-pai and Li Li-san (''left opportunists''); Wang Ming (''first 'left,' then right opportunist''); Chang Kuo-t'ao (who ''split the Red Army''); P'eng Te-huai, Kao Kang, Jao Shu-shih, and others (''right opportunist anti-party bloc''); and, ''after long years of struggle,'' Liu Shao-ch'i (''counterrevolutionary revisionist''). The chief culprits were Ch'en Tu-hsiu, who advocated a ''capitulationist'' line toward Chiang Kai-shek; Wang Ming, who switched from the extreme leftist line of ''all struggle and no alliance'' to the extreme rightist line of ''all alliance and no struggle''—i.e., submitting to the authority of the CCP-Kuomintang united front following the Japanese invasion in 1937; and Liu Shao-ch'i, who, like Ch'en and Wang, became ''capitulationist,'' and later adopted extreme rightist attitudes in economic and international affairs.

Though Ch'en, Wang, and Liu were the ostensible targets of this editorial, its intensity, as well as that of other recent references to the three, suggested that the attacks were aimed at contemporary ideological deviates. The charge that many of the ''rightist errors'' had actually been made under the guise of an ''ultra-leftist'' line indicated that the campaign was directed primarily at those who were currently exhibiting extreme leftist attitudes. The most logical target on the Politburo was Ch'en Po-ta, head of the Cultural Revolution group and former editor of *Hung ch'i*, who was presumed to have been removed at the Ninth Central Committee's Second Plenum, in August

1970, when he last appeared. A number of erroneous traits and activities condemned in the 1 July editorial and in later publications were suspiciously similar to those associated with Ch'en Po-ta (see *Current Scene*, Hong Kong, 7 November). Particularly suggestive was the editorial's attack on the "type of person who claims to be a 'humble little commoner' but is actually a big careerist." According to a March 1967 statement by Chiang Ch'ing, this self-deprecatory phrase (*hsiao-hsiao lao-pai-hsing*) had been used by Ch'en. The editorial attacked "sham Marxists" who "talked about Marxism-Leninism and even pretended to be Marxist theoreticians but only to bluff and hoodwink worker-peasant cadres and innocent young people." Ch'en's "errors" appeared to have been committed during the Cultural Revolution, and the allusion to "young people" may have referred to his leadership in the Red Guard movement, which had pursued policies now denounced.

Press statements during the year appeared also to associate Ch'en with the so-called "May 16" (or "516") group which received renewed attention in 1971. The "May 16" group took its name from a Central Committee circular of 16 May 1966 that installed the Cultural Revolution group headed by Ch'en. The "May 16" leaders, who the following year apparently took the circular as a cue to launch severe attacks—physical and verbal—against the PLA and the Foreign Ministry in particular, were accused of having been rightists masquerading as leftists. The movement was denounced as a conspiracy that, by resorting to these excesses, attempted to discredit the party leadership and thereby bring it down.[1]

Also apparently eliminated along with Ch'en, possibly as one of his supporters, was Li Hsüeh-feng, a Politburo alternate, "responsible person" of the Peking Military Region, vice-chairman of the Standing Committee of the National People's Congress (which met last in 1965), and chairman of the Hopei Revolutionary Committee. Li had not been seen since 1 October 1970 and his failure to be elected to the Hopei Party Committee leadership on 20 May 1971 gave further indication that he had been dismissed. Three other members of the Politburo, who were also leading the Cultural Revolution and might therefore have been expected to be removed with Ch'en, were Mao's wife, Chiang Ch'ing, and Chang Ch'un-ch'iao and Yao Wen-yüan, first and second secretaries, respectively, of the Shanghai Municipal Party Committee (which has the status of a provincial committee). None of these three has been affected, however, and they apparently continue to exert a leftist influence on the Politburo.

The July editorial did not go into great length on the historical importance of the Cultural Revolution, explaining that this had been adequately covered by Lin Piao in his report to the Ninth Congress. It did attempt to answer the question, presumably currently being posed by some in China, of whether or not it had been necessary:

> At first many of our comrades had a very poor understanding of this revolution. When the masses rose and split into two groupings, and even struggle by force occurred, everything under heaven seemed to be in chaos for a time. Some people ask: Since Liu Shao-ch'i and his handful usurped part of the power of the dictatorship of the proletariat, it needs only an order from Chairman Mao to dismiss them from office. Why should the present method be adopted? Practice shows that the other method, dismissal from office, could not solve the problem, though it was adopted on many occasions. This revolution is not merely about the dismissal of a few people from office;

---

[1]See *YICA*, 1968, p. 104. A former diplomat, Yao Teng-sheng, was reported to have been subjected to a "mass trial" on 11 June 1971 and sentenced to a long term of imprisonment for his role in the conspiracy and his subsequent recalcitrance (*New York Times*, 21 June; see also, *Far Eastern Economic Review*, Hong Kong, 17 July). Some have suggested that the "May 16" conspiracy had been contrived by party leaders to absolve themselves of the responsibility for the excesses of the Cultural Revolution (see Barry Burton, *Asian Survey*, Berkeley, November 1971).

it is a great revolution in the realm of the superstructure. Liu Shao-ch'i not only had a revisionist political line but also had an organizational line which served his political line. The leadership in quite a number of our units was not in the hands of Marxists and the worker and peasant masses. Only by arousing the broad masses to expose our dark aspect openly, in an all-round way and from below, would it be possible to clean out the Liu Shao-ch'i renegade clique."

Party Reconstruction. The completion of the campaign to reestablish province-level party committees, which had registered its first success in Hunan in December 1970, was announced in a *Jen-min jih-pao* editorial on 27 August 1971. The important role the party committees were to take was emphasized in the editorial: "The Chinese Communist Party is the core of leadership of the whole Chinese people. Without this core, the cause of socialism cannot be victorious. Once established, the new party committees at all levels must effectively strengthen centralized leadership by the party."

The composition of the new committees indicated a continuation of a trend established at the county level: a preponderance of military representation in the committee secretariats to the detriment of the often radical "mass organizations," the ranks of the latter being filled largely by Red Guard elements. The "three-way alliance" formula that was intended to give equal representation to the veteran party cadres, the PLA, and the mass organizations was apparently abandoned when the province-level party committees began forming. In its place, a new "three-in-one combination" of old, middle-aged, and young people, which persisted throughout 1971, was evidently aimed at permitting smaller representation of the mass organizations. These latter, which included workers, peasants, Red Guards, and others, had been associated with radical excesses during the Cultural Revolution and, despite statements to the contrary, seemed to have come into disfavor when party reconstruction began. Thus, the *Jen-min jih-pao* editorial stated that along with veteran cadres, the new committees were taking in "new blood" in the form of young people, workers, peasants, and cadres at the grass-roots level; however, according to one calculation, of 158 known province-level party committee leaders, 59.5 per cent were military men (including political commissars), 34.8 per cent were veteran civilian cadres, and only 5.7 per cent represented the "masses" (*New York Times*, 28 August). Others with poor representation were national minority groups, who accounted for only nine of the 158, and women, of whom there were five.

Among the new first secretaries of the 29 committees, only three were not military men (and two of these—Chang Ch'un-ch'iao and Hsieh Fu-chih—were on the party's Politburo); seven were commanders of military regions (there are 13 in China). Nine were political commissars at the military region or district level. Five were members of the Politburo: Chang Ch'un-ch'iao, Ch'en Hsi-lien (missing since 6 June 1971), Hsieh Fu-chih (missing since 3 June 1971), Hsü Shih-yu, and Li Te-sheng (an alternate), and all but two of the rest were members of the Central Committee (four as alternates). All held simultaneously leading positions in the parallel provincial revolutionary committees (within the government hierarchy), twenty-three as chairmen, two as first vice-chairmen, and four as lower ranking vice-chairmen.

In a few other provinces—mainly those in which the party committee leadership was not duplicative of the respective revolutionary committee or where there was a delay in holding the provincial party congress—there was evidence of factional disputes. In the first 17 province-level party committees to be established (4 December 1970-3 April 1971) all first secretaries continued to hold long-standing positions as provincial revolutionary committee chairmen (in Hunan, site of the first provincial party committee, the original revolutionary committee chairman was last seen in April 1970). Of the last 12 (5 April-19 August) only five were simultaneously chairmen of the respective revolutionary committees, and three of these chairmen had received their positions since 1969. Timing was also an indicator of difficulties. Although party committees were being established rather regularly (an average of one a week) until June, there was a gap of more than two months, with only four provinces left—Heilungkiang, Ninghsia, Szechwan, and Tibet—when no new committees were formed. Also, interestingly, the first province to create a revolutionary committee—Heilungkiang, in January 1967—was the last to form a party committee. Eight provincial leaders severely criticized during the Cultural Revolution reappeared in leading province-level party positions; four of these were transferred to provinces other than those where they had been leaders.

The dominant role of military men in the new party committees appeared to come under attack at the end of September—after the purge of the four leading members of the central military elite. A series of broadcasts citing examples of how PLA representatives on local revolutionary committees supported majority decisions suggested that the army was being admonished for high-handedness in opposing the majority elsewhere in local administration. A Sian radio broadcast on 25 September, for example, stated in regard to Hua county that "in order to ensure the unified leadership of the county party committee," the PLA representatives "resolutely sought instructions from the county party committee on important questions and have refrained from making arbitrary decisions." The broadcast added that the PLA should "act constantly as little pupils and servants" of the masses. Again, by negative inference, an indication of what probably was not happening in the three-in-one combinations of revolutionary committees at basic levels was provided by a New China News Agency report on 17 October, using examples of PLA cadres in industrial enterprises in Liaoning: in committee work the PLA representatives were said to "support strongly the resolutions adopted by the majority," "act consciously as models in implementing the party's decisions, especially when their opinions are rejected," and at all times "act as ordinary party members in the party organization."

The Absence of Lin Piao and Related Events. Since mid-September 1971, when Defence Minister Lin Piao, Chief of Staff Huang Yung-sheng, Air Force Commander Wu Fa-hsien, First Political Commissar of the Navy Li Tso-p'eng, and other military leaders were last seen, it was generally suspected that a purge had taken place against the PLA leadership. The targets of this apparent purge were unexpected. The current campaign against left and right extremism, which brought down Ch'en Po-ta and possibly others, would not presumably have touched the relatively moderate military element, which had been instrumental in subduing the Red Guard movement during the Cultural Revolution. On 20 September foreign correspondents were told by Foreign Ministry officials that the annual Peking parade celebrating China's twenty-second National Day on 1 October had been canceled for "reasons of economy." Most observers understood this to mean that there had been changes in China's top leadership that would have become apparent by absences at such an event, and that those remaining were not yet prepared to divulge the nature of these changes. Once evidence of a number of other possibly related events began to accumulate, it became apparent that a major incident had occurred sometime between 11 and 13 September. The sudden disappearance of Huang, Wu, and Li,[2] followed on the night of 12 September by the crash of a Chinese plane (apparently military) in Mongolia, the simultaneous grounding for three days of all Air Force and civilian planes and the placing of China's military on alert status, and the absence of all Politburo members on 12-16 September created a situation that encouraged rampant speculation. Rumors arose, sparked by quasi-authoritative reports in the foreign press, that Mao had died (he had not been seen since 7 August); that Lin had become seriously ill or had died; that Lin had been discovered in an attempt to bolster his position and his plane was shot down in Mongolia en route to the

[2]Last seen 10, 8, and 9 September, respectively. All except Lin had been very active until that time. Huang had made six public appearances earlier in the month; and between 1 January and 30 June 1971 Huang, Wu and Li had been cited by the Chinese news media 47, 21, and 26 times, respectively, in connection with public appearances.

Soviet Union where he had expected to gain some sort of support; that Lin, betrayed by his daughter in an assassination plot against Mao, had attempted to flee to the Soviet Union with his wife and members of the central military elite, but his plane had crashed in Mongolia; that because of the presumed ages of the passengers on board the plane, Lin could not have been among them; that Liu Shao-ch'i, under house arrest, had escaped or attempted to escape to the Soviet Union, possibly with the help of Huang Yung-sheng; or that China was facing a renewed military threat from the Soviet Union. At the end of the year the most widely held theory outside China was that Lin, sensing that his political resources were being whittled away, had attempted to consolidate his position in a major political move that involved members of the central military elite.

Whatever Lin's physical fate, there was little doubt at the end of the year that he had suffered a political death. References to him began to dwindle in mid-September and ceased by 8 October. At a banquet for Emperor Haile Selassie of Ethiopia on 6 October, Tung Pi-wu's welcoming statement omitted the customary reference to Lin, and, although Lin's name was mentioned among the toasts in Haile Selassie's speech, these were not carried in the NCNA report on 6 October. Similarly, on 11 October, at a reception for the opening of a Romanian industrial exhibition, the Romanians toasted Mao and Chou but omitted Lin, presumably on advice from Chinese officials (Agence France Presse, 12 October). Other indications during October of Lin's political demise included a toast to him during the visit to North Korea of a Chinese radio and television delegation (carried by the Korean Central News Agency on 16 October) that was omitted in the brief NCNA report of the same event (15 October). Telegrams on 27 October from the Albanians and Romanians on the occasion of China's admission to the United Nations also omitted Lin's name. On 12 September NCNA announced the publication of 50 color photographs of Mao (more than ten of which included Lin, according to Tsingtao radio, 30 September). They began to be distributed to the provinces ten days later, but sluggishly and not uniformly, judging from provincial radio broadcasts.

Although Lin's name was not specifically mentioned, he was obliquely implicated in various misdeeds by statements appearing in China's news media after September. One "error" is thought to be his persistence in perpetuating the "cult of Mao Tse-tung." In December 1970 in an interview with U.S. writer Edgar Snow, Mao revealed that he had resorted to the "cult" as a "necessary nuisance" (in the words of Snow) during the Cultural Revolution. Mao criticized the "ritualism" of the cult and stated that his various glorifying titles (such as "Great Helmsman") would be eliminated "sooner or later." (*Life* magazine, New York, 30 April.) During the latter part of 1971 portraits and statues of Mao in public places became increasingly less in evidence. Beginning with its 5 November issue, *Peking Review* no longer devoted its inside cover to quotations of Mao Tse-tung, reverting to the original format (in use before February 1967) of using that page for the table of contents. In early November *Quotations from Chairman Mao Tse-tung* suddenly became difficult to obtain in Peking. The disappearance of the "little red book" may not have been the result of the deceleration of the cult of Mao, but rather because of Lin's association with its compilation, including a preface by him. Other publications in which Lin had a hand, such as documents of the Ninth Congress and his 1965 policy statement "Long Live the Victory of People's War," were also reported to be unobtainable.

In the past Lin had referred to Mao as the "great genius of the present era" and to his "thoughts" as having been the product of this genius rather than a spontaneous outgrowth from among the working people. The timing and the parallel between this attitude and the remarks—now condemned—allegedly made by Liu Shao-ch'i, defending the role of "geniuses," "heroes," and "prophets," clearly suggest that Lin was the principal target. In the November issue of *Hung ch'i* an attack ostensibly on "Liu Shao-ch'i's reactionary theory of human nuture" accused Liu and "other political swindlers" (no doubt including Lin Piao) of having "denied that the masses have boundless creative power, and advocated the idealist conception that heroes decide everything." "The minds of millions of those who are doing things," the article stated, "create something infinitely loftier than the greatest genius can foresee."

In the campaign that began after the events of September, the most severe attack against those newly disfavored appeared in the joint editorial of *Hung ch'i*, *Jen-min jih-pao*, and *Chieh-fang chün-pao* on 1 December. The editorial denounced "senior party cadres" who were engaged in "splitting activities," "conspiracies and intrigues," and "illicit relations with foreign countries." Refering to those who were "bent on plotting," it stated: "Even now there are such persons at it. That there are persons plotting is an objective fact. It is not a question of whether we like it or not." Four former party leaders were specifically identified: Kao Kang and Jao Shu-shih, who were accused in the mid-1950's of attempting to establish an independent state in Manchuria, possibly with Soviet support; and P'eng Teh-huai and Huang K'o-ch'eng, former chief of staff and his deputy, who were dismissed in 1959 for their pro-Soviet sentiments and opposition to Mao's economic policies of the Great Leap Forward. The "errors" of these four apparently were being repeated by current party leaders, very possibly those of the central military elite. The editorial affirmed that the "incorrigible" elements were few and that the "overwhelming majority of good people, who committed mistakes in political line, are able to return to the correct line through criticism and self-criticism."

The removal of Huang Yung-sheng, Wu Fa-hsien, and Li Tso-p'eng, all three of whom had been elevated to full membership on the Politburo at the Ninth Congress, became apparent largely because of their record of frequent appearances, rather than because references to them had been omitted or because oblique criticisms of peculiar traits of one or the other had appeared in the news media, as had happened with Lin Piao. Their absence was most conspicuous at a rally celebrating the thirtieth anniversary of the Albanian Party of Labor on 8 November in Peking (NCNA, 8 November). The appearance of all other active Politburo members indicated that one purpose of the rally was to inform the Chinese public of the current status of that body. The coincidence of their apparent removal and the attacks against Lin suggested that all four had cooperated in the same "conspiracy." The involvement of Ch'iu Hui-tso, director of the PLA Logistics Department, was not so easily ascertained; his last public appearance was 24 September, almost two weeks after the incident that brought down the others.

The removal of five of the central military elite left the Politburo with only one senior PLA representative: Yeh Chien-ying. Yeh, who is 73 years old and had been considered to be on the verge of retirement, is one of the ten former marshals, vice-chairman of the Central Committee's Military Affairs Commission, and vice-chairman of the National Defence Council, but has not held any active post in the central PLA departments for fifteen years. With the exception of Li Te-sheng, a Politburo alternate, director of the General Political Department, and a provincial PLA commander, Yeh is the only active Politburo member representing the PLA. Yeh's relative isolation may indicate the proportion of military influence the party leadership seeks for the Politburo.

Although it is often difficult to distinguish the relative influences of the PLA and the CCP, differences over a number of domestic and international policies offered, from the benefit of hindsight, plausible explanations for the possibility that a power play had been attempted by the military elite. One such difference concerned the PLA's relation to economic policy (see Leo Goodstadt, *Far Eastern Economic Review*, 20 and 27 November). The fourth five-year economic plan, officially announced by NCNA on 13 January 1971, continued the policy, evident in 1970, of increasing provincial economic autonomy. It emphasized rural economy over industrial economy, and included a drive toward greater mechanization of agriculture, which implied the building of rural industrial complexes. To effect this policy, financial resources would have to be diverted to rural areas, draining potential funds away from heavy industry. This direction, military leaders may have feared, would have the effect of weakening the PLA, which had relied on the heavy industries of the urban centers for sophisticated equipment. At the same time, China's rapidly expanding international contacts, including improved relations with the United States, may have caused concern among military leaders. A relaxation of international tensions in those areas affecting China might detract from the prestige China's military establishment enjoyed internally, just as the Sino-Soviet border clashes before the opening of the Ninth Congress may have enhanced this prestige. It was speculated that, forseeing these threats to the authority of the PLA, military leaders combined their political resources to make a bid for greater control over domestic and foreign policy (*ibid.*; and Harry Harding, "China: The Fragmentation of Power," *Asian Survey*, January 1972).

The ideological balance on the new Politburo suggested possible sources for conflict in the future. Of the nine active members (in addition to Mao), three (Chiang Ch'ing, Chang Ch'un-ch'iao, and Yao Wen-yüan) have had common experiences in leading the Red Guard movement during the Cultural Revolution, and are generally considered to represent the Politburo's far left. Many observers have pointed to the differences in ideological background between these and another group of three (Chou En-lai, Yeh Chien-ying, and Li Hsien-nien) that is often labeled "pragmatist." The remaining three (Chi Teng-k'uei, Li Te-sheng, and Wang Tung-hsing) have no distinct affiliation to either group and could conceivably control the balance in controversial issues.

International Views and Positions. In 1971 China continued the rapid diplomatic expansion that began in May 1969 when it started to replace the ambassadors recalled during the Cultural Revolution (they had been withdrawn from every country but the U.A.R.). In 1970 the emphasis was on restoring these disrupted diplomatic ties, while seeking new ties with five countries.[3] In 1971 the emphasis shifted to new contacts. Diplomatic relations were established with 12 countries: Nigeria (10 February; the Chinese ambassador left to fill the post on 31 July), Kuwait (22 March; the ambassador left on 3 August), Cameroun (26 March; the ambassador left on 21 August), Austria (28 May; the ambassador left on 8 September), Sierra Leone (29 July), Turkey (5 August), Belgium (25 October), Peru (2 November), Lebanon (9 November), Rwanda (12 November), Senegal (7 December), Iceland (8 December); consular relations were established with San Marino on 6 May. Seven ambassadors returned to posts in countries where diplomatic relations had been broken: Norway (the ambassador left China on 6 February), Denmark (6 February), Morocco (16 February), Burma (21 March), Bulgaria (25 March), Mongolia (19 August), and Czechoslovakia (the current chargé d'affaires in Prague presented his credentials as ambassador on 2 June). Thus, since 1969, ambassadors had returned to 42 countries, leaving four posts (India, Kenya, Laos, and Uganda) still vacant or filled by chargés d'affaires.

Evident in these contacts was the development of a shift in China's foreign policy from supporting internal dissident movements to improving state relations. Where state relations had been established, subversive movements often received cautious, if any, attention from the Chinese.

The two highlights of the year in China's foreign affairs, both in line with the country's more extravert stance, were the announcement in July that U.S. President Nixon would visit China and the admission in October of the PRC to the United Nations. Better relations between China and the United States—one facet of which was the United States' qualified endorsement of the

---

[3]Equatorial Guinea, Italy, Ethiopia, Chile, and Canada. In 1971 Chinese ambassadors left to take up posts in these countries on 6 March, 10 April, 3 May, 5 June, and 19 July, respectively.

PRC's entry into the U.N.—almost assured the mainland's representation in the U.N. Once a member, the PRC increased its rate of establishing diplomatic relations. Within two months following admission (25 October), China established relations with six countries.

Soviet Union. Since the hard-hitting Lenin Centenary (22 April 1970) attack by the Chinese against various aspects of Soviet "social imperialism," Sino-Soviet relations had thawed slightly, symbolized by the exchange of ambassadors in 1970 and the relatively low-level polemics during that year. On 21 March 1971 a relatively high-level meeting took place in Peking between Chou En-lai and the Soviet Union's ambassador to China, V. S. Tolstikov, and its deputy foreign minister, Leonid Ilichev, the last having been in China since August 1970 as the Soviet representative to the Sino-Soviet border negotiations (TASS, 23 March). The topics of the four-hour talk were not divulged; but it occurred following a reception at the Nepalese Embassy at which the three were present, suggesting the meeting may have been spontaneous.

On 12 March a Soviet broadcast in Mandarin, calling China's claim to be applying the experience of the Paris Commune an "insult to the fighters of 1871," opened the wounds of the Lenin Centenary offensive. China responded on 18 March in a joint *Jen-min jih-pao, Hung ch'i, Chieh-fang chün-pao* editorial challenging the position of the Communist Party of the Soviet Union (CPSU) in the world communist movement and reaffirming the ideological differences between the two countries. With the dual purpose of discrediting Soviet policies and reaffirming China's adherence to the strategy of revolutionary violence to balance its new flexible international stance, the editorial stressed China's obligation to "continue to promote the proletarian world revolution and the criticism of modern revisionism with Soviet revisionism at its center." It saw the "frenzied opposition" of the CPSU to revolutionary violence as "another concentrated expression of the betrayal of the principles of the Paris Commune." Criticizing CPSU domestic policy, the editorial stated:

> From Khrushchev to Brezhnev all have tried to mask their dictatorship of the bourgeoisie as the "state of the whole people." ... The Soviet revisionist renegades have turned the Soviet Union into a paradise for a handful of bureaucrat monopoly-capitalists of a new type.

Two weeks after the editorial appeared, the CPSU opened its Twenty-fourth Congress, on 30 March. In the renewed polemics provoked by the editorial, the Soviet Union charged that it had been timed to supplement "imperialist propaganda" on the eve of the CPSU congress. In his speech to the congress, CPSU General Secretary Leonid Brezhnev mentioned the slight improvement in inter-state relations during the past 18 months, but accused the Chinese leaders of splitting the international communist movement and distorting Marxism-Leninism. He placed the Soviet party and government in the role of moderator, attempting to normalize relations. He described the border talks in Peking as "proceding slowly" and implied that the Chinese were hindering progress. (Moscow radio, 30 March.)

In his speech (and more formally on 15 June) Brezhnev proposed the convening of a conference of the five nuclear powers—the Soviet Union, the United States, China, France, and Great Britain—at which the "problems of nuclear disarmament as a whole should be considered." The Chinese reply was a relatively moderate reiteration of an established policy:

> The prevention of nuclear war, the elimination of nuclear threats, and the complete prohibition and thorough destruction of nuclear weapons are matters affecting the peace and security of all countries of the world and a few nuclear countries have no right to brush aside the majority of countries in the world and arbitrarily hold a conference to consider and decide upon matters of such great importance. (Dated 30 July; carried by NCNA 7 August.)

The Chinese statement referred to what it termed the failure of previous similar negotiations between the Soviet Union, the United States, and others to settle questions of disarmament. It defended China's own development of nuclear weapons as a defensive measure designed to break the "imperialist nuclear monopoly." It declared that China's nuclear weapons were "still in the experimental stage," and that the country would never become a "nuclear superpower."

The statement, apparently for the first time, appealed specifically to the United States and the Soviet Union to:

> issue statements separately or jointly to undertake openly the obligation not to be the first to use nuclear weapons at any time or in any circumstances; and to dismantle all nuclear bases set up on the territories of other countries and withdraw to their own countries the nuclear weapons stock-piled and nuclear armed forces stationed on those territories.

Soviet reaction to the scheduled visit of President Nixon to China (announced 15 July), slow in appearing, described it first as "sensationalism" and "unusual though not particularly unexpected" (*Komsomolskaya Pravda*, Moscow, 18 July); and later as part of an effort to "provoke a military conflict between the Soviet Union and the United States ... and then build on the ruins ... leaving China as the only superpower" (*Izvestiia*, Moscow, 8 September). The Chinese response to the Soviet attacks was generally restrained. On 9 September, however, NCNA described TASS as a "scandal-mongering news agency," for spreading anti-PRC rumors that originated in Taiwan. The article in question was a 6 September allegation that during talks in Peking in early July, Nixon's assistant for national security affairs, Henry Kissinger, had proposed Sino-American cooperation in the exploitation of oil deposits discovered under the bed of the Pohai Gulf in Northeast China and in the construction by the United States of an aircraft factory in China.

Romania. On 1-9 June, Secretary-General Nicolae Ceaușescu of the Romanian Communist Party visited China, one year after a similar visit by Emil Bodnăras, member of the Romanian party's Presidium. The rapidly growing relations between the two countries, as exemplified by the visits and trade and loan agreements, placed Romania firmly in the position of independence in the international movement, a stand it had been promoting since the early 1960's.

In November 1970, a large Chinese loan, estimated at $244 million, was negotiated. Three protocols signed in March 1971 covered the building and equipping of factories in Romania by the Chinese. In Februury trade agreements for the year 1971 included the supply by Romania to China of oil products, steel pipes, aluminum, and other commodities, and an unspecified increase in the exchange of goods during 1972-75.

Ceaușescu's visit to East Asia (which included also North Korea, North Vietnam, Mongolia, and the Soviet Union), accompanied by Premier Ion Gheorghe Maurer, elicited the response from the Soviet Union that Soviet-bloc coordination of policy did not in any way infringe the sovereignty and national interests of any communist countries (Moscow radio, 31 May). In a welcoming editorial on 1 June, *Jen-min jih-pao* praised Romanian opposition to foreign (i.e., Soviet) interference in defense of its state sovereignty and its example to "small and medium" countries in withstanding "big-power hegemony."

Despite the mutually expressed interest in international "noninterference," differences were evident in the speeches and joint communiqué. China, for instance (as mentioned above) does not hold the view expressed in Ceaușescu's speeches favoring disarmament. Ceaușescu did not go to the extent, as Chou En-lai had, of attacking the Soviet Union as a "superpower." He did contend that there was no single center of the communist movement and that all parties were free to devise their own political line. He referred also to the "victory" of China's Cultural Revolution and in the communiqué he praised the PRC's "valuable contribution" to the communist movement.

The visit was reciprocated, at a lower level, during Romania's National Day celebrations. On 22 August Li Te-sheng, Politburo alternate and director of the General Political Department of the PLA, arrived in Bucharest as head of what was identified as a "military friendship delegation." At the National Day reception in Peking, acting Foreign Minister Chi Peng-fei used the occasion to castigate the Soviet Union: "Those who pursue a policy of hegemony are again creating tension in the Balkans. They have repeatedly carried out military maneuvers, making a show of force and bringing pressure to bear on other countries." (*Peking Review*, 27 August.)

Vietnam. The impending visit of President Nixon to China in February 1972 exerted strains on the relations between China and North Vietnam, although earlier in the year exchanges of high-level delegations served to strengthen the "fraternal unity and militant friendship" of the two countries. On 4-8 March, Chou En-lai made an unannounced visit to Hanoi, which appeared timed to serve as a warning that the recent U.S.-supported incursion of South Vietnamese troops into Laos posed a serious threat to China and might require countermeasures. Chou, who was accompanied by two military leaders in the CCP Politburo, Yeh Chien-ying and Ch'iu Hui-tso (the latter since purged), stated during his visit that China was "prepared ideologically and militarily to eliminate any enemy that endangers its territory." At a rally on 6 March Chou quoted a previously undisclosed statement of Mao Tse-tung: "If anyone among us should say that we should not help the Vietnamese people in their struggle against U.S. aggression and for national salvation, that would be a betrayal, betrayal of the revolution" (*Jen-min jih-pao*, 11 March). To some observers this statement suggested there were persons in China who did not completely adhere to PRC support of the war effort, and that this lack of unanimity might be used to bring pressure to bear on North Vietnam through the threat of diminished aid.

First Secretary Le Duan of the (North) Vietnamese Workers' Party (VWP) stopped in Peking on his way to and from the Soviet Union, where during his six-week visit he attended the Twenty-fourth Congress of the CPSU. During his visits in China (25-28 March and 10-16 May) the Chinese reaffirmed their support for the "wars of liberation" in Indochina. Chou En-lai told Le Duan: "The Chinese people will always stand on the side of the peoples of Vietnam, Laos, Cambodia, Korea, and the people the world over. Together we unite, together we fight, and together we will win victory." (NCNA, 11 May.)

The announcement concerning Nixon's visit evoked no open criticism in the North Vietnamese press, but evidence of disagreement was discernable. On 19 July, four days after the announcement, the VWP organ *Nhan Dan* accused the United States of "dividing the socialist countries, winning over one section und pitting it against another in order to oppose the national liberation movement," referring, apparently, to the effect the Sino-American détente would have on Sino-Vietnamese relations. The article added: "Nixon's policy also consists of trying to achieve a compromise between the big powers in an attempt to make smaller countries bow to their arrangements." Later, on 3 August, an article in the daily organ of the Vietnamese People's Army, *Quan Doi Nhan Dan*, charged that the United States pursued a "policy of reconciliation with some countries in some areas," a major result of which was, by means of the Nixon Doctrine, to "infiltrate and subvert socialist countries" and to "sabotage the socialist camp and the world communist movement." Again the visit by Nixon to China was implied.

Throughout this period, China's press went to great lengths to reassure the North Vietnamese on the continuation of China's pledge of providing a "reliable rear area" for North Vietnam. These efforts were also observed during the visit to Peking on 20-27 November by North Vietnamese Premier Pham Van Dong (who is third in the VWP hierarchy). The visit produced no variations in the press reports, although Pham Van Dong may have been advised of the precise timing of Nixon's trip, announced publicly two days after his departure.

China's economic and military assistance agreement with North Vietnam for 1972, signed in Hanoi on 27 September, was negotiated by Li Hsien-nien, who led a delegation that under normal circumstances would have included a high-ranking military person, such as Huang Yung-sheng. The purge of the latter and other military leaders earlier in the month may have accounted for the choice of Hanoi for the signing, a reversal of past practice. No details on the agreement were given.

North Korea. Relations between China and North Korea, which began to thaw in late 1969 and warmed rapidly during 1970, continued to grow friendlier in 1971. On 8 February the twenty-third anniversary of the Korean People's Army (KPA) was celebrated with greater enthusiasm than the same event in 1970. A reception given by the North Korean military attaché in Peking was attended by Huang Yung-sheng, PLA chief of staff, who ranked higher than the PLA representative sent to the 1970 reception.

On 15 June the Korean Central News Agency reported the appointment of a new Chinese member on the joint Sino-North Korean delegation to the United Nations Military Armistice Commission at Panmunjom. After five years without such representation, China's renewed interest reflected the improved relations between the two countries. It also indicated China's desire to reassert its role in international negotiations.

A "China-Korea Friendship Week" began in Peking and Pyongyang on 9 July to mark the tenth anniversary of the Sino-North Korean treaty of friendship, cooperation, and mutual assistance. The main preoccupation of the two countries, as revealed in the exchange of messages on 10 July, was the fear of revived Japanese "militarism." High-level delegations were exchanged, on the Chinese side represented by Politburo member Li Hsien-nien and on the Korean side by Kim Chung-nin, secretary of the Korean Workers' Party. In a speech at a banquet in Peking on 10 July, Huang Yung-sheng said that "historical experience has proved that when the enemy invades China, it invariably invades Korea first and when it invades Korea, it invariably further invades China," referring to both Japan and the United States (NCNA, 10 July).

The major event in Sino-North Korean relations during 1971 was the signing in Peking on 6 September of an agreement that China would supply an undisclosed amount of free military aid to North Korea. This was the first time since the Korean War that such an agreement had been made. Although North Korea had been receiving a small amount of military aid from China before the agreement, the overwhelming bulk of such assistance had come from the Soviet Union.

Also significant were the circumstances surrounding the negotiations. The high-level North Korean delegation was led by General O Chin-u, KPA chief of staff, and included the KPA air force, navy, and artillery commanders. The Chinese negotiators were led by Huang Yung-sheng and other high-ranking military leaders for whom this was their last important function before their purge in mid-September. Despite the length of the visit (18 August-7 September), few reports were provided by NCNA, suggesting either that most of the time was taken up with negotiations or that the impending purge of the Chinese negotiators may have had some effect on news dissemination. At a banquet on the day of his delegation's arrival, O Chin-u referred in his speech to the PRC as North Korea's "closest comrade-in-arms," adding to the evidence that China was beginning to weigh heavier in the balance of North Korea's relations with China and the Soviet Union.

South Asia. Two separate rebellions in South Asia created dilemmas for the Chinese government during the year. Its reaction to the secessionist movement in East Pakistan, which broke into open rebellion at the end of March 1971, took some time to formulate. On 12 April, a Pakistan domestic broadcast announced that a message from Chou En-lai had, within the context of a condemnation of India, offered Chinese support to the Pakistan government in its "struggle to safeguard the state sovereignty." Thereafter, its attacks were leveled against what was described as Indian interference in an internal affair. In the final days of the war that inevitably developed between Pakistan and India (lasting from 3 to 17 December), the PRC delegation to the United Nations issued a statement placing almost all the blame on India and distributing the remainder among the Soviet Union and various "imperialist powers." Referring to India's problems with its own nationality groups, the statement declared:

> Many countries in the world have nationality problems, which need to be solved properly and reasonably in conformity with the desire and interests of the people, but these are internal affairs of the respective countries, which can be solved only by their own governments and people, and in which no foreign country has the right to interfere. (*New York Times*, 17 December.)

An appeal to Mao Tse-tung in April by the moderately pro-Chinese East Pakistan leader Maulana Bhashani to support the secessionist movement was apparently ignored by the Chinese, despite Bhashani's warning that the world might think Mao was "not a friend of the oppressed" (*Far Eastern Economic Review*, 1 May). Neither has the CCP offered any kind of recognition to the pro-Chinese Communist Party of East Pakistan (Marxist-Leninist), although it recognizes the latter's Indian counterpart, and the East Pakistan party has generally opposed the secessionist aspect of the movement in favor of transforming the upsurge into a "class struggle" under its leadership. The Chinese stand is explained partly by its characterization of the secessionist leader, Sheik Mujibur Rahman, as an "American agent" and a "bourgeois leader," but mostly by its desire to maintain a South Asian ally in opposition to India.

The rebellion in Ceylon, which began about the same time as that in East Pakistan but was aimed more at redressing grievances of the educated unemployed, created a similar reaction in Peking. The main force of the uprising, the People's Liberation Front, consisted of a number of diverse groups, among which there were some pro-Chinese sympathizers, but was for the most part nationalist. Opposing the rebellion was a three-party coalition government of socialists, Trotskyists, and pro-Soviet communists. Eventually the PRC established itself firmly on the side of the government. Its support went to the extent of an agreement in May for an interest-free loan, evidently to cover the costs of the insurrection and its suppression. The letter by Chou En-lai to Ceylonese Prime Minister Sirimavo Bandaranaike announcing China's agreement to the loan contained assurances that the Chinese government had always opposed "acts of rebellion" and the creation of chaotic situations by ultra-left or ultra-right "opportunists." (*Le Monde*, Paris, 26 May; Colombo radio, 26 May.)

There is some similarity of views between the CCP and Ceylon's pro-Chinese communist party (which the former party recognizes) in that both opposed the rebellion. However, tensions must ultimately have developed because of the failure of the Ceylonese party to support the government and the latter's arrest of the party's leader in April 1971. In any case China's efforts to seek good relations with the government have relegated the party to the background.

Africa. Much of the PRC's activities in the Middle East and Africa during 1971 concerned the establishment of diplomatic relations, particularly in Africa. Such relations were established during the year with Kuwait and Lebanon in the Middle East. China also recognized two new Middle Eastern states, Bahrein and Qatar, on 20 August and 10 September, respectively. In Africa China established diplomatic relations with Cameroun, Nigeria, Rwanda, and Senegal, and reestablished ambassadorial-level contacts with Morocco. Uganda and Kenya are two of the four countries that still await the return of Chinese ambassadors.

The main methods used by the Chinese to gain footholds in Africa, in addition to diplomatic advances, have been to offer economic aid on the one hand and to support guerrilla groups on the other. Its largest aid project in Africa is for the building of the Tanzania-Zambia railway, construction on which was formally inaugurated in 1970. In 1971 economic aid was extended in the form of economic and technical cooperation to Equatorial Guinea in January, Mauritania in April, the Somali Republic in June, Sierra Leone in July, Ethiopia in October, and Sudan in December. In July an economic and technical cooperation agreement was signed with Algeria, but this amounted to an extension of a little-used 1963 offer of $50 million. On 14 September a military aid agreement with Congo (Brazzaville) was signed to cover defense problems and the acquisition of heavy military equipment for the army. This was the only such agreement known to have been signed with a non-communist country in 1971.

During the second half of 1971 China began to renew its involvement with the "liberation struggles" in southern Africa. China not only increased the level of assistance, but also began to extend it to parties that had sided with the Soviet Union during the extensive factional disputes of the mid-1960's. China's main effort now is with movements in the Portuguese territories, particularly Mozambique's FRELIMO (Frente de Liberação de Moçambique). The pro-Chinese faction within the front, which suffered a setback in 1970 with the expulsion of a pro-Chinese leader, apparently regained influence over the pro-Soviet element in August 1971 when a FRELIMO delegation led by the movement's president, Samora Machel, spent six weeks touring China, North Korea, and North Vietnam.

While giving substantial military aid to FRELIMO, the PRC has at the same time assisted a number of FRELIMO minority breakaway groups, including the Mozambique Revolutionary Committee (COREMO), and a COREMO splinter group.

China has exercised caution in its involvement with dissident movements in countries with which it has recently established diplomatic relations. One example is Ethiopia, where China has in the past been the only communist country to give direct assistance to the secessionist Eritrean Liberation Movement. On 2 November one of the movement's leaders, Omar Jaber, admitted that China no longer offered support, adding that "this may be explained by the policy of China to widen its international relations" (*Daily Star*, Beirut, 3 November). The state visit to China of Ethiopian Emperor Haile Selassie (5-13 October) underlined China's willingness to cultivate relations with established African leaders in the fight against "imperialism," a theme prominent in the speeches during the visit. Of interest to China was the fact that the headquarters for the Organization of African Unity—which recognizes only FRELIMO among the parties in Mozambique—is in Ethiopia.

Another, and more conspicuous, example was China's reaction to events in Sudan in the last half of 1971. An abortive coup d'état by the Sudanese Communist Party (SCP) against Sudanese President Ja'far Muhammad al-Numairi on 19 July and the subsequent executions of SCP leaders evoked scant comment in the Chinese press. The first reference to the events was an NCNA report of 26 July that the "coup clique" had been crushed by government forces. This implicit support of Numairi's role drew criticism from the Soviet Union (TASS, 30 July). In a message to Mao Tse-tung and Chou En-lai on China's Army Day, Numairi expressed the hope that the "excellent relations" between the two countries would continue to strengthen, "thanks to our mutual understanding and cooperation and our joint struggle for the dignity of mankind against aggression" (Omdurman radio, 29 July). In October, the Chinese congratulated Numairi on his election as president and wished him success in "safeguarding national independence and state sovereignty" (NCNA, 13 October).

United States. Sino-U.S. relations underwent a remarkable transformation during 1971. In April China invited several table tennis teams—representing Canada, Colombia, Great Britain, Nigeria, and the United States at the world table tennis championships in Japan—to play good-will matches in Peking. On 14 April Chou En-lai held a reception for the players at which time he told the U.S. team that their visit "had opened a new page in the history of relations of the American and Chinese peoples" (*New York Times*, 15 April). The Chinese players, relaying the invitation to the Americans, stressed, according to Kyodo News Service (7 April), that the Chinese were making a distinction between the government and the people of the United States.

On the same day (14 April), President Nixon made five proposals for improving Sino-American relations. These were: relaxation of currency controls, permission for U.S. oil firms to refuel Chinese ships and planes, permission for U.S. ships to transport Chinese cargoes between non-communist ports and for U.S.-owned foreign flag ships to call at Chinese ports, establishment of a list of nonstrategic goods that could be exported to China under a general license, and an effort to expedite visas for Chinese intending to visit the United States. A White House statement of 10 June announced the removal of the 21-year-old embargo against trade with the PRC. This opened the door for exportation to China of such commodities as automobiles (except those with four-wheel drive), television sets, food grains, furniture, clothing, and agricultural, dairy, and textile machinery. Also suspended was the requirement that 50 per cent of exports of grain to foreign countries be carried in U.S. ships, which in the past had made the cost of such transactions prohibitive.

Meanwhile, the Chinese news media continued to attack policies of the U.S. government. May Day celebrations in China were accompanied by the publication of 32 slogans capsulizing Chinese policies on current domestic and foreign issues. "U.S. imperialism" was attacked in the majority of those slogans dealing with foreign affairs. In the beginning of the summer, the PRC renewed its offensive against the "U.S. occupation of Taiwan." NCNA on 27 June accused the United States of collusion with Japan in committing aggression against Taiwan.

On 15 July, the Chinese and U.S. governments simultaneously announced that President Nixon would visit the PRC before the spring of 1972. The announcement came as a result of a secret trip to Peking by Nixon's assistant, Henry Kissinger, the same month. Later preparations for the visit included a second visit by Kissinger in October.

That China had taken a controversial step was becoming increasingly clear, with open attacks from the Soviet Union and veiled criticisms from the North Vietnamese. China provided its theoretical justification for the move in a September *Hung ch'i* article. Quoting from an article written by Mao in 1940 to justify all forms of temporary alliance to defeat a common enemy (Japan in 1940), the *Hung ch'i* article emphasized the value of shifting alliances in such a way as to isolate enemies one by one and eliminate them. The application of this strategy to the current situation implied that the United States, no longer the principal enemy, could be treated as a temporary ally against, for instance, the Soviet Union. The article stressed: "Our principles must be firm, [but] we must also have all permissable and necessary flexibility to serve our principles."

The North Korean interpretation of the visit, published in the KWP organ *Nodong Sinmun* on 8 August, was that it demonstrated the "bankruptcy" of U.S. policy in Asia and in such circumstances it was "not the march by a 'victor' but a trip of the defeated." While the Chinese have not gone this far in their own declarations, the Chinese domestic broadcast (on 10 August) of the Korean analysis probably helped to reduce any confusion that may have arisen in China as a result of the scheduled visit.

United Nations. On 25 October the PRC replaced the Nationalist government on Taiwan as China's representative in the United Nations. Before its admission, the PRC strongly and frequently denounced all efforts by other countries to arrive at a compromise solution. The United States, controlling a large bloc of countries previously opposed to admission of the PRC, was most heavily criticized for its shift earlier in the year to a position calling for the seating of the PRC in the General Assembly and the Security Council, while the Nationalists would retain a seat as representatives of Taiwan. This "dual representation" solution was seen by the PRC as an attempt to keep Taiwan separate from China, and it seemed all the more threatening because its adoption appeared a distinct possibility. The Chinese press attacked the United States for the attitude that "the status of Taiwan remains to be determined," and also for allegedly instigating a demonstration in New York by the "Taiwan Independence Movement" on the eve of the opening of the General Assembly (NCNU, 22 September).

Chinese news media reported extensively on the General Assembly debate. When the PRC's admission to the General Assembly and Security Council became fact, acting Foreign Minister Chi Peng-fei, speaking at a reception given in Peking by the Iranian chargé d'affaires on 26 October, described the vote on the resolution for admission as a "victory of the people of the whole world" and expressed thanks to Albania, Algeria, and the 19 other co-sponsors of the resolution (NCNA, 26 October).

The Albanian-led resolution to seat China and expel Taiwan was adopted by a vote of 76 to 35 with 17 abstentions. Earlier the General Assembly rejected by a vote of 59 to 55 with 15 abstentions the U.S. procedural resolution requiring a two-thirds majority vote for a resolution to succeed in expelling Taiwan. The second U.S. resolution, to seat the PRC in the General Assembly and Security Council while retaining representation for Taiwan, was dropped following the success of the Albanian draft.

Countries which at the time had relations with Taiwan but voted for the Albanian resolution included Botswana, Ecuador, Peru, Portugal, Senegal, Mexico, Rwanda, Libya, and Togo. Bolivia and the Central African Republic shifted from abstention in the 1970 vote on the same Albanian resolution to a negative vote in 1971. Those that switched from a negative to a positive vote were Israel, Turkey, Mexico, Rwanda, Sierra Leone, and Togo.

With the admission to the U.N., the PRC immediately became eligible for admission to a number of international organizations, although such membership was not automatic. Beginning with the U.N. Educational, Scientific, and Cultural Organization (UNESCO) on 29 October, most of the international organizations soon voted for the PRC's admission and the Nationalists' expulsion. The PRC did not respond immediately to these organizations, perhaps to take time to become better acquainted with their functions and to select suitable representatives.

Publications. The official and most authoritative publication of the CCP is the newspaper *Jen-min jih-pao*, published in Peking. The theoretical journal of the CCP Central Committee, *Hung ch'i*, is published approximately once a month. The daily paper of the PLA is *Chieh-fang chün-pao*. *Ta kung pao* is a national daily, which also has Chinese- and English-language editions published in Hong Kong. The *Peking Review* is a weekly published in English, French, Spanish, Japanese, and German editions; it carries translations of important articles, editorials, and documents from *Jen-min jih-pao*, *Hung ch'i*, and *Chieh-fang chün-pao*.

The official news agency of the party and government is the New China News Agency (Hsin-hua she; NCNA).

Eric Stromquist

India

Indian communists give 26 December 1925 as the founding date of the Communist Party of India (CPI). Although Western sources usually put the founding in December 1928, there were regional Marxist groups in various parts of India earlier.

After the death of CPI Secretary-General Ajoy Gosh, in 1962, and the Sino-Indian border conflict of the same year, the struggle between right and left factions within the party greatly intensified. This culminated in a formal split in 1964, when two separate congresses were held, each claiming to be the Seventh All-India Party Congress. Since that time, two parties have existed independently. One is commonly referred to as the "right" or pro-Soviet party, and the other as the "left" or nonaligned party. They call themselves, respectively, the Communist Party of India—the CPI, and the Communist Party of India (Marxist)—the CPI(M). In 1969 a new, Maoist communist party, the Communist Party of India (Marxist-Leninist)—the CPI(M-L), was created, largely by defectors from the CPI(M). This group derives its inspiration from the peasant revolt it instigated in 1967 in Naxalbari, West Bengal; its members, along with other numerous but smaller Maoist organizations, continue to be referred to popularly as Naxalites.

On a nationwide basis the two larger parties, the CPI and the more militant CPI(M), have been competing against each other on more or less equal bases of strength. Active membership is probably about 80,000 in each, despite much higher claims by the parties themselves. The population of India is 554,000,000 (estimated 1970).

Geographically both the CPI and the CPI(M) are rather concentrated. The CPI holds 88 per cent of its membership is six states (in decreasing size of membership): Bihar, Andhra Pradesh, Kerala, West Bengal, Uttar Pradesh, and Madras—the last now called Tamilnadu. The CPI(M) is even more concentrated, having 70 per cent of its members in the three states of West Bengal, Kerala, and Andhra Pradesh. The strength of the latter party was further focused in West Bengal as a result of elections to the Lower House of Parliament (Lok Sabha) in March 1971 (see below).

In terms of parliamentary strength, the March 1971 national elections gave the two parties almost equal shares (about 4 per cent for each) of the seats of the Lok Sabha. As a result of the most recent elections for the more than 3,000 state and territory legislative assembly seats (held variously between 1967 and 1971), the CPI had a total of about 110 and the CPI(M) 160 at the end of 1971, as compared with 120 and 140 a year earlier.

The CPI(M-L), the most militant of the three communist parties, opposes parliamentary participation and boycotted the March elections. Its members are believed to number between 5,000 and 10,000.

In addition to these three parties there are a number of smaller communist parties, generally to the left of the CPI. These include the various Naxalite factions which are scattered throughout the country, and several parties, such as the Trotskyist Socialist Workers' Party, which are comparatively insignificant.

The CPI and the CPI(M) operate legally, though members of both parties have been arrested from time to time. The intense governmental campaign against members and followers of the CPI(M-L)—which went underground shortly after its establishment in April 1969—continued in 1971 and severely damaged the party and other Naxalite groupings.

The CPI. Estimates of the active membership of the Communist Party of India vary so much as to be of limited significance. A renewal of memberships at the beginning of 1970 produced a figure of 243,238 (compared with 172,902 announced at the party's Eighth Congress, in February 1968). The same number was repeated at the Ninth Congress on 3-10 October 1971, but on 13 October Moscow's "Radio Peace and Progress" put membership at "more than 250,000."

Leadership and Organization. The central leadership of the CPI, elected at its Ninth Congress, includes the party chairman, Shripad Amrit Dange; the general secretary, Chandra Rajeshwar Rao; the Central Secretariat (chairman, general secretary, and 7 secretaries), the Central Executive Committee (25 members), the Control Commission (9 members), and the National Council (101 full members and 10 candidate members). There are also party secretariats and state councils in each state in India. The Central Secretariat, elected at the 1971 congress, included Bhupesh Gupta, N. K. Kirshnan, and Bhowani Sen, in addition to Dange and Rao. The remaining four Secretariat positions (filled by Avtar Singh Malhotra, C. Achutha Menon, S. G. Sardesai, and Yogindra Sharma at the 1968 congress) were to be determined at a future meeting of the National Committee, as were five of the 25 Central Executive Committee positions (*New Age*, 17 October).

Chief among the CPI's major fronts is the All-India Trade Union Congress (AITUC), in which the CPI and the CPI(M) exercised joint leadership until the two parties' differences led to a formal split of the AITUC in 1970. The CPI retained control of the original AITUC, leaving the CPI(M) to form a new organization. CPI Chairman S. A. Dange remained as secretary-general of the AITUC. The size of the AITUC was indicated by the number of unions represented at its January 1970 annual conference, held in disregard of an appeal of the CPI(M) to boycott the conference: of the 2,878 unions affiliated as of January 1970 (representing a total of 1,860,000 members), 1,906 (representing 1,355,023 members) were reported to have sent delegates. The state with the greatest representation was West Bengal, followed at some distance by Tamilnadu, Andhra Pradesh, and Kerala.

Another important front, the All-India Kisan Sabha (Peasants' Association; AIKS), split in 1969 into two separate organizations—one controlled by the CPI and the other (the larger one) controlled by the CPI(M), both continuing the AIKS name. The AIKS of the CPI is led by Z. A. Ahmed, the organization's secretary-general, who is also a member of the CPI Central Executive Committee. Other major mass organizations dominated by the CPI include the All-India Youth Federation (Joginder Singh Dayal, president, and C. K. Chadrappan, general secretary); the All-India Student Federation (Sudhkar Reddy, president, Ranjit Guha, general secretary); the National Federation of Women (Aruna Asaf Ali, president, Vilma Farooqui, general secretary); and, for agricultural laborers, the Bharatiya Khet Mazdoor Union (Khadaghari Misra, president, Guru Prasad, general secretary).

Party Internal Affairs. The CPI's assessment of its own strengths and weaknesses, contained in reports on the Ninth Congress and the preparatory state council conferences, revealed satisfaction with the party's role in various mass actions, including a number of strikes and the land occupation movement of 1970 (see *YICA*, 1971, pp. 573-74), in the campaign that culminated in the nationalization of 14 banks, in the defeat of "reactionary" parties at the 1971 elections, and in the formation of a CPI-led government in Kerala. The organizational report (published along with other congress documents in a supplement to *New Age* on 31 October) recorded "partial improvements" of the party's journals and their circulation, its mass organizations, and the state and central party organizations.

On the negative side, the organizational report complained that the growth of the party's "mass influence" had not been accompanied by a commensurate consolidation of its organizational functions. Further: "All the serious weaknesses and failings in the field of organization nailed down in the organizational reports of the Bombay [1964] and Patna [1968] congresses persist even today and the flabbiness of the organization has not been overcome."

The report castigated those in the party who had adopted a "revisionist" interpretation of the party program's call for the achievement of socialism by peaceful means. The program, it emphasized, rather than obligate the party to use peaceful means merely recommended this direction. To a "section of comrades" the "peaceful path" had been transposed from the realm of possibility into one of certitude, where it was "wrongly" seen as equivalent to the parliamentary path. "As a result," the report acknowledged, "electioneering and parliamentary combinations and manipulations become the main form of activity, while mobilising and organising the masses ... get regulated to the background."

The source of this attack on strictly parliamentary activities was in part the result of the March Lok Sabha elections in which the CPI suffered some losses and would undoubtedly have suffered more had it not entered into electoral arrangements with the ruling Indian National Congress Party of Prime Minister Indira Gandhi, or Congress(R). The alliances between the two parties, which so far have occurred only at the state level and below, have intensified divisions within each of them. Reportedly, sections of the CPI, particularly from West Bengal, strongly opposed the current trend toward what appeared to be conciliation with the Congress(R) (*India Express*, Delhi, 1 May; Delhi radio, 10 October). In Punjab state, party leader Satya Pal Dang was said to have complained that such collaboration would make the CPI no more than a "tail of the Indian government" (*Far Eastern Economic Review*, Hong Kong, 23 October). In its political resolution and organizational report on the Ninth Congress, the CPI emphasized extraparliamentary "mass struggles" to complement alliances that might "sometimes include the Congress organisation as a whole."

While the political resolution of the Eighth Congress advocated the overthrow of the Congress Party by a union of leftist forces, the Ninth Congress documents sought to maintain the Congress(R) in power and to push it gradually leftward. Although such a change could be explained partly by the new leftward shift of the Congress(R) after the "reactionary" Congcess(O) faction broke away in 1969, it did not have universal acceptance within the CPI. The 1971 political resolution explained that the "old concept of anti-Congressism has proved a barren and reactionary concept." The party's experience over the last two years had shown that the "rightist bid for power could not be defeated by the unity of the non-Congress left and democratic forces alone." This did not mean, however, that the CPI would not fight the "anti-people policies" of the Congress governments. In view of this combination of "unity and struggle," the resolution stated that the CPI would adopt a "flexible attitude from state to state, taking the concrete situation of each into account."

This approach appeared to be designed to satisfy both pro- and anti-alliance factions within the CPI. It had been necessitated largely by the predicament in which the party found itself after the March elections. It was able to retain its strength with only slight reductions (except in the West Bengal state assembly) to a great extent because of cooperation with the congress(R). At the same time, the unexpectedly large electoral gains by the Congress(R) severely weakened the CPI's position in any negotiations and in its influence on Congress (R) policy. Paradoxically it was primarily through support by the CPI and the regional Dravida Munnetra Kazhagam of Tamilnadu that the Congress(R) was able to survive in the Lok Sabha without a majority since its split in mid-1969.

Domestic Views and Attitudes. The long-range goal of the CPI is the establishment in India of a "national democratic government" (following Soviet guidelines), composed of a coalition of "left and democratic forces" led by the communist party and based on a worker-peasant alliance. The coalition would be composed of the "patriotic" elements of the national bourgeoisie, the intelligentsia, the peasants (including "rich peasants"), and the workers, with the working class gradually rising to a position of leadership under the guidance of the communist party, ultimately forming a "genuinely socialist" society. Such coalitions have been only partly successful and only at the state level (the current leadership of the government of Kerala—the "National Democratic Front"—is an example). At the national level the CPI has not yet been able to form a single alliance with another party, despite constant appeals for a coalition of "progressive" parties in the Lok Sabha.

To help shift India's political tide to the left and simultaneously to create a "left and democratic unity," the Ninth Congress put forth a 27-point "broad platform" around which a mass movement should be formed. Among its salient demands were those for nationalization of "monopoly concerns," expansion of the public sector for the economy, increased credit to small-scale industry and agriculture, radical land reforms, aid to the unemployed, more power to the states, repeal of "repressive laws," opposition to religious communalism and casteism, abolition of privy purses and privileges for princes, a moratorium on foreign debts, and stronger links with the communist countries (China not included).

Elections. By dissolving Parliament 14 months before the next scheduled elections, Prime Minister Gandhi evidently chose to take advantage of the favorable political climate existing for her party at the time rather than submit to the fate of an uncertain future. She was well rewarded for the move when the elections, held during 1-10 March 1971 after a brief two-month campaign period, reseated the Congress(R) with an unexpected two-thirds majority in the Lok Sabha, approaching the 1962 election results. In 1967 the party was reduced to a bare majority (279 seats in a total of 520), and the split in 1967 left it with a minority of about 226 seats (as of December 1970). Most pre-election predictions in 1971 gave the Congress(R) somewhere between 230 and 270 seats, rarely exceeding 300.

The final results, reseating the ruling party with a strength of 350, meant that large numbers of seats had been lost by other parties. Much to the satisfaction of the communists, the greatest loss was suffered by the "reactionary" Grand Alliance of the breakaway opposition Congress Party—or Congress (O), the Swatantra Party, the Jana Sangh, and the Samyukta Socialist Party (SSP), which together fell from a total of 150 pre-election seats to 49 seats. (For a tabular analysis of the voting shifts see Stanley J. Heginbotham, "The 1971 Elections in India," *Asian Survey*, Berkeley, December 1971.)

The defeat of the right wing, the gains of the Congress(R), and the relatively slight decline of the leftist parties caused the CPI Central Executive Committee to declare that the elections had resulted in a "big victory for the democratic forces in the country." The committee saw the Congress(R) victory as the result of the image created by the latter's "progressive" policies, by the isolation of the "reactionary combine," and by the "complete disarray and disunity in the camp of the left forces, the opportunism of many of the left parties and the failure and collapse of the left united front governments in Kerala [i.e., in October 1969] and West Bengal due to the policy of the CPI(M)." The biggest failure on the part of the leftist parties, according to the committee, was the refusal of the CPI(M) and the SSP to cooperate with the CPI. As for its own performance in the elections, the CPI expressed disappointment. Its decline in votes and loss of one seat in the Lok Sabha and more than half its seats in the West Bengal state assembly (see tables) was explained by the National Council:

> The main reasons for our failure in this respect are to be sought in the basic defects and shortcomings of our mass political work, [in the] failure to build strong and expanding bases [and] in the serious weaknesses of Party organisation. (*New Age*, 2 May.)

1971 LOK SABHA ELECTIONS

Party	Seats held prior to elections	Seats won	Per cent of 1967 vote	Per cent of 1971 vote
CPI	24	23	5.2	4.7
CPI(M)	19	25	4.2	5.1
PSP	15	2	3.1	1
DMK	24	23	3.8	—
Congress(R)	226	350 }	40.7	43
Congress(O)	65	16		10.5
Jana Sangh	33	22	9.4	7.4
Swatantra	35	8	8.7	3.1
SSP	17	3	4.9	2.4

Sources: W. H. Morris-Jones, "India Elects for Change—and Stability," *Asian Survey*, August 1971; U.S. Department of State, *World Strength of the Communist Party Organizations*, 1971.

The CPI(M)'s reaction to the elections was much the reverse. It did not exhibit any enthusiasm about the victory of the Congress(R), but was generally satisfied with its own results. Though its gains were accompanied by a further concentration of strength in the state of West Bengal, its new holdings (an increase from 19 to 25) made it the largest single party in the Lok Sabha outside the Congress(R). The consequences of the Congress(R) victory were assessed by the CPI(M) Politburo:

> Indira Gandhi, by her wordy talk of Socialism, her pretensions to fight Right reaction, has not only defeated her electoral rivals on the Right, she has also undermined and dispersed to some extent the strength of the democratic opposition in the House of the People....
> The victory of Indira Gandhi cannot be considered to be a victory of the people. (*People's Democracy*, 21 March.)

Activities in the States. 1. *West Bengal.* Simultaneously with elections to the Lok Sabha, elections were held also for the state assemblies of Orissa, Tamilnadu, and West Bengal (see table). West Bengal, which had been under the rule of the central government since the dissolution of its assembly in March 1970, has long suffered considerable instability. The proliferation of parties, excessive political violence—often involving the CPI(M-L) and CPI(M), and economic burdens have contributed to the frequent turnover of governments during the past four years. Before the 1967 general elections, the state had been dominated by the Congress(R) since India's independence. After 1967 it had been governed on two separate occasions for a total of 22 months by coalitions in which the CPI and CPI(M) together were dominant. Inter-party strife caused the coalitions to disintegrate, however, giving way to "president's rule."

1971 STATE ASSEMBLY ELECTIONS

	Most recent elections	Total Assembly seats	CPI				CPI(M)			
			Seats won		Percentage of votes		Seats won		Percentage of votes	
			1971	Previous	1971	Previous	1971	Previous	1971	Previous
West Bengal	1969	280	13	30	8.6	7	111	80	33.8	20
Tamilnadu	1967	234	8	2	2.5	1.8	0	11	1.5	4.1
Orissa	1967	140	4	7	4.2	5.2	2	1	1.2	1.2

The March 1971 elections created an even more unstable situation by producing no majority party or coalition in the 280-seat assembly. (Elections were to only 277 seats as a result of the deaths by assassination of candidates in three constituencies.) Efforts by the CPI(M)-led United Left Front, with the largest number of seats (123), to form a minority government (as the CPI had done in Kerala) met with strong opposition in view of the CPI(M)'s alleged disruptive record in the state. In the search for alliances that ensued, the CPI-dominated United Left Democratic Front (25 seats) fell apart over the issue of alliance with the Congress(R). Eventually, a six-party coalition government was formed, composed of the Congress(R)—the second biggest winner (105 seats), parties associated in a coalition with the Bangla Congress Party (seven seats), and two others (nine seats), for a total of 121 seats. The CPI and three other parties, including the Congress(O), which remained outside the government, pledged the aggregate support of their 20 assemblymen, raising the government's effective strength to 141 in an assembly of 277. This bare majority survived from its inception on 2 April to the government's resignation on 28 June, brought about by factional disputes.

2. *Kerala.* In Kerala the CPI continued in 1971 its shaky leadership over the state government. With 16 seats in a governing coalition that held a total of 36 seats in the 133-member Assembly, the CPI counted on the support of the 32 Congress(R) assemblymen to achieve a majority. The minority position of the CPI-led National Democratic Front, the threatened loss of one of its parties (see below), and pressure from the Congress(R) operated to force the CPI to include the Congress(R) in the government.

Negotiations between the coalition and the Congress(R) were deadlocked over the issues of the size of the expanded cabinet and its ratio of coalition parties to the Congress(R). The Congress(R) had demanded a cabinet with a maximum of 11 ministers—seven for the coalition (a drop from the nine it held at the time) and four for itself. On 8 September the CPI agreed to a compromise of an eight-to-five ratio and volunteered to drop one of its own four ministers.

The need to bolster the weak ministry was necessitated by the potential loss of the Praja Socialist Party (PSP) which had contributed three seats and one minister to the coalition in 1970 (see *YICA*, 1971, p. 576). An agreement in June to merge the PSP and the Samyukta Socialist Party (SSP) created concern for the CPI as revealed in a Central Secretariat statement issued on 2 June. The specific threat to the CPI in Kerala was the condition that upon merging the parties would surrender their positions in the ministries of certain states. A directive of the PSP National Executive Committee that its Kerala branch withdraw from the government drew a strong negative reaction from the party's Kerala State Council that was given broad coverage in *New Age* (25 July). The SSP and PSP nevertheless merged to form the Socialist Party on 9 August, absorbing also the Indian Socialist Party and splinter parties in three states. According to a *New Age* commentary (19 September), the anti-merger forces in the Kerala PSP were strong enough to maintain the PSP identity and to retain its place in the coalition government.

In elections to the 19 Lok Sabha seats allotted to Kerala, the biggest gain was made by the Congress(R). (See table.) Despite a decline in parliamentary strength in the state's Lok Sabha constituencies, the CPI(M) maintained a strong electoral position, demonstrating that in this respect it was not becoming exclusively a party of West Bengal. According to a *People's Democracy* analysis on 28 March, the CPI's National Democratic Front won 53 per cent of the vote and the CPI(M), together with candidates sponsored or supported by it, won 40 per cent.

1971 LOK SABHA ELECTIONS: KERALA (19 SEATS)

	Seats held prior to elections	Seats won	Percentage of vote
CPI	3	3	9
CPI(M)	9	2	26
Congress(R)	1	6	19

International Views and Positions. *Pakistan.* The East Pakistan secessionist movement, proclaiming an independent Bengal nation or "Bangladesh," received immediate support from the CPI when hostilities began on 25 March 1971. On 4 April, *New Age* carried a Central Secretariat appeal for immediate recognition of Bangladesh by India and for "rendering all assistance to the people of Bangladesh in the hour of their supreme ordeal." It also demanded the withdrawal of Pakistan armed forces and the lifting of martial law to give the people of Bangladesh "freedom to decide their own destiny."

A CPI National Council meeting in April called on the Indian government and people to send all necessary aid, including arms, to the government and people of Bangladesh "in order to save them from slavery and extermination" (*New Age*, 2 May). On 26 October the CPI foresaw war as imminent between India and Pakistan, despite the fact that the CPI had "always stood for avoiding war between the two countries" (*ibid.*, 31 October). Following the conclusion of the inevitable war (lasting from 3 to 17 December), the party emphasized the role of the Soviet Union, whose "unwavering help made this victory possible" and "saved India" (*ibid.*, 26 December).

According to one party leader, the Bangladesh victory was the third most important event in the Asian continent since World War II, following behind the Chinese revolution and the conflict in Vietnam. He predicted that it would have to be given at least as much study by present and future revolutionaries as the Cuban revolution. Its effect on Indian politics was to inspire an "advance to the left." It had advanced also the ideals of "anti-U.S. imperialism and pro-Sovietism." (*Ibid.*)

Ceylon. The CPI opposed—but with some qualifications—the insurrection that broke out in Ceylon early in the year. According to a series of articles in *New Age* during June, the insurrection, involving many highly diverse groups primarily of young and educated unemployed persons, was sparked by the failure of the coalition government (composed of socialist, Trotskyist, and pro-Soviet communist parties) to carry out effective political, social, and economic policies, although ironically it had occurred at a time that the government had begun to "deal more decisively" with various socioeconomic problems.

Despite their grievances, the insurrectionists were not " 'revolutionaries' fighting for an ideology, for a programme, or for the liberation of the people from under the yoke of an oppressive rule," the *New Age* articles stated. The strongest criticism was indirect, in the form of a quotation from a 20 May statement by the Ceylon Communist Party's general secretary, Pieter Keuneman, who described the rebels' training as one in which "petty-bourgeois nationalism and even racism were combined with concepts drawn from Maoism, from anarchism, and from various brands of petty-bourgeois ultra-left adventurism currently fashionable in certain circles in Western Europe and America." The articles suggested also that the rebels were in fact "only the expendable front-line for more sinister rightwing forces." Nevertheless, the movement had one positive aspect: "the heightened political consciousness among the progressive forces, and [primarily] among the working class which has been in the forefront of the struggle against the terrorists."

Soviet Union. The CPI is a staunch supporter of Soviet policies with regard to the international communist movement, despite differences that have occurred from time to time. The Soviet Union, in its efforts to win the friendship of the Indian government, has on occasion appeared more conciliatory toward that government than the CPI, and may have exerted some influence in the decisions of the CPI and the Congress(R) to seek limited alliances.

The major events concerning Indian and (CPI) relations with the Soviet Union during 1971 were the Twenty-Fourth Congress of the Communist Party of the Soviet Union (CPSU) (March-April), the Indo-Soviet treaty of peace, friendship, and cooperation (signed 9 August, ratified 18 August), and the East Pakistan secessionist movement. The congress, attended by General Secretary Rao, received a considerable amount of publicity in the CPI organ, much of it contributed by Rao himself.

The treaty, the significance of which was primarily symbolic, seemed to have been precipitated by events in East Pakistan, although there were rumors that it had been in preparation since 1969. It appeared to stand as a warning to Pakistan and China, and to ensure that any Sino-Indian rapprochement would not damage Soviet interests. In its report on the international situation, the Ninth Congress of the CPI declared:

> The historic treaty is a bulwark of peace on our subcontinent, Asia, and the world.... [It] is an important factor in cementing the unity of all anti-imperialist, democratic and peace-loving forces and aiding their advance in India and elsewhere.

Different attitudes were apparent in the CPI and Soviet Union's reactions to the hostilities in East Pakistan. In contrast to the CPI's immediate support for the secessionist movement and appeal for weapons aid, the Soviet Union took some time before making its own public analysis of the conflict, reprinting in the meantime reports taken mainly from the Pakistan news services. Gradually, the Soviet press placed responsibility for the bloodshed on the Pakistan government, without, however, declaring support for Bangladesh.

China. Open support by the Chinese government of the Pakistan government in putting down the secessionist movement added fuel to the CPI's anti-Chinese propaganda effort. While China was accusing India of intervening in Pakistan's "internal affair," the CPI spoke of China's "intervention in the internal affairs of Bangladesh on the side of the occupying and invading troops of [Pakistan President] Yahya Khan" (*ibid.*, 18 April). By comparison, "for all their affection for Yahya Khan even the imperialists [were] hesitating to openly support him" (*New Age*, 18

April). The CPI used the situation also to discredit the CPI(M) by pointing to what it saw as the latter party's gradual movement toward China and the Chinese position since March.

The CPI Central Secretariat interpreted the scheduled visit of U.S. President Richard Nixon to China in 1972 as having the objectives of (1) seeking a favorable political solution in Vietnam with the help of the Chinese, (2) attempting to isolate the Soviet Union and provoke a war between it and China, and (3) bolstering the prestige of Nixon's "discredited regime" (*ibid*., 25 July).

The admission of the People's Republic of China (PRC) to the United Nations in October and the simultaneous expulsion of the Republic of China was welcomed by the CPI Central Executive Committee as a "victory of the socialist countries, progressive governments and all anti-imperialist forces" (*ibid*., 31 October). The CPI did not expect the PRC's experiences in the United Nations to soften its "anti-Sovietism," however, as this could only be accomplished when a battle was "fought and won within the PRC itself."

Other Areas. The CPI boasted the attendance at its Ninth Congress of delegations from 22 foreign parties—more than at any previous congress. Parties were represented from Bulgaria, Czechoslovakia, France, East Germany, West Germany, Great Britain, Greece, Hungary, Israel, Italy, Jordan, Mongolia, Nepal, New Zealand, East Pakistan, Poland, Romania, the Soviet Union, Spain, the United States, and Yugoslavia.

Among the tasks the party set for itself in the international sphere at the congress were increased efforts to strengthen India's foreign policy in a "consistent anti-imperialist direction." This meant increasing the level of support for the Bangladesh movement and enhancing Indo-Soviet friendship. It also involved an intensification of the party's campaign for Indian recognition of the Provisional Revolutionary Government of South Vietnam; raising from consular to ambassadorial level India's relations with the governments of East Germany, North Korea, and North Vietnam; and establishing closer economic and cultural ties with Cuba.

*   *   *

The CPI(M). Membership figures for the Communist Party of India (Marxist) are subject to question, but it is generally estimated that the party has about 80,000 active members. The CPI(M)'s own figure, given at its Eighth Congress in December 1968, was 76,233. A decline in membership preceding the congress was chiefly the result of the breaking off of the party's extreme left in 1967-68. As in the case of the CPI, the power of the CPI(M) lies in the non-Hindi states, particularly in Kerala and West Bengal.

Leadership and Organization. The CPI(M) leadership consists of party Secretary-General P. Sundarayya, the politburo (9 members), the Central Committee (28 members), and state secretariats and committees. Politburo members, elected at the Eighth Congress, are P. Sundarayya, B. T. Ranadive, M. Basavapunnaiah, E. M. S. Namboodiripad, Promode Das Gupta, Jyoti Basu, P. Ramamurti, Harkishan Singh Surjeet, and Avilliath Kutteri Gopalan. An aging founder member of the original CPI, Muzaffar Ahmad, occupies an honorary position above that of Sundarayya on the Central Committee.

The CPI(M) acquired its own trade-union federation in 1970, after having shared the leadership of the AITUC with the CPI since the parties' division in 1964. A CPI(M)-dominated "All-India Trade Union Conference" was held in May 1970 from which the new organization, the Centre of Indian Trade Unions, emerged. B. T. Ranadive and P. Ramamurti—both CPI(M) leaders in the undivided AITUC—were elected president and general secretary, respectively. The Credentials Committee report claimed that the conference represented 804,637 members in 1,759 affiliated trade unions. In addition, about 200 unions in various states, with a total of 150,000 members, were said to have expressed a desire to become affiliated.

The CPI(M) is somewhat stronger than the CPI in organizing the peasantry; its AIKS claimed very close to a million members in 16 states in 1969. Activity in the CPI(M) peasant front centered primarily in West Bengal and Kerala, with about 60 per cent of its AIKS membership located in West Bengal. Its leadership includes Politburo member A. K. Gopalan as president and Central Committee member Harekrishna Konar as general secretary. The CPI(M) also controls an agricultural laborers' union which has a membership of about 300,000. The CPI(M)'s former student organization (AISF) was reorganized in December 1970 as the Students' Federation of India.

Domestic Attitudes and Activities. The CPI(M) was originally formed, when it broke from the CPI in 1964, as a Stalinist pro-Chinese party that favored armed revolt by workers and peasants and accepted parliamentary participation only as a temporary means to build its base of power. Gradually, the "parliamentary path" appeared to become a more permanent feature of the party's strategy. With the adoption in 1967 of the "Madurai line" (referring to a meeting of the Central Committee in Madurai, Tamilnadu), the CPI(M) assumed an internationally independent policy, abandoning its pro-Chinese sentiments and many of their domestic ramifications. Since 1969, when it no longer held positions in the governments of Kerala and West Bengal, the party began to place even greater emphasis on its extra-parliamentary activities. (An exception was the massive election campaign in West Bengal early in 1971.)

The party's long-range goal is the establishment of a "People's Democratic India." It seeks a "voluntary union of the peoples of various nationalities of India," but one in which the nationalities would forfeit their right to secession.

In the party program adopted at its Seventh Congress—i.e., the one that formalized the CPI-CPI(M) division in 1964—the CPI(M) decided to omit reference to the "right of all nationalities to self-determination," embodied in the CPI program, pending further discussion on the matter. In documents prepared for the party's Ninth Congress (originally scheduled for 28 December 1971-2 January 1972, but later postponed indefinitely) a draft amendment to the party program proposed the following formulation: "The Communist Party of India (Marxist) works for the preservation and promotion of the unity of the Indian Union on the basis of real equality and autonomy for the different nationalities that inhabit the country, and to develop a democratic State structure.... It is opposed to all disruptive secessionist movements." (Supplement to *People's Democracy*, 28 November.) The amendment included also a rearranged outline of the envisaged state structure.

The new policy followed a lengthy justificatory explanation that cited Marxist theory and various precedents. Lenin's article, "The Right of Nations to Self-Determination," according to the statement, did not adequately cover the kind of situation that now prevailed in India. Its current multi-national character did not contain the requisite "oppressor" and "oppressed" nations; the oppression in India was said to be more in the form of class exploitation of one Indian nation over another.

The immediate significance of this policy was not defined, although it may have helped to allay fears that the CPI(M) was instigating a pan-Bengali movement by taking advantage of the Bangladesh uprising. While according to the CPI(M) formula East Pakistan was justified in attempting secession, West Bengal evidently would not be. The CPI(M)'s motives in Bengal were questioned by the CPI, which castigated the former party for comparing the situation in West Bengal with that of East Bengal (East Pakistan), and for Promode Das Gupta's reported statement that the border between Bangladesh and West Bengal had disappeared and that the struggles of the two Bengals were the same. (*New Age*, 9 May.)

The political resolution drafted for the postponed congress offered a number of demands to form the basis of common action by the "left and democratic forces." Most salient were those for immediate recognition of the provisional government of Bangladesh; the holding of elections to the West Bengal assembly in February 1972, along with the rest of the states; opposition to the oppression of castes, tribes, and Muslim minorities and to Hindu and Muslim chauvinism; a need-based minimum wage; radical land reforms; nationalization of all foreign businesses; and a moratororium of foreign debts for five years.

International Views and Positions. The CPI(M) maintains a policy of strict independence among the world's communist parties, refusing to align itself with either the Chinese Communist Party (CCP) or the CPSU. Although in 1964 it broke from the CPI as a pro-Chinese party, since 1967 it has condemned with equal intensity the errors of Chinese "left-sectarianism" and Soviet "revisionism." During 1971 CPI(M) statements on China and the Soviet Union seemed to indicate a shift to a more positive attitude toward both countries.

The CPI(M), which has not been accorded international recognition by either the CPSU or the CCP, has centered its efforts on establishing relations with nonaligned parties, particularly those of Cuba, North Korea, Romania, and North Vietnam.

Prominent among the international concerns of the CPI(M) was the secessionist Bangladesh movement. The CPI(M) did not hesitate to express support for the Bangladesh government that was formed in April, and on 29 March it organized a mass meeting in Calcutta to pressure the government of India immediately to accord full recognition to Bangladesh and to "render it effective diplomatic and material help" (*People's Democracy*, 4 April). The CPI(M) continued to campaign relentlessly through its party organ for the recognition of Bangladesh.

This position led the party to take issue with an article in the Peking *People's Daily* (11 April), which characterized the events in East Pakistan as a domestic issue and therefore suggested that foreign supporters of the movement were intervening in the internal affairs of Pakistan. The CPI(M) replied that failure to support Bangladesh was to "renounce the heritage of the communist movement" and concluded that the Chinese stand had brought "discredit to Marxism-Leninism" (*ibid.*, 16 May). At a press statement on 6 December the CPI(M) welcomed the decision by the government of India to recognize the People's Republic of Bangladesh.

The CPI(M) also devoted attention to the rebellious movement in Ceylon early in the year. Noting that the Ceylonese government had been able to suppress the uprising with arms from India, Pakistan, the Soviet Union, and the United States, a *People's Democracy* article (9 May) interpreted the events in Ceylon as an "uprising of the middle classes fast getting disillusioned with a Government which talks incessantly of a welfare State and Socialism but does everything only to further the interests of the planters and capitalists, native and foreign." The same article found that the uprising had taken an incorrect form since its leaders, as "petty-bourgeois adventurists," failed to organize the working class, build an alliance with the peasantry, and mobilize all the forces interested in "fulfilling the tasks of the democratic revolution." The CPI(M) maintained also that the uprising was a "purely internal affair" with no foreign involvement and condemned the Ceylonese government for attempting to implicate North Korea by expelling the officials and staff of the North Korean Embassy on "grounds of internal security." (*Ibid.*) Its attitude toward the parties of Ceylon's coalition government was expressed in a 30 May article in *People's Democracy*:

> By being a part of the bourgeois-landlord government of [the socialist Sri Lanka Freedom Party leader] Mrs. Bandaranaike, these parties like the [Trotskyist] Lanka Sama Samaja Party and the [pro-Soviet] Communist Party of Ceylon joined hands with the bourgeois-landlord classes to implement the anti-people policies of the government and refused to understand or fulfill the aspirations of the people.

A CPI(M) Politburo meeting on 23-26 July adopted a resolution welcoming the proposed visit of President Nixon to China. The same resolution rejected a campaign in India, waged especially by the CPI, to portray this development as a "ganging up of the People's Republic of China and the U.S. against the Soviet Union and other socialist countries and a sell-out of the liberation struggles of the oppressed peoples, especially the Vietnamese people." Also expressing a positive CPI(M) attitude toward China was its welcome of the PRC's admission to the United Nations: a "development which gladdens the anti-imperialist and socialist world" and also a "recognition, though belated, of the fact that the People's Republic of China is a world Power and [that] none of the problems concerning the world can be solved without its participation." (*Ibid.*, 31 October.)

Following the treaty of peace, friendship, and cooperation signed by the governments of India and the Soviet Union, the CPI(M) Secretary-General Sundarayya issued a press statement hailing it as a development which "should help India to resist the U.S. imperialist pressure and blackmail and call Yahya Khan's war [threats] a bluff" (*ibid.*, 15 August). At a Central Committee meeting on 24-29 August the CPI(M) reiterated support for the Indo-Soviet pact, expressing disappointment that it had not yet helped to "overcome all hesitations on the part of the Government of India to come forward to accord immediate recognition to Bangladesh" (*ibid.*, 12 September).

In its efforts to maintain contacts with the non-aligned communist parties, the CPI(M) sent at least two delegates abroad in 1971. Politburo member Jyoti Basu attended the fiftieth anniversary celebrations of the Romanian Communist Party in April. Secretary-General Sundarayya and Politburo member Harkishan Singh Surjeet made an extended visit to Cuba (1-12 October), where they held talks with leaders of the Communist Party of Cuba, including Politburo members Juan Almeida and Armando Hart.

*   *   *

The Naxalites. The left-extremist movement in India derives its inspiration from the Naxalbari, West Bengal, peasant uprising in 1967. The uprising was led by dissident CPI(M) members, who later left, or were expelled from, the party, taking with them a large number of sympathizers who subsequently formed the core of the Chinese-oriented "Naxalite" movement. The movement has attracted a number of unemployed college graduates, university students, landless peasants, and workers in tea plantations. It has suffered substantial atomization since its beginnings, particularly in 1969 and 1970, when a number of parties emerged promoting divergent tactics and strategies. Since the end of 1970, a government campaign against the Naxalites substantially reduced the size of the movement and eliminated almost all its leadership. Naxalites exist in almost every state, but are most numerous in West Bengal and Andhra Pradesh.

The largest of the Naxalite parties—and evidently the first to be established—is the Communist Party of India (Marxist-Leninist), which gives its founding date as 22 April 1969. It is recognized by the Chinese Communist Party, and articles from the CPI(M-L) monthly English-language periodical *Liberation* appear in *Peking Review*. Charu Mazumdar (one of the few leaders not yet arrested or killed) is the secretary-general and main theoretician; Kanu Sanyal (currently in prison), the leader of the peasant revolt in Naxalbari, is reportedly its strategist. Before the formation of the CPI(M-L), the loose organization from which it was derived—the All-India Coordination Committee of Communist Revolutionaries (AICCCR)—suffered a division between its West Bengal base and the important branch in the state of Andhra Pradesh. The latter group, led by Tarimela Nagi Reddi, did not join the CPI(M-L). It is not recognized by the Chinese, but neither is it denounced by them. According to the *Hindu* (Tamilnadu, 14 April 1970), there were in 1970 about 10,000 hard-core followers in the CPI(M-L) and 6,000 in Nagi Reddi's Andhra Pradesh Revolutionary Communist Committee (APRCC).

The difficulties between the CPI(M-L) and the APRCC originated in Andhra Pradesh over differences between the state Coordination Committee and the Coordination Committee of the Srikakulam District, where the Naxalites have registered their greatest successes. When the state committee affiliated with the AICCCR in December 1968, the Srikakulam committee, rejecting the former's insistence on building a defensive force before engaging in armed struggle, began to deal directly with the AICCCR in West Bengal. The state committee disassociated itself from the district committee and subsequently formed the APRCC, while the district committee became a branch of the CPI(M-L). (See Mohan Ram, "Maoism in India: Two Tactical Lines," in *The Institute for Defence Studies and Analyses Journal*, New Delhi, January 1971.)

Current differences between the two continue to revolve around armed resistance and mass participation, and armed offensive action by small guerrilla groups, the former adopted by the APRCC, and the latter by the CPI(M-L). While the APRCC advocates beginning the "liberation struggle" with an agrarian revolutionary program and the creation of a mass-based "red army," the CPI(M-L) postpones the agrarian revolution until the state machinery is destroyed by a program of selected "annihilation" of landlords, forcing the "class enemies" to flee the countryside and thereby "liberating" the villages. The latter seeks to consolidate its gains by establishing "revolutionary committees" (on the Chinese model).

This emphasis on rural areas was temporarily disrupted when in March 1970 the clandestine CPI(M-L) publication *Liberation* proposed a campaign among urban workers. As a result, the party became almost isolated in Calcutta, its headquarters, where the "annihilation" campaign, directed mainly at members of the CPI(M), aggravated the city's unstable condition and provoked the central government to retaliate with disastrous consequences for the party. The new line also fragmented the CPI(M-L) internally, and its district committees, including that of Srikakulam, began to assert their autonomy.

The urban campaign was apparently abandoned in favor of the original rural emphasis when, in the May issue of the clandestine Bengali publication, *Deshabrati*, Charu Mazumdar claimed that a "liberation army" had been formed and would soon begin its "long march" from the towns to the rural areas. A campaign of expropriating weapons—largely from citizens, rather than police, and mainly outside the urban areas—began at about the same time.

According to a CPI(M-L) statement reported in *New Age* (19 September), the West Bengal State Committee of the party split into two separate committees at the beginning of September. Followers of Charu Mazumdar were reported to have formed the new committee, labeling their erstwhile internal foes as "revisionists," and dissolving the party's Calcutta District Committee and the regional committee of the Bihar-Orissa-West Bengal border area. The statement, issued by Charu Mazumdar's committee, stressed the latter's determination to save the CPI(M-L) from the "pseudo-revolutionaries" and "revisionist cliques" who are "accustomed to [using the] pistol freely and who show utter contempt [for] the working class and landless peasantry." Those under attack, who owe their allegiance to Ashim Chatterjee, have apparently maintained their own state committee and reportedly declared themselves as the "correct followers of China's path."

The attitude of China, judging from its silence on the CPI(M-L) between autumn 1970 and autumn 1971, was to reject Mazumdar's urban line. On 7 October, the New China News Agency reported on an article in the April-June issue of *Liberation* which declared that in West Bengal "armed struggle" was being linked with the "mass movement" in the countryside, a claim that appears to approach the APRCC line. The article stated that nine revolutionary committees had been formed in the Naxalbari area, and that an unspecified number had been formed in the Burduan District.

*   *   *

Publications. Indian communists have a network of dailies, weeklies, and monthlies throughout the country, in English and various vernacular languages. The central organization of the CPI publishes the English weekly *New Age* in New Delhi (circulation, 7,500). Bhupesh Gupta is the editor. It also publishes the weekly *Party Life* and has dailies in five states: two in Kerala, and one each in Andhra Pradesh, West Bengal, Punjab, and Manipur.

The central organ of the CPI(M) is the English weekly *People's Democracy*, published in Calcutta and edited by B. T. Ranadive (circulation 9,000 to 10,000). The CPI(M) also publishes dailies in Kerala, West Bengal, and Andhra Pradesh, and weeklies in Madras, Karnataka, West Bengal, Punjab, and Jammu and Kashmir.

The CPI(M-L) publishes a monthly in English, *Liberation*, edited by Sushital Ray Chaudhury until his death on 13 March 1971, and a Bengali weekly, *Deshabrati*. Both were banned by the government after March 1970, but continued to appear clandestinely since then. Other extremist publications are, in Hindi, the weekly *Lok Yuddha* (People's War), issued since 1968, and, in English, the monthly *People's Path* and biweekly *Commune*.

Eric Stromquist

Indonesia

The Communist Party of Indonesia (Partai Komunis Indonesia; PKI) was founded on 23 May 1920 when the Indies Social Democratic Association (formed in 1914) decided to join the Third International (Comintern). Declared illegal in November 1926 after an unseccessful uprising, the PKI operated until 1945 with most of its leaders in Moscow or in Yenan, China. In October 1945, shortly after the proclamation of an independent Indonesian republic, the PKI resumed legal activity. In 1946 the exiled leaders returned and assumed direction of the party. On 18 September 1948, in response to the government's decision to demobilize many of the army's communist-led units, communist and pro-communist army officers and civilians launched a rebellion at Madium in East Java. Madium was recaptured in two weeks, and by the time the rebellion was crushed two months later many PKI leaders had been killed.

On the night of 30 September 1965, six senior generals of the Indonesian army were abducted and murdered in the course of an attempted coup mounted by a group of air force and army officers led by Lieutenant Colonel Untung. PKI involvement in the attempt apparently was extensive. Members of the PKI and of PKI-directed front organizations, such as the People's Youth and the Women's Movement, supported the attempt, which was described as "patriotic and revolutionary" in an editorial in the party newspaper. General Abdul Haris Nasution and Major General (now President) Suharto succeeded in escaping and proceeded to crush the insurgency.

On 12 March 1966 the PKI and all its affiliate organizations were banned, and the acceptance of former PKI members into other political organizations was declared illegal. On 5 July 1966 the Indonesian parliament formally outlawed the studying and teaching of Marxism-Leninism. Former PKI members were forbidden to participate in the 3 July 1971 general elections. In 1955, during Indonesia's only previous election, the PKI polled 16 per cent of the vote (*Christian Science Monitor*, 8 July 1971).

Before the 1965 coup attempt, the PKI was considered to be the third largest communist party in the world, with a claimed membership of 3,000,000. The party also controlled a number of fronts (see *YICA*, 1970, pp. 584-85). PKI members presently at large and engaging in political activity are thought to number no more than a few thousand. Afew hundred additional Indonesian communists reside in China, the U.S.S.R., and other communist countries. (U.S. Department of State, *World Strength of the Communist Party Organizations*, Washington, D.C., 1971). The population of Indonesia is 121,200,000 (estimated 1971).

The PKI has apparently split into three groups, consisting of (1) those elements who operate chiefly in Central and East Java and refer to themselves as the "Politburo of the PKI Central Committee," (2) the Peking-based "Delegation of the PKI Central Committee," and (3) the Moscow-based "Marxist' Leninist Group of the PKI." An "Indonesian People's Liberation Army" (Tentara Pembebasam Rakjat Indonesia; TPRI) was reportedly formed in mid-1966 from various PKI guerrilla and terrorist remnants.

The Politburo of the PKI Central Committe. The number of remaining PKI members in Indonesia is unknown, but according to Southeast Asian sources there are about 170,000 at large in Central Java and 8,000 in West Borneo. Following the 1965 coup attempt, an estimated 300,000 communist suspects were killed and about 100,000 jailed. Those imprisoned have been classified in categories reflecting the government's assessment of the degree of their participation in the coup attempt. In 1971 a total of 50,000 Category C prisoners (minor suspects) were released, leaving about 5,000 "prime suspect" Category A and 25,000 to 30,000 "hard-core activist" Category B prisoners in Indonesian jails (*New York Times*, 10 November 1971). Complaints of mistreatment of these prisoners were countered by statements by the chief medical officer of the International Red Cross, who inspected several of the prisons in early 1971. He reported that he had "discovered no signs of inhumanity or brutality," and concluded that "compared to the life of the average Indonesian, conditions in the detention centres were satisfactory" (*Far Eastern Economic Review*, Hong Kong, 13 March).

Communist elements in Java suffered setbacks during 1971 through the capture of several important leaders. The alleged leader of the pro-Soviet faction of the PKI in Central Java, Dr. Soegiono, was reportedly captured early in the year. Former PKI regional assemblyman Machtubhadi was arrested in May (*Djakarta Times*, 24 May), as was a PKI cadre named Soeharto who had managed to infiltrate the Indonesian Muslim Party (Antara, Indonesian news agency, Djakarta, 28 and 29 May). Four other PKI leaders—including former Central Committee member Margono and Central Java greater regional committeewoman, Mrs. Sugijone—were arrested early in the year (Djakarta radio, 9 March). Dr. Thung Tiong Tie, who after the coup attempt was given the task of organizing a Marxist-Leninist group in Semarang, Central Java, was tried by the government in July for his role in the coup. He disclosed that his Semarang group was under the leadership of Engineer Kuntjoro and that its headquarters in Bandung was headed by Hadi Sugandi. He reported that the PKI had been successful in recruiting many students from the Institute of Technology at Bandung. Dr. Thung identified Ismail Bakri as the leader of the "new style" PKI in West Java (Antara, 26 July).

In February the Indonesian government reported the arrest of Widagdo, the number two man of the outlawed "Communist University Student Organization," who was apprehended in Djakarta (Agence France Presse, AFP, 16 February). In August the head of the Information Service of the Djakarta Regional Security and Order Restoration Command, Lieutenant Colonel Mugni, stated the PKI remnants under the leadership of Jusman (alias Broto, Parto) were attempting to rebuild the Djakarta committee of the PKI. An attempt to establish a new PKI central committee by the end of December was reported in a Bandung daily. This "December plan" apparently envisioned a central committee which would remain underground for the immediate future. (*Pikiran Rakjat*, quoted by Djakarta radio, 31 March.)

In addition to the PKI proper, communists in Indonesia work through the Indonesian People's Liberation Army; the "Police and Army Training Center" and People's Liberation Army in Lampung, South Sumatra; the People's Youth (Permuda Rakjat); and GEMPAR (Movement of Revolutionary Pantjasilaist University Students). The exact relationship between the PKI and guerrilla bands operating in Kalimantan (Indonesian Borneo) is unknown. PKI Central Committee member M. A. Sofian reportedly crossed into Sarawak in July and took control of the ideological bureau of the Sarawak People's Guerrilla Army and North Kalimantan People's Armed Forces. These organizations, however, do not appear to be closely connected to the PKI (see *Malaysia*).

Domestic Attitudes and Activities. Although there was little first-hand information available, statements by communist prisoners and broadcasts by Soviet and Chinese radio stations made it clear that in 1971 the leadership of the PKI was still much divided by questions of strategy and by allegiances in the Sino-Soviet split. The Soviet position was echoed by the Marxist-Leninist

Group of the PKI (see below), and was apparent in the Soviet statement commemorating the fifty-first anniversary of the founding of the PKI:

> Today members of the banned Indonesian communist party continue their hard and selfless struggle. They want to rebuild their party on a Marxist-Leninist basis, want to build a national unity front of all patriotic forces and want to expand political work among the masses of people. Program statements of the Communist Party of Indonesia stress the importance of unity with the world communist and workers' movement. They stress the need to fight against the harmful Maoist influence and its adventuristic ideas.... Acting together with progressive and democratic forces in the country, the Indonesian communists will win their valiant struggle for the working people's cause. (Moscow radio, 23 May.)

The Soviets contrasted their program of political struggle through a united front with the "adventurism" of the Maoists:

> The national liberation movement in Indonesia is now facing serious difficulties.... The Maoists and their agents [have] stubbornly urged the Indonesian people to launch an armed struggle without delay. They assert that the situation for revolution is splendid in Indonesia. The fact that such provocative instigations by the Maoists could subject the remnant and scattered democratic forces in Indonesia to attacks by the reactionaries is apparently of no concern to the Maoists. In fact, this adventurous call is not based on the actual situation in Indonesia but on the selfish desire of the Maoists [to] show off their so-called "truth" that "political power grows out of the barrel of a gun." (*Ibid.*, 24 August.)

The PKI leaders found themselves in something of a dilemma: to instigate an armed struggle when both greatly outnumbered and out-organized by the Suharto government would court destruction; on the other hand, the tactic of the united front and political struggle was discredited in the minds of many PKI members in 1965—the communists had been adhering to just such a program before the coup attempt.

Indonesia's second general election reflected to a degree the differences between pro-Soviet and pro-Chinese communists. Although 1.7 million potential voters were removed from the election rolls because of alleged communist activities (*Far Eastern Economic Review*, 24 July), there were apparently large numbers of communists who escaped detection and were eligible to participate in the election. The attitudes of the two communist factions toward the elections were noted by the official Indonesian radio service a month before the voting:

> According to the general election laws, Indonesian communists [are] not allowed to take part in the general elections. They can neither run for a seat in the legislative assemblies nor cast their vote in the forthcoming general elections. In this connection, those who have followed Moscow radio's commentaries ... can draw the conclusion that communists in our country want to take part in the forthcoming general elections.... Unlike the Peking-oriented communists, the Moscow-oriented elements have been ordered to take part in the general election. Peking-oriented communists do not entertain the belief that the goal of their revolution can be attained through general elections.... The Moscow-oriented communists, however, entertain the belief that the goal of their revolution can be attained through general elections.... After the elections [the] communists are required to be an opposition party ... unless the elected government is entirely controlled by communists. The communists want to take part in the general elections only for propaganda purposes, making empty and lofty promises. (Djakarta radio, 5 June.)

The pro-Soviet faction apparently chose to support the Indonesian Nationalist Party (PNI). At least, it would seem that the Soviet Union favored this course, from references to the PNI's "big contribution to the national liberation movement" (*New Times*, Moscow, 29 July 1970) and, during the election campaign, to the PNI as a "progressive political party" (Moscow radio, 27 April 1971). Indonesian sources reported in January that the first secretary of the Polish Embassy had given a dinner party for the general chaiman of the PNI (Antara, 19 January). The biggest surprise of the election was the very poor showing of the PNI (*Far Eastern Economic Review*, 17 and 24 July; *New York Times*, 7 August), which fielded 506 candidates but polled only 11.5 per cent of the total vote. The party of President Suharto, with 538 candidates, won 226 of the 360 contested seats while the PNI was able to claim only 20. The death of the general chairman shortly before the election was probably a factor in the PNI's surprisingly low showing.

Communist activity during the election campaign was not limited to support for the PNI. There were numerous Indonesian press and radio reports of communist plots and activities aimed at disrupting the elections, or influencing them by infiltrating legal political parties. According to the military commander in East Java, the communists were trying to disrupt the elections by "playing-off tactics, distortion of facts, psychological warfare, and common crimes" (Antara, 3 May). A plot was reportedly uncovered in North Celebes which resulted in the arrest of 157 suspected communists; authorities reported that the communists had planned to kill all army officers in the province before the election (Djakarta radio, 1 May). The army daily, *Beritasyudha* (19 March) reported that other communist tactics included acts of sabotage, such as derailing trains.

PKI infiltration efforts have not been restricted to political parties. An investigation of communist infiltration into senior positions in the army led to the arrest of at least eight army generals during 1970, and to the suicide on 6 January 1971 of Lieutenant General Hartono (former ambassador to North Korea). PKI agents have reportedly infiltrated non-communist mass organizations and religious groups as well, apparently with Soviet guidance. (*Frankfurter Allgemeine Zeitung*, 5 February.)

Although there are strong differences of opinion within the PKI, the Java-based "Politburo of the PKI Central Committee" reportedly still favors the *Tripandji* (Three Banners) doctrine of former party chief Sudisman, who was executed by the government in 1967: "(1) formation of a Marxist-Leninist party free of opportunism and revisionism, (2) armed revolution by the farmers under the leadership of the working class, (3) formation of a united front under the leadership of the working class" (*Frankfurter Allgemeine Zeitung*, 4 February).

Communist guerrillas have been active for several years along the Malaysian-Indonesian border between Sarawak and Kalimantan, primarily under the leadership of Sawawak communist leaders (see *Malaysia*). In January the Indonesian military commander in West Kalimantan stated that captured materials indicated that the guerrillas were planning a protracted "Viet Cong-style" war in West Kalimantan (*Straits Times*, Singapore, 4 January). The commander combined a campaign to relocate ethnic Chinese (relied upon by the almost exclusively Chinese guerrillas for assistance) away from the border area with a series of major offensives against the insurgents. In one of the security operations, the Indonesian forces reported that "at least 100 communist terrorists were either captured or had surrendered" (Antara, 1 April). The success of the two-pronged offensive resulted in the flight of almost all of the communist guerrillas into Sarawak. New agreements were reached between Malaysian and Indonesian armed forces during 1971, providing for increased cooperation and joint operations "against the common enemy of Malaysia and Indonesia" (*San Francisco Chronicle*, 4 September).

International Views and Activities. As noted above, Sino-Soviet rivalries for the allegiance of PKI remnants continued during 1971. The Chinese position was usually expressed in statements by leaders of the "Delegation of the PKI Central Committee" in Peking (see below). Soviet statements included the broadcasting of articles from publications of the Moscow-based "Marxist-Leninist Group of the PKI" (see below), and Soviet attacks on the Chinese communists, using the Maoist position on Indonesia as an example of Chinese "adventurism." Although both sides had supporters within the PKI, the majority of PKI leaders were thought to favor the Maoist approach (Ruth T. McVey, "PKI Fortunes at Low Tide," *Problems of Communism*, January-April).

In July a communist leader on trial in Bandung, the aforementioned Dr. Thung Tiong Tie, reported that the Marxist-Leninist group to which he belonged had made contacts with North Vietnam and Cuba (Antara, 26 July). This was consistent with earlier government reports that North Vietnamese ships had entered Indonesian territorial waters, apparently trying to smuggle weapons to Indonesian and Sawawak communists (see *Malaysia*). In April, the commander in West Kalimantan announced that he had "concrete proof that arms were smuggled from a certain country" into that province (*ibid.*, 10 April). A Kalimantan news bulletin quoted "competent sources" as saying that the country in question was North Vietnam (*Kalimantan Barat Press*, 31 March). North Vietnam denied the charges, however, and in August the president of that country sent a message to President Suharto on the twenty-sixth anniversary of the founding of the Republic of Indonesia, concluding: "May the friendship between the Vietnamese and Indonesian peoples further consolidate and develop day by day" (Vietnam News Agency, Hanoi, 18 August).

*   *   *

The Delegation of the PKI Central Committe. The relationship of the Peking-based "Delegation of the PKI Central Committee" with the PKI Politburo is unclear. While the two groups usually advocate similar strategies, tactics, and programs, the Delegation places considerably more emphasis on the thoughts of Mao Tse-tung.

Headed by Jusuf Adjitorop, the Delegation of the PKI Central Committee reportedly comprises 700 persons, including former Indonesian ambassadors (mostly to communist capitals), pre-coup PKI members, and former front leaders. In Peking, the Delegation extends its influence through the Federation of Indonesian Students, the Indonesian People's Youth League, and the Indonesian Organization for Afro-Asian People's Solidarity.

In 1967 there were reports that the former Indonesian ambassador to Peking, Djawoto, would replace Adjitorop as the leader of the Delegation. During 1971 statements continued to be issued in the name of Adjitorop, a member of the PKI Politburo at the time of 1965 coup attempt. A small "revisionist" faction of the Delegation has been reported to be under the leadership of Ali Hanafiah, former Indonesian ambassador to Ceylon. Hanafiah was thought to be in Moscow during 1971.

Domestic Attitudes and Activities. The Delegation of the PKI Central Committee supports the Maoist line of armed struggle and opposes the "revisionist" position of the Soviet Union. In a message to the Central Committee of the Chinese Communist Party on 30 June, the Delegation stated:

> The teachings of the new-democratic revolution summed up by Comrade Mao Tse-tung have not only a Chinese significance, but also a world one, especially for colonial, semi-colonial and semi-feudal countries.... The experience of the Chinese revolution shows that by firmly upholding the principles of violent revolution, the proletarian political party must arouse mass struggle on the broadest scale, especially the masses of the peasantry, establish revolutionary bases in the rural areas, use the countryside to encircle and finally capture the cities.

The Delegation asserted that the Chinese experience showed the correct strategy for revolution in Indonesia.

> After having summed up the experience of the temporary setback of the Indonesian revolution and drawn lessons from the errors of the "peaceful road" in the past, the Political Bureau of the Central Committee of the Communist Party of Indonesia has stressed that "the Indonesian revolution, in order to achieve its complete victory, must also traverse the road of the Chinese revolution." (*Peking Review*, no. 31, 30 July.)

The 3 July 1971 general elections in Indonesia were the target of several attacks by the Peking-based Delegation. A pre-election statement referred to the election as a "fraud" which was "aimed at maintaining and consolidating Suharto's fascist military rule so as to better serve its imperialist masters," and asserted:

> General elections under the rule of the bourgeoisie cannot produce a people's political power. Particularly, the sham general election under the rule of the Suharto fascist regime which serves the interests of imperialism ... will at most be a fig-leaf to cover up their fascist nature and traitorous acts. The Indonesian revolutionary people under the leadership of the Indonesian communist party have, in accordance with their experiences won at the cost of blood, discarded the revisionist road of "peaceful transition" peddled by the Soviet revisionist renegade clique, and realized that the road to liberation will be possible only through revolutionary armed struggle. (NCNA, 5 July.)

The Indonesian Organization for Afro-Asian People's Solidarity charged: "The election has nothing to do with democracy; rather it is being carried out at bayonet point in order to further tighten the fascist rule." It denounced as "pure treachery" the "trash spread by the revisionists that 'armed struggle is premature,' and that 'the general election would provide the Communists with a platform for propaganda activities.' " (*Peking Review*, no. 27, 2 July.)

*   *   *

The Marxist-Leninist Group of the PKI. The Marxist-Leninist Group of the PKI appears to consist of exiles in Moscow led by Ali Hanafiah, former Indonesian ambassador to Ceylon. While there were groups of communists in Indonesia sympathetic to the goals of the Moscow-based organization, the relationship remained obscure. It is not clear whether the Marxist-Leninist Group is in opposition to the Politburo of the PKI Central Committee or whether the two are merely conflicting factions of the Indonesian communist movement. What evidence there is suggests that they are separate.

Domestic Attitudes and Activities. The Marxist-Leninist Group of the PKI played an increasingly important role in Soviet anti-Suharto propaganda during 1971—especially during the election campaign. One month prior to the election, Djakarta radio (2 June) charged:

> In its anti-Indonesian campaign, Radio Moscow has changed its tactics lately; instead of employing Soviet commentators, it now uses Indonesian communist fugitives in the Soviet Union whom we call members of the Moscow-oriented faction within the communist movement in our country. Every day Radio Moscow carries commentaries by Indonesian communist fugitives in the Soviet Union, particularly in connection with the coming general elections.

Three days later the same source asserted that Indonesian communists had "unlawfully entered the current election campaign through Moscow radio broadcasts." On the 44th anniversary of the founding of the Indonesian Nationalist Party (PNI), Moscow radio (4 July) carried a long commentary praising the PNI for having "constantly held aloft the anticolonialist and anti-imperialist banner," and concluding that: "All friends of Indonesia hope that the PNI, which once played a most important role in Indonesia's national liberation movement, will return to its proper position." While the broadcast was not presented as a PKI position, it was consistent with the general position of the Moscow-based PKI Group. It is possible that the PKI label was omitted out of fear that the Suharto government would use any "official" PKI endorsement of the PNI as grounds for suppression of the party.

In October the magazine of the group, *Tekad Rakjat*, was reported by Moscow radio (4 October) as proposing "(1) to revive the Indonesian communist party on the basis of Marxism-Leninism; (2) to promote the work of the Executive Committee among the masses; (3) to struggle for the creation of a national united front and the formation of a democratic government in the country; and (4) to restore strong unity and cooperation with the international communist movement.''

International Views and Positions. Being closely aligned with the Soviet Union, the Marxist-Leninist Group has been condemned by the People's Republic of China. Responding in kind, the group has strongly opposed the application of Maoism to the situation in Indonesia. After proposing the four-point program noted above, *Tekad Rakjat* stressed that "the Indonesian communist party's future directly depends on its quick and open disassociation from the adventurers and the party's capability to stand on its own feet and free itself from Mao's harmful influence" (Moscow radio, 4 October). Another *Tekad Rakjat* article commented:

> Besides facing ideological enemies from the outside and anti-communist ideologies in all forms, we also face schools of thought that are hostile to Marxism-Leninism within the ranks of workers' and communist movements, namely, rightist and leftist opportunism. These two schools of opportunism are harmful to workers' [and] communist movements, and our revolutionary struggle. Therefore, we must remain vigilant against those two schools of thought, we must fight them, defeat them, and cast them out of our ranks. ("Radio Peace and Progress," Moscow, 26 October.)

The Moscow-based group has expressed support for various revolutionary struggles around the world.

Publications. The PKI Politburo publishes a clandestine monthly, *Mimbar Rakjat*. Clandestine publications of the GEMPAR (student organization) also express PKI positions. Publications issued by or carrying statements of the Delegation of the PKI Central Committee include *Suara Rakjat Indonesia* (Voice of the Indonesian People), the organ of the Indonesian Afro-Asian Solidarity Organization, and *Voice of the Indonesian Youth*, the monthly organ of the Indonesian Students' Association, both published in Peking. The Marxist-Leninist Group of the PKI publishes *Tekad Rakjat* (People's Determination); a youth organ, *O.P.I.*; and a magazine, *Surat-Surat Dari Tanah Air* (Letters from the Fatherland). According to Djakarta radio (2 June 1971), these publications are printed on Soviet presses with funds provided by the Soviet government.

PKI Politburo statements are frequently publicized in Chinese, East German, North Korean, North Vietnamese, and Albanian media. Statements by the Delegation of the PKI Central Committee are publicized by Chinese and Albanian news media, and both countries have regular broadcasts in Indonesian. Statements by the Marxist-Leninist Group of the PKI are often carried by publications in the Soviet Union, East Germany, and by the pro-Soviet Communist Party of India.

Robert F. Turner

Japan

The Japan Communist Party (Nihon Kyosanto; JCP) celebrates the fiftieth anniversary of its founding on 15 July 1972. Free to organize and operate as a legal political party only after the end of the war in 1945 and with the advent of the Allied Occupation, the JCP experienced in the postwar period the vicissitudes of changing party lines and fluctuating membership and parliamentary representation. Party members numbered 7,500 in 1946, rose to 150,000 by 1949, but had declined to 40,000 by 1958 (see *YICA*, 1971, p. 594). Membership rose in the 1960s and by the time of the party's Eleventh Congress (July 1970) totaled 280,000. Following the congress, the party lost some adherents, but by mounting a vigorous campaign to expand the rolls it succeeded in bringing the figure back to 280,000 by the end of 1971. The JCP is the largest non-ruling communist party outside Europe and vies with the French Communist Party for second place among such parties in the world (the Italian Communist Party is first). The population of Japan is about 104,000,000 (estimated 1971).

Parliamentary Strength. The JCP reached a peak in parliamentary strength when it elected 35 candidates to the House of Representatives in 1949. All these seats were lost in the succeeding election in 1952 and not for twenty years was the party able again to break the "two-digit barrier" by winning 14 of the 486 seats in the House of Representatives in the elections of December 1969. The JCP held seven seats in the 250-member House of Councillors (Upper House) until 27 June 1971 when this figure was raised to 10. In eleven years (June 1960 to June 1971) the JCP increased its Diet representation six-fold, from four seats in both houses in 1960 to 24 in 1971.

Other elections in 1971 resulted in substantial gains for the JCP. Cooperation with the Japan Socialist Party (JSP) brought "reformist" governors to the two largest cities, Tokyo and Osaka. Including Kyoto, where a JCP-JSP "united front" candidate for governor was elected the previous year, three of Japan's most important cities were now administered by governors elected with JCP support. Communist-supported candidates were strikingly successful in the April local elections. The JCP won 105 seats in the prefectural assemblies, three times the number previously held, and became the third party in number of seats controlled, after the ruling Liberal Democratic Party (LDP) and the JSP. Similar gains were made in city, town, and village assemblies. The JCP returned 1,250 candidates for city and town assemblies—an increase of 467 over seats held from previous elections. A comparison of JCP strength in local assemblies in 1960 and 1971 reveals representation in the latter year 3.7 times that of 1960: 2,501 against 677.

The Autonomy Ministry report on receipts and expenditures of political parties during the first half of 1971 showed that the JCP was second in total funds received and disbursed, after the LDP. JCP registered income for the six months period was 2.1 billion yen ($5.8 million): somewhat more than a third of the amount received by the LDP (5.86 billion yen, or $16.3 million).

515

Leadership and Organization. Miyamoto Kenji, chairman of the Standing Committee of the Presidium, maintained his firm control of the JCP during 1971. No changes in the organization and personnel as established by the Eleventh Congress in July 1970 were announced. Nosaka Sanzo, chairman of the Central Committee, aged 79 and occupying a more honorary than active party post, was said to spend most of his time writing his memoirs, of which the first volume was published in 1971; nevertheless he made some public appearances, and in June he was reelected to the House of Councillors. Nosaka was to have headed a JCP delegation to the congress of the Communist Party, USA in New York in February 1972, but the trip was canceled when he and those to accompany him were found ineligible to receive visas for entry into the United States.

Fuwa Tetsuzo, director of the Central Committee Secretariat, continued to symbolize the "image change" to a "soft, smiling JCP" which Miyamoto was trying to propagate. A popular weekly magazine described Fuwa as "the most popular, trusted man in the JCP," and as the "Prince of Yoyogi"[1] who represents the new "youth group" (Fuwa is 41) of politicians now taking over party leadership from their elders (Ichikawa Ken in *Mantime*, September 1971).

The Standing Committee of the Presidium consists of Miyamoto Kenji (chairman), Hakamada Satomi and Ota Masayoshi (vice-chairmen), Fuwa Tetsuzo, Kurahara Korehito, Matsuhara Harushige, and Nishizawa Tomio.

Party Auxiliaries and Front Organizations. *The Youth Movement.* The JCP-supported youth organization is the Minshu Seinen Domei (Minseido), or Democratic Youth League. Its membership of 140,000 in January 1972 represented a drop of 40,000 since the 1970 congress. Its publication *Minsei Shimbun* had a reported circulation of 240,000 (300,000 in 1970).

The planned efforts of Minseido to increase its membership were unsuccessful: the JCP-oriented youth groups suffered from the same apathy that affected the student movement in Japan, turning it away from mass activities to factional disputes. Violence highlighted the actions of numerically small groups of ultra-radicals, invariably affiliated with anti-JCP factions. The policy of the JCP, carried out through all of its related fronts and organizations, continued to be one of seeking ends through nonviolent means.

Minseido, doubtless because of the failure of its membership drives, postponed until 1972 its Twelfth Congress, scheduled for 1971. The stated purpose of the delay was to allow more time to build up the organization in preparation for the congress. During 1971 Minseido directed its activities supporting JCP candidates in the local and upper house elections, organizing opposition to the Okinawa reversion treaty, disseminating propaganda, and preparing petitions to the Diet.

The National Federation of Students' Self-Government Associations (Zengakuren) loosely embraced 572 associations in 1971, with a total nationwide membership of 1,025,000 representing 59 per cent of all students in the country. In previous years Zengakuren split almost equally between the pro-JCP "mainstream" and anti-JCP radical factions, with the JCP-supported groups in the majority. The weight shifted in 1971, the ultra-radicals gaining at the expense of the JCP; as a result, anti-JCP groups controlled 51 per cent of the members, as opposed to 49 per cent for the JCP. The so-called "activists" in the JCP-affiliated organizations increased, however, from 16,000 in 1970 to 18,400 in 1971, while the numbers of anti-JCP activists dropped from 12,500 to 7,500. (*Koan Joho* [Public Safety Report], December, monthly magazine published by Social Problems Research Institute, Tokyo, and utilizing materials from government security agencies.)

Peace Movement. The JCP-sponsored Nihon Gensuikyo (Japan Council Against Atomic and

---

[1]Yoyogi is the name of the quarter of Tokyo where JCP headquarters are located and is often used as a synonym for the party.

Hydrogen Bombs) held its seventeenth national congress at Hiroshima on 5-6 August 1971. The press reported 10,000 persons in attendance, including 34 representatives from 11 countries and five organizations. For the first time in seven years, two delegates from North Vietnam received government permission to enter the country and attended the conference. Fuwa Tetsuzo spoke at the meeting for the JCP. Simultaneously the rival JSP-supported Gensuikin (People's Council Against Atomic and Hydrogen Bombs) met in Hiroshima with 8,000 in attendance, including representatives from eight countries. Officials of the Japan General Council of Trade Unions (Sohyo) and the JSP addressed the meetings. Approximately 1,400 anti-JCP student radicals staged a demonstration during the congresses to protest Prime Minister Sato's visit to Hiroshima to attend a memorial service for the victims of the nuclear bombing of the city. A clash with the police resulted in the arrest of 22 demonstrators.

Labor. The economic slowdown which Japan experienced in 1971 prolonged the annual "spring struggle" to obtain higher wages and increased the number of strikes. The JCP exploited this disturbed labor situation by intensifying its efforts to influence young workers and expand the party's influence in the trade unions and among unorganized urban labor. The April elections, in which the JCP and JSP joined to elect candidates for local offices, provided useful opportunities. The JCP organized "support groups" for candidates among young workers and in factories, employed aggressive tactics to influence trade union leaders, and even managed to infiltrate some unions affiliated with the JSP.

The "dollar shock" of U.S. President Nixon's economic policy, announced on 15 August, provided a new issue which the JCP called proof of the "bankruptcy of a policy of subservience to the United States." The JSP-affiliated Japan General Council of Trade Unions (Sohyo) also seized upon the "dollar crisis" and the Okinawa reversion treaty as twin issues to inspire a series of strikes, rallies, and demonstrations. The JCP cooperated with the JSP and Sohyo in these and in so-called one-day struggles, held 28 April, 19 May, and 21 October. The climax of these peaceful activities was reached in mid-November (see below).

The Japanese labor movement continued to be divided among Sohyo, largest federation of trade unions in the country with approximately 12 million members, the pro-DSP Domei Kaigi (Japan United Congress of Labor), and two smaller associations, Churitsu Roren (Federation of Independent Unions) and Shin Sanbetsu (New Congress of Industrial Unions).

The only labor organization in which the JCP has been able to exert influence is Sohyo. During 1971 the party tried to stimulate trade unions to assume more active roles in support of political parties and to engage in political action; the obvious purpose of these efforts was to lure Sohyo unions away from commitments to the JSP and to more friendly association with the JCP. The elections in 1971 furnished the impetus for these efforts and the united front with the JSP improved the opportunities to make contacts with unions previously uniquely loyal to the JSP.

Other Organizations. The JCP wholly or partly controls numerous organizations, including a miscellany of study circles, professional groups, labor unions based on individual memberships, cultural societies for music, drama, and literature, and groups formed for sports, peace, and friendship.

The General Federation of Korean Residents in Japan (Zainichi Chosenjin Sorengokai—or Chosen Soren) is pro-North Korean and claims to represent the majority of Koreans living in Japan. It is not controlled by the JCP, but relations between the JCP and the Chosen Soren reflect the kind of relationship existing at any given time between the JCP and the governing party of the Democratic People's Republic of Korea (DPRK), the Korean Workers' Party (KWP).

The Ninth Congress of Chosen Soren, held in the latter part of January, unanimously approved the report of Prime Minister Kim Il-song of the DPRK to the Fifth Congress of the KWP and determined a policy for action which called for a strengthened organization to look to the unification of Korea in the 1970s. This would include aid to the formation of a united revolutionary party, and the forging of a stronger alliance with leftist forces for "the struggle against Japanese militarism." Attacks were made on a dissident faction of the KWP under the slogan of "Strengthen the Armor of the Thought of Kim Il-song-ism!"

Among activities supported by Chosen Soren were the Red Cross-sponsored meetings between representatives of North and South Korea, the promotion of freer travel between Japan and North Korea, and the establishment of a "people's united front" among Koreans in Japan aimed at the United States, President Park of the Republic of Korea (ROK), and against Japanese militarism. Goals were the normalizations of relations between the two Koreas, the defense of civil rights, and the strengthening of cooperation between Koreans and Japanese of all classes and groups.

Movement toward one of the objectives of Chosen Soren—to speed up the repatriation to North Korea of North Koreans living in Japan—was slow; from May to October only 1,081 out of 15,000 still to be repatriated actually left Japan.

Relations between the JCP and Chosen Soren were good on the surface but sharp differences of opinion remained, especially over the "deification" of Kim Il-song. These differences were kept quiescent because of the greater desire of the JCP to tighten liaison with the Chosen Soren in common activities suggested by the slogan "Oppose American and Japanese militarism!"

Party Internal Affairs. The Central Committee of the JCP met four times in plenary session during the year. The Third Plenum (numbered from the Eleventh Congress in July 1970), on 31 January-2 February, considered reports on the upcoming local and upper house elections and on party construction and popular movements. The Fourth Plenum (11-13 May) assessed the results of the April elections and set plans and policies for the forthcoming June elections for the House of Councillors. Reports were heard from the JCP representatives stationed in Czechoslovakia and North Vietnam and from members who had attended international conferences. The Fifth Plenum (13-15 July) analyzed recent trends in party strength as revealed in the elections and heard reports on proposed actions to oppose the Okinawa reversion treaty, both inside and outside the Diet, and on plans to expand the party, improve its effectiveness, and prepare for the celebration of the fiftieth anniversary and general elections in 1972. The final meeting of the Central Committee for the year, the Sixth Plenum (3-6 December) issued a communiqué and approved resolutions on the party's future tasks and expansion. The resolution "On the current situation, party tasks, and party construction," included, among other exhortations, an appeal to improve the activities of party organizations with the aim of "developing into a strong mass vanguard party of hundreds of thousands of communists who can actually control Japan's politics." Specifically the resolution warned all party organizations against expelling members for petty reasons and condemned "erroneous administrative measures." (*Akahata*, 8 December.)

Party Expansion. The JCP in 1971 set expansion goals to be achieved by the date of the Twelfth Congress, scheduled for 1973. These called for a membership of 500,000 (as compared to 280,000 at the time of the Eleventh Congress) and a daily *Akahata* circulation of 700,000 (420,000 in 1970), with 2,500,000 on Sunday (1,500,000 in 1970). Since party membership and *Akahata* circulation in fact decreased after the 1970 congress and only in 1971 regained their former levels, the party would within one year have to raise membership by about 78 per cent and *Akahata* circulation by more than 66 per cent in order to achieve the set goals.

One reason for the drop in membership following the Eleventh Congress was the large number of expulsions carried out by both local and national party organs. Although more than 20,000 new members were admitted to the JCP during the 18 months subsequent to the 1970 congress, as many as 36,000 were expelled, largely because of over-zealous application of party regulations, during the first 12 months after the congress. In April 1971 the circulation of *Akahata* fell below that of the previous July, after which the party took immediate steps to boost sales. In the period October-November the party admitted 4,000 new members but expelled 3,500 members, thus achieving a net gain of only 500.

With the dual goals of the fiftieth anniversary and general elections in 1972, the party leadership put extraordinary force behind the campaign for membership expansion. The Central Committee ordered analyses made of the reasons for resignations from the party and issued directives to stop expelling members for "trivial" causes and to establish review procedures for those recommended for expulsion. Plans were laid to attack special "target groups" as potential sources for new members; these included *Akahata* subscribers, Minseido members, and persons affiliated with or sympathetic to organizations under communist influence. A principal aim was the stimulation and improvement of party educational and indoctrination activities.

The party's aim for the elections to the House of Representatives, expected in 1972, was a total popular vote of 4 million and from 20 to 30 out of a total of 486 seats.

Party Policy. The JCP continued to present the image of a benign party, dedicated to peaceful revolution and the achievement of power through the parliamentary process. In a speech on 26 February to the Foreign Correspondents Club in Tokyo, where no Japanese communist had ever appeared before, Miyamoto Kenji restated the basic principles which he said guided the JCP. Miyamoto declared that the realization of an independent, democratic, neutral Japan would lead to a socialist Japan, but that for the present the JCP did not aim for a socialist revolution but rather a program of a democratic character. A three-point minimum program would (1) establish Japanese independence by breaking the military alliance with the United States, (2) protect the people's livelihood by blocking the economic policies of "monopoly capitalists who create environmental damage and are responsible for soaring prices and traffic congestion," and (3) strongly oppose the "revival of militarism" and aim for the establishment of democratic, parliamentary administration. (*Akahata*, 27 February.)

For some years the JCP has been propagating its "soft line," attempting to erase the image in the Japanese popular mind of a party dedicated to terrorist tactics and violent revolution. In further pursuit of this objective, Miyamoto in June 1971—not long before the upper house elections—proposed several "vocabulary changes" to correct, as he said, certain misconceptions about the meaning of communist doctrine. Specifically, he objected to the Japanese translation of the word "dictatorship" as used in the phrase "dictatorship of the proletariat." He contended that the Japanese *dokusai* was too harsh a term and did not convey the correct nuance of the original Latin *dictatura*; he proposed a weaker word *shihai*, which can be translated as "control." Miyamoto also found fault with the translation of "violent" (as used in "violent revolution") as *boryaku* and suggested instead the word *kyoseiteki*, meaning "forceful" or "by force." Critics of the JCP ridiculed Miyamoto's efforts to camouflage doctrine by word changes, pointing out that the original translations were accurate and that no amount of vocabulary juggling would conceal the truth. Some cited statements from party tracts written by Miyamoto himself which suggested that the non-violent line might not be forever immutable. (*Koan Joho*, June 1971.) The controversy illustrates the importance which the party leadership now accords to achieving the popularity designed to produce victories at the polls.

Party Anniversary. The JCP celebrated the forty-ninth anniversary of its founding on 15 July with a lecture meeting on the 14th and a reception on the 15th. Representatives of the JSP, the Okinawa People's Party (OPP), Sohyo, and Chosen Soren attended the reception, and also the ambassadors or chargés d'affaires of Bulgaria, Czechoslovakia, Hungary, Poland, Romania, and the Soviet Union. The Soviet ambassador attended for the first time in three years. The party celebrated simultaneously the tenth anniversary of the enactment of the Party Program. The lecture meeting was addressed by Fuwa Tetsuzo and Nishizawa Tomio, member of the Presidium. Nishizawa praised the correctness of the "autonomous independent line" followed by the party and noted that while obstacles to normal relations with the Communist Party of the Soviet Union (CPSU) had been removed, so far no signs of reconciliation with the Chinese Communist Party (CCP) had appeared.

Domestic Attitudes and Activities. *United Front.* The brilliant victory in 1970 of the incumbent governor of Kyoto, Ninagawa Torazo, with combined JCP-JSP support inspired a continuing united front between these two parties in the 1971 local elections. The JCP declared the united front with the JSP a basic election policy and proceeded to recommend "renovationist" candidates who would run under the aegis of both parties. In the end the JCP judged the enterprise an outstanding success; the JSP, for understandable reasons, was less enthusiastic and it seemed uncertain whether the two parties would soon again cooperate in elections on such an extensive scale.

The results for the united front were impressive. Candidates jointly supported by the JCP and JSP contested five out of 18 elections for prefectural governors, won the two most important—Tokyo and Osaka, and lost Hokkaido by only 13,000 votes. The two-party coalition captured 11 out of 31 elections for mayors of cities and eight out of 18 for mayors of towns and villages. One election result was the remarkable increase in JCP representation in the local assemblies of municipalities in the urban Pacific Belt extending from Tokyo to Osaka, including the port city of Yokohama and the industrial city of Kawasaki. Governments of Tokyo, Osaka, and Kawasaki are headed by united-front-elected officials (Yokohama's mayor is a member of the JSP.)

The united front strategy brought greater success to the JCP than to the JSP. Although JCP seats in prefectural assemblies tripled, from 35 to 105, those held by the JSP declined from 505 to 401. Similar trends appeared in the popular vote; the proportion for the JSP in local assemblies went down from 22.0 to 19.0 per cent, that of the JCP rose from 4.0 to 7.5 per cent. The disillusionment of the JSP dictated its refusal to continue cooperation with the JCP in the June elections for the House of Councillors. Instead, the JSP accepted cooperation from the Democratic Socialist Party (DSP) and the Komeito (Clean Government Party) in three contests. Miyamoto declared that, regardless of JSP policy, the JCP would continue to pursue the united front as a matter of practical politics.

As in 1970 the JCP joined the JSP in sponsoring one-day joint struggles; on 28 April (anniversary of the San Francisco peace treaty according Okinawa's administration to the United States), 19 May (strike to protest the Okinawa reversion treaty), and 21 October (international anti-war day). The two parties also participated in a series of largely symbolical one-day joint strikes beginning 19 November which were staged to oppose the Okinawa reversion agreement. The JCP plan to organize a unified popular movement "from the bottom up" achieved some success, especially among factory workers; to these groups the JCP-JSP united front seemed to have greater appeal than the proposed coalition among the JSP, DSP, and Komeito.

Elections. The party program approved by the Eleventh Congress in July 1970 made clear that a principal task for the JCP in the succeeding months would be preparation for the local and upper house elections scheduled for 1971. So long as the program stressed the doctrine that power should be achieved by parliamentary means, the extension of JCP influence in local and national legislative bodies was of paramount importance. The 1971 elections indeed brought remarkable successes to the party, although in relative terms JCP strength in the total Japanese parliamentary spectrum was still minuscule. The JCP was, in fact, the only party which increased its votes as compared to previous local elections.

Elections for prefectural governors were held 11 April, those for mayors and local assemblies on 25 April. As a result, JCP-supported candidates now govern Japan's two most populous city-prefectures (Tokyo and Osaka), 11 other cities (as compared with seven previously), and eight towns and villages (an increase of six). Furthermore, the JCP tripled its seats in the prefectural assemblies, from 35 to 105 (total seats:2,558). Before the elections the party lacked representation in about half of these bodies; now only three are without JCP members. The party's voting strength in the prefectural assemblies of Tokyo, Osaka, and Kyoto is 11.2, 9.4, and 10.6 per cent respectively. The combined JCP-JSP vote for assembly members in five major cities (Osaka, Kyoto, Nagoya, Kobe, and Yokohama) was ahead of that garnered by the LDP in all but Kobe. The JCP added 49 new seats to its representation in the Tokyo ward assemblies, bringing the party's present total to 128 (out of a total of 1,091 seats in all). The JCP election record for city and town mayors and assemblies was equally noteworthy. Eleven out of 34 candidates for city mayors were elected and eight out of 17 candidates for mayors of towns and villages. Although both the LDP and JSP lost seats in the elections for city and town assemblies, the JCP won a total of 1,250 and thereby increased its holdings by 467. The 97 municipal assemblies lacking JCP membership were reduced to 18 by the April elections.

JCP candidates did well in districts near large industrial centers, in cities afflicted with problems of pollution, and in communities near military bases. At the same time the party made small but nevertheless surprising inroads in rural areas, long considered impregnable domains of the conservatives. Several largely agricultural prefectures gave remarkable numbers of votes to communist candidates. Comparisons with previous elections in 1967 showed a fourfold increase in predominantly rural Kagoshima Prefecture, a threefold rise in Oita, and a doubling of the JCP vote in Mie, to name only a few examples.

The elections for the House of Councillors (upper house) were held on 27 June. Since the JSP had refused to join the JCP in a united front, the two parties competed energetically for votes. The elections were characterized by a low turnout of voters, less than 60 per cent, which is unusual for Japan. As in April, the JCP bettered its previous record, with a gain of more than two million votes over those obtained in the upper house elections of 1968. In fact, the local constituencies turned out the largest vote for the JCP in its history, even beyond the 1949 record when 35 JCP candidates were elected to the House of Representatives. In numbers of seats, the party's attainments were less spectacular: five seats in the national and one in the local constituencies. The latter was the seat long held by the venerable chairman of the Central Committee, Nosaka Sanzo. An unusual and unexpected result of the election was the poor showing made in Tokyo by the veteran Nosaka. The only JCP local constituency candidate to be elected, he was fourth and last among the successful contenders. Various factors apparently contributed to his weak showing: his age (79), the apathy of Tokyo voters, and the greater attraction of "talent" candidates, who included personalities from the entertainment world with large followings among young persons and uncommitted voters.

The JCP now controls 10 seats (out of 250) in the House of Councillors, thereby acquiring the right of consultation as a party group but not the hoped-for right to initiate bills which would have come with one more seat. Nevertheless, the elections brought both the highest number and the highest percentage of votes in JCP history. National constituency candidates received a total of 3.2 million votes, or 8.1 percent, as compared to 2.0 million, or 5 percent, in 1968. The percentage in the local constituencies was even greater, although only one seat was won: 4.8 million votes, 12.1 per cent (1968: 3.5 million; 8.3 per cent).

The explanation for the JCP appeal was similar to that for the local successes in April. The aggressive emphasis on day-to-day problems of environment, housing, prices, and traffic combined with a widespread general dissatisfaction with LDP policies to improve chances for the JCP. Additionally the "image change" had removed much of the traditional fear which had alienated support in the past. JCP gains seemed to confirm Miyamoto's success in conveying to many Japanese the impression of an independent JCP, beholden neither to the Soviet Union nor to the People's Republic of China (PRC) but, as he said, to the "homeland of the workers of Japan." (Kondo Hitoshi in *Chuo Koron*, Tokyo, June 1971, p. 180).

International Views and Policies. Relations with the Soviet and Chinese communist parties dominated the JCP view of the world, continuing to form the principal elements affecting the international policies of the party. A marked change occurred in attitudes toward the Soviet party as significant steps were taken toward restoring party relationships to a normal basis. The Chinese Communist Party (CCP) remained an object of enmity and vituperative polemics. The JCP leadership faced a dilemma which their protestations served only to accentuate. It was unthinkable to oppose the normalization of government-to-government relations between Japan and the PRC and the admission of the latter into the United Nations, yet the position of the JCP as one of the "four enemies" of the CCP and the bitterness of the inter-party conflict presented to the public a contradiction difficult to explain away. The JCP found itself in the unenviable position of being the sole Japanese political party absolutely anathema to the CCP in a period when the "China mood" was growing in the country and when the announced visit to China of U.S. President Nixon was creating unprecedented changes in popular attitudes toward the Chinese communist regime. The louder the JCP leaders denounced as false the charges that they were being isolated in the Japanese political spectrum by their China policy, the more difficult their position became. Some observers concluded that the JCP was searching for a way out and would in reality welcome a diminution of tensions with the CCP, but mutual hostility had become so openly intense that a reversal of the trend seemed unlikely in the near future. In the meantime the motivation to better relations with the CPSU was understandably enhanced.

JCP-CCP Relations. The leaders of the PRC left no doubt about their feelings toward the JCP. Although JCP Presidium members had declared that the Japanese government should recognize the PRC and remove all obstacles to trade between Japan and China, Premier Chou En-lai made it quite clear to visitors that JCP representatives would not be welcome in Peking. What was particularly galling was to be ranked with such "right-wing reactionaries" as Prime Minister Sato and his brother Kishi Nobusuke in being declared *persona non grata*. Chou En-lai told former LDP Foreign Minister Fujiyama Aiichiro, who visited China in late February and early March, that any of his friends would be welcome in Peking *except* Kishi, Nosaka Sanzo, and Miyamoto Kenzo (*Yomiuri*, Tokyo, 8 March). A vice-chairman of the party secretariat, Kaneko Mitsuhiro, retaliated immediately with a statement that Chou's remarks were "high-handed interference in party affairs" and an "impermissible attack on the party" (*Kyodo News Service*, Tokyo, 8 March). China's premier infuriated JCP leaders even more when, in an interview with James Reston of the *New York Times* in August, he linked the LDP and the JCP as the only political parties which refused to recognize that militarism was reviving in Japan. In discussing the interview *Akahata* (18 August) quoted Chou as telling Reston: "the JCP supports Sato on this question."

Three Peking newspapers, the *People's Daily, Red Flag,* and *Liberation Army Daily*, published on 18 March a joint article commemorating the anniversary of the Paris Commune and incidentally attacking the JCP as "Miyamoto's revisionist clique." The JCP retorted in an *Akahata* editorial on 8 May referring to previous rebuttals of Chinese attacks and again insisting that the Maoists had no understanding of the role of elections and parliamentary competition in advanced industrial nations. *Akahata* quoted Lenin's denunciation of "anti-parliamentarians" and termed Chinese policy a "class crime of the Mao faction" by Lenin's standards. The editorial defended the restudy of the Japanese translation of "dictatorship of the proletariat" against Chinese charges that such action was "revisionism" and "mere playing with words." Insisting that research into the correct rendition of the expression was natural and an "internal question of the Japanese revolution," *Akahata* declared indignantly that no one would think of questioning how the CCP translated "dictatorship of the proletariat" into Chinese. The editorial returned to the heritage of the Paris Commune and to the teachings of Marx, Engels, and Lenin, which clearly showed that armed struggle was not absolute, as the Maoists proclaimed, but that political forms were necessarily diversified according to varying conditions in different countries. The JCP, according to *Akahata*, benefited from the historical lessons of the international communist movement, including those of the Paris Commune, and would seek to fulfill as its immediate task the establishment of a democratic parliamentary system in which the supreme organ of the state would be the Diet, both in name and in substance.

The announcement on 15 July that President Nixon would visit Peking proved an even greater shock to the JCP than to the Japanese government. Alone in its persistent quarrel with the Chinese party, the JCP outdid itself in trying to explain its stand and in condemning even more stridently than before the "deceit" and "big-powerism" of the CCP. Far from seeing the forthcoming visit as contributory to peace in Asia, as did Japan's other opposition parties, the JCP interpreted it as a deception designed to break the deadlock caused by U.S. intervention in Vietnam. *Akahata* published in quick succession articles originating in North Korea and North Vietnam which, although not mentioning the Nixon move toward China, denounced the "big powers" for trying to settle the problems of small countries. The JCP position was soon established: (1) Nixon's announcement was not a surprise, (2) his objective was to break the stalemate for the United States in the domestic and international situation, (3) the visit was a bargaining transaction made over the heads of small and medium-sized countries which recalled the Khrushchev-Eisenhower meeting at Camp David which "beautified" Eisenhower, (4) China's invitation to the U.S. president revealed the contradictions in the "four enemies theory": while welcoming the greatest enemy of the four, the PRC at the same time refused to invite the JCP to China, (5) Japan should engage in independent diplomacy, i.e., the Japanese people should insist that the government change its "slavish" following of U.S. policy in order to become truly independent (*Chugai Tokuho*, 20 August).

Beginning in August, the JCP launched a campaign attacking the CCP. Miyamoto in a press conference on 13 August stated that reconciliation between the JCP and CCP would be impossible unless the Chinese party changed its attitude of "big-power intervention." From then on a series of articles appeared in *Akahata* playing on the points of conflict between the parties. The titles of a few suggest the content: "Continuous Intervention and Attacks by One Group within the Chinese Communist Party" (15-16 August); "Chou En-lai's Irresponsible Theories of Japanese Political Parties" (18 August); "Nixon and American Imperialism" (21 August); "The Japan-China Question and the Japan Communist Party" (9 September).

The two-part series written by Tachiki Hiroshi and published on 15-16 August was typical of JCP treatment of the Chinese party. It continued the suggestion that attacks on the JCP originated with a minority within the CCP, usually called in the past the "Mao faction." Recognizing the two Chinese attacks on the JCP during the year—the joint editorial of 18 March and a *People's Daily* article of 24 May—Tachiki made three principal points: first, that the JCP was not "isolated" in its China policy and that it had always made a clear distinction between inter-party and inter-government relations; second, that the CCP had begun to escalate attacks on the JCP, with impermissible slanders and denunciations made by party leaders such as Chou En-lai and Kuo Mo-jo to numerous visitors to Peking; and third, that the CCP had perpetrated malicious intervention in the internal affairs of the JCP by encouraging and supporting anti-party elements. (These "anti-party elements" were the splinter pro-CCP parties which were receiving continuous publicity in Peking publications.)

The most comprehensive review of the party's China policy published during the year was the two-and-a-half page article entitled "The Japan-China Question and the Japan Communist Party" which appeared in *Akahata* on 9 September. It surveyed the history of the rift between the JCP and the CCP from the beginning in 1966 and traced the five succeeding years of relations between the parties, placing the blame for continued hostility squarely on the "interventionists in the CCP" (the term "Mao Tse-tung faction" was not used). The article again attacked the CCP on one of the issues which had been a principal cause of the break-up with the JCP: the insistence by Mao Tse-tung that "U.S. imperialism" and "Soviet revisionism" were inseparably linked targets of equal importance to be faced by any United front which would be formed. The CCP, according to *Akahata*, completely contradicted its own position by failing to include Soviet revisionism in numerous public statements condemning American imperialism, while continuing to regard the JCP as one of the "four enemies." Such action was termed a tactic of the "great power chauvinists of the CCP" to avoid isolation. Yet Chou En-lai, as quoted by *Akahata*, had told a Japan Socialist Party delegation that the Soviet revisionists were "not only puppets but even partners of the U.S. imperialists."

The JCP welcomed the entry of the PRC into the United Nations and continued to insist that the party favored the establishment of full diplomatic relations with the government in Peking. The party found nothing to praise in the forthcoming Nixon visit to China, seeing it as a deceitful tactic, in which the Chinese were happy to collude, intended to draw attention away from the "people's struggle" in Vietnam and from the urgent problems of the removal of all "U.S. imperialist" forces from Asia and the abolition of the security treaty, in order to exalt relations with China itself to first and only priority. Chinese propaganda directed against the JCP seemed less frenetic than the barrage aimed from Yoyogi. Except for the two articles (18 March and 24 May), the disparaging statements made to visitors by Chou En-lai and other leaders, and the activities of the rather insignificant pro-CCP splinter groups, the Chinese seemed to pay rather moderate attention to the JCP. There were no signs yet, however, that a reconciliation between the JCP and CCP was imminent.

JCP-CPSU Relations. Before accepting an invitation to send representatives to the Twenty-fourth Congress of the CPSU, the JCP insisted upon holding preliminary talks with the Soviet party. Consequently, a delegation headed by Nishizawa Tomio, member of the Presidium of the Central Committee, met in Moscow on 15-19 March with CPSU representatives to discuss the normalization of party relationships. The principal obstacles for the JCP were the encouragement which the CPSU had allegedly extended to the splinter "Voice of Japan" group, formed by Shiga Yoshio after his expulsion from the JCP in 1964, and the interference by the CPSU in the internal affairs of fraternal parties, by the invasion of Czechoslovakia and through the subsequently proclaimed Brezhnev doctrine. Nosaka Sanzo was to have headed a JCP delegation to the Twenty-third Congress, in April 1966, but party relations were broken by March—largely because of differences over the nuclear test ban treaty—and no JCP member attended the CPSU congress of that year. Although the parties made an effort in 1968 to resolve their differences, relations again deteriorated, as witnessed by the exchange of polemics in 1970 (see *YICA*, 1971, pp. 604-6), and it was not until early in 1971 that Miyamoto hinted publicly that the door was open for a reconciliation.

The preliminary March meetings were satisfactory and the parties issued a communiqué repeating the formula for normalizing relations: "independence, equality, and non-interference in each other's internal affairs.'' JCP leaders assured the party membership on their return to Japan that this time the CPSU was serious in its promise to sever all relations with the Shiga group and all other ''anti-party elements.'' A two-man delegation attended the Twenty-fourth Congress and normalization appeared once more to be in effect.

The JCP was clearly on the defensive in explaining the new turn in its policy. As in the case of relations with the CCP, the charges of international isolation touched a sensitive spot and party apologists belabored the arguments that moves to repair the ties with the CPSU were in no sense a tactical maneuver to break out of isolation. A writer in *Akahata* (16 April) listed friends of the JCP to prove his point: the communist parties of Vietnam, Korea, Romania, Italy, and Australia, not to mention the 40 parties that sent messages of solidarity at the time of the Eleventh Congress.

The CPSU responded with praise for the JCP. A writer in *Pravda* (20 May) began an article on JCP successes in the April elections with the affirmation that ''the Japanese communists are in the front ranks of the progressive forces in their country.'' He did not miss the opportunity to record that Chinese communist leaders regarded both the JCP and the CPSU as their principal enemies.

Preliminary meetings for a top-level JCP-CPSU conference were held in Moscow between 3 and 22 August by a JCP delegation headed by Fujii Sadaharu, member of the Central Committee. Miyamoto Kenji, accompanied by high-ranking members of the Central Committee, stopped over in Moscow on 19 August on his way to Romania, when final arrangements were doubtless made for the later visit in September.

The most significant inter-party meetings occurred in Moscow 19-26 September during the four-nation tour of Miyamoto Kenji and five other high-ranking party officials, including four members of the Central Committee. Talks were held with a CPSU group headed by General Secretary Leonid I. Brezhnev and including Secretariat member M. A. Suslov. A report of the conference, noting the prevailing ''frank and comradely atmosphere''—always a clue to some disagreements—emphasized that both sides confirmed the Marxist-Leninist principles of ''independence, equality, non-interference in each other's internal affairs, and international solidarity,'' hailed the ''struggles of the Indochinese peoples'' against U.S. ''imperialist aggression,'' affirmed that aid and support to the Indochinese should be increased, and called for a broad anti-imperialist front.

Miyamoto created consternation in the Japanese Foreign Office and headlines in the newspapers when he announced on his return home that Brezhnev had agreed to ''give serious consideration'' to Japan's claim to the Soviet-held northern islands ''as a diplomatic issue.'' No Soviet official had up to that time ever agreed to discuss the territorial problem, let alone admit that it was open for consideration; the Brezhnev statement, if reported accurately, was a total reversal of policy. Two weeks after the JCP visit to Moscow, an LDP delegation attempted to confirm with Soviet officials Miyamoto's startling report. A Soviet deputy foreign minister denied a change in the Soviet attitude toward the northern islands, declared that such a problem was one for governments to settle and never for discussion by political parties, and termed Miyamoto's interpretation a ''misunderstanding.'' The JCP—temporarily embarrassed, but not to be so easily contradicted—waited more than a month and then firmly rejected the denial. Kikunami Hiroshi, who had been a member of the delegation to visit Moscow, wrote in *Akahata* (28 November) that while the Soviet and Japanese parties differed on how to resolve the territorial issue, the CPSU delegation had unmistakably been willing to discuss it in Moscow and had promised to study the JCP position and refer the matter to the Soviet government for consideration. The Japanese government and press, convinced by the hard line taken consistently by Soviet officials with the LDP and the Japanese government, were quick to dismiss Miyamoto's report as indeed a ''misunderstanding'' and not a sign of a true change of policy. The later unexpected agreement of Soviet Foreign Minister Gromyko during his January 1972 Tokyo visit to negotiate a peace treaty within a year, and his failure specifically to exclude the Japanese-claimed northern territories as a subject for consideration, suggested that Miyamoto may have heard correctly after all. In any case, the new friendly atmosphere established by the September conversations in Moscow prepared the way not only for improved relationships between the JCP and the CPSU, but were perhaps symptomatic of a closer cooperation which the Soviet government hoped to achieve with the conservative government of Japan.

Other International Issues. In an interview with the Italian Communist Party organ *L'Unita* (13 September) during his visit to Rome, Miyamoto Kenji listed the three "most urgent" international tasks of the JCP: (1) full support to the seven-point proposal of the Provisional Revolutionary Government of South Vietnam, (2) the total return of Okinawa to Japan, including all military installations, and (3) the abrogation of the security treaty between Japan and the United States.

Throughout the year the JCP sounded the alarm against the escalation of U.S. "aggression" in Indochina and denounced U.S. defense policy in Asia. The party issued on 3 February an appeal for unified action in Japan and throughout the world against the aggression; on 18 February the Presidium denounced the invasion of Laos as a new intensification of the situation in Indochina, violating the Geneva Agreement of 1962, drawing Thai troops into the fighting, and exposing the Nixon doctrine as a plot to expand aggressive war rather than to reduce hostilities in Vietnam or to promote "non-intervention in Asia" (Japan Press Service, Tokyo, 19 February). The JCP saw the U.S. defense secretary's July visit to Japan as part of a U.S. plan to get Japan to expand its defense role in East Asia and carry out the aim of the Nixon doctrine to get "Asians to fight Asians." The visit, according to *Akahata* (9 July) would "undoubtedly mark the opening of a 'dangerous era' in which a closely coordinated joint Japanese-American military setup [would] be formed."

Okinawa was both a domestic and an international issue for the JCP and in a year of both local and national (upper house) elections, and in which the reversion treaty would be signed by the government and debated and ratified by the Diet, received continuing and massive attention. A major article in *Akahata* (24 April) set forth the party position in the greatest detail, starting with the resolution of the Eleventh Congress and treating each controversial point in the agreement to be signed. The philosophy portrayed was that of a subservient government abjectly submitting to the unjust and imperious demands of an imperialist United States, insistent on forging an invincible Japanese-American military alliance. The article described the reversion agreement as a "tool for more directly incorporating the whole of Japan into Nixon's plan for aggression, with the spearhead focused on Asia through self-serving negotiations to subordinate Japan to the United States—the opposite from being a first step toward true independence for Japan." The real purpose of the treaty was to solidify the American bases on Okinawa and to continue to operate special units for conducting subversive operations in Asia, spy flights, and broadcasts via the Voice of America, the latter in contravention of Japanese law. *Akahata* discussed at great length the damages to life and property suffered by Okinawans during the U.S. administration and demanded compensation for these losses; it ridiculed the idea of Japan's being forced to "buy" the administrative rights over the islands under guise of a "transfer of assets." The article concluded by appealing for victory for the "democratic forces" in the local and upper house elections as a protest against the "treacherous Okinawa reversion agreement and the strategem by Japanese and American ruling circles for strengthening the Japan-United States military alliance." As was to be expected, the JCP denounced the signing of the Okinawa treaty which took place on 17 June and called for its immediate cancellation (*Akahata*, 27 June).

The JCP renewed its opposition to the United States-Japan security treaty on the anniversary of its automatic extension on 23 June. Officials of both the JCP and JSP simultaneously appealed for a nationwide united front to achieve abrogation; the JCP linked the Okinawa and security treaties in the same declaration. The San Clemente conference between President Nixon and Prime Minister Sato inspired the JCP to attack the security treaty once again, noting the confirmation in the joint declaration by the prime minister and the president of the "important role" played by the treaty in relations between Japan and the United States. The communiqué itself was seen as a "dangerous milestone in the reorganization of the Japanese-American military alliance for aggressive purposes." (*Ibid.*, 9 January 1972.)

International Party Contacts. To enhance the prestige of the JCP and to counteract charges of international isolation, Miyamoto Kenji undertook to visit four countries in August and September: the Soviet Union (see above), Romania, Italy, and North Vietnam. In the course of the tour Miyamoto also managed to meet the secretary-general of the illegal Communist Party of Spain. The sojourn in Romania was the longest (20 August-3 September) and possibly considered the most important by the JCP. As a kindred party following the "independent" line, the Romanian communists had much in common with their Japanese colleagues, but JCP spokesmen denied vigorously that the Romanian party was being asked to intervene in the dispute between the JCP and the CCP. Miyamoto and the secretary-general of the Romanian party, Nicolae Ceaușescu, both stressed in their respective speeches the principles of equality, independence, and non-interference in each other's affairs, and both declared forcefully that there could be no question of any world "center" for communist parties. All of these points were included in the lengthy joint communiqué issued at the end of the talks.

According to an announcement of the JCP on 6 September Miyamoto and his group met during the "last part of August" with a delegation from the Spanish communist party headed by its secretary-general, Santiago Carrillo. The usual solidarity on questions of "U.S. imperialism" and the "struggle of the peoples of Indochina," and a call for the removal of military bases from Japan and Spain were mentioned in the joint communiqué, which also referred to the invasion of Czechoslovakia and the necessity for independence of communist parties. (*Akahata*, 13 September.) Although the place of the meetings with the Spanish party was not announced, it was surmised that the conference took place in Bucharest.

From Bucharest Miyamoto and his delegation traveled to Rome, where from 3 to 8 September they "exchanged wide-ranging information on political, economic, and social situations in their own countries, on policies and struggles of the two parties, and on the struggles of the workers and general masses" (*ibid.*, 9 September). The two parties have much in common in that they both operate in advanced capitalist nations and are at present seeking power through parliamentary processes.

From Italy Miyamoto moved on to Hanoi where he held meetings with North Vietnamese government and party officials from 10 to 18 September. The joint communiqué condemned the United States for its policies in Vietnam, including Vietnamization, and supported fully the seven-point peace proposal of the Provisional Revolutionary Government of South Vietnam, demanding the unconditional withdrawal of U.S. bases and forces and the cessation of support for the "war-loving fascist group" led by President Thieu of South Vietnam. The communiqué made no mention of China or of President Nixon's announced visit to Peking. (*Ibid.*, 20 September).

Upon his return to Japan, Miyamoto called the visits "inspiring" and labeled the five parties whose leaders he had met as of "particular importance in the international communist movement." He said that he returned with a stronger belief than ever before in the course the JCP was taking toward autonomy and independence. He noted that the question of the revival of Japanese militarism had been discussed "everywhere" and that he had found three mistaken views on this problem. One was a tendency to underestimate Japan's self-defense forces, a second was the simplistic view that militarism had *already* revived in Japan, and the third was that Japanese militarism was a greater danger in Asia than American imperialism. (*Ibid.*, 28 September).

During the period Miyamoto and his delegation were traveling abroad, a French Communist Party delegation headed by Rene Piquet, member of the Central Committee, was in Japan from 6 to 13 August at the invitation of the JCP. The chairman of the host committee was Fuwa Tetsuzo. A joint communiqué issued at the end of the visit included the usual references to solidarity against "U.S. imperialism" and "confirmed that an individual communist party knows best the situation in its own country" (*ibid.*, 16 August).

Publications. The circulation of *Akahata* (Red Flag), the JCP's official daily newspaper, was estimated at 420,000 for the daily edition in 1971 (the same as the 1970 figure) and at 1,620,000 for the Sunday edition, a slight increase over the 1.5 million reported in 1970. *Minsei Shimbun*, the organ of the Democratic Youth League (Minseido) dropped to 240,000 in 1971, from about 250,000 in 1970. The weekly *Shinfujin Shimbun* (New Woman's News) had a circulation of about 200,000 and the monthly *Gakushu no Tomo* (Students' Friend), 100,000. Other party publications, with estimated circulation figures, include: *Zenei* (Vanguard), a monthly theoretical magazine (100,000); *Sekai Seiji Shiryo* (World Political Documents), a bi-monthly magazine (30,000); *Gekkan Gakushu* (Student Monthly) (115,000). Numerous local weekly newspapers are published at the prefectural, district, and city level by JCP units.

*   *   *

Splinter Parties. The Japan Communist Party (Left)—Nihon Kyosanto (Saha)—is a small dissident group centered in Yamaguchi Prefecture in southeastern Japan. It was formed after the break between the JCP and CCP in 1966 and is headed by Fukuda Masayoshi. The CCP gives extensive publicity to this party, its statements and activities, and Chou En-lai received a delegation in Peking on 20 September. The party's Central Committee publishes a periodical, *Jimmin no Hoshi* (People's Star), which is frequently quoted by Chinese news media. Party membership is estimated at 700.

The Japan-China Friendship Association (Orthodox) is a pro-PRC organization with close ties to the left wing of the JSP. It sent a delegation to Peking to attend the celebrations of China's National Day at the invitation of its counterpart organization, the China-Japan Friendship Organization. This group split into two factions in 1969 but was reunited in 1971; the leaders of the two factions, JSP Diet member Kuroda Hisao and Miyazaki Semin, led the delegation to Peking (28 September-18 October).

The JCP reacted angrily to the active support given by the CCP to the "anti-party elements," most of whom had been expelled from the JCP. An article in *Akahata* (15 August) noted that "anti-party elements" had participated in eight out of fifteen Japanese delegations to visit China during the six months before August 1971. The article complained that *People's Daily* continuously reprinted articles from the publications of the anti-JCP groups and gave every possible support to their activities while never once reporting any activity of the JCP, "the vanguard of the Japanese people," no matter how big or important.

The second splinter party of some concern to the JCP is the pro-Soviet Voice of Japan (*Nihon no Koe*), organized by Shiga Yoshio after his expulsion from the JCP in 1964. The encouragement given this party by the CPSU was one of the principal obstacles to normalization of relations between the Soviet and Japanese parties and, following the meetings of March preceding the CPSU congress, the JCP felt that this problem had been solved, although trust in the CPSU was probably not completely restored. Meanwhile membership in the Voice of Japan declined to about 300 by the end of 1971. The agreement by the Soviet Union to withdraw support from Shiga's supporters has affected the membership of the Japan-Soviet Friendship Society, which included some persons expelled from the JCP. A controversy developed in May when the question arose of the continuation in office of the secretary-general, Inoue Tadao, and of 20 directors, all of whom had at one time or another been expelled from the JCP. A decision was finally reached that Inoue would voluntarily resign, but the directors would remain in office. The JCP announced that it would continue to take a "firm attitude ... toward anti-party elements."

John K. Emmerson

Korea: Democratic People's Republic of Korea

The Korean Communist Party (Choson Kongsan-dang; KCP) was formed at Seoul in 1925 during the time of the Japanese rule. It ceased to operate in 1928. Shortly after World War II, a revived KCP appeared briefly in Seoul. Control of the communist movement in Korea soon shifted to the northern part of the country, then occupied by Soviet forces, where the "North Korean Central Bureau of the KCP" was formed in October 1945 under Soviet auspices. The three major factions of the movement—comprising Korean communists who during the Japanese period had gone to China, or to the Soviet Union, or had remained in Korea—subsequently merged, and on 24 June 1949 the Korean Workers' Party (Choson Nodong-dang; KWP) was established. The KWP is the ruling party of the former Soviet-occupied area, which in 1948 became the Democratic People's Republic of Korea (DPRK).

The size of the KWP was not revealed at the party's Fifth Congress, held in November 1970, but during the preceding five years a membership of about 1,600,000 was claimed. Since the population of the DPRK is put at 13,900,000 (estimated 1970), the KWP may have the highest membership ratio of any communist party.

Leadership and Organization. The KWP is organized along highly centralized lines under the leadership of its secretary-general, Kim Il-song, who is also DPRK premier and commander in chief of the Armed Forces. Kim's nearly absolute power is largely the result of several substantial purges whereby he eliminated or severely weakened the aformentioned three factions, leaving himself surrounded by loyal followers, most of whom had accompanied him in anti-Japanese guerrilla operations in Manchuria and eastern Siberia before and during World War II. These and other purges have given the KWP a predominantly military leadership (see *YICA*, 1971, pp. 611-12). The party's Political Committee, elected at its Fifth Congress (November 1970) consists of full members (in order of rank) Kim Il-song,* Choe Yong-kon,* Kim Il,* Pak Song-chol, Choe Hyon, Kim Yong-chu,* O Chin-u,* Kim Tong-kyu,* So Chol, Kim Chung-in,* and Han Ik-su,* and candidates Hyon Mu-kwang,* Chong Chun-taek, Yang Hyong-sop,* and Kim Man-kum. The Secretariat has 10 members (designated by asterisks) and the Central Committee, 172.

The party's youth auxiliary, the League of Socialist Working Youth of Korea (LSWY), celebrated its twenty-fifth anniversary on 17 January 1971. The Sixth Congress of the LSWY—the first in seven years—opened in Pyongyang on 21 June and was attended by 1,550 delegates and many foreign observers, including representatives of some 20 foreign groups devoted to the study of the work of Kim Il-song; also present was a delegation of the "South Korean Revolutionary Youth Organization," in the Republic of Korea. Elections were carried out for the LSWY Central Committee (75 members), Central Auditing Committee (7), and Central Executive Committee (15). Kim Si-hak heads the LSWY as chairman of the Central Committee; the seven vice-chairmen are Kim Chong-suk,

Choe Tong-sok, Yi Nam-kyu, Kim Sang-un, Yi Hwa-chong, Mun Pyong-nok, and O Kwang-taek. The LSWY claims a membership of 2,700,000.

The Korean Democratic Women's Union held its Fourth Congress on 5-10 October. Kim Song-ae, the wife of Kim Il-song, was elected chairman of the Central Committee; the Secretariat consists of Kim Tok-nan (general secretary), Wang Ok-hwan, Ho Chang-suk, Yu Un-po, and Yi Chong-sun. Other important mass organizations include the General Federation of Trade Unions of Korea, headed by Chon Chang-chol and claiming 2,000,000 members, and the Union of Agricultural Working People, headed by Yi Nim-su.

Through the General Federation of Korean Residents in Japan (Chongnyong; known also by its Japanese name, Chosen Soren), the KWP competes with the organization of the Republic of Korea residents in Japan for the loyalty of the half-million or so Koreans who are in that country (South Koreans, citing Japanese sources, claim that 352,000 are registered as citizens of the Republic of Korea). At the Chongnyon's Ninth Congress, held in Tokyo on 29-31 January, Han Tok-su was reelected to head its 245-member Central Committee. Nosaka Sanzo, chairman of the Japan Communist Party, attended the congress. The DPRK allocated 1.52 billion won—an increase of 30 per cent over the previous year—to be sent to Chongnyon in 1971, primarily for educational purposes.

At least two subordinate political movements exist in North Korea: the Korean Democratic Party (Choson Minju-dang), headed by Kang Yang-uk, and the Young Friends of Chondogyo Party (Chondogyo Chong-u-dang), led by Pak Sin-tok (Chondogyo: the Heavenly Way Society). The function of these movements is to enhance acceptance of the United Democratic Fatherland Front (Choguk Tongil Minjujuui Chonson). The front, created in June 1949 and involving 71 political and social organizations, has the task of uniting, under the leadership of the KWP, "all the revolutionary forces of North and South Korea" in order to implement the "peaceful unification and complete independence of the country." There is also a "Committee for the Peaceful Unification of the Fatherland," led by Yi Kuk-no and consisting of representatives of the KWP, the Korean Democratic and Chondogyo parties, and various mass organizations.

Domestic Attitudes and Activities. Almost all aspects of life in North Korea are pervaded by Kim Il-song's efforts to promote the country's independence in its politics, economy, and defense. Although the end goal is to enhance the DPRK's international stature, the domestic aspects are equally significant. Kim's "unitary ideology" of *chuche* (national self-reliance) seeks the weeding out of all deleterious tendencies such as "revisionism," "dogmatism," "opportunism," and "flunkeyism" through which national independence would assertedly be lost in search of an easy road to national development. Chuche calls for heavy personal sacrifice so that capital production may expand at an ever increasing rate. It also means that a large share of investment capital must go to military development in order to lessen reliance on other communist-governed states.

In a major article released on 5 August 1971 by the Korean Central News Agency (KCNA), the concept of chuche was reaffirmed as an instrument for uniting the people. Within the KWP, it was claimed, "unity and cohesion" had become "indestructible." Emphatic references to the danger of misunderstandings and deviations from chuche seemed to indicate that the ideology had perhaps not been so firmly planted in everyone's mind. The article gave warning of what would happen if one should "lose chuche and fall into flunkeyism." His "independent thinking" would be paralyzed, he would be "unable to display any initiative and distinguish right from wrong," and he would "follow others blindly." Without independence, the article added, "one cannot have a faith in the strength of his people in revolution and construction or mobilize inner reserves of his country"; such a person would "depend upon others for everything."

To get the new six-year economic plan (1971-76) off to a fast start, a "100-day battle" was announced, with the object of achieving the goals of the first year before the twenty-third anniversary of the DPRK on 9 September. Moreover, the goals of the second year were to be reached before 15 April 1972 and the entire plan was to be completed two years ahead of schedule. The major thrust of the plan involves a three-point "technical revolution" which is intended (1) to eliminate the gap between heavy and light labor by increasing production of machine tools, (2) to narrow the gap between agricultural and industrial labor by the mechanization of agriculture, and (3) to relieve women of much of their housework and incorporate them in the labor force by developing the food industry and providing more laundries and similar aids.

Reporting on the 1971 budget to the Supreme People's Assembly, Finance Minister Choe Yun-su spoke of the necessity of strengthening "communist education" to consolidate and develop the self-sustaining economy: "We must wage a staunch struggle against all shades of counterrevolutionary ideological elements, including revisionism, dogmatism, bourgeois ideas, and feudal Confucian ideas, which run afoul of the party's unitary ideology." Choe admonished all functionaries and workers to "correct the mistaken attitude of dismissing as insignificant any reckless management or waste of state property," and to adhere strictly to a program of financial discipline, which would be enforced by intensified control efforts on the part of financial and banking organizations. (Pyongyang radio, domestic broadcast, 13 April.)

The budget allocated 30 per cent of its 1971 expenditures for military development (as compared with 26.4 per cent in South Korea). Although this was a reduction of only one per cent below the amount allocated in 1970, Kim Il-song declared that defense costs anticipated for the six-year plan had been "drastically reduced." Consequently, he said, the strain caused by the effort for parallel development of defense and the economy would be alleviated and greater emphasis could be placed on elevating living standards, which were expected to equal those of Western Europe upon the successful completion of the six-year plan. (*Asahi Evening News*, Tokyo, 28 September.)

South Korea. The DPRK's efforts to attain unification of the two Korean states have been promoted with an intensity equal to that of chuche—the drive for self-reliance. Although North Koreans have offered specific proposals for a peaceful settlement with the Republic of Korea, in the south, they have usually added that such a solution cannot be possible unless President Pak Chong-hui of the Republic of Korea is removed from office and the U.S. and other U.N. armed forces leave South Korea. An essential element in the unification campaign is the establishment in South Korea of clandestine revolutionary bases. On numerous occasions DPRK "agents" have been sent south for purposes ranging from intelligence gathering, guerrilla activities, and terrorism (sharply increased between 1966 and 1969) to political activities primarily designed for winning adherents to the philosophy of Kim Il-song. The illegal Revolutionary Party for Reunification (RPR)—formed in 1964 as the United Revolutionary Party and reconstituted as the RPR in 1969—provides the main base for DPRK activities in South Korea. The RPR clandestinely transmits radio broadcasts (the "Voice of the RPR Front") and publishes *Hyokmyong Chonson* (Revolutionary Front). It also issues a monthly publication, *Chongmaek*, and has a number of auxiliary organizations.

The RPR has suffered considerably from intensive surveillance by the South Korean Army Security Command. On 8 January 1971, fourteen persons were tried and sentenced (six condemned to death) for subversive activities in Pusan and elsewhere. Attacking the trial and saying those convicted had not committed crimes, the KCNA (10 January) described the fourteen as "revolutionaries and patriotic people" who "formed an underground revolutionary organization and strove to arm themselves with the great revolutionary ideas of the respected and beloved leader, comrade Kim Il-song.''

In April the Army Security Command announced the capture of eight alleged spies—among them a man and wife who were said to be following North Korean directives for organizaing an underground party in the areas around Seoul and Inchon and in North and South Cholla provinces to "inflame the popular passion with anti-war, anti-U.S., and anti-Japanese agitation and propaganda activities." The man reportedly had entered South Korea illegally in 1970 after seventeen months of "intensive espionage training" in North Korea. The couple allegedly had been ordered to frustrate the reelection of President Pak and lead public opinion to support another (unnamed) candidate. (Seoul radio, domestic broadcast, 8 April.)

The biggest blow to the South Korean revolutionaries came on 17 April with the arrests of 52 persons in Seoul, Pusan, and Cheju. Some of these were charged with establishing bases at universities in Seoul, others with attempting to organize fishermen and factory workers in Pusan. The KCNA (21 April) called the arrests a challenge to students and others who had "risen up in a just national-salvation struggle for freedom and democracy and for the unification and independence of the country." Two more arrests followed on 22 April. An announcement by Seoul radio on 23 April reported the capture eleven days earlier of a 13-member group operating in North Cholla and South Kyongsang provinces and allegedly engaged in building guerrilla bases.

Information obtained from arrested persons indicated that North Korea had fifty training centers for espionage and guerrilla warfare in the vicinity of Pyongyang and had shifted its tactical emphasis from guerrilla warfare in mountainous areas to uprisings in the cities.

Preliminary steps toward discussions between the two Korean states were initiated in August when the Republic of Korea issued a proposal, which the DPRK accepted, for the establishment of communications between members of families separated by the closed border (see below). Earlier in the year, speaking at the opening of the fifth session of the Fourth Supreme People's Assembly on 12 April, DPRK Foreign Minister Ho Tam offered an eight-point proposal for national reunification. Ho Tam called for withdrawal of U.S. troops from South Korea; reduction of troops by the Republic of Korea and the DPRK to a maximum of 100,000 each; abrogation of South Korea's treaties with the United States and Japan; establishment of a unified central government on the basis of general elections throughout the Korean Peninsula; or, if a unified government were not immediately feasible, creation of a confederation in which both sides would retain existing social systems; freedom of political activity for all groups and individuals; cooperation at economic, scientific, and cultural levels; travel and the exchange of letters between citizens on both sides; and a "political consultative meeting" to discuss these possibilities. Ho Tam proposed formally that representatives of North and South Korea meet on the border at Panmunjom or in a third country for a "heart-to-heart consultation." Referring to statements by some South Korean political figures favoring an interchange, he declared: "We express support for such policy statements, [which] are of affirmative significance for easing the prevailing tension and accomplishing the historic cause of the North-South unification." (*Pyongyang Times*, 17 April.) On 5 July the KWP newspaper *Nodong Sinmun* attacked President Pak's inaugural address, contending that he continued to talk about "reunification by prevailing over communistm."

On 12 August, the president of the South Korean Red Cross, Choe Tu-son, proposed that organizations from both sides enter into direct talks on locating members of separated families. Two days later the head of the North Korean Red Cross, Son Song-pil, replied that the proposal was "in accord with the reasonable proposals consistently advanced" by the DPRK (KCNA, 14 August). He suggested that the questions of travel and the exchange of letters also be discussed. Preliminary contacts begun in Panmunjom on 20 August were followed by talks which began on 20 September.

Later in the year the North Koreans began a campaign denouncing "attempts by the Pak Chong-hui puppet hordes," at the "instigation of U.S. imperialism," to frustrate the forthcoming talks. On 6 December Pak declared a state of emergency, asserting that an alleged intensification of war preparations in North Korea and changing international conditions were endangering South Korea's security. His powers were broadened when he signed the controversial "Special Measures Law for National Security and Defense" on 27 December. Although the South Korean defense minister disclosed at a press conference on 30 November that the government had "concrete evidence" to show that North Korea was "more eager than before to launch military provocations against the South," the threat was not apparent to outside observers, and even to many in South Korea (*New York Times*, 8 December). Some speculated that Pak had sought the extraordinary powers to stem internal difficulties (mostly economic), that would be aggravated by a detente between the North and South, i.e., by the loss of the cohesive force of a military threat from the North (*ibid.*, editorial, 28 December). The North Koreans interpreted the move as an effort to sabotage the reunification movement and to provide a "smokescreen" for preparations for a "fratricidal war" (KCNA, 8 December).

International Views and Positions. In accordance with the principle of chuche, North Korea carefully avoids leaning toward either the Soviet Union or China. It is militant in seeking the preservation of political independence and advocates a similar stand by other "Third World" countries. Though it calims that the concept of chuche cannot be exported, there is constant reference in the North Korean press to the value attached by others to chuche and the "teachings of Kim Il-song." On 15 January 1971, *Nodong Sinmun* reported, presumably for domestic benefit, that the "great revolutionary thought and strategies" of Kim Il-song were gaining acceptance among the world's revolutionaries:

> Today, progressive political activists and revolutionary people throughout the world are expressing unqualified faith in and support for our respected and beloved leader, Comrade Kim Il-song, who founded the chuche idea and who not only leads the Korean Revolution to victory but also contributes greatly to the cause of developing the international communist movement and the world revolution. They infinitely respect him, admire him, and draw inspiration and immense strength from his great revolutionary thought and anti-imperialist ideas.

When Nicolae Ceauşecu, first secretary of the Romanian Communist Party, visited Pyongyang on 9-12 June, Kim reasserted the importance of attaining self-sufficiency within the international communist movement. Praising Romania's independent development of its national economy, Kim stated: "Our experiences, too, show that ... the socialist countries ... should have political sovereignty under all circumstances; and political sovereignty can be guaranteed only when they have a solid, independent national economy, and a powerful self-defensive capacity" (KCNA, 14 June).

Relations with the Soviet Union. Currently, the chuche policy draws its inspiration mainly from the DPRK's opposition, in the first place, to Soviet "revisionism" and, closely following in second place, to the "left opportunism" or "dogmatism" of the Chinese communists. Thus, while attempting to maintain a strict policy of neutrality between its two giant neighbors, the DPRK has in fact fluctuated considerably in its attitude, being influenced by such developments as the de-Stalinization policy of former Premier Khrushchev in the Soviet Union and the Cultural Revolution in China.

Relations with the Soviet Union continued in 1971 to be warm, though overshadowed by a certain degree of mistrust and occasionally punctuated by conflicting interests. On 11 September, for example, the KCNA called attention to the arrival in Seoul of a Soviet citizen who was serving as the athletic coach of an Iranian soccer team. Quoting a South Korean claim that the incident would become a precedent for the permission of entry into the Republic of Korea by citizens of other communist states, the KCNA statement concluded: "Our people and public circles are surprised at the 'visit' of South Korea by Soviet citizen [Igor Aleksandrovich] Neto, regarding it as something hardly understandable.''

On 5 February the KCNA reported the signing of the DPRK's annual trade protocal with the Soviet Union. The omission of any reference to increased trade led some observers (e.g., *Far Eastern Economic Review*, Hong Kong, 24 April) to predict serious economic consequences for North Korea, since transactions with the Soviet Union account for more than half of its total foreign trade. Later, an article in *Trud* (Moscow, 24 July) claimed that under a long-term agreement the trade between the two countries would increase 55 per cent during 1971-75 as compared with the previous five-year period.

Relations with China. Relations between the DPRK and China, which had cooled considerably during the Cultural Revolution, thawed dramatically in 1969 and 1970. This trend continued in 1971. After an absence of five years, a Chinese delegate returned on 9 July to sit beside the North Korean delegation in the United Nations talks at Panmunjom, where delegates representing the interests of North and South Korea have met since the end of the Korean War to discuss disagreements.

The simultaneous announcement by the Chinese and U.S. governments on 15 July that President Nixon would visit China had a profound impact on North Korea. In a speech at a Pyongyang rally welcoming the former Cambodian head of state, Prince Norodom Sihanouk, Kim Il-song stated that Nixon would arrive in China with a "white flag" on a "trip of the defeated" (KCNA, 8 August). The text of the speech was subsequently broadcast by the New China News Agency. A few days later, the agreement by North and South Korean Red Cross organizations to meet for talks suggested that the North Koreans interpreted the prospective visit by Nixon as an indication of reduced tensions in East Asia. Other actions by the North Koreans also indicated the adoption of a more relaxed attitude toward Americans and their allies. In the second week of August, when a North Korean vessel arrived in Japan to carry Korean nationals who had decided to take up residence in North Korea, *Washington Post* correspondent Selig S. Harrison was invited on board with other foreign newspapermen. He was the first American to be allowed to board a North Korean ship under friendly circumstances. On 25 September, Kim Il-song granted an interview with the editor of the Tokyo *Asahi Evening News*. Since Japan is held by the DPRK to occupy a position close to that of the United States as the primary enemy, this was also an unusual gesture. In the course of the interview, which lasted for five and a half hours, Kim spoke of the international impact of Nixon's anticipated visit: "My view is that as a result of the China visit by President Nixon, the international situation will move in the direction of easing tensions, albeit temporarily" (*Asahi Evening News*, 28 September). Shortly after the announcement of the visit and following a three-week visit to China on 18 August-7 September by the DPRK army chief of staff, O Chin-u (also member of the KWP Political Committee), an agreement was reached by which China would provide nonrefundable military assistance to North Korea. Though the North Koreans will probably continue to turn to the Soviet Union for sophisticated equipment, the offer was significant in that they had received no major military aid from China since the 1950s. It was believed by some observers that a likely recipient of the aid would be the paramilitary forces that fall under the "all-people and all-nation defense system," which is designed to "convert the whole country into a strong fortress while strengthening the standing army." Suggesting that Sino-Korean relations had fully recovered from the bitter feelings expressed during the Cultural Revolution, O Chin-u spoke of China during his visit as North Korea's "closest comrade-in-arms" (NCNA, 18 August).

Publications. The KWP publishes a daily newspaper, *Nodong Sinmun*, and a journal, *Kulloja*. *Choson Inminkun* is the organ of the Porean People's Army; *Nodongja Sinmun*, of the General

Federation of Trade Unions of Korea; *Nongop Chongnyon*, of the LSWY; and *Choguk Tongil*, of the Committee for the Peace Unification of the Fatherland. *Pyongyang Times* and *People's Korea* are weekly English-language publications. The official news agency is the Korean Central News Agency.

Eric Stromquist

Laos

"Following the Communist International's instructions," the first session of the Vietnam Communist Party, meeting in October 1930, "decided to change the Party's name to Indochinese Communist Party becase 'the Vietnamese, Cambodian and Laotian proletariat have politically and economically to be closely related in spite of their difference in language, customs and race' " (*Thirty Years of Struggle of the Party*, Hanoi: Foreign Languages Publishing House, 1960, I, 27). For propaganda reasons, the Indochinese Communist Party was officially dissolved in November 1945. The communist Laotian People's Party (Phak Pasason Lao; PPL) was secretly founded in 1946, and was openly founded in 1955. Although it has not been outlawed, it chooses to operate clandestinely through the Laotian Patriotic Front (Neo Lao Hak Xat; NLHX—also known as NLHS), which replaced the Free Laos Front (Neo Lao Issara) in 1954. The NLHX held its First Congress on 6 January 1956 and became a legal party as a result of the Vientiane agreements of 1957. It is at present the communist component of the Tripartite National Union Government (often referred to by the communists as the Tripartite National Coalition Government), headed by neutralist Souvanna Phouma (half-brother of Prince Souphanouvong, chairman of the NLHX). The government was recognized by the Geneva agreements of 23 July 1962, and previously by the Zurich agreement of June 1961 and the Plain of Jars agreement of June 1962.

The NLHX was initially granted four of the 19 cabinet posts in the Tripartite National Union Government (four leftists, four rightists, and 11 neutralists). It has, however, refused active government participation since 1963, when it withdrew its cabinet members. The NLHX boycotted the 1967 elections, and during 1971 made it clear that it would not participate in the 1972 elections (see below).

The exact membership of the PPL is unknown. An estimate in 1964 placed the number at about 700. The NLHX, which is controlled by the PPL, is estimated to have between 1,500 and 3,000 members. The military arm of the NLHX, known as the Laotian People's Liberation Army (PLA—formerly and still commonly known as the Pathet Lao), was founded in 1949. It numbers between 30,000 and 40,000 (*New York Times*, 31 January 1971). It has approximately 2,500 supporters and the further support of some 2,000 to 3,000 dissident "neutralists" who comprise the Patriotic Neutralist Forces (see below). The Pathet Lao are supplemented by a sizable North Vietnamese contingent of an estimated 80,000 to 100,000 regulars (*Christian Science Monitor*, 8 December 1971; *The Economist*, 13 February). There are also 14,000 to 20,000 Communist Chinese soldiers in northern Laos guarding and building a major road project from Yunan Province in South China toward the Mekong River (*Washington Post*, 6 April; *Christian Science Monitor*, 5 August). The population of Laos is 3,000,000 (estimated 1971).

Leadership and Organization. Little is known about the leadership of the Phak Pasason Lao, except that it controls and to some extent overlaps the Central Committee of the NLHX. The

PPL secretary-general is Kaysone Phomvihan, who is also vice-chairman of the NLHX Central Committee. He appears to operate mainly from Hanoi and is apparently the most important person in the Laotian communist movement. Reports also indicate that he is a member of the Vietnam Workers' Party.

The chairman of the PPL Central Committee, Nouhak Phoumsavanh, is also NLHX Central Committee secretary and Vietnam Workers' Party high commissioner in Laos, acting as liaison between Hanoi and the NLHX. Other known PPL members include Sithon Khommandam, who is also NLHX Central Committee vice-chairman; Phoumi Vongvichit, NLHX secretary-general; General Phoume Sipraseuth, NLHX Politburo member; and Khampohouane Tounalom, NLHS Politburo member. It is thought that General Sinkapo Chounlamany, NLHX Politburo member, belongs also to the PPL.

NLHX leadership consists of Phoumi Vongvichit, secretary-general; Prince Souphanouvong, chairman of the Central Committee; and Sithon Khommandam, Kaysone Phomvihan, and Faydang Lobliayao (sometimes identified as Fayang), NLHX Central Committee vice-chairmen. Politburo members include Kaysone Phomvihan, General Phoume Sipraseuth, Sithon Khommandam, General Sinkapo Sikhoy Chounlamany, Nouhak Phoumsavanh, Khamphouane Tounalom, and Phoumi Vongvichit. Additional members of the Central Committee are Maysouk Saysompheng, Tiao Souk Vongsak, Meune, Saly Vongkhamsao, Kong My, Say, Sanan Southichak, Kiao Sik Phaisomphone, Sisana Sisane, Khampheng Boupha, Pheng Phang, Lo Foung, May Chit, Apheuy Keobounheuang, Phao Phimphachanh, Chanh My, Mme Bounthay, Mme Khampheng Boupha, Mme Phaiboun Pholesna, Nhia Vu Lobliayao (also listed as Nhia Vu), and Somsak.

The PLA (Pathet Lao) is headed by Khamtay Siphandone, commander in chief. Other key Pathet Lao figures include generals Phoume Sipraseuth and Sinkapo Sikhoy Chounlamany.

Communist influence is exercised through a number of mass organizations. The most important are: the National Laotian Women's Federation, headed by Mme Phaiboun Pholesna; the Laotian Patriotic Teacher's Union and the Laotian Afro-Asian Solidarity Committee, both headed by Tiao Souk Vongsak; the Laotian Patriotic Cultural Workers' Union, headed by Phoumi Vongvichit; the National Patriotic Women's Association, founded and organized by Mme Khampheng Boupha; the Laotian Patriotic Workers' Union, the Patriotic Youth League; and the Laotian Buddhists' Association.

There have been reports in the past of an internal split in the Laotian communism movement, between a pro-Soviet faction led by Souphanouvong and Phoumi Vongvichit and a pro-Chinese element under Nouhak Phoumsavanh and Kaysone Phomvihan. Statements during 1971 offered no evidence of this, and were apparently designed to maintain a balance between the two views. Evidence was abundant during 1971 of a split between many Pathet Lao soldiers at all levels and their North Vietnamese "advisers" (see below).

Domestic Attitudes and Activities. In January 1971, Laotian Premier Souvanna Phouma announced that he was "convinced that the North Vietnamese were beginning a general offensive against Laotian Government positions." The Prince said that the North Vietnamese strategy was to "attempt the conquest of...Laos now and leave South Vietnam to be dealt with later." (*New York Times*, 31 January.) Nine days later South Vietnamese troops, with U.S. air support, crossed into southern Laos commencing a six-week-long drive against communist forces along the Ho Chi Minh trail. The operation, code-named Lam Son 719, was greeted by a "mild protest" from Premier Souvanna Phouma, who said that "primary responsibility for the situation lies with North Vietnam" (*Washington Post*, 9 February). The reaction of the communists—in Laos, Vietnam, China, and the U.S.S.R. — was not so mild (see below). When the operation was over, the PLA Supreme Command issued a special communiqué asserting that the operation "has ended in complete defeat" for the South Vietnamese (quoted in *Peking Review, no.* 14, 2 April). Although the South Vietnamese government reported 5,755 killed, wounded, or missing and claimed to have killed over 13,000 communists (*New York Times*, 24 March; *Pacific Stars & Stripes*, Tokyo, 11 April), the Pathet Lao claimed to have "put out of action" over 15,000 "enemy troops" and to have captured another thousand (*Peking Review*, 2 April). Military claims and comments continued to dominate Laotian communist broadcasts throughout 1971. The year was one of successes and failures. In May the communists — primarily North Vietnamese regulars, but since neither North Vietnam nor the Pathet Lao admits the presence of Vietnamese communist soldiers in Laos, the credit was given to the Pathet Lao — seized virtual control of the strategically important Bolovens Plateau in southern Laos (*Economist,* 29 May). This led a senior Laotian general to comment: "Ce n'est plus une situation, c'est une guerre!" (*ibid.*). In July, following a reorganization of the Laotian Army, the government launched a series of military operations in various parts of the country. The strategic Plain of Jars in northern Laos was recaptured (see *YICA*, 1970, p. 623), and in southern Laos a number of important towns were recaptured from the communists. On 28 April, the town of Saravane was recaptured; on 2 September Lo Ngam was retaken, and on 16 September Paksong fell. By October the only highland town of strategic importance still under communist control was Attopeu. In December the communists were making progress in an attempt to capture the northern Laos military base at Long Tieng. They had succeeded in capturing Muong Poun, and were attempting to encircle Long Tieng (*New York Times*, 31 December). Several hundred Pathet Lao soldiers defected to the Laotian government during 1971, many giving as their primary reason mistreatment at the hands of the North Vietnamese (see below).

On 6 March 1970, the NLHX put forth a five-point peace plan (see *YICA*, 1970, p. 623). While continuing to support this proposal, the NLHX offered two new two-point plans during 1971. On 27 April, Central Committee Chairman Prince Souphanouvong proposed:

> (1) The U. S. imperialists must cease all acts of intervention and aggression against Laos. First of all they must immediately and unconditionally cease their bombing throughout the territory of Laos.
> (2) Immediately following cessation of the bombing, all armed forces in Laos must hold a cease-fire and cease all acts of violations and nibbling operations against the zone under the control of the other side. At the same time, the Lao parties concerned must immediately hold discussions on the formation of a provisional coalition government and on other questions of common concern, including a guarantee to strictly abide by the neutrality of the kingdom of Laos, as stated in the 1962 Geneva accord on Laos. (Hanoi radio, 12 May.)

On 22 June, Souphanouvong proposed, "on the basis of the 6 March 1970 five-point political solution and 27 April 1971 proposal," a new two-point proposal:

> (1) To achieve at once a cease-fire throughout the territory of Laos, including the cessation of U.S. bombing as well as all hostile military activities on the ground and in the air, and all acts of violation or nibbling operations against the zone under the control of the other side.
> (2) After a cease-fire throughout Laos, the Lao parties concerned will meet immediately to discuss all questions dealing with peace and national concord in Laos. As for the meeting site, this will, in turn, be the Plain of Jars and Vientiane." (Pathet Lao radio, clandestine, 2 July.)

Souvanna Phouma rejected both proposals, countering with one of his own calling for immediate discussions without major preconditions. This was rejected by the communists. (Vientiane radio, 31 May; Pathet Lao radio, 6 August). The Pathet Lao also rejected a Japanese proposal calling for the Soviet Union and Britain (co-chairmen of the 1962 Geneva conference on Laos), and the International Control Commission to take measures to ensure Laos's neutrality, independence, and territorial integrity (Kyodo news service, Tokyo, 24 February).

The NLHX opposed the participation of Premier Souvanna Phouma in the U.N. General Assembly, charging: "The Vientiane puppet administration has no right to and is not in a position to represent the Lao people at the United Nations or anywhere else" (Pathet Lao radio, 26 September).

In September the government invited the NLHX to participate in the general elections scheduled for 2 January 1972 (Vientiane radio, 21 and 22 September 1971). As was the case in the 1967 elections, the communists have refused to participate (Patriotic Neutralist Forces radio, 30 November).

During 1971 Laotian communist spokesmen again affirmed support for the NLHX twelve-point program, formulated in 1968 (see *YICA*, 1969). This program is extremely close to the 1967 program of the National Liberation Front in South Vietnam, probably too much so to be coincidental. (Justus M. van der Kroef, "Peking, Hanoi, and Guerrilla Insurgency in Southeast Asia," *Southeast Asian Perspectives*, no. 3, 1971, p. 23).

International Views and Positions. The Laotian communist movement continued during 1971 to be dominated by North Vietnam (for information on the Vietnamese communists' role in the establishment of the Pathet Lao, see Paul F. Langer and Joseph J. Zasloff, *North Vietnam and the Pathet Lao*, Cambridge, Mass., Harvard University Press, 1970). During July and August there was a "month of solidarity with Vietnam" (Pathet Lao radio, 26 July), and there were frequent statements in support of both the North and South Vietnamese communists. The relationship between Souphanouvong and the North Vietnamese leaders has been illustrated on several occasions in the past when the apparent interests of the Pathet Lao and Vietnamese communists have clashed. Souphanouvong has usually been willing to "place vital North Vietnamese interests above those of the Pathet Lao" (*Far Eastern Economic Review*, Hong Kong, 12 June 1971). During 1971 there were numerous reports of friction between North Vietnamese soldiers and advisers and Pathet Lao troops. In June, Laotian Finance Minister Prince Sisouk na Champassak asserted:

> Divisions in the Pathet Lao Party really exist; however, these are not divisions among the Pathet Lao but between the Pathet Lao and Vietnamese. The Vietnamese are persecuting the Pathet Lao forces and are not taking good care of them. They will immediately kill Pathet Lao people who argue with them. After talking to some senior Pathet Lao officers who defected, I feel that hatred for the Vietnamese is found from the highest to the lowest levels in the southern Pathet Pao forces ... even in their political command. (Vientiane radio, 25 June.)

This assertion finds support in numerous interviews with Pathet Lao defectors. One officer who defected in July charged: "Organizationally they [the North Vietnamese] have directly commanded us since 1970. As regards political rights, we have district officers and provincial governors, but they are regarded as puppets who implement North Vietnamese plans." (Vientiane radio, 6 August.) Among the many Pathet Lao officers that were said by defectors to have been executed by the North Vietnamese for questioning policy was the widely respected commander in southern Laos, General Phomma Doungmala, who was reportedly assassinated towards the end of 1970 (*Baltimore Sun*, 18 April; Vientiane radio, 5 May). In a Constitutional Day speech on 11 May, Premier Souvanna Phouma referred to the mass defections of hundreds of Pathet Lao troops and said that it was necessary for the Pathet Lao to "break away from the control of their masters." The North Vietnamese chargé d'affaires walked out in protest and part of the waiting crowd attacked his automobile as he left. (Vientiane radio, 11 May.) The North Vietnamese were apparently having difficulties with non-communist Laotians too. In March, they reportedly burned down a Lao village east of Savannakhet as a reprisal for information provided by the villagers about North Vietnamese positions (*Los Angeles Times*, 17 March). On 17 October the Royal Laotian Government published a fifth "White Book on the Violations of the 1962 Geneva Accords by the Government of North Vietnam," summarizing direct North Vietnamese involvement in the fighting in Laos.

The Laotian communists appeared to take a neutral position in the Sino-Soviet dispute, maintaining friendly relations with both giants. the Chinese sent warm greetings on the anniversary of the founding of the NLHX (*Peking Review*, no. 3, 15 January 1971), and the PLA (Pathet Lao News Agency, 23 January), promising: "The struggle of the Lao people is our struggle. The Chinese people and the Chinese People's Liberation Army ... will duly give support to and assist the Lao people ... in their war against U.S. aggression." During the South Vietnamese drive into Laos in February and March, Prince Souvanna Phouma expressed a fear that "it is highly possible that Communist Chinese troops will cross [Laotian] borders if the South Vietnamese appear to be on the verge of cutting the Ho Chi Minh trail" (*Washington Post*, 12 February). Although the Chinese verbally attacked the United States and South Vietnam for the Lam Son 719 operation, and afterward praised the "splendid victory of the Lao Patriotic Army and people" (*Peking Review*, no. 13, 26 March), they did not involve their troops in the conflict. During 1971 the primary Chinese interest in Laos appeared to be the roads they have been building in northern Laos since the early 1960s. Intelligence sources reported that Chinese military strength in Laos nearly doubled during 1971, rising to between 18,000 and 20,000 men (*Washington Post*, 6 April). During the same period sophisticated anti-aircraft defenses increased dramatically (*Christian Science Monitor*, 5 August). One segment of the road was heading in the general direction of Thailand (*Washington Post*, 12 February), supporting the interpretation that "the Chinese road construction through northern Laos seems to have long-range implications for the security of Thailand and Burma" and that "both those countries are considered targets for Chinese-backed guerrilla insurgency" (*Washington Post*, 6 April).

The Chinese endorsed the five-point political solution and the two-point peace proposal of the Pathet Lao (*Jen-min jih-pao*, 12 October). In August the Pathet Lao broadcast a statement supporting "the restoration of the People's Republic of China's legal rights in the United Nations" (Pathet Lao radio, 5 September).

The Laotian communists also exchanged fraternal greetings with the Soviet Union on several occasions. On Soviet Army Day the Pathet Lao News Agency (24 February) announced: "We are deeply moved by the generous assistance which the Soviet party and state, army and people have given us to increase our strength and defeat the enemy." In April Souphanouvong stated:

> The Lao patriotic forces and people have always won the increasing support and assistance from the party, government and people of the Soviet Union....The Lao people greatly rejoice over the splendid achievements which the Soviet people, through their creative ingenious labor and under the leadership of the glorious Communist Party of the Soviet Union, have recorded in socialist construction....We regard the great achievements of the Soviet Union as a source of inspiration. (Pathet Lao News Agency, 9 April.)

The Soviet Union endorsed the five-point political settlement proposal and the two-point 1971 proposal (TASS, 11 February, 13 July; *Pravda*, 22 May). In May the Soviets observed a "week of solidarity with the Laotian people" (*Izvestiia*, 22 May).

The Laotian communists exchanged frequent messages with the other Indochinese states, including commemoration of the first anniversary of the Indochinese People's Summit Conference (Liberation Press Agency, 24 April). The Pathet Lao peace proposal was endorsed by the government in exile of former Cambodian chief of state Sihanouk, and by the Provisional Revolutionary Government, National Liberation Front, and Alliance of National, Democratic and Peace Forces in South Vietnam. In February, Souphanouvong reportedly held a conference "in the frontier region of Laos" with Sihanouk, where a joint statement was issued asserting that "the Khmer and Laotian people are as close as brothers" and promising "to forever stand side-by-side, strengthen unity, and sincerely and whole-heartedly help and support each other" (NCNA, 11 February).

The NLHX sent several messuges of support to the government of North Korea, and observed a "month of solidarity with the Korean people" in June and July (Pathet Lao radio, 26 June). Messages of support and solidarity also were sent to Cuba (Pathet Lao News Agency, 4 January), and Mongolia (Pathet Lao radio, 11 November).

Next to the United States and South Vietnam, Thailand was the target of the strongest attacks by Laotian communist radio sources. The attacks varied between denouncing the Thai "reactionaries" (Pathet Lao radio, 31 August, 4 December), and praising "the Thai people's vigorous struggle" (Pathet Lao News Agency, 4 January; Pathet Lao radio, 4 June).

International Activities. In May an NLHX delegation, led by Prince Souphanouvong, paid a friendship visit to North Vietnam (Pathet Lao News Agency, 3 June). While this was taking place, a "heroes and model workers" delegation of the NLHX visited China (NCNA, 30 May). In mid-May General Chounlamany led a delegation of the Lao Committee for the Defense of World Peace to the World Peace Council congress in Budapest (Pathet Lao radio, 15 June). Shortly thereafter, a delegation of the Lao Patriotic Youth League attended the congress of the Socialist Working Youth League of [North] Korea and paid a visit to China en route home (NCNA, 15 July). In December a delegation of the Lao Patriotic Federation of Trade Unions attended the General Council meeting of the World Federation of Trade Unions, in Berlin, while another NLHX delegation was attending the World Conference on Medicine and the War in Indochina, in Paris.

Publications. NLHX directives and policy statements are disseminated by the Pathet Lao's clandestine radio station, believed to be in Sam Neua Province, and by the Pathet Lao News Agency (Khaosan Pathet Lao). The NLHX publishes two newspapers, *Kongthap Potpoi Passon* — the organ of the Pathet Lao — and *Lao Hak Xat*. The Laotian Information Service of the NLHX publishes *Laotian News*. The NLHX has an information bureau in Hanoi affiliated with the Vietnam Fatherland Front. North Vietnamese, Chinese, and Soviet media often carry NLHX statements.

The PNF. Founded in 1960, the Patriotic Neutralist Forces openly broke with the Laotian government in 1963 and allied themselves with the NLHX, which had withdrawn from the Tripartite National Union government that year. The NLHX has sought to present the PNF as the organization of "authentic neutralists" in Laos and thus to reduce Souvanna Phouma's neutralist following.

Leadership and Organization. The 2,000 to 3,000 PNF members are headed by Colonel Deuane Sounarath. The PNF appears, however, to be divided into two groups: one under Colonel Sounarath, commander in chief and also PNF supreme commander in the Plain of Jars; the other under General Khampheng Boupha, PNF supreme commander in northern Laos. At its First National Conference, in April 1969, the PNF set up the "Alliance Committee of the Laotian Patriotic Neutralist Forces," headed by Khamsouk Keola, to consolidate the PNF organization and take charge of short-term tasks.

Domestic Attitudes and Activities. Emphasis was placed during 1971 on the great unity between the NLHX and the PNF (Pathet Lao radio, 23 February), and several of the important statements by Laotian communists were joint statements of the two groups. A special "extraordinary meeting between the standing committees of the NLHX Central Committee and the PNF Alliance Committee" was held on 22 February, for the apparent purpose of denouncing the South Vietnamese drive into southern Laos (Pathet Lao radio, 23 February).

The PNF endorsed the various peace proposals of the NLHX:

> The peaceful settlement of the Laotian problem in accordance with the five-point political stance of the NLHS corresponds to the wishes of the nation and the interests of the people of all levels in Laos. The PNF wholeheartedly supports this stance. (*Ibid.*, 11 January.)

When Premier Souvanna Phouma rejected the Pathet Lao's 27 April two-point peace proposal, he was attacked by the PNF:

> Prince Souvanna Phouma's reply is merely an act which serves U.S. imperialism's designs of intensifying the war of agreession against Laos. It will endlessly prolong the bloodshed among the Lao people. The people are clearly aware of the unreasonable characteristics of Prince Souvanna Phouma's reply. The Patriotic Neutralist Forces Alliance Committee solemnly protests and condemns Prince Souvanna Phouma's attitude and his reply, which is lacking in good will, and demands that he ... sincerely accept the new reasonable NLHX peace proposals. (Pathet Lao radio, 15 June.)

The 22 June NLHS peace proposal also received the unqualified endorsement of the PNF (Patriotic Neutralist Forces radio, 10 August).

The general elections scheduled for 2 January 1972 were the subject of PNF condemnation on several occasions:

> On the order of the U.S. imperialists, the Vientiane puppet power-holders are preparing to hold a so-called parliamentary election on 2 January 1972. The election farce is another trick aimed at deceiving public opinion both at home and abroad into believing that its administrative system is "democratic." ... It will be held under the guns of the U.S. imperialists, and will be full of cheating and deception because the voters and candidates have been deprived of democratic rights and freedom....To conceal these tricks, the Vientiane puppet administration pretentiously invited the NLHX to participate in the election.... The PNF Alliance Committee strongly condemns and opposes the election ... and considers it illegal, undemocratic and irrelevant to the current realities in Laos (*Ibid.*, 30 November.)

International Views and Positions. The PNF has declared its intention to establish diplomatic relations with all countries of the world, regardless of their political ideologies, on a basis of mutual respect, and to welcome all aid without political ties as a contribution to the development of Laos. It has supported the Vietnamese and Cambodian "people's struggle against U.S. aggression" and their opposition to U.S. actions in Laos. In a lengthy article on "neo-colonialism," Alliance Committee Chairman Khamsouk Keola severely criticized the United States and referred to the Southeast Asian Treaty Organization as "a military clique whose duties are to launch aggression in Southeast Asian countries" (Patriotic Neutralist Forces radio, 16 August). On more than one occasion, the PNF denounced the "Thai reactionaries" for their involvement in Laos (*ibid*; Pathet Lao radio, 11 December).

Publications. PNF statements are broadcast by the clandestine PNF radio station, and frequently by the Pathet Lao News Agency and Pathet Lao radio station.

Robert F. Turner

Malaysia

The communist movement in Malaysia is divided into two virtually independent groups: the Communist Party of Malaya (CPM), which operates in West Malaysia and Singapore,[1] and the terrorist groups organized within the Sarawak Communist Organization (SCO) in East Malaysia. Both have a predominantly Chinese ethnic composition and maintain a pro-Chinese stance, which is reflected in their domestic activities.

The CPM originated in 1928 as the South Seas Communist Party, whose mission was to direct communist activities in most of Southeast Asia; it was composed exclusively of overseas Chinese, with headquarters in Singapore. On 28 April 1930 this organization was transformed into the Communist Party of Malaya and put under the direction of the Comintern's Far Eastern Bureau in Shanghai. By 1945 the CPM had attained a strong position through its anti-Japanese activities during World War II. In 1948, when the CPM initiated a campaign of armed struggle against British rule, the government outlawed the party and declared a state of emergency, which was not terminated until July 1960—three years after the independent Federation of Malaysia was established. As a result of government measures during this long period, the CPM was reduced to small, scattered groups on the Malay Peninsula and along the Thai-Malaysian border. The party has its headquarters in the border area, where it exercises varying degrees of territorial control.

The CPM is estimated to have between 1,700 and 2,500 members. Those in West Malaysia include 500 in urban centers, chiefly in the states of Penang, Johore, and Negri Sembilan, and 1,200 to 1,500 operating as insurgents along both sides of the 361-mile-long border with Thailand (*Washington Post*, 7 October 1971; *Christian Science Monitor*, 4 March). In East Malaysia, communist militants are estimated to number between 500 and 1,000 in Sarawak (*Washington Post*, 31 January; *New York Times*, 19 March), of whom 150 or so normally operate across the Indonesian border in West Kalimantan. The SCO is thought to have between "a few thousand" and 20,000 sympathizers (*New York Times*, 19 March). No communist activity has been reported in Sabah. In August 1970 Malaysia held its first census, which reported a population of 10,434,034. Of this total, 8,801,399 were in West Malaysia and 1,632,635 in East Malaysia (*Far Eastern Economic Review*, Hong Kong, 8 May 1971).

The CPM remains illegal. Besides conducting nationwide anti-communist campaigns, the government of Malaysia engages in coordinated and joint operations with the governments of Thailand and Indonesia against communist insurgents operating along border areas.

On 19 February 1971 the government ended a 21-month-old state of emergency—which had resulted from severe anti-Chinese rioting in which hundreds of people were killed on 13 May

---

[1]Singapore's communists nominally belong to the CPM, which regards Singapore as an integral part of Malaya (meaning all of the Malay Peninsula formerly part of the British Empire).

1969—but emphasized that "the country would continue to take firm and immediate action against subversive elements" (Kuala Lumpur radio, 22 February).

The CPM. Leadership and Organization. Little is known about the structure of the CPM, but what evidence there is suggests that it is organized along traditional communist lines. The party's secretary-general has since 1947 been Chin Peng, whose anti-Japanese exploits during World War II earned him the Order of the British Empire (rescinded in 1948). He joined the party at the age of eighteen years and at twenty-five led a successful purge and became secretary-general, arguing that the peaceful united-front policy was a failure and calling for armed struggle. As one of the senior guerrilla leaders in Southeast Asia, he has become something of a legend in Malaysia (*Christian Science Monitor*, 15 September 1971). The party chairman is Musa Ahmad; the third-ranking leader is Abdul Rashid Bin Maidin—now under detention in Perak. There are thought to be about ten Central Committee members and four Politburo members (including Chin Peng and Li On Tung). Chen Tien has been identified as chief of propaganda. Lam Fung Sing, Liew Yit Fun, Chiam Chung Him, Eu Chooi Yip, Lu Cheng, and Siew Chong are thought to be prominent CPM members residing in Communist China.

The military arm of the CPM is the Malayan National Liberation Army (MNLA)—usually referred to by the Malaysian government as the Communist Terrorist Organization (CTO)—which is currently composed of three regiments. The Eighth Regiment operates along the western section of the Thai-Malaysian border in the Sadao District, north of the state of Kedah. The Tenth Regiment —which unlike the others reportedly consists of mostly Malays rather than Chinese—operates on the eastern portion of the border in the Thai province of Weng, near the state of Kelantan. The Twelfth Regiment operates primarily in the mountainous central section of the border and reportedly is headquartered in Betong (Yala Province). During periods of intensive joint-operations by Thai-Malaysian forces, insurgents of the MNLA and their commander, Chin Peng, have been forced to move deeper into Thailand—a situation which has reportedly concerned the Communist Party of Thailand (see *Thailand*). According to a government white paper published on 2 October 1971, *The Resurgence of Armed Communism in West Malaysia*, a surrendered terrorist reported that during his training he was lectured on "military theories/tactics regarding the Vietnam War; Viet Cong tactics in shooting aircraft; methods of constructing tunnels; and Viet Cong anti-personnel devices." The paper makes it clear, however, that the CPM continues to draw its main inspiration from Mao Tse-tung's thought and its main support from China.

The CPM has in the past operated through two fronts—the Malayan National Liberation League (MNLL) and the Partai Persaudaraan Islam (Islamic Brotherhood Party; PPI)—and has extensively penetrated two left-wing legal political parties, the predominantly Chinese "Labor Party of Malaya" and the predominantly Malay "Socialist People's Party of Malaya" (Partai Sosialis Rakyat Malaya). According to the white paper cited above, however, a secret directive dated 1967 ordered the transfer of all the CPM's open united-front activities into clandestine preparations for armed struggle. By 1971 the fronts had virtually ceased to exist, and the two penetrated parties had dropped from some 300 branches in 1967 to only a handful. The CPM's youth organization is the Malayan Communist Youth League (MCYL), which provides the bulk of new party members and assists the party in communications, logistics, and intelligence work.

Domestic Attitudes and Activities. During 1971 the extremely heavy emphasis given to armed struggle by the CPM—a policy which it has publicly supported since September 1963—suggested the existence of serious disagreement within the party over the correct road to power. Beginning on 30 January with a broadcast over its clandestine radio station—the "Voice of the Malayan

Revolution'' (VMR)—commemorating the twenty-second anniversary of the MNLA, the party stressed that "historical experiences proved that whenever the road of using the countryside to surround the cities and seizing power by armed force was upheld, the revolution grew and advanced,'' while "if there was wavering over the road, the revolution suffered setbacks.'' This "precious experience'' was gained "at the cost of our blood, and all our comrades must always remember this.'' The broadcast concluded with an appeal for unity: "All commanders and fighters of the National Liberation Army must unite closely round the Central Committee of the Communist Party of Malaya [and] develop deeply the movement of studying and applying Mao Tse-tung Thought.'' On 28 April a broadcast to celebrate the forty-first anniversary of the founding of the CPM was devoted almost entirely to the theme armed struggle:

> From its long struggle ... the Malayan Communist Party has gained valuable experience, particularly that of surrounding the cities with the countryside and seizing political power with armed force. It has also learned that the revolution will meet with setbacks whenever we fail to apply this principle.... From our long struggle, we fully understand that to overthrow the bureaucratic state apparatus of the enemy's colonial rule, we must depend on our guns. We must not give up the use of guns and instead try to persuade our enemy to give more consideration to democracy in the hope of so-called reforms.

These broadcasts set a tone which was continued throughout 1971. The CPM used the occasions of the twenty-third anniversary of the start of the "anti-British war'' on 19 June, "Martyr's Day'' on 1 September, the twenty-second anniversary of the founding of the People's Republic of China on 1 October, and the thirtieth anniversary of the "war of national liberation against Japan'' on 8 December to give extensive attention to the correctness of the policy of "armed struggle.'' The last of these broadcasts asserted:

> Our party was unable to fully appreciate the necessity of the new democratic revolution of our country or to follow the path of encircling the cities from the countryside and seizing political power through force of arms. When the Japanese surrendered, because of setbacks ... our party was deceived by enemy secret agents who led the party into adopting the revisionist line, which resulted in burying the fruits of our success.

The broadcast concluded by calling on the people to rally around the party and uphold the "great red banner of the armed struggle.''

Government reports indicated a noticeable increase in insurgent activity—especially in the provinces of Kedah, Perlis, Perak, and Kelantan along the Thai-Malaysian border and in the western province of Penang, where the communist threat was officially termed "very real'' (*Straits Times*, Kuala Lumpur, 29 June). The first serious incident of 1971 occurred in early March, when communist terrorists blew up a railway bridge on the line from Thailand to Butterworth, forty-five miles south of the border on the west coast of Malaysia. On 23 April, to mark the anniversary of the CPM, terrorists bombed a government telecommunications building on the island of Penang, while CPM flags and posters were displayed in various areas of the country. An explosive charge was set to destroy another railway bridge near Butterworth, but was discovered and disarmed. In mid-June a terrorist camp was discovered in the jungle near Chemor (Perak Province), only nine miles from Ipoh and seventy miles south of the main communist bases on the Thai-Malaysian border. The camp, which could accommodate perhaps fifty persons, had a large quantity of dynamite and other explosives, Mao Tse-tung books, and a large drawing of Mao. The seriousness of the situation in Perak was illustrated on 16 June, when a curfew was imposed and tin mining in the northern part of the province ceased "because of security reasons'' (*Far Eastern Economic Review*, 3 July). According to government figures released in October, nine members of the Malaysian security forces and up to thirty communist terrorists had been killed along the Thai-Malaysian border in the previous eighteen months (*Far Eastern Economic Review*, 23 October). Communist claims for the twelve months of 1971 alone were considerably higher: "According to preliminary statistics, our army wiped out over 300 men of the Malayan and Thai reactionary forces; wiped out over 30 secret agents and running dogs; damaged two fighter-bombers; destroyed three military vehicles, and captured a large quantity of weapons, ammunition, and food supplies" (VMR, 1 January 1972).

A major hope for communist success in Malaysia has been the tense racial situation between the Malays and the generally more affluent Chinese. The government has concluded that a major cause of the 1969 race riots was this economic imbalance, which it is trying to overcome (*Washington Post*, 7 October 1971). The communists are undoubtedly hoping that this policy will increase their successes in recruitment among the Chinese, although because of the booming economy "most Malaysian Chinese [are] doing well enough economically to be uninterested in becoming communist guerrilla recruits" (*ibid.*, 3 January 1972). Past recruiting successes among the Chinese may explain the fact that the communist probes southward from the Thai-Malaysian border have kept to the western, more Chinese, part of the peninsula (*The Economist*, London, 10 July 1971). Thus it was not surprising that the CPM was concerned when in February the Malaysian Chinese Association (MCU) attempted to establish a Chinese unity movement to organize the 37 per cent of the Malaysian people who belong to the Chinese community. The MCU's proposed measures for reducing racial hostility between Chinese and Malays later drew strong criticism from the CPM:

> In order to maintain its fascist rule, the [Prime Minister Tun] Razak clique finds it necessary to … use Chinese bourgeoisie as its accomplices…. The profit-grabbing chieftans of the Malaysian Chinese Association have fully satisfied these demands of the Razak clique…. They advocate that it is necessary to respect unconditionally all privileges of the Malay bureaucrat-capitalist class and that no attempt should be made to waste efforts winning the right of equality of all nationalities. [Their] proposals can by no means serve the purpose of reviving the Malaysian Chinese Association, which is already a political corpse. On the contrary, the Chinese at all strata have seen more clearly from this [MCU] congress the reactionary servile nature of the Chinese bourgeoisie. (VMR, 11 September.)

Similarly, the Malaysian Indian Congress was attacked as "a reactionary political party which represents the interests of the Indian bourgeoisie and the Indian moneylenders" (*ibid.*, 4 August). The communists did not ignore the Malay population, and reportedly "made some propaganda headway among Malay rural dwellers by winning over aggrieved Muslims in Thailand's southern provinces and using them to work among their fellow Muslims in the Malaysian State of Kelantan" (*Christian Science Monitor*, 8 July). Evidence of success in recruiting Muslim Malay support was provided during 1971 on several occasions when Malaysian police and army elements captured jungle camps with two kitchens—one for Chinese cuisine, utilizing pork, and the other for Malays adhering to Muslim dietary laws (*Guardian*, London, 8 September). The CPM has attempted to offset Malay fears that communism is incompatable with religion by asserting that "religion need not prevent people from being Communists," and saying that communist supporters do not necessarily have to subscribe to communist ideology (*Straits Times*, 3 July).

International Views and Positions. The CPM ardently supports the strategy and policies of the Chinese Communist Party. In a greeting to the Chinese party on the fiftieth anniversary of its founding, the CPM stated:

> Powerful socialist China now has become the hope of mankind for emancipation and the impregnable base area for the world revolution. [We] extend our heartfelt thanks to Chairman Mao, the Chinese Communist Party, and the Chinese people for their enormous aid and support to the people of our country in carrying out our revolutionary struggle. (VMR, 30 June).

China and Malaysia exchanged unofficial trade delegations during 1971 for the first time, the Malaysian trade delegation was informed that it was the policy of China to "maintain a policy of non-interference and mutual respect for territorial sovereignty and integrity" (*Straits Times*, 19 May), and Peking radio on occasion, departing from usual Chinese and CPM practice, referred to Malaysia by its proper name rather than as "Malaya." Nevertheless there was little to suggest that Peking had given up its support of the CPM. The VMR's regular broadcast appeals for armed struggle were frequently publicized by Chinese media.

The CPM has in recent years followed the Chinese line in criticism of the Soviet Union. Because of this, it may be significant that the aforementioned 30 January and 28 April anniversary broadcasts omitted the usual attack on "Soviet revisionism." These omissions, coupled with the apparent indications of a split within the CPM (see above), led some observers to infer that perhaps one faction was "pro-Soviet." Others, however, interpreted the omission as indicating that the "Soviet position" was not a factor in the dispute. In other broadcasts the Soviet Union was referred to as the "most heinous enemy of the workers" and a "wolf in sheep's clothing," and in June the CPM asserted:

> The Communist Party of China [was] the first to perceive the perniciousness of Khrushchovian revisionism to the world revolution and [has] waged an uncompromising and principled struggle against modern revisionism with the Soviet revisionist renegade clique as the center. The great polemics carried out by the Communist Party of China against Khrushchovian revisionism have safeguarded the purity of Marxism-Leninism and created conditions for the victorious development of the international communist movement ideologically, theoretically and politically. (Quoted in *Peking Review*, 23 July, p. 18.)

The CPM predictably took the Chinese position when the Soviet Union proposed a five-nation nuclear power conference. The Chinese rejection was termed a "just and solemn statement" which had "once again exposed the ugly faces of the two superpowers, U.S. imperialism and Soviet revisionist social-imperialism." According to the CPM, "the development of nuclear weapons by China has been enthusiastically acclaimed and resolutely supported by the people of various countries." (VMR, 14 August.)

CPM statements supported the various communist movements in other Southeast Asian countries (e.g., VMR, 8 September), and branded the proposal by Prime Minister Tun Razak for the neutralization of all of Southeast Asia under the guarantee of the United States, the Soviet Union, and China as a "criminal plan" aimed at protecting "colonialist rule."

Publications. The CPM has no regular official publication. Its statements are circulated through numerous pamphlets and by the Chinese media, and since 15 November 1969 through the "Voice of the Malayan Revolution" (*Suara Revolusi*), a clandestine radio station based in South China. The VMR transmits for approximately 40 hours per week in Chinese, Malay, and Tamil, to West Malaysia and Singapore. The *Malayan Monitor and General News* (founded 1947), is a mimeographed monthly issued in London. Although not an official CPM publication, it prints CPM policy statements. Choong Wai Koh of West Malaysia is the news editor.

*   *   *

The SCO. The communist movement in East Malaysia is concentrated in Sarawak. All clandestine groups in the state[2] are organized within the multi-front Sarawak Communist Organization, which

---

[2] The SCO (formerly known as the Clandestine Communist Organization) includes the Sarawak Liberation League, the Sarawak Advanced Youth Association, the Sarawak Farmers' Association, and the North Kalimantan National Liberation League. All these groups are illegal.

works for the establishment of a communist state in Sarawak, Sabah, and Brunei and is believed to be directed by the somewhat nebulous Borneo Communist Party. Although the SCO operates along the border between Sarawak and Kalimantan (the Indonesian part of the island of Borneo), it has no known official ties with either the CPM or the Communist Party of Indonesia. Most of the reported 500 to 1,000 SCO insurgents are on the Sarawak side of the border.

The SCO has been described by the government as "100 per cent Chinese." It recruits especially among disenchanted urban youths. Malays represent only 17 per cent of the population of Sarawak, and the Chinese more than 30 per cent. The fact that they are the largest racial group probably accounts for a certain sympathy among the Chinese toward communist "anti-Malaysia" campaigns.

Leadership and Organization. Below the SCO's Central Committee are its area and town committees, branches, and cells. According to government sources, the Central Committee operates through four work departments: Labor Movement, Peasantry, Students, and Political Party. Although the SCO has used the Sarawak United Peoples Party (SUPP)—a left-wing but non-communist legal political party—as a front, the 7 July 1970 decision of the moderate leadership of the SUPP to join in a coalition government resulted in a reduction in communist influence within the party. The SUPP polled the largest number of votes (28.6 per cent) in the 1970 parliamentary election.

The military arms of the SCO, referred to collectively in Chinese reports as the Sarawak People's Armed Forces, are said to be (1) the Sarawak People's Guerrilla Army (Pertahanan—or Pasokan—Gerilja Rakjat Sarawak; PGRS), operating in the west under a leader known as Jahaj, and (2) the North Kalimantan People's Armed Force (Pakosan Ra'ayat Kalimantan Utara; Paraku) in the east under the leadership of Peking-trained Wong Kee Chok (also known as Wong Ki-chok, Wong Khi Chock, or "Sam"). According to Indonesian intelligence sources, the only remaining member of the Central Committee of the Communist Party of Indonesia, M. A. Sofian, crossed the border into Sarawak in July 1971 and took control of the PGRS-Paraku ideological bureau (*Guardian*, 21 August). Wong Kee Chok was reported in 1971 to be the supreme commander of all communist military forces in East Malaysia (*ibid.*) and to have been formerly "a Chinese diplomat at the Embassy in Jakarta before he turned guerrilla" (*New York Times*, 15 August). In clashes with SCO insurgents during 1971, government forces seized pictures of both Mao Tse-tung and Wong Kee Chok (Associated Press dispatch, 25 March).

In March 1970 the Communist Party of North Kalimantan (CPNK), announced its formation. So far, the CPNK apparently operates only in Sarawak. Its relationship to the SCO is not clear, but it may have replaced the Sarawak Liberation League, which had been the principal body within the SCP (see footnote 2). The only announced leader is Wong Kee Chok, identified as "Secretary, (Eastern) Bureau of the Central Committee of the CPNK." The CPNK is thought to maintain contact with the Chinese Communist Party through a "representative," named Wen Ming Chuan, who apparently has lived in Peking for several years and has been identified by the New China News Agency (9 August 1966) as "the North Kalimantan writer."

Domestic Attitudes and Activities. Like the CPM in West Malaysia, the SCO accepts the Maoist doctrine of armed struggle. Whereas in years past the insurgents relied primarily on propaganda and tried to avoid direct clashes with government forces, a party directive in January 1971 "led to the blowing up of bridges, attacks on isolated police posts and even the ambushing of army patrols" (*Washington Post*, 31 January). One of the most serious encounters in recent years occurred on 21 January, when a patrol of crack Malaysian rangers was hit by a 21-man communist river ambush in the Sungei (Patebah) area of Sarawak. Six rangers were killed, two were wounded, one was reported missing, and two communists were killed (Kuala Lumpur radio, 21 January; *Christian Science Monitor*, 4 March). During May, Malaysian forces killed 14 communists within four days and a total of 19 during the month; eleven more were captured, and six surrendered during May (Kuala Lumpur radio, 3 June). By June a total of 80 terrorists reportedly had been killed or captured, or had surrendered to government forces (*Straits Times*, 15 June). On 8 March security forces captured a large communist terrorist camp in the Sungai Buda Pegong area; the camp included an armory, an arms dump, a training center, and a food storage facility (*ibid.*, 11 March).

Malaysian problems with communist guerrillas in Sarawak were increased by an effective anti-communist campaign south of the border in Borneo. In an attempt to separate the "water from the fish," the Indonesian army commander of West Kalimantan Province moved to evacuate 40,000 Chinese from the border area to southern districts (*Guardian*, 21 August). The predominantly Chinese SCO guerrillas had long depended on the large Chinese population in the border area for intelligence, supplies, and shelter. While evacuating the Chinese from the troubled area, giving them time to sell their farms or businesses (*New York Times*, 19 March), the Indonesians had some success in enlisting local Dyak tribesmen into civil defense units to fight the insurgents. This forced the communists to retreat into Sarawak, where insurgency activities increased.

International Views and Activities. The communist movement in Sarawak is basically pro-Chinese and is believed to receive not only propaganda but also material assistance from China. Despite the exchange of unofficial trade missions with Malaysia during 1971, China continued to voice support for the communists in both East and West Malaysia. For example, on 19 May the New China News Agency claimed that the "People's Revolutionary Armed Forces of North Kalimantan" had become "stronger in the course of fighting in the past year." They had "repeatedly smashed the military 'encirclement and repression' operations" launched by the Malaysian and Indonesian "reactionaries." In Sarawak, they had "extended the guerrilla areas and promoted the widespread development of the North Kalimantan people's revolutionary movement."

On 14 April the official Indonesian news agency (Antara) quoted "competent sources" as reporting that a "North Vietnamese ship had entered Indonesian territorial waters" in March with a suspected cargo of weapons—a report which was immediately denied by the North Vietnamese. Later a "foreign vessel which had tried to smuggle weapons into West Kalimantan to help the communist movement there" was said to have been sunk (Antara, 5 June). In July a Djakarta weekly, *Chas*, said that for some time North Vietnamese ships disguised as merchant vessels had shadowed the West Kalimantan coast, but that "thanks to the vigilance of the coast guard and civil defense their attempts to land rubber boats were foiled" (quoted by Djakarta radio, 8 July). Shortly thereafter the Indonesian foreign minister accused China of sending Chinese agents into Indonesia through Sarawak (Antara, 17 and 26 July). Incidents such as these led the *Guardian* (21 August) to note:

> One of the biggest problems faced by the security forces on both sides of the border at the moment is the clandestine inflow of weapons and equipment. During the last few months unidentified ships have landed [their] cargoes on the Kalimantan and Sarawak coasts.

Publications. Sarawak communist groups have at least two publications, *Liberation News*, and *News Bulletin*. Other communist or communist-oriented newspapers known to circulate in Sarawak include the *Workers' and Farmers' News*, *National Independence*, and *Masses News*.

Robert F. Turner

Mongolia

The Mongolian People's Party was founded in 1921 as a fusion between two revolutionary groups, led by Damdiny Sukhe-Bator and Horloogiyn Choybalsan. Its First Congress was held in March of that year under Soviet Army protection. Since the Third Congress (1924), it has been known as the Mongolian People's Revolutionary Party (Mongol Ardyn Huuvisgalt Nam; MPRP). The MPRP exercises a monopoly of power in the Mongolian People's Republic (MPR). At its Sixteenth Congress, in June 1971, it claimed a membership of 58,048 (a growth of 9,478 since the Fifteenth Congress, in 1966), or slightly more than 4 per cent of the total population, estimated at 1,300,000 in 1970.

Organization and Leadership. The MPRP is organized approximately along the same lines as the Communist Party of the Soviet Union (CPSU). In contrast, however, with the separation between the highest party and state offices in the U.S.S.R., the posts of first secretary and premier are held by one person, Yumzhagiin Tsedenbal. The congress is in theory the party's supreme body, but more important are its Central Committee (85 full and 55 candidate members), the Politburo (7 full and 2 candidate members), and the Secretariat (5 members). The party dominates the government. The premier and seven deputies in the Council of Ministers belong to the party's Central Committee and four of these men are also members of the Politburo.

In 1971, the Sixteenth Congress reelected the same top party leadership that the 1966 congress had installed. The Secretariat is composed of Nyamyn Jagvaral, Demchigiyn Molomjamts, Badamyn Lhamsuren, Tsaganlamyn Dugersuren, and the first secretary, Tsedenbal. Full members of the Politburo are Tsedenbal, Jagvaral, Dugersuren, Molomjamts, Damdinjavyn Maydar, Sonomyn Lubsan, and Jamsrangiyn Sambuu; candidate members are Namsrayn Lubsanrabdan (also chairman of the Control Commission) and Lhamsuren.

Between the two congresses, the Central Committee was increased from 75 to 85 full members and from 51 to 55 candidate members. During this time the party grew by 9,478 members (12,366 persons joined and 2,888 for one reason or another left). In the second half of 1970 all party levels were affected by an exchange of membership cards, the first since 1947. Tsedenbal, in his report to the 1971 congress, emphasized that the intent had not been to purge, but added: "It helped, however, to conduct on a Party-wide scale a check-up and a principled appraisal of the political and business-like qualities of Communists, reveal shortcomings in some Party organizations with respect to the admission and education of new members, enhance the vanguard role of Communists, rid our ranks of unworthy individuals, and improve and streamline party documentation and records" (*IB*, no. 14-15, 1971).

Tsedenbal reported to the congress that 30.0 per cent of the party members were workers, 20.4 per cent were from farming cooperatives, and 49.6 per cent were office clerks and intellectuals. This indicated an increase in workers since 1970, when Tsedenbal stated that 26 per cent were workers and 24 per cent were farmers. The number of women in the party increased from 19.4 per cent in 1966 to 21.6 per cent in 1971. Of the 12,366 persons admitted to the party since the previous congress, some 63 per cent were between twenty and thirty years of age. Of the 784 delegates to the 1971 congress, about 60 per cent had a higher, incomplete higher, or specialized secondary education. In ages, 5.1 per cent were under thirty years and 23.3 per cent were past fifty. There were 619 who had joined the party since 1945, and 644 were attending a congress the first time. Ethnically, the delegates included 610 Khalkhas, 39 Kazakhs, and 30 Buryats; the remaining 105 were of other nationalities.

Auxiliary party organizations include the Mongolian Revolutionary Youth League (MRYL), with some 80,000 members. Its secretary is Choyjiljavyn Purevjav. Children are enrolled in the Young Pioneers, which has a membership of about 90,000. Both are modeled after their counterparts in the Soviet Union. Also important is the Central Council of Trade Unions (CCTU), whose chairman is Dovchingiyn Yadamsuren. The CCTU claimed during 1969-70 to have 170,000 members, drawn from among agricultural, industrial, trade and transport, construction, and cultural-education workers.

Domestic Attitudes and Activities. The major domestic concern of the MPRP is the progress of Mongolia's predominantly pastoral economy. At the beginning of the fifth five-year economic plan (1971-75), the country was still recuperating from a series of natural calamities. In the devastating 1967/68 winter large numbers of livestock perished and other sectors of farming suffered, as did Mongolia's industries, which are based on local agricultural raw materials.

The goal of creating by 1970 an "industrial-agrarian" economy, in which industry would provide more than half of the gross national product, was postponed in 1966 until "about the end of the 1970's." Tsedenbal in his 1971 congress speech identified this objective as the "initial step" toward the establishment of a material and techinical basis for socialism, but stated only that it would be accomplished in the "near future." Delay in industrial development arose in part from the continued emphasis on the agrarian sector, evident in the allocations of the new five-year plan. Agriculture was to receive 35 per cent of the total capital investment during 1971-75, as opposed to 24 per cent in 1966-70 plan. Industry was allocated 22 per cent, a decline of 2 to 3 per cent from the previous plan, but nevertheless was to increase its contribution to the GNP from the current 34 per cent to 40 per cent by the end of 1975.

International Views and Positions. *Relations with the Soviet Union.* Military and economic as-sistance from the U.S.S.R. has been extensive. Defense against China is augmented by the presence of Soviet troops and, reportedly, tank and antiaircraft missile units and possibly IRBM's. The U.S.S.R. underwrites about 45 per cent of Mongolia's capital investment (Radio "Peace and Progress," Moscow, 6 June 1971). It reportedly accounts for more than nine-tenths of the country's foreign trade, in which imports are between 70 and 80 per cent higher than exports (*Far Eastern Economic Review*, Hong Kong, 17 April).

Much of the Soviet Union's interest in assisting Mongolia—apart from incentives offered by the latter's strategic location and ethnic ties across the Chinese border—centers on building a model for the "non-capitalist path of development." This concept is a relatively recent Soviet elaboration of an alleged idea of Lenin. It holds that an underdeveloped "feudal" country, with the assistance of communist-governed states, can bypass the capitalist stage of development and advance directly from feudalism to socialism within decades, rather than waiting centuries. It is designed for Asia, Africa, and Latin America. The phrase "non-capitalist path" has been used by the U.S.S.R. to describe the economic development of India. Indicating the importance attached to the concept, an editorial in *Unen* (8 May), commenting on the MPRP Central Committee theses for the party congress, declared:

> The main result of the past 50 years has been that in a historically short period of time Mongolia has been able to overcome many centuries of economic and cultural backwardness and to accomplish the transition from feudalism to socialism, bypassing the capitalist stage of development.

When Soviet Premier Kosygin visited Ulan Bator in July to attend the celebrations commemorating the fiftieth anniversary of the MPR, he spoke of the "non-capitalist path" and stressed the importance of Mongolia's role as a model. Many nations of Asia and Africa, he said, were at the same stage of development as Mongolia had been in 1921, and added:

> The vitality of the non-capitalist path to development is confirmed by the Mongolian people's experience, and this is also its outstanding contribution to the history of all mankind.... It is a convincing indication of the fact that the successful development of liberated countries becomes possible thanks to the close alliance with the socialist countries. (Domestic radio broadcast, Moscow, 10 July).

This role, and other ties of mutual interest, including common enemies, have inspired frequent and strong declarations of friendship between the two countries at the expense of relations with China. An occasion for such declarations was provided by the twenty-fifth anniversary of their treaty of the friendship and mutual assistance. Mongolia's foreign minister, Lodongiyn Rinchin, stated in a Soviet publication (*New Times*, Moscow, 20 January): "The Mongolian people regard the firm friendship with the Soviet people, the fraternal unity and the solid internationalist ties between the Mongolian People's Revolutionary Party and the Communist Party of the Soviet Union as the greatest gain of the Mongolian People's Revolution." MPRP secretary Tsaganlamyn Dugersuren accompanied Tsedenbal to the Twenty-fourth Congress of the CPSU in April and stated (*ibid.*, 14 April), presumably with China in mind: "We are determined to resist any attempt from whatever quarter to undermine [Soviet-Mongolian] friendship." Although Mongolia is active in the Council for Mutual Economic Assistance, its considerable dependence on the Soviet Union in foreign trade seems to have prompted efforts to justify their situation. A Soviet broadcast in Mandarin to China asserted:

> The fraternal friendship and cooperation between the Soviet and Mongolian peoples thoroughly repudiates the lies fabricated by the Chinese propaganda machinery about Soviet relations with other socialist countries being unequal. The example of Soviet-Mongolian relations also demonstrates the extent of the falsity of the Peking propaganda machinery's allegation that the Soviet Union is obstructing the industrial development of the MPR and other socialist countries. (Radio "Peace and Progress," 6 June.)

Relations with China. Sino-Mongolian polemics reached in intense level during the Cultural Revolution but had died down considerably by 1971, although strong undercurrents of mutual distrust continued. At the Sixteenth Congress of the MPRP, differences in attitude concerning China were apparent in the speeches by CPSU Politburo delegate Andrei Kirilenko and by Tsedenbal. While Kirilenko confined his remarks to describing Soviet efforts to bring China back into the "world communist movement," Tsedenbal leveled sharp criticisms:

> Our party ... is waging a principled struggle against the anti-Marxist political line of the Chinese leaders. By their splitting actions the leaders of China are trying to divide the socialist countries, undermine and split the ranks of the Communist movement, disarm the working class and the working people of different countries in the face of rabid attacks launched by imperialist reactionaries. The course of the Chinese leaders, who have assumed bellicose nationalism and anti-Sovietism as their weapon, has resulted in China's breakaway from the socialist countries, in armed provocations against the USSR, country of Lenin. This policy radically contradicts the interests of the revolutionary

struggle of the peoples, including the vital interests of the Chinese peoples themselves. (*IB*, no. 14-15, 1971.)

Although Kirilenko's speech was more conciliatory, this section of Tsedenbal's speech constituted almost the whole of a Chinese-language broadcast on the congress by Moscow radio (8 June).

Despite occasional harsh statements, tensions between the two countries have eased. In June, a protocal on the mutual supply of goods was signed at Ulan Bator. Diplomatic relations were reinstated at the ambassadorial level when Hsu Wen-i presented his credentials in Ulan Bator on 25 August. (A Chinese ambassador had arrived in Moscow nine months earlier to fill a vacant position.)

Publications. The MPRP daily newspaper *Unen* (Truth) is edited by Tsendijn Namsray and has a circulation of about 82,000. A monthly, *Namyn Amdral* (Party Life), is also edited by Namsray. Other newspapers include *Zaluchuudyn Unen* (Young People's Truth), the MRYL organ, which has 144 issues each year (circulation 60,000); *Khudulmur* (Labor), the CCTU organ, with 156 issues per year; and *Ulan Od* (Red Star), the army organ, appearing twice a week, edited by Colonel J. Yadma. Montsame (Mongol tsahilgaan medeeniy agentlag; Mongolian Telegraph Agency) is the official MPR news agency.

Eric Stromquist

Nepal

The Communist Party of Nepal (CPN) was founded during September 1949 in West Bengal, India, by a small number of Nepalese members of the Indian Communist Party. In 1952 the CPN was banned. In 1955 the party softened its politically unrewarding anti-monarchial policy and the following year, in exchange for its temporary acceptance of constitutional monarchy, the ban was lifted. In 1960 King Mahendra proscribed all political parties, dissolved the short-lived Parliament, and assumed all governmental powers. Though the ban on political parties continues, limited legislative powers are held by a panchayat (assembly) system, established in 1962, that extends from the village level to the national level and in which a few CPN members (technically, former members) participate.

The CPN Central Committee's decision in 1955 to drop its strongly anti-monarchial stance split the party between the "moderate" supporters of the new line under the general secretary, Keshar Jang Rayamajhi, and dissident "extremists," led by Pushpa Lal Shrestha. In 1962, following a number of crises within the party during which the leadership of the Pushpa Lal group moved to India, each group "expelled" the other's leaders. The Sino-Indian conflict of October 1962 contributed to a split among the extremists: Pushpa Lal's group, though often labeled "Maoist," adopted an attitude critical of China, while a minority faction led by Tulsi Lal Amatya expressed support. Disagreements over policy led to further minor divisions within the party.

Though it is more accurate to regard Nepali communists simply as moderates or extremists, the former are often designated "pro-Soviet" and the latter "pro-Chinese." The moderates, most of whom remain in Nepal, advocate a temporary accommodation with the existing political system in order to improve the communist position. The extremists, while agitating against the partyless panchayat system, contend also that only by working toward a revolutionary overthrow of the king can they adhere to the true principles of communism.

Before the 1960 ban on parties, the CPN claimed to have 6,000 full members and 2,000 cadets or candidates (*Samiksha*, 11 June 1963). Current estimates vary widely. A U.S. government source (*World Strength of the Communist Party Organizations*, Washington, D.C., 1971) puts the total membership at 9,000 and adds that the party's own claim is twice this figure. Other estimates are in the range of 1,000 to 2,000 members. In any case, the number of those active in party work is small. The relative strength of the factions cannot be ascertained accurately, but it is believed that the extremists are the more numerous. The population of Nepal is 11,100,000 (estimated 1971).

Despite the ban on political parties, the moderate faction of the CPN has been able to function more or less openly. Even the extremists have benefited from King Mahendra's efforts to achieve a balance between the CPN and the other major party (also, of course, banned), the Nepali Congress Party, a faction of which has been more outspoken than the CPN extremists in calling for an end to the panchayat system. How many of the 125 deputies in the National Panchayat are CPN members is unknown, but it is estimated that 10 to 15 per cent are sympathizers (*World Strength of the Communist Party Organizations*, 1971).

Leadership and Organization. Little is known of the leadership of the moderate CPN faction. A report on its "Third Congress" (see *YICA*, 1969, p. 614) gave no information other than to state that a Central Committee of 15 full and 7 alternate members had been elected. Rayamajhi is known to be the secretary-general; another leader, and member of the Politburo of the Central Committee, is Kamar Shah. Though officially disbanded, the faction's organizational structure includes, in addition to the aforementioned central bodies, regional committees and local cells.

Similarly, little is known of the leadership of the two extremist factions, except that Pushpa Lal is the leader of one faction and Tulsi Lal of the other. Tulsi Lal was elected general secretary, along with a nine-member Politburo, at his faction's "Third Congress" in 1962 (see *YICA*, 1971, p. 643).

Other prominent members (or "former members") of the CPN representing various shades of the party's political spectrum, and who may or may not be associated with the three leaderships mentioned above, are: Shailendra Kumar Upadhyaya, a moderate who in April 1971 lost his year-old position as head of the Home Ministry; D. P. Adhikari, reportedly back from residence in India; Man Mohan Adhikari (one of the most popular communist leaders) and Shambu Ram Shrestha, both of whom upon their release in 1969 after lengthy imprisonments expressed pro-Chinese sentiments.

Domestic Attitudes and Activities. Because of the moderate faction's general support of the monarchy and the panchayat system, recent communist-related activities in Nepal have mainly involved the extremists, who are referred to as "Maoists" in the Nepali press. This is particularly true among the students, who constitute the most active political element in the country. Campaigning for annual student government elections is carried out more along political than educational lines, in contrast to the partyless panchayat system, where political issues are relatively more subdued. While party politics are technically not permitted, the student population has divided itself into four major political organizations that in many respects perform the functions of parties. Pro-Chinese students, who have formed the All Nepal Free Student Union (ANFSU), vastly outnumber pro-Soviet students, who are represented by the minor Nepal National Federation of Students (NNFS). The pro-Chinese students' main rivals are those aligned with the Nepali Congress Party, who in 1970 formed the Nepal Students' Union (NSU). The fourth organization, and the only one officially registered, is the pro-government Nationalist Independent Student Union (NISU).

In efforts to gain control of the Tribhuvan University Students' Union (the student government of Nepal's only university), the ANFSU-backed slate of "progressive" candidates has in recent years waged a seesaw battle against the pro-Nepali Congress students, who have backed the "democrat" slate. In 1971, before the 6 August elections to the student leadership at Tribhuvan, ANFSU students divided into two factions: the "organizational" faction, whose campaign concentrated its attacks on the United States, the Soviet Union, and India, and on the democrats and the Congress Party; and the "revolutionary" faction, which focused on domestic problems and the overthrow of the monarchy as a prerequisite to "class struggle," avoiding strong statements against the democrats. Each of the two factions put up separate slates of candidates, which weakened the ANSFU position against the NSU-backed democrats. Thus, the democrats claimed a victory with an unusually wide margin of 113 votes (there were 552 valid ballots), winning all five key positions, a gain from the previous year when they had won only one such position. The NSU, whose slate of democrats won 49 per cent of the votes, claimed that even if the ANFSU had presented a unified slate it would still have been defeated by a margin of 13 votes. (The pro-Soviet NNFS did not present a slate; the minor pro-government NISU presented a slate for the first time, but lost.) (*IIEE Bulletin*, organ of the Institut International d'Etudes sur l'Education, Brussels, 31 August.)

Despite their losses at Tribhuvan University, pro-Chinese students won in a number of elections at colleges in Nepal, where violent clashes between them and other student groups were reported throughout the year. Many schools in the Koshi and Mechi zones in eastern Nepal were said to be dominated by "Maoist" elements.

Mohan Bikran Singh, a former CPN leader who was imprisoned in the early 1960s, was released in April 1971. He promptly expressed pro-Chinese sympathies and leveled attacks against the Congress Party. Condemning the governments of the United States, South Vietnam, South Korea, and India, he told a rally of students on 15 May: "Gone are the days when it was widely believed that one becomes a democrat the moment one expresses faith in parliamentary democracy." A similar position was taken at the rally by former CPN member Shambu Ram Shrestha. (*Asiali Awaj*, Kathmandu, 19 May.)

Nepali Congress Party members charge that the government has permitted communists to entrench themselves in important positions where they take advantage of the situation by allowing subversive communist activities to go unchecked. The communists gain this comparative advantage, they say, by raising the bugbear of the threat posed by India and by the Congress Party (a large faction of which does, indeed, advocate armed rebellion along nationalistic lines. (E.g., *Arati*, Kathmandu, 19 February, and *Dainik Nepal*, Kathmandu, 27 July.)

Throughout the year there were reports that subversive elements, usually identified as "Maoists," were organizing in Nepal, particularly near the Indian border in the southeast. Some of these, presumably supporters of Pushpa Lal and Tulsi Lal, were said to have cooperated with outlawed pro-Chinese "Naxalites" from India (see *India*) who had sought refuge in Nepal. Together they organized disturbances in five districts: Jhapa, Dharan, Dhankuta, Ilan, and Tehrathum. Journals warned the Nepal government that if no action were taken against these activities, a situation might develop in which a rebel group commanded large areas of the country, as had happened in Ceylon (see *Ceylon*). In the eastern areas of the Koshi zone, according to the pro-Soviet *Samiksha* (10 September), the spirit of the pro-Chinese movement had been "spontaneous but negative." The movement was said to be divided into a number of groups, including Naxalites and "Che Guevarists," who looked upon one another with distrust, but were "united in opposing the banned Nepali Congress, in securing support from the government, and in singing the praises of Mao Tse-tung."

On 30 April-1 May a "revolutionary congress," attended by some 1,500 Indian and Nepalese "Maoists" and "Chinese friends," including more than 500 Indian Naxalites who crossed the border to take part, was reported to have been held in Mari, a village near Janakpur, close to the border with the Indian state of Bihar. The meeting was said to have passed a resolution calling for the execution of big landowners, moneylenders, and pawnbrokers. (*Motherland*, Kathmandu, 5 May; *Naya Sandesh*, Kathmandu, 7 and 14 May.)

International Views and Positions. The international issues which receive attention from Nepal's political forces are mainly concerned with the country's relations with its two giant neighbors, India and China. At the end of 1970 a ten-year trade and transit treaty with India expired and negotiations to reach a new agreement became stalemated. Because 90 per cent of Napal's foreign trade is with India and much of the rest depends on land transit routes through India, in 1971 the issue led to the most heated debate of the year, evoking bitter criticism of India from most quarters in Nepal even after the conclusion of a new treaty in August. *Samiksha* (especially, 8 and 15 January) cautioned against aggravating the tense relations with India by making retaliatory gestures such as a boycott of Indian goods.

The CPN extremists were at least partly critical of India. Mohan Bikran Singh stated after his release from prison: "Friendship with India is of importance for this nation. However, our friendship with India does not mean that we have friendship with India's monopoly capital and India's reactionaries who are interested only in imposing their colonial policies in the name of friendship.... Struggle against them is therefore inevitable." He criticized Soviet policy toward Nepal as one of either directly supporting or remaining neutral to the interference of Indian "monopolists" in Nepal. (*Asiali Awaj*, 19 May.)

China, on the other hand, was applauded by Mohan Bikran Singh for its support of "national liberation movements" throughout the world and of Nepal's efforts to check the "reactionary policy being pursued by Indian monopolists and American imperialists." "It is therefore necessary," he said, "that we should maintain a friendly attitude towards the People's Republic of China." (*Ibid.*) The attitude of *Samiksha* toward China was critical. Even in its statement welcoming China's entry into the United Nations (1 November), the pro-Soviet paper noted a similarity in approach and behavior on the part of China and the United States (which it said had refrained from obstructing China's entry into the U.N.) toward the "socialist camp" and "national liberation movements," and toward newly emerging countries. Both were identified as "expansionist nations."

Developments in East Pakistan were closely watched during the year. Shambu Ram Shrestha, who supports China, acknowledged that it was natural for the people of East Pakistan, who had lived under a military government since the creation of the country, to launch a "struggle for democracy," but he condemned "imperialists" who had tried to exploit the people's discontent with the objective of bringing about the dismemberment of the country (*Asiali Awaj*, 19 May). *Samiksha* (21 December) applauded the victory of the East Pakistan secessionists and criticized China and the United States for being interested only in maligning India while remaining indifferent to "tyranny being perpetrated on the people of East Bengal."

Although there was no public mention of a CPN delegate attending the Twenty-fourth Congress of the Communist Party of the Soviet Union (30 March-8 April), the CPN may have been represented as an unidentified observer, as it had been at previous international meetings. A CPN delegation attended the Soviet party's Twenty-third Congress in 1966, and there was evidence to indicate that Rayamajhi had represented the CPN at the International Meeting of Communist and Workers' Parties in Moscow in 1969.

Publications. Until political parties were banned in 1960, the CPN had an official organ called *Navayug* (New Age). The pro-Soviet weekly *Samiksha* (Analysis) is published in Kathmandu and edited by "former communist" Madan Dixit, a close associate of S. K. Upadhyaya. Pushpa Lal Shrestha's faction is reported to have a publication, *Nepal Patra*. *Samiksha* and other Nepali journals are reviewed in the English-language weekly *Nepal Press Digest*, published in Kathmandu and edited by Mahesh C. Regmi.

Eric Stromquist

New Zealand

The Communist Party of New Zealand (CPNZ) was founded in December 1920. Since 1963 the party has followed a pro-Chinese line. There exist also a pro-Soviet splinter organization, the Socialist Unity Party (SUP), formed in 1966, and the Socialist Action League (SAL), a Trotskyist party established in 1969. All have legal status. The combined membership of the three parties is not more than 500—about 250 for the CPNZ, 100 for the SUP, and perhaps 150 for the SAL. The population of New Zealand is 2,857,000 (estimated 1970).

CPNZ membership has declined steadily from a high of about 2,000 at the end of World War II, and the party has played a negligible role in the country's political life. No communist candidate has ever been elected to political office. In the November 1969 Parliamentary election the CPNZ received 364 votes, compared with 1,207 in 1966 and 2,868 in 1963. Some 30 communists in all—estimated at 15 each for the CPNZ and SUP—are believed to hold executive positions in the trade union movement. Preempting worker support, the opposition Labour Party has effectively robbed the CPNZ of any real hopes for electoral success. In response to this situation, the CPNZ, instead of watering down its revolutionary goals, as many communist parties elsewhere have done, has chosen to break completely with social-democratic movements and to disavow any expectation of a possible transition to socialism through electoral processes.

The CPNZ. Leadership and Organization. The leading organs of the CPNZ are the National Committee and its Political Committee and Secretariat; below this level are district committees in the major cities. The general secretary and leading figure is Victor Wilcox. The National Committee includes also Ron Taylor (acting CPNZ chairman, resident in Tirana, Albania), John Foulds, Ralph Hegman, Hugh McLeod, Ray Nunes, and A. Rait. The Political Committee includes Nunes (also a Secretariat member), Hegman, and R. Wolf; William McAra retired from the Political Committee in August 1971. The party press provides only fragmentary information concerning the CPNZ leadership, and contributors are seldom identified.

Party Internal Affairs. Throughout its existence, the CPNZ has been torn by factional strife between those determined to maintain an ideologically "pure" and elite core of revolutionaries—even at the expense of possible electoral gain—and those bent on pragmatic political advance. Frequent purges have failed to consolidate the party, and the CPNZ's constant emphasis on the necessity to "weed out the fifth columnists" in the party's ranks—"traitors, collaborators, and opportunists"—has contributed considerably to its numerical decline. The purges, moreover, have resulted in the establishment of extra-party, rival organizations harmful to the CPNZ. More recently, the formation in 1969 of a "Revolutionary Committee within the CPNZ" by an Auckland district group led to the expulsion of its leader, S. W. Taylor, and a number of his adherents. A new purge undertaken in October 1970 in the Wellington district removed the entire six-member leadership headed by Jack Manson (a member of both the National and Political Committees) and R. Bailey. The CPNZ dissolved and reorganized the Wellington committee, but the opposition appears to have retained control of the party district, and continues to present itself as the Wellington district CPNZ.

This latest purge has seriously affected the base of the CPNZ; the dissidents, actively opposing the CPNZ, have frequently joined forces with other communist groupings including the pro-Soviet SUP, the Trotskyist SAL, and the Taylor group in Auckland. The CPNZ has defended its expulsion of the "Manson-Bailey group" on the basis that its members are "opponents of Mao Tse-tung Thought which means they are opponents of Marxism-Leninism" and that their activities underline "the urgent truth of Lenin's words" that the "fight against imperialism is a sham and humbug unless it is inseparably bound up with the fight against opportunism" (*People's Voice*, 24 March). A later attack on the group (*ibid.*, 28 April) charged that since 1966 they had been engaged in a bid to "stack the National Committee with their own agents," pursued a "conspiratorial organizational line ... in tune with Trotskyism," and worked to restrict class struggle to "levels acceptable to the trade union bosses"—"agents of the class enemy in the workers' ranks." Since its "exposure," the group, by "deliberate distortions," "suppression of certain documents," and "physically preventing national leaders from speaking to the Wellington members," had succeeded in misleading "some good people inside and outside the party."

Ideological Orientation. Early in 1971, in a statement commemorating the fiftieth anniversary of the founding of the CPNZ, Wilcox spoke of the party's success in resisting the "dangers involved in revising the basic philosophical theories of Marxism-Leninism." It was because of its ideological consistency that the CPNZ had emerged in the "Western Imperialist World" as the "only party refusing to follow the revisionist lead of the traitorous leadership of the Communist Party of the Soviet Union." It was current CPNZ policy, he said, to "apply Marxism-Leninism, the Thought of Mao Tse-tung, to the objective conditions of our country, realizing that the era of imperialism is drawing to a close." He stressed the necessity of bringing the people to an understanding that the inroads by both international and domestic "monopolists" demanded "preparation for revolutionary mass struggle." The CPNZ rejected concepts that "leave struggle at the economic level within the framework of capitalism," and the "fallacy of parliamentarianism and of attempting to outcompete capitalism on the economic front in order to achieve socialism, as advocated by Khrushchevism." The Soviet Union and those who followed its leadership, Wilcox added, were returning to "a new form of capitalism basically the same as that of the old imperialist world." Conditions for revolutionary activity in New Zealand were increasing, according to Wilcox. On the industrial front workers were showing signs of revolt against "reformist and revisionist sellouts," while youth was developing "its own" methods of revolt against the "establishment," and now smaller farmers were "talking of action." It was imperative that the party raise its own level of understanding so as to be able to give "correct leadership" to all those exploited. (*New Zealand Communist Review*, March.)

In an editorial purporting to show the "vital difference between socialist and capitalist armed forces," the CPNZ declared that in a capitalist country the armed forces protect the "rule and system of a minority capitalist class which exploits the working people." In China, on the other hand, the armed forces were said to "protect the rule and system of the majority working class which exploits no one." Capitalist armed forces stood for "oppression and aggression," socialist ones for "liberation and national self-defense." Pacifism and nonviolence, the editorial concluded, could "only end up helping the capitalist class" by "disarming the class it exploits." (*People's Voice*, 7 July.) Despite such statements rejecting pacifism and nonviolence, the CPNZ does not directly advocate (or practice) the carrying of arms, and, as on other issues, its words far exceed its actions.

Domestic Views and Activities. The CPNZ declared that the New Zealand economy was "heading for a deeper crisis," regardless of whether it entered the European Economic Community. Imperialism, the party argued, has already gained a "large measure" of control over the country "with the aid of the government and the ruling class generally." With full control once achieved, imperialism would dictate price policies. The most that EEC membership could do, would be to "paste over the cracks for a year or two," but even this "brief respite" would give foreign capital time to "tighten its stranglehold on the livelihoods of the New Zealand people." (*People's Voice*, 2 June.)

On the labor front, the party urged workers to "combat any scheme for so-called 'wage restraints.' " Measures to halt inflation and boost the economy by restricting wages, it said, favored primarily "big business, led by United States monopoly"—which, in the CPNZ view, dominates New Zealand's economy and consequently its political, cultural, and military life. It was the design of the class enemy ("monopolism") to "extend its grip over the entire New Zealand people, making the country more and more an impoverished neo-colony for providing cheap land, cheap resources, cheap labor, and cheap cannon fodder for imperialist profit." The party told workers, furthermore, that to agitate for a higher income was "an essential part of the world struggle against U.S. imperialism ['Enemy No. 1'] and its agents against exploitation and aggression." The struggle, however, must not be confined to efforts for improved wages and conditions—that would be only to seek a "better share" inside the capitalist system. In order to be able to seize political power, it would be necessary to expose "those in the labor movement who peddle the idea that capitalism by arrangement and planning can provide stable and improving conditions for the working people it robs," and to correct those union leaders who aid in "the struggle for improvements within capitalism," but who, because they "accept the permanence of capitalism, ... end up collaborating with the class enemy of the working people." (*Ibid.*, 10 February.)

The party continued to present itself as the only New Zealand political entity seeking to further the interests of the Maori minority, alleging that, notwithstanding the 1840 Waitangi Treaty on the safeguarding of their rights, the Maoris had been exploited in a bid to assimilate them into New Zealand capitalist society and to corrupt their traditional from of communal life. The communists pointed to the "land grab" allegedly perpetrated against the Maoris in violation of the treaty, and termed the government's general treatment of them a "modified and prettied-up apartheid" which would not be eliminated "this side of socialism." The Maoris, according to the CPNZ, received none of the rights pledged by the treaty, whether with regard to equal pay, housing, or education. Only within the armed forces—to which they were driven by lack of opportunities in civilian life—were they permitted to be "more than equal" and encouraged to aid foreign powers in "stealing the land of others." The CPNZ urged Maoris and "Pakehas" (the white New Zealand population) to fight "shoulder to shoulder" against U.S., British, Japanese, and other foreign monopolies and to preserve their "common heritage." (*Ibid.*)

The party entered no candidates in the November municipal and local elections, explaining its abstention as a "saving of time, effort, and money on a campaign which, at best, could reach only a few people and which, through the mere fact of [CPNZ] participation, would add to the illusion that something worthwhile can be accomplished through the 'establishment.' " Participation in the elections would not help, but obstruct, the party's aim—"the winning of revolutionary consciousness and revolutionary action"—which was best served "outside of the capitalist institutions." (*Ibid.*, 22 September.)

International Views and Positions. The CPNZ's international position faithfully reflects that of the Chinese Communist Party, which in turn gives much prominence to CPNZ articles and statements, and never fails to give New Zealand communists a cordial reception in Peking.

CPNZ activity in the anti-war movement declined in 1971, largely because of the party's inability to find a common front with other forces opposed to the Western role in the Vietnam war, but also because New Zealand's combat role was winding down. The party charged that the anti-war movement throughout the Western world had been sabotaged by Trotskyists inasmuch as they had couched their protest in terms of a mere demand for the withdrawal of foreign troops from Vietnam, rather than condemnation of the U.S. for its "global imperialist strategy." The U.S. "countertactic" of Vietnamization, said the CPNZ, had thus met the demand of the anti-war movement and so "deprived it of its steam." The CPNZ assailed the National Anti-War Conference, which convened in Wellington in March and organized the largest anti-war demonstrations yet held in New Zealand (drawing an estimated 35,000 persons on 30 April and 32,000 on 30 July). CPNZ opposition to the conference stemmed largely from the fact that the SAL and SUP became active in the conference organization at a time (late 1970) when the CPNZ was vacillating as to a "correct" stance. The CPNZ accused the conference of "foisting undemocratically and unfraternally on the New Zealand left an anti-war movement which in effect totally endorses the war policies of [U.S. President] Nixon and [New Zealand Premier] Holyoake" (*People's Voice*, 24 March). It urged "progressives" to participate in demonstrations, but not to "blindly follow the lead of those who seek to sow illusions and weaken effective protest" (*ibid.*, 21 April.)

The party warned that with the impending withdrawal of U.S. forces from Vietnam, imperialism was trying to "mend its fences." SEATO activities were being tailored to support a "counter-subversion program" against any movement for national liberation, anti-monopolism, or anti-imperialism. Having failed to isolate China, the "moribund" SEATO, through its "counter-subversion program" was seen as making a "desperate last-ditch attempt in view of the fact that China must obviously soon take her place in world councils." (*Ibid.*, 5 May.) The invitation of the U.S. table tennis team to China "most certainly" did not mean a "reversal of Mao Tse-tung's 1970 call for the people of the world to "unite and defeat the U.S. aggressors and all their running dogs.' " It was, rather, "a gesture to the ordinary people of the U.S., most of whom oppose the aggression of their monopoly ruling class," and thus it accorded with China's desire for "normal relations with every country wishing to have peaceful relations." (*Ibid.*, 21 April.) The Labour Party, which was then advocating closer relations with China, was accused by the CPNZ of a "leap onto the China-trade wagon." Never having "made a stand of any sort against imperialism," it was "trying to get into the act twenty-five years late." Class-conscious workers, nevertheless, should not object to any advocacy of improved relations with China, "however reactionary the source." (*Ibid.*, 2 June.)

The party called China's seating in the United Nations a "blow to the prestige of U.S. imperialism and its shameless stooges like the Holyoake government who persisted, along with a motley cluster of fascist regimes, in trying to preserve the myth of 'two Chinas.' " It showed that U.S. imperialism "no longer dominates the members of the United Nations to the extent it did when it used that organization for aggression against the Korean people and for other nefarious purposes." The "reseating of China and the unseating of the Taiwan pretenders" had been achieved by the "application of firm uncompromising working class principles by Albania and China," with "no concession made to imperialism in the guise of 'peaceful coexistence' as is so shamelessly done by the Soviet revisionist leaders." (*Ibid.*, 3 November.)

Wilcox, who was in China in April-May, noted upon his return that "in discussions with Chou En-lai and others," the "menace of the new growth of Japanese imperialism" had been stressed. The U.S., they had agreed, was encouraging the "warlike military preparation of Japan's ruling class to attack Asia, particularly China." Soon to be "removed" from Indochina, "U.S. imperialism" would not have been eliminated from the Asiatic scene, but would "fall back on a second line of attack through Japan." New Zealand, "in one way or another," would be involved, said Wilcox. Japanese "imperialism," he added, was to New Zealand "second only to U.S. imperialism working in cooperation with Soviet revisionism—not forgetting, on a world scale, the increasing menace of West German military preparations." (*Ibid.*, 19 May.) The announcement, in July, of U.S. President Nixon's forthcoming visit to China was described by the CPNZ as a "tactical retreat." China's "acceptance" of the U.S. request to visit China was made "from a position of proletarian strength." (*Ibid.*, 21 July.)

The New Zealand government has been continually scored by the CPNZ for its alleged support of the South African apartheid policy. An article in 1971 commented that many anti-apartheid resolutions had been passed by the United Nations, but on no occasion had New Zealand cast a vote against "any aspect of South African racism." It was thus "obvious" that the two governments had a mutual "understanding." New Zealand's abstention on anti-apartheid votes, in the CPNZ view, denoted "tolerance of it anywhere—including New Zealand," based on the "profit motive" of retaining "cheap colored labor." (*Ibid.*, 17 March.)

Wilcox and Political Committee member R. Wolf were in Australia from 29 June to 2 July for talks with the Communist Party of Australia (Marxist-Leninist). "Complete agreement" was noted "on all questions" (*Ibid.*, 7 July). Wilcox and Ron Taylor attended the Albanian party congress in November. Wilcox's address there praised the "great achievements in the building of a socialist Albania" as a "shining example to the world" (*ibid.*, 1 December).

Party Media. The CPNZ's weekly newspaper, *People's Voice*, and its monthly journal, *New Zealand Communist Review*, are published in Auckland. In addition, Ron Taylor broadcasts to New Zealand in a "Letter from Albania" over Tirana radio.

*   *   *

The SUP. The Socialist Unity Party's national president, Alex Drennan, died in November 1971. The leading figure in the party is the national secretary, George Jackson. Other leading members include George Andersen, vice-president, who was named acting president after Drennan's death, and F. McNulty. The party's activity continues to be principally within organized labor (Andersen is secretary of the Northern Drivers' Union, and McNulty is general secretary of the New Zealand Freezing Workers' Union). The party participates in national and municipal elections, but has never won an office. As with the CPNZ, the average age of SUP members is high, and the party appears to hold little appeal for young persons.

The SUP's consistent loyalty to Soviet policies was finally rewarded in 1971 when Jackson and Drenan were invited to represent the SUP at the Twenty-fourth Congress of the Communist Party of the Soviet Union (CPSU). A post-congress editorial in the *New Zealand Tribune* (May) denied that the SUP was a "Moscow aligned" party—"the problems of New Zealand society can only be solved in N.Z., not Moscow, Peking, Washington or anywhere else"—but praised the CPSU for "its fulfilment of its duty to the international working class and the various liberation movements." Drennan and Jackson went from Moscow to Sofia, where they attended the Tenth Congress of the Bulgarian Communist Party.

The party claims 1921 as the founding year of its party. Celebrating its fiftieth anniversary in 1971, it received messages from pro-Soviet parties in both East and West.

The SUP monthly newspaper, the *New Zealand Tribune*, is issued in Wellington.

*   *   *

The SAL. Socialist Action League leaders include George Fyson, the national secretary, and Hugh Fyson, editor of the SAL biweekly newspaper *Socialist Action*, wich currently claims 4,000 readers. The party, which has declared its support for the Trotskyist Fourth International, is composed for the most part of considerably younger elements than either the CPNZ or SUP, and it appears to have increased its strength in 1971, not least because of its anti-war activities. It frequently supports the Labour Party (although not endorsing its basic policies) on the basis that that party embraces the overwhelming majority of the working class; it condemns "ultra-leftist" tactics, seeing no "short cuts" to socialist transformation. Basing its policies on "present realities," it hopes for the gradual building of a mass revolutionary movement.

The SAL entered Mike Goodger, a twenty-two-year-old anti-war activist, in the mayoral election in Auckland. Goodger, who pledged unconditional support for the Labour slate for city council, promised also to withdraw should the Labour Party decide to enter a mayoral candidate (it did not). He polled 4.7 per cent of the vote. (*Socialist Action*, 10 September; *Intercontinental Press*, New York, 8 November.)

Valerie Bloom

Pakistan

Communist origins in Pakistan go back to the early 1920's and the movement that established the Communist Party of India. In 1948 the Communist Party of Pakistan (CPP) was formed from sections of the Indian party functioning in those areas from which the predominantly Moslem state of Pakistan had been created by partition in the previous year. By that time the originally Moslem character of the CPP had been lost and Hindu elements controlled the party. Its strength was severely reduced in the early 1950's by governmental suppression and by cultural differences which caused many Hindu members to seek refuge in India. Proscription followed in 1954.

In 1969, at least partly in response to the passing of the Pakistan government from the hands of Ayub Khan to those of Yahya Khan, the Pakistani communists began to resurface, displaying numerous divisions that reflected the Sino-Soviet rift and domestic controversies. The strength of the movement over the past few years has probably held at about 3,000 members, of whom 2,500 are estimated to be in East Pakistan, where political and economic grievances have created a high degree of political awareness. (see Marcus F. Franda, "Communism and Regional Politics in East Pakistan," *Asian Survey*, Berkeley, July 1970). The population of Pakistan is 136,900,000 (estimated 1970).

Most of Pakistan's communists are associated with education, either as teachers or as students. They have been involved only to a limited degree in the trade union movement. After the banning of the CPP in 1954, party members who sought to influence the country directly through political activities entered various legal leftist parties in both East and West Pakistan which, three years later, merged to form the National Awami (People's) Party (NAP) under the leadership of Maulana Abdul Hamid Khan Bhashani.

The NAP, a relatively small nationalist party with a strongly socialist program, suffered from the Sino-Soviet conflict and in early 1968 began functioning as two separate parties, each calling itself the NAP. The NAP led by Khan Abdul Wali Khan in West Pakistan and by Professor Muzaffar Ahmed in East Pakistan tends to lean internationally toward the Soviet Union. This group has retained the Soviet recognition accorded the united NAP as the most "progressive" legal party in the country. The other NAP, led by Maulana Bhashani, operates almost exclusively in East Pakistan and is the more active and militant of the two in that province. Often labeled as pro-Chinese, it has been weakened by a series of divisions since 1969. These have led to the creation of at least three communist parties, each exhibiting some degree of adherence to the Maoist line.

Background to Developments in 1971. The rebellion that eventually led to the creation of an independent state of Bangladesh in December began with President Yahya Khan's postponment of the first meeting of Pakistan's newly elected (as of 7 December 1970) National Assembly, which had been scheduled to convene on 3 March 1971 for the purpose of drafting a constitution.

The two big winners in the elections were a West Pakistan party led by Zulfiqar Ali Bhutto, the Pakistan People's Party, and the Awami League led by Sheik Mujibur Rahman, which won all but two seats in East Pakistan and thereby obtained a majority in the full Assembly. Postponement resulted from their inability to agree on the issue of autonomy for East Pakistan. Mujibur Rahman, who insisted on autonomy in all but diplomatic and defense matters, was opposed by both Bhutto and Yahya Khan. Negotiations that began on 16 March between Mujib and Yahya failed to achieve a solution.

Angered by Mujib's lack of success, the Bengalis launched a protest movement, resulting in a series of bloody clashes between them and the government's military forces in East Pakistan. The demand for autonomy meanwhile shifted to a call for complete independence, although Mujibur Rahman continued to seek a political settlement. On 25 March there was a heavy attack by army troops against the secessionist Bengalis. When open rebellion broke out the next day, the province was placed under martial law, the Awami League was banned, and Sheik Mujib, declared a traitor by Yahya, was arrested.

A Bangladesh army, called "Mukti Fouj" (Liberation Army; renamed "Mukti Bahini," or Liberation Force, after August), was soon formed by rebel Bengali members of the Bengal Regiment (attached to the Pakistan armed forces), the East Pakistan Rifles (a paramilitary group), and local police. On 13 April, despite the reported arrest or death of almost all of Mujib's associates in the leadership, the secessionist government proclaimed its sovereignty and appointed a four-man cabinet. Mujib, still in prison, was designated president, and the next highest ranking Awami League leader, General Secretary Tajuddin Ahmed, became prime minister. Although an appeal for recognition and assistance from "all democratic countries" was unsuccessful, the government of India offered "wholehearted sympathy and support" by a unanimous vote in both houses of the Indian Parliament.

The Awami League, although powerful as a political force, was not prepared to operate on an underground basis, and the Mukti Fouj, trained in conventional warfare, was forced to shift to unfamiliar guerrilla tactics by the overwhelming strength of the government troops. The situation acted to the advantage of the various communist parties, as well as Bhashani's NAP. Some of the leftist parties in East Pakistan—all, in fact, except a Maoist group, the Communist Party of East Pakistan (Marxist-Leninist) — attempted to transform this advantage into political gain by advocating the creation of an all-party "liberation front," rather than continuance of exclusive support for the popular Awami League, which is avowedly anti-communist. The Awami League, however, was initially reluctant to participate in such a front. Mujib clarified his attitude toward the communists in an interview with the Agence France Presse sometime before Yahya's troops struck in March. Still pressing for an autonomy short of complete independence, he said:

> Why won't the West Pakistan Government understand that I am the only one who can save East Pakistan from Communism? If they decide to fight I will be removed from power and the Naxalities [i.e., pro-Chinese communists] will intervene. If I give way, if I make too many concessions, I will lose my authority. I am in a very difficult situation. (Quoted in *Morning Star*, organ of the Communist Party of Great Britain, London, 21 April.)

Mutual military provocations between Pakistan and India, including guerrilla incursions into Pakistan from India that increased during October-November, led to war between the two countries. India's goal was to separate East from West Pakistan, which it did in only two weeks of fighting (3-17 December).

Communist Party of Bangladesh. The emergence of the pro-Soviet Communist Party of East Pakistan — which adopted its current name, Communist Party of Bangladesh (CPB), during the early period of the rebellion — was first revealed when it sent an unnamed delegate to the June 1969 International Meeting of Communist and Workers' Parties in Moscow. Before this time many pro-Soviet communists existed as a faction within the NAP. In this connection, it may be significant that they surfaced shortly after the Muzaffar Ahmed-Bhashani split in early 1968. Although there is little overt association between Muzaffar Ahmed's "pro-Soviet" NAP and the CPB, the two have similar programs.

The leader ot the CPB is the seventy-year-old veteran communist Moni Sing, who during early April 1971 escaped from a Mymensingh prison with the help of rebel forces. Its general secretary is Abdus Salam. Among the party's mass fronts is the Bangladesh Students' Union, which claims to have 30,000 members. It is also said to have a large following among the peasantry.

In May 1971 the CPB adopted an 18-point "Proposed Program of the National Liberation Front" (full text in *Political Affairs*, theoretical journal of the Communist Party, USA, New York, October). This was offered as a minimum program to serve as the platform for a "liberation front." The most salient points concerned the complete "liberation" of Bangladesh as an "independent, soverign democratic republican state with a view to advancing along the path of socialism"; the guarantee of parliamentary democracy and the establishment of a secular state; and an independent and neutral foreign policy. The plan would nationalize banks, insurance companies, the jute industry, transportation, and foreign trade, but at the same time would encourage capitalists, "particularly owners of small capital," to develop areas outside the public sector. An extensive land reform would be carried out and peasants would be encouraged to adopt cooperative farming; owners of land acquired through the reform would be adequately compensated. On the other hand, those who "collaborated with the reactionary ruling clique of Pakistan" or "acted against the people" during the "liberation struggle" would be punished and their property would be confiscated. Further, the program sought a policy of full cooperation and support for the "just and democratic struggle of the exploited people and oppressed nations [i.e., ethnic groups or provinces] of West Pakistan." Abroad, it called for closer trade relations with the neighboring countries, especially India; establishment of relations with the Afro-Asian countries, the "Socialist Camp, and all friendly countries;" support and cooperation for "anti-imperialist national liberation" struggles throughout the world; and efforts to avoid becoming dependent on "imperialist capital."

A CPB Central Committee statement on 18 April declared the Party's full support for the new government, formed five days earlier. At the same time it pressed for a broad-based united front.

After long advocating the formation of a body for united political action, the CPB welcomed the announcement on 8 September of the creation of a "Cabinet Consultative Committee for the Bangladesh Liberation Struggle." The eight-member organization, established for the purpose of guiding the "liberation struggle," was composed of four Awami Party members (led by Tajuddin Ahmed, who presided over its meetings), Muzaffar Ahmed (representing the pro-Soviet NAP), Maulana Bhashani (representing the pro-Chinese NAP), Moni Singh (representing the CPB), and the leader of one other party. At its first meeting it called for the release of Mujibur Rahman and declared that the proposal of any political solution short of complete independence would be rejected by the people of Bangladesh (*New Age*, organ of the Communist Party of India, 12 September.)

International Views and Positions. The 18 April meeting of the CPB Central Committee appealed to "all democratic, progressive and socialist governments of the world" to recognize the Bangladesh government and give it "all possible help in repulsing the brutal aggression of the reactionary fascist ruling junta of Pakistan" (*Morning Star*, 22 April). The request, not unsimilar to those made by other parties in East Pakistan, became a source of embarrassment for the Soviet Union and China, both of which placed great value on maintaining friendly relations with Pakistan. This relationship presumably had to be weighed by the Soviet Union against its obligation to support a "liberation movement" in which a recognized fraternal party stood to gain heavily. Acting against recognition of the Bangladesh government were the "bourgeois" nature of the Awami League (which received more Soviet sympathy than it might have under other conditions) and the very real threat of war between Pakistan and India created by the secession attempt. (The U.S.S.R. has expended great diplomatic effort to avert such a war, and has emphasized its role in the successful mediation leading to the 1965 Tashkent Declaration.)

Soviet reaction to the events in Pakistan displayed extreme caution. Most of the early reports in the Soviet press consisted of releases by the Associated Press of Pakistan, which often referred to victories of the Pakistan army in controlling "anti-state" elements. Gradually, it placed responsibility for the situation—the mass killings and the intolerable refugee problem in India—on the Pakistan government, without, however, declaring support for the secessionist movement. Alexander Ulansky, writing in the October issue of *New Times* (Moscow) stated: "What the people of East Pakistan are now experiencing through the fault of the Pakistani authorities is a real tragedy. . . . It is absolutely essential immediately to achieve a political settlement in East Pakistan that would respect the will of the East Pakistani population."

A delicate situation was created by the attendance of a CPB representative at the Twenty-fourth Congress of the Communist Party of the Soviet Union in April. Two versions of the unnamed delegate's speech to the congress were given: one in *Pravda*, the other by Moscow radio (in English, to South and Southeast Asia), both on 8 April. The radio version apparently gave the full text; *Pravda* toned down or omitted the delegate's strong condemnations of the Pakistan government. A reference to the "massacre of thousands of unarmed innocent people by the reactionary military government" appeared in *Pravda* as the "murders in East Pakistan of innocent people." In the full text the delegate expressed "heartfelt gratitude" for Podgorny's 2 April message to Yahya Khan, which showed "grave concern of the Soviet government and the Soviet people about the killings, arrests, and repression of the people of East Pakistan and their leaders by the military forces of Pakistan" and appealed for a "political democratic solution of the constitutional problems of the country." *Pravda* eliminated the references to killings, arrests, repression, East Pakistani leaders, and a democratic solution of constitutional problems. Thus Podgorny's expression of concern became one regarding the "use of armed force by the military administration against the population of East Pakistan" and his appeal was "for an end to bloodshed, and for a political decision [to settle] the complex problems of the country."

Reporting on a CPB Central Committee meeting, *Ananda Bazar Patrika* (Calcutta, 28 May) related that the party was "shocked and surprised" by the attitude of the People's Republic of China toward Bangladesh. The Calcutta Paper's summary of the committee's resolutions stated: "The Central Committee cannot understand on what grounds China is supporting the military regime in Pakistan."

Pro-Chinese Parties. Maulana Bhashani's NAP acted as an umbrella for all communist factions until 1968, when Muzaffar Ahmed and Wali Khan and their pro-Soviet supporters broke away, leaving it a predominantly Chinese-oriented party. In 1970, Bhashani's party began to splinter in various directions when its secretary-general left to form the pro-Chinese Communist Party of East Pakistan (Marxist-Leninist), or CPEP(M-L). Other factions appeared, though they remained within the NAP into 1971. Two minor groups apparently left during 1971 to form separate organizations, both using the name Communist Party of East Bengal (CPEB).

At the end of the the year, four distinct parties exhibiting varying degrees of deference to China and the Chinese Communist Party were recognizable.

NAP (Bhashani). Though Bhashani claims not to be a Marxist, many communists find his program compatible with theirs on most issues. Their main points of disagreement have been on Bhashani's advocacy of "Islamic socialism" and, for a time, electoral participation. Some, such as those in the CPEP(M-L), contend that Bhashani does not go far enough and that his nationalism overrides the more important matter of class struggle. Bhashani appears to have an ideological outlook similar to that of the nonaligned Communist Party of India (Marxist), whose weekly organ, *People's Democracy*, refers to him as the "leader of the oppressed people of Bangladesh." He remains an outspoken leader of the leftist forces, however, and his party, though weakened, is still probably the largest of those on the left.

At the beginning of the year Bhashani was advocating complete independence and rejecting any compromise political solution. Within the Bangladesh movement he seemed to vacillate between seeking a multi-party "liberation front" and giving sole support to the Awami League. On 25 April his NAP, meeting with the two CPEB organizations and some leaders of peasants' and workers' unions, sought to establish a liberation front, which would have had the effect of weakening the Awami League and building up the smaller, more militant parties (*Far Eastern Economic Review*, Hong Kong, 15 May).

On 1 June a "Communist Revolutionaries' East Bengal Coordination Committee" was formed, with Bhashani as its leading figure. Established three months before its evidently more moderate counterpart, the Cabinet Consultative Committee of the Bangladesh Liberation Struggle, it included a number of parties and groups closely identified with Bhashani, including the CPEB (that led by Deben Sidkar) and the East Bengal Revolutionary Students' Union. Declaring its intention to coordinate fully its activities with those of the Awami League and the Mukti Bahini, it called for the creation of a peasant-based "people's army" that would engage in guerrilla warfare in the rural areas. Its immediate goals were set forth in a 15-point program that began with the creation in every village of all-party "People's Liberation Councils" to take over political, administrative, social, and other responsibilities.

The secessionist movement put China in a position similar to that of the Soviet Union. Initially silent, the Chinese press soon began to level all its attacks against alleged interference in Pakistan's internal affairs by India. On 12 April, a Pakistani domestic broadcast announced that a message from Chou En-lai had, within the context of a condemnation of India, offered Chinese support to the Pakistan government in its "struggle to safeguard the state sovereignty."

About the same time, Bhashani reportedly wrote to Chou and Mao Tse-tung expressing surprise at the Chinese attitude and hope that it would eventually become a condemnation of the Pakistan authorities (Press Trust of India, 22 April). On 23 April he appealed both to Mao and to President Nixon of the United States for recognition by their countries and for an effort to stop President Yahya from using weapons supplied by them (*New York Times*, 24 April). In the same appeal to Mao, Bhashani remarked that if the Chinese leader refused to protest the "atrocities of the military junta," the world might think that he was "not a friend of the oppressed" (*Far Eastern Economic Review*, 1 May).

CPEP(M-L). In mid-1970, Mohammed Toaha, a trade union leader and secretary-general of Bhashani's NAP, left the party with Abdul Huq, a peasant union leader, to form the CPEP(M-L) as the only orthodox pro-Chinese party in Pakistan. This event was not reciprocated by Chinese recognition. The party is small, but has an extremely well organized underground network. It is most active in the Sylhet and Mymensingh areas in the north, where Bhashani is also strong.

The party has characterized Mujibur Rahman as an "American agent" and a "bourgeois leader," accusing him of sabotaging the class struggle by raising the secessionist demand for an independent Bangla Desh (*Intercontinental Press*, New York, 5 July). Unlike the Chinese leadership, it did not openly offer support to Yahya's government. Its main immediate goal in East Pakistan appeared to be a transformation of the Bangladesh movement into a class struggle under its leadership. This presumably meant that much of its activity would be directed against landlords and various remnants of the feudal system.

The CPEP(M-L) has ties with the Communist Party of India (Marxist-Leninist). The latter party, unlike the CPEP(M-L), has been recognized by the Chinese, and its pronouncements have been disseminated extensively in the Chinese news media. Some of its members were reported to have joined the struggle in East Pakistan.

Publications. The weekly organ of the CPB, *Ekata*, reappeared in February 1972 after a ten-month lapse during the secessionist movement. Another weekly journal, *Muktiyudda*, began publication in July 1971; reportedly it has continued to be distributed clandestinely, even after the Bangladesh victory in December. The NAP of Bhashani controls a Bengali weekly, *Janata*, and Muzaffar Ahmed's NAP has a Bengali daily, *Sangbad*, both printed in Dacca. All publications in East Pakistan were affected by the imposition of martial law and strict press censorship on 26 March.

Eric Stromquist

Philippines

The Philippine Communist Party (Partido Komunista ng Pilipinas; PKP) was organized on 26 August 1930, with Crisanto Evangelista as secretary-general and a claimed membership of 3,000 people. In May 1931 the party organized demonstrations against the government. Shortly thereafter the key leaders were arrested and sent to prison, and in September the party was declared illegal. Following the instructions of the Seventh Congress of the Comintern (1935), calling for a united front against fascism, the PKP merged with the Socialist Party in October, 1938. On 29 March 1942 the PKP assumed the leading role in the formation of a "broad coalition of guerrilla resistance organizations" known as the People's Anti-Japanese Army (Hukbong Bayan Laban sa Hapan), commonly known as the Huks and later renamed the People's Liberation Army (Hukbong Mapagag-palaya ng Bayan). Following the defeat of Japan, the Huks refused to surrender their arms. In March 1948 the government outlawed the Huks. In January 1950 the PKP Politburo passed a resolution declaring the existence of a "revolutionary situation" and calling for armed struggle to overthrow the government. The Huks became the military arm of the PKP. Philippine National Defense Secretary Ramon Magsaysay directed the counter-insurgency campaign against the PKP-Huks, and by the end of 1956 most of the PKP leaders had surrendered or been killed, and only a few hundred armed Huks remained. In June 1957 the PKP, the Huks, and "any successors of such organizations" were outlawed by the Anti-Subversion Act.

Ever since its founding, the PKP had been divided by a dispute over tactics. In 1957 the pro-Soviet faction of the PKP—headed by Jesús Lava—switched to "parliamentary struggle" and renounced "armed struggle." As PKP secretary-general, Lava continued through the 1960s to lead the party along a pro-Soviet path. In December 1968 a pro-Chinese faction broke with the PKP and formed a Maoist-oriented PKP—here designated the PKP(M) (see below)—which in some reports is called the PKP, Marxist-Leninist. The following year the Huk organization split along parallel lines.

There are generally thought to be about 1,500 to 2,000 PKP members, whose activities include forming front organizations, infiltrating already existing non-communist organizations, and supporting the Huk movement. According to the Philippine government, the PKP has a mass base of about 37,000 sympathizers, backed by 100 armed men and 100 combat support troops. Estimates of Huk strength range from 200-300 (*San Francisco Examiner-Chronicle*, 29 August 1971) to just over 1,000 (*Christian Science Monitor*, 27 August). There is reportedly a Philippine branch of the Chinese Communist Party (CCP), also founded in 1930, with an estimated strength of 300 to 500. The population of the Philippines is 38,000,000 (estimated 1971).

An additional Marxist organization, the Democratic Union of Filipino Youth (Malayang Pag-kakaisang Kabataan Philipino; MPKP), was founded by former leaders of the Nationalist Youth Movement (see below) who were expelled from that body in 1967 because of ideological differences. The MPKP contends that, "as of now, the masses are not politicalized enough to be relied upon as a base for an armed struggle against the government'' (*Philippines Free Press*, Manila, 3 April 1971). The best-known founding member of the MPKP is Francisco Nemenzo, Jr., a political scientist at the University of the Philippines. Nemenzo denies charges that the MPKP is Soviet-oriented, contending that revolutionary action in the Philippines must conform with the local situation and not with a borrowed model.

The PKP. Leadership and Organization. Little information is available regarding the current leadership and organization of the PKP. Jesús Lava is still the secretary-general. In 1970 the government released several PKP leaders who had served sentences for rebellion, murder, and arson. These included former secretary-general José Lava (brother of Jesús), former treasurer Simeon Rodríguez, former chief of special warfare Angel Baking, and former chief of intelligence Federico Bautista. José Lava declared that he remained a communist, and the others reportedly shared his sentiments.

The People's Liberation Army (Huks), military arm of the PKP, was apparently still suffering from the loss of its two top leaders in 1970. Secretary-General Pedro Taruc was killed by government troops on 17 October, and Faustino del Mundo (alias ''Commander Sumulong'')—Taruc's second-in-command—was captured on 16 September. The loss of these men resulted in mass surrenders. Del Mundo was reportedly succeeded by George Ocampo and Fortunato Salak, who were both killed in November 1970. Their successors have not been identified.

In May and June of 1971 the political science students at the University of San Carlos conducted a public opinion poll of more than a thousand Filipinos representing a broad cross-section of the population. Although 72 per cent of the respondents approved of the increase in student activism through peaceful rallies and demonstrations, only 8 per cent favored violent revolution and 72 per cent indicated they were strongly opposed to it. Slightly less than 8 per cent said that they favored the communist system of government, while 82 per cent refused to shift from the existing government to any other type (*Philippines Free Press*, 21 August).

Domestic Attitudes and Activities. Although supporting the ''protracted struggle'' of the Huks, the PKP has placed primary emphasis on ''legal'' and ''parliamentary'' forms of struggle in an effort to form a broad united front. No PKP program has been made public in recent years, but some indication of party attitudes can be found in occasional Moscow radio broadcasts and in interviews with captured or surrendered PKP personnel. Faustino del Mundo (''Commander Sumulong'') was interviewed shortly after his capture and was described as believing in ''the classic gradualist approach to the seizure of power, relying on the step-by-step process of organizing and conditioning the people until they are ready and chafing for action'' (*Philippines Free Press*, 8 May 1971). When asked about the activities of the student radicals—who in early 1971 barricaded the University of the Philippines and fought the police with homemade bombs (*New York Times*, 3 February)—Sumulong accused them of ''short-circuiting'' real revolution, and said:

> Modern insurgents, or *revolutionaries*, as you fondly call them these days, must distinguish myth from reality. They don't know where they're going. Why can't they stop being romantic anarchists? The cities and capitals are their pitfalls; the countrysides and only the countrysides can provide the bases for a truly effective revolution! (*Ibid*. Emphasis in original.)

Although opposing the Maoist policy of immediate armed struggle, Sumulong subscribed to Mao Tse-tung's theory of encircling the cities from the countryside, giving three reasons for his belief. First, he argued that the local government was unable to provide solutions to nagging economic problems—problems which created restlessness and insecurity in the provinces. Second, he claimed that a large number of peasants were living under feudal conditions, still saddled with superstition, illiteracy, and backward traditions. He described these people as easily "manipulable." Sumulong's third, and most important, reason was the great inequality in the distribution of land. By posing as their champion on the land reform issue, the guerrilla would easily be able to win the support of the people. At the time of his capture, Sumulong said that he only had 50 armed followers in his organization, but claimed extensive mass support. He said: "Our paramount concern is the formation of cadres, recruits and scattered small groups to carry out our purposes, although our long-range objective is to organize large segments of the masses." (*Ibid*.)

International Views and Positions. The PKP has no regular outlet for pronouncements on international issues. Communist Chinese media virtually ignore the non-Maoist PKP, and Soviet comments are few. Unlike Peking, Moscow does not broadcast in Tagalog. The only international statement of significance by the PKP during 1971 was a message to the Twenty-fourth Congress of the Communist Party of the Soviet Union in April. The PKP attributed its defeat in the Huk rebellion during the 1950s to its "self-isolation from the international communist movement". It attacked the PKP(M) as "a revolutionary force ... guided by the counter-revolutionary concept serving the Maoist leadership's aspiration to dominate in Southeast Asia." The attack on the PKP(M) continued:

> This group has a negative attitude to the Soviet communist party's efforts to create the material and technical basis for communism. Ignoring the basic points of Marxism-Leninism, the group considers poverty as a built-in feature of the working class. The members of the group claim that improved living standards in the socialist countries turn them into bourgeois states. These assertions have nothing in common with the teaching of Lenin, a man always concerned with the benefit of the people. (Moscow radio, 12 April.)

Publications. Although the PKP has no regular publication, its positions are frequently reported in the *Chinese Commercial News*, a Chinese-language daily, and *The Graphic*, a weekly in English, both published in Manila.

The PKP(M). the Maoist-oriented PKP(M) is headed by José Maria Sison ("Amado Guerrero"), a former University of the Philippines lecturer who is chairman of the Central Committee. Little else is known about the leadership of this "revitalized" party.

The armed wing of the PKP(M) was formed in March 1969 when the Huk organization split along ideological lines paralleling the rift in the PKP. Several Huk units operating primarily in Tarlac Province broke away and formed the New People's Army (NPA), under Bernabe Buscayno ("Commander Dante"), a self-educated peasant who had once been the "understudy" of Huk leader Sumulong (*Philippines Free Press*, 8 May 1971). Estimates of NPA strength vary greatly. Sumulong claimed that the Dante group only had 40 to 45 diehard followers at the end of 1970 (*ibid*.). Government military sources quoted in August 1971 said that the NPA once claimed a membership of 10,000 but their forces now consisted of only about 300 armed regulars which constituted less of a threat to the government than the student radicals in the cities (*Washington Post*, 24 August). Less than two weeks later, however, President Marcos said that the NPA had about 1,000 members, 2,000 active supporters, and a "mass base" of 50,000 (*New York Times*, 3 September). The NPA is thought to be organized into twelve groups, one led by "Commander Berning" and another by Lieutenant Victor Corpuz—a former instructor at the Philippines military academy who led an attack on the school armory in December 1970, and then fled into the countryside to join the NPA. Another key NPA leader was Ernesto Miranda ("Commander Panchito"), who was thought to be a top aide to Commander Dante and NPA territorial commander in Zambales Province prior to his death in a fight with a government commando team on 1 October.

During 1971 the PKP(M) strengthened its ties with radical students in Manila and other cities and towns (*Washington Post*, 26 August). Early in 1970 the Movement for a Democratic Philippines (MDP), an umbrella organization, was formed to coordinate radical student activities with those of workers and peasants. The new organization was apparently dominated by the Democratic Youth Association (Samahang Domekratikong Kabataan; SDK) and its parent organization, the Patriotic Youth Movement (Kabataang Makabayan; KM). The KM was founded in 1964 by José Lansang and the PKP(M) Central Committee chairman, José Sison. It claims to have 6,000 members. Western observers put the membership at between 3,000 and 5,000. The Women's Bureau of the KM claims to have 200 hard-core members.

Domestic Attitudes and Activities. The emphasis placed by the PKP(M) on "armed struggle" was apparent in a book published during 1971, *Philippine Society and Revolution*, written by party Central Committee chairman "Amado Guerrero" (José Sison). He wrote:

> The main force of the Philippine revolution is the peasantry. It is the largest mass force in a semi-colonial country.... There is no solution to the peasant problem but to wage armed struggle, conduct agrarian revolution and build revolutionary base areas.... It would be erroneous for a Communist party in a semi-colonial and semi-feudal country to put the principal stress on its mass work in the cities instead of in the countryside. (Quoted in the *Guardian*, New York, 15 September.)

In March the NPA issued a statement commemorating the second anniversary of its founding and asserting that the non-Maoist PKP had collapsed:

> The complete collapse of the Taruc-Sumulong [PKP] gangster clique in less than two years after mass criticism and repudiation has totally vindicated the correctness of the establishment of the New People's Army under a Communist Party inspired by Marxism-Leninism-Mao Tse-tung Thought. (*Peking Review*, no. 17, 23 April).

The NPA statement also stressed the need to build a united front. A PKP(M) statement in September asserted:

> What is needed today [is] to gradually build up a revolutionary, militant, anti-chauvinist, anti-imperialist united front on the foundation of worker-peasant alliance irrespective of religious differences. This united front should include revolutionary people of various strata in society and should recognize rights of autonomy and self-determination of the Moslem minority nationalities. (Radio "Voice of the Malayan Revolution," 15 September.)

One of the organizations that the PKP(M) wanted to bring into the united front was the Liberal Party (*Guardian*, 6 October). The Liberal Party was the big winner in the 8 November off-year election, winning 7 of the 8 senate races. Part of the large Liberal vote was attributed to sympathy resulting from a terrorist attack on 21 August against a Liberal party rally in downtown Manila. Two fragmentation hand grenades were thrown into the large crowd, killing 10 and wounding 94 people, including all but one of the key Liberal party candidates. President Marcos charged that the terrorist attack was the work of the NPA, "supported by a foreign power" which he did not identify but which aides later identified as Communist China (*New York Times*, 25 August). Marcos said that the attack was part of a "July-August Plan" of the NPA to assassinate national leaders and bomb installations (*ibid.*, 19 September). On 23 August he declared a state of rebellion to be in existence and suspended the writ of habeas corpus (*Christian Science Monitor*, 4 September). While the communists clearly benefited from the attack—it injured key opposition leadership which could be expected to oppose the PKP(M)'s attempt to control the Liberal Party through a united front, and further exaccerbated the already serious "contradiction" between the Marcos government and its opposition—both the Liberal Party leaders and much of the world press suggested that the government was a more likely culprit (*Far Eastern Economic Review*, Hong Kong, 28 August;

Economist, 28 August; *Christian Science Monitor*, 2 September). According to a newspaper poll, only 8 per cent of the people thought the bombing was the work of President Marcos or his followers, while two-thirds of them attributed it to "enemies of the opposition," "the dissident movement," or "student activists" (*Far Eastern Economic Review*, 4 September). The president apparently thought that the Maoist Patriotic Youth (Kabataang Makabayan) might have been involved, as one of the first people arrested before the writ of habeas corpus was restored was the group's secretary-general, Luzvimindo David.

Although NPA activity is limited primarily to Central Luzon, during 1971 there was significant action both north and south of the traditional stronghold. In its second anniversary statement, the NPA asserted:

> Despite wild enemy assaults, the New People's Army continues to grow beyond expectations. The concentration of enemy [government] forces in Central Luzon since the founding of the [NPA] has not destroyed the revolutionary forces there but has furthermore allowed those elsewhere to grow rapidly, especially in Northern Luzon. Armed and unarmed propaganda teams are indefatigably working in such other regions as Southern Luzon, Visayan and Mindanao to develop guerrilla warfare. (*Peking Review*, no. 17, 23 April.)

Assassination of "local tyrants and bad elements" (*ibid*.) played an important role in NPA tactics during 1971. On 22 June, for example, the mayor of Benito Soliven and two other townsmen were killed for refusing to cooperate with the NPA. Military authorities in Isabela Province reported receiving complaints from residents and minor governmental officials in various parts of the province that they had been threatened with death if they refused to cooperate with the NPA. The off-year election probably increased the number of NPA assassinations. On 27 October, less than two weeks before the election, an NPA terrorist squad killed a candidate for mayor in Bamban, Tarlac Province.

On 26 August there were two relatively large NPA attacks. In Isabela Province, northern Luzon, NPA guerrillas attacked the forward headquarters of "Tast Force Lawin," the main government military unit operating against the NPA in the area. A group of about 35 guerrillas succeeded in destroying two Air Force helicopters and wounding one government soldier before withdrawing (*New York Times*, 3 September). On the same day a band of about 50 NPA guerrillas attacked a government patrol in the southeastern Luzon province of Camarines Sur, resulting in the deaths of one government soldier and two Maoist guerrillas. This was the first encounter with the NPA in the region, which is about 300 miles south of the traditional communist strongholds. On 19 September an army patrol engaged a small NPA force, killing two and capturing the remaining five. Among the weapons found was an AK-50, the latest in Soviet assault rifles.

During 1971 the "Revolutionary School of Mao Tse-tung's Thought" was reportedly moved from Tarlac to Isabela Province.

International Views and Positions. The PKP(M) is vigorously pro-Chinese and correspondingly hostile toward the Soviets. The party chairman referred to "Mao Tse-tung Thought" as "Marxism-Leninism of the present era," and said: "The living study and application of Marxism-Leninism-Mao Tse-tung Thought in Philippine conditions is today the main concern of the Communist Party of the Philippines" (*Peking Review*, no. 33, 13 August 1971).

Although some observers doubt that there is any direct connection between the PKP(M)-NPA and the Chinese government (*Washington Post*, 26 August; *Far Eastern Economic Review*, 16 October), there was a very noticeable increase during 1971 in Peking propaganda on behalf of the Maoist movement in the Philippines. In the month of January alone, Peking released more statements on the NPA than during all of 1970.

In its second anniversary statement the NPA set forth its position on the Soviet Union, Vietnam, the Middle East, and the world situation in general:

> Based on the revolutionary spirit of proletarian internationalism, the New People's Army under the leadership of the Communist Party of the Philippines considers itself as part of the world revolution against U.S. imperialism, modern revisionism centered around the Soviet Union and all reactionary forces. It has the highest hopes for the revolutionary triumph of the peoples of Viet Nam, Cambodia and Laos in Indochina, the Southeast Asian peoples in general, the Palestinian and Arab peoples, the Japanese and Korean peoples, the American people, and all other peoples of the world. There is no stepping back in the march of world revolution; China stands as the invincible and most reliable bulwark of socialism and the anti-imperialist struggle. (*Peking Review*, no. 17, 23 April.)

Publications. The clandestine organ of the PKP(M), *Ang Bayan* (Our Nation), appears sporadically in English, Tagalog, and Pampanga. The irregular *Progressive Review*, published in English, is the organ of the KM. It frequently reflects PKP(M) positions and was originally edited by Sison. PKP(M) and NPA statements are usually reprinted in *Peking Review* and carried over Peking radio, which broadcasts to the Philippines in Tagalog.

Robert F. Turner

Singapore

The communist movement in Singapore is theoretically part of the Communist Party of Malaya (CPM), whose headquarters and leaders are based along the Thai-Malaysian border (see *Malaysia*). The movement has, however, a certain degree of independence, considerably enhanced in recent years by the reduction of the CPM to a guerrilla movement and the separation of Singapore from the Federation of Malaysia in 1965. In view of Singapore's predominantly Chinese population —some 75 per cent (*Christian Science Monitor*, 3 March)—which in many respects identifies itself with the achievements of mainland China, distinction between communist groups and others with similar aims and sympathies is blurred. The Singapore branch of the CPM is thought to have about 200 members. Like its parent organization to the north, it is illegal. The population of Singapore is about 2,000,000 (estimated 1971).

Leadership and Organization. Because of its illegal status, communist activity in Singapore has been of a twofold nature: underground, and through front organizations and parties. The clandestine organization is difficult to delineate, owing to the communists' strict adherence to a policy of virtual elimination of all records and files and the replacement of party organs by "front publications."

The leadership of the Singapore communist movement appears to be split into two major contending factions: those favoring — at least for the present — a nonviolent approach to communist goals, and those advocating immediate armed struggle. The principal front organization, the Barisan Sosialis (Socialist Front), appears to be split similarly. There are two small left-wing parties in Singapore, the "People's Party" founded in 1956, and the "People's Front" founded in 1971 (*New York Times*, 4 April 1971).

The Barisan Sosialis was founded on 26 July 1961 by former members of the People's Action Party (PAP) — the ruling party in Singapore. Its relationship to the CPM became apparent on May Day, 1968, when its chairman admitted that the front "unquestionably recognized the leadership and vanguard role played by the Malayan proletarian political party in the whole Malayan liberation struggle." Although he could not mention the illegal CPM by name, his intent was clear. The Barisan Sosialis receives support from the 29 trade unions associated with it and has the occasional cooperation of the People's Party, which has been described as a Barison satellite with a Malay appeal.

The current Barisan Sosialis Central Cimmittee, elected in 1967, includes Lee Siew Choh (chairman), See Cheng Kiong (vice-chairman), Koo Yung (assistant secretary-general),* Taycheng Kang (treasurer), Chai Kuen Fak (assistant treasurer), Fong Swee Suan,* Poh Soo Kai,* Yang Ya Wu, Liang Li Ing,* Chang Tek Suen, Li Chen Min, Chen Ru Pen, and Hsieh Chin Chen. (Those designated by an asterick were under arrest and in detention during 1971). Lim Chin Siong, founder and first secretary-general of the Barisan Sosialis, resigned his post upon release from detention in 1969 and apparently has not been replaced. Barisan membership is thought to be under 1,000 (*Christian Science Monitor*, 3 March). Although it has been the most active of the opposition groups, "its leadership is regarded as inept" and the discipline of its members is "poor." One reason for this is that some of its best men are among the 69 political detainees held in jail indefinitely under the Internal Security Act. At least 11 of these prisoners are said to be hard-core communists. (*Ibid.*)

Domestic Attitudes and Activities. Because of the movement's clandestine nature, attitudes of Singapore communists are difficult to ascertain. It is thought that the most important difference between them and the CPM is on reunification as against "liberation." The Barisan Sosialis regards reunification of Singapore and Malaysia as the primary task, while the CPM emphasizes armed struggle to bring about the communization of both countries, to be followed by reunification. This does not mean that the Barisan is opposed to armed struggle. The party chairman, Lee Siew Choh, has on several occasions made it clear that the communists' extra-parliamentary struggle would lead to armed struggle in the future.

The fact that the majority of the Singapore population is Chinese is viewed with alarm by Prime Minister Lee Kuan Yew, whose government tolerates neither Nationalist nor Communist Chinese propaganda or political activity (*Ibid.*). During 1971 the government closed down several newspapers, justifying the moves on the grounds that "communists inside and outside the republic [were] trying to subvert it" (*New York Times*, 10 June). In May the English-language daily *Eastern Sun* was closed, and the owners were charged with having accepted a million dollars from communist agents in Hong Kong. When the owners refused to answer the charges, the editors of the newspaper walked out, declaring that they had no alternative but to believe that they had been working for a "Communist front organization" (*ibid.*, 17 May and 10 June). The prime minister reportedly has been disturbed by the diplomatic gestures between the United States and Communist China, fearing that they could lead to an outburst of Chinese chauvinism in Singapore (*Far Eastern Economic Review*, Hong Kong, 28 August). Speaking at a seminar on communism and democracy, Lee referred to the new developments in Sino-American relations and stressed that "Singapore citizens of Chinese descent must never forget they are Singaporeans." He went on to forecast China's long-term policy and its influence on Singapore, which he said would include trade "and, of course, help [for] insurgency movements" (*Sunday Times*, Singapore, 9 May).

The January "Singapore Conference" meeting of heads of state of Commonwealth nations was the target of several attacks by the CPM's China-based radio station, the "Voice of the Malayan Revolution" (VMR):

> British imperialism had an ulterior motive in choosing Singapore as the site for this conference. As is known by all, Lee Kuan Yew is a faithful lackey of British imperialism, and his regime is a puppet which the British imperialists have fostered....Since November 1970, the Lee Kuan Yew clique has gone all out to prepare for the conference....[It] has blatantly invented an excuse to arrest many leaders of trade unions and mass organizations and to step up its suppression of the mass struggle for the purpose of rendering meritorious service to its master. Acting on the will of its master, the Lee Kuan Yew clique also has taken measures since early January to apply discrimination against the black people. As a rule, all Negro passengers and seamen in transit through Singapore have been subject to crude treatment. (VMR, 16 January.)

Another broadcast charged that Lee had "acted throughout the meeting as an apologist for British imperialism" and had, under British direction, "vigorously attacked the People's Republic of China and slandered China as pursuing an expansionist policy in Southeast Asia" (*ibid.*, 27 January).

Conditions at the Changi prison, where eight Barisan members reportedly had been on a hungar strike, was another target of Singapore communist protest. The Barisan chairman at a press conference in early February denounced the treatment of Barisan detainees and demanded abolishment of punishment for detainees who refused to work the required five hours a day, an increase in visiting rights, and an end to the "demoralizing" Western music broadcast throughout the day in the prison (*Far Eastern Economic Review*, 13 February).

British military bases in Singapore have been a target of communist criticism from outside the country. The Barisan and its trade unions generally avoided the subject because many Singapore workers were employed at the bases.

International Views and Positions. Since Singapore is claimed by the CPM to be within its area of jurisdiction, the Singapore communists do not normally attend international meetings or make statements on international problems. They support the CPM's pro-Chinese position in the Sino-Soviet dispute and presumably in other issues as well. CPM broadcasts frequently include Prime Minister Lee Kuan Yew's "clique" along with that of Malaysian Prime Minister Tun Razak in their attacks. In November both governments were criticized for their positions on the admission of Communist China to the United Nations:

> When the resolution [for admission] was put to a vote, the Razak clique and the Lee Kuan Yew clique, which are beset with troubles internally and externally, were compelled to endorse it under the pressure of the international situation. As everybody knows, these two puppet cliques which were exclusively groomed and brought up by British imperialism have consistently acted as a hireling of imperialism in international affairs. Over a long period of time, [they] openly opposed the restoration of the People's Republic of China's lawful rights in the United Nations. (VMR, 6 November.)

In October the CPM combined an attack on the Lee government with a denunciation of "Japanese militarism":

> Japanese militarism, which has been revived with the support of U.S. imperialism, has always held ambitions toward our country's Singapore island which is strategically situated in Southeast Asia. Thus, while expanding its influence on the Malaya Peninsula, Japanese militarism has also increased its influence in Singapore both economically and politically. The expansionist activities of Japanese militarism have received support and cooperation from its former stooges Lee Kuan Yew and his ilk, thus seriously threatening the security of the people of our country....Under the reactionary rule of the Lee Kuan Yew puppet clique, Singapore's raw materials are cheaply priced [and] the worker movement has been cruelly suppressed and wages have been scaled to the lowest level....Japanese monopoly finanical groups have already infiltrated Singapore's shipbuilding, textile, lumber, metal production, cement, electronics, tire manufacturing, [and] other industries. (*Ibid.*, 27 October.)

Publications. The Singapore communists have no official publications. *Barisan* (or *Chern Sian Pau*) is published weekly by the Barisan Sosialis, and has a distribution of about 12,000 (*Christian Science Monitor*, 3 March 1971). Pro-communist publications include the *Plebian, News Bulletin* and *Rakyat*, together with *Mimbar Rakyat*, issued by the People's Party, and *People's Tribune*, the official organ of the People's Party. The *Malayan Monitor and General News*, a mimeographed monthly published in London, carries CPM policy statements.

Robert F. Turner

Thailand

Although a communist party was formed in Thailand as early as 1929 by the Siam Special Committee of the South Seas Communist Party, which had been founded by the Comintern in 1928, the present Communist Party of Thailand (CPT) was not founded until 1 December 1942. In October 1946 the Anti-Communist Act of 1933 was rescinded and two months later the party emerged into the open. It was outlawed again in 1952 and has remained illegal since then.

On 17 November 1971 the Revolutionary Party, under the leadership of Premier Thanom Kittikachorn, seized administrative power in Thailand in a bloodless coup and declared martial law. The 1968 constitution—which, while prohibiting the CPT and all communist front organizations, had provided for legal opposition political parties—was annulled, and the Thai legislature and Cabinet Council were abolished. All political gatherings of more than five persons were outlawed. (Bangkok radio, 17 November.) Among the reasons given for the coup d'état were the "communist insurrection in northern Thailand ... terrorism, and subversion" (*New York Times*, 18 November).

Non-communist estimates of CPT membership strength vary greatly, ranging from a few hundred to as many as 2,000 hard-core members. There are thought to be between 3,600 and 5,500 full-time armed insurgents under communist leadership: 1,200 to 1,800 in the northeast, 1,300 to 1,900 in the north, 100 to 400 in central Thailand, and 1,000 to 1,400 in the south (John W. Henderson et al., *Area Handbook for Thailand*, Washington, D. C., 1971, p. 207). The population of Thailand is 37,800,000 (estimated 1971).

Leadership and Organization. The CPT has received little support from the ethnic Thai people. A long history of national independence (Thailand was the only country in Southeast Asia to avoid colonialization), a common language, and the unifying influences of the Buddhist religion and the king, are perhaps some of the reasons for this. The highest positions in the party are thought to be held by Chinese, Sino-Thais, and Vietnamese. In recruiting guerrillas the communists have had their main successes among the Chinese population and the ethnic hill tribesmen, such as the Meo in northern Thailand. The predominately non-Thai composition of CPT leadership is a possible explanation for the party's failure to publish even a partial list of its Central Committee membership. Indeed, although a central committee was reportedly formed at the Second Congress of the CPT, in 1952, only one member (a Thai woman) has been identified in communist broadcasts in recent years, and even she seems not to have been mentioned since 1968.[1] The CPT is assumed to be organized along traditional lines, with a secretariat and politburo as well as a Central Committee.

In 1967 1967 Thai authorities arrested Thong Jamsri, a Thai citizen of Vietnamese descent who may have been the secretary-general of the CPT at that time. He was reportedly the coordinator

---

[1] Miss Nit Phuongdaphet, who reportedly lives in Peking and has written for Peking's *People's Daily* under the nom de plume of "Nita de Thailand," was up to 1968 frequently cited in announcements concerning the CPT.

of CPT activities in northeastern Thailand, and was thought to be responsible for liaison between the CPT and the communist parties of China and North Vietnam. On 19 July 1971 Thai police captured Kusol Surasen, the head of the communist psychological warfare campaign in the north. He reportedly received 18 months of training in psychological warfare in North Vietnam before returning to Thailand in mid-1970. (*Bangkok Post*, 19 July.) Two months later Thai officials announced the capture, in Chiang Mai Province in northwestern Thailand, of Phairoh Sae Darn, a woman who reportedly had spent six years in Hanoi and Peking studying politics and was, at the time of capture, "holding a high position among communist terrorists" (*The Nation*, Bangkok, 15 September).

During 1964 and 1965 the CPT created two united-front organizations, the "Thailand Independence Movement" (TIM) and the "Thailand Patriotic Front" (TPF), both headquartered in Peking, and a number of "mass organizations" and "patriotic groups."[2] In the years which followed, however, the CPT took a more open role in the insurgency and references to the TIM, TPF, and other front organizations decreased. During 1971 there were no significant references to any fronts in Thai communist propaganda.

Domestic Attitudes and Activities. Traditionally, the CPT has relied primarily on Communist China and North Vietnam for leadership training.[3] In October 1971, the Thai Ministry of the Interior announced that communist terrorists had established a "top-level military training school for guerrilla leaders with Communist Chinese and North Vietnamese instructors" in Nakhom Phanom Province near Laos. There were thought to be 10 to 20 foreign instructors, and more than 100 students. The Ministry regarded the establishment of the school as a "shift of tactics on the part of communist terrorists, who formerly sent local recruits to Peking and Hanoi for training." (*Bangkok World*, 25 October.) Lower-level terrorist training camps have existed in Thailand for several years and have frequently been the subject of attack by Thai police and military forces. Six large communist terrorist camps, and numerous smaller ones, were captured by government forces during 1971. In May government troops captured the largest such camp ever found, in Phatthalung Province in southern Thailand. The camp was thought to have held about 200 terrorists, and was identified by a sign saying "The National Liberation Front of Thailand." (*Bangkok Post*, 27 May.) Later in the year three even larger camps were captured in the south, each believed to have accommodated about 500 terrorists (*The Nation*, 26 August, 8 September, and 30 October).

Communist guerrilla activities in Thailand continued at a high level throughout 1971. According to a broadcast on December 1 by the CPT's "Voice of the People of Thailand" (VPT) radio station, the insurgents had "wiped out" more than 1,400 of the "enemy" and downed or damaged 50 aircraft during the first 11 months of the year. The chief communist military successes occurred in the northeast, especially in Nakhon Phanom Province. Thai government sources admitted in August that "communist terrorists" had "seized control of almost all the villages in Nakae and Khamcha-E districts in Nakhon Phanom Province," where they had "taken control of about 100

---

[2] For more information about communist fronts, mass organizations, and patriotic groups in Thailand see YICA, 1968, pp. 566-67.

[3] In the mid-1950's the Chinese set up a school in Chunking solely for the training of Thai communists, and in the 1960's the Foreign Language Institute in Peking began offering a three-year intensive course in the Thai language to prepare political cadres for work with Thai communists. In 1961 the "Political and Military School of the Thai Communist Party" was established in Hoa Binh Province of North Vietnam. By 1967 defectors reported that other training centers for Thai communists existed in the Phu Tho area and the Tay Bac autonomous region of North Vietnam. There were thought to be at least seven such schools. In 1968 the Hoa Binh school was reportedly closed following bombing by U.S. aircraft and subsequently most of the others reportedly were either closed or converted to other purposes.

villages" (*Bangkok Post*, 16 August). The communists had established "liberated areas" and reportedly were "making headway quietly, setting up village infra-structure and avoiding contact with government forces" (*ibid.*, 28 August). In October, Interior Ministry sources reported that "nearly 1,000 men" from ten villages in Tak Province had joined the communist terrorists and were "receiving weapons training in jungle camps" (*Bangkok World*, 4 October). The deterioration of security in the northeast, where insurgents were receiving assistance from North Vietnam and China and from communists in Laos, was described by one observer as "a throwback to the situation of six years ago" (*Far Eastern Economic Review*, Hong Kong, 11 September). Communist successes in the northeast were partly offset by losses in the north following a series of large-scale government operations. The same observer — generally skeptical of government claims — was sufficiently impressed by the progress in the north to conclude that there was "some truth" to optimistic government reports, but added: "Progress ... has been made [but] a full-scale guerrilla war is being fought in the north, and enemy forces may have the last word" (*ibid.*).

Unity continued to be an important theme in CPT propaganda during 1971: "Although ... the people's unity has become more and more consolidated, all patriotic forces must still strengthen their solidarity, consolidate their struggle in order to make it more effective" (VPT, 17 May). The necessity for armed struggle was also a recurring theme. A major broadcast commemorating the twenty-ninth anniversary of the founding of the CPT declared:

> Our revolution must be carried out through the seizure of political power by the people's armed struggle and through the bold and determined desire to use revolutionary violence to oppose ... counter-revolutionary violence....The Communist Party of Thailand has led our people to carry out courageously the armed struggle....The people have learned from experience that the armed struggle is the only correct way to solve the problems of the country and the people. (*Ibid.*, 1 December.)

Deprived of the traditional anti-colonialist sentiment prevalent in other Southeast Asian countires, the CPT has attempted to engender nationalistic support by protraying the United States as the "master" of the Thai government. Thai soldiers fighting in South Vietnam were referred to as "mercenaries" whom the government's "fascist piratic clique" had "sold" to the United States for use in the "dirty U.S. war" in Indochina (*ibid.*, 26 September). The "depraved influence" of the U.S. "cultural invasion" of Thailand was a frequent subject of attack:

> People have ... written to newspapers, expressing their great concern for our youth who, they say, are falling under the hippies' influence. They wear their hair long, smoke marijuana, and cast seductive glances. The future of the nation is at stake if the hippie movement cannot be checked. (*Ibid.*, 18 April.) The deterioration of our culture and society caused by the U.S. military occupation of our country, has greatly angered and disturbed people in various circles....Bars, nightclubs, massage parlors, hotels, and motels have appeared. Many Thai women have become "hired wives" to American soldiers....Orphans fathered by U.S. soldiers will cause future burdens for Thai society. (*Ibid.*, 23 May.)

Thai involvement in the Indochina conflict was also a frequent target: "While the United States and the Saigon puppet clique are moving their forces to invade southern Laos, the Thanom clique has sent thousands of its troops to participate in the invasion" (*ibid.*, 21 February). A month-long visit by British counter-insurgency expert Sir Robert Thompson drew this comment:

> Recently the clique ... invited Robert Thompson, Nixon's special adviser on people's suppression, [to] help the clique plan and direct suppression operations against the Thai people....This is further evidence of of the traitorous crime of the Thanom-Praphat clique in allowing U.S. imperialism to direct the suppression operations against the Thai people.(*Ibid.*, 4 October.)

The 17 November coup d'état, naturally a major target of communist propaganda, was denounced as a move by the Thanom government to "extend its treacherous, fascist distatorial, and people-plundering administration," (*ibid.*, 20 November) and was said to have been ordered by the United States: "To further its aggression, occupation and exploitation ... U.S. imperialism made its lackey, the Thanom-Praphat clique, put on the 'self-coup' show on 17 November ... in an effort to forestall the vigorously developing struggle of the patriotic and democratic people of Thailand" (*ibid.*, 26 November).

During 1971 there was an increase in assassinations of government officials by communist terrorists (*Far Eastern Economic Review*, 11 September). This practice was explained by the CPT (VPT, 12 January) as nothing more than elimination of "corrupt government officials" by "liberation soldiers."

International Views and Positions. During 1971 the CPT continued to praise Communist China and the doctrine of Mao Tse-tung. On the occasion of the fiftieth anniversary of the founding of the Chinese Communist Party, the CPT Central Committee hailed it as "the most mature Marxist-Leninist Party" and stated:

> "At the time of the emergence of modern revisionism in the international sphere, the Communist Party of China under the leadership of Chairman Mao Tse-tung ... has waged an uncompromising struggle against modern revisionism, safeguarded the purity of Marxism-Leninism and defended revolution and socialism."(*Peking Review*, no. 30, July 23.)

In a broadcast commemorating the twenty-second anniversary of the People's Republic of China, the CPT declared: "The great people of China have firmly and resolutely carried out Chairman Mao Tse-tung's solemn teaching that people who have won their revolution should help people who are struggling for their liberation" (VPT, 30 September). The announcement that U.S. President Nixon would visit China during 1972 was greeted as proof "that the U.S. imperialist policy to contain and isolate the People's Republic of China has crumbled to pieces, and that the international prestige of socialist China has soared high" (*ibid.*, 20 August).

As relations between the Thai government and the Soviet Union increased during 1971, anti-Soviet pronouncements by the CPT became more frequent. In a May Day article calling for stepped up insurgency, the CPT charged: "As for ... the revisionist renegades led by the Soviet revisionists, and all reactionaries in various countries, including the Thanom-Praphat clique, their positions are deteriorating" (*ibid.*, 1 May).

Several CPT broadcasts expressed "militant solidarity" with the people of China, Vietnam, Laos, and Cambodia as well as support for communist movements in countries in Southeast Asia not directly involved in the Indochina War. In a review of the situation in September, the CPT asserted:

> "At present, the revolutionary situation, the armed struggle waged by the people in the various Southeast Asian countries, [is] developing victoriously....Inspired by the present excellent world situation, the peoples of Burma, Malaya, the Philippines, Indonesia, and North Kalimantan have fanned the flames of their armed struggle. [They] clearly understand that only by taking the road of armed struggle ... as pointed out by Chairman Mao Tse-tung ... can they cause their revolution to advance from one victory to another. (*Ibid.*, 15 September.)

Intelligence reports cited by Thai government officials indicated some friction between the CPT and other communist movements active in the northeast and southern sections of Thailand. The army commander in chief reported in February: "Disagreement has arisen between the CPT and the Hanoi-directed communist terrorists [in the northeast] over how domination of Thailand should be achieved" (*Bangkok Post*, 3 February). The Hanoi-trained leaders, he said, favored a more Maoist line. This conclusion was based on a study of documents captured when two Japanese communists — apparently bringing material to the CPT from an international communist conference in Hanoi — were arrested by Thai authorities on 6 December 1970. Other intelligence reports suggested that there were differences between CPT leaders and Chin Peng (see *Malaysia*), the communist leader of Chinese guerrillas in the south along the Thai-Malaysian border. Combined Thai-Malaysian security operations along the border during 1971 reportedly forced the guerrillas — who traditionally operate only along the border region — to penetrate deep into Thai territory and "close ranks with the communist terrorists in the inner-southern provinces" (*The Nation*, 7 October). According to Thai government officials, "the Thai communists want Chin Peng out of Thailand so that they can set up their authority in the southern provinces" (*ibid.*, 13 November).

Publications. The CPT publishes an irregular clandestine journal, *Ekkarat* (Independence). Party policy statements are broadcast by the "Voice of the People of Thailand" (*Siang Pracheachon*), a clandestine radio station which began broadcasting in March 1962 and is thought to be located in South China. The VPT transmits for 28 hours a week in Thai, 14 in Laotian, and 4 in Mung. Peking radio devotes about 21 hours a week to Thai-language broadcasts, and both Peking and Hanoi media frequently carry CPT statements.

Robert F. Turner

Vietnam: Democratic Republic of Vietnam

The Vietnam Workers' Party (*Dang Lao Dong Viet Nam*; VWP) is an outgrowth of the Indochinese Communist Party founded on 3 February 1930. On 19 May 1941 the Eighth Congress of the party created the "League for Vietnamese Independence" (*Viet Nam Doc Lap Dong Minh Hoi*), known as the Viet Minh. While presented as a nationalistic front of all anti-French and anti-Japanese forces in Vietnam, the Viet Minh was in fact completely controlled by communists. For propaganda purposes, the Indochinese Communist Party was officially dissolved in November 1945. Party functions were carried on clandestinely by the "Association for Marxist Studies," under the leadership of Truong Chinh. On 11 February 1951 "The second national congress of party delegates ... decided to change the name of the party to the Vietnamese Lao Dong Party" (*Hanoi Moi*, 22 January 1970), and the VWP—although still illegal—began to operate publicly. At the same time, the Viet Minh was absorbed into the "United Vietnam Nationalist Front" (*Mat Tran Lien Hiep Quoc Dan Viet Nam*), better known as the Lien Viet, a front organization created in 1946. In September 1955 the Lien Viet was absorbed by the Vietnam Fatherland Front (*Mat Tran To Quoc Viet Nam*), which remains active today. One knowledgeable Vietnamese observer has asserted that "the frequent changes of names were symptomatic of a gradual decline in the popularity of the 'front' rather than of any major change in policy" (Hoang Van Chi, *From Colonialism to Communism—A Case History of North Vietnam*, New York: Praeger, 1964, p. 70).

At the Third National Congress of the VWP, in September 1960, a decision was announced to create "a broad National United Front" under the leadership of the party in South Vietnam. Shortly thereafter, the "National Liberation Front [NLF] of South Vietnam" came into being, and the party in the South temporarily adopted a new name, the "People's Revolutionary Party" (see *Vietnam: Republic of Vietnam*). The VWP has on several occasions referred to the NLF policy in South Vietnam as a "cleverly applied tactic" of the party, and has listed "the struggle for the liberation of the south at present" as a "valuable experience" of "our party" (e.g., "Let Us Step Up the Theory-Formulating Task of the Party," *Hoc Tap*, no. 9, September 1966). Despite this, communists in both North and South Vietnam present the PRP as an "indigenous southern proletarian party."

According to the 1960 constitution of the Democratic Republic of Vietnam (DRV), the highest organ of state power is the National Assembly, which in theory enacts laws, supervises the enforcement of the provisions of the constitution, and elects the president and vice-president. The first National Assembly elections in seven years were held in April 1971 (see below). Although the constitution vests all legislative power in the hands of the National Assembly, in practice the VWP dictates and supervises the administrative, legislative, judicial, military, cultural, and economic aspects of the government through parallel but separate hierarchial organizations extending to the lowest territorial units. All key positions in the government are held by senior VWP leaders.

The VWP claimed a membership of 1,100,000 in 1970. Since that time there has been a major drive to recruit a "Ho Chi Minh class of party members" (see below), and tens of thousands of new party members have reportedly been admitted. The population of North Vietnam is about 22,000,000 (estimated 1971).

Leadership and Organization. According to the "Statute of the VWP," published by *Nhan Dan* on 4 November 1960, "the highest leading organ of the party is the National Delegates' Congress." Although "the National Delegates' Congress usually meets once every four years, faced with special circumstances, the Central Executive Committee may ... postpone its meetings during a certain period." The last such congress was held in September 1960. The party statute provides for a politburo, elected by the Central Committee, which shall "lead party activities during the interval between two plenary conferences of the Central Executive Committee." In practice, the Politburo is the most powerful group in North Vietnam. The post of Central Committee chairman has been vacant since the death of Ho Chi Minh.

There are nine announced full members of the Politburo. Although relative positions sometimes change, they are usually ranked as follows: Le Duan, Truong Chinh, Pham Van Dong, Pham Hung, Vo Nguyen Giap (senior general), Le Duc Tho, Nguyen Duy Trinh, Le Thanh Nghi, and Hoang Van Hoan. The two announced alternate members are Tran Quoc Hoan and Van Tien Dung (colonel general).

In addition to the 11 Politburo members listed above, there are 30 announced full members of the Central Committee, and 28 alternate members. Full members are Hoang Anh, Le Quang Ba, Nguyen Luong Bang, Duong Quoc Chinh, Nguyen Con, Tran Huu Duc, Vo Thuc Dong, Ha Huy Giap, Song Hao (lt. gen.), To Huu, Nguyen Van Kinh, Nguyen Khang, Ung Van Khiem, Nguyen Lam, Le Van Luong, Tran Luong (maj. gen.), Le Hien Mai (maj. gen.), Chu Huy Man, Do Muoi, Ha Thi Que, Bui Quang Tao, Chu Van Tan (col. gen.), Phan Trong Tue (maj. gen.), Hoang Van Thai (lt. gen.), Ton Duc Thang, Nguyen Thi Thap, Le Quoc Than, (Nguyen) Xuan Thuy, Nguyen Van Tran, and Hoang Quoc Viet. Announced alternate members are Ly Ban, Nguyen Thanh Binh, Dinh Thi Can, Nguyen Tho Chan, Le Quang Dao (maj. gen.), Tran Do (maj. gen.), Nguyen Don (maj. gen.), Tran Quy Hai (maj. gen.), Tran Quang Huy, Le Hoang, Nguyen Khai, Nguyen Huu Khieu, Hoang Van Kieu, Le Liem, Ngo Minh Loan, Nguyen Van Loc, Nguyen Huu Mai, Ha Ke Tan, Nguyen Khanh Toan, Hoang Tung, Tran Danh Tuyen, Le Thanh, Dinh Duc Thien, Ngo Thuyen, Tran Van Tra (lt. gen.), Bui Cong Trung, Nguyen Van Vinh (maj. gen.), and Nguyen Trong Vinh.

The most important mass organization is the Vietnam Fatherland Front, of which the VWP is the leading component. Founded on 5 September 1955, the front has continued to advance a program maintaining that Vietnam is indivisible but allowing for different conditions in the North and South. DRV President Ton Duc Thang is chairman of the Central Committee Presidium of the Fatherland Front. Other Presidium members include Truong Chinh, Hoang Van Hoan, Hoang Quoc Viet, Xuan Thuy, Nghiem Xuan Yem, Tran Dang Khoa, Nguyen Xien, Hoang Minh Giam, Phan Ke Toai, Chu Van Tan (col. gen.), Le Quang Dao (maj. gen.), Pham Kiet (maj. gen.), Nguyen Thi Thap, Ha Thi Que, Nguyen Duc Thuan, Vu Quang, Y Wang, Ven. Thich Tri Do, Vu Xuan Ky, Nguyen Van Huong, Nguyen Van Huyen, Dang Thai Mai, Ton That Tung, Tran Huu Duyet, Nguyen Thi Luu, Bo Xuan Luat, Nguyen Hoang Khoan, Duong Thi Thau, Pham Kieu, Nguyen Van Hieu, Pham Van Bach, Nguyen Van Hieu, and Hoang Mau. The secretary-general is Tran Huu Duyet, and the deputy secretary-general is Nguyen Thi Luu.

The Third Congress of the Vietnam Fatherland Front opened in Hanoi on 14 December 1971, and lasted for three days. Important mass organizations affiliated under the Fatherland Front are the Vietnam General Federation of Trade Unions, headed by Hoang Quoc Viet; the Ho Chi Minh

Working Youth Union, headed by Vu Quang; and the Vietnam Women's Union, headed by Mme Nguyen Thi Thap.

Party Internal Affairs. Prior to the death of Ho Chi Minh, it was common for analysts of North Vietnamese affairs to divide the Politburo into factions—usually pro-Chinese and pro-Soviet groups—or into "dogmatic" and "pragmatic" elements. While either approach oversimplifies, both have some merit. Truong Chinh, the fomer VWP secretary-general and leading theoritician, is clearly more "pro-Chinese" than General Vo Nguyen Giap and more "dogmatic" than First Secretary Le Duan. "Truong Chinh" is Vietnamese for "Long March," and is the party name taken by Dang Xuan Khu, selected because it reflects his identification with the Chinese communists. Chinh was responsible for the brutal "land reform" which took place in North Vietnam between 1954 and 1956, and which is estimated to have taken as many as 500,000 lives (see Hoang Van Chi, *op. cit.*, pp. 72, 205). The popular revulsion to the "land reform" was so great that Truong Chinh was forced to step down as VWP secretary-general. Ho Chi Minh held the position for a short while, and then gave the job to Le Duan, changing the title to first secretary. Partly because of this, there have been reports of a personal quarrel between Chinh and Duan. There have also been reports of friction between Chinh and General Giap, a former history teacher who apparently holds strong reservations about becoming too closely involved with the Chinese—aware from his study of history that Chinese imperialism has traditionally been Vietnam's greatest enemy. Le Duan is reported to have a personal animosity with Le Duc Tho, with whom he is thought to have quarreled during the French-Viet Minh war over strategy in the South. (For additional information on conflicts within the Politburo see P. J. Honey, *Communism in North Vietnam*, Cambridge, Mass.: The MIT Press, 1963, pp. 19-39.)

Ho Chi Minh was able to command the complete allegiance of the various factions by refusing to name an heir apparent. His appointment of the elderly Ton Duc Thang (now DRV president) as vice-president was viewed as a move to keep from having to appoint a successor, as Thang was not considered a serious contender for real power. Upon Ho's death, party statements indicated that the VWP would be led by a "collective leadership." Five months afterward Le Duan stated: "The Party's leadership constantly rests upon *the principle of collective leadership*" (emphasis in original). He explained: "Only collective decisions taken on the strength of a collective mind can avoid subjectivism, which leads to errors with often dangerous consequences. Collective leadership is the highest principle in the Party's leadership." (Le Duan, *The Vietnamese Revolution: Fundamental Problems, Essential Tasks*, Hanoi: Foreign Languages Publishing House, 1970, p. 182.) This emphasis on "collective leadership" was widely interpreted as a new concept in Vietnamese communist thinking, and as evidence that neither Duan, Chinh, nor DRV Premier Pham Van Dong would emerge as a new Ho Chi Minh. In fact, the concept of "collective leadership" has been an important part of Vietnamese communism for many years. In 1956 Ho Chi Minh himself spoke of the need to check the "personality cult" of Stalinism, and stated: "In general, our Party has carried out the principle of collective leadership" (*Selected Works*, Hanoi: Foreign Languages Publishing House, 1962, IV, 179, 184). The preamble to the party statute states that "The party must continually keep a firm hold on collective leadership, which is the highest leading principle of the party" (*Nhan Dan*, 15 September 1960). Four years before Ho's death, Le Duan stressed the need to "strengthen the role of collective leadership" (Le Duan, *On The Socialist Revolution in Vietnam*, Hanoi: Foreign Languages Publishing House, 1965, II, 35), and in May 1967, an apparent attack on the "personality cult" of Mao Tse-tung, the party's theoretical journal, *Hoc Tap*, asserted that "Only by collective leadership can one-sided and erroneous decisions be prevented." Thus, while it may be true that no member of the Politburo has emerged to a position of clear superiority, the fact that the party is stressing "collective leadership" is not in itself convincing proof. The party was stressing "collective leadership" during the years when Ho Chi Minh was clearly the most powerful man in North Vietnam.

The fact that Ho's seat as chairman of the VWP Central Committee was still vacant at the end of 1971 was more convincing as proof that if a power struggle were in fact taking place, no one had emerged the undisputed winner. There were indications that Le Duan was in a powerful position, perhaps more powerful than that of any of his most likely challengers. One of the most important documents from North Vietnam in recent years was Le Duan's 14 February 1970 *Nhan Dan* article, later published in English as *The Vietnamese Revolution: Fundamental Problems, Essential Tasks* (see *YICA*, 1971, p. 680). This lengthy article was given extensive coverage in all party media, and special instructions were published to assist party members in studying the document. During 1971 it continued to receive wide publicity and extensive quotation in theoretical articles. Several *Nhan Dan* editorials cited the document (e.g., 8 February, 26 March), and one article in the March-April issue of *Tuyen Huan* quoted from it at least seven times. In a *Hoc Tap* (January 1971) article on labor productivity, the chairman of the DRV Economic Affairs Board cited the 14 February 1970 Le Duan article and also a 1962 *Tuyen Huan* article by him. One *Nhan Dan* (26 March) editorial cited the February article twice, and quoted also from "Comrade Le Duan's teachings" in a 1966 speech.

In January 1971, Canadian journalist Michael Maclear—one of few Western journalists allowed to visit North Vietnam more than once—concluded that "at the end of a long power struggle it seems that Le Duan ... has finally established his supremacy over his rivals" (*Economist*, 23 January 1971). In May and June, there was speculation that perhaps Le Duan was in political trouble, and suggestions of possible "immenent changes in the constellation of the present North Vietnamese collective leadership" (*Far Eastern Economic Review*, Hong Kong, 12 June). This speculation was based primarily on Le Duan's lengthy stay in the Soviet Union following his attendance at the Soviet party congress—he was in the U.S.S.R. for six weeks—and the apparent secrecy of his activities during much of his stay. He was absent from Moscow during the May Day celebrations, and his name appeared in the news only once between 14 April and 9 May. He was absent from Hanoi during several important events which would normally require his presence. He was away during the 11 April National Assembly elections, but was reelected by 99.46 per cent of the vote in his precinct (surpassing the vote of any of his potential Politburo rivals, all of whom received over 99 per cent votes). Premier Pham Van Dong was the key speaker at the celebration of May Day, the anniversary of Ho Chi Minh's birthday on 19 May, and the party congress in Hanoi on 19 April, and Le Duan's name was not mentioned. (*Ibid.*) It is worth noting that Le Duan was one of the first foreign speakers to be allowed to address the Soviet party congress, and that his reception both in the U.S.S.R. and in China en route home were warm. Thus it may well be that his brief absence (during which he was reported to be in the Black Sea area, a location popular with communist leaders both for vacations and for medical treatment) was due to something other than a decline in power. Other possible explanations are that Le Duan was ill, or that he was having difficulty assuring continued support for the war by the DRV's communist allies (*ibid.*). Although the evidence is far from conclusive, it appears that during 1971 VWP First Secretary Le Duan was in a position of greater power than any of his rivals, but had not equaled the position of the late Ho Chi Minh and was still vulnerable and in need of the support of other Politburo leaders to maintain his position.

The VWP conducted a campaign to recruit a "Ho Chi Minh class of new party members" from 19 May 1970 until 19 May 1971 (the anniversary of Ho Chi Minh's birth). Considerable concern was expressed over the quality of the new party members. In the above-mentioned talk to the party congress Pham Van Dong noted: "The efficiency of a number of party basic units and of a number of party members is still low. This is one of the great problems that needs to be solved." Dong stated that in the immediate future the Hanoi party chapter must "step up the campaign to improve the quality of party members" and "persist in educating party members along with heightening the sense of discipline within the party." (*Nhan Dan*, 18 May.) The party daily complained that while "in the recent phases of recruiting the Ho Chi Minh class of party members, our party has admitted to its ranks tens of thousands of new members," there were a number of "shortcomings" (*ibid.*, 10 May). The paper asserted: "The number of party members who do not meet the prescribed recruiting norms represent a remarkably high percentage and ... the leadership of party echelons in certain places at certain times is loose." The editorial concluded that "under whatever circumstances, those who are admitted to the party must fulfill the prescribed norms." (*Ibid.*)

Domestic Attitudes and Activities. During recent years there has been a debate within the VWP over priorities—whether primary emphasis should be given the task of "liberating the South," or whether resources should be devoted first to strengthening the North, to be followed by liberating the South at some time in the near future. All of the senior VWP leaders acknowledge that both goals are important, but differ on the question of priorities. The faction which advocates strengthening North Vietnam first—generally thought to be headed by Truong Chinh—is apparently concerned about North Vietnam's ability to continue supporting the war without first building up its run-down economy, and about the willingness of the people to continue supporting the war effort. There have been reports of serious morale problems among the people and army in North Vietnam, and it is likely that at least one of the reasons for an emphasis on producing consumers' goods and raising the living standards of the people is to improve morale. The faction favoring primary emphasis on liberating the South—thought to be headed by Le Duan—is apparently concerned about morale also. Not only might the North Vietnamese population resist supporting the war effort if it is unnecessarily protracted, but the communists in South Vietnam might feel abandoned and give up the fight.

Public statements by party and governmental officials during 1971 indicated that both objectives were to receive about equal attention. A New Year's Day broadcast on the 1971 State Plan declared:

> North Vietnam's duty consists of [insuring] that the great frontline [South Vietnam] will receive full assistance in time under all circumstances and simultaneously stepping up economic and cultural activities, building the rear [North Vietnam] firmly and all-sidedly, and causing socialist construction in the North to progress strongly.... In accordance with this spirit, the 1971 State Plan must, on the one hand, aim at mobilizing manpower and material riches to urgently and timely provide all battlefields [South Vietnam, Laos, and Cambodia] with necessary aid.... On the other hand, it must aim at developing production, practicing thriftiness, restoring and developing the economy, and causing socialist construction to advance a new step. (Hanoi radio, 1 January 1971.)

Premier Pham Van Dong, in his March report to the seventh session of the National Assembly, explained: "Now, as the situation has become more urgent and our tasks heavier, we must ... increase the North's support to the South, [and] at the same time, we must endeavour to accelerate the building of socialism in the North politically, economically, and culturally" (Vietnam News Agency [VNA], 5 March). Central Committee member Do Muoi stated in an article on labor productivity: "In the present stage when we must perform two strategic tasks at the same time—struggling against U.S. aggression for national salvation and building socialism.... We have no other choice than [to] motivate all our people to boost production and practice economy, to 'tighten our belts,' to reduce unnecessary expenses ... while at the same time taking care of our people's livelihood and satisfying the basic needs of the people." (*Hoc Tap*, January.)

Do Muoi was one of many VWP leaders to complain of waste and corruption in North Vietnamese society. He charged that there were people who "did not exert their maximum efforts in fulfilling their tasks, did not practice economy, and even wasted or embezzled the state's property.'' He added:

> In agricultural and industrial production and in communications and transportation activities, there has been a wastage of human, material, and financial resources.... Machines and equipment have not been used to full efficiency.... The wastage of raw materials, fuel, and semifinished materials in the industrial branches has exceeded the prescribed norms. Labor output in the industrial branches has decreased. The official number of workdays and workhours has not been fulfilled. As a result, the cost of industrial goods has increased considerably. In agricultural cooperatives, the waste of manpower, the expenditures incurred in the use of materials, and the amount of money spent on a cultivated hectare of paddy have increased enormously. (*Hoc Tap*, January.)

In September, Pham Van Dong reported that North Vietnam had been hit by the worst floods in its history. The streets of Hanoi were reportedly waist-deep with water, and much of the dike system—essential to protect the country's rice bowl—had been destroyed. Although no casualty figures were released, the flood was considered worse than the 1945 flood which reportedly killed a million persons. U.S. intelligence specialists estimated that about 800,000 tons of North Vietnamese rice—10 per cent of the annual crop—were completely destroyed by the floods, which lasted for three months.

Morale and discipline problems were also present in the North Vietnamese Army (NVA or PAVN). In order to meet the requirements of fighting wars in South Vietnam, Laos, and Cambodia, the North Vietnamese conducted a number of recruitment drives during 1971 (*Christian Science Monitor*, 3 March). NVA prisoners and defectors in South Vietnam have reported that it is not uncommon for young men who receive conscription notices to move to neighboring villages where the population is usually willing to support them. The army daily newspaper complained in an editorial in January: ''Loose discipline has manifested itself in the following ways: orders and directives have not been strictly, properly and firmly implemented; combat readiness systems and regulations have not yet been correctly implemented; there is procrastination in the carrying out of orders and training of soldier's deportment.'' (*Quan Doi Nhan Dan*, 7 January.) Army discipline was the subject of several editorials in July. One argued that while ''leaders and commanders must not become militarist and mechanical,'' they must not ''be soft and irresolute with regard to the implementation of instructions and orders.... All cadres must closely maintain military discipline, be strict with the lower echelons and combatants, and absolutely must not relax discipline.'' (*Ibid.*, 7 July.) The paper complained that ''outside military billets, there still are soldiers who dress outlandishly, speak impolitely to others, behave themselves in an uncivilized manner, and violate state laws, discipline, and public sanitary regulations.'' (Quoted in *Christian Science Monitor*, 24 July.)

Soldiers were not the only North Vietnamese youths to ''dress outlandishly'' or ''behave themselves in an uncivilized manner.'' *Hanoi Moi* (12 January) carried an account of the trial of Phan Thang Toan and his ''gang.'' Toan had been charged with playing ''rock'' music which he had learned by listening to South Vietnamese ''psywar'' stations. According to *Hanoi Moi*, Toan and his friends ''enticed a certain number of young boys and girls who loved music but who were artistically immature, and caused them to follow their clique. [They] told each other about the dissolute, degrading, and orgy-filled life of the capitalist class.'' Toan was accused of injecting North Vietnamese youths with the ''poison of discontent'': ''the philosophy of an American-style 'free' life, the reactionary philosophy of 'art for art's sake.' '' Toan and his fellow musicians ''slandered our society, saying that there was no freedom and that in our society there was no room for artists to flourish.... They induced youths dreaming of an American or a Saigon life-style to oppose our regime and to avoid the labor task and military obligation.'' At his trial, ''Toan confessed [that] he did not like our regime [and] continually dreamed of a 'free' and dissolute life like that in the United States and Saigon." The article noted that "because of the seriousness of the case, the court sentenced Toan to fifteen years' imprisonment and the forfeiture of his citizenship rights for five years after his release."

During 1971 elections were held in North Vietnam for the Fourth Legislature of the National Assembly, and for People's Councils. The national assembly elections, and the subsequent first session of the Fourth Legislature, produced few surprises. In the first place, the National Assembly serves as nothing more than a rubber stamp for decisions made by the party. As *Nhan Dan* (6 March) observed, "Under the party's leadership, the National Assembly [has] always fulfilled its various functions and missions." While "the law states that mass organizations and political parties [can] introduce candidates ... in reality, the Fatherland Front suggests the list of candidates" (*Nhan Dan*, 13 February). The Fatherland Front is, as noted above, under the control of the VWP. "The national assembly has met on an average [of] only once every 14 months since 1965, and has been limited to approving actions already decided upon" (*Christian Science Monitor*, 14 April). For the 11 April 1971 election, there were 529 candidates for 420 seats. Voting was done openly, without the secrecy of booths. (*New York Times*, 12 April.) Although a detailed account of election procedures was not given, Hanoi radio (24 April) quoted Truong Chinh as urging "that the 'election cells' endeavor to perform well their task of concrete directions to the voters so that the latter would not make mistakes in the voting process." During the 1960 election, the function of these "election cells" was described as that of helping "the comrades who had difficulty in making out their ballot" (VNA, 9 May 1960). With the help of the election cells, all of the key party leaders were reelected by a vote of 99-plus per cent.

One of the most important results of the election was that the 89 surviving deputies representing constituencies in South Vietnam—elected in the 6 January 1946 election held by the Viet Minh, and allowed to retain their membership in the assembly during subsequent elections—were excluded from the assembly. The reason for their exclusion was given by Standing Committee's secretary-general, Ton Quang Phiet, in a report to the National Assembly:

> The southern deputies have constantly proved themselves worthy of the mission entrusted to them by the southern compatriots, [but] at present ... the southern revolution has undergone new developments. On 6 June 1969, the southern Vietnamese national delegates' congress elected the Republic of South Vietnam Provisional Revolutionary Government [PRG] and its Advisory Council.... At present, the [PRG] has been recognized by more than 20 countries.... In view of this situation, the National Assembly Standing Committee feels that it is no longer proper to continue to extend the term of the southern deputies in the DRV National Assembly. (Hanoi radio, 6 March.)

The first session of the Fourth Legislature met in Hanoi from 7 to 10 June. It devoted its activities primarily to approving resolutions and reports submitted by the Standing Committee, and to reelecting various senior governmental leaders (*ibid.*, 6 March). On 13 June *Nhan Dan* published a revised list of governmental leaders as approved by the assembly. There were few significant changes, but three omissions were noted by Western observers. Most importantly, VWP Politburo member Pham Hung was not reelected as a vice-premier. Since Hung is thought to have been heading the Central Office for South Vietnam (COSVN) for the past few years (see *Vietnam: Republic of Vietnam*), some observers concluded that he might be dead. A more likely explanation is that the VWP wants Pham Hung to play a more open role in the PRG in South Vietnam in the future. This theory is supported by the National Assembly's replacing Ung Van Khiem—a VWP Central Committee member—with Duong Quoc Chinh as Interior minister. Khiem was born in Cochin China (South Vietnam), and for more than twenty years was a key party expert on South Vietnam. In 1953 he was named chairman of the VWP's South Vietnam Sub-Committee for Finance and Economic Affairs. As a reward for his work in South Vietnam during the French-Viet Minh war, Khiem was named deputy foreign minister of the DRV in 1954 and foreign minister in 1961.

He had headed the Ministry of the Interior since 1963. It may well be that the VWP intends to utilize Ung Van Khiem in South Vietnam.

Another omission from the National Assembly list was the National Reunification Commission (NRC), and its former chairman, Major General Nguyen Van Vinh. The NRC had as its primary objective the promotion of the overthrow of the South Vietnamese government. General Vinh, while born in North Vietnam, spent the French-Viet Minh War in the South and for several years has been reported in South Vietnam with COSVN (see *Vietnam: Republic of Vietnam*). While taken alone the omissions of Pham Hung, Ung Van Khiem, and Nguyen Van Vinh may not be viewed as significant, when considered together and in light of the almost simultaneous exclusion of the 89 "southern deputies" from the National Assembly they suggest a change in Hanoi's strategy toward South Vietnam. It is quite possible that they will in the future become key figures in the PRG.

The Vietnam Fatherland Front held its Third Congress in Hanoi on 14-16 December 1971, ten years after the Second Congress. During the congress, Hoang Quoc Viet delivered a major address which stressed the importance of "strengthening the North in every way" while assisting the movement in South Vietnam. He asserted: "The rear base [North Vietnam] is one of the permanent factors deciding victory on the battlefield. The rear base is a source of human and material supplies and of political and spiritual encouragement for the frontline. The firmer and stronger the rear base is, the more victories the frontline will win." (*Nhan Dan*, 16 December.) The final act of the congress was to issue an appeal calling on everyone in North Vietnam to work harder and "to consolidate our strength in all fields, to completely defeat the U.S. aggressors, to supply the big front [South Vietnam] in time and adequately, to improve the livelihood of the northern people step by step, and to continue to build a strong and stable socialist North" (*ibid.*, 18 December). The Fatherland Front also announced a new Central Committee of 134 members instead of the original 81. The new Presidium (see above) consists of 34 members, almost triple the original 12.

International Views and Positions. Although forced by military and economic necessities to rely on the U.S.S.R. and China for vital supplies, North Vietnam has attempted to follow a middle path in the Sino-Soviet dispute, shifting slightly one way or the other depending upon the international situation from year to year. While appreciative of external aid, DRV leaders have stressed the need for self-sufficiency, frequently quoting the late President Ho Chi Minh: "Naturally, the assistance of friendly countries is important, but we must not rely on it nor expect it. A people who do not achieve self-sufficiency but who expect assistance from other peoples are not worthy of their independence." (Quoted by Do Muoi, *Hoc Tap*, January 1971.) DRV Foreign Minister Nguyen Duy Trinh, in a lengthy article on "The Diplomatic Task" in the party theoretical journal, stated:

> We are defeating the U.S. imperialists for the sake of the Vietnamese revolution and at the same time for the sake of the world revolution.... Our party has asserted [that] each party [has] the duty to contribute to the common revolutionary struggle of the people of the world. The revolution in our country is part of the world revolution. (*Ibid.*, April.)

He quoted from a speech made by Ho Chi Minh in 1964:

> The foreign policy of our party and state consists of strengthening solidarity with the brother socialist countries on the basis of Marxism-Leninism and proletarian internationalism ... of resolutely supporting the national liberation and national independence protection movement and of supporting the struggle movement of the working class and the world's people for peace, national independence, democracy, and socialism.

Trinh pledged that the DRV would "strive to strengthen [its] militant solidarity and friendly relations with the brother socialist countries, especially the Soviet Union and China," and asserted that the "militant solidarity" between the DRV and the U.S.S.R. and China had been strengthened:

"We have done and will do our best in supporting efforts aimed at making positive contributions to restoring and strengthening the solidarity of the socialist camp and the international communist movement . . . in a reasonable and sensible manner."

During 1971 the VWP and DRV appeared to have a very warm relationship with the Soviet Union. Although total aid figures are not normally released by the DRV, Soviet aid is thought to total at least 500 million dollars per year (*New York Times*, 11 March). As mentioned above, VWP First Secretary Le Duan spent six weeks in the Soviet Union in March, April, and May, and attended the Soviet party Congress. His name was listed first by *Pravda* in reporting on about 50 foreign delegations that had arrived for the congress (*ibid.*, 29 March). During the visit, a meeting between Duan and Soviet party leader Brezhnev was reported during which "the two party leaders reaffirmed the fervent, unswerving desire of both sides to further develop relations of militant friendship, solidarity, and comprehensive cooperation between the two parties" (Moscow radio, 10 May). In September a DRV National Assembly delegation led by Hoang Van Hoan paid a three-day friendship visit to the U.S.S.R. (VNA, 16 September). During October, Soviet head of state Podgorny made a widely publicized visit to Hanoi, which resulted in a Soviet pledge of "assistance on all levels—military, political and diplomatic" (*New York Times*, 5 October). This was the first visit to the DRV by a top-level Soviet leader in two years. In an editorial welcoming Podgorny, the army daily *Quan Doi Nhan Dan* (3 October) referred to the Soviet Union as "the strongest great socialist power" and asserted that "The brilliant achievements of the Soviet Union are of great encouragement to the working class and the revolutionary people throughout the world." At a banquet welcoming Podgorny DRV President Ton Duc Thang was equally high with his praise of Soviet accomplishments, but balanced his remarks with an expression of appreciation for Chinese aid as well (*New York Times*, 5 October). The U.S.S.R. continued to support a political settlement of the problems of Vietnam and Indochina during 1971 (e.g., Moscow radio, 11 February and 17 April). The Soviets observed a "month of solidarity with Vietnam" starting on 20 July.

VWP and DRV relations with China were warm during 1971, in spite of North Vietnamese concern over the upcoming visit to China by U.S. President Nixon. China is estimated to provide approximately 200 million dollars worth of aid annually to the DRV (*New York Times*, 11 March). On 15 February a new economic and military aid agreement was announced (NCNA, 15 February), but as is normally the case no figures were released. In June, on the occasion of the fiftieth anniversary of the founding of the Chinese Communist Party, the VWP Central Committee sent a message of congratulations which referred to Vietnam and China as being "neighbors as closely related as the lips and the teeth" (*Peking Review*, no. 28, 9 July).

Shortly after South Vietnamese soldiers began operations against the Ho Chi Minh trail in Laos, DRV Paris talks spokesman Nguyen Thanh Le stated: "I must affirm that intensification of aggression against the DRV, multiplication of acts of war against North Vietnam and Laos, constitute a grave threat to China which will not stand idle in the face of such aggression" (*Washington Post*, 19 February).

On 6 March Chinese Premier Chou En-lai led a party and governmental delegation to Hanoi which was warmly received. In a joint statement signed on 8 March, Chou En-lai announced: "Should U.S. imperialism go down the road of expanding its war of aggression in Indochina, the Chinese people are determined to take all necessary measures, not flinching even from the greatest national sacrifices, to give all-out support and assistance to the Vietnamese and other Indochinese peoples for the thorough defeat of the U.S. aggressors" (NCNA, 10 March). Later that month, when Le Duan stopped off in Peking en route to the Soviet party congress, Chou remarked that the "great victory" of the North Vietnamese campaign in Laos had "fully demonstrated the boundless might of the people's war," and Le Duan replied that the success could not "be disassociated from the devoted assistance of the fraternal Chinese people" (VNA, 28 March). Le Duan stopped in Peking en route home from Moscow, and received an equally warm reception.

In September a Chinese economic delegation visited the DRV and was warmly received. DRV Vice Premier Le Thanh Nghi referred to Vietnam and China as being as "closely related as the lips and the teeth," but balanced his remarks with a reference to "the great support and assistance of the Soviet people" (NCNA, 27 September). In November DRV Premier Pham Van Dong led a party and governmental delegation to Peking and stated: "On behalf of the delegation of the Vietnam Workers Party ... we wish to express our sincere and deep thanks to the peoples of the Soviet Union ... for their tremendous and valuable sympathy, support and assistance." In a plea for Sino-Soviet unity, he quoted Ho Chi Minh's will: "I wish that our party will do its best to contribute effectively to the restoration of unity among the fraternal parties on the basis of Marxism-Leninism and proletarian internationalism" (VNA, 24 November).

The announcement that President Nixon would visit China during 1972 was greeted with alarm in Hanoi. On 19 July a *Nhan Dan* editorial—entitled "The Nixon Doctrine Will Surely Fail"—accused the United States of trying to divide the socialist camp, "winning over one section and pitting it against another," and of "trying to achieve a compromise between the big powers in an attempt to make smaller countries bow to their arrangements." A similar editorial in the army daily was branded by some observers as "Hanoi's strongest attack on Peking to date" (*Washington Post*, 14 August). In August, *Hoc Tap* stated: "If the Nixon Administration truly wants to find a solution to the Vietnam problem, there is no alternative but to talk directly with the genuine representatives of the people of South and North Vietnam. Only those who are fighting the Americans can raise a decisive voice about the future of their own country." In an attempt to reassure the Vietnamese people, the newspaper *Thong Nhut* published a letter describing "the worries ... of compatriots in Saigon as to whether international support will lessen as a result [of the Nixon visit] and whether Nixon will be successful in his global diplomatic [attempts] to disengage himself from Vietnam." In reply, the paper assured the readers that the U.S.S.R. and China would never let the Vietnamese communists down, and cited recent pledges of aid from both countries. The paper also stressed that the most important thing was self-reliance and not depending on others. (*Christian Science Monitor*, 23 November.)

North Vietnam and the VWP continued during 1971 to support both materially and through propaganda the activities of communists in South Vietnam, Laos, and Cambodia. Toward the end of the year there were signs of a decrease in publicity for the South Vietnamese communists—for example, the usual slogan supporting the PRG or the NLF on the anniversary of the "August Revolution" was absent (*Baltimore Sun*, 22 September). This may have been another part of an overall program to separate the southern communists from the VWP for propaganda purposes. From Laos, Pathet Lao leaders stopped in Hanoi en route to and from the Soviet party congress (Pathet Lao News Agency, 24 March; VNA, 10 May). In February, Prince Norodom Sihanouk, chairman of the Peking-based National United Front of Kampuchea (NUFK), made a friendship visit to North Vietnam (Hanoi radio, 11 February).

North Vietnam and the VWP maintained close relations with all of the Eastern European communist states, and during 1971 signed military and economic aid agreements with several of them. In March trade relations were established with Chile (VNA, 31 March). In October the DRV and Switzerland established diplomatic relations (Hanoi radio, 11 October). Relations with Cuba and North Korea continued to be cordial; delegations from both countries visited the DRV.

There were frequent expressions of appreciation for the anti-war movements throughout the world, especially in the United States. The "spring offensive" against the war in the United States received extensive coverage in English-language broadcasts directed at U.S. soldiers, and also in Vietnamese broadcasts both for domestic consumption and beamed to South Vietnam. The "Pentagon papers''—a collection of stolen classified government documents published by several U.S. news-papers—also were widely reported, and were cited as further proof that the United States was the aggressor in Vietnam (*New York Times*, 18 June). Hanoi radio asserted: "The important point lies in the publication by U.S. newspapers of these secret documents, which gives evidence of the deep contradictions within the U.S. ruling groups ... due to the effects of the Vietnam war.... This publication also demonstrates the awakening of the Americans' conscience and their intense weariness of the war of aggression [which] is leading to opposition against and unmasking of the U.S. government by all means.'' (Hanoi radio, 29 June.)

Publications. VWP policy statements and directives are carried primarily in the daily organ of its Central Committee, *Nhan Dan* (The People), whose editor in chief is Hoang Tung; in *Hoc Tap* (Studies), the VWP monthly theoretical journal edited by Dao Duy Tung; and in *Quan Doi Nhan Dan* (People's Army), the daily organ of the army. Other major publications include *Tien Phong* (Vanguard), the organ of the Central Committee of the Ho Chi Minh Working Youth Union; *Lao Dong* (Labor), the organ of the Vietnam General Federation of Trade Unions; *Cuu Quoc* (National Salvation), the weekly organ of the Central Committee of the Vietnam Fatherland Front; *Doc Lap* (Independence), the weekly organ of the Central Committee of the Vietnam Democratic Party; and *To Quoc* (Motherland), the bimonthly organ of the Vietnam Socialist Party. International publications include *Vietnam Courier*, a weekly published in English and French by the Committee for Cultural Relations with Foreign Countries, and *Vietnam*, an illustrated monthly published in English, French, Russian, Chinese, and Vietnamese.

Party statements are also broadcast by the Vietnam News Agency, which is headed by Dat Tung.

Robert F. Turner

Vietnam:
Republic of Vietnam

Prior to the division of Vietnam at the seventeenth parallel by the Geneva Conference of 1954, the communist movement throughout the country was under the control of the Indochinese Communist Party, renamed the Vietnam Workers' Party (VWP) in 1951 (see *Democratic Republic of Vietnam*). After partition, the party went underground in the South but still received instructions from the VWP leadership in Hanoi. Utilizing the "united front" strategy which had been highly successful for Vietnamese communists during years past, the VWP Central Committee announced in September 1960: "To ensure the complete success for the revolutionary struggle in South Vietnam, our people there, under the leadership of the Marxist-Leninist Party of the working class, must strive [to] bring into being a broad National United Front" (Le Duan, in *Third National Congress of the Viet Nam Workers' Party*, Hanoi: Foreign Languages Publishing House, I, 62-63). Three months later, on 20 December, the National Liberation Front of South Vietnam (Mat Tran Dan Toc Giai Phong Mien Nam Viet Nam; NLFSV or NLF) was founded.

For propaganda reasons, the VWP decided to establish an "independent" Marxist-Leninist party in the South. On 18 January 1962, the Hanoi-based Vietnam News Agency (VNA) announced that the People's Revolutionary Party (Dang Nhan Dan Cach Mang; PRP) had been formally established on 1 January. The relationship between this "new" Marxist-Leninist party and the VWP was made clear by an internal party document captured in Ba Xuyen Province, dated 7 December 1961: "The People's Revolutionary Party has only the appearance of an independent existence; actually, our party is nothing but the Lao Dong Party of Vietnam [VWP], unified from North to South, under the direction of the Central Executive Committee of the party, the chief of which is President Ho [Chi Minh]." Although the two parties disclaim any official connection in their external propaganda, it is noteworthy that the international communist movement does not recognize the independent existance of the PRP, dealing directly with the North Vietnamese government and party in matters concerning material aid and supplies. The PRP and all communist organizations are illegal in South Vietnam.

On 8 June 1969 a "Congress of People's Representatives" met in "liberated areas" of South Vietnam and established the "Provisional Revolutionary Government of the Republic of South Vietnam" (PRG). Shortly thereafter, the PRG assumed all state functions of the NLF, internal and external—including the seat at the Paris peace talks. During 1971 most nonmilitary communist activity in South Vietnam was conducted in the name of the PRG. The term "Viet Cong"—a condensation of Viet Nam Cong San, "Vietnamese Communist"—is often used to identify the military and political elements of the South Vietnamese communist movement as distinct from the movement in North Vietnam and those North Vietnamese Army (NVA) regulars fighting in South Vietnam.

In 1951 the activities of the VWP in southern Vietnam were organized under a six-man "Central Office for South Vietnam (Trung Uong Cuc Mien Nam: COSVN), and were headed by Le Duan, who is now first secretary of the VWP in Hanoi. COSVN was phased out in 1954, but its function was assumed by the Nam Bo Regional Committee. In late 1960 Hanoi decided to reactivate COSVN, and sent Major General Tran Luong, a member of the VWP Central Committee, to South Vietnam to be in command. Since then, actual military command of Viet Cong forces has been in the hands of senior North Vietnamese military and political leaders, who are in close contact with the VWP in Hanoi.

Accurate estimates of PRP membership are not available, but most authorities place the figure at between 75,000 and 100,000. Viet Cong military forces include perhaps 40,000 main force regulars, and another 100,000 guerrillas or administrative personnel. There were thought to be about 100,000 NVA soldiers in South Vietnam during 1971. The population of South Vietnam is about 18,000,000 (estimated 1971).

Leadership and Organization. The chairman of the PRP Central Committee is Vo Chi Cong, who is thought to be also known as Nguyen Van Cuc. The secretary-general is Tran Nam Trung, who is thought to be Tran Van Tra, an NVA lieutenant general and VWP Central Committee alternate member. The deputy secretary-general is thought to be Nguyen Van Lien, and the secretary, Van Han Hau. Other members of the PRP leadership reportedly include: Nguyen Huu Tho (NLF chairman), Huynh Tan Phat (PRG president), Tran Do (NVA major general), Pham Xuan Thai (Liberation Worker's Association chairman and NLF Central Committee Presidium member), Pham Trong Dan, Ybih Aleo (NLF Central Committee Presidium vice-chairman and PRG Advisory Council member), Tran Bach Dang (NLF Central Committee Presidium member and Liberation Youth Association president), Dang Tran Thi (NLF Central Committee Presidium member and Liberation Workers' Association vice-chairman), Rochom Thep (Central Trung Bo PRG vice-chairman), Le Thanh Nam (NLF Central Committee member), Huynh Van Tam (NLF Central Committee member), Tran Van Thanh (NLF Central Committee member), Tran Hoai Nam (NLF Central Committee member), and Tran Van Binh. (For details of PRP organizational structure see Douglas Pike, *Viet Cong: The Organization and Techniques of the National Liberation Front of South Vietnam*, Cambridge, Mass.: The M.I.T. Press, 1966, pp. 145-150.)

The NLF is represented at the hamlet and village level by the "administrative liberation associations," which themselves are composed of "functional liberation associations" and political parties (see Pike, *op. cit.* pp. 109-18). Nominally, authority runs from the NLF Central Committee down through a number of administrative levels to the village administrative liberation associations, but in fact all command authority and reporting passes vertically through PRP channels to COSVN. The NLF Central Committee was intended to have 64 members, but at the time of its founding 11 seats were reserved for representatives of political parties and other organizations or forces which might join the NLF at a later date. The chairman of the Presidium of the Central Committee of the NLF is Nguyen Huu Tho. Vice-chairmen include Ybih Aleo, Dr. Phung Van Cung, Vo Chi Cong, Venerable Thom Me The Nhem, Huynh Tan Phat, and Tran Nam Trung. Other Presidium members are: General (Mrs.) Nguyen Thi Dinh, Tran Bach Dang, Bonze Thich Thien Hao, Tran Buu Kiem, Nguyen Ngoc Ngoi, Pham Xuan Thai, Nguyen Huu The, Nguyen Van Dang, and Dang Tran Thi. The NLF Central Committee Secretariat is composed of Huynh Tan Phat (secretary-general), Professor Le Van Huan (deputy secretary-general), Ho Xuan Son, and Ung Ngoc Ky.

The PRG leadership consists of Huynh Tan Phat (chairman), Phung Van Cung (vice-chairman), Nguyen Van Kiet (vice-chairman), Nguyen Doa (vice-chairman), Tran Buu Kiem (minister to the chairman's office), Tran Nam Trung (minister of defense), Nguyen Thi Binh (minister of foreign affairs), Phung Van Cung (minister of the interior), Luu Huu Phuoc (minister of information and culture), Nguyen Van Kiet (minister of education and youth), Duong Quynh Hoa (minister of health, social action, and disabled soldiers), Truong Nhu Tang (minister of justice), Ung Ngoc

Ky (vice-minister to the chairman's office), Dong Van Cong and Nguyen Chanh (vice-ministers, defense), Le Quang Chanh and Hoang Bich Son (vice-ministers, foreign affairs), Nguyen Ngoc Thuong (vice-minister, interior), Nguyen Van Trieu (vice-minister, economy and finance), Hoang Trong Qui and Le Phuong (vice-ministers, information and culture), Le Van Tri and Ho Huu Nhut (vice-ministers, education and youth), Ho Van Hue and Bui Thi Me (vice-ministers, health, social action and disabled soldiers), and Le Van Tha (vice-minister, justice). The minister of economy and finance, Cao Van Bon, died 28 April 1971.

The PRG Advisory Council is chaired by Nguyen Huu Tho, and Trinh Dinh Thao is the vice-chairman. Members include Ybih Aleo, Huynh Cuong, Venerable Thich Don Hau, Bonze Huynh Van Tri, Nguyen Cao Phuong, Lam Van Tet, Vo Van, Le Van Giap, Lucien Pham Ngoc Hung, and (Mrs.) Nguyen Dinh Chi.

The Viet Cong organization about which the least is known is COSVN. According to high-ranking Viet Cong and NVA defectors, COSVN—often referred to as "R" by Vietnamese communists—was headed during 1971 by VWP Politburo member Pham Hung. This information is consistent with other intelligence sources, which report that Pham Hung replaced NVA Senior General Nguyen Chi Thanh, an alternate member of the VWP Politburo, when the latter was killed during an air attack in South Vietnam in July 1967. Hung's deputy is thought to be Nguyen Van Cuc known also as Muoi Ut. The important Military Affairs Committee is reportedly chaired by Lieutenant General Hoang Van Thai (a vice-minister of national defense in North Vietnam and member of the VWP Central Committee). Members of the Military Affairs Committee include: Lieutenant General Tran Van Tra and Major General Tran Do (VWP Central Committee alternate members), and Major General Tran Luong (reportedly also PRG minister of defense under the alias Tran Nam Trung, which has also been attributed to NVA Lieutenant General Tran Van Tra and others).

Regular NVA units operating in South Vietnam do not normally report through COSVN. All other communist military elements—main force and paramilitary—belong to the People's Liberation Armed Forces (PLAF). VWP Politburo member Pham Hung is reported to serve as both commanding officer and political officer of the PLAF. The senior military official is NVA Lieutenant General Hoang Van Thai, who is assisted by Lieutenant Generals Tran Van Tra and Nguyen Hau Xuyen, and Major Generals Le Trong Tan and Hoang Duc Anh. Major General Tran Do is thought to be the assistant political officer. Mrs. Nguyen Thi Dinh, the head of the Women's Liberation Association, has been presented by Viet Cong propagandists as a general in charge of all guerrilla warfare in the South. While this may be true, statements by senior defectors indicate that her position is devoid of actual power and that her function is primarily for propaganda purposes.

Another Viet Cong front is the Vietnam Alliance of National, Democratic, and Peace Forces (Lien Mien Dan Toc Dan Cav va Hoa Binh a Viet Nam; VANDPF), formed during the 1968 Tet offensive and announced in April 1968. The VANDPF is headed by Trinh Dinh Thao (vice-chairman, PRG Advisory Council): vice-chairmen are Lam Van Tet and Thich Don Hau. Most of the important VANDPF leaders hold positions in the NLF or PRG, and the organization has announced its "unanimity with the NLF on all subjects" (See *YICA*, 1969, pp. 907-9). The announced purpose of the VANDPF is to serve as an alliance of "intellectuals, students, civil servants, and others who despite their different political leanings and religious colors are identified with one another in their hatred for the unbearable rule of the U.S. puppets."

Domestic Attitudes and Activities. The PLAF claims that during 1971 it "wiped out nearly 250,000 enemy troops" and "shot down and destroyed on the ground 1,800 aircraft, demolished or captured nearly 8,000 military vehicles, sank 700 war vessels and combat launches, and seized 15,000 guns" (Liberation Press Agency [LPA], 4 January 1972). In spite of these claims, the year was a rough one for PLAF forces. In a major broadcast on "Some problems on the Ideological

Task of the South Vietnam PLAF." "Cuu Long" (thought to be a pseudonym of the PLAF assistant political officer, Tran Do) stated: "The combat of our armed forces ... has now become increasingly critical, difficult, and fierce. The demands of the resistance have become increasingly numerous." (Liberation Radio, 27 April 1971). "Cuu Long" warned against "rightist phenomena" which had "at times appeared in different forms in every unit, locality, and individual." He explained:

> The rightist ideology is the ideology of the small bourgeois, and ideology that is influenced by remnants of the bourgeois and feudal ideology that have remained in our persons. It can easily cause us to lose our spirit of self-reliance ... to evaluate the enemy incorrectly, to erroneously believe in an easy success at some times, to fear length and hardships at other times, and to fail to resolutely fulfill our tasks at still other times. Therefore, more than ever, it is at present necessary to further strengthen political education and ideological leadership in a constantly critical and active manner and on a widespread basis. (*Ibid.*)

In the same article, which was broadcast in five installments, "Cuu Long" revealed some of the difficulties facing the Viet Cong on the military front, where many units had to fight " ... in extremely difficult conditions with a shortage of everything." These shortages, combined with the political unreliability of some cadres, had led to "acts that are not truly revolutionary. They still fear difficulties and hardships and are afraid of making sacrifices." One of the methods used by the Vietnamese communists to encourage personal sacrifice by soldiers is the "hero emulation movement." Stories of the heroism of certain NVA or PLAF soldiers are told and retold through lectures, posters, songs, poems, and any other propaganda media available, and other soldiers are encouraged to emulate their examples. One of the most famous of all Viet Cong "emulation heroes" way young Nguyen Van Be, whose face appeared on the front page of nearly every communist periodical in Vietnam. A "Nguyen Van Be" hero medal was created in his memory, and songs were written detailing his exploits. Be was reported to have been taken prisoner by U.S. forces in the Mekong Delta. When questioned about the workings of an anti-tank mine, he grabbed the mine and smashed it against a nearby armored personnel carrier, killing himself and 69 "U.S. aggressor troops." In fact, Be was found in a prison camp shortly after the emulation campaign began, and was identified by the mother and neighbors of the "dead hero" Nguyen Van Be. Viet Cong propaganda cadres had been informed that Be was killed in an ambush, and had created the story of his "heroic sacrifice" to motivate other soldiers. In early October 1971 the PLAF held an "Eastern Nam Bo and Saigon PLAF Heroes' and Emulation Combatants' Congress," which claimed that in the past ten years the PLAF had "built a broad emulation movement and created 149 heroes, 77 heroic units, and tens of thousands of emulation combatants and outstanding valiant combatants" (Liberation Radio, 8 October).

Along with efforts to inspire and motivate their own soldiers, the Viet Cong have devoted much attention to military proselyting activities. An important part of this program is played by Liberation Radio, which frequently encourages South Vietnamese Army (ARVN) soldiers to desert. "Don't follow the enemy ... because you will die uselessly. Turn your guns on him and return to the people's side. You will be treated kindly and humanely." (*Ibid.*, 27 February.) A broadcast claimed: "Puppet troops [have] staged mass desertion and revolt movements everywhere. The movement to oppose recruitment has been seethingly conducted." (*Ibid.*, 10 April.)

There were two major elections in South Vietnam during 1971: 1,240 candidates competed for 159 lower house seats on 29 August; and President Nguyen Van Thieu ran unopposed for reelection on 3 October. Prohibited from running in either election, communists were strongly critical of both. The Viet Cong described the House elections as "a rigged, deceitful farce" and declared: "Being aware of the true nature of these elections, our compatriots have firmly boycotted them.... As in previous times, our compatriots have firmly refused ... to go to the polls." (*Ibid.*, 29 August.) Two days before the presidential election, a broadcast asserted: "If we desire peace and a bountiful life we will certainly not vote for Thieu and allow him to continue to rule this country'' (*ibid.*, 1 October). The day following the election, the PRG delegation to the Paris conference charged that the "election farce" had "taken place with the most cheating tricks and the most barbarous terrorist and repressive measures" (VNA, 5 October).

As in the past, the holding of elections brought an increase in communist terrorism (*New York Times*, 30 August and 4 October). Terrorism—assassinations, bombings, kidnaping, etc.—has always played a major role in Viet Cong strategy (see Douglas Pike, *The Viet-Cong Strategy of Terror*, Saigon: United States Mission, Vietnam, 1970). The most serious terrorist attack since 1965 occurred on 17 September when the Tu Do nightclub in downtown Saigon was blown up. The bombing attack resulted in more than 75 casualties, including 19 persons killed. Among the more than 50 casualties of Viet Cong terrorism on National Assembly election day were two election officials and five villagers killed in Binh Dinh Province when a hand grenade was thrown into a polling booth. Every year since 1966 thousands of South Vietnamese citizens have been assassinated by Viet Cong terrorists (*ibid.*, p. 117). Typical targets are village and hamlet administrative officials, schoolteachers, pacification cadres, members of nationalist political parties, religious leaders, and relatives of such persons who refuse to pressure them to work for or cooperate with the Viet Cong: in short, all potential opposition leadership. While in general this strategy is aimed at the middle- and lower-level supporters of the government, occasionally a more prominent individual is assassinated. An example was the assassination of Professor Nguyen Van Bong in early November. Bong was the leader of the Progressivist Nationalist Party and considered himself part of the "loyal opposition." While supporting the war against the communists, Bong was a frequent critic of President Thieu on domestic issues. He was highly respected, and was considered a serious candidate for premier in 1971 and possibly for president in the future (*New York Times*, 11 November). In addition to trying to eliminate potential opposition through terrorism, the Viet Cong have reportedly made an extensive effort to infiltrate the South Vietnamese government. Estimates of the extent of this effort range from 6,000 or 7,000 to more than 30,000 (*Christian Science Monitor*, 6 January).

A common element in many Viet Cong appeals is the call for "unity." In May, for example, a joint meeting of the PRG, NLF, and VANDPF was held to celebrate the birthday of the late North Vietnamese president, Ho Chi Minh. At the ceremony PRG President Huynh Tan Phat said:

> The key to our success resides in the fact that we have correctly implemented President Ho's teaching which is condensed in these golden letters and which has been engraved forever in our minds: "Unity, unity, great unity." The resistance undertaking is that of our entire people. Unity constitutes a strength to defeat all enemies. (Liberation Radio, 18 May.)

Considerable attention was devoted to criticizing the economy of South Vietnam and stressing its problems. Although the rate of inflation was reduced by more than 50 percent from 1970 to 1971 (*New York Times*, 29 January 1972), South Vietnam still faced serious economic problems. A frequent target was the reduction of jobs created by the withdrawal of U.S. forces from Vietnam. In May the communists charged that "American capitalist bosses at a number of ... worksites are arrogantly continuing to lay off workers" (Liberation Radio, 22 May). A number of broadcasts were devoted to attacks on Tran Quoc Buu, the secretary-general of the Trade Union Federation—the largest labor organization in South Vietnam. In June Liberation Radio charged that Buu had "exerted an unbearable control over trade unions" and was "trampling on the starving workers and laborers with a view of becoming 'chief of state' " (*ibid.*, 28 June).

Few subjects received as much attention in Viet Cong propaganda as "Vietnamization"—the program of withdrawing U.S. troops from Vietnam and replacing them with properly trained and equipped Vietnamese. In October "Cuu Long" issued a five-part article, entitled "The U.S. Vietnamization Strategy Has Been and Will Certainly Be Defeated," which concluded that "Nixon's Vietnamization is a roundabout, deadlocked, and outdated strategy.... The realities on the various battlefronts have clearly proven this fact." (Liberation Radio, 17 October.)

Relations with North Vietnam. As noted above, the communist movement is an integral part of the Lao Dong Party—the VWP—of North Vietnam. Major decisions are made by the party in Hanoi, and there are VWP Politburo and Central Committee members in the South to handle other problems. While considerable effort is made to conceal the actual extent of control by the North Vietnamese, a close association is apparent from propaganda broadcasts. Early in 1971 a broadcast stated:

> Recently, answering the "be determined to fight and defeat U.S. aggression" appeal of the VWP and the DRV [North Vietnam] government, the Central Committee of the South Vietnam Liberation Peasants Association issued an appeal urging all cadres, members, and peasants to increase their revolutionary acts in combat and production ... to step up the armed, political, and military proselyting struggles, to destroy tyrants ... to accelerate the guerrilla warfare movement [and] to fulfill the duty of contributing human and material resources. (Liberation Radio, 12 January.)

Following the 1971 National Assembly elections in North Vietnam (see *Vietnam: Democratic Republic of Vietnam*), Liberation Radio (14 June) announced: "We are deeply convinced that the present [North Vietnamese] National Assembly ... is a determined-to-fight-and-win National Assembly that represents the will and aspirations of our Vietnamese people from north to south."

To say that the movement in South Vietnam is controlled and directed from the North is not to suggest that there are no differences between the two groups. Despite continuous declarations of solidarity, there were indications during 1971 of friction between North and South Vietnamese communist forces over a number of issues. The NVA soldiers often tended to regard themselves as superior in training and discipline to their southern counterparts, and neither liked to be placed under the command of the other. Inadequate supplies of food and matériel increased the friction, as PLAF troops resented the arrival of better-equipped NVA units. There have also been problems between the NVA soldiers and the local population of South Vietnam, which is much more likely to protect or assist local communist guerrillas than soldiers from North Vietnam. On 7 June, a former Viet Cong battalion commander told a press conference in Saigon that there had been considerable friction between North and South Vietnamese communists in the war zone. He said that many southerners felt that they were not completely trusted by the party, because younger and lower-ranking North Vietnamese cadres were often allowed to supervise them.

International Views and Positions. Indochinese solidarity was a major theme in Viet Cong statements throughout 1971. When the South Vietnamese government launched "Operation Lam Son 719" into southern Laos, Liberation Radio (10 February) condemned the move as "an extremely brazen invasion that tramples upon the independence, sovereignty, territorial integrity, and neutrality of the Laotian Kingdom" and demanded the total withdrawal of all "Saigon puppet troops" in order to "allow the Laotian people to solve their own affairs free from foreign intervention." When the operation was concluded, it was branded a "bitter defeat" for the government (LPA, 28 March). In May, Laotian Prince Souvanna Phouma, during a "Constitutional Day" speech, referred to the large number of North Vietnamese soldiers in Laos. The North Vietnamese chargé d'affaires in Vientiane walked out of the meeting in protest (see *Laos*). The Liberation Press Agency (13 May) reported that "Prince Souvanna Phouma once again rehashed absurd allegations and slanders about [North Vietnam's] 'invasion of Laos.' " and concluded: "The Vientiane authorities must bear full responsibility for the serious consequences of their acts of provocation and slanders against the Vietnamese people."

In the Sino-Soviet dispute, the Viet Cong have attempted to steer a middle course. To side publicly with one or the other might risk the loss of essential military aid. In June the NLF sent a delegation to China. At a banquet in Peking on 5 June to commemorate the second anniversary of the founding of the PRG, the chief of the general staff of the Chinese Peoples' Liberation Army, Huang Yung-sheng, stated in a solidarity speech: "Chairman Mao has taught us: If anyone among us should say that we should not help the Vietnamese people in their struggle against U.S. aggression and for national salvation, that will be betrayal, betrayal of the revolution" (*Peking Review*, 11 June). An editorial in the Peking *Jen-min jih-pao* on 6 June asserted: "The Vietnamese people's heroic and staunch fighting spirit is a model from which the Chinese people should learn. Supporting the Vietnamese and other Indochinese peoples in their war against U.S. aggression and for national salvation is the bounden internationalist duty of the Chinese people." On 26 June the Central Committee of the NLF sent a congratulatory message to the Chinese Communist Party on the fiftieth anniversary of its founding.

In March, an NLF delegation attended the Twenty-fourth Congress of the Communist Party of the Soviet Union (CPSU), bringing "most affectionate greetings of freindship and solidarity" to the "glorious CPSU" and the "heroic Soviet people" (VNA, 31 March). On the second anniversary of the founding of the PRG, Soviet party leaders Brezhnev, Podgorny, and Kosygin sent a message of "warmest fraternal greetings," and stated: "The Soviet people ... declare [their] unswerving and firm support to the freedom-loving Vietnamese people" (LPA, 7 June). Four months later Podgorny asserted, during a visit to North Vietnam:

> The Soviet Communist Party and Government, constantly abiding by Lenin's principles of internationalism and of support to the national liberation movement, have always supported and are supporting in every aspect the South Vietnamese patriots and the entire South Vietnamese people in their just struggle against the encroachment by the imperialist aggressors. (VNA, 11 October.)

The Podgorny visit was hailed as "a new development of the close and unbreakable relations between the Vietnamese people and the brother Soviet people," and as a "historic visit of far-reaching importance" (LPA, 10 October).

Nguyen Thi Binh, PRG foreign minister and head of the Viet Cong delegation to the Paris talks, made a number of visits to East European communist countries, including Romania (VNA, 16 March), Hungary (LPA, 14 May), and Yugoslavia (NCNA, 20 May). Nguyen Van Hieu led NLF delegations to the congress of the Communist Party of Czechoslovakia (Liberation Radio, 20 May) and to the congress of the (East) German Socialist Unity Party (*ibid.*, 12 June). Cuba, North Korea, Mongolia, Chile, and Algeria also received propaganda support from Viet Cong sources during 1971. In June the NLF sent a delegation headed by Dr. Dang Quanh Minh to the congress of the Mongolian People's Revolutionary Party (LPS, 3 June).

While the Japanese government was the subject of attacks (e.g., LPA, 1 October), the Japanese people were commended for their anti-war activities (*ibid.*, 27 October). Thailand was strongly criticized for having sent troops into Laos (*ibid.*, 22 February), and for the "repression of Vietnamese" in Thailand (LPA, 27 May).

Psychological warfare has been an extremely important weapon for the Viet Cong, and perhaps the most important target has been the U.S. public. Major anti-war conferences and demonstrations in the United States received messages of appreciation from Nguyen Thi Binh, Nguyen Huu Tho, or other important PRG and NLF leaders (e.g., LPA, 13 January and 9 February). Reports of anti-war demonstrations were broadcast in Vietnamese to encourage the PLAF and demoralize South Vietnamese forces.

The Viet Cong sent delegations to the Afro-Asian Solidarity Conference in Damascus, Syria (Liberation Radio, 26 June), and to the Vietnam Fatherland Front congress in North Vietnam (Hanoi radio, 23 December).

At the 119th session of the Paris peace talks, on 1 July, PRG Foreign Minister Nguyen Thi Binh presented a seven-point peace plan, which was immediately endorsed by North Vietnam. Point one stated that once the U.S. set a terminal date for the withdrawal of all forces from South Vietnam, agreement could be reached on the safety of the withdrawing troops and the release of prisoners of war (including American pilots held in North Vietnam). A cease-fire between PLAF and U.S. forces would begin as soon as agreement was reached on total U.S. withdrawal. Point two provided for the establishment of a "government of national concord" in South Vietnam, followed by a cease-fire between the PLAF and "the armed forces of the Saigon administration." "Free" elections were to be held following the establishment of the coalition government. Point three provided that "the question of Vietnamese armed forces in South Vietnam" would be settled "without foreign interference". Point four provided for the "peaceful reunification of Vietnam" to be achieved "step by step, by peaceful means, and again prohibited "foreign interference"—which Viet Cong officials have in the past explained prohibits United Nations supervision—in "all questions concerning the two zones." Point five provided for a foreign policy of "peace and neutrality," and for relations with all countries "in accordance with the five principles of peaceful coexistence." Point six provided that "the U.S. Government must bear full responsibility for the losses and destruction it has caused to the Vietnamese people in the two zones." The final point states that "the parties will find agreement on the forms of respect for and international guarantee of the accords that will be concluded." (LPA, 1 July; *Peking Review*, No. 28, 9 July).

Publications. The main publications of the PRP are *Tien Phong* (Vanguard), and *Nhan Dan* (The People), a weekly newspaper patterned after the North Vietnamese party daily of the same name. The "central organ" of the NLF is *Giai Phong* (Liberation), and the "official mouthpiece" of the NLF Central Committee is *South Vietnam in Struggle*, published three times each month in English and French. The main PLAF newspaper is *Quan Giai Phong* (Liberation Army). The VANDPF organ is *Lien Minh* (Alliance).

Viet Cong statements are carried by the Liberation Press Agency—the official press agency of the NLF—and by Liberation Radio. Statements are also frequently carried by Hanoi radio.

Robert F. Turner

INTERNATIONAL COMMUNIST FRONT ORGANIZATIONS

Afro-Asian Writers' Permanent Bureau

The Afro-Asian Writers' Permanent Bureau (AAWPB) was originally set up by the Soviets at an "Afro-Asian Writers' Conference" in Tashkent in October 1958. Following a second conference, in Cairo in February 1962, a "Permanent Bureau" was established with headquarters in Colombo, Ceylon. The Chinese communists gained control of the organization at a meeting of its Executive Committee in Bali, Indonesia, in July 1963, and established a new Executive Secretariat in Peking on 15 August 1966. Thus, while the AAWPB is still officially based in Colombo, it operates exclusively from Peking. A pro-Soviet faction—the AAWPB-Cairo—broke away after the Chinese began to dominate the organization. The AAWPB-Cairo, now planning its Fifth Conference is the more active of the two, while the AAWPB-Peking, which has not yet held a third conference, appears to have no activities outside its irregular publication, *The Call*, and occasional statements carried by New China News Agency.

The AAWPB-Cairo. the pro-Soviet faction of the AAWPB was founded on 19-21 June 1966 at an "extraordinary meeting" attended by delegations from Cameroun, Ceylon, India, Sudan, the Soviet Union, and the U.A.R. Its relatively successful "Third Afro-Asian Writers' Conference," held at Beirut in 1967 and attended by some 150 delegates from 42 countries, was the first serious blow to the pro-Chinese AAWPB. Since then, the pro-Soviet organization appears to have consolidated and augmented its base of support.

The secretary-general of the AAWPB-Cairo is Yusuf el-Sebai (U.A.R.), who is also secretary-general of the Afro-Asian People's Solidarity Organization and a member of the Presidential Committee of the World Peace Council. The assistant secretary-general is Edward el-Kharat (U.A.R.). The AAWPB-Cairo has a ten-member Permanent Bureau, with members from India, Japan, Lebanon, Mongolia, the Portuguese colonies, Senegal, South Africa, the Soviet Union, Sudan, and the U.A.R. There is also a 30-member Executive Committee.

Views and Activities in 1971. The "seventh session" of the AAWPB-Cairo took place in Moscow on 5-8 July. Among the delegates were representatives from Algeria, India, Japan, Lebanon, Mongolia, South Africa, the U.A.R., and the U.S.S.R. Secretary-General Yusuf el-Sebai gave a report on the organization's work since the Fourth Conference, in November 1970 (see *YICA*, 1971, pp. 753-54). Among the topics discussed were the publication of works of Afro-Asian writers and the preparation of a history of the twelve years of the Afro-Asian writers' movement.

Resolutions adopted by the session expressed satisfaction with the work of the editors of the organization's magazine *Lotus*; approved a document condemning racial discrimination; adopted a declaration hailing the lead taken by writers in African and Asian countries in the struggle against "imperialism" and in the service of "peace, democracy, and progress"; awarded prizes for 1971 to Sonomyn Udval (Mongolia), Semben Usman (Senegal), and Tawfiq al-Hakim (U.A.R);

approved the holding of an Afro-Asian poets' seminar in Khartoum and a seminar on African dramatic literature in Cairo, both in 1972 (*Ogonyok*, Moscow, no. 30, July; *Egyptian Gazette*, Cairo, 5 August).

A broadcast to Asia on 3 May by Moscow's "Radio Peace and Progress" referred to preparations for the Fifth Conference of the AAWPB-Cairo (due to be held in the U.S.S.R. in 1973) and the important organizational role that *Lotus* should play in such preparations. The broadcast stated that meetings of the AAWPB-Cairo Secretariat and the *Lotus* editorial staff would be held during the summer months to discuss the expansion of the Afro-Asian writers' movement and questions connected with the publication and circulation of *Lotus*. Literary works, articles, and other material appearing in the magazine, the broadcast commented, enabled readers to acquire a deeper knowledge of the culture and life of people living in different continents but linked together by common aims and interests in opposing the "bitterest enemies of humanity," namely, "imperialism, colonialism, and racism."

The main organ of the AAWPB-Cairo is the "literature, arts and sociopolitical quarterly" *Lotus* (formerly *Afro-Asian Literature*), which appears in English, French, and Arabic editions. In addition, books by various "Afro-Asian men of letters" have been published by the AAWPB-Cairo in the Soviet Union.

The AAWPB-Peking. The pro-Chinese AAWPB, the continuation of the original body, is led by Frederik L. Risakotta (Indonesia), a member of the Peking-based Delegation of the Communist Party of Indonesia Central Committee, who is identified as "acting head ad interim" of the AAWPB Secretariat. (The former secretary-general, Rathe Deshapriya Sananayake returned to his native Ceylon in mid-1968; in April 1970, Kinkazu Saionji of Japan was identified by the NCNA as "acting head ad interim," but returned home the following August.) The AAWPB-Peking claims to have affiliates in some 40 countries, which probably includes individual as well as organizational memberships.

Views and Activities in 1971. No activities were reported for the AAWPB-Peking during the year, and with the exception of a couple of minor statements it was silent. On 11 February its Executive Secretariat "sternly denounced" U.S. "imperialism" for its "new crime of invading Laos and expanding and intensifying aggression in Indochina" (NCNA, 11 February). The statement reiterated the organization's "unreserved support" for the efforts of the people of Laos, Vietnam, and Cambodia to "carry to the end their struggles against U.S. aggression." It called upon the "revolutionary and progressive writers" of Asia and Africa to continue "denouncing with their sharp pens the crimes and dark plots of aggression of U.S. imperialism."

The Executive Secretariat congratulated the Chinese Communist Party (CCP) on its fiftieth anniversary. In a statement carried by the NCNA on 9 July, great praise was heaped upon the CCP for its accomplishments. As a result of the Cultural Revolution, for example, "the revolutionary writers and artists of China, guided by the proletarian revolutionary line of Chairman Mao in literature and art, launched successful attacks on bourgeois literature and art." The CCP and the Chinese people, the statement continued, would always "march hand in hand with the people of the world" to defeat the "two superpowers" (the United States and the Soviet Union) and all their "lackeys" for the "liberation of all mankind."

The AAWPB-Peking bulletin, *The Call*, is issued from Peking at irregular intervals in English, French, and Arabic.

Eric Stromquist

International Association
of Democratic Lawyers

The International Association of Democratic Lawyers (IADL) was founded at an "International Congress of Jurists" held in Paris in October 1946 under the auspices of a para-communist organization, the Mouvement National Judiciaire, and attended by lawyers from 25 countries. Although the movement originally included elements of various political orientations, the leading role was played by leftist French lawyers, and by 1949 most non-communists had resigned.

The IADL was originally based in Paris but was expelled by the French government in 1950. It then moved to Brussels, where it remains; some organizational work has also been carried out from Warsaw.

Membership is open to lawyers' organizations or groups and to individual lawyers, and may be on a "corresponding", "donation," or "permanent" basis. Lawyers holding membership through organizations or individually are estimated to number about 25,000. The IADL claims to be supported by membership fees and donations; no details of its finances are published.

The IADL holds consultative status, Category C, with the U.N.'s Economic and Social Council (ECOSOC).

Structure and Leadership. The highest organ of the IADL is the Congress, in which each member organization is represented. There have been nine congresses to date, the latest at Helsinki in July 1970. The Congress elects the IADL Council, which is supposed to meet yearly and consists of the Bureau, the Secretariat, and a representative of each member organization and of the co-opted members.

The key officers of the IADL are the president, Pierre Cot (France), the honorary president, Dennis Nowell Pritt (Britain), and the secretary-general, Joë Nordmann (France). There are believed to be between 15 and 20 vice-presidents, from Bulgaria, Czechoslovakia, Hungary, North Korea, Poland, Romania, the Soviet Union, North and South Vietnam, and four Arab nations including Jordan. Several Greek lawyers in political detention are honorary members of the Bureau.

Views and Activities in 1971. Fifty lawyers from 20 countries, including the United States, the U.S.S.R., Britain, Italy, Czechoslovakia, Brazil, and India, and a representative from the United Nations, attended a meeting of the IADL Bureau in Budapest on 7-9 May 1971. Pierre Cot and Mihaly Korom, the Hungarian Minister of Justice, spoke at the opening session. The participants discussed: Vietnam, the Middle East, the twenty-fifth anniversary of the Nuremberg trials, the international petroleum situation, European security and cooperation, and racial discrimination. Plans for future activities included: a world conference on human rights, a meeting on "the legal questions of European security," a colloquium on oil rights, a colloquium on "the economic and political struggle" in Latin American countries, and a world conference on Indochina. (MTI, Hungarian news agency, 7, 10, and 11 May.)

The decisions of the Bureau meeting were submitted to a "lawyers' working group" at the World Peace Assembly convened by the World Peace Council (WPC) in Budapest on 13-16 May, which endorsed IADL projections. (WPC *Assembly Documents*.)

Lawyers from 18 European countries attended the IADL's meeting, in East Berlin on 24-26 September, on "The Legal Aspects of European Security and Cooperation." Heinrich Toeplitz (East Germany), IADL treasurer, opening the meeting, declared that the signing of the four-power agreement on West Berlin had "deprived the enemies of a European security conference of the last pretext for delaying their approval of such a conference." The final resolution included a psoposal to European governments for "a permanent organization for security and cooperation, open equally to all states." Such an organization "could also be concerned with the operating of the legal principles, the study of disarmament, and with the coordination of economic, cultural, scientific, and technical activities." (ADN, East German news agency, 24 September; *L'Humanité*, Paris, 27 September.)

IADL propaganda and protests continued to be anti-West in general and anti-United States in particular. An IADL statement issued in connection with the murder-conspiracy trial of "anti-racist leader" Angela Davis appealed for popular pressure on the U.S. government to "save Angela Davis" and for protest against the U.S. "policy of racial discrimination ... contrary to the international laws approved by the United Nations" (*L'Humanité*, 8 January).

The United States was similarly attacked by the IADL for "escalating the war in Indochina," in "crying violation of the U.N. Charter and the Geneva agreements of 1954 and 1962." It appealed to signatories of the 1962 Geneva agreements to "bring their influence to bear on the U.S. administration in order to end that criminal war." (TASS, 9 February.) Lev Smirnov (Soviet Union), an IADL Council member, led a delegation of Soviet lawyers to North Vietnam in April. They had working meetings with the Vietnam Lawyers' association, the North Vietnamese "Commission for Investigating U.S. War Crimes in Vietnam," and met also with "Laotian and Cambodian representatives" in Hanoi. (Vietnam News Agency, 27 April.) The IADL organized a "World Conference of Lawyers on Indochina" in Algiers on 26-28 November. The conference, similar to one held by the IADL in Grenoble in July 1968, discussed alleged U.S. violations of the rules of international law, "the people's right to self-determination," and "action for the withdrawal of all U.S. military forces." Henri Rolin (Belgium), the conference chairman, and Boualem Benhamouda, the Algerian Minister of Justice, welcomed the 150 lawyers attending from 43 countries and associations. Other speakers included Joë Nordmann, Lev Smirnov, Peter Weiss (United States), and Lelio Basso (Italy). (Basso is a member of the WPC-dominated Stockholm Conference Vietnam War Crimes Commission.) There were five working commissions of the conference, headed by Bogdan Zlatarik (Yugoslavia), IADL vice-president and World Peace Council member Shafiq Irsheidat (Jordan), (first name unknown) Mazon (Spain), Mostefa Barabey (U.A.R.), and IADL secretary Harish Chandra (India). (Algiers radio, 22 November; *El Moudjahid*, 26-29 November; *L'Humanité*, 1 December.)

The final communiqué of the conference contained an indictment of "atrocious American aggression in Indochina," supported the "realistic peace proposals" of the Provisional Revolutionary Government of South Vietnam, the Hanoi government, the United National Front of Cambodia, and the Laotian Patriotic Front. It recommended synchronization of actions in the U.S. against the war with those of the rest of the world, protection of deserters and other Americans opposing the war, and action in defense of the Vietnamese, Cambodian, and Laotian 'patriots.' A separate resolution expressed satisfaction with the "unceasing efforts of the U.S. peace movement and lawyers to end U.S. aggression in Indochina." (*El Moudjahid*, 28-30 November; *L'Humanité*, 1 December.)

Pierre Cot and 50 IADL members attended an "International Colloquium on the Rights of Oil-Producing Countries," in Algiers on 20 October (*El Moudjahid*, 21 October). The IADL held that Britain bore responsibility under international law for its actions in Ulster which, "in violating human rights and even the Irish Republic's territory, were international and a breach of the U.N. Charter" (Moscow radio, 13 September, speech by Igor Blichenko, IADL secretary). R. Zalles (Bolivia) represented the IADL at a forum on "The Application of Human Rights in Latin America," held in Montevideo on 5-11 September and organized by the Uruguayan National Workers' Convention and the Latin American Confederation of Christian Trade Unions (*El Popular, Uruguay*, 12 September). René Blum (France) led an IADL "mission of inquiry" to Greece in support of Greek communists on trial for subversive activities (*L'Humanité*, 20 February). The IADL condemned the "worsening of repression in Iran of any kind of democratic opposition" (*ibid.*, 28 June). An IADL appeal to the king of Morocco urged him to intervene in the trial of 193 Moroccan "democrats" (*ibid.*, 24 September).

Publications. The IADL's two principal publications, both in English and French editions, are the *Review of Contemporary Law*, edited by Pierre Cot, which is supposed to appear semiannually but does not always do so, and the *Information Bulletin*, issues of which appear irregularly and are frequently devoted to a single topic. The IADL also issues pamphlets on questions of topical interest.

Valerie Bloom

International Federation of Resistance Fighters

The International Federation of Resistance Fighters (Fédération Internationale des Résistants; FIR) was founded in 1951 in Vienna as a successor to the International Federation of Former Political Prisoners (Fédération Internationale des Anciens Prisonniers Politiques; FIAPP). With the name change, membership eligibility was widened to include not only political prisoners, but also former partisans, resistance fighters, and all victims of Nazism and fascism and their descendants.

In 1959 the FIR had a membership of four million; no more recent figures have been announced, but as it celebrated its twentieth anniversary in 1971 the FIR claimed 55 affiliated groups and representation in every country of Europe (*Résistance unie*, no. 14, Vienna, April-June 1971). Federation headquarters are located in Vienna; a small secretariat is maintained in Paris.

Aims and Political Involvement. The FIR claims to be independent of all parties and governments, and its charter outlines the following basic aims: to unite the members in order to secure the independence of their homelands and the freedom and peace of the world; to defend freedom and human dignity and to fight against racial, political, ideological, and religious discrimination and any renaissance of fascism and Nazism; to honor the martyrs of underground fighting and to keep alive the memories of their ideals and the horrors of prisons and concentration camps; to represent the material and moral interests of resistance fighters and their heirs; and to work for friendly and peaceful relations between nations in accord with the U.N. Charter.

In spite of these very general stated goals, the FIR has always subordinated its interests to the policies of the Soviet Union. The most conspicous examples of political motivation include the expulsion of the Yugoslav affiiate after Tito's break with the Soviet Union, tolerance for the disregard shown to Polish-Jewish survivors of concentration camps by the Polish affiliate, discrimination by the FIR leadership toward Israeli members after the Arab-Israeli war in 1967, and "purges" by the Czechoslovak Association of Anti-Fascist Fighters of a number of veteran resistance fighters who had supported the reforms of Alexander Dubček prior to the military occupation of Czechoslovakia in 1968.

Although it persists in attempts to establish working relationships with non-communist organizations, and especially with the United Nations, the FIR still lacks U.N. representation and in general has made little headway among non-communist groups. It maintains close relations with other communist front organizations, especially the World Peace Council and the International Association of Democratic Lawyers.

Organization and Leadership. The organs of the FIR are the Congress, General Council, Bureau, and Secretariat. Until the Sixth Congress (its latest), held in Venice in November 1969, the Congress was convened every three years. It was then decided that this body should meet every four years. The congress elects the FIR president, the vice-presidents, and the members of the Bureau, and determines the number and ratifies members of the General Council after they have been nominated by national associations. The General Council is supposed to meet at least once a year between congresses and assign the tasks of the Bureau; it is composed of the members of the Bureau and one representative from each affiliated organization. Holding great power, the Bureau supervises the implementation of decisions by the Congress and the General Council, and is also responsible for the budget. It is headed by the FIR president, and from among its members it elects the Secretariat.

Arialdo Banfi (Italy) has been FIR president since 1965. The Sixth Congress elected 15 vice-presidents: Jacques Debû-Bridel (France), Dimo Dichev (Bulgaria), Petr Dudáš (Czechoslovakia), Albert Forcinal (France), Istvan Gabor (Hungary), Nicolae Guina (Romania), Helge Theil Kierulff (Denmark), Włodzimierz Lechowicz (Poland), Alexei Petrovich Maresiev (Soviet Union), André de Raet (Belgium), Josef Roussaint (West Germany), Ludwig Soswinski (Austria), Georg Spielmann (East Germany), Umberto Terracini (Italy), and Pierre Villon (France).

Jean Toujas (France) serves as secretary-general of the Secretariat, Gustav Alef-Bolkowiak (Poland) is deputy secretary-general, and Guiseppe Gaddi (Italy) and Wolfgang Bergold (East Germany) are secretaries; Theodor Heinisch (Austria) was reelected treasurer by the 1969 congress.

Views and Activities in 1971. Trying to support Soviet policies, the FIR from its inception was highly critical of the Federal Republic of Germany and accused its government of "revanchism." After the West German elections of September 1969 resulted in a more liberal coalition government under Chancellor Willy Brandt, the FIR toned down its attack on the government and concentrated on the more conservative non-governmental elements in West Germany. In 1971, however, the FIR noted "weekly evidence of growing Nazi activity" and called for the dissolution and prohibition of all neo-Nazi or extreme right-wing groups. A statement issued in Vienna expressed serious concern with announced plans for "Sudeten German Day" in Nüremberg and charged that right-wingers intended to stage rallies that would be a "massive provocation against the easing of tension in Europe." It added that since the conclusion of the German-Soviet and German-Polish treaties in 1970 several demonstrations of similar nature had been held with the avowed aim of preventing the ratification of the treaties. (FIR press release, 27 April; *Volksstimme*, Vienna, 18 April). On the other hand, the FIR expressed approval of the Berlin agreement concluded by the ambassadors of Great Britain, the United States, France, and the Soviet Union and expressed the hope that it would promote ratification of the treaties and the holding of an all-European security conference (Moscow radio, 31 August).

On the occasion of its anniversary the FIR announced its most important future tasks: (1) to make a contribution to the creation of a European security system; (2) to continue opposition to neo-Nazism and persecution of former resistance fighters in West Germany; and (3) to encourage historians in all countries to include the resistance struggle in the teaching of history. Discussions for an FIR-sponsored security conference had begun in Belgrade in October 1970.· Subsequently a preparatory meeting in Paris on 27-28 April 1971 decided on Rome and 18-20 November as the site and date of a "Meeting on Security, Friendship, and Peace" to be open to any national or international veterans' group (*Réistance unie*, no. 14, April-June). This conference took place as scheduled and representatives from more than 100 organizations from 19 countries attended. It was the first time since World War II that veterans of that war convened for a common cause, regardless of whether they had been allies or enemies (*Neues Deutschland*, East Berlin, 20 November).

Events in Greece continued to be an object of FIR protests. On 19 April a telegram to the government demanded the release of all political prisoners and raised particular objections against the treatment of Manolis Glezos, a leader of the United Democratic Left, who had been granted a twenty-day temporary release from prison and thereafter was to be sent into exile (*Informationsdienst*, Vienna, no. 4, April).

Organized FIR memorial celebrations and pilgrimages, once numerous and stricly observed, have steadily decreased in number. However, monuments and museums on the sites of the most notorious former concentration camps — Mauthausen, Dachau, Auschwitz, Buchenwald, and others — continued to attract millions of visitors in 1971.

FIR delegates participated in special celebrations in various European countries. In April, Gustav Alef-Bolkowiak and Guiseppe Gaddi of the Secretariat attentded several events organized by the Czechoslovak Federal Committee of the Union of Anti-Fascist Fighters, an FIR affiliate. In Hradec Kralove they addressed a rally "against fascism and war, for socialism and peace, for the policy of the Czechoslovak Communist Party and Government," in Bratislava, Alef-Bolkowiak emphasized the importance of the meeting on security which was then in the planning stage (CTK, 14 and 15 April). Secretary-General Jean Toujas attended a conference in Sofia on 19 March called by the Bulgarian Committee of Fighters against Fascism and Capitalism to mark the FIR anniversary. Vice-president Josef Roussaint headed a West German delegation from the Association of Victims of Nazi Persecution which went to Moscow at the invitation of the Soviet Committee of Veterans of the Second World War to discuss methods of further cooperation between the two organiztions in rallying "progressive forces" in support of European security (TASS, 31 August).

Publications. The FIR publishes a journal in French and German, *Résistance unie-/Widerstandskämpfer*; changes in the number of annual issues have been made without announcement. News reports are also disseminated through the irregularly distributed French-language *Service d'Information de la FIR* and its German counterpart, *Informationsdienst der FIR*.

Edith Wyden

International Organization of Journalists

The International Organization of Journalists (IOJ) was founded in June 1946 in Copenhagen. The International Federation of Journalists (IFJ) and the International Federation of Journalists of Allied and Free Countries were both formally disbanded and merged with the IOJ, so that for a time it was representative of journalists over the world. By 1950, all non-communist unions had withdrawn from the IOJ in order to refound, in 1952, the IFJ. Since 1955 the IOJ has made unsuccessful overtures to the IFJ for cooperation and for eventually forming a new world organization of journalists. It was for the purpose of bridging differences with the IFJ that the IOJ in that year founded the International Committee for Cooperation of Journalists (ICCJ). No IFJ member is known to have affiliated with the ICCJ, however, and most ICCJ officers are also leading members of the parent IOJ. The IOJ headquarters, originally in London, moved to Prague in 1947.

In 1963 pro-Chinese journalists established a rival organization, the Afro-Asian Journalists' Association (AAJA; see below).

The IOJ was awarded consultative and informational Category B status with UNESCO in 1969, after having held consultative Category C status since 1962. It also holds consultative status, Category II, with UNESCO's Economic and Social Council.

Structure and Leadership. National unions and groups of journalists are eligible for membership in the IOJ, as are also individual journalists. The organization claims to have some 150,000 members, representing 67 organizations and groups in 58 countries (TASS, 14 June; *Trybuna Ludu*, Warsaw, 6 February). It professes to be financed entirely by affiliation fees; no accounts are published.

The highest body of the IOJ is the Congress, which is supposed to meet every four years. The Congress elects the Executive Committee, which includes the Presidium (president, vice-presidents, and secretary-general), other officers (secretaries and treasurer), and ordinary members.

Elections at the Seventh Congress, held in 1971 (see below), reseated the three top leaders despite speculation as to changes in the Presidium broadcast from Havana on 10 January. Jean-Maurice Hermann (France) was reelected as president (his fifth term), Jiří Kubka (Czechoslovakia) as secretary-general, and Norbert Siklósi (Hungary), as treasurer. Among the 50 representatives elected to the Executive Committee, showing some changes from the previous composition (see *YICA*, 1970, p. 770), were 15 vice-presidents: Ernesto Vera (Cuba), Alfredo Olivares (Chile), Jaime Figueroa (Peru), Ahmad Baha' al-Din (U.A.R.), and representatives from France, East Germany, North Korea, Poland, Mongolia, Finland, the Provisional Government of South Vietnam, North Vietnam, the Soviet Union, Angola, Cape Verde Islands, and Guinea. The five-member Secretariat presumably remained unchanged. Among those new to the Executive Committee were James Aldridge (Great Britain) and Madeleine Riffaud (France), both appointed as a result of a regulation, approved by the congress, that winners of IOJ awards be included on the committee. Thanasis Georgiou (Greece) was elected to the committee. (*Granma*, Havana, 12 January; TASS, 12 January; Radio

"Voice of Truth" of the Communist Party of Greece, 12 January; and *al-Ahram*, Cairo, 29 January.)

The IOJ's Auditing Commission, Permanent Professional Commission (based in Bucharest), and Permanent Social Commission (based in Sofia) are headed, respectively, by Pekto Koradelko (Bulgaria), Nestor Ignat (Romania), and Radi Vasilev (Bulgaria).

New IOJ members, accepted by the congress, were organizations from Argentina, Bolivia, Chile, Cyprus, Spain, the United States, Greece (two groups), Japan (two groups), Jordan, Laos, Madagascar, Palestine, Peru, Sierra Leone, Somalia, Sudan, Venezuela, and Yemen (*Democratic Journalist*, no. 4, April).

Aims and Policies. Although the avowed aims of the IOJ include "defense of the right of every journalist to write according to his conscience and conviction," its duties, according to a Secretariat statement, are to expose the "demagogism of imperialist propaganda," promote the cohesion of all "anti-imperialist" forces, and spread the "truth about the great success of the socialist countries" (TASS, 14 June 1971). Secretary-General Kubka, who appealed to delegates at the Seventh Congress to strengthen the IOJ as a "centre of all anti-imperialist and democratic journalists," stated:

> Our mission is the defence of peace and the strengthening of friendship among nations, the promotion of international understanding, the flow of free, true and honest information. Our mission is the struggle against the spread of war psychosis and war propaganda, against national and racial hatred, against the creation of international tension. It is our purpose to fully support, defend and protect all journalists who are fulfilling this noble mission. (*Democratic Journalist*, no. 4, April.)

IOJ schools for training journalists, drawing mostly journalists from developing countries, have been set up in Hungary, East Germany, and Czechoslovakia. A resolution of the Seventh Congress recommended that the IOJ prepare with UNESCO a program on teaching journalism and that correspondence courses be organized.

The Seventh Congress. The Seventh Congress of the IOJ was its first to be held outside of Europe. Originally planned for December 1970, the meeting took place on 4-11 January 1971 in Havana. The conclusion, scheduled for 9 January, was delayed two days by the preparation of a resolution on the Middle East. Arab delegations insisted that it call for complete withdrawal of Israeli forces from occupied areas and for support of the "struggle" and full rights of the Palestine Arabs. The resolution as adopted was called by the head of the Jordanian delegation the "strongest international resolution supporting Arab rights in Palestine." (*al-Dustour*, Amman, 19 January.) The opening of the congress was delayed briefly when the Arab delegations refused to enter the hall until an Israeli delegation was expelled (*ibid.*).

A total of 326 journalists (187 delegates, 71 guests, and 68 observers) attended the congress, drawn from 21 countries in Africa, 18 in Asia, 23 in the Americas and Australia, and 21 in Europe (*Democratic Journalist*, no. 4; *Trybuna Ludu*, 6 February). The IOJ sent a protest to the Japanese government for its refusal to allow Korean journalists working in Japan to go to Cuba. Fode Berete, editor of *Horoya* (Guinea), informed the IOJ that Guinea would not be represented at the congress because of the people's "general mobilization to face Portuguese aggression" (Conakry radio, 31 December 1970). Delegations attended from various "liberation movements": the Laotian Patriotic Front, the Provisional Revolutionary Government of South Vietnam, the African Party for the Independence of Guinea and the Cape Verde Islands (PAIGC) and the Front for the Liberation of Mozambique (FRELIMO).

The general themes of the speeches included solidarity with the peoples of Indochina, and moral support for "freedom fighters." Delegates from "capitalist" countries gave accounts of difficulties encountered by "progressive" journalists in their homelands. President Hermann referred particularly to difficulties encountered by Greek, South Vietnamese, and some African journalists, and urged all the journalists attending to apply themselves to the "task of awakening revolutionary will and intelligence" (*Democratic Journalist*, no. 4). The delegates welcomed a proposal by the Finnish delegation that the next congress be held in Finland.

Hector J. Collins, a delegate from Venezuela, wrote on his return in the Caracas journal *Elite* (19 February) that he had wanted to bring up the case of Venezuelan journalist Ali Lameda but was told that if he did so he would have to "face the consequences." Lameda had not been heard from since his imprisonment in 1967 in North Korea, where he had been working for two years. Collins also wrote of unfavorable treatment accorded his and other delegations in Moscow (the Venezuelans had to surrender their passports, which were given back only when they boarded the plane on their return trip) and in Havana (delegates were isolated and no outsiders were allowed into their hotel without permission).

Resolutions adopted at the congress referred to the large role of journalists in the "ideological struggle." The delegates supported the revolutionary struggles of the Indochinese, Arab, African, and Latin American peoples, and called for a strengthening of European security. An annual "Week of Solidarity of Progressive Journalists with the Heroic Struggle of the Vietnamese People," to be held in 1971 on 15-20 December, was approved, and tribute was paid to Che Guevara as a "real revolutionary intellectual" and "model of fidelity to revolutionary convictions" (Havana radio, 12 January).

Chairmen Nestor Ignat (Romania) of the Permanent Professional Commission and Radi Vasilev (Bulgaria) of the Permanent Social Commission reported on activities of their commissions, both created since the Sixth Congress in 1966. The Permanent Professional Committee had worked at improving the quality of journalists by coordinating such events as seminars, courses, symposiums, and by awarding scholarships. Ignat proposed that the IOJ organize a symposium on the communication media in the scientific revolution, in which journalists, sociologists, psychologists, and economists would participate. Vasilev told the congress that his commission had been active in preventing repression of the press and in establishing social and welfare facilities for journalists. Ly Van Sau (South Vietnam), presiding at the plenary session which approved the report, suggested that the Permanent Social Commission pay more attention to journalists of the Third World who were working under difficult circumstances "with their pen in one hand and a gun in the other." (*Granma*, 7 and 12 January.)

Other Activities. The first Latin American journalists' congress was held in Santiago, Chile, on 23-25 September 1971. One of the meeting's main purposes was to set up a regional organization of the IOJ in Latin America, the Latin American Journalists' Federation. The idea—suggested at the Seventh National Convention of the Venezuelan Association of Journalists in September 1970—was taken into consideration by Latin American delegates at the Havana congress, but no decisions were made (*El Siglo*, Santiago, 6 January.)

Publications. The IOJ issues a monthly journal, *The Democratic Journalist*, in English, French, Russian, and Spanish editions, edited by Oldrich Bures, and a fortnightly *Information Bulletin*.

*   *   *

The AAJA. The Afro-Asian Journalists' Association was set up in Djakarta in April 1963, with an Afro-Asian press bureau and a permanent Secretariat. Until the attempted communist coup in Indonesia (1965), the AAJA appeared to represent a possibly serious rival to the pro-Soviet IOJ, particularly in developing countries. At that juncture, AAJA headquarters were "temporarily" moved to Peking. Djawoto, the AAJA's Indonesian secretary-general, who was dismissed from his post as Indonesia's ambassador to China, has since headed the Secretariat in Peking, which has become the permanent seat of AAJA operations.

The AAJA Secretariat, in addition to Djawoto, includes Supeno and Umar Said (both of Indonesia), Yang I (China), Sugiyama Ichihei (Japan), Said Salim Abdullah (Tanzania), Ahmed Gora Ebrahim (South Africa), and D. Manuweera (Ceylon). The AAJA claims members in 53 countries, but this distribution would seem to reflect individual memberships as well as formal participating organizations.

There is no indication that the AAJA has succeeded in winning over the allegiance of IOJ members or member organizations. Few journalists' organizations and governments have expressed open support for the AAJA or indicated that they would send delegates to an eventual AAJA conference. Unable to make pragmatic headway, the AAJA devotes its energies mainly to propagating the Chinese line in international political affairs.

Views and Activities in 1971. Like the IOJ, the AAJA sponsors training programs for journalists. Aimed at "aspiring young people of the Afro-Asian nations," courses have been conducted in Peking for students of journalism from South Africa, South-West Africa, Mozambique, Lesotho, Zimbabwe (Rhodesia), and Ceylon. The sixth course to be sponsored took place from 16 March to 16 July 1971 and was attended by 13 journalists from Congo (Brazzaville). The leader of the group, Marcel Eta, stated at a welcoming reception in Peking:

> The Congolese Party of Labour, conscious of the need to educate the Congolese masses, had decided ... to send young journalist fighters to the AAJA's practical school where the weapon for struggle against imperialism, colonialism, and neo-colonialism is given.... The AAJA, staunch organization for struggle against the forces of oppression, is stimulating revolution in the whole world." (NCNA, 16 March.)

On 23 April the Secretariat celebrated Afro-Asian Journalists' Day by holding a meeting attended by Djawoto, members of the Executive Secretariat of the Afro-Asian Permanent Writers' Bureau, "progressive journalists and friends in Peking of Asian and African countries and other countries and regions, Congolese friends at the sixth training course sponsored by the AAJA and leading members of Chinese journalistic and other organizations." Diplomatic envoys of Asian, African, and other countries and Chinese officials were also present. At the meeting Djawoto denounced the "predatory performance of U.S. imperialism" in Asia and reiterated the AAJA promise of wholehearted support for the fighting people of the world. (NCNA, 23 April.)

Publications. The AAJA's main publication, *Afro-Asian Journalist*, appears irregularly. Pamphlets on specific issues are published from time to time.

Eric Stromquist

International Union
of Students

The International Union of Students (IUS) was founded in August 1946 at a congress in Prague attended by students of varying political and religious persuasions. In its constitution the union was described as a "representative organization of the democratic students of the whole world who work for progress." By 1951 most non-communists had left the IUS because of its domination by pro-Soviet elements. The IUS has headquarters at Vocelova 3, Prague.

Full or associate membership in the IUS is open to national student unions and to other student organizations in countries where no national union exists. The IUS claims to have 92 affiliated organizations.

The IUS has consultative Category C status with UNESCO; applications for Category B status have been repeatedly deferred.

Structure and Leadership. The highest governing body of the IUS is its Congress, which is supposed to meet every two years and to which affiliated and associated organizations send delegates. The Congress elects the Executive Committee, comprising the Secretariat, Finance Committee, and individual members. The National student organizations represented on the Executive Committee are chosen by the Congress, but each designated organization selects its own representative. The Executive Committee usually meets at least twice a year. (See *YICA*, 1968, pp. 720-21 for a list of organizations elected to the Executive Committee at the Ninth Congress, in 1967, which was valid until 1971.)

In 1971, the IUS's twenty-fifth anniversary year, its Tenth Congress was held in Bratislava on 3-11 February. Dusan Ulcak (Czechoslovakia) was reelected president and Fathi Muhammad al-Fadl (Sudan) became secretary-general. (A Prague radio report on 12 February mistakenly announced the reelection of Mahdi al-Hafid as secretary-general.) The new Secretariat has 23 members; these, and an additional 24 persons, comprise the Executive Committee. Vice-presidents represent member organizations in Senegal, Portuguese Africa (designated by the IUS as "Black Africa under Portuguese Colonial Domination"), Cuba, Panama, Chile, North Korea, India, Iraq, the Soviet Union, Bulgaria, and Poland. (*Ibid.*)

The Tenth Congress. The congress was preceeded by a preparatory meeting of the Executive Committee on 28-29 January 1971 in Prague. Representatives from 37 countries approved an agenda, a report on the development of the IUS since the previous congress and the union's future tasks, and applications for IUS membership. All member organizations (in 87 countries) and 65 other student organizations were invited to send delegations to the congress. It was attended by 214 delegates and 138 observers who together represented 58 national student unions, 12 international organizations, and 8 national liberation movements.

Discussions at the congress—focused on the "struggles of the people and students" in Indochina, the Middle East, Latin America, Portugal and Portuguese Africa, Spain, and Greece, and also apartheid, European security, and democratization and reform in education—occupied thirty-six hours and resulted in the approval of 127 resolutions. Students were urged to close their ranks, while uniting with the working class, in order to "fight against imperialism, colonialism, and neo-colonialism" and support "struggles for liberation" in Indochina, the Middle East, and Africa; to support Cuba; and to fight against NATO in favor of a strictly European security system. Condemnation was expressed for the "racist regimes" in southern Africa, West German "revanchism," and Greek, Spanish, and Portuguese "fascism," and for militarism of education in the highly developed capitalist countries. (Rudé Právo, Prague, 12 February.) Che Guevara was upheld as the "most faithful form of the revolutionary ideal" (El Siglo, Santiago, Chile, 14 February).

At the 7 February session, the congress ratified the Executive Committee's decision to admit as full members the General Union of Students of the U.A.R., the Union of Students of Somalia, the Union of Students of East Pakistan, the National Union of Syrian Students, the Association of Guatemalan University Students, the National Union of Mozambican Students, the General Association of University Students of El Salvador, and the Council of Presidents of Chilean University Federations; associate membership was approved for the National Union of Finnish Students. The application of the National Union of Israeli Students (NUIS), which had applied for membership also at the two previous congresses, was rejected because the NUIS "had not changed its policy of approval of Israeli aggression against the Arab people" CTK, Czechoslovak news agency, 8 February).

Evidence of some discord was given in a 25 February Pravda report by Soviet delegate Vladimir Zhitenev, who stated: "The enemies of the democratic student movement hoped that they could organize anti-Soviet and anti-socialist speeches at the congress, but their hopes were in vain." A reporter for the radical Guardian (New York, 12 February), after apparently having spoken with dissident delegates, was told that some "nasty moments" arose over the 1968 Warsaw Pact intervention in Czechoslovakia and its consequences: the Belgian delegation refused to stand and applaud the "collaborationist" Slovak premier and stated that they would not have attended the session had they known that a government spokesman would address it; the Irish delegates "regretted" the events of 1968. The same article attributed to Czechoslovak politics the repeated accusations that the organizers of the congress had been guilty of "formalism" and restricting the agenda.

Henri Verley, a French student who attended the congress, reported in Politique Hebdo (published in Paris by dissident communists and others) on 25 February that tight security and restricted disclosure of information were imposed to give the appearance of unity.[1] He stated that the organizers, further, had assured harmony by the selection of delegations: with the help of the Czechoslovak government they turned back the Congo (Kinshasa) delegation at the airport, expelled the Greek student representatives (who had already settled in their hotel), and refused entry visas to delegates from France,[2] Guadeloupe, and Martinique. In other cases, Verley said, delegates were treated unjustly: the organizers "forgot" to send transportation tickets (normally supplied by the IUS) to Guatemalan and Honduran delegations; two Belgian delegates were detained by police for four hours on the

[1]Although Rudé Právo (21 January) spoke of arrangements for some 40 journalists who were expected to cover the congress, the accounts in the Guardian and the Politique Hebdo stated that only two reporters—from the Soviet Komsomol's Komsomolskaia Pravda, who were included in the Soviet delegation—actually attended the congress. Reportedly, only certain delegates were available for interview.

[2]The National Union of French Students (UNEF) was not represented because the Czechoslovak government denied visas to two members of the "Permanent Delegation of the UNEF" (dominated by Trotskyist and New Left groups) on the grounds that they did not represent the UNEF. The "UNEF Renouveau," supported by the French Communist Party, had recently resigned from the IUS. (Le Monde, Paris, 5 February.)

night of their arrival for allegedly having scattered anti-Czechoslovak leaflets in the streets, and were released only when they threatened to make an issue of the arrest at the congress; the Belgian and Argentine[3] delegations, both full members of the IUS and also members of the Secretariat, were classified as observers by the Accreditations Committee.

In opposition to these "anti-democratic practices and manipulations," nine delegations—Argentina, Mexico, Spain, El Salvador, Ireland, Belgium (both Flemish and Walloon), the Union of Black African Students in France, and the Federation of Madagascar Students in France—protested on the second day to the congress Presidium in a joint eight-point resolution referring to the above complaints. The Presidium, according to Verley, ignored the resolution—which also contended that the congress did not have the quorum needed for valid proceedings—and tried thereafter to prevent its sponsors from gaining the floor.

Verley noted the development of an anti-Soviet bloc that included the delegations from Spain, Mexico, Belgium (both), El Salvador, Bolivia, the Union of Black African Students in France, and Madagascar. It gained support from Romania, Yugoslavia,[4] North Korea, Japan, Venezuela, and, on several occasions, Cuba and North Vietnam. Verley cited instances in which evidence of the bloc was apparent. The Soviet bloc rejected two Spanish proposals, one for a commission to be set up to look into the students' struggle in the Western capitalist countries and another for the words "[the struggle] for national and social liberation" to be included in the section of the agenda describing the tasks of the IUS. A third proposal by the Spanish delegation, expressing solidarity with the Arabs' "anti-imperialist struggles" and "especially with the struggle of the Palestinian people and students," was adopted by 21 votes (including those of Spain, Romania, Cuba, North Vietnam, and Yugoslavia) to 18 (the Soviet Union and others). The Soviet delegation also unsuccessfully opposed a Cuban amendment denoucing "imperialist penetration" in the universities. During the course of the debates, Verley said, many of these "rebels" challenged the IUS bureaucracy, criticizing what they regarded as its limited and superficial definition of anti-imperialist struggle and its ineffective action, especially regarding solidarity. On the last day several delegations (particularly those from Venezuela and the Dominican Republic) protested strongly against the single list of candidates for election to IUS posts. The Spanish delegation walked out as a protest.

An article in the Slovak socialist youth newspaper Smena (Prague, 19 February) explained that much of the opposition to the Spanish proposal (presumably the first mentioned above) concerned the relationship between the students and the working class:

> Students will succeed in asserting their demands only in a joint struggle with the workers class; anything else is illusory. Only one draft resolution appeared at the Bratislava congress, drawn up by Spanish and Belgian delegates, which overrated the possibilities of the student movement and strove to place it above the revolutionary struggle of the workers class. The draft referred to the ability of students to create a "revolutionary situation in the country," to "play a leading role in the revolutionary struggle," and to "make impossible the normal functioning of capitalism and

---

[3]Which of the two Belgian delegations, he did not specify. Two rival delegations were competing for representation of the Argentine University Federation (FUA) membership. One, the "15 November FUA," led by adherents of the pro-Soviet Communist Party of Argentina, represented (according to Verley) only nine university centers, while the "5 December FUA," dominated by the secessionist Communist Party of Revolutionary Recovery, claimed 60. The Cuban delegation proposed sending a commission to Argentina to investigate, but during discussions on this point the simultaneous translation cable "conveniently broke at the level of the Soviet delegation." Eventually, the "5 December FUA" took the seats, but when a Soviet speaker later accused them of "anti-Sovietism" they left the congress in protest, applauded by some delegations and accompanied to the door by the Spanish delegation.

[4]Yugoslavia has apparently not applied for readmission to the IUS since its expulsion in 1950, although here its delegation seems to have been permitted to vote. An editorial in Borba (Belgrade, 8 July), while "unofficially" disclosing that participation in the organization was being considered by the Croatian student organization, stated that the Yugoslav Student Federation already belonged to the IUS.

finally even to destroy it.'' The resolute rejection of this seemingly tempting draft congress resolution testifies to the political realism and maturity of the progressive student movement.

"Political adventurism" and "ultra-left radicalism" were not permitted by the congress, the article said. Thus, the congress rejected the "isolated view" of a Latin American delegate who urged adoption of the principle that the "language of guns should in turn be answered only with guns." The article cited the recently elected Marxist government in Chile as an example of the "effectiveness of other ways."

Other Activities. Immediately following the congress, the IUS in conjunction with the National Union of Finnish Students (SYL) convened an international conference on "Students and the African Liberation Movement," a theme popular at the congress. It was held in Helsinki on 14-19 February and attended by delegations from student organizations of more than 60 countries of Europe, Asia, Africa, and Latin America. A delegate from the Liberation Front for South Sudan was refused admission on the grounds that the front was a separatist movement in an independent country, was not recognized by the Organization of African Unity, and was not included on the list of participants prepared in advance (*Helsingin Sanomat*, Helsinki, 15 February). The Finnish Foreign Ministry rejected an SYL request for financial support for the conference on the grounds that the principles of international justice and the U.N. Charter prevented Finland from supporting groups and movements using violence. In the final communiqué, the conference called on student organizations to sponsor campaigns, conferences, and meetings to make the aims of the African "liberation" movements better known. Students were urged to collect money, medicine, food, and clothing for the "freedom fighters."

A "European seminar," sponsored by the Swedish National Union of Students (SFS), was held in Lund, Sweden, on 14-18 June. Attended by delegates from 21 national student organizations of West and East Europe, it was the most representative European student conference in a number of years. The main purpose of the meeting was to seek means of cooperation and to break the deadlock in preparations for the Tenth European Meeting of students. The preparations had been progressing slowly for more than two years because of disputes concerning representation of certain organizations, especially the Czechoslovak government-sponsored Czechoslovak Student Center (CSC). Some members objected to participation by the CSC in the European Meeting, and the SFS agreed to invite it to the seminar only on the understanding that this would not imply SFS recognition of the group. Conditions prevailing at the seminar indicated that the mandate given to the SYL (Finland) to hold the Tenth European Meeting within a year could be fulfilled.

The twenty-fifth anniversary of the IUS was celebrated by the organization's Secretariat at a two-day meeting in Moscow. This meeting took place in conjunction with the Fifth International Student Summer School on the "Scientific-Technological Revolution, Students, and Society," held under the auspices of Komsomol and UNESCO on 23 August-2 September.

Publications. The principal IUS publications are a monthly magazine, *World Student News*, edited by Mazin Husaini (Jordan) and published in English, French, German, and Spanish editions, and a fortnightly bulletin, *IUS News Service*, issued in English, French, and Spanish editions.

Eric Stromquist

Women's International Democratic Federation

The Women's International Democratic Federation (WIDF) was founded in Paris in December 1945 at a "Congress of Women" organized by the communist-dominated "Union des Femmes Françaises."The WIDF was headquartered in Paris until 1951, when it was expelled by the French government. It then moved to East Berlin.

Organization and Leadership. The WIDF Congress meets every four years and holds ultimate responsibility for the plans and activities of the federation. The Sixth Congress met in Helsinki in June 1969. Next in authority is the Council, which meets annually and is in control between congresses; it elects the Bureau and the Secretariat. The Bureau meets at least twice a year and implements decisions taken by the Congress and the Council; it is assisted by the Secretariat.

The Sixth Congress of the WIDF elected Hertta Kuusinen (Finland) as president and Cécile Hugel (France as secretary-general. National member organizations from around the world are represented on the Council and lesser organizational bodies. (For details see *YICA*, 1971, pp. 731-32.)

Membership in the WIDF is open to women's organizations and groups anywhere in the world and in exceptional cases to individuals. Total membership is estimated to be in excess of 200 million and in 1971 included 107 affiliated and associated organizations in 95 countries (*Vietnam*, no. 3, 1971). The WIDF tries to maintain contact with non-affiliated women's groups through its International Liaison Bureau, which has headquarters in Copenhagen and a secretariat in Brussels.

The WIDF has close relations with such other communist-front organizations as the World Peace Council, the World Federation of Trade Unions (WFTU), and the World Federation of Democratic Youth. It continually strives to expand its contacts with agencies of the United Nations and has Category A status with ECOSOC and Category B with UNESCO.

Aims and Policies. According to its charter, the WIDF aims to unite all the women of the world regardless of race, nationality, religion, or political belief, so that they may work together to defend their rights as citizens, mothers, and workers; protect children; ensure peace, democracy and national independence; and establish bonds of friendship and solidarity among themselves.

Views and Activities in 1971. President Hertta Kuusinen was the WIDF's leading spokesman in 1971. Writing in *World Marxist Review* (March) on the new role of women, she claimed that "only socialism leads to woman's complete liberation and offers the most favorable conditions for maximum use of her rights as mother, worker and citizen." She also recalled that for twenty-five years the WIDF had "consistently supported peoples fighting imperialist aggression, militarism, colonialism, neo-colonialism and racism, reactionary terror and persecution of democrats" because it was "part of the grand effort to promote peace and security, democracy and the basic human rights."

In accord with these basic ideas the WIDF observed its annual International Women's Day on 8 March, celebrating the "gains women have already made through hard work and sacrifice" and pledging to continue the fight for equal rights as an "integral part of the struggle for peace, democracy, and independence." (WIDF circular letter.) International Children's Day on 1 June was marked by a WIDF call for cooperation by all women and all "progressive forces," and the request that all governments recognize the U.N. Declaration of Children's Rights published eleven years ago. A special statement dealt with the suffering of children in the "war ravaged countries, in South Africa, the Portuguese colonies, in Spain and Greece, in the developing Asian, African and American countries, that continued to be in need of solidarity in the widest measure"; it further noted that in Indochina parents and children were subjected to bombing attacks and that in the United States "the ruling classes intend white children to hate their colored contemporaries" (ADN, East German news agency, 27 May).

Protests and appeals were characteristic of WIDF activities throughout 1971. In January the Secretariat expressed deep sympathy with the Democratic Union of Cameroun Women after the public execution of three "patriots" and the conviction that the Cameroun affiliate would redouble its efforts to win the struggle against neo-colonialism and thus honor the dead (ibid., 20 January). In a telegram to Premier Golda Meir of Israel, the WIDF demanded that she stop all actions on the part of Israel that were hostile to détente, and work for a peaceful settlement of the Middle East conflict in accordance with suggestions by mediator Gunnar Jarring and the U.N. Security Council resolution of November 1967 (MTI, Hungarian news agency, 18 January). President Kuusinen sent birthday wishes to U.S. communist Angela Davis and expressed solidarity with her "struggle against racial discrimination and the oppression of national minorities" (ADN, 21 January). In February Secretary-General Cécile Hugel wrote to the Portuguese Minister of Justice to demand immediate release of ten "Angolan patriots" on trial in Lisbon (ibid., 17 February). In March a special statement condemned U.S. policies and declared that "Laos is yet another illustration that the policy of so-called Vietnamization ... is a complete failure of U.S. global strategy" (ibid., 30 March). On African Women's Day, 31 July, the WIDF welcomed "the resolute stand of women in the young national states of Africa and their success in fighting neo-colonialist machinations endangering the independence of their countries and in building a new life"(ibid., 30 July). The federation expressed great alarm at the persecution of "democratic forces" in Sudan following the abortive communist coup and particularly at the arrest of Fatima Ahmad Ibrahim. She was described by the French communist newspaper L'Humanité (29 July) as an "eminent personality in the international women's movement, a member of the WIDF Bureau, and President of the Sudanese Women's Union." Her husband, WFTU vice-president al-Shaf'i Ahmad al-Shaikh, one of Sudan's leading communists, was executed. The WIDF tried to enlist the aid of the U.N. Commission on Human Rights to effect the release of Mrs. Ngo Ba Thanh, a lawyer and chairman of the "Women's Committee for the Defense of the Right to Live" in Saigon and Huynh Lien, a Buddhist priestess, both of whom were arrested by the government of the Republic of Vietnam on 27 May, together with about sixty "freedom fighters" (Vietnam, no. 3).

The WIDF expressed profound concern with the grave position in East Pakistan and the growing stream of refugees to India. It sent a message to the president of Pakistan asking an end to the trail of Sheik Mujibar Rahman, head of the Awami League, and the creation of conditions that would ensure the population of East Pakistan political, social, economic, and cultural rights in accord with the principles of the Universal Declaration of Human Rights (TASS, 5 October). The WIDF Bureau, meeting in East Berlin on 23-26 November, passed a resolution calling on the government of Pakistan to end "military repression in Bangla Desh" and to seek a political solution. The women of the world were asked to aid the refugees and to work for a peaceful settlement of the "grave problem" caused by "crushing the legitimate democratic rights" of the people of Bangla Desh (*Patriot*, New Delhi, 3 December).

WIDF representatives traveled widely and participated in a number of conferences in various parts of the world. President Kuusinen visited Cuba and Venezuela. Secretary-General Hugel spent three months in Africa, visiting Sudan, Morocco, Algeria, Mali, Guinea, Congo (Brazzaville), Zambia, the "liberated areas of Angola," and Zanzibar. In Zanzibar she announced that the WIDF planned to establish a training center in Sudan so that women could receive "health and cooperative education" (*Nationalist*, Dar es Salaam, 14 May). Ilse Thiele, a WIDF vice-president from East Germany, was a speaker at a Baltic Week women's conference (ADN, 11 July).

Publications. The WIDF publishes an illustrated quarterly magazine, *Women of the Whole World*, in English, German, Spanish, French, and Russian. The WIDF for many years issued numerous brochures, pamphlets, and bulletins, but cutbacks have recently become obvious. In 1971, *Vietnam*, a circular published by the International Viet Nam Solidarity Committee attached to the WIDF, was distributed several times.

Edith Wyden

World Federation of Democratic Youth

The World Federation of Democratic Youth (WFDY) was founded in November 1945 at a "World Youth Conference" convened in London by the World Youth Council. At first the WFDY appeared to represent varying shades of political opinion, but the key positions were taken by communists. By 1950 most of the non-communists had left to found their own organization, the World Assembly of Youth (WAY). Originally based in Paris, the WFDY was expelled by the French government in 1951. Since then it has maintained headquarters in Budapest. It holds category C status with UNESCO and is on the register of ECOSOC.

According to the WFDY constitution, all youth organizations and other bodies that contribute to the safeguarding of the activities of young persons are eligible for membership. A total membership of some 100 million persons in 200 organizations in 90 countries is claimed (TASS, 12 October 1970); the vast majority of members live in communist-ruled countries. The WFDY claims to be financed entirely by affiliation fees; no details are published.

Structure. The highest governing body of the WFDY is the Assembly, which is supposed to convene every three years, and to which all affiliated organizations may send representatives. The Eighth Assembly was held in Budepast in October-November 1970. The Executive Committee is elected by the Assembly and is supposed to meet at least twice a year, while day-to-day work at the headquarters is conducted by the Bureau of the Executive Committee, which meets when necessary. The Bureau controls the WFDY Secretariat and its various departments and regional commissions.

The Eighth Assembly elected a 57-member Executive Committee (with places reserved for an additional three to come from Chile, Peru, and China), which formed a 26-member Bureau. Angelo Oliva (Italy), who acceded to the presidency in 1969, was replaced by Roberto Viezzi (Italy) in October 1971, and Alain Therouse (France) succeeded Michel Jouet (France) as secretary-general, the latter having held the office since 1968 (see below). There are seven vice-presidents, two deputy secretaries-general, 13 secretaries, and a four-member Auditing Commission. (See *YICA*, 1971, p. 720, for countries represented in these offices.)

WFDY subsidiaries include the International Committee of Children's and Adolescents' Movements (CIMEA), which organizes international camps and film festivals; the International Bureau of Tourism and Exchanges of Youth (BITEJ), charged with planning and supervising work camps, meetings, and conferences for young tourists (BITEJ is an associate member of the Coordinating Committee for International Voluntary Service, which works under the aegis of UNESCO); the International Sports Committee for Youth, which arranges special events in connection with WFDY-IUS World Youth Festivals; the International Voluntary Service for Friendship and Solidarity of Youth (SIVSAJ), geared to increasing WFDY influence in developing countries by sending "young volunteers" to work with the people of these countries; and various "International Committees of Solidarity."

Aims and Policies. The avowed aims of the WFDY are to contribute to the education of young persons in the spirit of freedom and democracy; to raise the living standard of the young; to end colonialism; to ensure peace and security in the world; to promote the active participation of young persons in economic, social, cultural, and political life; to ensure in all countries and for all young persons full freedom of speech, the press, religious belief, assembly, and organization; and to further the spirit of international friendship and support the principles of the United Nations. In practice, strong support of the Soviet Union and its policies has been evident in WFDY pronouncements and actions. Since the emergence of the Sino-Soviet dispute, the Chinese have not participated in WFDY activities.

Views and Activities in 1971. Preparations for the three-year international "Youth Accuses Imperialism" campaign, a joint undertaking by the WFDY and the International Union of Students (IUS) which was initiated at the Eighth Assembly, were evident in various parts of the world during 1971. In Latin America the campaign began in August with a meeting in Chile under the title "Youth and Students of Latin America and North America Accuse Imperialism in Solidarity with the Peoples of Vietnam, Laos and Cambodia." The meeting, held in Santiago on 31 August-3 September, was attended by some 300 young persons from 58 countries. Themes taken into consideration included the strengthening of solidarity among Latin American and North American young people and students; Latin American support for antiwar efforts in North America; and support for Latin American struggles for independence, social progress, defense of natural resources and national sovereignty, and release of political prisoners (*Tribuna Popular*, Santiago, 10 June). Resolutions adopted concerned, among other things, support for the Bolivian people (whose government had come under rightist control through a coup two weeks earlier) and an appeal for the release of political prisoners—particularly in Paraguay, Greece, Portugal, Spain, and Haiti. Another outlined a plan of action for aiding the hoped for defeat of the United States in Vietnam to include supporting the campaign to build the Nguyen Van Troi Hospital in Hanoi; mobilizing people in support of North Vietnam on 20 December and of the revolutionary forces of Laos and Cambodia on 12 October and 9 November, respectively; and arranging tours of Latin America by Vietnamese young people and members of the Vietnam War Crimes Commission (*El Siglo*, Santiago, 1-5 September).

Following the Santiago meeting, the WFDY Executive Committee convened in Valparaiso, Chile, on 6-8 September. Its sessions drew a reported attendance of 248 young persons from 58 countries. Resolutions were adopted which called for worldwide support for the "revolutionary process" in Cuba and Northern Ireland (*ibid.*, 12 and 19 September).

The committee agreed that Roberto Viezzi (Italy), a member of the Directorate of the Federation of Italian Communist Youth, should replace Angelo Oliva as WFDY president, Oliva having been "called by the Italian Communist Party to another appointment." Rene Martinek (replacing Siegfried Diener—both from East Germany) and Naomi Chesman (United States) were appointed secretaries, and Ireneusz Matela (Poland) became BITEJ executive director. Ryszard Tyrluk (Poland) lost his position as secretary. (*WFDY News*, no. 7; *L'Unità*, Rome, 18 September.)

The committee granted full membership in the WFDY to ten groups. Four were former "observer" member organizations in Nigeria, Argentina, Bolivia, and Chile. The other six were organizations in Chile, Honduras, Peru, Dominican Republic, El Salvador, and Uruguay. (*El Siglo*, 26 September.)

The selection of Chile as the site for the two WFDY meetings seemed designed, as the speeches and resolutions indicated, to show approval of and gain support for the year-old government of Marxist president Salvador Allende. Earlier in the year, WFDY secretary-general Michel Jouet, in Chile to promote the "Youth Accuses Imperialism" campaign, stated at a press conference:

> Imperialism was building up its attack on the deeply renovationary Chilean method through rightists' plots involving the [U.S.] Central Intelligence Agency to a campaign of lies on an international

scale. The campaign was particularly violent in some of the reactionary press organs, but it could not hide the truth. Never had Chile enjoyed so much prestige on the international scale. (*Ibid.*, 7 March.)

Support for liberation movements in Portuguese Africa was the central theme of a WFDY-sponsored "International Meeting of Solidarity with the Struggle of the peoples and Youth of the Portuguese Colonies" held at Brazzaville in the People's Republic of Congo, on 22-24 April. A strongly worded resolution condemned "exploitation and oppression" by the Portuguese colonists, citing the "Lisbon-Salisbury-Pretoria alliance," the November 1970 attack on Guinea by forces from Portuguese Guinea, and the alleged Portuguese bombing raids on neighboring countries which supported "patriots" fighting Portuguese colonialism. It praised the "liberation struggles" being conducted by the Popular Movement for the Liberation of Angola (MPLA), the African Party for the Independence of Guinea and the Cape Verde Islands (PAIGC), and the Front for the Liberation of Mozambique (FRELIMO), and called on all "progressive and democratic youth organizations" to mark the anniversaries of the beginnings of armed struggle by the three movements with demonstrations of solidarity and a dialogue with South Africa. (TASS, 23 April.)

For future activities the meeting entrusted the WFDY and the Pan African Youth Movement to: send youth delegations to Latin America, the United States, Canada, and Western Europe to gain support for the liberation movements in the Portuguese colonies; arrange for a WFDY delegation to tour the "liberated zones" of those colonies; and launch an international youth campaign from 3 August 1971 to 4 September 1972 to collect funds (Brazzaville radio, 25 April).

In Europe the WFDY was active in its attempts to forge European unity among young people and to promote support for the European collective security system proposed by the Soviet Union. WFDY representatives from 21 European countries held a consultative meeting in Marianske Lazne, Czechoslovakia, on 14-16 April to assess the organization's activities in Europe since its Eighth Assembly and the role of youth in the "struggle for European security and cooperation."

The idea of convening a European youth meeting in 1971 was discussed in Marianske Lazne and given additional impetus at meetings in Cesky Krumlov and Susice, Czechoslovakia, on 15-17 and 18-20 June, respectively, co-sponsored by the Czechoslovak Socialist Youth Union, the WFDY, and IUS. A preparatory conference was held in Florence, Italy, on 28-29 July for the all-European meeting which was scheduled to take place in the same city on 2 December. Some 800 delegates from Eastern and Western Europe accepted the invitation. Four commissions were set up to prepare for discussions of European security, international cooperation, the defense and development of democracy, and the Mediterranian as a sea of peace. (*L'Unità*, 1 August.)

An attempt was made to achieve some degree of cooperation between the WFDY and a European competitor, the Council of European National Youth Committees (CENYC). Representatives of the two organizations met at the Seventh Congress of the CENYC, held in Salzburg, Austria, on 22-25 April, to discuss such cooperation. WFDY secretary-general Michel Jouet (writing in *WFDY News*, no. 5-6) declared that, despite differences between the two groups,

> the Salzburg meeting laid the foundations for the development of joint work on many issues, particularly with regard to the rights and responsibilities of youth in all fields.... It underlined the common will of WFDY and CENYC to work together for the preparation and convening of a European youth meeting.... In our opinion this meeting would be an event within the framework of efforts made by youth in support of an All-European Conference of States.... More generally speaking the contacts begun two years ago ... were further developed at the Salzburg meeting which was characterized by increased recognition and mutual trust and by a determination to promote joint work.

According to a joint communiqué the CENYC and WFDY delegates agreed to set up a working group to prepare a European youth meeting (*ibid.*).

Publications. The WFDY publishes a bimonthly magazine, *World Youth*, in English and French, and "in a number of national editions." Its monthly newssheet, *WFDY News*, appears in English, French, and Spanish editions. Other publications are directed to specific areas of interest, including special magazines and pamphlets to commemorate congresses, festivals, and other events.

Eric Stromquist

World Federation
of Scientific Workers

The World Federation of Scientific Workers (WFSW) was founded in London in 1946 at the initiative of the British Association of Scientific Workers. Eighteen organizations of scientists from 14 countries were represented at the inaugural meeting. Although the WFSW purported to be a scientific rather than a political organization, communists succeeded in obtaining most of the official posts at the start, and have retained control ever since. The WFSW headquarters is in London, but the office of the secretary-general is in Paris.

Membership in the WFSW is open to organizations of scientific workers everywhere and to individual scientists from countries where no affiliated groups are active. The WFSW claims to represent 300,000 scientists in 30 countries; most of the membership is derived from 14 groups in communist-ruled countries. The only large non-communist affiliate is the British Association of Scientific Workers, which has 21,000 members. Scientists of distinction who do not belong to an affiliated organization may be nominated for "corresponding membership." The WFSW has a constitution and a "Charter for Scientific Workers" to which its affiliates must subscribe (see *YICA*, 1968, p. 736).

Structure and Leadership. The governing body of the WFSW is the General Assembly, in which all affiliated organizations are represented. Nine General Assembly meetings have been held to date, the last in April 1969, in Paris. The Executive Council is theoretically responsible for controlling the activities of the WFSW between assemblies, but it is the WFSW Bureau which actually conducts day-to-day work. The Bureau consists of the WFSW president, vice-presidents, and treasurer, the Executive Council chairman and vice-chairman, the chairman of the Editorial Board, and the heads of regional centers.

The president of the WFSW is Eric Burhop (Britain). Vice-presidents include Hermann Budzislawski (East Germany), I. I. Artobolevsky (Soviet Union), and S. H. Zaheer (India). John K. Dutton (Britain) is organizing secretary and William Wooster (Britain) is treasurer. The WFSW Secretariat includes Pierre Biquard (France), secretary-general, and assistants to the secretary-general Grigori Kotovsky (Soviet Union), Mohammed el-Lakany (U.A.R.), Anita Rimel (Britain), and P. L. Marger (France). The WFSW's regional centers in New Delhi, Cairo, and Prague are headed respectively by N. P. Gupta, S. Hedayat, and I. Malek.

The WFSW has consultative Category B status with UNESCO. It exchanges information with such U.N. groups as the International Labor Organization (ILO) und the World Health Organization (WHO).

Views and Activities in 1971. Burhop indicated in *Scientific World* (no. 1, 1971) that the WFSW planned "to keep in the public view the whole question of weapons of mass destruction," and would sponsor a conference on ABC (atomic, biological, and chemical) weapons. It would also organize an international symposium on the problems of young scientists, "as a forerunner of a much larger one on 'the scientist in society' which is to be held in Moscow during 1972."

Over 100 delegates from some 20 countries attended the "Symposium of Young Scientific Workers in Contemporary Society," held on 14-16 July at Enschede, Netherlands. UNESCO sent two observers. Burhop told delegates that a "Charter on the Rights of Scientific Workers," being prepared by representatives of the WFSW's British, French, Czechoslovak, and Soviet affiliates, had been discussed with UNESCO and ILO representatives. The WFSW, he said, had been invited to "discuss the next steps" with those organizations and with representatives of "other non-governmental organizations." Burhop spoke also of the need to update the twenty-five-year-old WFSW constitution. A committee set up for that purpose could report to the Executive Council, which could consider whether to suggest modifications to the next General Assembly to take place in 1973). Burhop thanked UNESCO for providing travel grants to some symposium participants, and noted that UNESCO attached sufficient importance to the "problems we are discussing" to "have asked us to form a working group inside the symposium to formulate recommendations to UNESCO on the preparation, and proposals for the agenda, of an international conference on youth, to be organized in the period 1973-4." He also thanked the East German and Soviet affiliates for their "generous donations" to the symposium travel fund. (*Scientific World*, no. 5.)

The WFSW Conference on ABC Weapons convened in East Berlin on 21-23 November, with some 150 scientists from 21 countries and 12 "important international organizations" attending. The conference studied the Soviet proposal for convening a world governmental disarmament conference. It also discussed a European security conference, regional conferences on peace, security, and disarmament, and the "economic and social consequences of disarming." A resolution was adopted calling upon the United States to "cease chemical warfare against the people of Indochina immediately and unconditionally, to withdraw its troops, and to cease supporting the Thieu regime in South Vietnam." (ADN, East German news agency, 20-23 November.) Immediately before the conference, WFSW Bureau members met to discuss "disarmament and the responsibility of scientists," and the Executive Council met during the conference and formed a "committee to direct scientists in the disarmament struggle" (TASS, 23 November). On 23 November, East German Foreign Minister Otto Winzer told Burhop and Biquard that the goals pursued by socialist states were "in complete accord with the aims of the conference and of the WFSW" (ADN, 23 November).

Publications. The official publication of the WFSW is *Scientific World*, issued bimonthly in English, French, Russian, German, Spanish, and Czechoslovak editions. The WFSW *Bulletin*, which appears irregularly and is issued only to members, is published in English, French, German, and Russian editions. "Science and Mankind" is the general title of a series of WFSW booklets that have appeared in several languages. The WFSW also publishes pamphlets on particular subjects from time to time.

Valerie Bloom

World Federation of Trade Unions

The World Federation of Trade Unions (WFTU) was set up at the initiative of the British Trade Union Congress (TUC). After a preparatory conference in London earlier in the year, the founding congress was held in October 1945 in Paris, where the first headquarters of the organization was established. Since then the WFTU has had to move its base of operations twice after expulsion for subversive activities - to Vienna in 1951 and to Prague in 1956.

In recognition of Britain's leadership in establishing the WFTU, Sir Walter Citrine was elected the federation's first president. At Soviet insistence, Louis Saillant of France was elected secretary-general. Saillant is generally considered responsible for bringing the Secretariat and other ruling bodies of the WFTU under communist control. He was so effective that some members charged in 1948 that the WFTU was "rapidly becoming nothing more than another platform and instrument for furtherance of Soviet policy." Rebelling against political control, some non-communist affiliates in 1949 gave up their membership to found an alternative organization, the International Conference of Free Trade Unions (ICFTU).

Organization and Leadership. The highest authority of the WFTU is the Congress; it meets every four years and is composed of delegates from affiliates in proportion to the number of their members. The latest congress met at Budapest in October 1969. The 461 delegates, observers, and guests from 97 countries were said to be representative of 153 million workers, organized in more than 50 national affiliated organizations and almost as many non-affiliated groups.

Congresses have no policy-making function and are too large to transact much specific business. They elect the federation's General Council, Executive Bureau (newly established in 1969), and the Secretariat. The 1969 meeting elected a General Council of 66 regular and 68 deputy members, representing not only the national affiliates, but also 11 "Trade Union Internationals" (TUIs). It chose an Executive Bureau composed of newly elected WFTU President Enrique Pastorino (Uruguay), Secretary-General Pierre Gensous (France), and twenty-three members representing every part of the world; two seats were left vacant to be filled by representatives of China and Indonesia respectively. The Executive Bureau has been compared to a Politburo and is the most powerful body of the WFTU. It has assumed much of the authority which before 1969 was enjoyed by the Secretariat. The Secretariat itself was revamped by the congress and reduced in size to a total of six members, including the secretary-general.

The Trade Union Internationals represent workers of particular trades or crafts. One of the main purposes of the TUIs is to recruit local unions which do not, through their national centers, belong to the WFTU itself. Though the TUIs are in theory independent — each TUI has its own offices and officials, holds its own meetings, and publishes its own bulletin — their policies and finances are controlled by the WFTU department having supervision over their particular areas. The General Council meeting of the WFTU in December 1966 decided that each TUI should have its own constitution; this move for bolstering the appearance of independence had the purpose of allowing the TUIs to join international bodies as individual organizations.

The WFTU has set up a number of subsidiary organizations to deal with specific problems and to achieve collaboration with non-communist trade unionists in solving them. One of the most important subsidiaries is the "Special Commission on U.N. Agencies," which was established in 1967 to try to expand WFTU activities in the United Nations. The WFTU is permanently represented at the U.N. headquarters in New York, at the International Labor Organization (ILO) in Geneva, the Food and Agriculture Organization (FAO) in Rome, and UNESCO in Paris, and enjoys Category A status with a number of other U.N. agencies.

Aims and Policies. The WFTU constitution states that the federation exists "to improve the living and working conditions of the people of all lands." It also details the prime purposes of the WFTU: (1) to organize and unite within its ranks the trade unions of the whole world irrespective of considerations of race, nationality, religion, or political opinion; (2) to assist, whenever necessary, the workers of socially or industrially less-developed countries in setting up their trade unions; (3) to carry on the struggle for the extermination of all fascist forms of government and every manifestation of fascism, under whatever form it operates and by whatever name it may be known; and (4) to combat war and the causes of war and work for a stable and enduring peace.

The constitution clearly endorses political activity by the WFTU, but this has at times led to serious friction. Non-communist unions have complained that the WFTU is subservient to the Soviet Union and that it supports Soviet causes around the world, while reserving criticism for the Western countries or those politically at odds with the Soviet Union. Political controversy has been at the root of the inactivity of the Chinese trade unions in the WFTU since 1966, and of the Yugoslavs' refusal to reaffiliate after their expulsion in 1950 at the height of the Stalin-Tito antagonism.

Views and Activities. The WFTU held two of its most important meetings of 1971 — the Fourth Session of the Executive Bureau and the Twenty-first General Council Meeting — in East Berlin late in the year.

The agenda for the Bureau meeting, held on 8-9 December contained two items: (1) the experience gained in trade union activities in the socialist countries and (2) preparations for the meeting of the General Council, scheduled for 10-13 December. President Enrique Pastorino opened the session by paying tribute to the memory of al-Shaf'i Ahmed al-Shaikh, former WFTU vice-president, Lenin Prize winner, and secretary-general of the Federation of Sudanese Trade Unions, who was executed in Sudan on 26 July following the roundup of communists in the aftermath of their abortive coup. Pastorino then described the first topic of the day as dealing with "ideological work." He urged intensification of propaganda activities in order to inform workers in the capitalist countries of the experiences of trade unionists in the socialist states, "where the working people share in the leadership of the nation and are masters of their destiny." A communiqué issued at the conclusion of the meeting characterized the growing role of the trade unions in socialist countries as a special result of "socialist reality" and as "evidence of the superiority of socialism over capitalism." (ADN, East Berlin, 9 December.)

The General Council Meeting considered a broader range of topics and dealt with such administrative matters as admission of new affiliates — the United Trade Union Federation of El Salvador and the Trade Union Federation of Laos — and personnel changes in the General Council, the Executive Bureau, and the Secretariat. It adopted a general resolution on thw world situation and a statement of principles. The statement endorsed the holding of a European security conference, welcomed the quadripartite agreement on Berlin; appealed for greater solidarity with the people of Indochina; asked for trade union participation in the preparation for the "World Conference against the War in Indochina" to be convened in Versailles in February 1972; issued a declaration concerning the situation on the Indian subcontinent, asking for an immediate end to the bloodshed in Pakistan and a political solution of the conflict "based on the legitimate rights and interests of the East Pakistani people"; and reaffirmed "absolute solidarity with the Korean people" in their fight for immediate withdrawal of U.S. troops from South Korea. In general the Council dealt with the "complicated and contradictory international situation" and the "exacerbation of the class struggle" and viewed them as requiring "constant vigilance and new initiatives for carrying out concerted and powerful actions in which all trade union forces must take part, regardless of their orientation." (*Ibid.*, 10 December.)

Earlier in the year the Bureau met in Paris (21-23 April). The occasion was noteworthy because it was the first time since the WFTU's expulsion from France in 1951 that the organization had returned for a meeting. The opening session was devoted to marking the centenary of the Paris Commune as an event of international importance and especially for the development of the "socialist system." Other sessions examined relations with U.N. orgainzations, working-class struggles in capitalist countries, the Indochina war, and the Middle East. Virgil Trofin, the Romanian delegate, discussed the proposal to organize an Asian trade union conference, but cautioned that preparations should be delayed until "success of the venture" and "participation of the trade unions of all the socialist countries of the Asian continent" seemed assured (Agerpress, Romanian news agency, 23 April). In his closing speech Secretary-General Gensous took up the question of unity within the WFTU and praised a "more profound agreement" to continue more resolutely in pursuit of that goal. (*L'Humanité*, Paris, 24 April; *World Trade Union Movement*, no. 5-6, May-June.)

The WFTU not only scheduled its own meetings, but sent delegates to numerous conferences organized by other groups, and issued declarations, statements, and appeals on topics of international interest or even on behalf of a few individuals. In January, General Council member Abd al-Quadir Amin (South Yemen) represented the WFTU at an Iraqi Trade Union Federation conference in support of Palestine, while a high-level delegation led by President Pastorino attended the Cairo congress of the All-African Trade Union Federation, where resolutions condemned Israeli "penetration of Africa" and alleged that U.S. aid to Israel was part of an imperialist plan to dominate the continent (TASS, 21 and 23 January; Cairo radio, 24 January).

The International Labor Organization and the role of trade unions in it were discussed at a February meeting in Brussels with representatives of the World Conference of Labor (WCL). The International Confederation of Free Trade Unions (ICFTU) had refused an invitation, ignoring a WFTU General Council appeal of October 1970 for cooperation of the three organizations and for a free exchange of views between them without prior conditions (*PCB Informations*, Belgium, 18 February). Unity of action by trade unions figured prominently again when WFTU-affiliated European organizations met in Sofia on 3 March, to consider European security. It was also an important topic in Geneva on 5 June at the 56th Session of the ILO, where Secretary-General Gensous in a major speech urged that the ILO initiate necessary changes to allow all the unions of the world to participate in international dialogue and to include the unions of the German Democratic Republic on an equal footing (*World Trade Union Movement*, no. 7, July).

An "International Conference in Support of Palestine" attracted 71 delegations from 61 countries to Sofia in September for a meeting jointly organized by the WFTU and ICATU (International Confederation of Arab Trade Unions). The conference decided to appeal to the workers of the world for support of the "just struggle of the Arab people, and particularly of the people of Palestine, in defense of their legitimate and human right to independent national existence on their native soil." It also resolved to send a memorandum to U.N. Secretary U Thant seeking "firm measures" to stop "Israeli aggression" and to send a separate memorandum to the U.N. Commission on Human Rights. (Bulgarian Telegraphic Agency, 14 September.)

WFTU preoccupation with Vietnam continued to be pronounced in 1971. In August a large delegation led by Gensous visited Hanoi to offer moral and financial aid to the Vietnamese trade unions. The WFTU expressed support for the Stockholm Conference on Vietnam and whatever plans it might make for an international meeting to be held in Montreal or Stockholm.

Statements issued by the WFTU covered a broad range of interests or problems. In January the federation criticized the British government for passage of its Industrial Relations Bill; the WFTU saw the bill as limiting the rights of trade unionists to conduct their own affairs and as facilitating rationalization of production by "big monopolies" at the expense of the workers (*Press Release*, no. 1, 8 January).   Early in the year a WFTU statement welcomed the United Nations' initiative to make 1971 "the international year for action to combat racism and racial discrimination" (CTK, Czechslovak news agency, 11 January). Another urged dismissal of criminal charges against "the black political militant Angela Davis" because of "reactionary and racist forces seek to intimidate the growing anti-racist and democratic movement" in the United States (*L'Humanité*, 19 January). In March the WFTU joined several other international organizations with consultative status in the United Nations in a joint appeal to the government of Brazil for a mission of inquiry to investigate "systematic violations of human rights" in that country (*Le Monde*, Paris, 27 March). The *World Trade Union Movement* (no. 3, March) reported on "Terrorism, Pillar of the Military Dictatorship," and referred to scores of victims of "medieval torture methods" in Brazil. In June a statement issued in Prague protested "unwarranted and brutal attacks against Algerian workers in France following the nationalization of French oil companies operating in Algeria." The WFTU charged that nationalization, although welcomed by the people of Algeria, was used by "reactionary and neo-colonalist circles in France as a pretext for an intensification of the racialist campaign" against Algerian immigrant workers. (CTK, 10 June.)

Ranging far afield, the WFTU was concerned with the international monetary crisis, citing it as evidence of the deep-seated problems of capitalism; agreed to support a demand by the "Central Commission for the Repatriation of Greek Political Refugees" for the release of Nikolaos Kaloudhis, imprisoned Politburo member of the Communist Party of Greece; expressed support for striking textile workers in Bombay, India, and for the Japanese struggle against "U.S. imperialism" on Okinawa (*News in Brief*, nos. 41 and 44); protested the "undemocratic action" and the "arbitrary dissolution of the General Federation of Jordanian Trade Unions (*ibid.*, no. 42); expressed concern about trade union rights in Senegal, and demanded the release of all union leaders in prison there (*ibid.*); and asked that trade unions exert pressure at the United Nations to force Israel to respect UN decisions (CTK, 30 November).

The WFTU faced unusual developments affecting a number of its affiliates. Without specific comment it reported on the resignation of Executive Bureau member Ignacy Loga-Sowinski from his post as chairman of the Central Council of Polish Trade Unions "in full understanding of the necessity for a basic change in the activity of the trade unions" (PAP, Polish Press Agency, 15 January). The announcement that the Central Council of the Czechoslovak Revolutionary Trade Union Movement had "relieved Jan Pillar [WFTU Executive Bureau member], at his own request, of the function of chairman and of his other functions in the Central Council" was received with similar official WFTU silence (CTK, 10 March). As Italian trade unions negotiated to achieve unity "despite the existence of important divergences of views," the WFTU was left to ponder the implications, if the huge and powerful Italian General Confederation of Labor (CGIL) were to leave the WFTU for the sake of such unity. The CGIL, in turn, left little doubt concerning its own views, originally presented to the WFTU General Council in October 1970: "The CGIL considers that the new unified union must remain outside both the WFTU and the International Confederation of Free Trade Unions....The CGIL, rejecting the idea of isolation, proposed a search for new possibilities and the construction of new, non-discriminatory organizational structures, beginning with Western Europe, through bilateral and multinational connections, on the basis of new notions of international policy, which shall be the expression of the real problems of the workers of the various countries" (*L'Unitá*, Rome, 9 July). The WFTU protested the disbandment of the trade unions in Sudan (TASS, 9 August) and ignored a request that it expel Secretariat member Ibrahim Zakaria for "publishing fabrications and misleading allegations, making use of the information services in Prague, and for having been elected by the defunct Sudanese Communist Party. (Omdurman radio, 12 September).

Moscow radio (30 October) in a Chinese-language broadcast strongly in contrast to previous recriminations, expressed the hope that China would return as an active affiliate of the WFTU and end the "abnormal situation ... detrimental to the struggle for the unity of the workers' movement." The broadcast recalled the important role China once played in the WFTU and the dissolution of the Chinese organization during the Cultural Revolution, when China "did not give up its intention to split the workers of the world" and the WFTU had expelled a number of individuals "falsely representing the Chinese working people."

Publications. The most important publication of the WFTU is the illustrated magazine *World Trade Union Movement*. In 1971 there were eleven issues, circulated in some 70 countries in English, French, Spanish, German, Russian, and other foreign-language editions. The monthly bulletin *News in Brief* is published in four languages. Leaflets, pamphlets, brochures, or booklets are issued as activities or interests warrant, but there has been a cutback in such publications in recent years.

Edith Wyden

World Peace Council

The "world peace" movement headed by the World Peace Council (WPC) dates from August 1948, when a "World Congress of Intellectuals for Peace" in Wroclaw, Poland, set up an organization called the "International Liaison Committee of Intellectuals." This committee in April 1949 convened a "First World Peace Congress" in Paris. (Part of the meeting was held in Prague because the French government refused visas to delegates from communist countries.) The congress launched a "World Committee of Partisans of Peace," which in November 1950 was renamed the "World Peace Council." Originally based in Paris, it was expelled in 1951 by the French government, moving first to Prague and then, in 1954, to Vienna — where it adopted the name "World Council of Peace." Although outlawed by Austria in 1957, the World Council of Peace continued its operations in Vienna under the cover of an ostensibly new organization, the International Institute for Peace (IIP). In September 1968, World Council of Peace headquarters were transferred to Helsinki, while the IIP remained in Vienna. Although no formal announcement was made, the World Council of Peace has reverted to its designation as the World Peace Council.

Structure and Membership. The WPC is organized on a national basis, with "peace committees" in some 80 countries. No figure of the total number of members has ever been disclosed, but the WPC has members from more than 100 countries, most of them representing national peace committees. The highest authorities of the WPC are its 460-member Council, the Council-elected 59-member Presidential Committee, and the Committee-elected 15-member Secretariat. The Council has held nine congresses or "peace assemblies" to date; the latest, the "World Peace Assembly," convened in Budapest on 13-16 May 1971. The Presidential Committee and Secretariat control the WPC between Council sessions. Secretary-General is Romesh Chandra (India); Presidential Committee member Isabelle Blume (Belgium) appears to have stepped down as chairman of that body, a post she held until 1971. The executive bodies of the IIP — ostensibly independent of those of the WPC but, in fact, elected by the WPC Council — are the 7-member Presidium and the 30-member Executive Committee.

A number of structural changes adopted by the 1971 assembly, enacted in the name of the need "to adapt the WPC to the realities of the situation in the present world," in most instances resulted in increased centralization of authority and control over peace committees and even individual members. A permanent "working group" of the Presidential Committee, composed of the chairman, secretary-general, and "certain other members," would meet between regular Presidential Committee meetings. On the question of finance, it was directed that every national organization, movement, or group represented in the WPC make an annual contribution "in accordance with its possibilities and in agreement with the Secretariat." Similarly, each Council member would be required to contribute an amount "to be decided by each member himself, in accordance with his possibilities, personally or through his national committee." (*Assembly Documents.*)

Principles and Aims. The WPC, according to its stated tenets, favors general disarmament; elimination of all forms of colonialism and racial discrimination; and respect for the territorial integrity, popular sovereignty, and independence of every state. From its inception, however, the WPC has defended the policies of the Soviet Union and attacked those of the Western powers in every instance where such issues were at stake. Recent activities have focused primarily upon "U.S. aggression" in Southeast Asia and support of the Soviet call for a new European security system. Increasingly, the WPC is attempting to broaden and coordinate the efforts of its members and affiliates in various parts of the world by linking, as joint objects of attack, what it characterizes as (1) "racism" and "neo-colonialism" — from the United States to the Portuguese colonies and to South Africa and Rhodesia; (2) "imperialism" — the United States, West Germany, and Israel; and (3) "fascism" — Greece, Portugal, and Spain. Although a broad segment within the WPC disapproved of the 1968 Soviet-led invasion of Czechoslovakia, the WPC as an organization has remained firm in its support of the Soviet Union. The People's Republic of China has not participated in WPC activities for several years.

Views and Activities in 1971. An appeal issued by the WPC on 30 January (TASS) in connection with the announcement of the ninth World Peace Assembly indicated the WPC's major current interests. In Europe, it charged, the United States and the "aggressive circles of NATO" were continuing the arms drive and "creating obstacles" to the holding of a conference on security and cooperation, while the United States was "forcing higher war budgets" on NATO countries. The "imperialist threat to peace was growing in Indochina and the Middle East, while "neo-colonialism" threatened the sovereignty of African states and "the work of African national liberation movements." In Latin America, the United States was accused of trying to hold back "the movement for emancipation."

There was considerable movement among WPC officials in the months preceding the Assembly. Secretary-General Romesh Chandra took part in a meeting of "peace movements" from Denmark, Finland, Iceland, Norway, and Sweden in Stockholm on 24 January. The same month Khalid Muhyi al-Din (U.A.R.), a Presidential Committee member, headed a delegation that visited Italy, Britain, and West Germany. In February, WPC delegations met with representatives of the Organization of African Unity (OAU) in Addis Ababa, the National Union of Tanganyikan Workers (NUTA) and the All-African Trade Union Federation (AATUF) in Dar es Salaam. (TASS, 14, 24 February.) A WPC delegation including Chandra, Alfred Varela (Argentina, WPC secretary), and Canon Raymond Goor (Belgium; not a WPC member, but a "Permanent Observer" on its Presidential Committee, and head of Pax Christi), toured Venezuela, Chile, Peru, Bolivia, Uruguay, and Argentina. Chandra said in Caracas that they had come to "show solidarity with the wishes of the Latin American countries to attain real development while exercising their complete sovereignty." In Chile the delegation was received by (WPC member) President Allende, who was reported to have expressed his solidarity with the WPC program "because it accorded with the program of Popular Unity (Allende's coalition)." Chandra told Peruvians that the WPC was "fully behind" the Peruvian government and people in their efforts to achieve "economic emancipation." (*El Nacional*, Venezuela, 4, 7 March; *El Siglo*, Chile 5, 9 March; *La Crónica*, Peru, 14 March.) Chandra headed a delegation that visited Cuba on 19-24 February and met with President Dórticos and various labor and "peace" groups (*Granma*, Havana, 2 March).

As preparations for the Assembly advanced, however, it became apparent that European security was to be the dominant theme. The IIP convened a "Scientific Conference on Questions of European Security" on 19-21 February in Vienna. IIP Vice-President Georg Fuchs (Austria) afterward termed it "the first representative meeting of prominent scientists from the West and the East at which the main political, economic, and cultural problems in Europe were thoroughly discussed" (**TASS,**

22 February). The European Security Commission of the WPC (set up after the eighth World Peace Assembly, East Berlin, June 1969) met in Helsinki on 14-15 April. Finnish President Kekkonen expressed to delegates his regret that multilateral preparations for a governmental conference had not yet begun, while Chandra praised Finland's offer to be host to it as "a valuable contribution to the cause of peace affecting all nations." The commission urged exploration by the Assembly of "the possibilities for concrete actions by European public opinion toward the rapid preparation and convocation, multilaterally and without prior conditions, of a Conference on European Security and Cooperation." (*Helsingin Sanomat*, 15, 16 April; *Press Release*, no. 5, 15 April.)

Some 800 delegates from 124 countries and 30 international organizations attended the Assembly. These included, besides communist front organizations, two U.N. committees (on apartheid and decolonization), the OAU, the Afro-Asian Peoples' Solidarity Organization (AAPSO), the AATUF; the International Committee for the Recognition of the German Democratic Republic (Sweden); the Conference for European Security and Cooperation (Belgium); the Christian Peace Conference (CPC); and the International Confederation of Arab Trade Unions (ICATU). In the keynote speech, Chandra spoke of the changing world attitude toward "the problems of peace," and of WPC efforts to end the "cold war" among different peace organizations by means of the "Stockhom spirit" (referring to the continuing Stockholm Conference on Vietnam, an originally independent anti-war movement which is now dominated by the WPC; see also below). The peace movement today, he said, not only led the "counterattack against imperialism and war" but was "inextricably linked with the struggle of all peoples for independence, justice, and social progress." He cited as examples on the national level the U.S. Peoples' Coalition for Peace and Justice (on whose executive WPC Presidential Committee member Carlton Goodlett sits) and "national liberation movements ... in Southern Africa and elsewhere." Escalation of "imperialist aggression," meanwhile, was "clearly seen" in recent events in Laos, North Vietnam, Guinea, Sierra Leone, Somalia, Uganda, East Pakistan, Japan, North Korea, Cuba, Chile, Peru, and Bolivia. In the Middle East, the United States was encouraging Israel's "aggressive positions" rather than pressing it to cooperate with the United Nations over a political solution, and was plotting to "split the anti-imperialist forces" in the Arab countries. European security was vital for the whole world, Chandra emphasized, for the "fangs of NATO" supported Portuguese colonialism, South African racism, and the system of "linked imperialist military pacts" such as CENTO, SEATO, ANZUS, and the projected South Atlantic and Pacific Asia Treaty Organizations. He noted a "weakness in peace movement actions on European security compared with actions on Vietnam where the dangers to world peace are more apparent but are in fact no greater than in the Europe of NATO." The leading Soviet delegate, Presidential Committee member Aleksandr Korneichuk, accused "U.S. imperialist circles" of attempting to "resurrect the bogey of the mythical Soviet threat as an excuse to unleash a new round of the arms race." (*Assembly Documents*.)

A manifesto adopted by the Assembly considered the treaties between West Germany and the U.S.S.R. and Poland, respectively, as "proof of the consistent efforts by socialist countries in pursuit of peace," and found "U.S. imperialism" seeking to "impose its will in whole regions of the world." The manifesto called for a world conference on disarmament, a conference of the five nuclear powers on nuclear disarmament, "an end to chemical and bacteriological weapons and to foreign military bases and military alliances," "reduction of military expenditure and the application of U.N. resolutions on colonialism and on racial discrimination," and recognition of "de facto frontiers" in Europe, adherence to the rules of international law by all countries, and the "universality of the U.N., by admitting countries not yet members." (*Ibid.*)

WPC Lambrakis medals were awarded, among others, to Angela Davis, ("an outstanding figure in the fight against racial persecution in the U.S."), to the Black Panther Organization, ("fighting for colored peoples' rights"), to President Sekou Touré of Guinea, to "victims of apartheid" in South Africa, to Jordanian "victims of Israeli aggression," and to the Auschwitz museum (for preserving "the memory of the martyrs of fascism"). Joliot-Curie medals went to President Salvador Allende of Chile, "the people of Laos fighting for freedom and independence," the U.S. Coalition for Peace and Justice, and the OAU. The late President Nasser of the U.A.R. had been awarded the medal earlier in the year. The medal awarded in 1970 to the late Martin Luther King was received by his successor, the Reverend Ralph Abernathy. (*Budapress Bulletin*, 26 May.)

Belgians Raymond Goor and Maurice Lambiliotte, an IIP Executive Committee member, together head the recently formed Conference for European Security and Cooperation, whose first meeting, in Brussels on 22-24 June, "attended by personalities representing various shades of opinion and different organizations from most European countries," moved to set up an international preparatory committee to organize an "Assembly of Peoples of Europe" (*L'Humanité*, Paris, 28 June). WPC instrumentality was manifest at the outset. So as to give a "mass character" to the preparatory work for the Assembly of Peoples of Europe, the WPC convened a meeting of some 20 European national peace committees in Saarbrücken, West Germany on 11-12 September. A result of the Saarbrücken meeting was an enlarged session of the WPC Commission on European Security, held in Oslo on 18-19 December. The delegates, from 18 countries, included members of the British Labour Party, German and Scandinavian Social Democratic parties, and the Liberal and Center Parties of Norway and Finland. The meeting directed an appeal to all governments for an immediate start to preparations for a governmental European security conference in 1972, and a letter to U.N. members urging acceptance of both German states. The Assembly of Peoples of Europe was tentatively set for June 1972 in Brussels. (TASS, 20, 22 December.)

The Fourth General Assembly of the Christian Peace Conference was held in Prague on 30 September-3 October, with observers from the WPC, the World Council of Churches, the World Lutheran Federation, the All-African Conference of Churches, and UNESCO. According to *Le Figaro* (Paris, 1 October), "following the 1968 events in Czechoslovakia deep repercussions have occurred within the CPC so that it has become an instrument of Soviet policy, with new leaders in place of those opposing the Soviet action in 1968." Furthermore, "all who meet in Prague will have accepted beforehand the decisions taken for the CPC's future under the presidency of Metropolitan Nikodim (U.S.S.R.) and with Janusz Makovski as Secretary-General." Final resolutions—on "Christians seeking a peaceful future for all mankind," Vietnam, European security, racism, the Middle East, East Pakistan, and South Africa—all reflected Soviet positions. WPC Presidential Committee members Richard Andriamanjato (Malagasy Republic), Tibor Bartha (Hungary), and Herbert Mochalski (West Germany; WPC member), were elected to the CPC Working Group. (CPC *Information*, no. 79, October.)

An extraordinary session of the Presidential Committee opened in Helsinki on 15 December with an address by Albert Norden (East Germany). A statement welcomed the agreements between East and West Germany, and between East Germany and the Senate of West Berlin; pressed for ratification of West Germany's treaties with the U.S.S.R. and Poland, the putting into force of the four-power agreement on West Berlin, and the immediate, multilateral preparation of the European Conference on Security and Cooperation; and demanded international recognition of East Germany, including its admission to the United Nations (ADN, East German News agency, and TASS, 15 December.)

Following a "consultative meeting" in Helsinki on 19-21 January between Chandra and other WPC Secretariat members and an AAPSO delegation led by Deputy Secretary-General Kamal Bahya Eddin (U.A.R.), a joint communiqué was issued in which the two organizations agreed to coordinate their campaigns and activities in 1971 (*Press Release*, no. 2, 21 January). They did not succeed, however, in their attempt to stage their most important planned joint endeavor to date, a "Conference on Peace and Justice in the Middle East." Originally scheduled to have been held in Italy in the spring of 1971, it was postponed a number of times and at year's end was set for spring 1972. At a preparatory meeting for the conference, in Rome on 19-20 April, it was agreed that it should be "neither a peace negotiation, nor a bridge for various views, but rather a place for open discussion and confrontation." Israelis, Arabs, and "Palestinians" should be invited to take part, for example. A statement was drawn up inviting to the conference "everyone interested in discussing the possibility of a Middle East settlement by peaceful means." (*Avanti*, Italy, 25 April.) In telegrams to the Palestine Liberation Organization and the Jordanian prime minister, the WPC expressed its solidarity with the "Palestine Resistance — an important part of the Arab peoples' struggle against Israeli aggression — and for the national legitimate rights of the Palestinian people," and demanded "an end to Jordanian acts of repression" (*Letter to National Committees*, no. 14, 8 April).

WPC operations in Africa saw a similar effort to gain co-sponsorship of regional "anti-imperialist" or "anti-colonialist" activities with existing non-communist organizations. In a *Letter to Members* (no. 1, 21 January), the WPC claimed that the OAU had solicited its cooperation in the preparation of a "World Conference on Racism and Colonialism" which, it said, would be held somewhere in Europe in the fall (but which has not yet taken place). The WPC was to "carry out a number of visits in order to meet members of African governments with whom we have had little or no contact up to now, such as Zambia, Tanzania, Somalia, Mali, and Sierra Leone." It was reported that AAPSO would take part in the conference. A *Letter to National Committees* (no. 5, 26 January) called upon affiliates to undertake actions during the week of 4-11 February condemning "the criminal actions of Portuguese colonialists in the war of genocide which they have undertaken against Angola, Mozambique, and Guinea Bissau," as well as NATO assistance to them, and asking for material aid for the "national liberation movements" in the area. In a statement observing an "International Day for the Elimination of Racial Discrimination," 21 March, the WPC urged peace committees to intensify their actions for the liberation of the people of "Namibia" (South-West Africa), declaring that the arms embargo on South Africa should be "observed absolutely," "all links" with South Africa severed, and the "lawfulness of the struggle of the South African peoples against racial discrimination universally recognized" (Helsinki radio, 20 March). A statement issued in connection with the "Day of Solidarity with Zimbabwe [Rhodesia] Peoples," 17 March, termed the Ian Smith government in Rhodesia a "serious danger to international peace and security." Britain, it claimed, "plans to recognize the Smith regime, as has been shown by the renewal of talks between [British Prime Minister] Heath and Smith, and the use of the British veto against the Afro-Asian resolution in the U.N. Security Council," and all of this was leading "deliberately to a policy of connivance in South Africa's armed intervention in Zimbabwe." The WPC appealed to all "peace-lovers" to "support morally, politically, and materially, the people of Zimbabwe under the direction of ZAPU [Zimbabwe African Peoples Union]."

WPC agitation against U.S. participation in the Vietnam war took its most active form through the ostensibly non-aligned Stockholm Conference on Vietnam. A *Letter to National Committees* (no, 2, 12 January) quoted the "appeal" of the Sixth Stockholm Conference (November 1970) for solidarity with the "victims of repression in the United States ... in their efforts to bring independence in Indochina." Affiliates were asked to "take action in the form of speeches on human rights, appeals to President Nixon and to U.S. journalists, and public demonstrations." On 5 February the WPC circulated a statement on the "intrusion of U.S. and Saigon troops into Laos," protesting that the action had "increased the danger for the people in that area and the whole world," and calling on all "peace-loving peoples to support the "Indochinese struggle for freedom, independence, and peace" (TASS, 5 February.) Chandra and Isabelle Blume headed a WPC delegation that met with leaders of the Provisional Revolutionary Government of South Vietnam and North Vietnamese delegates to the Paris talks, and with representatives of Cambodian and Laotian students in

France. A WPC statement following the meetings asked "peace forces throughout the world" to "show their full support of the activities of the joint U.S. peace forces." (*L'Humanité*, Paris 4 March.)

In a *Letter to National Committees* (no. 15, 7 April), the WPC said that the "progressive rebirth of Japanese militarism under the Sato government" and in "collusion with the U.S. imperialists" was "giving rise to growing concern among the peoples of Asia and the world peace forces." The WPC and its Japanese affiliate campaigned against the U.S.-Japanese security treaty and for the return of Okinawa to Japan, and staged an "international week against the rebirth of Japanese militarism" beginning 28 April. Declaring that "the Americans have shown that their overall strategy is to dominate Asia with the help of Japanese militarists," the WPC designated 30 April and 19 May "days of solidarity" with the Cambodian and Vietnamese "people" respectively. The International Commission of Inquiry into U.S. War Crimes (established in 1970 by the Stockholm Conference) convened its second session in Oslo on 20 June, and found the United States "guilty" of war crimes in Vietnam, Cambodia, and Laos (*L'Humanité*, 26 June). John Takman, a member of the commission (and a leading member of the communist party of Sweden), was elected to the WPC Presidential Committee in 1971. The WPC announced in a *Letter to National Committees* on 9 November that a "World Conference against the War in Indochina" would be held in Versailles on 11-13 February 1972, with more than 1,000 delegates expected to attend.

The WPC appeared to make little headway in Latin America in 1971, and its influence there remains inconsiderable. In an "Appeal against Terrorism in Guatemala" *Press Release*, no. 1, 1 March), the WPC said that the only crime of the many Guatemalans killed in recent months had been "to declare themselves true patriots for peoples' rights ... and for the emancipation of the country from U.S. imperialism." It asked affiliates to direct protests to the president of Guatemala and to the U.N. Commission on Human Rights. It was reported in *Peace Courier* (no. 9, September/October) that the Guatemala-based Executive Council of the Federation of Central American Students would "coordinate with the WPC activities throughout Central America." Elsewhere in Latin America, Alberto Casella (Argentina), WPC Presidential Committee member, represented the WPC at an international seminar for lawyers on the "Application of Human Rights in Latin America" organized by the Uruguayan Confederation of Labor (CNT) and other organizations in Montevideo on 5-12 September (*El Popular*, Montevideo, 12 September). In a statement expressing "solidarity with the Bolivian people against the fascist coup" the WPC said that "the responsibility of the United States in the coup through its Embassy in La Paz and the Central Intelligence Agency was undeniable," and that Hugo Banzer had also been "helped to power" by "the military dictatorships closely tied to the U.S., those of Brazil and Paraguay" (*Press Release*, no. 29, 3 September).

The WPC's application for Category B status (Information and Consultation) in UNESCO was granted on 14 May 1971. It had acquired Consultative Status C in 1969, and had been actively campaigning for the higher association. The WPC sits on three "special committees" of the Non-Governmental Organizations (NGO) Conference attached to the U.N.: Human Rights, Disarmament, and the Second Development Decade. It was represented by Jerzy Markiewicz (Poland), secretary, at a meeting in Geneva on 16-17 February of the NGO Committee on Disarmament, at which the WPC proposed that a world conference on disarmament be held in 1972 or 1973 (*Peace Courier*, no. 3, 31 March). On 10 September a 12-member WPC delegation including Krishna Menon (India), one of three WPC Honorary Presidents—the others being Pablo Picasso (Spain) and Louis Saillant (France)—together with Romesh Chandra and Presidential Committee members Isabelle Blume, Aziz Sherif (Iraq), Guido Fanti (Italy), Camara Damantang (Guinea), Evgeny Fedorov (U.S.S.R.), Raymond Guyot (France), and Carlton Goodlett (United States) met with then U.N. Secretary-General U Thant. They "informed him of possibilities to expand mutual contacts" and handed him "a memorandum on the principles of the WPC." (*Pravda*, 22 September.) In his report on the meeting, sent to members on 20 September, Chandra claimed that no non-governmental organization had done as much as the WPC to "implement U.N. decisions." U Thant, he said, had "agreed on the importance of greater U.N. cooperation with the WPC and thought that the WPC could play a significant role in shaping human society." At meetings with the U.N. Special Committees on Decolonization and Apartheid the WPC had presented proposals for closer cooperation, "preferably continuous and permanent, and associated with the day-to-day work"; it had invited both committees to take part in the next session of the Presidential Committee, and had proposed a joint meeting between the U.N. Committee on Apartheid and the WPC Commission on Racism, in New York, possibly in 1972. The WPC delegation had, in this connection, "referred to its cooperation with the OAU and to the OAU's plans for a "Conference on Colonialism and Racism" in Oslo in 1972. "In principle," said Chandra, both U.N. committees had "accepted the idea of regular cooperation on concrete issues." The WPC had proposed regular consultations with the U.N. at its New York headquarters, and had suggested "the participation of the U.N." in the "World Conference of Non-Governmental Organizations on Disarmament" (proposed by the WPC Assembly and currently envisaged for September 1972, probably in Geneva), and in "other important conferences sponsored by the WPC and others."

Delegates from 20 countries attended an "enlarged meeting" of the WPC Commission on Disarmament in Moscow, 30-31 October, presided over by Evgeny Fedorov. Speakers included Romesh Chandra, Josef Lukas (Czechoslovakia), Martin Niemöller (West Germany), K.D. Malaviya (India, president of the commission). The delegates recommended making 1972 "a year of intensive actions for disarmament," and sent a message to the U.N. General Assembly asking it to make "firm arrangements" for a world conference. (TASS, 31 October, and 1 November.)

Publications. The WPC issues a semimonthly bulletin, *Peace Courier*, in English, French, Spanish, and German, and a quarterly journal, *New Perspectives*, in English and French. The WPC also distributes occassionally a *Letter to National Committees*, and a *Letter to Members*, and issues *Documents*, *Statements*, and *Press Releases* in connection with its conferences and campaigns. A special booklet was issued in connection with the 1971 World Assembly of Peace.

Valerie Bloom

CHRONOLOGY

Chronology

JANUARY

Iran	Central Committee plenum replaces Reza Radmanesh as chairman of Tudeh Party with Iradj Eskanderi.
	Confederation of Iranian Students Abroad declared illegal and members subject to arrest on return to Iran.
Luxembourg	Communist party celebrates fiftieth anniversary.
1 Australia	Moscow's *New Times*, charges party leadership with "deviation from views common to communist movement."
Jordan	Party dissension confirmed by Politburo announcement that "Leninist Cadre" group has withdrawn and established provisional Central Committee.
4 Indonesia	Military commander quotes captured materials on communist guerrilla plan for protracted "Viet Cong-style" war in West Kalimantan.
4-11 International Organization of Journalists	IOJ holds congress, first outside Europe, in Havana.
14 Czechoslovakia	Central Committee document, "Lessons from the Crisis Development of Party and Society since the 13th Party Congress," claims present leadership approved military intervention in August 1968.
14-17 Venezuela	New faction of communist party, Movement toward Socialism, holds first congress.
15 Algeria	National Union of Algerian Students dissolved by Interior Ministry because it "served as cover for a counter-revolutionary movement." Eight students arrested.

22 France	Roger Garaudy and 68 other dissidents ratify six-point "Declaration of Intent" of new Centers for Communist Initiative.
23-28 Venezuela	Communist Party of Venezuela holds congress.
24 World Peace Council	Meeting of Danish, Finnish, Icelandic, Norwegian, and Swedish "peace movements" held at Stockholm to stimulate popular demand for European security conference.
25-26 Albania	Central Committee replaces Xhafer Spahiu with Haki Toska on Secretariat.
26-9 February Cambodia/Vietnam: Democratic Republic of Vietnam	Exiled Royal Government of National Union head Sihanouk with friendship delegation to DRV.

FEBRUARY

Greece	Communist party plenum in East Europe adopts amended draft program for congress and approves recent purge of opposition to secretary-general.
3-11 International Union of Students	IUS holds congress at Bratislava, with some discord from anti-Soviet group.
4 Germany: West Berlin	Chairman of West Berlin communist party meets premier of East Germany.
5 Albania/Yugoslavia	Albania and Yugoslavia raise diplomatic representation to ambassadorial level.
Hungary	Death in Soviet Union reported of former party leader, Mátyás Rákosi.
Uruguay	Formation of Broad Front (Frente Amplio) officially announced.
8 Finland	Communists precipitate major union strike over rejection of wage contract proposals.
9 Bolivia	Open letter by member of Bolivian Communist Party (Marxist-Leninist) indicates probable emergence of rival group.

Cambodia/Laos	Sihanouk reportedly talks with Souphanouvong, Central Committee chairman of Laotian Patriotic Front, in "frontier region of Laos." Joint statement of solidarity issued.
14 Australia	Young Communist Movement is formed by 80-member group as autonomous organization of young workers and students, generally supporting the communist party.
U.S.S.R.	Publication of directives for ninth Five-Year Plan (1971-75).
mid-February Poland	Strike shuts down seven textile plants at Lódz.
15 Morocco	Government seizes two major opposition daily newspapers: *al-Alam*, and its French edition *L'Opinion*.
18-19 Romania/Warsaw Pact	Meeting of Warsaw Pact foreign ministers at Bucharest.
19 Morocco/U.S.S.R.	U.S.S.R.-Moroccan Friendship Society is founded.
19-21 World Peace Council	International Institute for Peace, associated with WPC, convenes "Scientific Conference on Questions of European Security" in Vienna.
26 Germany: Federal Republic of Germany	Social Democratic Party demands of all members respect for resolution on "incompatibility of action" with communist organizations.
27 Ceylon	Anti-government rally of People's Liberation Front in Colombo.
Israel	MAKI party chairman presents "Four Bases for Peace," program to settle Arab-Israeli conflict and develop Middle East.

MARCH

Sweden	Communist party adopts dual stance in protracted strikes by civil servants and professionals, supporting pay demands of lower and medium white-collar workers, but opposing increases for top functionaries.
1-10 India	In elections, nonaligned Communist Party of India (Marxist) becomes strongest national communist group and wins 80 per cent of con-

stituencies in West Bengal, making it strongest regional party. Pro-U.S.S.R. Communist Party of India suffers slight loss in parliament but loses more than half of its seats in West Bengal Assembly.

3
World Federation of Trade Unions

Affiliates meet at Sofia to discuss plans for European security.

4
Switzerland

Party of Labor celebrates fiftieth anniversary.

5-7
France

UNEF (Union Nationale des Etudiants de France) splits, and communist faction (UNEF-Renouveau) holds own congress in Paris.

6
Ceylon

Armed assault on U.S. embassy by self-styled "Mao Youth Movement."

11
Austria

Communist party's Central Committee resolution revises previous condemnation of Czechoslovak invasion as "incorrect," in view of later developments.

14
Germany: West Berlin

With 2.3 per cent of vote, Socialist Unity Party of West Berlin denied representation in city government.

15
U.S.S.R./Romania

Vasilii Drozdenko, new Soviet ambassador, arrives in Bucharest.

15-19
Japan/U.S.S.R.

Delegation of Japan Communist Party meets with leaders in Soviet Union to normalize relations.

16
Ceylon

Emergency declared, following assault on U.S. Embassy and other activities by People's Liberation Front.

16-20
Romania

Ceauşescu visits Sweden and Denmark.

17
Finland

Communist-dominated Finnish People's Democratic League withdraws from government coalition in protest against economic stabilization policies.

19-21
Belgium

Communist Party of Belgium holds congress.

20
Ceylon

Explosives found at Peradeniya campus of Ceylon University.

22 China/Romania	Chinese-Romanian trade protocol signed in Peking.
23-27 Romania	Federation of Romanian Trade Unions holds congress.
24-26 Czechoslovakia	Higher Military Court sentences former head of security, justice and army department of Central Committee, General Václav Prchlík, to three years in prison.
25-29 Yugoslavia	Tito visits Italy and Vatican.
26 Pakistan	Rebellion breaks out in East Pakistan.
28 Burma	Ceremony in Ingaby township welcomes 200 White Flag communists who surrendered.
30-9 April U.S.S.R.	CPSU congress held at Moscow.

APRIL

Latin America	*World Marxist Review* editorial board sponsors round table conference in Santiago, attended by communist leaders from Argentina, Brazil, Chile, Colombia, Peru, Venezuela.
Paraguay	Communist party clandestinely holds congress sometime in April.
1 Czechoslovakia/ U.S.S.R.	Secretary-general Husák repeats "invitation thesis" at Soviet party congress.
4 Japan	Candidates supported by Japan Communist Party elected governors of two most populous prefectures, Tokyo and Osaka.
5-6 Ceylon	Night attacks on some 25 police stations throughout country by People's Liberation Front; movement outlawed.
9 Burma/China	"Voice of the People of Burma" radio inaugurated from southern China in name of communist party (White Flag).

11 Bolivia	People's Assembly officially formed by coalition of leftist labor and political organizations, including communist and Trotskyist parties.
Vietnam: Democratic Republic of Vietnam	First National Assembly elections since 1964. Key party leaders reelected by 99-plus per cent of vote.
12 Finland/ U.S.S.R.	Communist party discussions with Soviet party leaders followed by economic treaty and agreement to consider closer Finnish association with Council for Mutual Economic Assistance.
13 Pakistan	Secessionist government of Bangladesh proclaims sovereignty.
16 Ceylon/Korea: Democratic People's Republic of Korea	North Korean ambassador to Ceylon and entire staff expelled for alleged complicity in the March-June uprising, though diplomatic ties not severed.
20-25 Bulgaria	Bulgarian Communist Party holds congress.
21 Czechoslovakia	Preliminary data from 1970 census indicates around 100,000 persons fled the country in 1968.
21-23 World Federation of Trade Unions	Bureau meeting at Paris marks first return of administrative unit to France since 1951 expulsion.
23-25 Norway	Communist Party holds congress, with chairman and supporters consolidating positions. Maoist bloc quits party to join earlier secessionists.
23-30 Cuba	First National Congress on Education and Culture held in Havana.
25 Hungary	General elections for National Assembly and local councils.
26 Argentina	National Assembly of the Argentines, electoral front established by pro-Soviet communist party and dissidents from five other parties, holds rally in Buenos Aires attended by 25,000 persons.
Ceylon/China	Chou En-lai offers interest-free loan of 150 million rupees for purchase of rice.
27 Cuba	Heberto Padilla, poet arrested on 20 March, released after signing "confession" that repudiates "insults and defamations" of Cuban Revolution. International controversy develops.

Laos	Patriotic Front Central Committee chairman, Souphanouvong, proposes new two-point peace plan.
28 Netherlands	Communist party with 3.9 per cent of vote in elections to parliament wins one seat, bringing total to six.
28-30 Yugoslavia	LCY Presidium discusses internal party crisis, particularly Serbo-Croatian relations, at Brioni.
30 New Zealand	Communist Party plans minor role in extensive anti-war demonstrations, charging sabotage by Trotskyists through dilution of revolutionary principles.

MAY

Germany: Federal Republic of Germany	Spartakus-Association of Marxist Students holds founding congress in Bonn at a time of growing influence in universities and colleges.
United Arab Republic	President Anwar Sadat arrests high-ranking government, party, and army leaders on charge of planning overthrow of government.
3 Germany: German Democratic Republic	Walter Ulbricht resigns as first secretary of Socialist Unity Party and is succeeded by Erich Honecker.
6 Albania/Greece	Albania and Greece restore diplomatic relations.
7 Romania	Fiftieth anniversary of communist party celebrated.
11 Luos/Vietnam: Democratic Republic of Vietnam	Premier Souvanna Phouma denounces North Vietnamese involvement in Laos during constitution day speech. DRV chargé d'affaires walks out in protest and is attacked by crowd.
13 Syria/Lebanon/ Jordan/Iraq	Communist parties of Syria, Lebanon, and Jordan denounce Iraq government for "measures of suppression and terror" against Iraqi communist party.
13-15 Czechoslovakia	Communist Party of Slovakia congress meets and calls for collectivization of remaining private agriculture.

13-16 World Peace Council	Ninth "World Peace Assembly" convenes in Budapest, with 800 delegates from 124 countries and 30 international organizations.
14 World Peace Council	WPC granted Category B status (Information and Consultation) in UNESCO.
14-16 Czechoslovakia	Party celebrates fiftieth anniversary.
14-18 Costa Rica	People's Vanguard Party holds congress.
16 Bulgaria	New constitution adopted by referendum.
Jordan	Communist party reportedly expells dissident group led by Fahmi Salfiti and Rushdi Shahin.
17 Morocco	The progressive National Union of Moroccan Students in communiqué calls on students to make 17 May a day of struggle and solidarity with militants accused at Marrakesh trial.
19 New Zealand/China	Following talks in Peking with Chou En-lai and others, communist party leader Wilcox reports "the menace of the new growth of Japanese imperialism" as major topic of mutual concern.
Vietnam: Democratic Republic of Vietnam	Year-long campaign to recruit "Ho Chi Minh class" of new party members ends amid concern over high percentage not meeting prescribed norms.
22 Yugoslavia/Vietnam	Diplomatic relations established with Provisional Revolutionary Government of South Vietnam.
22-23 Germany: Federal Republic of Germany	Socialist German Workers' Youth, organization of German Communist Party, holds congress.
23 Argentina	Trotskyist People's Revolutionary Army kidnaps British consul in Rosario and releases him in exchange for food and other supplies distributed in ten slum areas.
Dominican Republic	Maximiliano Gómez, leader of pro-Chinese Dominican People's Movement, found dead in Brussels.

France	Some 50,000 communists and supporters celebrate centenary of Paris commune; 27 countries represented at Maurice Thorez Institute conference to commemorate event.
25-29 Czechoslovakia	Party congress meets in Prague.
25-29 Italy	Italian party delegate prevented from delivering speech to party congress in Czechoslovakia.
27 United Arab Republic/U.S.S.R.	Fifteen-year treaty of friendship and cooperation signed with Soviet Union.

JUNE

Honduras	Honduran Communist Party clandestinely holds congress.
Yugoslavia	Federal Assembly adopts constitutional amendments.
1-9 Romania/China	Ceauşescu visits China.
4 Hungary	Death of György Lukács, foremost Marxist philosopher and literary critic.
6 Central America	Conference of communist parties of Central America, Mexico, and Panama held at undisclosed location.
7-10 Vietnam: Democratic Republic of Vietnam	First session of newly elected National Assembly in Hanoi.
7-11 Mongolia	Mongolian People's Revolutionary Party holds congress, concentrating mainly on economic matters.
9-10 Yugoslavia/China	Foreign Secretary Tepavac visits Peking at invitation of Chinese government.
11 France	New, enlarged socialist party emerges from Epinay-sur-Seine congress, with François Mitterand as leader.

11-12 Bolivia	Pro-Soviet Communist Party of Bolivia holds congress, seven years after the previous one.
12 and 13 Switzerland	Party of Labor holds congress, without major change in party leadership.
13 Iceland	Labor Alliance receives 17.1 per cent of popular vote and 10 of 60 parliamentary seats. Communist offshoot, Organization of Liberals and Leftists, in first attempt wins 9 per cent and 5 seats.
U.S.S.R.	Elections to soviets give candidates 98.4 per cent endorsement with 99.96 per cent of electorate participating.
13-14 Italy	Communist party registers small loss in local elections, largely in southern Italy.
15-19 Germany: German Democratic Republic	Socialist Unity Party holds congress in East Berlin.
20 World Peace Council	"International Commission of Inquiry into U.S. War Crimes" convenes second session in Oslo and finds United States "guilty" of war crimes in Indochina.
22 Laos	Souphanouvong proposes second two-point peace plan.
23 Germany: German Democratic Republic	Five-Year Plan directive published, after amendments and commitment not to raise consumer prices during plan period.
Poland	Legislation passed transferring former German church property to Polish episcopate.
24 Germany: German Democratic republic	Erich Honecker elected chairman of National Defense Council.
25 Poland/U.S.S.R.	Zenon Nowak appointed ambassador to U.S.S.R.
Poland	Mieczyslaw Moczar is transferred from party secretariat to government Supreme Control Chamber.
27 Bulgaria	National Elections.

Japan	Japan Communist Party wins six seats and highest percentage of votes ever in upper house elections: 8.1 per cent in national constituencies and 12.1 per cent in local constituencies.
29 June-1 July Albania	Central Committee plenum approves draft directives of fifth Five-Year Plan.
29 June-3 July Romania/Finland	Caeușescu visits Finland.
30 Yugoslavia	Federal Assembly adopts constitutional amendments.

JULY

1 China	Chinese Communist Party celebrates fiftieth anniversary. Joint editorial in three leading journals condemns left and right extremism.
Vietnam	Provisional Revolutionary Government of South Vietnam foreign minister, Nguyen Thi Binh, presents seven-point peace plan in Paris.
3 Lebanon	Gorges Hawi, influential leader of communist party, arrested for alleged slander of army and government; released after several days.
5 Lebanon	Two splinter groups from communist party merge into Organization for Communist Action, critical of Soviet Union and Lebanese party.
10 Iceland	Labor Alliance and Organization of Liberals and Leftists join Progressive Party in coalition to succeed conservative social-democratic government.
Morocco	Communists, National Union of Popular Forces, and Istiqlal Party accused of connection with unsuccessful Army mutiny attempt to overthrow King.
14-16 World Federation of Scientific Workers	"Symposium of Young Scientific Workers in Contemporary Society" meets at Enschede, Netherlands, with over 100 delegates from 20 countries.
mid-July Iceland	New government program envisages unilateral extension of Iceland's fishing limit and ouster of U.S.-NATO defense force.

15 China/ United States	Chinese and U.S. governments announce simultaneously that President Nixon will visit China before spring 1972.
19 Israel/U.S.S.R.	*Jerusalem Post* reveals Soviet contacts with MAKI party, excluded since 1967 from international communist activities because of pro-Israeli stand.
19 Thailand	Police capture Kusol Surasen, head of communist psychological warfare campaign in northern Thailand.
19-22 Sudan	Left-wing officers, led by Hashim al-'Attah, fail in attempt to seize power from Ja'far Muhammad al-Numairi.
20 Ceylon	Parliament told 1,200 persons killed and 14,000 arrested during April insurgency.
Turkey	Ban on leftist Turkish Labor Party protested by clandestine communist party, which calls for general strike and mass resistance against government.
22-11 August Cambodia/Korea: Democratic People's Republic of Korea	Sihanouk makes friendship visit to DPRK at invitation of Kim Il-Song.
27-28 Sudan	'Abd al-Khaliq Mahjub, secretary-general of communist party, is hanged.
27-29 Eastern Europe	CMEA adopts plan for closer economic integration.
29 Yugoslavia	Composition of new collective state presidency (23 members) announced.

AUGUST

United Arab Republic/U.S.S.R.	Best-known communist, Muhyi al-Din, placed under house arrest (but released three weeks later, allegedly after Soviet pressure).
2 Romania/Western Europe	Ceauşescu entertains secretaries of several West European communist parties at Black Sea resort.

U.S.S.R./ East Europe	Secretaries of East European communist parties meet in Crimea without Ceauşescu of Romania.
6 Nepal	Elections to Tribhuvan University student union, barometer of political climate, result in pro-Chinese student organization's loss of year-old leadership.
7 Germany: Federal Republic of Germany	German Communist Party presents ideology and tasks in theses for November congress.
8-12 United States	Socialist Workers' Party holds national convention in Cleveland.
9 India/U.S.S.R.	Soviet Union and India sign treaty of peace, friendship, and cooperation.
11 Czechoslovakia	Press joins in denouncing absence of Romania from East European meeting in Crimea.
12 Morocco	Authorities seize for second time French edition of Istiqlal Party newspaper, *L'Opinion*.
14 Korea	Red Cross of North Korea agrees with Red Cross of South Korea proposal (12 August) to enter talks on locating separated family members.
20-29 Japan/Italy/Romania/ Vietnam: Democratic Republic of Vietnam/ U.S.S.R.	Miyamoto Kenji, Japan Communist Party chairman, leads delegation to four countries (Romania, Italy, DRV, Soviet Union) to bolster JCP international prestige.
21 Philippines	Two hand grenades thrown at Liberal Party rally kill 10 persons and wound 94, including all but one of key candidates. President Marcos attributes incident to Maoist "New People's Army."
29 Peru	Pro-Soviet Communist Youth of Peru holds first congress, attended by delegates from four foreign parties.

SEPTEMBER

Germany: Federal Republic of Germany	Max Reimann, secretary-general of banned Communist Party of Germany, applies for membership in legal German Communist Party.

Latin America	Representatives of communist parties in Argentina, Bolivia, Brazil, Chile, Paraguay, Peru, and Uruguay meet at undisclosed location, probably in Chile.
4 Belgium	Belgian Communist Party celebrates fiftieth anniversary.
11 U.S.S.R.	Nikita S. Khrushchev dies at age of 77 years.
11-12 World Peace Council	European peace committees meet at Saarbrücken, West Germany, to discuss preparation for an "Assembly of Peoples of Europe," tentatively in June 1972.
15 Peru	Hugo Blanco, leader of Trotskyist Movement of Revolutionary Left, is deported to Mexico.
Thailand	Officials announce capture of Hanoi- and Peking-trained communist leader, Phairoh Sae Darn.
17 Brazil	Carlos Lamarca, most popular revolutionary leader, killed by police at Pintada (Bahia).
17 Morocco	Verdict announced in Marrakesh trial of 193 political opponents, charged with conspiracy to overthrow government.
20 China	Foreign correspondents informed that National Day parade on 1 October is canceled. Other events suggest purge of Lin Piao and others.
21 Denmark	Communist Party receives 1.4 per cent of vote in election and loses its one parliamentary seat.
22-25 U.S.S.R./Yugoslavia	Brezhnev visits Yugoslavia.
23 Algeria	Release of students arrested in January.
24-26 International Association of Democratic Lawyers	Lawyers from 18 countries attend meeting in East Berlin sponsored by IADL on "Legal Aspects of European Security and Cooperation."
28 Ceylon	Upper house of parliament abolished.
Hungary	Cardinal Mindszenty leaves asylum in U.S. Embassy at Budapest for exile in Vienna.

29-1 October U.S.S.R.	Ideological conference underscores CPSU congress emphasis on party authority.

OCTOBER

Lebanon	Lebanese communist party publishes "Action Program" for congress, scheduled for January 1972.
1 Philippines	Important leader of Maoist "New People's Army," Ernesto Miranda ("Commander Panchito") killed in fight with government commando team.
2 Malaysia	Government publishes white paper on *Resurgence of Armed Communism in West Malaysia*.
2-9 Yugoslavia	"Freedom-71" army maneuvers in western party of country.
3-10 India	Communist party holds congress and adopts policy of "unity and struggle" against ruling Congress Party.
4-8 Algeria/U.S.S.R.	Visit by U.S.S.R. Premier Kosygin to Algeria.
10 Austria	In elections, communist party receives 1.4 per cent of vote and remains without a parliamentary seat.
12 France	Communist party publishes 200-page *Program for a Democratic Government and Popular Unity*.
13-21 Yugoslavia/ Middle East	Tito visits Iran, India, and Egypt.
16-17 Ireland	Communist party holds congress.
21 Czechoslovakia/ U.S.S.R.	Central Committee reiterates thesis that "attitude to Soviet Union is touchstone of socialist and progressist character of any party or government."
25 China/United Nations	U.N. General Assembly adopts resolution to recognize People's Republic of China and expel Republic of China by vote of 76 to 35, with 17 abstentions.

Greece	Government arrests Dimitrios Partsalides, Kharalambos Drakopoulos, and 30 others from dissident faction of communist party.
26-29 Poland/Warsaw Pact	Military Council of Warsaw Pact meets in Poland.
26-30 Cuba/U.S.S.R.	Soviet Premier Kosygin visits Cuba.
27-2 November Yugoslavia/ United States	Tito visits United States.
30-31 Switzerland	In national elections, Party of Labor polls 2.7 per cent of vote and retains five seats in the 200-deputy lower house.
October-November China/Spain	Five members from Communist Party of Spain, led by Santiago Carrillo, reported in China to establish inter-party relations.

NOVEMBER

New Zealand	Communist party enters no candidates in municipal and local elections, saying participation would obstruct revolutionary goals, best served "outside capitalist institutions."
1-7 Albania	Party of Labor congress reelects Enver Hoxha as first secretary and approves fifth Five-Year Plan.
8 Albania	Enver Hoxha addresses mass rally in Tirana on thirtieth anniversary of Party of Labor.
9 Ceylon	Five-year plan prepared by finance minister, ex-Trotskyite Dr. N. M. Perera, submitted to parliament.
10 Iran	'Abd al-Samad Kambakhsh, second secretary of Tudeh Party, dies of heart attack.
10-4 December Chile/Cuba	Cuban Premier Castro visits Chile.
13-16 Great Britain	Communist party holds congress, at which "Stalinist" minority opposition generates 20 per cent support.

14 Germany: German Democratic Republic	In elections, 99.85 per cent of votes cast for National Front candidates.
18-20 International Federation of Resistance Fighters	Representatives of 19 veterans' organizations meet in Rome to discuss security, friendship, and peace.
19-21 Puerto Rico	National Assembly of the Movement for Independence meets in San Juan, as founding convention of Puerto Rican Socialist Party (PSP).
21-23 World Federation of Scientific Workers	"Conference on ABC [Atomic, Biological, and Chemical] Weapons" convenes in East Berlin, with 150 scientists present from 21 countries.
22 Yugoslavia	Student strike at Zagreb University leads to major shakeup in Croatian party leadership.
23-24 Yugoslavia/Romania	Tito and Ceauşescu meet in Romania.
25 Syria	Beirut newspaper reports Khalid Bakdash, Syrian communist party first secretary, forced to resign. Denial issued by party Politburo, but rumors to contrary persist.
Italy	Three major trade unions, including communist-dominated General Confederation of Italian Labor, announce last separate congresses for 1972 and development of guidelines for unification.
25-28 Germany: Federal Republic of Germany	German Communist Party holds congress. Kurt Bachmann reelected chairman and Max Reimann, secretary-general of banned Communist Party of Germany, named honorary president.
26 Germany: German Democratic Republic	Walter Ulbricht elected chairman of State Council.
26-27 Czechoslovakia	Parliamentary elections give candidates of National Front 99.81 per cent of vote and bring out 99.45 per cent of voters.
26-28 International Association of Democratic Lawyers	"World Conference of Lawyers on Indochina" meets in Algiers and accuses United States of violating international law.

| 27-29 Canada | Communist party holds convention. |

DECEMBER

Iraq	After government-announced National Action Charter, communist party expresses willingness to cooperate in "National Front" if political restrictions are lifted.
1-2 Yugoslavia	LCY Presidium meets after purge of Croatian party leadership.
3-17 India/Pakistan	War ends in independence of Bangladesh (East Pakistan).
6 Korea: Democratic People's Republic of Korea/ Republic of Korea	South Korean president, Pak Chong-hui, citing alleged war preparations by North Korea, declares emergency. North Korea charges that Pak sabotages reunification movement and prepares "fratricial war."
6-10 Colombia	Pro-Soviet communist party holds congress.
6-11 Poland	Polish United Workers' Party holds congress.
8-9 World Federation of Trade Unions	Bureau meeting in East Berlin pays tribute to memory of former vice president al-Shaf'i Ahmad al-Shaikh, executed in Sudan after abortive coup.
11 December Germany: German Democratic Republic/ Federal Republic of Germany	Transit agreement signed.
14-17 Vietnam: Democratic Republic of Vietnam	Congress of Fatherland Front held in Hanoi.
24 Italy	Giovanni Leone, moderate Christian Democrat, elected president of Italy despite vigorous opposition from communist party.
29 Ceylon	Final draft of new constitution presented to Constituent Assembly.

BIBLIOGRAPHY

General on Communism

Besse, Guy. *Lenine, la philosophie et la culture*. Paris, Editions Sociales, 1971. 191 pp.

Colletti, Lucio. *Bernstein und der Marxismus der Zweiten Internationalen*. Frankfurt am Main, Europäische Verlagsanstalt, 1971. 90 pp.

Dallin, Alexander, and Breslauer, George W. *Political Terror in Communist Systems*. Stanford, Stanford University Press, 1971. 144 pp.

Deutscher, Isaac. *Marxism in Our Time*. Berkeley, Ramparts Press, 1971. 312 pp.

Ellul, Jacques. *Autopsy of Revolution*. New York, Knopf, 1971. 300 pp.

Fejtö, François. *Dictionnaire des partis communistes et des mouvements révolutionnaires. Précédé d'un Essai sur la crise actuelle de l'internationalisme marxiste*. Paris, Tournai Casterman, 1971. 235 pp.

Fikentscher, Wolfgang. *Zur politischen Kritik an Marxismus und Neomarxismus als ideologische Grundlagen der Studentenunruhen 1965 bis 1969*. Tübingen, Mohr [Siebeck], 1971. 62 pp.

Gerassi, John (comp.). *Towards Revolution*. London, Weidenfeld and Nicholson, 1971. 2 vols.

Haak, Ernst. *Grundkurs zu Lenins Werk "Der Imperialismus als höchstes Stadium des Kapitalismus."* Berlin, Dietz Verlag, 1971. 238 pp.

Humbert-Droz, Jules. *Memoires: De Lénine à Staline, 1921-1931*. Neuchâtel, Editions de la Baconnière, 1971. 507 pp.

Jackson, W. A. Douglas (ed.). *Agrarian Policies and Problems of Communist and Non-Communist Countries*. Seattle, University of Washington Press, 1971. 488 pp.

Kanet, Roger E. (ed.). *The Behavioral Revolution and Communist Studies*. New York, Free Press, 1971. 376 pp.

Lengyel, Emil. *Nationalism: The Last Stage of Communism*. New York, Funk & Wagnalls, 1971. 352 pp.

Lingner, K. *Sozialistischer Internationalismus und nationale Interessen: Lenin und die Dialektik von Nationalem und Internationalem im Sozialismus*. Berlin, Staatsverlag der DDR, 1971. 96 pp.

Lukacs, George. *History and Class Consciousness: Studies in Marxist Dialectics*. Cambridge, MIT Press, 1971. 356 pp.

McSherry, James E. *Khrushchev and Kennedy in Retrospect*. Palo Alto, Open Door Press, 1971. 233 pp.

Miller, Norman and Roderick, Aya (eds.). *National Liberation: Revolution in the Third World*. New York, Free Press, 1971. 307 pp.

Neuberg, A. (pseud.). *Armed Insurrection*. New York, St. Martin's Press, 1971. 285 pp.

Orfei, Ruggero. *Marxismo e Umanesimo*. Rome, Coines Edizioni, 1971. 464 pp.

Orth, Robert. *Hilfsorganisationen des Weltkommunismus*. Pfaffenhofen/Ilm, Ilmgau Verlag, 1971. 388 pp.

Paloczi-Horvath, George. *Youth up in Arms; A Political and Social World Survey, 1955-1970.* New York, David McKay, 1971. 349 pp.

Parkin, Frank. *Class Inequality & Political Order: Social Stratification in Capitalist and Communist Societies.* New York, Praeger, 1971. 205 pp.

Ploss, Sidney I. (comp.). *The Soviet Political Process: Aims, Techniques, and Examples of Analysis.* Waltham, Mass., Ginn, 1971. 304 pp.

Portal, Roger. *Die Slawen.* München, Kindler Verlag, 1971. 806 pp.

Röchlin, Peter R., and Hagemann, Ernst. *Die Kollektivierung der Landwirtschaft in der Sowjetunion und der Volksrepublik China: Eine vergleichende Studie.* Berlin, Deutsches Institut für Wirtschaftsforschung, 1971. 175 pp.

Smith, Donald Eugene (ed.). *Religion, Politics, and Social Change in the Third World.* Riverside, Calif., Free Press, 1971. 304 pp.

Spulber, N. *Socialist Management and Planning: Topics in Comparative Socialist Economics.* Bloomington, Indiana University Press, 1971. 235 pp.

Staar, Richard F. (ed.). *1971 Yearbook on International Communist Affairs.* Stanford, Hoover Institution Press, 1971. 803 pp.

Swearingen, Rodger (ed.). *Leaders of the Communist World.* New York, Free Press, 1971. 632 pp.

Teruel-Mania, Pierre. *De Lénine au panzer-communisme.* Paris, F. Maspero, 1971. 233 pp.

Trapeznikov, Sergei Pavlovich. *Na krutykh povorotakh istorii: iz urokov bor'by s revizionizmom vnutri marksistsko-leninskogo dvizheniia.* Moscow, Mysl, 1971. 271 pp.

U.S. Department of State. *World Strength of the Communist Party Organizations.* Washington, D.C., 1971. 248 pp.

Wagenlehner, Günter. *Staat oder Kommunismus: Lenins Entscheidung gegen die kommunistische Gesellschaft.* Stuttgart, Seewald Verlag, 1971. 260 pp.

Wiles, Peter J. D. (ed.). *The Prediction of Communist Economic Performance.* Cambridge, Cambridge University Press, 1971. 390 pp.

EAST EUROPE AND THE SOVIET UNION

General

Adams, Arthur E., and Adams, Jan S. *Men versus Systems: Agriculture in the USSR, Poland and Czechoslovakia.* New York, Free Press, 1971. 327 pp.

Bender, Peter. *6 X Sicherheit.* Cologne, Kiepenheuer, 1971. 250 pp.

Benz, Ernst. *Geist und Leben der Ostkirche.* Munich, Wilhelm Fink Verlag, 1971, 2d, rev. ed. 206 pp.

Boltho, Andrea. *Foreign Trade Criteria in Socialist Economies.* London, Cambridge University Press, 1971. 176 pp.

Domes, Alfred (ed.). *Reformen und Dogmen in Osteuropa.* Cologne, Verlag Wissenschaft und Politik, 1971. 269 pp.

Fejtö, François. *A History of the People's Democracies: Eastern Europe Since Stalin.* New York, Praeger, 1971. 374 pp.

Gumpel, Werner, and Vogel, Heinrich. *Die Wirtschaft Ungarns, Bulgariens und Rumäniens: Lage und Aussichten.* Munich, Olzog Verlag, n.d. 160 pp.

Kintner, William R., and Klaiber, Wolfgang. *Eastern Europe and European Security.* New York, Dunellen Company, 1971. 394 pp.

Lange-Prollius, Horst. *Ostwesthandel für die 70er Jahre.* Bad Harzburg, Verlag für Wissenschaft, Wirtschaft und Technik, 1971. 467 pp.

Lendvai, Paul. *Anti-Semitism without Jews: Communist Eastern Europe.* Garden City, N.Y., Doubleday, 1971. 393 pp.

Lindner, Walter. *Aufbau des Sozialismus oder kapitalistische Restauration? Zur Analyse der Wirtschaftsreformen in der DDR und der CSSR.* Erlangen, Politladen, 1971. 100 pp.

Mellor, R. E. H. *Comecon: Challenge to the West.* New York, Van Nostrand-Reinhold, 1971. 152 pp.

Raupach, Hans, et al. (eds.). *Jahrbuch der Wirtschaft Osteuropas.* Munich, Günter Olzog Verlag, 1971, vol. 2. 556 pp.

Remington, Robin Alison. *The Warsaw Pact: Case Studies in Communist Conflict Resolution.* Cambridge, MIT Press, 1971. 268 pp.

Sabaliunas, Leonas. *Lithuania in Crisis: Nationalism to Communism, 1939-1940.* Bloomington, Indiana University Press, 1971. 320 pp.

Staar, Richard F. *The Communist Regimes in Eastern Europe.* Stanford, Hoover Institution Press, 1971, 2d, rev. ed. 304 pp.

Stupperich, Robert (ed.). *Kirche und Staat in Bulgarien und Jugoslawien: Gesetze und Verordnungen.* Witten, Luther Verlag, 1971. 56 pp.

Weber, Eckhard. *Stadien der Aussenhandelsverflechtung Ostmittel-und Südosteuropas.* Stuttgart, Fischer, 1971. 308 pp.

Albania

Anon. *The History of the Party of Labor of Albania.* Tirana, Naim Frashëri State Publishing House, 1971. 746 pp.

Prifti, Peter R. *Albania and Sino-Soviet Relations, 1971.* Cambridge, MIT Center for International Studies, 1971. 35 pp.

Bulgaria

Oren, Nissan. *Bulgarian Communism: The Road to Power, 1934-1944.* New York, Columbia University Press, 1971. 293 pp.

Czechoslovakia

Hamšik, Dušan. *Writers against Rulers.* London, Hutchinson, 1971. 208 pp.

Jancar, Barbara Wolfe. *Czechoslovakia and the Absolute Monopoly of Power: A Study of Political Power in a Communist System.* New York, Praeger, 1971. 330 pp.

Journalist, M. *A Year is Eight Months.* Garden City, N.Y., Doubleday, 1971. 260 pp.

Kusin, Vladimir V. *The Intellectual Origins of the Prague Spring: The Development of Reformist Ideas in Czechoslovakia, 1956-1967.* Cambridge, Cambridge University Press, 1971. 153 pp.

Pelikan, Jiři (ed.). *The Czechoslovak Political Trials, 1950-1954: The Suppressed Report of the Dubcek Government's Commission of Inquiry, 1968.* Stanford, Stanford University Press, 1971. 360 pp.

Pelikan, Jiři (ed.). *The Secret Vysočany Congress.* London, Allen Lane, Penguin Press, 1971. 303 pp.

Salomon, Michel. *Prague Notebook: The Strangled Revolution*. Boston, Little, Brown, 1971. 361 pp.

Shawcross, William. *Dubcek*. New York, Simon & Schuster, 1971. 317 pp.

Svitak, Ivan. *The Czechoslovak Experiment, 1968-1969*. New York, Columbia University Press, 1971. 243 pp.

Szulc, Tad. *Czechoslovakia Since World War II*. New York, Viking, 1971. 503 pp.

Tigrid, Pavel. *Why Dubcek Fell*. London, Macdonald, 1971. 229 pp.

Germany: Democratic Republic of Germany

Baumgart, Hildegard (ed.). *Briefe aus einem anderen Land: Briefe aus der DDR*. Hamburg, Hoffmann & Campe, 1971. 304 pp.

Bröll, Werner, Heisenberger, Wolfgang, and Sühlo, Winifred. *Der andere Teil Deutschlands*. Munich, Günter Olzog Verlag, 1971, 3d ed. 268 pp.

Germany, Democratic Republic of, Amt für Jugendfragen. *Jugendpolitik in der DDR*. Berlin, Staatsverlag der DDR, 1971. 400 pp.

Graf, H., and Seiler, G. *Wahlen und Wahlrecht im Klassenkampf*. Berlin, Staatsverlag der DDR, 1971. 384 pp.

Hoffmann, Ursula. *Die Veränderungen in der Sozialstruktur des Ministerats der DDR, 1949-1969*. Düsseldorf, Droste, 1971. 100 pp.

Immler, Hans. *Agrarpolitik in der DDR*. Cologne, Verlag Wissenschaft und Politik, 1971. 222 pp.

Kreusel, Dietmar. *Nation und Vaterland in der Militärpresse der DDR*. Stuttgart, Seewald, 1971. 340 pp.

Lades, Hans, and Burrichter, Christian. *Produktivkraft Wissenschaft: Sozialistische Sozialwissenschaften in der DDR*. Hamburg, Drei Mohren Verlag, 1971. 415 pp.

Laschitza, Annelies, and Radczun, Gunter. *Rosa Luxemburg: Ihr Wirken in der deutschen Arbeiterbewegung*. Berlin, Dietz Verlag, 1971. 600 pp.

Lippmann, Heinz. *Honecker: Portrait eines Nachfolgers*. Cologne, Wissenschaft und Politik, 1971. 272 pp.

Ludz, Peter Christian (ed.). *Studien und Materialien zur Soziologie der DDR*. Opladen, Westdeutscher Verlag, 1971, 2d ed. 540 pp.

Mewis, Karl. *Im Auftrag der Partei*. Berlin, Dietz Verlag, 1971. 320 pp.

Reisberg, A. *An den Quellen der Einheitsfrontpolitik: Der Kampf der KPD um die Aktionseinheit in Deutschland 1921-1922*. Berlin, Dietz Verlag, 1971. 720 pp.

Siebert, Herd. *Mitbestimmung drüben: Aus der überbetrieblichen Arbeit der Gewerkschaften in der DDR*. Frankfurt, Nachrichten-Verlag, 1971. 159 pp.

Socialist Unity Party of Germany. *Dokumente des VIII. Parteitages der SED*. Berlin, Dietz Verlag, 1971. 208 pp.

Ulbricht, Walter. *Die historische Mission der Sozialistischen Einheitspartei Deutschlands*. Berlin, Dietz Verlag, 1971. 96 pp.

Weber, Hermann. *Die sozialistische Einheitspartei Deutschlands, 1946-1971*. Hannover, Verlag für Literatur und Zeitgeschehen, 1971. 220 pp.

Weber, Hermann, and Oldenburg, Fred. *25 Jahre SED: Chronik einer Partei*. Cologne, Verlag Wissenschaft und Politik, 1971. 160 pp.

Hungary

Shagvari, A., and Muchi, F. (eds.). *Dvadsat' piat' let svobodnoi Vengrii*. Budapest, Akadémiai Kiadó, 1971. 378 pp.

Volgyes, Ivan (ed.). *Hungary in Revolution 1918-1919: Nine Essays*. Lincoln, University of Nebraska Press, 1971. 219 pp.

Poland

Feiwel, George R. *Poland's Industrialization Policy: A Current Analysis*. New York, Praeger, 1971. 455 pp.

Feiwel, George R. *Problems in Polish Economic Planning: Continuity, Change and Prospects*. New York, Praeger, 1971. 454 pp.

Fitzgibbon, Louis. *Katyn: A Crime without Parallel*. New York, Scribner, 1971. 285 pp.

Karsov, Nina. *In the Name of Tomorrow: Life Underground in Poland*. New York, Schocken Books, 1971. 286 pp.

Lammich, Siegfried. *Das Sozialistische Parlament Polens*. Cologne, Verlag Wissenschaft und Politik, 1971. 112 pp.

Romania

Hale, Julian A. S. *Ceausescu's Romania: a Political Documentary*. London, Harrap, 1971. 208 pp.

Jowitt, Kenneth. *Revolutionary Breakthroughs and National Development: The Case of Romania 1944-1965*. Berkeley, University of California Press, 1971. 317 pp.

U.S.S.R.

Allworth, Edward (ed.). *Soviet Nationality Problems*. New York, Columbia University Press, 1971. 296 pp.

Aspaturian, Vernon V. *Process and Power in Soviet Foreign Policy*. Boston, Little, Brown, 1971. 939 pp.

Bordeaux, Michael. *Faith on Trial in Russia*. New York, Harper & Row, 1971. 192 pp.

Browne, Michael (ed.). *Ferment in the Ukraine*. New York, Praeger, 1971. 267 pp.

Cohen, Richard (ed.). *Let My People Go! Today's Documentary Story of Soviet Struggle to be Free*. New York, Popular Library, 1971. 286 pp.

Communist Party of the Soviet Union. *XXVI syezd Kommunisticheskoi Partii Sovetskogo Soyuza*. Moscow, Politizdat, 1971, 2 vols.

Conklin, David W. *An Evaluation of the Soviet Profit Reforms: With Special Reference to Agriculture*. New York, Praeger, 1971. 192 pp.

Conquest, Robert. *The Great Terror: Stalin's Purge of the Thirties*. New York, Macmillan, 1971. 633 pp.

Dmytryshyn, Basil. *USSR: a Concise History*. New York, Scribner, 1971, 2d ed. 584 pp.

Ellman, Michael. *Soviet Planning Today: Proposals for an Optimally Functioning Economic System*. New York, Cambridge University Press, 1971. 219 pp.

Fireside, Harvey. *Icon and Swastika: The Russian Orthodox Church under Nazi and Soviet Control*. Cambridge, Harvard University Press, 1971. 242 pp.

Heer, Nancy Whittier. *Politics and History in the Soviet Union*. Cambridge, MIT Press, 1971. 319 pp.

Hingley, Ronald. *The Russian Secret Police*. New York, Simon & Schuster, 1971. 313 pp.

Hoffmann, Erik P., and Fleron, Frederick J., Jr. *The Conduct of Soviet Foreign Policy*. Chicago, Aldine-Atherton, 1971. 512 pp.

Hudson, G. F. *Fifty Years of Communism: Theory and Practice, 1917-1967*. Baltimore, Penguin Books, 1971. 229 pp.

Hyde, H. Montgomery. *Stalin: the History of a Dictator*. New York, Farrar, Straus and Giroux, 1971. 679 pp.

Inkeles, Alex. *Social Change in Soviet Russia*. New York, Simon & Schuster, 1971. 475 pp.

Koutaissoff, Elizabeth. *The Soviet Union*. New York, Praeger, 1971. 288 pp.

Lane, David. *Politics and Society in the USSR*. New York, Random House-Alfred A. Knopf, 1971. 624 pp.

Lawrence, John. *Russians Observed*. Lincoln: University of Nebraska Press, 1971. 192 pp.

Marko, Kurt. *Dogmatismus und Emanzipation in der Sowjetunion: Sowjetphilosophie, Reformdenken, Opposition*. Stuttgart, Kohlhammer, 1971. 224 pp.

Medvedev, Zhores A. *The Medvedev Papers: The Plight of Soviet Science*. New York, St. Martin's Press, 1971. 471 pp.

Medvedev, Zhores A., and Medvedev, Roy A. *A Question of Madness*. New York, Knopf, 1971. 223 pp.

Mikoian, Anastas I. *Dorogoi bor'by*. Moscow, Politizdat, 1971. 590 pp.

Millar, James R. (ed.). *The Soviet Rural Community: A Symposium*. Urbana, University of Illinois Press, 1971. 420 pp.

Mohrenschildt, Dimitri von (ed.). *The Russian Revolution of 1917: Contemporary Accounts*. New York, Oxford University Press, 1971. 320 pp.

Morozow, Michael. *Das Sowjetische Establishment*. Stuttgart, Seewald, 1971. 198 pp.

Murarka, Dev. *The Soviet Union*. New York, Walker, 1971. 240 pp.

Pennar, Jean, Bakalo, Ivan I., and Bereday, George Z. F. *Modernization and Diversity in Soviet Education: With Special Reference to Nationality Groups*. New York, Praeger, 1971. 400 pp.

Ponomarev, Boris N., et al. *Istoriia Kommunisticheskoi Partii Sovetskogo Soiuza: Uchebnik*. Moscow, Politizdat, 1971, 4th ed. 752 pp.

Ponomarev, B. N., Gromyko, A. A., and Khvostov, V. M. (eds.). *Istoriia Vneshnei Politiki SSSR, 1945-1970*. Moscow, Izdatel'stvo Nauka, 1971. 519 pp.

Pospelov, Petr. N. (ed.). *Istoriia Kommunisticheskoi Partii Sovetskogo Soiuza*. vol. 4, pt. 2 (1929-1937), vol. 5, pt. 1 (1938-1945). Moscow, Politizdat, 1971.

Pospielovsky, Dimitry. *Russian Police Trade Unionism*. London, Weidenfeld and Nicolson, 1971. 189 pp.

Reshetar, John S. *The Soviet Polity; Government and Politics in the U.S.S.R.* New York, Dodd, Mead, 1971. 412 pp.

Roberts, Paul Craig. *Alienation and the Soviet Economy*. Albuquerque, University of New Mexico Press, 1971. 121 pp.

Scammell, Michael (ed.). *Russia's Other Writers: Selections from Samizdat Literature*. New York, Praeger, 1971. 216 pp.

Schapiro, Leonard. *The Communist Party of the Soviet Union*. New York, Random House, 2d rev. ed., 1971. 704 pp.

Skilling, H. Gordon, and Griffiths, Franklyn (eds.). *Interest Groups in Soviet Politics*. Princeton, Princeton University Press, 1971. 433 pp.

Smolar, Boris. *Soviet Jewry Today and Tomorrow*. New York, Macmillan, 1971. 228 pp.

Strong, John W. *The Soviet Union under Brezhnev and Kosygin: The Transition Years*. New York, Van Nostrand-Reinhold, 1971. 277 pp.

Valentinov (Vol'sky), N. *Novaia ekonomicheskaia politika i krizis partii posle smerti Lenina: Gody raboty v VSNKH vo vremia NEP vospominaniia*. Stanford, Hoover Institution Press, 1971. 256 pp.

Weaver, Kitty D. *Lenin's Grandchildren: Preschool Education in the Soviet Union*. New York, Simon and Schuster, 1971. 254 pp.

Wesson, Robert G. *Soviet Foreign Policy in Perspective*. Homewood, Ill., Dorsey Press, 1971. 480 pp.

Yugoslavia

Adizes, Ichak. *Industrial Democracy: Yugoslav Style*. New York, Free Press, 1971. 297 pp.

Dedijer, Vladimir. *The Battle Stalin Lost: Memoirs of Yugoslavia, 1948-1953*. New York, Viking, 1971. 341 pp.

Milenkovitch, Deborah D. *Plan and Market in Yugoslav Economic Thought*. New Haven, Yale University Press, 1971. 323 pp.

Palmer, Stephen E. Jr., and King, Robert R. *Yugoslav Communism and the Macedonian Question*. Hamden, Conn., Archon Books, 1971. 247 pp.

Pavlowitch, Stevan K. *Yugoslavia*. New York, Praeger, 1971. 416 pp.

Dorothy Atkinson and Milorad Popov

WEST EUROPE

General

Amendola, Giorgio. *I comunisti e l'Europa*. Rome, Editori Riuniti, 1971. 98 pp.

Lange-Prollius, Horst. *Ostwesthandel fur die 70er Jahre*. Bad Harzburg, Verlag für Wissenschaft, Wirtschaft und Technik, 1971. 467 pp.

Austria

Hautmann, Hans. *Die verlorene Raeterepublik: Am Beispiel der Kommunistischen Partei Deutsch-österreichs*. Wien, Europa-Verlag, 1971, 2d ed., 286 pp.

Belgium

Belgian Communist Party. *Perspectives de la lutte des classes en Belgique*. Brussels, 1971.

Cyprus

Adams, T W. *Akel: The Communist Party of Cyprus*. Stanford, Hoover Institution Press, 1971. 284 pp.

Finland

Wagner, Ulrich. *Finlands Kommunisten: Volksfrontexperiment und Parteispaltung 1960-1970*. Stuttgart, Kohlhammer Verlag, 1971. 198 pp.

France

Dansette, Adrien. *Mai 1968*. Paris, Plon, 1971. 473 pp.

Dubois, Pierre. *Grèves revendicatives ou grèves politiques? Acteurs, pratiques, sens du mouvement de mai*. Paris, Editions Anthropos, 1971. 551 pp.

Dupleix, André. *Le socialism de Roger Garaudy et le problème religieux*. Toulouse, Privat, 1971. 111 pp.

Enkiri, Gabriel. *Militant de base*. Paris, Mercure de France, 1971. 151 pp.

Figuères, Léo. *Jeunesse Militante*. Paris, Editions Sociales, 1971. 302 pp.

Fremontier, Jacques. *La Forteresse ouvrière: Renault*. Paris, Fayard, 1971. 380 pp.

French Communist Party. Colloque de l'Institut Maurice Thorez. *La fondation du parti communiste français et la pénétration des idées léninistes en France*. Paris, Editions Sociales, 1971. 312 pp.

French Communist Party. *Le Programme pour un gouvernement démocratique d'union populaire*. Paris, Parti Communiste Français, 1971. 251 pp.

Garaudy, Roger. *Reconquête de l'espoir*. Paris, Grasset, 1971. 148 pp.

Jedermann. *La "bolchevisation" du parti communiste français*. Paris, F. Maspero, 1971. 117 pp.

Jourdain, Henri, Fabre, Jean, Quin, Claude, et al. *Capitalisme monopoliste d'état*. Paris, Editions Sociales, 1971, 2 vols.

Moneta, Jacob. *La politique du parti communiste français dans la question coloniale 1920-1963*. Paris, F. Maspero, 1971. 307 pp.

Semaine de la pensée marxiste. 22-29 Avril 1971. *Problèmes de la révolution socialiste en France. Cent ans après la commune*. Paris, Editions Sociales, 1971. 285 pp.

Tillon, Charles. *Un "procès de Moscou" à Paris*. Paris, Seuil, 1971. 192 pp.

Wilson, Frank L. *The French Democratic Left, 1963-1968: Toward a Modern Party System*. Stanford, Stanford University Press, 1971. 258 pp.

Germany: Federal Republic of Germany

Bachman, Kurt and Mies, Herbert. *Kommunisten und Sozialdemokraten in der Bundesrepublik*. Hamburg, Blinkfür Verlag, 1971. 37 pp.

German Communist Party. 8. Tagung. *Demokratisches Bauernprogramm der Deutschen Kommunistischen Partei*. Düsseldorf, Parteivorstand, 1971. 49 pp.

Germany, Federal Republic. Bundestag. *Materialien zum Bericht zur Lage der Nation 1971*. Bonn, 1971. 374 pp.

Sywottek, A. *Deutsche Volksdemokratie: Studien zur politischen Konzeption der KPD 1935-1946*. Düsseldorf, Bertelsmann-Universitäts Verlag, 1971.

Waldmann, Eric. *Die sozialistische Einheitspartei Westberlins. Ein Instrument der sowjetischen Aussenpolitik*. Boppard, Boldt, 1971. 300 pp.

Whetten, Lawrence L. *Germany's Ostpolitik: Relations between the Federal Republic and the Warsaw Pact Countries*. New York, Oxford University Press, 1971. 244 pp.

Windsor, Philip. *Germany and the Management of Détente*. New York, Praeger, 1971. 207 pp.

Italy

Badaloni, Nicola. *Il marxismo italiano degli anni sessanta*. Rome, Editori Riunti, 1971. 122 pp.

De Feo, Italo. *Tre anni con Togliatti*. Milan, Mursia, 1971. 2d ed. 304 pp.

De Rosa, Giuseppe. *Chiesa e comunismo in Italia*. Rome, Coines Edizioni, 1971. 208 pp.

Fiori, Giuseppe. *Antonio Gramsci: Life of a Revolutionary*. New York, Dutton, 1971. 304 pp.

Spain

Carrillo, Santiago. *Libertad y socialismo, informe pronunciado ante el Pleno ampliado del Comite central del Partido comunista de España, septiembre de 1970*. Paris, Editions Sociales, 1971. 104 pp.

Hermet, Guy. *Les Communistes en Espagne*. Paris, Armand Colin, 1971. 216 pp.
Ibarruri, Dolores. *Espana, estado multinacional*. Paris, F. Maspero, 1971. 61 pp.

Switzerland
Senn, Alfred Erich. *The Russian Revolution in Switzerland 1914-1917*. Madison, University of Wisconsin Press, 1971. 250 pp.

Denise McRary

MIDDLE EAST AND AFRICA

General
Agwami, M. S. *Communism in the Arab East*. New York, Asia Publishing House, 1971. 259 pp.
Chamieh, Jebran (ed.). *Record of the Arab World: Documents, Events, Political Opinions*. Beirut, Research and Publishing House, 1971, 3 vols.
Gann, Lewis H. *Central Africa: The Former British States*. Englewood Cliffs, N.J., Prentice-Hall, 1971. 180 pp.
Grundy, Kenneth W. *Guerrilla Struggle in Africa*. New York, Grossman, 1971. 204 pp.
Haddad, George M. *Revolutions and Military Rule in the Middle East. Vol. II: The Arab States–Iraq, Syria, Lebanon and Jordan*. New York, Robert Speller, 1971.
Hirschmann, Ira Arthur. *Red Star over Bethlehem; Russia Drives to Capture the Middle East*. New York, Simon and Schuster, 1971. 192 pp.
Joint Publications Research Service. *Political Parties of Africa: A Soviet Study*. Arlington, Va., 1971. 340 pp.
Larkin, Bruce D. *China and Africa 1949-1970: The Foreign Policy of the People's Republic of China*. Berkeley, University of California Press, 1971. 268 pp.
Lyautey, Pierre. *Proche Orient, la Guerre de Demain?* Paris, Juliard, 1971. 224 pp.
Middle East Record 1967. Jerusalem, Israel Universities Press for the Shiloah Center for Middle Eastern and African Studies, Tel-Aviv University, 1971. 637 pp.
Mokgatle, Naboth. *The Autobiography of an Unknown South African*. Berkeley, University of California Press, 1971. 348 pp.
Padmore, George. *Pan-Africanism or Communism*. Garden City, N.Y., Doubleday, 1971. 439 pp.
Solodovnikov, V. *Africa Fights for Independence*. Moscow, Novostii Publishing House, 1971. 141 pp.
Page, Stephen. *The USSR and Arabia*. London, Central Asian Research Centre, 1971. 152 pp.
Rustow, Dankwart A. *Middle Eastern Political Systems*. Englewood Cliffs, N.J., Prentice-Hall, 1971. 114 pp.
Taylor, Alice (comp.). *Focus on the Middle East*. New York, Praeger, 1971. 223 pp.

Egypt
Dekmejian, R. Hrair. *Egypt Under Nasir: A Study in Political Dynamics*. Albany: State University of New York Press, 1971. 368 pp.

Kerr, Malcolm H. *The Arab Cold War; Gamal 'Abd Al-Nasir and His Rivals, 1958-1970.* New York, Oxford University Press, 1971. 169 pp.
Mayfield, James B. *Rural Politics in Nasser's Egypt; a Quest for Legitimacy.* Austin, University of Texas Press, 1971. 288 pp.

Israel
Avineri, Shlomo. *Israel and the Palestinians.* New York, St. Martin's Press, 1971. 168 pp.
Forrest, Alfred Clinton. *The Unholy Land.* Toronto, McClelland and Stewart, 1971. 173 pp.
Landmann, Michael. *Das Israelpseudos der Pseudolinken.* Berlin, Colloquium Verlag, 1971. 147 pp.

Syria
Mahr, Horst. *Die Baath-Partei.* Munich: Olzog, 1971. 181 pp.

Yemen
O'Ballance, Edgar. *The War in the Yemen.* Hamden, Conn., Archon Books, 1971. 218 pp.

Susan Hillback and Lewis Gann

NORTH AMERICA

Alinsky, Saul David. *Rules for Radicals.* New York, Random House, 1971. 196 pp.
Anon. *Towards an American Socialist Revolution: A Strategy for the 1970's.* New York, Pathfinder Press, 1971. 207 pp.
Baritz, Loren (ed.). *The American Left: Radical Political Thought in the Twentieth Century.* New York, Basic Books, 1971. 522 pp.
Beeching, William. *Farmers! Fight for Your Future: The Communist Party's Answer to Ottawa's Failing Farm Policy.* Toronto, Progress Books, 1971. 22 pp.
Brustein, Robert. *Revolution as Theatre: Notes on the New Radical Style.* New York, Liveright, 1971. 170 pp.
Cannon, James Patrick. *Speeches for Socialism.* New York, Pathfinder Press, 1971. 462 pp.
Green, Gil. *The New Radicalism: Anarchist or Marxist?* New York, International Publishers, 1971. 189 pp.
Mazlish, Bruce (ed.). *Revolution.* New York, Macmillan, 1971. 533 pp.
Morris, George. *Rebellion in the Unions: A Handbook for Rank and File Action.* New York, New Outlook Publishers, 1971. 160 pp.
Widener, Alice. *Teachers of Destruction: Their Plans for a Socialist Revolution.* Arlington, Va., Citizen's Evaluation Institute, 1971. 257 pp.

Danica Bacciocco

LATIN AMERICA

General

Alegria, Fernando. *Literatura y revolución*. Mexico City, Fondo de Cultura Económica, 1971. 244 pp.

Aviles, René. *Educación y revolución*. Mexico City, Costa-Amic, 1971. 128 pp.

Barreiro, J. *Violencia y política en América Latina*. Mexico City, Siglo XXI Editores, 1971. 208 pp.

Bell, J. Bowyer. *The Myth of the Guerrilla: Revolutionary Theory and Malpractice*. New York, Knopf, 1971. 285 pp.

Bishop McClave, Jordan. *Cristianismo radical y marxismo*. Mexico City, Editorial Nuestro Tiempo, 1971. 107 pp.

Câmara, Hélder. *Revolution through Peace*. Translated from the Portuguese by Amparo McLean. New York, Harper & Row, 1971. 149 pp.

Cardoso, Fernando Henrique. *Ideología de la burguesía industrial en sociedades dependientes*. Mexico City, Siglo XXI, 1971. 242 pp.

Castro Villagrana, Bernardo. *La iglesia, el subdesarrollo y la revolución*. Mexico City, Editorial Nuestro Tiempo, 1971. 248 pp.

Crow, John A. *The Epic of Latin America*. Garden City, N.Y., Doubleday, 1971. Rev. ed. 879 pp.

Depestre, René. *Por la revolución, por la poesía*. Montevideo, Semanario Marcha, 1971. 205 pp.

García, T. R. *El catoli-comunismo*. Mexico City, Editores Mexicanos Unidos, 1971? n.p.

Goldenberg, Boris. *Kommunismus in Latein Amerika*. Stuttgart, W. Kohlhammer, 1971. 369 pp.

Gott, Richard. *Guerrilla movements in Latin America*. Garden City, N.Y., Doubleday, 1971. 626 pp.

Gott, Richard. *Las guerrillas en América Latina*. Santiago, Editorial Universitaria, 1971. 477 pp.

Haverstock, Nathan A., and Schroeder, Richard C. *Dateline Latin America: A Review of Trends and Events of 1970*. Washington, D.C., Latin American Service, 1971. 106 pp.

Huberman, Leo. *Debray y la revolución latino-americana*. Mexico City, Editorial Nuestro Tiempo, 1971. 120 pp.

Iribarne, Eduardo P. *Marx, científico de la revolución*. Santiago, Universidad Católica, 1971. 424 pp.

Jalée, P. *El imperialismo en 1970*. Mexico City, Siglo XXI Editores, 1971. 304 pp.

Lipschütz, Alejandro. *Lenín en América Latina*. Santiago, Zamorano y Caperán (dist.), 1971. 56 pp.

MacEoin, Gary. *Revolution next Door: Latin America in the 1970s*. New York, Holt, Rinehart and Winston, 1971. 243 pp.

McDonald, Ronald H. *Party Systems and Elections in Latin America*. Chicago, Markham Publishing Co., 1971. 324 pp.

Marini, R. M. *Subdesarrollo y revolución*. Mexico City, Siglo XXI Editores, 1971. 2d ed. 172 pp.

Martínez Ocaranza, Ramón. *Poesía insurgente*. Mexico City, UNAM, 1971. 177 pp.

Miranda, José Porfirio. *Marx y la Biblia*. Mexico City, Editorial Porrúa (dist.), 1971. 263 pp.

Moreno, Francisco José, and Mitrani, Barbara (eds.). *Conflict and Violence in Latin American Politics*. New York, Crowell, 1971. 452 pp.

Ranis, Peter. *Five Latin American Nations: A Comparative Political Study*. New York, Macmillan, 1971. 337 pp.

Ratliff, William E. (ed.). *Yearbook on Latin American Communist Affairs, 1971*. Stanford, Hoover Institution Press, 1971. 194 pp.

Szulc, Tad. *The United States and the Caribbean*. Englewood Cliffs, N.J., Prentice-Hall, 1971. 212 pp.

Argentina

Abad de Santillan, Diego. *La F.O.R.A.: ideología y trayectoría del movimiento obrero revolucionario en la Argentina*. Buenos Aires, Editorial Proyección 1971. 2d rev. ed. 293 pp.

Cuenca, E. *El militarismo en la Argentina*. Buenos Aires, Editorial Independencia, 1971. 90 pp.

Ferrer, Gustavo. *Los partidos políticos*. Buenos Aires, Centro Editor de América Latina, 1971. 111 pp.

McGregor, J. F. *La red y la tijera*. Buenos Aires, Abece Ediciones, 1971. 255 pp.

Solomonoff, Jorge N. *Ideologías del movimiento obrero y conflicto social*. Buenos Aires, Editorial Proyección, 1971. 314 pp.

Bolivia

Assman, Hugo. *Teoponte; una experiencia guerrillera*. Cochabamba, Los Amigos del Libro, 1971. 277 pp.

Justo, Liborio. *Bolivia; una revolución derrotada*. Buenos Aires, Juárez Editor, 1971. 326 pp.

Lara, Jesús. *Guerrillero Inti*. Cochabamba, Los Amigos del Libro, 1971. 260 pp.

Musselman, James A. *Communist insurgency in Bolivia: Origin, Development, Decline; Causes of Failure*. Maxwell AFB, Ala., Air University, Air Command and Staff College, 1971. 71 pp.

Peredo, Inti. *Mi campaña con el Che*. Mexico City, Editorial Diógenes, 1971. 118 pp.

Rojas, Marta, and Rodríguez Calderón, Mirta. *Tania la guerrillera*. Mexico City, Editorial Diógenes, 1971. 143 pp.

Villarroel Claure, Ramiro. *Prensa y revolución*. Cochabamba, Los Amigos del Libro, 1971. 30 pp.

Brazil

Dressel, Heinz. *Das reiche Land der Armen; Brasilien-heute und morgen*. Neuendettelsau, Freimund, 1971. 152 pp.

Julião, Francisco. *Brasil, antes y después*. Mexico City, Editorial Nuestro Tiempo, 1971. 128 pp.

Marighella, Carlos. *For the Liberation of Brazil*. Baltimore, Penguin, 1971. 191 pp.

Chile

Banks, Marlon C. *An Analysis of the Political System of Chile: Chile at the Crossroads*. Maxwell AFB, Ala., Air University, Air Command and Staff College, 1971. 45 pp.

Chambers, James E. *Dynamic Forces and a Changing Chile*. Maxwell AFB, Ala., Air University, Air Command and Staff College, 1971. 51 pp.

Debray, Régis. *Conversación con Allende; logrará Chile implantar el socialismo*. Mexico City, Siglo XXI, 1971. 150 pp.

Dorfman, Ariel, and Mattelart, Armand. *Para leer al pato Donald*. Santiago, Quimantu, 1971. 161 pp.

Echaíz, René Léon. *Evolución histórica de los partidos políticos chilenos*. Buenos Aires, Francisco de Aguirre, 1971. 200 pp.

Foxley, Alejandro. *Chile: Búsqueda de un nuevo socialismo*. Santiago, Zamorano y Caperán (dist.), 1971. 266 pp.

Grayson, George. *El Partido Demócrata Cristiano Chileno*. Buenos Aires, Francisco de Aguirre, 1971. n.p.

Labarca, Eduardo. *Chile al rojo: Reportaje a una revolución que nace*. Santiago, Ediciones de la Universidad Técnica del Estado, 1971. 398 pp.

Lya Payro, Ana. *Chile ¿Cambio de gobierno o toma del poder?* Mexico City, Editorial Porrúa, 1971. 204 pp.

Nix, Billy G. *The 1970 Chilean Presidential Election: A Study of the Factors Involved*. Maxwell AFB, Ala., Air University, Air Command and Staff College, 1971. 140 pp.

Obispos de Chile. *Evangelio, política y socialismo*. Santiago, Zamorano y Caperán (dist.), 1971. 96 pp.

Colombia

Rojas, Robinson. *Colombia; surge el primer Vietnam en América Latina*. Montevideo, Nativa Libros, 1971. 100 pp.

Cuba

Acosta, Maruja, and Hardoy, Jorge E. *Reforma urbana en Cuba revolucionaria*. Caracas?, Sintesis 2000, 1971. 152 pp.

Bernardo, Robert M. *The Theory of Moral Incentives in Cuba*. University, University of Alabama Press, 1971. 159 pp.

Bonsal, Philip Wilson. *Cuba, Castro and the U.S*. Pittsburgh, University of Pittsburgh Press, 1971. 318 pp.

Castro, Fidel. *History Will Absolve Me*. London, Cape, 1971. 110 pp.

Cinco documentos. Havana, Editorial de Ciencias Sociales, 1971. 207 pp.

Clytus, John, and Rieker, Jane. *Mi vida en Cuba roja*. Mexico City, Editorial Diana, 1971. 150 pp.

Galindo, Roberto. *An Analysis of Cuban Policy Concerning Insurgency Movements in Latin America*. Maxwell AFB, Ala., Air University, Air Command and Staff College, 1971. 62 pp.

García Regueiro, Ovidio. *Cuba, raíces y frutos de una revolución*. Montevideo, I.E.P.A.L. (Instituto de Estudios Políticos para América Latina), 1971. 281 pp.

Karol, K. S. *Guerrillas in Power: The Course of the Cuban Revolution*. New York, Hill & Wang, 1971. 624 pp.

Levinson, Sandra, and Brightman, Carol (eds.). *Venceremos Brigade: Young Americans Sharing the Life and Work of Revolutionary Cuba*. New York, Simon & Schuster, 1971. 412 pp.

Lowy, Michael. *El pensamiento del Che Guevara*. Mexico City, Editorial Siglo XXI, 1971. 160 pp.

Mesa-Lago, Carmelo (ed.). *Revolutionary Change in Cuba*. Pittsburgh, University of Pittsburgh Press, 1971. 544 pp.

Monreal, Manuel. *Cuba, el comunismo y el caos*. Mexico City, Costa-Amic, 1971. 416 pp.

Reckord, Berry. *Does Fidel Eat More Than Your Father?: Conversations in Cuba*. New York, Praeger, 1971. 192 pp.

Salkey, A. *Havana Journal*. Baltimore, Penguin, 1971. 320 pp.

Silverman, Bertram (ed.). *Man and Socialism in Cuba*. New York, Atheneum, 1971, 382 pp.

Thomas, Hugh. *Cuba, or The Pursuit of Freedom*. London, Eyre & Spottiswoode, 1971. 696 pp.

Torres Ramírez, Blanca. *Las relaciones cubano-soviéticas*. Mexico City, Colegio de México, 1971. 142 pp.

El Salvador

Anderson, Thomas P. *Matanza: El Salvador's Communist Revolt of 1932*. Lincoln, University of Nebraska Press, 1971. 175 pp.

Mexico

Abascal, Salvador. *La secta socialista en México*. Mexico City, Editorial Ser, 1971. 334 pp.

Carrion, Jorge. *Tres culturas en agonía (el conflicto estudiantil de México de 1968)*. Mexico City, Editorial Nuestro Tiempo, 1971. 292 pp.

Díaz Soto y Gama, Antonio. *La revolución agraria del sur y Emiliano Zapata, su caudillo*. Mexico City, Editores Mexicanos Unidos, 1971. n.p.

Ehrenreich, Barbara, and Ehrenreich, John. *Itinerario de la rebelión juvenil*. Mexico City, Editorial Nuestro Tiempo, 1971. 152 pp.

García Cantú, Gastón. *El socialismo en México; siglo XIX*. Mexico City, Ediciones Era, 1971. n.p.

Mateos, Juan A. *El cerro de las campañas; memorias de un guerrillero*. Mexico City, Editorial Porrúa, 1971. 427 pp.

Medina, Claudio. *Las llagas de la revolución y la nueva reforma; memorias de un mexicano cero*. Mexico City, Editores Mexicanos Unidos, 1971. n.p.

Mondragón, M. *Cuando la revolución se cortó las alas*. Mexico City, Editores Mexicanos Unidos, 1971? n.p.

Tarik, Ali. *Los nuevos revolucionarios; la oposición de izquierda*. Mexico City, Editorial Grijalbo, 1971. 463 pp.

Valadés, José C. *La revolución mexicana*. Mexico City, Editores Mexicanos Unidos, 1971. Vols. 1-10.

Peru

Angeles Caballero, César. *Poemas a Tupac Amarú*. Lima, Librería Juan Mejía Baca (dist.), 1971. 98 pp.

Hilliker, Grant. *The Politics of Reform in Peru; the Aprista and Other Mass Parties of Latin America*. Baltimore, Johns Hopkins Press, 1971. 201 pp.

Letts, Ricardo [Américo Pumaruna]. *Pérou, révolution socialiste our caricature de révolution?* Paris, F. Maspero, 1971. 107 pp.

Lewin, Boleslao. *Tupac Amaru*. Montevideo, Semanario Marcha, 1971. 183 pp.

Paredes Macedo, Saturnino. *Política sindical y tareas del partido*. Montevideo, Nativa Libros, 1971. 90 pp.

Valcárcel, Carlos Daniel. *Tupac Amaru; el revolucionario*. Lima, Francisco Moncloa Editores, 1971. 328 pp.

Velasco Alvarado, Juan. *Velasco, la voz de la revolución; discursos del Presidente de la República General de División, 1968-1970*. Lima, Ediciones Peisa, 1971? 284 pp.

Uruguay

Uruguay

Actas tupamaras. Buenos Aires, Schapire Editorial, 1971. 260 pp.

Actas Tupamaras; M.L.N. (Movimiento Tupamaro). Buenos Aires, Tres Américas, 1971. n.p.

Costa, Omar. *Los tupamaros.* Mexico City, Era, 1971. 284 pp.

Frente amplio (cristianos y marxistas). Montevideo, Semanario Marcha, 1971. 2 vol.

Labrousse, Alain. *Les Tupamaros; guérilla urbaine en Uruguay.* Paris, Editions du Seuil, 1971. 201 pp.

Mercader, Antonio, and Vera, Jorge. *Los tupamaros.* Mexico City, Editorial Porrúa (dist.), 1971. 167 pp.

Partido Socialista. *Tésis del P.S.* Montevideo, Editorial Brigada, 1971. 92 pp.

Venezuela

Alexander, Robert J. *El partido comunista de Venezuela.* Mexico City, Editorial Diana, 1971. 235 pp.

Chacon, Alfredo. *La izquierda cultural venezolana, 1958-1968; ensayo y antología.* Caracas, Librería Politécnica Moulines, 1971. 431 pp.

Vicki Cunningham

ASIA AND THE PACIFIC

General

Beech, Keyes. *Not Without the Americans: A Personal History.* Garden City, N.Y., Doubleday, 1971. 343 pp.

Bell, J. Bowyer. *The Myth of the Guerrilla: Revolutionary Theory and Malpractice.* New York, Knopf, 1971. 285 pp.

Braeker, Hans. *Kommunismus und Weltreligionen Asiens: Kommunismus und Islam.* Tuebingen, Mohr, 1971. 546 pp.

Dareff, Hal. *From Vietnam to Cambodia: A Background Book about the Struggle in Southeast Asia.* New York, Parents Magazine Press, 1971. 196 pp.

Kirk, Donald. *Wider War: The Struggle for Cambodia, Thailand, and Laos.* New York, Praeger, 1971. 305 pp.

Cambodia

Dudman, Richard. *Forty Days with the Enemy: The Story of a Journalist Held Captive by Guerrillas in Cambodia.* New York, Liveright, 1971. 182 pp.

Grant, J., Moss, L., and Unger, J. (eds.). *Cambodia: The Widening War in Indochina.* New York, Washington Square Press, 1971. 355 pp.

China

Asian Peoples' Anti-Communist League. *An Analysis of the Draft of the Revised Constitution of the Chinese Communist Regime.* Taipei, APACL, 1971. 137 pp.

Barrymaine, Norman. *The Time Bomb: Today's China from the Inside.* New York, Taplinger, 1971. 214 pp.

Baum, Richard, with Bennett, Louise B. (eds.). *China in Ferment: Perspectives on the Cultural Revolution.* Englewood Cliffs, N.J., Prentice-Hall, 1971. 245 pp.

Bennett, Gordon A., and Montaperto, Ronald N. *Red Guard: The Political Biography of Dai Hsiao-Ai.* Garden City, N.Y., Doubleday, 1971. 267 pp.

Bianco, Lucien. *Origins of the Chinese Revolution, 1915-1949.* Stanford, Stanford University Press, 1971. 223 pp.

Boorman, Scott A. *The Protracted Game: A Wei-ch'i Interpretation of Maoist Revolutionary Strategy.* London, Oxford University Press, 1971. 242 pp.

Chang, Kuo-t'ao. *The Rise of the Chinese Communist Party, 1921-1927: Vol. I of the Autobiography of Chang Kuo-t'ao.* Lawrence, University Press of Kansas, 1971. 756 pp.

Cheng, Chu-yuan. *The Machine-Building Industry in Communist China.* Chicago, Aldine-Atherton, 1971. 339 pp.

Elegant, Robert S. *Mao's Great Revolution.* New York, World Publishing, 1971. 478 pp.

Feng, Hai. *An Account of the Cultural Revolution in the Canton Area.* Hong Kong, Union Research Institute, 1971. 450 pp.

Fitzgerald, C. P. *Communism takes China.* New York, American Heritage, 1971. 128 pp.

Fujimoto, Kozo (ed.). *Collected Writings of Mao Tse-tung.* Tokyo, Hokuba-sha, 1971. 10 vols.

Grey, Anthony. *Hostage in Peking.* Garden City, N.Y., Doubleday, 1971. 365 pp.

Hawkins, John N. *Educational Theory in the People's Republic of China: The Report of Ch'ien Chún-Jui.* Honolulu, University of Hawaii Press, 1971. 122 pp.

Herzer, Christine. *Die Volksrepublik China.* Wiesbaden, Harrassowitz, 1971. 384 pp.

Hinton, Harold C. *The Bear at the Gate: Chinese Policymaking under Soviet Pressure.* Washington, D.C.: American Enterprise Institute and Hoover Institution, 1971. 112 pp.

Howe, Christopher. *Employment and Economic Growth in Urban China, 1949-1957.* London, Cambridge University Press, 1971. 224 pp.

Hsiao, Katherine Huang. *Money and Monetary Policy in Communist China.* New York, Columbia University Press, 1971. 305 pp.

Hsu, Francis L. K. *Under the Ancestors' Shadow: Kinship, Personality and Social Mobility in China.* Stanford, Stanford University Press, 1971. 349 pp.

Hsueh, Chun-tu. *Revolutionary Leaders of Modern China.* New York, Oxford University Press, 1971. 608 pp.

Kan, David. *The Impact of the Cultural Revolution on Chinese Higher Education.* Hong Kong, Union Research Institute, 1971. 183 pp.

Klein, Donald W., and Clark, Anne B. *Biographic Dictionary of Chinese Communism, 1921-1965.* Cambridge, Harvard University Press, 1971. 2 vols.

Lewis, John (ed.). *The City in Communist China.* Stanford, Stanford University Press, 1971. 480 pp.

Leys, Simon. *Les Habits Neufs du Président Mao.* Paris, Editions Champ Libre, 1971. 310 pp.

Li, Yu-ning. *The Introduction of Socialism into China.* New York, Columbia University Press, 1971. 138 pp.

Lindbeck, John M. H. (ed.). *China: Management of a Revolutionary Society.* Seattle, University of Washington Press, 1971. 394 pp.

Liu, Alan P. L. *Communications and National Integration in Communist China.* Berkeley, University of California Press, 1971. 225 pp.

Michael, Franz. *The Taiping Rebellion.* Seattle, Washington University Press, 1966-1971. 3 vols.

Moorsteen, Richard, and Abramowitz, Morton. *Remaking China Policy*. Cambridge, Harvard University Press, 1971. 128 pp.

Myrdal, Jan, and Kessle, Gun. *China: The Revolution Continued*. New York, Pantheon, 1971. 219 pp.

Nee, Victor. *The Cultural Revolution at Peking University*. New York, Monthly Review Press, 1971. 90 pp.

Pye, Lucian W. *Warlord Politics: Conflict and Coalition in the Modernization of Republican China*. New York, Praeger, 1971. 212 pp.

Ravenal, Earl C. (ed.). *Peace with China?* New York, Liveright, 1971. 248 pp.

Ridley, Charles P., Goodwin, Paul H. B., and Doolin, Dennis J. *The Making of a Model Citizen in Communist China*. Stanford, Hoover Institution Press, 1971. 404 pp.

Robinson, Thomas W., Baum, Richard, Dorrill, William F., Gurtov, Melvin, and Harding, Harry, Jr. *The Cultural Revolution in China*. Berkeley, University of California Press, 1971. 528 pp.

Selden, Mark. *The Yenan Way in Revolutionary China*. Cambridge, Harvard University Press, 1971. 311 pp.

Service, John S. *The Amerasian Papers: Some Problems in the History of U.S.-China Relations*. Berkeley, Center for Chinese Studies, 1971. 214 pp.

Shewmaker, Kenneth E. *Americans and Chinese Communists, 1927-1945: A Persuading Encounter*. Ithaca, Cornell University Press, 1971. 346 pp.

Solomon, Richard H. *Mao's Revolution ana the Chinese Political Culture*. Berkeley, University of California Press, 1971. 624 pp.

Tan, Chester C. *Chinese Political Thought in the Twentieth Century*. Garden City, Doubleday, 1971. 390 pp.

Thomson, George. *From Marx to Mao Tse-tung*. London, China Policy Study Group, 1971. 192 pp.

Union Research Institute. *Documents of the Chinese Communist Party Central Committee 1956-1969*. Hong Kong, 1971. Vol. I. 838 pp.

U.S.S.R. Academy of Sciences, Far East Institute. *The Foreign Policy of the CPR*. Moscow, International Relations Publishers, 1971. 191 pp.

Urban, George R. (comp.). *The Miracles of Chairman Mao: A Compendium of Devotional Literature, 1966-1970*. London, Tom Stacey Ltd., 1971. 182 pp.

Waller, D. J. *The Government and Politics of Communist China*. New York, Hillary House Publishers, 1971. 192 pp.

India

Adhikari, G. (ed.). *Documents of the History of the Communist Party of India, Volume I (1917-22)*. New Delhi, People's Publishing House, 1971. 650 pp.

Fic, Victor M. *Kerala: Yenan of India*. Bombay, Nachiketa Publication Ltd., 1971. 555 pp.

Franda, Marcus F. *Radical Politics in West Bengal*. Cambridge, MIT Press, 1971. 287 pp.

Ghose, Sankar. *Socialism and Communism in India*. Bombay, Allied Publishers, 1971. 468 pp.

Haithcox, John Patrick. *Communism and Nationalism in India: N. M. Roy and Comintern Policy 1920-1939*. Princeton, Princeton University Press, 1971. 299 pp.

Kaushik, Devendra. *Soviet Relations with India and Pakistan*. New York, Barnes & Noble, 1971. 119 pp.

Maxwell, Neville. *India's China War*. New York, Pantheon, 1971. 475 pp.

Nizami, Taufig Ahmad. *The Communist Party [of India] and India's Foreign Policy*. New Delhi, Associated Publishing House, 1971. 282 pp.

Ram, Mohan. *Maoism in India*. New York, Barnes & Noble, 1971. 196 pp.

Indonesia

Dahm, Bernhard. *History of Indonesia in the Twentieth Century*. New York, Praeger, 1971. 321 pp.

Jones, Howard P. *Indonesia: The Possible Dream*. New York, Harcourt Brace Jovanovich, 1971. 473 pp.

Kahin, George McTurnan. *Nationalism and Revolution in Indonesia*. Ithaca, Cornell University Press, 1971. 490 pp.

Sloan, Stephen. *A Study in Political Violence: The Indonesian Experience*. New York, Rand, McNally, 1971. 107 pp.

Japan

Emmerson, John K. *Arms, Yen and Power: The Japanese Dilemma*. New York, Dunellen Publishing Company, 1971. 420 pp.

Kahn, Herman. *The Emerging Japanese Superstate: Challenge and Response*. Englewood Cliffs, N.J., Prentice-Hall, 1971. 274 pp.

Langer, Paul F. *Communism in Japan: A Case of Political Naturalization*. Stanford, Hoover Institution Press, 1971. 112 pp.

Weinstein, Martin E. *Japan's Postwar Defense Policy, 1947-1968*. New York, Columbia University Press, 1971. 158 pp.

Korea

Cole, David C., and Lyman, Princeton N. *Korean Development: The Interplay of Politics and Economics*. Cambridge, Harvard University Press, 1971. 254 pp.

Kim, Il-song. *Revolution and Socialist Construction in Korea*. New York, International Publishers, 1971. 225 pp.

Park, Chung Hee. *To Build a Nation*. Washington, D.C., Acropolis Books, 1971. 216 pp.

Laos

Dommen, Arthur J. *Conflict in Laos: The Politics of Neutralization*. New York, Praeger, 1971. Rev. ed. 454 pp.

Langer, Paul F., and Zasloff, Joseph J. *North Vietnam and Pathet Lao: Partners in the Struggle for Laos*. Cambridge, Harvard University Press, 1971. 262 pp.

Malaysia

Barber, Noel. *The War of the Running Dogs: How Malaya Defeated the Communist Guerrillas, 1948-60*. London, Collins, 1971. 284 pp.

Mongolia

Axelbank, Albert. *Mongolia*. Tokyo, Kodansha International, 1971. 138 pp.

Stolypine, Arcady, with Stolypine, Dimitri. *La Mongolie Entre Moscou et Pékin*. Paris, Stock, 1971. 238 pp.

Nepal

Rose, Leo F. *Nepal: Strategy for Survival*. Berkeley, University of California Press, 1971. 310 pp.

Rose, Leo F., and Fisher, Margaret W. *The Politics of Nepal*. Ithaca, Cornell University Press, 1971. 197 pp.

Philippines

Lachica, Eduardo. *Huk: Philippine Agrarian Society in Revolt*. New York, Praeger, 1971. 159 pp.

Vietnam

Cameron, Allan W. (ed.). *Viet-Nam Crisis: A Documentary History, Volume 1: 1940-1956*. Ithaca, Cornell University Press, 1971. 452 pp.

Halberstam, David. *Ho*. New York, Random House, 1971. 118 pp.

Le Duan. *Selected Articles and Speeches (1965-1970)*. Moscow: Politizdat, 1971. 359 pp.

Le Duan. *The Vietnamese Revolution*. New York, International Publishers, 1971. 151 pp.

Maneli, Mieczyslaw. *War of the Vanquished: A Polish Diplomat in Vietnam*. New York, Harper & Row, 1971. 228 pp.

N. Khac, Huyen. *Vision Accomplished? The Enigma of Ho Chi Minh*. New York, Macmillan, 1971. 377 pp.

Oberdorfer, Don. *Tet!* Garden City, N.Y., Doubleday, 1971. 385 pp.

Race, Jeffrey. *War Comes to Long An: Revolutionary Conflict in a Vietnamese Province*. Berkeley, University of California Press, 1971. 350 pp.

Sansom, Robert L. *The Economics of Insurgency in the Mekong Delta of Vietnam*. Cambridge, MIT Press, 1971. 282 pp.

Woodside, Alexander B. *Vietnam and the Chinese Model*. Cambridge, Harvard University Press, 1971. 294 pp.

John Ma

INDEX

INDEX

INDEX OF PERSONS